D1582985

MILNER'S CASES AND MATERIALS ON CONTRACTS

MILNER'S
CASES AND
MATERIALS ON
CONTRACTS

Edited by

S. M. WADDAMS

Faculty of Law
University of Toronto

Third Edition

UNIVERSITY OF TORONTO PRESS
TORONTO BUFFALO LONDON

First edition 1963
© *University of Toronto Press 1963*

Second edition 1971
© *University of Toronto Press 1971*
Toronto and Buffalo

Third edition 1977
© *University of Toronto Press 1977*
Toronto and Buffalo
Reprinted 1979

Printed in Canada

ISBN 0—8020—2272—3 (Lib.)
ISBN 0—8020—2273—1 (Coll.)
LC 75—151396

TO PRATT

PREFACE TO THE THIRD EDITION

The law of contracts seems to be in a process of quite rapid and fundamental change. The aim of this revision of Milner's casebook is to reflect that change.

Several recent decisions reflect what seems to be a new judicial attitude to the role of the courts in law reform. *Miliangos* v. *George Frank (Textiles) Ltd.*, *New Zealand Shipping Co. Ltd.* v. *A. M. Satterthwaite & Co. Ltd.*, *Macaulay* v. *A. Schroeder Music Publishing Co. Ltd.*, *Steadman* v. *Steadman*, and *Cehave N. V.* v. *Bremer Handelgesellschaft m.b.H.* are the most striking examples. All these have been included.

The materials on enforceability have been reorganized with two ends in view. First, materials on offer acceptance and consideration are put together, in order to emphasize that they are all components of the idea of bargain. Second, the materials on enforcement of non-bargain promises have been separated from the bargain materials, with greater emphasis on reliance as a reason for enforcement.

Another significant change is in the organization of the materials on the protection of weaker parties. This topic has been elevated to the status of a chapter, and includes the recent cases on unconscionability, and a considerable amount of statutory material on consumer protection.

The chapters on assignment and agency have been reduced with the object of providing merely the background information necessary for the study of contracts and third parties, rather than a full study of assignment and agency in their own right. Other reductions have been made in the materials on conditions and on frustration.

A substantial number of questions and problems have been added in the belief that students and instructors find them useful.

S. M. WADDAMS
TORONTO 1977

SUMMARY TABLE OF CONTENTS

ANALYTICAL TABLE OF CONTENTS

TABLE OF CASES

INTRODUCTION TO FIRST EDITION

This collection of "cases and materials" is one version of what is commonly called a "casebook" and is intended as a teaching aid in a process commonly called teaching by the "case method." A definition of the "case method" is better not attempted; it should be sufficient to warn any of you who may have heard talk about the case method that there is no such thing—if anything, the reference should be to "case methods," in the plural, and you should expect to find as many methods as you have teachers. With this warning in mind a few words may be said about this book, which is admittedly a casebook.

It is first of all a portable library, designed to prevent the excessive wear and tear on library books when a hundred students are sent to read the same six or seven pages in the same volume, year after year. It consists of extensively reproduced reports of law suits (about 250) usually in the higher courts, but sometimes in the trial court. There are some less extensive excerpts. And there are some excerpts that can best be described as notes of reports. The word "materials" covers these lesser excerpts, but it also covers a variety of other "legal" things, sections of statutes, clauses from contracts, text notes, and questions and problems. Some explanation of what you are expected to do with all these cases and materials is offered in this short introduction.

WHAT DOES THE CASE STAND FOR? Early in their legal education many law students pick up a virus from some unknown source that drives them to ask of each case, what does it stand for? They seem to assume that the cases are building blocks, that each has an understandable shape and will fit neatly into a little wall of law, snugly and certainly. The correct answer to the question is that the case "stands for" what it is, a little segment of human history, history of an event or of an idea, or of both. The important question is: What is to be done with this case? The answer can really only be fully appreciated by experiencing the study of law, but a few suggestions may be helpful.

The importance of the facts. If the case is regarded as the history of an event the event consists of a set of facts. Although, as we shall see, your interest will centre mainly around the ideas also included in most cases, an understanding of the facts of a case is vital to an understanding of the idea —any principle is better understood if it is thought about in the context of a specific situation. This is one of the great merits of the so-called "case method," that it tends to keep the discussion in an understandable framework of the reasonably familiar.

The facts of cases are not always fully known or available for study. The report of the case sometimes quotes from the "record." These facts are the proven facts, and under the common law system the judge is supposed to confine himself to proven facts and not to act on his own knowledge. Indeed, if he has any personal knowledge of the facts he should consider seriously whether he should disqualify himself and get some other judge to handle the case.

Our trial system is far from perfect and you need not assume that the record will necessarily show all the facts that might have been proven.

Witnesses are not perfect: their powers of perception may be very limited, they may have poor memories, sometimes they are simply inarticulate and fail to communicate, and, of course, some lack veracity. The lying witness is not the most frequent cause of an inaccurate record, however. Witnesses are more often likely to tell the truth than most law students seem to believe. The other three dangers are much greater threats to an accurate record.

But even if the record is fairly complete, we do not, usually, have access to it in the reports. We have to rely on the abstract of the facts that the judges write in their decisions, and there is always a possibility, sometimes quite real, that the abstracting by the judge will, deliberately or otherwise, omit reference to facts that other judges or students might have considered of value. Clearly then we deal with an imperfect set of facts.

Sometimes we haven't even an abstraction from the trial record, because the issue of law is tried, not on proven facts, but on alleged facts which may or may not be proven in the subsequent trial. Such a trial of an issue was said in the old pleadings to be on a "demurrer." An illustration of a case where the facts alleged, which were assumed on the demurrer, apparently did not get proved at the trial, which came to an opposite decision, may be seen in *Angell* v. *Duke*, on page 445.

Sometimes the judge may not repeat the facts at all, or too briefly to be of use to us, and the reporter of the case may then summarize the facts himself, which may or may not be accurate. *Hadley* v. *Baxendale*, on page 35, illustrates this possibility, as does *Dickinson* v. *Dodds*, on page 193. The reporter may be content to reproduce at length the pleadings in the case which, of course, give a perfectly accurate account of the allegations. The difficulty with this method is that it is wasteful of space, since the older pleadings particularly were repetitious. I have, therefore, taken the liberty in some cases of writing a note about the facts myself, and I hope these shorter statements, which are designed to save you time, are sufficiently complete and accurate for their purpose. In any case, where my summary is inadequate, one citation of the case is immediately available and the full report may easily be consulted. I should like, however, to avoid this inadequacy in another edition and I hope you will bring your complaints to my attention.

Variations of the facts. The discipline of the case lies in its facts. Law students show a very human tendency to want to change the facts, ever so slightly perhaps, to make them "fit" an idea, usually a preconceived idea with which the student is familiar. The student must resist this temptation in discussion in class, and especially in answering examination questions! Intellectual honesty demands that the facts be considered as they are, not as we would like them to be. This distortion, consciously or unconsciously, of the facts on record, is sometimes observed in judges as well as law students, and it is no more admirable on the bench than in the classroom. In classroom discussion it is a commonplace to consider many variations of the facts but each variation must be dealt with honestly, especially if the "logical" result is disturbing. It is just this disturbance that may lead to a new insight or understanding of the problem being considered.

One other aspect of the facts may be mentioned. In considering variations on the original theme, students sometimes ask, "How can you prove such a fact? It's only the plaintiff's word against the defendant's." Discussion on the merits would bog down pretty quickly if one had to imagine, not only the variant of the facts, but the kind of evidence that would be necessary to prove it. Let it suffice that most facts can be proved, and many a lawsuit has been won by a plaintiff because the judge or jury believed his testimony and rejected the defendant's. The problem of proof is best left to the course on Evidence, where problems of this sort form the main core of the subject.

One qualification is, however, necessary here. There are some kinds of facts that may be considered incapable of proof and a rule of law based on such a fact is always suspect. A typical example is the proof of "intention," a "fact" frequently considered relevant in the law of contracts. As Brian C.J. put it in 1477, "The thought of man is not triable, for the Devil himself knoweth not the thought of man." (Y.B. (1477) P. 17 E. 4. 2a, pt. 2.) He intended to imply, I think, that if the Devil, with all his satanic powers, couldn't find out, for mere man the task would be hopeless. Modern psychiatry is making headway, admittedly, but so far the psychiatrist's methods do not appear to have too much value in the trial process. Meanwhile, you may look with some scepticism on rules that purport to give effect to the "intention of the parties." You will find, however, that notions of "intent" play a useful and important part in the law of contracts.

Facts that are not on the record, but which nevertheless exist, are assuming an increasing importance in the study of law. These background facts, which are sometimes rather specific and intimate facts, sometimes rather large general facts, may be purposely kept out of the record, perhaps because of desire by one party and ignorance by the other or because they are so extensive their proof becomes too inconvenient or expensive. These facts about the facts, what really happened, sometimes point up the real problem. *Jacob and Youngs, Inc.* v. *Kent*, on page 682, is a case where one is tempted to think that the real dispute has been carefully hidden from the court. Here the background facts, undisclosed, were probably highly personal. In *Hadley* v. *Baxendale*, on page 35, the background facts that obviously influenced the thinking of the court were very general. You may even wonder whether they were "facts." Facts of this latter class are frequently invoked by students who want to settle a dispute by reference to the "custom of the trade." It is often quite difficult to convince beginning law students that the "custom" may not be very customary, and that proof may be impossible because the custom simply doesn't exist. There may be almost as many "customs" as there are "traders." Professor Fuller has a very nice account of this problem in a note on "Proving the business background of a contract" in his *Basic Contract Law*.

The importance of facts may be appreciated from a remark made in my presence by a distinguished member of the Supreme Court of Canada some ten years ago. He said, "I sometimes feel that when I have mastered the facts I have done seventy-five per cent of my job." He was expressing a familiar experience of lawyers, that the facts have a habit of dictating a solution. It might be said to be one of the principal tasks of the lawyer to try to explain why that solution seems to be so irresistibly indicated. The law has been described as the perfection of reason and no lawyer, or at least no judge, likes to leave his decision without the crutches of reason if only because he wants the respect of his colleagues and he thinks, quite rightly, that a reasoned decision will earn it more quickly than a hunch, no matter how acceptable.

The sources of the ideas. The principal sources of ideas in this casebook are the reports of judges' decisions in actual litigation. These reports have been appearing since shortly after the Norman conquest. Originally their reporting was the work of private individuals, sometimes the judges themselves, and much later, series of reports were started by commercial publishers who retained reporters, usually young and unemployed barristers, to report cases for them. The early reports are known by the names of the reporters. In 1865 the English profession set up the Incorporated Council of Law Reporting, which has since been responsible for what are sometimes called the "official reports," although they have no other "official" status. Both English and Canadian governments have been loath to publish law reports, although Canada does publish, through the Queen's Printer, the *Canada Law Reports*, better known as the *Exchequer Court Reports* and the *Supreme Court Reports*. The best coverage of Canadian cases is to be found in the *Dominion Law Reports*, a privately published series commenced in 1911 by the Canada Law Book Company and covering all of Canada, but with relatively less emphasis on Quebec. Not all cases are reported; the choice is made by the editor, who uses his own criteria. No accurate information is available, but one could hazard a guess that not fifty per cent of the cases are reported. Yet hundreds of thousands of cases have been reported over the centuries, and in the United States the number is over the million mark.

The reports in this casebook are not exclusively from any one jurisdiction. The largest number from any one jurisdiction are from England. This should not surprise you. Except for the province of Quebec, Canada is a "common law" country and it has its legal roots deep in the common law as it originated and developed in England. Naturally enough, the next largest number come from Canada, particularly from Ontario. There is no chauvinistic influence whatever in this selection. The English cases are chosen sometimes because they have historical importance and enable you to trace the history of an idea, sometimes because they have rather striking sets of facts, or rather well expressed statements of law, or novel notions worth reflecting about. The Canadian cases have been chosen for the same reasons. Generally speaking the earlier Canadian courts frequently tended not to discuss a problem on its merits, but merely recited English cases thought to have a bearing, or even to be binding on the Canadian courts. Such cases have little teaching value. In more recent years the tendency has started the other way, and Canada has a rather enviable position in the Commonwealth in that it has had a "new" Supreme Court since appeals to the Privy Council were abolished, and the possibilities of a renaissance in the Canadian common law, though hardly probable, are not to be ignored.

I do not apologize for any undue number of Canadian cases. Others may think there are too few. But since this book is intended for use in a Canadian law school it is only sensible, I think, to present as full a picture of Canadian contracts, in and out of courts, as it is possible to do, simply because Canadian law students are likely to understand the Canadian background of Canadian cases better than they will understand either English or American backgrounds. And there seems to be some virtue in concentrating study in one familiar area rather than spreading one's self too thinly. Nevertheless I have not hesitated to take advantage of cases from any common law country, particularly the United States, and even, in one case, from a civil law country. I hope the richness of variety of ideas presented has not suffered from the shortage of American decisions, but American casebooks and textbooks are fortunately readily available if it does.

Some references have been made to code provisions from civil law jurisdictions. These are not presented with any naive notion that Canadian common law students can learn the civil law from a half dozen excerpts, but

I do hope that these few glimpses will alert you to the fact that there exists another major legal system with different ideas from those of the common law. If you are interested in the relation of law to society you may note that the people of some civil law countries seem to be both happy and prosperous.

Further ideas are to be found in the occasional excerpts from the statute law. There probably should be more of these. First year law students can too easily get the impression that life in the law is just one continuous lawsuit. Case study falsely emphasizes this impression. The cases are almost always cases in courts, and the constant reading of cases may tend to drive out of mind the other areas in which law is equally operative. Perhaps some figures about law practice may help to improve your sense of proportion. The number of lawyers in practice in Canada is something over 14,000. It would not be too far from the fact to say that not as many as 500 of these lawyers earn their living exclusively from court practice. In England, where the legal profession is divided into solicitors (office lawyers) and barristers (court lawyers), the ratio is about ten to one. There are something like 20,000 solicitors and 2,000 barristers, and in fact only about half of the barristers are actively engaged in their profession. This slight apology for so many cases is not quite abject, because first year law students are expected to learn thoroughly the judicial process, how and why it works and what its limitations are, and this can best be done by a thorough examination of the results of the process. As I shall point out later, in law practice *predicting* the outcome of possible litigation underlies most of the lawyer's general office practice. *Influencing* the outcome is his task in court.

The statute law is not only important as a second source of ideas, but also as a source of ideas of a very different kind. The statute represents, usually, an attempt to solve a problem by a general rule, rather than by the settlement of a single dispute. This approach carries with it a different set of ground rules, and you are invited to investigate the principles of legislation as you go along. The statute is a special device for solving special problems, and like contract and adjudication, it has its special limitations.

There are interspersed throughout the cases, and in special separate notes, a few clauses from contracts. These clauses are useful sources of ideas that have often been tried because the ideas worked out by the courts or legislatures are unsatisfactory. Probably there should be more of these examples, but I trust that there are enough to alert you to the possibilities of drafting better solutions for familiar and unfamiliar problems.

Among the other sources of ideas should be mentioned the few examples of private opinion, from textbooks and periodical literature, and the great American Law Institute *Restatement of the Law of Contracts*, something rather like a code of the law, compiled by a group of practising and teaching lawyers. The *Restatement* has no official status, but it has received considerable favourable notice in American courts.

Finally, but in a place of honour at the bottom of the list, comes you, the law student. It is you who will be shaping the law twenty years from now, and the ideas you have now, or that you develop as you proceed with your study of the law, are not unimportant. At the beginning you may feel that you know too little to contribute, but before you have been completely brain washed I hope you may add to the intellectual ferment that ought to characterize any lively classroom of beginning law students.

Supplementary reading. Let me give you one word of advice. You will find in the casebook relatively few references to other reading. I have not even included all the citations to the full reports of the cases in this book! Needless to say, there is an incredible amount of material to which you might be sent. There is much too much. You may easily become overwhelmed at the prospect of it, and you may believe that somewhere in there is the answer to your problem. Don't look for it. Think it out for yourself, or in collaboration with your friends in your class. Discussion with them will be surprisingly profitable. Take some comfort from these words of Professor I. A. Richards, who says, in his *Speculative Instruments*, at pages 61-2, "Modern scholarship positively gets in the way. The critical apparatus of approach to the great things keeps them from their would be student. He is daunted incessantly by the thought that somewhere there is something which would, if he only knew it, help him to understand better. He comes to distrust the direct appraoch, and lives in an unhealthy terror of his ignorance—which will anyhow for all men to time's end be infinite. He forgets that we do not help ourselves or others by collecting more facts and comments, but by understanding more clearly our problems and theirs. We learn best to do this by reflecting upon such problems and by seeing them through the eyes of the best minds." Believe me, this is not just an excuse for not knowing everything.

How to read a case. May I leave this topic with an attempt to state shortly what I think you, as a beginning law student, are expected to do with these facts and ideas? I think you have to try to do two rather irreconcilable things. You have to get to know the best which has been thought and said about the law of contracts, and you must turn a stream of fresh and free thought upon our stock notions and habits. I apologize to Matthew Arnold. You have to know what judges and legislatures have said but you also have to know that there are other, and sometimes better, ideas that they might have expressed; and you have to know the legal system, how and why it works, or doesn't work, so that you, as future law reformers, may have some hope that your better ideas will be adopted.

I believe it is futile to try to tell other people how to study, and any attempt to explain how to read a case is likely to meet with little success. You must work out your own methods of study, which you will doubtless modify as you increase your understanding of the study of law. Here are some general suggestions that may help in that understanding. Remember that a case is the settlement of a dispute by a third person and if you are to understand the settlement you must know the issue. Who is suing whom for what? Before what court? What happened, what are the facts? Who won? What was the remedy? What were the reasons given? These questions represent the minimum you must know about the case, where that minimum is given in the casebook. Sometimes only the facts are given, in which case you are obviously expected only to speculate how those facts might have been treated by a court. Judgments or opinions have sometimes been omitted so that you don't come to rely wholly on what you may regard as so superior a source of ideas that it stultifies your own analysis and creative thought.

There are, of course, other matters to be noticed in a case. Are the reasons consistent with other judgments you have read? Do you agree with the judge's interpretation of earlier decisions or statutes? Are his reasons consistent within themselves? Has the judge used words ambiguously? Has he disclosed an attitude inconsistent with the ideal detachment of a judge? Sometimes I have pointed to some of these matters by inserting questions after the case. Where there are no questions you should develop the habit of asking your own. I have not put questions after every case because you may not bother to ask your own if you spend too much time wondering about mine. Your own efforts will be more rewarding in the long run. Take nothing for granted until you are forced to. Ask yourself whether you fully understand the judge's point of view before you attempt to criticise it, but do not hesitate to criticise it constructively. Reading the case is important, and it must *precede* class discussion if you are to get the most out of the discussion. But reading and thinking cannot occupy the same space at the same time, and much of the editing of these cases and materials has been directed to cutting down the reading time necessary for you to get the facts and ideas to think about. This is especially true of the first three chapters, which have been pruned to the limit, so that you could get an early start with your own thinking. The cases in the later chapters are more extensively reported because by then you should be able to read and absorb a judgment more quickly.

After you have read the case, what should you remember? Students frequently ask whether they have to memorize the names of cases, the facts, the decisions, the reasons for judgment or the names of the judges, or any of these, for "examination purposes." It seems to me that most students tend to remember the essentials as a by-product of their reading, thinking and discussion. Particular facts can usually be forgotten. The particular facts that prove to be crucial in distinguishing situations must be remembered, I suppose, but they can often be stated in more general terms, and fitted into the statement of principle that one wants to remember in any event.

The names of the cases stay in some minds without effort, in others no amount of effort seems to work. But the names are only useful as a short-hand means of referring to the case and a longer description of some high-light will usually be as good, althouth expensive in time during the writing of examinations. Some lawyers sometimes indulge in a kind of gamesman-ship with case names, but I doubt whether the gamesmanship is very im-portant. Canadian and English lawyers probably tend to learn more of the same cases in their law schools. The Americans have a much greater pool to draw from, and I suspect that few Americans remember many cases by names.

The names of judges are a bit of a luxury, but the position of the court in the judicial hierarchy is a very important matter in estimating the weight that will be attached to the decision. Obviously the fact that the idea you are promoting comes from a Supreme Court of Canada judge or from an inex-perienced trial judge may justify no inference about its quality but the source may matter a great deal about its acceptability in some circles!

IS THIS CASE RIGHTLY DECIDED? Early in your legal education many of your teachers will have picked up a virus from some unknown source that drives them to ask you, of each case, is it rightly decided? You may be tempted to ask, if you have been bitten by the bug of semantics, "What do you mean by 'right'?" The question is a fair one, and no law teacher or law student should try to dodge it, even if you or they may occasionally feel you are poised on the brink of philosophical chaos. To ask this question is to introduce the element of ethics into the rather more precise world of legal propositions. Nevertheless by asking and trying to answer the question, you may gain a very useful insight into the legal system. In England, where all litigation points toward one final court, in the House of Lords, one can understand the tendency to judge "rightness" by reference to what the House of Lord has said, or will say. Of course the element of prediction involved in guessing what the House *will* say opens the door just a little bit to the question of "rightness," although the House may shut it in counsel's face if it has spoken on the subject before. See, however, the rather interesting view of Viscount Simonds on this subject, in *Midland Silicones Ltd.* v. *Scruttons Ltd.*, on page 389, and in *Director of Public Prosecutions* v. *Shaw*, on page 391.

In Canada there is a somewhat different attitude, although there may be a tendency for Canadians (and Americans) to overstate the conservatism of English courts and the liberality of their own. As I have already mentioned, Canada is at a rather interesting stage in the development of her national judiciary. We have, in effect, a new Supreme Court whose judges, many of them only appointed since the "new" Court came into being in 1950, may prove to be more aware of the truly creative role a supreme court can play, not only in constitutional matters, but generally in the application and development of the common law. They may yet be moved by the boast of the great English judge, Lord Mansfield, who said in 1744, "the common law . . . *works itself pure* by rules drawn from the fountains of justice." (*Omychund* v. *Barker* (1744), 1 Atk. 21 at page 33; E. R. 15 at pages 22-3.)

In Canada we have ten separate provinces, and, for some purposes, each of those provinces is a separate law district, or jurisdiction. This is obviously the case in matters of legislation. The legislature of Ontario does not make law for the province of Nova Scotia or British Columbia. But when it comes to the statement of the common law, it is possible in most cases to take an important issue of law to the Supreme Court of Canada, and that Court has usually taken the view that the common law (as distinct from statute law) is common to all provinces except Quebec, and that there isn't a common law of Ontario, another of British Columbia and so on throughout the nine common law provinces. In the United States, another federal state, the system works the other way, and fifty states have fifty sovereign common law jurisdictions. When, in proper circumstances, a case from a state gets to the United States Supreme Court, that Court now takes the view that it must decide first which state law to apply and then to decide it according to its view of that state law. Earlier it had taken the view that there were individual state laws and a federal common law as well. It apparently never thought it a good idea to try to make uniform the state common law as the Supreme Court of Canada does. Hence the degree of intellectual boiling-over in the United States is higher than in Canada because the lid is constantly off. In Canada, while nine common law provincial courts of appeal may boil at their pleasure, the Supreme Court may at any time put on the lid.

What, then, is the answer to the teacher's question, "Is the case 'right'?" Can there be any less of an answer than an examination of the possible reasonable and practical alternatives? The answer to the question may be a qualified "yes, but" in some cases, because on a proper view of the problem of the case it may appear that there are other legal processes better adapted to its solution than the adjudicative. While the case as presented may be "rightly" decided, the problem of the case, which is also the law student's concern, is not satisfactorily solved. It is admittedly a dangerous question, one that opens up large and exciting vistas, and yet, in a *university*, no matter how modern, can one properly refuse to consider it?

WHAT IS THE LAW OF THIS *JURISDICTION*? Early in their legal education many law students pick up a second virus from some unknown source that drives them to ask after the discussion of cases from other jurisdictions, what is the local law? Some English critics of North American casebooks have been heard to say that they present the law of nowhere. This criticism is more aptly applied to national casebooks in American schools, where it is quite possible that cases from every state may be included in the assigned casebook. The alternative, presumably, would be to select cases from only one state. It would be interesting to speculate about the student enrolment at Harvard (which is representative of every state in the Union and many foreign countries) if it professed to teach only the law of Massachusetts! The question I think arises from two related sources of student concern, at least at the beginning of his law studies.

What is law? The first source is the uncertainty in the law, which he probably did not anticipate. He probably expected the law to consist of a long series of settled rules which he was expected to memorize and to understand. The second source is the dilemma in which he finds himself once he discovers that law is not all that settled. He soon learns that he is expected to "know the law" and, at the same time, to have explored the "unknown," not to say the "unknowable." He has to become an *educated* as well as an *informed* student of the law. On the whole it is a perfectly natural intellectual state for any student. He must accept the discipline of his subject and yet he must try to think creatively and imaginatively. From the teacher's point of view this dilemma has only one unfortunate aspect: the chronic pressure of examinations, which the student may think, and sometimes rightly, will stress more the knowledge of the law than the creative or imaginative attack of problems. This is a weakness of the examination system, not of the conflicting objectives of legal education, and if it will comfort, encourage or scare the student, there is an ever present possibility that the examination system may be improved! On this depressing thought that the examination plays too great a role in university education let me return to the first concern.

Beginning law students come with only a vague notion about what law is. They expect to find somewhere a set of rules. If they have heard of the "case method" they probably expect to find the rules buried in the cases. Some of them become impatient with this tedious method of extracting them. They hurry off to a library to read a text book written by someone they suppose has already done the tedious work and will tell them what the law is. Text writers sometimes say, in their introduction, "The law is presented as of January 31, 1963." One is tempted to ask who is going to change it or add to it after that date? How can the law "be" at a date that is now past? Why this continuous temporal limitation? What *is* the law?

Attempts to fix a final single meaning for the word "law" have occupied the time of many scholars and filled many books, but the attempts are surprisingly barren or incomplete. If you now think of law as a series of rules laid down (by whom?) to govern human behaviour, you have some distinguished scholars on your side. But for a student who looks forward to the practice of law a collection of rules is far from a complete qualification. Recent graduates are often heard to complain that no client ever asks them anything they learned in the law school. Of course a client rarely asks a lawyer what the law is (and when he does he is often sidetracked); he asks more commonly what can he do, or not do, in particular circumstances. He wants advice on how to act in a situation that presents a variety of courses of action. He does not want an abstract statement of what the law is, or what some lawyer believes it to be. It does not follow that the lawyer can think only in terms of what Tennyson, in *Aylmer's Field*, called

> ". . . the lawless science of our law
> That codeless myriad of precedent,
> That wilderness of single instances."

To begin with, there are large areas of what might be called "accepted doctrine," with which any lawyer can quickly familiarize himself from text books, once he has gained sufficient insight into the legal system to enable him to use text books intelligently. Relatively few of a lawyer's problems, however, can be settled by reference to accepted doctrine, and it is surprising how much doctrine (accepted or unaccepted) a business man knows that his lawyer may not. The business man does not consult his lawyer about such matters. When he needs a lawyer his accepted doctrine has failed him: he is either in trouble, or, less frequently, but increasingly more commonly, he wants to avoid trouble and he is not sure what to do. He wants advice.

Law as prediction. If the trouble is far enough advanced a lawsuit may be inevitable and the lawyer may be asked to anticipate what a court will do in the circumstances. One famous definition of the law is limited to just this. Oliver Wendell Holmes, a distinguished American judge, said "The prophecies of what the courts will do in fact, and nothing more pretentious, are what I mean by the law." ("The Path of the Law" (1897), 10 *Harvard Law Review* 457.) The definition is far too limited to be useful; not even Holmes himself entirely agreed, for he said later on, in the same talk, "Still it is true that a body of law is more rational and more civilized when every rule it contains is referred articulately and definitely to an end which it subserves, and when the grounds for desiring that end are stated or are ready to be stated in words. . . . For the rational study of the law the black letter man may be the man of the present, but the man of the future is the man of statistics and the master of economics."

Even predicting what a court will do is obviously much more than merely mastering a series of rules, for if it were certain what rule the court would follow "prediction" would not result in the parties financing two or more opposing lawyers through a trial court, a court of appeal, and the Supreme Court of Canada.

So far as the law consists of prediction, it may be likened to weather predictions in the daily papers. The short, overly simplified "black letter" version usually appears on the front page in an upper corner. The Toronto *Globe and Mail* announced there, on August 30, 1954: "Sunny, Warm, High Here 80." Anyone interested in the conflicting influences which led to the summary statement could turn to page two, where an incomprehensible map showing these influences was supposed to make everything clear. As a matter of interest, and to complete the analogy with law as prediction, the forecast turned out, in this instance, to be rather misleading. On page two of the same paper, on August 31, the maximum temperature for the day before was said to be 68 and 0.65 inches of rain fell. It was explained that "the disturbance over Lake Ontario was retarded in its eastward trek by the slow northward motion of the hurricane off the North Carolina coast." The corresponding situations in law would probably be called black letter law, functional analysis, and the law-in-action. We are, I think, still lagging behind the other social sciences in our study of the law-in-action, yet that is where the functional analysis receives its only important testing. Obviously, the analogy with weather prediction falls down when we remember that the lawyers in a case influence the court's decision, so that the prediction of law becomes a complex purposive activity of man, not an observation of inanimate elements having no known purpose.

This limited definition of law as prediction led Benjamin Cardozo, another well known American judge, to say, derisively, of it, "Law never *is*, but is always about to be." (*The Nature of the Judicial Process* (1921), page 126.) Curiously, one can give his words quite another meaning, in which I think they convey a greater insight into the common law. Compare them with Lord Mansfield's remark I quoted above, that the common law works itself pure by drawing on the fountains of justice. It is *always* about to be. That, I think, is a great idea.

Law as process. The weakness of the definition of law as prediction is that it limits our sights too restrictively. As I have already pointed out, most lawyers are not employed as barristers, and although to a very important degree they have to base all their actions on at least an educated guess at what a court might, in the long run, say about their advice and solution, they have an infinite variety of short run problems in which the ultimate judicial decision, which they may hope will not have to be sought, will play a secondary role. Their professional action will be based on their predictions, but it may take the form of, for example, drafting clauses in a contract, persuading an administrative official to vary a regulation, or a legislative committee to recommend an amendment to a statute, or organizing a new corporation. All of these activities are in a sense legislative, rather than adjudicative, and they justify, in my view, an even greater emphasis on the legislative area than our legal education presently offers.

For the student about to study the law of contract, the prediction definition is peculiarly inapt or incomplete, because it suggests that "law" is limited to the occasion when contract disputes are litigated. Yet contract is in fact the principal means whereby individuals make private arrangements to control their affairs *without* the interference of the state. If "law" is limited to judicial action, the law student would presumably have little concern with the many problems of drafting contracts in order that the parties may achieve their purposes. Yet almost every lawyer may be asked to help his clients draft contracts as well as get them out of difficulties resulting from their own insufficient planning. The "law" of contracts, therefore, it seems to me, consists about equally of understanding how, when and, above all, *why* the state may interfere in private arrangements and of understanding how private arrangements may be made more effective, and what the limits of effective action through private arrangements may be. An understanding of contract, as a legal process, can, I think, be gained by studying the results of litigation, for in this way you may acquire experience vicariously, but you must use this experience to think about the problems of planning private affairs, as well as the problems of state interference. All of this should make apparent to you the importance to the law of human purposes. These purposes are many, varied, and conflicting; the task of the law is to sort them out and promote those that should be promoted and suppress those that should be suppressed. We might call the difficult task of selection the basic problem of justice.

The legal discipline. Can it be said, in view of this combination of elements, that the law has any claim to be called an intellectual discipline, entitled to a place in the classical university? I think it has. It may be impossible to explain what that discipline is to students who haven't yet immersed themselves in it, but I am going to suggest some guides to which you may return as you gain the insight of experience.

It seems to me that the law may be regarded as consisting of three basic processes having as their objective what might be called "justice." Each process has its place in the sun, and because this is a casebook on contracts, I put the contract process, of negotiation, promise and exchange, as the first. It doesn't matter whether it is more or less important than the other two, but I think a lawyer has to know what can be done by contract, or private arrangement, and what can not. That is the first branch of his discipline.

The second basic process is adjudication, of which the judicial process is an instance, but so is arbitration. The study of cases is the study of the judicial process in itself, as well as a study of the substantive field with which the cases deal. Just as there are limitations on what you can do by way of private arrangement, so there are on what you can do by way of adjudication and the important subclass, the judicial process. The second branch of the discipline is the process of adjudication.

The third basic process is legislation, or the exercise of power by a body authorized to make rules for general application or decisions in particular cases, but without the incidents of adjudication. How, when and why a social or individual problem should be solved by the exercise of some authority by a private individual or an official of the state is the peculiar subject matter of the process of legislation. This allocation of authority should not be thought of as exclusively the function of a state legislative body because private individuals may be given a great deal of power by contract, or private arrangement. The obvious illustration of this private power is that given by contract to their employer by a group of employees, whose affairs are managed by the employer for a large part of their waking life. The obvious example is the modern collective agreement.

THE ORGANIZATION OF THESE MATERIALS. The materials presented here may be divided into two parts, although no such formal breakdown has been indicated in the table of contents. The first part deals chiefly with the interference of the state in private arrangements, and attempts to search out the purposes sought by the individual contracting parties and the purposes of the state in interfering. The second part deals chiefly with the planning of private arrangements and the drafting of contracts to serve them, but since the materials are still judicial decisons, they are also illustrative of judicial, or state interference.

Throughout all of these materials the thing being closely examined is the *promise.* The word is used in its ordinary sense, with one exception. We ordinarily think of a promise as being a personal prediction that a stated event over which the person promising has some control will come to pass. My Concise Oxford Dictionary defines a promise as an "assurance given to a person that one will do or not do something or will give or procure him something." In most contexts this is all that is meant by "promise" in these cases and materials. But in some commercial contexts it is common for a man to give an "assurance" that a particular state of affairs, or quality of a thing, exists, or is true. We may thus assure a person that a car we are about to sell him is a "good" car. If we admit this meaning, then we can say that, thus supplemented, the word "promise" is used with its ordinary meaning. The course might then be called the law about, and the social use of, promises. I shall not now attempt any definition of contract; you may do that yourself whenever you feel ready for it.

The first chapter deals with the remedies the state offers for the breach of a promise. There are two reasons for starting here. First, the essential situation is simple and familiar since everyone has experienced the disappointment of a broken promise and nearly everyone has caused such disappointment at some time or other. To keep the discussion under reasonable control, you must assume that there is a promise and that it is enforceable. In later chapters both of these assumptions are examined.

The second reason for starting with remedies is that it will give you an excellent perspective of the purposes of the law in enforcing contracts. Later, when you are asked to decide whether a court would interfere in particular negotiations or how a particular clause should be drafted, you must know what kind of interference is possible and probable before you try to answer the questions. Hence the study of remedies gets at a most fundamental aspect of the "law" of contracts: the extent of the legal protection given to private arrangements. Throughout the book emphasis is constantly laid on the fact that contract is a purposive activity and that the state in turn interferes in private arrangements only for good reason, and it is, I think, very important to get this perspective at the start of the course. I think you will find that Chapter 1 gives you an introduction to many aspects of the law that you later learn in more detail.

Chapter 2 assumes only the existence of a promise, and asks why it should be enforced. Unless there is an absolute rule that all promises be enforced, or none, there are bound to be differences between reasonable men about drawing the line. The fact that drawing the line in individual cases may be difficult is not in itself a sufficient reason for reverting to absolute rules, but you must reconcile yourself to the prospect of unsatisfactory solutions in some cases, and you must examine closely the process by which the line is drawn. Where the law does not have a rule, the *process* of drawing the line is the heart of the law.

This chapter asks the most difficult of the questions in the first three chapters: when, in the intricacies of contract negotiation, should the state interfere and take sides? When has the negotiation matured to the point where one of the parties should be able to call for help? This question involves so much of life beyond the experience of most law students that the cases probably seem much simpler than they really are.

INSTEAD OF A DEFINITION. A casebook on contracts might be expected to start with a definition of "contracts" as a frequently recurring word whose meaning ought to be understood. A satisfactory legal definition at this point would be almost meaningless, and by the time the reader has reached the end of the book he ought to be able to write his own. Meanwhile, instead of a definition of "contract" the following paragraphs attempt to explain in non-legal terms something about the area of human conduct involved in contract situations.

A large part of human affairs is successfully conducted by private arrangements that do not involve the State in any immediate way. It is with this area of private arrangement that this book is concerned. A little reflection will make it apparent that there are certain disadvantages in trying to keep such arrangements of personal and business affairs entirely private. This is particularly obvious when the arrangements do not work out as planned. One party had defaulted on his side of the arrangement and the other party has been put to a good deal of trouble for which he expects some settlement. If he cannot get satisfaction by further resort to another private arrangement, a settlement, he may want to invoke the State.

The circumstances under which the State can be and should be invoked are at the heart of contract law. In the early development of England, and later, of Canada, the needs of private arrangers for State assistance were largely met by the courts, the judges and the administrative officials who are closely associated. The "law" of contracts was thus judge-made law until the end of the nineteenth century, and rules emerged from judicial decisions guiding private arrangements and their consequences in terms of remedies, the kinds of arrangements that were enforceable, the times when the courts would intervene, that is, when an arrangement could be said to have become enforceable. In the relatively simple and commercially stable period of the Victorians, these questions were apparently satisfactorily answered by the courts.

At the same time, the courts carried on another important aid to private arrangements—they settled disputes that arose over the meaning of the contract and in some cases they determined disputes about what the terms were, let alone what they meant. So the courts both developed contract doctrine (a "legislative" role) and settled contract disputes over the facts and their interpretation. (an "adjudicative" role).

In the next years, especially after the social dislocation following the first world war, the problems to be settled by private arrangement became more and more complex and less and less amenable to private solution. Businesses became larger. The distinction between "private" and "public" arrangements became somewhat indistinct. It soon became obvious that problems were emerging that the courts were hardly able to solve by themselves. Courts are dependent upon the existence of litigants, who come at random. The social problems of our time demand a less haphazard timing of their solution. As a result, the courts have been, if not replaced, at least substantially supplemented in their control of private arrangement by legistive and administrative techniques. The legislatures have been able to provide more generalized solutions and from a strategically more effective point of view.

A simple example may help. Over the years the courts worked out "rules" to be applied to a contract for the sale of goods, so that the goods must be up to their contract description and fit for the purpose for which they are sold. Thus the courts could provide a remedy for a person who contracted to buy a hundred five grain tablets of acetyl salicylic acid— "aspirin." If, on chemical analysis, the purchaser found that his quarter's worth of aspirin contained only three grains in each tablet, he could recover "damages" in a lawsuit—if he could afford such an action. Today, a government department will protect his interest much more cheaply and effectively. If the product sold as five grains of acetyl salicylic acid contains only three grains, the government's agent may seize the product and refuse to reimburse the seller. With this threat in the background, the seller and the manufacturer are both likely to take greater care to produce a product that meets its technical description and will do the job it is supposed to do.

At present the various governments in Canada are reluctant to extend this kind of protection to the market generally. It is available only in the limited area of "pure food and drugs." The extent to which the consumer should be further protected is currently being studied by lawyers, economists, and sociologists. Today's law students may expect to be deeply involved in this movement toward even greater interference in, or control of, private arrangements.

Private arrangements are changing their character in another way. They are beginning to reflect in a major way the use of one-sided arrangements made by a large entrepreneur who offers them on a "take-it-or-leave-it" basis. Such arrangements are commonly called "standard-form" contracts and their use is currently presenting courts and legislatures with new problems of justice.

These newer social problems are giving rise to new rules of contract law, or rules respecting private arrangement that are announced by the legislature and take the form of prohibition of certain arrangements or of new standards that arrangements must meet. This does not mean that private arrangements are of less importance in our society. It merely means that we must now look beyond the courts for the regulation of our affairs.

Judicial doctrine in contract, private ordering, or private arrangement has not changed much in the last half century, but the "law" of private arrangement has not stood still. It has moved in two ways. Outside the courts, private arrangements have been greatly affected by new legislation. In some cases businessmen have ceased to use contract altogether. In other cases they have modified their contracts to meet "new law." Within the courts litigation has continued to serve a basic need for arbitration—interpretation of disputed terms and settlement of disputed facts.

DIGRESSION ON INTERPRETATION. The interpretation of contracts and contractual behaviour generally is perennial in the life of the law. No chapter in this casebook is devoted to the subject, but most of the cases raise questions of interpretation and sometimes attention is drawn to them, although more often it is not. The student of contract law should try to understand fully the problems of interpretation and the judicial and other solutions for them. To return to the matter of the changing role of private arrangements, while all of this provides new problems for lawyers, they need not be unduly concerned. Private arrangement has simply moved beyond judicial control to legislative and administrative control, and in some cases, to administrative replacement. The lawyer simply has to widen his horizon to include in his understanding of contract law, not only judge-made law but legislative and administrative controls as well. He must also know more about the changing reliance in business and domestic arrangements, on private ways of settling disputes rather than on litigation in a State court. Use of the courts for even simple settlements of disputes will be avoided where continuing business relations make resort to the emotionally charged atmosphere of the courts undesirable. The lawyers will increasingly work out sensible settlements without the judges' supervision. All of this is meant to protect the reader from over-exposure to judicial opinions.

One final word. This introduction has been deliberately written in the first person because I intend it primarily for my own classes. I should warn any other reader that the objectives of legal education and the consequent arrangement of topics in a course are highly personal, and my views may very well not be shared by other law teachers.

J. B. MILNER

Faculty of Law
University of Toronto,
1963 and 1968

ACKNOWLEDGEMENTS

I am glad to acknowledge the kind permission generously given by the authors and publishers to reproduce the following copyright matter: The Incorporated Council of Law Reporting for England and Wales for material from *The Law Reports* and *The Weekly Law Reports*; Butterworth & Co. (Publishers) Ltd., for material from *The All England Law Reports*, and *The Law Times*; Sweet and Maxwell, Ltd., for material from the *Law Journal Reports*; the Times Publishing Co. Ltd., for material from *The Times Law Reports* and the *Commerical Cases*; the Canada Law Book Company for material from the *Dominion Law Reports*; the Law Book Company of Australia for an extract from *Australian Law Journal Reports*; Lloyds of London for an extract from *Lloyd's Law Reports*; the West Publishing Company for extracts from two cases and from *Corbin on Contracts*; the Northwestern University Press for an extract from Havighurst, *The Nature of Private Contract*; Professor Lon L. Fuller and the West Publishing Company, as copyright holder, for the material from *Basic Contract Law*, and the *Yale Law Journal* for extracts from three articles and the *Columbia Law Review*, as original publisher, for part of "Consideration and Form"; the many sections from the *Restatement of the Law of Contracts,* Copyright 1932, reprinted with the permission of The American Law Institute; Ward-Price, Limited, for permission to reproduce their auction sale contract, the Canadian Construction Association and The Royal Architectural Institute of Canada for permission to use parts of the standard form Canadian construction contract. I have made every attempt to obtain necessary permission to use copyright material but if any such material has been used improperly by oversight I hope the error will be brought to my attention so that suitable acknowledgement can be made in a later revision.

MILNER'S CASES AND MATERIALS ON CONTRACTS

CHAPTER 1

REMEDIES FOR BREACH OF PROMISE

In discussion and reflection about the materials in this chapter the existence of an enforceable promise should be assumed. The question is, what happens when that promise is broken? The basic fact situations are essentially simple. A promise has been made and broken. The problems are concerned with the kind and extent of protection the state ought to give to the interests of the aggrieved and of the defaulting parties.

How can these interests be protected? Is the payment of some amount of money enough? How do you determine the amount? Should a promise-breaker be penalized? Why is the interest being protected? Should the defaulting party be made to perform his promise? When you have brought your horse to the well, how do you make him drink? Can you ever put the parties back where they were at the start? When ought the protection of the state to become available? For how long? As you read these first cases, keep these questions in mind, and keep in mind the practical limitations on the realization of justice.

1. THE INTERESTS PROTECTED

FULLER AND PERDUE, "THE RELIANCE INTEREST IN CONTRACT DAMAGES"
1936. 46 Yale Law Journal 52, 53-54, 56-57, 61-63

It is convenient to distinguish three principal purposes which may be pursued in awarding contract damages. These purposes, and the situations in which they become appropriate, may be stated briefly as follows.

First, the plaintiff has in reliance on the promise of the defendant conferred some value on the defendant. The defendant fails to perform his promise. The court may force the defendant to disgorge the value he received from the plaintiff. The object here may be termed the prevention of gain by the defaulting promisor at the expense of the promisee; more briefly, the prevention of unjust enrichment. The interest protected may be called the *restitution interest*. For our present purposes it is quite immaterial how the suit in such a case be classified, whether as contractual or quasi-contractual, whether as a suit to enforce the contract or as a suit based upon a rescission of the contract. These questions relate to the superstructure of the law, not to the basic policies with which we are concerned.

Secondly, the plaintiff has in reliance on the promise of the defendant changed his position. For example, the buyer under a contract for the sale of land has incurred expense in the investigation of the seller's title, or has neglected the opportunity to enter other contracts. We may award damages to the plaintiff for the purpose of undoing the harm which his reliance on the defendant's promise has caused him. Our object is to put him in as good a position as he was in before the promise was made. The interest protected in this case may be called the *reliance interest*.

Thirdly, without insisting on reliance by the promisee or enrichment of the promisor, we may seek to give the promisee the value of the expectancy which the promise created. We may in a suit for specific performance actually compel the defendant to render the promised performance to the plaintiff or, in a suit for damages, we may make the defendant pay the money value of this performance. Here our object is to put the plaintiff in as good a position as he would have occupied had the defendant performed his promise. The interest protected in this case we may call the *expectation interest*. . . .

It is obvious that the three "interests" we have distinguished do not present equal claims to judicial intervention. It may be assumed that ordinary standards of justice would regard the need for judicial intervention as decreasing in the order in which we have listed the three interests. The "restitution interest," involving a combination of unjust impoverishment with unjust gain, presents the strongest case for relief. If, following Aristotle, we regard the purpose of justice as the maintenance of an equilibrium of goods among members of society, the restitution interest presents twice as strong a claim to judicial intervention as the reliance interest, since if A not only causes B to lose one unit but appropriates that unit to himself, the resulting discrepancy between A and B is not one unit but two.

On the other hand, the promisee who has actually relied on the promise, even though he may not thereby have enriched the promisor, certainly presents a more pressing case for relief than the promisee who merely demands satisfaction for his disappointment in not getting what was promised him. In passing from compensation for change of position to compensation for loss of expectancy we pass, to use Aristotle's terms again, from the realm of corrective justice to that of distributive justice. The law no longer seeks merely to heal a disturbed status quo, but to bring into being a new situation. It ceases to act defensively or restoratively, and assumes a more active role. With the transition, the justification for legal relief loses its self-evident quality. It is as a matter of fact no easy thing to explain why the normal rule of contract recovery should be that which measures damages by the value of the promised performance. Since this "normal rule" throws its shadow across our whole subject it will be necessary to examine the possible reasons for its existence. It may be said parenthetically that the discussion which follows, though directed primarily to the normal measure of recovery where damages are sought, also has relevance to the more general question, why should a promise which has not been relied on ever be enforced at all, whether by a decree of specific performance or by an award of damages? . . .

[The reference is to Aristotle, *Nicomachean Ethics*, 1132a-1132b.]

. . . the rule measuring damages by the expectancy may also be regarded as a prophylaxis against the losses resulting from detrimental reliance. Whatever tends to discourage breach of contract tends to prevent the losses occasioned through reliance. Since the expectation interest furnishes a more easily administered measure of recovery than the reliance interest, it will in practice offer a more effective sanction against contract breach. It is therefore possible to view the rule measuring damages by the expectancy in a quasi-criminal aspect, its purpose being not so much to compensate the promisee as to penalize breach of promise by the promisor. The rule enforcing the unrelied-on promise finds the same justification, on this theory, as an ordinance which fines a man for driving through a stop-light when no other vehicle is in sight.

In seeking justification for the rule granting the value of the expectancy there is no need, however, to restrict ourselves by the assumption, hitherto made, that the rule can only be intended to cure or prevent the losses caused by reliance. A justification can be developed from a less negative point of view. It may be said that there is not only a policy in favor of preventing and undoing the harms resulting from reliance, but also a policy in favor of promoting and facilitating reliance on business agreements. As in the case of the stop-light ordinance we are interested not only in preventing collisions but in speeding traffic. Agreements can accomplish little, either for their makers or for society, unless they are made the basis for action. When business agreements are not only made but are also acted on, the division of labor is facilitated, goods find their way to the places where they are most needed, and economic activity is generally stimulated. These advantages would be threatened by any rule which limited legal protection to the reliance interest. Such a rule would in practice tend to discourage reliance. The difficulties in proving reliance and subjecting it to pecuniary measurement are such that the business man knowing, or sensing, that these obstacles stood in the way of judicial relief would hesitate to rely on a promise in any case where the legal sanction was of significance to him. To encourage reliance we must therefore dispense with its proof. For this reason it has been found wise to make recovery on a promise independent of reliance, both in the sense that in some cases the promise is enforced though not relied on (as in the bilateral business agreement) and in the sense that recovery is not limited to the detriment incurred in reliance. . . .

The inference is therefore justified that the ends of the law of contracts and those of our economic system show an essential correspondence. One may explain this either on the ground that the law (mere superstructure and ideology) reflects inertly the conditions of economic life, or on the ground that economic activity has fitted itself into the rational framework of the law. Neither explanation would be true. In fact we are dealing with a situation in which law and society have interacted. The law measures damages by the expectancy *in part* because society views the expectancy as a present value; society views the expectancy as a present value *in part* because the law (for reasons more or less consciously articulated) gives protection to the expectancy.

SALLY WERTHEIM v. CHICOUTIMI PULP COMPANY
Quebec. Privy Council. [1911] A.C. 301

LORD ATKINSON: . . . And it is the general intention of the law that, in giving damages for breach of contract, the party complaining should, so far as it can be done by money, be placed in the same position as he would have been in if the contract had been performed. . . . That is a ruling principle. It is a just principle.

BOLLENBACK v. CONTINENTAL CASUALTY COMPANY
(1965) 414 P. 2d 802 (Oregon S.C.)

HOLMAN J.: Plaintiff was the holder of a policy issued by defendant under a group health and accident plan. The effective date of the policy was August 10, 1954. Premiums were due every six months and were paid by plaintiff. On September 28, 1963, while the policy was in full force and effect, plaintiff was hospitalized for six days with a back injury.

On November 12 he filed a claim with defendant for $107.33. He received no answer. On December 12 he wrote to the defendant calling to its attention that he had filed the claim and had received no acknowledgment. He still received no answer. On January 6, 1964, he wrote to the defendant a third time calling to its attention the filing of his claim and his previous correspondence. On January 20 both plaintiff and defendant wrote to each other. Plaintiff wrote to the assistant to the president of defendant, calling his attention to the plaintiff's payment of premiums, protesting the manner in which he was being ignored, enclosing copies of his previous letters, and asking for action. Defendant's correspondence was an answer to plaintiff's letter of January 6, informing plaintiff that his policy had lapsed in 1959 for nonpayment of premiums. On January 30 defendant wrote again to plaintiff. This letter specified that it was an answer to plaintiff's letter of January 20 to the assistant to the president of defendant. This letter contained the same information previously given plaintiff about the lapse of his policy and called to his attention their previous notification to this effect.

On January 25, plaintiff wrote two more letters to the defendant, one to the accounting department requesting information from its records concerning the premiums it had received from him and the other to the claims department requesting information about the reason for the policy's lapse. Plaintiff had received no answer to these letters when, on February 4, he filed the present case stating that he had elected to rescind the contract because of its repudiation by defendant and requesting judgment against defendant for all premiums previously paid under the policy in the sum of $2,166.50.

To plaintiff's complaint defendant filed an answer denying its repudiation of the contract, pleading the affirmative defense of mistake and tendering the amount of plaintiff's claim into court. A trial without a jury ensued which resulted in findings and conclusions by the judge to the effect that defendant had repudiated the contract by nonpayment of plaintiff's claim, that it had done so because of mistake and that plaintiff was entitled to recover as prayed for in his complaint.

Defendant assigns as error the court's denial of judgment in its favor at the close of testimony, its denial of a conclusion of law that plaintiff was not entitled to rescission, and the entering of the conclusion of law that plaintiff was entitled to recover. . . .

(5) Defendant contends plaintiff has adequate redress in an action for damages and that rescission is an extraordinary remedy available only in exceptional cases. The right to rescission and restitution is an alternative remedy where there has been repudiation or a material breach of the contract. 5 Williston, *Contracts* § 1455, at 4064 (Rev. ed. 1937) states as follows:

"The right of rescission and restitution generally exists as an alternative remedy to an action for damages where there has been repudiation or a material breach of contract. . . . This choice of remedies . . . has been developed very largely under cover of the fictitious declaration of *indebitatus assumpsit.* . . ."

In *Mohr* v. *Lear*, supra, 239 Or. at page 48, 395 P.2d at page 120, Justice Rossman stated for this court as follows:

"... When one party repudiates a contract or commits a total breach thereof, the injured party has an election to pursue one of three remedies: he may treat the contract as at an end and sue for restitution, he may sue for damages, or he may sue for specific performance in certain cases. *Armsby* v. *Grays Harbor Commercial Co.,* 62 Or. 173, 123 P. 32; *Massey* v. *Becker,* 90 Or. 461, 176 P. 425; *Cornely* v. *Campbell,* 95 Or. 345, 186 P. 563, 187 P. 1103; *Paine* v. *Meier & Frank Co.,* 146 Or. 40, 27 P.2d 315, 29 P.2d 531; *Macomber* v. *Waxbom,* 213 Or. 412, 325 P.2d 253."

(6) Before a party to a contract is justified in rescinding it because of its breach by the other party, the breach must be substantial. Rescission is not warranted when the breach is not substantial and does not defeat the objects of the parties. *Walton* v. *Denhart,* 226 Or. 254, 262, 359 P.2d 890 (1961); *Mohr* v. *Lear,* supra, 239 Or. at 48, 395 P.2d 117. Have the ends the contract was designed to subserve been effectively frustrated? *Mohr* v. *Lear,* supra at 50, 395 P.2d 117.

The purpose of the contract, in so far as plaintiff was concerned, was to obtain protection in the form of defendant's promise to pay claims in case of his disability. It would hardly seem arguable but that defendant's refusal to pay claims, based upon its position that the policy has lapsed, effectively frustrated this purpose and was a substantial breach. ...

The defendant next contends the return of all the premiums is not the proper measure of relief. The law relative to relief that can be secured by the insured when the insurer wrongfully repudiates the contract is in much confusion. One reason is the failure to distinguish an action for restitution upon rescission of the contract from an action for damages for its breach. The first is based on an annulment of the contract, the latter upon an assertion of the contract. As an illustration of the confusion the Annotation, 48 A.L.R. 107 (1927), uses the following language at page 110:

"As concerns the *measure of damages* for the wrongful cancellation, repudiation, or termination of the contract of insurance by the insurer, there seems to be an irreconcilable conflict between two principal lines of authority, as well as variations from these two rules. The first of these rules is to the effect that the insured may *recover as damages* the amount of premiums paid or premiums, with interest, where there has been a wrongful repudiation of the contract by the insurer, *and the assured has elected to rescind the contract rather than have it enforced.* The other of these two rules is to the effect that, if the assured is still in such a state of health that he can secure other insurance of like nature and kind, his measure of damages would be the difference between the cost of carrying the insurance which he has for the term stipulated for, and the cost of new insurance at the rate he would then be required to pay for a like term...." (Emphasis added.) See also Annotation 107 A.L.R. 1233, at 1235 (1937).

The fact is that recovery in each case is based upon a different theory. The purpose of rescission and restitution is to return the parties as near as possible to their respective positions prior to the formation of the contract so that each of the parties will be free to obtain his desired performance elsewhere. The purpose of an action for damages is to put the injured party as near as possible to the position where he would have been had the contract actually been performed. See 5 Corbin, Contracts § 996 (1964); *Federici* v. *Lehman,* supra, 230 Or. at 72-73, 368 P.2d 611. A more consistent adherence by the courts to this distinction would enable a more accurate analysis and classification of cases.

Whether relief for wrongful repudiation of an insurance contract is granted by way of restitution upon rescission or upon an action for damages for breach of contract, there is a split in authority whether or not a proper measure of recovery is the return of *all* premiums. Probably the majority opinion in the United States is that all premiums may be recovered. At least, it is referred to as the majority rule. See Annotation 48 A.L.R. 107, at 111. Oregon is among the jurisdictions having recognized this rule. In *Hinkson* v. *Kansas City Life Ins. Co.,* supra, the defendant issued several policies of life insurance to plaintiff and subsequently wrongfully canceled them, claiming the premiums had not been paid when in fact they had. Plaintiff brought an action for restitution of premiums paid under the policies and received a jury verdict. Upon appeal this court affirmed, stating at 93 Or. at page 500, 183 P. at page 33 as follows:

"The verdict was for the full amount of each alleged payment, with accrued interest. Upon the theory that the policies were in force until such time as they were canceled and that the plaintiff had the benefit of insurance, the defendant claims that it was entitled to a reduction or an offset. 2 Bacon on Benefit Societies and Life Insurance (3 ed. [1904]) § 376, lays down this rule:

" 'If a company wrongfully declares the policy forfeited and refuses to accept the premium when duly tendered, and to give the insured the customary renewal receipt, evidencing the continued life of the policy, the assured has his choice of three courses: He may tender the premium and wait until the policy becomes payable by its terms and then try the question of forfeiture; or he may sue in equity to have the policy continued in force; or he may elect to consider the policy at an end and bring an action to recover the just value of the policy, in which case the measure of damages is the amount of the premiums paid with interest on each from the time it was made.' "

It is apparent that this court at times has also failed to distinguish between an action for restitution upon rescission and one for damages.

One of the cases which makes the best argument for the position that the insured is entitled to the recovery of all premiums is *American Life Ins. Co.* v. *McAden*, 109 Pa. 399, 1 A. 256 (1885), which states at pages 404-405, 1 A. at 258, as follows:

"In the case at bar, the rights of the parties under the contract of insurance had attached, but the plaintiffs had never received any actual benefit from it. They may, in some sense perhaps, be said to have enjoyed the protection which the policy afforded in the event of the husband's death; but as that event did not occur, the policy had as yet been of no appreciable actual advantage to the plaintiff, and no real disadvantage to the defendant. The parties for anything that appears, upon the plaintiffs' recovery are placed precisely in the same situation they were in before the contract was made; for, although the company carried the risk, and the plaintiff Mary F. McAden, at all times during the continuance of the contract upon the happening of the event provided against was entitled to the indemnity it secured, yet the company has paid nothing and the plaintiffs have received nothing. As in the case of any other contract, the parties were each entitled during its continuance according to its terms.

"The policy when made was admittedly valid; the premiums which were paid were voluntarily paid upon that policy; the risk had been running for 10 years; the obligations of the contract were long since in force on both sides; and it is clear that the plaintiffs could not on their own mere motion rescind it, so as to recover back the premiums paid; but if after receiving these several premiums, the company, without right, refuse to receive further premiums as they mature, deny their obligation, and declare the contract at an end, the plaintiff, we think, may take the defendants at their word, treat the contract as rescinded, and recover back the premiums paid as so much money had and received for their use. Rescission or avoidance, properly so called, annihilates the contract and puts the parties in the same position as if it had never existed. . . ."

There are also cases which hold that upon rescission there should be offset against the recovered premiums the value of the coverage actually received by the insured. The case which best illustrates the argument for this position is *Watson v. Massachusetts Mut. Life Ins. Co.,* 78 U.S.App. D.C. 248, 140 F.2d 673 (1943), cert. den. 322 U.S. 746, 64 S.Ct. 1156, 88 L.Ed. 1578 (1944). It states, at page 677, as follows:

". . . Therefore, when the defendant disclaimed liability it committed an immediate, not an anticipatory, breach of its contract to furnish insurance protection. Had the plaintiff chosen to do so he could have sued for damages, which ordinarily would have been the difference in cost between the repudiated policy and other insurance taken out at the advanced age of the subject of the policy.

"However, instead of seeking damages plaintiff has elected to rescind. We must, therefore, consider the second question—whether his right to rescission entitles him to return of the premiums. Some cases permit the recovery of premiums when an insurance company repudiates its liability, without reduction for the benefit of the insurance afforded while the policy was in force. This is in conflict with the well-established rule that if a party seeks restitution after rescinding on account of a breach of an executory contract he must deduct the benefits, if any, which he has received under such contract.

"Only a total failure of consideration should entitle the plaintiff to recover all his premiums. In this case the plaintiff was actually receiving full insurance protection prior to defendant's repudiation. It would require the application of the principle of punitive damages to permit him to recover the premiums which represented what it cost the defendant to carry the insurance for his benefit. A rule allowing the recovery of all premiums upon repudiation of an insurance contract can logically apply only to a case of intentional misrepresentation where it is shown that the defendant was at no time during the life of the policy willing to meet its obligation. There are no facts alleged which show such an intentional misrepresentation. So far as we can determine from the complaint, plaintiff received full value for all premiums paid prior to the disclaimer. *His right to rescind the contract does not carry with it the right to recover such premiums to the extent that they represent the cost of carrying insurance protection actually furnished the plaintiff.* No payments in excess of such costs are alleged" (Emphasis added).

(9) The theory of relief on an action for restitution is placing both parties in statu quo ante. Because insurance protection cannot be returned to defendant, the theory of recovery necessarily means the return to plaintiff of all premiums less the value of any benefits the plaintiff has

actually received under the contract. *Watson* v. *Massachusetts Mutual Life Ins. Co.*, supra; *Lovell* v. *St. Louis Mut. Life Ins. Co.*, 111 U.S. 264, 274, 4 S.Ct. 390, 395, 28 L.Ed. 423, 427 (1884). Defendant contends plaintiff received the value of the protection for the ten year period which, upon loss, could have been asserted by plaintiff at any time despite defendant's subsequent disavowal of the contract. Defendant's assertion upon repudiating the contract was that the policy had lapsed in 1959. There is no reason to believe that after that date defendant would have been any more willing to honor claims by plaintiff than it was in 1964 when it refused payment. By its own assertion that the policy lapsed in 1959 defendant demonstrated its unwillingness to meet contractual obligations since that time. Plaintiff therefore could not have been receiving the protection for which his premiums were being paid.

(10) It is our opinion that *Watson* v. *Massachusetts Mutual Life Ins. Co.*, supra, and similar cases correctly state the amount recoverable in restitution by an action for money had and received upon rescission of the insurance contract because of repudiation by the other party. To the extent that *Hinkson* v. *Kansas City Life Ins. Co.*, supra, is in conflict, it is hereby expressly overruled. There must be deducted from the amount of premiums which are returned to him the value of the protection plaintiff has received.

Plaintiff has not claimed that the amount of premiums paid were in excess of the cost to defendant of carrying the risk of his policy. As was stated in *Watson* v. *Massachusetts Mut. Life Ins. Co.*, supra 78 U.S. App.D.C. 248, 140 F.2d at 677, "No payments in excess of such costs are alleged." Defendant, on the other hand, has not stated, nor did it prove when in 1959 it terminated plaintiff's policy. Not having shown this, it should be considered as terminated on January 1, 1959, or the time most unfavorable to defendant.

(11) As a result, plaintiff is not entitled to recover for those premiums paid prior to the year 1959 because it appears from the record that he received the protection these payments afforded. It would be inequitable for him to recover them. Defendant having wrongfully terminated plaintiff's policy in 1959, plaintiff is entitled to recover all premiums paid subsequent to January 1, 1959.

Finally, defendant claims as error the court's failure to admit into evidence certain questions and answers in a written interrogatory of one of defendant's witnesses. We have examined the interrogatory, and the contention has no merit.

(12) The case is remanded to the trial court with directions to modify the judgment to include only those sums paid by plaintiff to defendant subsequent to January 1, 1959. Interest on such payments is to be computed from the time the payments were actually made. The case of *Schuler* v. *Humphrey*, 198 Or. 458, 496-497, 257 P.2d 865 (1953), is not applicable because the policy was terminated by defendant in 1959 and thereafter plaintiff received no coverage for his premiums.

ANGLIA TELEVISION LTD. v. *REED*
[1972] 1 Q.B. 60 (C.A.)

LORD DENNING M.R.: Anglia Television Ltd., the plaintiffs, were minded in 1968 to make a film of a play for television entitled "The

Man in the Wood." It portrayed an American man married to an English woman. The American has an adventure in an English wood. The film was to last for 90 minutes. Anglia Television made many arrangements in advance. They arranged for a place where the play was to be filmed. They employed a director, a designer and a stage manager, and so forth. They involved themselves in much expense. All this was done before they got the leading man. They required a strong actor capable of holding the play together. He was to be on the scene the whole time. Anglia Television eventually found the man. He was Mr. Robert Reed, the defendant, an American who has a very high reputation as an actor. He was very suitable for this part. By telephone conversation on August 30, 1968, it was agreed by Mr. Reed through his agent that he would come to England and be available between September 9 and October 11, 1968, to rehearse and play in this film. He was to get a performance fee of £1,050, living expenses of £100 a week, his first class fares to and from the United States, and so forth. It was all subject to the permit of the Ministry of Labour for him to come here. That was duly given on September 2, 1968. So the contract was concluded. But unfortunately there was some muddle with the bookings. It appears that Mr. Reed's agents had already booked him in America for some other play. So on September 3, 1968, the agent said that Mr. Reed would not come to England to perform in this play. He repudiated his contract. Anglia Television tried hard to find a substitute but could not do so. So on September 11 they accepted his repudiation. They abandoned the proposed film. They gave notice to the people whom they had engaged and so forth.

Anglia Television then sued Mr. Reed for damages. He did not dispute his liability, but a question arose as to the damages. Anglia Television do not claim their profit. They cannot say what their profit would have been on this contract if Mr. Reed had come here and performed it. So, instead of claim for loss of profits, they claim for the wasted expenditure. They had incurred the director's fees, the designer's fees, the stage manager's and assistant manager's fees, and so on. It comes in all to £2,750. Anglia Television say that all that money was wasted because Mr. Reed did not perform his contract.

Mr. Reed's advisers take a point of law. They submit that Anglia Television cannot recover for expenditure incurred *before* the contract was concluded with Mr. Reed. They can only recover the expenditure *after* the contract was concluded. They say that the expenditure *after* the contract was only £854.65, and that is all that Anglia Television can recover.

The master rejected that contention: he held that Anglia Television could recover the whole £2,750; and now Mr. Reed appeals to this court.

Mr. Butler, for Mr. Reed, has referred us to the recent case of *Perestrello & Companhia Limitada* v. *United Paint Co. Ltd.*, The Times, April 16, 1969, in which Thesiger J. quoted the words of Tindal C.J. in *Hodges* v. *Earl of Litchfield* (1835) 1 Bing. N.C. 492, 498: "The expenses preliminary to the contract ought not to be allowed. The party enters into them for his own benefit at a time when it is uncertain whether there will be any contract or not." Thesiger J. applied those words, saying: "In my judgment pre-contract expenditure, though thrown away, is not recoverable."

I cannot accept the proposition as stated. It seems to me that a plaintiff in such a case as this has an election: he can either claim for loss of profits; or for his wasted expenditure. But he must elect between them. He cannot claim both. If he has not suffered any loss of profits—or if he cannot prove what his profits would have been—he can claim in the alternative the expenditure which has been thrown away, that is, wasted, by reason of the breach. That is shown by *Cullinane* v. *British "Rema" Manufacturing Co. Ltd.* [1954] 1 Q.B. 292, 303, 308.

If the plaintiff claims the wasted expenditure, he is not limited to the expenditure incurred *after* the contract was concluded. He can claim also the expenditure incurred *before* the contract, provided that it was such as would reasonably be in the contemplation of the parties as likely to be wasted if the contract was broken. Applying that principle here, it is plain that, when Mr. Reed entered into this contract, he must have known perfectly well that much expenditure had already been incurred on director's fees and the like. He must have contemplated—or, at any rate, it is reasonably to be imputed to him—that if he broke his contract, all that expenditure would be wasted, whether or not it was incurred before or after the contract. He must pay damages for all the expenditure so wasted and thrown away. This view is supported by the recent decision of Brightman J. in *Lloyd* v. *Stanbury* [1971] 1 W.L.R. 535. There was a contract for the sale of land. In anticipation of the contract—and before it was concluded—the purchaser went to much expense in moving a caravan to the site and in getting his furniture there. The seller afterwards entered into a contract to sell the land to the purchaser, but afterwards broke his contract. The land had not increased in value, so the purchaser could not claim for any loss of profit. But Brightman J. held, at p. 547, that he could recover the cost of moving the caravan and furniture, because it was "within the contemplation of the parties when the contract was signed." That decision is in accord with the correct principle, namely, that wasted expenditure can be recovered when it is wasted by reason of the defendant's breach of contract. It is true that, if the defendant had never entered into the contract, he would not be liable, and the expenditure would have been incurred by the plaintiff without redress; but, the defendant having made his contract and broken it, it does not lie in his mouth to say he is not liable, when it was because of his breach that the expenditure has been wasted.

I think the master was quite right and this appeal should be dismissed.

PHILLIMORE L.J.: I agree.

MEGAW L.J.: I also agree.

Appeal dismissed with costs.

A. I. OGUS, "DAMAGES FOR PRE-CONTRACT EXPENDITURE" (1972) 35 Mod. Law Rev. 423

. . . Three questions arise for consideration.

(1) *Should the plaintiff have the right to elect between his reliance interest and his expectation interest?* The principle of election is stated broadly without qualification and yet concealed behind the question is a

policy issue of fundamental importance. If the plaintiff is allowed recovery on the basis of his reliance interest the award will seek to put him in the position he would have been in if the contract had not been made. He may as a result be put in a better position than if the defendant had performed his contract. He may, in short, be able to protect himself against the consequences of having made a bad bargain. It may be sought to defend this result on the ground that it does not lie in the mouth of a person who has broken his contract to complain if the plaintiff is put in the position he would have been in if he had not entered into a contract with the defendant. But this view involves, by implication, a punitive consideration. The opposing view, that a plaintiff should never be put in a better position than if the contract had been performed, seems to be more consistent with the doctrine of compensation. If this latter view were to be preferred then the principle of election enunciated by Lord Denning M.R. would be subject to the qualification that recovery of reliance interest damages should not exceed the value of the expectation.

(2) *Should pre-contract expenditure form part of the reliance interest award*? Having allowed the plaintiff to elect between the reliance and expectation interests, Lord Denning M.R. decided that an award of reliance interest damages might include pre-contract expenditure. This is, with respect, a doubtful proposition. The measure of damages so envisaged would not put the plaintiffs in the position they would have been in if the contract had not been made, for the expenses would still have been incurred. The expenses were incurred not in reliance on the defendant's promise to perform—they were incurred merely in the hope that agreement with the defendant would be secured. There was indeed no causal connection between the loss (the wasted expenses) and either the making of the contract or its breach. In the United States of America these theoretical objections have proved decisive: all attempts to recover pre-contract expenditure (where there was no special agreement binding the defaulting party to pay) have failed. . . .

PITCHER v. SHOEBOTTOM
[1971] 1 O.R. 106 (Ont. H.C.)

Prior to August, 1958, the plaintiff made an oral agreement with the defendant S to buy certain land. This agreement was reduced to writing in the summer of 1959, and the plaintiff made some payments to S under the agreement. In 1960, S, in breach of the agreement, sold the land to a third person.

The plaintiff brought an action against S for specific performance of the agreement for the sale of land, for a declaration that the subsequent purchasers had no interest in the land, or, alternatively, for damages against all the defendants. The claims for specific performance and for damages against the other purchasers were dismissed, but the claim for damages against S was allowed.

LIEFF J.: . . . I find Shoebottom liable to the plaintiff for breach of contract but I also find that there is not sufficient evidence before me to ascertain the damages which the plaintiff suffered as a result of the breach. The only evidence led in this regard was contained in Kingshott's testimony where he stated that the value of the Pitcher lands is now more than $8,000 and in 1958 the value was $2,000. I therefore think it is necessary to direct a reference to the local Master at Parry Sound to ascertain the quantum of damage suffered by the plaintiff. . . .

Therefore in the present case the Master must ascertain the value of the Pitcher lands at the date when the Pitcher agreement was to close, and the difference between that value and the contract price represents the loss of bargain damage to which I find the plaintiff to be entitled. The plaintiff is also entitled to the return of the moneys which he paid on account of the purchase price but he is not entitled to any expenditures relating to investigating title or any other expenditures which had been necessary if the transaction had been closed as planned. On the other hand, the cost of the survey which the plaintiff would have acquired must be deducted if in fact he did not need to have that survey made as a result of the vendor's breach. These items all flow from the principle that damages are being awarded to put the plaintiff in the same position he would have been in at the time when the contract was breached by the vendor. Thus any items of expenditure which would have been necessary in order to close the deal must be taken into consideration.

The last problem relates to the problem that the agreement of purchase and sale did not specify a closing date. In such a circumstance, a reasonable time is implied. (*Shackleton* v. *Hayes*, [1954] 4 D.L.R. 81 at p. 89, *per* Cartwright J.) Hence, a reasonable time for closing the transaction would have been early 1960. It is a fact that a survey could not have been carried out prior to the spring of 1959 due to weather conditions. Therefore, early 1960 is the date which the Master should use in ascertaining the market value of the land at the date of the breach. . . .

QUESTION. Assuming that the land had increased in value between 1960 and 1970, why was the plaintiff not entitled to recover that increase? This aspect is discussed in section 7, below.

PROBLEM. In April, A agreed to sell 2,000 bushels of wheat to B at $1.03 a bushel, to be delivered July 25. On July 13, A sold the wheat to C at $1.16 a bushel. By July 25, the market price of wheat had dropped to $0.97 a bushel. B claims damages for breach of contract. Will he succeed?

See *Acme Mills & Elevator Co.* v. *Johnson* 133 S.W. 784 (1911).

NOTE. The measure of damages applied in *Pitcher* v. *Shoebottom*, based on the object of putting the plaintiff in as good a position, so far as money can do it, as performance, is often called the "normal" rule. The following cases deal with an exception to that rule where a vendor of land fails, without his fault, to give good title. The exception is often known as the rule in *Bain* v. *Fothergill*.

ONTARIO ASPHALT BLOCK CO. v. MONTREUIL
Ontario. Supreme Court of Canada. 1915. 52 S.C.R. 541

Ontario Asphalt Block Co. leased from Montreuil certain land and a water lot on a lake for ten years from 1903 with an option to purchase for $22,000, Montreuil promising to deliver a deed in fee simple free of incumbrances. Ontario Asphalt agreed to pay a rent of $1,000 a year and to construct a dock costing at least $6,000, which was to become Montreuil's property unless the option to purchase was exercised. In fact the Company

built a dock costing about $200,000. In 1908 it discovered that Montreuil
had only a life estate in the land, and that his children, all of whom were
over twenty-one in 1903, were entitled to the remainder. The water lot belonged to Montreuil in fee. At this time at least $80,000 had been spent
on the dock and factory. At a later trial Mr. Fleming, a lawyer and secretary of Ontario Asphalt, testified: "A. . . . we had not any idea but what
when we spent the first dollar on the property that we had purchased under
the option we could not afford to spend the money without doing that. . . .
Q. Why did you take the lease instead of buying out-right at the first? A.
Because $1,000 a year is less than 5% on the purchase price of $22,000,
and in addition to that $22,000 meant a lot to us in establishing a plant of
this sort. . . . His Lordship: And then you went right on after the discovery; after 1908 you went on? A. Yes, my Lord, we had to take care of
the business; it was a case of necessity. Mr. Rodd: What position would
your client have been in if you had not gone on? A. We would not have
been able to have taken care of the increase of business; business has to
grow or go back, we could not stand still." Attempts by the Company to
have Montreuil persuade his children to join in a deed were ignored. An
action was commenced for specific performance of the promise to convey
and for damages. Lennox J. at the trial awarded specific performance of the
promise to convey with an abatement or reduction in the purchase price
in the proportion in which a fee simple exceeded Montreuil's life estate in
value at the end of the term. He also awarded damages beyond the abatement because Montreuil "by his deliberate and continuous silence invited
and encouraged the plaintiff company to continue its improvements and
expenditures and to believe, as it evidently did believe, that the defendant
would be able to and would in fact carry out his contract." The Court of
Appeal varied the judgment by refusing the damages beyond the abatement.
Meredith C.J.O. said, for the Court, ". . . It is, I think, clear, upon principle,
that a purchaser who elects to take what the vendor can convey, with an
abatement of the purchase-money for a deficiency in title is not entitled to
anything beyond that. He is not bound to take what the vendor can give,
but may rescind the contract or claim damages for the breach of it. . . . To
give to the purchaser in a case such as this . . . damages for not getting that
which the vendor cannot convey, would be, I think, directly contrary to
what was decided in *Bain* v. *Fothergill*. . . ." Ontario Asphalt appealed to
the Supreme Court of Canada.

FITZPATRICK C.J. (dissenting): The judgment of the appeal court proceeds on the rule established by the jurisprudence of the English courts
that the contract for sale of real property is an exception to the ordinary
rules of law applicable to the question of the damages recoverable upon a
breach of contract.

This rule, first laid down in the case of *Flureau* v. *Thornhill* (1776), 2 W.
Bl. 1078; 96 E.R. 635, is that upon a contract for the purchase of real
estate if the vendor, without fraud, is incapable of making a good title the
intended purchaser is not entitled to any compensation for the loss of his
bargain. . . .

The rule in *Flureau* v. *Thornhill* finds little favour in the United States.
In Sedgwick on Damages, 9th ed., vol. 3, at p. 2121, we read:—

"If the defendant fails to convey because he has not a good title, he is
always liable in substantial damages. This is commonly called the United
States Supreme Court Rule, and represents one extreme of the series of

principles of which the highest English court has adopted the other extreme. It seems to be the correct one on principle."

I have thought it well to make the foregoing remarks as perhaps affording support to the appeal, but the real ground on which I rest my judgment is that in any event this case is outside the transactions to which in its widest interpretation the rule making exception to the general law of contracts has any application. . . .

Is it not obvious that the damages sustained by the appellant by reason of the failure of the respondent to implement his agreement are altogether special and by no means such loss of a bargain as alone is contemplated by the rule in *Flureau* v. *Thornhill*?

I think it is impossible to hold that such an agreement is to be governed by an admittedly anomalous rule of law in England, one based on reasons which may have little application here; presupposing entirely different conditions and intended to have application not to any damage sustained by the purchaser, but solely to the possible loss of his prospective profit on a resale of the property.

It cannot, I think, be necessary to treat this very special rule as absolutely inflexible regardless of all attendant conditions. . . .

Then as to the remarks of Chief Justice Meredith concerning the appellants' means of knowledge of the respondent's title. The latter being only tenant for life could, of course, make no demise to endure beyond his own life and, therefore, was in no position to make the lease for ten years, still less to covenant for its renewal for a further term of ten years. The lessee could not call for or dispute the lessor's title and until the option to purchase was exercised there was no contract for sale which would have entitled the appellant to call for the title.

The Chief Justice says that the appellant had the same opportunity of knowing what the nature of the respondent's title was as the respondent himself had. I think this must be going too far in any case; the respondent must surely as devisee under the will of his father be credited with better knowledge than the appellant. But in any case such knowledge would have been accidental in this particular case and cannot, I think, affect the principle involved.

That it would have been the more prudent course for the appellant when making the contract to have insisted on immediate preliminary proof of the respondent's title may be admitted and perhaps the company may have to suffer loss in any event as a consequence of not doing so, but that is no reason for relieving the respondent from the liability for failure to fulfil his contractual obligations. . . .

DAVIES J. (dissenting): The question in this case to be determined is whether the facts bring it within the rule of law laid down in *Bain* v. *Fothergill* (1873), L.R. 7 H.L. 158, that if a vendor of land without fraud is incapable of making a good title the intending purchaser is not entitled to recover compensation in damages for the loss of his bargain.

That rule has for many years been adopted as part of their jurisprudence by the Ontario courts and it is not my desire or intention to call that adoption in question.

The question arising in this appeal is not whether that rule is in force in Ontario, but whether the facts of this case bring it within the rule.

I understand a majority of the court holds that the rule applies and I desire to state very shortly my reasons for dissenting.

In the case of *Day* v. *Singleton*, [1899] 2 Ch. 320, the Court of Appeal held that:

"A purchaser of leasehold property which the vendor cannot assign without a licence from his lessor, is entitled to damages (beyond return of the deposit, with interest and expenses) for loss of his bargain by reason of the vendor's omission to do his best to procure such licence."

In delivering the judgment of the court, Lord Lindley M.R. said, p. 328:—

"Singleton never asked the lessors to accept Day as their tenant without a bar and consequently it would be for him, Singleton, to show that if he had asked them they would have refused."

Now, in the present case, it is contended that when the respondent Montreuil ascertained that he could not give the Ontario Asphalt Company a good title and that he had only a life estate, the remainder being in his children, it became his duty as between him and the Asphalt Company with whom he had covenanted to give a good title to do all that lay in his power to enable him to carry out his contract and to shew that he had applied to his children to join with him in conveying to the Asphalt Company and that they had refused to do so.

There was evidence that they did join with him upon request in the conveyance of other portions of the same property, but no evidence that he had applied to them to do so with respect to the property in dispute.

I confess I was much struck with this argument. If it was Montreuil's duty "to do all that lay in his power" to give appellants a good title, then it seems reasonable that it would be part of his duty to the Asphalt Company under the peculiar facts of this case to try and obtain the signature of his children to the deed and so complete his contracts with them. . . .

I do not desire, however, to rest my judgment upon that ground, but rather upon the ground that the special facts of this case and the special terms of the lease to the company with the option of purchase at the end of the term of ten years, provided six months' notice of the lessee's intention to purchase was given, together with the covenant on the lessor, Montreuil's part to convey a good title in fee simple, and a covenant from the lessee to build a dock on the demised premises within a year from the granting of the lease at a cost of *at least* $6,000, which dock was to become the property of the lessor at the end of the demised term, unless the lessee purchased under his option, all combine to convince me that this is not a case in which the rule in *Bain* v. *Fothergill* should be applied, but rather one in which on the neglect, refusal or inability of the lessor to comply with his covenant to give a good title free from incumbrance substantial damages should be awarded.

The evidence shewed that the company had after entering upon the lands under the lease erected an expensive manufacturing plant and docks partly on the leased upland and partly on the water lot in front of it as to which latter lot Montreuil had obtained a grant from the Crown, the whole expenditure aggregating $200,000, besides yearly betterments and improvements. A part of this expenditure at least was made in pursuance of respondent's covenant in the lease to expend at least $6,000 in dock construction.

The Appellate Division, reversing the trial judge, who had decreed specific performance and an abatement in the price amounting to substantial damages the latter to be determined on a reference, directed that the abatement in the purchase money should be based upon the value of the interest in the lands which the defendant could convey, having regard to the "purchase price" of the whole and refusing other damages beyond the abatement.

I cannot accede to the principle on which the Appellate Court has directed the abatement, basing it upon the stipulated purchase price and limiting it to that while ignoring the expenditure which as part of the consideration for the granting of the lease the lessees covenanted to make in building a dock on the lands.

This expenditure, the minimum amount of which was placed at $6,000 and the maximum of which might reach $60,000 or more, was really and substantially as much a part of the purchase price as the $22,000 mentioned and has just as much right to be considered in determining what abatement should be made as the latter sum.

But over and beyond that I do not think the case is one within the principle of *Bain* v. *Fothergill*, nor that substantial damages should be denied the vendee. That principle is as Lindley M.R. says in *Day* v. *Singleton*, "an anomalous rule based upon and justified by difficulties in shewing a good title to real property in this country, *but one which ought not to be extended in cases to which the reasons on which it is based do not apply.*"

Now, I take it that one of the reasons on which the rule is based is that it is not within the contemplation of both parties in the ordinary case of a contract for sale of land, that if the vendor is incapable of making a good title the intending purchaser is to receive compensation for the loss of his bargain beyond the expenses he has incurred.

But if there are special facts in the case shewing that it was and must have been in contemplation of both parties that failure on the part of the vendor to carry out his covenant to

"execute and deliver to the purchaser a good and sufficient deed in fee simple of the land."

must inevitably cause the intending purchaser great damage, as was the case here; and if, in addition, the purchaser has bound himself on the faith of this covenant to expend very large sums of money on dock and other improvements as the purchaser did here, then I say in the event of the vendor failing to give the good title he covenanted to give, the common law rule as to damages for breach of contract applies and the "anomalous rule" laid down in *Bain* v. *Fothergill*, relating to ordinary contracts between vendor and vendee with respect to the sale of lands does not apply.

I do not contend that any damages can be recovered in respect of anything that the purchaser did or incurred after he discovered the defect in the title; I limit my observations to those incurred by him before such discovery.

For these reasons, I would allow the appeal.

IDINGTON J.: I think the judgment appealed from is right for the reasons assigned in support thereof by the learned Chief Justice for Ontario.

The case seems a hard one, but that is no reason for our adopting bad law and disturbing the minds of those who prefer that well-settled law should be upheld. . . .

ANGLIN J.: Admitting the applicability of the rule laid down in *Bain* v. *Fothergill* to the original option in this case, the appellants have sought to bring it within the qualifications upon that rule recognized in *Day* v. *Singleton*. But in the latter case the Court of Appeal, as the judgment of Lord

Lindley shews (p. 328), took the view that the correspondence between Singleton's solicitors and the lessor established that if Singleton (the vendor of the leasehold) did not actually procure the refusal of the lessors' assent to the assignment to Day, he
"certainly made no effort to obtain it . . . as it was his duty to do . . . and it ought to be inferred as against Singleton that the lessors would have accepted Day if Singleton had asked him to do so."

The decision there proceeded upon the fact, held to have been sufficiently proven, that it was within the vendor's powers to carry out his contract and that he refused or neglected to take the means available. Here the plaintiffs rely upon the fact that the defendant maintained silence after his inability to make title had become known and they had asked him to obtain confirmation of the option from the remaindermen, the fact that the remaindermen had (under what circumstances, or for what consideration does not appear) confirmed the title of some other grantees of the defendant who were in like plight with the plaintiffs, and the further fact that, in answer to the plaintiff's suit for specific performance, other defences were set up in addition to that of inability to make title. I am quite unable to find in these bald facts—and the plaintiffs have nothing else—enough to warrant an inference that the defendant after discovery of the defect in his title made no effort to procure the concurrence of the remaindermen; still less do I find enough to warrant the inference that such an effort, if made would have been successful.

The appeal, in my opinion, fails and should be dismissed with costs.

[The opinion of Idington J. is drastically cut. Duff and Brodeur JJ. agreed in dismissing the appeal. The decision is thus four to two for dismissal.]

NOTE. In *Bain* v. *Fothergill*, upon which the majority relied, the defendants paid into Court a sum sufficient to cover the deposit, interest and expenses. What happened to that money is not apparent from the report, but it would appear that the Court made no decision of the question of damages based on reliance. Is there good reason for distinguishing between the expectation interest and the reliance interest here? Is there good reason for following *Bain* v. *Fothergill* in Canada, where questions of title are somewhat simpler due to the widespread use of the registry system or the Torrens system?

MONTREUIL v. *THE ONTARIO ASPHALT BLOCK COMPANY.* 1922. 63 S.C.R. 401. After getting their order for specific performance of the conveyance of the water lot. and the estate pur autre vie in the land, Ontario Asphalt remained in possession until August of 1918. Montreuil having died in January of 1918 the children brought an action for ejectment. Ontario Asphalt relied on what is now section 38 (1) of *The Conveyancing and Law of Property Act*, R.S.O. 1960, c. 66, which provides:

"38. (1) Where a person makes lasting improvements on land under the belief that it is his own, he or his assigns are entitled to a lien upon it to the extent of the amount by which its value is enhanced by the improvements, or are entitled or may be required to retain the land if the court is of opinion or requires that this should be done, according as may under all circumstances of the case be most just, making compensation for the land, if retained, as the court directs."

The Court held, Idington and Duff JJ. dissenting, that a lessee with an option to purchase was not an "owner" within the meaning of the section.

Anglin J. said, at p. 426, "This statute gives the court the extraordinary power of depriving a lawful owner of his property against his will, although for a compensation. . . . The condition on which a jurisdiction so much in derogation of common law right is conferred must be strictly construed and fully satisfied."

THE VENDORS AND PURCHASERS ACT
Ontario. Revised Statutes. 1970. Chapter 478

4. Every contract for the sale and purchase of land shall, unless other-wide stipulated, be deemed to provide that . . .

(c) the vendor has thirty days in which to remove any objection made to the title, but if he is unable or unwilling to remove any objection that the purchaser is not willing to waive, he may cancel the contract and return any deposit made but is not otherwise liable to the purchaser . . .

[This section was first introduced in 1926, The Vendors and Purchasers Act, 1926 (Ontario, c. 41). What effect, if any, would this section have had in the Ontario Asphalt case?]

WROTH v. TYLER
[1974] Ch. 30

The Plaintiffs, a young married couple, made an agreement to purchase defendant's house. The day after the agreement was made, the defendant's wife registered a charge against the title under the Matrimonial Homes Act, 1967, an English statute designed to protect the wife from eviction from the matrimonial home. The registration of such a charge was binding on a subsequent purchaser. The plaintiffs consequently demanded removal of the charge. The defendant's wife refused to remove the charge and the plaintiffs sued for specific performance with compensation, or damages. One of the issues in connection with the claim for damages was whether or not the rule in *Bain* v. *Fothergill* applied.

[The case is further reported in section 7, below.]

MEGARRY J.: . . . I turn to damages. The fourth main point is whether the damages are limited to those recoverable under the rule in *Bain* v. *Fothergill*, L.R. 7 H.L. 158. The rule is conveniently stated in Williams, *The Contract of Sale of Land* (1930), p. 128:

"Where the breach of contract is occasioned by the vendor's inability, without his own fault, to show a good title, the purchaser is entitled to recover as damages his deposit, if any, with interest, and his expenses incurred in connection with the agreement, but not more than nominal damages for the loss of his bargain."

What is said by Mr. Lyndon-Stanford is, quite simply, that the statutory charge in favour of the defendant's wife is a defect in title within the rule, just as much as any other charge would be, whether legal or equitable, and so the rule applies.

In *Bain* v. *Fothergill* itself, a distinction was drawn between matters of conveyancing and matters of title. Lord Hatherley said, at p. 209:

"Whenever it is a matter of conveyancing, and not a matter of title, it is the duty of the vendor to do everything that he is enabled to do by force of his own interest, and also by force of the interest of others whom he can compel to concur in the conveyance."

This was said in relation to *Engell* v. *Fitch*, L.R. 4 Q.B. 659, where the principle of *Bain* v. *Fothergill*, as exemplified in its ancestor, *Flureau* v. *Thornhill* (1776) 2 Wm.Bl. 1078, was held not to apply to mortgagees who sold with vacant possession but refused to evict the mortgagor who was in possession. The right to vacant possession may be regarded as a matter of conveyancing rather than of title, in that vacant possession is required to be delivered only on completion, and a title may be in perfect order eevn though the vendor is out of possession. By contrast, in *Bain* v. *Fothergill*, L.R. 7 H.L. 158, the vendor had a mere equitable title to the lease of the mining royalty that he had contracted to sell, and he unexpectedly failed to obtain the lessor's consent to the assignment that would have enabled him to convey what he had contracted to sell. That was plainly a matter of title, and the rule applied. That in turn may be contrasted with *Day* v. *Singleton* [1899] 2 Ch. 320, where the lessor's consent was requisite for the assignment of the lease which had been sold, and, as I have mentioned, the vendor either did not really try to obtain the consent, or else had induced the lessors to withhold it. The Court of Appeal held that damages for loss of the bargain were recoverable in that the vendor had failed in his duty to obtain the lessor's consent. At p. 329, Lord Lindley M.R. and Rigby L.J. said of the rule in *Bain* v. *Fothergill* that it was "an anomalous rule based upon and justified by difficulties in showing a good title to real property in this country, but one which ought not to be extended to cases in which the reasons on which it is based do not apply."

Certainly the courts have proved ready to find grounds for holding that cases do not fall within the rule. In *In re Daniel* [1917] 2 Ch. 405 a testator had, before his death, contracted to sell land which, with other property, was comprised in a mortgage. The mortgagee refused to release the land upon payment of an appropriate fraction of what was due under the mortgage, and the testator's estate was insufficient to pay off the entire mortgage. Sargant J. held that the rule in *Bain* v. *Fothergill*, L.R. 7 H.L., 158 did not apply, for the failure of the executors to perform the contract was due not to any defect in title, but to the insufficiency of the testator's estate, and he refused to extend the anomalous rule in *Bain* v. *Fothergill* (or *Flureau* v. *Thornhill*, 2 Wm.Bl. 1078) to a case which was not within the spirit of the rule. In *Braybrooks* v. *Whaley* [1919] 1 K.B. 435, a mortgagee contracted to sell land, but without obtaining, either before or after the contract, the leave of the court made requisite by the Courts (Emergency Powers) Act 1914. Again the rule was held not to apply. Horridge J. said that the failure to seek leave of the court was not a matter of title within the rule, but a matter of completing the contract by conveyance, and Salter J. held that the contention that the application, if made, would have failed had not been established. Mr. Lyndon-Stanford submitted that this decision was wrong, at all events in so far as it proceeded on the footing that the vendor was under a duty to take proceedings to remove the obstacle to completion, for he had no clear right to the grant of leave by the court but merely a hope or prospect that the discretionary powers of the court would be exercised in his favour.

Various other cases were cited, including *Thomas* v. *Kensington* [1942]

2 K.B. 181 and *J. W. Cafés Ltd.* v. *Brownlow Trust Ltd.* [1950] 1 All E.R. 894, but I do not think I need discuss them. None of the cases cited to me plainly covers the facts of the present case, or answers the question whether the wife's right is a defect in title within the principle of *Bain* v. *Fothergill*, L.R. 7 H.L. 158. At one stage Mr. Lyndon-Stanford observed that her right was a very strange right, but whatever it was, it was a defect in title within the rule: and Mr. Blackburne was constrained to accept that it constituted some sort of defect in title, though he said that it was not a defect of a type which brought *Bain* v. *Fothergill* into play, particularly as the rule was anomalous and ought not to be extended.

Let me consider the consequences of holding that the rule applies, in days when a new verb of doubtful etymology has been attracting considerable attention, namely, the verb "to gazump." The most helpful approach seems to be to take the matter by stages. First, if the mere existence of the wife's charge, before registration, creates a defect in title within the rule, then Parliament has at a blow imposed a defect in title on many millions of homes vested in one or other of the parties to a marriage. On January 1, 1968, millions of perfectly good titles became defective. I should be slow indeed to impute to Parliament any intention to produce this result. This is all the more striking in the case of registered land, where the operation of the rule in *Bain* v. *Fothergill*, L.R. 7 H.L. 158 might be expected to be minimal; for the main purpose of the Land Registration Acts is to simplify titles and conveyancing. Furthermore, if the mere existence of an unregistered charge under the Act constitutes a defect in title, it is a singularly impotent defect, for on completion of a sale it will be void against the purchaser for want of registration. If instead the vendor refused to complete, plainly he would be refusing to take a step which would remove the defect from his title; and on the principle of *Day* v. *Singleton* [1899] 2 Ch. 320 he would appeal to *Bain* v. *Fothergill* in vain. As at the date of the contract in this case, I therefore cannot see how the rule in *Bain* v. *Fothergill* could have applied. In other words, looking at matters immediately after the contract had been made, the case could not, in my judgment, be said to fall within either the spirit or the letter of the rule in *Bain* v. *Fothergill*.

When in this case the wife's rights were registered the day after the contract had been made, a different situation arose; for then her rights could no longer be destroyed by completing the sale. On the footing that the wife's rights thereupon became capable of attracting the rule in *Bain* v. *Fothergill*, does the rule apply to cases where, at the date of the contract, the necessary conditions for the application of the rule did not exist, but those conditions first came into being after the contract had been made? It has not been suggested that there is any authority bearing directly on this point. The action is an action for damages for breach of contract, and I should be slow to hold that some supervening event could bring within the rule a case initially outside it. Furthermore, the basis of the rule is that of the contract having been made against a background of the uncertainty of titles to land in England: see, for example, *Bain* v. *Fothergill*, L.R. 7 H.L. 158, 210, *per* Lord Hatherley. In *Engell* v. *Fitch*, L.R. 4 Q.B. 659, 666, Kelly C.B. said that the rule was "founded entirely on the difficulty that a vendor often finds in making a title to real estate, not from any default on his part, but from his ignorance of the strict legal state of his title."

As I have indicated, a rule laid down for defects in title which lay concealed in title deeds which were often, in the phrase attributed to Lord Westbury, "difficult to read, disgusting to touch, and impossible to understand," seems singularly inapposite to the effect of a modern statute upon registered land, with its aseptic certainty and clarity of title.

Furthermore, the rule is anomalous, and, as was shown by the Court of Appeal in *In re Compton* [1945] Ch. 123, 139, 140 (in an entirely different field), where the court encounters an anomalous rule, it is in general better to confine the anomaly within its established sphere than to extend the anomaly to analogous cases. Here, the wife's rights are the creature of statute, imposed generally, and in no way dependent upon the vicissitudes of a particular title to property. The charge itself is sui generis. The wife has personal rights of occupation which she cannot deal with, thus differing greatly from other charges, such as legal or equitable charges for money. If her rights are rights of property at all, they are at least highly idiosyncratic. They do not seem to me to fall within the spirit or intendment of the rule in *Bain* v. *Fothergill*, L.R. 7 H.L. 158; and I so hold. . . .

2. PROBLEMS IN MEASURING DAMAGES

COTTER v. GENERAL PETROLEUMS LTD.
Alberta. Supreme Court of Canada. [1950] 4 D.L.R. 609

A lease for 160 acres contained a covenant on the part of the lessee (the plaintiff, and appellant) to commence drilling for oil within six months and to drill to a depth of 5,500 feet. He could obtain an extension of six months on payment to the lessor of $1,000. The lessee sublet 80 acres to the respondents who agreed to drill the well, the cost of drilling to be recovered as a share in the sale of the product of the well. In May and June, 1948, wells about a mile away were abandoned after being drilled to about 5,500 feet and the respondents decided at the end of June, 1948, not to commence drilling. The appellant lessee took the position that the respondents were bound to drill a well, and the respondents replied that in view of the location it would be a needless waste of money. On August 31, 1948, the appellant sued for $100,000 damages. The trial judge held that the respondents were obliged to drill by August 1, 1948 and were in breach. He assessed damages at $54,500, being $53,500, the admitted cost of the drilling, and $1,000 paid by the appellant for an extension of the lease. Geologists gave evidence on the likelihood of there being any oil, and the finding was that the chances were far from favourable but couldn't be completely ruled out. The Court of Appeal reversed on other grounds.

CARTWRIGHT J.: . . . I respectfully agree with the learned trial judge that the respondents are liable in damages to the appellant for failure to drill a well to the prescribed depth. . . . It remains to be considered on what principle and at what amount the damages should be assessed. . . . In the case at bar if the respondents had carried out the contract the appellant would not have had to pay the $1,000 for a 6 months' extension which he did in fact pay to the head-lessor. The circumstances as to the necessity of making such payment were known to the parties and I agree with the learned trial Judge that that sum is recoverable. What further benefits would have resulted to the appellant from the performance of the contract? If the respondents had drilled the well to the prescribed depth and it had proved a producer, the appellant would have received, (a) his share of the proceeds and, (b) the benefit of having the head lease validated, by the performance of the lessee's covenant to drill, not only as to the 80 acres described in the sublease but as to the whole 160 acres described in the head lease. If on the other hand, as, from the evidence of the geologists, would seem much more probable, the well had proved a failure the appellant would not have received benefit (a) but would have received benefit (b). It must be remembered however that as a result of the respondents' breach the appellant holds the whole 160 acres free from any claim of the respondents. No part of the consideration which under the contract would have passed to the respondents has passed, except that from April 21, 1948, until some time in June, 1948, when they repudiated the agreement, the respondents had rights in the 80 acres and the appellant was not free to deal therewith. Under these circumstances, I do not think that the cost of drilling is the proper measure of damages. Suppose that instead of the consideration set out in the contract the appellant had agreed to pay the respondents $53,500 to drill the well and the respondents had repudiated the contract before the date set for the commencement of the work and before any monies had been paid to them. In such a case by analogy to the rule in the case of building contracts the measure of damages would seem to be the difference (if any) between the price of the work agreed upon and the cost to which the appellant was actually put in its completion. I think it will be found that those cases in which it has been held that the cost of drilling is the proper measure of damages are cases where the consideration to be given for the drilling had actually passed to the defendant. Examples of such cases are *Cunningham* v. *Insinger*, [1924], 2 D.L.R. 433, S.C.R. 8, and *Pell* v. *Shearman* (1855), 10 Exch. 766, 156 E.R. 650 (a contract to sink a shaft).

The appellant did not seek to put his case on the ground that by reason of the breach he stood to lose the head lease, but rather that he intended to make and was in process of making other arrangements to have a well drilled. In my view, the proper measure of his damages under the circumstances of this case is the difference between the value to him of the consideration for which the respondents agreed to drill the well and the value to him of the consideration which, acting reasonably, he should find it necessary to give to have the well drilled by others. I am unable to find in the record evidence on which the damages can be assessed on this basis. It is well settled that the mere fact that the damages are difficult to estimate and cannot be assessed with certainty does not relieve the party in default of the necessity of paying damages and is no ground for awarding only nominal damages, but the onus of proving his damages still rests upon the plaintiff. The evidence of the appellant given at the trial on December 3, 1948, was to the effect that he and his associates had been and still were in negotiation with an oil company but that they had found themselves forced to deal with the whole 160 acres instead of 80 acres. As Mr. Steer pointed out there is no evidence as to the terms offered by such company and such terms may have been more or less advantageous to the appellant than those in the contract sued on. It would have been open to the appellant to have delayed bringing his action until the completion of his arrangements to have the well drilled by which time the damages, if any, would have been more easily ascertained. But the appellant, as he had a right to do, brought his action to trial before that date. There is no complaint that any evidence he wished to tender in support of his claim for damages was rejected, nor was there any request made for a reference to fix the damages and the case must be decided upon the evidence in the record. In my view, there is no evidence to support an award of damages other than the $1,000 paid for the extension of the time for drilling. If the evidence showed that the appellant had suffered or must of necessity suffer substantial damages, over and above the $1,000 already mentioned, by reason of the respondents' breach, the Court should, I think, seek some means of arriving at a proper assessment, but in my view the most that the evidence can be said to indicate is a probability of some loss. It is possible that there has been no loss at all. . . .

[Appeal allowed. Rinfret C.J.C. joined with Kerwin J. in a judgment allowing the appeal, and Fauteux J. joined with Cartwright J. Locke J. dissented on other grounds.]

CARSON v. WILLITTS
(1930) 65 O.L.R. 456 (Ont. Appellate Division)

A contract to bore three oil wells. The defendant bored one well and refused to carry on. MASTEN J.A.: "Then what is the basis on which this court should now direct the damages to be assessed? In my opinion, what the plaintiff lost by the refusal of the defendant to bore two more wells was a sporting or gambling chance that valuable oil or gas would be found when the two further wells were bored. If the wells had been bored and no oil or gas of value had been found, the effect would be that the plaintiff has lost nothing by the refusal of the defendant to go on boring. On the other hand, if valuable oil or gas had been discovered, by the boring of these two wells, he had lost substantially. It may not be easy to compute what that chance was worth to the plaintiff, but the difficulty in estimating the quantum is no reason for refusing to award any damages.

"In *Mayne on Damages*, 10th ed., p. 6, it is said:

" 'A distinction must be drawn between cases where absence of evidence makes it impossible to assess damages, and cases where the assessment is difficult because of the nature of the damage proved. In the former case only nominal damages can be recovered. In the latter case, however, the difficulty of assessment is no ground for refusing substantial damages.' "

GROVES v. JOHN WUNDER CO.
Minnesota. Supreme Court. 1939. 286 N.W. 235

STONE J.: Action for breach of contract. Plaintiff got judgment for a little over $15,000. Sorely disappointed by that sum, he appeals.

In August, 1927, S. J. Groves & Sons Company, a corporation (hereinafter mentioned simply as Groves), owned a tract of 24 acres of Minneapolis suburban real estate. It was served or easily could be reached by railroad trackage. It is zoned as heavy industrial property. But for lack of development of the neighborhood its principal value thus far may have been in the deposit of sand and gravel which it carried. The Groves company had a plant on the premises for excavating and screening the gravel. Near by defendant owned and was operating a similar plant.

In August, 1927, Groves and defendant made the involved contract. For the most part it was a lease from Groves, as lessor, to defendant as lessee; its term seven years. Defendant agreed to remove the sand and gravel and to leave the property "at a uniform grade, substantially the same as the grade now existing at the roadway . . . on said premises, and that in stripping the overburden . . . it will use said overburden for the purpose of maintaining and establishing said grade."

Under the contract defendant got the Groves screening plant. The transfer thereof and the right to remove the sand and gravel made the consideration moving from Groves to defendant, except that defendant incidentally got rid of Groves as a competitor. On defendant's part it paid Groves $105,000. So that from the outset, on Groves' part the contract was executed except for defendant's right to continue using the property for the stated term. (Defendant had a right to renewal which it did not exercise.)

Defendant breached the contract deliberately. It removed from the premises only "the richest and best of the gravel" and wholly failed, according to the findings, "to perform and comply with the terms, conditions, and provisions of said lease . . . with respect to the condition in which the surface of the demised premises was required to be left." Defendant surrendered the premises, not substantially at the grade required by the contract "nor at any uniform grade." Instead, the ground was "broken, rugged, and uneven." Plaintiff sues as assignee and successor in right of Groves.

As the contract was construed below, the finding is that to complete its performance 288,495 cubic yards of overburden would need to be excavated, taken from the premises, and deposited elsewhere. The reasonable cost of doing that was found to be upwards of $60,000. But, if defendant had left the premises at the uniform grade required by the lease, the reasonable value of the property on the determinative date would have been only $12,160. The judgment was for that sum, including interest, thereby nullifying plaintiff's claim that cost of completing the contract rather than difference in value of the land was the measure of damages. The gauge of damage adopted by the decision was the difference between the market value of plaintiff's land in the condition it was when the contract was made and what it would have been if defendant had performed. The one question for us arises upon plaintiff's assertion that he was entitled, not to that difference in value, but to the reasonable cost to him of doing the work called for by the contract which defendant left undone.

1. Defendant's breach of contract was wilful. There was nothing of good faith about it. Hence, that the decision below handsomely rewards bad faith and deliberate breach of contract is obvious. That is not allowable. Here the rule is well settled, . . . that where the contractor wilfully and fraudulently varies from the terms of a construction contract he cannot sue thereon and have the benefit of the equitable doctrine of substantial performance. That is the rule generally. . . .

2. In reckoning damages for breach of a building or construction contract, the law aims to give the disappointed promisee, so far as money will do it, what he was promised. . . .

Never before, so far as our decisions show, has it even been suggested that lack of value in the land furnished to the contractor who had bound himself to improve it any escape from the ordinary consequences of a breach of the contract. . . .

Even in case of substantial performance in good faith, the resulting defects being remediable, it is error to instruct that the measure of damage is "the difference in value between the house as it was and as it would have been if constructed according to contract." The "correct doctrine" is that the cost of remedying the defect is the "proper" measure of damages. . . .

Value of the land (as distinguished from the value of the intended product of the contract, which ordinarily will be equivalent to its reasonable cost) is no proper part of any measure of damages for wilful breach of a building contract. The reason is plain.

The summit from which to reckon damages from trespass to real estate is its actual value at the moment. The owner's only right is to be compensated for the deterioration in value caused by the tort. That is all he has lost. But not so if a contract to improve the same land has been breached by the contractor who refuses to do the work, especially where, as here, he has been paid in advance. The summit from which to reckon damages for that wrong is the hypothetical peak of accomplishment (not value) which would have been reached had the work been done as demanded by the contract.

The owner's right to improve his property is not trammeled by its small value. It is his right to erect thereon structures which will reduce its value. If that be the result, it can be of no aid to any contractor who declines performance. As said long ago in *Chamberlain* v. *Parker*, 45 N.Y. 569, 572:

"A man may do what he will with his own, . . . and if he chooses to erect a monument to his caprice or folly on his premises, and employs and pays another to do it, it does not lie with a defendant who has been so employed and paid for building it, to say that his own performance would not be beneficial to the plaintiff."

To the same effect is *Restatement, Contracts*, s. 346, p. 576, Illustrations of Subsection (1), par. 4.

Suppose a contractor were suing the owner for breach of a grading contract such as this. Would any element of value, or lack of it, in the land have any relevance in reckoning damages? Of course not. The contractor would be compensated for what he had lost, i.e., his profit. Conversely, in such a case as this, the owner is entitled to compensation for what he has lost, that is, the work or structure which he has been promised, for which he has paid, and of which he has been deprived by the contractor's breach.

To diminish damages recoverable against him in proportion as there is presently small value in the land would favor the faithless contractor. It would also ignore and so defeat plaintiff's right to contract and build for the future. To justify such a course would require more of the prophetic vision than judges possess. This factor is important when the subject matter is trackage property in the margin of such an area of population and industry as that of the Twin Cities. . . .

[Under] a construction contract, the thing lost by a breach such as we have here is a physical structure or accomplishment, a promised and paid for alteration in land. That is the "injury" for which the law gives him compensation. Its only appropriate measure is the cost of performance.

It is suggested that because of little or no value in his land the owner may be unconscionably enriched by such a reckoning. The answer is that there can be no unconscionable enrichment, no advantage upon which the law will frown, when the result is but to give one party to a contract only what the other has promised; particularly where, as here, the delinquent has had full payment for the promised performance.

3. It is said by the Restatement, Contracts, s 346, Comment b:

"Sometimes defects in a completed structure cannot be physically remedied without tearing down and rebuilding, at a cost that would be imprudent and unreasonable. The law does not require damages to be measured by a method requiring such economic waste. If no such waste is involved, the cost of remedying the defect is the amount awarded as compensation for failure to render the promised performance."

The "economic waste" declaimed against by the decisions applying that rule has nothing to do with the value in money of the real estate, or even with the product of the contract. The waste avoided is only that which would come from wrecking a physical structure completed, or nearly so, under the contract. . . . Absent such waste, as it is in this case, the rule of the Restatement, Contracts, s 346, is that "the cost of remedying the defect is the amount awarded as compensation for failure to render the promised performance." That means that defendants here are liable to plaintiff for the reasonable cost of doing what defendants promised to do and have wilfully declined to do. . . .

The judgment must be reversed with a new trial to follow.

JULIUS J. OLSON J. (dissenting): . . . Since there is no issue of fact, we should limit our inquiry to the single legal problem presented: What amount in money will adequately compensate plaintiff for his loss caused by defendant's failure to render performance? . . .

As the rule of damages to be applied in any given case has for its purpose compensation, not punishment, we must be ever mindful that, "if the application of a particular rule for measuring damages to given facts results in more than compensation, it is at once apparent that the wrong rule has been adopted." *Crowley* v. *Burns Boiler Co.*, 110 N.W. 969, 973.

We have here then a situation where, concededly, if the contract had been performed, plaintiff would have had property worth, in round numbers, no more than $12,000. If he is to be awarded damages in an amount exceeding $60,000 he will be receiving at least 500 per cent more than his property, properly leveled to grade by actual performance, was intrinsically worth when the breach occurred. To so conclude is to give him something far beyond what the parties had in mind or contracted for. There is no showing made, nor any finding suggested, that this property was unique, specially desirable for a particular or personal use, or of special value as to location or future use different from that of other property surrounding it. Under the circumstances here appearing, it seems clear that what the parties contracted for was to put the property in shape for general sale. And the lease contemplates just that, for by the terms thereof defendant agreed "from time to time, as the sand and gravel are removed from the various lots . . . leased, it will surrender said lots to the lessor" if of no further use to defendant "in connection with the purposes for which this lease is made."

The theory upon which plaintiff relies for application of the cost of performance rule must have for its basis cases where the property or the improvement to be made is unique or personal instead of being of the kind ordinarily governed by market values. His action is one at law for damages, not for specific performance. As there was no affirmative showing of any peculiar fitness of this property to a unique or personal use, the rule to be applied is, I think, the one applied by the court. The cases bearing directly upon this phase so hold. Briefly, the rule here applicable is this: Damages recoverable for breach of a contract to construct is the difference between

dissenting
judges' claim

the market value of the property in the condition it was when delivered to and received by plaintiff and what its market value would have been if defendant had fully complied with its terms. . . .

No one doubts that a party may contract for the doing of anything he may choose to have done (assuming what is to be done is not unlawful) "although the thing to be produced had no marketable value." In *Restatement, Contracts*, s. 346, pp. 576, 577, Illustrations of Subsection (1), par. 4, the same thought is thus stated:

"A contracts to construct a monumental fountain in B's yard for $5,000, but abandons the work after the fountain has been laid and $2,800 has been paid by B. The contemplated fountain is so ugly that it would decrease the number of possible buyers of the place. The cost of completing the fountain would be $4,000. B can get judgment for $1,800, the cost of completion less the part of price unpaid."

But that is not what plaintiff's predecessor in interest contracted for. Such a provision might well have been made, but the parties did not. They could undoubtedly have provided for liquidated damages for nonperformance. . . or they might have determined in money what the value of performance was considered to be and thereby have contractually provided a measure for failure of performance.

The opinion also suggests that this property lies in an area where the owner might rightly look for future development, being in a so-called industrial zone, and that as such he should be privileged to so hold it. This he may of course do. But let us assume that on May 1, 1934, condemnation to acquire this area had so far progressed as to leave only the question of price (market value) undetermined; that the area had been graded in strict conformity with the contract but that the actual market value of the premises was only $12,160, as found by the court and acquiesced in by plaintiff, what would the measure of his damages be? Obviously, the limit of his recovery could be no more than the then market value of his property. In that sum he has been paid with interest and costs; and he still has the fee title to the premises, something he would not possess if there had been condemnation. In what manner has plaintiff been hurt beyond the damages awarded? As to him "economic waste" is not apparent. Assume the defendant abandoned the entire project without taking a single yard of gravel therefrom but left the premises as they were when the lease was made, could plaintiff recover damages upon the basis here established? The trouble with the prevailing opinion is that here plaintiff's loss is not made the basis for the amount of his recovery but rather what it would cost the defendant. No case has been decided upon that basis until now. Plaintiff asserts that he knows of no rule "giving a different measure of damages for public contracts and for private contracts in case of nonperformance." It seems to me there is a clear distinction to be drawn with respect to the application of the rule for recoverable damages in case of breach of a public works contract from that applicable to contracts between private parties. The construction of a public building, a sewer, drainage ditch, highway, or other public work, permits of no application of the market value doctrine. There simply is and can be no "market value" as to such. And for this cogent reason there can be but one rule of damages to apply, that of cost of completion of the thing contracted to be done. I think the judgment should be affirmed.

[Stone J. delivered the judgment of the Court save that Hilton and Loring JJ. took no part, and Holt J. joined in the dissenting judgment.]

NOTE. If the "reasonable value of the property on the determinative date would have been only $12,160," why is the plaintiff entitled to $15,000 representing the $12,160 plus interest? The defendant surrendered the land to the plaintiff, must it not have some value? Should this value not be deducted from the $12,160? Professors Dawson and Harvey in their casebook on *Contracts and Contract Remedies* (1959) report (p. 28) that the case was compromised and the defendant paid $55,000 in cash settlement. In 1953 three fifths of the land was sold for $45,000 after $6,000 had been spent on levelling that portion. It was left at a higher level than planned, but still suitable for a railroad siding.

See also *Peevyhouse* v. *Garland Coal & Mining Co.* (1963) 382 P. 2d. 109, in which the Supreme Court of Oklahoma refused to follow *Groves* v. *John Wunder Co.* in a case where the plaintiff sought damages for breach of a promise to restore a strip mining site.

PROBLEM 1. J owned a 1950 Austin car to which he was sentimentally attached and which he referred to affectionately as "Esmerelda". As the result of an accident, Esmerelda's fender was in need of repair, and K agreed to repair it for $50. K now finds that the cost of repair will actually be $200 and in breach of contract he refuses to do the repairs. J has the repairs done elsewhere for $200, and sues K for $150. It is proved that the market value of the car now (as repaired) is $100; in its damaged condition it was $80, but J was so attached to Esmerelda that he wouldn't consider buying another car. Advise K.

See *O'Grady* v. *Westminster Scaffolding Ltd.* [1962] 2 Ll.R.238, *Darbishire* v. *Warran* [1963] 3 All E.R. 310, *Nu West Homes, Ltd.* v. *Thunderbird Petroleums, Ltd.* (1975) 59 D.L.R. (3d) 292, 307-8.

PROBLEM 2. A, a carpenter, agreed with B, acting on behalf of a church organization, to build pews for a church. When the work was completed it was discovered that the pews did not meet specifications; they were too narrow, and made of weak material. To replace the pews with the proper ones would cost $200. The difference in cost between the material used and that specified is about $50. B sues for damages. Advise A.

See *Wood* v. *Stringer* (1890) 20 O.R. 148 (Ch. Div.).

PROBLEM 3. C entered a newspaper contest run by D, the terms of which were that 50 applicants would be chosen for personal interviews, and out of those 50, 12 would be picked to receive theatrical engagements. C was one of the 50 chosen for interviews, but the letter from D giving the time of the interview reached her too late to enable her to attend. As a result she was not among the 12 winners. C sues for damages.

See *Chaplin* v. *Hicks* [1911] 2 K.B. 786.

THE SALE OF GOODS ACT
R.S.O. 1970. Chapter 421

48 (1) Where the buyer wrongfully neglects or refuses to accept and pay for the goods, the seller may maintain an action against him for damages for non-acceptance.

(2) The measure of damages is the estimated loss directly and nat-

urally resulting in the ordinary course of events from the buyer's breach of contract.

(3) Where there is an available market for the goods in question the measure of damages is *prima facie* to be ascertained by the difference between the contract price and the market or current price at the time or times when the goods ought to have been accepted, or, if no time was fixed for acceptance, then at the time of the refusal to accept.

49 (1) Where the seller wrongfully neglects or refuses to deliver the goods to the buyer, the buyer may maintain an action against the seller for damages for non-delivery.

(2) The measure of damages is the estimated loss directly and naturally resulting in the ordinary course of events from the seller's breach of contract.

(3) Where there is an available market for the goods in question, the measure of damages is *prima facie* to be ascertained by the difference between the contract price and the market or current price of the goods at the time or times when they ought to have been delivered, or, if no time was fixed, then at the time of the refusal to deliver.

THOMPSON (W.L.) LTD. v. ROBINSON (GUNMAKERS) LTD.

[1955] Ch. 177. The defendants had contracted to buy a standard model car from the plaintiffs, who were dealers in cars. The defendants, in breach of contract, refused to accept delivery of the car, and the plaintiffs returned it to their suppliers, who took it back. The plaintiffs claimed that they had lost the profit which they would have made if the defendants had bought the car; the defendants relied on section 48 of the Sale of Goods Act (s. 50 of the English Act).

UPJOHN J.: This action raises a question of some importance to the motor trade as to the true measure of damages where the buyer of a motorcar, in this case a Standard "Vanguard," refuses to complete his bargain and take delivery.

[His Lordship stated the facts and continued:] The law is not really in doubt; it is set out in section 50 of the Sale of Goods Act, 1893. That section was declaratory of the existing law, and the general principle which has been observed in all cases [is this:] "Subject to these observations I think that there are certain broad principles which are quite well settled. The first is that, as far as possible, he who has proved a breach of a bargain to supply what he contracted to get is to be placed, as far as money can do it, in as good a situation as if the contract had been performed." That is the general rule.

Apart altogether from authority and statute it would seem to me on the facts which I have to consider to be quite plain that the plaintiffs' loss in this case is the loss of their bargain. They have sold one "Vanguard" less than they otherwise would. The plaintiffs, as the defendants must have known, are in business as dealers in motor-cars and make their profit in buying and selling motor-cars, and what they have lost is their profit on the sale of this "Vanguard". . . .

The main case, however, put by the defendants is this: they submit that subsection (3) of section 50 applies, because they say that there is an available market for the goods in question, and in that available market we know that the price of the "Vanguard" is fixed. It is fixed by the manufacturers. Therefore, they say, the measure of damages must necessarily be

nominal damages

little more than nominal. Had the plaintiffs kept the car and sold it to another at a later stage, no doubt they would have been entitled to the costs of storage in the meantime, possibly interest on their money laid out, and so on, but as they had in fact mitigated their damages by getting out of the contract, damages are nil. . . .

Had the matter been res integra I think that I should have found that an "available market" merely means that the situation in the particular trade in the particular area was such that the particular goods could freely be sold, and that there was a demand sufficient to absorb readily all the goods that were thrust on it, so that if a purchaser defaulted, the goods in question could readily be disposed of. Indeed, such was the situation in the motor trade until very recently. It was, of course, notorious that dealers all over the country had long waiting lists for new motor-cars. People put their names down and had to wait five or six years, and whenever a car was spared by the manufacturer from export it was snatched at, and if any purchaser fell out there were many waiting to take his place, and it was conceded that if those circumstances were still applicable to the "Vanguard" motor-car the claim for damages must necessarily have been purely nominal. But on the assumed facts circumstances had changed in relation to "Vanguard" motor-cars, and in March of this year there was not a demand in the East Riding which could readily absorb all the "Vanguard" motor-cars available for sale. If a purchaser defaults, that sale is lost, and there is no means of readily disposing of the "Vanguard" contracted to be sold so that there is not even on the extended definition an available market. But there is this further consideration: even if I accepted Mr. Platts-Mills's broad argument that one must now look at the market as being the whole conspectus of trade, organization and marketing, I have to remember that subsection (3) provides only a prima facie rule, and if on investigation of the facts one finds that it is unjust to apply that rule, in the light of the general principles mentioned above, then it is not to be applied. In this case, as I said in the earlier part of my judgment, it seems to me plain almost beyond argument that in fact the loss to the plaintiffs is the sum of £61. Accordingly, however one interprets subsection (3), it seems to me on the facts that I have to consider one reaches the same result.

[Judgment for the plaintiffs.]

CHARTER v. *SULLIVAN* [1957] 2 Q.B. 117 (C.A.). The defendant refused to accept delivery of a standard model car which he had contracted to buy from the plaintiff car dealer. There was evidence that the plaintiff could sell all the cars of this sort which he could get, and he did in fact resell the particular car in question.

JENKINS L.J.: I turn now to consider what, on the undisputed facts of the case, is in the eye of the law the true measure of the damages, if any, over and above merely nominal damages, which the plaintiff has suffered through the defendant's failure to take and pay for the car he agreed to buy.

Consideration of this question must inevitably begin with a reference to section 50 of the Sale of Goods Act, 1893. [His Lordship read section 50 and continued:] Mr. Collard, for the defendant, argued that in the present case there was an available market for "Hillman Minx" de luxe saloon cars within the meaning of section 50 (3) of the Act, and accordingly that the measure of damages ought, in accordance with the prima facie rule laid down by that subsection, to be ascertained by the difference between the contract price and the market or current price at the time of the defendant's refusal to perform his contract.

The result of this argument, if accepted, would be that the plaintiff could claim no more than nominal damages, because the market or current price could only be the fixed retail price, which was necessarily likewise the price at which he sold to the defendant and resold to Wigley.

But the plaintiff is a motor-car dealer whose trade for the present purpose can be described as consisting in the purchase of recurrent supplies of cars of the relevant description from the manufacturers, and selling the cars so obtained, or as many of them as he can, at the fixed retail price. He thus receives, on each sale he is able to effect, the predetermined profit allowed by the fixed retail price, and it is obviously in his interest to sell as many cars as he can obtain from the manufacturers. The number of sales he can effect, and consequently the amount of profit he makes, will be governed, according to the state of trade, either by the number of cars he is able to obtain from the manufacturers, or by the number of purchasers he is able to find. In the former case demand exceeds supply, so that the default of one purchaser involves him in no loss, for he sells the same number of cars as he would have sold if that purchaser had not defaulted. In the latter case supply exceeds demand, so that the default of one purchaser may be said to have lost him one sale. . . .

In *Thompson (W. L.) Ltd.* v. *Robinson (Gunmakers) Ltd.* Upjohn J. had before him a claim for damages in a case resembling the present case to the extent that the damages were claimed in respect of the defendants' refusal to perform a contract with the plaintiffs for the purchase from the plaintiffs of a car (in that instance a "Standard Vanguard" car) which, like the car in the present case, could only be sold by the plaintiffs at a fixed retail price. It is, however, important to note that the case to which I am now referring proceeded on certain admissions, including an admission to the effect that in the relevant district at the date of the contract (which was also the date of the breach) "there was no shortage of 'Vanguard' models to meet all immediate demands in the locality," which I take to mean, in effect, that the supply of such cars exceeded the demand. In these circumstances the plaintiffs by agreement with their suppliers rescinded their contract with them, and returned the car. In the ensuing action the plaintiffs claimed from the defendants damages amounting to the profit the plaintiffs would have made on the sale of the car to the defendants if the defendants had duly completed their purchase of it, and the judge held them entitled to those damages. The defendants raised the same argument as had been raised by the defendant in the present case, namely, that there was an available market for a car of the kind in question, within the meaning of section 50 (3), that there was a market or current price in the shape of the fixed retail price, and that as the fixed retail price was the same as the contract price the plaintiffs had suffered no damage. . . .

It remains, therefore, to ascertain the loss (if any) "naturally resulting, in the ordinary course of events" from the defendant's breach of contract, and the measure of that loss must, in my opinion, be the amount, if any, of the profit the plaintiff has lost by reason of the defendant's failure to take and pay for the car he agreed to buy. This accords with the view taken by Upjohn J. in *Thompson (W. L.) Ltd.* v. *Robinson (Gunmakers)*

Ltd., and also with the principle stated in *In re Vic Mill Ltd.* which Upjohn J. applied.

I should next refer to evidence of which I have deferred consideration earlier in this judgment. . . .

Notwithstanding Mr. Aldous's submission to the contrary on the plaintiff's behalf, I think we should assume that the judge accepted as accurate the plaintiff's sales manager's own description of the state of the plaintiff's business in "Hillman Minx" cars. Moreover, I think we should take that description as signifying, according to the ordinary meaning of the language used, that the plaintiff could always find purchasers for all the "Hillman Minx" cars he was able to get. . . .

The matter therefore stands thus. If the defendant had duly performed his bargain, the plaintiff would have made on that transaction a profit of £97 15s. The calculation accordingly starts with a loss of profit, through the defendant's default, of £97 15s. That loss was not cancelled or reduced by the sale of the same car to Wigley, for if the defendant had duly taken and paid for the car he agreed to buy, the plaintiff could have sold another car to Wigley, in which case there would have been two sales and two profits: see *In re Vic Mill Ltd.*, and particularly *per* Hamilton L.J. and Buckley L.J. But the matter does not rest there. The plaintiff must further show that the sum representing the profit he would have made if the defendant had performed his contract has in fact been lost. Here I think he fails, in view of Winter's evidence to the effect that the plaintiff could sell all the "Hillman Minx" cars he could get.

I have already expressed my opinion as to the meaning of this statement. It comes, I think, to this, that according to the plaintiff's own sales manager the state of trade was such that the plaintiff could always find a purchaser for every "Hillman Minx" car he could get from the manufacturers; and if that is right it inevitably follows that he sold the same number of cars and made the same number of fixed profits as he would have sold and made if the defendant had duly carried out his bargain.

Upjohn J.'s decision in favour of the plaintiff dealers in *Thompson's* case was essentially based on the admitted fact that the supply of the cars in question exceeded the demand, and his judgment leaves no room for doubt that if the demand had exceeded the supply his decision would have been the other way.

[Appeal allowed. Damages reduced to nominal sum.]

NOTE. The problem in *Thompson* v. *Robinson* and *Charter* v. *Sullivan*, sometimes called the "lost volume" problem, is not confined to contracts for the sale of goods. See, for example, *Inter-office Telephones, Ltd.* v. *Robert Freeman Co., Ltd.*, [1958] 1 Q.B. 190. (C.A.), which concerned a contract for the hire of goods.

3. REMOTENESS

BRITISH COLUMBIA SAW MILLS CO. v. NETTLESHIP
(1868) L.R. 3 C.P. 499 at 508

WILLES J.: "Cases of this kind [involving remoteness of damages] have always been found to be very difficult to deal with, beginning with a case said to have been decided about two centuries and a half ago, where a man going to be married to an heiress, his horse having cast a shoe on the journey, employed a blacksmith to replace it, who did the work so unskilfully that the horse was lamed, and, the rider not arriving in time, the lady married another; and the blacksmith was held liable for the loss of the marriage. The question is a very serious one. . . .''

On this example F. E. Smith commented as follows: "It is hardly necessary to observe that the man of the anvil, even with notice of his customer's errand, could hardly have apprehended in the bride an animus nubendi so imperious and undiscriminating" (1900) 16 L.Q.R. 279.

HADLEY v. BAXENDALE
(1854) 9 Exch. 341, 156 E.R. 145

The plaintiff owned a steam powered mill at Gloucester. The shaft having broken, the plaintiff had to send it to Greenwich, near London, to serve as a pattern for the manufacture of a new one. The defendant was in the business of carrying goods. The plaintiff sent the shaft for an agreed price, but its delivery at Greenwich was delayed beyond what was found to be a reasonable delivery time. The final delivery of the new shaft to the plaintiff was consequently delayed, and the plaintiff brought an action against the defendant for the profits lost due to the mill standing idle during that period of delay. At the trial, the jury awarded a sum of money in respect of the lost profits. The defendant sought an order [a "rule"] for a new trial.

ALDERSON B.: We think that there ought to be a new trial in this case; but, in so doing, we deem it to be expedient and necessary to state explicitly the rule which the Judge, at the next trial, ought, in our opinion, to direct the jury to be governed by when they estimate the damages.

It is indeed, of the last importance that we should do this; for, if the jury are left without any definite rule to guide them, it will, in such cases as these, manifestly lead to the greatest injustice. . . .

Now we think the proper rule in such a case as the present is this: Where two parties have made a contract which one of them has broken, the damages which the other party ought to receive in respect of such breach of contract should be such as may fairly and reasonably be considered either arising naturally, i.e., according to the usual course of things, from such breach of contract itself, or such as may reasonably be supposed to have been in the contemplation of both parties, at the time they made the contract, as the probable result of the breach of it. Now, if the special circumstances under which the contract was actually made were communicated by the plaintiffs to the defendants, and thus known to both parties, the damages resulting from the breach of such a contract, which they would reasonably contemplate, would be the amount of injury which would ordinarily follow from a breach of contract under these special circumstances so known and communicated. But, on the other hand, if these special circumstances were wholly unknown to the party breaking the contract, he, at the most, could only be supposed to have had in his contemplation the amount of injury which would arise generally, and in the great multitude of cases not affected by any special circumstances, from such a breach of contract. For, had the special circumstances been known, the parties might have specially provided for the breach of contract by special terms as to damages in that case; and of this advantage it would be very unjust to deprive them. Now the above principles are those by which we think the jury ought to be guided in estimating the damages arising out of any breach of contract. It is said, that other cases, such as breaches of contract in the non-payment of money, or in the not making a good title to land, are to be treated as exceptions from this, and as governed by a conventional rule. But as, in such cases, both parties must be supposed to be cognisant of that well-known rule, these cases may, we think be more properly classed under the rule above enunciated as to cases under known special circumstances, because there both parties may reasonably be presumed to contemplate the estimation of the amount of damages according to the conventional rule.

Now, in the present case, if we are to apply the principles above laid down, we find that the only circumstances here communicated by the plaintiffs to the defendants at the time the contract was made, were, that the article to be carried was the broken shaft of a mill, and that the plaintiffs were the millers of that mill. But how do these circumstances shew reasonably that the profits of the mill must be stopped by an unreasonable delay in the delivery of the broken shaft by the carrier to the third person? Suppose the plaintiffs had another shaft in their possession put up or putting up at the time, and that they only wished to send back the broken shaft to the engineer who made it; it is clear that this would be quite consistent with the above circumstances, and yet the unreasonable delay in the delivery would have no effect upon the intermediate profits of the mill. Or again, suppose that, at the time of the delivery to the carrier, the machinery of the mill had been in other respects defective, then, also, the same results would follow. Here it is true that the shaft was actually sent back to serve as a model for a new one, and that the want of a new one was the only cause of the stoppage of the mill, and that the loss of profits really arose from not sending down the new shaft in proper time, and that this arose from the delay in delivering the broken one to serve as a model. But it is obvious that, in the great multitude of cases of millers sending off broken shafts to third persons by a carrier under ordinary circumstances, such consequences would not, in all probability, have occurred; and these special circumstances were here never communicated by the plaintiffs to the defendants. It follows, therefore, that the loss of profits here cannot reasonably be considered such a consequence of the breach of contract as could have been fairly and reasonably contemplated by both parties when they made this contract. For such loss would neither have followed naturally from the breach of this contract in the great multitude of such cases occurring under ordinary circumstances, nor were the special circumstances, which, perhaps, would have made it a reasonable and natural consequence of such breach of contract, communicated to or known by the defendants. The Judge ought, therefore, to have told the jury that, upon the facts then before them, they ought not to take the loss of profits into consideration at all in estimating the damages. There must therefore be a new trial in this case.

[Rule absolute.]

J.H. JACKSON, CONTRACT LAW IN MODERN SOCIETY, pp. 10-11

... The role of the jury has always had considerable effect on the law of contract. Before the eighteenth century, writes one noted scholar,

"... the jury by and large, had a free discretion when money damages were claimed, to determine the amount of the award." In theory the amount of damages was a "question of fact" and in England the itinerant trial justice sent out from London was little disposed to challenge the "yeoman of the neighborhood" who had knowledge of the affair. Because of outrageous or excessive verdicts, however, judges began to exercise control over the jury by rulings on evidence, by granting new trials, and by instructing the jury about the amount which was proper. Thus legal doctrine began to grow. The famous 1854 case of *Hadley* v. *Baxendale*, ..., demonstrates this tendency and it is commonly said that the modern law of contract damages dates only from the middle of the nineteenth century. ...

QUESTIONS. Suppose that the plaintiffs had taken their shaft in at ten o'clock in the morning, and that at eleven o'clock the plaintiffs' servant came in again and said, "The mill is stopped; we can't make any flour until we get that shaft back. Please hurry it." Then suppose that at twelve noon Samuel Stranger came in and the defendants agreed to take a chest in the only available conveyance to Penzance in time for his daughter's wedding the next day. Suppose that he offered to pay £5, twice the usual rate. If the defendants accepted this proposal and returned the plaintiffs their £2 4s., should this deliberate breach of the promise after the work stoppage was known affect the calculation of damages? *Corbin on Contracts* (vol. 5, s. 1008) suggests that we distinguish between wilful and non-wilful breach, and in the former case make the material time for notice of unusual loss the time the defendant chose to commit the wilful breach. The distinction hàs not been adopted in Canadian or English cases.

Who, of Hadley and Baxendale, could more easily insure against the loss that occurred? Should such a question be relevant to the court's conclusion?

PROBLEM. Able, a farmer, ordered tractor headlights from Baker's Department Store Ltd., at their usual price. He told the clerk in the store that he needed the lights to operate his tractor to harvest his crop at night, and that if the lights were not supplied he would lose his crop. The clerk promised that the lights would be supplied in time. The lights were not supplied, and Able lost his crop, being unable to procure substitute lights in time. Is Baker's Department Store liable for the loss?

See *Lamkins* v. *International Harvester Co.* 182 S.W. 2d 203 (1944) (Ark. S.C.).

FULLER AND PERDUE, "THE RELIANCE INTEREST
IN CONTRACT DAMAGES"
(1936) 46 Yale L.J. 52, 84-88

Before we discuss the relation between the reliance interest and *Hadley* v. *Baxendale* it will be necessary to state briefly what seems to us to be involved in that famous case, considering it not so much as an event in legal history but as the accepted symbol for a set of problems. The case may be said to stand for two propositions: (1) that it is not always wise to make the defaulting promisor pay for all the damage which follows as a consequence of his breach, and (2) that specifically the proper test for determining whether particular items of damage should be compensable is to inquire whether they should have been foreseen by the promisor at the time of the contract. The first aspect of the case is much more important than the second. In its first aspect the case bears an integral relation to the very bases of contract liability. It declares in effect that just as it is wise to refuse enforcement altogether to some promises (considerationless, unaccepted, "social" promises, etc.) so it is wise not to go too far in enforcing those promises which are deemed worthy of legal sanction. The answer to the question of *Hadley* v. *Baxendale* (where shall we stop?) must inevitably be as complex as the answer to the question (where shall we begin?) which is implicit in the law of mutual assent, consideration and the rules governing the formation of contracts generally.

In its second aspect *Hadley* v. *Baxendale* may be regarded as giving a grossly simplified answer to the question which its first aspect presents. To the question, how far shall we go in charging to the defaulting promisor the consequences of his breach, it answers with what purports to be a single test, that of foreseeability. The simplicity and comprehensiveness of this test are largely a matter of illusion. In the first place, it is openly branded as inappropriate in certain situations where the line is drawn much more closely in favor of the defaulting promisor than the test of foreseeability as normally understood would draw it. There are, therefore, exceptions to the test, to say nothing of authorities which reject it altogether as too burdensome to the defaulter. In the second place, it is clear that the test of foreseeability is less a definite test itself than a cover for a developing set of tests. As in the case of all "reasonable man" standards there is an element of circularity about the test of foreseeability. "For what items of damage should the court hold the defaulting promisor? Those which he should as a reasonable man have foreseen? But what should he have foreseen as a reasonable man? Those items of damage for which the court feels he ought to pay." The test of foreseeability is therefore subject to manipulation by the simple device of defining the characteristics of the hypothetical man who is doing the foreseeing. By a gradual process of judicial inclusion and exclusion this "man" acquires a complex personality; we begin to know just what "he" can "foresee" in this and that situation, and we end, with not one test but with a whole set of tests. This has obviously happened in the law of negligence, and is happening, although less obviously, to the reasonable man postulated by *Hadley* v. *Baxendale*.

Even if the reasonable man who does the foreseeing is a juristic construct, endowed precisely with those qualities which the court feels he ought to have for the purpose at hand, it does not seem that there is a complete *petitio principii* in the test of foreseeability. When we import into a question of liability the "reasonable man" standard we do at least two things. In the first place we increase the chance that the case will ultimately be determined by the jury. Though the court may define the reasonable man, it cannot be sure that its definition will be regarded by the jury, and any test which speaks of the reasonable man decreases the court's chance of removing the case from the jury. In the second place, whether the case is ultimately decided by the judge or the jury, stating the problem in terms of the reasonable man creates a bias in favor of exempting *normal* or *average* conduct from legal penalties. The reasonable man is not necessarily the average man, but he tends to be, and the notion of what is normal and average puts a bridle on the judicial power of defining reasonableness. But the restraint is far from complete. It becomes illusory in those situations where the concepts "normal" and "average" are without definite content; where the "average man" is as much a juristic construct as the "reasonable man." The restraint is often thrown off even in those fields where, because rather definite lay ways of thought and action are discoverable in them, the notion of the "normal" and "average" has some objective reality. The courts have not hesitated to invest the reasonable man with capacities either greater or less than those of the average man. For an example of this judicial autonomy within the reign of fact one need look no further than the case which originated the test of foreseeability, *Hadley* v. *Baxendale* itself. ("Thus, in *Hadley* v. *Baxendale* itself, the carrier was told of the use to which the broken shaft was to be put and that the mill was shut down, but it was held that this was not enough, since it was not told that another shaft was not available!" McCormick, *Damages* (1935) § 140.)

HORNE v. *THE MIDLAND RAILWAY COMPANY.* 1873 L.R. 8 C.P. 131 (England. Exchequer Chamber). The plaintiffs, shoe manufacturers in Kettering, were under contract to supply a quantity of shoes to a firm in London for the use of the French army, at the unusually high price of 4s. per pair. By the terms of the contract with the London firm, the plaintiff was bound to deliver the shoes by the 3rd of February, 1871, and to meet this provision he sent the shoes to the defendant's station at Kettering in time to be delivered in the usual course in the evening of that day, when they would have been accepted and paid for by the consignees. Notice was given to the station-master (which notice was, for the purpose of the case, deemed to be notice to the company) at the time the shoes were delivered to him that the plaintiffs were under contract to deliver the shoes by the 3rd, and that unless they were so delivered they would be thrown upon the plaintiffs' hands. The shoes were not delivered in London until the morning of the 4th of February, when the consignee refused them, and the plaintiffs were obliged to sell them at the best price obtainable, namely 2s. 9d. per pair.

In an action against the defendants for the delay in delivering the shoes, they paid into court a sum of £20 which would be sufficient to cover any ordinary loss such as expenses incidental to the re-sale, but the plaintiffs further claimed the sum of £267 as the difference between the price at which they had contracted to sell the shoes and the price which they ultimately received.

On a stated case to the Court of Common Pleas, the defendant received a judgment (L.R. 7 C.P. 583), which was affirmed in this appeal.

BLACKBURN J.: ". . . Then if there was no special contract, what was the effect of the notice? In the case of Hadley v. Baxendale it was intimated that, apart from all question of a special contract with regard to the amount of damages, if there were a special note of the circumstances the plaintiff might recover the exceptional damages. This doctrine has been adverted to in several subsequent decisions with more or less assent, but they appear to have all been cases in which it was held that the doctrine did not apply because there was no special notice. It does not appear that there has been any case in which it has been affirmatively held that in consequence of such a notice the plaintiff could recover exceptional damages. The counsel for the plaintiff could not refer to any such case, and I know of none. If it were necessary to decide the point, I should be much disposed to agree with what my Brother Martin has suggested, viz., that in order that the notice may have any effect, it must be given under such circumstances, as that an actual contract arises on the part of the defendant to bear the exceptional loss. Before, however, deciding the point, I should have wished to take time to consider . . . "

HYDRAULIC ENGINEERING CO. LTD. v. *McHAFFIE.* 1878. 4 Q.B.D. 670 (England). BRAMWELL L.J.: "It has occurred to me that the true explanation is that a person contemplates the performance and not the breach of his contract; he does not enter into a kind of second contract to pay damages, but he is liable to make good those injuries which he is aware that his default may occasion to the contractee." COTTON L.J.: "It cannot be said that damages are granted because it is part of the contract that they shall be paid; it is the law which imposes or implies the term that upon breach of a contract damages must be paid."

RIVERS v. *GEORGE WHITE & SONS CO.* [1919] 2 W.W.R. 189 (Saskatchewan Court of Appeal). HAULTAIN C.J.S.: "It may be observed that this theory 'of a kind of second contract to pay damages' has been mainly developed in actions against carriers, on the ground that a common carrier has no discretion to decline a contract."

KINGHORNE v. *THE MONTREAL TELEGRAPH CO.* 1859. 18 U.C.Q.B. 60 (Ontario. Queen's Bench). In an action for failure to deliver a telegram that cost sixty cents and might have led to a contract that might have been carried out the jury awarded £57 13s. 7d. as damages. On a motion for a non-suit, held, for the defendant. McLEAN J.: "It is, in my opinion, extremely doubtful whether in any such case a party who avails himself of the facilities afforded in communicating by telegraph can expect that a telegraph company shall be responsible for all damages, no matter what amount, which may arise in the hurry of transmitting a message from any verbal inaccuracy of an operator, or from an omission in forwarding or delivering it when received. It ought not to be expected that so great facilities are to be afforded for so small a remuneration, and at a risk which might bring ruin upon any company if obliged to indemnify for every possible loss."

VICTORIA LAUNDRY LTD. v. *NEWMAN INDUSTRIES LTD.*
[1949] 1 All E.R. 997 (C.A.)

ASQUITH L.J. read the following judgment of the court.: This is an appeal by the plaintiffs against a judgment of Streatfeild J., in so far as that judgment limited the damages to £110 in respect of an alleged breach of contract by the defendants which is now uncontested. The breach of contract consisted in the delivery of a boiler sold by the defendants to the plaintiffs some twenty odd weeks after the time fixed by the contract for delivery. The short point is whether, in addition to the £110 awarded, the plaintiffs were entitled to claim in respect of loss of profits which they say they would have made if the boiler had been delivered punctually.

The defendants are and were at all material times a limited company which described itself on its invoices as "Electrical and Mechanical Engineers and Manufacturers." They did not manufacture the boiler in question. They just happened to own it. The plaintiffs were at all material times a limited company carrying on the business of laundrymen and dyers in the neighbourhood of Windsor. In January, 1946, the plaintiffs were minded to expand their business, and to that end required a boiler of much greater capacity than the boiler they then possessed. . . . Seeing an advertisement by the defendants on Jan. 17, 1946, of two boilers, which appeared suitable . . . they negotiated for the purchase of one of them, and by Apr. 26, 1946, had concluded a contract for its purchase at a price of £2,150, loaded free on transport at Harpenden.

Seeing that the issue is as to the measure of recoverable damages and the application of the rules in *Hadley* v. *Baxendale* it is important to inquire what information the defendants possessed at the time when the contract was made as to such matters as the time at which, and the purpose for which, the plaintiffs required the boiler. The defendants knew before and at the time of the contract that the plaintiffs were laundrymen and dyers and required the boiler for purposes of their business as such. They also knew that the plaintiffs wanted the boiler for immediate use. On the latter point the correspondence is important. The contract was concluded by, and is contained in, a series of letters . . . and finally, on Apr. 26, in the concluding letter of the series by which the contract was made: "We are most anxious that this" (that is, the boiler) "should be put into use"—we call attention to this expression—"in the shortest possible space of time." Hence, up to and at the very moment when a concluded contract emerged, the plaintiffs were pressing on the defendants the need for expedition, and the last letter was a plain intimation that the boiler was wanted for immediate use. This is none the less so because when, later, the plaintiffs encountered delays in getting the necessary permits and licences, the exhortations to speed come from the other side, who wanted their money, which, in fact, they were paid in advance of delivery. The defendants knew the plaintiffs needed the boiler as soon as the delays should be overcome, and they knew by the beginning of June that such delays had by then, in fact, been overcome. The defendants did not know at the material time the precise role for which the boiler was cast in the plaintiffs' economy, *e.g.,* whether (as the fact was) it was to function in substitution for an existing boiler of inferior capacity, or in replacement of an existing boiler of equal capacity, or as an extra unit to be operated side by side with and in addition to any existing boiler. It has, indeed, been argued strenuously that, for all they knew, it might have been wanted as a "spare" or "standby," provided in advance to replace an existing boiler, when, perhaps some time hence, the latter should wear out, but such an intention to reserve it for future use seems quite inconsistent with the intention expressed in the letter of Apr. 26 to "put it into use in the shortest possible space of time." In this connection, certain admissions made in the course of the hearing are of vital importance. The defendants formally admitted what in their defence they had originally traversed, namely, the facts alleged in para. 2 of the statement of claim. That paragraph reads as follows:

"At the date of the contract hereinafter mentioned the defendants well knew as the fact was that the plaintiffs were launderers and dyers carrying on business at Windsor and required the said boiler for use in their said business and the said contract was made upon the basis that the said boiler was required for the said purpose."

On June 5, the plaintiffs, having heard that the boiler was ready, sent a lorry to Harpenden to take delivery. Mr. Lennard, a director of the plaintiff company, preceded the lorry in a car. He discovered on arrival that four days earlier the contractors employed by the defendants to dismantle the boiler had allowed it to fall on its side, receiving damage. Mr. Lennard declined to take delivery of the damaged boiler in its existing condition and insisted that the damage must be made good. He was, we think, justified in this attitude, since no similar article could be bought on the market. After a long wrangle, the defendants agreed to perform the necessary repairs, and, after further delay through the difficulty of finding a contractor who was free and able to perform them, completed the repairs by Oct. 28. Delivery was taken by the plaintiffs on Nov. 8 and the boiler was erected and working by early December. The plaintiffs claim, as part —the disputed part—of the damages, loss of the profits they would have earned if the machine had been delivered in early June instead of November.

Evidence was led for the plaintiffs with the object of establishing that, if the boiler had been punctually delivered, then, during the twenty odd weeks between then and the time of actual delivery (1) they could have taken on a very large number of new customers in the course of their laundry business, the demand for laundry services at that time being insatiable—they did, in fact, take on extra staff in the expectation of its delivery—and (2) that they could and would have accepted a number of highly lucrative dyeing contracts for the Ministry of Supply. In the statement of claim, para. 10, the loss of profits under the first of these heads was quantified at £16 a week and under the second at £262 a week. The evidence, however, which promised to be voluminous, had not gone very far when counsel for the defendants submitted that in law no loss of profits was recoverable at all, and that to continue to hear evidence as to its *quantum* was mere waste of time. He suggested that the question of remoteness of damage under this head should be decided on the existing materials, including the admissions to which we have referred. The learned judge accepted counsel's submission, and on that basis awarded £110 damages under certain minor heads, but nothing in respect of loss of profits, which he held to be too remote. It is from that decision that the plaintiffs now appeal. It was a necessary consequence of the course which the case took that no evidence was given on behalf of the defendants, and only part of the evidence available to the plaintiffs. It should be observed parenthetically that the defendants had added as third party the contractors who, by dropping the boiler, so causing the injuries to it, prevented its delivery in early June and caused the defendants to break their contract. Those third party proceedings have been adjourned pending the hearing of the present appeal as between the plaintiffs and the defendants. The third party, nevertheless, was served with notice of appeal by the defendants and argument was heard for him at the hearing of the appeal.

The ground of the learned judge's decision . . . may be summarised as follows. He took the view that the loss of profit claimed was due to special circumstances, and, therefore, recoverable, if at all, only under the second rule in *Hadley* v. *Baxendale*, and not recoverable in the present case because such special circumstances were not at the time of the contract communicated to the defendants. He also attached much significance to the fact that the object supplied was not a self-sufficient profit-making article, but part of a larger profit-making whole. . . . Before commenting on the learned judge's reasoning, we must refer to some of the authorities. The authorities on recovery of loss of profits as a head of damages are not easy to reconcile. At one end of the scale stand cases where there has been non-delivery or delayed delivery of what is on the face of it obviously a profit-earning chattel, for instance, a merchant or passenger ship; . . . or some essential part of such a ship for instance, a propellor, . . . or engines. . . . In such cases loss of profit has rarely been refused. A second and intermediate class of case in which loss of profit has often been awarded is where ordinary mercantile goods have been sold to a merchant with knowledge by the vendor that the purchaser wanted them for re-sale, at all events, where there was no market in which the purchaser could buy similar goods against the contract on the seller's default. . . . At the other end of the scale are cases where the defendant is not a vendor of the goods, but a carrier. In such cases the courts have been slow to allow loss of profit as an item of damage. This was not, it would seem, because a different principle applies in such cases, but because the application of the same principle leads to different results. A carrier commonly knows less than a seller about the purposes for which the buyer or consignee needs the goods or about other "special circumstances" which may cause exceptional loss if due delivery is withheld.

Three of the authorities call for more detailed examination. First comes *Hadley* v. *Baxendale* itself. . . .

British Columbia, etc., Saw Mill Co. v. *Nettleship* (1868), L.R. 3 C.P. 499, annexes to the principle laid down in *Hadley* v. *Baxendale* a rider to the effect that, where knowledge of special circumstances is relied on as enhancing the damages recoverable, that knowledge must have been brought home to the defendant at the time of the contract and in such circumstances that the defendant impliedly undertook to bear any special loss referable to a breach in those special circumstances. The knowledge which was lacking in that case on the part of the defendant was knowledge that the particular box of machinery negligently lost by the defendant was one without which the rest of the machinery could not be put together and would, therefore, be useless.

Cory v. *Thames Ironworks Co.* (1868), L.R. 3 Q.B. 181—a case strongly relied on by the plaintiffs—presented the peculiarity that the parties contemplated respectively different profit-making uses of the chattel sold by the defendants to the plaintiff. It was the hull of a boom derrick and was delivered late. The plaintiffs were coal merchants, and the obvious use, and that to which the defendants believed it was to be put, was that of a coal store. The plaintiffs, on the other hand, the buyers, in fact intended to use it for transhipping coals from colliers to barges, a quite unprecedented use for a chattel of this kind, one quite unsuspected by the sellers, and one calculated to yield much higher profits. The case, accordingly, decides, *inter alia*, what is the measure of damages recoverable when the parties are not *ad idem* in their contemplation of the use for which the article is needed. It was decided that in such a case no loss was recoverable beyond what would have resulted if the intended use had been that reasonably within the contemplation of the defendants, which in that case was the "obvious" use. This special complicating factor, the divergence between the knowledge and contemplation of the parties respectively, has somewhat obscured the general importance of the decision, which is in effect that the facts of the case brought it within the first rule of *Hadley* v. *Baxendale* and enabled the plaintiff to recover loss of such profits as would have arisen

from the normal and obvious use of the article. The "natural consequences," said Blackburn J. (L.R. 3 Q.B. 191), of not delivering the
derrick was that £420 representing those normal profits was lost. Cockburn
C.J., interposing during the argument (ibid., 187), made the significant
observation:

"No doubt, in order to recover damage arising from a special purpose
the buyer must have communicated the special purpose to the seller; but
there is one thing which must always be in the knowledge of both parties,
which is, that the thing is bought for the purpose of being in some way or
other profitably applied."

This observation is apposite to the present case. These three cases have
on many occasions been approved by the House of Lords without any
material qualification.

What propositions applicable to the present case emerge from the authorities as a whole, including those analysed above? We think they include the
following: (1) It is well settled that the governing purpose of damages is to
put the party whose rights have been violated in the same position, so far
as money can do so, as if his rights had been observed. This purpose, if
relentlessly pursued, would provide him with a complete indemnity for all
loss *de facto* resulting from a particular breach, however improbable, however unpredictable. This, in contract at least, is recognised as too harsh a
rule. Hence, (2) In cases of breach of contract the aggrieved party is only
entitled to recover such part of the loss actually resulting as was at the
time of the contract reasonably foreseeable as liable to result from the
breach. (3) What was at that time reasonably foreseeable depends on the
knowledge then possessed by the parties, or, at all events, by the party who
later commits the breach. (4) For this purpose, knowledge "possessed" is
of two kinds—one imputed, the other actual. Everyone, as a reasonable
person, is taken to know the "ordinary course of things" and consequently
what loss is liable to result from a breach of that ordinary course. This is
the subject-matter of the "first rule" in *Hadley* v. *Baxendale*, but to this
knowledge, which a contract-breaker is assumed to possess whether he
actually possesses it or not, there may have to be added in a particular case
knowledge which he actually possesses of special circumstances outside the
"ordinary course of things" of such a kind that a breach in those special
circumstances would be liable to cause more loss. Such a case attracts the
operation of the "second rule" so as to make additional loss also recoverable. (5) In order to make the contract-breaker liable under either rule it
is not necessary that he should actually have asked himself what loss is
liable to result from a breach. As has often been pointed out, parties at the
time of contracting contemplate, not the breach of the contract, but its performance. It suffices that, if he had considered the question, he would as a
reasonable man have concluded that the loss in question was liable to
result. . . . (6) Nor, finally, to make a particular loss recoverable, need it
be proved that on a given state of knowledge the defendant could, as a
reasonable man, foresee that a breach must necessarily result in that loss. It
is enough if he could foresee it was likely so to result. It is enough . . . if the
loss (or some factor without which it would not have occurred) is a
"serious possibility" or a "real danger." For short, we have used the word
"liable" to result. Possibly the colloquialism "on the cards" indicates the
shade of meaning with some approach to accuracy.

If these, indeed, are the principles applicable, what is the effect of their
application to the facts of the present case? We have, at the beginning of

this judgment, summarised the main relevant facts. The defendants were an engineering company supplying a boiler to a laundry. We reject the submission for the defendants that an engineering company knows no more than the plain man about boilers or the purposes to which they are commonly put by different classes of purchasers, including laundries. The defendant company were not, it is true, manufacturers of this boiler or dealers in boilers, but they gave a highly technical and comprehensive description of this boiler to the plaintiffs by letter of Jan. 19, 1946, and offered both to dismantle the boiler at Harpenden and to re-erect it on the plaintiffs' premises. Of the uses or purposes to which boilers are put, they would clearly know more than the uninstructed layman. Again, they knew they were supplying the boiler to a company carrying on the business of laundrymen and dyers, for use in that business. The obvious use of a boiler, in such a business, is surely to boil water for the purpose of washing or dyeing. A laundry might conceivably buy a boiler for some other purpose, for instance, to work radiators or warm bath water for the comfort of its employees or directors, or to use for research, or to exhibit in a museum. All these purposes are possible, but the first is the obvious purpose which, in the case of a laundry, leaps to the average eye. If the purpose then be to wash or dye, why does the company want to wash or dye, unless for purposes of business advantage . . . ?

Since we are differing from a carefully reasoned judgment, we think it due to the learned judge to indicate the grounds of our dissent. . . . The answer to [his] reasoning has largely been anticipated in what has been said above, but we would wish to add, first, that the learned judge appears to infer that because certain "special circumstances" were, in his view, not "drawn to the notice of" the defendants, and, therefore, in his view, the operation of the "second rule" was excluded, *ergo*, nothing in respect of loss of business can be recovered under the "first rule." This inference is, in our view, no more justified in the present case than it was in *Cory* v. *Thames Ironworks Co.*

Secondly, while it is not wholly clear what were the "special circumstances" on the non-communication of which the learned judge relied, it would seem that they were or included the following:—(a) the "circumstance" that delay in delivering the boiler was going to lead "necessarily" to loss of profits, but the true criterion is surely not what was bound "necessarily" to result, but what was likely or liable to do so, and we think that it was amply conveyed to the defendants by what was communicated to them (plus what was patent without express communication) that delay in delivery was likely to lead to "loss of business"; (b) the "circumstance" that the plaintiffs needed the boiler "to extend their business." It was surely not necessary for the defendants to be specifically informed of this as a precondition of being liable for loss of business. Reasonable persons in the shoes of the defendants must be taken to foresee, without any express intimation, that a laundry which, at a time when there was a famine of laundry facilities, was paying £2,000 odd for plant and intended at such a time to put such plant "into use" immediately, would be likely to suffer in pocket from five months' delay in delivery of the plant in question, whether they intended by means of it to extend their business, or merely to maintain it, or to reduce a loss; (c) the "circumstance" that the plaintiffs had the assured expectation of special contracts, which they could only fulfil by securing punctual delivery of the boiler. Here, no doubt the learned judge had in mind the particularly lucrative dyeing contracts to which the plaintiffs looked forward. . . . We agree that in order that the plaintiffs should recover specifically and as such the profits expected on these contracts, the defendants would have had to know, at the time of their agreement with the plaintiffs, of the prospect and terms of such contracts. We also agree that they did not, in fact, know these things. It does not, however, follow that the plaintiffs are precluded from recovering some general (and perhaps conjectural) sum for loss of business in respect of dyeing contracts to be reasonably expected any more than in respect of laundering contracts to be reasonably expected. Thirdly, the other point on which Streatfeild J., largely based his judgment was that there is a critical difference between the measure of damages applicable when the defendant defaults in supplying a self-contained profit-earning whole and when he defaults in supplying a part of that whole. In our view, there is no intrinsic magic, in this connection, in the whole as against a part. The fact that a part only is involved is only significant is so far as it bears on the capacity of the supplier to foresee the consequences of non-delivery. If it is clear from the nature of the part (or the supplier of it is informed) that its non-delivery will have the same effect as non-delivery of the whole, his liability will be the same as if he had defaulted in delivering the whole. The cases . . . so strongly relied on . . . were all cases in which, through want of a part, catastrophic results ensued, in that a whole concern was paralysed or sterilized—a mill stopped, a complex of machinery unable to be assembled, a threshing machine unable to be delivered in time for the harvest, and, therefore, useless. In all three cases the defendants were absolved from liability to compensate the plaintiffs for the resulting loss of business, not because what they had failed to deliver was a part, but because there had been nothing to convey to them that want of that part would stultify the whole business of the person for whose benefit the part was contracted for. There is no resemblance between these cases and the present, in which, while there was no question of a total stoppage resulting from non-delivery, yet there were ample means of knowledge on the part of the defendants that business loss of some sort would be likely to result to the plaintiffs from the defendants' default in performing their contract.

We are, therefore, of opinion that the appeal should be allowed and the issue referred to an official referee as to what damage, if any, is recoverable in addition to the £110 awarded by the learned trial judge. The official referee would assess those damages in consonance with the findings in this judgment as to what the defendants knew or must be taken to have known at the material time, either party to be at liberty to call evidence as to the *quantum* of the damage in dispute.

[Appeal allowed with costs. Costs on the issue of profit damages to be reserved to the official referee. No order as to third party costs of appeal.]

QUESTIONS. ASQUITH L.J. cited the *British Columbia Saw-Mill* case, but he did not quote Bovill C.J. who said, "It is to be observed that the defendant is a carrier, and not a manufacturer of goods supplied for a particular purpose." STUART J. drew attention to this distinction in *Canada Foundry Co. Ltd.* v. *Edmonton Portland Cement Co. Ltd.*, [1913] 1 W.W.R. 382 (Alberta), and he also said, "There are indeed numbers of cases in which loss of profits has been awarded for breach of contract. . . . In actions against carriers the Courts have perhaps hesitated more than they have in actions against manufacturers and builders." Is the distinction valid? Should a distinction be made between a carrier, a seller and a manufacturer?

MUNROE EQUIPMENT SALES LTD. v. *CANADIAN FOREST PRODUCTS LTD.* 1961. 29 D.L.R. (2d) 730 (Manitoba. Court of Appeal). The plaintiff agreed early in December, 1956, to rent a second-hand Allis Chalmers HD15 tractor to the defendant at the rate of $1,500 a month. The defendant wanted the tractor to be used along with his other equipment (including other tractors) in road clearing operations that winter, so that his pulpwood could be brought to market. When the contract was made the defendant stressed that the tractor was needed to open roads, that time was short and that frost had set in. Nevertheless the contract was made on December 13 when the defendant's superintendent "accidentally bumped into" a salesman of the plaintiff. The tractor broke down within two days and thereafter its performance was sporadic and it was not much used until January 20, 1957. During this time the defendant made no effort to get a replacement largely because the plaintiff's salesman thought the tractor could be repaired sooner than it could be replaced. Two subcontractors got additional equipment "when they became tired of waiting for the HD 15." The final breakdown occurred on February 20 and from then until the end of the season the tractor was abandoned. By agreement no rent was charged for the month ending January 17, but in this action the plaintiff claimed $6,667.99. The trial Judge allowed him $2,075.00 made up of $1,500 for one month's rent and freight charges. But he also allowed a counterclaim of $6,958.37 (the defendant asked for $14,298.12) most of which was based on lost profits because the defendant was prevented from removing 3,500 cords of pulpwood. He relied on *Hadley* v. *Baxendale* and found the defendant's loss "was a natural and probable consequence that ought to have been in plaintiff's contemplation." On appeal the Court divided three to two in modifying the verdict by reducing the plaintiff's award to $1,826.43 and dismissing the counterclaim altogether. MILLER C.J.M.: "With respect, I do not think *Victoria Laundry (Windsor) Ltd.* v. *Newman Industries Ltd.*, [1949] 1 All E.R. 997, 2 K.B. 528, quoted by the learned trial Judge, is of much help to defendant. In any event, that decision is not binding on this Court. I prefer the reasoning of the trial Judge to that of the Judges of Appeal so far as the application of the law to the facts is concerned. . . . [*Anson on Contract*, 21st ed., pp. 460-3, quoted and adopted.]

"It seems to me that in the case at bar the defendant cannot succeed on its counterclaim unless it establishes that the special circumstances in connection with the use of the tractor were communicated and made known to the plaintiff company. There was nothing discussed in the negotiations for the tractor which would indicate whether the defendant company intended to remove 100 cords or 100,000 cords of wood; nor, so far as the knowledge of, or the knowledge imparted to, the plaintiff company was concerned, how much wood was cut and ready to be moved. Nor was it in any way indicated to the plaintiff that all the wood which the defendant company had cut by itself or its subcontractors had to be moved that year. The fact that the defendant had labour trouble in the fall of 1956, as deposed by Knelman the general manager of defendant, was not disclosed to plaintiff, or that, as a result thereof, the defendant was going to attempt to remove all wood that season, As stated above, it is not uncommon in the business in question to leave a substantial portion of 1 year's cut in the bush for removal in another year. Neither was it made known to the plaintiff company that the defendant company had a sale for any specific quantity of wood. The rental contract covering the HD 15 was of indeterminate duration and presumably could have been determined by either party at virtually any time.

"It seems to me that the defendant company was seeking—and urgently seeking—a tractor, and was glad to obtain this rebuilt tractor. The defendant (not the plaintiff) was the originator of the contract in issue.

"It appears to me that if it were a matter of such urgency to the defendant company that this tractor should bear the brunt of the roadwork, the defendant company would not have left the securing of same until as late as December 1956 when hauling operations were ready to begin. It also seems logical to me that if the defendant company were going to hold the plaintiff company responsible in such large damages for any failure of a second-hand rebuilt unit, the defendant company should have made clear to the plaintiff the extent of the work to be done. I do not believe the plaintiff acted in any improper way and I do believe that any representations the salesman of the plaintiff company may have made were made innocently, in good faith, and were not intended as a guarantee: but, as above pointed out, the learned trial Judge found that the salesman had guaranteed the tractor to be in good mechanical condition—whatever that may have meant with respect to a second-hand unit. There is no warranty or guarantee in the written rental agreement ex. 3.

"In my opinion it is unreasonable to expect that such a burden of responsibility for damages as now claimed by the defendant should be assumed from the rental of a second-hand unit. Surely no reasonable person could contemplate, under the circumstances of the renting of this machine, that the lessor of one second-hand tractor was underwriting and virtually insuring the removal of all this pulpwood from the bush. . . .

"Had the plaintiff contemplated possible liability for such damage as claimed by the counterclaim, it is scarcely conceivable that it would have risked letting a second-hand tractor bear such responsibility; nor would any reasonable person do so. Such damages do not ordinarily flow from the fact that a second-hand tractor does not "stand-up", and therefore in order to fix the plaintiff with responsibility for such damages the defendant, at the time of making the contract, should have made clear its version of the extraordinary responsibility the defendant might seek to impose upon the plaintiff. At least it should have warned the plaintiff of its (defendant's) intention to remove all wood that season, the quantity involved, the sale contracts for wood that defendant had made, and such like. If this had been done it is probable the defendant would not have secured the tractor or the plaintiff would have insisted upon contracting itself out of any liability. . . ."

SCYRUP v. ECONOMY TRACTOR PARTS LTD.
(1963) 40 D.L.R. (2d) 1026 (Man. C.A.)

MILLER C.J.M. (dissenting): This is an appeal from the judgment of Maybank J., who allowed plaintiff judgment for $2,001.14 damages. The damages were agreed upon as being out-of-pocket expenses amounting to $541.14 (against which there was a credit of $190, leaving a balance of $351.14) plus loss of profits of $1,650.

The action arose out of a purchase by plaintiff from defendant of a second-hand La Plante Hydraulic attachment for a D8 caterpillar tractor.

Plaintiff had, or expected to secure, a contract from Supercrete Limited to do certain work with this equipment in a gravel pit. His equipment was needed to replace that owned and operated by Supercrete during a period when Supercrete's equipment was being repaired. Plaintiff testified that he had entered into the contract before he ever attempted to purchase the equipment from defendant, although some doubt was raised on this point by the evidence of an employee of Supercrete Ltd., who indicated the deal between plaintiff and Supercrete was made just a few days before July 10, 1961, whereas the equipment was ordered by plaintiff in May or early in June, 1961.

With a view to obtaining the desired equipment the plaintiff approached defendant company in Winnipeg, but as suitable equipment was not available from defendant in Winnipeg, plaintiff was referred to defendant's parent company in Fargo, North Dakota, called Surplus Tractor Parts Inc., from which it was finally secured.

After delivery was made to plaintiff, he settled with defendant for the equipment at around $1,000, plus import duty. Plaintiff duly assembled the attachment and placed it on his tractor but when he commenced to work with it in July it did not operate properly and it now appears that various parts, including hoses and pumps, were either missing or were practically useless. When plaintiff communicated with defendant regarding these deficiencies, the defendant or its parent company co-operated and supplied the missing parts. The pumps were immediately replaced (actually during the course of the trouble the pumps were replaced more than once). The defendant company, under instructions from the parent company in Fargo, made an adjustment of $40 for hoses and a further $150 was later paid plaintiff in compensation for the repairs made, including repairs to defective pumps. Finally Supercrete became impatient because plaintiff's equipment was not in proper condition and hired someone else to do the job, with the result that plaintiff lost the contract.

Plaintiff testified that he had told defendant and also Surplus Tractor Parts Inc. that he had this contract and needed the equipment for the purpose of the contract. The following appears on pp. 13 and 14 of the evidence:

"Q. What did you tell the Defendant? A. I told him I needed the hydraulic dozer as soon as possible. I had picked out one down in Fargo."

"Q. Before we get to there, what did you tell the Defendant while you were in Winnipeg? A. I told him I had a job to go to with a hydraulic dozer. He told me fine, we have dozers like that in Fargo, North Dakota. . . ."

"Q. I believe this was a conversation with Mr. Swartz you are still referring to? A. Yes, I am."

"Q. Did you tell him who your job was with? A. Yes I did."

And at p. 19 of the evidence:

"Q. What happened then? A. I explained to Mr. Goodman that I had to have this piece of equipment in quite a hurry and it had to be in good working order. He showed me this one that I have purchased and it was not all . . . there was pieces missing here and there which he said. . . ."

"A. Yes, but he said he had those parts to go with it and that it would be all checked over before delivery in good working order."

And at p. 22 of the evidence:

"Q. What did he say? Tell us what he said, not just what you understood but what was actually said. A. I explained to him that I did not want it unless it was going to be in good working order and he agreed with me that it would be all checked over and in good working order. There wasn't a pump at the time on the machine that the hydraulic system was on but he said if they did not have one they would make up a good pump for it. And I explained the necessity of having all parts because I would be quite a ways from the city putting this machine together when it did arrive."

This does not indicate too clearly that much information was given defendant as to the scope of the contract, including whether it was a small or large contract, what type of work was involved, where or when it was to be performed, or its duration. In other words, the paucity of essential information communicated to defendant by plaintiff seems to me to be fatal to plaintiff's claim for profits.

The representative of the Surplus Tractor Parts in Fargo gave evidence that plaintiff only intimated to him that he possibly had a contract; but the learned trial Judge believed plaintiff and it must therefore be assumed by this Court that the communication, to the extent set out in the quoted evidence at least, was made by plaintiff to defendant.

The learned trial Judge found as follows:

"I have no doubt that judgment herein should be for the plaintiff. I accept the evidence of him and his witnesses wherever it is in conflict with other evidence. The defendant sold to the plaintiff the equipment detailed in the statement of claim and warranted it fully. The machinery was quite defective. It would not work. The defendant was apprised at the time of the purchase that the plaintiff wanted the apparatus for use on a contract of work he had just obtained. When the apparatus was found to be inoperative this contract was lost to the plaintiff. Such loss was clearly foreseeable at the time the plaintiff dealt with the defendant for the purchase of the said machinery."

These are strong findings, conclusions, and inferences in favour of plaintiff. I am of the opinion that the "foreseeability" inferred by the learned trial Judge is not supported by the evidence, and that indeed on the evidence it is not supportable in law.

With respect, I feel it is very doubtful that this second-hand machinery should be saddled with a claim for damages for loss of profits unless it was clearly indicated to defendant at the time the equipment was purchased exactly what kind of contract was being entered into by plaintiff, the type of work that was to be done and the magnitude of the operation. All the evidence in this case discloses is that plaintiff wanted the equipment because he had a contract. It might have been a contract of a very minor nature so far as the evidence is concerned; it might have been a contract involving $100 or one involving $100,000; or a contract that would take a week or a month, or two years. In other words, it is doubtful whether the evidence discloses that sufficient information was given defendant to indicate the responsibilities to be assumed by this second-hand equipment.

This Court recently dealt with a somewhat similar problem in *Munroe Equipment Sales Ltd.* v. *Canadian Forest Products Ltd.* (1961), 29 D.L.R. (2d) 730. (This was not cited to the learned trial Judge nor incorporated in either factum, but was referred to us in defendant's oral submission.) In that case the various decisions dealing with the principle involved in such claims, particularly *Hadley* v. *Baxendale* (1854), 9 Exch. 341, 156 E.R. 145, were examined. *Hadley* v. *Baxendale* first established the rule or rules governing liability for damages in circumstances such as existed in the instant case.

The following quotations from the *Munroe Equipment* case, seem pertinent to the appeal now before us page 731 (headnote):

"*Held*, on appeal by a majority, defendant hirer failed to establish the damages which would ordinarily flow from the failure of the tractor to come up to expectations, and the large damages awarded were not reasonably foreseeable as flowing from the failure of the tractor. No reasonable person could contemplate in the circumstances that the owner of the second-hand tractor was virtually insuring the removal of the timber from the bush.

"Nor was it established that the special circumstances in connection with the use of the tractor were communicated and made known to the owner, either as to the amount of wood cut, or the amount to be removed. Since the tractor broke down almost immediately, defendant hirer was under a duty to mitigate damages and it was its duty in the circumstances to seek another tractor from plaintiff or elsewhere rather than pin its faith on a broken down article for a short winter season when so much was at stake."

Page 739: "It seems to me that in the case at bar the defendant cannot succeed on its counterclaim unless it establishes that the special circumstances in connection with the use of the tractor were communicated and made known to the plaintiff company. There was nothing discussed in the negotiations for the tractor which would indicate whether the defendant company intended to remove 100 cords or 100,000 cords of wood; nor, so far as the knowledge of, or the knowledge imparted to, the plaintiff company was concerned, how much wood was cut and ready to be moved. Nor was it in any way indicated to the plaintiff that all the wood which the defendant company had cut by itself or its subcontractors had to be moved that year."

Pages 741-2: "I cannot see how any person or company dealing in second-hand machinery would contemplate for a moment that if the rebuilt machine broke down the vendor or lessor thereof would be liable for the type of damages claimed and allowed in this action.

Had the plaintiff contemplated possible liability for such damage as claimed by the counterclaim, it is scarcely conceivable that it would have risked letting a second-hand tractor bear such responsibility; nor would any reasonable person do so. Such damages do not ordinarily flow from the fact that a second-hand tractor does not "stand-up," and therefore in order to fix the plaintiff with responsibility for such damages the defendant, at the time of making the contract, should have made clear its version of the extraordinary responsibility the defendant might seek to impose upon the plaintiff. At least it should have warned the plaintiff of its (defendant's) intention to remove all wood that season, the quantity involved, the sale contracts for wood that defendant had made, and such like. If this had been done it is probable the defendant would not have secured the tractor or the plaintiff would have insisted upon contracting itself out of any liability."

The rule referred to in the *Baxendale* case is discussed in *Hammond & Co.* v. *Bussey* (1887), 20 Q.B.D. 79, and a quotation from the latter appears in the *Munroe Equipment Sales* case, supra. *Burrard Dry Dock Co.* v. *Canadian Union Line Ltd.*, [1954] 3 D.L.R. 561, [1954] S.C.R. 307; *Victoria Laundry (Windsor), Ltd.* v. *Newman Industries, Ltd.*, [1949] 1 All E.R. 997, [1949] 2 K.B. 528; *Anson on Contract*, 21st ed., pp. 460-3 and *Overseas Tankship (U.K.), Ltd.* v. *Morts Dock & Engineering Co.*, [1961] 1 All E.R. 404, were all reviewed in *Munroe Equipment Sales*, supra, and clearly established the tests to be applied on such a claim for damages as the one with which we now have to deal.

Counsel for plaintiff argued before us that these damages for loss of profit naturally flow from breach of contract by defendant and therefore come under the first rule in the *Baxendale* case; that these would be in the same category as damages for the repair costs of the defective parts. I am unable to accept this argument. I do not think that damages for loss of profit naturally flow from the defective character of the equipment or that they could have been reasonably foreseen or anticipated by defendant, because, as I have said above, defendant was not given sufficient information regarding the actual contract in which plaintiff was interested to permit it to determine the scope of its liability if the machine did not work satisfactorily. Defendant was not given an opportunity, by full disclosure or communication, to be put in the position where it could reasonably have anticipated damages for loss of profit by plaintiff on this particular contract and had no opportunity to contract itself out of liability if unwilling to be subjected to damages of unascertained magnitude. That being so, I would not allow the judgment against defendant for loss of profits of $1,650 to stand. The damages, $351.14, allowed to plaintiff for the balance of the repair costs is proper because they flow naturally from the breach of contract disclosed in the evidence.

I would therefore allow the appeal and vary the judgment by reducing the amount awarded from $2,001.14 to $351.14. Defendant should have its costs of appeal in this Court.

[Schultz J.A. concurs with Freedman J.A.]

FREEDMAN J.A.: This is an appeal by the defendant from a judgment of Maybank J., holding the defendant liable to the plaintiff for damages for breach of contract arising from the sale of a hydraulic dozer attachment for the plaintiff's D8 caterpillar tractor.

There was contradiction in the testimony concerning the facts. The learned trial Judge resolved this in favour of the plaintiff, saying "I accept the evidence of him and his witnesses wherever it is in conflict with other evidence." The brief recital of facts which follows takes due account of that finding.

Prior to the matters in question in this case the plaintiff had entered into a contract, requiring the use of his tractor, with a company known as Supercrete Ltd. It was to make the tractor fit and suitable for the Supercrete job that the plaintiff needed the hydraulic dozer attachment. It is common ground that he purchased this attachment from the defendant. The plaintiff's evidence establishes that he made known to the defendant the fact that the attachment was for a tractor which was to be used by him on a job with Supercrete Ltd. He also made it plain that he needed this equipment in a hurry and that it had to be in good working order.

The attachment was duly sold and delivered by the defendant to the plaintiff. But the learned trial Judge found, on substantial evidence, that the equipment did not measure up to the terms of the contract. The plaintiff first discovered that certain parts were missing. Then, after these were replaced, it was found that the hydraulic attachment would not function. Tests showed that the hydraulic pump did not generate sufficient pressure to operate the unit. The plaintiff later received in turn, three replacing pumps, not one of which proved adequate. Finally the plaintiff had to rebuild one of the pumps in order to make the attachment operable.

In consequence of the attachment equipment being defective the caterpillar could not function. For Supercrete Ltd., it was imperative to have a tractor effectively working at its gravel pit. Since the plaintiff's tractor, in the condition it then was, could not do the job, Supercrete cancelled the contract with the plaintiff and hired another tractor from a third party to do the work. The plaintiff's loss of profit, which he would have earned on the Supercrete contract, represents the main item of the damages which he now claims from the defendant.

Both plaintiff and defendant referred to *Hadley* v. *Baxendale*, 9 Exch. 341, 156 E.R. 145, and to several of the cases which later considered that earlier decision, including *Victoria Laundry (Windsor), Ltd.* v. *Newman Industries Ltd.*, [1949] 1 All E.R. 997, [1949] 2 K.B. 528. I do not think it necessary in the present case to make any lengthy examination of the jurisprudence on this subject. The guiding principles are clear. It is usual to think of *Hadley* v. *Baxendale* as enunciating two rules, or, at all events, one rule with two branches. Under the first rule (or branch) damages for breach of contract should be such as arise naturally—that is, according to the usual course of things—from the breach of contract itself, or such as may reasonably be supposed to have been in the contemplation of the parties, at the time they made the contract, as the probable result of its breach. Under the second rule, if there are special circumstances relating to the contract—and these are actually communicated by the plaintiff to the defendant—damages reasonably contemplated would be the amount of injury which would ordinarily follow from a breach of contract under these special circumstances so known and communicated.

The *Victoria Laundry* v. *Newman* case, in considering the *Hadley* v. *Baxendale* rules, made it clear that damages for breach of contract should be measured by what was reasonably foreseeable as liable to result from the breach. That in turn would depend on the knowledge possessed by the parties or, at all events, by the party who later commits the breach. Knowledge could be either imputed or actual. Imputed knowledge is sufficient to bring into play the first rule; actual knowledge is required for the second.

Reasonable foreseeability is the test under both rules. Indeed it is not always easy to make a rigid division between the two rules, and one writer comments that "the modern restatement of the rule as a totality is a salutary trend": *vide Mayne & McGregor on Damages*, 12th ed., p. 127.

It seems to me that whether we say there is one rule or two, or one rule with two branches, the test of reasonable foreseeability in either case operates here in favour of the plaintiff. For if imputed knowledge under the first rule is sufficient, it is not unrealistic to ascribe to the defendant an awareness that his breach of contract in selling this defective equipment to the plaintiff would in the ordinary course of events result in damages in the form of loss of profits as here sustained. If, on the other hand, actual knowledge of special circumstances attaching to the contract is required, the evidence on the record shows that the defendant had such knowledge.

I would accordingly agree with the learned trial Judge that the defendant is liable as claimed. The amount of the damages had been agreed to, subject to liability being established.

I would therefore dismiss the appeal and affirm the judgment of the Court below, with costs.

Guy J.A. (dissenting) concurs with Miller C.J.M.

Monnin J.A., concurs with Freedman J.A.

[Appeal dismissed.]

KOUFOS v. C. CZARNIKOW, LTD.
(*The Heron II*)
[1967] 3 W.L.R. 1491 (H.L.)

LORD REID: My Lords, by charterparty of October 15, 1960, the respondents chartered the appellant's vessel, *Heron II*, to proceed to Constanza, there to load a cargo of 3,000 tons of sugar; and to carry it to Basrah, or, in the charterer's option, to Jeddah. The vessel left Constanza on November 1, 1960. The option was not exercised and the vessel arrived at Basrah on December 2, 1960. The umpire has found that "a reasonably accurate prediction of the length of the voyage was twenty days." But the vessel had in breach of contract made deviations which caused a delay of nine days.

It was the intention of the respondents to sell the sugar "promptly after arrival at Basrah and after inspection by merchants." The appellant did not know this, but he was aware of the fact that there was a market for sugar at Basrah. The sugar was in fact sold at Basrah in lots between December 12 and 22, 1960, but shortly before that time the market price had fallen, partly by reason of the arrival of another cargo of sugar. It was found by the umpire that if there had not been this delay of nine days the sugar would have fetched £32 10s. 0d. per ton. The actual price realised was only £31 2s. 9d per ton. The respondents claim that they are entitled to recover the difference as damage for breach of contract. The appellant admits that he is liable to pay interest for nine days on the value of the sugar and certain minor expenses but denies that fall in market value can be taken into account in assessing damages in this case.

McNair J., following the decision in *The Parana*, (1877) 2 P.D. 118, decided this question in favour of the appellant. He said: "In those circumstances, it seems to me almost impossible to say that the shipowner must have known that the delay in prosecuting the voyage would probably result, or be likely to result, in this kind of loss."

The Court of Appeal by a majority (Diplock and Salmon L.JJ., Sellers L.J. dissenting) reversed the decision of the trial judge. The majority held that *The Parana* laid down no general rule, and, applying the rule (or rules) in *Hadley* v. *Baxendale* as explained in *Victoria Laundry* (*Windsor*) *Ltd.* v. *Newman Industries Ltd.* they held that the loss due to fall in market price was not too remote to be recoverable as damages.

It may be well first to set out the knowledge and intention of the parties at the time of making the contract so far as relevant or argued to be relevant. The charterers intended to sell the sugar in the market at Basrah on arrival of the vessel. They could have changed their mind and exercised their option to have the sugar delivered at Jeddah but they did not do so. There is no finding that they had in mind any particular date as the likely date of arrival at Basrah or that they had any knowledge or expectation that in late November or December there would be a rising or a falling market. The shipowner was given no information about these matters by the charterers. He did not know what the charterers intended to do with the sugar. But he knew there was a market in sugar at Basrah, and it appears to me that, if he had thought about the matter, he must have realised that at least it was not unlikely that the sugar would be sold in the market at market price on arrival. And he must be held to have known that in any ordinary market prices are apt to fluctuate from day to day; but he had no reason to suppose it more probable that during the relevant period such fluctuation would be downwards rather than upwards—it was an even chance that the fluctuation would be downwards.

So the question for decision is whether a plaintiff can recover as damages for breach of contract a loss of a kind which the defendant, when he made the contract, ought to have realised was not unlikely to result from a breach of contract causing delay in delivery. I use the words "not unlikely" as denoting a degree of probability considerably less than an even chance but nevertheless not very unusual and easily foreseeable.

For over a century everyone has agreed that remoteness of damage in contract must be determined by applying the rule (or rules) laid down by a court including Lord Wensleydale (then Parke B.), Martin B. and Alderson B. in *Hadley* v. *Baxendale*. But many different interpretations of that rule have been adopted by judges at different times. So I think that one ought first to see just what was decided in that case, because it would seem wrong to attribute to that rule a meaning which, if it had been adopted in that case, would have resulted in a contrary decision of that case.

In *Hadley* v. *Baxendale* the owners of a flour mill at Gloucester which was driven by a steam engine delivered to common carriers, Pickford & Co., a broken crankshaft to be sent to engineers in Greenwich. A delay of five days in delivery there was held to be in breach of contract and the question at issue was the proper measure of damages. In fact the shaft was sent as a pattern for a new shaft and until it arrived the mill could not operate. So the owners claimed £300 as loss of profit for the five days by which resumption of work was delayed by this breach of contract. But the carriers did not know that delay would cause loss of this kind.

Alderson B., delivering the judgment of the court, said: "We find that the only circumstances here communicated by the plaintiffs to the defendants at the time the contract was made, were, that the article to be carried was the broken shaft of a mill, and that the plaintiffs were the millers of that mill. But how do these circumstances show reasonably that the profits of the mill must be stopped by an unreasonable delay in the delivery of the broken shaft by the carrier to the third person? Suppose the plaintiffs had another shaft in their possession put up or putting up at the time, and that they only wished to send back the broken shaft to the engineer who made it; it is clear that this would be quite consistent with the above circumstances, and yet the unreasonable delay in the delivery would have no effect upon the intermediate profits of the mill. Or, again, suppose that at the time of the delivery to the carrier, the machinery of the mill had been in other respects defective, then, also, the same results would follow." Then, having said that in fact the loss of profit was caused by the delay, he continued: "But it is obvious that, in the great multitude of cases of millers sending off broken shafts to third persons by a carrier under ordinary circumstances, such consequences would not, in all probability, have occurred."

Alderson B., clearly did not and could not mean that it was not reasonably foreseeable that delay might stop the resumption of work in the mill. He merely said that in the great multitude—which I take to mean the great majority—of cases this would not happen. He was not distinguishing between results which were foreseeable or unforeseeable, but between results which were likely because they would happen in the great majority of cases, and results which were unlikely because they would only happen in a small minority of cases. He continued: "It follows, therefore, that the loss of profits here cannot reasonably be considered such a consequence of the breach of contract as could have been fairly and reasonably contemplated by both the parties when they made this contract." He clearly meant that a result which will happen in the great majority of cases should fairly and reasonably be regarded as having been in the contemplation of the parties, but that a result which, though foreseeable as a substantial possibility, would only happen in a small minority of cases should not be regarded as having been in their contemplation. He was referring to such a result when he continued: "For such loss would neither have flowed naturally from the breach of this contract in the great multitude of such cases occurring under ordinary circumstances, nor were the special circumstances, which perhaps, would have made it a reasonable and natural consequence of such breach of contract, communicated to or known by the defendants."

I have dealt with the latter part of the judgment before coming to the well known rule because the court were there applying the rule and the language which was used in the latter part appears to me to throw considerable light on the meaning which they must have attached to the rather vague expressions used in the rule itself. The rule is that the damages "should be such as may fairly and reasonably be considered either arising naturally, i.e., according to the usual course of things, from such breach of contract itself, or such as may reasonably be supposed to have been in the contemplation of both parties, at the time they made the contract, as the probable result of the breach of it."

I do not think that it was intended that there were to be two rules or that two different standards or tests were to be applied. The last two passages which I quoted from the end of the judgment applied to the facts before the court which did not include any special circumstances communicated to the defendants; and the line of reasoning there is that because in the great majority of cases loss of profit would not in all probability have occurred, it followed that this could not reasonably be considered as having been fairly and reasonably contemplated by both the parties, for it would not have flowed naturally from the breach in the great majority of cases.

I am satisfied that the court did not intend that every type of damage which was reasonably foreseeable by the parties when the contract was made should either be considered as arising naturally, i.e., in the usual course of things, or be supposed to have been in the contemplation of the parties. Indeed the decision makes it clear that a type of damage which was plainly foreseeable as a real possibility but which would only occur in a small minority of cases cannot be regarded as arising in the usual course of things or be supposed to have been in the contemplation of the parties: the parties are not supposed to contemplate as grounds for the recovery of damage any type of loss or damage which on the knowledge available to the defendant would appear to him as only likely to occur in a small minority of cases.

In cases like *Hadley* v. *Baxendale* or the present case it is not enough that in fact the plaintiff's loss was directly caused by the defendant's breach of contract. It clearly was so caused in both. The crucial question is whether, on the information available to the defendant when the contract was made, he should, or the reasonable man in his position would, have realised that such loss was sufficiently likely to result from the breach of contract to make it proper to hold that the loss flowed naturally from the breach or that loss of that kind should have been within his contemplation.

The modern rule of tort is quite different and it imposes a much wider liability. The defendant will be liable for any type of damage which is reasonably foreseeable as liable to happen even in the most unusual case, unless the risk is so small that a reasonable man would in the whole circumstances feel justified in neglecting it. And there is good reason for the difference. In contract, if one party wishes to protect himself against a risk which to the other party would appear unusual, he can direct the other party's attention to it before the contract is made, and I need not stop to consider in what circumstances the other party will then be held to have accepted responsibility in that event. But in tort there is no opportunity for the injured party to protect himself in that way, and the tortfeasor cannot reasonably complain if he has to pay for some very unusual but nevertheless foreseeable damage which results from his wrongdoing. I have no doubt that today a tortfeasor would be held liable for a type of damage as unlikely as was the stoppage of Hadley's Mill for lack of a crankshaft: to anyone with the knowledge the carrier had that may have seemed unlikely but the chance of it happening would have been seen to be far from negligible. But it does not at all follow that *Hadley* v. *Baxendale* would today be differently decided.

As long ago as 1872 Willes J. said in *Horne* v. *Midland Railway Co.*: "The cases as to the measure of damages for a tort do not apply to a case of contract. That was suggested in a case in Bulstrode but the notion was corrected in *Hadley* v. *Baxendale*. The damages are to be limited to those that are the natural and ordinary consequences which may be supposed to have been in the contemplation of the parties at the time of making the contract." And in *Cory* v. *Thames Ironworks Co.* (1868) L.R. 3 Q.B. 181, Blackburn J. said: "I think it all comes round to this: The measure of damages when a party has not fulfilled his contract is what might be reasonably expected in the ordinary course of things to flow from the non-fulfilment of the contract, not more than that, but what might be reasonably expected to flow from the non-fulfilment of the contract in the ordinary state of things, and to be the natural consequences of it. The reason why the damages are confined to that is, I think, pretty obvious, viz. that if the damage were exceptional and unnatural damage, to be made liable for that would be hard upon the seller, because if he had known what the consequences would be he would probably have stipulated for more time, or, at all events, have used greater exertions if he knew that that extreme mischief would follow from the non-fulfilment of his contract." It is true that in some later cases opinions were expressed that the measure of damages is the same in tort as it is in contract, but those were generally cases where it was sought to limit damages due for a tort and not cases where it was sought to extend damages due for breach of contract, and I do not recollect any case in which such opinions were based on a full consideration of the matter. In my view these opinions must now be regarded as erroneous.

For a considerable time there was a tendency to set narrow limits to awards of damages. Such phrases were used as that the damage was not "the immediate and necessary effect of the breach of contract". . . . But later a more liberal tendency can be seen. I do not think it useful to review the authorities in detail but I do attach importance to what was said in this House in *R. & H. Hall Ltd.* v. *W. H. Pim (Junior) & Co. Ltd.*, [1928] All E.R. Rep. 763.

In that case Pim sold a cargo of wheat to Hall but failed to deliver it. Hall had resold the wheat but as a result of Pim's breach of contract lost the profit which they would have made on their sub-sale. Three of their Lordships dealt with the case on the basis that the relevant question was whether it ought to have been in the contemplation of the parties that a resale was probable. The finding of the arbitrators was: "The arbitrators are unable to find that it was in the contemplation of the parties or ought to have been in the contemplation of Messrs. Pim at that time that the cargo would be resold or was likely to be resold before delivery; in fact, the chances of its being resold as a cargo and of its being taken delivery of by Messrs. Hall were about equal." On that finding the Court of Appeal had decided in favour of Pim, saying that, as the arbitrators had stated as a fact that the chances of the cargo being resold or not being resold were equal, it was therefore "idle to speak of a likelihood or of a probability of a resale."

Viscount Dunedin pointed out that it was for the court to decide what was to be supposed to have been in the contemplation of the parties, and then said: "I do not think that 'probability' . . . means that the chances are all in favour of the event happening. To make a thing probable, it is enough, in my view, that there is an even chance of its happening. That is the criterion I apply; and in view of the facts, as I have said above, I think there was here in the contemplation of parties the probability of a resale." He did not have to consider how much less than a 50 per cent chance would amount to a probability in this sense.

Lord Shaw of Dunfermline went further. He said: "To what extent in a contract of goods for future delivery the extent of damages is in contemplation of parties is always extremely doubtful. The main business fact is that they are thinking of the contract being performed and not of its being not performed. But with regard to the latter if their contract shows that there were instances or stages which made ensuing losses or damage a not unlikely result of the breach of the contract, then all such results must be reckoned to be within not only the scope of the contract, but the contemplation of parties as to its breach."

Lord Phillimore was less definite and perhaps went even further. He said that the sellers of the wheat knew that the buyers "might well sell it over again and make a profit on the resale"; and that being so they "must be taken to have consented to this state of things and thereby to have made themselves liable to pay" the profit on a resale.

It may be that there was nothing very new in this but I think that *Hall's* case must be taken to have established that damages are not to be treated as too remote merely because, on the knowledge available to the defendant when the contract was made, the chance of the occurrence of the event which caused the damage would have appeared to him to be rather less than an even chance. I would agree with Lord Shaw that it is generally sufficient that that event would have appeared to the defendant as not unlikely to occur. It is hardly ever possible in this matter to assess probabilities with any degree of mathematical accuracy. But I do not find in that case or in cases which preceded it any warrant for regarding as within the contemplation of the parties any event which would not have appeared to the defendant, had he thought about it, to have a very substantial degree of probability.

But then it has been said that the liability of defendants has been further extended by *Victoria Laundry (Windsor) Ltd.* v. *Newman Industries Ltd.* I do not think so. The plaintiffs bought a large boiler from the defendants and the defendants were aware of the general nature of the plaintiffs' business and of the plaintiffs' intention to put the boiler into use as soon as possible. Delivery of the boiler was delayed in breach of contract and the plaintiffs claimed as damages loss of profit caused by the delay. A large part of the profits claimed would have resulted from some specially lucrative contracts which the plaintiffs could have completed if they had had the boiler: that was rightly disallowed because the defendants had no knowledge of these contracts. But Asquith L.J. then said: "It does not, however, follow that the plaintiffs are precluded for recovering some general (and perhaps conjectural) sum for loss of business in respect of dyeing contracts to be reasonably expected, any more than in respect of laundering contracts to be reasonably expected."

It appears to me that this was well justified on the earlier authorities. It was certainly not unlikely on the information which the defendants had when making the contract that delay in delivering the order would result in loss of business: indeed it would seem that that was more than an even chance. And there was nothing new in holding that damages should be estimated on a conjectural basis. . . .

But what is said to create a "landmark" is the statement of principles by Asquith L.J. This does to some extent go beyond the older authorities and in so far as it does so, I do not agree with it. In paragraph (2) it is said that the plaintiff is entitled to recover "such part of the loss actually resulting as was at the time of the contract reasonably foreseeable as liable to result from the breach." To bring in reasonable foreseeability appears to me to be confusing measure of damages in contract with measure of damages in tort. A great many extremely unlikely results are reasonably foreseeable: it is true that Lord Asquith may have meant foreseeable as a likely result, and if that is all he meant I would not object further than to say that I think that the phrase is liable to be misunderstood. For the same reason I would take exception to the phrase "liable to result" in paragraph (5). Liable is a very vague word but I think that one would usually say that when a person foresees a very improbable result he foresees that it is liable to happen.

I agree with the first half of paragraph (6). For the best part of a century it has not been required that the defendant could have foreseen that a breach of contract must necessarily result in the loss which has occurred. But I cannot agree with the second half of that paragraph. It has never been held to be sufficient in contract that the loss was foreseeable as "a serious possibility" or "a real danger" or as being "on the cards." It is on the cards that one can win £100,000 or more for a stake of a few pence— several people have done that. And anyone who backs a hundred to one chance regards a win as a serious possibility—many people have won on such a chance. And the *Wagon Mound (No. 2)*, [1967] 1 A.C. 617, could not have been decided as it was unless the extremely unlikely fire should have been foreseen by the ship's officer as a real danger. It appears to me that in the ordinary use of language there is a wide gulf between saying that some event is not unlikely or quite likely to happen and saying merely that it is a serious possibility, a real danger, or on the cards. Suppose one takes a well-shuffled pack of cards—it is quite likely or not unlikely that the top card will prove to be a diamond: the odds are only 3 to 1 against. But most people would not say that it is quite likely to be the nine of diamonds for the odds are then 51 to 1 against. On the other hand I think that most people would say that there is a serious possibility or a real danger of its being turned up first and of course it is on the cards. If the tests of "real danger" or "serious possibility" are in future to be authoritative then the *Victoria Laundry* case would indeed be a landmark because it would mean that *Hadley* v. *Baxendale* would be differently decided today. I certainly could not understand any court deciding that, on the information available to the carrier in that case, the stoppage of the mill was neither a serious possibility nor a real danger. If those tests are to prevail in future then let us cease to pay lip service to the rule in *Hadley* v. *Baxendale*. But in my judgment to adopt these tests would extend liability for breach of contract beyond what is reasonable or desirable. From the limited knowledge which I have of commercial affairs I would not expect such an extension to be welcomed by the business community and from the legal point of view I can find little or nothing to recommend it.

LORD PEARCE: . . . The underlying rule of the common law is that "where a party sustains a loss by means of a breach of contract, he is, so far as money can do it, to be placed in the same situation with regard to damages, as if the contract had been performed". . . . But since so wide a principle might be too harsh on a contract-breaker in making him liable for a chain of unforeseen and fortuitous circumstances, the law limited the liability in ways which crystallised in the rule in *Hadley* v. *Baxendale*. This was designed as a direction to juries but it has become an integral part of the law.

Since an Olympian cloud shrouded any doubts, difficulties and borderline troubles that might arise in the jury room and the jury could use a common sense liberality in applying the rule to the facts, the rule worked admirably as a general guidance for deciding facts. But when the lucubrations of judges who have to give reasons superseded the reticence of juries, there were certain matters which needed clarification. That service was well performed by the judgment of the Court of Appeal in the case of *Victoria Laundry (Windsor) Ltd.* v. *Newman Industries Ltd.* I do not think that there was anything startling or novel about it. In my opinion it represented (in felicitous language) the approximate view of *Hadley* v. *Baxendale* taken by many judges in trying ordinary cases of breach of contract.

It is argued that it was an erroneous departure from *Hadley* v. *Baxendale* in that it allowed damages where the loss was "a serious possibility" or "a real danger" instead of maintaining that the loss must be "probable," in the sense that it was more likely to result than not. But, over twenty years before, in *R. & H. Hall Ltd.* v. *W. H. Pim (Junior) & Co. Ltd.* Viscount Dunedin had said that it was enough if there was an even chance of the loss happening. Lord Shaw of Dunfermline said that the two parts of the rule need not be antithetically treated but might run into each other and be one; and he read "probable" as meaning a "not unlikely" result. Lord Phillimore said: "[They] are called damages in the contemplation of the parties, not because the parties contemplate a breach of contract, but because they recognise that a breach is possible, and they reckon that these damages may flow from that breach. I designedly use the word 'may.' There may be cases where the word to be used might be 'will,' but there are also cases, and more common cases, where the word to use is 'may.'" Lord Blanesburgh expressed agreement with the others, and presumably did not dissent from the views set out above. Viscount Haldane dealt with the matter as one of construction: "Whether such a resale was likely or not does not matter if, as I think, the buyers stipulated for power to make it being provided. . . ."

Accordingly in my opinion the expressions used in the *Victoria Laundry* case were right. I do not however accept the colloquialism "on the cards" as being a useful test because I am not sure just what nuance it has either in my own personal vocabulary or in that of others. I suspect that it owes its attraction, like many other colloquialisms, to the fact that one may utter it without having the trouble of really thinking out with precision what one means oneself or what others will understand by it, a spurious attraction which in general makes colloquialism unsuitable for definition, though it is often useful as shorthand for a collection of definable ideas. It was in this latter convenient sense that the judgment uses the ambiguous words "liable to result." They were not intended as a further or different test from "serious possibility" or "real danger."

The whole rule in *Hadley* v. *Baxendale* limits damages to that which may be regarded as being within the contemplation of the parties. The first part deals with those things that "may fairly and reasonably be considered as arising naturally, i.e. according to the usual course of things." Those are presumed to be within the contemplation of the parties. . . . Even the first part of the rule however contains the necessity for the knowledge of certain basic facts, e.g. in *Hadley* v. *Baxendale* the fact that it was a mill shaft to be carried. On this limited basis of knowledge the horizon of contemplation is confined to things "arising naturally, i.e. according to the usual course of things."

Additional or "special" knowledge, however, may extend the horizon to include losses that are outside the natural course of events. And of course the extension of the horizon need not always *increase* the damages; it might introduce a knowledge of particular circumstances, e.g., a subcontract, which show that the plaintiff would in fact suffer *less* damage than a more limited view of the circumstances might lead one to expect. According to whether one categorises a fact as basic knowledge or special knowledge the case may come under the first part of the rule or the second. For that reason there is sometimes difference of opinion as to which is the part which governs a particular case and it may be that both parts govern it.

I do not think that Alderson B. was directing his mind to whether something resulting in the natural course of events was an odds-on chance or not. A thing may be a natural (or even an obvious) result even though the odds are against it. Suppose a contractor was employed to repair the ceiling of one of the Law Courts and did it so negligently that it collapsed on the heads of those in court. I should be inclined to think that any tribunal (including the learned baron himself) would have found as a fact that the damage arose "naturally, i.e., according to the usual course of things." Yet if one takes into account the nights, weekends, and vacations, when the ceiling might have collapsed, the odds against it collapsing on top of anybody's head are nearly ten to one. I do not believe that this aspect of the matter was fully considered and worked out in the judgment. He was thinking of causation and type of consequence rather than of odds. The language of the judgment in the *Victoria Laundry* case was a justifiable and valuable clarification of the principles which *Hadley* v. *Baxendale* was intending to express. Even if it went further than that, it was in my opinion right.

Nor do I consider that the *Victoria Laundry* case is inconsistent with the actual decision on the facts in *Hadley* v. *Baxendale*. The carriers were asked (without special directions, as the court found) to transport a broken shaft away from a mill. "In the great multitude of cases" (to quote the learned baron's own phrase) one would not expect the whole working of a mill to be stopped by a delay in transportation. The mere absence of urgent instructions spoke strongly against such a contingency. The fact that the shaft was to be used immediately by engineers for measurements (which one would have rather expected to go on paper by post) for making a new shaft would not, I think, have been in the contemplation of the carriers, on the meagre information available.

The facts of the present case lead to the view that the loss of market arose naturally i.e., according to the usual course of things, from the shipowner's deviation. The sugar was being exported to Basrah, where, as the respondents knew, there was a sugar market. It was sold on arrival and fetched a lower price than it would have done had it arrived on time. The fall in market price was not due to any unusual or unpredictable factor. . . .

NOTE. The other Law Lords in *The Heron II* were more restrained than Lord Reid in their criticisms of the language used in *Victoria Laundry* v. *Newman*. The effect of the speeches was summed up in *Aruna Mills Ltd.* v. *Dhanrajmal Gobindram*, [1968] 1 Q.B. 655, at 668 by DONALDSON J.: In the course of the speeches in the *Czarnikow* case their Lordships expressed varying degrees of enthusiasm for the *Victoria Laundry* case; but, subject to two possible qualifications, it seems to me to remain unimpaired as the classic authority on the topic. These two qualifications are as follows. First, reference in the judgment in the *Victoria Laundry* case to a loss being "reasonably foreseeable" should perhaps be taken as referring to the loss having been within "actual or assumed contemplation" (see the speech of Lord Reid). Second, the phrase "liable to result" is not correctly paraphrased by the use of the expression "on the cards," but conveys the relevant shade of likelihood by its own wording (Lord Hodson) or when defined (as it was in proposition (6) in the *Victoria Laundry* case) as indicating that a loss is a "serious possibility" or "real danger" (see Lord Pearce and Lord Upjohn), words which amongst others had the approval of Lord Morris of Borth-y-Gest.

NOTE. In *Freedhof* v. *Pomalift Industries Ltd.* [1971] 2 O.R. 723 (Ont. C.A.), the plaintiff, a ski resort operator, took out a mortgage to finance the purchase of a new skilift from the defendant. The lift proved defective; in consequence the plaintiff lost all his customers, defaulted on the mortgage, and had his land and equipment seized and sold by the mortgagee. The Court of Appeal disallowed an award of damages for the loss of the property, holding that such loss did not meet the test of foreseeability, despite the fact that the defendant was aware of the plaintiff's financial status when the contract was made.

PROBLEM 1. A bought a ticket on the midnight train to Sudbury. The train did not go on to Sudbury as it was supposed to do, but stopped several miles outside the city, and A was forced to disembark. Since no transport or accommodation was available, A walked the 5 miles to his home through freezing rain. As a result, he caught a severe cold, and was off work for several days. A sues for pain and suffering and loss of wages. Will he succeed?

See *Hobbs* v. *London & S.W. Rlwy.* (1875) L.R. 10 Q.B. 111.

PROBLEM 2. C visits horse shows in order to display and promote the sale of his products. At the London fair, he met the agent of D, a railway company, who was at the fair for the purpose of delivering and receiving goods. C delivered his samples to the agent for delivery at the Toronto fair, and marked the consignment note "must be at Toronto by Monday certain." The samples were not delivered in time for the fair. C sues for loss of profits. Will he succeed?

See *Simpson* v. *London & N.W. Rlwy* (1876) 1 Q.B.D. 274.

PROBLEM 3. X contracted to employ Y for 5 years at a salary of $10,000 a year plus any bonuses X might give, as he saw fit. After 2 years, X wrongfully dismissed Y. The next year, X discontinued his bonus system, and increased his employees' salaries by $1,000 a year, instead. Y claims that his damages should include the extra $2,000 he would have received. Advise him.

See *Lavarack* v. *Woods of Colchester, Ltd.* [1967] 1 Q.B. 278.

4. INTANGIBLE INJURIES

ADDIS v. *GRAMOPHONE COMPANY LIMITED*
England. House of Lords. [1909] A.C. 488

The plaintiff was employed by the defendants as manager of their business in Calcutta at £15 per week as salary, and a commission on the trade done. He could be dismissed by six months' notice.

In October, 1905, the defendants gave him six months' notice, but at the same time they appointed Mr. Gilpin to act as his successor, and took steps to prevent the plaintiff from acting any longer as manager. In December, 1905, the plaintiff came back to England.

The plaintiff brought this action in 1906, claiming an account and damages for breach of contract. That there was a breach of contract is quite clear. If what happened in October, 1905, did not amount to a wrongful dismissal, it was, at all events, a breach of the plaintiff's right to act as manager during the six months and to earn the best commission he could make.

When the action came to trial it was agreed to refer the matters of account to arbitration. The causes of action for breach of contract were tried by Darling J. and a jury. The jury found for the plaintiff in respect of wrongful dismissal £600, and £340 in respect of excess commission over and above what was earned by the plaintiff's successor between October, 1905, and April, 1906.

The Court of Appeal by a majority held that upon their views of the facts there was (apart from the account which must be taken) no cause of action, and they entered judgment for the defendants.

LORD ATKINSON: My Lords, I entirely concur with the judgment of my noble and learned friend on the woolsack. Much of the difficulty which has arisen in this case is due to the unscientific form in which the pleadings, as amended, have been framed, and the loose manner in which the proceedings at the trial were conducted.

The rights of the plaintiff, disembarrassed of the confusing methods by which they were sought to be enforced, are, in my opinion, clear. He had been illegally dismissed from his employment. He could have been legally dismissed by the six months' notice, which he, in fact, received, but the defendants did not wait for the expiry of that period. The damages plaintiff sustained by this illegal dismissal were (1) the wages for the period of six months during which his formal notice would have been current; (2) the profits or commission which would, in all reasonable probability, have been earned by him during the six months had he continued in the employment; and possibly (3) damages in respect of the time which might reasonably elapse before he could obtain other employment. He has been awarded a sum possibly of some hundreds of pounds, not in respect of any of these heads of damage, but in respect of the harsh and humiliating way in which he was dismissed, including, presumably, the pain he experienced by reason, it is alleged, of the imputation upon him conveyed by the manner of his dismissal. This is the only circumstance which makes the case of general importance, and this is the only point I think it necessary to deal with.

I have been unable to find any case decided in this country in which any countenance is given to the notion that a dismissed employee can recover in the shape of exemplary damages for illegal dismissal, in effect damages for defamation, for it amounts to that, except the case of *Maw* v. *Jones* (1890), 25 Q.B.D. 107.

In that case Matthew J., as he then was, during the argument, while counsel was urging . . . that the measure of damages for the improper dismissal of an ordinary domestic servant was a month's wages and nothing more, no doubt interjected in the shape of a question the remark, "Have you ever heard the principle applied to a case where a false charge of misconduct has been made?" But the decision was that the direction of the judge at the trial was right.

Now, what was the character of that direction? The defendant had power to dismiss his apprentice, the plaintiff, on a week's notice, and had also power to dismiss him summarily if he should show a want of interest in his work. He dismissed the apprentice summarily without notice, assigning as a reason that he had been guilty of frequent acts of insubordination and that he had gone out at night without leave.

The judge at the trial told the jury that they were not bound to limit the damages to the week's notice he had lost, but that they might take into consideration the time the plaintiff would require to get new employment— the difficulty he would have as a discharged apprentice in getting employment elsewhere—and it was on this precise ground the direction was upheld I do not think that this case is any authority what ever for the general proposition that exemplary damages may be recovered for wrongful dismissal, still less, of course, for breach of contract generally; but, such as it is, it is the only authority in the shape of a decided case which can be found upon the first-mentioned point.

I have always understood that damages for breach of contract were in the nature of compensation, not punishment. . . .

There are three well-known exceptions to the general rule applicable to the measure of damages for breach of contract, namely, actions against a banker for refusing to pay a customer's cheque when he has in his hands funds of the customer's to meet it, actions for breach of promise of marriage, and actions like that in *Flureau* v. *Thornhill* (1776), 2 W.Bl. 1078, where the vendor of real estate, without any fault on his part, fails to make title. I know of none other.

The peculiar nature of the first two of these exceptions justified their existence. Ancient practice upholds the last, though it has often been adversely criticized as in *Bain* v. *Fothergill* (1873), L.R. 7 H.L. 158. If there be a tendency to create a fourth exception it ought, in my view, to be checked rather than stimulated; inasmuch as to apply in their entirety the principles on which damages are measured in tort to cases of damages for breaches of contract would lead to confusion and uncertainty in commercial affairs, while to apply them only in part and in particular cases would create anomalies, lead occasionally to injustice, and make the law a still more "lawless science" than it is said to be.

For instance, in actions of tort, motive, if it may be taken into account to aggravate damages, as it undoubtedly may be, may also be taken into account to mitigate them, as may also the conduct of the plaintiff himself who seeks redress. Is this rule to be applied to actions of breach of contract? There are few breaches of contract more common than those which arise where men omit or refuse to repay what they have borrowed, or to pay for what they have bought. Is the creditor or vendor who sues for one of such breaches to have the sum he recovers lessened if he should be shown to be harsh, grasping, or pitiless, or even insulting, in enforcing his demand, or lessened because the debtor has struggled to pay, has failed because of misfortune, and has been suave, gracious, and apologetic in his refusal? On the other hand, is that sum to be increased if it should be shewn that the debtor could have paid readily without any embarrassment, but refused with expression of contempt and contumely, from a malicious desire to injure his creditor?

Few parties to contracts have more often to complain of ingratitude and baseness than sureties. Are they, because of this, to be entitled to recover from the principal, often a trusted friend, who has deceived and betrayed them, more than they paid on that principal's behalf? If circumstances of aggravation are rightly to be taken into account in actions of contract at all, why should they not be taken into account in the case of the surety, and the rules and principles applicable to cases of tort applied to the full extent?

In many other cases of breach of contract there may be circumstances of malice, fraud, defamation, or violence, which would sustain an action of tort as an alternative remedy to an action for breach of contract. If one should select the former mode of redress, he may, no doubt, recover exemplary damages, or what is sometimes styled vindictive damages; but if he should choose to seek redress in the form of an action for breach of contract, he lets in all the consequences of that form of action. One of these consequences is, I think, this: that he is to be paid adequate compensation in money for the loss of that which he would have received had his contract been kept, and no more.

I can conceive nothing more objectionable and embarrassing in litigation than trying in effect an action of libel or slander as a matter of aggravation in an action for illegal dismissal, the defendant being permitted, as he must in justice be permitted, to traverse the defamatory sense, rely on privilege, or raise every point which he could raise in an independent action brought for the alleged libel or slander itself.

In my opinion, exemplary damages ought not to be, and are not according to any true principle of law, recoverable in such an action as the present, and the sums awarded to the plaintiff should therefore be decreased by the amount at which they have been estimated, and credit for that item should not be allowed in his account.

KOLAN v. SOLICITOR
(1969) 7 D.L.R. (3d) 481 (Ont. H.C.)

The plaintiff brought an action for damages against her solicitor. The solicitor failed to discover that premises purchased by the plaintiff were subject to a City demolition order. The plaintiff proved that consequent anxiety had caused injury to her health. On the question of damages, LACOURCIERE J. said: "In the present case the plaintiff relies on *Cook* v. *S.*, [1967] 1 All E.R. 299, a decision of the Court of Appeal dealing with the measure of damages against a solicitor as a result of his negligence. It had been pleaded that the plaintiff suffered an anxiety state and could not work, and that the defendant knew that she was peculiarly liable to nervous shock. The plaintiff was awarded damages but nothing with respect to her claim for mental distress. It was held as summarized in the headnote: ". . . the plaintiff's breakdown in health owing to anxiety was not a reasonably foreseeable consequence of the defendant's negligence, and, although damages for reasonably foreseeable injury in health due to nervous shock or anxiety could be recovered for breach of duty to use care and skill where, as in the present case, the cause of action lay in contract, yet in this case the ruling of the trial judge that the damage was too remote should stand. . . ."

The following dictum appears in the judgment of Lord Denning, M.R., at p. 303: "In these circumstances I think that, just as in the law of tort, so also in the law of contract, damages can be recovered for nervous shock or anxiety state if it is a reasonably foreseeable consequence. So the question became this: when a client goes to a solicitor, is it a reasonably foreseeable consequence that, if anything goes wrong with the litigation owing to the solicitor's negligence, there will be a breakdown in health? It can be foreseen that there will be injured feelings; mental distress; anger, and annoyance. But for none of these can damages be recovered. It was so held in *Groom* v. *Crocker* on the same lines as *Addis* v. *Gramophone Co., Ltd.* ([1908-10] All E.R. Rep. 1, [1909] A.C. 488). Is it reasonably foreseeable that there may be an actual breakdown in health? I do not think so. It was suggested in this case that there were special circumstances in that the plaintiff was peculiarly liable to nervous shock. I am afraid that she was. The history of her life shows one nervous breakdown after another. If this special circumstance was brought home to the defendant, it might enlarge the area of foreseeability so as to make him liable; but it was not pleaded. Moreover when counsel for the plaintiff put questions to the defendant, he did not succeed in showing that special circumstances were brought home to him. All the defendant knew was that she was a woman obviously highly strung and worried as any woman would be in the circumstances. That does not mean, however, that he should foresee that, if he was negligent, she would suffer injury to health. In all these cases of nervous shock and breakdown in mental health, it is very difficult to draw the line. In *King* v. *Phillips* ([1953] 1 All E.R. 617 at p. 624) I asked: "Where is the line to be drawn?" I found the answer given by Lord Wright: "Only where 'in the particular case the good sense of the . . . judge, decides'." In this present case the judge thought that the damages for the breakdown in health were too remote. I am not prepared to disturb his ruling. On this point the appeal fails."

In the case at bar, it is undisputed that the plaintiff did suffer physical illness, and the question is therefore whether such illness was reasonably foreseeable to the defendant at the time of the contract. Mr. Starr argued that such consequence was foreseeable in that Mrs. Kolan was a widow of modest means who was using her limited cash reserve to complete the purchase of an old potentially substandard house, and that a demolition order of the Housing Standards Board would therefore place her in a critical position where a woman of her age and in her position would suffer illness. I am not prepared to find that the health breakdown of the plaintiff was a reasonably foreseeable consequence of the defendant's negligence, and I am not prepared to award the plaintiff any damages under that heading or refer any for assessment."

D. v. *B.* 1917. 40 O.L.R. 112 (Ontario Court of Appeal). Plaintiff and defendant were engaged to be married and the defendant broke the engagement. Plaintiff sued and recovered a verdict for $5,000. She did not prove any actual damage. The $5,000 was almost entirely sentimental and in the middle of the war may have unduly reflected the defendant's Austrian background. He was an Austrian by birth but had been educated in Canada and had been admitted to the Bar two years before the action. He worked for a legal firm for $1,500 a year and had dependent relatives for whom he was morally if not legally responsible. Plaintiff was a Russian, had been in the country for only a year, and was expected to return to Russia, in which case "her prospects of future marriage will not probably be affected." On appeal a new trial was ordered. FERGUSON J.A.: "The principles of law and rules governing the trial of an action for breach of promise are considered in *Smith* v. *Woodfine* (1857), 1 C.B.N.S. 660; 140 E.R. 272. In that case Mr. Justice Willes, at p. 667, quotes with approval from the American work, Sedgwick on Damages, 2nd ed., p. 368, as follows: "The action for breach of promise of marriage . . . though nominally an action founded on the breach of an agreement, presents a striking exception to the general rules which govern contracts. This action is given as an indemnity to the injured party for the loss she has sustained, and has always been held to embrace the injury to the feelings, affections, and wounded pride, as well as the loss of marriage. . . . From the nature of the case, it has been found impossible to fix the amount of compensation by any precise rule; and as in tort, the measure of damages is a question for the sound discretion of the jury in each particular instance . . . subject, of course, to the general restriction that a verdict influenced by *prejudice, passion*, or corruption, will not be allowed to stand. Beyond this the power of the Court is limited, as in cases of tort, almost exclusively to questions arising on the admissibility of evidence when offered by way of enhancing or mitigating damages. . . .' In my opinion, the verdict, is, under all the circumstances, excessive. . . ."
MEREDITH C.J.O.: ". . . The prejudice to the appellant was, I think, greatly aggravated by the contrast between the parties, evidently sought to be impressed upon the jury by painting the respondent as a refugee from our ally Russia, while the appellant was of Austrian enemy origin. . . . I am always reluctant to interfere with the finding of a jury, and endeavour to be on my guard against usurping the functions of a jury in a case in which they have come to a conclusion different from that which I have formed as to the result of the evidence; but, at a time like this, when the minds of the

people are rightly inflamed against the German and Austrian peoples, it is, I think, incumbent on the Court to guard against that feeling being used to the detriment of a litigant who comes or is brought into a Court of Justice, and to be astute to see that, where it has been played upon by the successful litigant, he is deprived of any advantage thus unfairly obtained; and it is not, I think, unfair to presume against such a litigant that his effort has had the desired effect."

NOTE. The exception to the rule limiting damages to compensation made in what are sometimes called "heart balm" cases has led to frequent abuse. Compare the two legislative solutions reproduced below, both as to substance and as to form and style. Can you suggest other, and perhaps better ways of dealing with excessive damage awards? What is the purpose of section 61-a in the New York Laws? Is it necessary in Ontario? Is it a Good Thing?

THE EVIDENCE ACT
Ontario. Revised Statutes. 1970. Chapter 151

13. The plaintiff in an action for breach of promise of marriage shall not recover unless his or her testimony is corroborated by some other material evidence in support of the promise.

NEW YORK LAWS
New York. Statutes. 1935. Chapter 263

61-a. *Declaration of public policy of state.* The remedies heretofore provided by law for the enforcement of actions based upon alleged alienation of affections, criminal conversation, seduction and breach of contract to marry, having been subjected to grave abuses, causing extreme annoyance, embarrassment, humiliation and pecuniary damage to many persons wholly innocent and free of any wrongdoing, who were merely the victims of circumstances, and such remedies having been exercised by unscrupulous persons for their unjust enrichment, and such remedies having furnished vehicles for the commission or attempted commission of crime and in many cases having resulted in the perpetration of frauds, it is hereby declared as the public policy of the state that the best interests of the people of the state will be served by the abolition of such remedies. Consequently, in the public interest, the necessity for the enactment of this article is hereby declared as a matter of legislative determination.

61-b. *Certain causes of action hereafter accruing abolished.* The rights of action heretofore existing to recover sums of money as damage for the alienation of affections, criminal conversation, seduction, or breach of contract to marry are hereby abolished.

61-d. *Legal effect of certain acts hereafter occurring.* No act hereafter done within this state shall operate to give rise, either within or without this state, to any of the rights of action abolished by this article. No contract to marry, hereafter made or entered into in this state shall operate to give rise, either within or without this state, to any cause or right of action for the breach thereof. . . .

HERBERT CLAYTON AND JACK WALLER LTD. v. *OLIVER*
England. House of Lords. [1930] A.C. 209

Barrie Oliver, a young actor, agreed with Messrs. Clayton and Waller, producers, "to play one of three leading comedy parts" in a musical production at the London Hippodrome for £55 a week for six weeks certain. Oliver considered that the part offered to him did not meet this test and declined to appear in it. His view was accepted by the House of Lords, Lord Buckmaster remarking, "Making all necessary allowances for the fact that the kind of humour of such a play seems melancholy in print, the part assigned to the plaintiff is so trivial that even in relation to this play the verdict is fully warranted." No other part was offered and Oliver commenced this action for damages for loss of salary and for loss of the advertisement and reputation he would have enjoyed had the contract been performed. The jury awarded £165 for loss of salary and £1,000 for loss of advertisement. The Court of Appeal learned that Oliver had obtained service at an equivalent remuneration elsewhere and refused the £165, but confirmed the £1,000.

LORD BUCKMASTER: ... The next question is what was the measure of the damage? It is true that as a general rule the measure of damage for breach of contract is unaffected by the motives or manner of its breach. What are known as vindictive or exemplary damages in tort find no place in contract nor accordingly can injury to feelings or vanity be regarded. The action of breach of promise of marriage is an exception to the general rule, for, strictly assessed, the loss to a woman as a husband of a man who declines with insult to marry her might be assumed to be nil, but that is not the way such damages are determined.

In the present case the old and well established rule applies without qualification, the damages are those that may reasonably be supposed to have been in the contemplation of the parties at the time when the contract was made, as the probable result of its breach, and if any special circumstances were unknown to one of the parties, the damages associated with and flowing from such breach cannot be included. Here both parties knew that as flowing from the contract the plaintiff would be billed and advertised as appearing at the Hippodrome, and in the theatrical profession this is a valuable right.

In assessing the damages, therefore, it was competent for the jury to consider that the plaintiff was entitled to compensation because he did not appear at the Hippodrome, as by his contract he was entitled to do, and in assessing those damages they may consider the loss he suffered (1) because the Hippodrome is an important place of public entertainment and (2) that in the ordinary course he would have been "billed" and otherwise advertised as appearing at the Hippodrome. The learned judge put the matter as a loss of reputation, which I do not think is the exact expression, but he explained that as the equivalent of loss of publicity and that summarizes what I have stated as my view of the true situation.

As to the amount, that was for the jury; the damages appear to me extravagant ... but they are not so extravagant as to vitiate the verdict ....

[Lords Blanesburgh and Tomlin agreed with Lord Buckmaster. Viscount Dunedin gave a short concurring judgment. Lord Warrington of Clyffe agreed.]

JARVIS v. *SWANS TOURS LTD.*
[1973] Q.B. 233 (C.A.)

LORD DENNING M.R.: Mr. Jarvis is a solicitor, employed by a local authority at Barking. In 1969 he was minded to go for Christmas to Switzerland. He was looking forward to a skiing holiday. It is his one fortnight's holiday in the year. He prefers it in the winter rather than in the summer.

Mr. Jarvis read a brochure issued by Swans Tours Ltd. He was much attracted by the description of Mörlialp, Giswil, Central Switzerland. I will not read the whole of it, but just pick out some of the principal attractions:

"House Party Centre with special resident host. . . . Mörlialp is a most wonderful little resort on a sunny plateau . . . Up there you will find yourself in the midst of beautiful alpine scenery, which in winter becomes a wonderland of sun, snow and ice, with a wide variety of fine ski-runs, a skating rink and exhilarating toboggan run . . . Why did we choose the Hotel Krone . . . mainly and most of all because of the 'Gemütlichkeit' and friendly welcome you will receive from Herr and Frau Weibel. . . . The Hotel Krone has its own Alphütte Bar which will be open several evenings a week. . . . No doubt you will be in for a great time, when you book this house-party holiday . . . Mr. Weibel, the charming owner, speaks English."

On the same page, in a special yellow box, it was said:

"Swans House Party in Mörlialp. All these House Party arrangements are included in the price of your holiday. Welcome party on arrival. Afternoon tea and cake for 7 days. Swiss dinner by candlelight. Fondue party. Yodler evening. Chali farewell party in the 'Alphütte Bar.' Service of representative."

Alongside on the same page there was a special note about ski-packs. "Hire of Skis, Sticks and Boots . . . Ski Tuition . . . 12 days £11.10."

In August, 1969, on the faith of that brochure, Mr. Jarvis booked a 15-day holiday, with ski-pack. The total charge was £63.45, including Christmas supplement. He was to fly from Gatwick to Zurich on December 20, 1969, and return on January 3, 1970.

The plaintiff went on the holiday, but he was very disappointed. He was a man of about 35 and he expected to be one of a house party of some 30 or so people. Instead, he found there were only 13 during the first week. In the second week there was no house party at all. He was the only person there. Mr. Weibel could not speak English. So there was Mr. Jarvis, in the second week, in this hotel with no house party at all, and no one could speak English, except himself. He was very disappointed, too, with the skiing. It was some distance away at Giswil. There were no ordinary length skis. There were only mini-skis about 3 ft. long. So he did not get his skiing as he wanted to. In the second week he did get some longer skis for a couple of days, but then, because of the boots, his feet got rubbed and he could not continue even with the long skis. So his skiing holiday, from his point of view, was pretty well ruined.

There were many other matters, too. They appear trivial when they are set down in writing, but I have no doubt they loomed large in Mr. Jarvis's mind, when coupled with the other disappointments. He did not have the nice Swiss cakes which he was hoping for. The only cakes for tea were potato crisps and little dry nut cakes. The yodler evening consisted of one man from the locality who came in his working clothes for a little while, and sang four or five songs very quickly. The "Alphütte Bar" was an unoccupied annex which was only open one evening. There was a representative, Mrs. Storr, there during the first week, but she was not there during the second week.

The matter was summed up by the judge: "During the first week he got a holiday in Switzerland which was to some extent inferior . . . and, as to the second week, he got a holiday which was very largely inferior" to what he was led to expect.

What is the legal position? I think that the statements in the brochure were representations or warranties. The breaches of them give Mr. Jarvis a right to damages. It is not necessary to decide whether they were representations or warranties: because since the Misrepresentation Act 1967, there is a remedy in damages for misrepresentation as well as for breach of warranty.

The one question in the case is: What is the amount of damages? The judge seems to have taken the difference in value between what he paid for and what he got. He said that he intended to give "the difference between the two values and no other damages" under any other head. He thought that Mr. Jarvis had got half of what he paid for. So the judge gave him half the amount which he had paid, namely, £31.72. Mr. Jarvis appeals to this court. He says that the damages ought to have been much more.

There is one point I must mention first. Counsel together made a very good note of the judge's judgment. They agreed it. It is very clear and intelligible. It shows plainly enough the ground of the judge's decision: but, by an oversight, it was not submitted to the judge, as it should have been: see *Bruen* v. *Bruce (Practice Note)* [1959] 1 W.L.R. 684. In some circumstances we should send it back to the judge for his comments. But I do not think we need do so here. The judge received the notice of appeal and made notes for our consideration. I do not think he would have wished to add to them. We will, therefore, decide the case on the material before us.

What is the right way of assessing damages? It has often been said that on a breach of contract damages cannot be given for mental distress. Thus in *Hamlin* v. *Great Northern Railway Co.* (1856) 1 H. & N. 408, 411 Pollock C.B. said that damages cannot be given "for the disappointment of mind occasioned by the breach of contract." And in *Hobbs* v. *London & South Western Railway Co.* (1875) L.R. 10 Q.B. 111, 122, Mellor J. said that "for the mere inconvenience, such as annoyance and loss of temper, or vexation, or for being disappointed in a particular thing which you have set your mind upon, without real physical inconvenience resulting, you cannot recover damages."

The courts in those days only allowed the plaintiff to recover damages if he suffered physical inconvenience, such as having to walk five miles home, as in *Hobbs'* case; or to live in an over-crowded house, *Bailey* v. *Bullock* [1950] 2 All E.R. 1167.

I think that those limitations are out of date. In a proper case damages for mental distress can be recovered in contract, just as damages for shock can be recovered in tort. One such case is a contract for a holiday, or any other contract to provide entertainment and enjoyment. If the contracting party breaks his contract, damages can be given for the disappointment, the distress, the upset and frustration caused by the breach. I know that it is difficult to assess in terms of money, but it is no more difficult than the assessment which the courts have to make every day in personal injury cases for loss of amenities. Take the present case.

Mr. Jarvis has only a fortnight's holiday in the year. He books it far ahead, and looks forward to it all that time. He ought to be compensated for the loss of it.

A good illustration was given by Edmund Davies L.J. in the course of the argument. He put the case of a man who has taken a ticket for Glyndbourne. It is the only night on which he can get there. He hires a car to take him. The car does not turn up. His damages are not limited to the mere cost of the ticket. He is entitled to general damages for the disappointment he has suffered and the loss of the entertainment which he should have had. Here, Mr. Jarvis's fortnight's winter holiday has been a grave disappointment. It is true that he was conveyed to Switzerland and back and had meals and bed in the hotel. But that is not what he went for. He went to enjoy himself with all the facilities which the defendants said he would have. He is entitled to damages for the lack of those facilities, and for his loss of enjoyment.

A similar case occurred in 1951. It was *Stedman* v. *Swan's Tours* (1951) 95 S.J. 727. A holiday-maker was awarded damages because he did not get the bedroom and the accommodation which he was promised. The county court judge awarded him £13.15. This court increased it to £50.

I think the judge was in error in taking the sum paid for the holiday £63.45 and halving it. The right measure of damages is to compensate him for the loss of entertainment and enjoyment which he was promised, and which he did not get.

Looking at the matter quite broadly, I think the damages in this case should be the sum of £125. I would allow the appeal, accordingly.

[Edmund Davies and Stephenson L.J.J. agreed.]

HEYWOOD v. *WELLERS*
[1976] 2 W.L.R. 101 (C.A.)

H, a woman, instructed a firm of solicitors to seek an injunction to restrain a man, M, from molesting her. The solicitors failed to institute the proper proceedings, and M continued to molest H. H sued the solicitors for the return of the fees she had paid and for damages for negligence. The trial judge ordered repayment of the fees, but refused to award further damages. H appealed (conducting the appeal in person).

LORD DENNING M.R.: So the solicitors were entitled to nothing for costs; and Mrs. Heywood could recover the £175 as money paid on a consideration which had wholly failed. She was, therefore, entitled to recover it as of right. And she is entitled to recover as well damages for negligence. Take this instance. If you engage a driver to take you to the station to catch a train for a day trip to the sea, you pay him £2—and then the car breaks down owing to his negligence. So that you miss your holiday. In that case you can recover not only your £2 back but also damages for the disappointment, upset and mental distress which you suffered: see *Jarvis* v. *Swan's Tours Ltd.* [1973] Q.B. 233 and *Jackson* v. *Horizon Holidays Ltd.* [1975] 1 W.L.R. 1468.

So here Mrs. Heywood employed the solicitors to take proceedings at law to protect her from molestation by Mr. Marrion. They were under a duty by contract to use reasonable care. Owing to their want of care she was molested by this man on three or four occasions. This molestation caused her much mental distress and upset. It must have been in their contemplation that if they failed in their duty she might be further molested and suffer much upset and distress. This damage she suffered was within their contemplation within the rule in *Hadley* v. *Baxendale* (1854) 9 Exch. 341. That was the test applied by Lawson J. in the recent case of *Cox* v. *Philips Industries Ltd.* (October 15, 1975) reported only in The Times, October 21, 1975. Mr. Keith Simpson urged that damages for mental distress were not recoverable. He relied on *Groom* v. *Crocker* [1939] 1 K.B. 194 and *Cook* v. *Swinfen* [1967] 1 W.L.R. 457, 461. But those cases may have to be reconsidered. In any case they were different from this. Here the solicitors were employed to protect her from molestation causing mental distress—and should be responsible in damages for their failure.

It was suggested that even if the solicitors had done their duty and taken the man to court he might still have molested her. But I do not think they can excuse themselves on that ground. After all, it was not put to the test: and it was their fault that it was not put to the test. If they had taken him to court as she wished—and as they ought to have done— it might well have been effective to stop him from molesting her any more. We should assume that it would have been effective to protect her, unless they prove that it would not: see *Coldman* v. *Hill* [1919] 1 K.B. 443, 457 by Scrutton L.J. and *Scottish Co-operative Wholesale Society Ltd.* v. *Meyer* [1959] A.C. 324, 367.

So the remaining question is: What damages should be awarded to Mrs. Heywood for the molestation she suffered on three or four occasions and the mental distress and upset she suffered? The judge, unfortunately, did not quantify the damages. In her claim as amended she put them at £150. I would allow her that sum.

[James and Bridge L.J.J. agreed.]

5. MITIGATION OF LOSS

PAYZU LIMITED v. *SAUNDERS*
England. Court of Appeal. [1919] 2 K.B. 581

By a contract in writing dated November 9, 1917, the defendant, who was a dealer in silk agreed to sell the plaintiffs 200 pieces of crepe de chine at 4s. 6d. a yard and 200 pieces at 5s. 11d. a yard, "delivery as required January to September, 1918; conditions 2½ per cent 1 month," which meant that payment for goods delivered up to the twentieth day of the month should be made on the twentieth day of the following month, subject to 2½ per cent discount. At the request of the plaintiffs, the defendants delivered, in November 1917, a certain quantity of the goods under the contract, the price of which amounted to £76 less 2½ per cent discount. On December 21st the plaintiffs drew a cheque in favor of the defendant in payment of these goods, but the cheque was never received by the defendant. Early in January, 1918, the defendant telephoned to the plaintiffs asking why she had not received a cheque. The plaintiffs then drew another cheque, but owing to a delay in obtaining the signature of one of the plaintiffs' directors, this cheque was not sent to the defendant until January 16th. On that day the plaintiffs gave an order by telephone for further deliveries under the contract. The defendant in the belief, which was in fact erroneous, that the plaintiff's financial position was such that they could not have met the cheque which they alleged had been drawn in December, wrote to the plaintiffs on January 16, refusing to make any further deliveries under the contract, unless the plaintiffs paid cash with each order. The plaintiffs refused to do this, and after some further correspondence brought this action claiming damages for breach of contract. The damages claimed were the difference between the market price in the middle of February 1918, and the contract price of the two classes of goods, the difference alleged being respectively 1s. 3d. and 1s. 4d. a yard.

McCARDIE J.: . . . in my opinion, the defendant's letter of January 16 did in fact and in law amount to an unjustifiable refusal by her to carry out her contractual obligations, for she announced in clear terms that she would thenceforth deliver no further goods to the plaintiffs under the contract unless the plaintiffs paid cash to cover each invoice. The market price of these goods was rising from the beginning of January and continued to rise up to the middle of February. The plaintiffs claim to be entitled to damages based on the market price at that date. I find as a fact that the market prices in February were respectively 6d. and 7d. per yard in excess of the contract prices. The plaintiffs did not in fact purchase goods as against their contract with the defendant. They asserted that the market was so bare of goods as to render purchases impracticable.

Now a serious question of law arises on the question of damages. I find as a fact that the defendant was ready and willing to supply the goods to the plaintiffs at the times and places specified in the contract, provided the plaintiffs paid cash on delivery. Mr. Matthews [of counsel for the plaintiffs] argued with characteristic vigour and ability that the plaintiffs were entitled to ignore that offer on the ground that a person who has repudiated a contract cannot place the other party to the contract under an obligation to diminish his loss by accepting a new offer made by the party in default.

The question is one of juristic importance. What is the rule of law as to the duty to mitigate damages? I will first refer to the judgment of Cockburn C.J., in *Frost* v. *Knight*, (1872), L.R. 7 Ex. 111, 115, where he said: "In assessing the damages for breach of the performance, a jury will of course take into account whatever the plaintiff has done, or has had the means of doing and, as a prudent man, ought in reason to have done, whereby his loss has been or would have been, diminished." . . .

The question, therefore, is what a prudent person ought reasonably to do in order to mitigate his loss arising from a breach of contract. I feel no inclination to allow in a mercantile dispute an unhappy indulgence in farfetched resentment or an undue sensitiveness to slights or unfortunately worded letters. Business often gives rise to certain asperities. But I agree that the plaintiffs in deciding whether to accept the defendant's offer were fully entitled to consider the terms in which the offer was made, its bona fides or otherwise, its relation to their own business methods and financial position, and all the circumstances of the case; and it must be remembered that an acceptance of the offer would not preclude an action for damages for the actual loss sustained. Many illustrations might be given of the extraordinary results which would follow if the plaintiffs were entitled to reject the defendant's offer and incur a substantial measure of loss which would have been avoided by their acceptance of the offer. The plaintiffs were in fact in a position to pay cash for the goods but instead of accepting the defendant's offer, which was made perfectly bona fide, the plaintiffs permitted themselves to sustain a large measure of loss which as prudent and reasonable people, they ought to have avoided. But the fact that the plaintiffs have claimed damages on an erroneous principle does not preclude me from awarding to them such damages as they have in fact suffered, calculated upon the correct bases. . . . They have suffered serious and substantial business inconvenience, and I conceive that I am entitled to award them damages for that. . . . Moreover, even if the plaintiffs had accepted the defendant's offer, they would nevertheless have lost a very useful period of credit which the contract gave them. Taking into consideration all the circumstances of the case I have come to the conclusion that the right sum to award as damages is £50. I give judgment for the plaintiffs for that amount, and in view of the important points involved, I give costs on the High Court Scale.

[The plaintiffs appealed to the Court of Appeal on the question of damages.]

BANKS L.J.: At the trial of this case the defendant, the present respondent, raised two points: first, that she had commited no breach of the contract of sale, and secondly that, if there was a breach, yet she had offered and was always ready and willing to supply the pieces of silk, the subject of the contract, at the contract price for cash; that it was unreasonable on the part of the appellants not to accept that offer, and that therefore they cannot claim damages beyond what they would have lost by paying cash with each order instead of having a month's credit and a discount of 2½ per cent. We must take it that this was the offer made by the respondent. The case was fought and the learned judge has given judgment on that footing. It is true that the correspondence suggests that the respondent was at one time claiming an increased price. But in this court it must be taken that the offer was to supply the contract goods at the contract price except that payment was to be by cash instead of being on credit.

In these circumstances the only question is whether the appellants can establish that as a matter of law they were not bound to consider any offer made by the respondent because of the attitude she had taken up. . . .

It is plain that the question what is reasonable for a person to do in mitigation of his damages cannot be a question of law but must be one of fact in the circumstances of each particular case. There may be cases where as matter of fact it would be unreasonable to expect a plaintiff to consider any offer made in view of the treatment he had received from the defendant. If he had been rendering personal services and had been dismissed after being accused in presence of others of being a thief, and if after that his employer had offered to take him back into his service, most persons would think he was justified in refusing the offer and that it would be unreasonable to ask him in this way to mitigate the damages in an action of wrongful dismissal. But that is not to state a principle of law, but a conclusion of fact to be arrived at on a consideration of all the circumstances of the case. Mr. Matthews complained that the respondents had treated his clients so badly that it would be unreasonable to expect them to listen to any proposition she might make. I do not agree. In my view each party was ready to accuse the other of conduct unworthy of a high commercial reputation and there was nothing to justify the appellants in refusing to consider the respondent's offer. I think the learned judge came to a proper conclusion on the facts, and that the appeal must be dismissed.

SCRUTTON L.J.: I am of the same opinion. Whether it be more correct to say that a plaintiff must minimize his damages, or to say that he can recover no more than he would have suffered if he had acted reasonably, because any further damages do not reasonably follow from the defendant's breach, the result is the same. . . . In certain cases of personal service it may be unreasonable to expect a plaintiff to consider an offer from the other party who has grossly injured him; but in commercial contracts it is generally reasonable to accept an offer from the party in default. However, it is always a question of fact. About the law there is no difficulty. *Appeal dismissed.*

[Parts of the opinions reproduced, as well as Eve J.'s, are omitted.]

ROTH & CO. v. *TAYSEN, TOWNSEND & CO.*
England. Court of Appeal. 1896. 1 Comm. Cas. 306

This was an action for damages for the non-acceptance by the defendants, Grant and Grahame, of a cargo of maize. The alleged contract was contained in telegrams which passed between the parties on May 23, 1895, and the trial judge and the Court of Appeal found it to be a contract to ship the cargo by a named boat, the ship to be ready to load on July 15, and the buyers to have the power of cancelling on Aug. 15 if the ship was not ready to load by that day. On May 29 defendants repudiated. The plaintiff did not sue until July 24 and did not resell the cargo until September 5, the last day in which a delivery might have been made under the contract. The resale on September 5 was at a loss of £3807 3s. 8d. The trial court (Mathew J.) fixed the damages at £1557 which would have been the amount of the loss if the cargo had been sold on July 24, when the plaintiffs issued the writ.

Against this judgment the defendants, Grant & Grahame, appealed on the ground that there was no binding contract between the parties, and that the damages were excessive. The damages, they contended, if payable, were £688 only, the amount of the loss if the cargo had been sold on May 29, when they repudiated the contract. The plaintiffs entered a cross-appeal, claiming by way of damages £3807 3s. 8d., the amount of the loss sustained by the sale of the cargo on September 5.

Lord Esher M.R.: . . . Then comes the question of damages. When there is a repudiation which the other party chooses to treat as a breach, the primary rule is that the damages are the difference between the contract price and the market price of the goods at the date of the breach. If the repudiation takes place before the day of delivery, the other party has the right to bring an action immediately, and it follows that he has the right to have his damages assessed at the time he brings his action. In such a case the damages are not the difference between the contract and market price on the day the action is brought. It is the duty of the jury to assess them, having regard to, and making allowance for, the fact that the party plaintiff is receiving damages before the date of delivery has arrived. There is this further rule. The party who has treated a repudiation as a breach is bound to do what is reasonable to prevent the damages from being inflamed or increased. Now, did the plaintiffs do what was unreasonable in declining to sell till September 5? . . .

The evidence before the judge was that the market was falling steadily from day to day and from week to week, and was still falling when the writ was issued. Any one acquainted with the market must have seen the strong probability that the market would continue to fall. The plaintiffs had no right to suppose that the market would begin to rise, and no ordinary business man who was not a speculator would have thought that it was likely to do so. Buyers were refusing to come forward, being of opinion that they would have to sell.at a still lower price. The judge had the right to come to the conclusion, 'as a jury, that ordinary business men (such as the plaintiffs), who were desirous of diminishing the loss, would have sold the maize at an earlier date, and I cannot undertake to say that his finding was wrong. The appeal and the cross-appeal therefore fail.

LOPES L.J.: . . . What are the plaintiff's rights? Ever since the case of *Hochster* v. *De La Tour* (1852), 118 E.R. 922, it has been the rule that if a payor repudiates a contract and the payee accepts his repudiation, the payee may bring an action. If no time has been fixed for the fulfilment of the contract, the plaintiff is entitled to such damage as he has sustained calculated at the date of the breach; if a time has been fixed for fulfilment, the damages are the loss of the plaintiff calculated as at the date of fulfilment. Here the breach was on July 24. The plaintiffs were bound to take reasonable steps to mitigate the damages; and, if they could have sold the cargo at any time previous to the date of fulfilment of the contract, or about the time of the breach, they ought to have done so. The learned judge held that they might have sold, and that they ought to have done so, about July 24. It is said for the plaintiffs that, though there is that rule of law, there was no evidence upon which a judge or jury could hold that it would have been prudent for the plaintiffs to sell. Of course, it is true that if the plaintiffs had sold and the market had then risen, they might have been told that they were wrong to sell; but I think that they were indiscreet in holding on when the market was falling, and that they would have been well advised if they had sold at an earlier date. The learned judge has held that they did not act reasonably, and I am not prepared to say that he was wrong. I think the amount of damages which he awarded was right.

RIGBY L.J.: . . . The only question, then, is as to the measure of damages. Now, taking in its full effect in favour of the plaintiffs the rule laid down in *Roper* v. *Johnson* (1873), L.R. 8 C.P. 167, it may be that prima facie, this being the breach of a contract to deliver goods, the damages are to be assessed as at the agreed date of delivery. But here the plaintiffs put an end to the contract at an earlier date. Judges have always held that a person availing himself of his right to accept repudiation of a contract must take measures to mitigate the damages which he has sustained by the breach. It is true that by so doing he may take some risk upon himself, but the tribunal will take that fact into consideration. In the present case there seems to be sufficient evidence though it is not conclusive, to justify the learned judge in holding that the plaintiffs ought to have sold the cargo when they put an end to the contract by accepting the defendants' repudiation. I gather that there was evidence that the market was falling, and that the state of things did not render a recovery of prices probable within a reasonable time. I cannot accept the argument of Mr. Bigham [of counsel for the plaintiffs] that it is sufficient to show that the plaintiffs acted to the best of their judgment. The standard which one must use in these cases is the conduct of an ordinary prudent man under similar circumstances. The result is that both appeals must be dismissed.

Appeal and cross-appeal dismissed.

[Only that part of the case dealing with the question of damages is reproduced.]

PROBLEM 1. C bought a house with the assistance of his solicitor, D. A year later, a defect in the title of the house came to light, and C sued D for negligence. D admitted the negligence, but on the question of damages, claimed that C should have mitigated his loss by suing the vendor, E. Advise C.
See *Pilkington* v. *Wood* [1953] Ch. 770.

PROBLEM 2. P was employed as general manager of Q Company. He had an employment contract for 5 years at $5,000 a year. After 3 years, Q Co. went bankrupt and P was dismissed. At this point, P bought certain goods from Q Company, and sold them to make $11,000 profit. P now sues for damages for wrongful dismissal. Advise Q Company.
See *Cockburn* v. *Trusts & Guarantee Co.* (1917) 37 D.L.R. 701 (S.C.C.).

PROBLEM 3. Pharmacist B negligently supplied tranquilizers instead of birth control pills to C, a married woman with 7 children. As a result, an unwelcome eighth child was born. B claims that C has suffered no damages, or alternatively, that she should have mitigated her loss either by abortion or by giving the child up for adoption. Advise C.
See *Troppi* v. *Scarf*, 187 N.W. 2d 511 (1971, Mich. C.A.).

PROBLEM 4. F, who operated a ski resort, bought a ski lift from P. The lift proved defective, F lost all his customers, and his business was ruined. He could not mitigate those losses because he had no money to purchase another ski lift. Is P liable for the loss of the business?
See *Freedhof* v. *Pomalift Industries Ltd.* [1971] 2 O.R. 773 (C.A.).

PROBLEM 5. A, in breach of contract, delivers defective goods to B, who has agreed to supply them to C, an old customer. The contract between B and C contains a clause in fine print exempting B from liability to C, and obliging C to pay for the goods even if defective. B buys sound goods and delivers them to C. In B's action against A, A argues that B should have mitigated his loss by foisting the defective goods on C in accordance with B's strict rights. B replies that he could not so treat an old and valued customer. Advise A.
See *James Finlay & Co.* v. *N. V. Kwik Hoo Tong H.M.* [1929] 1 K.B. 400.

WHITE & CARTER (COUNCILS), LTD. v. McGREGOR
Scotland. House of Lords. [1961] 3 All E.R. 1178

LORD REID: My Lords, the pursuers supply to local authorities litter bins which are placed in the streets. They are allowed to attach to these receptacles plates carrying advertisements and they make their profit from payments made to them by the advertisers. The defender carried on a garage in Clydebank and in 1954 he made an agreement with the pursuers under which they displayed advertisements of his business on a number of these bins. In June, 1957, his sales manager made a further contract with the pursuers for the display of these advertisements for a further period of three years. The sales manager had been given no specific authority to make this contract and when the defender heard of it later on the same day he at once wrote to the pursuers to cancel the contract. The pursuers refused to accept this cancellation. [The contract, itself, stated that it could not be cancelled by the advertiser.] They prepared the necessary plates for attachment to the bins and exhibited them on the bins from Nov. 2, 1957, onwards. [It was found by the Court of Session and the Sheriff Court that the appellants made no effort to minimise their loss by procuring another advertiser to take up the advertising space included in the contract.]

The defender refused to pay any sums due under the contract and the pursuers raised the present action in the Sheriff Court craving payment of £196 4s. the full sum due under the contract for the period of three years. After sundry procedure the sheriff-substitute on Mar. 15, 1960, dismissed the action. He held that the sales manager's action in renewing the contract was within his apparent or ostensible authority and that is not now disputed. The ground on which he dismissed the action was that in the circumstances an action for implement of the contract was inappropriate. He relied on the decision in *Langford & Co., Ltd.* v. *Dutch,* [1952] S.C. 15, and cannot be criticised for having done so.

The pursuers appealed to the Court of Session and on Nov. 29, 1960, the Second Division refused the appeal. The present appeal is taken against their interlocutor of that date. That interlocutor sets out detailed findings of fact and, as this case began in the Sheriff Court, we cannot look beyond those findings. The pursuers must show that on those findings they are entitled to the remedy which they seek.

The case for the defender (now the respondent) is that, as he repudiated the contract before anything had been done under it, the appellants were not entitled to go on and carry out the contract and sue for the contract price: he maintains that in the circumstances the appellants' only remedy was damages, and that, as they do not sue for damages, this action was rightly dismissed.

The contract was for the display of advertisements for a period of 156 weeks from the date when the display began. This date was not specified but admittedly the display began on Nov. 2, 1957, which seems to have been the date when the former contract came to an end. The payment stipulated was 2s. per week per plate together with 5s. per annum per plate both payable annually in advance, the first payment being due seven days after the first display. The reason why the appellants sued for the whole sum due for the three years is to be found in cl. 8 of the conditions:

"8. In the event of an instalment or part thereof being due for payment, and remaining unpaid for a period of four weeks or in the event of the advertiser being in any way in breach of this contract then the whole amount due for the 156 weeks or such part of the said 156 weeks as the advertiser shall not yet have paid shall immediately become due and payable."

A question was debated whether this clause provides a penalty or liquidated damages but on the view which I take of the case it need not be pursued. The clause merely provides for acceleration of payment of the stipulated price if the advertiser fails to pay an instalment timeously. As the respondent maintained that he was not bound by the contract he did not pay the first instalment within the time allowed. Accordingly, if the appellants were entitled to carry out their part of the contract notwithstanding the respondent's repudiation, it was hardly disputed that this clause entitled them to sue immediately for the whole price and not merely for the first instalment.

The general rule cannot be in doubt. It was settled in Scotland at least as early as 1848 and it has been authoritatively stated time and again in both Scotland and England. If one party to a contract repudiates it in the sense of making it clear to the other party that he refuses or will refuse to carry out his part of the contract, the other party, the innocent party, has an option. He may accept that repudiation and sue for damages for breach of contract whether or not the time for performance has come; or he may if he chooses disregard or refuse to accept it and then the contract remains in full effect. . . .

I need not refer to the numerous authorities. They are not disputed by the respondent but he points out that in all of them the party who refused to accept the repudiation had no active duties under the contract. The innocent party's option is generally said to be to wait until the date of performance and then to claim damages estimated as at that date. There is no case in which it is said that he may, in face of the repudiation, go on and incur useless expense in performing the contract and then claim the contract price. The option, it is argued, is merely as to the date as at which damages are to be assessed. Developing this argument, the respondent points out that in most cases the innocent party cannot complete the contract himself without the other party doing, allowing or accepting something, and that it is purely fortuitous that the appellants can do so in this case. In most cases by refusing co-operation the party in breach can compel the innocent party to restrict his claim to damages. Then it was said that even where the innocent party can complete the contract without such co-operation it is against the public interest that he should be allowed to do so. An example was developed in argument. A company might engage an expert to go abroad and prepare an elaborate report and then repudiate the contract before anything was done. To allow such an expert then to waste thousands of pounds in preparing the report cannot be right if a much smaller sum of damages would give him full compensation for his loss. It would merely enable the expert to extort a settlement giving him far more than reasonable compensation.

The respondent founds on the decision of the First Division in *Langford & Co., Ltd.* v. *Dutch*. There an advertising contractor agreed to exhibit a film for a year. Four days after this agreement was made the advertiser repudiated it but, as in the present case, the contractor refused to accept the repudiation and proceeded to exhibit the film and sue for the contract price. The sheriff-substitute dismissed the action as irrelevant and his decision was affirmed on appeal. In the course of a short opinion the Lord President (LORD COOPER) said:

"It appears to me that, apart from wholly exceptional circumstances of which there is no trace in the averments on this record, the law of Scotland does not afford to a person in the position of the pursuers the remedy which is here sought. The pursuers could not force the defender to accept a year's advertisement which she did not want, though they could of course claim damages for her breach of contract. On the averments the only reasonable and proper course, which the pursuers should have adopted, would have been to treat the defender as having repudiated the contract and as being on that account liable in damages, the measure of which we are, of course, not in a position to discuss."

The Lord President cited no authority and I am in doubt what principle he had in mind. In the earlier part of the passage which I have quoted he speaks of forcing the defender to accept the advertisement. Of course, if it had been necessary for the defender to do or accept anything before the contract could be completed by the pursuers, the pursuers could not and the court would not have compelled the defender to act, the contract would not have been completed, and the pursuers' only remedy would have been damages. But the peculiarity in that case, as in the present case, was that the pursuers could completely fulfil the contract without any co-operation of the defender. The Lord President cannot have meant that because of non-acceptance the contract had not been completely carried out, because that in itself would have been a complete answer to an action for the contract price. He went on to say that the only reasonable and proper course which the pursuers should have adopted would have been to treat the defender as having repudiated the contract, which must, I think, mean to have accepted the repudiation. It is this reference to "the only reasonable and proper course" which I find difficult to explain. It might be, but it never has been, the law that a person is only entitled to enforce his contractual rights in a reasonable way and that a court will not support an attempt to enforce them in an unreasonable way. One reason why that is not the law is no doubt because it was thought that it would create too much uncertainty to require the court to decide whether it is reasonable or equitable to allow a party to enforce his full rights under a contract. The Lord President cannot have meant that. . . .

Langford & Co., Ltd. v. *Dutch* is indistinguishable from the present case. Quite properly the Second Division followed it in this case as a binding authority and did not develop LORD COOPER's reasoning: they were not asked to send this case to a larger court. We must now decide whether that case was rightly decided. In my judgment it was not. It could only be supported on one or other of two grounds. It might be said that, because in most cases the circumstances are such that an innocent party is unable to complete the contract and earn the contract price without the assent or co-operation of the other party, therefore in cases where he can do so he should not be allowed to do so. I can see no justification for that.

The other ground would be that there is some general equitable principle or element of public policy which requires this limitation of the contractual rights of the innocent party. It may well be that, if it can be shown that a person has no legitimate interest, financial or otherwise, in performing the contract rather than claiming damages, he ought not to be allowed to saddle the other party with an additional burden with no benefit to himself. If a party has no interest to enforce a stipulation he cannot in general enforce it: so it might be said that if a party has no interest to insist on a particular remedy he ought not to be allowed to insist on it. And, just as a party is not allowed to enforce a penalty, so he ought not to be allowed to penalise the other party by taking one course when another is equally advantageous to him. If I may revert to the example which I gave of a company engaging an expert to prepare an elaborate report and then repudiating before anything was done, it might be that the company could show that the expert had no substantial or legitimate interest in carrying out the work rather than accepting damages. I would think that the de minimis principle would apply in determining whether his interest was substantial and that he might have a legitimate interest other than an immediate financial interest. But if the expert had no such interest then that might be regarded as a proper case for the exercise of the general equitable jurisdiction of the court. But that is not this case. Here the respondent did not set out to prove that the appellants had no legitimate interest in completing the contract and claiming the contract price rather than claiming damages, there is nothing in the findings of fact to support such a case, and it seems improbable that any such case could have been proved. It is, in my judgment, impossible to say that the appellants should be deprived of their right to claim the contract price merely because the benefit to them as against claiming damages and reletting their advertising space might be small in comparison with the loss to the respondent: that is the most that could be said in favour of the respondent. Parliament has on many occasions relieved parties from certain kinds of improvident or oppressive contracts, but the common law can only do that in very limited circumstances. Accordingly, I am unable to avoid the conclusion that this appeal must be allowed and the case remitted so that decree can be pronounced as craved in the initial writ.

LORD MORTON OF HENRYTON (dissenting): My Lords, the facts of this case have already been fully stated. It is plain that the respondent (defender in the action) repudiated the contract of June 26, 1957, immediately after his sales manager had entered into it and some months before the time for performance of it by the appellants, and persisted in his repudiation throughout. Notwithstanding this, the appellants proceeded with the preparation of plates advertising the respondent's garage business and, as the sheriff-substitute held, they

"made no effort to procure another advertiser to take up the advertising space included in said contract and thus minimise their loss."

The plates were first exhibited on the litter bins on Nov. 2, 1957, and they remained on display during the whole of the contract period of 156 weeks. The respondent throughout made it clear that he did not want the advertisements and refused to pay for them. The present action is brought to recover £196 4s., the full sum payable under the contract. Alternatively, the appellants claim the same sum as liquidated damages. The respondent contends that in the circumstances of the present case the only remedy of the appellants was damages, to be assessed according to ordinary principles.

My Lords, I think that this is a case of great importance, although the claim is for a comparatively small sum. If the appellants are right, strange consequences follow in any case in which, under a repudiated contract, services are to be performed by the party who has not repudiated it, so long as he is able to perform these services without the co-operation of the repudiating party. Many examples of such contracts could be given. One, given in the course of the argument and already mentioned by my noble and learned friend, LORD REID, is the engagement of an expert to go abroad and write a report on some subject for a substantial fee plus his expenses. If the appellants succeed in the present case, it must follow that the expert is entitled to incur the expense of going abroad, to write his unwanted report, and then to recover the fee and expenses, even if the other party has plainly repudiated the contract before any expense has been incurred.

It is well established that repudiation by one party does not put an end to a contract. The other party can say "I hold you to your contract, which still remains in force". What, then, is his remedy if the repudiating party persists in his repudiation and refuses to carry out his part of the contract? The contract has been broken. The innocent party is entitled to be compensated by damages for any loss which he has suffered by reason of the breach, and in a limited class of cases the court will decree specific implement. The law of Scotland provides no other remedy for a breach of contract, and there is no reported case which decides that the innocent party may act as the appellants have acted. The present case is one in which specific implement could not be decreed, since the only obligation of the respondent under the contract was to pay a sum of money for services to be rendered by the appellants. Yet the appellants are claiming a kind of inverted specific implement of the contract. They first insist on performing their part of the contract, against the will of the other party, and then claim that he must perform his part and pay the contract price for unwanted services. In my opinion, my Lords, the appellants' only remedy was damages, and they were bound to take steps to minimise their loss, according to a well-established rule of law. Far from doing this, having incurred no expense at the date of the repudiation, they made no attempt to procure another advertiser, but deliberately went on to incur expense and perform unwanted services with the intention of creating a money debt which did not exist at the date of the repudiation.

The only cases cited in which a claim of the kind now put forward has been considered are *Langford & Co., Ltd.* v. *Dutch* when it was rejected by the Court of Session, and *White & Carter (Councils), Ltd.* (that is, the present appellants) v. *A. R. Harding* (May 21, 1958; unreported). The latter case is, I think, distinguishable from the present case but if it cannot be distinguished it was, in my opinion, wrongly decided by the Court of Appeal. The former case is directly in point, and was, in my opinion, rightly decided, and rightly followed by the Court of Session in the present case.

The facts in Langford's case have been stated by my noble and learned friend, LORD REID. The Court of Session held that the law of Scotland did not "afford to a person in the position of the pursuers the remedy which is here sought." These words are quoted from the short opinion of the Lord President (LORD COOPER), and he continued:

"the pursuers could not force the defender to accept a year's advertisement which she did not want, though they could of course claim damages for her breach of contract."

These two sentences embodied, I think, the basis of the learned Lord President's opinion, but he added:

"On the averments the only reasonable and proper course, which the pursuers should have adopted, would have been to treat the defender as having repudiated the contract and as being on that account liable in damages, the measure of which we are, of course, not in a position to discuss."

My Lords, I think that this last sentence was merely a comment on the behaviour of the pursuers, which applies with equal force to the appellants in the present case. The course of action followed by the appellants seems to me unreasonable and oppressive, but it is not on that ground that I would reject their claim. I would reject it for the reasons which I have already given. . . .

I would dismiss the appeal.

LORD KEITH OF AVONHOLM (dissenting): . . . The contract was to come into operation on Nov. 2, 1957, when the previous contract expired. But it involved, in the absence of other advertising matter supplied by the defender, the display by the appellants of at least the name, business and address of the advertiser. I should hesitate to say that any contractor was entitled to display these particulars of the defender against his wish, even if the withholding of his assent be in breach of contract.

Some play was made by counsel for the appellants with an expression

used by ASQUITH L.J., in *Howard* v. *Pickford Tool Co., Ltd.*, [1951] 1
K.B. 417 at p. 421 that "An unaccepted repudiation is a thing writ in
water . . ." A graphic phase, or expression, has its uses even in a law report
and can give force to a legal principle, but it must be related to the circumstances in which it is used. Howard was a managing director with a six
years contract of service. He thought that the company with which he was
serving had shown by the conduct of its chairman that it no longer intended
to be bound by its agreement. He brought an action which, as amended,
sought a declaration that the company by so acting had repudiated the
contract and excused the plaintiff from further performance of his obligations under it. EVERSHED M.R., said at p. 420:

"It is quite plain . . . that if the conduct of one party to a contract amounts
to a repudiation, and the other party does not accept it as such but goes on
performing his part of the contract and affirms the contract, the alleged act
of repudiation is wholly nugatory and ineffective in law."

ASQUITH L.J., said:

"An unaccepted repudiation is a thing writ in water and of no value to
anybody: it confers no legal rights of any sort or kind."

The declaration was held to be academic and the claim struck out. These
observations must be read in the light of the facts which they relate. They
were directed to an alleged repudiation unaccepted by the man who said
there was a repudiation before any cause of action had arisen. At best the
case was no more than one of an intended repudiation, for performance was
going on. The servant was still serving and the employer was continuing to
employ him. What the court was saying was that the plaintiff had at that time
no cause of action. But in the case of repudiation of a contract when performance is tendered, or due to be given by the other party, the repudiation
cannot be said to be writ in water. It gives rise immediately to a cause of
action. This does not involve acceptance of the repudiation. There has been
a breach of contract which the complaining party denies the other had any
right to commit. I know of no authority for saying that the offended party
can go quietly on as if the contract still continued to be fully operative
between both parties. He is put to his remedy at the date of the breach. It has
been said that when an anticipatory repudiation is not treated as a cause of
action the contract remains alive. It does until the contract would become
operative, when the repudiation, if still maintained, then becomes a cause
of action and all pleas and defences then existing are available to the
respective parties.

The party complaining of the breach also has a duty to minimize the
damage he has suffered, which is a further reason for saying that after the
date of breach he cannot continue to carry on his part of an executory contract. A breach of a contract of employment will serve to illustrate the
nature of this duty. A person is engaged to serve for a certain period, say
three months, to commence at a future date. When that date arrives the
prospective employer wrongfully refuses to honour the engagement. The servant is not entitled to see out the three months and then sue the recalcitrant
employer for three months' wages. He must take steps by seeking other
employment to minimize his loss. It is true, of course, that a servant cannot
invoke a contract to force himself on an unwilling master, any more than a
master can enforce the service of an unwilling servant. But if the appellants'
contention is sound, it is difficult to see why, by parity of reasoning, it
should not apply to a person who keeps himself free to perform the duties
of his contract of service during the whole period of the contract and is

prevented from doing so by the refusal of the other contracting party. Yet in *Hochster* v. *De La Tour*, from which the whole law about anticipatory repudiation stems, LORD CAMPBELL C.J., plainly indicated that if the courier in that case, instead of accepting as he did the repudiation of his engagement as a cause of action, before it was due to commence, had waited till the lapse of the three months of the engagement he could not have sued as for a debt. The jury, he said, would be entitled to look at all that might "increase or mitigate the loss of the plaintiff down to the day of trial." There is no difference in this matter between the law of England and the law of Scotland. . . .

This brings me to *Langford & Co., Ltd.* v. *Dutch*. I took part in the judgment in that case, though the only opinion delivered in the case was given by the Lord President (Lord Cooper), with whom I and the other judges of the division concurred. The judgment was not a reserved judgment and the case was not, I think, so fully argued as the case now before your Lordships. It is, if rightly decided, determinative of the present appeal and is, so far as I am aware, the only other case in which the question raised on this appeal has ever been considered. . . . I have reconsidered the decision in *Langford & Co., Ltd.* v. *Dutch* in the light of the further argument on this appeal. I have come to the conclusion that it was rightly decided and that the Second Division in the present case was bound to follow it. . . .

[Lord Tucker agreed with Lord Hodson, whose decision is omitted, in allowing the appeal. The opinion of Lord Keith is considerably cut.]

NOTE. White & Carter v. *McGregor* was criticised by Professor Goodhart in 78 L.Q.R. 263. Professor Goodhart gives the example of an order placed for the building of an expensive machine, and then immediately cancelled. If the law is that the seller can disregard the cancellation, build the machine (now useless to the buyer) and claim the full price, it follows that the seller would be in the position to demand a very large sum from the buyer as payment for the surrender of the right to build the machine. Professor Goodhart points out that American authority almost unanimously holds that the innocent party to an anticipatory breach of contract must take reasonable steps to mitigate his loss, and that the Restatement of Contracts by the American Law Institute is to this effect (s. 388). Professor Goodhart concludes: "In the present case there can be no question that if the pursuers had sued the defender on the day when he gave notice of repudiation they could have recovered as damages only the reasonable profits they would have made; it seems odd that by deliberately doing something that was of no value to the defender they could increase the damages he had to pay."

FINELLI et al. v. *DEE et al.*
(1968) 67 D.L.R. (2d.) 393 (Ont. C.A.)

LASKIN J.A. (orally): This case arises out of a written contract between the plaintiffs and the male defendant, for the paving of the driveway at the defendants' home. The contract was made on June 18, 1966, and while a price was fixed and other terms included, it did not fix any particular time for the commencement or completion of the work. It appears from the evidence that the parties agreed that the work would not begin immediately because the defendant was then in no position to pay for it, but that it would be performed sometime in October or about that time, in 1966.

There is evidence, which was accepted by the trial judge, that the defendant telephoned the office of the plaintiffs, after the contract was made and before any performance was contemplated, cancelling the contract, and that the plaintiff's sales manager at the office who received the telephone call, agreed that it would be cancelled. On or about November 1, 1966, when the defendants were away from home, the plaintiffs carried out the contract and the defendants were confronted with the completed work on their return to their premises in the evening. The plaintiffs sued for the price of the work done under the contract but their claim was rejected by the trial judge.

On appeal, a question was raised whether the cancellation of the contract amounted to rescission or simply represented a repudiation by the defendant. Of course, if there was rescission (and I should say that, notwithstanding the contrary argument of the plaintiffs' counsel, rescission could be effected by oral agreement even though the contract in question was in writing), then there would be no basis on which an action to enforce the provision as to price could be founded. If, on the other hand, the cancellation amounted to repudiation, a question arises as to the applicability of the principles canvassed by the House of Lords in *White & Carter (Councils), Ltd.* v. *McGregor*, [1961] 3 All E.R. 1178. It was the view of the majority of that Court that a repudiation by one party to a contract does not preclude the innocent party from carrying out the contract and suing for the price, at least where this can be done without the assent or cooperation of the party in breach. I am not, of course, bound by this judgment, but, respecting as I do the considered opinion of the majority, I must say that I am attracted by the reasons of the two dissenting members of the Court. Repudiation is not something that calls for acceptance when there is no question of rescission, but merely excuses the innocent party from performance and leaves him free to sue for damages. But, even accepting the majority view in the *McGregor* case, I should point out that it was a case in which the innocent party could carry out the contract notwithstanding the repudiation, without the assent or cooperation of the party in breach. This is not the situation here.

In the first place, it was necessary for the plaintiffs to enter upon the defendants' land in order to perform; and without wishing to embark on any issue as to trespass, the plaintiffs, in my view, were obliged to give previous intimation to the defendant that they were prepared to do the work called for by the contract and proposed to do it on a certain day. This, of course, was not done.

It follows that whether the cancellation amounts to rescission or merely to repudiation by the defendant, the plaintiffs are not entitled to recover the contract price. Accordingly, I would dismiss the appeal with costs and with a counsel fee of $25 to the defendants.

[Appeal dismissed.]

NOTE. In *Hounslow London Borough Council* v. *Twickenham Garden Developments Ltd.* [1971] 1 Ch 233, the defendant, a building contractor, refused to leave the plaintiff's building site and continued to work, despite the council's demand that he depart. The plaintiff's repudiation was found to be in breach of contract, but the plaintiff sought an interim injunction to keep the defendant off the site. The court, although holding that *White & Carter* v. *McGregor* did not apply, refused to grant the injunction on the basis that equity would not assist a breach of contract.

PROBLEM. C delivered some pictures to M, to be cleaned. After M had begun work on the pictures, C changed his mind, and asked M to stop. M refused, completed cleaning the pictures, and now sues C for the full price agreed. Advise C. Would it make any difference if C's repudiation was based on expert advice that cleaning the pictures would reduce their value on the art market? Would M be liable in tort for that reduction in value?

See *Clark* v. *Marsiglia* (1843) 43 Am. Dec. 670 (N.Y.S.C.).

6. SPECIFIC PERFORMANCE

In the preceding sections the remedy awarded by the courts ultimately resulted in the payment of money damages except in the *Ontario Asphalt* case. It was not an "order" to pay a particular sum promised in a contract, although in some cases of course the award may have been calculated by direct reference to such a sum. The successful litigant "recovered" damages. If the defendant failed to pay the damages the state's long arm could reach out and seize his property (if any) to be sold to raise the amount. Generally speaking this was the extent of the remedy and its sanction in the common law courts.

However, along with the development of the "law" in the common law courts, there also developed a supplementary system commonly called "equity." If an aggrieved party wanted to have his expectation interest more specifically satisfied, if he wanted to have the promise actually performed, he could turn to equity. This "law" was administered by the Court of Chancery. Generally speaking its remedies were available when it considered the remedies of the common law inadequate. The Chancery Court commonly ordered specific performance of contracts for the sale of land on the theory that any land, including a jerry-built house on a sub-division lot indistinguishable from its next fifty neighbours on either side, is unique, and no amount of damages could compensate for its loss! If the defendant refused to execute the conveyance when so ordered, he might be sent to prison for contempt.

Today in most jurisdictions the two systems have been merged by merging the courts and providing that where the rules of law and equity conflict, the rules of equity prevail. But just as the rules of law developed through analysis of fact situations, from case to case, so did the rules of equity, and the equitable remedies in our modern legal system are not applied generally, but only to the kinds of fact situation to which the Court of Chancery had applied them. (This broad statement is of course subject to considerable reservation but the reservations can wait until you are ready to deal with them.) To understand the equitable remedies, therefore, you must know the historical processes (accidents?) that took some kinds of disputes into the Chancery Courts but not others.

STEWART v. *KENNEDY*. 1890. 15 App. Cas. 75 (Scotland. House of Lords). LORD WATSON: ". . . I do not think that upon this matter any assistance can be derived from English decisions; because the laws of the two countries regard the right to specific performance from different standpoints. In England the only legal right arising from a breach of contract is a claim of damages; specific performance is not a matter of legal right, but a purely equitable remedy, which the Court can withhold when there are sufficient reasons of conscience or expediency against it. But in Scotland the breach of a contract for the sale of a specific subject such as landed estate, gives the party aggrieved the legal right to sue for implement, and, although he may elect to do so, he cannot be compelled to resort to the alternative of an action of damages unless implement is shewn to be impossible, in which case, *loco facti imprestabilis subit damnum et interesse.* Even where implement is possible, I do not doubt that the Court of Session has inherent power to refuse the legal remedy upon equitable grounds, although I know of no instance in which it has done so. It is quite conceivable that circumstances might occur, which would make it inconvenient and unjust to enforce specific performance of a contract of sale; but I do not think that any such case is presented in this appeal. The fact that the construction of a term in the contract is attended with doubt and difficulty, evidenced it may be by the different meanings attributed to it by Courts or individual judges, ought not, in my opinion, to prevent its receiving its full legal effect, according to the interpretation finally put upon it by a competent tribunal. The argument that, in this case, a decree for specific performance would necessarily impose upon the appellant the duty of performing a long series of personal acts under the supervision of the Court does not appear to me to have a solid basis in fact. The acts which such a decree enjoins would be entirely within his power, and practically might be performed *uno flatu, viz.*, by his signing a conveyance in favour of the respondent, and at the same time giving instructions to his agents to take the necessary steps for obtaining its approval by the Court."

FALCKE v. GRAY
England. Chancery. 1859. 29 L.J. Ch. 28

In a suit for specific performance of a contract giving Mr. Falcke the option of purchasing two valuable china jars it appeared that Mr. Falcke had rented a house from Mrs. Gray and had accepted an option to buy some furniture including what Mr. Falcke's counsel described as "a couple of large Oriental jars, with great ugly Chinese pictures upon them." The jars were valued by agreement at £40. Later Mrs. Gray was offered £200 by Messrs. Watson, to whom she promptly sold them. Mrs. Gray stated the jars were left her by a lady who had been offered £100 for them by King George IV. Mr. Falcke was a dealer in the same trade as Messrs. Watson and should have known the actual value of the jars.

KINDERSLEY V.C.: The defendants insist, in the first place, that this bill cannot be maintained on the ground that the plaintiff can have no right to the specific performance of a contract relating solely to chattels. On this question, my opinion is entirely in favour of the plaintiff, that the Court will not refuse such relief. In the eye of this Court, there is no difference between real and personal estate in the performance of a contract; and a contract for one stands in no position different from a contract for the other. The principle upon which this Court decrees specific performance, as enunciated by Lord Redesdale, in *Harnett v. Yielding*, 2 Sch. & Lef. 549, is, that a Court of laws deals with the contract, and gives such a decree as it is competent to give in consequence of non-performance— that is, by giving compensation in the shape of damages for the non-performance. But a Court of equity says that it is not enough; and in many cases the mere remuneration and compensation in damages is not sufficient satisfaction. Apply that principle to chattels—and why is it less applicable to them than to real estate? In ordinary contracts, as for the purchase of ordinary articles of use and consumption, such as coals, corn or consols, this Court will not decree specific performance. And why? Because you have only to go into the market and buy another equally good article, and so you can get your compensation. It is not because it is a chattel, but because you can get adequate compensation for it. Now, here these articles are of unusual distinction and curiosity, if not unique; and it is altogether doubtful what price they will fetch. I am of opinion, therefore, that this is a contract which this Court can enforce; and if the case stood alone upon that ground I would decree specific performance. . . .

[The bill was dismissed on another ground, and part of the judgment of the Vice-Chancellor is omitted.]

CARTER v. *LONG AND BISBY*. 1896. 26 S.C.R. 430. STRONG C.J.: "Although not ordinarily interfering in the case of chattels, courts of equity would always take jurisdiction in two cases viz., where the chattel was of particular value so that damages would be no adequate compensation. . . . The other ground was where a fiduciary relationship existed between the parties; there, irrespective altogether of the nature and value of the property, the jurisdiction of equity could always be invoked for the protection of the *cestui que trust*."

> person holding the character of a trustee

COHEN v. *ROCHE*
England. King's Bench Division. [1927] 1 K.B. 169

At an auction sale Hepplewhite chairs (lot 145) which belonged to the auctioneer, the defendant, himself were knocked down to the plaintiff. After the sale the auctioneer refused to hand over the chairs to the plaintiff. Thereupon the plaintiff brought an action against the defendant in which he claimed for the delivery up of the chairs and alternatively damages for alleged breach of contract.

McCARDIE J.: . . . I now take the final point in the case. The plaintiff sued in detinue only. The writ and statement of claim contain no alternative demand for damages for breach of contract. They ask (a) for delivery up of the chairs or payment of their value, and (b) damages for detention. I have however allowed an amendment whereby the statement of claim asks damages for breach of contract. The plaintiff vigorously contends that he is entitled as of right, once a binding contract is established, to an order for the actual delivery of the chairs, and that he is not limited to damages for breach of bargain. This point raises a question of principle and practice. Here I may again state one or two of the facts. The Hepplewhite chairs in lot 145 possessed no special feature at all. They were ordinary Hepplewhite furniture. The plaintiff bought them in the ordinary way of his trade for the purpose of ordinary resale at a profit. He had no special customer in view. The lot was to become a part of his usual trade stock.

The form of order in detinue cases for the delivery of goods is, in substance, this: "It is this day adjudged that the plaintiff do have a return of the chattels in the statement of claim mentioned and described (here set out description) or recover against the defendant their value (here set out value). . . . and damages for their detention.". . . By order XLVIII., r. 1, however, the Court has power to direct that execution shall issue for the delivery of the goods without giving to the defendant the option to retain the property upon payment of the assessed value. Now in the case before me, the plaintiff desires to secure a warrant for the compulsory and specific delivery of the chairs to him. . . .

But at this point there arise other considerations. In *Chinery* v. *Viall*

(1860), 5 H. & N. 288, it was laid down that as between buyer and seller the buyer cannot recover larger damages by suing in tort instead of contract. . . . Bearing *Chinery* v. *Viall* in mind, it is necessary to mention next s. 52 of the *Sale of Goods Act,* 1893, which provides that in any action for breach of contract to deliver specific or ascertained goods the Court may, if it thinks fit, on the application of the plaintiff, direct by its judgment that the contract shall be performed specifically without giving the defendant the option of retaining the goods on payment of damages. It has been held that s. 52 applies to all cases where the goods are ascertained, whether the property therein has passed to the buyer or not: see Parker J. in *Jones* v. *Earl of Tankerville,* [1909] 2 Ch. 440, 445. It seems clear that the discretionary provisions of s. 52 cannot be consistent with an absolute right of a plaintiff to an order for compulsory delivery under a detinue judgment in such a case as the present. How, then, does the law stand as to detinue? In my view the power of the Court in an action of detinue rests upon a footing which fully accords with s. 52 of the Sale of Goods Act, 1893. In *Whitely, Ld.* v. *Hilt,* [1919] 2 K.B. 808, 819, (an action of detinue) Swinfen Eady, M.R. said: "The power vested in the Court to order the delivery up of a particular chattel is discretionary, and ought not to be exercised when the chattel is an ordinary article of commerce and of no special value or interest, and not alleged to be of any special value to the plaintiff, and where damages would fully compensate." In equity, where a plaintiff alleged and proved the money value of the chattel, it was not the practice of the Court to order its specific delivery: see *Dowling* v. *Betjemann* (1862), 2 J. & H. 544. The law is thus, I am glad to find, consistent in its several parts. In the present case the goods in question were ordinary articles of commerce and of no special value or interest and no grounds exist for any special order for delivery. The judgment should be limited to damages for breach of contract. The plaintiff in his evidence said that the chairs were worth from £70 to £80. With this I agree. I assess the damages at the sum of £15.

For the reasons given I therefore enter judgment for the plaintiff for £15 damages for breach of contract. . . .

[The statement of facts is abridged, and part of the judgment of McCardie J. dealing with the *Statute of Frauds* is omitted. Section 50 of *The Sale of Goods Act,* R.S.O. 1960, c. 358, is substantially the same as s. 52 of the English Act, which has been adopted in all the common law provinces of Canada.]

QUESTION. Suppose the plaintiff buyer in *Cohen* v. *Roche* had agreed to sell the chairs to someone else at a specially lucrative price, which, naturally enough, he had not mentioned to the defendant seller. Should specific performance be granted to enable the plaintiff to take advantage of the contract at no extra expense to the defendant where the advantage might not be accounted for in calculating damages?

SKY PETROLEUM LTD. v. V.I.P. PETROLEUM LTD.
[1974] 1 W.L.R. 576

The plaintiffs had entered into a contract with the defendants to purchase from the defendants, at fixed prices, their entire requirements of motor gasoline and diesel fuel for the plaintiffs' filling stations, with a minimum annual quantity being stipulated. At a time when the supply of petroleum was restricted and the plaintiffs had no prospect of finding an alternative source of supply, the defendants purported to terminate the contract on the ground that the plaintiffs had exceeded the credit provisions in the contract.

GOULDING J.: This is a motion for an injunction brought by the plaintiff company, Sky Petroleum Ltd., as buyer under a contract dated March 11, 1970, made between the defendant company, VIP Petroleum Ltd., as seller of the one part and the plaintiffs of the other part. That contract was to operate for a period of ten years, subject to certain qualifications, and thereafter on an annual basis unless terminated by either party giving to the other not less than three months' written notice to that effect. It was a contract at fixed prices, subject to certain provisions which I need not now mention. Further, the contract obliged the plaintiffs—and this is an important point—to take their entire requirement of motor gasoline and diesel fuel under the contract, with certain stipulated minimum yearly quantities. After the making of the agreement, it is common knowledge that the terms of trade in the market for petroleum and its different products changed very considerably, and I have little doubt that the contract is now disadvantageous to the defendants. After a long correspondence, the defendants, by telegrams dated November 15 and 16, 1973, have purported to terminate the contract under a clause therein providing for termination by the defendants if the plaintiffs fail to conform with any of the terms of the bargain. What is alleged is that the plaintiffs have exceeded the credit provisions of the contract and have persistently been, and now are, indebted to the defendants in larger amounts than were provided for. So far as that dispute relates, as for the purposes of this motion it must, to the date of the purported termination of the contract, it is impossible for me to decide it on the affidavit evidence. It involves not only a question of construction of the contract, but also certain disputes on subsequent arrangements between the parties and on figures in account. I cannot decide it on motion, and the less I say about it the better.

What I have to decide is whether any injunction should be granted to protect the plaintiffs in the meantime. There is trade evidence that the plaintiffs have no great prospect of finding any alternative source of supply for the filling stations which constitute their business. The defendants have indicated their willingness to continue to supply the plaintiffs, but only at prices which, according to the plaintiffs' evidence, would not be serious prices from a commercial point of view. There is, in my judgment, so far as I can make out on the evidence before me, a serious danger that unless the court interferes at this stage the plaintiffs will be forced out of business. In those circumstances, unless there is some specific reason which debars me from doing so, I should be disposed to grant an injunction to restore the former position under the contract until the rights and wrongs of the parties can be fully tried out.

It is submitted for the defendants that I ought not to do so for a number of reasons. It is said that, on the facts, the defendants were entitled to terminate and the plaintiffs were in the wrong. That, of course, is the very question in the action, and I have already expressed my inability to resolve it even provisionally on the evidence now before me. Then it is said that there are questions between the parties as to arrangements subsequent to the making of the contract, in particular regarding the price to be paid, and that they give rise to uncertainties which would make it difficult to enforce any order made by way of interlocutory relief. I do not think I ought to be deterred by that consideration, though I can see it has some force. In fact, during September and October, to go no further back, the defendants have gone on supplying and the plaintiffs have gone on paying. There has been nothing apparently impracticable in the contract, although the defendants say, of course, that the plaintiffs have not been paying large enough sums quickly enough.

Now I come to the most serious hurdle in the way of the plaintiffs which is the well known doctrine that the court refuses specific performance of a contract to sell and purchase chattels not specific or ascertained. That is a well-established and salutary rule, and I am entirely unconvinced by Mr. Christie, for the plaintiffs, when he tells me that an injunction in the form sought by him would not be specific enforcement at all. The matter is one of substance and not of form, and it is, in my judgment, quite plain that I am, for the time being, specifically enforcing the contract if I grant an injunction. However, the ratio behind the rule is, as I believe, that under the ordinary contract for the sale of non-specific goods, damages are a sufficient remedy. That, to my mind, is lacking in the circumstances of the present case. The evidence suggests, and indeed it is common knowledge that the petroleum market is in an unusual state in which a would-be buyer cannot go out into the market and contract with another seller, possibly at some sacrifice as to price. Here, the defendants appear for practical purposes to be the plaintiffs' sole means of keeping their business going, and I am prepared so far to depart from the general rule as to try to preserve the position under the contract until a later date. I therefore propose to grant an injunction.

Dealing first with its duration, it will restrain the defendants (in terms I will come to in a moment) until judgment in the action or further order, but not in any event beyond June 30, 1974, without further order of the court. I say that because of a provision in the contract which requires further steps to be taken in relation to the price of supply after that date. The terms which I suggest must, with certain qualifications, follow the notice of motion. If counsel are able to arrive at something more convenient and easier to enforce, they may mention the matter to me at an early date and the wording can be reconsidered, but for the moment I will order that the defendants by themselves, or their servants or agents, in the usual form be restrained from withholding supplies of "motor gasoline and DERV" from the plaintiffs in accordance with the terms of the contract dated March 11, 1970, and such other arrangements, if any, as were agreed between the parties before the issue of the writ in this action. There will be a proviso that the plaintiffs are not to require delivery of more than a specified number of gallons in any one month, and that number is to be ascertained by taking the arithmetical mean of the three months of supply, August, September, and October. That will, I hope, prevent any abuse of the injunction by the plaintiffs.

I would be sympathetic to any application by the defendants for the provision of security in some particular sum and form. I do not know whether the plaintiffs can make any specific offer in that respect, or whether the best thing is that all the details should be considered by counsel.

[Order accordingly.]

BEHNKE v. *BEDE SHIPPING CO., LTD.* [1927] 1 K.B. 649. An action for specific performance of a contract for the sale of a ship. WRIGHT J.: "In the present case there is evidence that the *City* was of peculiar and practically unique value to the plaintiff. She was a cheap vessel, being old, having been built in 1892, but her engines and boilers were practically new and such as to satisfy the German regulations, and hence the plaintiff could, as a German shipowner, have her at once put on the German register. A very experienced ship valuer has said that he knew of only one other comparable ship, but that may now have been sold. The plaintiff wants the ship for immediate use, and I do not think damages would be an adequate compensation. I think he is entitled to the ship and a decree of specific performance in order that justice may be done." It had been contended that the plaintiff had the option of inspecting the vessel and of requiring the sellers to repair any damages found and since the Court would not order performance of a contract to do work the option constituted a bar to specific relief. Wright J. rejected the contention. The sellers were not dry dock owners nor ship-repairers and anyway the plaintiff might not require the inspection.

GILBERT v. BARRON
Ontario. High Court. 1958. 13 D.L.R. (2d) 262

WILSON J.: ... The company, Amerwood (Eastern) Canada Ltd., is incorporated as a public company under the Ontario *Companies Act* by letters patent of this Province dated October 26, 1948. Under agreement with an American company it manufactures and sells a plywood product known as Amerwood, and since 1954 it also manufactures and distributes another product known as Cellotex. The dispute in this action arises out of a struggle for control of the ownership of the shares of the Ontario company, hereinafter called Amerwood.

The plaintiff MacDonald, a successful salesman who resides in the City of Toronto, is responsible for the organization of Amerwood. He sold much treasury stock at Owen Sound, where the company, when organized, carried on its manufacturing operations. As was natural, he became one of the principal shareholders. The other two principal shareholders were one Parkes and the plaintiff Gilbert, an investment broker of many years' standing, who resides in Toronto. Gilbert became a shareholder in 1948, and at the annual meeting in February 1950 he was elected a director. In June 1954 he was elected president, an office he held until he was succeeded by Barron in 1956 in the circumstances hereinafter related. Shortly after his election as a director in 1948, he and Parkes, who was the general manager of the company from its inception until his resignation and retirement on account of ill-health on January 2, 1954, and MacDonald, who was a director and vice-president from the organization of the company until the annual meeting in 1957, entered into an agreement with the object of holding and preserving among the three of them stock control of the company. The terms of this agreement were that if any one of the three should purchase shares in the company, he would offer one-third to each of the other two at cost price. The agreement did not necessarily require the two shareholders to take up the offer but at least they had this right to purchase. This agreement was acted upon when Parkes' son sold his shares to his father. Gilbert and MacDonald agreed that they should be sold to Parkes Sr. because the quantity of shares made no real difference as to the balance of control.

Early in 1953 Parkes became ill, and subsequent to his resignation in January 1954, he died. In January 1954, before his resignation, he sold most of his shares to the defendant Barron, with the approval of Gilbert and MacDonald, after Barron agreed to the same arrangement with respect to the acquisition of future shares as had existed among Parkes, Gilbert and MacDonald. This agreement was made before Barron acquired his shares. The exact date of the agreement is not of great importance. I am satisfied it was made before Barron acquired Parkes' shares. Moreover, as appears later, the agreement was acted upon, and, later again, acknowledged on a Sunday in February 1955 at a meeting, at which Barron, MacDonald and Gilbert were present in Barron's office at Port Credit. I find that Barron acted upon the agreement when he purchased in December 1954 the shares which were known as the 500 Russell shares. This number did not lend itself to an even division, and after negotiation among the three they were divided 150 shares to each of Gilbert, MacDonald and Barron and 50 shares to a member of the staff, Miss Dorothy Gilbank.

By February 1956, without the knowledge of his two fellow shareholders Gilbert and MacDonald, Barron had decided to secure control of the company. He purchased options to buy enough shares to give him voting control of the company and at the annual meeting he had enough proxies and shares in his name to give him voting control of it. After the meeting he took up the options thus acquiring stock control.

Gilbert and MacDonald learned of this control just before the annual meeting and in due course made demands upon Barron for their shares in accordance with the agreement among them. These demands were not replied to, and on February 8, 1957, this action was commenced. In the interval between this annual meeting and the commencement of the action the plaintiffs were acting upon legal advice. . . .

[After considering and rejecting three defences: (1) a denial of the agreement, (2) no consideration, and (3) the *Statute of Frauds*, Wilson J. continued:

The plaintiffs are entitled to specific performance of the agreement in respect of all shares claimed by them. He must tender one-third—that is to say, 816 common and 816 preferred—to each of the plaintiffs who will, upon such tender, pay for them in accordance with the agreement. . . .

The plaintiffs also ask an injunction restraining the defendants from voting the shares to which they are entitled, and from selling, pledging or transferring them. They will have judgment for this relief (directly and indirectly) in respect of Barron. He has apparently placed the shares in the name of Port Credit Lumber Co., of which he has voting share control. However, it is quite apparent that Barron was only using this company as well as his co-defendants as his agent to break the agreement with the plaintiffs. In any event, Barron has not pleaded that it is impossible for him to comply with the contract.

The plaintiffs also ask damages. To this they are entitled as against Barron. No evidence was adduced to prove the amount of damages suffered. I should think there would be some at least loss of salary as directors, but I am unable to conclude there was more. I think the sum of $200 to each of the plaintiffs as nominal damages would suffice. These are the directors' fees they appear to have lost. In other circumstances, even though the task seems an impossible one from the practical point of view, the damages could be assessed at a much higher figure.

In addition to the costs already dealt with, the plaintiffs will have their costs of the action against the defendant Barron which includes the costs they have incurred against the other defendants.

TANENBAUM v. W. J. BELL PAPER CO. LTD.
Ontario. High Court. 1956. 4 D.L.R. (2d) 177

The W. J. Bell Paper Co. Ltd., in October, 1951, purchased a parcel of land, marked A on the sketch, from one Tanenbaum, as a site for its new head office and plant. Tanenbaum retained the parcel C on the sketch, and the contract of sale contained a promise by the Bell Co. that it would construct "a roadway not less than twenty-eight feet in width, similar to that at present constructed on Wicksteed Avenue" along the western boundary

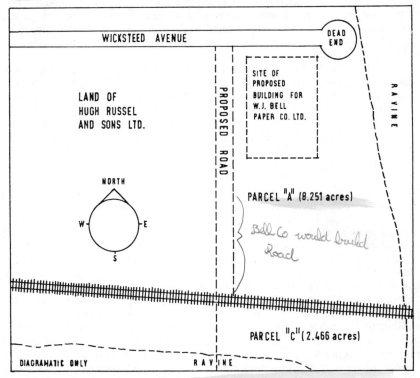

of parcel A, and that Tanenbaum should have a right of way over it. The Bell Co. also agreed to install sewer and water pipes of unspecified size along the new road to provide service for parcel C which was to be used for "industrial operations." Wicksteed Avenue, a street built by the Town of Leaside, is twenty-eight feet wide, without sidewalks. It had an eight inch Portland cement base with two and one half inches of asphalt "hot-mix" top. The surface was twenty-six feet wide and on each side were twelve inch brick gutters and concrete curbs. After some delay the Bell Co. actually constructed a road with an eight inch crushed stone base and with one and one half to three inches of asphalt, hot or cold mix, on top, with no gutters or curbing. The road was finished in May, 1953, at a cost of about $25,000. The Bell Co. also installed a two inch water main from its own plant to the northern limits of parcel C. The road proved trouble-

some and in this action for specific performance and damages the court interpreted the contract as calling for a road like Wicksteed Avenue, with a
concrete base and gutters and curbs, and a water main at least six inches
in diameter.

GALE J.: . . . The defendant must, therefore, be held accountable for the
breach of contract. The plaintiff asks for specific performance of the
covenants but the defendant urges that such relief would be inappropriate and too drastic in the circumstances of this case.

Generally the Court will not order a contract to build or to repair to be
specifically performed. But an exception to that rule is now recognized and
it is my understanding of the authorities that specific performance ought to
be decreed where a person undertakes accommodation works on lands possessed by him in consideration for obtaining those lands or in consideration
of the purchase-price of other lands sold by him, if the particulars of the
work are sufficiently clear and defined and the Court comes to the conclusion that damages will not provide an adequate remedy for the breach of
the contract. . . .

That the Court will enforce building contracts in certain circumstances
was firmly established in *Wolverhampton Corp.* v. *Emmons*, [1901] 1
K.B. 515. That was a decision of the English Court of Appeal and may
well be regarded as the leading modern authority on the subject. In pursuance of a scheme of improvement the plaintiffs, an urban sanitary authority, conveyed to the defendant some lands abutting on a street. The
defendant covenanted that he would erect buildings thereon within a certain time. Subsequently the nature and particulars of the houses to be
erected were agreed upon, but the defendant failed to fulfil his covenant
to build. The plaintiffs thereupon brought the action and were held entitled
to a decree of specific performance. That was not a case involving a railway
company. Romer L.J. at pp. 524-5 describes the exception to which I have
alluded as follows: "There is no doubt that as a general rule the Court will
not enforce specific performance of a building contract, but an exception
from the rule has been recognised. It has, I think, for some time been held
that, in order to bring himself within that exception, a plaintiff must establish three things. The first is that the building work, of which he seeks to
enforce the performance, is defined by the contract; that is to say, that the
particulars of the work are so far definitely ascertained that the Court can
sufficiently see what is the exact nature of the work of which it is asked to
order the performance. The second is that the plaintiff has a substantial
interest in having the contract performed, which is of such a nature that he
cannot adequately be compensated for breach of the contract by damages.
The third is that the defendant has by the contract obtained possession of
land on which the work is contracted to be done."

The exception so defined by Romer L.J. was considered and expanded
somewhat by Farwell J., as he then was, in *Carpenters Estates Ltd.* v.
Davies, [1940] Ch. 160. In that case the defendant sold certain land to
the plaintiffs for building development and agreed to install roads, mains,
sewers and drains on other lands retained by her. The covenant having
been broken, the plaintiffs succeeded in an action for specific performance.
After setting out, *inter alia*, the passage in the *Emmons* case which I have
quoted above, Farwell J. seemed to express himself as being of the view
that if the conditions as to clarity and inadequacy of damages were present,
the plaintiff would be entitled to succeed on his quest for a decree by showing merely that the defendant was in possession of the lands upon which the

work was to have been done, and the exception may now perhaps be regarded as being as broad as that. I do not have to settle that question here.

It may be that the learned Judge did not intend to carry the extension of the exception so far because later in his judgment he said at p. 165: "The defendant has contracted to do the work on her own land in consideration of the purchase price of other land belonging to her, and if the other two conditions are fulfilled, I am unable to see why the Court should be debarred from granting relief by way of specific performance." He was not, however, prepared to accept as being completely exhaustive the statement of Romer L.J. and for the moment, therefore, I prefer to express the exception to the general rule as I have done.

Perhaps it is scarcely necessary to add that the exception which I have outlined has been worked into the fabric of the law of Canada. It was acknowledged and applied by two of the three Judges in *Colton* v. *Rookledge* (1872), 19 Gr. 121, and was reasserted by Idington J. in one of the judgments of the Supreme Court of Canada in *Gross* v. *Wright*, [1923], 2 D.L.R. 171, S.C.R. 214. In the latter case the litigants entered into a party-wall agreement under which the defendant was to build a wall 2 ft. or more in thickness with its middle line to coincide with the boundary-line. The wall erected by the defendant complied with the agreement to the level of the second storey but was narrowed from there up on the defendant's side, while remaining perpendicular on the plaintiff's side. The latter discovered this situation some years after the wall formed part of the defendant's building and sued for a mandatory injunction to compel the latter to pull down that which had been erected and for specific performance of the agreement. The majority of the Court granted a mandatory injunction on the theory that having obtained a licence to enter on the land for a particular purpose and having breached that licence, the defendant was committing a trespass. However, Idington J. expressly awarded the decree which was sought on the ground that the Court had jurisdiction to grant specific performance of the agreement itself. Indeed at p. 176 D.L.R., p. 219 S.C.R., he stated that in his opinion specific performance was the only appropriate remedy in the circumstances and certainly the other members of the Court did not take the position that the relief being ordered could not have been based on the claim for specific performance of the contract between the parties.

Here the defendant argues that specific performance is not available to the plaintiff, firstly because the terms of the agreement, ex. 1, as to the road and watermain are not sufficiently explicit, secondly, because the plaintiff can be appropriately compensated in damages if those works do not comply with the provisions of the agreement; and lastly, because the plaintiff has had some performance from the defendant.

As already indicated, I am of the opinion that the road and watermain which were to have been installed by the defendant were sufficiently described by the contract and that the defendant failed to fulfil its obligations in that respect. It is very difficult, if not impossible, to set down a general formula as to what degree of certainty is required in a contract before the Court will enforce its performance, so much depends upon the facts of each case. But I think it may be said with confidence that the certainty which is essential must be a reasonable one, having regard to the nature and subject-matter of the undertaking and the attendant conditions under which and with regard to which it was entered into. The authorities on this point substantiate such a conclusion. . . .

All the defendant had to do here was to have copied the essential elements of a named street and to have installed a main which, in view of what must have been in the minds of the parties, would be at least 6 ins. in diameter. There was no room for doubt as to what was to be done and accordingly I hold that the plaintiff is not to be denied his decree by reason of any suggestion of uncertainty or ambiguity as to the nature of the work.

Probably the most serious objection to the granting of specific performance comes from the submission that if the road and watermain do not meet the terms of the agreement, the plaintiff can be properly and sufficiently compensated in damages. Let me say at once, however, that it is my view that such relief, even if capable of being calculated, would be quite inadequate to atone for the inadequacy of the watermain. As long as that pipe remains its sole source of water, parcel "C" cannot be put to its full use and certainly its potential sale value cannot be realized. I suspect that counsel for the defendant was aware of the hopelessness of his arguments that a pecuniary award could counterbalance the lack of a suitable main, because, while stoutly resisting all efforts to have the road replaced, he conceded that the installation of a new watermain would not be a very serious matter.

The question whether damages ought to be substituted for performance with respect to the road has not been easy to decide but here again I do not subscribe to the idea that an award of damages would give the proper relief. It would be futile to attempt to lay down a general rule as to when damages will be ordered in lieu of enforcing performance. . . .

The best statement on the subject that I have been able to find appears in Williston on Contracts, rev. ed., vol. 5, s. 1423, pp. 3976-7, where this appears: "In contracts other than those ordinarily designated as contracts of service, it is generally true so far as affirmative relief is concerned, that 'Equity will not award specific performance where the duty to be enforced is continuous and reaches over a long period of time, requiring constant supervision by the court.' Therefore, 'There is no doubt that as a general rule the Court will not enforce specific performance of a building contract.' The basis of equity's disinclination to enforce building contracts specifically is the difficulty of enforcing a decree without an expenditure of effort disproportionate to the value of the result. But where the inadequacy of damages is great, and the difficulties not extreme, specific performance will be granted and the tendency in modern times has been increasingly towards granting relief, where under the particular circumstances of the case damages are not an adequate remedy."

In this instance certainly the difficulties which would follow a decree of specific performance would not be extreme. The present roadway would have to be taken up and replaced with what should have been installed there in the first place and that would, of course, be an expensive undertaking. Indeed, the defendant protests strenuously that the cost of having to supplant the present road would not only be substantial but would also be out of all proportion to the advantages to be achieved by doing so. However, in many judgments upon the subject it has frequently been declared that mere hardship on the party in default should not be allowed to overcome the exercise of the Court's discretion in favour of ordering performance. Needless to say, if damages could be easily ascertained and were relatively insignificant in amount, I would pause long before making an order which might seriously prejudice the defendant's existence. Obviously that is not the situation here. As I shall point out in a moment, any attempt to assess damages is likely to prove abortive and the cost of building a proper road, while heavy by some standards, will by no means cripple the defendant company. And it must never be forgotten that if the decree were withheld the Court would, in one sense, be permitting the defendant to take advantage of its own wrong. . . .

If for no other reason . . . the conduct of the defendant and its contractor would probably induce me to grant that relief, for, as I have already mentioned, the reckless and almost wilful manner in which the plaintiff's rights were put aside would cause any Court to deal with the defendant quite dispassionately.

It strikes me too that the inadequacy of damages would be of significance here for the added reason that the full enjoyment of worth of the plaintiff's land is permanently impaired while the road is allowed to remain as it is.

However, perhaps the most formidable obstacle to the granting of damages comes from the fact that to try to calculate those damages would be an almost insuperable task. They arise in several ways. The plaintiff should have an amount equivalent to the difference between the estimated cost of repairing the private roadway and that of repairing one like Wicksteed Ave. during the life span of the latter. Counsel for the defendant urged that a monetary allowance for that difference would represent the full loss sustained by its adversary, but I do not agree, for clearly the enjoyment of parcel "C" and its disposal-value will continue to be adversely affected so long as the present road is there. I propose to examine those two sources of damages to determine whether either can be properly ascertained.

In the first place, it is questionable who will be making any future repairs. Certainly the defendant has the right to rebuild or repair the road but it is not obliged to do so since the agreement contains no covenant to that effect. Conversely, the plaintiff has no right to alter or rebuild that which is there. But can he repair the road? On behalf of the defendant it was said that Mr. Tanenbaum could enter upon it to make minor repairs at his own expense and counsel for the plaintiff concurred in that suggestion. It is extremely difficult to say, however, to what extent that privilege can be exercised. For example, the plaintiff could not close off the road at any time for that purpose without obtaining permission, for the defendant has already granted further rights of way over it to the Russell company and perhaps to others. It occurs to me, therefore, that it would not be easy to define in advance the scope of the repairs which the plaintiff might make; assuredly he could not make material alterations to that which is there.

Even assuming that the plaintiff is at liberty to mend the surface of the road as it deteriorates, how could the present value of the cost of doing so be reckoned? The evidence proved beyond doubt that Wicksteed Ave. would not require as much in the way of maintenance as the private road but that on occasions when repairs will have to be made the cost of doing so will exceed that which will have to be expended for individual repairs to the private road. That being so, anyone fastened with the unenviable duty of assessing damages would be required to determine the life-expectancy of a cement-based road and then try to estimate what the repairs to this road over that period of time would amount to. I am completely convinced that it would be quite impossible to do that with any degree of accuracy because the extent of future repairs and their frequency will depend on the volume and weight of the traffic the road will be called upon to carry and the speeds at which the vehicles will pass over it. Even if the

[margin note: too difficult to estimate damages]

magnitude and volume of repairs could be predicted, how could anyone come to a conclusion as to what those repairs would cost, bearing in mind that no one can know when they will be needed? Prices ten years hence may bear no relation to to-day's prices. And if all of these data could in some miraculous way be calculated, they would still have to be compared with similar data concerning an imaginary cement-based road.

If the damages relating to the comparative cost of repairs could be determined the struggle would not be over, for there would still have to be a decision as to the amount of damages accruing to the plaintiff because the present road causes and will continue to cause some reduction in the disposal-value of parcel "C". . . .

The defendant finally contended that specific performance ought not to be granted because the plaintiff has been provided with a hard-surfaced road which can be used. In other words, counsel suggested that since the plaintiff has had some measure of performance, he is precluded from obtaining anything but damages. Once again I do not agree and I am substantiated by the authorities. In *Lane* v. *Newdigate* (1804), 10 Ves. 192, 32 E.R. 818, the decree was made and again in *Gross* v. *Wright*, [1923], 2 D.L.R. 171, S.C.R. 214, the Court, and particularly Idington J., did not hesitate to order the demolition of a substantial part of an existing building and the reconstruction of a wall which had been built but did not comply with the agreement between the parties. If it were otherwise, it would mean that a person who has determined upon non-observance of a contract could arbitrate on what was to be done. I concede, of course that specific performance would probably be refused if the disparity of execution were slight, but that is not the situation here. The differences between the two roads are notable and the fact that the plaintiff will always be out of possession of the lands on which the road is laid and that he has no certain or clear right to effect even minor repairs to it is one which should never be overlooked.

For those reasons I order the defendant to cause to be installed along the westerly boundary of its lands a roadway similar to Wicksteed Ave. and by that I have in mind that there should be laid a road at least 28 ft. wide, having an 8-in. Portland cement base, a 2½-in. asphaltic standard highway hot-mix top, two brick gutters 12 ins. in width and consisting of 3 courses of brick and cement curbs. That roadway should extend, of course, from the southerly limit of Wicksteed Ave. to the north rail of the present railway siding. In addition, the defendant must also cause to be installed a 6-in. watermain leading from or close to the defendant's hydrant which is approximately 363 ft. south of the Town main to parcel "C". If the plaintiff desires to have an 8-in. main he will have to pay the difference between the installation of one of that dimension and the 6-in. main I have ordered. I see no reason why both of these works cannot be completed within 4 months from the date of this judgment. . . .

[A large part of the judgment dealing with damages arising from the delay in performance and the resulting inaccessibility of steel stored on Tanenbaum's land is omitted.]

RYAN v. MUTUAL TONTINE WESTMINSTER CHAMBERS ASSOCIATION

England. Chancery Division. [1893] 1 Ch. 116

KAY L.J.: . . . This remedy by specific performance was invented, and has been cautiously applied, in order to meet cases where the ordinary remedy by an action for damages is not adequate compensation for breach of contract. The jurisdiction to compel specific performance has always been treated as discretionary, and confined within well-known rules. In this case the Plaintiff is the lessee of a flat, which forms portion of a large building. In the lease is a covenant to the effect that the premises are taken by the lessee subject to certain regulations made by the lessors with respect to the duties of the resident porter and other matters, which are set out in a schedule. By the schedule it is stated that the building is divided into blocks, and the rooms in each block are, together with the entrance and staircase belonging to it, in charge of a resident porter, appointed and removeable by the lessors, but who shall be and act as the servant of the tenants of the several rooms in the block. The tenants are to have the right to the general services of the porter resident in their block within the scope of his general duties, as defined by rule 6. They are also to have the right to the special services of such porter, as defined by rules 8, 9 and 10. The Plaintiff's right under this covenant appears to me to be to have the advantage of the performance of the specified duties by the resident porter. In this case a man was appointed as porter, and held office; the complaint really was that he was not a proper porter, and the tenant did not get the advantage of the services stipulated for in the schedule; that he was not constantly in attendance; but, being engaged elsewhere, was not on the premises as much as he should be; and that, when he was there, he did not perform his duties himself. When one looks at that which was the real gravamen of the action, the contention seems rather odd that we ought to divide the contract into two parts—one that a porter should be appointed, the other that he should perform the duties specified. The lessor's covenant being in substance that the lessee should have the advantage of the performance of certain services by the porter, a covenant which I cannot conceive to be divisible, as was ingeniously suggested, the Plaintiff's claim is shaped thus. It is alleged that the lessee took possession under the lease, but that a porter was not appointed, and the lessee does not get the advantage of the performance of the porter's duties. He therefore asks for some remedy by means of which he may have these duties performed. That is really the nature of the action. But now it is sought to overlook that, and to say that, though a contract that the lessee shall have the benefit of the performance by the porter of his duties is not the sort of contract of which the Plaintiff can have specific performance, yet he can claim to have the contract performed specifically to this extent; he can ask the Court to compel the appointment of a proper porter, though, when he is appointed, the Court is not asked to compel performance of his duties. As I have said, the contract is really a single contract—viz., that the Plaintiff shall have the advantage of performance by the porter of his duties; and I dissent entirely from the notion that this contract can be divided into two parts in the way suggested, and the Court asked to grant specific performance of one part, but not of the other.

There are, no doubt, certain cases where a contract may be treated as divisible for the purpose of specific performance. The common case is where there is a contract like that in *Lumley v. Wagner* (1852), 1 De G.M. & G. 604; 42 E.R. 687, in which case the contract was to sing for the plaintiff, and not to sing for others. The Court says in such cases, though we cannot enforce performance of the contract to sing for a particular person, and so cannot enforce the whole contract; nevertheless, there being the independent negative stipulation against singing for others, we can enforce that by injunction. In the case of *Lumley* v. *Wagner*, the Lord Chancellor . . . expressly said that if he had to deal with the affirmative covenant only that the defendant would sing for the plaintiff, he would not have granted an injunction. That is one exception to the rule.

There is another exception to the general rule as to the specific performance. Ordinarily the Court will not enforce specific performance of works, such as building works, the prosecution of which the Court cannot superintend; not only on the ground that damages are generally in such cases an adequate remedy, but also on the ground of the inability of the Court to see that the work is carried out. . . . An exception to this rule has been established in cases where a railway company has taken lands from a landowner on the terms that it will carry out certain works. In those cases, because damages are not adequate remedy, the Court has gone to great lengths, and has granted specific performance of the definite works—they must be definite works—which the company that has taken the lands has contracted to do. This case does not come within either of the exceptions to which I have alluded. Therefore, for the reasons stated by the Master of the Rolls, this case is not one in which the Court could compel specific performance.

There appears to me to be also another reason for our decision which is quite sufficient. At the time when the action was brought there had been a breach of covenant. The learned Judge found no difficulty in assessing damages for breach of the contract down to that time. Why should there be any difficulty with regard to future breaches of contract? I have heard no sufficient reason adduced in the argument. If for the breach of contract down to action brought adequate compensation may be given by damages, that appears to me to be a reason for the Court not exercising its extraordinary jurisdiction. A sufficient reply to this argument is not afforded by the mere fact that these damages are not compensation for future breaches of contract. If that were sufficient, I cannot conceive of any case of a continuing contract where specific performance might not be granted. For these reasons I differ respectfully from the learned Judge, and think that nothing but a judgment for the damages found by him should be given.

[The opinions of Lord Esher M.R. and Lopes L.J. are omitted. The trial judge awarded specific performance but in case he was wrong he also assessed damages at £25.]

WARNER BROS. PICTURES INCORPORATED v. NELSON
England. King's Bench. [1937] 1 K.B. 209

BRANSON J.: The facts of this case are few and simple. The plaintiffs are a firm of film producers in the United States of America. In 1931 the defendant then not well known as a film actress [Miss Bette Davis], entered into a contract with the plaintiffs. Before the expiration of that contract the present contract was entered into between the parties. Under it the defendant received a considerably enhanced salary, the other conditions being substantially the same. This contract was for fifty-two weeks and contains options to the plaintiffs to extend it for further periods of fifty-two weeks at ever-increasing amounts of salary to the defendant. No question of construction arises upon the contract, and it is not necessary to refer to it in any great detail; but in view of some of the contentions raised it is desirable to call attention quite generally to some of the provisions contained in it. It is a stringent contract, under which the defendant agrees "to render her exclusive services as a motion picture and/or legitimate stage actress" to the plaintiffs, and agrees to perform solely and exclusively for them. She also agrees, by way of negative stipulation, that "she will not, during such time"—that is to say, during the term of the contract—"render any services for or in any other phonographic, stage or motion picture production or productions or business of any other person . . . or engage in any other occupation without the written consent of the producer being first had and obtained."

With regard to the term of the contract there is further clause, clause 23, under which, if the defendant fails, refuses or neglects to perform her services under the contract, the plaintiffs "have the right to extend the term of this agreement and all of its provisions for a period equivalent to the period during which such failure, refusal or neglect shall be continued."

In June of this year the defendant, for no discoverable reason except that she wanted more money, declined to be further bound by the agreement, left the United States and, in September, entered into an agreement in this country with a third person. This was a breach of contract on her part, and the plaintiffs on September 9 commenced this action claiming a declaration that the contract was valid and binding, an injunction to restrain the defendant from acting in breach of it, and damages. The defence alleged that the plaintiffs had committed breaches of the contract which entitled the defendant to treat it as at an end; but at the trial this contention was abandoned and the defendant admitted that the plaintiffs had not broken the contract and that she had; but it was contended on her behalf that no injunction could as a matter of law be granted in the circumstances of the case.

At the outset of the considerations of law which arise stands the question, not raised by the pleadings but urged for the defendant in argument, that this contract is unlawful as being in restraint of trade. The ground for this contention was that the contract compelled the defendant to serve the plaintiffs exclusively, and might in certain circumstances endure for the whole of her natural life. No authority was cited to me in support of the proposition that such a contract is illegal, and I see no reason for so holding. Where, as in the present contract, the covenants are all concerned with what is to happen whilst the defendant is employed by the plaintiffs and not thereafter, there is no room for the application of the doctrine of restraint of trade. . . .

I turn then to the consideration of the law applicable to this case on the basis that the contract is a valid and enforceable one. It is conceded that our Courts will not enforce a positive covenant of personal service; and specific performance of the positive covenants by the defendant to serve the plaintiffs is not asked in the present case. The practice of the Court of Chancery in relation to the enforcement of negative covenants is stated on the highest authority by Lord Cairns in the House of Lords in *Doherty* v. *Allman* (3 App. Cas. 709). His Lordship says: "My Lords, if there had been a negative covenant, I apprehend, according to well-settled practice, a Court of equity would have had no discretion to exercise. If parties, for valuable consideration, with their eyes open, contract that a particular thing shall not be done, all that a Court of Equity has to do is to say, by way of injunction, that which the parties have already said by way of covenant, that the thing shall not be done; and in such case the injunction does nothing more than give the sanction of the process of the Court to that which already is the contract between the parties. It is not then a question of the balance of convenience or inconvenience, or of the amount of damage or of injury—it is the specific performance, by the Court, of that negative bargain which the parties have made, with their eyes open, between themselves."

That was not a case of a contract of personal service; but the same principle had already been applied to such a contract by Lord St. Leonards in *Lumley* v. *Wagner* (1852), 1 De G.M. & G. 604; 42 E.R. 687. The Lord Chancellor used the following language: "Wherever this Court has not proper jurisdiction to enforce specific performance, it operates to bind men's consciences, as far as they can be bound, to a true and literal performance of their agreements; and it will not suffer them to depart from their contract at their pleasure, leaving the party with whom they have contracted to the mere chance of any damages which a jury may give. The exercise of this jurisdiction has, I believe, had a wholesome tendency towards the maintenance of that good faith which exists in this country to a much greater degree perhaps than in any other; and although the jurisdiction is not to be extended, yet a judge would desert his duty who did not act up to what his predecessors have handed down as the rule for his guidance in the administration of such an equity.". . . .

The defendant, having broken her positive undertakings in the contract without any cause or excuse which she was prepared to support in the witness-box, contends that she cannot be enjoined from breaking the negative covenants also. The mere fact that a covenant which the Court would not enforce, if expressed in positive form, is expressed in the negative instead, will not induce the Court to enforce it. . . . The Court will attend to the substance and not to the form of the covenant. Nor will the Court, true to the principle that specific performance of a contract of personal service will never be ordered, grant an injunction in the case of such a contract to enforce negative covenants if the effect of so doing would be to drive the defendant either to starvation or to specific performance of the positive covenants. . . .

[In] *Rely-a-Bell Burglar and Fire Alarm Co., Ltd.* v. *Eisler*, [1926] Ch. 609 which was strongly relied upon by the defendant, . . . Russell, J., as he then was, said, . . . "It was said that the covenants . . . were so framed that the servant, if the covenants were enforced, could make his living neither by serving nor by carrying on business independently; whereas in the present case the covenant only prohibited serving. Therefore, it was said, he was still free to start in business on his own account, and it could not be said, if an injunction were granted in the terms of the covenant, that he would be forced to remain idle and starve. That distinction seems to me somewhat of a mockery. It would be idle to tell this defendant, a servant employed at a wage. that he must not serve anybody else in that capacity, but that the world was still open to him to start business as an independent man. It seems to me that if I were to restrain this man according to the terms of the covenant, he would be forced to remain idle and starve." Had it not been for that view of the facts, I think that the learned Judge would have granted an injunction in that case.

The conclusion to be drawn from the authorities is that, where a contract of personal service contains negative covenants the enforcement of which will not amount either to a decree of specific performance of the positive covenants of the contract or to the giving of a decree under which the defendant must either remain idle or perform those positive covenants, the Court will enforce those negative covenants; but this is subject to a further consideration. An injunction is a discretionary remedy, and the Court in granting it may limit it to what the Court considers reasonable in all the circumstances of the case.

This appears from the judgment of the Court of Appeal in *William Robinson & Co., Ltd.* v. *Heuer*, [1898] 2 Ch. 451. The particular covenant in that case is set out at p. 452 and provides that "Heuer shall not during this engagement, without the previous consent in writing of the said W. Robinson & Co., Ltd.," and so forth, "carry on or be engaged either directly or indirectly, as principal agent, servant, or otherwise, in any trade, business or calling, either relating to goods of any description sold or manufactured by the said W. Robinson & Co., Ltd. . . . or in any other business whatsoever.". . .

Before parting with that case, I should say that the Court there proceeded to sever the covenants and to grant an injunction, not to restrain the defendant from carrying on any other business whatsoever, but framed so as to give what was felt to be a reasonable protection to the plaintiffs and no more. The plaintiffs waived an option which they possessed to extend the period of service for an extra five years, and the injunction then was granted for the remaining period of unextended time. . . .

The case before me is, therefore, one in which it would be proper to grant an injunction unless to do so would in the circumstances be tantamount to ordering the defendant to perform her contract or remain idle or unless damages would be the more appropriate remedy.

With regard to the first of these considerations, it would, of course, be impossible to grant an injunction covering all the negative covenants in the contract. That would, indeed, force the defendant to perform her contract or remain idle; but this objection is removed by the restricted form in which the injunction is sought. It is confined to forbidding the defendant, without the consent of the plaintiffs, to render any services for or in any motion picture or stage production for anyone other than the plaintiffs.

It was also urged that the difference between what the defendant can earn as a film artiste and what she might expect to earn by any other form of activity is so great that she will in effect be driven to perform her contract. That is not the criterion adopted in any of the decided cases. The defendant is stated to be a person of intelligence, capacity and means, and no evidence was adduced to show that, if enjoined from doing the specified acts otherwise than for the plaintiffs, she will not be able to employ herself both usefully and remuneratively in other spheres of activity, though not as remuneratively as in her special line. She will not be driven, although she may be tempted to perform the contract, and the fact that she may be so tempted is no objection to the grant of an injunction. This appears from the judgment of Lord St. Leonards in *Lumley* v. *Wagner*, where he used the following language: "It was objected that the operation of the injunction in the present case is mischievous, excluding the defendant J. Wagner from performing at any other theatre while this Court had no power to compel her to perform at Her Majesty's Theatre. It is true, that I have not the means of compelling her to sing, but she has no cause of complaint, if I compel her to abstain from the commission of an act which she has bound herself not to do, and thus possibly cause her to fulfil her enagagement. The jurisdiction which I now exercise is wholly within the power of the Court and being of the opinion that it is a proper case for interfering, I shall leave nothing unsatisfied by the judgment I pronounce. The effect, too, of the injunction, in restraining J. Wagner from singing elsewhere may, in the event"—that is a different matter—"of an action being brought against her by the plaintiff, prevent any such amount of vindictive damages being given against her as a jury might probably be inclined to give if she had carried her talents and exercised them at the rival theatre: the injunction may also, as I have said, tend to the fulfilment of her engagement; though, in continuing the injunction, I disclaim doing indirectly what I cannot do directly."

With regard to the question whether damages is not the more appropriate remedy, I have the uncontradicted evidence of the plaintiffs as to the difficulty of estimating the damages which they may suffer from the breach by the defendant of her contract. I think it is not inappropriate to refer to the fact that, in the contract between the parties, in clause 22, there is a formal admission by the defendant that her services, being "of a special, unique, extraordinary and intellectual character" gives them a particular value "the loss of which cannot be reasonably or adequately compensated in damages" and that the breach may "cost the producer great and irreparable injury and damage," and the artist expressly agrees that the producer shall be entitled to the remedy of injunction. Of course, parties cannot contract themselves out of the law; but it assists, at all events, on the question of evidence as to the applicability of an injunction in the present case, to find the parties formally recognizing that in cases of this kind injunction is a more appropriate remedy than damages.

Furthermore, in the case of *Grimston* v. *Cunningham*, [1894] 1 Q.B. 125, which was also a case in which a theatrical manager was attempting to enforce against an actor a negative stipulation against going elsewhere, Wills, J., granted an injunction and used the following language: "This is an engagement of a kind which is pre-eminently subject to the interference of the Court by injunction, for in cases of this nature it very often happens that the injury suffered in consequence of the breach of the agreement would be out of all proportion to any pecuniary damages which could be proved or assessed by a jury. This circumstance affords a strong reason in favour of exercising the discretion of the Court by granting an injunction."

I think that that applies to the present case also, and that an injunction should be granted in regard to the specified services.

Then comes the question as to the period for which the injunction should operate. The period of the contract, now that the plaintiffs have undertaken not as from October 16, 1936, to exercise the rights of suspension conferred upon them by clause 23 thereof, will, if they exercise their options to prolong it, extend to about May, 1942. As I read the judgment of the Court of Appeal in *Robinson* v. *Heuer* the Court should make the period such as to give reasonable protection and no more to the plaintiffs against the ill effects to them of the defendant's breach of contract. The evidence as to that was perhaps necessarily somewhat vague. The main difficulty that the plaintiffs apprehend is that the defendant might appear in other films whilst the films already made by them and not yet shown are in the market for sale or hire and thus depreciate their value. I think that if the injunction is in force during the continuance of the contract or for three years from now, whichever period is the shorter, that will substantially meet the case.

The other matter is as to the area within which the injunction is to operate. The contract is not an English contract and the parties are not British subjects. In my opinion all that properly concerns this Court is to prevent the defendant from committing the prohibited acts within the jurisdiction of this Court, and the injunction will be limited accordingly.

BETTE DAVIS, THE LONELY LIFE. 1962. Chapter eleven and the first of chapter twelve of this autobiography tell in some detail the story of *Warner Brothers* v. *Nelson* from Mrs. Nelson's point of view. When she left the United States she had already won an Academy Award, and felt confined by her contract and convinced that Warner Brothers had no serious intention of letting her choose her own parts or find parts she would approve. A few other actors and actresses were also battling the restrictive terms of the standard form of actor's contract. Mrs. Nelson mentions familiar names, James Cagney, Margaret Sullivan, Carole Lombard and Eddie Cantor. In a comparatively new industry, the "stars" were beginning to realize their contribution and were rebelling against the "slavery" of the contract designed to serve the convenience of a more experienced business management. Apparently Mrs. Nelson thought she could not be stopped from working abroad. The litigation cost Mrs. Nelson over $30,000. Sir William Jowitt, retained for the defence, had "recommended" that Mrs. Nelson immediately give him a $10,000 retainer. At this time Mrs. Nelson was, of course, under suspension and receiving no salary. Her decision not to appeal was largely influenced by the actor George Arliss, who had said, "I admire your courage in this affair but now—go back and face them proudly." In fact, Warner Brothers welcomed Mrs. Nelson with open arms and graciously assumed their share of the costs and part of hers. Their standard form had received a shot in the arm that gave assurance to the management side of the whole film industry. In recent years several Hollywood actors have assumed the added role of producer in order to overcome the restraints of the older standard forms.

DETROIT FOOTBALL CO. v. *DUBLINSKI.* 1957. 7 D.L.R. (2d) 9 (Ontario Court of Appeal). The Detroit Football Club applied on June 16, 1955, for an injunction restraining Dublinski from playing football with the Toronto Argonauts and alleging irreparable damage if Dublinski's breach of his contract with the Club were not restrained. Dublinski deposed that his livelihood was solely dependent on his playing professional football and if restrained he would be unable to earn a livelihood. This "evidence, however strange it may seem, stands unimpeached and uncontradicted." An interlocutory injunction was refused by WELLS J. ([1955] 4 D.L.R. 176). By the time the action came on for trial before McRUER C.J.H.C. on July 26, 1956 (4 D.L.R. (2d) 688) the contract and the renewal had expired. The action was for damages and a declaration that the Club was entitled to have Dublinski restrained. McRUER C.J.H.C. said, referring to the *Warner Brothers* case: "This is a decision of a single Judge and I do not think it applies to this case. If it purports to hold that a Court of equity will enforce a negative covenant attached to a contract of employment by granting an injunction where the injunction will protect no interest by enforcing the negative covenant apart from the interest flowing from the positive covenant, I decline to follow it. But a careful examination of the argument in that case shows that what the plaintiff wished to be protected against was the exploitation of the defendant's services by a company competing with it that had a world market. . . . All through the cases runs the thread of the principle that a Court of equity will only protect a plaintiff for a period against *likely damage* by reason of the breach of a negative covenant, express or implied. . . ." Since the Detroit Club and the Toronto Argonauts played in separate and distinct leagues, for different audiences, and the Detroit Club had broken off its relationship with Dublinski, the

ratio of Davis cas

fact that "the defendant played football or was likely to play football for the Argonaut Club during the playing season of 1955 did the plaintiff no more harm than if he had remained idle." The plaintiff Club appealed. The Court of Appeal did not deal with the question of the injunction, but awarded damages in the amount of $6,950. ROACH J. A. said, "It requires only a mathematical calculation to demonstrate that, leaving out of consideration the value of the players traded to the Washington Red Skins [there was no evidence on this point], it cost the plaintiff $6,950 to fill the gap caused by the defendant breaking his contract. That calculation is as follows:

'To paid in acquiring the substitute $10,000.00
'To paid salary of substitute 11,200.00
'By credit—Salary of defendant .... $ 7,750.00
'By credit—Salary of one traded player 6,500.00
                                                    21,200.00 $14,250.00
                                                    14,250.00
'Net cost to plaintiff ....$ 6,950.00' "

ROACH J.A. accepted the submission that this calculation did not adequately account for the heavy investment of the plaintiff Club in training Dublinski. "It is very much like the case of the owner of a thoroughbred colt. . . . If the animal should break its legs the day before the race, all the money spent on it is a dead loss. Here, the defendant broke his contract, and it seems reasonable to me that the plaintiff, like the owner of the colt, has suffered some loss." However there was no evidence on this point to enable the court to assess the amount. "It is possible that [the club] suffered a greater loss. The Court however, cannot fix a sum that would amount to perfect compensation and I have concluded that on all evidence, justice would probably be done by fixing the damages at $6,950."

PAGE ONE RECORDS LTD. v. BRITTON
[1968] 1 W.L.R. 157

On February 1, 1966, Charles Christopher Britton, Ronald James Bullis, Reginald Maurice Ball, and Peter Lawrence Staples, a group of "pop" musicians known as "The Troggs," appointed Page One Records Ltd. (the first plaintiff) to be their managers and on April 22 and 25 they made two further agreements, one an agency and the other a recording agreement, with the plaintiff. On January 3, 1967, they made a publishing agreement with the second plaintiff, Dick James Music Ltd. In March, 1967, the first plaintiff appointed Harvey Block Associates Ltd. as booking agents for the Troggs for ballrooms but subsequently the Troggs considered inviting that company to become their manager and agent in place of the first plaintiff. On June 19, 1967, by two letters written one to the first plaintiff and the other to the second plaintiff, the Troggs purported to determine the four agreements they had made with the plaintiffs.

The first plaintiff sought an injunction to restrain the Troggs until trial from engaging anyone else as their manager or agent or from publishing any music performed by them otherwise than through the medium of the plaintiffs. The plaintiffs also sought an injunction against the second defendant restraining it from inducing any breaches of the agreements between the plaintiffs and the Troggs.

The defendants alleged that, even if the plaintiffs had acted impeccably towards the group at all times, which they denied, no injunction amounting to specific performance of a contract for personal services could be granted. Nor should any employer be prevented by injunction from dismissing an agent who occupied a fiduciary position. They also claimed that since the group could not have brought an action against their manager for specific performance of its agreement, no injunction could be granted against them. (MUTUALITY)

The facts are stated more fully in the judgment.

STAMP J.: The defendants have not, in my judgment, established a prima facie case for the view that there were such breaches by the first plaintiff of its duty to the Troggs as to justify the Troggs in repudiating the agreements they made with it. If all I had to do was to determine whether the plaintiffs had made out a prima facie case of breach of contract entitling them to damages. I would hold that they had, entitling the plaintiffs to make a heavy claim for damages against the defendants.

But it does not follow that because the plaintiffs have made out a prima facie case for succeeding in recovering damages in the action, that they have made out a prima facie case, or any case, for an interlocutory, or any, injunction.

The plaintiffs, relying on *Lumley* v. *Wagner* and the cases which followed it, claim, as regards the first plaintiff, an order that the first four defendants and each of them be restrained until trial from engaging as their managers or agents, or personal representatives in the branches of the entertainment industry referred to in clause 1 of the agreement of February 1, 1966, or from engaging as their managers conducting all their affairs relating to their professional careers in any medium of professional entertainment, any person, firm or corporation other than the first named plaintiff, and further, an injunction restraining each of the four Troggs acting as a group, from publishing or causing to be published any music performed by them, otherwise than through the medium of the first or second named plaintiffs. Then for an order that the second named defendant be restrained until the trial from inducing or procuring any breach or further breach by the Troggs as a group or otherwise of agreements between the plaintiffs and the Troggs for the management of the Troggs by the first plaintiff or the publication by either plaintiff of the music of the first named defendants in accordance with the terms of the four written agreements, to which I have referred.

Sir Andrew Clark submits that even if the plaintiffs had throughout acted impeccably towards the Troggs, no such injunction as is asked for ought to be granted. He advances three propositions on behalf of the Troggs. (1) Specific performance is never granted to enforce a contract for personal services. (2) An injunction is never granted which would have the effect of preventing an employer discharging an agent who is in a fiduciary position vis-à-vis the employer. He emphasises that here the first plaintiff, as manager and agent of the Troggs, is in the position of an employee. (3) An injunction is never granted at the suit of the party against whom the party to be restrained could not obtain specific performance.

It is urged—and, in my judgment, correctly—that the Troggs could have no action for specific performance of the management or agency agreements against the first plaintiff.

The present case is clearly distinguished, in principle, from such cases as *Lumley* v. *Wagner*, for there the only obligation on the part of the plaintiffs seeking to enforce the negative stipulation was an obligation to pay remuneration and an obligation which could clearly be enforced by the defendants. But here the obligations of the first plaintiff, involving personal services, were obligations of trust and confidence and were obligations which, plainly, could not be enforced at the suit of the Troggs. Here, indeed, so it seems to me, the totality of the obligations between the parties are more a joint venture, almost approaching the relationship of partners than anything else, involving mutual confidence and reciprocal obligations on all sides.

For the purposes of consideration of equitable relief, I must, I think, look at the totality of the arrangements, and the negative stipulations on which the plaintiffs rely, are, in my judgment, no more or less than stipulations designed to tie the parties together in a relationship of mutual confidence, mutual endeavour, and reciprocal obligations. These considerations, in the view of Knight Bruce L.J. in *Johnson* v. *Shrewsbury and Birmingham Railway Co.*, and *Pickering* v. *Ely (Bishop of)*, on which that Lord Justice relied in the former case, distinguish *Lumley* v. *Wagner*. I quote from his Lordship's judgment:

"It is clear in the present case that, had the defendants been minded to compel the plaintiffs to perform their duties against their will, it could not have been done. Mutuality therefore is out of the question, and, according to the rules generally supposed to exist in courts of equity, that might have been held sufficient to dispose of the matter; cases however have existed where, though the defendant could not have been compelled to do all he had undertaken to do by the contract, yet as he had contracted to abstain from doing a certain thing the court has interfered reasonably enough.

"A case, lately much referred to on this point is that of a German singer, who, having found probably that more could be obtained by breaking her promise than by keeping it, determined to obtain the larger sum and accordingly to break her promise. She could not be compelled to sing as she had contracted to do, but as she had contracted not to sing at any other place than the one specified in the agreement, she was (and very properly in my opinion) restrained from singing at any other place. There all the obligations on the part of the plaintiff could have been satisfied by the payment of money, but not so those of the defendant. Here the parties are reversed. Here all the obligations of the defendants can be satisfied by paying money; but not so the obligations of the plaintiffs, who come here for the purpose of compelling the defendants by a prohibitory or mandatory injunction, to do or abstain from doing certain acts, while the correlative acts are such as the plaintiffs could not be compelled to do."

But apart altogether from the lack of mutuality of the right of enforcement, this present case, in my judgment, fails, on the facts at present before me, on a more general principle, the converse of which was conveniently stated in the judgment of Branson J. in *Warner Brothers Pictures, Inc.* v. *Nelson*. Branson J. stated the converse of the proposition and the proposition, correctly stated, is, I think, this, that where a contract of personal service contains negative convenants the enforcement of which will amount either to a decree of specific performance of the positive covenants of the contract or to the giving of a decree under which the defendant must either remain idle or perform those positive covenants, the court will not enforce those negative covenants.

In the *Warner Brothers* case Branson J. felt able to find that the injunction sought would not force the defendant to perform his contract or remain idle.

1) Davis Case

I quote from the report:

"It was also urged that the difference between what the defendant can earn as a film artiste and what she might expect to earn by any other form of activity is so great that she will in effect be driven to perform her contract. That is not the criterion adopted in any of the decided cases. The defendant is stated to be a person of intelligence, capacity and means, and no evidence was adduced to show that, if enjoined from doing the specified acts otherwise than for the plaintiffs, she will not be able to employ herself both usefully and remuneratively in other spheres of activity, though not as remuneratively as in her special line. She will not be driven, although she may be tempted, to perform the contract, and the fact that she may be so tempted is no objection to the grant of an injunction."

Davis Case

So it was said in this case that if an injunction is granted the Troggs could, without employing any other manager or agent, continue as a group on their own or seek other employment of a different nature. So far as the former suggestion is concerned, in the first place I doubt whether consistently with the terms of the agreements which I have read, the Troggs could act as their own managers; and, in the second place, I think I can, and should, take judicial notice of the fact that these groups, if they are to have any great success, must have managers. Indeed, it is the plaintiffs' own case that the Troggs are simple persons, of no business experience, and could not survive without the services of a manager. As a practical matter on the evidence before me, I entertain no doubt that they would be compelled, if the injunction was granted, on the terms that the plaintiffs seek, to continue to employ the first plaintiff as their manager and agent and it is, I think, on this point that this case diverges from *Lumley* v. *Wagner* and the cases which have followed it, including the *Warner Brothers* case: for it would be a bad thing to put pressure upon these four young men to continue to employ as a manager and agent in a fiduciary capacity one who, unlike the plaintiff in those cases (who had merely to pay the defendant money) has duties of a personal and fiduciary nature to perform and in whom the Troggs, for reasons good, bad or indifferent, have lost confidence and who may, for all I know, fail in its duty to them.

On the facts before me on this interlocutory motion, I should, if I granted the injunction, be enforcing a contract for personal services in which personal services are to be performed by the first plaintiff. In *Lumley* v. *Wagner*, Lord St. Leonards, in his judgment, disclaimed doing indirectly what he could not do directly; and in the present case, by granting an injunction I would, in my judgment, be doing precisely that. I must, therefore, refuse the injunction which the first plaintiff seeks. The claim of the second plaintiff seems to me to be inextricably mixed up with the claim by the first plaintiff and no separate argument has really been addressed to me on the basis that the second plaintiff might succeed although the first plaintiff failed to obtain an injunction at the trial.

[Motion dismissed.]

7. TIME OF MEASURING DAMAGES

WROTH v. TYLER
[1974] Ch. 30

The facts have been stated in section 1. The portion of the judgment reproduced here concerns the proper time for measurement of damages, an important question since the value of the house rose dramatically between the date agreed for conveyance and the date of the trial. The contract price was £6,000, the value at the date agreed for conveyance, £7,500, and the value at the date of trial, £11,500. The plaintiff's action for specific performance was dismissed on the ground that a decree of specific performance would split the family (the wife, only, being entitled by statute to stay in the house).

MEGARRY J.: It was common ground that the normal rule is that the general damages to which a purchaser is entitled for breach of a contract for the sale of land are basically measured by the difference between the contract price and the market price of the land at the date of the breach, normally the date fixed for completion. On the facts of this case, the damages under this rule would be of the order of £1,500. The real issue was whether that rule applies to this case, or whether some other rule applies.

Now the principle that has long been accepted is that stated by Parke B. in *Robinson* v. *Harman* (1848) 1 Exch. 850, in which, incidentally, the rule in *Flureau* v. *Thornhill*, 2 Wm.Bl. 1078, was considered. Parke B. said, at p. 855: "The rule of the common law is, that where a party sustains a loss by reason of a breach of contract, he is, so far as money can do it, to be placed in the same situation, with respect to damages, as if the contract had been performed."

In the present case, if the contract had been performed, the plaintiffs would at the date fixed for completion have had the house, then worth £7,500 in return for the contractual price of £6,000. If in lieu of the house they had been paid £1,500 damages at that date, they could, with the addition of the £6,000 that they commanded, have forthwith bought an equivalent house. I am satisfied on the evidence that the plaintiffs had no financial resources of any substance beyond the £6,000 that they could have put together for the purchase of the defendant's bungalow, and that the defendant knew this when the contract was made. The plaintiffs were therefore, to the defendant's knowledge, unable at the time of the breach to raise a further £1,500 in order to purchase an equivalent house forthwith, and so, as events have turned out, mitigate their loss. Today, to purchase an equivalent house they need £5,500 in addition to their £6,000. How, then, it may be asked, would the award today of £1,500 damages place them in the same situation as if the contract had been performed? The result that would have been produced by paying £1,500 damages at the date of the breach can today be produced only by paying £5,500 damages, with in each case the return of the deposit. On facts such as these, the general rule of assessing damages as at the date of the breach seems to defeat the general principle, rather than carry it out. In the ordinary case of a buyer of goods which the seller fails to deliver, the buyer can at once spend his money in purchasing equivalent goods from another, as was pointed out in *Gainsford* v. *Carroll* (1824)

2 B. & C. 624, and so the rule works well enough; but that is a very different case. It therefore seems to me that on the facts of this case there are strong reasons for applying the principle rather than the rule. The question is whether it is proper to do so.

I do not think that I need inquire whether such an award could be made at common law. It may be that it could. The rule requiring damages to be ascertained as at the date of the breach does not seem to be inflexible, and in any case the rule may be one which, though normally carrying out the principle, does on occasion fail to do so; and on those occasions the rule may have to be modified so as to accord with the principle. However, as I have said, I do not think I need explore that; for it seems to me that this case, in which there is a proper claim for specific performance, falls within the Chancery Amendment Act 1858 (better known as Lord Cairns' Act), and that damages assessed under that Act are to be ascertained in accordance with that Act on a basis which is not identical with that of the common law. That Act provides, by section 2:

"In all cases in which the Court of Chancery has jurisdiction to entertain an application for an injunction against a breach of any covenant, contract, or agreement, or against the commission or continuance of any wrongful act, or for the specific performance of any covenant, contract, or agreement, it shall be lawful for the same court, if it shall think fit, to award damages to the party injured, either in addition to or in substitution for such injunction or specific performance, and such damages may be assessed in such manner as the court shall direct. [Section 21 of the Ontario Judicature Act is in similar terms]. . . .

On the wording of the section, the power "to award damages to the party injured, . . . in substitution for such . . . specific performance," at least envisages that the damages awarded will in fact constitute a true substitute for specific performance. Furthermore, the section is speaking of the time when the court is making its decision to award damages in substitution for specific performance, so that it is at that moment that the damages must be a substitute. The fact that a different amount of damages would have been a substitute if the order had been made at the time of the breach must surely be irrelevant. In the case before me, I cannot see how £1,500 damages would constitute any true substitute for a decree of specific performance of the contract to convey land which at the time of the decree is worth £5,500 more than the contract price. A choice between the inadequate and the equivalent seems to me to be no real choice at all. It may seem strange that nearly 115 years should have elapsed before this aspect of Lord Cairns' Act should have emerged; but the economic conditions which reveal its significance have not been with us long.

There are dicta in *Leeds Industrial Co-operative Society Ltd.* v. *Slack* [1924] A.C. 851 which support this view, or are at least consistent with it. In a speech with which the Earl of Birkenhead expressed his agreement, Viscount Finlay said, at p. 859: ". . . the power to give damages in lieu of an injunction must in all reason import the power to give an equivalent for what is lost by the refusal of the injunction; for this purpose compensation only for what has passed would be futile."

He added: "It has been urged that the word 'damages' must be used as denoting compensation for what has already happened. It is, of course, true that a court of common law gives damages as compensation for past wrongs, but the word 'damages' is perfectly apt to denote compensation for the damage which will be sustained if a building is allowed to proceed so as to obstruct ancient lights. If an injunction is granted the obstruction will never take place. If damages are given instead of the injunction, they must be in respect of an injury which is still in the future."

Lord Dunedin expressly concurred in Lord Finlay's speech; but he also said, at p. 865, that the words referring to damages in substitution for an injunction "clearly point to a pecuniary payment equalling the loss to be occasioned by the act against which, but for the provision in question, an injunction would have been obtained. . . ."

I must, of course, have care in applying dicta uttered in a case where the problem before me was obviously not in view, even though section 2 of the Act lays down the same rule for injunctions and specific performance alike. Yet on principle I would say simply that damages "in substitution" for specific performance must be a substitute, giving as nearly as may be what specific performance would have given. There are, moreover, certain other authorities which provide assistance. In *Fritz* v. *Hobson* (1880) 14 Ch.D. 542 it was held that damages awarded under the Act in substitution for an injunction were not confined to damages down to the issue of the writ, as at law, but included damages down to the hearing. Fry J. said, at p. 556: "Now it is manifest that damages cannot be an adequate substitute for an injunction unless they cover the whole area which would have been covered by the injunction, . . ."

In *Chapman, Morsons & Co.* v. *Guardians of Auckland Union* (1889) 23 Q.B.D. 294, the Court of Appeal approved the view taken by Fry J. in *Fritz* v. *Hobson*, 14 Ch.D. 542, 556. In *Dreyfus* v. *Peruvian Guano Co.* (1889) 43 Ch.D. 316, 342, Fry L.J. said of Lord Cairns' Act: "I am clear that the statute often enables the court, where a wrong has been done, to give damages upon a different scale from what was done by the Courts of Common Law, because it may give them in substitution for an injunction; . . ."

Cotton L.J., who had previously delivered the leading judgment, then said that he agreed with what Fry L.J. had said about Lord Cairns' Act.

I should say at once that these additional authorities were not discussed before me, but as they support the view which I took without their aid, it seems proper for me to cite them without incurring the costs and delay of restoring the case for further argument. There seems to me to be adequate authority for the view that damages under Lord Cairns' Act may be awarded in cases in which there is no claim at all at law, and also that the quantum of damages is not limited by the rules at law. No doubt in exercising the jurisdiction conferred by the Act a court with equitable jurisdiction will remember that equity follows the law, and will in general apply the common law rules for the assessment of damages; but this is subject to the overriding statutory requirement that damages shall be "in substitution for" the injunction or specific performance. In the words of Cardozo C.J., "Equity follows the law, but not slavishly nor always": *Graf* v. *Hope Building Corporation* (1930) 254 N.Y. 1, 9. Obedience to statute, whether in its precise words or in its spirit, is an excellent and compelling reason for not following the law.

In my judgment, therefore, if under Lord Cairns' Act damages are awarded in substitution for specific performance, the court has jurisdiction to award such damages as will put the plaintiffs into as good a position as if the contract had been performed, even if to do so means awarding damages assessed by reference to a period subsequent to the date of the breach. This seems to me to be consonant with the nature of specific performance, which is a continuing remedy, designed to secure (inter alia) that the purchaser receives in fact what is his in equity as soon as the contract is made, subject to the vendor's right to the money, and so on. On the one hand, a decree may be sought before any breach of contract has occurred, and so before any action lies for common law damages; and on the other hand the right to a decree may continue long after the breach has occurred. On the facts of this case, the damages that may be awarded are not limited to the £1,500 that is appropriate to the date of the breach, but extend to the £5,500 that is appropriate at the present day, when they are being awarded in substitution for specific performance. I should add that no contention has been advanced (in my judgment, quite rightly) that the case does not fall within Lord Cairns' Act. The sale of a house is a case par excellence in which the court "has jurisdiction to entertain an application . . . for the specific performance" of a contract, and the plaintiffs have done nothing to disentitle themselves to a decree. The undesirability of granting the decree if any suitable alternative exists springs from the position of the defendant and his wife.

That brings me to a subsidiary point which Mr. Lyndon-Stanford urged upon me. He contended that an award of damages of the order of £5,500 was precluded by the operation of what is often called the "second rule" in *Hadley* v. *Baxendale* (1854) 9 Exch. 341, relating to what was in the contemplation of the parties. I was very properly referred to that case in the light of the discussion in later cases set out in *McGregor on Damages*, 13th ed. (1972) principally at pp. 124-132. It was beyond question that a rise in the price of houses was in the contemplation of the parties when the contract was made in this case. But Mr. Lyndon-Stanford took it further. He contended that what a plaintiff must establish is not merely a contemplation of a particular head of damage, but also of the quantum under that head. Here, the parties contemplated a rise in house prices, but not a rise of an amount approaching that which in fact took place. A rise which nearly doubled the market price of the property was, as the evidence showed, outside the contemplation of the parties, and so it could not be recovered. Thus ran the argument.

I do not think that this can be right. On principle, it seems to me to be quite wrong to limit damages flowing from a contemplated state of affairs to the amount that the parties can be shown to have had in contemplation, for to do this would require evidence of the calculation in advance of what is often incalculable until after the event. The function of the so-called "second rule" in *Hadley* v. *Baxendale*, 9 Exch. 341, seems to me to be not so much to add to the damages recoverable as to exclude from them any liability for any type or kind of loss which could not have been foreseen when the contract was made. No authority was put before me which appeared to me to provide any support for the alleged requirement that the quantum should have been in contemplation. So far as it went, the language used in the authorities that were cited seems to me to have been directed to the heads of damage rather than to quantum. Thus one finds phrases such as "special circumstances" and the "type" or "kind" of damage. I would therefore on principle reject the defendant's contention, and hold that a plaintiff invoking the so-called "second rule" in *Hadley* v. *Baxendale*, 9 Exch. 341, need show only a contemplation of circumstances which embrace the head or type of damage in question, and need not demonstrate a contemplation of the quantum of damages under that head or type. Accordingly, in my judgment, this subsidiary contention of the defendant's fails, even if it is one that would apply, either directly or by analogy, to damages under Lord Cairns' Act.

During the argument it seemed to me surprising that the point should not be covered by authority; yet the only authority put before me that seemed to bear on the point was *Vacwell Engineering Co. Ltd.* v. *B.D.H. Chemicals Ltd.* [1971] 1 Q.B. 88. Mr. Lyndon-Stanford referred me to this case in performance of his duty of assisting the court, although it was against him. The point does not seem to have been argued there in terms, but it was held that where the parties to a contract could reasonably have foreseen that there might be a small or minor explosion, with some damage to property, if a proper warning was not given as to the precautions to be taken in handling the chemical sold, but could not reasonably have foreseen the major explosion which in fact occurred, killing a scientist and doing extensive damage to property, the vendors were nevertheless liable for the whole of the damage done. As Rees J. said, at p. 110: "... the explosion and the type of damage being foreseeable, it matters not in the law that the magnitude of the former and the extent of the latter were not." An appeal was settled: see [1971] 1 Q.B. 111, 112 (note)

That case, however, does not stand alone. In *Great Lakes Steamship Co.* v. *Maple Leaf Milling Co. Ltd.* (1924) 41 T.L.R. 21, the respondents, in breach of contract, had failed "to lighter immediately" the appellants' vessel on its arrival at the respondents' wharf on Lake Erie. Three days later, before any lightering had taken place, the vessel settled on the bottom as a result of a fall in the level of the water in the lake that was within the contemplation of the parties. Unknown to either party, a large anchor was resting on the bottom at that point, projecting two feet above the rock floor which there formed the bottom. This anchor caused serious injuries to the hull, for which the appellants claimed over $40,000 damages. In delivering the advice of the Judicial Committee, Lord Carson said, at p. 23:

"There can be no doubt that it was from breach of the contract immediately to lighter that the vessel grounded by reason of the lowering of the water, the very thing which it was anticipated might occur and which rendered the immediate lightering so important, and it must, in their Lordship's opinion, be held that it was the breach of contract in not lightering the vessel which was the immediate cause of the damage, and the fact that such damage might not have occurred if the anchor had not been sunk can make no difference. If grounding takes place in breach of contract, the precise nature of the damage incurred by grounding is immaterial."

That case seems to me to provide strong support for the view that I take. In the present case, the argument is directed purely to quantum. The precise head of damage, a general rise in the price of houses, was admittedly in contemplation: all that could be said to be outside the contemplation was the full amount, or the higher stages of the rise from £6,000 to £11,500. In *Great Lakes Steamship Co.* v. *Maple Leaf Milling Co. Ltd.*, 41 T.L.R. 21, what was in contemplation was the fact that delay in lightering might cause the vessel to rest on the bottom by the wharf, a bottom consisting of rock; nobody contemplated the anchor, yet the damages recoverable included those stemming from the anchor. On the authority of that case, the case before me seems a fortiori. I therefore find confirmation in that case of the view that at the hearing I took without its aid.

The conclusion that I have reached, therefore, is that as matters stand I ought to award damages to the plaintiffs of the order of £5,500, in substitution for decreeing specific performance, with all the doubts and difficulties and probably undesirable consequences that a decree in either form would produce. An award of damages on this scale, I accept, will bear hardly on the defendant. Though able in one way or another to raise £1,500 without selling his bungalow. £5,500 is another matter; in all probability he could not raise that sum without selling the bungalow with vacant possession, and he has no power to do this. If, however, he becomes bankrupt, then his trustee in bankruptcy can sell the bungalow free from the wife's rights, even though they are registered: see section 2 (5) of the Act of 1967. With the money so raised, the trustee in bankruptcy will then be able to pay the plaintiffs their damages, one hopes in full; or it may be possible for the plaintiffs to take the bungalow in satisfaction of their claim. This is a dismal prospect for the defendant, but if the plaintiffs obtain neither a decree of specific performance nor £5,500 by way of damages, theirs also is a dismal prospect. Having made a binding contract to purchase for £6,000 a bungalow now worth £11,500, they would recover neither the bungalow nor damages that would enable them to purchase anything like its equivalent. It is the plaintiffs who are wholly blameless. Nothing whatever can be said against them, or has been, save as to the contention that delay barred them from a decree of specific performance; and that I have rejected. Nor do I think that there was any delay on their part that could affect the measure of damages.

The ultimate truth as between the defendant and his wife I do not know. As the evidence stands, his wife did nothing whatever to warn the plaintiffs that she was not willing to leave the bungalow, but conducted herself so as to lead them to believe that she concurred in the sale. So far as the defendant was concerned, his wife was very cool about the move, and it may well be that the move was one which a strong-willed husband was in effect imposing on a reluctant yet secretive wife. Nevertheless, the consequences of disputes between husband and wife, whether open or concealed, ought not to be visited upon innocent purchasers.

In these circumstances, I think that what I ought to do is to make no order today, but, subject to what counsel may have to say, to adjourn the case until the first day of next term. In ordinary circumstances, I would adjourn the case for only a week, but unfortunately the impending vacation makes this impossible. During the adjournment I hope that the defendant and his wife will take advice, separately or together. When I resume the hearing, it may be that the defendant's wife will not have changed her mind about her charge. In that case, I shall award the plaintiffs damages against the defendant of the order of £5,500, even though the probable consequence will be the bankruptcy of the defendant and the sale of the bungalow with vacant possession by his trustee in bankruptcy, free from the wife's rights. On the other hand, the defendant's wife may by then have changed her mind, and rather than force her husband into bankruptcy without avoiding having to vacate the bungalow, she may have taken effective steps to enable the defendant to convey the bungalow to the plaintiffs free from her rights. In that case I shall decree specific performance of the contract. In this way the plaintiffs will obtain either the bungalow that they bought or else an amount of damages which will enable them to purchase its equivalent. I may add that of course I give each side liberty to apply in the meantime; and I should say that I shall be available until 4 p.m. today. As I have indicated, I feel much sympathy for the defendant as well as for the plaintiffs at being embroiled in this way. Yet as between the two sides both the law and the merits seem to me to point to the plaintiffs as being the parties who should be as little hurt as possible; and they have already suffered considerably, not least in relation to their temporary accommodation pending these proceedings. Counsel will no doubt assist me with any submissions that they may have on this proposed adjournment, which was not mooted during the argument.

January 11, 1973. The defendant's wife refused to remove the notice. Damages of £5,500 assessed as at January 11, 1973, were awarded in lieu of specific performance, with costs.

[Order accordingly.]

QUESTION. What if the land is an apartment building, and the purchaser has ample funds on hand to purchase another as soon as the vendor defaults? See *A.V.G. Management Science Ltd.* v. *Barwell Developments, Ltd.* (1976) 69 D.L.R. (3d) 741 (B.C.S.C.).

R.G. LAWSON, DAMAGES — AN APPRAISAL OF *WROTH* v. *TYLER* (1975) 125 N.L.J. 300

Damages for breach of contract, Parke B. once suggested, should place the innocent party in the position he would have occupied had the contract been performed (*Robinson* v. *Harrian* (1848) 1 Ex. 850, 855). Generally speaking, this is done by awarding a measure of compensation based on the difference in sale price and market price at the date of breach. A buyer fortified with such damages, the theory goes, is able to purchase equivalent goods in the market, and so occupy the position originally promised him by the seller.

Of course, if the market price at the date of judgment exceeds the market price at the date of breach, compensation based on the earlier date may be unsatisfactory. The objection that the buyer should mitigate his loss by making a substitute purchase before the date of judgment is valid only if he has sufficient cash in hand. This may not be so; particularly if he paid the defaulting seller in advance.

The situation canvassed above had rarely engaged authoritative attention. In *Gainsford* v. *Carroll* (1824) 2 B & C 624, the buyer was denied the rate prevailing at judgment: he had not prepaid, and could have made a replacement purchase at the date of breach. Although this indicates that the latter date would have been apposite where advance payment had been made, a later court ruled otherwise where precisely this had happened: *Startup* v. *Cortazzi* (1835) 2 C.M. & R. 165.

When the matter later arose, the facts, as Megarry J. put it, were "as simple as the law is complex" (*Wroth* v. *Tyler* [1973] 1 All E.R. 897, 901). Put briefly, the plaintiff sought specific performance of a contract for the sale of land. This was refused. Megarry J. then proceeded to award damages: but the date chosen was not the £7,500 at the date of breach, but the £11,500 which the land was worth at the date of judgment.

In *Wroth* v. *Tyler*, the damages were assessed under the Chancery Amendment Act, 1858 ("Lord Cairns' Act"). They were not awarded as common law damages, but were awarded under this statute in lieu of specific performance. Section 2 speaks of damages being awarded "in substitution" for specific performance which "at least envisages that the damages awarded will in fact constitute a true substitute for specific performance. Furthermore, the section is speaking of the time when the court is making its decision to award damages in substitution, so that it is at that moment that the damage must be a substitute" (*ibid.* at p. 920).

Perhaps an even clearer statement had come from Sholl J. in *Bosaid* v. *Andrey* [1963] V.L.R. 465. Damages would be given by a Chancery Court in lieu of specific performance, he believed, "on the hypothesis that the contract came to an end by the act of the Court itself in withholding specific performance—that is to say, at the time (usually of the decree) when the Court substituted an order for damages, even if it did not at once assess them."

If it follows inexorably from this reasoning that damages under Lord Cairns' Act are based as at the date of judgment, it is not self-evident that the same approach would obtain at law. Megarry J. was content to say only that it might; but he did add that the "rule requiring damages to be ascertained as at the date of breach does not seem to be inflexible," and that the normal principle of common law damages "may have to be modified so as to accord with the principle."

In *Horsler* v. *Zorro* [1973] 2 W.L.R. 183, Megarry J. was content once more to leave open the question whether damages at law could be awarded as at the date of judgment. Goff J., too, in *Grant* v. *Dawkins* [1973] 3 All E.R. 897, 900, has gone no further than to say that "there may be exceptions" to the normal date of assessment for damages at law. But in *Souster* v. *Epsom Plumbing Contractors Ltd.* [1974] 2 N.Z.L.R. 515 McMullin J. put the view, *obiter dicta*, that the same measure of damages would be allowable at common law since Lord Cairns' Act was merely a procedural section designed to permit the employment of common law remedies in Courts of Equity.

This is doubtless so; but it is no support for the further argument that damages at law may also be assessed as at the date of judgment. The special factor in Lord Cairns' Act, and this was recognised by McMullin J. as well as Megarry and Sholl JJ., is that the contract is terminated only when the Court judges that specific performance is inappropriate. Such considerations are absent when damages are sought at law.

There is, furthermore, the flatly contradictory decision in *Chitholie* v. *Nash & Co.* (1974) 229 E.G. 786. This was an action where the defendants conceded that they had no authority to act for the vendor in the sale of a dwelling-house. Talbot J. refused to award damages on the higher rate prevailing at the date of judgment. He was bound, so the report runs, "to follow the normal common law rule as to the measure of damages for breach of a contract for sale of land . . . to depart from that normal rule would be to place upon the shoulders of the defendants the burden of a higher award of damages due not to their breach, but to events which had occurred after the breach and over which they had no control."

MILIANGOS v. GEO. FRANK (TEXTILES) LTD.
[1976] A.C. 443 (H.L.)

LORD WILBERFORCE: My Lords, the facts in this case are as simple as in *In re United Railways of Havana and Regla Warehouses Ltd.* [1961] A.C. 1007 they were complex. It is concerned with a contract made in May, 1971 for the sale of 90,718 kilogrammes of polyester yarn at a price of 12.56 Swiss francs per kilogramme, price to be paid within 30 days of invoice. The proper law of this contract was Swiss law and the money of account and of payment was Swiss francs. The respondent, the seller, is a national of Switzerland and the yarn was produced by his firm in Switzerland. It was delivered in the autumn of 1971 under five invoices, each of which stated the price in Swiss francs, payment to be made within 30 days to a Swiss bank. The appellant company did not pay any part of the price. It accepted, by way of part payment, two bills of exchange drawn in Switzerland for a total sum of 300,000 Swiss francs payable on January 31, 1972, but these were dishonoured on presentation.

The action was begun by writ on April 20, 1972. In his statement of claim the respondent claimed the amount of the price or, alternatively, the amount due on the bills expressed, in each case, in the sterling equivalent of the sum due in Swiss francs as at the dates when payment should have been made. The appellant delivered a defence and a counter-claim alleging that the yarn was defective and there followed a number of interlocutory steps arising out of this allegation. But on November 22, 1974, just before the action was due to come on for trial the appellant wrote to say that it abandoned the defence and counterclaim and would submit to judgment.

Thereafter the proceedings took a remarkable course. On November 26, 1974, the Court of Appeal (Lord Denning M.R., Lawton L.J., and Foster J.) announced their decision in a case involving a claim in German currency—*Schorsch Meier G.m.b.H.* v. *Hennin* [1975] Q.B. 416. Although they were faced with a unanimous decision of this House in *In re United Railways of Havana and Regla Warehouses Ltd.* [1961] A.C. 1007 that, on a foreign currency claim, judgment can only be given in sterling, to which the foreign currency must be converted as at the date when the debt became due, the court held by a majority that an English court could give a money judgment in a foreign currency, when that currency was the currency of the contract. Lawton L.J., dissenting, considered that he was bound by the *Havana Railways* case. Unanimously, as a second ground of decision, the court held that where the creditor resided in an E.E.C. country, an English court was obliged [sic] by article 106 of the Treaty of Rome to give a judgment in the currency of the creditor, if that was the currency of the contract.

This decision was naturally welcomed by the respondent. So when this action came on for hearing on December 2, 1974, he applied to amend his statement of claim so as to claim the amount due to him in Swiss francs. This amendment was allowed by Bristow J. so that the claim became one for 415,522.45 Swiss francs for the price plus 621.75 the cost of protesting the two bills, making together 416,144.20 Swiss francs. Since, between the date in 1971 when payment was due and the date of the hearing, sterling had fallen in value as against the Swiss franc from Sw.Frs. 9.90 to 6.00 (approximately) to the £, this meant that if the respondent could obtain judgment in Swiss francs he could recover in sterling terms some £60,000, whereas if he had to accept the sterling equivalent at the 1971 rate he could recover only some £42,000.

This amendment having been made, the action (together with a second action into which it is unnecessary to enter) came for trial. The learned judge found himself in a difficult position. On the one hand there was the decision of this House in the *Havana Railways* case [1961] A.C. 1007 which clearly precluded him from giving judgment in Swiss francs or from awarding the sterling equivalent of the sum due converted at any other date than the date when the sum claimed was due. On the other hand there was the decision of the Court of Appeal in *Schorsch Meier* [1975] Q.B. 416, which had declined to apply the *Havana Railways* decision. In these circumstances he decided that he ought to follow the decision of this House and that the decision in *Schorsch Meier* was given *per incuriam*.

An appeal was brought to the Court of Appeal and was heard in February 1975 by Lord Denning M.R., Stephenson, and Goeffrey Lane L.JJ. It was submitted that the court, on indistinguishable facts, was bound by and should follow the *Havana Railways* case, but the court declined to do so. It held that the majority decision in *Schorsch Meier* was not given per incuriam (the unanimous alternative was not directly relevant since Switzerland is not an E.E.C. member) and that it was binding upon the court. It therefore varied the judgment of Bristow J. so as to give judgment for the respondent for the sum claimed in Swiss francs. From this judgment appeal has come to this House. There has been no appeal in the *Schorsch Meier* case but since it was applied by the Court of Appeal in these proceedings I shall have to comment upon it.

My Lords, it is clear from this account that some distortion of the judicial process has been brought about. As Bristow J. said [1975] Q.B. 487, 492:

"I am faced with a judgment of a majority of the Court of Appeal, which in its application to the issue raised before me says that a rule of English law taken for granted by the Court of Appeal and the House of Lords for some 350 years is no longer a rule of English law. The speeches of the House of Lords in *Broome* v. *Cassell & Co. Ltd.* [1972] A.C. 1027 constrain me in the circumstances to hold that the rule of law that my judgment can only be expressed in sterling is still of full force and effect, since Parliament has not altered it, nor has the House of Lords itself under its 1966 declaration: see *Practice Statement (Judicial Precedent)* [1966] 1 W.L.R. 1234."

It has to be reaffirmed that the only judicial means by which decisions of this House can be reviewed is by this House itself, under the declaration of 1966. Whether it can or should do so is a difficult enough question, which I shall now examine.

My Lords, although the "breach date rule" has a long history, possibly, but, I think, not clearly, extending back to the Year Books, consideration of it at the present time as regards foreign money debts must start from the *Havana Railways* case [1961] A.C. 1007. For that was a case of a money debt as to which it was sought to persuade this House that a different rule should be applied from that which was admitted to be relevant to claims for damages for tort or for breach of contract. The claim there was for a debt (or debts) in U.S. dollars, due under a contract the proper law of which was held to be the law of Pennsylvania. The debtor (the United Havana Railways Co.) was English: the creditor was American. The proceedings were by way of proof in the liquidation of the debtor, not by action by writ, but it was not suggested that this made any difference, and I say at once that I do not think that any distinction can be drawn on this ground. On the arguments presented which were at least strenuous, and after examination of the cases extending over a long period, the House unanimously decided that the provable sum in U.S. dollars had to be converted into sterling at the rates of exchange prevailing when the relevant sums fell due and were not paid. They rejected the counter-suggestion that conversion should be made at the date of judgment. They did not take up or accept suggestions which had been made in some earlier cases that a separate rule applied to foreign money claims.

My Lords, even if I were inclined to question some of the arguments used in the speeches, I should find it inappropriate and unnecessary to say that, in the circumstances of the time and on the arguments and authorities presented, the decision was wrong or is open to distinction or explanation.

What we can do, and what is our responsibility, is to consider whether this decision, clear and comparatively recent, should be regarded as a binding precedent in today's circumstances. For that purpose it is permissible to examine the speeches in order to understand the considerations upon which the opinions there reached were based, for the ultimate purpose of seeing whether there have emerged fresh considerations which might have appealed to those who gave those opinions and so may appeal to their successors. . . .

[His Lordship then examined the *Havana Railways* case.]

My Lords, I have quoted extensively from these opinions, not only because they embody the standing authority on the question now at issue, but also in order to make clear what, I think, appears from all of them to be the basic presupposition. This is that procedurally an action cannot be brought here for recovery or payment of a sum expressed in foreign currency, and that, in effect, it can only be brought for a sum expressed in sterling, recoverable by way of damages. I now have to ask, what is the position at the present time? Have any fresh considerations of any substance emerged which should induce your Lordships to follow a different rule? I will endeavour to state those which appear to me to be significant.

1. The courts have evolved a procedure under which orders can be made for payment of foreign currency debts in the foreign currency. The Court of Appeal has given its approval to the form: "It is adjudged . . . that the defendant do pay to the plaintiff [the sum in foreign currency] or the sterling equivalent at the time of payment." (See *Schorsch Meier G.m.b.H.* v. *Hennin* [1975] Q.B. 416, 425 *per* Lord Denning M.R.). I can find no reason in principle why such orders cannot be made. The courts have generally power to order delivery in specie whenever, in their opinion, damages are an inadequate remedy. In cases such as the present, indeed, one of the arguments against making orders for payment of foreign currency in specie has been that damages are an adequate remedy (see particularly *Lloyd Royal Belge S.A.* v. *Louis Dreyfus & Co.* (1927) 27 Ll.L.Rep. 288, 294 *per* Romer J.). But if, in the circumstances of today, damages are not an adequate remedy, as they clearly may not be if the breach date rule is applied in times of floating currencies, this argument, in any case nothing more than an appeal to

discretion, loses its force. The jurisdiction is clear, on general principle: how the courts' discretion is to be exercised depends on the circumstances. I return to this later. Further, I can find nothing in the Rules of the Supreme Court which prevents such orders being made: indeed, though I do not attach the same importance to the change as did the learned Master of the Rolls, the present form of the rules (R.S.C., Ord. 42, r. 1, Ord. 45 and Forms 45 et seq., Appendix A) is somewhat more favourable to the making of orders in this form than was the version in force in 1961. Lord Denning M.R. adhered to this position in the present case after further argument upon the rules, by which time any serious inconveniences or practical difficulties would have come to light. I shall return to this subject later with particular reference to the question of the date of conversion. At the present stage what is relevant is that orders in this form are jurisdictionally legitimate and procedurally workable.

2. The situation as regards currency stability has substantially changed even since 1961. Instead of the main world currencies being fixed and fairly stable in value, subject to the risk of periodic re- or devaluations, many of them are now "floating," i.e., they have no fixed exchange value even from day to day. This is true of sterling. This means that, instead of a situation in which changes of relative value occurred between the "breach date" and the date of judgment or payment being the exception, so that a rule which did not provide for this case could be generally fair, this situation is now the rule. So the search for a formula to deal with it becomes urgent in the interest of justice. This leads to the next point.

3. The state of facts referred to under 2 has become recognised in those commercial circles which are closely concerned with international contracts. The reaction to them appears in the field of arbitration. In 1969 two of the most experienced arbitrators in the City of London made an award expressed in terms of U.S. dollars and the validity of this came to be tested in the courts: *Jugoslavenska Oceanska Plovidba* v. *Castle Investment Co. Inc.* [1974] Q.B. 292. In reserved judgments the Court of Appeal (Lord Denning M.R., Cairns and Roskill L.JJ.), disagreeing with observations made in that court in *The Teh Hu* [1970] P. 106, 129, held that the award was valid. What is more, and relevant in the present context, they held that it could be enforced under section 26 of the Arbitration Act 1950 which enables an award to be enforced "in the same manner as a judgment or order to the same effect." They pointed out that this was also the case as regards foreign awards which under section 36 (1) of the same Act "shall be enforceable" in the same manner as an award "is enforceable under section 26." Roskill L.J., who has great experience in these matters, said that awards of this kind made in the City have been entirely satisfactory and honoured all over the world. He also referred to inquiries made by Kerr J., at first instance, of the Central Office of the High Court which showed that there is no difficulty in practice in enforcing foreign currency awards: the foreign currency is simply converted into sterling at the rate prevailing at the date of the award.

I regard this development as of great importance for two reasons. First, it goes a long way towards removing the practical objections as regards enforcement which weighed so heavily in the *Havana Railways* case [1961] A.C. 1007. If an award in a foreign currency case can be readily enforced, after conversion into a sterling sum, and since an award is enforceable as a judgment, it should follow that a judgment in a foreign currency can be similarly enforced, after conversion into a sterling sum. Secondly, it would be an intolerable situation if a different rule were to prevail as regards arbitrations upon debts expressed in foreign currency on the one hand and actions upon similar debts on the other. Counsel for the appellants was therefore obliged to argue that if he was to succeed the decision in the *Jugoslavenska* case [1974] Q.B. 292 must either be overruled, or narrowly confined. I can find no limits within which it can be confined which would not still enclose the present case, so, if the appeal were to be allowed, the case would have to be overruled. But if I am faced with the alternative of forcing commercial circles to fall in with a legal doctrine which has nothing but precedent to commend it or altering the doctrine so as to conform with what commercial experience has worked out, I know where my choice lies. The law should be responsive as well as, at times, enunciatory, and good doctrine can seldom be divorced from sound practice.

4. Further recognition of the need for, and practicality of, making orders in terms of foreign currencies was given in *The Halcyon the Great* [1975] 1 W.L.R. 515, where an order was made in Admiralty for the sale of a ship for U.S. dollars, and for the lodgment of the price in a separate dollar account. The judgment of Brandon J. contains a clear acceptance (contrary to the appellant's arguments here) of the proposition that U.S. dollar currency may be regarded as "money" within the meaning of English procedural rules and that the courts can easily adapt their procedure so as to give effect to foreign money claims in specie. The case indeed prompts the reflection that a similar procedure might have been regarded as acceptable in the *Havana Railways* case, the factual situation (i.e., a debt in foreign currency secured upon a sum expressed in foreign currency) being in many respects similar.

5. I should mention at this stage the argument based upon article 106 of the E.E.C. Treaty of Rome. I can understand the temptation, in the search for an argument why the *Havana Railways* case should not now be followed, to fasten upon the important development which the treaty represents. Although Switzerland is not an E.E.C. member, the argument unanimously accepted by the Court of Appeal in *Schorsch Meier* [1975] Q.B. 416 was invoked by the respondent in this appeal and correspondingly attacked by the appellants. It cannot therefore be passed over in silence, all the less since there is a risk that it may be quoted as a precedent. There are two reasons for dealing with it here with restraint. First, there is no direct appeal against the decision in *Schorsch Meier*: secondly, the issue of the applicability and interpretation of article 106, if it were to be considered by this House, would necessitate a reference to the European Court under article 177 of the treaty. But nevertheless I feel bound to say that I entertain the strongest reservations concerning the use made by the Court of Appeal of article 106 in the present context, and I cannot believe that, if the court had heard argument on the other side (corresponding to that of the present appellants), very weighty arguments would not have been brought forward concerning such questions as the direct applicability of this article, its bearing on any question of the currency in which claims may be made in the courts of member States or its relevance at all to the ascertainment of the date of conversion of such claims, which arguments seem to have been unappreciated.

Any other court in which such issues may arise would be well advised to refer them to the European Court for clarification. In this appeal, in my opinion, no argument based directly or indirectly upon article 106 of the treaty should be considered as available to the respondent.

6. Finally, I wish to express my agreement as to what my noble and learned friend Lord Simon of Glaisdale has said about the maxim "cessante ratione," etc. [cessante ratione, cessat ipsa lex; when the reason for it ceases, the rule itself must cease.]

My Lords, before attempting the task of deciding where, in the end, this House should stand as regards the *Havana Railways* [1961] A.C. 1007 rule there are some other general observations I think should be made.

First, I do not for myself think it doubtful that, in a case such as the present, justice demands that the creditor should not suffer from fluctuations in the value of sterling. His contract has nothing to do with sterling: he has bargained for his own currency and only his own currency. The substance of the debtor's obligations depends upon the proper law of the contract (here Swiss law): and though English law (lex fori) prevails as regards procedural matters, it must surely be wrong in principle to allow procedure to affect, detrimentally, the substance of the creditor's rights. Courts are bound by their own procedural law and must obey it, if imperative, though to do so may seem unjust. But if means exist for giving effect to the substance of a foreign obligation, conformably with the rules of private international law, procedure should not unnecessarily stand in the way.

There is, unforunately, as Lord Radcliffe pointed out in the *Havana Railways* case, a good deal of confusion in English cases as to what the creditor's rights are. Appeal has been made to the principle of nominalism, so as to say that the creditor must take the pound sterling as he finds it. Lord Denning said so in the *Havana Railways* case (pp. 1069-70) and I can safely and firmly disagree with him in that because he has himself, since then, come to hold another view. The creditor has no concern with pounds sterling: for him what matters is that a Swiss franc for good or ill should remain a Swiss franc. This is substantially the reasoning of Holmes J. in the important judgment of the U.S. Supreme Court in *Deutsche Bank Filiale Nürnberg* v. *Humphrey* (1926) 272 U.S. 517. Another argument is that the "breach date" makes for certainty whereas to choose a later date makes the claim depend on currency fluctuations. But this is only a partial truth. The only certainty achieved is certainty in the sterling amount—but that is not in point since sterling does not enter into the bargain. The relevant certainty which the rule ought to achieve is that which gives the creditor neither more nor less than he bargained for. He bargained for 415,522.45 Swiss francs; whatever this means in (unstipulated) foreign currencies, whichever way the exchange into those currencies may go, he should get 415,522.45 Swiss francs or as nearly as can be brought about. That such a solution, if practicable, is just, and adherence to the "breach date" in such a case unjust in the circumstances of today, adds greatly to the strength of the argument for revising the rule or, putting it more technically, it adds strength to the case for awarding delivery in specie rather than giving damages. . . .

[His Lordship then examined the line of cases disallowing judgments in foreign currency.]

This brings me to the declaration made by this House in 1966. Under it, the House affirmed its power to depart from a previous decision when it appears right to do so, recognising that too rigid adherence to precedent might lead to injustice in a particular case and unduly restrict the proper development of the law. My Lords, on the assumption that to depart from the *Havana Railways* case would not involve undue practical difficulties, that a new and more satisfactory rule is capable of being stated, I am of opinion that the present case falls within the terms of the declaration. To change the rule would, for the reasons already explained, avoid injustice in the present case. To change it would enable the law to keep in step with commercial needs and with the majority of other countries facing similar problems. The latter proposition is well vouched by Dr. F. A. Mann's work, *The Legal Aspect of Money*, 3rd ed. (1971), Chapter X.

I return then to the two preconditions.

1. Can a better rule be stated? I would make it clear that, for myself, I would confine my approval at the present time of a change in the breach-date rule to claims such as those with which we are here concerned, i.e., to foreign money obligations, sc. obligations of a money character to pay foreign currency arising under a contract whose proper law is that of a foreign country and where the money of account and payment is that of that country, or possibly of some other country but not of the United Kingdom.

I do not think that we are called upon, or would be entitled in this case, to review the whole field of the law regarding foreign currency obligations: that is not the method by which changes in the law by judicial decision are made. In my opinion it should be open for future discussion whether the rule applying to money obligations, which can be a simple rule, should apply as regards claims for damages for breach of contract or for tort. It is only because it has been thought that the same rule need apply to all these situations that we have been forced into straitjacket solutions based on concepts, or on forms of action ("archaic legalistic nonsense" in the words of Lawton L.J. in *Schorsch Meier* [1975] Q.B. 416, 430). But the principles on which damages are awarded for tort or breach of contract are both very intricate and not the same in each case, involve questions of remoteness (cf. the speech of Lord Parmoor in *S.S. Celia (Owners)* v. *S.S. Volturno (Owners)* (*The Volturno*) [1921] 2 A.C. 544) and have no direct relevance to claims for specific things, in which I include specific foreign currency. To take one familiar point. Whereas in the case of the inevitable contract to supply a foreign cow, the intending purchaser has to be treated as going into the market to buy one as at the date of breach, this doctrine cannot be applied to a foreign money obligation, for the intending creditor has nothing to buy his own currency with—except his own currency. I therefore see no need to overrule or criticise or endorse such cases as *The Volturno* [1921] 2 A.C. 544 or *Di Ferdinando* v. *Simon, Smits & Co. Ltd.* [1920] 3 K.B. 409. I would only say, in agreement with Scrutton L.J. (*The Baarn* [1933] P. 251, 266), that the former case leaves a number of difficulties unsolved and that the mere fact that as a general rule in English law damages for tort or for breach of contract are assessed as at the date of the breach need not preclude, in particular cases, the conversion into sterling of an element in the damages, which arises and is expressed in foreign currency, as at some later date. It is for the courts, or for arbitrators, to work out a solution in each case best adapted to giving the injured plaintiff that amount in damages which will most fairly compensate him for the wrong which he has suffered. As examples in which acceptance of this principle might have led to a juster result I may refer to *The Teh Hu* [1970] P. 106 and *Nederlandsch-Amerikaansche Stoomvaart Maatschappij N.V.* v. *Royal Mail Lines Ltd.* [1958] 1 Lloyd's Rep. 412, and as an example where it did so to *In re Dawson, decd.* [1966] 2 N.S.W.R. 211.

As regards foreign money obligations (defined above), it is first necessary to establish the form of the claim to be made. In my opinion acceptance of the argument already made requires that the claim must be specifically for the foreign currency—as in this case for a sum stated in Swiss francs. To this may be added the alternative "or the sterling equivalent at the date of . . ." (see below). As regards the conversion date to be inserted in the claim or in the judgment of the court, the choice, as pointed out in the *Havana Railways* case [1961] A.C. 1007, is between (i) the date of action brought, (ii) the date of judgment, (iii) the date of payment. Each has its advantages, and it is to be noticed that the Court of Appeal in *Schorsch Meier* and in the present case chose the date of payment meaning, as I understand it, the date when the court authorises enforcement of the judgment in terms of sterling. The date of payment is taken in the convention annexed to the Carriage of Goods by Road Act 1965 (article 27 (2)). This date gets nearest to securing to the creditor exactly what he bargained for. The date of action brought, though favoured by Lord Reid and Lord Radcliffe in the *Havana Railways* case, seems to me to place the creditor too severely at the mercy of the debtor's obstructive defences (cf. this case) or the law's delay. It may have been based on an understanding of the judgment of Holmes J. in the *Deutsche Bank* case (272 U.S. 517) now seen to be probably mistaken (see Mann, *The Legal Aspect of Money*, 3rd ed. (1971), p. 355 and cases cited). The date of judgment is shown to be a workable date in practice by its inclusion in the Carriage by Air Act 1961 which gave effect to the Hague Convention of 1965 varying, on this very point, the Warsaw Convention of 1929, but, in some cases, particularly where there is an appeal, may again impose on the creditor a considerable currency risk. So I would favour the payment date, in the sense I have mentioned. In the case of a company in liquidation, the corresponding date for conversion would be the date when the creditor's claim in terms of sterling is admitted by the liquidator. In the case of arbitration, there may be a minor discrepancy, if the practice which is apparently adopted (see the *Jugoslavenska* case [1974] Q.B. 292, 305) remains as it is, but I can see no reason why, if desired, that practice should not be adjusted so as to enable conversion to be made as at the date when leave to enforce in sterling is given.

2. A rule in the form suggested above would not, in my opinion, give rise to any serious procedural difficulty. Suggestions were made at the Bar that as regards such matters as set off, counterclaim, payment into court, it would be difficult or impossible to apply. I would say as to these matters that I see no reason why this should be so: it would be inappropriate to discuss them here in detail and unnecessary since the Court of Appeal has assessed the procedural implications and has not been impressed with any difficulty. I have no doubt that practitioners,

with the assistance of the Supreme Court, can work out suitable solutions —not overlooking the provisions of the Exchange Control Act 1947. I would only add that while the rule I have suggested would fit perfectly well into such a situation as existed in *Société des Hôtels Le Touquet Paris-Plage* v. *Cummings* [1922] 1 K.B. 451 it would not be reconcilable with the later case of *Madeleine Vionnet et Cie.* v. *Wills* [1940] 1 K.B. 72. I do not think that case can any longer be followed.

My Lords, in conclusion I would say that, difficult at this whole matter undoubtedly is, if once a clear conclusion is reached as to what the law ought now to be, declaration of it by this House is appropriate. The law on this topic is judge-made: it has been built up over the years from case to case. It is entirely within this House's duty, in the course of administering justice, to give the law a new direction in a particular case where, on principle and in reason, it appears right to do so. I cannot accept the suggestion that because a rule is long established only legislation can change it—that may be so when the rule is so deeply entrenched that it has infected the whole legal system, or the choice of a new rule involves more far-reaching research than courts can carry out. A recent example of the House changing a very old established rule is *West Midland Baptist (Trust) Association (Inc.)* v. *Birmingham Corporation* [1970] A.C. 874. Lord Reid thought that it was proper to re-examine a judge-made rule of law based on an assumption of fact (as to the stability of money) when the rule was formulated but which was no longer true and which in many cases caused serious injustice. So in that case the House selected a new date and did not think it necessary or right to wait for legislation and I would not think it necessary or right here. Indeed, from some experience in the matter, I am led to doubt whether legislative reform, at least prompt and comprehensive reform, in this field of foreign currency obligation, is practicable. Questions as to the recovery of debts or of damages depend so much upon individual mixtures of facts and merits as to make them more suitable for progressive solutions in the courts. I think that we have an opportunity to reach such a solution here. I would accordingly depart from the *Havana Railways* case and dismiss this appeal.

LORD SIMON OF GLAISDALE (dissenting): My Lords, ". . . if there is one thing clear in our law, it is that the claim must be made in sterling and the judgment given in sterling," said Lord Denning in *In re United Railways of Havana and Regla Warehouses* [1961] A.C. 1007, 1068-69. This was apparently still the law when *Jugoslavenska Oceanska Plovidba* v. *Castle Investment Co. Inc.* [1974] Q.B. 292 was decided on July 6, 1973 (see especially Lord Denning M.R. at p. 299D-F). But by the time the judgments in *Schorsch Meier G.m.b.H.* v. *Hennin* [1975] Q.B. 416 came to be delivered by the Court of Appeal some 17 months later the things that had been clearest in our law were no longer apparent: in fact the rules of law had been clearly reversed; and it was held that a claim could be made in our courts in a foreign currency and judgment could be given in that currency by an English court. Of course, the fact that a rule of law is clear and of long standing and has been reiterated by a long series of great lawyers does not preclude its abrogation when it is found to work injustice or no longer to accord with changed social or economic conditions or with changed ideologies or sensibilities or with newly dominant theories. But it has been generally accepted that a revolutionary change in the law prompted by such factors is within the proper and exclusive province of Parliament advised by the executive (and often, appropriately, by a Royal Commission or a departmental or interdepartmental committee); because Parliament, so advised, is in general the constitutional organ best fitted to weigh such factors. It is true that since 1966 your Lordships have power to depart from a previous decision of your Lordships' House; although, in view of the limited resources available to decision-making by a court of law, it is a power which your Lordships have exercised with due restraint. But the statement of Lord Gardiner L.C. of July 26, 1966 [*Practice Statement (Judicial Precedent)* [1966] 1 W.L.R. 395], expressly asserted that it was "not intended to affect the operation of the rule of precedent elsewhere than" in your Lordships' House; and it is clear law that the Court of Appeal is bound by a decision of your Lordships' House and (at least on its civil side) by a previous decision of the Court of Appeal itself. . . . Any change in this respect would require legislation. . . .

Notwithstanding the great authority and the high lineage of the *Havana* case, notwithstanding all its juridical adhesions, notwithstanding my lack of confidence that I am capable of weighing the full potentialities of the situation and the full repercussions of the decision, I might be tempted to join in overruling *Havana* if I were convinced that that would on balance conduce to justice. I do not think that the *Havana* rules do justice in the present case—it was envisaged that they (like all others put forward) might not in every case. But take the following example.

John Mitchell is a newly and greatly enriched dividend-stripper and property speculator in England. He conceives that a notable art collection would be a desirable adjunct and mark of his new position in society. His art agent learns that Count Commenus has the finest collection in Central Europe, accumulated by his enlightened family over the centuries; and that the estates of the count are so heavily encumbered that he is reluctantly faced with the necessity of selling his family collection. The deal is clinched. John Mitchell agrees to buy the collection for 10 million Ruritanian talers. The taler is gold-backed, and the sum is equivalent to £1 million. The collection is duly shipped to England, but the purchaser fails to pay on the due date. It is not his fault. War has broken out, and strict exchange control has been imposed. Towards the end of the war a revolution takes place in Ruritania. Count Commenus is glad to escape with his bare life, and arrives penniless in this country. In the meantime, the Ruritanian taler, no longer gold-backed, has become worth only the accumulating paper it is printed on. Count Commenus remembers his debt from Mr. Mitchell and that his magnificent collection is now the principal ornament of the Mitchell mansions. He claims £1 million. Mr. Mitchell tenders him a lorry filled with 10 million worthless Ruritanian talers. Is it justice that Mr. Mitchell should succeed, the proud possessor of a valuable collection acquired for nothing, and that the count should starve? . . .

Afterword. There are three more general questions which are raised by this important appeal.

(1) Overruling *Havana* [1961] A.C. 1007 involves that the law must be deemed always to have been as my noble and learned friends now

declare it. This may affect the vires of some Rules of Court; but beyond this there has been, so far as I can see, no consideration of what consequences the retrospective alteration of the law (for, let us face it, that is the reality) may have. I would be more ready to go along with my noble and learned friends if the decision had prospective effect only. One of the several reasons why radical law reform is in general more appropriately carried out by Parliament is that a statute can (and usually does) operate prospectively. I venture once again to plead that consideration should be given to the various forms of prospective overruling such as obtain in some other common law systems.

(2) The type of law reform by the judiciary which is here exemplified, and which has been exemplified in some other recent cases, is a very considerable social responsibility. Of course, no worthwhile judge is afraid of responsibility. But I presume to suggest that consideration should be given to the desirability of the Lords of Appeal sitting in banc in such circumstances—at least where the overruling of a *recent* decision of your Lordships' House is in question.

(3) The main ground of my dissent from the opinions of my noble and learned friends is that this type of issue is unsuitable for law reform by the judiciary. It is the sort of case where, in my view, a wide range of advice, official especially but also commercial, is required. The training and experience of a judge is unsuitable for this type of decision-making unaided; his circumspection is too narrow; his very qualities of keen perception of his immediate problem tend to militate against sound judgment of the wider and more general issues involved. But if courts are to undertake legislative responsibilities, something might be done to equip them better for the type of decision-making which is involved. Official advice and a balanced executive view might be made available by a law officer or his counsel acting as amicus curiae. I venture to suggest consideration of some such machinery.

NOTE. It appears that in Canada, legal judgments must be given in Canadian currency, by s.11 of the Currency, Mint and Exchange Fund Act (see *Baumgartner* v. *Carsley Silk Co. Ltd.,* (1971) 23 D.L.R. (3d) 225); however, the choice must still be made between date of breach and date of judgment. The Ontario High Court held in *Quartier* v. *Farah* (1921) 64 D.L.R. 37 (where the domestic currency had appreciated) that the applicable exchange rate for the foreign currency was the rate prevailing at the date of judgment.

8. RESTITUTION

Instead of claiming to be put into the position he would have been in had the contract been performed, the injured party may claim, instead, to be put into the position he was in before the contract was made. That is, he may seek restitution of the benefits conferred on the other party. A disappointed buyer, for example, might wish to recover back his price from the defaulting seller. It is clear that if such a claim is to succeed, the buyer must be ready to return the goods, if he has received them, to the seller. This restoration of benefits by the injured party is known as restitutio in integrum.

ERLANGER v. *THE NEW SOMBRERO PHOSPHATE COMPANY.* 1878. 3 App. Cas. 1218. Baron Erlanger, a Paris banker, headed a syndicate (or partnership) that on August 30, 1871, acquired for £55,000 a lease of an island in the West Indies believed to contain valuable phosphate mines. He proceeded to organize a corporation with directors of his own choosing and the corporation bought the mines for £110,000 on September 20, 1871. At the first ordinary general meeting of the Company on February 2, 1872, a shareholder queried the sale, which the first directors had already confirmed, but no action was taken. At the first annual general meeting on June 19, 1872, a committee was appointed to investigate rumours about the sale. The committee reported on August 29, and on December 24 the Company filed suit against Erlanger and others asking to have the contract set aside, the £110,000 repaid to the Company, the Company to deliver up the island and to account for profits (if any) made by working it. It was so ordered. Most of the judgments are taken up with the question of the duty of promoters in equity to make full disclosure, and with the question of the separate identities of the promoters, the Company, and its handful of shareholders on September 20, 1871, and on June 19, 1872. On the question of restitution, LORD BLACKBURN said: "It is, I think, clear on principles of general justice, that as a condition to a rescission there must be a *restitutio in integrum*. The parties must be put *in statu quo*. . . . It is a doctrine which has often been acted upon both at law and in equity. But there is a considerable difference in the mode in which it is applied in Courts of Law and Equity, owing, as I think, to the difference of the machinery which the Courts have at command. I speak of these Courts as they were at the time when this suit commenced, without inquiring whether the Judicature Acts make any, or if any, what difference.

"It would be obviously unjust that a person who has been in possession of property under the contract which he seeks to repudiate should be allowed to throw that back on the other party's hands without accounting for any benefit he may have derived from the use of the property, or if the property, though not destroyed, has been in the interval deteriorated, without making compensation for that deterioration. But as a Court of Law has no machinery at its command for taking an account of such matters, the defrauded party, if he sought his remedy at law, must in such cases keep the property and sue in an action for deceit, in which the jury, if properly directed, can do complete justice by giving as damages a full indemnity for all that the party has lost. . . .

"But a Court of Equity could not give damages, and, unless it can rescind the contract, can give no relief. And, on the other hand, it can take accounts of profits, and make allowance for deterioration. And I think the practice has always been for a Court of Equity to give this relief whenever, by the exercise of its powers, it can do what is practically just, though it cannot restore the parties precisely to the state they were in before the contract. And a Court of Equity requires that those who come to it to ask its active interposition to give them relief, should use due diligence, after there has been such notice or knowledge as to make it inequitable to lie by. And any change which occurs in the position of the parties or the state of the property after such notice or knowledge should tell much more against the party *in morâ*, than a similar change before he was *in morâ* should do."

DEGLMAN v. GUARANTY TRUST CO. AND CONSTANTINEAU
Ontario. Supreme Court of Canada. [1954] 3 D.L.R. 785

RAND J.: In this appeal the narrow question is raised as to the nature of part performance which will enable the Court to order specific performance of a contract relating to lands unenforceable at law by reason of s. 4 of the *Statute of Frauds*, R.S.O. 1950, c. 371. The respondent Constantineau claims the benefit of such a contract and the appellant represents the next-of-kin other than the respondent of the deceased, Laura Brunet, who resist it.

The respondent was the nephew of the deceased. Both lived in Ottawa. When he was about 20 years of age, and while attending a technical school, for 6 months of the school year 1934-35 he lived with his aunt at No. 550 Besserer St. Both that and the house on the adjoining lot, No. 548, were owned by the aunt and it was during this time that she is claimed to have agreed that if the nephew would be good to her and do such services for her as she might from time to time request during her lifetime she would make adequate provision for him in her will, and in particular that she would leave to him the premises at No. 548. While staying with her the nephew did the chores around both houses which, except for an apartment used by his aunt, were occupied by tenants. When the term ended he returned to the home of his mother on another street. In the autumn of that year he worked on the national highway in the northern part of Ontario. In the spring of 1936 he took a job on a railway at a point outside of Ottawa and at the end of that year, returning to Ottawa, he obtained a position with the city police force. In 1941 he married. At no time did he live at the house No. 548 or, apart from the 6 months, at the house No. 550.

The performance consisted of taking his aunt about in her own or his automobile on trips to Montreal and elsewhere, and on pleasure drives, of doing odd jobs about the two houses, and of various accommodations such as errands and minor services for her personal needs. . . .

[RAND J. considered the argument of part performance, which he rejected, reversing the courts below, and holding the contract unenforceable under the *Statute of Frauds* and continued:]

There remains the question of recovery for the services rendered on the basis of a *quantum meruit*. On the findings of both Courts below the services were not given gratuitously but on the footing of a contractual relation: they were to be paid for. The statute in such a case does not touch the principle of restitution against what would otherwise be an unjust enrichment of the defendant at the expense of the plaintiff. This is exemplified in the simple case of part or full payment in money as the price under an oral contract; it would be inequitable to allow the promisor to keep both the land and the money and the other party to the bargain is entitled to recover what he has paid. Similarly is it in the case of services given.

This matter is elaborated exhaustively in the Restatement of the Law of Contract issued by the American Law Institute and Professor Williston's monumental work on Contracts, 1936, vol. 2, s. 536 deals with the same topic. On the principles there laid down the respondent is entitled to recover for his services and outlays what the deceased would have had to pay for them on a purely business basis to any other person in the position of the respondent. The evidence covers generally and perhaps in the only way possible the particulars, but enough is shown to enable the Court to make a fair determination of the amount called for; and since it would be to the benefit of the other beneficiaries to bring an end to this litigation, I think we should not hesitate to do that by fixing the amount to be allowed. This I place at the sum of $3,000.

The appeal will therefore be allowed and the judgment modified by de-

claring the respondent entitled to recover against the respondent administrator the sum of $3,000; all costs will be paid out of the estate, those of
the administrator as between solicitor and client.

CARTWRIGHT J.: . . . I agree with the conclusion of my brother Rand that
the respondent is entitled to recover the value of these services from the
respondent administrator. This right appears to me to be based, not on the
contract, but on an obligation imposed by law.

In *Fibrosa Spolka Akcyjna* v. *Fairbairn Lawson Combe Barbour Ltd.*,
[1943] A.C. 32 at p. 61, Lord Wright said: "It is clear that any civilized
system of law is bound to provide remedies for cases of what has been
called unjust enrichment or unjust benefit, that is to prevent a man from
retaining the money of or some benefit derived from another which it is
against conscience that he should keep. Such remedies in English law are
generically different from remedies in contract or in tort, and are now recognized to fall within a third category of the common law which has been
called quasi-contract or restitution."

And at p. 62: "Lord Mansfield does not say that the law implies a
promise. The law implies a debt or obligation which is a different thing.
In fact, he denies that there is a contract; the obligation is as efficacious
as if it were upon a contract. The obligation is a creation of the law, just
as much as an obligation in tort. The obligation belongs to a third class,
distinct from either contract or tort, though it resembles contract rather
than tort."

Lord Wright's judgment appears to me to be in agreement with the view
stated in Williston on Contracts referred to by my brother Rand. . . .

In the case at bar all the acts for which the respondent asks to be paid
under his alternative claim were clearly done in performance of the existing
but unenforceable contract with the deceased that she would devise 548
Besserer St. to him, and to infer from them a fresh contract to pay the
value of the services in money would be . . . to draw an inference contrary
to the fact.

In my opinion when the *Statute of Frauds* was pleaded the express contract was thereby rendered unenforceable, but the deceased having received
the benefits of the full performance of the contract by the respondent, the
law imposed upon her, and so on her estate, the obligation to pay the
fair value of the services rendered to her.

If this is, as I think, the right view of the nature of the obligation upon
which the respondent's claim rests it follows that the *Limitations Act* can
have no application. . . . In my opinion the obligation which the law imposes upon the respondent administrator did not arise until the deceased
died intestate. It may well be that throughout her life it was her intention
to make a will in fulfilment of the existing although unenforceable contract
and until her death the respondent had no reason to doubt that she would
do so. The statutory period of limitation does not commence to run until
the plaintiff's cause of action has accrued; and on the facts of the case at
bar the cause of action upon which the respondent is entitled to succeed
did not accrue until the death of the deceased intestate.

For the above reasons I would dispose of the appeal as proposed by my
brother Rand.

[Rinfret C.J.C. and Taschereau J. concurred with Rand J. and Estey,
Locke and Fauteux JJ. concurred with Cartwright J.]

QUESTION. What would have been the result if the value of the nephew's services had exceeded the value of the house?

See *Boomer* v. *Muir* (1933) 24 P. 2d. 570 (District Court of Appeal, California).

BOONE v. *COE.* 1913. 154 S.W. 900 (Kentucky Court of Appeals). The plaintiffs Boone and J. T. Coe were farmers in Kentucky. The defendant J. F. Coe, a farmer in Texas, orally promised them a lease of his farm for a year, to commence on their arrival at the farm in Texas. He also promised to build them a dwelling ready for occupancy on their arrival, to provide materials for a stock and grain barn, and to share with them a portion of the crop which the plaintiffs were to sow and cultivate. The plaintiffs did move to Texas, with their families, wagons, horses, and camping outfit, taking about fifty-five days, at an expense of $1,387.80 including $8 a day for the fifty-five days, and twenty-two days while they remained in Texas, cash outlay en route $361.80, $100 for loss of time on the return trip, which took four days and $150 for losses suffered in abandoning their homes and businesses in Kentucky. They returned because the defendant J. F. Coe failed to carry out any of his promises. In an action for damages the court held the contract was unenforceable under the *Statute of Frauds*, which required a promise for a lease for more than a year to be in writing and refused relief. CLAY C. said: ". . . In the case under consideration the plaintiffs merely sustained a loss. Defendant received no benefit. Had he received a benefit, the law would imply an obligation to pay therefore. Having received no benefit, no obligation to pay is implied. The statute says that the contract of defendant made with plaintiffs is unenforceable. Defendant therefore had the legal right to decline to carry it out. To require him to pay plaintiffs for losses and expenses incurred on the faith of the contract, without any benefit accruing to him, would, in effect, uphold a contract upon which the statute expressly declares no action shall be brought. The statute was enacted for the purpose of preventing frauds and perjuries. That it is a valuable statute is shown by the fact that similar statutes are in force in practically all, if not all, of the states of the Union. Being a valuable statute, the purpose of the lawmakers in its enactment should not be defeated by permitting recoveries in cases to which its provisions were intended to apply. . . . ."

[Why is the Statute of Frauds not intended to apply when the plaintiff confers a benefit, but is intended to apply when the plaintiff confers no benefit? The history, interpretation, and effect of the Statute of Frauds are set out briefly in Chapter 12.]

MOSES v. *MACFERLAN.* 1760. 2 Burr. 1005; 97 E.R. 676. Lord Mansfield said: "If the defendant be under an obligation, from the ties of natural justice, to refund; the law implies a debt, and gives this action, founded in the equity of the plaintiff's case, as it were upon a contract (*quasi ex contractu*, as the Roman law expresses it). . . . This kind of equitable action, to recover back money, which ought not in justice to be kept, is very beneficial, and therefore much encouraged. It lies only for money which, *ex aequo et bono*, the defendant ought to refund . . . it lies for money paid by mistake; or upon a consideration which happens to fail; or for money got through imposition, (express or implied); or extortion; or oppression; or an undue advantage taken of the plaintiff's situation, contrary to laws made for the protection of persons under those circumstances.

"In one word, the gist of this kind of action is that the defendant, upon the circumstances of the case, is obliged by the ties of natural justice and equity to refund the money."

NOTE. The category of cases in which the "ties of natural justice and equity" call forth the remedy of restitution is not limited to those involving breach of contract, or repayment of money, but extends to cover other situations as well.

J. D. McCAMUS, "RESTITUTIONARY REMEDIES" LAW SOCIETY OF UPPER CANADA, SPECIAL LECTURE SERIES, 1975

A second misconception more directly traceable to *Deglman* is the view, occasionally evidenced in the reported cases, that restitution and the unjust enrichment principle relate only to situations like that arising in *Deglman* where there is a contract between the parties which, for some reason, cannot be enforced. This is simply not so. From the point of view of authority, a number of cases may be cited to illustrate judicial reliance on the unjust enrichment principle in claims in which there is not an unenforceable contract in the background. To obtain a more complete picture of the breadth of the subject one might turn to the table of contents of the American Law Institute's *Restatement of Restitution* or the more recent English text, Goff and Jones, *The Law of Restitution.* At the risk of over-simplification, the substantive grounds for restitutionary relief might be summarized as follows: the recovery of benefits conferred by the plaintiff, (a) by mistake, (b) under ineffective transactions, (c) to preserve the life, health or property of another or (d) to discharge a duty owed by another, and, additionally, the broad range of rules which have as their object the recovery of benefits obtained by the defendant as a result of some form of wrongdoing.

CHAPTER 2

THE KINDS OF PROMISES LEGALLY ENFORCED

COHEN, "THE BASIS OF CONTRACT"
(1932) 56 Harvard L. R. 553, 571-75

THE JUSTIFICATION OF CONTRACT LAW: The Sanctity of Promises. Contract law is commonly supposed to enforce promises. Why should promises be enforced?

The simplest answer is that of the intuitionists, namely, that promises are sacred *per se*, that there is something inherently despicable about not keeping a promise, and that a properly organized society should not tolerate this. This may also be said to be the common man's theory. Learned writers ignore this because of their interest in showing the evil consequences of allowing promises to be broken. But the intuitionists can well object that to judge the goodness of an act by its consequences is an obvious evasion by postponing the issue. For when we inquire which consequences are good and which are bad, we face the same question over again. If the terms "good" and "bad" have any meaning, there must be some ultimate character of action that makes them so, just as there is some ultimate character or nature of objects that makes them blue or beautiful. To say that the blueness or beauty of an object depends upon "the observer" only means that a complete answer involves an additional factor that "the observer" brings into the case. There can be no sense at all in speaking of the quality of an object that the observer beholds if there is no object or there are no qualities to behold.

Now there can be no doubt that common sense does generally find something revolting about the breaking of a promise, and this, if a fact, must be taken into account by the law though it may be balanced by other factors or considerations. In any case, let us not ignore the fact that judges and jurists, like other mortals, do frequently express this in the feeling that it would be an outrage to let one who has broken his promise escape completely.

It is not a sufficient answer to the foregoing position to show that common sense is not consistent, that in many cases we approve the breaking of promises, that the promises which we think ought not to be broken depend on the relation in which people stand to us, and that all these factors vary from time to time. I do not always have the same appetite or aversion for the same food, but when I do like or dislike a given dish, that is a fact which is not to be read out of existence because something else was true on another occasion. If, then, we find ourselves in a state of society in which men are, as a matter of fact, repelled by the breaking of promises and feel that such practice should be discouraged or minimized, that is a primary fact which the law must not ignore.

While the intuitionist theory contains an element of truth, it is clearly inadequate. No legal system does or can attempt to enforce all promises. Not even the canon law held all promises to be sacred. And when we come to distinguish between promises which should be and those which should not be enforced, this theory gives us no light or guiding principle.

Similar to the intuitionist theory is the view of Kantians like Reinach that the duty to keep one's promise is one without which rational society would be impossible. There can be no doubt that from an empirical or historical point of view, the ability to rely on the promises of others adds to the confidence necessary for social intercourse and enterprise. But as an absolute proposition this is untenable. The actual world, which assuredly is among the possible ones, is not one in which all promises are kept, and there are many people—not necessarily diplomats—who prefer a world in which they and others occasionally depart from the truth and go back on some promise. It is indeed very doubtful whether there are many who would prefer to live in an entirely rigid world in which one would be obliged to keep *all* one's promises instead of the present more viable system in which a vaguely fair proportion is sufficient. Many of us indeed would shudder at the idea of being bound by every promise, no matter how foolish, without any chance of letting increased wisdom undo past foolishness. Certainly, some freedom to change one's mind is necessary for free intercourse between those who lack omniscience.

For this reason we cannot accept Dean Pound's theory that all promises in the course of business should be enforced. He seems to me undoubtedly right in his insistence that promises constitute modern wealth and that their enforcement is thus a necessity of maintaining wealth as a basis of civilization. My bank's promise to pay the checks drawn to my account not only constitutes my wealth but puts it into a more manageable form than that of my personal possession of certain goods or even gold. Still, business men as a whole do not wish the law to enforce every promise. Many business transactions, such as those on a stock or produce exchange, could not be carried on unless we could rely on a mere verbal agreement or hasty memorandum. But other transactions, like those of real estate, are more complicated and would become too risky if we were bound by every chance promise that escapes us. Negotiations would be checked by such fear. In such cases men do not want to be bound until the final stage, when some formality like the signing of papers gives one the feeling of security, of having taken proper precautions. The issue obviously depends upon such factors as the relative simplicity of a given transaction, the speed with which it must be concluded, and the availability of necessary information.

At various times it has been claimed that mere promises as such received legal force in Hebrew, Greek, early German, and canon law. None of these claims can be justified.

All biblical references to binding promises are either to those involving an oath or promise to God or else they assume, as a matter of course, some formality such as striking of hands and pledge or security. Greek covenants, or agreements, had to be in writing or to be recorded and were not free from other formalities. The binding character of promises could not have been absolute to a people to whom Odysseus was a hero.

Though the great authority of Gierke, following Tacitus and Grotius, can be cited for the view that the early Germans attached great importance to keeping one's word, the evidence collected by such men as Brunner, Von Amira, Heusler, and Brissaud shows that the Germans, like other peoples, held promises binding only if some real object passed hands or some formal ceremony took place. Otherwise, pledge or security was required.

More substantial is the case for the canon law, which undoubtedly went further than any other system to enforce bare promises. The Council of Carthage in 348 B.C. made all written agreements binding and this later led to the action *ex nudo pacto* before the courts of the Church. But the use of the oath was a distinctive ceremony and as it was binding in conscience, that is, in one's relation to God, it did not always afford relief to the promisee. The latter was at times even compelled by the ecclesiastical judge to release the promisor. And through the extension of the power of temporal rulers, as well as of bishops, to pass on the validity of the promise under oath, the legal effectiveness of the latter was whittled away.

NOTE. The materials in this chapter are divided into bargains and non-bargain promises. A bargain is an agreed exchange, and the existence of a bargain is the chief criterion of enforceability of promises. The constituent parts of a bargain are mutual assent (commonly called offer and acceptance) and an exchange of value (commonly called consideration). In the nineteenth century the view developed that all contracts were bargains, that is, that the existence of a bargain was the *only* reason for enforcement. This view is still held by some writers. The materials in section 3, below, however, suggest that the bargain theory is not a full account of contract law, and that there are other reasons for enforcement of promises.

The question of enforceability cannot be dissociated from the question of remedies. Without doubt, the bargain theory of contract formation tends to support the "normal" rule of contract damages, for one of the reasons for securing to the promisee the value of performance is that he has paid the agreed equivalent of it. Once it is accepted that there are other reasons, besides bargain, for enforcement, the question arises whether the measure of damages should be limited. If the reason for enforcement is the reliance of the promisee, should not reliance be also the measure of his damages?

1. BARGAINS

A. Preliminary Negotiations

DENTON v. GREAT NORTHERN RAILWAY COMPANY
England. Queen's Bench. 1856. 5 E. & B. 860; 119 E.R. 701

The plaintiff being in London in March, 1855, and having business at Peterborough on the 25th March, 1855, and at Hull on the 26th March, 1855, consulted the printed time tables issued in the usual way by the defendants for that month. In these time tables a train was advertised to leave London at 5 p.m. and reach Peterborough about 7 p.m. and thence to proceed, amongst other towns, to Hull, to arrive there about midnight. At the bottom of the time tables was the following notice:

exculpatory clause "The Companies make every exertion that the trains shall be punctual, but their arrival or departure at the times stated will not be guaranteed, nor will the companies hold themselves responsible for delay or any consequences arising therefrom."

The time tables advertising this train were, till after 26th March, exhibited by the defendants at their stations, where the plaintiff had seen them, and were printed and circulated; and on the 25th March the plaintiff had one in his possession.

The plaintiff, having made his arrangements on the faith of these time tables, went down to Peterborough by an early train of the defendants, transacted his business at Peterborough, and went to the defendants' station at Peterborough in due time to take a ticket to Hull by the evening train so advertised: but there was no such train to Hull; nor had there been one during any part of the month of March. The explanation of this was that the whole line of railway from Peterborough to Hull was not the property of the defendants, their line ending at Askerne on the route from Peterborough to Hull. They had running power over the line of the Lancashire and Yorkshire Railway Company from Askerne to Milford Junction, where the line of the North Eastern Railway Company joins that of The Lancashire and Yorkshire Railway Company. There had been, in February, an arrangement between the three companies by which passengers booked at the stations on the line of The Great Northern Railway Company were carried in the carriages of that company to Milford Junction, and thence were conveyed by The North Eastern Railway Company to Hull by a train departing a few minutes after the arrival of the train leaving Peterborough about 7 p.m. Toward the end of February, prior to the publication by the defendants of their time tables, but after they had been prepared and printed, The North Eastern Railway Company gave notice to the defendants that, after the 1st day of March, the train from Milford Junction to Hull would be discontinued. The defendants nevertheless made no alteration in their time tables, which were published and issued for March. The plaintiff consulted them and was misled as above stated. In consequence of the absence of this train the plaintiff could not get to Hull in time for an appointment which he had made for the morning of the 26th March, and sustained damage to the amount of £5 10s. It did not appear in or by the time tables whether the train from Peterborough to Hull was or was not entirely under the control of the defendants. . . .

LORD CAMPBELL C.J.: This is a case of some importance, both as regards the public and the railway companies. It seems to me that the representations made by railway companies in their time tables cannot be treated as mere waste paper; and in the present case I think the plaintiff is entitled to recover, on the ground that there was a contract with him and also on the ground that there was a false representation by the Company.

It seems to me that, if the Company promised to give tickets for a train, running at a particular hour to a particular place, to any one who would come to the station and tender the price of the ticket, it is a good contract with any one who so comes. I take it to be clear that the issuing of the time tables in this way amounts in fact to such a promise; any one who read them would so understand them. Then, is it a good contract in law? The consideration is one which is a prejudice to the person who makes his arrangements with a view to the fulfilment of the contract, and comes to the station on the faith of it. Is it not then within the principle of those cases in which it has been held that an action lies on a contract to pay a reward? There the promise is to the public at large, exactly as it is here; it is in effect the same as if made to each individual conditionally; and, on an individual fulfilling the condition, it is an absolute contract with him, and he may sue. That being so, there is, I think, a contract: and there is no excuse shown for breaking it. It is immaterial that the defendants are not owners of the line the whole way to Hull. It is admitted to have been often rightly held that, where there is a ticket taken out to go to a station, the contract binds the company issuing the ticket, though it is not specified how much of the line over which the journey is to be belongs to that company. Then reliance is placed on the class of cases which decide that an absolute contract must be fulfilled whatever happens, which, it is said, shows that there cannot be a contract here. But from the nature of the contract I think that there might be implied exceptions. A carrier by sea excepts the perils of the sea. It may be from the nature of this contract that the perils of the railroad are excepted. I see no inconvenience likely to arise from holding this a contract. It is put, as an example of inconvenience, that a shipowner who has advertised that his ship is bound for Calcutta as a general ship, and that he will take on board goods brought to her, would be liable to an action if when goods were brought on the faith of the advertisement he said he had got a better freight, and was now bound for Jamaica; but I see no reason why he should not be liable. It seems to me, therefore, that this is a contract, and that the plaintiff who has acted on it has his remedy on that ground. But on the other ground there is no doubt. The statement in the time tables was untrue, and was made so as to be what the law calls a fraudulent representation. It was not the original printing that was blameable; but, after notice that the train was withdrawn, the defendants continue, down to the 25th March, to issue these tables. Was not that a representation that there was such a train? And, as they knew it had been discontinued for some time, was it not a false representation? It is all one as if a person, duly authorized by the company, had, knowing it was not true, said to the plaintiff: "There is a train from Milford Junction to Hull at that hour." The plaintiff believes this, acts upon it, and sustains loss. It is well established law that, where a person makes an untrue statement, knowing it to be untrue, to another who is induced to act upon it, an action lies. The facts bring the present case within that rule.

WIGHTMAN J.: It seems to me that the publication of these time tables amounted to a promise to any one of the public who would come to the station and pay for a ticket, that he shall have one by the train at seven. It is said that this will make the Company liable though there be inevitable accidents. But the provision at the foot of the time tables protects the Company in cases of delay by accident, though the proviso does not apply to the present case where the train is altogether taken off.

But, whether there be a contract or not, the defendants are liable as having induced the plaintiff by a continued knowingly false representation to believe that there was a train at seven to Hull, which he, believing, acted upon to his prejudice. All the essentials for an action for a false representation are here. The representation is untrue; it is known by the persons making it to be untrue; it is calculated to induce the plaintiff to act; and he, believing it, is induced to act accordingly.

CROMPTON J.: I think also that the plaintiff is entitled to judgment.

I entirely agree in what has been said by my Lord and my brother Wightman, that an action in the nature of an action for deceit lies here. The Company make a fresh statement at every moment whilst they continue to hold out these time tables as theirs. I am besides much inclined to think that they are liable also on the ground that they have committed a breach of their duty as public carriers. A public carrier of goods must carry according to his public profession; I think, however, that there has been no decision that carriers of passengers are under the same obligation: though in *Story on Bailments*, s. 591, it is said they are. I cannot doubt that the defendants publicly professed to be carriers of passengers by this train; and therefore I am inclined to think an action would lie on that ground.

But I am not prepared to say that there is a contract. As I agree that the defendants are liable, there is no occasion to decide this; and it is true that the cases as to the recovery of rewards have an analogy to this case. But there is a difference; where a reward if offered, it is generally offered to procure a service which is entirely performed by the party claiming the reward. I never was able to see any good reason why in such cases he might not sue for work and labour done at the request of the defendant. But in the present case, or in that which might be put of a shopkeeper advertising that he had cheap goods in his shop, I doubt if the labour of coming to the station, or of crossing the threshold of the shop, really is part of the consideration at all. If it be, it is a very small one. I agree, however, that any consideration, however small, will support a promise; and perhaps the difference between me and my Lord and my brother Wightman is rather as to the fact than the law. I doubt whether the promise here in fact was in consideration of coming to the station. If it was, I see difficulty in saying that the shopkeeper does not promise to have his wares for those who will take the trouble to leave the street and come into his shop. But it is quite unnecessary for the decision of this case to come to a determination on that. I am clearly of opinion that the action lies as for a false representation. I think, though less decidedly, that it lies on the ground of their duty as public carriers of passengers to act up to their public profession. But I doubt whether they are answerable on a contract to do all that may be found in the time tables, if there be anything there beyond what would be implied as part of their duty as carriers.

[Judgment for the plaintiff.]

QUESTIONS ON LEGAL METHOD. What is the *ratio decidendi* of this case? Can there be two *rationes*?

ANDERSON v. *WISCONSIN CENTRAL RAILWAY CO.*
Minnesota. Supreme Court. 1909. 120 N.W. 39

ELLIOTT J.: The Wisconsin Central Railway Company, having acquired certain real property in the city of Duluth through condemnation proceedings, advertised that at a time and place stated the buildings thereon would be sold at public auction. Bids for a certain house had been made until the amount offered amounted to $675. Anderson then increased his bid $5, making his offer $680. The auctioneer refused to consider this bid, because, as he stated, the amount of the raise was too insignificant. After waiting for a time to give Anderson an opportunity to increase it, the auctioneer announced that the house was sold to the last previous bidder for $675. An entry of this sale was made by the auctioneer in his entry book, as required by section 2815, Rev. Laws 1905. Anderson demanded to know why the auctioneer had not accepted his bid, and on the same day he tendered the $680, and it was refused. Before this tender was made a bill of sale of the building had been executed and delivered to the party to whom the building had been knocked down. Anderson then brought this action for damages, and recovered a verdict for $1,500. The defendant appealed from an order denying its motion for judgment notwithstanding the verdict or for a new trial.

The conflicting contentions of the parties arise out of fundamentally different conceptions of the nature of an auction. The appellant contends that the advertisement of a sale at auction is a mere declaration of intention which does not bind the owner to sell, or to sell to any particular bidder, and that the contract is not made until the bid is accepted. The complaint charges the defendant with liability for damages resulting to the plaintiffs from its unlawful refusal to sell the building to them and to carry out the terms and conditions of the auction sale. It proceeds upon the theory that, notwithstanding the bid, no sale was in fact made to them, because the defendant refused to recognize their right to purchase. The claim, as stated in the brief, is that "the advertisement constitutes a complete memorandum of contract, not of sale, but to sell, to the person who shall comply with its conditions, i.e., become the highest bidder at the auction provided for in the writing. The proposal became a binding contract to sell to that person the building at his bid." While the action was thus brought for the breach of an agreement to sell to the highest bidder, the argument proceeds upon the theory that under such conditions a contract has its inception in the announcement or advertisement of the owner's intention to sell the designated property at public aution to the highest bidder; that, unless the contrary is expressly stated in the announcement, the sale is to be without reserve; that the bid of the highest bidder is the acceptance of the offer; that the fall of the hammer is an announcement by the agent of the owner that he will wait no longer for the higher bid; and that the one whose bid was highest when the hammer fell is the purchaser without reference to the action of the auctioneer in announcing that some other bidder is the purchaser. Reduced to its lowest terms, this means that' the offer to sell is made in the advertisement of intention to sell at auction, and that the contract is completed by the acceptance of that offer by the bidder. There is some ground for this theory, but the decided weight of authority sustains the view that the announcement is a mere statement of intention to hold an auction, and that no contract of any character is made until the offer to purchase is accepted by the auctioneer.

The jury, under proper instructions, found that the property was offered without express reservations as to the amount of the bids, that the bid of $5 was made in good faith, and that under the circumstances the amount was not so small as to justify the auctioneer in declining to consider it on that ground. No exceptions were taken to the instructions which submitted these questions to the jury, and on this appeal we accept the conclusions of the jury as final. The issue is also simplified by the fact that the case involves no question of puffing or by-bidding by the owner, or of fraud or misrepresentation in the announcement of the sale. For the purpose of the argument, we assume the correctness of the respondent's claim that an advertisement or announcement of an auction sale which does not state limitations and conditions is equivalent to the announcement that the sale will be without reserve. The issue of law is thus clearly defined. . . .

In view of the general prevalence of the custom of selling by auction, it is remarkable that no very early cases are found in the English reports. The parent case of *Payne* v. *Cave* (1789), 3 Term R. 148; 100 E.R. 502, was decided by Lord Kenyon C.J., sitting at Guildhall in 1788. The plaintiff offered a distilling apparatus for sale including a pewter worm, at public auction, on the usual conditions that the highest bidder should be the purchaser. There were several bidders for the worm, of whom Cave, who bid £40, was the last. The auctioneer dwelt on this bid for some time, until Cave said: "Why do you dwell? You will not get more." The auctioneer stated that he was informed that the worm weighed at least 1,300 hundred-weight, and was worth more than £40. The bidder then asked him if he would warrant it to weigh so much, and receiving an answer in the negative, he declared that he would not take. The worm was then resold on a subsequent day for £30 and an action was brought against Cave for the difference. Lord Kenyon ruled that the bidder was at liberty to withdraw his bid at any time before the hammer fell, and nonsuited the plaintiff. On motion to set aside the nonsuit, it was contended that a bidder is bound by the conditions of the sale to abide by his bid, and could not retract; that the hammer is suspended, not for the benefit of the bidder, or to give him an opportunity for repenting, but for the benefit of the seller; and that in the meantime the person who bid last is a purchaser, conditional upon no one bidding higher. But the court thought otherwise, and held that the auctioneer was the agent of the vendor, and that the assent of both parties was necessary to make the contract binding, and "That is signified on the part of the seller, by knocking down the hammer, which was not done here until the plaintiff retracted." "An auction," said the court, "is not inaptly called a *locus poenitentiae*. Every bidding is nothing more than an offer on one side, which is not binding on the other side until assented to."

The idea that an action will lie for the breach of an implied undertaking to sell to the highest bidder was advanced in *Warlow* v. *Harrison* (1859), 1 El & El. 309; 120 E.R. 925 and dicta supporting it will be found in *Harris* v. *Nickerson* (1873), L.R. 8 Q.B. 288, *Spencer* v. *Harding* (1870), L.R. 5 C.P. 563, *Re Agra & Masterman Bank* (1867), 2 Ch. App. 391, 397, and *Johnson* v. *Boyes*, [1899] 2 Ch. 73. These cases assume that an offer to sell property at auction is indistinguishable from the case of an offer to the general public, such as a reward for the return of lost property, where it is held that contract rights are created in favour of one who complies with the conditions of the offer. *Carlill* v. *Carbolic Smoke Ball Co.*, [1893] 1 Q.B. 256. Langdell seems to be the only text-writer who takes this view of what the law should be. In his *Summary of the Law of Contracts* (page 24) it is stated that the correct view is "that the seller makes the offer when the article is put up, namely, to sell it to the highest bidder, and when a bid is made there is an actual sale, subject to the condition that no one else shall bid higher.". . .

Warlow v. *Harrison*, the source of all the uncertainty, was an action against an auctioneer who had advertised that he would sell certain horses, "the property of a gentleman, without reserve," at auction. Warlow bid 60 guineas for one of the horses, whereupon the owner bid 61 guineas. Warlow refused to increase his bid, and the horse was announced as sold for 61 guineas to the owner. Warlow, claiming to be the highest goodfaith bidder, tendered the amount of his bid to the auctioneer and demanded the horse, and, on this being refused, brought an action against the auctioneer, alleging that the defendant was his agent to complete the contract, that he had refused to do so, and that he had thereby lost certain money in attending the auction and had been deprived of the benefit of his contract. The defendant pleaded (1) not guilty; (2) that the plaintiff was not the highest bidder; and (3) that the auctioneer did not become the bidder's agent to complete the sale. The plaintiff recovered a verdict, but the Common Pleas (Lord Campbell C.J., Wightman J., and Erle J.) ordered a nonsuit on the ground that the plaintiff's allegation as to the agency of the defendants and the duty of the defendant to complete the contract on behalf of the plaintiff was not sustained. It was urged in argument that an auctioneer is the agent of the bidder to receive the bid; that the bidder is a conditional purchaser; that, when the sale by the conditions is without reserve, the bidder is absolutely the purchaser, unless, there be a bona fide higher bidding; and that the auctioneer, in consideration of the bidding by which a commission will come to him, promises the highest bidder to knock down the article to him and to do all that is necessary to complete the sale. "But this reasoning," said Lord Campbell, "is wholly at variance with the case of *Payne* v. *Cave*, which has been considered good law for nearly 70 years. That case decided that a bidding at an auction, instead of being a conditional purchase, is a mere offer, that the auctioneer is the agent of the vendor, that the assent of both parties is necessary to the contract, that his assent is signified by knocking down the hammer, and that until then either party may retract. This is quite inconsistent with the notion of a conditional purchase by a bidding, and with the notion of there being any personal promise by the auctioneer to the bidder that the bidding of an intending purchaser shall absolutely be accepted by the vendor. The vendor himself and the bidder being respectively free till the hammer is knocked down, the auctioneer cannot possibly be previously bound." Holding, thus, that no action would lie against the auctioneer, the court found it unnecessary to consider whether there was any remedy against a vendor who had violated a condition that the property would be sold to the highest bona fide bidder without reserve. In the Exchequer Chamber the decision was affirmed; but, as the plaintiff might amend his declaration, the court discussed the merits of the case which might be made. Barons Martin, Byles, and Watson were of the opinion that the plaintiff was entitled to recover from the auctioneer, because the auction was announced to be "without reserve," which meant that neither the owner nor any one in his behalf should bid at the auction, and that the property would be sold to the highest bidder, whether the sum bid was equivalent to the real value or not. On the principle which creates a contract between the loser of property who offers a reward for its return and the finder, or a railway company which advertises a time-table and one who purchases a ticket, it was said that an auctioneer who put the property up for sale upon such conditions pledges himself that the sale shall be without reserve, and that the contract is made with the highest bidder, who, in case of a breach thereof, has a right of action against the auctioneer. "We think," said Baron Martin, "that the auctioneer has contracted that the sale shall be without reserve, and that the contract is broken upon a bid being made by or on behalf of the owner, whether it be during the time the property is under the hammer or it be the last bid upon which the article is knocked down. In either case the sale is not 'without reserve' and the contract of the auctioneer is broken. We entertain no doubt that the owner may, at any time before the contract is legally complete, interfere and revoke the auctioneer's authority; but he does so at his peril, and if the auctioneer has contracted any liability in consequence of his employment and the subsequent revocation or conduct of the owner he is entitled to be indemnified." Baron Bramwell and Willes J. preferred to rest the judgment upon the ground that the auctioneer had undertaken to have, and yet there was evidence that he had not, authority to sell without reserve. . . .

In *Harris* v. *Nickerson*, the nature of the advertisement was considered, and it was held that it should be construed as a mere declaration of intention, which did not amount to a contract with any one who might act upon it, or constitute a warranty that the articles advertised would be offered for sale. Certain articles were not offered, and a party who attended for the purpose of bidding brought an action to recover for his loss of time and expense. Blackburn J. said: "This is certainly a startling proposition, and would be excessively inconvenient if carried out. It amounts to saying that any one who advertises a sale by publishing an advertisement becomes responsible to every one who attends the sale for his cab hire and travelling expenses." Referring to *Warlow* v. *Harrison*, the learned judge remarked that "there the majority of the judges held that an action would lie for not knocking down the property to the highest bidder when the sale was advertised as without reserve; that in such a case there is a contract to sell to the highest bidder, and if the owner bids there is a breach of the contract." Quinn J. was also of the opinion that the particular action could not be maintained without going to the extent of saying that where an auctioneer issued an advertisement of the sale of goods, if he withdraws any part of them without notice, the persons attending may all maintain actions against him. He was of the opinion, however, that when a sale is advertised without reserve, and a lot is put up and bid for, there is a ground for saying, as was said in *Warlow* v. *Harrison*, that a contract is entered into between the auctioneer and the highest bona fide bidder. But that rule was not applicable to the case under consideration, as the property was never put up for sale, and it was to say that there was a contract with every one attending the sale. The real point in the case was brought out by Justice Archibald, who said: "This is an attempt on the part of the plaintiff to make a mere declaration of intention a binding contract. He has utterly failed to show authority or reason for the proposition. If a false and fraudulent representation had been made, it would have been quite another matter. But to say that a mere advertisement that certain articles are to be sold at auction amounts to a contract to indemnify all who attend, if the sale of any part of the articles does not take place, is a proposition without authority or ground for supporting it.". . .

In *Johnson* v. *Boyes* it appeared that Boyes had advertised the freehold of a public house for sale at auction under conditions providing that the highest bidder should be the purchaser. The plaintiff, a married woman of financial standing, sent her husband to bid for her, but did not supply him with the necessary funds. The property was knocked down to him; but the auctioneer, who knew that he was financially irresponsible, refused to accept his check for the amount of the required deposit and sold the property to another person. The husband assured the auctioneer that his wife would furnish the money to make the check good, and the court found that his statement was true. The plaintiff sued the vendors for breach of the contract that the highest bidder should be the purchaser. It was held that the bidder had not complied with the conditions of sale, which required that the deposit should be in cash. This disposed of the case; but the court stated the action could have been maintained, had the deposit been tendered in cash and the highest bidder been refused the property. "A vendor," said Cozens-Hardy J., "who offers property for sale by auction on the terms of the printed conditions can be made liable to a member of the public who accepts the offer, if those conditions be violated"—citing *Warlow* v. *Harrison*, and *Carlill* v. *Carbolic Smoke Ball Co.*

But the doctrine of *Warlow* v. *Harrison* was never generally acquiesced in, and in Lord Halsbury's *Laws of England*, vol. 1. p. 511 (n), doubt is expressed as to its correctness. In a recent English edition of *Benjamin on Sale* (1906), the learned editors say that "two points were involved in

Warlow v. *Harrison*: (1) Is an announcement that a sale will be without reserve, or will be made to the highest bidder, an offer of a contract with the highest bona fide bidder, and accepted by his bid? (2) When an auctioneer, acting for an undisclosed principal, makes such an announcement, does he thereby offer to contract personally? Although technically *Warlow* v. *Harrison* may not have been an actual decision upon these points, yet there was the strongest intimation of opinion in the affirmative on both points on the part of three judges, from which the other two did not dissent, and the case has been subsequently treated as actually deciding them. On the second point, however, of the personal liability of the auctioneer acting for an undisclosed principal, the case was doubted by Cockburn C.J. and Shee J., in *Mainprice* v. *Westley* (1865), 6 Best & S. 420; 122 E.R. 1250 because the employment of an auctioneer necessarily involves the character of agent only, and therefore, prima facie, he does not contract personally. . . . As pointed out by a learned writer (*Pollock on Contracts*, pp. 17-19, *Warlow* v. *Harrison* involves the theory that bidding at an auction advertised to be without reserve is not, as in other cases, a mere offer, but a conditional acceptance; the condition being that no higher bidder presents himself. But this theory cannot hold good under section 58(2) of the Code, as the sale is not complete until the fall of the hammer, so that, until then, neither party is bound. Yet, when once the goods are put up, there may, perhaps, be an implied contract not to withdraw them"—citing *Johnson* v. *Boyes*.

In commenting on *Warlow* v. *Harrison* Sir Frederick Pollock says that "opinions expressed by the judges, therefore, are not equivalent to the actual judgment of a court of error, and have, in fact, been regarded with some doubt in a later case, where the Court of Queen's Bench decided that, at all events, an auctioneer whose principal is disclosed by the conditions of sale does not contract personally that the sale shall be without reserve." Pollock, Contracts (Williston Ed.) p. 18, citing *Mainprice* v. *Westley*. It is now settled that the fact of disclosure or nondisclosure of the principal is immaterial. *Wolfe* v. *Thorne*, (1877), 2 Q.B.Div. 355; *Rainbow* v. *Hawkins*, [1904] 2 K.B. 322.

Sale of Goods Act, 1893 (56 & 57 Vict. c. 71) s. 58(2), provides that ". . . (2) a sale by auction is complete when the auctioneer announces its completion by the fall of the hammer or in other customary manner. Until such announcement is made, any bidder may retract his bid." It was held in the Scotch case of *Fenwick* v. *MacDonald*, [1904] 6 F. (Ct. of Sess.) 850, that, whatever may have been the law formerly, this statute entitles a bidder to withdraw his bid at any time before the fall of the hammer, and the vendor must be equally free to withdraw his offer to sell, because one party cannot be bound while the other is free. But in the recent case of *McManus* v. *Fortescue*, [1907] 2 K.B. 1, some support was again given to *Warlow* v. *Harrison*. . . .

The Canadian cases of *McAlpine* v. *Young*, 2 Ch. Chamb. Rep. (Ont.) 85, and *O'Connor* v. *Woodward*, 6 Ont. Rep. [P.R.?] 223, seems to approve the doctrine of *Warlow* v. *Harrison*; but *Hilder* v. *Jackson*, 11 U. C.C.P. 543, is to the contrary. The plaintiff there rested his claim on the theory that an auctioneer at a public auction must receive the bid of any person and does a wrong to any person whose bid he refuses to receive. After conceding, on the authority of *Warlow* v. *Harrison*, that, when the sale is advertised to be without reserve, the auctioneer cannot receive a higher bid on the behalf of the owner to the prejudice of the preceding bidder, the court said; "But in such a sale as is stated in this count I do not understand on what ground any person can claim as a right to be allowed to bid—to offer to become the purchaser. It will be going beyond any authority I have seen to hold that by holding an auction under such circumstances there is an implied duty or contract to deal with any person who presents himself, and that the auctioneer, with due regard to his responsibilities to his principal, has not a right to refuse to deal with any particular person. The principal might refuse from mere caprice to sell to A, B, or C, and might direct the auctioneer to refuse to sell to certain parties; and I can see no reason why the auctioneer (his agent) is bound by law to accept offers or bids, any more than his principal would be." See *Cull* v. *Wakefield*, 6 U.C.Q.B. (O.S.) 178. . . .

On principle and authority the correct rule is that an announcement that a person will sell his property at public auction to the highest bidder is a mere declaration of intention to hold an auction at which bids will be received: that a bid is an offer which is accepted when the hammer falls, and until the acceptance of the bid is signified in some manner neither party assumes any legal obligation to the other. At any time before the highest bid is accepted, the bidder may withdraw his offer to purchase, or the auctioneer his offer to sell. The owner's offer to sell is made at the time through the auctioneer, and not when he advertises the auction sale. A merchant advertises that on a certain day he will sell his goods at bargain prices; but no one imagines that the prospective purchaser, who visits the store and is denied the right to purchase, has an action for damages against the merchant. He merely offers to purchase, and if his offer is refused, he has no remedy, although he may have lost a bargain, and have incurred expense and lost time in visiting the store. The analogy between such a transaction and an auction is at least close. As the advertisement in this case was a mere statement of intention to offer the property for sale at public auction to the highest bidder, the respondent's bid did not complete either a contract of sale or a contract to make a sale. . . .

The order is therefore reversed, with directions to enter judgment for the defendant.

[Section 58(2) of the English Sale of Goods Act is reproduced as s. 56, R.S.O. 1970, c. 421.]

PROBLEM. A advertises the sale by auction of a clock and a piano "without reserve." B is the highest bidder for the clock, but A withdraws it from the sale when no higher bid is forthcoming. The piano is withdrawn before bidding for it starts. Advise B, and C who has travelled 100 miles especially to bid for the piano.

SPENCER and ANOTHER v. HARDING and OTHERS
England. Common Pleas. 1870. L.R. 5 C.P. 561

The second count of the declaration stated that the defendants by their agents issued to the plaintiffs and other persons engaged in the wholesale trade a circular in the words and figures following, that is to say:

"28 King Street, Cheapside, May 17th 1869.
We are instructed to offer to the wholesale trade for sale by tender the stock in trade of Messrs. G. Eilbeck & Co. of No. 1 Milk Street, amounting as per stock-book to £2,503 13s. 1d., and which will be sold at a discount in one lot. Payments to be made in cash. The stock may be viewed

on the premises. No. 1 Milk Street, up to Thursday, the 20th instant, on which day, at 12 o'clock at noon precisely, the tenders will be received and opened at our offices. Should you tender and not attend the sale, please address to us, sealed and enclosed, 'Tender for Eilbeck's stock.' Stockbooks may be had at our office on Tuesday morning.

Honey, Humphreys & Co."

And the defendants offered and undertook to sell the said stock to the highest bidder for cash, and to receive and open the tenders delivered to them or their agents in that behalf, according to the true intent and meaning of the said circular. And the plaintiffs thereupon sent to the said agents of the defendants a tender for the said goods, in accordance with the said circular, and also attended the said sale at the time and place named in the said circular. And the said tender of the plaintiffs was the highest tender received by the defendants or their agents in that behalf. And the plaintiffs were ready and willing to pay for the said goods according to the true intent and meaning of the said circular. And all conditions were performed, etc., to entitle the plaintiffs to have their said tender accepted by the defendants, and to be declared the purchasers of the said goods according to the true intent and meaning of the said circular; yet the defendants refused to accept the said tender of the plaintiffs, and refused to sell the said goods to the plaintiffs, and refused to open the said tender or proceed with the sale of the said goods, in accordance with their said offer and undertaking in that behalf, whereby the plaintiffs had been deprived of profit.

Demurrer, on the ground that the count showed no promise to accept the plaintiffs' tender to sell them the goods. Joinder.

WILLES J.: I am of opinion that the defendants are entitled to judgment. The action is brought against persons who issued a circular offering a stock for sale by tender, to be sold at a discount in one lot. The plaintiffs sent in a tender which turned out to be the highest, but which was not accepted. They now insist that the circular amounts to a contract or promise to sell the goods to the highest bidder,—that is, in this case, to the person who should tender for them at the smallest rate of discount; and reliance is placed on the cases as to rewards offered for the discovery of an offender. In those cases, however, there never was any doubt that the advertisement amounted to a promise to pay the money to the person who first gave information. The difficulty suggested was that it was a contract with all the world. But that, of course, was soon overruled. It was an offer to become liable to any person who, before the offer should be retracted, should happen to be the person to fulfil the contract of which the advertisement was an offer or tender. That is not the sort of difficulty which presents itself here. If the circular had gone on "and we undertake to sell to the highest bidder," the reward cases would have applied, and there would have been a good contract in respect of the persons. But the question is, whether there is here any offer to enter into a contract at all, or whether the circular amounts to anything more than a mere proclamation that the defendants are ready to chaffer for the sale of goods, and to receive offers for the purchase of them. In advertisements for tenders for buildings it is not usual to say that the contract will be given to the lowest bidder, and is not always that the contract is made with the lowest bidder. Here there is a total absence of any words to intimate that the highest bidder is to be the purchaser. It is a mere attempt to ascertain whether an offer can be obtained within such a margin as the sellers are willing to adopt.

[Keating and Montague Smith JJ. concurred.]

JOHNSTON BROTHERS v. ROGERS BROTHERS
Ontario. Divisional Court. 1899. 30 O.R. 150

An appeal by the defendants from the judgment of William Elliott, senior Judge of the County Court of Middlesex, in favour of the plaintiffs in an action in that Court, the facts of which are fully set out in the following [portion of the] opinion delivered by that Judge:

The plaintiffs are bakers, and seek to recover damages from the defendants for breach of a contract for the sale and delivery of a quantity of flour.

The following letter is the basis of the plaintiff's claim:

"Toronto, April 26, 1898.

Dear Sir,—We wish to secure your patronage, and, as we have found the only proper way to get a customer is to save him money, we therefore are going to endeavour to save you money.

It is hardly prudent for us to push the sale of flour just now, as prices are sure to advance at least 50 cents per barrel within a very few days, and to give you the advantage of a cut from 20 to 25 cents per barrel seems a very foolish thing, but nevertheless we are going to do it, just to save you money and secure your patronage.

We quote you (R.O.B. or F.O.B.) your station, Hungarian $5.40, and strong Bakers $5.00, car lots only, and subject to sight draft with bill of lading.

We would suggest your using the wire to order, as prices are so rapidly advancing that they might be beyond reach before a letter would reach us.

Yours respectfully,
Rogers Bros."

This communication was received by the plaintiffs on the 27th April. The plaintiffs telegraphed the defendants the same morning as follows:

"London, April 27, 1898.

To Rogers Bros., Confederation Life Building, Toronto.
We will take two cars Hungarian at your offer of yesterday.
Johnston Bros."

On the same day, namely, the 27th April, the plaintiffs received the following communication by telegraph:

"Toronto, Ont., April 27, 1898.

Flour advanced sixty. Will accept advance of thirty on yesterday's quotations. Further advance certain.
Rogers Bros."

Then followed a letter, dated the 28th April, from Messrs. Hellmuth &

Ivey, solicitors for the plaintiffs, calling upon the defendants to fulfil the order "according to the offer contained in your letter of the 26th and duly accepted by them by wire on April 27th; and upon your refusal damages will be demanded."

FALCONBRIDGE J. delivered the judgment of the Court.: . . . The real crux of the case is whether there is a contract.

Leaving out the matters of inducement (in both the legal and the ordinary sense) in the letter of the 26th, the contract, if there is one, is contained in the following words:

Letter, Defendants to Plaintiffs

"27th April, 1898.

We quote you, F.O.B. your station, Hungarian $5.40, and strong Bakers $5.00, car lots only, and subject to sight drafts with bills of lading."

Telegram, Plaintiffs to Defendants

"27th April, 1898.

We will take 2 cars Hungarian at your offer of yesterday."

I should expect to find American authority as to the phrase "we quote you" which must be in very common use among brokers, manufacturers, and dealers in the United States; but we were referred to no decided case, and I have found none where that phrase was used.

In the *American and English Encyclopedia of Law*, 2nd ed., vol. 7, p. 138, the law is stated to be: "A quotation of prices is not an offer to sell, in the sense that a complete contract will arise out of the mere acceptance of the rate offered or the giving of an order for merchandise in accordance with the proposed terms. It requires the acceptance by the one naming the price, of the order so made, to complete the transaction. Until thus completed there is no mutuality of obligation."

Of the cases cited in support of this proposition, *Mouton* v. *Kershaw* (1884), 59 Wis. 316, 48 Am. Rep. 516, is the nearest to the present one, but in none is the word "Quote" used.

The meaning of "quote" is given in modern dictionaries as follows:

Standard (Com.)—To give the current market price of, as bonds, stocks, commodities, etc.

Imperial, ed. 1884—In com., to name as the price of an article; to name the current price of; as, what can you quote sugar at?

Century (Com.)—To name as the price of stocks, produce, etc.; name the current price of.

Webster (Com.)—To name the current price of.

Worcester—To state the price as the price of merchandise.

See also Black's *Law Dictionary, sub tit.* "Quotation."

There is little or no difference between any of these definitions. Now if we write the equivalent phrase into the letter—"We give you the current or market price, F.O.B. your station, of Hungarian Patent $5.40—" can it be for a moment contended that it is an offer which needs only an acceptance in terms to constitute a contract?

The case of *Harty* v. *Gooderham* (1871), 31 U.C.R. 18, is principally relied on by the plaintiffs. But that case presents more than one point of distinction. There the first inquiry was from the plaintiff, which, I think, is an element in the case. He writes the defendants to let him "know your lowest prices for 50 O.P. spirits," etc. To which defendants answered, mentioning prices and particulars: "Shall be happy to have an order from you, to which we will give prompt attention," which the court held to be equivalent to saying "We will sell it at those prices. Will you purchase from us and let us know how much?" And so the contract was held to be complete on the plaintiff's acceptance.

But there is no such offer to sell in the present defendant's letter. *Harvey* v. *Facey*, [1893] A.C. 552, is strong authority against the plaintiffs.

I have not overlooked the concluding paragraph of the letter, viz., "We would suggest your using the wire to order, as prices are so rapidly advancing that they might be beyond reach before a letter would reach us." The learned Judge considers this to be one of the matters foreign to a mere quotation of prices. I venture, on the contrary, to think that this suggestion is more consistent with a mere quotation of prices, which might vary from day to day or from hour to hour. There could be no question of the prices becoming "beyond reach" in a simple offer to sell at a certain price.

In my opinion, the plaintiffs have failed to establish a contract, and this appeal must be allowed with costs, and the action dismissed with costs. . . .

QUESTIONS. Suppose the Plaintiff in *Harty* v. *Gooderham* had ordered more "spirits, etc." than the Defendant could reasonably have possessed or acquired? Is *Harvey* v. *Facey* such a strong authority against the plaintiffs? What is *Harvey* v. *Facey* authority for? See (1923), 1 *Can. Bar Rev.* at pp. 398ff., and 694, 713.

HARVEY v. FACEY
Jamaica. Privy Council [1893] A.C. 552

LORD MORRIS: The appellants are solicitors carrying on business in partnership at Kingston, [Jamaica], and it appears that in the beginning of October, 1891, negotiations took place between the respondent L. M. Facey and the Mayor and Council of Kingston for the sale of the property in question; that Facey had offered to sell it to them for the sum of £900; that the offer was discussed by the Council at their meeting on the 6th of October, 1891, and the consideration of its acceptance deferred; that on the 7th of October, 1891, L. M. Facey was travelling in the train from Kingston to Porus, and that the appellants caused a telegram to be sent after him from Kingston addressed to him "on the train for Porus," in the following words: "Will you sell us Bumper Hall Pen? Telegraph lowest cash price—answer paid"; that on the same day L. M. Facey replied by telegram to the appellants in the following words: "Lowest price for Bumper Hall Pen £900"; that on the same day the appellants replied to the last-mentioned telegram by a telegram addressed to L. M. Facey "on train at Porus" in the words following: "We agree to buy Bumper Hall Pen for the sum of nine hundred pounds asked by you. Please send us your title deed in order that we may get early possession." The above telegrams were duly received by the appellant and by L. M. Facey. . . . Their Lordships concur in the judgment of Mr. Justice Curran that there was no concluded contract between the appellants and L. M. Facey to be collected from the aforesaid telegrams. The first telegram asks two questions. The first question is as to the willingness of L. M. Facey to sell to the appellants; the second question asks the lowest price, and the word "Telegraph" is in its collocation addressed to that second question only. L. M. Facey replied to the second question only, and gives his lowest price. The third telegram from the appellants treats the answer of L. M. Facey stating his lowest price as an unconditional offer to sell to them at the price named. Their Lordships cannot treat the telegram from L. M. Facey as binding him in any respect, except to the extent it does by its terms, viz., the lowest price. Everything else is left open, and the reply telegram from the appellants cannot be treated as an acceptance of an offer to sell to them; it is an offer that required to be accepted by L. M. Facey. The contract could only be completed if L. M. Facey had accepted the appellant's last telegram. It has been contended for the appellants that L. M. Facey's telegram should be read as saying "yes" to the first question put in the appellants' telegram, but there is nothing to support that contention. L. M. Facey's telegram gives a precise answer to a precise question, viz., the price. The contract must appear by the telegrams, whereas the appellants are obliged to contend that an acceptance of the first question is to be implied. Their Lordships are of the opinion that the mere statement of the lowest price at which the vendor would sell contains no implied contract to see at that price to the persons making the inquiry. . . .

PROBLEM. What if Facey's telegram had said, "I am prepared to offer you Bumper Hall Pen for £900?"
See *Clifton* v. *Palumbo* [1944] 2 All. E.R. 497 (C.A.).
In another case, the vendor's letter said, "For a quick sale I would accept £26,000." Was that an offer?
See *Bigg* v. *Boyd Gibbons Ltd.* [1971] 1 W.L.R. 913 (C.A.).

GRAINGER & SON v. *GOUGH.* [1896] A.C. 325 (House of Lords). LORD HERSCHELL: "The transmission of such a price list does not amount to an offer to supply an unlimited quantity of the wine described at the price named, so that so soon as an order is given there is a binding contract to supply that quantity. If it were so, the merchant might find himself involved in any number of contractual obligations to supply wine of a particular description which he would be quite unable to carry out, his stock of that wine being necessarily limited."

BOYER AND CO. v. *D. & R. DUKE.* [1905] 2 Ir.R. 617. MADDEN J.: "It is a matter of common knowledge that quotations of prices are scattered broadcast among possible customers. Business could not be carried on if each such recipient of a priced catalogue offering a desirable article —say a rare book—at an attractive price, were in a position to create a contract of sale by writing that he would buy at the price mentioned. The catalogue had probably reached many collectors. The order of one only can be honoured. Has each of the others who write for the book the right of action? Wholesale dealers have not in stock an unlimited supply of the articles the price of which they quote to the public at large. This stock usually bears some proportion to the orders which they may reasonably expect to receive. Transactions of the kind under consideration are intelligible and business-like, if we bear in mind the distinction between a quotation, submitted as a basis of a possible order, and an offer to sell which, if accepted, creates a contract for the breach of which damages may be recovered.

"These observations seem to apply with special force to a quotation furnished by a manufacturer, in the position of the defendants, stating the terms on which he is prepared to work, as to price and time for completion. He may receive and comply with many applications for quotations on the same day. If his reply in each case can be turned into a contract by acceptance, his looms might be burdened with an amount of work which would render it impossible for him to meet his engagements. In my opinion, a merchant, dealer, or manufacturer, by furnishing a quotation invites an offer which will be honoured or not according to the exigencies of the business. A quotation based on current prices usually holds good for a limited time. But it remains a quotation on the basis of which an offer will not be entertained after a certain date."

ROOKE v. *DAWSON*. [1895] Ch.D. 480 (England). The defendants announced an examination for a scholarship which they administered. The plaintiff and one other candidate competed and the plaintiff wrote the better paper. He claimed the scholarship, which the defendants refused to him. Held, for the defendants. CHITTY J.: "It is plain the plaintiff could not state that the announcement included the term that the scholarship would be awarded, in all events, to the boy who got the highest number of marks. That would be a most improbable announcement to be made by trustees in the position of these defendants." [Why?]

STORER v. MANCHESTER CITY COUNCIL
[1974] 3 All E.R. 825 (C.A.)

LORD DENNING M.R.: In May, 1971 there was a change in the control of the defendants, Manchester Corporation. Previously the Conservatives had been in control. Afterwards it was Labour. The change had legal repercussions. During the Conservative administration the policy of the corporation was to sell their council houses to tenants on favourable terms. They were willing to sell to any sitting tenant who had been in occupation more than a year. The sale price was to be the market value of the house if sold with vacant possession, but with a reduction for the tenant according to the length of time he had been in the premises as a tenant. He might get a reduction of from ten to 20 per cent on the price. Furthermore, the corporation were ready to give him a 100 per cent mortgage.

When the Labour administration took over in May, 1971 that policy was reversed. The Labour-controlled administration decided that they would not sell council houses to tenants. But they realised that they could not go back on existing contracts. So they gave instructions to their officers that they were to fulfil existing contracts but not to make any fresh contracts. Now in many cases tenants had filled in various forms applying to buy their houses, but the contracts of sale had not been exchanged. The tenants claim that firm contracts had been made even though the contracts had not been exchanged. But the town clerk thought that the contracts were only binding when contracts of sale had been exchanged. So he wrote this letter to the tenants: "At their meeting on the 7th July, 1971 the Council decided to discontinue the Scheme for the sale of

Council houses, and to proceed only with those cases where Contracts have been exchanged. As Contracts have not been formally exchanged in this case, I am unable to proceed with the proposed sale." Now the plaintiff, Mr. Storer, one of the tenants, has brought this action to test that ruling.

The facts are these. Mr. Storer was a tenant of a council house, 167 Moorcroft Road, Wythenshawe. On 15th November 1970 he filled in a request for information asking for the price and details of any mortgage. On 14th January 1971 the corporation wrote saying that they "may be prepared to sell the house to you at the purchase price of £2,750," less a discount of 17 per cent (as he had had a council house for several years), making a net sum of £2,282. If he were granted a mortgage, it would be for £2,279 repayable over 25 years. They said in their letter: "This letter should not be regarded as a firm offer of a mortgage." Later on, however, they did make a firm offer, as I will show.

On 11th February 1971 Mr. Storer filled in an application form to buy a council house. He said: "I . . . now wish to purchase my Council house." In it he asked for a loan on mortgage. On 9th March 1971 the city treasurer wrote to him: "The Corporation will lend £2,279 repayable over 25 years with interest at 8½% . . . the total monthly instalment payable will be . . . £14.98." On the same day, 9th March 1971, the town clerk himself wrote a letter which is of crucial importance in the case:

"Dear Sir,

Sale of Council Houses

"I understand you wish to purchase your Council house and enclose the Agreement for Sale. If you will sign the Agreement and return it to me I will send you the Agreement signed on behalf of the Corporation in exchange. From the enclosed list of Solicitors, who are prepared to act for you and advise you on the purchase, please let me know the name of the firm that you select, as soon as possible."

Enclosed with that letter there was a form headed: "City of Manchester. Agreement for Sale of a Council House." The corporation had filled in various details, such as the name of the purchaser, the address of the property, the price, the mortgage, amount, and the monthly repayments. There was this item left blank: "7. Date when your tenancy ceases and mortgage repayments will commence," followed by these clauses:

" 8. *Freehold* to be conveyed or transferred by the Corporation.

" 9. There will be no abstract or investigation of title . . .

"10. *Deeds* of Conveyance or Transfer and Mortgage to be in the Corporation's standard forms including conditions against use except as a private dwelling-house and against advertising and a restriction not to sell or lease the property for five years.

"11. *Warning.* As from the date mentioned in 7 above the property is at your risk. If you are taking a mortgage from the Corporation it will be insured for you but the cost recharged to you. *If you are not taking a Mortgage insure it at once.* Your responsibility for repairs and for payment of rates also start from that day. My solicitors are . . ."

Mr. Storer filled in that form. He filled in the name of solicitors, Messrs Hargreaves & Co. He signed the form himself and returned it on 20th March 1971. So he had done everything which he had to do to bind himself to the purchase of the property. The only thing left blank was the date when the tenancy was to cease.

The sale would have gone through, no doubt, within a short time but for the corporation and the town clerk's office being so pressed. The housing manager passed a note to the town clerk suggesting that the sale be completed with effect from Monday 22nd March or Monday 12th April. But nothing more was done before the election which brought a change of control in the corporation. The town clerk's staff were, apparently, overworked and did not deal with the matter in time. Then in May, 1971 there was the election. In July, 1971 the corporation, under the new control, resolved that there were to be no more sales to council tenants; but the corporation recognised that they had to go on with the cases where the corporation were legally bound.

Thereupon the town clerk wrote to Mr. Storer and other tenants in like situation a letter saying: "As Contracts have not been formally exchanged in this case, I am unable to proceed with the proposed sale." Mr. Storer took the advice of Messrs Hargreaves & Co. Some 120 other tenants also took advice. They were advised that there was a binding contract, even though formal contracts had not been exchanged. So this case of Mr. Storer has come as a test case for Manchester Corporation. It is to decide whether or not "exchange" is necessary in order to form a concluded contract.

When parties arrange for a sale "subject to contract," that means, as a rule, that there is no binding contract until the contracts of sale have been formally exchanged. That is clear from *Eccles* v. *Bryant*. But where there is no arrangement "subject to contract," the only question is whether a contract has been concluded: see *Bigg* v. *Boyd Gibbins Ltd.* One example is where one solicitor is acting for both sides, such as in *Smith* v. *Mansi*. It is "artificial nonsense," Danckwerts LJ said, to have an exchange of contracts where there is only one solicitor acting. The present case is, I think, another example. The corporation put forward to the tenant a simple form of agreement. The very object was to dispense with legal formalities. One of the formalities—exchange of contracts—was quite unnecessary. The contract was concluded by offer and acceptance. The offer was contained in the letter of 9th March in which the town clerk said: "I . . . enclose the Agreement for Sale. If you will sign the Agreement and return it to me I will send the Agreement signed on behalf of the Corporation in exchange." The acceptance was made when the tenant did sign it, as he did, and return it, as he did on 20th March. It was then that a contract was concluded. The town clerk was then bound to send back the agreement signed on behalf of the corporation. The agreement was concluded on Mr. Storer's acceptance. It was not dependent on the subsequent exchange.

I appreciate that there was one space in the form which was left blank. It was cl. 7 for "Date when your tenancy ceases." That blank did not mean there was no concluded contract. It was left blank simply for administrative convenience. A similar point arose in *Smith* v. *Mansi* where Russell L.J. said:

"There was nothing left for the parties themselves to do but agree the date. Its insertion in the already signed document—in the hands of the common solicitor—could surely be nothing but an administrative tidying up to be done, if at all, at the solicitor's convenience."

So here the filling in of the date was just a matter of administrative tidying up, to be filled in by the town clerk with a suitable date for the change-over—the date on which the man ceased to be a tenant and became a purchaser.

A further point was taken. It was said that the town clerk had not actually signed the form of agreement. No matter. He had signed a letter of 9th March 1971 and that was sufficient. It was a note or memorandum sufficient to satisfy the Law of Property Act 1925, s. 40.

The final point was this. Counsel for the corporation said that the town clerk did not intend to be bound by the letter of 9th March 1971. He intended that the corporation should not be bound except on exchange. There is nothing in this point. In contracts you do not look into the actual intent in a man's mind. You look at what he said and did. A contract is formed when there is, to all outward appearances, a contract. A man cannot get out of a contract by saying: "I did not intend to contract," if by his words he has done so. His intention is to be found only in the outward expression which his letters convey. If they show a concluded contract that is enough.

It seems to me that the judge was quite right in holding that there was a binding contract in this case, even though there was no exchange. It is a proper case for specific performance; and I would dismiss the appeal.

PHARMACEUTICAL SOCIETY OF GREAT BRITAIN v. BOOTS CASH CHEMISTS (SOUTHERN) LTD.
England. Court of Appeal. [1953] 1 Q.B. 401

The Pharmaceutical Society is charged with the enforcement of the *Pharmacy and Poisons Act, 1933*, section 18 of which provides in part that no person shall "sell any poison included in Part I of the Poisons List, unless ... the sale is effected by, or under the supervision of, a registered pharmacist." "Boots," well known chain store druggists (chemist's shops) in England, operated a shop in Edgware where substances included in Part I of the Poisons List were displayed in a self service area. A customer taking one of these substances could only escape from the area by passing a cashier's desk which was near and under the supervision of the pharmacist. The cashier and the pharmacist were instructed to prevent any customers from removing any drug from the shop if the pharmacist thought fit. The Pharmaceutical Society brought this action on an agreed statement of facts to determine whether, as the Society contended, the sale took place when the customer helped himself from the shelf, or as "Boots" maintained, the sale took place when the cashier decided whether she would accept the payment. The society supposed that if the sale had already taken place it had not taken place under the supervision of a registered pharmacist and that Boots could not, therefore, refuse to accept payment or stop the customer from leaving with the prescribed drugs. Lord Goddard C.J. decided that the sale took place when the cashier accepted payment and under proper supervision. The Society appealed.

SOMERVELL L.J.: It is not disputed that in a chemist's shop where this self-service system does not prevail a customer may go in and ask a young woman assistant, who will not herself be a registered pharmacist, for one of these articles on the list, and the transaction may be completed and the article paid for, although the registered pharmacist, who will no doubt be on the premises, will not know anything himself of the transaction, unless the assistant serving the customer, or the customer, requires to put a question to him. It is right that I should emphasize, as did the Lord Chief Justice, that these are not dangerous drugs. They are substances which contain very small portions of poison, and I imagine that many of them are the type of drug which has a warning as to what doses are to be taken. They are drugs which can be obtained, under the law, without a doctor's prescription.

The point taken by the plaintiff is this: it is said that the purchase is complete if and when a customer going round the shelves takes an article and puts it in the receptacle which he or she is carrying, and that therefore, if that is right, when the customer comes to the pay desk, having completed the tour of the premises, the registered pharmacist, if so minded, has no power to say: "This drug ought not to be sold to this customer." Whether and in what circumstances he would have that power we need not inquire, but one can, of course, see that there is a difference if supervision can only be exercised at a time when the contract is completed.

I agree with the Lord Chief Justice in everything that he said, but I will put the matter shortly in my own words. Whether the view contended for by the plaintiffs is a right view depends on what are legal implications of this layout—the invitation to the customer. Is a contract to be regarded as being completed when the article is put into the receptacle, or is this to be regarded as a more organized way of doing what is done already in many types of shops—and a bookseller is perhaps the best example—namely, enabling customers to have free access to what is in the shop, to look at the different articles, and then, ultimately, having got the ones which they wish to buy, to come up to the assistant saying "I want this"? The assistant in 999 times out of 1,000 says "That is all right," and the money passes and the transaction is completed. I agree with what the Lord Chief Justice has said, and with the reasons which he has given for his conclusion, that in the case of an ordinary shop, although goods are displayed and it is intended that customers should go and choose what they want, the contract is not completed until, the customer having indicated the articles which he needs, the shop-keeper, or someone on his behalf, accepts that offer. Then the contract is completed. I can see no reason at all, that being clearly the normal position, for drawing any different implication as a result of this layout.

The Lord Chief Justice, I think, expressed one of the most formidable difficulties in the way of the plaintiffs' contention when he pointed out that, if the plaintiffs are right, once an article has been placed in the receptacle the customer himself is bound and would have no right, without paying for the first article, to substitute an article which he saw later of a similar kind and which he perhaps preferred. I can see no reason for implying from this self-service arrangement any implication other than that which the Lord Chief Justice found in it, namely, that it is a convenient method of enabling customers to see what there is and choose, and possibly put back and substitute, articles which they wish to have, and then go up to the cashier and offer to buy what they have so far chosen. On that conclusion the case fails, because it is admitted that there was supervision in the sense required by the Act and at the appropriate moment of time. For these reasons, in my opinion, the appeal should be dismissed.

[The judgments of Birkett and Romer L.JJ., who agreed are omitted.]

QUESTIONS. If the decision had gone the other way, would it follow, as Lord Goddard seems to have thought, that once a customer had handled a product he would have to pay for it, even if he saw another product he preferred? Is not one of the purposes of a self service system to permit customers to make more informed choices of products after comparison, without involving the time of a clerk? If this is a purpose, is there any real difficulty in interpreting the situation as one of an offer to sell acceptable only by taking the finally selected product to the cashier?

Does the *Boots* case offer any help in solving the vexing case of the window lure? During World War II shopkeepers sometimes placed scarce articles, such as nylon stockings, in their windows, hoping to induce customers to come into the shop. Of course this end would be defeated if this sole remaining pair of nylons were sold to the first customer. Has the first, or any customer who wants to buy at the stated price, and produces the money, a contractual right? If so, and the shopkeeper refuses to sell, what damages will the customer be awarded? Will the practical result that more customers will be annoyed than will be pleased by this practice be a sufficient discouragement to shopkeepers? Has the customer any "moral right" not to be lured into a shop?

PROBLEM. Able, a shopper in Baker's supermarket, is injured when a bottle of ginger ale explodes as he removes it from his shopping cart and puts it on the checkout counter. The explosion is caused by a latent and indetectable defect in the bottle. Can Able sue Baker for breach of the implied warranty of fitness in section 15 of the Sale of Goods Act (Ont.)?

FISHER v. *BELL* [1960] 3 All E.R. 731 (England. Queen's Bench Division). A 1959 statute made it an offence for anyone to "manufacture, sell or hire or offer for sale or hire, or lend or give to any other person" a spring blade knife, commonly known as a "flick knife". Respondent had such a knife displayed in his shop window, with a price tag "Ejector knife —4s." attached. A police constable gave the respondent his opinion that it was a flick knife to which the respondent said, "Why do the manufacturers still bring them round for us to sell?" The constable told the respondent he would be reported for offering for sale a flick knife, to which he said, "Fair enough." On a prosecution, held, for the respondent. The display of the knife was a mere invitation to treat, not an "offer for sale." LORD PARKER C.J.: ". . . I think that most lay people would be inclined to the view (as, indeed, I was myself when I first read these papers), that if a knife were displayed in a window like that with a price attached to it, it was nonsense to say that that was not offering it for sale. The knife is there inviting people to buy it, and in ordinary language it is for sale; but any statute must be looked at in the light of the general law of the country, for Parliament must be taken to know the general law. It is clear that, according to the ordinary law of contract, the display of an article with a price on it in a shop window is merely an invitation to treat. . . . [In] many statutes and orders which prohibit selling and offering for sale of goods, it is very common, when it is so desired, to insert the words, 'offering or exposing for sale', 'exposing for sale' being clearly words which would cover the display of goods in a shop window. . . . I, for my part, though I confess reluctantly, am driven to the conclusion that no offence was here committed."

R. v. *BERMUDA HOLDINGS LTD.* (1969) 9 D.L.R. (3d) 595 (B.C.S.C.) A regulation under the British Columbia Motor Vehicle Act provided as follows: "No person who is engaged in the business of selling motor vehicles shall keep for sale, or sell or offer for sale, any new or used motor vehicle unless the motor vehicle is equipped as required by these regulations." The accused, who was in the business of selling motor vehicles, exhibited on his lot a number of cars which failed to comply with the regulations. A policeman asked whether the cars were "for sale" and was told that they were. The accused was charged with unlawfully "offering for sale" the cars in question. It was convicted, and appealed on the ground that it had not made an "offer for sale."

WOOTTON J. cited several cases, including *Fisher* v. *Bell* and *Pharmaceutical Society* v. *Boots*, and continued: "What is apparent to the casual observer of the words "offer for sale" has not the general meaning those words appear to have. There must be something more than mere exhibition, for if that is all there is the exposure is only an invitation to treat. There is no definition in the Act regarding offer for sale or anything of that kind. What was done here was not an offering for sale, but the goods, viz., the motor vehicles, were exposed for sale and the exposure was merely an invitation to treat as laid down in the foregoing authorities. I must answer the question raised in the stated case in the following manner. . . . The answer to the question raised is that the presence of the automobiles around the front of the appellant's premises, amplified by the statement of one of the officers of the appellant company that such cars were for sale, did not constitute a valid offer for sale at law. At best there was merely an invitation to treat."

QUESTION. Is there any reason why the decision in these quasi-criminal cases should depend on the contractual concept of "offer"? Are not the Courts here dealing with entirely different problems?

SWISS FEDERAL CODE OF OBLIGATIONS

7. . . . The display of merchandise with a price tag is considered as a rule as an offer.

PROBLEM. A newspaper advertisement, placed by M Department Store, read as follows: "Saturday, 9 a.m. one fur stole worth $139.50, for $1.00. First come, first served." B saw the advertisement and was first at the counter on Saturday morning, dollar in hand. The store refused to sell him the stole, saying that the advertisement was only meant for women. Advise B.

See *Lefkowitz* v. *Great Minneapolis Surplus Store* (1957) 86 N.W. 2d. 689 (Minn. S.C.).

COMBINES INVESTIGATION ACT
R.S.C. 1970 C-23, amended 1976

37(2) No person shall advertise at a bargain price a product that he does not supply in reasonable quantities having regard to the nature of the market in which he carries on business, the nature and size of the business carried on by him, and the nature of the advertisement.

(4) Any person who violates subsection (2) is guilty of an offence and is liable on summary conviction to a fine not exceeding twenty-five thousand dollars or to imprisonment for one year or both.

31(1) Any person who has suffered loss or damage as a result of conduct that is contrary to any provision of Part V [s. 37 is in Part V] ... may, in any court of competent jurisdiction, sue for and receive from the person who engaged in the conduct ... an amount equal to the loss or damage proved to have been suffered by him, together with any additional amount that the court may allow not exceeding the full cost to him of any investigation in connection with the matter and of proceedings under this section.

BRISTOL, CARDIFF, AND SWANSEA AERATED BREAD COMPANY v. MAGGS
England Chancery Division. 1890. 44 Ch.D. 616

This was an action by the Plaintiffs, the Bristol, Cardiff, and Swansea Aërated Bread Company (Limited), against the Defendant, a baker and confectioner carrying on business at 15, Duke Street, Cardiff, for the specific performance of a contract alleged to be constituted by two letters. The first was written by the Defendant to Colonel Guthrie, a director of the Plaintiff company, and was as follows:

"Cardiff, 29th of May, 1889
Dear Sir,—I beg to submit to you the following conditions for disposal of my business carried on at 15, Duke Street, Cardiff. Lease and goodwill, £450 (lease from the 29th of September, 1888, for fourteen years). All fixtures, fittings, utensils, &c., stock-in-trade connected with the premises to be taken at valuation.
Yours truly,
R. Maggs.
This offer to hold good for ten days."

The letter did not on the face of it shew to whom it was written. Colonel Guthrie, writing with the authority of the board of directors of the company, replied as follows:

"Cardiff, 1st of June, 1889.
Dear Sir,—On behalf of the Bristol, Cardiff, and Swansea Aërated Bread Company (Limited), I accept your offer for shop and lease, &c., 15, Duke Street, Cardiff.
Yours truly,
John Guthrie,
For B., C., and S. Aërated Bread Company.
Mr. R. Maggs,
15, Duke Street, Cardiff."

On the 2nd of June, 1889, the Defendant's solicitor sent Colonel Guthrie a formal memorandum of agreement for approval, with an accompanying letter. This memorandum was altered by the plaintiff's solicitors, mainly by the insertion of a clause preventing the vendor for five years from carrying on a like business within the borough of Cardiff or within a distance of five miles from the Townhall. The memorandum so altered was returned on the 4th of June, with a letter of the Plaintiff's solicitors. On the 5th of June the Defendant's solicitor wrote sending the draft again to the Plaintiffs' solicitors, with a modification of the proposed additional clause. On the 6th of June the Plaintiffs' solicitors wrote that they could not themselves agree to the proposed modification, but that they had asked Colonel Guthrie to call about it.

On the 7th the Defendant's solicitor wrote that he regretted the Plaintiffs' solicitors had not agreed to the terms of the draft contract, and continued: "Colonel Guthrie has not been near me, and by my client's instructions I beg to inform you that he declines to proceed further in the matter."

On the 8th Colonel Guthrie saw the Defendant's solictor and said he had come to settle the agreement which had been returned to him. The answer was that he was too late; the Defendant had made other arrangements. Colonel Guthrie replied he was prepared to sign the agreement leaving out the disputed clause. The solicitor declined; and Colonel Guthrie went immediately to the Defendant, who told him that he wished to have the agreement cancelled, because his son was very much against his parting with the shop. The Defendant, it appeared, did not suggest that there was no agreement, but asked Colonel Guthrie to use his influence with his co-directors to get the sale cancelled. The memorandum of agreement contained several terms not expressed in the letters; for example, it provided for the book debts and books of account being reserved to the vendor and for the payment of a deposit of £45; it fixed the 24th of June as the day for completion of the purchase and delivery of possession; it provided for delivery of abstract of title and the date from which it was to commence, and for other matters, all of which were more or less of a formal nature.

KAY J. (after stating the facts, continued): The contested stipulation in the memorandum of agreement as to restricting the vendor from carrying on a like business to that which he had sold was not by any means a matter of form. After some conflict of opinion, it has been decided by the Court of Appeal, in *Pearson* v. *Pearson* (1884), 27 Ch.D. 145, that a man who sells the goodwill of a business may not only set up a similar business next door and say that he is the person who carried on the old business, but that he may also solicit the customers of the old business to continue to deal with him, although by these proceedings he might not only destroy all benefit to the purchaser of the thing which he had bought, but might recover to himself the actual possession of it. Such a fraudulent proceeding, according to the decision, cannot be prevented by any Court of Law or Equity. It follows that the stipulation which the company's solicitors introduced into the draft was one which they were not entitled to insert if the two letters which I have read were a complete contract. In other words, they were trying to obtain an additional and most important concession from the vendor. Now ... suppose this to pass in conversation: A. offers to B. his business, lease, and goodwill for £450 B. says, "I accept." A day or two afterwards B. asks A. to engage not to carry on a similar business within a distance of five miles. A. answers, "I cannot agree to that, but I will if you say three miles." B. takes time to consider, saying he will send an agent next day to settle the terms. The agent does not go next day, and A. accordingly says to B., "I put an end to the matter." No one could doubt that would be a continuous negotiation, and that B. could not say, "I will disregard all that followed the acceptance of the first offer, and insist on there being a complete contract by that acceptance." Well, then, still leaving out of sight the statute and authorities suppose all this to take place by letters between A. and B. instead of conversation; it is obvious the result must be the same. Some of the letters being by the principals and some by the solicitors could not make any difference. . . .

It was suggested that the ten days during which the offer was to remain open had not expired when it was withdrawn. But this can make no difference. The offer was not a contract, and the term that it should remain open for ten days was therefore not binding. It has often been held that such an offer may, notwithstanding, be withdrawn within the time limited. . . .

I decide this case against the Plaintiffs upon the ground, that although the two letters relied on would, if nothing else had taken place, have been sufficient evidence of a complete agreement, yet the Plaintiffs have themselves shewn that the agreement was not complete by stipulating afterwards for an important additional term, which kept the whole matter of purchase and sale in a state of negotiation only, and that the Defendant was therefore at liberty to put an end to the negotiations, as he did, by withdrawing his offer. . . .

[Part of the opinion dealing with the Statute of Frauds has been omitted.]

BELLAMY v. *DEBENHAM*. 1890. 45 Ch. D. 481. NORTH J.: . . . "Some of the phrases used by Mr. Justice Kay, in *Bristol, Cardiff, and Swansea Aërated Bread Co.* v. *Maggs* seem to me to go further than that. By way of illustration he put a case of a definite offer to sell a business, lease, and goodwill, and a definite acceptance, and after that negotiations between the parties as to whether a new term, limiting the area within which the vendor of the business was to carry on a similar business, should be introduced, and said that in such a case he thought that the purchaser could not disregard all that followed the acceptance of the prior offer, and insist on there being a complete contract by that acceptance. . . .

"In my opinion, subsequent negotiations, first commenced on new points after a contract complete in itself has been signed, cannot be regarded as constituting a part of the negotiations going on at the time when it was signed, because, *ex hypothesi*, the Court has arrived at the conclusion that they were not going on then—that they were not thought of at that time, but related to matters first thought of subsequently.

"I do not in any way dissent from the view which Mr. Justice Kay took of the case then before him; but those remarks of his, if they meant as much as they might possibly mean, seem to me to go too far, and I should not be prepared to follow them. . . ."

HARVEY v. *PERRY* [1953] 2 D.L.R. 465 (Alberta. Supreme Court of Canada). Negotiations were spread over several months leading to an alleged contract for the sale of eight oil leases in Alberta. Correspondence starting in January, 1950, included a letter from Perry dated May 2, rejecting terms so high "we cannot handle it at all" and continuing, "However, you might consider the following and if you feel that you could accept these terms, I am sure we could put a deal over for you. . . ." On May 8, Harvey wrote, "I will accept your proposition. . . ." On May 15, Perry wrote, "We will proceed immediately to try and consummate a deal for you at the earliest possible moment. There will, in all probability, be a counter proposal or two from our clients, and if such is the case, we will submit them to you at once." On August 24, Perry's solicitor wrote that "Mr. A. C. Perry . . . advises that he is in a position to take these leases under the terms and conditions contained in his letter to you of the 2nd May and your letter to his firm dated May 8th, 1950. Mr. Perry has asked us to prepare the Assignment . . . it will be necessary that we have access to the above leases now in your possession." In due course Harvey forwarded the leases. On August 26, the solicitor again wrote, "some discussion between you will be necessary before adequate instructions can be given to draw such an Agreement." On the same day Perry himself wrote that, "Mr. Howatt of Howatt and Howatt, my solicitor, is sending through a copy of the proposed agreement. However you and I will get together and complete the terms." The "get together" took place on September 1, when, Perry contended, "we had made a deal . . . and we shook hands on that deal right there and then in front of the Hotel." On September 2 Perry's solicitor sent a letter and draft agreement with some variations from the oral agreement, which Harvey's solicitors objected to on September 7, and to the correction of which Perry's solicitor agreed, on September 9, saying, "the terms are acceptable." On September 13 Perry forwarded a second agreement in identical terms with the first, and containing another variation from the oral agreement of September 1. Neither Harvey nor his solicitors made any further communication and Perry's letters remained unanswered. About September 15 Harvey announced that he would drill his own wells, which concluded the negotiations. The trial judge found a contract in the letters of May 2, 8, 15 and August 24 and in Harvey's sending the leases. The Alberta Court of Appeal agreed. The Supreme Court of Canada, following the *Maggs* case, reversed, ESTEY J. saying, "The letter of September 2nd, the proposed agreement enclosed therewith and respondent's solicitors' letter of September 9th, might support a conclusion that the parties had agreed, but, when read, as they must be, with respondent's solicitors' letter of September 13th and the proposed agreement enclosed therewith, it is clear that the respondent had not agreed. . . . There was no consensus ad idem because the respondent was still negotiating for better terms."

PINSONNEAULT v. *LESPERANCE.* 1925. 58 O.L.R. 375 (Ontario Appellate Division). A document (in French) relating to the sale of land by Lesperance to Pinsonneault stated: "I acknowlege having received one hundred dollars ($100.00) on account of my house No. 812 Assumption, which I sell to L.P. Pinsonneault for the price of five thousand dollars ($5,000.00) on the following condition—$900 on execution of contract; $500 or more a year on principal with interest at 7%." A few days later Lesperance sold the property to his nephew for $5,500 and Pinsonneault brought this action for $1,000 damages. Held, for Pinsonneault. WRIGHT J.:". . . I think the document itself contains all the essentials necessary for a concluded agreement, and that the contract referred to was intended merely to put in more formal language the agreement between the parties. . . ." Wright J. was affirmed on appeal, Mulock C.J.O. dissenting (same citation). The deposit of $100 was ordered returned and damages were fixed at $500, the difference between the two selling prices.

SPOTTISWOODE, BALLANTYNE & CO. LTD. v. DOREEN APPLIANCES LTD. and G. BARCLAY (LONDON), LTD.
England. Court of Appeal. [1942] 2 All E.R. 65

Appeal by the plaintiffs from the judgment of Atkinson J., who dismissed the action for recovery of possession of certain premises and allowed the defendants' counterclaim for specific performance of an agreement to grant the defendants a lease of the premises.

LORD GREENE M.R.: The question involved is a very short one and one which, to my mind, with all respect to the judge, has a clear answer. Some time before the end of July, 1941, the parties had been in negotiation with regard to the granting of a lease. On August 1, 1941, the first defendants wrote making an offer, and on the same day Messrs. Farebrother, Ellis & Co., who were agents for the plaintiffs, wrote a letter upon the true construction of which the whole question turns. It was as follows:

"We are obliged by your letter of to-day's date, making an offer to take the first and second floors as inspected. We have submitted this to our clients who are prepared to proceed with the letting, subject in the usual way to your references being satisfactory and to the terms of a formal agreement to be prepared by their solicitors. We have today applied for the references and as soon as these are approved by our clients we will ask you to let us have your cheque for one quarter's rent in advance, viz., £68 15s. 0d., when our client will give instructions for the necessary work to be put in hand, and will be willing for you to enter into possession, provided the rent is paid from the date you take it over and you give an undertaking to vacate when called upon, if no agreement is entered into."

The last paragraph of the letter I need not read. The defendants went in; they paid the rent in advance. The necessary alterations, I think, were not done, but the premises were whitewashed or distempered by the plaintiffs, and on August 13 the plaintiffs' solicitors sent to the defendants a draft of the agreement. On August 20 there was a meeting between Mr. Woolf of Farebrother, Ellis & Co. and Mr. Blockheart of the first defendant company, at which certain discussion took place, and eventually, on August 28, the plaintiffs wrote a letter saying that they were not willing to proceed with the agreement. It was the contention of the defendants that a binding agreement was in existence and that accordingly they were entitled to have that agreement specifically performed.

The whole question turns on the meaning of the letter of August 1, 1941, which I have read. The crucial words are those which refer to the formal agreement. It is said that those words mean nothing more than this, that as soon as the solicitors for the plaintiffs had put into formal shape the matters on which the parties weere in agreement a binding unconditional contract would come into existence, notwithstanding that the formal document in which those terms were to be set out was never signed and exchanged by the parties. On the other hand, it is said by the plaintiffs that this language means, on its true construction, that unless and until a formal agreement has been entered into, no contract was to exist between the parties. The problem is one which is familiar to all of us. In my opinion, the second construction is unquestionably the right one. I am quite unable to construe the words "subject to the terms of a formal agreement to be prepared by their solicitors" as meaning that "a formal agreement" there referred to is not one which is to be executed by the parties in the usual way. An unexecuted document would not be a formal agreement. Even if any doubt could remain as to the true construction of that phrase, the matter is entirely settled, in my judgment, by the words referring to the undertaking to vacate when called upon if no agreement is entered into. It is manifest that the agreement there referred to is the same thing as the formal agreement referred to in the earlier passage; and how a formal agreement is to be entered into unless it is executed and exchanged in the usual way, I for one am unable to discover. The real fact of the matter is that the language used here is equivalent to the common and more concise phrase "subject to contract," and, if anything is settled, it is that that phrase is one which makes it clear that the intention of the parties is that neither of them is to be contractually bound until a contract is signed in the usual way.

That really disposes of the whole case, but I must say a word or two with regard to the manner in which the judge dealt with a large number of authorities which he reviewed at length. It is with no disrespect to him that I venture to suggest that the examination has prevented him from seeing clearly the true nature of the question before him. Inspired, no doubt, by a desire to protect the defendants from treatment which he may have thought was high-handed, he endeavoured to draw fine distinctions between the language used in this case and that used in other cases. I do not propose to follow him by examining those authorities at length, but I am going to make a very short reference to three of them. The first is *Lockett* v. *Norman-Wright*, [1925] 1 Ch. 56. The relevant words there were: "Subject to suitable agreements being arranged between your solicitors and mine." The solicitors had come to an agreement between themselves; the draft was settled; they were ready to complete; and then the plaintiff refused to go on. Tomlin J., said this, at p. 61:

"The question is one primarily of construction. Is there any real distinction between the language used here and such phrases as "subject to a formal contract," "subject to contract," "subject to a proper contract to be prepared by the vendor's solicitor." The plaintiff urges that the phrase here means: "I agree to take a lease at the rent and for the term mentioned in the letter and upon such other terms as the solicitors of the parties may settle between themselves"; and that when once the draft lease had been approved by the solicitors the condition was fulfilled and there was an absolute contract. I do not think I can place any such construction upon the language. I think the natural meaning of the language is that the execution of a suitable agreement or suitable agreements in a form approved by the solicitors on both sides is a condition of any concluded bargain. The construction suggested on behalf of the plaintiff is artificial, and I do not think that the court should place an artificial meaning on the language employed in order to make a contract of that which would otherwise be no contract."

The next case is *Raingold* v. *Bromley*, [1931] 2 Ch. 307. There the phrase was "subject to the terms of a lease" and an exactly similar argument was put forward. Lawrence L.J., said this, at p. 316:

"The matter, however, does not rest there, for in my opinion the true construction of the expression 'subject to the terms of a lease' is that contended for on behalf of the defendant. The expression, I think, means 'subject to the terms to be contained in a lease executed by the lessor,' and therefore, implies that a lease has to come into existence and has to be executed by the lessor before any binding agreement is reached. The expression 'subject to the terms of a lease' is in my opinion at least as strong as 'subject to contract,' and was inserted in the letter of December 9, in order to keep the matter open until a lease had actually been executed by the defendant."

The last case is *Berry, Ltd.* v. *Brighton and Sussex Building Society,*

[1939] 3 All E.R. 217. There the words were "subject to a lease to be drawn up by our clients' solicitors." Farwell J., said this, at p. 219:

"Counsel for the plaintiffs says that that means, as a matter of construction, that, the moment the solicitors have agreed as to the form of the lease the condition is fulfilled, and the contract is a binding contract, which his clients are entitled to enforce. On the other hand, it is said that this in effect is nothing more than a contract to enter into a contract, which, the authorities have established now quite plainly, is not a binding contract at all."

He then refers to the decision of Lawrence L.J., in *Raingold* v. *Bromley*, with the reasoning of which he says he entirely agrees, and, after quoting the passage which I have read, he proceeds as follows at p. 220:

"In my judgment, the reasoning of that passage in the judgment is conclusive in this case. It is said on behalf of the plaintiffs, however, that in that case the condition was 'subject to the terms of a lease,' and that those words differ from the words which I have before me—'subject to . . . a lease to be drawn up by our client's solicitors'—and that that is different, in that it imports into this letter a term that this is to be a binding contract, subject to a condition, which condition is fulfilled as soon as the solicitors on each side agree as to the terms of the lease."

It seems to me that the judges who decided those cases were putting a manifestly correct construction on the language before them. I am quite unable to draw between that language and the language which we have here any such fine distinctions as the judge found it possible to draw, and, as I have said, we have in this case the additional phrase "if no agreement is entered into." The appeal must be allowed and judgment entered for the plaintiff for possession and for mesne profits; and the counterclaim must be dismissed. The plaintiffs will have their costs here and below.

[Mackinnon and Goddard L.JJ. agree. A short opinion by Goddard L.J. is omitted.]

BRITISH AMERICAN TIMBER CO. v. ELK RIVER TIMBER CO.
[1933] 4 D.L.R. 286 (B.C.C.A.)

MACDONALD, C.J.B.C.: The parties entered into what is contended to be a binding and enforceable contract, as far as it went, to purchase timber limits, dated June 15, 1931. The said contract has been partially performed. Shortly it provides for a survey and cruise of the limits as preliminary, it is contended, to a formal agreement of sale to be drawn up in fulfilment of cl. 10 of the agreement. That clause reads as follows:

"10. So soon as the cruise and survey as hereinbefore provided for shall have been completed, a formal contract shall be executed between the parties hereto according to the usual form adopted in such cases in the Province of British Columbia and containing inter alia, such of the provisions of this agreement as shall be applicable."

The formal agreement was not drawn up and the plaintiff sues for specific performance of the executed agreement of June 15, 1931. The appellant submits that the execution of the formal agreement was a condition precedent to the respondent's right to sue. It is necessary to consider the said agreement and particularly the said cl. 10. It will be noted that that clause provides that so soon as the cruise and survey have been completed, and this was on September 5, 1931, "a formal contract shall be executed between the parties according to the usual form adopted in such cases in the Province of British Columbia and containing inter alia, such of the provisions of this agreement as shall be applicable." I do not think that there is any such thing as a "usual form" of agreement in cases of this kind in British Columbia. The parties have agreed to the terms of such a form whether it exists or not and have not left any of the terms of the formal agreement for further negotiation. That usual form of agreement may be merely an imaginary one, but whatever it is its terms have been agreed upon by both parties. But in addition to that usual form it is to include "such of the provisions of this agreement (that of June 15) as shall be applicable."

The provisions of "this agreement" show an agreement of sale and purchase describing the timber to be sold; the parties to the agreement; the purchase-price; and the time of payment of the purchase-price. Leaving cl. 10 out of consideration for the moment, I think that agreement would be a complete and enforceable agreement of sale. Clause 10 does not permit of anything being introduced into the formal agreement except what they have assented to, namely, terms usual in formal agreements of that character to which with the added terms of June 15, the parties are in actual accord. There is to be embodied in that agreement the terms of the agreement of June 15, 1931, which are applicable to the transaction and nothing more. It was contended, however, on the argument by appellant's counsel that the agreement of June 15 did not specify a time fixed for payment of the purchase-money. This submission, I think, is not sustainable.

By cl. 2 of said agreement the purchase-money is "to be payable as to $25,000.00 in cash so soon" as the survey and cruise have been completed which was on September 5, 1931; and the balance in annual instalments the times of payment whereof were already agreed upon. I think, therefore the times of payment are clearly established. Those provisions of cl. 2 are clearly applicable to the formal agreement. There being no formal agreement what is left is the agreement of June 15 and nothing additional which must be supposed to be included in it. The purchase-money is to be paid in cash upon the execution of the formal agreement and the formal agreement is to be executed so soon as a cruise and survey have been made. This, I think sufficiently fixes the time for payment of the purchase-money. All the other provisions, except those already performed are, I think, applicable to the formal agreement and are to be deemed to be incorporated in it.

Therefore, I think, it is clear that the parties have agreed to all the terms of the sale. Nothing has been left for further negotiation and in these circumstances the Courts have had regard to the fact that the parties were *ad idem* with regard to the essentials of their contract. The agreement of June 15 is the whole agreement and includes all they agreed upon or intended to agree upon. When an agreement is complete in itself the fact that a formal contract is to be drawn up embodying its terms does not render it unenforceable.

We have been referred to a very large number of authorities which I do not think it necessary to consider in detail, but I shall refer to one or two as reflecting substantially the others. One of very high authority indeed is that of the House of Lords—*Love & Stewart Ltd.* v. *Instone & Co. Ltd.* (1917), 33 T.L.R. 475, at p. 476. In that case the agreement had been come to by correspondence except in one particular. Lord Loreburn, in his opinion said that he had come to the conclusion "that the parties agreed on price and quantity and period of delivery and time of payment, and he thought also on the port of shipment. It seemed also that they intended to make a firm bargain and not to make it conditional upon the completion of the formal document. But had come to the conclusion that they also bound themselves to have a strike clause in the formal contract.

"The inclusion of such a term would make no difficulty if it could be said that by usage or by previous dealing or by law these parties, in binding themselves to a strike clause, bound themselves to something certain, because *id certum est quod certum reddi potest*. But no one said, and no proof was given, that it was so. There might be various kinds of strike clauses. No doubt both parties would have agreed as to the strike clause to be inserted in the formal document had the business . . . . [eventuated], but they had not agreed upon such a clause at the time when the business came to be broken off. If, therefore, their Lordships were to say these parties had made a binding contract not subject to the completion of the formal document they must hold that a contract could be binding when the parties were not *ad idem* with regard to one of the intended terms of it," and he held that the contract was not complete in the absence of a formal agreement including a strike clause. The same view was taken by the other members of the House.

In *Chinnock* v. *Marchioness of Ely*, 4 De G.J. & S. 638, at pp. 645-6, 46 E.R. 1066, the Lord Chancellor said:

"I entirely accept the doctrine contended for by the Plaintiff's counsel, and for which they cited the cause of *Fowle* v. *Freeman* (9 Ves. 351 [32 E.R. 638]), *Kennedy* v. *Lee* (3 Mer. 441 [36 E.R. 170]), and *Thomas* v. *Dering* (1 Keen, 729 [48 E.R. 488]), which establish that if there had been a final agreement, and the terms of it are evidenced in a manner to satisfy the Statute of Frauds, the agreement shall be binding, although the parties may have declared that the writing is to serve only as instructions for a formal agreement, or although it may be an express term that a formal agreement shall be prepared and signed by the parties. As soon as the fact is established of the final mutual assent of the parties to certain terms, and those terms are evidenced by any writing signed by the party to be charged or his agent lawfully authorized, there exist all the materials, which this Court requires, to make a legally binding contract."

It was held in that case that the agent who had made the contract had no authority to make it and that therefore it could not be enforced, but that the mutual assent to terms of an informal agreement may be sufficient where a formal agreement is contemplated notwithstanding the failure to execute it.

In this case there is a contract to which all the parties assented and intended to be bound by. It was intended to be put in legal form which was not done but no term in the contract was left as a matter for negotiation and further their informal agreement was complete. The rule of law is also referred to in *Chitty on Contracts*, 18th ed., at p. 13, in these words:

rule "If the terms in which the proposal is accepted show that the parties intended that a formal instrument should be prepared and agreed upon between them, and that, until that be done, no contract should arise: they will not be bound, until such formal instrument has been agreed upon. But where certain terms have been mutually assented to, the mere fact that the parties have expressly stipulated that a formal instrument shall be prepared, embodying those terms, does not, by itself, show that they have not come to a final agreement, nor does the fact that the acceptance contains a statement that the acceptor has instructed his solicitor to prepare the necessary documents."

In support of that is cited *inter alia Rossiter* v. *Miller* (1878), 3 App. Cas. 1124, and *Chinnock* v. *Marchioness of Ely, supra.* There are cases in our own Courts which show that a contract which has been duly assented to by the parties but in which they stipulate for a formal agreement has been itself enforceable. In *Horsnail* v. *Shute* (1919) 27 B.C.R. 474, at p. 478, this is quoted with approval from *Rossiter* v. *Miller* (p. 1149):

" 'But when an agreement embracing all the particulars essential for finality and completeness, even though it may be desired to reduce it to shape by a solicitor, is such that those particulars must remain unchanged, it is not, in my mind, less coercive because of the technical formality which remains to be made'."

To the same effect are quotations made by McPhillips, J.A., from *Love & Stewart Ltd.* v. *Instone & Co. supra.* It was argued that where an informal agreement is made *subject* to a formal contract being drawn up it cannot be enforced unless the condition is performed. I am not sure that that is strictly correct. It is not correct when all the terms have been assented to according to law. But it does not matter in this case since the drawing up of the formal contract was provided for by agreement and not put in the form of a condition.

I therefore think that the appeal must be dismissed since the parties, I am convinced, came to a concluded contract and the respondent's attempt to now recede from it cannot be countenanced.

[MacDonald J.A. agreed. He made this comment on the appellant's motives]:

Appellant, rueing its bargain, doubtless because of depressed economic conditions, refused to execute the formal contract and claims that, without it, and a consensus as to its terms, the agreement cannot be enforced. In reality it submits that it may capriciously refuse to agree to terms and resist performance. That is the true deduction notwithstanding any contrary pretentions. I do not overlook the fact that appellant professed willingness to discuss a formal contract on the basis that it was not already bound and that its terms should be mutually agreed to. If it ever had in mind the arrival at a consensus in this regard (and I doubt it) it would be, not by carrying out the terms of the main contract but by materially altering it. That could not be considered by respondent. I make no further comment; we are concerned with the legal aspect of the case.

GREEN v. *AINSMORE CONSOLIDATED MINES LTD.* [1951] 3 D.L.R. 632 (British Columbia. Supreme Court). A letter outlining in some detail clauses for an agreement was approved by the plaintiff and signed by the appropriate officers of the defendant company. It requested that the plaintiff "submit to us a draft form of agreement" and concluded with the words: "This memorandum shall be subject to a formal agreement of sale and undertaking being prepared, satisfactory in form to the solicitors of both parties...." WILSON J. found that the agreement submitted by the plaintiff, prepared by overzealous attorneys, did not conform to the meaning of the letter but that this difficulty might have been overcome by further honest discussion, and that the refusal of the defendant company to execute a written agreement was entirely due to advice given it by its solicitor that the chief disadvantage to the company arose out of resulting income tax liability. He held that the letter was not an enforceable contract, following *Chillingworth* v. *Esche*, [1924] 1 Ch. 97. "It is [not] open to me to review the reasonableness or *bona fides* of the refusal to execute a formal contract."

PROBLEM. A signed an agreement to purchase B's farm. The document ended: "This is a provisional agreement until a fully legalized agreement, drawn up by a solicitor, and embodying all the conditions herewith stated, is signed." No "legalized" agreement was ever signed. Do A and B have a contract?

See *Branca* v. *Cobarro* [1947] K.B. 854 (C.A.).

MAY and BUTCHER, LIMITED v. THE KING
England. House of Lords. 1929. [1934] 2 K.B.17

The suppliants, May & Butcher, Ltd., who were general contractors, alleged in a Petition of Right that it was mutually agreed between them and the Controller of the Disposals Board for the purchase by the suppliants of the whole of the tentage which might become available in the United Kingdom for disposal up to March 31, 1923. The material letters for the purposes of the case were dated June 29, 1921, and January 7, 1922. By the earlier of these letters writtten by the Controller to the suppliants it was stated that "in consideration of your agreeing to deposit with the [Disposals & Liquidation] Commission the sum of £1000 as security for the carrying out of this extended contract, the Commission hereby confirm the sale to you of the whole of the old tentage which may become available . . . up to and including December 31, 1921, upon the following terms:

"(1) The Commission agrees to sell and [the suppliants] agree to purchase the total stock of old tentage. . . .

"(3) The price or prices to be paid, and the date or dates on which payment is to be made by the purchasers to the Commission for such old tentage shall be agreed upon from time to time between the Commission and the purchasers as the quantities of the said old tentage become available for disposal, and are offered to the purchasers by the Commission.

"(4) Delivery . . . shall be taken by the purchasers in such period or periods as may be agreed upon between the commission and the purchasers when such quantities of old tentage are offered to the purchasers by the Commission. . . .

"(10) It is understood that all disputes with reference to or arising out of this agreement will be submitted to arbitration in accordance with the provisions of the Arbitration Act, 1889."

By the second letter dated January 7, 1922, the Disposals Controller, referring to verbal negotiations that had taken place for an extension of the agreement between the Commission and the suppliants, confirmed the sale to the latter of the tentage which might become available for disposal up to March 31, 1923. This letter, which varied in certain respects the earlier terms, stated that "the prices to be agreed upon between the Commission and the purchasers in accordance with the terms of clause 3 of the said earlier contract shall include delivery free on rail . . . nearest to the depots at which the said tentage may be lying. . . ."

Some time later the proposals made by the suppliants for purchase were not acceptable to the Controller, and in August, 1922, the Disposals Board said they considered themselves no longer bound by the agreement, whereupon the suppliants filed their petition of right claiming an injunction restraining the Commission from disposing elsewhere than to the suppliants of the remainder of the tentage; an account of the tentage that had become available; and compensation for the damage done to them.

By the demurrer, answer and plea the Attorney-General said that the petition of right disclosed no sufficient and binding contract for the sale to the suppliants of any tentage, and further that it was a term of the contract (if any) that the suppliants should pay a reasonable price for the tentage and that the suppliants were not at the material time ready and willing to pay a reasonable price.

Rowlatt J. held that the letters of June 29, 1921, and January 7 and 18, 1922, constituted no contract but contained merely a series of clauses for adoption if and when contracts were made, because the price, date of payment and period of delivery had still to be agreed: and that the arbitration clause did not apply to differences of opinion upon these questions. The Court of Appeal (Scrutton L.J. dissenting) affirmed Rowlatt J.'s decision. The suppliants appealed.

LORD BUCKMASTER: . . . In my opinion there never was a concluded contract between the parties. It has long been a well recognized principle of contract law that an agreement between two parties to enter into an agreement in which some critical part of the contract matter is left undetermined is no contract at all. It is of course perfectly possible for two people to contract that they will sign a document which contains all the relevant terms, but it is not open to them to agree that they will in the future agree upon a matter which is vital to the arrangement between them and has not yet been determined. It has been argued that as the fixing of the price has broken down, a reasonable price must be assumed. That depends in part upon the terms of the Sale of Goods Act, which no doubt reproduces, and is known to have reproduced, the old law upon the matter. That provides in s. 8 that

"the price in a contract of sale may be fixed by the contract, or may be left to be fixed in manner thereby agreed, or may be determined by the course of dealing between the parties. Where the price is not determined in accordance with the foregoing provisions the buyer must pay a reasonable price";

while, if the agreement is to sell goods on the terms that the price is to be fixed by the valuation of a third party, and such third party cannot or does not make such valuation, s. 9 says that the agreement is avoided. I find myself quite unable to understand the distinction between an agreement to permit the price to be fixed by a third party and an agreement to permit the price to be fixed in the future by the two parties to the contract themselves. In principle it appears to me that they are one and the same thing. . . .

The next question is about the arbitration clause, and there I entirely agree with the majority of the Court of Appeal and also with Rowlatt J. The clause refers "disputes with reference to or arising out of this agreement" to arbitration, but until the price has been fixed, the agreement is not there. The arbitration clause relates to the settlement of whatever may happen when the agreement has been completed and the parties are regularly bound. There is nothing in the arbitration clause to enable a contract to be made which in fact the original bargain has left quite open. . . .

VISCOUNT DUNEDIN: . . . In the system of law in which I was brought up, that was expressed by one of those brocards of which perhaps we have been too fond, but which often express very neatly what is wanted: "Certum est quod certum reddi potest." Therefore, you may very well agree that a certain part of the contract of sale, such as price, may be settled by some one else. As a matter of the general law of contracts all the essentials have to be settled. What are the essentials may vary according to the particular contract under consideration. We are here dealing with sale, and undoubtedly price is one of the essentials of sale, and if it is left still to be agreed between the parties, then there is no contract. It may be left to the determination of a certain person, and if it was so left and that person either would not or could not act, there would be no contract because the price was to be settled in a certain way and it has become impossible to settle it in that way, and therefore there is no settlement. No doubt as to goods, the Sale of Goods Act, 1893, says that if the price is not mentioned and settled in the contract it is to be a reasonable price. The simple answer in this case is that the Sale of Goods Act provides for silence on the point and here there is no silence, because there is a provision that the two parties are to agree. As long as you have something certain it does not matter. For instance, with regard to price it is a perfectly good contract to say that the price is to be settled by the buyer. I have not had time, or perhaps I have not been industrious enough, to look through all the books in England to see if there is such a case; but there was such a case in Scotland in 1760, where it was decided that a sale of a landed estate was perfectly good, the price being left to be settled by the buyer himself. . . .

[Lord Warrington of Clyffe also delivered reasons for dismissing the appeal.]

W. N. HILLAS AND CO., LIMITED v. ARCOS, LIMITED
England. House of Lords. 1932. 38 Com. Cas. 23

On May 21, 1930, Hillas and Company agreed "to buy 22,000 standards softwood goods of fair specification" from Arcos, Limited "over the season 1930 under the following conditions. . . ." The conditions provided that "Buyers shall also have the option of entering into a contract with sellers for the purchase of 100,000 standards for delivery during 1931. Such contract to stipulate that whatever the conditions are the buyers shall obtain the goods on conditions and at prices which show to them a reduction of 5 per cent on the f.o.b. value of the official price list at any time ruling during 1931. Such option to be declared before the 1st January 1931." On December 22, 1930, Hillas and Company took up the option to purchase "100,000 standards of softwood of fair specification." Arcos, Limited replied pointing out that the May agreement had been cancelled, and refused to deliver the goods. In the ensuing action Mackinnon J. found that the agreement had not been cancelled. He interpreted the agreement as a contract to sell, first, 22,000 standards of a *reasonable and* fair specification": and then, 100,000 standards of the same *reasonable* specification. He conceded that "the task of ascertaining what specification answers the description of a fair specification may be one of extra-ordinary difficulty. . . ." Arcos, Limited appealed, successfully. In the Court of Appeal, Scrutton L.J. said, in part: ". . . In my view, apart from authority, considering the number of things left undetermined, kinds, sizes and quantities of goods, times and ports and manner of shipment, as will be seen from the detailed terms in contracts which were agreed, but which had in this case to be determined by agreement after negotiation, the option clause was not an agreement, but what Lord Parker called in *Van Hatsfeldt's* case, 'an agreement to make an agreement,' which is not an enforceable agreement. I should have arrived at this view in the present case without further authority, but in my opinion the decision of the House of Lords in *May and Butcher* v. *The King* (not reported; decided February 22, 1929) to which the attention of the Courts below was unfortunately not drawn, binds me to take this view. We have been furnished with the Lords' record and judgment in this case, which I thought, and still think, showed very unsatisfactory behaviour on the part of a Government Department. . . . I took the view, for the reasons stated in my judgment, that there was a contract; that if no price was agreed, the price under the Sale of Goods Act would be a reasonable price, or there would be a dispute arising out of the agreement which should be settled under the arbitration clause. My brothers Sargant and Eve took Lord Parker's view that there could not be a contract to make a contract, and that, in spite of the language of absolute sale used in the document, there was no enforceable contract. The three members of the House of Lords who heard the appeal thought there was no need to call on the respondents. They said the price should be agreed and was not agreed, and when the arbitration clause spoke of disputes arising out of the contract, its framers forgot that there was no contract. I refer to the judgment for its terms. I am afraid I remain quite impenitent. I think I was right and that nine out of ten business men would agree with me. But of course I recognize that I am bound as a Judge to follow the principles laid down by the House of Lords. But I regret that in many commercial matters the English law and the practice of commercial men are getting wider apart, with the result that commercial business is leaving the Courts and being decided by commercial arbitrators with infrequent reference to the Courts. Commercial men carry on an enormous mass of business under the system of 'string contracts,' under which A, who has made a contract with B, goes to arbitration with Z, of whom he never before heard and with whom he has in the eyes of the law no contractual relations. Their view of damages as a sufficient remedy for breach of contract entirely differs from the law's remedy of rejection. The commercial man does not think there can be no contract to make a contract when every day he finds a policy 'premium to be agreed' treated by law as a contract.

"I have great sympathy with Mackinnon J.'s judgment on that point, which I think proceeds on the lines of my dissentient judgment in the 'tentage' case, but I think if he had had cited to him the decision of the House of Lords he must have held that in the present case there was no contract enforceable in the King's Courts. . . ."

[Hillas and Company then appealed to the House of Lords.]

LORD WRIGHT: . . . The document of May 21st, 1930 cannot be regarded as other than inartistic, and may appear repellant to the trained sense of an equity draftsman. But it is clear that the parties both intended to make a contract and thought they had done so. Business men often record the most important agreements in crude and summary fashion; modes of expression sufficient and clear to them in the course of their business may appear to those unfamiliar with the business far from complete or precise. It is accordingly the duty of the Court to construe such documents fairly and broadly, without being too astute or subtle in finding defects; but, on the contrary, the Court should seek to apply the old maxim of

English law, *Verba ita sunt intelligenda ut res magis valeat quam pereat*. That maxim, however, does not mean that the Court is to make a contract for the parties, or to go outside the words they have used, except in so far as there are appropriate implications of law, as for instance, the implication of what is just and reasonable to be ascertained by the Court as matter of machinery where the contractual intention is clear but the contract is silent on some detail. Thus in contracts for future performances over a period, the parties may neither be able to nor desire to specify many matters of detail, but leave them to be adjusted in the working out of the contract. Save for the legal implication I have mentioned, such contracts might well be incomplete or uncertain: with that implication in reserve they are neither incomplete nor uncertain. As obvious illustrations I may refer to such matters as prices or times of delivery in contracts for the sale of goods, or times for loading or discharging in a contract of sea carriage. Furthermore, even if the construction of the words used may be difficult, that is not a reason for holding them too ambiguous or uncertain to be enforced if the fair meaning of the parties can be extracted. . . .

[Clause 9] must not be construed as if it stood by itself; it is an integral part of the whole agreement; the option under it is given as one of the conditions under which the appellants agree to buy the 22,000 standards, and is part of the consideration for their agreeing to do so. It is accordingly a binding offer, which the appellants are entitled by accepting before January 1, 1931, to turn into a contract if other objections do not prevail. Some confusion has been imported, as I think, into the question by dwelling on the exact words—"The option of entering into contract," and it is said that this is merely a contract to enter into a contract. The phrase is epigrammatic, but may be either meaningless or misleading. A contract *de praesenti* to enter into what, in law, is an enforceable contract, is simply that enforceable contract, and no more or no less; and if what may not very accurately be called the second contract is not to take effect till some future date but is otherwise an enforceable contract, the position is as in the preceding illustration, save that the operation of the contract is postponed. But in each case there is *eo instanti* a complete obligation. If, however, what is meant is that the parties agree to negotiate in the hope of effecting a valid contract, the position is different. There is then no bargain except to negotiate, and negotations may be fruitless and end without any contract ensuing yet even then, in strict theory, there is a contract (if there is good consideration) to negotiate, though in the event of repudiation by one party the damages may be nominal, unless a jury think that the opportunity to negotiate was of some appreciable value to the injured party. However, I think the words of clause 9 in this case simply mean that the appellants had the option of accepting an offer in the terms of clause 9, so that when it was exercised a contract at once came into existence, unless indeed the terms of the option embodied in the clause were not sufficiently certain and complete: before considering this matter I ought to deal with a further contention based on a construction of the second paragraph of clause 9, which is in these terms: "such contract to stipulate that, whatever the conditions are, buyers shall obtain the goods on conditions and at prices which show to them a reduction of 5 per cent on the f.o.b. value of the official price list at any time ruling during 1931."

It is argued that these words read with the preceding paragraph confirm the view that the option was merely for the preparation and agreeing of a formal contract, because the words "whatever the conditions are" mean "whatever the conditions of the contract are." Such an argument involves adding the words "of the contract," which are not expressed, and on the other grounds I do not think that it is correct. I think the word "conditions" refers to conditions affecting other people in the trade, primarily as regards price, and such analogous advantages as are dealt with in clause 8 in connection with the 1930 season. What the appellants are stipulating is that they are to have, throughout the year 1931, such conditions of this character and such prices as will secure to them in any event a clear 5 per cent advantage over other buyers who might compete. On a fair reading of the words, I think the contract is clear and complete in its stipulations as to price. It was contended that no official price list might be issued in 1931, so that the contract price was in that way uncertain and contingent. But in past years in the conduct of this business it had been an invariable practice of the respondents to issue such a list: the evidence and finding in the present case are that an official price list was issued in 1931; indeed it is difficult to see how the respondents could carry on the business unless it was issued. I think that as regards the definition of the machinery for fixing the price there is sufficient certainty here for a business transaction; the issue in 1931 of the official price list is not a mere contingency but a practical certainty: it is unnecessary to consider what would have been the legal position if the respondents had ceased to carry on business or had been dispossessed by war or revolution. Such considerations are not relevant to determining whether there is a good contract or not, but relate to such questions as frustrations or breach of the contract.

The description of the goods offered to be sold in 1931, in clause 9, is also in my judgment sufficient in law ... In practice, under such a description, the parties will work out the necessary adjustments by a process of give and take in order to arrive at an equitable or reasonable apportionment on the basis of the respondents' actual available output, according to kinds, qualities, sizes and scantlings: but, if they fail to do so, the law can be invoked to determine what is reasonable in the way of specification, and thus the machinery is always available to give the necessary certainty. As a matter of strict procedure, the sellers would make a tender as being of fair specification, the buyers would reject it, and the Court or an arbitrator decide whether it was or was not a good tender. It is, however, said that in the present case the contract quantity is too large, and the range of variety in description, qualities, and sizes is too complicated to admit of this being done. But I see no reason in principle to think that such an operation is beyond the powers of an expert tribunal, or of a judge of fact assisted by expert witnesses. . . .

Accordingly I see no reason to think that, as regards the quality and description of the goods, the contract is either uncertain or incomplete. Nor can it justly be objected that the ascertainment of a reasonable specification is impossible. The law, in determining what is reasonable, is not concerned with ideal truth, but with something much less ambitious, though more practical. . . .

In the result I arrive at the same conclusion as Mackinnon J., viz., that the contract is valid and enforceable and that the appellants are entitled to recover damages from the respondents for its repudiation. The judgment of the Court of Appeal was otherwise. Apart from their conclusion that clause 9 was no more than an arrangement to negotiate in the future terms of a new contract for 1931, they held that in any view clause 9 was uncertain and incomplete. Scrutton L.J. held that, "Considering the number of things left undetermined, kinds, sizes, and quantities of goods, times and ports and manner of shipment . . . which had in this case to be determined by agreement after negotiation," the option clause was not an enforceable agreement. With respect to the learned Lord Justice, and for the reasons I have already explained, I cannot agree with that conclusion. He seems to base his conclusion in part at least on the evidence of Mr. Hillas as to how in working out the contract in practice there would be mutual concessions and arrangements. I do not question that, as I have already explained, this would be so, but I prefer the statement of the learned Lord Justice at another part of his judgment that witnesses "were not entitled to construe the agreement or give their opinion as to how it could or ought to be worked." The conclusion of Scrutton L.J., would, in very many cases, exclude in law the possibility of business men making big forward contracts for future goods over a period, because in general in such contracts it must be impossible, as I have already indicated, to specify in advance all the details of a complicated performance. Indeed, Greer L.J. expressly states the view that such contracts are impossible in law, though he regrets the conclusion. He holds that "if there are any essential terms of a contract of sale undetermined and therefore to be determined by a subsequent contract, there is no enforceable contract"; he adds that the Courts have not power to make for parties a contract which in its view it is probable they would have made if there had been further negotiation to deal with matters not already decided. This latter proposition stated in general terms may be correct, but I have already explained why, in my judgment, this contract was complete and enforceable without further negotiation. It must always be a matter of construction of the particular contract whether any essential terms are left to be determined by a subsequent contract.

When the learned Lord Justice speaks of essential terms not being precisely determined, i.e.—by express terms of the contract—he is, I venture with respect to think, wrong in deducing as a matter of law that they must therefore be determined by a subsequent contract; he is ignoring, as it seems to me, the legal implication in contracts of what is reasonable, which runs throughout the whole of modern English law in relation to business contracts. To take only one instance, in *Hoadly* v. *M'Laine* (1834), 10 Bing. 482; 131 E.R. 982, Tindal C.J. (after quoting older authority) said: "What is implied by law is as strong to bind the parties as if it were under their hand. This is a contract in which the parites are silent as to price and therefore leave it to the law to ascertain what the commodity contracted for is reasonably worth." It is unnecessary, in my judgment, to multiply illustrations of this principle, which goes far beyond matters of price. After all, the parties being business men ought to be left to decide what degree of precision it is essential to express in their contracts, if no legal principle is violated. The learned Lord Justices (for Romer L.J. took the same view) relied, I think mainly in regard to this aspect of the case on *May and Butcher, Limited* v. *The King* which Scrutton L.J. thought compelled him to decide as he did. There was there a contract for the sale of certain goods, somewhat inelegantly called "tentage," with an option to buy futher quantities at prices to be agreed upon between the parties when the material was ready for sale. Scrutton L.J. had taken the view in the Court of Appeal that there was an effective intention to contract to sell and buy, on the terms that if the parties did not agree the price it was by implication to be a reasonable price; but he was in a minority in the Court of Appeal, and this House held that there was no binding contract there till prices had been agreed. A somewhat similar decision on another contract was given in the Court of Appeal in the case of *Loftus* v. *Roberts*, where the rule was summed up as being "Promissory expressions reserving an option as to performance do not create a contract." No one would dispute such a rule, and its application to the instrument before the House in *May and Butcher, Limited* v. *The King* has been finally determined in that case; but, in my judgment, the Court of Appeal were not justified in thinking that this House intended to lay down universal principles of construction or to negative the rule that it must be in each case a question of the true construction of the particular instrument. In my judgment, the parties here did intend to enter into, and did enter into, a complete and binding agreement, not dependent on any future agreement for its validity. But in any event the cases cited by the Court of Appeal do not, in my judgment, apply here, because this contract contains no such terms as were considered in those cases; it is not stipulated in the contract now in question that such matters as prices or times or quantities were to be agreed. I should certainly share the regret of the Lords Justices if I were compelled to think such important forward contracts as the present could have no legal effect and were mere "gentlemen's agreements" or honourable obligations. But for the reasons given I feel constrained to dissent from their conclusions—I have only with great diffidence arrived at this conclusion—but I am supported by reflecting that I am in agreement with a learned Judge very experienced in these questions.

[Appeal allowed. Lord Tomlin also gave a judgment for the plaintiffs, in which Lords Warrington and Macmillan concurred. Lord Thankerton's judgment is also omitted.]

PROBLEM. M, a dealer in mustard seed, agreed with G, a mustard farmer, to buy his entire 1961 crop. In the contract, the only price specified was for "Grade #1 seed *only*." G found that his seed was not Grade #1, and, believing that the contract was therefore not enforceable, he sold his crop on the open market at an increased price. Advise M.

See *Montana Mustard Seed Co.* v. *Tates* (1963) 42 W.W.R. 303 (Sask. Q.B.).

FOLEY v. CLASSIQUE COACHES, LIMITED
England. Court of Appeal. [1934] 2 K.B. 1

The plaintiff was a retail dealer in petrol and the defendants were the owners of motor coaches who carried on business at premises adjoining those of the plaintiff at 481 Lea Bridge Road, Leyton.

By an agreement in writing dated April 11, 1930, it was agreed that the plaintiff should sell and the defendants should purchase for £1,100 the freehold property which immediately adjoined that retained by the plaintiff. The sale was made subject to certain conditions, among others that the defendants would enter into an agreement with the plaintiff as to the sale of petrol and/or oil, the terms of which had been agreed between them. On the same date the agreement as to the sale of petrol and/or oil was signed. It recited that it was "supplemental to an agreement bearing even date herewith and made between the same parties as are parties thereto and whereby the vendor has agreed to sell and the company to purchase" the property in the already mentioned agreement, and "whereas the vendor and his present wife are the proprietors of a petrol and oil filling station at his said address and the company are proposing to carry on the business of a char-à-banc and garage proprietors on the said adjoining land and it has been agreed that the vendor shall supply to the company and the company will take from the vendor all petrol as shall be required by the company as hereinafter mentioned. Now it is hereby agreed as follows:—

"1. The vendor shall sell to the company and the company shall purchase from the vendor all petrol which shall be required by the company for the running of their said business at a price to be agreed by the parties in writing and from time to time.

"2. The vendor shall deliver the said petrol to the company from the vendor's pumps now or hereafter on his said land.

"3. This agreement shall remain in force during the life of the vendor and his present wife if she survives him."

Clause 4 dealt with the contingecy of a strike or lock-out.

"5. In the event of the company being wound up . . . the vendor may determine this agreement at any time after the commencement of such winding-up by giving one week's notice in writing of his intention so to do . . . and upon the expiration of such notice this agreement shall cease . . . but without prejudice to the right of action of the vendor in respect of any breach of the company's agreements herein contained.

"6. The company shall not purchase any petrol from any other person or corporation so long as the vendor is able to supply them with sufficient petrol to satisfy their daily requirements and nothing herein contained shall prevent the vendor from selling petrol and/or oil to any other person or corporation to be used for any purposes whatever provided that the company and their servants shall be at liberty to purchase such petrol as may be found necessary to complete the particular journey when engaged on journeys over a distance necessitating the re-fueling of their vehicles.

"7. The vendor shall supply the said petrol of a standard and quality at present supplied by the vendor or such other standard and quality as the company may reasonably approve.

"8. If any dispute or difference shall arise on the subject matter or construction of this agreement the same shall be submitted to arbitration in the usual way in accordance with the provisions of the Arbitration Act, 1889."

The land, the subject of the first agreement, was duly conveyed to the company, and from April 26, 1930, till October 7, 1933, the defendants bought petrol from the plaintiff in pursuance of the agreement at prices charged by the plaintiff in accounts delivered by him to the defendants each week.

Disputes then arose between the parties as to the price and quality of the petrol, and eventually the defendants' solicitor wrote this letter to the plaintiff dated September 29, 1933:

"It appears that although you have supplied petrol to my clients as and when they have required it no agreement in writing as to price has ever been made, nor any agreement of any sort thereunder. My clients have from time to time sent you their cheque in payment of statements of account rendered by you. Having considered this alleged agreement and the aforesaid facts, I have advised my clients that this document is of no force or effect, and therefore, acting on their behalf, I hereby give you notice that my clients do not intend to be bound by any of the provisions contained in this alleged agreement. As from October 8, 1933, my clients will be purchasing their petrol supplies elsewhere."

The plaintiff thereupon issued a writ claiming (1) a declaration that the petrol agreement was valid and binding upon the parties; (2) an injunction to restrain the defendants from purchasing any petrol required by them for the carrying on of their said business from any persons other than the plaintiff; (3) an account of all petrol bought by the defendants in breach of the said petrol agreement from any person other than the plaintiff; and (4) damages for breach of contract.

The defendants pleaded that no price at which petrol should be sold to them by the plaintiff had been agreed; that the provision relating to the supply of petrol did not constitute a binding and/or complete agreement; that clause 6 of the agreement was an unreasonable and unnecessary restraint of the defendants' trade and was contrary to public policy and illegal; and further, or in the alternative, that that provision was applicable when, and only so long as, the parties agreed the price at which petrol was to be supplied. . . .

Lord Hewart C.J. granted an injunction restraining the defendants, their agents and servants from any breach of clause 6 and awarded an amount of damages to be ascertained. The defendants appealed.

SCRUTTON L.J.: In this appeal I think that the Lord Chief Justice's decision was right, and I am glad to come to that conclusion, because I do not regard the appellant's contention as an honest one.

The nature of the case is this: the respondent, the plaintiff in the action, had some land, part of which was occupied by petrol pumps. Adjoining that land was some vacant land belonging to him which the appellants wanted to use as the headquarters for their char-a-bancs, and they approached the respondent, who was willing to sell on the terms that the appellants obtained all their petrol from him. It is quite clear that unless the appellants had agreed to this they would never have got the land. There was a discussion whether this term about the petrol and the agreement to purchase the land should be put in one document or in two, but ultimately it was decided to put them in two documents of even date. One relates specifically to the sale and purchase of the land, and that was to go through on condition that the appellants undertook to enter into the petrol agreement, the terms of which had been already agreed. On the same day the second agreement was signed reciting that it was supplemental to the agreement of even date, that is the agreement for the sale of the land. The petrol agreement included a clause that if any dispute or difference should arise on the subject-matter or construction "the same shall be submitted to arbitration in the usual way." It is quite clear that the parties intended to make an agreement, and for the space of three years no doubt entered the mind of the appellants that they had a business agreement, for they acted on it during that time. The petrol supplied by the respondent was non-combine petrol, but he had also combine petrol pumps. The non-combine petrol was supplied to the appellants at a price lower than that paid by the public, and an account was rendered periodically in writing and paid. In the third year some one acting for the appellants thought he could get better petrol elsewhere, and on September 29, 1933, their solicitor, thinking he saw a way out of the agreement, wrote on behalf of the appellants the letter of September 29, 1933, repudiating the agreement. Possibly the solicitor had heard something about the decision of the House of Lords in *May and Butcher, Limited* v. *The King* but probably had not heard of *Braithwaite* v. *Foreign Hardwood Co.* [1905] 2 K.B. 543, in which the

Court of Appeal decided that the wrongful repudiation of a contract by one party relieves the other party from the performance of any conditions precedent. If the solicitor had known of that decision he would not have written the letter in the terms he did. Thereafter the respondent brought his action claiming damages for breach of the agreement, a declaration that the agreement is binding, and an injunction to restrain the appellants from purchasing petrol from any other person. The Lord Chief Justice decided that the respondent was entitled to judgment, as there was a binding agreement by which the appellants got the land on condition that they should buy their petrol from the respondent. I observe that the appellants' solicitor in his letter made no suggestion that the land would be returned, and I suppose the appellants would have been extremely annoyed if they had been asked to return it when they repudiated the condition.

A good deal of the case turns upon the effect of the two decisions of the House of Lords which are not easy to fit in with each other. The first of these cases is *May and Butcher, Limited* v. *The King* which related to a claim in respect of a purchase of surplus stores from a Government department. In the Court of Appeal two members of the Court took the view that inasmuch as there was a provision that the price of the stores which were to be offered from time to time was to be agreed there was no binding contract because an agreement to make an agreement does not constitute a contract, and that the language of clause 10 that any dispute as to the construction of the agreement was to be submitted to arbitration was irrelevant, because there was not an agreement, although the parties thought there was. In the second case, *Hillas & Co.* v. *Arcos*, there was an agreement between Hillas & Co. and the Russian authorities under which Hillas & Co. were to take in one year 22,000 standards of Russian timber, and in the same agreement they had an option to take in the next year 100,000 standards, with no particulars as to the kind of timber or as to the terms of shipment or any of the other matters one expects to find dealt with on a sale of a large quantity of Russian timber over a period. The Court of Appeal, which included Greer L.J. and myself, both having a very large experience in these timber cases, came to the conclusion that as the House of Lords in *May and Butcher, Limited* v. *The King* considered that where a detail had to be agreed upon there was no agreement until that detail was agreed, we were bound to follow the decision in *May and Butcher, Limited* v. *The King* and hold that there was no effective agreement in respect of the option, because the terms had not been agreed. It was, however, held by the House of Lords in *Hillas & Co.* v. *Arcos* that we were wrong in so deciding and that we had misunderstood the decision in *May and Butcher, Limited* v. *The King*. The House took this line: it is quite true that there seems to be considerable vagueness about the agreement but the parties contrived to get through it on the contract for 22,000 standards, and so the House thought there was an agreement as to the option which the parties would be able to get through also despite the absence of details. It is true that in the first year the parties got through quite satisfactorily; that was because during that year the great bulk of English buyers were boycotting the Russian sellers. In the second year the position was different. The English buyers had changed their view and were buying large quantities of Russian timber, so that different conditions were then prevailing. In *Hillas & Co.* v. *Arcos* the House of Lords said that they had not laid down universal principles of construction in *May and Butcher, Limited* v. *The King*, and that each case must be decided on the construction of the particular document, while in *Hillas & Co.* v. *Arcos* they found that the parties believed they had a contract. In the present case the parties obviously believed they had a contract and they acted for three years as if they had; they had an arbitration clause which relates to the subject-matter of the agreement as to the supply of petrol, and it seems to me that this arbitration clause applies to any failure to agree as to the price. By analogy to the case of a tied house there is to be implied in this contract a term that the petrol shall be supplied at a reasonable price and shall be of reasonable quality. For these reasons I think the Lord Chief Justice was right in holding that there was an effective and enforceable contract, although as to the future no definite price had been agreed with regard to the petrol.

It was said, secondly, on behalf of the appellants that the contract was bad, as para. 6 was in restraint of trade. In my view that contention is clearly untenable. The contract is an ordinary one to purchase petrol from a particular person, and as long as petrol of a reasonable price and quality is supplied—and there is an implied term that it shall be so supplied—there is no undue restraint of trade. It is suggested, however, that the injunction granted to restrain a breach of clause 6 might have this result, that if the appellants moved their coaching business, say to Edinburgh, they would still be required to purchase their petrol in London from the respondent. That, no doubt, would be a ridiculous agreement if it had been made, but it is quite clear that the appellants' obligation to take their supplies of petrol from the respondent applies only to the business carried on by them on the land adjoining the respondent's petrol pumps, and has no application to a business carried on in Edinburgh or Aberdeen or any other place remote from London.

The appeal therefore fails, and no alteration is required in the form of the injunction that has been granted.

[The judgments of Greer and Maugham L.JJ. have been omitted.]

SCAMMELL (G.) AND NEPHEW, LIMITED v. OUSTON
England. House of Lords. [1941] A.C. 251

On December 8, 1937, Ouston agreed to purchase a Commer van from Scammell and Nephew, Limited for £268 in exchange for a 1935 Bedford van and "the balance of purchase price . . . on hire-purchase terms over a period of two years." Later Scammell wrote to Ouston, ". . . we have now received advice from the United Dominion Trust Co. Ltd. of their acceptance of the hire-purchase in connection with the vehicle we are supplying, and we will, in due course, forward the documents to you." A few days later on February 10, 1938 Scammell reported that the van would be ready for collection in a few days "subject to mutual acceptance of the hire-purchase agreement." He added, "We make it a condition of the supply of vehicles on hire-purchase terms that we approve terms of agreement before supply." Before the hire-purchase agreement was entered into, Scammell refused to go ahead on the ground that the Bedford van was a 1934 model and not in satisfactory condition. This ground was abandoned at the subsequent trial. Tucker J. awarded damages, the Court of Appeal dismissed the appeal, and Scammell accordingly appealed to the House of Lords.

LORD WRIGHT [after a careful review of the conflicting views of

Tucker J. and Slesser, MacKinnon and Goddard L.JJ., as well as of both counsel for the Oustons in the House, as to the "true meaning" of the words "on hire-purchase terms"]: . . . There are in my opinion two grounds on which the court ought to hold that there was never a contract. The first is that the language used was so obscure and so incapable of any definite or precise meaning that the court is unable to attribute to the parties any particular contractual intention. The object of the court is to do justice between the parties, and the court will do its best, if satisfied that there was an ascertainable and determinate intention to contract, to give effect to that intention, looking at the substance and not mere form. It will not be deterred by mere difficulties of interpretation. Difficulty is not synonymous with ambiguity so long as any definite meaning can be extracted. But the test of intention is to be found in the words used. If these words, considered however broadly and untechnically and with due regard to all just implications, fail to evince any definite meaning on which the court can safely act, the court has no choice but to say that there is no contract. Such a position is not often found. But I think that it is found in this case. My reason for so thinking is not only based on the actual vagueness and unintelligibility of the words used, but is confirmed by the startling diversity of explanations, tendered by those who think there was a bargain, of what the bargain was. I do not think it would be right to hold the appellants to any particular version. It was all left too vague. There are many cases in the books of what are called illusory contracts, that is, where the parties may have thought they were making a contract but failed to arrive at a definite bargain. It is a necessary requirement that an agreement in order to be binding must be sufficiently definite to enable the court to give it a practical meaning. Its terms must be so definite, or capable of being made definite without further agreement of the parties, that the promises and performances to be rendered by each party are reasonably certain. In my opinion that requirement was not satisfied in this case.

But I think the other reason, which is that the parties never in intention nor even in appearance reached an agreement, is a still sounder reason against enforcing the claim. In truth, in my opinion, their agreement was inchoate and never got beyond negotiations. They did, indeed, accept the position that there should be some form of hire-purchase agreement, but they never went on to complete their agreement by settling between them what the terms of the hire-purchase agreement were to be. The furthest point they reached was an understanding or agreement to agree upon hire-purchase terms. But as Lord Dunedin said in *May & Butcher, Limited* v. *The King,* [1934] 2 K.B. 17, reported in a note to *Foley* v. *Classique Coaches, Ld.* [1934] 2 K.B. 1, "To be a good contract there must be a concluded bargain and a concluded contract is one which settles everything that is necessary to be settled and leaves nothing to be settled by agreement between the parties. Of course it may leave something which has still to be determined but then that determination must be a determination which does not depend upon the agreement between the parties." MacKinnon L.J. thought that in this case the agreement of the parties was complete and nothing was left for them to agree. Whatever was lacking in their agreement could and should, he thought, be supplied by the court by invoking the standard of reasonableness, on the principles laid down by this House in *Hillas & Co.* v. *Arcos,* a decision which has not found a place in the Law Reports, even in a Note, but is reported in 147 L.T. 503, and in 36 Com. Cas. 353 and 38 Com. Cas. 23. The Lord Justice's view, as I have already indicated, was, if I have understood correctly, that there was a contract for a hire-purchase agreement and that no further agreement of the parties was necessary because the court could determine for the parties what was a reasonable hire-purchase agreement and thus the contract would be complete. I am unable to concur in this conclusion. In the first place the appellants at least in their letter of February 10, 1938, expressly stated that the transaction was subject to mutual acceptance of the hire-purchase agreement. This was not demurred to by the respondents. The letter was written before any difficulty had arisen about the condition or description of the Bedford van. It seems to me that this attitude was sensible both from the point of view of business and of law. It is here necessary to remember what a hire-purchase agreement is. It is not a contract of sale, but of bailment. The owner of the chattel lets it out on hire on a periodic rent on the terms that on completion of the agreed number of payments, and on due compliance with the various terms of the agreement, the hirer is to have the option to buy the chattel on payment of one shilling or some nominal sum. . . . While the bailment continues the property remains in the letter. Such a transaction, though not a contract of sale, is used in practice to carry out a sale transaction, with the advantage to the buyer of credit facilities. Though the property in the chattel does not pass while the agreement is current, the hirer gets the use of it. What would be the price if it were a contract of sale has to be increased by whatever sum is necessary for interest and bank charges until the periodic instalments have been discharged. Terms must accordingly be arranged in respect of the period of the bailment as to user, repairs, insurance, rights of retaking possession on the hirer's default and various other matters. A hire-purchase agreement is therefore in practice a complex arrangement. Thus when in the letter of December 8, 1937, the condition of hire-purchase was introduced into what had seemed on the letters to be proceeding as a contract of sale, there was a complete change in the character of the transaction and a complex arrangement had necessarily to be substituted for a simple agreement to sell. It was not even clear who were to be parties to the hire-purchase agreement or what their respective roles were to be. The respondents it is clear were necessary parties. The appellants also were necessary parties because it was their chattel which was being dealt with. The finance company was also a necessary party. But there were at least two possible ways of carrying out the deal. The hire-purchase agreement might be in such terms that the appellants were the letters and the respondents the hirers, and the purchase price was to be discharged by periodic instalments in the form of negotiable instruments, payable to the appellants, thus enabling the appellants to discount the bills with the finance company, who on the security of the bills drawn by the respondents and endorsed by the appellants, would pay the appellants the purchase price at once, keeping as their eventual profit the extra amount which was added to the price for interest and bank charges. Such an arrangement must obviously involve the making of a special tripartite agreement. Another possible method would be for the appellants to agree with the respondents to sell the van to the finance company on the stipulation that the latter should agree to let the van to the respondents under a hire-purchase agreement. Clearly in that case also a special tripartite agreement would be necessary. There was, perhaps, a third possible mode under which the appellants sold the van for cash (at least as regards the balance, for the transaction was, in part, barter) to the respondents, who, having become purchasers, then transferred the van to the finance company on a hire-purchase agreement in consideration of the company advancing the price. Even in such a case the appellants would, I think, in practice be a necessary party because the finance company would require the undertaking of the appellants to transfer the van direct to them and the respondents' concurrence in that undertaking. Otherwise the finance company would be paying cash without at once obtaining their security in the form of the van. Thus a tripartite agreement would be necessary. But I need not consider that case because it was clearly not contemplated by the parties. The correspondence shows that the terms of the hire-purchase agreement were to be matters of joint concern to the three parties who were to agree upon them. What is clear is that while a hire-purchase agreement was being demanded, its exact form and its exact terms were left for future agreement. The true view may be that the letter of December 8, 1937, amounts to nothing more than an announcement that the deal is only to proceed upon a hire-purchase basis, the parties anticipating that the terms of such an agreement would be settled between them in due course.

What I have said will sufficiently explain why I do not feel able to agree with MacKinnon L.J. that there was a complete and enforceable agreement concluded between the parties. He cited *Hillas & Co.* v. *Arcos*, (1932), 38 Com. Cas. 23, in support of his view, but that was a quite different case. There was in that case a contract for the supply of Russian timber in 1930, which also gave an option to the buyers to purchase a further supply of 100,000 standards in the ensuing year. The option clause was extremely bare and meagre, but it was held as a matter of construction that the 100,000 standards were to be soft wood goods of fair specification for delivery during 1931. It was decided by this House, reversing the judgment of the Court of Appeal and restoring the judgment of MacKinnon J., as he then was, that no further agreement was necessary or contemplated. The court could not, indeed, make a contract for the parties or go outside the words they had used except in so far as there were appropriate implications of law, as, for instance, the implication of what was just and reasonable where the contractual intention was clear but the contract was silent in some detail which the court could thus fill in. Thus the condition of "fair specification over the season" 1931 enabled the court with the help of expert evidence to identify what was a fair and reasonable specification and a fair and reasonable distribution by way of instalment deliveries of the contract quantity. Certain other matters were similarly dealt with. In the same way the court has in proper circumstances found itself able to determine what is a reasonable price when the price is not specified in the contract as was done in *Foley*'s case, rightly, as I think, distinguishing *May & Butcher's* case, or to determine what is a reasonable time, or what are reasonable instalments. Many other examples of this principle might be given. And in addition the court may import terms on the proof of custom or by implication. But it is in my opinion a very different matter to make an entire contract for the parties as the court would be doing if the course suggested by MacKinnon L.J. was adopted. That is simply making a contract for the parties. The analogy he cited of a c.i.f. contract is in my opinion no true analogy. These initial letters have a definite and complete meaning under the law merchant, just as much as the meaning of a bill of exchange, or the general effect of a marine contract, is determined by the law merchant. The law has not defined and cannot of itself define what are the normal and reasonable terms of a hire-purchase agreement. Though the general character of such an agreement is familiar, it is necessary for the parties in each case to agree upon the particular terms. It may, perhaps, be that this might be done in particular circumstances by general words of reference. For instance if it were stipuated that there should be "a usual" hire-purchase agreement, the court might be able if supplied with appropriate evidence to define what are the terms of such an agreement. But there was nothing of the sort in this case.

I think this appeal should be allowed because I am of opinion upon either of the main grounds which I have explained, or on both of them, that there was no concluded contract between the appellants and respondents.

[The judgments of Viscount Simon L.C., Viscount Maugham, and Lord Russell of Killowen, who concurred in allowing the appeal, are omitted.]

CALVAN CONSOLIDATED OIL & GAS LTD. v. *MANNING.* 1959. 17 D.L.R. (2d) 1 (Alberta. Supreme Court of Canada). An agreement provided for the exchange of part interests in petroleum and natural gas permits. Calvan was to have power to deal with a permit in which Manning had a 20% interest. The possibility was envisaged that Calvan might itself want to develop the land instead of selling or farming it out. In such a case it was provided that an operating agreement would be drawn up, and if the terms of such an operating agreement could not be agreed on, they were to be settled by arbitration. The agreement concluded: "It is also agreed that a formal agreement will be drawn up as soon as possible." A few days later a clause was added: "It is agreed that the terms of the formal agreement are to be subject to our mutual agreement, and if we are unable to agree, the terms of such agreement are to be settled for us by arbitration by a single arbitrator, pursuant to The Arbitration Act of the Province of Alberta." It was argued that the agreement was unenforceable, first because the terms of the envisaged operating agreement had not been settled, and, second, because the reference to a later formal contract indicated that the present agreement was not meant to be binding. On the first point, JUDSON J. for the Supreme Court, said, "The learned trial Judge was of the opinion that the provision for arbitration in relation to a possible operating agreement was meaningless and unenforceable. If this were so, the consequence would be that contracting parties in the position of Calvan and Manning who do not know what their ultimate intentions may be if they retain the property must provide in detail for a contingency that may never arise unless they wish to run the risk of having the rest of their contractual efforts invalidated and declared unenforceable. I agree with the opinion of the Court of Appeal that such a situation may be dealt with by an agreement to arbitrate and I can see no legal or practical difficulty in the way. No more could the learned author of Russell on Arbitration, 16th ed., p. 10, when he said: 'Since an arbitrator can be given such powers as the parties wish, he can be authorised to make a new contract between the parties. The parties to a commercial contract often provide that in certain events their contract shall be added to or modified to fit the circumstances then existing, intending thereby to create a binding obligation although they are unwilling or unable to determine just what the terms of the new or modified agreement shall be. To a court such a provision is ineffective as being at most a mere "agreement to agree"; but a provision that the new or modified terms shall be settled by an arbitrator can without difficulty be made enforceable. . . .' On the second point, JUDSON J. said:

"Only two questions remain to be considered and these arise from the provision in the amending agreement for arbitration on the terms of the formal agreement. The questions are, first, whether this indicates an intention not to be bound until the formal agreement is executed, and, second, what terms may be incorporated in the formal agreement by the arbitrator. My opinion is that the parties were bound immediately on the execution of the informal agreement, that the acceptance was unconditional and that all that was necessary to be done by the parties or possibly by the arbitrator was to embody the precise terms, and no more, of the informal agreement in a formal agreement. This is not a case of acceptance qualified by such expressed conditions as 'subject to the preparation and approval of a formal contract', 'subject to contract' or 'subject to the preparation of a formal contract, its execution by the parties and approval by their solicitors'. Here we have an unqualified acceptance with a formal contract to follow. Whether the parties intend to hold themselves bound until the execution of a formal agreement is a question of construction and I have no doubt in this case."

F.O. SYKES (WESSEX) LTD. v. FINE FARE, LTD. [1967]
1 Lloyd's Rep. 53 (C.A.)

The plaintiff and defendant entered into a contract whereby the plaintiff was to supply chickens for the defendant's processing plant. The contract contained a clause specifying the number of chickens per week to be supplied during the first year, and stating that quantities thereafter were to be agreed between the parties. Provision was made for submission to arbitration, should the parties not come to an agreement. The defendant repudiated the contract after 18 months, and the plaintiff sued for damages. The defendant argued that the contract was void for uncertainty in that the number of chickens was not specified. The Court held, however, that a reasonable number could be set by arbitration, and therefore the contract was not void.

LORD DENNING M.R.: On this point we have once more gone through all the cases from *May and Butcher, Ltd. v. The King*, [1934] 2 K.B. 17n; *Hillas & Co., Ltd. v. Arcos, Ltd.*, (1932) 38 Com. Cas. 23; (1932) 43 Ll.L. Rep. 359; *Foley v. Classique Coaches, Ltd.*, [1934] 2 K.B. 1; *British Bank for Foreign Trade, Ltd. v. Novinex, Ltd.*, [1949] 1 K.B. 623; and others. I would just say this. In a commercial agreement the further the parties have gone on with their contract, the more ready are the Courts to imply any reasonable term so as to give effect to their intentions. When much has been done, the Courts will do their best not to destroy the bargain. When nothing has been done, it is easier to say there is no agreement between the parties because the essential terms have not been agreed. But when an agreement has been acted upon and the parties, as here, have been put to great expense in implementing it, we ought to imply all reasonable terms so as to avoid any uncertainties. In this case there is less difficulty than in others because there is an arbitration clause which, liberally construed, is sufficient to resolve any uncertainties which the parties have left.

THOMSON GROCERIES LTD. v. *SCOTT* [1943] 3 D.L.R. 25 (Ontario Court of Appeal). An action was brought for specific performance of an agreement for the purchase of premises described in a lease between the parties. The lease contained the following clause:

"It is understood that Thomson Groceries Limited are given the option to purchase these premises for the sum of seven thousand three hundred and seventy-five dollars during the life of this lease. Terms Four thousand dollars cash, balance 1st mortgage. Interest at five per cent. per annum."

The plaintiff exercised the option by letter to which the defendant did not reply. The defendant contended that as the terms and duration of the mortgage were not provided for, the agreement was too indefinite to be considered in law a completed agreement. Held, for the plaintiff. KELLOCK J.A. said, ". . . The case is not one of an agreement incomplete in fact because of something left to be the subject-matter of future discussion, or future arrangement, nor is it one where there is a dispute as to what had in fact been agreed upon . . . With regard to the form of the mortgage, apart from the time for payment . . . [it] should be according to the *Short Forms of Mortgages Act*, R.S.O. 1937, c. 160. . . The mortgage will be payable on demand. Where an implied liability arises from the existence of the debt in cases where there is no covenant for payment in the mortgage, such liability is enforceable on demand. . . . There is no evidence as to what the parties had in mind, apart from what they put in writing. The question then is merely as to what follows in law from that. The act of the appellant's solicitor in drawing a five year mortgage does not affect the matter."

BUYERS v. *BEGG* [1952] 1 D.L.R. 313 (British Columbia. Court of Appeal). The appellant signed an interim receipt in which he agreed to purchase a piece of property from the respondent for $7,000. having paid a deposit of $500. The receipt provided for payment of $2,000 cash, and the balance "$50 per month including interest at 6%. Vendor has the privilege of mortgaging his interest giving precedence over agreement for sale; purchaser to assume cost of mortgage. Purchaser to have the privilege of paying off the difference between cash payment and mortgage at any time without notice or bonus."

The agreement also provided: "An agreement for sale containing the usual covenants in agreements of sale of land within the Province of British Columbia to be entered into on the terms hereof."

Appellant became dissatisfied with his bargain, repudiated it, and sued to recover his deposit on the ground that there was no contract or that there was a contract to make a contract, which is unenforceable. The trial judge dismissed the action. O'Halloran and Robertson JJ.A. allowed the appeal, Sidney Smith J.A. dissenting in agreement with the trial judge. The *Jackson* case was applicable. O'HALLORAN J.A. said: ". . . In this province there is no form of agreement for sale that can properly be described as 'usual'; if there is asserted to be such a thing, evidence ought to have been adduced to that effect. Furthermore even if there were a 'usual' form of agreement for sale the unusual stipulation that the vendor should be allowed to mortgage the land in priority to his purchaser's interest (and the agreement being silent regarding mortgage terms and conditions, its assumption by purchaser, remedies upon default, and protection of purchaser in respect to his instalments paid the vendor mortgagor), in itself made it legally impossible to adopt any 'usual' form of agreement for sale." ROBERTSON J.A. distinguished between cases where the mortgage is to be given by the purchaser: legal rate of interest would apply, the form of the *Short Forms of Mortgages Act*, R.S.B.C. 1948, c. 308 would apply and if no time is fixed payment would be on demand and *Thomson Groceries* is cited with approval. "It seems to me that all the appellant has agreed to is that if a mortgage is given by the respondent, it shall have precedence over the agreement for sale, but he has not agreed as to the terms of the mortgage."

UNIFORM COMMERCIAL CODE
American Law Institute, 1962

2.204. Formation in General.

... (3) Even though one or more terms are left open, a contract for sale does not fail for indefiniteness if the parties have intended to make a contract and there is a reasonably certain basis for giving an appropriate remedy.

PROBLEM. In a contract for the sale of land, the purchaser promised to pay part of the purchase price in cash, and the balance by "Mortgage and/or Agreement of Sale." The vendor subsequently refused to complete the sale. Advise the purchaser.

See *Block Bros. Realty Ltd.* v. *Occidental Hotel Ltd.* (1971) 19 D.L.R. (3d) 194 (B.C.C.A.).

NICOLENE, LIMITED v. *SIMMONDS*. [1953] 1 Q.B. 543 (England. Court of Appeal). In a contract for the sale of 3,000 tons of steel reinforcing bars one clause stated: "We are in agreement that the usual conditions of acceptance apply." DENNING L.J.: "There were no usual conditions of acceptance at all, so the words are meaningless. There is nothing to which they can apply. On that account it is said that there was never a contract at all between the parties. In my opinion a distinction must be drawn between a clause which is meaningless and a clause which is yet to be agreed. A clause which is meaningless can often be ignored, whilst still leaving the contract good; whereas a clause which has yet to be agreed may mean that there is no contract at all, because the parties have not agreed on all the essential terms.

"I take it to be clear law that if one of the parties to a contract inserts into it an exempting condition in his own favour, which the other side agrees, and it afterwards turns out that that condition is meaningless, or what comes to the same thing, that it is so ambiguous that no ascertainable meaning can be given to it, that does not mean that the whole contract is nullity. It only means that the exempting condition is a nullity and must be rejected. It would be strange indeed if a party could escape from every one of his obligations by inserting a meaningless exception from some of them."

DARLEEN
294-4248
∠ 12:00

B. The Power of Acceptance

SHATFORD v. B.C. WINE GROWERS LTD.
British Columbia. Supreme Court. [1927] 2 D.L.R. 759

MURPHY J.: Plaintiff's case, on his pleadings, is, that the letter of April 21, 1926 (ex. 3) with enclosure is an offer from the defendants to plaintiff for the purchase of loganberries. . . I think plaintiff's action must fail because he did not accept this offer within a reasonable time. The causes of this delay are immaterial. The facts are that ex. 3 was mailed on April 22, and was received probably on the 23rd, or, at latest, on the 24th. Plaintiff did not sign the contract enclosed with ex. 3 until April 30—a delay of at least some six days. He mailed the signed document to defendant on the evening of April 30. Ordinarily a proposal sent by mail calls for an acceptance, if not by return of post, at least during business hours of the day on which such offer is received (*Dunlop* v. *Higgins* (1848), 1 H.L. Cas. 381, 9 E.R. 805). In all cases the offer must be accepted within a reasonable time. Here, having regard to the commodity being bargained for, the time of year of the offer, and the necessity, under the circumstances, as shown by the evidence of prompt decision, as to whether an offer would be accepted or not, I hold the plaintiff did not accept defendants' offer within a reasonable time. Action dismissed with costs.

6 day delay

MANCHESTER DIOCESAN COUNCIL FOR EDUCATION v. COMMERCIAL & GENERAL INVESTMENTS LTD.
[1969] 3 All E.R. 1593

BUCKLEY J.: . . . It has long been recognised as being the law that, where an offer is made in terms which fix no time limit for acceptance, the offer must be accepted within a reasonable time to make a contract (*Chitty on Contracts* (22nd edn.), vol. 1, p. 47, para. 89; *Williams on Vendor and Purchaser* (4th edn.), vol. 1, p. 16; 8 *Halsbury's Laws of England* (3rd edn.), p. 71, para. 124) There seems, however, to be no reported case in which the reason for this is explained.

There appear to me to be two possible views on methods of approaching the problem. First, it may be said that by implication the offer is made on terms that, if it is not accepted within a reasonable time, it must be treated as withdrawn. Alternatively, it may be said that, if the offeree does not accept the offer within a reasonable time, he must be treated as having refused it. On either view the offer would cease to be a live one on the expiration of what in the circumstances of the particular case should be regarded as a reasonable time for acceptance. The first of these alternatives involves implying a term that if the offer is not accepted within a reasonable time, it shall be treated as withdrawn or lapsing at the end of that period if it has not then been accepted; the second is based on an inference to be drawn from the conduct of the offeree, that is, that having failed to accept the offer within a reasonable time he has manifested an intention to refuse it. If, in the first alternative, the time which the offeror is to be treated as having set for acceptance is to be such a time as is reasonable at the date of the offer, what is reasonable must depend on circumstances then existing and reasonably likely to arise during the continuance of the offer; but it would be not unlikely that the offeror and offeree would make different assessments of what would be reasonable even if, as might quite possibly not be the case, they based those judgments on identical known and anticipated circumstances. No doubt a court could resolve any dispute about this, but this approach clearly involves a certain degree of uncertainty about the precise terms of the offer. If on the other hand the time which the offeror is to be treated as having set for acceptance is to be such a time as turns out to be reasonable in the light of circumstances then existing and of circumstances arising thereafter during the continuance of the offer, whether foreseeable or not, an additional element of uncertainty is introduced. The second alternative on the other hand involves simply an objective assessment of facts and the determination of the question whether on the facts the offeree should in fairness to both parties be regarded as having refused the offer.

It does not seem to me that either party is in greater need of protection by the law in this respect than the other. Until his offer has been accepted it is open to the offeror at any time to withdraw it or to put a limit on the time for acceptance. On the other hand, the offeree can at any time refuse the offer or, unless he has been guilty of unreasonable delay, accept it. Neither party is at a disadvantage. Unless authority constrains me to do otherwise, I am strongly disposed to prefer the second alternative to the first.

PROBLEM 1. On November 15, B wrote to C, offering to sell C his farm for $15,000. The letter said that the deal could be closed immediately, and that the title would be transferred on January 1st, and ended, "Trusting to hear from you as soon as possible." C was away when the letter arrived, and did not accept the offer until December 10. Meanwhile, B sold the farm to H. Both C and H claim the farm. Advise C.

See *Clark* v. *Barrick* [1949] 2 W.W.R. 1009 (Sask. C.A.).

PROBLEM 2. A sends an offer to B to sell goods, asking for a reply within a week. Eight days after receiving the offer, B replies accepting it. Two days later B changes his mind and withdraws his acceptance. Advise A, who has incurred expense in preparing the goods for shipment.

DOMINION BUILDING CORPORATION, LTD. v. *THE KING,* [1933] 3 D.L.R. 577 (Canada. Privy Council). One Forgie on July 27, 1925, offered in writing to purchase from His Majesty property at the corner of King and Yonge Streets in Toronto. The offer concluded with these words: "This offer of purchase, if accepted by Order of His Excellency the Governor General in Council, shall constitute a binding contract of purchase and sale, subject to all the terms and provisions thereof and which contract shall enure to the benefit of the undersigned [Forgie], his heirs, etc. and to the benefit of His Majesty, etc." An Order in Council was duly passed and a certified copy sent to Forgie, who could not remember when he received it or whether he had received a covering letter with it. The Exchequer Court held there was a binding contract, which decision the Supreme Court unanimously reversed on the ground that there was no written acceptance. LORD TOMLIN: "Their Lordships think that if any notification of acceptance of the offer was necessary, the only possible inference upon the evidence is that there was a notification of acceptance by the sending to the appellant Forgie of a certified copy of the Order in Council.

"But in fact, in their Lordships' opinion, there was not upon the true construction of the contract any need for a notification of acceptance. The language of the offer is . . . not the language of precision, but the meaning which can most naturally be and ought, in their Lordships' opinion, to be attributed to it, is that the offer shall be deemed to have been accepted when the necessary Order in Council has been made."

ration

LARKIN v. GARDINER
Ontario. High Court. 1895. 27 O.R. 125

This was an action for the specific performance of a contract for the sale of land, brought by Jane Larkin, alleging herself to be the vendor, against the defendant, who had, as she alleged, entered into a contract with her.

The defendant denied the making of any contract, and alleged a want of title in the vendor and a cancellation of the contract if any existed.

The property had been placed in the hands of one Nesbitt, a land agent, by the plaintiff for sale on her behalf. The defendant went to Nesbitt and offered $1,900 for the property. Nesbitt stated, as the fact was, that he was not authorized to sell at that price, but that if the defendant would sign an agreement to purchase at that price, he would submit the matter to the plaintiff. Thereupon Nesbitt prepared a form of agreement, beginning "I, Jane Larkin of Toronto, married woman, agree to sell, through John A. Nesbitt as my agent, and I, David Gardiner of the city of Toronto, baker, agree to buy, all that certain parcel." etc.

This was signed by the defendant at about seven p.m. on the 22nd April, 1895, and left by him with Nesbitt. Early next morning Nesbitt went to the plaintiff's house and she signed the agreement. At about one o'clock on the same day, the defendant gave written notice to Nesbitt withdrawing from the offer he had made. At the time he received this notice, Nesbitt had taken no step to communicate to the defendant the fact that the plaintiff had accepted his offer or had signed the agreement. The agreement with the two signatures attached to it, had simply remained in his possession as agent for the plaintiff without communication to any one of the fact that the plaintiff had completed it by her signature. Subsequently the defendant, while always repudiating the existence of any agreement on his part to purchase, and expressly without prejudice to that position, upon being served with an abstract of title, made objections to it, and upon these not being satisfactorily answered, refused to do anything further, whereupon the present action was brought.

never conveyed acceptance

STREET J.: The instrument signed by the defendant, although drawn in the form of an agreement, must, in my opinion, be treated as a mere offer to purchase which might be withdrawn before it had been accepted by the plaintiff; and the only question to be determined is, whether the mere signature of the plaintiff without anything more was a sufficient acceptance.

issue

In *Brogden* v. *Metropolitan R. W. Co.* (1877), 2 App. Cas. 666, Lord Blackburn, at p. 691, says: "I have always believed the law to be this, that whenever an offer is made to another party, and in that offer there is a request express or implied that he must signify his acceptance by doing some particular thing, then as soon as he does that thing, he is bound." And he goes on to say, at p. 692, "But when you come to the general proposition which Mr. Justice Brett seems to have laid down, that a simple acceptance in your mind, without any intimation to the other party, and expressed by a mere private act, such as putting a letter into a drawer, completes a contract, I must say I differ from that."

general rule

exception

Now, I think it would be unreasonable to hold in the present case that the defendant having made his offer to purchase, did not impliedly stipulate that in some form or other he should be made aware of the plaintiff's decision with regard to it—either by a letter informing him of the fact, or by the delivery to him of the contract signed by the plaintiff. I do not think it would be consistent with what we must assume the intention of the parties to have been that the mere signature of the plaintiff not communicated to him, should convert his offer into a binding contract. If I am right in so viewing the matter, then it follows that until the plaintiff had done something irrevocable towards communicating to him her acceptance of his offer, he was at liberty to withdraw it. The posting of a letter to him, or the verbal communication to him, of the fact that she had signed the contract, would have been sufficient. But the delivery to her own agent of the contract with her signature to it, was a revocable act until it had been communicated to the defendant, and was of no more force than if she had kept the instrument in her own drawer after signing it. If it had been possible to hold that Nesbitt was agent for the defendant to receive notice of the completion of the contract, his knowledge that the plaintiff had signed, would of course have bound the defendant, but there is not the slightest ground for any such finding.

In my opinion, therefore, the defendant was within his rights when he withdrew the offer he had made, and no contract binding upon either party ever existed. . . .

[The judgment of Armour C.J. is omitted. Falconbridge J. concurred.]

POWELL v. *LEE* 1908. 99 L.T. 284; 24 T.L.R. 606. The plaintiff applied for the position of head master of a school conducted by the defendants, who were members of the board of country school managers. The board passed a resolution appointing the plaintiff. One of the members of the board without any authority wrote the plaintiff telling him he had been appointed. At a subsequent meeting of the board, the earlier resolution was rescinded and another person appointed. The plaintiff sued for breach of contract. Held, no contract.

COOKE v. *OXLEY*. 1790. 3 T.R. 653; 100 E.R. 785 (King's Bench). The defendant offeror gave the plaintiff offeree until four o'clock in the afternoon to make up his mind whether to purchase 286 hogsheads of tobacco at a certain price. The plaintiff claimed to have accepted the offer before four o'clock, but the defendant refused to deliver the tobacco. Held, for the defendant. BULLER J.: "In order to sustain a promise, there must be either a damage to the plaintiff, or an advantage to the defendant; but here was neither when the contract was first made. Then, as to the subsequent time, the promise can only be supported on the ground of a new contract made at four o'clock; but there is no pretence for that. It has been argued that this must be taken to be a complete sale from the time when the condition was complied with; but it was not complied with, for it is not stated that the defendant did agree at four o'clock to the terms of the sale; or even that the goods were kept till that time." [*Cooke* v. *Oxley* is today regarded as obsolete. It can be best understood if it is supposed that the Court had no notion of a "power of acceptance" but had a notion that an *actual* meeting of minds at some instant of time was required before a contract could come into being. Suppose that when the offeree returned before four o'clock, the offeror had said before the offeree could accept "I know

I promised to wait until four o'clock, but you gave me nothing in exchange. I am not bound by that promise, and I revoke my offer"?]

DICKINSON v. DODDS
England. Court of Appeal. 1876. 2 Ch. D. 463

On Wednesday, the 10th of June, 1874, the defendant John Dodds signed and delivered to the plaintiff, George Dickinson, a memorandum, of which the material part was as follows:

"I hereby agree to sell to Mr. George Dickinson the whole of the dwelling houses, garden ground, stabling, and outbuildings thereto belonging, situated at Croft, belonging to me, for the sum of £800. As witness my hand this tenth day of June, 1874. John Dodds."

"P.S.—This offer to be left over until Friday, 9 o'clock, a.m. J.D. (the twelfth), 12th June, 1874. (signed) J. Dodds."

The bill alleged that Dodds understood and intended that the plaintiff should have until Friday, 9 a.m., within which to determine whether he would or would not purchase, and that he should absolutely have, until that time, the refusal of the property at the price of £800, and that the plaintiff in fact determined to accept the offer on the morning of Thursday, the 11th of June, but did not at once signify his acceptance to Dodds, believing that he had the power to accept it until 9 a.m. on the Friday.

In the afternoon of Thursday the plaintiff was informed by a Mr. Berry that Dodds had been offering or agreeing to sell the property to Thomas Allan the other defendant. Thereupon the plaintiff, at about half-past seven in the evening, went to the house of Mrs. Burgess, the mother-in-law of Dodds, where he was then staying, and left with her a formal acceptance, in writing, of the offer to sell the property. According to the evidence of Mrs. Burgess, this document never in fact reached Dodds, she having forgotten to give it to him.

On the following (Friday) morning, at about seven o'clock, Berry, who was acting as agent for Dickinson, found Dodds at the Darlington railway station, and handed to him a duplicate of the acceptance by Dickinson, and explained to Dodds its purport. He replied that it was too late, as he had sold the property. A few minutes later Dickinson himself found Dodds entering a railway carriage, and handed him another duplicate of the notice of acceptance, but Dodds declined to receive it, saying, "You are too late. I have sold the property."

It appeared that on the day before, Thursday, the 11th of June, Dodds had signed a formal contract for the sale of the property to the defendant Allan for £800, and had received from him a deposit of £40.

Bacon V.C., decreed specific performance in favour of the plaintiff, on the ground that by the original offer or agreement with the plaintiff, and by relation back of the acceptance to the date of the offer, Dodds had lost the power to make a sale to Allan. From this decision the defendants appealed.

JAMES L.J.: ... That shows it was only an offer. There was no consideration given for the undertaking or promise, to whatever extent it may be considered binding, to keep the property unsold until 9 o'clock on Friday morning; but apparently Dickinson was of opinion, and probably Dodds was of the same opinion, that he (Dodds) was bound by that promise, and could not in any way withdraw from it, or retract it, until 9 o'clock on Friday morning, and this probably explains a good deal of what afterwards took place. But it is clear settled law, on one of the clearest principles of law, that this promise, being a mere *nudum pactum*, was not binding, and that at any moment before a complete acceptance by Dickinson of the offer, Dodds was as free as Dickinson himself. Well, that being the state of things, it is said that the only mode in which Dodds could assert that freedom was by actually and distinctly saying to Dickinson, "Now I withdraw my offer." It appears to me that there is neither principle nor authority for the proposition that there must be an express and actual withdrawal of the offer, or what is called a retraction. It must, to constitute a contract, appear that the two minds were at one at the same moment of time; that is, that there was an offer continuing up to the time of the acceptance. If there was not such a continuing offer, then the acceptance comes to nothing. Of course it may well be that the one man is bound in some way to let the other know that his mind with regard to the offer has been changed; but in this case, beyond all question, the plaintiff knew that Dodds was no longer minded to sell the property to him as plainly and clearly as if Dodds had told him in so many words, "I withdraw the offer." This is evident from the plaintiff's own statements in the bill.

The plaintiff says, in effect that, having heard and knowing that Dodds was no longer minded to sell to him, and that he was selling or had sold to someone else, thinking that he could not, in point of law, withdraw his offer, meaning to fix him to it, and endeavoring to bind him, "I went to the house where he was lodging, and saw his mother-in-law, and left with her an acceptance of the offer, knowing all the while that he had entirely changed his mind. I got an agent to watch for him at 7 o'clock the next morning, and I went to the train just before 9 o'clock, in order that I might catch him and give him my notice of acceptance just before 9 o'clock, and when that occurred he told my agent, and he told me, you are too late, and he then threw back the paper." It is to my mind quite clear that, before there was any attempt at acceptance by the plaintiff, he was perfectly well aware that Dodds had changed his mind, and that he had in fact agreed to sell the property to Allan. It is impossible, therefore, to say there was ever that existence of the same mind between the two parties which is essential in point of law to the making of an agreement, I am of opinion, therefore, that the plaintiff has failed to prove that there was any binding contract between Dodds and himself.

[The decision of Mellish L.J. is omitted. Baggalley J.A. concurred.]

QUESTIONS. What are the facts of this case? Mellish L.J. remarked that "Berry does not tell us from whom he heard it, but he says that he did hear it, that he knew it, and that he informed Dickinson of it." Later he referred to the offeree receiving notice "in some way" that the property has been sold. Suppose that Mrs. Dodds, if there were one, told Mrs. Dickinson, if any, at a cocktail party, that Mr. Dodds had sold the Croft place to Smith for £900; and that that was Dickinson's only "knowledge" of the sale, would you say there was an effective revocation?

GERMAN CIVIL CODE

Section 145. An offer to contract is binding upon the offeror unless he has provided for the contrary.

QUESTIONS. If the business world knows of this provision, and customarily provides for the contrary, as is said to be the case, is this evidence that the section is misconceived? Why is an offer revocable? Is the business world more likely to know the terms of the Civil Code than of the Common Law?

UNIFORM COMMERCIAL CODE
American Law Institute, 1962

Section 2-205 Firm Offers

An offer by a merchant to buy or sell goods in a signed writing which by its terms gives assurance that it will be held open is not revocable for lack of consideration during the time stated or if no time is stated for a reasonable' time, but in no event may such period of irrevocability exceed three months; but any such term of assurance on a form supplied by the offeree must be separately signed by the offeror.

NOTE. It was held in *Dickinson* v. *Dodds* to be "clear settled law" that a promise to hold an offer open for a certain time is unenforceable unless there is consideration for the promise or unless it is under seal. James L.J. thought that both parties assumed the contrary, and it has often been suggested that business practice is not in accord with the law in this matter. The section of the Uniform Commercial Code, set out above, makes a limited exception to the rule in the American jurisdictions where it is in force. If a promise to hold an offer open is made under seal, it is enforceable even though there is no consideration for it. But the offeree may still not be in quite as good a position as he would have been in had he accepted the offer before revocation. For example, A makes an offer to B to sell his house, and promises under seal to keep the offer open for a month; in breach of his promise he then revokes his offer the next day. B is clearly entitled to damages for breach of a promise made under seal, but he may not be entitled to specific performance of an agreement to sell the house. This is because specific performance is an equitable remedy, which Equity will not grant in the absence of consideration. The seal makes the promise enforceable at Law, but is not recognised by Equity as a substitute for consideration. The problem was discussed in *Savereux* v. *Tourangeau* (1908) 16 O.L.R. 600.

DICKINSON v. *DODDS.* 1876. 2 Ch. D. 463 (reproduced above). MELLISH L.J.: "It is admitted law that, if a man who makes an offer dies, the offer cannot be accepted after he is dead, and parting with the property has very much the same effect as the death of the owner, for it makes the performance of the offer impossible."

BRADBURY v. *MORGAN*
England. Exchequer. 1862. 1 H. & C. 249; 158 E.R. 877

Leigh, the deceased, wrote Bradbury, Greatorex & Co. as follows: "I request that you will give credit in the usual way of your business to Henry Jones Leigh, of Leather Lane, Holborn; and in consideration of your doing so, I hereby engage to guarantee the regular payment of the running balance of this account with you, until I give you notice to the contrary, to the extent of one hundred pounds sterling. Limit £100." Bradbury gave credit from time to time to H. J. Leigh, whose account with Bradbury, before and after Leigh's death, and before Bradbury had notice of his death, reached £100, and remained unpaid. Morgan, Leigh's executor, refused to pay the guarantee, and in this action, on a demurrer argued that since all the goods sold to H. J. Leigh were sold after Leigh's death, Leigh's estate was under no obligation.

POLLOCK C.B.: We are all of the opinion that the plaintiff is entitled to judgment. No doubt, if this were merely an implied contract which arose from a request, it would be revoked by the death of either party. *Blades* v. *Free* (1829), 9 B. & C. 167; 109 E.R. 63, is an authority that a request is revoked, but a contract is not put an end to, by death. The language here used, "I request you will give credit," is a mere mode of civil expression, and the party using it never meant to request in that sense which Mr. Brown has suggested. Instead of saying "I will thank you to give credit;" or "you will oblige me by giving credit" he says, "I request you will give credit." Whether his death was contemplated, I do not know. The probability is, that if it had been suggested the plaintiffs would have required some notice before the guarantee was determined; but this is a contract and the question is whether it is put an end to by the death of the guarantor. There is no direct authority to that effect; and I think that all reason and authority, such as there is, are against that proposition, and that the plaintiffs are therefore entitled to judgment.

BRAMWELL B.: I am of the same opinion. The general rule is thus stated in *Williams on Executors*, p. 1559, 5th ed.: "The executors or administrators so completely represent their testator or intestate, with respect to the liabilities above mentioned, that every bond, or covenant, or contract of the deceased includes them, although they are not named in the terms of it; for the executors or administrators of every person are implied in himself." The only exception is where the contract is in respect of the personal qualification of the testator or intestate, and that does not apply to the present case. . . . [The opinion of Channell B. is omitted.]

QUESTIONS. Does *Bradbury* v. *Morgan* deal with the effect of death upon an offer? What is meant by a "request"?

OFFORD v. *DAVIES*. 1862. 12 C.B. (N.S.) 748; 142 E.R. 1336 (England. Common Pleas). The defendants wrote the plaintiff guaranteeing *"for the space of twelve calendar months* the due payment of . . . bills of exchange [discounted by the plaintiff at their request for Davies] to the extent of £600" and undertaking to "make good any loss . . . you may sustain or incur in consequence of advancing Messrs. Davies & Co. . . . moneys." The plaintiff discounted some bills which were duly paid, others were not, during the twelve month period. In an action to recover on the guarantee, it was pleaded that the bills discounted and sums advanced were discounted and advanced after the defendants had countermanded their guarantee. The plaintiff demurred that a party giving a guarantee for a definite period has no power to countermand it without assent. ERLE C.J. delivered the judgment of the Court for the defendants: ". . . This promise by itself creates no obligation. It is in effect conditioned to be binding if the plaintiff acts upon it, either to the benefit of the defendants or to the detriment of himself. But, until the condition has been at least in part fulfilled, the defendants have the power of revoking it. In the case of a simple guaranty for a proposed loan, the right of revocation before the proposal has been acted on did not appear to be disputed. Then are the rights of the parties affected either by the promise being expressed to be for twelve months, or by the fact that the same discounts had been made before that now in question, and repaid? We think not.

"The promise to repay for twelve months creates no additional liability on the guarantor, but, on the contrary, fixes a limit in time beyond which his liability cannot extend. And, with respect to other discounts, which had been repaid, we consider each discount as a separate transaction, creating a liability on the defendant till it is repaid, and after repayment leaving the promise to have the same operation that it had before any discount was made, and no more."

NOTE. In the case of a guarantee of a third person's debt, two analyses are possible. The guarantor may bind himself irrevocably for a certain period, or he may only be bound if and when the creditor advances money to the principal debtor. *Offord* v. *Davies* applies the second analysis.

FELTHOUSE v. BINDLEY
England. Common Pleas. 1862. 11 C.B. (N.S.) 869; 142 E.R. 1037

Action for the conversion of a horse. A verdict was found for the plaintiff, damages £33, leave being reserved to the defendant to move to enter a nonsuit. A rule nisi was obtained.

WILLES J.: I am of opinion that the rule to enter a nonsuit should be made absolute. The horse in question had belonged to the plaintiff's nephew, John Felthouse. In December, 1860, a conversation took place between the plaintiff and his nephew relative to the purchase of the horse by the former. The uncle seems to have thought that he had on that occasion bought the horse for £30, the nephew that he had sold it for 30 guineas: but there was clearly no complete bargain at that time. On the 1st of January, 1861, the nephew writes, "I saw my father on Saturday. He told me that you considered you had bought the horse for £30. If so, you are labouring under a mistake, for, 30 guineas was the price I put upon him, and you never heard me say less. When you said you would have him, I considered you were aware of the price." To this the uncle replies on the following day, "Your price, I admit, was 30 guineas. I offered £30; never offered more: and you said the horse was mine. However, as there may be a mistake about him, I will split the difference. If I hear no more about him, I consider the horse mine at £30 15s." It is clear that there was no complete bargain on the 2nd of January: and it is also clear that the uncle had no right to impose upon the nephew a sale of his horse for £30 15s. unless he chose to comply with the condition of writing to repudiate the offer. The nephew might, no doubt, also have retracted his offer at any time before acceptance. It stood an open offer: and so things remained until the 25th of February, when the nephew was about to sell his farming stock by auction. The horse in question being catalogued with the rest of the stock, the auctioneer (the defendant) was told that it was already sold. It is clear, therefore, that the nephew in his own mind intended his uncle to have the horse at the price which he (the uncle) had named, £30 15s.: but he had not communicated such his intention to his uncle, or done anything to bind himself. Nothing, therefore, had been done to vest the property in the horse in the plaintiff down to the 25th of February, when the horse was sold by the defendant. It appears to me, that, independently of the subsequent letters, there had been no bargain to pass the property in the horse to the plaintiff, and therefore that he had no right to complain of the sale. Then, what is the effect of the subsequent correspondence? The letter of the auctioneer amounts to nothing. The more important letter is that of the nephew, of the 27th of February, which is relied on as shewing that he intended to accept and did accept the terms offered by his uncle's letter of the 2nd of January. That letter, however, may be treated either as an acceptance then for the first time by him, or as a memorandum of a bargain complete before the 25th of February, sufficient within the statute of frauds. It seems to me that the former is the more likely construction: and if so, it is clear that the plaintiff cannot recover. But, assuming that there had been a complete parol bargain before the 25th of February, and that the letter of the 27th was a mere expression of the terms of that prior bargain, and not a bargain then for the first time concluded, it would be directly contrary to the decision of the Court of Exchequer in *Stockdale* v. *Dunlop* (1840), 6 M. & W. 224; 151 E.R. 391, to hold that that acceptance had relation back to the previous offer so as to bind third persons in respect of a dealing with the property by them in the interim. . . .

[Byles J. agreed, as did Keating J., who said, "Had the question arisen as between uncle and nephew, there would probably have been some difficulty." The record shows that Bindley simply forgot the horse had been sold. The decision was affirmed by the Court of Exchequer Chamber in (1863) 7 L.T. 835.]

LUCY v. *MOUFLET*. 1860. 5 H. & N. 229; 157 E.R. 1168. POLLOCK C.B.: "Now though it is true that if a stranger were to write and say to a person, 'If I do not hear I will send goods,' the omission to reply would be no evidence of a contract, yet it is different where two persons are actually engaged in dealing or under contract with each other. Then, if a proposal is made to which assent might be reasonably expected amongst men of business, and no answer is sent to it, acquiescence may be presumed."

WHEELER v. *KLAHOLT*
Massachusetts. Supreme Court. 1901. 59 N.E. 756

HOLMES C.J.: This is an action for the price of one hundred and seventy-four pairs of shoes, and the question raised by the defendants' exception is whether there was any evidence, at the trial, of a purchase by the defendants. . . .

The evidence of the sale was this. The shoes had been sent to the defendants on the understanding that a bargain had been made. It turned out that the parties disagreed, and if any contract had been made it was repudiated by them both. Then, on September 11, 1899, the plaintiffs wrote to the defendants that they had written to their agent, Young, to inform the defendants that the latter might keep the goods "at the price you offer if you send us net spot cash at once. If you cannot send us cash draft by mail, please return the goods to us immediately via Wabash & Fitchburg Railroad, otherwise they will go through New York City and it would take three or four weeks to get them." On September 15, the defendants enclosed a draft for the price less four per cent, which they said was the proposition made by Young. On September 18 the plaintiffs replied, returning the draft, saying that there was no deduction of four per cent, and adding, "if not satisfactory please return the goods at once by freight via Wabash & Fitchburg Railroad." This letter was received by the defendants on or before September 20, but the plaintiffs heard nothing more until

October 25, when they were notified by the railroad company that the goods were in Boston.

It should be added that when the goods were sent to the defendants they were in good condition, new, fresh, and well packed, and that when the plaintiffs opened the returned cases their contents were more or less defaced and some pairs of shoes were gone. It fairly might be inferred that the cases had been opened and the contents tumbled about by the defendants, although whether before or after the plaintiff's final offer perhaps would be little more than a guess.

Both parties invoke *Hobbs* v. *Massasoit Whip Co.* (1893), 33 N.E. 495, the defendants for the suggestion on page 495, that a stranger by sending goods to another cannot impose a duty of notification upon him at the risk of finding himself a purchaser against his own will. We are of opinion that this proposition gives the defendants no help. The parties were not strangers to each other. The goods had not been foisted upon the defendants, but were in their custody presumably by their previous assent, at all events by their assent implied by their later conduct. The relations between the parties were so similar to those in the case cited, that if the plaintiffs' offer had been simply to let the defendants have the shoes at the price named, with an alternative request to send them back at once, as in their letters, the decision would have applied, and a silent retention of the shoes for an unreasonable time would have been an acceptance of the plaintiffs' terms, or, at least would have warranted a finding that it was. . . .

The defendants seek to escape the effect of the foregoing principle, if held applicable, on the ground of the terms offered by the plaintiffs. They say that those terms made it impossible to accept the plaintiffs' offer, or to give the plaintiffs any reasonable ground for understanding that their offer was accepted, otherwise than by promptly forwarding the cash. They say that whatever other liabilities they may have incurred they could not have purported to accept an offer to sell for cash on the spot by simply keeping the goods. But this argument appears to us to take one half of the plaintiffs' proposition with excessive nicety, and to ignore the alternative. Probably the offer could have been accepted and the bargain have been made complete before sending the cash. At all events we must not forget the alternative, which was the immediate return of the goods.

The evidence warranted a finding that the defendants did not return the goods immediately or within a reasonable time, although subject to a duty in regard to them. The case does not stand as a simple offer to sell for cash received in silence, but as an alternative offer and demand to and upon one who was subject to a duty to return the goods, allowing him either to buy for cash or to return the shoes at once, followed by a failure on his part to do anything. Under such circumstances a jury would be warranted in finding that a neglect of the duty to return imported an acceptance of the alternative offer to sell, although coupled with a failure to show that promptness on which the plaintiffs had a right to insist if they saw fit, but which they also were at liberty to waive. *Exceptions overruled.*

DAY v. McLEA
England. Court of Appeal. 1899. 22 Q.B.D. 610

LORD ESHER M.R.: This was an action to recover damages for breach of contract. The plaintiffs were claiming a considerable sum as damages, and, before action brought, the defendants sent them ·a cheque for £102 18s.

6d., being less than the amount claimed, with a form of receipt, to be signed by the plaintiffs, that this sum was accepted in full satisfaction of the claim. The plaintiffs kept the cheque but refused to accept it in satisfaction, and sent a receipt on account. It was contended that the keeping of the cheque so sent was, as a matter of law, an accord and satisfaction of the claim, and that the plaintiffs were bound either to take it in full satisfaction or to return it. The contention, therefore, was that the plaintiffs having kept the cheque must be taken in law to have accepted it in satisfaction. Upon the other side it was contended that the keeping of the cheque could only be evidence of accord and satisfaction, and that whether or not it was taken in satisfaction was a question of fact to be determined according to the circumstances of the case. That argument raises the question whether the fact of keeping a cheque sent in satisfaction of a claim for a larger amount is in law conclusive that there had been an accord and satisfaction. It is said that that inference of law must be drawn even though the person receiving the cheque never intends to take it in satisfaction and says so at the time he receives it. All I can say is that if that is a conclusive inference it would be one contrary to the truth. I object to all such inferences of law. This very question, however, came before this Court in *Miller* v. *Davies*. (Not reported.) In that case the action was upon a solicitor's bill of costs for £50, and there was a plea of accord and satisfaction. Before action the defendant sent the plaintiff a cheque for £25, with a letter stating that, in order to put an end to the matter, he sent the cheque for £25, on the terms that the plaintiff would receive it in settlement. The plaintiff kept the cheque and cashed it, and wrote to the defendant that he declined to accept it in settlement and that he required a cheque for the balance. The defendant thereupon wrote in reply requesting the plaintiff to return the cheque if he would not accept it in satisfaction. The jury found that there was no accord and satisfaction. It was contended there as in the present case that the fact of the plaintiff keeping the cheque was conclusive in law that he had taken it in accord and satisfaction of the claim, inasmuch as it had been sent in satisfaction and the plaintiff was bound either to keep it upon the terms on which it had been sent or to return it. This Court, however, held that the fact of keeping the cheque was not conclusive in law, that the question was one of fact, and that the jury having found that there was no accord and satisfaction the Court would not interfere. That case is clearly in point. The question, therefore, whether there has been an accord and satisfaction is one of fact. It was for the judge to decide whether the plaintiffs agreed to take £102 18s. 6d. in satisfaction of their claim. The learned judge has found that fact in favour of the plaintiffs and consequently this appeal must be dismissed.

[The concurring opinions of Bowen and Fry L.JJ. are omitted.]

RESTATEMENT OF THE LAW OF CONTRACTS (SECOND) TENTATIVE DRAFT
American Law Institute 1964

72. (1) Where an offeree fails to reply to an offer, his silence and inaction operate as an acceptance in the following cases and in no others:

(a) Where an offeree takes the benefit of offered services with reasonable opportunity to reject them and reason to know that they were offered with the expectation of compensation.

(b) Where the offeror has stated or given the offeree reason to understand that assent may be manifested by silence or inaction, and the offeree in remaining silent and inactive intends to accept the offer.

(c) Where because of previous dealings or otherwise it is reasonable that the offeree should notify the offeror if he does not intend to accept.

(2) An offeree who does any act inconsistent with the offeror's ownership of offered property is bound in accordance with the offered terms unless they are manifestly unreasonable. But if the act is wrongful against the offeror it is an acceptance only if ratified by him.

NEWSPAPERS AND PERIODICALS SUBSCRIPTION ACT
Nova Scotia. Revised Statutes. 1954. Chapter 199

1. No person shall be liable to pay for any newspaper, or other periodical sent by post to such person, by reason of the fact that such person has taken such newspaper or other periodical so sent by post, from any post office or way office and kept the same.

2. (1) No person shall be liable to pay for any newspaper, or other periodical for which such person has subscribed after the expiration of the year for which such person is a subscriber; or after the expiration of any current year, if such person before the end of such year notifies the publisher of the newspaper, or other periodical, to discontinue sending the newspaper or other periodical.

(2) Notice of discontinuance may be given by mailing a registered letter or by notice otherwise given, to the publisher of the newspaper, or other periodical.

CONSUMER PROTECTION ACT
R.S.O. 1970 c. 82

46. (1) In this section, (a) "credit" means the advancing of money, goods or services to or on behalf of another for repayment at a later time, whether or not there is a cost of borrowing, and includes variable credit;

(b) "unsolicited goods" means personal property furnished to a person who did not request it and a request shall not be inferred from inaction or the passing of time alone, but does not include,

(i) personal property that the recipient knows or ought to know is intended for another person, or

(ii) personal property supplied under a contract in writing to which the recipient is a party that provides for the periodic supply of personal property to the recipient without further solicitation.

(2) No action shall be brought by which to charge any person upon any arrangement for the extension of credit evidenced by a credit card unless the person to whom credit is to be extended requested or accepted the credit arrangement and card in writing, and the obtaining of credit by the person named in the credit card shall be deemed to constitute such written acceptance by him.

(3) No action shall be brought by which to charge any person for payment in respect of unsolicited goods notwithstanding their use, misuse, loss, damage or theft.

(4) Except as provided in this section, the recipient of unsolicited goods

or of a credit card that has not been requested or accepted in accordance with subsection 2 has no legal obligation in respect of their use or disposal.

(5) This section applies in respect of credit cards and unsolicited goods received on or after the 3rd day of December.

PROBLEM 1. A orders from B 1,000 tons of no. 1 widgets at a price of $150,000. By mistake B delivers 1,000 tons of no. 2 widgets, worth $200,000. Is A entitled to keep them without payment?

PROBLEM 2. A orders goods from B, and B agrees to supply them. A then, in breach of contract, cancels the order. By mistake B delivers the goods. Can A keep them without paying?

PROBLEM 3. A writes to B. "I hereby offer to sell you volume 1 of the Acme Encyclopaedia for the bargain price of $39.99. If I do not hear from you by Monday I shall assume that you wish to buy it." B, who wishes to buy the volume, does nothing, but A refuses to supply it. Advise B.

PROBLEM 4. T made a contract with I, whereby T was to supply stand-by tugboat services at a specified pay rate. After the contract expired, T continued to supply the tugs and send invoices. I continued to use the service, but did not pay the bills. Advise T.

See *Saint John Tugboat Co. Ltd.* v. *Irving Refinery Ltd.* (1964) 49 M.P.R. 284 (S.C.C.).

ELIASON v. *HENSHAW*
United States. Supreme Court. 1819. 4 Wheaton 225

WASHINGTON J. delivered the opinion of the Court: . . . It is an undeniable principle of the law of contracts, that an offer of a bargain by one person to another imposes no obligation upon the former, until it is accepted by the latter according to the terms in which the offer was made. Any qualification of or departure from those terms invalidates the offer, unless the same be agreed to by the person who made it. Until the terms of the agreement have received the assent of both parties, the negotiation is open, and imposes no obligation upon either.

In this case, the plaintiffs in error offered to purchase from the defendant two or three hundred barrels of flour, to be delivered at Georgetown by the first water, and to pay for the same $9.50 per barrel. To the letter containing this offer they required an answer by the return of the wagon by which the letter was despatched. This wagon was at that time in the service of the defendant, and employed by him in hauling flour from his mill to Harper's Ferry, near to which place the plaintiffs then were. The meaning of the writers was obvious. They could easily calculate, by the usual length of time which was employed by this wagon in travelling from Harper's Ferry to Mill Creek, and back again with a load of flour, about what time they should receive the desired answer; and, therefore, it was entirely unimportant whether it was sent by that or another wagon, or in any other manner, provided it was sent to Harper's Ferry, and was not delayed beyond the time which was ordinarily employed by wagons engaged in hauling flour from the defendant's mill to Harper's Ferry. Whatever uncertainty there might have been as to the time when the answer would be received, there was none as to the place to which it was to be sent; this was distinctly indicated by the mode pointed out for the conveyance of the answer. The place, therefore, to which the answer was to be sent constituted an essential part of the plaintiff's offer.

It appears, however, from the bill of exceptions, that no answer to this letter was at any time sent to the plaintiffs at Harper's Ferry. Their offer, it is true, was accepted by the terms of a letter addressed Georgetown, and received by the plaintiffs at that place; but an acceptance communicated at a place different from that pointed out by the plaintiffs, and forming a part of their proposal, imposed no obligation binding upon them, unless they had acquiesced in it, which they declined doing.

It is no argument that an answer was received at Georgetown; the plaintiffs in error had a right to dictate the terms upon which they would purchase the flour; and, unless they were complied with, they were not bound by them. All their arrangements may have been made with a view to the circumstances of place, and they were the only judges of its importance. There was, therefore, no contract concluded between these parties; and the Court ought, therefore, to have given the instruction to the jury which was asked for. [Judgment reversed.]

NOTES AND QUESTIONS. If the offeree had personally met the offeror at Georgetown the day after receiving the offer and had handed him an acceptance, would there have been an acceptance? The defendant's letter was written on the 14th and dispatched on the first mail thereafter, on the 19th. The plaintiff acknowledged receipt on the 25th, all in the same month. Why does the Court practically disregard the delay?

If an acceptance is late, or does not comply with some stipulated condition, how can it be "acquiesced" in?

A writes to B making him an offer, calling for a reply "by return mail." B mails a letter of acceptance three days after receipt of the offer. When A receives B's letter he commences getting the goods together. B then wires "I will not take the goods." Result?

MANCHESTER DIOCESAN COUNCIL FOR EDUCATION v. COMMERCIAL & GENERAL INVESTMENTS LTD.
[1969] 3 All E.R. 1593

BUCKLEY J.: It may be that an offeror, who by the terms of his offer insists on acceptance in a particular manner, is entitled to insist that he is not bound unless acceptance is effected or communicated in that precise way, although it seems probable that, even so, if the other party communicates his acceptance in some other way, the offeror may by conduct or otherwise waive his right to insist on the prescribed method of acceptance. Where, however, the offeror has prescribed a particular method of acceptance, but not in terms insisting that only acceptance in that mode shall be binding, I am of opinion that acceptance communicated to the offeror by any other mode which is no less advantageous to him will conclude the contract. Thus in *Tinn* v. *Hoffman & Co.*, where acceptance was requested by return of post, Honeyman J. said: "That does not mean exclusively a reply by letter by return of post, but you may reply by telegram or by verbal message, or by any means not later than a letter written and sent by return of post . . ." If an offeror intends that he shall be bound only if his offer is accepted in some particular manner, it must be for him to make this clear.

HYDE v. WRENCH
England. Chancery. 1840. 3 Beav. 334; 49 E.R. 132

LORD LANGDALE M.R.: Under the circumstances stated in this bill, I think there exists no valid binding contract between the parties for the purchase of the property. The defendant offered to sell it for £1,000, and if that had been at once unconditionally accepted, there would undoubtedly have been a perfect binding contract; instead of that, the plaintiff made an offer of his own to purchase the property for £950, and he thereby rejected the offer previously made by the defendant. I think that it was not afterwards competent for him to revive the proposal of the defendant, by tendering an acceptance of it; and that therefore there exists no obligation of any sort between the parties; the demurrer must be allowed.

NOTE. Must a counter-offer of necessity reject a previous offer? Compare the following suggested by Oliphant, "The Duration and Termination of an Offer" (1920), 18 *Mich. L. Rev.* 201: "Suppose, in reply to an offer by A, B writes, 'I shall want to consider your offer for more than the time which you have allowed me for that purpose because I am so situated now that I cannot return an immediate answer. However, the situation is such that if you want to settle the matter at once, I will close with you now at 5% less than the price you name.'"

See also the following suggested in the same article: "Suppose the offerer says when making the offer, 'I expect you to reject this offer upon first consideration, but I want you to consider it further because I think you will accept when you have thought about it a while.' The offeree immediately sends a rejection which this offerer ignores. On further thought, the offeree sends an acceptance." Is the offeror bound?

STEVENSON, JACQUES & CO. v. McLEAN
England. Queen's Bench Division. 1880. 5 Q.B.D. 346

Action for non-delivery of a quantity of iron which it was alleged the defendant contracted to sell to the plaintiffs at 40s. per ton, net cash.

The plaintiff and defendant had been negotiating some time, and on the 27th September, the defendant wrote the plaintiff the following letter: "Mr. Fossick's clerk showed me a telegram from him yesterday mentioning 39s. for No. 3 as present price, 40s. for forward delivery. I instructed the clerk to wire you that I would now sell for 40s., net cash, open till Monday."

The plaintiff thus had on the 28th (Sunday) this letter. It was admitted that "open till Monday," meant that the defendant would hold it open all Monday.

On the Monday morning, at 9.42, the plaintiffs telegraphed to the defendant: "Please wire whether you would accept forty for delivery over two months, or if not, longest limit you would give."

This telegram was received at the office at Moorgate at 10 a.m., and was delivered at the defendant's office in the Old Jewry shortly afterwards.

No answer to this telegram was sent by the defendant, but after its receipt he sold the warrants, through Fossick, for 40s. net cash, and at

1.25 sent off a telegram to the plaintiffs: "Have sold all my warrants here for forty net today,"

This telegram reached Middlesborough at 1.46, and was delivered in due course.

Before its arrival at Middlesborough, however, and at 1.34, the plaintiffs telegraphed to defendant: "Have secured your price for payment next Monday—write you fully by post."

By the usage of the iron market at Middlesborough, contracts made on Monday for cash are payable on the following Monday.

At 2.06 on the same day after receipt of the defendant's telegram announcing the sale through Fossick, the plaintiffs telegraphed: "Have your telegram following our advice to you of sale, per your instructions, which we cannot revoke, but rely upon your carrying out."

The defendant replied: "Your two telegrams received, but your sale was too late; your sale was not per my instructions."

And to this the plaintiffs rejoined: "Have sold your warrants on terms stated in your letter of twenty-seventh."

The iron was sold by plaintiffs to one Walker at 41s. 6d., and the contract note was signed before 1 o'clock on Monday. The price of iron rapidly rose and the plaintiffs had to buy in fulfilment of their contract at a considerable advance on 40s.

LUSH J.: . . . The only question of fact raised at the trial was, whether the relation between the parties was that of principal and agent, or that of buyer and seller. The jury found it was that of buyer and seller, and no objection has been taken to this finding.

Two objections were relied on by the defendant: first, it was contended that the telegram sent by the plaintiffs on the Monday morning was a rejection of the defendant's offer and a new proposal on the plaintiffs' part, and that the defendant had therefore a right to regard it as putting an end to the original negotiation.

Looking at the form of the telegram, the time when it was sent, and the state of the iron market, I cannot think this is its fair meaning. The plaintiff Stevenson said he meant it only as an inquiry, expecting an answer for his guidance, and this, I think is the sense in which the defendant ought to have regarded it.

It is apparent throughout the correspondence, that the plaintiffs did not contemplate buying the iron on speculation, but that the acceptance of the defendant's offer depended on their finding some one to take the warrants off their hands. All parties knew that the market was in an unsettled state, and that no one would predict at the early hour when the telegram was sent how the prices would range during the day. It was reasonable that, under these circumstances, they should desire to know before business began whether they were to be at liberty in case of need to make any and what concession as to the time or times of delivery, which would be the time or times of payment, or whether the defendant was determined to adhere to the terms of his letter; and it was highly unreasonable that the plaintiffs should have intended to close the negotiation while it was uncertain whether they could find a buyer or not, having the whole of the business hours of the day to look for one. Then again, the form of the telegram is one of inquiry. It is not "offer forty for delivery over two months," which would have likened the case to *Hyde* v. *Wrench* (1840), 49 E.R. 132. . . .

Here there is no counter proposal. The words are, "Please wire whether you would accept forty for delivery over two months, or, if not, the longest limit you would give." There is nothing specific by way of offer or rejection, but a mere inquiry, which should have been answered and not treated as a rejection of the offer. This ground of objection therefore fails.

The remaining objection was one founded on a well-known passage in Pothier, which has been supposed to have been sanctioned by the Court of Queen's Bench in *Cooke* v. *Oxley* (1790), 100 E.R. 785, that in order to constitute a contract there must be the assent or concurrence of the two minds at the moment when the offer is accepted; and that if, when an offer is made, and time is given to the other party to determine whether he will accept or reject it, the proposer changes his mind before the time arrives, although no notice of the withdrawal has been given to the other party, the option of accepting it is gone. The case of *Cooke* v. *Oxley*, does not appear to me to warrant the inference which has been drawn from it, or the supposition that the judges ever intended to lay down such a doctrine. . . .

All that the judgment affirms is, that a party who gives time to another to accept or reject. a proposal is not bound to wait till the time expires. And this is perfectly consistent with legal principles and with subsequent authorities, which have been supposed to conflict with *Cooke* v. *Oxley*. It is clear that a unilateral promise is not binding, and that if the person who makes an offer revokes it before it has been accepted, which he is at liberty to do, the negotiation is at an end; see *Routledge* v. *Grant*, 4 Bing. 653. But in the absence of an intermediate revocation, a party who makes a proposal by letter to another is considered as repeating the offer every instant of time till the letter has reached its destination and the correspondent has had a reasonable time to answer it: . . ."Common sense tells us." said Lord Cottenham, in *Dunlop* v. *Higgins* (1848), 9 E.R. 805, "that transactions cannot go on without such a rule." It cannot make any difference whether the negotiation is carried on by post, or by telegraph, or by oral message. If the offer is not retracted, it is in force as a continuing offer till the time for accepting or rejecting it has arrived. But if it is retracted, there is an end of the proposal. *Cooke* v. *Oxley*, if decided the other way, would have negatived the right of the proposing party to revoke his offer.

Taking this to be the effect of the decision in *Cooke* v. *Oxley*, the doctrine of Pothier before adverted to, which is undoubtedly contrary to the spirit of English law, has never been affirmed in our Courts. Singularly enough, the very reasonable proposition that a revocation is nothing till it has been communicated to the other party, has not, until recently, been laid down, no case having apparently arisen to call for a decision upon the point. In America it was decided some years ago that "an offer cannot be withdrawn unless the withdrawal reaches the party to whom it is addressed before his letter of reply announcing the acceptance has been transmitted." *Tayloe* v. *Merchants Fire Insurance Co.* (1850), 9 How. 390, and in *Byrne & Company* v. *Leon Van Tienhoven* (1880), 5 C.P.D. 344, my brother, in an elaborate judgment, adopted this view, and held that an uncommunicated revocation is, for all practical purposes and in point of law, no revocation at all.

It follows, that as no notice of withdrawal of his offer to sell at 40s., net cash, was given by the defendant before the plaintiffs sold to Walker, they had a right to regard it as a continuing offer, and their acceptance of it made the contract, which was initiated by the proposal, complete and binding on both parties.

My judgment must, therefore, be for the plaintiffs for £1,900 but this amount is liable to be reduced by an arbitrator to be agreed on by the parties, or, if they cannot agree within a week, to be nominated by me. If no arbitrator is appointed, or if the amount be not reduced, the judgment will stand for £1,900. The costs of the arbitration to be in the arbiter's direction.

[Judgment for the plaintiffs.]

RE COWAN AND BOYD. 1921. 49 O.L.R. 335 (Ontario. Appellate Division). A's lease being about to expire, he wrote his landlord B on March 17th about a renewal. B replied on March 24th offering a renewal at an advanced rent of $75. A replied on March 31st saying that he was paying as high a rent as he felt he should pay, "so if you do not see your way clear to renew at the present rental we would appreciate an early reply." On April 5th B wrote that he would call and see A at the end of the month. On April 19th A wrote B, saying, "I have decided to accept your terms of $75. per month." Held, the letter of April 5th left the offer open.

PROBLEM 1. D offered to sell an airplane to N for £27,000, £5,000 payable in advance. No delivery time was specified. N replied accepting the offer, stipulating delivery within 30 days, and sending £5,000 to D's bank to be payable on delivery. D thought there was a contract but later repudiated. Advise N.

See *Northland Airliners Ltd.* v. *Dennis Ferranti Meters, Ltd.* (1970) 114. S.J. 845 (C.A.).

PROBLEM 2. E offered to sell his land to L for $1,800. L replied by telegram, saying, "Send lowest cash price. Will give $1,600 cash." E answered by telegram, "Cannot reduce price," upon which L wrote accepting the original offer. E refused to sell. Advise L.

See *Livingstone* v. *Evans* [1925] 4 D.L.R. 269 (Alta. S.C.).

BRITISH ROAD SERVICES LTD. v. ARTHUR V. CRUTCHLEY & CO. LTD.
[1968] 1 All E.R. 811 (C.A.)

The plaintiff carriers delivered a truck load of whisky to the defendants' warehouse. During the night, the whisky was stolen. The plaintiffs sought damages for the loss of whisky. The major issue in the case was the question of the defendants' negligence, but the defendants also claimed that their liability was limited to £800 per ton, according to the conditions under which they received the goods.

LORD PEARSON: . . . Now I come to the terms of the contract between the plaintiffs and the defendants. It was not proved that the plaintiffs' conditions of sub-contracting were ever sent to the defendants, and the defendants in evidence denied that they were sub-contractors to the plaintiffs. The plaintiffs' form of delivery note contained the words: "All goods are carried on the [plaintiffs'] conditions of carriage, copies of which can be obtained upon application to any office of the [plaintiffs]."

Under the long-established course of business between the parties, however, the plaintiffs' driver brought his delivery note into the defendants' office at the Cotton Street warehouse and asked in effect if he could bring his load into the warehouse. If there were room in the warehouse, the permission would be given, and the delivery note would be rubber-stamped by the defendants with the words "Received under A.V.C. conditions," followed by the date and the address of the warehouse. The delivery note, thus converted into a receipt note, would be handed back to the plaintiff's driver and he would bring his load into the warehouse as instructed by the warehouse foreman. If this had only happened once, there would have been a doubt whether the plaintiffs' driver was their agent to accept the defendants' special contractual terms. This, however, happened frequently and regularly over many years at this and other warehouses of the defendants. Also the defendants' invoices contained the words: "All goods are handled subject to conditions of carriage copies of which can be obtained on application." It may perhaps be material to add that the defendants' conditions of carriage were not peculiar to them, but were the conditions of carriage of Road Haulage Association, Ltd. At any rate, I agree with the decision of the judge that the plaintiffs' conditions were not, and the defendants' conditions were, incorporated into the contract between these parties. The effect was that, while the nature of the defendants' liability as bailees to the plaintiffs was un-affected, the liability was limited in amount to £800 per ton.

ANGLO-NEWFOUNDLAND FISH CO. v. SMITH & CO. LTD. 1902. 35 N.S.R. 267 (Nova Scotia Supreme Court *en banc*). The plaintiffs agreed to buy 2,000 to 3,000 quintals of cod "cleaned on the face, free from black skin and liver and blood marks" at twenty-five cents above the Halifax price for ordinary bank cod not cleaned free of black skin. The defendants couldn't "see that if the fish is cured, washed, and made clean in every respect, that the dark skin on napes would make any difference to any market." The plaintiffs answered, "It is done on all the codfish . . . that is caught and cured in Ireland, Shetland, and Faroe Island, and, for that one reason, codfish of these countries will sell at a fair price, when ours can't be sold at all." The defendants replied promising to furnish the fish at the price offered and concluded, "I will do my best in regard to removing the black skin." The plaintiffs then promised to take 2,500 quin-tals "according to previous arrangement as to quality and price." Defend-ants delivered no fish and in this action denied any contract. Townshend J. held for the plaintiffs and the Court *en banc* divided two to two in dis-missing the appeal. WEATHERBE J.: ". . . . Commerce could not be carried on, and no contract could ever be concluded if merchants were required to use the precision of solicitors in contracts with each other. All that is required is to find out what, in reading a letter, is the main idea intended to be conveyed. . . . after using words agreeing to supply the fish asked for, defendants merely expressed a determination not to be outdone by those of other countries. . . ." GRAHAM E.J.: ". . . . There is, in my opinion, a material difference between the plaintiffs' proposal and that of the defend-ants. The plaintiffs proposed that the defendants should enter into an un-conditional contract. . . . The defendants . . . would only undertake to do their best in regard to removing the black skin, etc. The removal of all black skin may have been physically possible, but it was, in their business, an untried thing; it was a question of degree in view of securing an entry into a new market, and might require such an amount of labour and care as to render it commercially impossible. And the defendants protected themselves. . . ."

UNIFORM COMMERCIAL CODE
American Law Institute, 1962

Section 2-207. Additional terms in Acceptance or Confirmation.

(1) A definite and seasonable expression of acceptance or a written confirmation which is sent within a reasonable time operates as an acceptance even though it states terms additional to or different from those offered or agreed upon, unless acceptance is expressly made conditional on assent to the additional or different terms.

(2) The additional terms are to be construed as proposals for addition to the contract. Between merchants such terms become part of the contract unless:

(a)   the offer expressly limits acceptance to the terms of the offer;

(b)   they materially alter it; or

(c)   notification of objection to them has already been given or is given within a reasonable time after notice of them is received.

(3) Conduct by both parties which recognises the existence of a contract is sufficient to establish a contract for sale although the writings of the parties do not otherwise establish a contract. In such case the terms of the particular contract consist of those terms of which the writings of the parties agree, together with any supplementary terms incorporated under any other provisions of this Act.

NOTE. Section 2-207 has given rise to much litigation, and to many conflicting interpretations. The fundamental' difficulty is that the basic provision of the section involves a contradiction. One court was driven to announce that its application would lead to an "absurdity" (*Roto-Lith Ltd.* v. *F.P. Bartlett & Co. Inc.* (1962) 297 F. 2d 497 (C.A.-1)). A definite expression of acceptance operates as an acceptance even though it states terms additional to or different from those offered. But what is an expression of acceptance? It is a manifestation of assent to the offeror's terms. The statement of terms "additional to or different from" the offeror's is, of course, a manifestation of dissent from those terms. So what meaning can be given to a provision that an assent operates as an assent even though it is not an assent. The use of the word "definite" does nothing to assist, and suggests that the draftsman was uneasy about the basic concept of the provision.

See Corman, "Formation of Contracts for the Sale of Goods" (1967) 42 Wash. L.R. 347.

C. Contracts Negotiated by Correspondence

Several kinds of problems arise where parties negotiate by correspondence. The cases below deal, first, with the problem of offers that cross in the mail, second, with the problem of delay in transmission of the offer, third, with the problem of loss or delay of a message of acceptance, fourth, with the problem of revocation of an offer. Reference is also made to the problem of overtaking communications with contradictory messages.

An entirely different type of problem arises when the contracting parties live in different provinces or countries. In legal matters the law of Ontario is not the law of British Columbia or of any other province or state. Each provincial jurisdiction is as foreign to the other as, say, a state of the United States is to France. Sometimes the question for the Court is which law to apply in case of a dispute. But more often the question of where a contract is made is relevant to the problem of whether the Court should take jurisdiction over the dispute. In some jurisdictions service of a writ outside the jurisdiction is only allowed if the contract was made within the jurisdiction, and for this purpose the Court may ask where a contract is made. The courts usually answer this by asking where the letter of acceptance was dispatched or received, on the theory that the contract was made where the last act necessary for its creation took place. Whether this is a sound test need not concern us now, but it is important to know that the court is deciding not when a contract comes into existence, but where, and for a very special purpose. The courts assume that the contractual analysis is relevant to the solution of the jurisdictional problem. Is this assumption justified?

See, on the problems of this section generally, Fuller, *Basic Contract Law*, pp. 181-6.

TINN v. HOFFMAN AND COMPANY
England. Exchequer Chamber. 1873. 29 L.T.R. 271

Tinn, a manufacturer of iron products, carried on an extended correspondence with Hoffman and Company, iron merchants, about the purchase of 800 tons of iron for which Hoffman wanted 69s. a ton. Tinn proposed to increase his order to 1200 tons if Hoffman would lower his price. On November 28, 1871, Hoffman wrote offering a "further 400 tons . . . at the same price we quoted you by ours of the 24th inst. . . . Kindly let us have your reply by return of post as to whether you accept our offers of together 1,200 tons. . . ." On the same day Tinn wrote, "You can enter me 800 tons on the terms and conditions named in your favour of the 24th inst., but I trust you will enter the other 400, making in all, 1,200 tons, referred to in my last, at 68s. per ton." The next day Hoffman wrote rejecting "your esteemed order for 1,200 tons . . . at a lower price than 69s., and even that offer we can only leave you on hand for reply by tomorrow before twelve o'clock." On December 1, Tinn wired, "Book other 400 tons pig iron for me, same terms and conditions as before." The views of two judges (only on the issue whether the letters of November 28 constituted a contract) are reproduced:

HONEYMAN J. (dissenting): . . . What, then is the effect when the two letters are written on the same day and crossed each other in the post? Does it make any difference? . . . I cannot see why the fact of the letters crossing each other should prevent their making a good contract. If I say I am willing to buy a man's house on certain terms, and he at the same moment says that he is willing to sell it, and these two letters are posted so that they are irrevocable with respect to the writers, why should that not constitute a good contract. The parties are *ad idem* at one and the same moment. On these grounds it appears to me that the judgment of the court below was wrong, and ought to be reversed, I speak with some hesitation in this case when I find that the opinion of the majority of my brothers is against me, and also when the question turns entirely on the construction of a somewhat ambiguously written letter.

BRETT J.: . . . If [the defendant's letter of November 28th] were a separate offer, which I should think it was not, it then would be a new offer with regard to 800 tons, and a separate offer with regard to 400 tons, but, even if it were so, I should think that the new offer with regard to the 800 tons had never been accepted, so as to make a binding contract. The new offer would not, in my opinion, be accepted, by the fact of the plaintiff's letter of November 28th crossing it. If the defendants' letter of November 28th is a new offer of the 800 tons, that could not be accepted by the plaintiff until it came to his knowledge, and his letter of November 28th could only be considered as a cross offer. Put it thus: If I write to a person and say, "If you can give me £6000 for my house, I will sell it to you," and on the same day, and before the letter reaches him, he writes to me saying, "If you will sell me your house for £6000 I will buy it," that would be two offers crossing each other, and cross offers are not an acceptance of each other, therefore there will be no offer of either party accepted by the other. That is the case where the contract is to be made by the letters, and by the letters only. I think it would be different if there were already a contract in fact made in words, and then the parties were to write letters to each other, which crossed in the post, those might make a very good memorandum of the contract already made, unless the Statute of Frauds intervened. But where the contract is to be made by the letters themselves, you cannot make it by cross offers, and say that the contract was made by one party accepting the offer which was made to him. It seems to me, therefore, in both views, that the judgment of the court below was right.

[The judgments of eight judges favoured the defendants, not always for the same reasons. Three judges dissented.]

NOTE. Is the debate over "cross offers" merely conceptual or is there a matter of substance involved? If, as it is sometimes said, especially in the older cases, the offeror is regarded as making his offer continually, then surely cross offers result in a "meeting of minds." Equally, the cross offer cannot be said to be an answer to the other offer. What then is the issue of substance? Is there a good reason for holding no contract? If one offeror, excepting that he has twenty-four hours before delivery of his offer, receives a better proposal, should he not be free to revoke his offer by telegraph or telephone? Reconsider why offers are revocable.

ADAMS v. LINDSELL
England. King's Bench. 1818. 1 B. & Ald. 681; 106 E.R. 250

Action for non-delivery of wool according to agreement. At the trial at the last Lent Assizes for the county of Worcester, before Burrough J., it appeared that the defendants, who were dealers in wool at St. Ives, in the county of Huntingdon, had on Tuesday, the 2nd of September, 1817, written the following letter to the plaintiffs who were woollen manufacturers residing in Bromsgrove, Worcestershire: "We now offer you eight hundred tods of wether fleeces, of a good fair quality of our country wool, at 35s. 6d. per tod, to be delivered at Leicester, and to be paid for by two months' bill in two months, and to be weighed up by your agent within fourteen days, receiving your answer in course of post."

This letter was misdirected by the defendants to Bromsgrove, Leicestershire, in consequence of which it was not received by the plaintiffs in Worcestershire till 7 p.m. on Friday, September 5th. On that evening the plaintiffs wrote an answer, agreeing to accept the wool on the terms proposed. The course of the post between St. Ives and Bromsgrove is through London, and consequently this answer was not received by the defendants till Tuesday, September 9th. On the Monday, September 8th, the defendants not having, as they expected, received an answer on Sunday, September 7th (which, in case the letter had not been misdirected would have been in the usual course of the post), sold the wool in question to another person. Under these circumstances the learned Judge held that the delay having been occasioned by the neglect of the defendants, the jury must take it that the answer did come back in due course of post; and that then the defendants were liable for the loss that had been sustained: and the plaintiffs accordingly recovered a verdict.

Jervis having in Easter Term obtained a rule nisi for a new trial, on the ground that there was no binding contract between the parties.

Dauncy, Puller, and Richardson showed cause. They contended that, at the moment of the acceptance of the offer of the defendants by the plaintiffs, the former became bound. And that was on Friday evening, when there had been no change of circumstances. They were then stopped by the Court, who called upon Jervis and Campbell in support of the rule. They relied on *Payne* v. *Cave* (1789), 100 E.R. 502, and more particularly on *Cooke* v. *Oxley* (1790), 700 E.R. 785. So here the defendants who have proposed by letter to sell this wool, are not to be held liable, even though it be now admitted that the answer did come back in due course of post. Till the plaintiffs' answer was actually received, there could be no binding contract between the parties; and before then the defendants had retracted their offer by selling the wool to other persons.

But the Court said, that if that were so, no contract could ever be completed by the post. For if the defendants were not bound by their offer when accepted by the plaintiffs till the answer was received, then the plaintiffs ought not to be bound till after they had received the notification that the defendants had received their answer and assented to it. And so it might go on *ad infinitum*. The defendants must be considered in law as making, during every instant of the time their letter was travelling, the same identical offer to the plaintiffs; and then the contract is completed by the acceptance of it by the latter. Then as to the delay in notifying the acceptance, that arises entirely from the mistake of the defendants, and it therefore must be taken as against them that the plaintiffs' answer was received in the course of post.

[Rule discharged.]

QUESTIONS. Do you agree with the Court's "ad infinitum" argument? Because a sequence of events may appear to go on forever is that a sufficient reason for cutting off the sequence after the first event? Why not the second? Is there good reason for preferring the offeree's convenience to the offeror's?

HOUSEHOLD INSURANCE CO. v. GRANT
England. Court of Appeal. 1879. 4 Ex.D. 216

THESIGER L.J.: In this case the defendant made an application for shares in the plaintiffs' company under circumstances from which we must imply that he authorized the company, in the event of their allotting to him the shares applied for, to send the notice of allotment by post. The company did allot him the shares, and duly addressed to him and posted a letter containing the notice of allotment, but upon the finding of the jury it must be taken that the letter never reached its destination. In this state of circumstances Lopes J. has decided that the defendant is liable as a shareholder.

He based his decision mainly upon the ground that the point for his consideration was covered by authority binding upon him, and I am of opinion that he did so rightly, and that it is covered by authority equally binding upon this Court.

The leading case upon the subject is *Dunlop* v. *Higgins* (1848), 9 E.R. 805. It is true that Lord Cottenham might have decided that case without deciding the point raised in this. But it appears to me equally true that he did not do so, and that he preferred to rest and did rest his judgment as to one of the matters of exception before him upon a principle which embraces and governs the present case. If so the Court is as much bound to apply that principle, constituting as it did a *ratio decidendi*, as it is to follow that exact decision itself. The exception was that the Lord Justice General directed the jury in point of law that, if the pursuers posted their acceptance of the offer in due time according to the usage of trade they were not responsible for any casualties in the post office establishment. This direction was wide enough in its terms to include the case of the acceptance never being delivered at all; and Lord Cottenham, in expressing his opinion that it was not open to objection, did so after putting the case of a letter containing a notice of dishonour posted by the holder of a bill of exchange in proper time, in which case he said, "Whether that letter be delivered or not is a matter quite immaterial, because for accidents happening at the post office he is not responsible." In short, Lord Cottenham appears to me to have held that, as a rule, a contract formed by correspondence through the post is complete as soon as the letter accepting an offer is put into the post, and is not put an end to in the event of the letter never being delivered. My view of the effect of *Dunlop* v. *Higgins* is that taken by James L.J., in *Harris' Case* (1872), 7 Ch. App. 587, where he speaks of the former case as "a case which is binding upon us, and in which every principle argued before us was discussed at length by the Lord Chancellor in giving judgment." He adds, the Lord Chancellor "arrived at the conclusion that the posting of the letter of acceptance is the completion of the contract; that is to say, the moment one man has made an offer, and the other has done something binding himself to that offer, then the contract is complete and neither party can afterwards escape from it.". . . Now, whatever in abstract discussion may be said as to the legal notion of its being necessary, in order to the effecting of a valid and binding contract, that the minds of the parties should be brought together at one and the same moment, that notion is practically the foundation of English law upon the subject of the formation of contract. Unless therefore a contract constituted by correspondence is absolutely concluded at the moment that the continuing offer is accepted by the person to whom the offer is addressed, it is difficult to see how the two minds are ever to be brought together at one and the same moment. This was pointed out by Lord Ellenborough in the case of *Adams* v. *Lindsell* (1818), 106 E.R. 250 which is a recognized authority upon this branch of the law. But on the other hand it is a principle of law, as well established as the legal notion to which I have referred, that the minds of the two parties must be brought together by mutual communication. An acceptance, which only remains in the breast of the acceptor without being actually and by legal implication communicated to the offeror, is no binding acceptance. . . . How then are these elements of law to be harmonized in the case of contracts formed by correspondence through the post? I see no better mode than that of treating the post office as the agent of both parties. . . . But if the post office be such common agent, then it seems to me to follow that, as soon as the letter of acceptance is delivered to the post office, the contract is made as complete and as final and absolutely binding as if the acceptor had put his letter into the hands of a messenger sent by the offeror himself as his agent to deliver the offer and receive the acceptance. What other principle can be adopted short of holding that the contract is not complete by acceptance until and except from the time that the letter containing the acceptance is delivered to the offeror, a principle which has been distinctly negatived. . . . The acceptor, in posting the letter, has, to use the language of Lord Blackburn, in *Brogden* v. *Directors of Metropolitan Ry. Co.* (1877), 2 App. Cas. 666, 691, "put it out of his control and done an extraneous act which clenches the matter, and shows beyond all doubt that each side is bound." How then can a casualty in the post, whether resulting in delay, which in commercial transactions is often as bad as no delivery, or in non-delivery, unbind the parties or unmake the contract? To me it appears that in practice a contract complete upon the acceptance of an offer being posted, but liable to be put an end to by an accident in the post, would be more mischievous than a contract only binding upon the parties to it upon the acceptance actually reaching the offeror, and I can see no principle of law from which such an anomalous contract can be deduced.

There is no doubt that the implication of a complete, final, and absolutely binding contract being formed, as soon as the acceptance of an offer is posted, may in some cases lead to inconvenience and hardship. But such there must be at times in every view of the law. It is impossible in transactions which pass between parties at a distance, and have to be carried on through the medium of correspondence, to adjust conflicting rights between innocent parties, so as to make the consequences of mistake on the part of a mutual agent fall equally upon the shoulders of both. At the same time I am not prepared to admit that the implication in question will lead to any great or general inconvenience or hardship. An offeror, if he chooses, may always make the formation of the contract which he proposes dependent upon the actual communication to himself of the acceptance. If he trusts to the post he trusts to a means of communication which, as a rule, does not fail, and if no answer to his offer is received by him, and the matter is of importance to him he can make inquiries of the person to whom his offer was addressed. On the other hand, if the contract is not finally concluded, except in the event of acceptance actually reaching the offeror, the door would be opened to the perpetration of much fraud, and, putting aside this consideration, considerable delay in commercial transactions, in which despatch is, as a rule, of the greatest consequence, would be occasioned; for the acceptor would never be entirely safe in acting upon his acceptance until he had received notice that his letter of acceptance had reached its destination.

Upon balance of conveniences and inconveniences it seems to me, applying with slight alterations the language of the Supreme Court of the United States in *Tayloe* v. *Merchants Fire Insurance Co.* (1850), 9 Howard S. Ct. Rep. 390, more consistent with the acts and declarations of the parties in this case to consider the contract complete and absolutely binding on the transmission of the notice of allotment through the post, as the medium of communication that the parties themselves contemplated, instead of postponing its completion until the notice had been received by the defendant. Upon principle, therefore, as well as authority, I think that the judgment of Lopes J. was right and should be affirmed, and that this appeal should therefore be dismissed.

BRAMWELL L.J. (dissenting): The question in this case is not whether the post office was a proper medium of communication from the plaintiffs to the defendant. There is no doubt that it is so in all cases where personal service is not required. It is an ordinary mode of communication, and every person who gives anyone the right to communicate with him, gives the right to communicate in an ordinary manner and so in this way and to this extent, that if an offer were made by letter in the morning to a person at a place within half-an-hour's railway journey of the offeror, I should say that an acceptance by post, though it did not reach the offeror till the next morning, would be in time. Nor is the question whether, when the letter reaches an offeror, the latter is bound and the bargain made from the time the letter is posted or despatched, whether by post or otherwise. The question in this case is different. I will presently state what in my judgment it is. Meanwhile I wish to mention some elementary propositions which, if carefully borne in mind, will assist in the determination of this case.

First. Where a proposition to enter into a contract is made and accepted, it is necessary, as a rule, to constitute the contract that there should be a communication of that acceptance to the proposer, per Brian C.J., and Lord Blackburn: *Brogden* v. *Metropolitan Ry. Co.*, 2 App. Cas. at p. 692.

Secondly. That the present case is one of proposal and acceptance.

Thirdly. That as a consequence of or involved in the first proposition, if the acceptance is written or verbal, i.e., is by letter or message, as a rule, it must reach the proposer or there is no communication, and so no acceptance of the offer.

Fourthly. That if there is a difference where the acceptance is by a letter sent through the post which does not reach the offeror, it must be by virtue of some general rule or some particular agreement of the parties. As for instance, there might be an agreement that the acceptance of the proposal may be sending the article offered by the proposer to be bought, or hanging out a flag or sign to be seen by the offeror as he goes by, or leaving a letter at a certain place, or any other agreed mode, and in the same way there might be an agreement that dropping a letter in a post pillar box or other place of reception should suffice.

Fifthly. That as there is no such special agreement in this case, the defendant, if bound, must be bound by some general rule which makes a difference when the post office is employed as the means of communication.

Sixthly. That if there is any such general rule applicable to the communication of the acceptance of offers, it is equally applicable to all communications that may be made by post. Because, as I have said, the question is not whether this communication may be made by post. If, therefore, posting a letter which does not reach is a sufficient communication of acceptance of an offer, it is equally a communication of everything else which may be communicated by post, e.g., notice to quit. It is impossible to hold, if I offer my landlord to sell him some hay and he writes accepting my offer, and in the same letter gives me notice to quit, and posts his letter which, however, does not reach me, that he has communicated to me his acceptance of my offer, but not his notice to quit. Suppose a man has paid his tailor by cheque or banknote, and posts a letter containing a cheque or banknote to his tailor, which never reaches, is the tailor paid? If he is, would he be if he had never been paid before in that way? Suppose a man is in the habit of sending cheques and banknotes to his banker by post, and posts a letter containing cheques and banknotes, which never reaches. Is the banker liable? Would he be if this was the first instance of a remittance of the sort? In the cases I have supposed, the tailor and banker may have recognized this mode of remittance by sending back receipts and putting the money to the credit of the remitter. Are they liable with that? Are they liable without it? The question then is, is posting a letter which is never received a communication to the person addressed, or an equivalent, or something which dispenses with it? It is for those who say it is to make good their contention. I ask why is it? My answer beforehand to any argument that may be urged is, that it is not a communication, and that there is no agreement to take it as an equivalent for or to dispense with a communication. That those who affirm the contrary say the thing which is not. That if Brian C.J. had had to adjudicate on the case, he would deliver the same judgment as that reported. That because a man, who may send a communication by post or otherwise, sends it by post, he should bind the person addressed, though the communication never reaches him, while he would not so bind him if he had sent it by hand, it is impossible. There is no reason in it; it is simply arbitrary. I ask whether anyone who thinks so is prepared to follow that opinion to its consequence; suppose the offer is to sell a particular chattel, and the letter accepting it never arrives, is the property in the chattel transferred? Suppose it is to sell an estate or grant a lease, is the bargain completed? The lease might be such as not to require a deed, could a subsequent lessee be rejected by the would-be acceptor because he had posted a letter? Suppose an article is advertised at so much, and that it would be sent on receipt of a post office order. Is it enough to post the letter? If the word "receipt" is relied on, is it really meant that that makes a difference? If it should be said let the offeror wait, the answer is, maybe he may lose his market meanwhile. Besides, his offer may be advertisement to all mankind. Suppose a reward for information, information posted does not reach, someone else gives it and is paid, is the offeror liable to the first man?

It is said that a contrary rule would be hard on the would-be acceptor, who may have made his arrangements on the footing that the bargain was concluded. But to hold as contended would be equally hard on the offeror, who may have his arrangements on the footing that his offer was not accepted; his non-receipt of any communication may be attributable to the person to whom it was made being absent. What is he to do but to act on the negative, that no communication has been made to him? Further, the use of the post office is no more authorized by the offeror than the sending an answer by hand, and all these hardships would befall the person posting the letter if he sent it by hand. Doubtless in that case he would be the person to suffer if the letter did not reach its destination. Why should his sending it by post relieve him of the loss and cast it on the other party? It was said, if he sends it by hand it is revocable, but not if he sends it by post, which makes the difference. But it is revocable when sent by post, not that the letter can be got back, but its arrival might be anticipated by a letter by hand or telegram, and there is no case to shew that such anticipation would not prevent the letter from binding. It would be a most alarming thing to say that it would. That a letter honestly but mistakenly written and posted must bind the writer if hours before its arrival he informed the person addressed that it was coming, but was wrong and recalled; suppose a false but honest character given, and the mistake found out after the letter posted, and notice that it was wrong given to the person addressed.

Then, as was asked, is the principle to be applied to telegrams? Further, it seems admitted that if the proposer said, "unless I hear from you by return of post the offer is withdrawn," that the letter accepting it must reach him to bind him. There is indeed a case recently reported in the Times before the Master of the Rolls, where the offer was to be accepted within fourteen days, and it is said to have been held that it was enough to post the letter on the 14th, though it would and did not reach the offeror till the 15th. Of course there may have been something in that case not mentioned in the report. But as it stands it comes to this, that if an offer is to be accepted in June, and there is a month's post between the places, posting the letter on the 30th of June will suffice, though it does not reach till the 31st of July; but that case does not affect this. There the letter reached, here it has not. If it is not admitted that "unless I hear by return the offer is withdrawn" makes the receipt of the letter a condition, it is to say an express condition goes for nought. If it is admitted, is it not what every letter says? Are there to be fine distinctions, such as, if the words are "unless I hear from you by return post, &c.," it is necessary the letter should reach him, but "let me know by return of post," it is not; or if in that case it is, yet it is not where there is an offer without those words. Lord Blackburn says that Mellish L.J. accurately stated that where it is expressly or impliedly stated in the offer, "you may accept the offer by posting a letter," the moment you post this letter the offer is accepted. I agree; and the same thing is true of any other mode of acceptance offered with the offer and acted on—as firing a cannon, sending off a rocket, give your answer to my servant the bearer. Lord Blackburn was not dealing with the question before us; there was no doubt in the case before him that the letter had reached. . . .

I am of opinion that this judgment should be reversed. I am of opinion that there was no bargain between these parties to allot and take shares, that to make such bargain there should have been an acceptance of the defendant's offer and a communication to him of that acceptance. That there was no such communication. That posting a letter does not differ from other attempts at communication in any of its consequences, save that it is irrevocable as between the poster and post office. The difficulty has arisen from a mistake as to what was decided in *Dunlop* v. *Higgins*, and from supposing that because there is a right to have recourse to the post as a means of communication, that right is attended by some peculiar consequences, and also from supposing that because if the letter reaches it binds from the time of posting, it also binds though it never reaches. Mischief may arise if my opinion prevails. It probably will not, as so much has been said on the matter that principle is lost sight of. I believe equal if not greater, will, if it does not prevail. I believe the latter will be obviated only by the rule being made nugatory by every prudent man saying, "your answer by post is only to bind if it reaches me." But the question is not to be decided on these considerations. What is the law? What is the principle? If Brian C.J. had had to decide this a public post being instituted in his time, he would have said the law is the same, now there is a post, as it was before, viz., a communication to affect a man must be a communication, i.e., must reach him.

[Judgment affirmed. The opinion of Baggallay L.J., who agreed with Thesiger L.J., is omitted.]

NOTE. The only "circumstances" from which Thesiger L.J. thought he must imply that the defendant had authorized the plaintiff Company to use the post would appear to be that the defendant *handed* to one Kendrick, the plaintiff Company's local agent, a written application for shares, which Kendrick duly forwarded, presumably by post, to his principals in London.

HENTHORN v. FRASER
England. Court of Appeal. [1892] 2 Ch. 27

After two futile attempts by Henthorn to purchase property in Birkenhead from Fraser, the secretary of the Huskisson Benefit Building Society in Liverpool (the two cities are across the mouth of the Mersey River from each other), Fraser, on July 7th orally offered to sell it for £750 and handed Henthorn a written note stating "I hereby give you the refusal of the Flamank Street property at £750 for fourteen days." On July 8 Fraser agreed to sell the same property to someone else, subject to his being able to cancel if he could not cancel his offer to Henthorn. Fraser posted a letter to Henthorn about noon that day, but it was not delivered to Henthorn's address until five o'clock and Henthorn did not in fact have it until he returned home about eight o'clock. Meanwhile Henthorn's solicitor had posted a letter in Birkenhead at ten to four that afternoon accepting the offer. The letter of acceptance was delivered at eight thirty that evening and was received by Fraser the next morning. Fraser denied the contract and Henthorn sued for specific performance in the Court of the County Palatine. His action was dismissed and he appealed.

LORD HERSCHELL: . . . If the acceptance by the plaintiff of the defendant's offer is to be treated as complete at the time the letter containing it was posted, I can entertain no doubt that the society's attempted revocation of the offer was wholly ineffectual. I think that a person who has made an offer must be considered as continuously making it until he has brought to the knowledge of the person to whom it was made that it is withdrawn. . . . The grounds upon which it has been held that the acceptance of an offer is complete when it is posted have, I think, no application to the revocation or modification of an offer. These can be no more effectual than the offer itself, unless brought to the mind of the person to whom the offer is made. But it is contended on behalf of the defendants that the acceptance was complete only when received by them, and not on the letter being posted. It cannot, of course, be denied, after the decision in *Dunlop* v. *Higgins* (1848), 9 E.R. 805, in the House of Lords, that where an offer has been made through the medium of the post, the contract is complete as soon as the acceptance of the offer is posted, but that decision is said to be inapplicable here, inasmuch as the letter containing the offer was not sent by post to Birkenhead, but handed to the plaintiff in the defendant's office at Liverpool. The question therefore arises in what circumstances the acceptance of an offer is to be regarded as complete as soon as it is posted. In the case of the *Household Insurance Company* v. *Grant* (1879), 4 Ex.D. 216, Lord Justice Baggallay said: "I think that the principle established in *Dunlop* v. *Higgins* is limited in its application to cases in which by reason of general usage, or of relations between the parties to any particular transactions, or of the terms in which the offer is made, the acceptance of such offer by a letter through the post is expressly or impliedly authorized." . . . Applying the law [there] laid down by the Court of Appeal I think in the present case an authority to accept by post must be implied. Although the plaintiff received the offer at the defendant's office in Liverpool, he resided in another town, and it must have been in contemplation that he would take the offer, which by its terms was to remain open for some days with him to his place of residence, and those who made the offer must have known that it would be according to the ordinary usages of mankind that if he accepted it he should communicate his acceptance by means of the post. I am not sure that I should myself have regarded the doctrine that an acceptance is complete as soon as the letter containing it is posted as resting upon an implied authority by the person making the offer to the person receiving it to accept by those means. It strikes me as somewhat artificial to speak of the person to whom the offer is made as having the implied authority of the other party to send his acceptance by post. He needs no authority to transmit the acceptance through any particular channel; he may select what means he pleases, the post-office no less than any other. The only effect of the supposed authority is to make the acceptance complete as soon as it is posted, and authority will obviously be implied only when the tribunal considers that it is a case in which this result ought to be reached.

I should prefer to state the rule thus: Where the circumstances are such that it must have been within the contemplation of the parties that, according to the ordinary usages of mankind, the post might be used as a means of communicating the acceptance of an offer, the acceptance is complete as soon as it is posted. It matters not in which way the proposition be stated, the present case is in either view within it. The learned Vice-Chancellor appears to have based his decision to some extent on the fact that before the acceptance was posted the defendants had sold the property to another person. The case of *Dickinson* v. *Dodds* (1876), 2 Ch.D. 463, was relied upon in support of that defence. In that case, however, the plaintiff knew of the subsequent sale before he accepted the offer, which, in my judgment, distinguishes it entirely from the present case. For the reasons I have given I think the judgment must be reversed, and the usual decree for specific performance made. The respondents must pay the costs of the appeal and of the action.

[The judgments of Lindley and Kay L.JJ. to the same effect are omitted.]

DUNLOP v. *HIGGINS*. 1848. 1 H.L.C. 381; 9 E.R. 805 (Scotland. House of Lords). Dunlop, in Glasgow, wrote to Higgins in Liverpool, offering to sell 2,000 tons of pig iron. Higgins mailed an acceptance on January 30th but not by the first post of that day. The letter was erroneously dated January 31st, and did not reach Glasgow until February 1st due to a delay in the mails. If the acceptance had been mailed 31st January the court indicated it would have been too late, but under the circumstances held a valid contract was completed. Higgins was not answerable for casualties in the Post Office.

[Suppose that Dunlop on receiving the letter and observing the date "January 31st" had sold the goods to a third party? (Lord Cottenham stated it was impossible to hold an erroneous date precluded the making of a contract "whether it produces mischief to the other party or not.") What difference if on the morning of February 1st Dunlop, not having received a reply when he was entitled to expect it, i.e. January 31st, had sold the goods to a third party?]

BYRNE & CO. v. LEON VAN TIENHOVEN & CO.
England. Common Pleas Division. 1880. 5 C.P.D. 344

LINDLEY J.: This was an action for the recovery of damages for the non-delivery by the defendants to the plaintiffs of 1000 boxes of tin plates, pursuant to an alleged contract, which I will refer to presently. The action was tried at Cardiff before myself without a jury; and it was agreed at the trial that in the event of the plaintiffs being entitled to damages they should be £375.

The defendants carried on business at Cardiff and the plaintiffs at New York, and it takes ten or eleven days for a letter posted at either place to reach the other. The alleged contract consists of a letter written by the defendants to the plaintiffs on the 1st of October, 1879, and received by them on the 11th, and accepted by telegram and letter, sent to the defendants on the 11th and 15th of October respectively. These letters and telegrams were as follows: [On the 1st of October, 1879, the defendants wrote the plaintiffs offering them 1000 boxes of tin plates at 15s. 6d. per box. The plaintiffs on the 11th of October, 1879 cabled the defendants accepting this offer, and on the 15th of October wrote the defendants confirming their previous cable of acceptance. On the 8th of October however the defendants wrote a letter to the plaintiffs informing them that as there had been a big run on the tinplate market in the last few days causing prices to rise considerably, they withdrew their offer and considered it cancelled from this date.]

... There is no doubt that an offer can be withdrawn before it is accepted, and it is immaterial whether the offer is expressed to be open for acceptance for a given time or not.... For the decision of the present case, however, it is necessary to consider two other questions, viz: 1. Whether a withdrawal of an offer has any effect until it is communicated to the person to whom the offer has been sent? 2. Whether posting a letter of withdrawal is a communication to the person to whom the letter is sent?

It is curious that neither of these questions appears to have been actually decided in this country. As regards the first question, I am aware that Pothier and some other writers of celebrity are of opinion that there can be no contract if an offer is withdrawn before it is accepted, although the withdrawal is not communicated to the person to whom the offer has been made. The reason for this opinion is that there is not in fact any such consent by both parties as is essential to constitute a contract between them. Against this view, however, it has been urged that a state of mind not notified cannot be regarded in dealings between man and man; and that an uncommunicated revocation is for all practical purposes and in point of law no revocation at all. This is the view taken in the United States: see *Tayloe v. Merchants Fire Insurance Co.* (1850), 9 How. Sup. Ct. Rep. 390, cited in *Benjamin on Sales*, pp. 56-58, and it was adopted by Mr. Benjamin. The same view is taken by Mr. Pollock in his excellent work on *Principles of Contract*, 2nd ed., p. 10, and by Mr. Leake in his *Digest of the Law of Contracts*, p. 43. This view, moreover, appears to me much more in accordance with the general principles of English law than the view maintained by Pothier.

I pass, therefore, to the next question, viz., whether posting the letter of revocation was a sufficient communication of it to the plaintiff. The offer was posted on the 1st of October, the withdrawal was posted on the 8th, and did not reach the plaintiff until after he had posted his letter of the

11th, accepting the offer. It may be taken as now settled that where an offer is made and accepted by letters sent through the post, the contract is completed the moment the letter accepting the offer is posted: *Harris' Case* (1872), 7 Ch. App. 587; *Dunlop* v. *Higgins* (1848), 1 H.L.C. 381; 9 E.R. 805, even although it never reaches its destination. When, however, these authorities are looked at, it will be seen that they are based upon the principle that the writer of the offer has expressly or impliedly assented to treat an answer to him by a letter duly posted as a sufficient acceptance and notification to himself, or, in other words, he has made the post office his agent to receive the acceptance and notification of it. But this principle appears to me to be inapplicable to the case of the withdrawal of an offer. In this particular case I can find no evidence of any authority in fact given by the plaintiffs to the defendants to notify a withdrawal of their offer by merely posting a letter; and there is no legal principle or decision which compels me to hold, contrary to the fact, that the letter of the 8th of October is to be treated as communicated to the plaintiff on that day or any day before the 20th, when the letter reached them. But before that letter had reached the plaintiffs they had accepted the offer, both by telegram and by post; and they had themselves resold the tinplates at a profit. In my opinion the withdrawal of the defendants on the 8th of October of their offer of the 1st was inoperative and a complete contract binding on both parties was entered into on the 11th of October, when the plaintiff accepted the offer of the 1st, which they had no reason to suppose had been withdrawn. Before leaving this part of the case it may be as well to point out the extreme injustice and inconvenience which any other conclusion would produce. If the defendants' contention were to prevail no person who had received an offer by post and had accepted it would know his position until he had waited such a time as to be quite sure that a letter withdrawing the offer had not been posted before his acceptance of it. It appears to me that both legal principles, and practical convenience require that a person who has accepted an offer not known to him to have been revoked, shall be in a position safely to act upon the footing that the offer and acceptance constitute a contract binding on both parties.

[The facts have been considerably abbreviated, and only that part of the case is given which deals with revocation of the offer.]

QUESTION. Is this case authority for the proposition that an acceptance by telegram takes effect upon dispatch?

HOLWELL SECURITIES LTD. v. *HUGHES*
[1974] I All E.R. 161 (C.A.)

By clause 1 of an agreement dated 19th October 1971 made between the defendant of the one part and the plaintiffs of the other, the plaintiffs were granted an option to purchase certain freehold property from the defendant. Clause 2 of the agreement provided: "The said option shall be exercisable by notice in writing to the [defendant] at any time within six months from the date hereof ... "On 14th April 1972 the plaintiffs' solicitors wrote a letter to the defendant giving notice of the exercise of the option. The letter was posted, properly addressed and prepaid, on 14th April, but it was never in fact delivered to the defendant or to his address. No other written communication of the exercise of the option was given or sent to the defendant before the expiry of the time limit on 19th April.

RUSSELL L.J.: It is not disputed that the plaintiffs' solicitors letter dated 14th April 1972 addressed to the defendant at his residence and place of work, the house which was the subject of the option to purchase, was posted by ordinary post in a proper way, enclosing a copy of the letter of the same date delivered by hand to the defendant's solicitors. It is not disputed that the letter and enclosure somehow went astray and never reached the house nor the defendant. It is not disputed that the language of the letter and enclosure would have constituted notice of exercise of the option had they reached the defendant. It is not contended that the handing of the letter to the solicitor constituted an exercise of the option.

The plaintiffs' main contention below and before this court has been that the option was exercised and the contract for sale and purchase was constituted at the moment that the letter addressed to the defendant with its enclosure was committed by the plaintiffs' solicitors to the proper representative of the postal service, so that its failure to reach its destination is irrelevant.

It is the law in the first place that prima facie acceptance of an offer must be communicated to the offeror. On this principle the law has engrafted a doctrine that, if in any given case the true view is that the parties contemplated that the postal service might be used for the purpose of forwarding an acceptance of the offer, committal of the acceptance in a regular manner to the postal service will be acceptance of the offer so as to constitute a contract, even if the letter goes astray and is lost. Nor, as was once suggested, are such cases limited to cases in which the offer has been made by post. It suffices I think at this stage to refer to *Henthorn v. Fraser.* In the present case, as I read a passage in the judgment below, Templeman J. concluded that the parties here contemplated that the postal service might be used to communicate acceptance of the offer (by exercise of the option); and I agree with that.

But that is not and cannot be the end of the matter. In any case, before one can find that the basic principle of the need for communication of acceptance to the offeror is displaced by this artificial concept of communication by the act of posting, it is necessary that the offer is in its terms consistent with such displacement and not one which by its terms points rather in the direction of actual communication. We were referred to *Henthorn v. Fraser* and to the obiter dicta of Farwell J. in *Bruner* v. *Moore*, which latter was a case of an option to purchase patent rights. But in neither of those cases was there apparently any language in the offer directed to the manner of acceptance of the offer or exercise of the option.

The relevant language here is, "The said option shall be exercisable by notice in writing to the Intending Vendor . . . ," a very common phrase in an option agreement. There is, of course, nothing in that phrase to suggest that the notification to the defendant could not be made by post. But the requirement of "notice . . . to," in my judgment, is language which should be taken expressly to assert the ordinary situation in law that acceptance requires to be communicated or notified to the offeror, and is inconsistent with the theory that acceptance can be constituted by the act of posting, referred to by Anson as "acceptance *without notification*."

It is of course true that the instrument could have been differently worded. An option to purchase within a period given for value has the characteristic of an offer that cannot be withdrawn. The instrument might have said "The offer constituted by this option may be accepted in writing within six months": in which case no doubt the posting would have sufficed to form the contract. But that language was not used, and, as indicated, in my judgment the language used prevents that legal outcome. Under this head of the case hypothetical problems were canvassed to suggest difficulties in the way of that conclusion. What if the letter had been delivered through the letterbox of the house in due time, but the defendant had either deliberately or fortuitously not been there to receive it before the option period expired? This does not persuade me that the artificial posting rule is here applicable. The answer might well be that in the circumstances the defendant had impliedly invited communication by use of an orifice in his front door designed to receive communications.

LAWTON L.J.: Counsel for the plaintiffs submitted that the option was exercised when the letter was posted, as the rule relating to the acceptance of offers by post did apply. The foundation of his argument was that the parties to this agreement must have contemplated that the option might be, and probably would be, exercised by means of a letter sent through the post. I agree. This, submitted counsel, was enough to bring the rule into operation. I do not agree. In *Henthorn* v. *Fraser* Lord Herschell stated the rule as follows: "Where the circumstances are such that it must have been within the contemplation of the parties that, according to the ordinary usages of mankind, the post might be used as a means of communicating the acceptance of an offer, the acceptance is complete as soon as it is posted." It was applied by Farwell J. in *Bruner* v. *Moore* to an option to purchase patent rights. The option agreement, which was in writing, was silent as to the manner in which it was to be exercised. The grantee purported to do so by a letter and a telegram.

Does the rule apply in *all* cases where one party makes an offer which both he and the person with whom he was dealing must have expected the post to be used as a means of accepting it? In my judgment, it does not. First, it does not apply when the express terms of the offer specify that the acceptance must reach the offeror. The public nowadays are familiar with this exception to the general rule through their handling of football pool coupons. Secondly, it probably does not operate if its application would produce manifest inconvenience and absurdity. This is the opinion set out in Cheshire and Fifoot's *Law of Contract*. It was the opinion of Bramwell B. as is seen by his judgment in *British & American Telegraph Co.* v. *Colson*, and his opinion is worthy of consideration even though the decision in that case was overruled by this court in *Household Fire and Carriage Accident Insurance Co. Ltd.* v. *Grant*. The illustrations of inconvenience and absurdity which Bramwell B. gave are as apt today as they were then. Is a stockbroker who is holding shares to the orders of his client liable in damages because he did not sell in a falling market in accordance with the instructions in a letter which was posted but never received? Before the passing of the Law Reform (Miscellaneous Provisions) Act 1970 (which abolished actions for breach of promise of marriage), would a young soldier ordered overseas have been bound in contract to marry a girl to whom he had proposed by letter, asking her to let him have an answer before he left and she had replied affirmatively in good time but the letter had never reached him? In my judgment, the factors of inconvenience and absurdity are but illustrations of a wider principle, namely, that the rule does not apply if, having regard to all the circumstances, including the nature of the subject-matter under consideration, the negotiating parties cannot have intended that there should be a binding agreement until the party accepting an offer or exercising an option had in fact communicated the acceptance or exercise to the other. In my judgment, when this principle is applied to the facts of this case it becomes clear that the parties cannot have intended that the posting of a letter should constitute the exercise of the option.

CHARLEBOIS v. BARIL
Quebec. Supreme Court of Canada. [1928] S.C.R. 88

On August 14, 1924, the defendant handed a written offer to purchase certain property to the plaintiff's representative for delivery. On August 25 the plaintiff wrote a letter of acceptance addressed to the defendant and gave it to his son to post. It was posted the same day. The defendant denied receipt of the letter. The Courts below, doubtless relying on *Magann* v. *Auger* (1901), 31 S.C.R. 186, made no finding on the question of receipt by the defendant. He denied liability and the action was commenced to compel performance.

ANGLIN C.J.C. delivered the judgment of the Court: ... The Courts below ... regarded the judgment of this Court in *Magann* v. *Auger* as determining that the mailing of the plaintiff's letter of acceptance to the defendant constituted communication of it to him. With great respect this is an erroneous view of the scope and effect of the decision of this court. That case was one of contract by correspondence, i.e., the offer was sent by mail and that was held to constitute a nomination by the sender of the post office as his agent to receive the acceptance for carriage to him. The civil law of Quebec was held to be the same in this regard as the law of England. But this decision has no application to a case where the offer is communicated, as here, not by mail, but by another means. To make a contract the law requires communication of offer and acceptance alike either to the person for whom each is respectively intended, or to his authorized agent.

Here there was nothing to constitute the post office the defendant's agent and a finding of actual receipt by him of the plaintiff's acceptance was, therefore, essential. The burden of procuring such a finding was upon the plaintiff. Without it he cannot succeed. ...

[A new trial was ordered because the Supreme Court of Canada was not in a position to pass on the now relevant issue of fact.]

NOTES AND QUESTIONS. Magann v. *Auger* was a case of a contract wholly negotiated by post, the offer having been mailed at Quebec, the letter of acceptance at Toronto, and the court talked about negotiations carried on by correspondence. Apparently the court in *Charlebois* v. *Baril* felt it should distinguish between "correspondence" consisting of letters posted and "correspondence" consisting of a letter handed over to the offeree's agent and a letter posted in reply. Is this distinction true in English law? Is *Charlebois* v. *Baril* a decision on the common law of Canada? If so, can it be assumed that the Supreme Court intended to "overrule" *Henthorn* v. *Fraser*? Is it open to a modern Canadian Court to reconsider the matter?

UNDERWOOD & SON, LTD. v. *MAGUIRE.* 1895. Q.R. 6 Q.B. 237
(Quebec. Queen's Bench on appeal from the Superior Court). Underwood
represented the plaintiff company in Canada and negotiated with Maguire
in Quebec for 200 tons of hay for delivery in England. An agreement was
reached and Maguire wrote Underwood in Kingston, Ontario, confirming it.
Underwood replied questioning the mode of payment and Maguire wrote
again, this time to Toronto, repeating his original view of the transaction.
Underwood posted a letter in Toronto accepting this arrangement. On the
same day Maguire wrote to Underwood withdrawing his offer because his
hay had been sold in Liverpool by his agents by mistake. Held, for
Maguire. WURTELE J.: ". . . when parties carry on their negotiations by
correspondence, it is only when the letter containing the acceptance has
reached the party who made the offer and that such party has had communication of it that the contract is formed, and that the power to retract
the offer has ceased to exist." French authors cited. The argument that
once a letter of acceptance was posted it belonged to the addressee was
rejected because "the acceptance contained in it remains nevertheless unknown to the proposer until it really comes into his hands." Two judges
dissented. [It is not clear from the report whether Maguire or Underwood
received the other's letter first. If Maguire had received Underwood's
acceptance first would he have lost his power to revoke? In *Magann* v.
Auger (1901), 31 S.C.R. 186, this case was effectively overruled by the
Supreme Court of Canada. That Court rejected the French authors cited
by Wurtele J. which they conceded to be in the majority, and preferred
others who "completely refute the reasoning upon which the contrary doctrine is based." What is the effect of *Charlebois* v. *Baril* on *Magann* v.
Auger and *Underwood* v. *Maguire*? Does it restore in part the French civil
law Wurtele J. considered that he was applying?]

POST OFFICE ACT
Canada. Revised Statutes. 1952. Chapter 212

39. Subject to the provisions of this Act and the regulations respecting
undeliverable mail, mailable matter becomes the property of the person to
whom it is addressed when it is deposited in a post office.
  [By section 2(1) (i) "post office" includes a "post box".]

NOTE. The unsuccessful argument of the *Post Office Act* in *Underwood* v.
Maguire was repeated in *Magann* v. *Auger*, but Taschereau J. speaking for the
Court does not mention it.

MILINKOVICH v. *CANADIAN MERCANTILE INSURANCE CO.*
1960. 25 D.L.R. (2d) 481 (Quebec. Supreme Court of Canada). Milinkovich had insured his house and furniture in Arntfield, Quebec, with
Canadian Mercantile for $8,000 and $2,000 respectively. In February,
1952, the house and furniture were totally destroyed by fire, the loss being
estimated at $43,220.45. One Callaghan, an adjuster, visited the premises
and confirmed the loss a few days later. Milinkovich signed a declaration
for the adjuster and asked what he had to do next. He was told, "Just
wait, the company will let you know." Milinkovich then moved to Niagara
Falls, Ontario, where in March he was interviewed by another adjuster,
who also had him sign a declaration. In April Milinkovich consulted Mr.
LaMarsh, a lawyer in Niagara Falls, who wrote the company and in reply

received a letter from Callaghan dated April 14 enclosing a Proof of Loss form and saying, "Kindly have Mr. Milinkovich complete and sign this form and return to us and we will forward it to his insurers for their consideration." Mr. LaMarsh personally mailed the letter containing the completed form correctly addressed to Callaghan. Nothing further was heard from Canadian Mercantile or Callaghan, and in December a Montreal lawyer "charged with looking after the insured's interest" commenced this action for $10,000. The sole defence was that action was premature in that the insurer had not received the Proof of Loss form. Held, for Milinkovich. The Supreme Court of Canada discussed *Magann* v. *Auger* and *Charlebois* v. *Baril* and quoted Lord Hershell in *Henthorn* v. *Fraser*. FAUTEUX J.: "In accordance with the law regulating the contract of insurance between the parties, the insurer had the right to require *delivery* of the proofs of loss. This position it could modify, or authorize an agent named by it to do so. And this is what, in my opinion, actually occurred. Mr. LaMarsh did not have to question the authority and the sole discretion which in his letter of 14th April, Callaghan informed him he had received from the company. In the execution of this authority and the exercise of this discretion, Callaghan virtually invited Mr. Lamarsh by his letter to return the forms to him by post, a service of which he himself made use to send them to him. Mr. LaMarsh's obligation ceased there, and he fulfilled this obligation. . . .

"Undoubtedly the point here is not the making of a contract, but of a modification, suggested and accepted, in the conditions of its execution. Evaluated against the background of all the circumstances peculiar to this case, Callaghan's letter to Mr. LaMarsh made it only reasonable for the latter to assume that the insurer was satisfied the proofs of loss would be entrusted to the postal service on which he had relied completely to obtain delivery of them. The silence and inaction of the respondent company and of its employee, both clearly notified by the lawyer of the insured's intention to ask for the execution of the contract, as also the nature of the sole argument pleaded in defence to the action, are, in the case with which we are concerned, incompatible with the good faith which should be present in the execution of this contract of insurance. . . ."

SMITH & OSBERG LTD. v. HOLLENBECK
British Columbia. Supreme Court. 1938. 53 B.C.R. 296

On July 13, 1938, Hollenbeck handed Smith & Osberg Ltd. in Vancouver an option for thirty days to purchase shares in a company. On August 12 Smith & Osberg Ltd. wired Hollenbeck in Seaside, Oregon, from Vancouver, accepting the offer. There was no evidence that Hollenbeck ever received the telegram. McDonald J. gave leave to issue a writ out of the jurisdiction and Hollenbeck applied to have the order discharged.

MANSON J.: . . . In *Charlebois* v. *Baril*, [1928] S.C.R. 88, it was held in the Supreme Court of Canada that where an acceptance of a contract is made by mail, the post office only becomes the agent of the offeror where the offer was originally sent by mail but not where the offer was communicated in some other way. In the latter case an acceptor by mail who desires to enforce the contract must prove actual receipt of the letter of acceptance by the offeror.

I have not been referred to any authority which lays down that the telegraph office becomes the agent of the offeror unless the offer has been made by telegram and an acceptance by telegram thereby impliedly authorized or unless the circumstances are such as to warrant the conclusion that an acceptance by telegram was impliedly authorized as in [*Bruner* v. *Moore*, [1904] 1 Ch. 305]. It is quite true that it is common practice in business to use the telegraph service for the purpose of carrying on business negotiations, but I am not prepared to hold that the practice has been so thoroughly established as to warrant me in finding that the offeror in the circumstances of the case at Bar had constituted the telegraph office his agent for the purpose of receiving an acceptance. *Cowan* v. *O'Connor* (1888), 20 Q.B.D. 640, to which counsel for the plaintiff refers is not inconsistent with the conslusion at which I have arrived.

Had it been established that the defendant received the plaintiff's telegram, the acceptance would have been effective on its receipt and the contract would have been one concluded out of the jurisdiction. . . .

[The order was discharged and the writ set aside.]

CAROW TOWING CO. v. The "ED McWILLIAMS"
Canada. Exchequer Court. 1919. 46 D.L.R. 506

Action for towage. The plaintiffs carry on business at Cheboygan, Mich., U.S.A. Negotiations were begun by wire from the ship owners at Sault Ste. Marie, Ont., to Cheboygan, Mich., and a return wire to Sault Ste. Marie. No contract was formed by the telegrams. Subsequently the plaintiff telephoned from Cheboygan to Captain Climie at Sault Ste. Marie, and the parties concluded the contract over the telephone.

A question of jurisdiction arose, in which it became necessary to determine the place where the contract was made.

HODGINS L.J.A.: . . . I think the contract was one made in Ontario, for, when Captain Climie went to his telephone, he then and there received an offer, or discussed terms, which, when accepted, formed the contract. In other words, the plaintiffs at Cheboygan, Mich., by using the long distance telephone, were able to reach Captain Climie in Ontario, just as if they telegraphed to him and he had received the telegram at the Soo. His reply at the telephone is of the same effect as if he had posted a letter or sent off a telegram from an office in Ontario. . . .

MELADY v. JENKINS STEAMSHIP CO. 1909. 18 O.L.R. 251 (Ontario.
MAGEE J.: ". . . in *Cowan* v. *O'Connor* (1888), 20 Q.B.D. 640, it was held that the telegraph was a mere means of communication, as if one were speaking to the other, and that a telegram sent from within the city of London accepting an order by telegraph from outside the city completed the contract within the city and gave jurisdiction to the mayor's court. On the same principle this contract, if any, was made in Toronto. . . ." [Can this be based on any "common agency" theory? Must the offeree use the same telegraph company the offeror used? In England the Post Office Department operates the telegraph service. Note that in the principal case and in *Melady* and *Cowan* the question was, *where* was the contract made? Should the questions *when* and *where* be answered by the same tests?]

ENTORES, LTD. v. MILES FAR EAST CORPORATION. [1955] 2 All
E.R. 493 (England. Court of Appeal). An offer by a London company was accepted by agents of an American corporation in Amsterdam, by means of

"Telex," a service set up by the Post Office by which the typewritten message in Holland could be read in London a minute or so later. To establish jurisdiction, it had to be shown that the contract was made in England. DENNING L.J.: "The problem can only be solved by going in stages. Let me first consider a case where two people make a contract by word of mouth in the presence of one another. Suppose, for instance, that I shout an offer to a man across a river or a courtyard but I do not hear his reply because it is drowned by an aircraft flying overhead. There is no contract at that moment. If he wishes to make a contract, he must wait till the aircraft is gone and then shout back his acceptance so that I can hear what he says. Not until I have his answer am I bound. . . .

Now take a case where two people make a contract by telephone. Suppose, for instance, that I make an offer to a man by telephone and, in the middle of his reply, the line goes "dead" so that I do not hear his words of acceptance. There is no contract at that moment. The other man may not know the precise moment when the line failed. But he will know that the telephone conversation was abruptly broken off, because people usually say something to signify the end of the conversation. If he wishes to make a contract, he must therefore get through again so as to make sure that I heard. Suppose next that the line does not go dead, but it is nevertheless so indistinct that I do not catch what he says and I ask him to repeat it. He then repeats it and I hear his acceptance. The contract is made, not on the first time when I do not hear, but only the second time when I do hear. If he does not repeat it, there is no contract. The contract is only complete when I have his answer accepting the offer.

Lastly take the Telex. Suppose a clerk in a London office taps out on the teleprinter an offer which is immediately recorded on a teleprinter in a Manchester office, and a clerk at that end taps out an acceptance. If the line goes dead in the middle of the sentence of acceptance, the teleprinter motor will stop. There is then obviously no contract. The clerk at Manchester must get through again and send his complete sentence. But it may happen that the line does not go dead, yet the message does not get through to London. Thus the clerk at Manchester may tap out his message of acceptance and it will not be recorded in London because the ink at the London end fails or something of that kind. In that case the Manchester clerk will not know of the failure but the London clerk will know of it and will immediately send back a message "not receiving". Then, when the fault is rectified, the Manchester clerk will repeat the message. Only then is there a contract. If he does not repeat it, there is no contract. It is not until his message is received that the contract is complete.

In all the instances I have taken so far, the man who sends the message of acceptance knows that it has not been received or he has reason to know it. So he must repeat it. But suppose that he does not know that his message did not get home. He thinks it has. This may happen if the listener on the telephone does not catch the words of acceptance, but nevertheless does not trouble to ask for them to be repeated: or if the ink on the teleprinter fails at the receiving end, but the clerk does not ask for the message to be repeated: so that the man who sends an acceptance reasonably believes that his message has been received. The offeror in such circumstances is clearly bound, because he will be estopped from saying that he did not receive the message of acceptance. It is his own fault that he did not get it. But if there should be a case where the offeror without any fault on his part does not receive the message of acceptance—yet the sender of it reasonably believes it has got home when it has not—then I think there is no contract.

My conclusion is that the rule about instantaneous communications between the parties is different from the rule about the post. The contract is only complete when the acceptance is received by the offeror: and the contract is made at the place where the acceptance is received."

QUESTION. The problem before the Court here is whether it should take jurisdiction over the dispute. For the purpose of solving that problem, is it relevant to consider whether an offeror is bound by an acceptance that fails to arrive? Is not the latter an entirely different problem?

RESTATEMENT OF CONTRACTS (SECOND)
American Law Institute, 1964 (Tentative Draft)

64. Unless otherwise provided,
    (a) an acceptance made in a manner and by a medium invited by an offer is operative and completes the manifestation of mutual assent as soon as put out of the offeree's possession, without regard to whether it ever reaches the offeror; but
    (b) an acceptance under an option contract is not operative until received by the offeror.
65. Acceptance by telephone or other medium of substantially instantaneous two-way communication is governed by the principles applicable to acceptances where the parties are in the presence of each other.
66. Unless circumstances known to the offeree indicate otherwise, a medium of acceptance is reasonable if it is the one used by the offeror or one customary in similar transactions at the time and place the offer is received.

PROBLEM 1. Wally Waffle carried on a lumber business in Halifax, Nova Scotia, and received an offer from Peter Pratt in Vancouver, British Columbia on Monday for the sale of Douglas Fir at a bargain price. Pratt's offer concluded, "Please reply by return mail." Waffle wrote Pratt Monday afternoon by surface mail accepting the offer. The course of post is four days. Tuesday morning Waffle wrote to Pratt by air mail saying, "Disregard letter of yesterday, your price is too high." Air mail from Halifax to Vancouver is, say, twenty-four hours. Later that morning Waffle unexpectedly found a buyer for the lumber, and sent a telegram to Pratt accepting the offer after all. Tuesday afternoon Waffle, having found that his buyer had repudiated his promise just after he had sent his wire, telephoned Pratt to disregard all communications, he, Waffle, was rejecting the offer. Is there a contract? See a note in 8 *Can. Bar Rev.* 615 (1930) reviewing the authorities and concluding, "If a letter of acceptance has once been posted, a telegram revoking such acceptance is inoperative though it reaches the offeror long before the letter arrives. . . . It is settled law that the contract is complete in cases of contracts by correspondence, at the moment of posting the acceptance. There is no reason for creating an exception to this rule. What really matters in commercial transactions is to have a definite settled rule (whatever it may be) and not to render it obscure by engrafting upon it a multiplicity of ultra-refined exceptions." Do you agree? How many exceptions would be necessary to put both Waffle and Pratt in an equally protected position?

PROBLEM 2. On May 11, D posted 2 letters offering to sell his hay, one to E and one to P. Both letters arrived on May 14. E replied on May 14, and P on May 15, both accepting the offer. The letters arrived together, and D sold the hay to E. Advise P.

See *Patterson* v. *Dolman* [1908] V.L.R. 354 (S.C. Vict.).

PROBLEM 3. X made an offer to Y through Z. Y wrote to Z accepting the offer, and Z forwarded the letter to X. Subsequently, Y wrote another letter to Z cancelling the acceptance. Z forwarded the second letter, and both letters reached X at the same time. Advise Y.

See *Countess of Dunmore* v. *Alexander* (1830) 9 S. 190.

PROBLEM 4. A, in answer to an offer, mails a rejection. An hour later he mails an acceptance.

If rejection were valid only when received, suppose the offeror on receipt of the rejection re-sold the goods offered?

Would the fact that the rejection was contained in a counter-offer only, affect your argument?

RESTATEMENT OF THE LAW OF CONTRACTS
(SECOND) Tentative draft
American Law Institute. 1964

39. Rejection or counter-offer by mail or telegram does not terminate the power of acceptance until received by the offeror, but limits the power so that a letter or telegram of acceptance started after the sending of an otherwise effective rejection or counter-offer is only a counter-offer unless the acceptance is received by the offeror before he receives the rejection or counter-offer.

D. Consideration: The Bargain Theory

CURRIE v. *MISA.* 1875. L.R. 10 Ex. 153, 162, affirmed, 1 App. Cas. 554. Lush J.: "A valuable consideration, in the sense of the law, may consist either in some right, interest, profit, or benefit accruing to the one party, or some forbearance, detriment, loss or responsibility, given, suffered, or undertaken by the other." [The definition has frequently been cited with approval in Canadian courts.]

DUNLOP PNEUMATIC TYRE CO. v. *SELFRIDGE & CO.* [1915] A.C. 847, 855. Lord Dunedin: "My Lords, I am content to adopt from a work of Sir Frederick Pollock, to which I have often been under obligation, the following words as to consideration: 'An act or forbearance of one party, or the promise thereof, is the price for which the promise of the other is bought, and the promise thus given for value is enforceable.' (Pollock on Contracts. 8th ed., p. 175)." [This definition seems not to have been cited in any Canadian court.]

WESTLAKE v. *ADAMS.* 1858. 5 C.B.N.S. 248; 141 E.R. 99, 106. Byles J.: "It is an elementary principle, that the law will not enter into an enquiry as to the adequacy of the consideration. . . ."

HOBBES, LEVIATHAN. 1651. "The value of all things contracted for is measured by the appetite of the contractors, and therefore the just value is that which they be contented to give."

VERNON v. *BETHELL*. 1762. 2 Eden 110; 28 E.R. 838, 839 (England, Chancery), Northington L.C.: ". . . necessitous men are not, truly speaking, free men, but, to answer a present exigency, will submit to any terms that the crafty may impose upon them." [This attitude is representative of a court of equity, in this case deciding that a mortgagee had made "an undue use of the influence of a mortgage."]

P.S. Atiyah, Consideration in Contracts, 1974. "To talk of abolition of the doctrine of consideration is nonsensical. Consideration means a reason for the enforcement of a promise. Nobody can seriously propose that all promises should become enforceable; to abolish the doctrine of consideration, therefore, is simply to require the courts to begin all over again the task of deciding what promises are to be enforceable."

NOTE ON LEGAL METHOD. Obviously numerous difficulties will arise in the application of these definitions: What is an exchange? Must it be equal in value to the promise? If so, who is to decide the relative values? Must it be contemporaneous with the promise? And so on. These difficulties are raised by the cases in this chapter. On thinking about them, it is important to remember that many people feel (as a matter of intuition) that a man who makes a serious promise ought to keep it, whether he exacted anything in exchange or not. The result is that courts are usually under some pressure to enforce a "barren" promise by "implying" a requested exchange, or "interpreting" the facts to show that there was one in circumstances where it is quite easy to reach the opposite conclusion.

A short tale from *Huckleberry Finn* may throw some light on this judicial peculiarity. The account is taken from Pound, "Law in Books and Law in Action" (1910) 44 American Law Review 12.

"When Tom Sawyer and Huck Finn had determined to rescue Jim by digging under the cabin where he was confined, it seemed to the uninformed lay mind of Huck Finn that some old picks the boys had found were the proper implements to use. But Tom knew better. From reading he knew what was the right course in such cases, and he called for case-knives. 'It don't make no difference,' said Tom, 'how foolish it is, it's the *right way*—and it's the regular way. And there ain't no other way that ever I heard of, and I've read all the books that gives any information about these things. They always dig out with a case-knife.' So, in deference to the books and the proprieties, the boys set to work with case-knives. But after they had dug till nearly midnight and they were tired and their hands were blistered, and they had made little progress, a light came to Tom's legal mind. He dropped his knife and, turning to Huck, said firmly, 'Gimme a case-knife.' Let Huck tell the rest:

" 'He had his own by him, but I handed him mine. He flung it down and says, "Gimme a *case-knife.*"

" 'I didn't know just what to do—but then I thought, I scratched around amongst the old tools and got a pickaxe and give it to him, and he took it and went to work and never said a word.

" 'He was always just that particular. *Full of principle.*'

"Tom had made over again one of the earliest discoveries of the law. When tradition prescribed case-knives for tasks for which pickaxes were better adapted, it seemed better to our forefathers, after a little vain struggle with case-knives, to adhere to principle—but use the pickaxes. They granted that law ought not to change. Changes in law were full of danger. But, on the other hand, it was highly inconvenient to use case-knives. And so the law has always managed to get a pickaxe in its hands, though it steadfastly demanded a case-knife, and to wield it in the virtuous belief that it was using the approved instrument."

NOTE ON THE HISTORY OF CONSIDERATION. The neat formulas defining consideration hide their mixed ancestry rather well, but some general understanding of the early development of the idea of consideration may help in grappling with modern problems. One word of warning may not be out of place. Legal history is frequently based on rather slim evidence; often there is only a sketchy report of a case separated from the next report by a number of years. What happened between these reports is largely a matter of guesswork.

In the late nineteenth century a major simplification of procedure in law suits was attempted, but before that, each action was commenced by the appropriate one of a number of writs each of which instituted a particular form of action having its own peculiarities. If a lawyer selected the wrong one, he might end up in failure and have to start from the beginning after making a red faced explanation to his client, whose money he had just wasted.

One of the earliest forms of action was *debt*, which lay for the recovery of a "sum certain" promised, as we would say today, but perhaps "granted" (but not yet handed over) might be closer to the ancient idea, in return for services rendered or goods supplied. If the promise was to deliver a specific chattel, the form of action was *detinue*. In each case the promise was enforceable only after the goods had been delivered or the services rendered. And there had to be an express promise of a stated amount of money. The remedy was therefore limited—it was of no use if the plaintiff's act still remained to be performed or if the amount of money was not agreed upon. This exchange of goods for a sum certain came to be called a *quid pro quo*, a sort of exchange of "grants," rarely thought of as a promise.

Another limitation lay in the fact that the defendant could "wage" his law, a curious defence in which the merits of the case could be avoided, and the defendant merely had to swear that he was not indebted. He then had to produce some number, usually a dozen, "compurgators" or "oath-helpers," men who were prepared to swear that the defendant's oath was trustworthy. They were a kind of character witness. They did not testify to facts. (See Plucknett, *A Concise History of the Common Law*, 5th ed., p. 115). This strange defence was not so easy as it sounds, nor so unequal to a trial on the merits. In those days the oath was a fearsome thing, and on the other hand, methods of fact-finding were primitive—parties could not testify, few people could read or write, and juries were not limited to the evidence produced before them. Wager of law was theoretically permissible in England until abolished in 1833.

One of the peculiarities of English legal development lay in the competition between courts. Supreme judicial tribunals are a relatively modern phenomenon, and they appear to be open to attack now by rival administrative tribunals, e.g. the Workmen's Compensation Board. In early days the action of debt with its defence of wager of law lay only in the Court of Common Pleas. Hence, if you could find a form of action that would let you into the Court of King's Bench, you could avoid wagers of law and be sure your case would be tried on its merits. And the Court was not unwilling to strain a point of practice to acquire the new business.

In the King's Bench, which had no great interest in contract, apart from formal covenants, the first appearance of contract was in a form of action that evolved very slowly from the favourite tort action of trespass, trespass on the case, in which it was alleged that something was undertaken (in Latin

Assumpsit—the name by which the writ came to be known) and performed in such a way as to injure the plaintiff. Injury to the plaintiff of the kind familiar in trespass actions was originally very important. Injury to an expectation interest came slowly, although in covenant it was quite familiar. This gradually developed in *assumpsit* for non-feasance, where the promise was not performed at all. In the development of the action of assumpsit the expression "in consideration of" which appears in early forms, seems to have led to the use of the word "consideration" to denote something done by the plaintiff in exchange for the undertaking. We would call this an "executed consideration" because the requested act had been performed before the action was brought. This, of course, was familiar to minds accustomed to the *quid pro quo* of debt. The next development lay in the recognition of a promise by the plaintiff as a sufficient "consideration."

The attractiveness of the growing *assumpsit* brought lawyers from the Court of Common Pleas into the King's Bench. The attempt was made to fit *assumpsit* to facts to which *debt* clearly applied. The original "grant" (or promise) to pay a sum certain seems not to have been acceptable as an *assumpsit* (undertaking) but if the debtor made a second promise later, this could be taken as the assumpsit, and thus, in effect, debt moved into the King's Bench. The action was called *indebitatus assumpsit*, "being indebted, he undertook." (Curiously enough, at this stage, it seems not to have troubled the Court that any consideration for the second promise must have been executed before that promise was made. This later, in 1615, did cause some trouble. See *Lampleigh* v. *Brathwait*, reproduced in section 3.B of this chapter.) Of course, the second promise would not always be made, and any debtor who hoped to wage his law would presumably be careful to avoid a second commitment. In a momentous decision in the Exchequer Chamber (a Court hearing appeals from the King's Bench, normally consisting of the judges of Common Pleas(!) and the Barons of the Exchequer) it was held, in effect, that the second promise need not be proved, it might be presumed. See *Slade's Case* (1602) 4 Co. Rep. 91a; 76 E.R. 1072.

On this whole subject, very sketchily presented here as a basis for discussion of the cases in class, see *Plucknett, A Concise History of The Common Law*, 5th ed., pp. 637-56. A short discussion of the basis of contractual liability is to be found in Fuller, *Basic Contract Law*, pp. 289-313. On mutual promises see pp. 391-5 of the same book.

WHITE (EXECUTOR) v. WILLIAM BLUETT
England. Court of Exchequer. 1853. 23 L.J. Ex. (N.S.) 36

Action upon a promissory note made payable to John Bluett; the testator: Plea that Bluett was the father of the defendant, and that in his lifetime, the defendant William Bluett complained to his father that he had not received at his hands so much money or so many advantages as the other children and controversies arose between them. Bluett afterward admitted the defendant's complaints were well founded, and it was agreed that the defendant should forever cease to make such complaints, and that in consideration thereof, and in order to do justice to the defendant, and also out of Bluett's natural love and affection toward the defendant, he, Bluett, would discharge the defendant of and from all liability in respect of the promissory note.

Demurrer and joinder.

[Parke B., during the argument, asked: "Is an agreement by a father in consideration that his son will not bore him, a binding contract?"]

POLLOCK C.B.: The plea is clearly bad. By the argument a principle is pressed to an absurdity, as a bubble blown until it bursts. Looking at the words merely, there is some foundation for the argument, and, following the words only, the conclusion may be arrived at. It is said the son had a right to an equal distribution of his father's property, and did complain to his father because he had not an equal share, and said to him, "I will cease to complain if you will not sue upon this note." Whereupon the father said, "If you will promise me not to complain I will give up the note." If such a plea as this could be supported, the following would be a binding promise: A man might complain that another person used the public highway more than he ought to do, and that the other might say, "Do not complain, and I will give you £5." It is ridiculous to suppose that such promises could be binding. So, if the holder of a bill of exchange were suing the acceptor, and the acceptor were to complain that the holder had treated him hardly, or that the bill ought never to have been circulated, and the holder were to say, "Now if you will not make any more complaints I will not sue you." Such a promise would be like that now set up. In reality, there was no consideration whatever. The son had no right to complain, for the father might make what distribution of his property he liked; and the son's abstaining from doing what he had no right to do can be no consideration. *Judgment for the plaintiff.*

QUESTIONS ON LEGAL METHOD. In the sentence beginning "The son had no *right* to complain . . . ," what does the word *right* mean? Is Pollock C.B. saying that the son could not succeed in an action against his father, or his father's estate, for a share of that estate; or is he saying that the son was not entitled to annoy his father with his complaints? If the word *right* involves this ambiguity, would it not be better to find two words instead of the one? Try *claim* for the first and *privilege* for the second. Could giving up a privilege at the request of the promisor constitute consideration?

SHARON v. *SHARON.* 1885. 8 P. 614 (California). An action based on the following writing. "Palace Hotel. San Francisco, Nov. 7, 1880. I hereby agree to pay Miss S. A. Hill 250 dollars for each and every month of the year A. D. 1883 [*sic*]. Wm. Sharon." Although the defendant denied any consideration for his note, he averred that "to induce the plaintiff to desist from making unwelcome visits and annoying and disturbing him in his rooms, and on the consideration that she would cease to disturb him, he executed the document in question. *Judgment for the plaintiff.*

DUNTON v. *DUNTON.* 1892. 18 Vict. L.R. 114 (Australia). The marriage of John and Louisa Dunton was dissolved on March 12, 1890. John Dunton, in a written agreement dated August 30, promised to pay Louisa £6 a month from September 1, 1890, during the continuance of the agreement. The agreement would be ended if Louisa committed any act to bring personal hate, contempt or ridicule on either of them, or if she did not conduct herself with sobriety, and in a respectable, orderly and virtuous manner. The agreement recited John Dunton's desire, notwithstanding the dissolution, to make provision for his former wife. In an action to recover payment of £6 under the agreement, the question of consideration was raised. Held, for the plaintiff. HIGINBOTHAM J.: ". . . But it was said this was only a promise to do that which the plaintiff was already bound to do, and that such a promise does not constitute a good consideration. . . . [A] promise not to do, or to do something which the promisor may lawfully and without wrong to the promisee do or abstain from doing, is a good consideration. . . . She was legally at liberty, so far as the defendant was concerned, to conduct herself in these respects as she might think fit, and her promise to surrender liberty and to conduct herself in the manner desired by the defendant constituted, in my opinion, a good consideration. . . ." WILLIAMS J.: ". . . She was under no legal obligation to the defendant, or to anyone, not to get drunk in her own or any friend's house. . . ." HOOD J., who dissented, said: "It was, however, contended that the real consideration is an implied promise by her that she will conduct herself with sobriety. . . . I cannot imply such a promise from the document but even if it were expressed therein it would not, in my opinion, constitute a consideration. . . . A promise in order to be good consideration must be such as may be enforced. It must, therefore, be not only lawful, and in itself possible, but it must also be reasonably definite. Now [this] promise . . . seems to me to be about as vague a promise as can well be imagined."

QUESTION. B, a married man, has been seen by A in public with a notorious prostitute, and promises A, "If you promise not to tell anyone you have seen us together, I will give you $1,000." A promises. B refuses to pay the money. Will A recover in an action for breach of the promise? See, on this question, Goodhart, "Blackmail and Consideration in Contracts" (1928), 44 *Law Quarterly Review* 436.

SCHNELL v. *NELL.* 1861. 17 Ind. 29 (Supreme Court of Indiana). Theresa Schnell made a will leaving $200 each to Nell and others. After her death it appeared that all of her property was jointly held with her husband Zacharias Schnell, and reverted to him on her death. In consideration of the love and respect he bore for his wife, etc., Zach promised to pay Nell and others $200 each, and in consideration Nell and the others "agree to pay the above-named sum of money (one cent), and to deliver up to said Schnell, and abstain from collecting any real or supposed claims upon him or his estate, arising from the said last will and testament of the said Theresa Schnell, deceased." Held, for Schnell. PERKINS J.: "The consideration of one cent will not support the promise of Schnell. It is true, that as a general proposition, inadequacy of consideration will not vitiate an agreement. . . . But this doctrine does not apply to a mere exchange of sums of money, of coin, whose value is exactly fixed, but to the exchange of something of, in itself, indeterminate value, for money, or perhaps for other thing of indeterminate value. In this case had the one cent mentioned been some particular one cent, a family piece, or ancient, remarkable coin, possessing an indeterminate value, extrinsic from its simple money value, a different view might be taken. As it is, the mere promise to pay six hundred dollars for one cent, even had the portion of that cent due from the plaintiff been tendered, is an unconscionable contract, void, at first blush upon its face, if it be regarded as an earnest one. . . . The consideration of one cent is, plainly, in this case, merely nominal, and intended to be so."

NOTE. Professor Fuller, in his *Basic Contract Law*, at p. 347 comments on the argument of counsel for the defendant in *Schnell* v. *Nell* and points out that he did not advance the argument about the inadequacy of the one cent consideration in the form adopted by the court. He referred to a text proposition that where an agreement is unconscionable a court of equity will not give specific performance and a court of common law will give only reasonable damages. As Schnell had apparently already paid Nell $98.67 that should be sufficient.

ELEANOR THOMAS v. BENJAMIN THOMAS
England. Queen's Bench. 1842. 2 Q.B. 851; 114 E.R. 330

The defendant was executor with Samuel Thomas (since deceased) of the will of John Thomas who had intended that his widow, the plaintiff, should have some further protection and orally expressed a wish that she should have the house he lived in, with all its contents, or £100 instead. Shortly after his death his executors attempted to put his wish into effect. A written agreement was executed by the parties reciting this desire and the desire of the executors to fulfil it, and the executors promised "in consideration of such desire and of the premises" to convey the house to the widow for life or as long as she continued unmarried, "provided nevertheless, and it is hereby further agreed and declared, that the said Eleanor Thomas . . . shall . . . at all times during which she shall have possession of the said dwelling house . . . pay to the . . . executors . . . the sum of £1 yearly towards the ground rent . . . and shall . . . keep the said . . . house . . . in good . . . repair." The plaintiff was left in possession for some time, but the defendant, after the death of the co-executor, refused to execute a conveyance and ejected the plaintiff. The plaintiff sued on the agreement. Verdict for plaintiff. A rule nisi was obtained to enter a non suit.

LORD DENMAN C.J.: There is nothing in this case but a great deal of ingenuity, and a little wilful blindness to the actual terms of the instrument itself. There was nothing whatever to show that the ground-rent was payable to a superior landlord; and the stipulation for the payment of it is not a mere proviso, but an express agreement. (His Lordship here read the proviso.) This is in terms an express agreement, and shows a sufficient legal consideration quite independent of the moral feeling which disposed the executors to enter into such a contract. Mr. Williams' definition of consideration is too large: the word *causa* in the passage referred to means one which confers what the law considers a benefit to the party. Then the obligation to repair is one which might impose charges heavier than the value of the life estate.

PATTESON J.: It would be giving *cause* too large a construction if we were to adopt the view urged for the defendant; it would be confounding consideration with motive. Motive is not the same thing with consideration. Consideration means something which is of some value in the eye of the law, moving from the plaintiff: it may be some detriment to the plaintiff, or some benefit to the defendant; but at all events it must be moving from the plaintiff. Now that which is suggested as the consideration here—a pious respect for the wishes of the testator—does not in any way move from the plaintiff: it moves from the testator; therefore, legally speaking, it forms no part of the consideration. Then it is said that, if that be so, there is no consideration at all, it is a mere voluntary gift: but when we look at the agreement we find that this is not a mere proviso that the donee shall take the gift with the burthens; but it is an express agreement to pay what seems to be a fresh apportionment of a ground-rent, and which is made payable not to a superior landlord but to the executors. So that this rent is clearly not something incident to the assignment of the house; for in that case, instead of being payable to the executors; it would be payable to the landlord. Then as to the repairs: these houses may very possibly be held under a lease containing covenants to repair, but we know nothing about it; for anything that appears, the liability to repair is created by this instrument. The proviso certainly struck me at first as Mr. Williams [one of counsel] put it, that the rent and repairs were merely attached to the gift of the donors; and, had the instrument been executed by the donors only; there might have been some ground for that construction; but the fact is not so. Then it is suggested that this would be held to be a mere voluntary conveyance as against a subsequent purchaser for value: possibly that might be so: but suppose it would: the plaintiff contracts to take it, and does take it, whatever it is, for better for worse: perhaps a bona fide purchase for a valuable consideration might override it, but that cannot be helped. *Rule discharged.*

[The opinion of Coleridge J. is omitted.]

QUESTIONS. Has Eleanor Thomas expressly or impliedly promised to take possession or keep possession? Is there mutuality of obligation here? If Eleanor had no right to possession, did she, by remaining in possession, incur a detriment such that might be good consideration?

VANBERGEN v. ST. EDMUNDS PROPERTIES, LTD.
England, Court of Appeal. [1933] 2 K.B. 233

The plaintiff, being indebted to the defendants in London, and threatened by them with bankruptcy, promised to pay the amount owing into a bank in Eastbourne for the credit of the defendants in London, if the defendants would withhold service of the bankruptcy notice. The defendants served the notice to the knowledge of business associates of the plaintiff in an alleged breach of their promise. Macnaghten J. allowed general damages of £500 by analogy to the cases where a banker refuses to honour a customer's cheque. On the question of consideration he said, [1933] 1 K.B. 45, at p. 348: "The plaintiff, by going to Eastbourne, obtaining the money and remitting it in the manner suggested, made it a binding contract on the part of Mr. Kennard that he would not serve the bankruptcy notice . . . according to the terms proposed, the plaintiff was not to pay his debt to his creditors, but was to secure the payment of the money to the account of Stanley Evans & Co. at the Law Courts branch of the Bank of England. He was under no obligation to do that, and there was, therefore, sufficient consideration to prevent the alleged contract being nudum pactum."

[The defendants appealed.]

ROMER L.J.: . . . The jury, having returned a verdict in favour of the plaintiff for £500, must be taken to have arrived at the conclusion that the agreement, sued upon by the plaintiff and alleged by him in para. 2 of the statement of claim, was in fact made. The agreement so stated in para. 2 is in these terms: "On the 6th day of July, 1932, the defendants, by their solicitor, Mr. Kennard, verbally agreed with the plaintiff that if the plaintiff would on the 7th day of July, 1932, pay into any bank at Eastbourne the sum of £208 6s. 3d. in cash for the credit of Messrs. Stanley Evans & Co., the defendants' solicitors, at the Law Courts branch of the Bank of England such payment would satisfy all sums which the plaintiff owed to the defendants and the bankruptcy notice which they had issued on June 24, 1932, for £140 8s. 5d. would not be served on him." That being the agreement alleged, and found by the jury to have been arrived at, the question is whether there was any good consideration for such an agreement. It was suggested by Mr. Comyns Carr [one of counsel] that the consideration is to be found in, and indeed consisted of, the obligation undertaken by the plaintiff to proceed to Eastbourne and there endeavour to borrow money from somebody—from whom was not stated, but from somebody—of a sufficient amount to enable him to pay his debt of £208 odd, which the plaintiff at that time was owing. In the first place, that is not the agreement alleged, and if it had been the agreement alleged there is no evidence to support such an agreement, that is to say, an agreement that the plaintiff at the request of the defendants should proceed to Eastbourne on any such errand. The evidence, to my mind, makes it perfectly clear what the arrangement come to on July 6 was. It must be remembered that the plaintiff had been given until July 7 to pay this £208 odd, and on July 6 he rang up the defendants' solicitor and explained that he was not able to find the money on the 7th. Mr. Kennard, the defendants' solicitor, was naturally annoyed, but on being pressed by the plaintiff he agreed to give him still further time—namely, up to 12 o'clock noon on the following day, Friday, July 8. He was induced to do that because the plaintiff said he had to go down to Eastbourne on the following day and he hoped when he got there he would be able to raise the money from some other source. Then he explained to Mr. Kennard, who had been insisting on being paid cash in London by 12 o'clock on the Friday, that there would be some difficulty in his getting back from Eastbourne on that day, and thereupon Mr. Kennard pointed out to the plaintiff that there was a very easy way of providing for payment in cash in London by 12 o'clock on Friday—namely, by paying the money into the bank at Eastbourne to the account of Mr. Kennard at the Bank of England. That was the suggestion made by Mr. Kennard to help the plaintiff out of the difficulty. In point of fact, what was done on July 6 was, as pointed out by Lawrence L.J., that Mr. Kennard made two concessions to the plaintiff: one was that he should have up to 12 o'clock to pay cash, and the other concession, if concession indeed it was, was that he should pay in this particular way instead of having to come and pay it personally. In my opinion, there is no consideration for the agreement to give time until 12 o'clock on the Friday, nor for the agreement which the jury find was concluded that if it was paid by 12 o'clock the bankruptcy notice should not be served.

For these reasons I agree that this appeal must be allowed with the consequences that have been indicated by the Master of the Rolls.

[The judgments of Lord Hanworth M.R. and Lawrence L.J. to the same effect, are omitted. Lawrence L.J. observed "Speaking for myself, I have had the greatest difficulty in this case in ascertaining the terms of the agreement."]

PROBLEM. Uncle promises Nephew to pay him $5,000 if he refrains from smoking until he is 21. Nephew promises to refrain and does so. Is Uncle liable? See *Hamer* v. *Sidway* (1891) 27 N.E. 256 (N.Y.C.A.).

E. Mutual Promises

THORP v. *THORP*, 1702. 12 Mod. 455; 88 E.R. 1448, 1450. HOLT C.J.: "... where the doing of a thing will be a good consideration, a promise to do that thing will be so too...."

HARRISON v. *CAGE*. 1698. 5 Mod. 411; 87 E.R. 736. A case of mutual promises to marry, breach by the woman. Action on the case. HOLT C.J.: "Why should not a woman be bound by her promise as well as a man is bound by his? Either all is *nudum pactum*, or else the one promise is as good as the other. You agree a woman shall have an action; now what is the consideration of a man's promise? Why, it is the woman's. Then why should not his promise be a good consideration for her promise, as well as her promise is a good consideration for his? There is the same parity of reason in the one case as there is in the other, and the consideration is mutual." TURTON J.: "This action is grounded on mutual promises."

NOTE ON LEGAL METHOD. The ease with which an eighteenth century judge could hold the exchange of a promise good consideration for a promise has not been characteristic of later centuries, notably the latter half of the nineteenth and the first half of the twentieth. Pollock, for example, in his *Contracts* (13th ed., p. 144), inclines to the view that an exchange of promises cannot be logically explained in terms of benefit and detriment. This rule, "the most important for the business of life" has "no conclusive reason other than the convenience of so holding." Unless the promise given in exchange is binding, how has the promisee suffered a legal detriment, or changed his position at the request of the promisor? It seems rather unconvincing to argue that the promisee is privileged to utter words or not, as he pleases, and that he gives up this privilege, because there is no reason to think that the promisor requests such an utterance. He requests a binding promise, that is, a legal thing, not a mere physical noise. On the other hand, if the promise is considered binding because of the exchanged promise, and the exchanged promise is binding because it, in turn, is given in consideration of the first promise, the circular argument is objectionable. A simple escape from this dilemma is to accept the existence of a bargain as a sufficient reason for enforcement and to include within the concept of bargain an executory exchange.

THE GREAT NORTHERN RAILWAY COMPANY v. *WITHAM*
England. Common Pleas. 1873. L.R. 9 C.P. 16

In October, 1871, the plaintiffs advertised for tenders for the supply of goods (amongst other things iron) to be delivered at their station at Doncaster, according to a certain specification. The Defendant sent in a tender as follows:-

I, the undersigned, hereby undertake to supply the Great Northern Railway Company, for twelve months from the 1st of November, 1871, to 31st of October, 1872, with such quantities of each or any of the several articles named in the attached specification as the company's storekeeper may order from time to time, at the price set opposite each article respectively, and agree to abide by the conditions stated on the other side.

(Signed) SAMUEL WITHAM.

The tender was accepted and several orders for iron were given by the company, which were from time to time duly executed by the defendant: but ultimately the defendant refused to supply any more, whereupon this action was brought.

A verdict having been found for the plaintiffs, Digby Seymour, Q.C., moved to enter a nonsuit, on the ground that the contract was void for want of mutuality. He contended that, as the company did not bind themselves to take any iron whatever from the defendant, his promise to supply them with iron was a promise without consideration. . . .

BRETT J.: The company advertised for tenders for the supply of stores such as they might think fit to order, for one year. The defendant made a tender offering to supply them for that period at certain fixed prices; and the company accepted his tender. If there were no other objection, the contract between the parties would be found in the tender and the letter accepting it. This action is brought for the defendant's refusal to deliver goods ordered by the company; and the objection to the plaintiff's right to recover is, that the contract is unilateral. I do not, however, understand what objection that is to a contract. Many contracts are obnoxious to the same complaint. If I say to another, "If you will go to York, I will give you £100" that is in a certain sense a unilateral contract. He has not promised to go to York; but if he goes it cannot be doubted that he will be entitled to receive the £100. His going to York at my request is a sufficient consideration for my promise. So, if one says to another, "If you will give me an order for iron, or other goods, I will supply it at a given price:" if the order is given, there is a complete contract which the seller is bound to perform. There is in such a case ample consideration for the promise. So, here, the company having given the defendant an order at his request, his acceptance of the order would bind them. If any authority could have been found to sustain Mr. Seymour's contention, I should have considered that a rule ought to be granted. But none has been cited. *Burton* v. *Great Northern Railway Company*, 9 Ex. 507, is not at all to the purpose. This is matter of every day's practice; and I think it would be wrong to countenance the notion that a man who tenders for the supply of goods in this way is not bound to deliver them when an order is given. I agree that this judgment does not decide the question whether the defendant might have absolved himself from the further performance of the contract by giving notice. *Rule refused.*

[The concurring opinions of Keating and Grove JJ. are omitted.]

QUESTIONS. Does Brett J. refer by "unilateral contract" to the same situation as Digby Seymour, Q.C., does with his expression "want of mutuality"? Did the court find a contract in this case? Was it unilateral or bilateral? What do these expressions mean? How do you "absolve yourself" from performance of a contract by giving notice unless the contract itself provides for notice, or notice can be reasonably implied? Under the contract found by the court, does the railway have to buy any iron? Is it free to buy iron from anybody else if it chooses?

Speaking of this case, Professor Corbin, in "The Effect of Options on Consideration" (1925), 34 *Yale Law Journal* 571, said: "In cases like this it may be reasonably argued that there was no contract because of lack of acceptance in accordance with the offer rather than for lack of consideration; orders were asked of the offeree and not illusory promises. Often however, the offeror does not so understand his own offer and makes no such contention;

lack of consideration is a good defense. If an order is given before the offer is withdrawn, a contract is made." Do you agree? What are the terms of the "contract" that is so made?

By "illusory promise" Professor Corbin means a "promise that is not a promise. ... the chief feature of contract law is that by an expression of his will today the promisor limits his freedom of voluntary choice in the future. ... To fall within this field, therefore, a promise must in its terms express a willingness to effect this limitation on freedom of choice. ... [An] illusory promise is neither enforceable against the one making it, nor is it operative as a consideration for a return promise."

Should a promise to sell the *entire output* of the promisor's plant be regarded as equally illusory? What about a promise to buy all the promisor's *needs* in a certain line from the promisee? Will the analysis differ if there are promises not to sell the *output* to third persons, or to buy *needs* from third persons?

PERCIVAL v. *LONDON ETC. COMMITTEE.* 1918. 87 L.J. K.B. 677. ATKIN J.: "One knows that these tenders are very often in a form under which the purchasing body is not bound to give the tenderer any order at all; in other words, the contractor offers to supply goods at a price, and if the purchasing body chooses to give him an order for goods during the stipulated time, then he is under an obligation to supply the goods in accordance with the order; but apart from that nobody is bound."

IN RE THE GLOUCESTER MUNICIPAL ELECTION PETITION. [1901] 1 K.B. 683. A tender ·to supply goods which the council might want in a certain period, when accepted was held to result in a contract. DARLING J.: "There is a good obligation to order from the respondent such of the goods included in his tender as the council might require ... for I do not think that the council would have been justified in treating the respondent's tender as a mere price list, and ordering the goods which they required from any one whom they might choose. ... There was a contract, because there was an obligation on both sides."

REGINA v. *DEMERS.* [1900] A.C. 103 (Quebec). On March 18, 1897, a contract was signed by Her Majesty represented by the Provincial Secretary of Quebec and Demers under which Demers covenanted to execute for Her Majesty for a term of eight years from January 1, 1897, at price Demers had received for the same work since 1892, the printing and binding of the public documents specified in the contract. The Government was defeated in the election shortly after and on May 28, 1897, their successors came into office. On June 30, the contract was cancelled. Demers sued to recover $85,000 for lost profits. Held, for the defendant province. LORD MACNAGHTEN: "The contract ... does not purport to contain any covenant or obligation of any sort on the part of the Crown. The respondent undertakes to print certain public documents at certain specified rates. For all work given to him on the footing of the contract the Government. was undoubtedly bound to pay according to the agreed tariff. But the contract imposes no obligation on the Crown to pay the respondent for work not given to him for execution. There is nothing in the contract binding the Government to give to the respondent all or any of the printing work referred to in the contract, nor is there anything in it to prevent the Government from giving the whole of the work, or such ·part as they think fit, to any other printer." [The Superior Court had held that the contract could not bind the Crown for payments extending over future years without legislative sanction. The Court of Queen's Bench held that because the printing was not unusual and the habit being to make such contracts for a term of years, the making of the contract was a matter of administration although, of course, the legislature might interfere if it chose. Damages granted in the Superior Court for the fiscal year were confirmed with future rights reserved.]

BERLIN MACHINE WORKS, LIMITED v. *RANDOLPH & BAKER, LIMITED.* 1917. 45 N.B.R. 201 (New Brunswick. Appeal Division). In an action for the purchase price of machinery sold to the defendant for his lumber mill the defendant counterclaimed for damages because the machinery proved unsatisfactory. One item of damage was the loss sustained by the defendant in performing his contract to deliver the output of his mill to a purchaser. The plaintiff was aware of the contract. To meet his supposed obligation the defendant went out and purchased 1,000,000 feet of lumber which he delivered to the purchaser for fifty cents a thousand less than he paid for it. This item of $500 was not allowed because the defendant was not "bound to deliver any specific quantity of logs" or "any other logs than those cut in his own mill." WHITE J.: "I think it quite clear that the allowance of the $500 could only be sustained by proof that the defendants were legally bound to make delivery to MacKay of this million feet which they purchased . . . there is no such proof."

GREENBERG v. *LAKE SIMCOE ICE SUPPLY CO.* 1917. 39 O.L.R. 32 (Ontario High Court). The Lake Simcoe Company, a dealer in coal, confirmed an arrangement with Greenberg, a retailer of coal, in these words: "We beg to confirm our quotation on coal taken by you at our Dupont or Florence street yards, namely, . . . $6.75 per ton for all coal taken from September 1st to April 30, 1917." No quantity of coal was agreed to be supplied and there was no undertaking to purchase any coal. In fact about forty tons were supplied before the Company sought to put aside the arrangement because of suspected dishonest dealings. Greenberg sued for damages. Held, no contract. LATCHFORD J.: "The plaintiff was not under the slightest obligation to purchase a single ton of coal from the defendants. There was no consideration from him to the defendants, and no acceptance . . . except in so far as the plaintiff from time to time prior to the revelation of his fraud, applied for and was supplied with coal. Until each such transaction was completed, there was no mutuality of obligation."

TOBIAS v. DICK AND T. EATON CO.
Manitoba. King's Bench. [1937] 4 D.L.R. 546

DYSART J.: The plaintiff sues John Dick and the T. Eaton Co. Ltd.,—the one for a breach of an alleged contract, and the other for interfering with his rights under that contract. He also charges both defendants with conspiracy, and asks for an injunction and damages.

The "contract" in question was originally drawn up by the plaintiff Tobias himself, who, by trickery, induced the defendant to sign it in its present changed form; but this defendant has by conduct since confirmed it, and cannot repudiate it. It reads thus—

"Morden, Manitoba, April   th., 1935.

AGREEMENT

"This is to confirm that A. M. Tobias of Morden, Manitoba has the exclusive selling agency, to sell and organize territory and appoint his own agents for the John Dick Crushers, from the above date, April   th., 1935 to December 31st., 1937, for all Manitoba, Saskatchewan and Alberta.

"John Dick reserves the right to sell in the district and tributary of Emerson, Manitoba, and for a radius of 30 miles East, West, North and South of the Town of Emerson, Manitoba.

"The cost of the grain grinders to A. M. Tobias is $43.00 F.O.B. Emerson. . . .

"At no time must there be more than five machines unpaid for, and all machines must be paid for in cash, unless with the consent of John Dick.
"Witness H. Dueck   A. M. Tobias
"Jno. E. Dick."

The parties to this litigation assumed to the very last day of the trial that this document constituted a contract binding on both parties thereto. In my opinion, it is not a contract at all. It has no mutuality—it is entirely a one-sided arrangement. By it, Tobias gets the exclusive right "to sell" Dick's machines within a stated territory for a stated time, but does not promise to sell any of the machines. The term "to sell" by implication gives Tobias the right first to *buy*, in order that he may then sell. In essence therefore, the document gives him the exclusive right to *buy* Dick's entire output of machines. This construction finds confirmation in the later provisions of the document fixing the price and terms upon which Tobias may buy the machines from Dick.

These provisions taken together clearly indicate that there is no control left in Dick over the machines, nor over Tobias' dealings in respect of the machines after Tobias has bought them; nor over the appointment of agents or the organization of a selling staff. Tobias' profits are not based on commission, but he is free to resell the machines at his own price and terms, and through his own appointed agents. Clearly, therefore, the agreement, notwithstanding an express declaration to that effect, does not create an agency.

The indirect promise by Dick "to sell" to Tobias is not supported by any consideration moving from Tobias, and so is not binding upon Dick. There is therefore no contract. The document evidences nothing more than an offer from Dick open for a given time. This offer of course remains open for acceptance until withdrawn, and has never been formally withdrawn. It is of such a nature, having regard to Dick's method of manufacturing, that it could be accepted in part, from time to time. And so far as it was accepted, it was accepted by instalments.

Tobias ordered a number of machines on two separate occasions, took delivery of them and paid for them. Some of these he is unable to sell, but he does not pretend that he can return them to Dick and have the price refunded, as he might do if he were an agent.

Apart from these two partial acceptances, Tobias has not requested any more machines, and there has therefore been no refusal by Dick to live up to his offer. Dick was only too anxious to sell more machines to Tobias, and repeatedly urged Tobias to take those that were already completed. Only after Dick had lost all hope of disposing of his machines to Tobias did he decide to ignore his "agreement" altogether and sell his machines elsewhere.

To sum up, there was no contract between these two parties, and therefore no breach. The plaintiff's action against Dick must be dismissed with costs. . . .

The plaintiff's action against the T. Eaton Co. will also be dismissed with costs. . . .

[Action dismissed.]

WOOD v. *LUCY, LADY DUFF-GORDON*. 1917. 222 N.Y. 88, 118 N.E. 214 (New York Court of Appeals). Wood was given the exclusive right for one year, renewable, subject to Lady Duff-Gordon's approval, to place her endorsement on dresses, hats and the like, and in return she was to have one-half of all profits and revenues from any contracts Wood might make. The agreement recited that "The said Otis F. Wood possesses a business organization adapted to the placing of such endorsements as the said Lucy, Lady Duff-Gordon, has approved." Lady Duff-Gordon broke the agreement, placed her endorsement without Wood's knowledge, and withheld profits. Wood sued and Lady Duff-Gordon denied consideration. Held, for plaintiff. CARDOZO J.: "It is true that he does not promise in so many words that he will use reasonable efforts to place the defendant's endorsements and market her designs. We think, however, that such a promise is fairly to be implied. The law has outgrown its primitive stage of formalism when the precise word was the sovereign talisman, and every slip was fatal. It takes a broader view today. A promise may be lacking, and yet the whole writing may be 'instinct with an obligation', imperfectly expressed. . . . If that is so, there is a contract. . . . His promise to pay the defendant one-half of the profits and revenues resulting from the exclusive agency and to render accounts monthly was a promise to use reasonable efforts to bring profits and revenues into existence."

QUESTIONS. If Lady Duff-Gordon were suing Wood because he failed to bring any profits and revenues into existence what standard of effort on Wood's part would she have to prove? How would the damages be measured? If Wood were also under the same "contract" with another equally prominent person, how would he have to divide his efforts? Is the business incentive on Wood's part enough to justify holding Lady Duff-Gordon to her promise? Could we say that Lady Duff-Gordon exchanged her promise for the chance, given her by Wood, that he would likely bring into existence profits and revenues?

HOLT v. *WARD CLARENCIEUX*. 1732. 2 Strange 937; 93 E.R. 954 (England, King's Bench). The plaintiff and defendant agreed to marry, the female plaintiff being fifteen years old. The defendant did not marry her but did marry someone else. In an action for £4,000 plaintiff obtained a verdict for £2,000 and demurred to the plea of infancy. LORD RAYMOND L.C.J.: "The objection in this case is, that, the plaintiff not being bound equally with the defendant, this is *nudum pactum*, and the defendant cannot be charged in this action. . . . [The] single question is, whether this contract, as against the plaintiff, was absolutely void. And we are all of opinion that this contract is not void, but only voidable at the election of the infant; and as to the person of full age it absolutely binds.

"The contract of an infant is considered in law as different from the contracts of all other persons. In some cases his contract shall bind him; such is the contract of an infant for necessaries, and the law allows him to make this contract as necessary for his preservation; and therefore in such case a single bill shall bind him, though a bond with a penalty shall not. . . .

"Where the contract may be for the benefit of the infant or to his prejudice, the law so far protects him as to give him an opportunity to consider it when he comes of age; and it is good or voidable at his election. . . . But though the infant has this privilege, yet the party with whom he contracts has not; he is bound in all events. And as marriage is now looked upon to be an advantageous contract, and no distinction holds whether the party suing be man or woman, but the true distinction is whether it may be for the benefit of the infant, we think that though no express case upon a marriage contract can be cited, yet it falls within the general reason of the law with regard to infants' contracts. And no dangerous consequence can follow from this determination, because our opinion protects the infant even more than if we rule the contract to be absolutely void. And as to persons of full age, it leaves them where the law leaves them, which grants them no such protection against being drawn into inconvenient contracts.

"For these reasons we are all of opinion that the plaintiff ought to have her judgment upon the demurrer."

F. Pre-Existing Duty

HARRIS v. WATSON
England. Nisi Prius, 1791. Peake 102; 170 E.R. 94

In this case the declaration stated that the plaintiff being a seaman on board the ship "Alexander," of which the defendant was master and commander, and which was bound on a voyage to Lisbon: whilst the ship was on her voyage, the defendant, in consideration that the plaintiff would perform some extra work, in navigating the ship, promised to pay him five guineas over and above his common wages. There were other counts for work and labour, &c.

The plaintiff proved that the ship being in danger, the defendant, to induce the seamen to exert themselves, made the promise stated in the first count.

LORD KENYON: If this action was to be supported, it would materially affect the navigation of this kingdom. It has been long since determined that when the freight is lost, the wages are also lost. This rule was founded on a principle of policy, for if sailors were in all events to have their wages, and in times of danger entitled to insist on an extra charge on such a promise as this, they would in many cases suffer a ship to sink, unless the captain would pay an extravagant demand they might think proper to make. The plaintiff was nonsuited.

STILK v. MYRICK
England. Nisi Prius. 1809. 2 Camp. 317; 170 E.R. 1168

This was an action for a seaman's wages, on a voyage from London to the Baltic and back.

By the ship's articles, executed before the commencement of the voyage, the plaintiff was to be paid at the rate of £5 a month; and the principal question in the cause was, whether he was entitled to a higher rate of wages. In the course of the voyage two of the seamen deserted; and the captain having in vain attempted to supply their places at Cronstadt, there entered into an agreement with the rest of the crew, that they should have the wages of the two who had deserted equally divided among them, if he could not procure two other hands at Gottenburgh. This was found impossible; and the ship was worked back to London by the plaintiff and eight more of the original crew, with whom the agreement had been made at Cronstadt.

Lord Ellenborough: I think *Harris* v. *Watson* [the preceding case] was rightly decided; but I doubt whether the ground of public policy, upon which Lord Kenyon is stated to have proceeded, be the true principle on which the decision is to be supported. Here, I say the agreement is void for want of consideration. There was no consideration for the ulterior pay promised to the mariners who remained with the ship. Before they sailed from London they had undertaken to do all they could under all the emergencies of the voyage. They had sold all their services till the voyage should be completed. If they had been at liberty to quit the vessel at Cronstadt, the case would have been quite different; or if the captain had capriciously discharged the two men who were wanting, the others might not have been compellable to take the whole duty upon themselves, and their agreeing to do so might have been a sufficient consideration for the promise of an advance of wages. But the desertion of a part of the crew is to be considered an emergency of the voyage as much as their death; and these who remain are bound by the terms of their original contract to exert themselves to the utmost to bring the ship in safety to her destined port. Therefore, without looking to the policy of this agreement, I think it is void for want of consideration, and that the plaintiff can only recover at the rate of £5 a month.

Verdict accordingly.

HARTLEY v. *PONSONBY*. 1857. 7 E. & B. 872; 119 E.R. 1471. The crew of a ship was so reduced in number that "for the ship to go to sea with so few hands was dangerous to life. If so, it was not incumbent on the plaintiff to perform the work; and he was in the condition of a free man." It was held there was consideration for the contract to pay him an additional sum to work the ship home.

QUESTIONS. Suppose the captain in *Stilk* v. *Myrick* had requested the seamen to give him a peppercorn (if they had one with them). Suppose he had put his promise in writing and under seal?

HOLMES, THE COMMON LAW (1881)

. . . The only universal consequence of a legally binding promise is, that the law makes the promisor pay damages if the promised event does not come to pass. In every case it leaves him free from interference until the time for fulfilment has gone by, and therefore free to break his contract if he chooses. . . .

If, when a man promised to labour for another, the law made him do it, his relation to his promise might be called a servitude *ad hoc* with some truth. But that is what the law never does. It never interferes until a promise has been broken, and therefore cannot possibly be performed according to its tenor. It is true that in some instances equity does what is called compelling specific performance. But, in the first place, I am speaking of the common law, and, in the next, this only means that equity compels the performance of certain elements of the total promise which are still capable of performance. . . .

NOTE. Holmes is suggesting that the duty of the promisor under a contract is *either* to perform his contract *or* to pay damages. It is then arguable that since the promisor has his choice, that is, this privilege of performing one duty or the other, by giving up this privilege and agreeing to perform the contract rather than pay damages he has given up a valuable legal right, called in technical terms a *privilege*. And that, of course, is a valid exchange constituting a legal detriment. On this basis *Stilk* v. *Myrick* must be wrongly decided, but *Harris* v. *Watson* may be right.

Does Holmes' theory not settle the whole legal character of a promise (or contract) by what happens in one type of case? He concedes that the equitable remedy of specific performance does not fit into his theory. Does *Stilk* v. *Myrick*? Has the common law not succeeded in denying the alternative here? Would it be true to say that the "law" requires a promisor to perform his promise, but administrative necessity sometimes (usually) permits him to escape by paying damages, but sometimes (rarely) obtains actual performance, and sometimes (more rarely, as in the principal cases) indirectly obtains actual performance by refusing to recognize the "right" to break a contract as the alternative to performance? In the last situation administrative necessity, which usually filters out specific performance, places no obstacle in the path of complete legal recognition of the duty to perform. In other words, the duty to perform is on what the semanticists might call a different level of abstraction from the duty to pay damages, and the two ought not to be considered as alternatives. Damages are supplementary to performance.

SMITH v. DAWSON
Ontario. Court of Appeal 1923. 53 O.L.R. 615

The plaintiffs agreed with the defendant to build her a house for $6,464. When the house was nearly finished, a fire took place in it doing considerable damage.

The defendant effected insurance on the house as it was being built. The plaintiffs effected no insurance. After the fire the defendant asked the plaintiffs to go ahead and complete the house. The plaintiffs said they would if the defendant promised to pay them the insurance monies.

RIDDELL J.: . . . The situation then seems quite clear—the plaintiffs, learning that the defendant had received some insurance money on the house, objected to go on without some kind of assurance that they were to get the insurance money—the defendant demurred, as she had lost considerably by the destruction of her furniture, but finally said, "All right, go ahead and do the work." If this constituted a contract at all, it was that she would give them the insurance money which she had received, if they would go ahead and do the work they were already under a legal obligation to do.

In some of the United States a doctrine has been laid down that (at least in building contracts) the contractor has the option either to complete his contract or to abandon it and pay damages. These Courts have accordingly held that the abandonment by the contractor of his option to abandon is sufficient consideration for a promise to pay an extra amount.

The Courts of Illinois, Indiana, and Massachusetts seem to have adopted this rule. . . . But such a course is to allow a contractor to take advantage of his own wrong, and other American Courts reprobate it: 9 *Corpus Juris*, 720; 13 *Corpus Juris*, 354, sec. 210, and cases cited in notes.

This is not and never was law in Ontario, as it is not and never was law in England. It has long been text-book law that "not the promise or the actual performance of something which the promisee is legally bound to perform" is a consideration for a promise.

Halsbury's *Laws of England*, 385, para. 798; "the performance of an existing contract by one of the parties is no consideration for a new promise by the other party": Leake on Contracts, 7th ed., p. 455, and cases cited.

I am of the opinion that the promise (if there was one) to pay for the work to be done was not binding for want of consideration, and would allow the appeal with costs here and below. If there be any difficulty in moulding the judgment, one of us may be spoken to.

[The judgments of Latchford and Middleton JJ. are omitted. Logie J. agreed with Riddell J.]

SHADWELL v. *SHADWELL*
England. Common Pleas. 1860. 30 L.J.C.P. 145

Charles Shadwell wrote from Gray's Inn, to his nephew, then unmarried, on August 11, 1838 as follows: "My dear Lancey, I am glad to hear of your intended marriage with Ellen Nicholl; and as I promised to assist you at starting, I am happy to tell you that I will pay to you £150 yearly during my life, and until your annual income derived from your profession of a Chancery barrister shall amount to 600 guineas, of which your own admission will be the only evidence that I shall receive or require." Lancey Shadwell married Ellen Nicholl and claimed to have earned eighteen yearly sums of £150 in his uncle's lifetime and that he never earned as much as 600 guineas. He had received twelve such sums and £12 on account of the thirteenth, but his uncle defaulted in paying the rest. On his uncle's death Lancey Shadwell commenced this action against his uncle's executor. On a demurrer it was contended that there was no consideration for the promise: Lancey was already engaged to be married when Charles Shadwell promised and had not been requested by him to marry, and, moreover, he had abandoned the practice of a Chancery barrister in 1858.

ERLE C.J.: . . . Now do these facts show that the promise was in consideration, either of the loss to be sustained by the plaintiff, or the benefit to be derived from the plaintiff to the uncle at his, the uncle's request? My answer is in the affirmative. First, do these facts show a loss sustained by the plaintiff at the uncle's request? When I answer this in the affirmative, I am aware that a man's marriage with the woman of his choice is in one sense a boon, and in that sense the reverse of a loss; yet, as between the plaintiff and the party promising an income to support the marriage, it may be a loss. The plaintiff may have made the most material changes in his position, and have induced the object of his affections to do the same, and have incurred pecuniary liabilities resulting in embarrassments, which would be in every sense a loss if the income which had been promised should be withheld; and if the promise was made in order to induce the parties to marry, the promise so made would be, in legal effect, a request to marry. Secondly, do these facts show a benefit derived from the plaintiff to the uncle at his requests? In answering again in the affirmative, I am at liberty

to consider the relation in which the parties stood, and the interest in the
status of the nephew which the uncle declares. The marriage primarily affects the parties thereto; but in the second degree it may be an object of
interest with a near relative, and in that sense a benefit to him. This benefit
is also derived from the plaintiff at the uncle's request, if the promise of the
annuity was intended as an inducement to the marriage; and the averment
that the plaintiff, relying on the promise, married, is an averment that the
promise was one inducement to the marriage. This is a consideration averred in the declaration, and it appears to me to be expressed in the letter,
construed with the surrounding circumstances. No case bearing a strong
analogy to the present was cited, but the importance of enforcing promises
which have been made to induce parties to marry has been often recognized. . . . I do not feel it necessary to add anything about the numerous
authorities referred to in the learned arguments addressed to us, because
the decision turns on a question of fact, whether the consideration for the
promise is proved as pleaded. I think it is, and therefore my judgment on
the first demurrer is for the plaintiff. The second demurrer raises the question, whether the plaintiff's continuing at the bar was made a condition
precedent to the right to the annuity. I think not. The uncle promises to
continue the annuity until the professional income exceeds the sum mentioned, and I find no stipulation that the annuity shall cease if the professional diligence ceases. My judgment on this demurrer is also for the
plaintiff, and I should state that this is the judgment of my Brother Keating
and myself, my Brother Byles differing with us.

BYLES J.: I am of opinion that the defendant is entitled to the judgment
of the court. . . . The inquiry . . . narrows itself to this question. Does the
letter itself disclose any consideration for the promise? The consideration
relied on by the plaintiff's counsel being the subsequent marriage of the
plaintiff, I think the letter discloses no consideration. . . . It is by no means
clear that the words "at starting" mean "on marriage with Ellen Nicholl,"
or with any one else. The more natural meaning seems to me to be "at
starting in the profession," for it will be observed that these words are used
by the testator in reciting a prior promise, made when the testator had not
heard of the proposed marriage with Ellen Nicholl, or, so far as appears,
heard of any proposed marriage. This construction is fortified by the consideration that the annuity is not, in terms, made to begin from the marriage, but, as it should seem, from the date of the letter. Neither is it in
terms made defeasible if Ellen Nicholl should die before marriage.
   But even on the assumption that the words "at starting" mean "on marriage," I still think that no consideration appears sufficient to sustain the
promise. The promise is one which, by law, must be in writing; and the
fourth plea shows that no consideration or request, dehors the letter,
existed, and, therefore, that no such consideration or request can be alluded
to by the letter. Marriage of the plaintiff at the testator's express request
would be, no doubt, an ample consideration, but marriage of the plaintiff
without the testator's request is no consideration to the testator. It is true
that marriage is, or may be a detriment to the plaintiff; but detriment to the
plaintiff is not enough, unless it either be a benefit to the testator or be
treated by the testator as such, by having been suffered at his request.
Suppose a defendant to promise a plaintiff, "I will give you £500 if you
break your leg," would that detriment to the plaintiff, should it happen, be
any consideration? If it be said that such an accident is an involuntary mis-

chief, would it have been a binding promise if the testator had said, "I will give you £100 a year while you continue in your present chambers"? I conceive that the promise would not be binding for want of a previous request by the testator.

Now, the testator in the case before the court derived, so far as appears, no personal benefit from the marriage. The question, therefore, is still further narrowed to this point. Was the marriage at the testator's request? Express request there was none. Can any request be implied? The only words from which it can be contended that it is to be implied are the words, "I am glad to hear of your intended marriage with Ellen Nicholl." But it appears from the fourth plea that that marriage had already been agreed on, and that the testator knew it. These words, therefore, seem to me to import no more than the satisfaction of the testator at the engagement as an accomplished fact. No request, can as it seems to me, be inferred from them.

And, further, how does it appear that the testator's implied request, if it could be implied, or his promise, if that promise alone would suffice or both together, were intended to cause the marriage, or did cause it, so that the marriage can be said to have taken place at the testator's request, or, in other words, in consequence of that request? It seems to me, not only that this does not appear, but that the contrary appears; for the plaintiff before the letter had already bound himself to marry by placing himself not only under a moral, but under a legal obligation to marry, and the testator knew it. The well known cases which have been cited at the bar in support of the position that a promise, based on the consideration of doing that which a man is already bound to do, is invalid, apply to this case; and it is not necessary, in order to invalidate the consideration, that the plaintiff's prior obligation to afford that consideration should have been an obligation to the defendant. It may have been an obligation to a third person. . . . The reason why the doing what a man is already bound to do is no consideration, is not only because such a consideration is in judgment of law of no value, but because a man can hardly be allowed to say that the prior legal obligation was not his determining motive.

But whether he can be allowed to say so or not, the plaintiff does not say so here. He does, indeed, make an attempt to meet this difficulty by alleging, in the replication to the fourth plea, that he married relying on the testator's promise; but he shrinks from alleging that though he had promised to marry before the testator's promise to him, nevertheless, he would have broken his engagement, and would not have married without the testator's promise. A man may rely on encouragements to the performance of his duty who yet is prepared to do his duty without those encouragements. At the utmost, the allegation that he relied on the testator's promise seems to me to import no more than that he believed the testator would be as good as his word. It appears to me, for these reasons, that this letter is no more than a letter of kindness, creating no legal obligation. In their judgment on the other portions of the record I agree with the rest of the Court.

[Judgment for the plaintiff.]

DE CICCO v. *SCHWEIZER*. 1917. 221 N.Y. 431; 117 N.E. 807 (New York, Court of Appeals). Joseph Schweizer promised Count Oberto Gulinelli in writing to pay to Schweizer's daughter Blanche, who was about to marry the Count, the sum of $2500 annually during her lifetime. The agreement recited the intended marriage as consideration for the promise. The first payment was made on the day of the marriage, January 20, 1902. Payments were continued until 1912. About then the Count and Blanche assigned the agreement to Attilio De Cicco, who brought this action to recover the installment due in 1912. Consideration was denied on the ground that the Count and Blanche were already engaged when Schweizer gave his promise. CARDOZO J.: "The courts of this state are committed to the view that a promise by A to B to induce him not to break his contract with C is void. . . . If that is the true nature of this promise, there was no consideration. We have never held, however, that a like infirmity attaches to a promise by A, not merely to B, but to B and C jointly, to induce them not to rescind or modify a contract which they are free to abandon. . . . It would not have been enough that the Count remained willing to marry. The plain import of the contract is that his bride also should be willing, and that marriage should follow. The promise was intended to affect the conduct, not of one only, but of both. This becomes the more evident when we recall that though the promise ran to the Count, it was intended for the benefit of the daughter. . . . The situation, therefore, is the same in substance as if the promise had run to husband and wife alike, and had been intended to induce performance by both. They were free by common consent to terminate their engagement or to postpone the marriage. If they forebore from exercising that right and assumed the responsibilities of marriage in reliance on the defendant's promise, he may not now retract it." Judgment for the plaintiff affirmed.

SCOTSON AND OTHERS v. PEGG
England. Exchequer. 1861 6 H. & N. 295; 158 E.R. 121

Plaintiffs, who were under contract with other persons to deliver a cargo of coal to the defendant, were promised by the defendant that if they would deliver the coal he, the defendant , would unload it at the rate of forty-nine tons a day. Plaintiffs delivered the coal but the defendant failed to unload it at the agreed rate, and in fact took five days longer. Plaintiffs claimed damages for having to maintain the ship and its crew for the extra time. Defendant pleaded that because the plaintiffs were already obliged to other persons (from whom the defendant had bought the coal) to deliver it to the defendant, there was no consideration in their promising the defendant to do what they were already obliged to do.

[In the argument the following comments were made. . . . WILDE B.: . . . A man may be bound by his contract to do a particular thing, but while it is doubtful whether or no he will do it, if a third person steps in and says, "I will pay you if you will do it," the performance is a valid consideration for the payment. Martin B. If a builder was under contract to finish a house on a particular day, and the owner promised to pay him a sum of money if he would do it, what is to prevent the builder from recovering the money?]

MARTIN B.: I am of opinion that the plea is bad, both on principle and in law. It is bad in law because the ordinary rule is, that any act done whereby the contracting party receives a benefit is a good consideration for a promise by him. Here the benefit is the delivery of the coals to the defendant. It is consistent with the declaration that there may have been some dispute as to the defendant's right to have the coals, or it may be that the plaintiffs detained them for demurrage; in either case there would be good consideration that the plaintiffs, who were in possession of the coals, would allow the defendant to take them out of the ship. Then is it any answer that the plaintiffs had entered into a prior contract with other persons to deliver the coals to their order upon the same terms, and that the defendant was a stranger to that contract? In my opinion it is not. We must deal with this case as if no prior contract had been entered into. Suppose the plaintiffs had no chance of getting their money from the other person, who might perhaps have become bankrupt. The defendant gets a benefit by the delivery of the coals to him, and it is immaterial that the plaintiffs had previously contracted with third parties to deliver to their order.

WILDE B.: I am also of opinion that the plaintiffs are entitled to judgment. The plaintiffs say, that in consideration that they would deliver to the defendant a cargo of coals from their ship, the defendant promised to discharge the cargo in a certain way. The defendant, in answer, says, "You made a previous contract with other persons that they should discharge the cargo in the same way, and therefore there is no consideration for my promise." But why is there no consideration? It is said, because the plaintiffs, in delivering the coals, are only performing that which they were already bound to do. But to say that there is no consideration is to say that it is not possible for one man to have an interest in the performance of a contract made by another. But if a person chooses to promise to pay a sum of money in order to induce another to perform that which he has already contracted with a third person to do, I confess I cannot see why such a promise should not be binding. Here the defendant, who was a stranger to the original contract, induced the plaintiffs to part with the cargo, which they might not otherwise have been willing to do, and the delivery of it to the defendant was a benefit to him. I accede to the proposition that, if a person contracts with another to do a certain thing, he cannot make the performance of it a consideration for a new promise to the same individual. But there is no authority for the proposition that where there has been a promise to one person to do a certain thing, it is not possible to make a valid promise to another to do the same thing. Therefore, deciding this matter on principle, it is plain to my mind that the delivery of the coals to the defendant was a good consideration for his promise, although the plaintiffs had made a previous contract to deliver them to the order of other persons.

[Judgment for the plaintiff.]

McDEVITT v. *STOKES.* 1917. 174 Ky. 515; 192 S.W. 681 (Kentucky, Court of Appeals). Mike McDevitt, a jockey, was hired by one Shaw, the owner of the mare Grace, to drive her in the Kentucky Futurity race. Stokes, who ran a stock farm and owned Peter the Great and Orianna, the sire and dam of Grace, afterwards promised McDevitt $1000 if he would drive in the race and win. He drove and won. Stokes paid $200 but failed to pay the balance. In this action to recover $800, Stokes denied any fresh consideration for his promise. McDevitt showed that the value of Peter the Great had increased by $10,000, of Orianna, by $5000, and of other horses in Stokes' farm by $5000 each. Held, "the petition fails to state a cause of action against appellee. The latter was, it is true, benefited by the winning of the Kentucky Futurity purse by the mare Grace, driven by appellant, but the benefit was purely incidental and one to which he was entitled regardless of appellant's undertaking. . . ." [In this context, what does the word "entitled" mean? Does it refer to a legal relationship?]

ENGLAND v. *DAVIDSON*. 1840. 11 Ad. & E. 856; 113 E.R. 640 (England. Queen's Bench). The defendant offered a reward of £50 to anyone giving information leading to the conviction of persons who broke into his house. The plaintiff, a police constable on duty in the area in which the defendant's house was located, did give such information and claimed the reward. The defendant paid him five guineas but failed to pay the balance. In an action to recover the balance it was objected that the plaintiff had given no consideration since as a police constable he was bound to give such information anyway. Judgment for the plaintiff. LORD DENMAN C.J.: "I think there may be services which the constable is not bound to render and which he may therefore make the ground of a contract. We should not hold a contract to be against the policy of the law, unless the grounds for so deciding were very clear."

NOTE. Martin, counsel for the defendant in the case just noted, had argued that the contract was against public policy. To what policy is it obnoxious? Do rewards operate to deflect a policeman's attention from his regular duties? Should this fact, if it is a fact, justify the promisor's failure to carry out his promise? Some police forces have a rule that any rewards earned by a member of the force must be pooled for the benefit of all members. Some forces do not allow members to accept awards. Should a court concern itself with such a question, or should it be left to the chief of police?

REIF v. *PAGE*. 1882. 55 Wisc. 496. A husband offered a reward to anyone who would rescue his wife, dead or alive, from a burning building. A fireman who took out the dead body was held entitled to recover. The court said that a fireman was not legally bound to risk his life in effecting a rescue.

LAW REVISION COMMITTEE, SIXTH INTERIM REPORT
England. 1937. Cmnd. 5449; 15 *Can. Bar Rev.* 585

In 1934 the Lord Chancellor appointed a committee "to consider how far, having regard to the Statute Law and to judicial decisions, such legal maxims and doctrines as the Lord Chancellor may from time to time refer to the Committee require revision in modern conditions." These excerpts are from the report on the *Statute of Frauds* and the Doctrine of Consideration. The Committee's general attitude toward reform is a realistic, if pessimistic one, and may be seen from the first of the following paragraphs:

27. Many of us would like to see the doctrine abolished root and branch. But a recommendation to this effect would probably be unwise. It is so deeply embedded in our law that any measure which proposed to do away with it altogether would almost certainly arouse suspicion and hostility. An opportunity should, however, be taken to prune away from the doctrine those aspects of it which can create hardship or cause unnecessary inconvenience. If the proposals which follow are accepted, the doctrine will survive, though deprived of most of its mischievous features. . . .

36. Three cases must be discussed:

(a) Where A makes a promise to B in consideration of B doing or primising to do something which he is already bound to do by reason of a duty imposed upon him by the law, whether by a Statute or otherwise; for instance, the duty of a local police authority to afford adequate protection to A and his property;

(b) Where A makes a promise to B in consideration of B doing or promising to do something which he is already bound to do under a contract with A;

(c) Where A makes a promise to B in consideration of B doing or promising to do something which he is already bound to do under a contract with C.

In cases (a) and (b) where the thing promised or performed is precisely the thing which the promisor is already bound to do, and no more, and there is no dispute that he is bound to do it, there is said to be no consideration or only illusory consideration for the new promise, and it is not enforceable. In case (c) the law is not so clear and frequently other factors are present out of which a consideration for the promise can be manufactured.

In our opinion, in all three cases, a promise made by A to B in consideration of B doing or promising to do something which he is already bound to do should be enforced by the law, provided that in other respects such as legality and compatibility with public policy it is free from objection; thus a promise in return for an agreement by a police authority to give precisely the amount of protection it was by law bound to give and no more should be unenforceable as being against public policy.

The dominant factor is that A thought it worth his while to make the promise to B in order that he should feel more certain that B would do the thing bargained for, and we can see no reason in general why A, having got what he wanted, should be allowed to evade his promise. Moreover, why did the promisor make a new promise if it was to have no legal effect? The connection between the general rule under discussion and the dictum in *Pinnel's Case*, which is a particular application of it, will not have escaped notice, and the observations by Lord Blackburn already quoted are equally relevant to the cases now under discussion.

RAGGOW v. *SCOUGALL AND CO.*
England. Divisional Court. 1915. 31 T. L. R. 564

This was an appeal by the defendants, Messrs. Scougall and Co., who were a firm of mantle-makers, from a decision of Judge Rentoul in the City of London Court, by which plaintiff, a mantle designer, recovered judgment for £58.

In August, 1913, the plaintiff by an agreement in writing agreed to become the defendants' designer for two years at a certain salary. It was provided that if the business should be discontinued during the period the agreement should cease to be of any effect. When the war broke out many customers cancelled orders which they had given to the firm, and the defendants had to consider whether they should close the business altogether. They called their employees together, and most of them agreed to a reduction of wages during the war if the defendants would continue the business. The plaintiff entered into a new agreement in writing, in which he, like other employees of the firm, agreed to accept a smaller salary for the duration of the war, provided that when the war was over the terms of the old agreement should be revived. He went on with his work and accepted the new salary until February last, when the defendants received a solicitor's letter claiming payment in full at the rate fixed in the old agreement; and as they refused to pay the excess this action was brought.

In the Court below judgment was given for the plaintiff on the ground that no consideration had been shown for the new agreement to accept a reduced payment. . . .

MR. JUSTICE DARLING said that the appeal must be allowed. It was clear from the provision in the new agreement that the terms of the old one should be reviewed when the war came to an end and that until the war ended the old agreement was dead. The parties had in fact torn up the old agreement and made a new one by mutual consent. They could have done it by recitals setting out the existence and rescission of the old agreement, but they had adopted a shorter course. The new agreement was an agreement contemplating employment on certain terms while the war lasted, and on certain other terms, which could be ascertained by reference to the older document, after the war had ended. The point, therefore, as to want of consideration failed and the appeal succeeded. He was the more glad to be able to arrive at this conclusion on the law, for it was evident that the plaintiff was trying to do a very dishonest thing.

[Coleridge J. agreed.]

PROBLEM. A, a builder, agrees with B, a supplier of steel, that B will supply 1,000 tons of steel beams, which A requires for a construction project, at an agreed price. While the project is in progress the market price of steel rises dramatically, and B demands a higher price for the steel beams still to be delivered. Knowing that no other supplier could make the immediate deliveries that he requires, A agrees to B's demand. The beams are supplied but A now refuses to pay more than the price originally agreed. Advise B.

See *Gilbert Steel Ltd.* v. *University Construction, Ltd.* (1976) 12 O.R. (2d) 19 (C.A.).

FOAKES v. *BEER*
England. House of Lords. 1884. L.R. 9 App. Cas. 605

In 1875 Mrs. Beer recovered judgment against Dr. Foakes for £2090 19s. including costs. In an agreement dated December 21, 1876, Dr. Foakes promised to pay "the whole sum," £500 down and the balance in fixed payments over some five years; and Mrs. Beer promised not to take any proceedings on the judgment. This in effect meant that Mrs. Beer would not claim any interest on the unpaid part of the judgment. In 1882 Mrs. Beer commenced this action on the judgment for the interest, the principal amount having been paid as agreed. Cave J. held Mrs. Beer was not entitled to judgment because of the agreement. The Queen's Bench Division discharged an order for a new trial on the ground of misdirection. The Court of Appeal reversed that decision and entered judgment for the respondent for the interest due, with costs. Dr. Foakes appealed to the House of Lords.

HOLL Q.C. for the appellant: Apart from the doctrine of *Cumber* v. *Wane* (1721), 1 St. 425; 93 E.R. 613, there is no reason in sense or law why the agreement should not be valid, and the creditor prevented from enforcing his judgment if the agreement be performed. It may often be much more advantageous to the creditor to obtain immediate payment of part of his debt than to wait to enforce payment, or perhaps by pressing his debtor to force him into bankruptcy with the result of only a small dividend. Moreover if a composition is accepted friends, who would not otherwise do so, may be willing to come forward to assist the debtor. And if the creditor thinks that the acceptance of part is for his benefit who is to say it is not? The doctrine of *Cumber* v. *Wane*, has been continually assailed, as in *Couldery* v. *Bartrum* (1880), 19 Ch. D. 394, by Jessel M.R. In the note to *Cumber* v. *Wane* (1 Smith L.C. 4th ed. p. 253, 8th ed. p. 367) which was written by J. W. Smith and never disapproved by any of the editors, including Willes and Keating JJ., it is said "that its doctrine is founded upon vicious reasoning and false views of the office of a Court of law, which should rather strive to give effect to the engagements which persons have thought proper to enter into, than cast about for subtle reasons to defeat them upon the ground of being unreasonable. Carried to its full extent the doctrine of *Cumber* v. *Wane* embraces the exploded notion that in order to render valid a contract not under seal, the adequacy as well as the existence of the consideration must be established. Accordingly in modern times it has been, as appears by the preceding part of the note, subjected to modification in several instances," *Cumber* v. *Wane* was decided on a ground now admitted to be erroneous, viz. that the satisfaction must be found by the Court to be reasonable. The Court cannot inquire into the adequacy of the consideration. *Reynolds* v. *Pinhowe* (1595), Cro. Eliz. 429; 78 E.R. 669, which was not cited in *Cumber* v. *Wane* . . . decided that the saving of trouble was a sufficient consideration; "for it is a benefit unto him to have his debt without suit or charge." . . . *Pinnel's Case* (1602), 5 Coke's Rep. 117a; 77 E.R. 237, was decided on a point of pleading; the dictum that payment of a smaller sum was no satisfaction of a larger, was extra-judicial, and overlooked all considerations of mercantile convenience, such as mentioned in *Reynolds* v. *Pinhowe*; and it is also noticeable that it was a case of a bond debt sought to be set aside by a parol agreement. It is every day practice for tradesmen to take less in satisfaction of a larger sum, and give discount, where there is neither custom nor right to take credit. . . . The result of the cases is that if *Cumber* v. *Wane* be right, payment of a less sum than the debt due, by a bill, promissory note or cheque is a good discharge; but payment of such less sum by sovereigns or Bank of England notes is not. Here the agreement is not to take less than the debt, but to give time for payment of the whole without interest. Mankind have never acted on the doctrine of *Cumber* v. *Wane*, but the contrary; nay few are aware of it. By overruling it the House will only declare the universal practice to be good law as well as good sense.

[EARL OF SELBORNE L.C.: Whatever may be the ultimate decision of this appeal the House is much indebted to Mr. Holl for his exceedingly able argument.]

EARL OF SELBORNE L.C.: . . . The question, therefore, is nakedly raised by this appeal, whether your Lordships are now prepared, not only to overrule, as contrary to law, the doctrine stated by Sir Edward Coke to have been laid down by all the judges of the Common Pleas in *Pinnel's Case* in 1602, and repeated in his note to Littleton, sect. 344. but to treat a prospective agreement, not under seal, for satisfaction of a debt, by a series of payments on account to a total amount less than the whole debt, as binding in law, provided those payments are regularly made; the case not being one of a composition with a common debtor, agreed to, *inter se*, by several creditors. I prefer so to state the question instead of treating it (as it was put at the Bar) as depending on the authority of the case of *Cumber* v. *Wane*, decided in 1718. It may well be that distinctions, which in later cases have been held sufficient to exclude the application of that doctrine, existed and were improperly disregarded in *Cumber* v. *Wane*; and yet that the doctrine itself may be law, rightly recognized in *Cumber* v. *Wane*, and not really contradicted by any later authorities. And this appears to me to be the true state of the case. The doctrine itself, as laid down by Sir Edward Coke, may have been criticised, as questionable in principle, by some persons whose opinions are entitled to respect, but it has never been judicially overruled; on the contrary I think it has always since the sixteenth century, been accepted as law. If so, I cannot think that your Lordships would do right, if you were now to reverse, as erroneous, a judgment of the Court of Appeal, proceeding upon a doctrine which has been accepted as part of the law of England for 280 years.

The distinction between the effect of a deed under seal, and that of an agreement by parol, or by writing not under seal, may seem arbitrary but it is established in our law; nor is it really unreasonable or practically inconvenient that the law should require particular solemnities to give to a gratuitous contract the force of a binding obligation. If the question be (as, in the actual state of the law, I think it is), whether consideration is, or is not, given in a case of this kind, by the debtor who pays down part of the debt presently due from him, for a promise by the creditor to relinquish, after certain further payments on account, the residue of the debt, I cannot say that I think consideration is given, in the sense in which I have always understood that word as used in our law. It might be (and indeed I think it would be) an improvement in our law, if a release or acquittance of the whole debt, or payment of any sum which the creditor might be content to receive by way of accord and satisfaction (though less than the whole), were held to be, generally, binding, though not under seal; nor should I be unwilling to see equal force given to a prospective agreement, like the present, in writing though not under seal; but I think it impossible, without refinements which partially alter the sense of the word, to treat such a release or acquittance as supported by any new consideration proceeding from the debtor. . . .

My conclusion is, that the order appealed from should be affirmed, and the appeal dismissed, with costs, and I so move your Lordships.

[The opinions of Lords Blackburn, Fitzgerald and Watson to the same effect are omitted.]

NOTE. Payment of a debt, or part of a debt, by a third person has been held to operate as a discharge of the original debtor. "The effect of such an agreement between a creditor and a third party with regard to the debt is to render it impossible for the creditor afterwards to sue the debtor for it. The way in which this is worked out in law may be that it would be an abuse of the process of the Court to allow the creditor under such circumstances to sue, or it may be, and I prefer that view, that there is an extinction of the debt; but whichever way it is put, it comes to the same thing, namely that, after acceptance by a creditor of a sum offered by a third party in settlement of the claim against the debtor, the creditor cannot maintain an action for the balance." Fletcher Moulton L.J. in *Hirachand* v. *Temple*.

Where several creditors agree with the debtor to accept a proportion of their claim in satisfaction, such composition agreements are held good. See *Good* v. *Cheesman* (1831), 2 B. & Ad. 328; 109 E.R. 1165. It is usually stated that the promise of each creditor is consideration for the promise of every other creditor. If the creditors promise not to sue the debtor, how can this avail the debtor? That it does operate in his favour is undoubted.

HISTORY AND SUBSEQUENT FATE OF FOAKES v. *BEER*. The House of Lords in the principal case relied on *Pinnel's Case*, which was decided in the Court of Common Pleas in 1602. The report is very brief:

"Pinnel brought an action of debt on a bond against Cole of £16 for payment of £8 10s. the 11th day of Nov. 1600. The defendant pleaded, that he at the instance of the plaintiff, before the said day, *scil.* 1 Octob. *anno* 44, *apud W. solvit querenti* £5 2s. 2d. *quas quidem* £5 2s. 2d. the plaintiff accepted in full satisfaction of the £8 10s. And it was resolved by the whole court, that payment of a lesser sum on the day in satisfaction of a greater, cannot be any satisfaction for the whole, because it appears to the Judges that by no possibility, a lesser sum can be a satisfaction to the plaintiff for a greater sum. But the gift of a horse, hawk, or robe, &c. in satisfaction is good. For it shall be intended that a horse, hawk, or robe, &c., might be more beneficial to the plaintiff than the money, in respect of some circumstances, or otherwise the plaintiff would not have accepted of it in satisfaction. But when the whole sum is due, by no intendment the acceptance of parcel can be a satisfaction to the plaintiff; but in the case at bar it was resolved, that the payment and acceptance of parcel before the day in satisfaction of the whole would be a good satisfaction in regard of circumstance of time; for peradventure parcel of it before the day, would be more beneficial to him than the whole at the day, and the value of the satisfaction is not material.

So if I am bound in £20 to pay you £10 at Westminster, and you request me to pay you £5 at the day at York, and you will accept it in full satisfaction of the whole £10 it is a good satisfaction for the whole: for the expenses to pay it at York is sufficient satisfaction: but in this case the plaintiff had judgment for the insufficient pleading; for he did not plead that he had paid the £5 2s. 2d. in full satisfaction (as by the law he ought) but pleaded the payment of part generally; and that the plaintiff accepted it in full satisfaction. And always the manner of the tender and of the payment shall be directed by him who made the tender on payment, and not by him who accepts it. And for this cause judgment was given for the plaintiff."

The House evidently took the view that this case was decided on its merits, although it seems that it might have been decided on deficiencies in the pleadings. It is to be noted that *Pinnel's Case* is an action in debt and the defence of accord and satisfaction is peculiar to this form of action. Is there any reason why the "law" of debt and accord and satisfaction should apply to *assumpsit* or to modern contract?

The House also relied on *Cumber* v. *Wane*, decided in the King's Bench, in 1721. It was an action *indebitatus assumpsit* for £15. The defendant pleaded that he give the plaintiff a promissory note for £5 in satisfaction and that the plaintiff received it in satisfaction. Pratt C.J. said, in part,

"We are all of the opinion that the plea is not good, and therefore the judgment must be affirmed: as the plaintiff had a good cause of action, it can only be extinguished by a satisfaction he agrees to accept and it is not his agreement alone that is sufficient, but it must appear to the court to be a reasonable satisfaction; or at least the contrary must not appear, as it does in this case. If £5 be (as is admitted) no satisfaction for £15 why is a simple contract to pay £5 a satisfaction for another simple contract of three times the value? In the case of a bond, another has never been allowed to be pleaded in satisfaction, without a bettering of the plaintiff's case, as by shortening the time of payment. . . ."

But the House did not mention the case of *Reynolds* v. *Pinhowe* decided in the Court of King's Bench in 1595 and obviously relied on heavily by Holl Q.C. That too, was an action in *assumpsit*. The available report is sketchy, but very much to the point:

"Whereas the defendant had recovered five pounds against the plaintiff; in consideration of four pounds given him by the plaintiff, that the defendant assumed to acknowledge satisfaction of that judgment before such a day; and that he had not done it. And it was thereupon demurred; for it was moved, that there was not any consideration; for it is no more than to give him part of the money which he owed him, which is not any consideration. But all the court held it to be well enough; for it is a benefit unto him to have it without suit or charge; and it may be there was error in the record; so as the party might have avoided it. Wherefore it was adjudged for the plaintiff."

Neither counsel nor the House mentioned *Bagge* v. *Slade*, another decision in the King's Bench, in 1616, 3 Bulst. 162; 81 E.R. 137, decided by Sir Edward Coke himself, and, of course, long before *Cumber* v. *Wane*. In that case Coke C.J. is reported to have said.

". . . if a man be bound to another by a bill in £1000 and he pays unto him £500 in discharge of this bill, the which he accepts of accordingly, and doth upon this assume and promise to deliver up unto him his said bill of £1000, this £500 is no satisfaction of the £1000 but yet this is good and sufficient to make a good promise, and upon a good consideration, because he had paid money, £500, and he had no remedy for this again. . . ."

Can *Pinnel's Case* and *Cumber* v. *Wane* be distinguished? If not, ought their 280 years of respectability to be left intact despite the admitted inconsistency with modern business practice?

THE MERCANTILE LAW AMENDMENT ACT
R.S.O. 1970 c. 272

16. Part performance of an obligation, either before or after a breach thereof, when expressly accepted by the creditor in satisfaction, or rendered in pursuance of an agreement for that purpose, though without any new consideration, shall be held to extinguish the obligation.

NOTE. This section was originally enacted in 1885 as s. 6 of the Administration of Justice Act. Like any statute, it is better understood when applied to specific facts. Would it have produced a different result in *Foakes* v. *Beer*? Suppose Mrs. Beer had commenced her action before Dr. Foakes had made the £500 down payment, could the statute have been invoked? Suppose after Dr. Foakes had completed all but the last payment Mrs. Beer had made her claim?

Some American states have adopted similar legislation. See, for example, *California Civil Code*, s. 1524. In some states an executory agreement is made binding if it is in writing. See, for example, *Michigan Compiled Laws of 1948*, s. 566.1.

ROMMERILL v. GARDENER
British Columbia. Court of Appeal. 1962. 35 D.L.R. (2d) 717

DAVEY, J.A.: By an oral judgment that was not recorded the learned County Court Judge found that the defendant (respondent) agreed to pay and the plaintiff (appellant) to accept $599.19 in full of his claim for commissions amounting to $1,187.23. There is ample evidence to support that finding.

From the learned Judge's notes of the evidence of the respondent and her husband it would appear that the respondent either told the appellant that she would pay the amount by Easter, 1960, or agreed that it was to be paid by that date. Appellant's evidence is no help on this point because he denied the agreement. The learned County Court Judge must have thought that the agreement to accept the $599.19 in full was not terminated by the failure to pay that amount by Easter. We are quite unable to say from the fragmentary notes of the evidence that the learned Judge was wrong in not regarding the promise to pay by Easter as a condition of the settlement.

The appellant wrote in October of that year demanding payment of $1,187.23. The respondent then sent him a cheque for $599.19, which he retained but did not cash; thereupon he commenced action for $1,187.23. Two days before trial the respondent paid appellant $599.19, which he accepted on account and proceeded to trial. The learned County Court Judge held, so counsel tell us, that the payment was as good as if made at Easter and dismissed the action. Appellant appeals.

Unless respondent can bring the payment of $599.19 within the terms of s. 2 (33) of the *Laws Declaratory Act*, R.S.B.C. 1960, c. 213, it is obvious that the payment of the lesser amount without new consideration will not satisfy the greater sum of $1,187.23 otherwise due.

The clause, which is substantially the same as enactments in Ontario, Saskatchewan and Alberta, and similar to one in Manitoba, reads as follows:

> (33)   Part performance of an obligation either before or after a breach thereof, when expressly accepted by the creditor in satisfaction or rendered in pursuance of an agreement for that purpose, though without any new consideration, shall be held to extinguish the obligation.

The first branch of the subsection may be dismissed at once for both counsel agree that the $599.19 was not accepted by the appellant in satisfaction of the greater amount. If the payment of $599.19 extinguished the obligation it must be because it was rendered in pursuance of the agreement that it be paid and accepted in full of the obligation.

To that appellant's counsel makes two submissions:

First: He says that the agreement mentioned in the clause means a contract under seal or supported by consideration, and that there was no consideration for the parol agreement in question.

Secondly: He contends that the appellant in October, 1960, had before payment demanded the whole amount of $1,187.23, and consequently effectively terminated any agreement to take the lesser amount in full.

In support of his first submission counsel relies upon the judgment of Gregory, J., in *Bell* v. *Quagliotti et al.* (1918), 25 B.C.R. 460 in which he held that the agreement mentioned in the clause means a binding agreement, supported by consideration when not under seal, *i.e.*, a contract, and consequently that a lesser sum paid in pursuance of an agreement not constituting a contract would not operate to extinguish an obligation to pay a greater sum. But this part of the judgment was *obiter*. The judgment of the Court of Appeal (1919), 26 B.C.R. 482, affirming his decision, cannot be taken to support that particular proposition.

Also, this dictum is contrary to several judgments of single Judges in the other Provinces. The Ontario section was discussed by Rose, J., in *Bank of Commerce* v. *Jenkins* (1888), 16 O.R. 215, but the reasons do not indicate whether Rose, J., regarded the agreement in that case as having been made without consideration. MacMahon, J., who sat with Rose, J., had some reservations about his construction of the section.

It is somewhat difficult to follow the reasoning of Beck, J., in *Goodchild* v. *Bethel* (1914), 19 D.L.R. 161, 8 A.L.R. 98, Scott and Simmons, JJ., agreeing, in holding that an immediate payment of part of arrears that otherwise would not have been paid at all, was valuable consideration for the agreement to take that part and certain other sums in full satisfaction of the debtor's obligations. It is not clear from the report what that learned Judge's opinion would have been if he had concluded there was no consideration for the agreement.

In *MacKiw* v. *Rutherford*, [1921] 2 W.W.R. 329, the agreement in question, although in writing, seems to have been made without legal consideration, but $100 was paid at once on account of the lesser sum to be ultimately paid in discharge of the full amount. Curran, J., without discussing the question of consideration, held that the payment of the $100 and a tender of the balance due under the agreement extinguished the original obligation.

In *A. R. Williams Machinery Co.* v. *Winnipeg Storage Ltd.* [1928] 1 D.L.R. 12 at p. 24, 37 Man. R. 187, Fullerton, J.A., in allowing an appeal upon the Manitoba section said that it required no consideration for the agreement. Perdue, C.J.M., allowed the appeal on another ground, and Dennistoun, Prendergast and Trueman, JJ.A., merely concurred in the result, so it cannot be said from the report that they concurred in the reasoning of Fullerton, J.A.

In *Hoolahan* v. *Hivon*, [1944] 4 D.L.R. 405 at p. 409, Ewing, J.A., sitting as a trial Judge, said that in his opinion the payment of $100 as the first payment due under an agreement made without consideration brought the case within the second branch of the statute so as to prevent the agreement being revoked while in the course of being performed.

The weight of subsequent authority seems to be against the view expressed by Gregory, J., in *Bell* v. *Quagliotti, supra*. As a matter of pure construction, I should think that for the purposes of the clause the agreement need not by itself be a binding contract, and consequently need not be supported by consideration. The words "though without any new consideration," while relating grammatically to the verbs "accepted" and "rendered," in my opinion point significantly to the purpose of the clause. Moreover a part performance rendered pursuant to a binding contract based upon a new consideration to accept that part performance in full would by that very fact constitute an accord and satisfaction at common law. When the clause says rendered without any new consideration, it must mean that there need not be consideration for the agreement upon which the part performance is rendered.

Appellant cannot succeed on that branch of his argument.

Turning to the second ground of appeal, the ·respondent admits that about October, 1960, the appellant demanded payment of the full sum of $1,187.23, in response to which she sent him the cheque for $599.19, which was never cashed. But the letter making that demand is not before us, and so far as the notes of evidence go there was no secondary evidence of its contents, consequently we do not know the tenor of the demand. It is unlikely that it was a demand terminating the unperformed agreement because of default, because the appellant denied at the trial that there was such an agreement. I suppose that under some circumstances a bare demand of the greater sum might terminate an unperformed agreement made without consideration to take a lesser sum in full satisfaction of the indebtedness, but it is by no means evident to me at the moment that such a bare demand would by itself necessarily terminate an agreement that the creditor denied. Without the letter I am unable to come to any conclusion upon this ground of appeal. This makes it unnecessary to consider whether under cl. (33) such a creditor can terminate at will a voluntary agreement before it has been partly performed; see *Bank of Commerce* v. *Jenkins*, 16 O.R. 215 at p. 225; *Mason* v. *Johnston* (1893), 20 O.A.R. 412 at p. 415; *MacKiw* v. *Rutherford*, [1921] 2 W.W.R. 329 at p. 333, and *Hoolahan* v. *Hivon*, [1944] 4 D.L.R. 405.

The learned County Court Judge dismissed the action without costs. Appellant contends that because tender was not made or pleaded he should have had the costs of the trial up to the time of the payment two days before the trial opened; but in that event he would have had to pay the costs of the trial.

The respondent's failure to make and plead tender were circumstances requiring a special direction as to costs within the meaning of s. 161 of the *County Courts Act*, R.S.B.C. 1960, c. 81, and I am quite unable to see anything wrong with the way the learned Judge exercised his discretion in those circumstances.

I would dismiss the appeal.

McMANUS v. *BARK*. 1870. L.R. 5 Exch. 65 (England, Exchequer). An action by the executor of John McManus, against John Bark, on Bark's promissory note for £520 with interest at 5 per cent. Bark relied on an agreement which provided: ". . . . The said John Bark owing the said John McManus the sum of £520 for which the said John McManus has already a promissory note, it has been mutually agreed this day that the principal shall be repaid at £25 each quarter, with interest after the rate of £5 per cent, per annum. . . ." KELLY C.B.: . . . We are all of opinion that the agreement constitutes no bar to the present action, inasmuch as it was made for no consideration whatever. It was argued that there was a consideration for it in one of two ways. The mode of payment of interest was varied, it was said, and a quarterly instalment secured to the deceased. But that circumstance cannot be relied on; for the note was payable with interest on demand, and at any moment the payment of the whole, with interest, could have been insisted on. Then, again, the counsel for the defendant contended that the agreement gave the deceased a secure investment for the amount of the note for a fixed time at a sufficient rate of interest. This, however, depends on whether the defendant was left at liberty to come at any time and tender the whole amount. We think he was at liberty to do so. There was no obligation upon him to remain indebted, unless he pleased. Nor, on the other hand, was the deceased under any obligation not to sue on the note after demand. There was, therefore, no consideration for the agreement relied on by the defendant, and the rule must be refused.

QUESTION. How might the agreement have been drafted to prove effective as a bar to this action?

COULDERY v. *BARTRUM.* 1880. 19 Ch. D.394. JESSEL M.R.: "According to English Common Law a creditor might accept anything in satisfaction of his debt except a less amount of money. He might take a horse, or a canary, or a tomtit if he chose, and that was accord and satisfaction; but, by a most extraordinary peculiarity of the English Common Law, he could not take 19s. 6d. in the pound; that was *nudum pactum.* Therefore, although the creditor might take a canary, yet, if the debtor did not give him a canary together with his 19s. 6d., there was no accord and satisfaction; if he did, there was accord and satisfaction. That was one of the mysteries of English Common Law."

LAW REVISION COMMITTEE, SIXTH INTERIM REPORT
England. 1937. Cmnd. 5449; 25 *Can. Bar Rev.* 585

34. In *Foakes* v. *Beer* Lord Blackburn was evidently disposed to hold that it was still open to the House of Lords to reconsider the rule based on the dictum [in *Pinnel's Case*], but in deference to his colleagues who were of a different opinion he did not press his views. In a few words (at p. 622) he summed up what appears to us to be a powerful argument for the abolition of the rule. He said:

"What principally weighs with me in thinking that Lord Coke made a mistake of fact is my conviction that all men of business, whether merchants or tradesmen, do every day recognize and act on the ground that prompt payment of a part of their demand may be more beneficial to them than it would be to insist on their rights and enforce payment of the whole. Even where the debtor is perfectly solvent, and sure to pay at last, this often is so. Where the credit of the debtor is doubtful it must be more so."

35. In our opinion this view is as valid as it was fifty years ago, and we have no hesitation in recommending that legislation should be passed to give effect to it. This legislation would have the additional value of removing the logical difficulty involved in finding a consideration for the creditor's promises in a composition with creditors when not under seal. It would be possible to enact only that actual payment of the lesser sum should discharge the obligation to pay the greater, but we consider that it is more logical and more convenient to recommend that the greater obligation can be discharged either by a promise to pay a lesser sum or by actual payment of it, but that if the new agreement is not performed then the original obligation shall revive.

G. Compromises

✗*COOK* v. *WRIGHT*
England. Queen's Bench. 1861. 1 B. & S. 559; 121 E.R. 822

BLACKBURN J.: In this case it appeared on the trial that the defendant was agent for a Mrs. Bennett, who was non-resident owner of houses in a district subject to a local act. Work had been done in the adjoining street by the commissioners for executing the act, the expenses of which, under the provisions of their act, they charged on the owners of the adjoining houses. Notice had been given to the defendant, as if he had himself been owner of them. He attended at a board meeting of the commissioners, and objected both to the amount and nature of the charges, and also stated that he was not the owner of the houses, and that Mrs. Bennett was. He was told that if he did not pay he would be treated as one Goble had been. It appeared that Goble had refused to pay a sum charged against him as owner of some houses, and the commissioners had taken legal proceedings against him, and he had then submitted and paid with costs. In the result it was agreed between the commissioners and the defendant that the amount charged upon him should be reduced, and that time should be given to pay it in three instalments; he gave three promissory notes for the three instalments; the first was duly honoured, the others were not, and were the subject of the present action. At the trial it appeared that the defendant was not in fact owner of the houses. As agent for the owner he was not personally liable under the act. In point of law, therefore, the commissioners were not entitled to claim the money from him; but no case of deceit was alleged against them. It must be taken that the commissioners honestly believed that the defendant was personally liable, and really intended to take legal proceedings against him, as they had done against Goble. The defendant, according to his own evidence, never believed that he was liable in law, but signed the notes in order to avoid being sued as Goble was. Under these circumstances the substantial question reserved (irrespective of the form of the plea) was whether there was any consideration for the notes. We are of opinion that there was.

There is no doubt that a bill or note given in consideration of what is supposed to be a debt is without consideration if it appears that there was a mistake in fact as to the existence of the debt, *Bell* v. *Gardiner* (1842), 4 M. & Gr. 11; 134 E.R. 5; and, according to the cases of *Southall* v. *Rigg* and *Forman* v. *Wright* (1851), 11 C.B. 481; 138 E.R. 560, the law is the same if the bill or note is given in consequence of a mistake of law as to the existence of the debt. But here there was no mistake on the part of the defendant either of law or fact. What he did was not merely the making an erroneous account stated, or promising to pay a debt for which he mistakenly believed himself liable. It appeared on the evidence that he believed himself not to be liable; but he knew that the plaintiffs thought him liable, and would sue him if he did not pay, and in order to avoid the expense and trouble of legal proceedings against himself he agreed to compromise; and the question is, whether a person who has given a note as a compromise of a claim honestly made on him, and which but for that compromise would have been at once brought to a legal decision, can resist the payment of the note on the ground that the original claim thus compromised might have been successfully resisted.

If the suit had been actually commenced, the point would have been concluded by authority. In *Longridge* v. *Dorville* (1821), 5 B. & A. 117; 106 E.R. 1136, it was held that the compromise of a suit instituted to try a doubtful question of law was a sufficient consideration for a promise. In *Atlee* v. *Blackhouse* (1838), 3 M. & W. 633; 150 E.R. 1298 where the plaintiff's goods had been seized by the excise, and he had afterwards entered into an agreement with the commissioners of excise that all proceedings should be terminated, the goods delivered up to the plaintiff, and a sum of money paid by him to the commissioners, Parke B., rests his judgment, p. 650, on the ground that this agreement of compromise honestly made was for consideration, and binding. In *Cooper* v. *Parker* (1855), 15 C. B. 822; 139 E.R. 650 the Court of Exchequer Chamber held that the withdrawal of an untrue defence of infancy in a suit, with payment of costs, was a sufficient consideration for a promise to accept a smaller sum in satisfaction of a larger.

In these cases, however, litigation had been actually commenced; and it was argued before us that this made a difference in point of law, and that though, where a plaintiff has actually issued a writ against a defendant, a compromise honestly made is binding, yet the same compromise, if made before the writ actually issues, though the litigation is impending, is void. *Edwards* v. *Baugh* (1843), 11 M. & W. 641; 152 E.R. 962, was relied upon as an authority for this proposition. But in that case Lord Abinger expressly bases his judgment (pp. 645, 646) on the assumption that the declaration did not, either expressly or impliedly, show that a reasonable doubt existed between the parties. It may be doubtful whether the declaration in that case ought not to have been construed as disclosing a compromise of a real bona fide claim, but it does not appear to have been so construed by the court. We agree that unless there was a reasonable claim on the one side, which it was bona fide intended to pursue, there would be no ground for a compromise; but we cannot agree that (except as a test of the reality of the claim in fact) the issuing of a writ is essential to the validity of the compromise. The position of the parties must necessarily be altered in every case of compromise, so that, if the question is afterward opened up they cannot be replaced as they were before the compromise. The plaintiff may be in a less favorable position for renewing his litigation, he must be at an additional trouble and expense in again getting up his case, and he may no longer be able to produce the evidence which would have proved it originally. Besides, though he may not in point of law be bound to refrain from enforcing his rights against third persons during the continuance of the compromise to which they are not parties, yet practically the effect of the compromise must be to prevent his doing so. For instance, in the present case, there can be no doubt that the practical effect of the compromise must have been to induce the commissioners to refrain from taking proceedings against Mrs. Bennett, the real owner of the houses, while the notes given by the defendant, her agent, were running; though the compromise might have afforded no ground of defence had such proceedings been resorted to. It is this detriment to the party consenting to a compromise arising from the necessary alteration in his position which, in our opinion forms the real consideration for the promise, and not the technical and almost illusory consideration arising from the extra cost of litigation. The real consideration therefore depends, not on the actual commencement of a suit, but on the reality of the claim made and the bona fides of the compromise.

In the present case we think that there was sufficient consideration for the notes in the compromise made as it was.

The rule to enter a verdict for the plaintiff must be made absolute.

CALLISHER v. *BISCHOFFSHEIM.* 1870. L.R. 5 Q.B. 449 (England). COCKBURN C.J.: "If the defendant's contention were adopted, it would result that in no case of a doubtful claim could a compromise be enforced. Every day a compromise is effected on the ground that the party making it has a chance of succeeding in it; and if he bona fide believes he has a fair chance of success, he has a reasonable ground for suing, and his forbearance to sue will constitute a good consideration. When such a person forbears to sue he gives up what he believes to be a right of action, and the other party gets an advantage; and, instead of being annoyed with an action, he escapes from the vexation incident to it."

MILES v. *NEW ZEALAND ALFORD ESTATE CO.* 1886. 32 Ch. D. 266 (England. Court of Appeal). COTTON L.J.: "Now, what I understand to be the law is this, that if there is in fact a serious claim honestly made, the abandonment of the claim is a good 'consideration' for a contract. . . . Now, by 'honest claim,' I think is meant this, that a claim is honest if the claimant does not know that his claim is unsubstantial, or if he does not know facts, to his knowledge unknown to the other party, which show that his claim is a bad one. Of course, if both parties know all the facts, and with the knowledge of those facts obtain a compromise, it cannot be said that that is dishonest. . . . The doubt of the Master of the Rolls [expressed in *Ex parte Banner* (1881), 17 Ch. D. 480] seems to have been whether a compromise would not be bad, or a promise to abandon a claim would be a good consideration if, on the facts being elicited and brought out, and on the decision of the Court being obtained, it was found that the claim which was considered the consideration for the compromise was a bad one. But if the validity of a compromise is to depend upon whether the claim was a good one or not, no compromise would be effectual, because if it was afterward disputed, it would be necessary to go into the question whether the claim was in fact a good one or not; and I consider notwithstanding the doubt expressed by the Master of the Rolls, that the doctrine laid down in *Cook* v. *Wright* and *Callisher* v. *Bischoffsheim* . . . is the law of this Court."

ALLIANCE BANK v. *BROOM.* 1864. 2 Dr. & Sm. 289; 62 E.R. 631. The plaintiffs, having lent £22,000 to the defendants, wrote the latter asking for security. The defendants, stating they were entitled to certain goods, wrote the plaintiffs' manager promising to hypothecate the goods to the bank. Subsequently, the defendant having refused to hypothecate the goods, the bank sued, asking for an order to the defendant to deliver the goods. The defendant pleaded that his promise was without consideration. The court overruled this objection stating that although forbearance was not promised, it was in effect given, and the defendant received the benefit of it. Moreover, the court stated that if the promise had not been given the creditor would have sued for the debt, therefore the fact that he did not "necessarily involved the benefit to the debtor of a certain amount of forbearance, which he would not have derived, if he had not made the agreement." [Did the defendant ask for forbearance as the price of his promise? Did the plaintiff offer forbearance in return for the promise? See the discussion of *Alliance Bank* v. *Broom*, in *Glegg* v. *Bromley*, [1912] 3 K.B. 474 at 481].

FAIRGRIEF v. *ELLIS*
British Columbia. Supreme Court. 1935. 49 B.C.R. 413

McDONALD J.: Defendant is a retired gentleman, 72 years of age, owning and residing upon a small parcel of land on Lulu Island, worth approximately $2,500. For some years his relations with his wife have been strained; she refused to live with him in British Columbia and maintained her residence in California.

Plaintiffs are sisters, cultured maiden ladies about 50 years of age, who until the year 1933 lived in Winnipeg where they had been employed in clerical work though in recent times they were for considerable periods out of employment. They had been close friends of the defendant over a period of some 25 years and their relations may be judged from the fact that they called him "Dad." In the spring of 1933 the plaintiff Cornelia Fairgrief came to British Columbia on an excursion and visited with the defendant for some three days. Following that occasion some letters passed between the defendant and the plaintiff Anne Fairgrief wherein the plaintiff Anne Fairgrief was invited to visit the defendant. This invitation she declined. In August of that year defendant's son, who had for some months been residing with him, departed for the United States whereupon defendant wrote the plaintiff Anne Fairgrief stating that he was alone and that he required a housekeeper and that he wished the plaintiffs to come and keep house for him, final arrangements to be made after their arrival. Plaintiffs thereupon came to the defendant's home and took up their residence with him upon a verbal agreement that if they would become his housekeepers and take charge of his home during his lifetime the home would become theirs upon his death.

Pursuant to the above agreement plaintiffs entered upon their duties, took full charge of the home, performed all the household duties and did a good deal of work outside including painting, cleaning up the ground and other works of a more or less permanent nature. In addition to being his housekeepers they were his congenial companions and the three lived comfortably and happily until August, 1934, when the defendant's wife (much to his surprise for he had expected nothing of the sort) suddenly arrived in Vancouver. Defendant requested the plaintiffs to remain and be kind to his wife while she should reside with them, he feeling quite assured that her stay would not be a lengthy one. At the end of about a month defendant told the plaintiffs that he was grieved to be obliged to tell them that his wife insisted that they should depart the premises as she intended to remain and take charge. Defendant, knowing of his obligation to the plaintiffs, promised them if they would give up their rights under the agreement already entered into, and would depart from his home he would on or about the 1st of October, 1934, pay them $1,000. That offer was accepted and plaintiffs removed themselves from the premises. The plaintiffs now bring action to recover that sum of $1,000. I have no doubt at all that the defendant's repudiation of his agreement resulted from the interference of his wife. Having persistently refused to live with him and assist him in making a happy and comfortable home, she was determined that the plaintiffs should not be allowed to render that assistance which she herself declined to render. Incidentally it may be said that her further actions justify to some extent this assumption for she again left her husband on November 2nd, 1934, and has not returned to him. Although there is a conflict of evidence I find the facts to be as above stated.

On the above facts, can the plaintiffs succeed? It is contended in the first instance that the agreement first made cannot be enforced by reason of the 4th section of the Statute of Frauds, the agreement being one relating to an interest in land. With that contention I agree and I also agree that the plaintiffs cannot rely upon the fact that they have partly performed their contract for the reason that the acts which they performed are not necessarily referable to the contract alleged by them but might equally be referable to the contract set out by the defendant, *viz*:

"That the agreement under which the plaintiffs came to reside with the defendant . . . was that in return for their board and lodging the plaintiffs were to keep house for the defendant until the defendant's wife came up from California."

See *Haddock* v. *Norgan* (1923), 33 B.C. 237; (1924), 34 B.C. 74.

Notwithstanding the above, however, I cannot understand why the plaintiffs cannot succeed on their claim for $1,000. When the agreement was made in September to pay the plaintiffs $1,000 the defendant thought that he was under an obligation to the plaintiffs and in order to be released from that obligation and so that the plaintiffs might agree to peacefully vacate his premises, he made the second agreement. Even although he was not in law bound to perform the first agreement nevertheless I think there was good consideration to support the promise to pay $1,000. . . .

There will be judgment for the plaintiffs for $1,000. . . .

2. INTENTION

Several of the cases in the preceding materials carry references to the intention of the parties, or one of them, to bind himself legally. Intention is an ambiguous word, and care must be taken that the intended meaning is understood when the word appears, as it does in this casebook, and indeed throughout the law, in a variety of different contexts where the purposes served by the word may be materially different.

If intention is to be relied upon as a test of the enforcement of promises, we should decide what kind of intention we mean. When the judges speak of a promisor who intends to be bound, are they speaking only of a promisor who, in his own mind, when he spoke, thought about the matter and consciously chose to be bound? Is it likely that a promisor thinks any more about the binding character of his promise than he does about the consequences in damages if he breaks it?

If the promisor does not have to have a conscious intention to be bound, is it sufficient that he appears to have such an intention? If so, what appearances will determine the question?

The extent to which the common law has openly acknowledged the relevance of intention is explored in the next cases.

WEEKS v. *TYBALD*. 1605. Noy 11; 74 E.R. 982. In this case it would appear that the plaintiff or his father was told by the defendant, whose daughter the plaintiff later married, that "he would give £100 to him that should marry his daughter with his consent." Held, for defendant. "It is not averred nor declared to whom the words were spoken, and it is not reason that the defendant should be bound by such general words spoken to excite suitors."

STAMPER v. *TEMPLE*. 1845. 6 Humph. 113 (Tennessee). TURLEY J.: "We are constrained to believe that what is called an offered reward of $200, was nothing but a strong expression of his feelings of anxiety for the arrest of those who had so severely injured him, and this greatly increased by the distracted state of his own mind, and that of his family; as we frequently hear persons exclaim, 'Oh, I would give a thousand dollars if such an event were to happen or vice versa'. No contract can be made out of such expressions; they are evidence of strong excitement, but not of a contracting intention."

BALFOUR v. BALFOUR
England. Court of Appeal. [1919] 2 K.B. 571

Appeal from a decision of Sargent J., sitting as an additional judge of the King's Bench Division.

The plaintiff sued the defendant (her husband) for money which she claimed to be due in respect of an agreed allowance of £30 a month. The alleged agreement was entered into under the following circumstances. The parties were married in August, 1900. The husband, a civil engineer, had a post under the Government of Ceylon as Director of Irrigation, and after the marriage he and his wife went to Ceylon, and lived there together until the year 1915, except that in 1906 they paid a short visit to this country, and in 1908 the wife came to England in order to undergo an operation, after which she returned to Ceylon. In November, 1915, she came to this country with her husband, who was on leave. They remained in England until August, 1916, when the husband's leave was up and he had to return. The wife however on the doctor's advice remained in England. On August 8, 1916, the husband being about to sail, the alleged parol agreement sued upon was made. The plaintiff, as appeared from the judge's note, gave the following evidence of what took place: "In August, 1916, defendant's leave was up. I was suffering from rheumatic arthritis. The doctor advised my staying in England for some months, not to go out till November 4. On August 8 my husband sailed. He gave me a cheque from 8th to 31st for £24, and promised to give me £30 per month till I returned." Later on she said: "My husband and I wrote the figures together on August 8; £34 shown. Afterwards he said £30." In cross-examination she said that they had not agreed to live apart until subsequent differences arose between them, and that the agreement of August, 1916, was one which might be made by a couple in amity. Her husband in consultation with her assessed her needs, and said he would send £30 per month for her maintenance. She further said that she then understood that the defendant would be returning to England in a few months, but that he afterwards wrote to her suggesting that they had better remain apart. In March, 1918, she commenced proceedings for restitution of conjugal rights, and on July 30 she obtained a decree nisi. On December 16, 1918, she obtained an order for alimony.

Sargent J. held that the husband was under an obligation to support his wife, and the parties had contracted that the extent of that obligation should be defined in terms of so much a month. The consent of the wife to that agreement was a sufficient consideration to constitute a contract which could be sued upon. He accordingly gave judgment for the plaintiff. The husband appealed.

Atkin L.J.: The defence to this action on the alleged contract is that the defendant, the husband, entered into no contract with his wife, and for the determination of that it is necessary to remember that there are agreements between parties which do not result in contracts within the meaning of that term in our law. The ordinary example is where two parties agree to take a walk together, or where there is an offer and an acceptance of hospitality. Nobody would suggest in ordinary circumstances that those agreements result in what we know as a contract, and one of the most usual forms of agreement which does not constitute a contract appears to me to be the arrangements which are made between husband and wife. It is quite common, and it is the natural and inevitable result of the relationship of husband and wife, that the two spouses should make arrangements between themselves—agreements such as are in dispute in this action—agreements for allowances, by which the husband agrees that he will pay to his wife a certain sum of money, per week, or per month, or per year, to cover either her own expenses or the necessary expenses of the household and of the children of the marriage, and in which the wife promises either expressly or impliedly to apply the allowance for the purpose for which it is given. To my mind those agreements, or many of them, do not result in contracts at all, and they do not result in contracts even though there may be what as between other parties would constitute consideration for the agreement. . . . Nevertheless they are not contracts, and they are not contracts because the parties did not intend that they should be attended by legal consequences. To my mind it would be of the worst possible example to hold that agreements such as this resulted in legal obligations and could be enforced in the Courts. It would mean this, that when the husband makes his wife a promise to give her an allowance of 30s. or £2 a week, whatever he can afford to give her, for the maintenance of the household and children, and she promises to apply it, not only could she sue him for his failure in any week to supply the allowance, but he could sue her for non-performance of the obligation, express or implied, which she had undertaken on her part. All I can say is that the small Courts of this country would have to be multiplied one-hundredfold if these arrangements were held to result in legal obligations. They are not sued upon, not because the parties are reluctant to enforce their legal rights when the agreement is broken, but because the parties, in the inception of the arrangements, never intended that they should be sued upon. Agreements such as these are outside the realm of contracts altogether. The common law does not regulate the form of agreements between spouses. Their promises are not sealed with seals and sealing wax. The consideration that really obtains for them is that natural love and affection which counts for so little in these cold Courts. The terms may be repudiated, varied or renewed as performance proceeds or as disagreements develop, and the principles of the common law as to exoneration and discharge and accord and satisfaction are such as find no place in the domestic code. The parties themselves are advocates, judges, Courts, sheriff's officer and reporter. In respect of these promises each house is a domain into which the King's writ does not seek to run, and to which his officers do not seek to be admitted. The only question in this case is whether or not this promise was of such a class or not. For the reasons given by my brethren it appears to me to be plainly established that the promise here was not intended by either party to be attended by legal consequences. I think the onus was upon the plaintiff, and the plaintiff has not established any contract. The parties were living together, the wife intending to return. The suggestion is that the husband bound himself to pay £30 a month under all circumstances, and she bound herself to be satisfied with that sum under all circumstances, and, although she was in ill-health and alone in this country, that out of that sum she undertook to defray the whole of her medical expenses that might fall upon her, whatever might be the development of her illness, and in whatever expenses it might involve her. To my mind neither party contemplated such a result. I think that the parol evidence upon which the case turns does not establish a contract. I think that the letters do not evidence such a contract, or amplify the oral evidence which was given by the wife, which is not in dispute. For these reasons I think the judgment of the Court below was wrong and that this appeal should be allowed. Appeal allowed.

WARRINGTON L.J.: . . . These two people never intended to make a bargain which could be enforced in law. The husband expressed his intention to make this payment, and he promised to make it, and was bound in honour to continue it so long as he was in a position to do so. The wife on the other hand, so far as I can see, made no bargain at all. That is in my opinion sufficient to dispose of the case. . . .

DUKE L.J.: . . . I am satisfied that there was no consideration moving from the wife to the husband or promise by the husband to the wife which was sufficient to sustain this action founded on contract.

[Is this case decided on the basis of "consideration" or "intent to contract"?]

McGREGOR v. *McGREGOR*, 1888, 21 Q.B.D. 424. An action on an agreement for separation. The plaintiff and defendant, who were wife and husband, took out cross-summonses against each other for assault, but, before the hearing, an oral agreement was entered into by them by which the summonses were to be withdrawn and the plaintiff and defendant were to live separate, the defendant, the husband, agreeing to pay the plaintiff, the wife, £1 a week for maintenance, and the plaintiff agreeing to maintain herself and her children and to indemnify the defendant against any debts contracted by her. The summonses were accordingly withdrawn, and the parties thenceforward lived separate. The defendant having failed to pay the weekly allowance, the plaintiff sued him for six weeks' arrears. Held, plaintiff may recover.

SIMPKINS v. *PAYS*. [1955] 3 All E.R. 10 (England. High Court). The defendant, a lady of eight-three, had living with her her grand-daughter and the plaintiff, who had been a boarder since 1950, in circumstances that had "some element of a family circle" about it, although the plaintiff was not related to the defendant. The three ladies competed regularly in a newspaper competition under a not very formal arrangement that if they won, they would "go shares." The defendant and her grand-daughter would put their guesses on a slip of paper and the plaintiff would fill in the coupon, putting her own guess first, then the grand-daughter's and the defendant's last. Whoever happened to have stamps handy seems to have supplied the trifling amount involved each week. When the weekly entry finally won £750 on the grand-daughter's entry, the defendant claimed the whole amount. The plaintiff sued to recover £250. Held, for the plaintiff. SELLERS J.: "It may well be there are many family associations where some sort of rough and ready statement is made which would not, in a proper estimate of the circumstances, establish a contract which was contemplated to have legal consequences, but I do not so find here. I think that in the present case there was a mutuality in the arrangement between the parties. . . . This was in the nature of a very informal syndicate so that they should all get the benefit of success."

MERRITT v. MERRITT
[1970] 2 All E.R. 760 (C.A.)

The husband and wife were married in 1941 and had three children. In 1966, the husband became attached to another woman and left the matrimonial home to live with her. At that time, the matrimonial home, a freehold house, was in the joint names of the husband and wife, and was subject to an outstanding mortgage of some £180. The wife pressed the husband to make arrangements for the future, and on 25th May 1966, they met and talked the matter over in the husband's car. The husband said that he would pay the wife £40 a month out of which she must make the outstanding mortgage payments on the house and he gave her the building society mortgage book. Before leaving the car the wife insisted that the husband should put down in writing a further agreement, and on a piece of paper he wrote: "In consideration of the fact that you will pay all charges in connection with the house . . . until such time as the mortgage repayment has been completed, when the mortgage has been completed I will agree to transfer the property in to your sole ownership." The husband signed and dated that agreement, and the wife took the piece of paper away with her. In the following months she paid off the mortgage, partly out of the husband's monthly payment to her and partly out of her own earnings. When the mortgage was paid off the husband refused to transfer the house to the wife.

This was an appeal by the husband, John Bertram Merritt, against the judgment of Stamp J., given on 14th May 1969, whereby he held that the wife, Millicent Joan Merritt, was entitled to a declaration that she was now the sole beneficial owner of the matrimonial home, a freehold property known as 133 Clayton Road, Hook, Surrey, and ordered the husband to join with the wife in transferring the property to her. Stamp J. also dismissed the husband's counterclaim that the property was owned by the parties in equal shares.

LORD DENNING M.R.: . . . The first point taken on his behalf by counsel for the husband was that the agreement was not intended to create legal relations. It was, he says, a family arrangement such as was considered by the court in *Balfour v. Balfour* and in *Jones* v. *Padavatton*. So the wife could not sue on it. I do not think that those cases have any application here. The parties there were living together in amity. In such cases their domestic arrangements are ordinarily not intended to create legal relations. It is altogether different when the parties are not living in amity but are separated, or about to separate. They then bargain keenly. They do not rely on honourable understandings. They want everything cut and dried. It may safely be presumed that they intend to create legal relations.

Counsel for the husband then relied on the recent case of *Gould* v. *Gould*, when the parties had separated, and the husband agreed to pay the wife £12 a week "so long as he could manage it." The majority of the court thought that those words introduced such an element of uncertainty that the agreement was not intended to create legal relations. But for that element of uncertainty, I am sure that the majority would have held the agreement to be binding. They did not differ from the general proposition which I stated: "When . . . husband and wife, at arm's length, decide to separate and the husband promises to pay a sum as maintenance to the wife during the separation, the court does, as a rule, impute to them an intention to create legal relations."

In all these cases the court does not try to discover the intention by looking into the minds of the parties. It looks at the situation in which they were placed and asks itself: would reasonable people regard the agreement as intended to be binding?

Counsel for the husband sought to say that this agreement was uncertain because of the arrangement for £40 a month maintenance. That is obviously untenable. Next he said that there was no consideration for the agreement. That point is no good. The wife paid the outstanding amount to the building society. That was ample consideration. It is true that the husband paid her £40 a month which she may have used to pay the building society. But still her act in paying was good consideration. Counsel for the husband took a small point about rates. There was nothing in it. The rates were adjusted fairly between the parties afterwards. Finally, counsel for the husband said that, under s. 17 of the Married Women's Property Act 1882, this house would be owned by the husband and the wife jointly; and that, even if this house were transferred to the wife, she should hold it on trust for them both jointly. There is nothing in this point either. The paper which the husband signed dealt with the beneficial ownership of the house. It was intended to belong entirely to the wife.

I find myself in entire agreement with the judgment of Stamp J. This appeal should be dismissed.

JONES v. PADAVATTON
[1969] 2 All E.R. 616 (C.A.)

DANCKWERTS L.J.: This is an action between the mother and the daughter, and one which is really deplorable. The points of difference between the two parties appear to be comparatively small, and it is distressing that they could not settle their differences amicably and avoid the bitterness and expense which is involved in this dispute carried as far as this court. Both the mother and the daughter come from Trinidad and appear to be of East Indian descent. At the opening of the story in 1961-62 the mother was resident in Trinidad. The daughter (who had been married to, and divorced from, a Mr. Wyatt) was living in a flat in Washington, D.C., in the United States, and was employed at a satisfactory salary, with pension rights, in the Indian embassy in Washington. She had one child by her marriage, a boy called Tommy. She had been on a holiday with her mother to England in 1957.

A suggestion was made that she might go to England in order to read for the Bar in England and, if she became a qualified barrister, then to go to Trinidad and practise as a lawyer there. There is a dispute as to which of the two parties initiated the idea, but the daughter gave evidence very strongly suggesting that it was the mother's idea. She points to her very satisfactory job with the Indian embassy in Washington and her flat, and claims to have been unwilling to go to England, and to have been induced by extreme pressure. The mother intimated that, if the daughter would go and read for the Bar as suggested, she would provide maintenance for her at the rate of $200 a month. Unfortunately, the mother (Mrs. Jones) was thinking in West Indian dollars in which $200 were equal to £42 a month, and the daughter, living in Washington, was thinking in United States dollars, in which $200 were equal to £70. The two were plainly not ad idem then, but the daughter, when she received only £42 per month, seems to have accepted that sum without anything much in the way of protest.

Anyhow, the daughter was entered with Lincoln's Inn as a student, and the necessary fees were paid by a Mr. Agimudie, a lawyer in Trinidad, as the mother's agent. Mr. Agimudie in a contemporary letter assured the daughter that, of course, maintenance would be provided for her. So the daughter went to England in November 1962 and entered on her studies for the Bar. She took her son, Tommy, with her. The precise terms of the arrangement between the mother and the daughter were difficult to discover completely. There is no doubt that the daughter gave consideration for a promise by her mother to provide maintenance at the rate of £42 per month so long as she was reading for the Bar in England by giving up her job and her other advantages in Washington, and by reading for the Bar. But various incidental matters appear never to have been thought out at all. There were no terms recorded in writing, no sort of businesslike statement of the parties' respective obligations, not even of how long the mother was to go on paying if the studies were prolonged or unsuccessful. In fact the daughter has passed all the examinations in Part I except one, but Part II is still to be taken.

The question therefore arises whether any binding legal contract was intended, or whether this was simply a family arrangement in which one member of the family relies on a promise given by another person and trusts that person to carry out the promise. But such an arrangement is not intended to create actionable legal rights. The situation so far has been called "step one." But in 1964 a new element was introduced. The daughter was experiencing some discomfort in England. She, with Tommy, was occupying one room in Acton, for which she had to pay £6 17s. 6d. per week. In 1964 the mother made a proposal that she should buy a house in London of some size so that the daughter and Tommy could live in a room or in rooms in the house, and the rest of the house could be let off to tenants, and the rents would cover expenses and provide maintenance for the daughter and Tommy in place of the £42 a month. It is not clear whether the mother had in mind a profitable investment in England, or wished to avoid the inconvenience of remitting £42 a month to England, or whether she simply had in mind the difficulties that her daughter was experiencing.

At any rate, a house, no. 181, Highbury Quadrant, was found, which was conveyed into the mother's name. The price was £6,000 and moneys were provided by the mother in several sums for this. But there were also expenses of the purchase, as well as other expenses, and furniture, as it was desirable that the tenancies should be of furnished rooms. The moneys provided by the mother were insufficient to provide for all these things; until furniture was provided, there could be no tenants. The purchase was completed in December 1964, and the daughter and Tommy went into occupation on 31st January 1965. Somehow money was found to buy furniture, and tenants began to arrive in February 1965. The daughter had a power of attorney from her mother. There was, of course, no written agreement, and lots of incidental matters remained open: In what order were the rents to be applied; were outgoings to be paid first, or did the daughter's maintenance come first? There was a doubt whether the daughter's rights were confined to one room, or could she occupy several? In fact she occupied not only one room but also a kitchen, and a so-called store room where various things were stored, but Tommy slept there. This has been called "step two." The question again arises: Was there any legally binding contract, or was it just an informal family arrangement?

The daughter had been married on 6th January 1965 to a Mr. Padavatton, who is a lecturer at the London School of Economics, I understand, but it is not clear what part he has played in these matters. The new arrangement, or the varied old arrangement, whatever it may be, continued until November 1967. The mother, who had also visited England in 1963, came again to England in August 1967. The mother, it should be observed, has never received any money from the rents of the house, and she was paying substantial interest on a mortgage on property in Trinidad by which she had raised money for the purchase of the house. There was a most peculiar incident when, on the mother's arrival in England, she was driven to the house by Mr. Rawlins, her solicitor, and could not get in. But nothing really depends on that.

The mother, who had complained that she could not get any accounts from her daughter, had consulted English solicitors, and before this a summons by the mother against the daughter had been taken out claiming possession of the house, and particulars of claim were delivered dated 4th July 1967. Of course, the house is the property of the mother. The mother had given notice to quit on 20th March 1967. A defence and counterclaim dated 11th August 1967 had been delivered, which was amended on 21st February 1968. In these are set out the daughter's version of the arrangements made between the parties, and she counterclaims £1,655 16s. 9d., which the daughter claims she has paid in respect of the house, and ought to be re-imbursed to her. On 11th January 1968 the learned county court judge decided against the mother and dismissed the claim for possession. He gave judgment on the counterclaim in favour of the daughter and referred the matter to the registrar. I do not find the grounds of the learned county court judge's decision easy to understand. He regarded both mother and daughter as very respectable witnesses, and he accepted the daughter's story in regard to the arrangements between them.

Before us a great deal of time was spent on discussions as to what were the terms of the arrangements between the parties, and it seemed to me that the further the discussions went, the more obscure and uncertain the terms alleged became. The acceptable duration of the daughter's studies was not finally settled, I think. There was a lack of evidence on the matter, and the members of the court were induced to supply suggestions based on their personal knowledge. At any rate, two questions emerged for argument: (i) Were the arrangements (such as they were) intended to produce legally binding agreements, or were they simply family arrangements depending for their fulfilment on good faith and trust, and not legally enforceable by legal proceedings? (ii) Were the arrangements made so obscure and uncertain that, though intended to be legally binding, a court could not enforce them?

Counsel for the daughter argued strenuously for the view that the parties intended to create legally binding contracts. He relied on the old case of *Shadwell* v. *Shadwell* (1860) 9 C.B.N.S. 159 and *Parker* v. *Clark* [1960] 1 All E.R. 93. Counsel for the mother argued for the contrary view that there were no binding obligations, and that if there were they were too uncertain for the court to enforce. His stand-by was *Balfour* v. *Balfour*. The

could not be considered a contract anyway

principles involved are very well discussed in *Cheshire and Fifoot on Contract* (6th Edn.), at pp. 94-96. Of course, there is no difficulty, if they so intend, in members of families entering into legally binding contracts in regard to family affairs. A competent equity draftsman would, if properly instructed, have no difficulty in drafting such a contract. But there is possibly in family affairs a presumption against such an intention (which, of course, can be rebutted). I would refer to ATKIN, L.J.'s magnificent exposition in regard to such arrangements in *Balfour* v. *Balfour*.

There is no doubt that this case is a most difficult one, but I have reached a conclusion that the present case is one of those family arrangements which depend on the good faith of the promises which are made and are not intended to be rigid, binding agreements. *Balfour* v. *Balfour* was a case of husband and wife, but there is no doubt that the same principles apply to dealings between other relations, such as father and son and daughter and mother. This, indeed, seems to me a compelling case. The mother and the daughter seem to have been on very good terms before 1967. The mother was arranging for a career for the daughter which she hoped would lead to success. This involved a visit to England in conditions which could not be wholly foreseen. What was required was an arrangement which was to be financed by the mother and was such as would be adaptable to circumstances, as it in fact was. The operation about the house was, in my view, not a completely fresh arrangement, but an adaptation of the mother's financial assistance to the daughter due to the situation which was found to exist in England. It was not a stiff contractual operation any more than the original arrangement.

In the result, of course, on this view, the daughter cannot resist the mother's rights as the owner of the house to the possession of which the mother is entitled. What the position is as regards the counterclaim is another matter. It may be, at least in honesty, that the daughter should be reimbursed for the expenditure which she had incurred. In my opinion, therefore, the appeal should be allowed.

SALMON L.J.: I agree with the conclusion at which DANCKWERTS, L.J., has arrived, but I have reached it by a different route. The first point to be decided is whether or not there was ever a legally binding agreement between the mother and the daughter in relation to the daughter's reading for the Bar in England. The daughter alleges that there was such an agreement, and the mother denies it. She says that there was nothing but a loose family arrangement which had no legal effect. The onus is clearly on the daughter. There is no dispute that the parties entered into some sort of arrangement. It really depends on: (a) whether the parties intended it to be legally binding; and (b) if so, whether it was sufficiently certain to be enforceable.

Did the parties intend the arrangement to be legally binding? This question has to be solved by applying what is sometimes (although perhaps unfortunately) called an objective test. The court has to consider what the parties said and wrote in the light of all the surrounding circumstances, and then decide whether the true inference is that the ordinary man and woman, speaking or writing thus in such circumstances, would have intended to create a legally binding agreement.

Counsel for the mother has said, quite rightly, that as a rule when arrangements are made between close relations, for example, between husband and wife, parent and child or uncle and nephew in relation to an allowance, there is a presumption against an intention of creating any legal relationship. This is not a presumption of law, but of fact. It derives from experience of life and human nature which shows that in such circumstances men and women usually do not intend to create legal rights and obligations, but intend to rely solely on family ties of mutual trust and affection. This has all been explained by Atkin L.J., in his celebrated judgment in *Balfour* v. *Balfour*. There may, however, be circumstances in which this presumption, like all other presumptions of fact, can be rebutted. Counsel for the daughter has drawn our attention to two cases, in which it was, *Shadwell* v. *Shadwell* and *Parker* v. *Clark*. The former was a curious case. It was decided by Erle C.J., and Keating J. (Byles J., dissenting) on a pleading point, and depended largely on the true construction of a letter written by an uncle to his nephew. I confess that I should have decided it without hesitation in accordance with the views of Byles J. But this is of no consequence. *Shadwell* v. *Shadwell* laid down no principle of law relevant to what we have to decide; it merely illustrated what could never, I think, be seriously doubted, viz., that there may be circumstances in which arrangements between close relatives are intended to have the force of law.

In the present case the learned county court judge, having had the advantage of seeing the mother and the daughter in the witness box, entirely accepted the daughter's version of the facts. He came to the conclusion that on these very special facts the true inference must be that the arrangement between the parties prior to the daughter's leaving Washington were intended by both to have contractual force. On the facts as found by the learned county court judge this was entirely different from the ordinary case of a mother promising her daughter an allowance whilst the daughter read for the Bar, or a father promising his son an allowance at university if the son passed the necessary examinations to gain admission. The daughter here was 34 years of age in 1962. She had left Trinidad and settled in Washington as long ago as 1949. In Washington she had a comfortable flat and was employed as an assistant accountant in the Indian embassy at a salary of $500 a month (over £2,000 a year). This employment carried a pension. She had a son of seven years of age who was an American citizen, and had, of course, already begun his education. There were obviously solid reasons for her staying where she was. For some years prior to 1962, however, the mother, who lived in Trinidad, had been trying hard to persuade her to throw up all that she had achieved in Washington and go to London to read for the Bar. The mother would have been very proud to have a barrister for a daughter. She also thought that her plan was in the interest of her grandson, to whom she was much attached. She envisaged that, after the daughter had been called to the Bar, she would practise in Trinidad and thereafter presumably she (the mother) would be able to see much more of the daughter than formerly. The daughter was naturally loath to leave Washington, and did not regard the mother's suggestion as feasible. The mother, however, eventually persuaded the daughter to do as she wished by promising her that, if she threw up her excellent position in Washington and came to study for the Bar in England, she would pay her daughter an allowance of $200 a month until she had completed her studies. The mother's attorney in Trinidad wrote to the daughter to confirm this. I cannot think that either intended that if, after the daughter had been in London, say, for six months, the mother dishonoured her promise and left her daughter destitute, the daughter would have no legal redress.

In the very special circumstances of this case, I consider that the true inference must be that neither the mother nor the daughter could have intended that the daughter should have no legal right to receive, and the mother no legal obligation to pay, the allowance of $200 a month.

The point was made by counsel for the mother that the parties cannot have had a contractual intention since it would be unthinkable for the daughter to be able to sue the mother if the mother fell on hard times. I am afraid that I am not impressed by this point. The evidence which the learned county court judge accepted showed that the mother was a woman of some substance, and prior to the agreement had assured the daughter that there would be no difficulty in finding the money. The fact that, if contrary to everyone's expectation the mother had lost her money the daughter would have been unlikely to sue her throws no light on whether the parties had an intention to contract. The fact that a contracting party is in some circumstances unlikely to extract his pound of flesh does not mean that he has no right to it. Even today sometimes people forbear from mercy to enforce their undoubted legal rights. . . .

[Salmon L.J. then went on to hold that the agreement was enforceable despite its uncertainties; the court could imply reasonable terms where the parties had left the details unsettled. However, he agreed in the result reached by Danckwerts L.J. on the ground that in the circumstances a reasonable time for the duration of the daughter's legal studies had elapsed, and hence that her right to stay in the house had expired. Fenton Atkinson L.J., the other member of the court, agreed with Danckwerts L.J. that there was no intent to enter into a legally binding contract.]

ROSE AND FRANK COMPANY v. J. R. CROMPTON & BROTHERS, LIMITED

England. Court of Appeal. [1923] 2 K.B. 261

J. R. Crompton and Brothers Ltd., were English manufacturers of carbonizing tissue papers. Rose and Frank Co. were merchants in the United States handling the product of the former firm. A series of contracts had been entered into by both parties dating from 1905 which contracts having been performed, the two companies in 1913 entered into negotiations for an arrangement which was to govern future dealings.

A lengthy document was drawn up and signed by both parties in July and August, 1913. This document provided *inter alia* for the duration of the arrangement, the method of determining it, the territory covered, the fixation of prices. In the body of the document there was inscribed the following paragraph:—

"This arrangement is not entered into, nor is this memorandum written, as a formal or legal agreement, and shall not be subjected to legal jurisdiction in the Law Courts either of the United States or England, but it is only a definite expression and record of the purpose and intention of the three parties concerned to which they each honourably pledge themselves with the fullest confidence, based on past business with each other, that it will be carried through by each of the . . . parties with mutual loyalty and friendly co-operation."

J. R. Crompton and Bros. Ltd., becoming dissatisfied with the manner in which the plaintiffs were conducting the business in America, refused to continue the arrangement. The plaintiffs then brought this action. At the trial Bailhache J. found for the plaintiffs, adjudging the agreement of 1913 to be a legally binding contract. The defendants appealed.

SCRUTTON L.J.: . . . Now it is quite possible for parties to come to an agreement by accepting a proposal with the result that the agreement concluded does not give rise to legal relations. The reason of this is that the parties do not intend that their agreement shall give rise to legal relations. This intention may be implied from the subject-matter of the agreement, but it may also be expressed by the parties. In social and family relations such an intention is readily implied, while in business matters the opposite result would ordinarily follow. But I can see no reason why, even in business matters, the parties should not intend to rely on each other's good faith and honour and to exclude all idea of settling disputes by any outside intervention, with the accompanying necessity of expressing themselves so precisely that outsiders may have no difficulty in understanding what they mean. If they clearly express such an intention I can see no reason in public policy why effect should not be given to their intention. Both legal decisions and the opinions of standard text writers support this view. . . . In the early years of the war, when a member of a club brought an action against the committee to enforce his supposed rights in a golf club competition, I nonsuited him for the same reason, that from the nature of the domestic and social relations I drew the inference that the parties did not intend legal consequences to follow from them: *Lens* v. *Devonshire Club*, (Unreported. See *The Times*, Dec. 4, 1914.) . . . Judged by this test, I come to the same conclusion as the learned judge, that the particular clause in question shows a clear intention by the parties that the rest of their arrangement or agreement shall not affect their legal relations, or be enforceable in a Court of Law, but in the words of the clause, shall be "only a definite expression and record of the purpose and intention of the three parties concerned to which they each honourably pledge themselves," "and shall not be subject to legal jurisdiction." If the clause stood first in the document, the intention of the parties would be exceedingly plain. The cases cited to us to the contrary were cases in which the form of the other part of the document, as a covenant in a deed, or a grant of a right in property in legal terms, clearly showed an intention to create a legal right, and where subsequent words, purporting not to define but to negative the creation of such a right, were rejected as repugnant. In *Ellison* v. *Bignold*, (1821), 2 Jac. & W. 503; 37 E.R. 720, where the parties under seal "resolved and agreed and did by way of declaration and not of covenant spontaneously and fully consent and agree," Lord Eldon laid aside "the nonsense about agreeing and declaring without covenanting." An agreement under seal is quite inconsistent with no legal relations arising therefrom. And in the present case I think the parties, in expressing their vague and loosely worded agreement or arrangement, having expressly stated their intention that it shall not give rise to legal relations but shall depend only on mutual honourable trust. This destroys the decision of Bailhache J. so far as it is based on the view that the document of 1913 gives rise to legal rights which can be enforced.

[The opinions of Bankes and Atkin L.JJ. are omitted and only the facts and the opinion as they relate to the validity of the written agreement as a contract are given. Insofar as the Court of Appeal declared the written agreement invalid as a contract their judgment was affirmed by the House of Lords in [1925] A.C. 445.]

JONES v. *VERNON'S POOLS, LTD.* [1938] 2 All E.R. 626 (England. King's Bench Division). The plaintiff claimed that he had accurately completed a coupon which he entered in the defendant's weekly pool on football matches, a lottery which paid large sums to the successful applicants. The defendant denied that it had received the plaintiff's coupon, and relied on a statement printed on the back of all its coupons, that "the sending in and acceptance of the coupon" should not "give rise to any legal relationship . . . but [be] binding in honour only." Held, for the defendant. AT-KINSON J.: ". . . I am told that there are a million coupons received every weekend. Just imagine what it would mean if half the people in the country could come forward and suddenly claim that they had posted and sent in a coupon which they never had, bring actions against the pool alleging that, and calling evidence to prove that they had sent in a coupon containing the list of winning teams, and if Vernon's had to fight case after case to decide whether or not those coupons had been sent in and received. The business could not be carried on for a day on terms of that kind. . . . There is to be no legal liability to pay. He has got to trust to them, and, if something goes wrong, as I say, it is his funeral, and not theirs."

UPTON-ON-SEVERN RURAL DISTRICT COUNCIL v. POWELL
England. Court of Appeal. [1942] 1 All E.R. 220

LORD GREENE M.R.: The appellant lives at Strensham, and in November 1939 a fire broke out in his Dutch barn; he thereupon telephoned to the police inspector at the Upton police office and told him that there was a fire and asked for a fire brigade to be sent. The police inspector telephoned a garage near to the fire station at Upton, which itself had no telephone, the Upton brigade was informed and immediately went to the fire, where it remained for a long time engaged in putting it out. It so happens that, although the appellant's farm is in the Upton police district it is not in the Upton fire district. It is in the Pershore fire district, and the appellant was entitled to have the services of the Pershore fire brigade without payment. The Upton fire brigade, on the other hand, was entitled to go to a fire outside its area, and, if it did so, quite apart from its statutory rights, it could make a contract that it would be entitled to repayment of its expenses.

The sole question here is whether or not any contract was made by which the Upton fire brigade rendered services on an implied promise to pay for them made by or on behalf of the appellant. It appears that some six hours after the arrival of the Upton fire brigade, the officer of the Pershore brigade arrived on the scene, but without his brigade; he pointed out to the Upton officer that it was a Pershore fire, and not an Upton fire, but the Upton fire brigade continued rendering services until the next day when the Pershore fire brigade arrived and took over. In the view that I take in this case, what happened in relation to the arrival of the Pershore officer and his conversation with the Upton officer and the subsequent arrival of the Pershore fire brigade has nothing what ever to do with the issue which we have to decide. The county court judge held that the appellant when he rang up the police inspector, asked for "the fire brigade" to be sent. He also held that the inspector summoned the local Upton fire brigade, which was perfectly natural, and that he took the order as being one for the fire brigade with which he was connected. It appears that neither the appellant, nor the police officer, nor the Upton fire brigade, until it was so informed by the Pershore officer, knew that the appellant's farm was, in fact, not in Upton area, but was in the Pershore area. The county court judge then goes on to find that the inspector passed on the order and sent his fire brigade, and that was the fire brigade, I have no doubt, which the appellant expected. The county court judge said:

"The defendant did not know that if he sent for the Pershore fire brigade what advantage he would have obtained. In my view, there is no escape from the legal liability the defendant has incurred. I think he gave the order for the fire brigade he wanted, and he got it."

Now those findings are attacked, because it is said that, as the defendant did not know what fire brigade area he was in, what he really wanted was to get the fire brigade of his area, whatever it might be. It does not seem to me that there is any justification for attacking the finding of the judge on that basis. What the defendant wanted was somebody to put out his fire, and put it out as quickly as possible, and in ringing up the Upton police he must have intended that the inspector at Upton would get the Upton fire brigade; that is the brigade which he would naturally ask for when he rang up Upton. Even apart from that, it seems to me quite sufficient if the Upton inspector reasonably so construed the request made to him, and, indeed, I do not see what other construction the inspector could have put upon that request. It follows, therefore, that on any view the appellant must be treated as having asked for the Upton fire brigade. That request having been made to the Upton fire brigade by a person who was asking for its services, does it prevent there being a contractual relationship merely because the Upton fire brigade, which responds to that request and renders the services, thinks, at the time it starts out and for a considerable time afterwards, that the farm in question is in its area, as the officer in charge appears to have thought? In my opinion, that can make no difference. The real truth of the matter is that the appellant wanted the services of Upton; he asked for the services of Upton—that is the request that he made—and Upton, in response to that request, provided those services. He cannot afterwards turn round and say: "Although I wanted Upton, although I did not concern myself when I asked for Upton as to whether I was entitled to get free serviccs, or whether I would have to pay for them, nevertheless, when it turns out that Upton can demand payment, I am not going to pay them, because Upton were under the erroneous impression that they were rendering gratuitous services in their own area." That, it seems to me, would be quite wrong on principle. In my opinion, the county court judge's finding cannot be assailed and the appeal must be dismissed with costs.

LUXMOORE L.J.: I agree.

GODDARD L.J.: I agree.

QUESTIONS. Did Powell intend to enter into a legally binding contract here? Did the Upton brigade? Suppose Powell had merely pulled a handle on a Pershore fire brigade call box and as a result of defective wiring called the Upton instead of the Pershore brigade? Who received the unpaid-for benefit in this case, Powell or the Pershore fire brigade? Could the Upton council recover from the Pershore council in the circumstances of this case? Should the case have been decided on the basis of contract at all? For a comment, see (1942) 20 *Can. Bar Rev.* 557.

POLLOCK ON CONTRACTS. 13th ed., p. 3, n. 5. "An appointment between two friends to go out for a walk or to read a book together is not an agreement in the legal sense: for it is not meant to produce, nor does it produce, any new legal duty or right or any change in existing ones. Nothing but the absence of intention seems to prevent a contract from arising in many cases of this kind. A asks B for dinner. Here is proposal of something to be done by B at A's request, namely, coming to A's house at the appointed time. If B accepts, there is in form a contract by mutual promises. . . . Why is A not legally bound to have meat and drink ready for B, so that if A had forgotten his invitation and gone elsewhere B should have a right for action? Only because no legal bond was intended by the parties."

WILLISTON ON CONTRACTS Students' ed. rev. sec. 21. "The further statement of Savigny, which has been popularized for English and American lawyers by Sir Frederick Pollock and others, that not only mental assent to a promise in fact, but an intent to form a legal relation is a requisite for the formation of contracts. . . . cannot be accepted. . . . In a system of law . . . which does not enforce promises unless some benefit to the promisor or detriment to the promisee has been asked and given, there is no propriety in such a limitation. The only proof of its existence will be the production of cases holding that, although consideration was asked and given for a promise, it is, nevertheless, not enforceable because a legal relation was not contemplated."

QUESTIONS. Do you see any point to this dispute? Would you prefer to say, with Atkin L.J., "In respect of these promises each house is a domain into which the King's writ does not seek to run"? Is it desirable to enforce "domestic arrangements"? Although Scrutton L.J. appears to agree with *Balfour* v. *Balfour*, see his observation in *Czarnikow* v. *Roth, Schmidt & Co.* [1922] 2 K.B. 478, "There must be no Alsatia in England where the King's writ does not run." Despite the *Upton-on-Severn* case, can it be said that in Anglo-Canadian law intention is still an element of a contract?

3. NON-BARGAIN PROMISES

A. The Seal

The oldest of the rules followed by the courts is the rule that an action may be brought on a promise in writing ending with a *testimonium*, or witnessing clause, that said, in substance: "In witness whereof I (or, "the parties hereto") have hereunto set my (or, "their") hand and seal." Below the *testimonium* the promisor (or promisors) signed the deed and opposite his signature he placed his seal. In addition to the *testimonium*, there was also an attestation clause, which said, "Signed, sealed, and delivered, in the presence of" and was followed by the signature of a witness to the execution of the deed.

The seal, in the early days, consisted of a blob of wax, usually red, upon which the promisor impressed his seal, if he had one. *Corbin on Contracts*

(p. 797) reports Edward III as reciting, "In witness that this is sooth, I bite this wax with my tooth, in the presence of Magge, Maud and Margery, and my third son Henry." Henry III is reported to have used William Marshall's seal because "We have no seal." The Chinese used a thumb print, although it is doubtful whether they appreciated its distinctive characteristic. Before the seal, a religious symbol, the mark of the Cross, was used. Sir Edward Coke, 1552-1633 (3 Inst. 169) said, *"Sigillum est cera impressa quia cera sine impressione non est sigillum."* Corbin comments (pp. 798-9), "The fact that this is an excellent example of begging the question, pompously concealed by putting it into a dead language, should not cause us to overlook the fact that Coke's statement may have been true. Indeed, Coke had so great an influence over English law that by merely stating it in Latin he could make it true for a century or more."

Of these three elements of form, signing, sealing, and delivering, little remains.

As to signing, it was never considered that the signature was as important as the sealing. See *Martin* v. *Barnes* (1863), 5 N.S.R. (1 Oldright) 291, esp. at pp. 304, 307. Plucknett, *A Concise History of the Common Law* (5th ed., 196), comments: "We do not commonly find signatures on deeds before the sixteenth century, and they did not become generally necessary until the Statute of Frauds." In medieval and renaissance England very few people could read or write.

As to sealing, Boyd C. said, in *Re Bell and Black* (1882), 1 O.R. 125 at p. 126,". . . the current of modern decisions has worn away every distinctive feature of this ancient definition. Neither wax, wafer, nor other adhesive substance is now required." The modern practice (1963) includes the use of the printed word "seal" inside a circle, opposite the space for the signature. More ambiguous is the use of the two letters "L.S." inside the circle. If these letters are taken to stand for "legal seal," as some suppose, it could properly be regarded as a sealed instrument. If the letters are taken to stand for the Latin *locus sigilli*, the place of the seal, and no seal has been put in the place, it could properly be regarded as not a sealed instrument.

As to delivering, it is clear that delivery is as much a symbol as a fact.

The use of the *testimonium* itself is not essential. See *Whittier* v. *McLennan* (1856), 13 U.C.Q.B. 638. Robinson C.J. said, ". . . we cannot say that it is indispensable to the creation of a specialty, that besides sealing the party should expressly affirm that he seals it." See, for interesting sets of facts, *Clauda* v. *Lodge*, [1952] 4 D.L.R. 570 (British Columbia), and *Ray* v. *Gillmore* (1957), 11 D.L.R. (2d) 443 (British Columbia).

The practical significance of a formal promise lies in the fact that no exchange of any sort is required. The court enforces what is sometimes called "a barren promise" or a "voluntary promise," or, putting it in Latin, a *nudum pactum*. Almost as practical is the extension of liability for breach of the promise from six to twenty years under the *Limitations Acts*.

EZRA AND EDWARD ZWICKER v. ERI ZWICKER
Canada. Supreme Court. 1899. 29 S.C.R. 527

This was an action brought by Eri Zwicker, as administrator of his father, Joseph Zwicker, intestate, seeking, among other things, the delivery up of certain personal property and a deed dated April 5, 1877, from Joseph Zwicker to Eri, Ezra, and Edward Zwicker. Ezra and Edward Zwicker, the defendants (appellants), denied having any personal property, or a deed, that belonged to Eri *as administrator*. Evidence was produced of the signing and sealing of the deed, but its delivery was disputed.

Strong C.J.: . . . At the trial before a judge without a jury, the facts appeared to be that the deed of the 5th of April, 1877, was an indenture made between Joseph Zwicker, the intestate, of the one part, and his three sons the respondent and the appellants of the other part, whereby the grantor purported to convey certain lands to his sons in fee. It also contained a disposition of chattel property in the following words:

"I also give unto my two sons, Ezra and Edward, all my stock of cattle, household furniture, farming implements, all personal property but the notes of hand and mortgages, and the house shall be jointly owned by my three sons.". . .

It is however urged, and the court below have given effect to the objection, that there is no proof of the delivery of the deed. It is assumed, and it is I think the proper conclusion from the evidence, that the deed was retained in the possession of the grantor until his death, and this fact has been considered sufficient to show that the deed never was so delivered as to take effect as a duly executed instrument. It is in the face of decided cases of the highest authority out of the question to say that a deed must be presumed to have been inoperative for want of delivery merely because the grantor has retained it in his possession for many years and up to the time of his death. . . .

In all these cases it was held that the retention of the deed after its signing and sealing by the grantor did not show that the execution was defective for want of delivery even in the case where the fact of its existence had never up to the grantor's death been communicated to the parties claiming under it. In *Fletcher* v. *Fletcher* (1844), 4 Hare 67; 67 E.R. 564, Wigram V.C. says:

"The case of *Doe* v. *Knight* (1826), 5 B. & C. 671; 108 E.R. 250, shows that if an instrument is sealed and delivered the retainer of it by the party in his possession does not prevent it from taking effect. No doubt the intention of the parties is often disappointed by holding them to be bound by deeds which they have kept back but such is unquestionably the law."

In *Xenos* v. *Wickham* (1866), L.R. 2 H.L. 296, Mr. Justice Blackburn in delivering his opinion to the House of Lords thus states the law:

"No partcular technical form of words or acts is necessary to render an instrument the deed of the party sealing it. . . . It is clear on the authorities as well as on the reason of the thing that the deed is binding on the obligor before it comes into the custody of the obligee, nay before he even knows of it."

In the same case Lord Cranworth says:

"In the first place the efficacy of a deed depends on it being sealed and delivered by the maker of it, not on his ceasing to retain possession of it. This as a general proposition of law cannot be controverted."

In *Moore* v. *Hazelton* (1864), 9 Allen (Mass.) 102, the court says:

"Execution of the deed in the presence of an attesting witness is sufficient evidence from which to infer a delivery."

Although these authorities are not referred to in the judgment under appeal I assume they were cited in the court below, and that their decision holding the deed inoperative proceeded on the ground that the facts in evidence rebutted the presumption in favour of the due execution of the instrument. These facts are said to consist not only in the retention of the deed by the grantor, but also in the fact that it comprised all the property which he possessed, and that it professed to dispose of this property immediately and that inconsistently with its tenor the grantor retained the possession and enjoyment of his property until his death. No case is referred to as warranting the proposition that this is sufficient to control the effect of the deed, and in the absence of authority I see nothing to authorise it. The circumstance of non-communication to those taking benefits under the deed (if we are to assume such to have been the fact), is shown by the cases referred to to be immaterial, and it may well be that the intestate thought fit to trust to the good feeling and affection of his sons not to disturb him in his enjoyment. At all events we could not disregard a rule of law sanctioned by such high authority and in so many reported decisions without making a precedent which we should be compelled to follow in other cases.

When Joseph Zwicker died in 1894 this deed came into the possession of his sons, and they, including the respondent, agreed to act upon it, and did act upon it by placing it upon the county registry of deeds in order to do which they had of course to treat it as a valid and subsisting instrument by proving it in the manner required by the law. The respondent, moreover, contributed his share of the expense of registration.

Further, it is out of the question to say that there was no communication of the deed to the sons during the grantor's lifetime. One of the documents sought to be recovered is the bond already mentioned dated the 2nd of October, 1884. By this instrument the three sons became bound to pay certain sums to three grandsons of the intestate named Ernst, sons of two of his daughters, both of whom were dead. These sums were duly paid on the testator's decease. To this bond there is appended a memorandum also under seal of the intestate himself. . . . The division referred to in this memorandum must be taken to have reference to the division effected by the deed as no other division is suggested. . . .

[How does this "deed" differ from a "will"?]

SHARINGTON v. *STROTTON*. 1566. 1 Plowden 298; 75 E.R. 454. BROMLEY, in argument: ". . . where the agreement is by deed, there is more time for deliberation. For when a man passes a thing by deed, first there is the determination of the mind to do it, and upon that he causes it to be written, which is one part of deliberation, and afterwards he puts his seal to it, which is another part of deliberation, and lastly he delivers the writing as his deed, which is the consummation of his resolution. . . . So that there is great deliberation used in the making of deeds, for which reason they are received as a *lien* final to the party, and are adjudged to bind the party without examining upon what cause or consideration they were made."

FULLER, "CONSIDERATION AND FORM"
1941. 41 Columbia L.R. 799, 800-1. (1941)

. . . *The Evidentiary Function.*—The most obvious function of a legal formality is, to use Austin's words, that of providing "evidence of the existence and purport of the contract, in case of controversy." The need for evidentiary security may be satisfied in a variety of ways: by requiring a writing, or attestation, or the certification of a notary. It may even be satisfied, to some extent, by such a device as the Roman *stipulatio*, which compelled an oral spelling out of the promise in a manner sufficiently ceremonious to impress its terms on participants and possible bystanders.

The Cautionary Function.—A formality may also perform a cautionary or deterrent function by acting as a check against inconsiderate action. The seal in its original form fulfilled this purpose remarkably well. The affixing and impressing of a wax wafer—symbol in the popular mind of legalism and weightiness—was an excellent device for inducing the circumspective frame of mind appropriate in one pledging his future. To a less extent any requirement of a writing, of course, serves the same purpose, as do requirements of attestation, notarization, etc.

The Channeling Function.—Though most discussions of the purposes served by formalities go no further than the analysis just presented, this analysis stops short of recognizing one of the most important functions of form. That a legal formality may perform a function not yet described can be shown by the seal. The seal not only insures a satisfactory memorial of the promise and induces deliberation in the making of it. It serves also to mark or signalize the enforceable promise; it furnishes a simple and external test of enforceability. This function of form Ihering described as "the facilitation of judicial diagnosis" and he employed the analogy of coinage in explaining it.

"Form is for a legal transaction what the stamp is for a coin. Just as the stamp of the coin relieves us from the necessity of testing the metallic content and weight—in short, the value of the coin (a test which we could not avoid if uncoined metal were offered to us in payment), in the same way legal formalities relieve the judge of an inquiry *whether* a legal transaction was intended, and—in case different forms are fixed for different legal transactions—*which* was intended."

In this passage it is apparent that Ihering has placed an undue emphasis on the utility of form for the judge, to the neglect of its significance for those transacting business out of court. If we look at the matter purely from the standpoint of the convenience of the judge, there is nothing to distinguish the forms used in legal transactions from the "formal" element which to some degree permeates all thinking. Even in the field of criminal law "judicial diagnosis" is "facilitated" by formal definitions, presumptions, and artificial construction of fact. The thing which characterizes the law of contracts and conveyances is that in this field forms are deliberately used, and are intended to be so used, by the parties whose acts are to be judged by the law. To the business man who wishes to make his own or another's promise binding, the seal was at common law available as a device for the accomplishment of his objective. In this aspect form offers a legal framework into which the party may fit his actions, or, to change the figure, it offers channels for the legally effective expression of intention. It is with this aspect of form in mind that I have described the third function of legal formalities as "the channeling function." . . .

CHILLIBACK v. PAWLIUK
Alberta. 1956. 1 D.L.R. (2d) 611

EGBERT J.: The plaintiff, who was a gratuitous passenger in the defendant's car, sues for damages arising out of injuries sustained in an accident allegedly caused by the gross negligence of the defendant.

The defence is twofold—that the defendant was not grossly negligent, and secondly, that if he did become liable to compensate the plaintiff, the latter subsequently released the defendant by signing a written release under seal.

At the conclusion of the trial I found on the evidence that the accident, and the plaintiff's consequent injuries had been caused by the gross negligence of the defendant. Counsel for the defendant then asked for leave to file a written argument on the second line of defence, relating to the alleged release. This leave was granted and both counsel have now filed written arguments on this point.

The accident occurred on June 10, 1953. This action was commenced on June 8, 1954. In the interval, on October 30, 1953, the plaintiff signed the alleged release.

The parties were on friendly terms before the accident and remained on similar terms after the accident, until at least some time after the execution of the alleged release at the end of October, 1953, although after the accident they did not see one another so frequently, since the plaintiff, because of his injuries, was unable to continue his work in Big Valley, where the defendant was also located, and where the parties frequently saw one another.

On October 30, 1953, the plaintiff went into the beer parlour of an hotel in Edmonton. According to his evidence he had some six glasses of beer with a friend who cannot now be located, when another friend, Mercer, came along. Each of the three men had another four or six beers. At this point, when the plaintiff had been in the beer parlour about three hours, the defendant entered, found the group, and said to the plaintiff, "I have a paper here I'd like you to sign, because I'd like to get my driver's licence back" (or very similar words). The plaintiff had once had his own driver's licence taken away for "impaired driving", and knew what the defendant was talking about. The plaintiff then signed a paper which the defendant handed to him. He received no money or other consideration for signing, and says that he signed to help the defendant get his licence back. He had consulted Mr. Dubensky, a solicitor in Edmonton, before this about the possibility of taking action against the defendant, but says that he did not know this paper had anything to do with the lawsuit. He admits that the defendant used no force, or threat or promise to induce him to sign the paper. He denies that he was drunk when he signed the document. The defendant made any insertions or alterations in the document that appear in hand-writing. (These consist of the insertion of the date, and the insertion of the word "nil" in two places.) The plaintiff signed the document and Mercer signed it as witness to the plaintiff's signature. The document itself is contained on one sheet of paper, and reads as follows:

RELEASE AND DISCHARGE

"IN CONSIDERATION of the payment or settlement of the sum of ($)   Nil   Dollars, the receipt whereof is hereby acknowledged), I   Fred Chilliback   do hereby release and forever discharge   William Pawliuk   from all and any actions, cause of actions, claims and demands for, upon or by reason of any damage, loss or injury which heretofore have been or which hereafter may be sustained by   in   in consequence of   the   accident of June 10th, 1953 IT BEING FURTHER AGREED AND UNDERSTOOD that the payment of the said ($)   nil   Dollars is not to be construed as an admission on the part of the said William Pawliuk of any liability whatever in consequence of said accident. I further state that I have carefully read the foregoing release, and know the contents thereof, and I sign the same of my own free will.

IN WITNESS WHEREOF, I have hereunto set my hand and seal this　30 day of　　October　　1953.

SIGNED, SEALED AND DELIVERED)
　　　IN THE PRESENCE OF　　　　　)
(Name) 'J. F. Mercer'　　　　　　(SIGNATURE)　　　'F. Chilliback'
(Address)　　10860—73 St.　　　)　　　　　　　　　　　(Seal)
　　　　　　　　　　　　　　　　　)　　To bear the signature of
　　　　　　　　　　　　　　　　　)　　Fred Chilliback.
　　　　　　Witness"

In the space in the right lower corner marked "Seal" is affixed a red wafer seal.

It appears to be common ground that this document was prepared by the Motor Vehicle Branch of the Highways Department, but it is not common ground that that Branch affixed the seal before the document was sent out, or, in fact, that the seal had actually been placed on the document before the plaintiff signed it. The evidence of both parties and of the witness Mercer, appears to be silent on this point. In the absence of evidence, and in the light of a statement made to me by counsel for the defendant, I think I must assume that the seal had been affixed to the document by the Motor Vehicle Branch, and was affixed to it at the time the plaintiff signed it, despite the suggestion of counsel for the plaintiff that it was affixed at some later time.

The defendant states in his evidence that the plaintiff read over the release before he signed it, and had no difficulty in understanding it, and himself suggested that the defendant write in the word "nothing" in the space relating to the consideration. This is not denied by the plaintiff. The defendant admits that he gave the plaintiff no consideration for the release.

The plaintiff's skull injuries affected his mental processes to some extent. His demeanour in the witness-box indicated a mental slowness, which other evidence substantiated, but there was no evidence on which a conclusion could be based that the plaintiff was unable to understand either the nature or the contents of the release.

Counsel for the plaintiff argues in the first place that the execution of the release was a case of *non est factum.* . . . It is not a case where the principle of *non est factum* is applicable. There is nothing to indicate that the minds of the parties did not meet. It may be that the plaintiff did not appreciate the full legal effect of the release, but that is not an unusual circumstance. How many men fully understand the complete legal effect of the contracts they sign?

The defence resolves itself into the sole question of whether the complete lack of consideration is offset by the presence of the red seal opposite the plaintiff's signature. I am left with no doubt that if there had been no seal the release would have been inoperative because of the absence of consideration. Does the presence of the small, red wafer seal make it operative?

I have no doubt on the evidence, or possibly I should say on the lack of evidence touching the matter of the seal, that both the plaintiff and the defendant were, at the time of the execution of the release, entirely oblivious to its existence, and to the effect of its presence. Indeed, counsel for the defendant states in his argument "neither the plaintiff nor the defendant were at all concerned, nor probably even cognizant of the fact that a seal was on the document or required to be on the document". With this statement I entirely agree. There is no evidence that the plaintiff said any word or did any act which in any way amounted to an adoption by him of the seal as *his* seal. So far as the plaintiff was concerned, he was *signing* a document submitted to him by the defendant—that was the transaction and the whole transaction insofar as he understood it. Nevertheless the document he signed did have affixed to it, opposite the space for his signature, the seal now in question, and the defendant now produces a release purporting to be signed and sealed by the plaintiff.

As is stated in most textbooks and in many ancient authorities, a seal was said to "import" consideration, so that a document under seal might be enforced even though no consideration appeared on the face of the instrument. In other words, the seal itself constituted *prima facie* proof that consideration had passed. . . . But how can it be said that a seal "imports" consideration when the document itself expressly states that there is no consideration? In this case we not only have an express negation of consideration in the instrument, but all the available evidence proves conclusively that no consideration passed from the defendant to the plaintiff, and that the plaintiff himself recorded that fact in the instrument.

In my view, the evidence discloses that the parties did not intend that this document should be executed as a sealed document.

Somewhat similar circumstances were discussed by Stuart J. in *Sawyer & Massey Ltd.* v. *Bouchard* (1910), 13 W.L.R. 394, when he arrived at the same conclusion. As Stuart J. said, after reviewing a number of authorities [p. 398]: "It will be seen, I think, from an examination of these cases, that the whole question is one of fact, and that the question is, not whether there is a seal on the instrument, but whether the person executing it affixed his seal thereto, either by doing so in fact or by doing something which the law will hold as equivalent thereto. The sealing must be either directly or indirectly the act of the party executing the instrument."

As Stuart J. points out, when a person signs his name to an instrument already sealed, he is presumed to have adopted the seal affixed—this is one of the equivalents above referred to accepted by the law. But it is only a presumption which is raised, and this presumption may be rebutted by evidence by which a contrary intention is proved or from which it may be inferred. In this case, as I have said, the evidence is, in my view, clear that both parties were quite oblivious to the presence of the seal, and that there was no intention on the part of either of them that the document should be sealed. It is true that in *Sawyer & Massey Ltd.* v. *Bouchard* there was no *testimonium* clause as there is here, and that Stuart J. refers to its absence, and says that had there been such a clause, it "would probably, though I refrain from expressing any decided opinion, have been enough to have shewn an intention to adopt the printed seal as his own" [p. 399]. It will be observed, however, that Stuart J. does refrain from expressing a decided opinion, and since, as he had previously observed, the question is one of intention, I think I am justified in holding that the mere presence of the *testimonium* clause is not sufficient if the evidence otherwise leads to a conclusion that the intention to execute the document under seal did not exist.

I accordingly hold, in the first place, that the release is not an instrument under seal, and therefore since no consideration passed to the plaintiff, it is not enforceable by the defendant.

In the second place, I hold that even if the document is under seal, it is, under the circumstances, not enforceable for want of consideration. As I have said, the document itself, as well as the surrounding evidence, negatives consideration, so that the mere presence of a seal cannot "import" consideration, or raise an irrebuttable presumption of a consideration which did not, in fact, exist. The Court, in the exercise of its equitable jurisdiction may look at the true bargain between the parties, and refuse to enforce an otherwise unenforceable agreement, merely because it is under seal. . . .

Having found that the release relied on by the defendant is unenforceable, it only remains to assess the plaintiff's damages. . . .

NOTE. Apart from Egbert J.'s point that Chilliback didn't intend to *seal*, but merely to *sign*, the instrument, the basis of his decision that the seal is merely presumptive evidence of consideration is quite without historical foundation. The formal promise was enforced long before the doctrine of consideration became current. But the earliest cases were cases where, even if there had been no seal, the facts disclosed sufficient consideration to enable a modern court to enforce the promise without the formality. Pollock and Maitland, in *The History of English Law* (2d ed., 1898, Vol. 2, 213-14) "doubt whether in the thirteenth century a purely gratuitous promise, though made in a sealed instrument, would have been enforced if its gratuitous character had stood openly revealed." For a comment on the principal case, see Weston, "Contracts under Seal—Enforceability—Necessity of Consideration" (1956), 34 *Can. Bar Rev.* 453. See also Milner, "The Common Law of Contract" in *Canadian Jurisprudence* (ed. McWhinney), 90-117.

As to Chilliback's intention, or lack of it, if the seal is there, should his intention be called into account? How might Ihering have dealt with this case?

MARTIN v. *BARNES.* 1863. 5 N.S.R. (1 Oldright) 291. Young C.J.: "[U]nless our legislature interferes, as they have done in Connecticut, (which I would not be understood, however, as approving,) and enact that conveyances and bonds shall be valid without seals, we must adhere to the common law rule . . . we ought to require evidence of some positive and serious public inconvenience, before we at one stroke annihilate so well established and venerable a practice as the use of seals in the authentication of deeds. Of the use of seals in the authentication of writs, we had a memorable instance in this Court in the recent case of *The Queen* v. *Burdell and Lane*, when the want of a bit of wafer reduced the crime of homicide from murder to manslaughter."

LINTON v. *ROYAL BANK OF CANADA*, (1966) 60 D.L.R. (2d.) 398 (Ont. H.C.) The plaintiff signed a guarantee in favour of the defendant bank, but omitted to seal it. The document had printed on it the legend "signed, sealed and delivered" and the word "seal" was printed in brackets opposite the space provided for signature. An employee of the bank later added a seal, and the plaintiff now argues that the document is void in that it has been materially altered. HARTT J.: When the guarantee in question was signed by Mr. Linton with the intention of constituting the document a deed, it became such. The important evidence in this regard was the markings on the document itself, namely "signed, sealed and delivered" and the word "seal" beside the space provided for signature. The document being a deed from the outset, the addition of a paper wafer by the bank cannot be considered a material alteration affecting the "legal incidence" of the document.

THE LAND TITLES ACT
Ontario. Revised Statutes. 1960. Chapter 204

81. Notwithstanding any statute or rule of law, a charge or transfer of registered land may be duly made by an instrument not under seal and, if so made, the instrument and every agreement, stipulation and condition therein has the same effect for all purposes as if made under seal.

NOTE ON THE ABOLITION OF SEALS. Canadian legislatures have not hastened to "abolish the seal," whatever that expression may mean, but legislatures in the United States have been quite active. For example, California, Idaho, Montana, North Dakota and Oklahoma have language like California's *Civil Code*, section 1629, "All distinctions between sealed and unsealed instruments are abolished." As a result of this section, are unsealed promises as enforceable as sealed ones used to be? Or are sealed instruments no longer enforceable unless consideration is proved?

The California *Code* also provided, in section 1614, "A written instrument is presumptive evidence of consideration."

Compare the *Uniform Written Obligations Act* approved by the Commissioners on Uniform State Laws in 1925. It is in force only in Pennsylvania:

"A written release or promise hereafter made and signed by the person releasing or promising shall not be invalid or unenforceable for lack of consideration, if the writing also contains an additional express statement, in any form of language, that the signer intends to be legally bound."

Williston, who advocated the model Act, says (*Williston on Contracts*, 3d ed., sec. 219, p. 794) "efforts to fill the gap created by statutory abolition of the seal have proved largely unsuccessful." See *Corbin on Contracts*, sec. 257, for a short criticism. Critics have also suggested that the form of words can become as sterile as the seal through mass reproduction in fine print on ready made forms of contracts and the further suggestion has been made that the model Act be modified to require that the words be in the handwriting of the promisor after the principle of holograph wills. See also Steele, "The Uniform Written Obligations Act—A Criticism" (1920), 21 *Illinois Law Review* 185.

No attempt has been made to reproduce the wide variety of American legislative attempts to "abolish the seal," but merely to indicate the kind of legislative drafting and interpretative problems involved in this apparently simple exercise.

QUEBEC CIVIL CODE

1208. A notarial instrument received before one notary is authentic if signed by all the parties. . . .
1210. An authentic writing makes complete proof between the parties to it and their heirs and legal representatives:
    1. Of the obligation expressed in it;
    2. Of what is expressed in it by way of recital, if the recital have a direct reference to the obligation or to the object of the parties in executing the instrument. . . .

COMPARATIVE LAW NOTE. A notary has no counterpart in the common law system. Although a private practitioner, with substantially the same training as a lawyer, his function in authenticating "notarial instruments" is a "public" one. Attention is drawn to this provision merely because it represents an alternative formal method of authenticating contracts. Its use in Quebec is limited and it is more cumbersome than the common law seal.

LAW REVISION COMMITTEE, SIXTH INTERIM REPORT
England. 1937. Cmnd. 5449; 15 *Can. Bar Rev.* 585

29. Basing themselves on the views of Lord Mansfield stated in *Pillans* v. *Van Mierop*, which we have quoted above, many judges and writers of textbooks (see, in particular, Professor Holdsworth, *History of English Law*, Vol. VIII, p. 48) have advocated that a promise in writing, though not under seal and not supported by consideration, should be enforceable. The only justification for the doctrine of consideration at the present day, it is said, is that it furnishes persuasive evidence of the intention of the parties concerned to create a binding obligation, but it does not follow from this that consideration should be accepted as the *sole* test of such intention. This intention ought to be provable by other and equally persuasive evidence such as, e.g., the fact that the promisor has put his promise in writing. We agree with this view, and we therefore recommend that consideration should not be required in those cases in which the promise is in writing.

We must make it clear when we speak of the promise being in writing we mean the promise which is being sued upon, and we do not mean that, in the case of a contract consisting of mutual promises both the promises must be in writing.

30. On the other hand we are of the opinion that the entire promise should be in writing to bring it within the rule and that no other evidence of the promise, whether in writing or partly in writing and partly oral, should be considered sufficient. Nor do we recommend that the written promise must be signed: all that is necessary is that the Court should be satisfied that the writing (which includes typescript and print) is that of the promisor or his agent. This can be proved in the same way as any other question of fact is proved. Thus the requirement of writing which we are now recommending has nothing to do with the old "memorandum or note" of the Statute of Frauds. It differs both in purpose and in content.

This recommendation does not mean that a promise in writing will be binding in every case. It will still be necessary for the Court to find that the parties intended to create a binding obligation. Just as the presence of consideration today does not convert a social engagement into a legal contract, so the presence of writing will not convert a gratuitous promise into a legally binding one unless the Court determines that the parties intended it to be legally binding.

B. Past Consideration

LAMPLEIGH v. BRATHWAIT
England. Common Pleas. 1615. Hobart 105; 80 E.R. 255

Anthony Lampleigh brought an assumpsit against Thomas Brathwait, and declared that, whereas the defendant had feloniously slain one Patrick Mahume, the defendant, after said felony done, instantly required the plaintiff to labor and do his endeavor to obtain his pardon from the king; whereupon the plaintiff upon the same request did, by all the means he could and many days' labor, do his endeavor to obtain the king's pardon for the said felony; viz., in riding and journeying at his own charges from London to Reiston, when the king was there, and to London back, and so to and from Newmarket, to obtain pardon for the defendant for the said felony. Afterwards in consideration of the premises, the said defendant did promise the said plaintiff to give him £100 and that he had not, to his damage £120.

To this, the defendant pleaded *non assumpsit*, and found for the plaintiff, damage £100. It was said in arrest of judgment that the consideration was past.

It was agreed that a mere voluntary courtesy will not have a consideration to uphold an assumpsit. But if that courtesy were moved by a suit or request of the party that gives the assumpsit, it will bind; for the promise, though it follows, yet it is not naked, but couples itself with the suit before, and the merits of the party procured by that suit, which is the difference. . . .

KENNEDY v. *BROUN.* 1863. 13 C.B.N.S. 677; 143 E.R. 268, 292. ERLE C.J.: "In *Lampleigh* v. *Brathwait*, it was assumed that the journeys which the plaintiff performed at the request of the defendant, and the other services he rendered, would have been sufficient to make any promise binding if it had been connected therewith in one contract; the peculiarity of the decision lies in connecting a subsequent promise with a prior consideration after it had been executed. Probably at the present day, such service or such request would have raised a promise by implication to pay what it was worth; and the subsequent promise of a sum certain would have been evidence for the jury to fix the amount."

STEWART v. *CASEY.* [1892] 1 Ch. 104 at 115. BOWEN L.J.: "That raises the old question—or might raise it, if there was not an answer to it— of *Lampleigh* v. *Brathwait*, a subject of great interest to every scientific lawyer, as to whether a past service will support a promise. . . . Even if it were true, as some scientific students of law believe, that a past service cannot support a future promise, you must look at the document and see if the promise cannot receive a proper effect in some other way. Now, the fact of a past service raises an implication that at the time it was rendered it was to be paid for, and, if it was a service which was to be paid for, when you get in the subsequent document a promise to pay, that promise may be treated either as an admission which evidences or as a positive bargain which fixes the amount of that reasonable remuneration on the faith of which the service was originally rendered."

QUESTION ON LEGAL METHOD. What is a "scientific lawyer"?

ROSCORLA v. THOMAS
England. Queen's Bench. 1842. 3 Q.B. 234; 114 E.R. 496

The plaintiff bought a horse from the defendant for £30. There was apparently no promise made at the time about the horse's qualities. Later the defendant did promise the plaintiff that the horse was not over five years old and was sound and free from vice. It then appeared that the horse was "very vicious, restive, ungovernable, and ferocious." In an action based on the later promise (assumpsit) there was a verdict for the plaintiff but the defendant obtained a rule nisi to arrest the judgment on the ground that there was no consideration.

LORD DENMAN C.J. delivered the judgment of the Court:... It may be taken as a general rule, subject to exception not applicable to this case, that the promise must be co-extensive with the consideration. In the present case, the only promise that would result from the consideration as stated, and be co-extensive with it, would be to deliver the horse upon request. The precedent sale without a warranty, though at the request of the defendant, imposes no other duty or obligation upon him. It is clear therefore that the consideration stated would not raise an implied promise by the defendant that the horse was sound or free from vice.

But the promise in the present case must be taken to be, as in fact it was, express and the question is, whether that fact will warrant the extension of the promise beyond that which would be implied by law; and whether the consideration, though insufficient to raise an implied promise, will nevertheless support an express one. And we think that it will not.

The cases in which it has been held that, under certain circumstances, a consideration insufficient to raise an implied promise will nevertheless support an express one, will be found collected and reviewed in the note (a) to *Wennall* v. *Adney*, (1802). 3 B. & P. 247: 127 E.R. 137 and in the case of *Eastwood* v. *Kenyon* [above]. They are cases of voidable contracts subsequently ratified, of debts barred by operation of law subsequently revived, and of equitable and moral obligations which, but for some rule of law, would of themselves have been sufficient to raise an implied promise. All these cases are distinguishable from, and indeed inapplicable to the present, which appears to us to fall within the general rule, that a consideration past and executed will support no other promise than such as would be implied by law.

The rule for arresting the judgment upon the first count must therefore be made absolute.

QUESTIONS. A, seeing B's house on fire, hires men to assist him in putting out the fire. B, who was absent at the time, hears of A's actions and promises to pay him $1,000. Can A recover?

B is taken ill at his club. A, a doctor, attends him. On recovering B promises to give A Blackacre, worth $10,000, for his services. Can A claim Blackacre? Suppose B's promise were to pay $100. Would it make any difference as to enforceability whether B were unconscious at the time A attended him?

NOTE. As indicated in the above cases, there was a school of thought in the eighteenth and early nineteenth centuries that maintained that the existence of a moral obligation should in itself be sufficient reason for enforcing a promise to fulfil that obligation. In *Lee* v. *Muggeridge*, (1813) 5 Taunt. 36: Lord Mansfield said: "It has long been established that where a person is bound morally and conscientiously to pay a debt, though not legally bound, a subsequent promise to pay will give a right of action." Since *Eastwood* v. *Kenyon* (1840) 11 A&E 438, this view has been regarded as overruled, but there are several situations where relics of the earlier view may still be found. One such relic is the rule, enacted by s. 53 of the Bills of Exchange Act, that an antecedent debt or liability constitutes sufficient consideration for a bill of exchange. Another principle is that promises to pay prior debts may sometimes be enforceable, even though the debt itself is for some reason unenforceable. This principle has been applied to debts unenforceable because contracted in infancy, and to debts barred by the statute of limitations; the following materials concern those situations.

EDMUNDS v. *MISTER*, 58 Miss. 765 (Miss. S.C., 1881). CHALMERS C.J.: "The executory contracts of infants for the payment of money, not for necessaries, impose no legal liability upon them. They furnish a sufficient consideration to support contracts thereafter made, so that if ratified in any way after majority they will be enforced; but they derive their vitality not from the original consideration, but from the new promise or ratification. They can be ratified at common law only by an act or agreement which possesses all the ingredients necessary to a new contract, save only a new consideration. The contract made during minority will furnish the consideration, but it will furnish nothing more. All else must be supplied by the new agreement. A mere acknowledgment of the debt is not sufficient, but there must be an express promise to pay, voluntarily made; and this is true under the common law authorities, without reference to the provisions of statute, which declares that the new promise or ratification must be in writing.

"There cannot be said to be any contract in any legitimate sense of the term until after the act of ratification, or until after the written promise under our statute. Before ratification, it is wholly unilateral in its bearing; that is to say, the consideration has been advanced by the adult, but there is no corresponding legal liability upon the minor. It stands, not upon the footing of a debt barred by the Statute of Limitations and afterwards revived by a new promise, because in such a case there has always been an existing, unextinguished right, since limitation affects only the remedy, and not the right; but it is rather like a debt wiped out by a discharge in bankruptcy. In such case there is no existing debt, but there is an outstanding consideration which will support a new contract. . . . It is an anomaly in pleading that the plaintiff declares upon the original contract, and to a plea of infancy replies the new promise, while all authorities declare that the recovery is not upon the original contract, but upon the new promise; and yet undoubtedly the anomaly exists. While this is true, it is clear that if the declaration should set out the whole facts,—that is, if it shewed that the articles were furnished to a minor, that they were not necessaries, and that there had been no new promise,—it would be demurrable; or if judgment by default was taken upon it, it would be reversed upon appeal. The reason is that it would show no cause of action, and it would shew no cause of action because of the absence of a new promise. It is the new promise, therefore, that makes the debt, and without it there is none."

STATUTE OF FRAUDS
Ontario. Revised Statutes. 1970. Chapter 444

7. No action shall be maintained whereby to charge a person upon a promise made after full age to pay a debt contracted during infancy or upon a ratification after full age of a promise or simple contract made during infancy, unless the promise or ratification is made by a writing signed by the party to be charged therewith or by his agent duly authorized to make the promise or ratification.

MACCORD v. *OSBORNE*. 1876. 1 C.P.D. 568. After attaining his majority the debtor had written, "I promise to pay the above as a debt of honor. . . ." Held not to be an acknowledgment of a debt for which he was legally liable. GROVE J., in the course of the argument, "To satisfy the statute [similar to the Ontario Statute above] it must be an enforceable promise, not a mere recognition of the debt."

THRUPP v. *FIELDER*. 1798. 2 Esp. 628; 170 E.R. 477. LORD KENYON: "The case of infancy differs from the Statute of Limitations: in the latter case a bare acknowledgement has been held sufficient. In the case of an infant, I shall hold an acknowledgement not to be sufficient, and require proof of an express promise to pay. . . . Payment of money is no such promise."

SPENCER v. *HEMMERDE*
England. House of Lords. [1922] 2 A.C. 507

VISCOUNT CAVE: In the year 1910 Mr. Joseph Benson (through whom the appellant claims) lent to the respondent, Mr. Hemmerde, a sum of £1000; and in a letter acknowledging the loan which was dated the 2nd of March, 1910, the respondent undertook to repay it in two months and to pay interest at 7 per cent. per annum, and added: "It is extremely kind of you to assist me at this juncture by a transaction which is quite outside the ordinary rules of business security, and which I recognize to be merely a generous and timely effort to help me over a very unpleasant financial crisis."

Certain securities were deposited with Mr. Benson as security for the loan, but these were subsequently given up at the respondent's request. No part of the principal or interest was in fact paid. Mr. Benson, to whom this advance appears to have caused some financial embarrassment, from time to time pressed for payment; and ultimately on the 4th November, 1915, he wrote to the respondent a letter in which he made formal application for payment of the £1000 and interest and stated that he would not stay his hand any further and the matter would have to be settled without further delay. The writer added: "I confess I am greatly surprised that you have treated the matter so coolly, no letter or personal word. You will remember your coming to me in your time of great need, and at great personal inconvenience I helped you because I believed you would honourably fulfil your promise and repay me on an early date."

In answer to this urgent application the respondent wrote to Mr. Benson a letter dated the 4th November in the following terms:

"I think it is a pity you write me in such a tone. Have you the slightest idea what these times mean to professional men? I have not been to see you because I had absolutely nothing to tell you but what you must know already. I will look in and see you some day next week, but I cannot at present hold out the slightest hope of paying you the capital. I will tell you exactly how things stand when I see you."

This did not satisfy Mr. Benson, who on the 5th November wrote a further letter stating that a call would be useless and that unless he had some definite proposal from the respondent he should ask his solicitor to take the matter in hand and to act promptly. The respondent thereupon wrote the following letter, upon which this case appears to me to turn:—

"1, Hare Court,
Temple, E.C.
November 7th.
My dear Mr. Benson,
It is not that I won't pay you, but that I can't do so. It is important that I should see you and explain the situation, and I shall therefore ring you up tomorrow to make an appointment.

What I wrote was not that I saw no prospect at present of being able to repay the capital, but that I saw no prospect of being able to repay the capital at present. The condition of things at the Bar is such that the vast majority of us will be getting into debt rather than out of it.

I have a good deal to talk to you about, and nothing can be gained by flying to solicitors.
Yours truly,
EDWARD G. HEMMERDE."

Mr. Benson accordingly stayed his hand, and it was not until the 22nd June 1920, that the appellant (the trustee under a deed of arrangement with creditors executed by Mr. Benson) issued his writ in this action, claiming payment of the principal and interest. The respondent pleaded the *Statute of Limitations* and the appellent in his reply relied on the above-mentioned two letters of the 4th and 7th November, 1915, and on other letters which are not now material, as containing a sufficient acknowledgment to take the case out of the statute. Bailhache J. held the letters to be sufficient for that purpose, and gave judgment for the appellant; but on appeal the Court of Appeal (Bankes and Atkin L.JJ.; Scrutton L.J. dissenting), . . . reversed his decision and dismissed the action. Hence the present appeal.

My Lords, the law relating to matters of this kind is not in doubt. The statute enacted that ". . . all actions of debt grounded upon any lending or contract without specialty . . . shall be commenced and sued . . . within six years next after the cause of such actions . . . and not after," and made no reference to any acknowledgment; but it was held in a series of cases that a promise by the debtor to pay the debt, if given within six years before action brought, was sufficient to create a new contract and so to take the case out of the operation of the statute, the existing debt being a sufficient consideration to support the promise. It was also held that simple acknowledgment of the debt, without any express promise was sufficient for the purpose, an acknowledgment implying a promise to pay. Some of the earlier cases went so far as to decide that an acknowledgment was sufficient, though coupled with a promise to pay at some future which had not arrived or upon some condition that had not been performed, or even with an absolute refusal to pay; but this was set right by the decision of the Court of King's Bench in *Tanner* v. *Smart* (1827), 6 B. & C. 603: 108 E.R. 573, where Lord Tenterden, in giving the judgment of the Court, said: "Upon a general acknowledgment, where nothing is said to prevent it, a general promise to pay may, and ought to be, implied; but where the party guards his acknowledgment, and accompanies it with an express declaration to prevent any such implication, why shall not the rule *expressum facit cessare tacitum* apply?"

No doubt the doctrine so established was originally judge-made law; but it has stood unchallenged for nearly a century, and indeed it has received statutory recognition. For the statute commonly called Lord Tenterden's Act, 9 Geo. 4, c. 14, after referring to the Statutes of Limitation, provides that: "In actions of debt or upon the case grounded upon any simple contract no acknowledgment or promise by words only shall be deemed sufficient evidence of a new or continuing contract, whereby to take any case out of the operation of the said enactments or either of them, or to deprive any party of the benefit thereof, unless such acknowledgment or promise shall be made or contained by or in some writing to be signed by the party chargeable thereby." This enactment refers to an "acknowledgment or promise" as if either would be sufficient to take a case out of the statute. But the words of the Act are negative only, and I think it clear that the acknowledgment there referred to must be an acknowledgment which but for this Act would have been sufficient to take the case out of the statute of James, that is to say, an acknowledgment implying a promise to pay; and it has always been so held.

Since the case of *Tanner* v. *Smart* the law as there laid down has been uniformly accepted, and it must be held to be settled law (1.) that a written promise to pay a debt given within six years before action is sufficient to take the case out of the operation of the statute of James I; (2.) that such a promise is implied in a simple acknowledgment of the debt; but (3.) that where an acknowlegment is coupled with other expressions, such as a promise to pay at a future time or on a condition or an absolute refusal to pay, it is for the Court to say whether those other expressions are sufficient to qualify or negative the implied promise to pay. The decisions upon the Act are very numerous; but in every one of them the law has been assumed to be as above stated and the decision has turned upon the meaning of the particular words used in the case. It is therefore unnecessary to refer to the authorities in detail. . . .

This being the law, I turn to the letters written in this case with a view to determining whether, according to the fair and natural meaning of those letters, they contain an express promise to pay or a clear acknowledgment of the debt, and in the latter case whether the acknowledgment is coupled with words which prevent the implication of an unconditional promise. The respondent's letter of November 4 contains neither promise nor clear acknowledgment; and its principal value to the appellant is that it serves to connect the later letters with Mr. Benson's letter of November 4, and so to identify the debt referred to in those letters as being the principal and interest payment of which was required by Mr. Benson's letter of November 4. It is on the interpretation of the respondent's letter of November 7 that the decision must turn.

What, then, does that letter mean? And, first, does it contain an acknowledgment of the debt? I think it does. The expression, "It is not that I won't pay you," appears to me to mean that the writer does not refuse to pay his debt, but on the contrary admits the debt and holds himself bound to pay it; and this interpretation is supported by the subsequent repudiation of any suggestion that he had professed to see no prospect of paying the capital, and by reference to getting out of debt. The words may not amount to an express promise to pay the principal and interest due, but at least they contain an admission of liability and a profession of the writer's willingness to discharge it, which, unless qualified by other expressions in the letters, carries with it a promise to pay.

Then, are the words, "I can't do so," and the statement that the writer sees no prospect of being able to pay the capital at present, so inconsistent with a promise to pay that they negative the implication of such a promise? I do not think they are. There is no promise to pay on a future date, or on the fulfilment of a condition, and still less is there a refusal to pay at all. There is only a profession of present inability to carry out the promise which is implied. It is urged that, when a man couples his acknowledgment of a debt with a statement that he cannot pay, it is difficult to read into his acknowledgment a promise that he will pay; and no doubt there is force in this observation, which appears to have commended itself to the Court of Appeal. . . . But it does not appear to me that the two things are really inconsistent. A debtor may well say at one and the same time: "I admit my obligation and promise to discharge it," and "I do not discharge it now, because I have not the money to do so." The important thing is that the present obligation to pay is admitted and the original promise to pay is renewed and affirmed without condition or qualification; and if that be done, there is a new promise to pay upon which an action may be founded. I do not doubt that in the present case the respondent intended his letter to be read in this sense, nor that Mr. Benson so understood it and upon the faith of the letter, so understood, delayed his proceedings; and if so, the respondent must be held to his promise. In my opinion there is a sufficient acknowledgment to prevent the statute from having effect.

My Lords, I have thought it right to deal with the letters relied upon according to their terms, and without reference to the countless decisions upon the meaning of other documents couched in different terms. . . .

Upon the whole I think that the appeal should be allowed and that the judgment of Bailhache J. should be restored with costs here and below, and I move your Lordships accordingly.

LORD SUMNER: My Lords, as Scrutton L.J. truly says, the practical question here is to decide whether the respondent's words, which it is conceded acknowledge that a debt has been contracted but has not been paid, are so coupled with words which prevent the possibility of the implication of a promise to pay it, as to destroy the effect of that acknowledgment, or whether, on the other hand, they are only accompanied by other words, which, though they are in themselves less than a promise to pay, do not necessarily put an end to such an implication. I do not propose to read the words used here in the light of words judicially interpreted elsewhere, for everybody agrees that comparison with the words of other debtors is of little use. Still less do I imagine it to be possible to extract anything that deserves to be called a principle from the decisions of three centuries, which have been directed to what is after all the task of decorously disregarding an Act of Parliament. Some "acknowledgments" save the statute and some do not. The whole doctrine is purely artificial. Acknowledgments under other Statutes of Limitations dealing with other subject matters than simple debts know nothing of these niceties about fresh promises. The only thing to be done is to ascertain what really are the tests, which have been applied by authority, for determining the class to which any given words belong. . . .

It is quite impossible that so many judges should have spoken of the old debt being the consideration for the new promise without their being fully aware that if a new cause of action is meant this is contrary to long settled rules of law as to consideration. They must have spoken of the new promise as something different from a new contract, binding in law as such. Sir William Anson does, it is true, say (*Contracts*, 14th ed., p. 128) that

the case is an exception to the general rule as to past executed consideration, and, while expressly disclaiming reliance on any moral obligation to
pay, suggests that in consideration of the creditor's having given everything
that the debtor could get out of the contract and being unable, owing to the
statute, to get anything which the contract was to have given to him, a
promise by the debtor to remove the bar and pay is legally binding. I confess I do not follow this. It is not a consideration that moves to the debtor;
it is a matter of honour, if it is anything, as to which one may say that the
creditor has only his good nature to thank for his loss, and in any case
it is a consideration inapplicable when the debt is not yet barred, though
the doctrine which it purports to explain applies equally to acknowledgments given before six years have run as to those given afterwards. I find
that the great preponderance of the cases is against regarding the new
promise as a new cause of action, and it seems to me that reason also is
against it. Surely the real view is, that the promise, which is inferred from
the acknowledgment and "continues" or "renews" or "establishes" the original promise laid in the declaration, is one which corresponds with and is
not a variance from or in contradiction of that promise. This alone seems
to accord with the language used in *Tanner* v. *Smart,* as reproduced in
Hart v. *Prendergast* (1845), 14 M. & W. 741, 743; 153 E.R. 674, where
after Mr. Lush had said in argument, "the questions are first, does this
letter taken altogether, amount to a promise to pay. Secondly, does it support the promise laid in the declaration, to pay on request?" the judges,
Parke, Alderson and Rolfe BB., said, respectively, that the promise must
"fit" or must "maintain" or must "support" the promise declared upon. If
so, there is no question of any fresh cause of action. . . .

Order of the Court of Appeal reversed, and judgment of Bailhache J.
restored.

[Lords Atkinson, Wrenbury and Carson also delivered opinions.]

THE LIMITATIONS ACT
Ontario. Revised Statutes. 1970. Chapter 246

50. (1) Where an acknowledgment in writing, signed by the principal
party or his agent, is made by a person liable upon an indenture, specialty,
judgment or recognizance, or where an acknowledgment is made by such
person by part payment, or part satisfaction, on account of any principal
or interest due on the indenture, specialty, judgment or recognizance, the
person entitled may bring an action for the money remaining unpaid and so
acknowledged to be due, within twenty years . . . after such acknowledgment in writing, or part payment, or part satisfaction, or where the person
entitled is, at the time of the acknowledgment, under disability aforesaid,
or the person making the acknowledgment is, at the time of making the
same, out of Ontario, then within twenty years . . . after the disability has
ceased, or the person has returned, as the case may be.

51. (1) No acknowledgment or promise by words only shall be deemed
sufficient evidence of a new or continuing contract whereby to take out of
the operation of this Part, any case falling within its provisions respecting
actions, . . .

(b) on simple contract or of debt grounded upon any lending or contract without specialty . . .

or to deprive any party of the benefit thereof, unless the acknowledgment
or promise is made or contained by or in some writing signed by the party

chargeable thereby, or by his agent duly authorized to make the acknowledgment or promise.

(2) Nothing in this section alters, takes away or lessens the effect of
any payment of any principal or interest by any person.

NOTE ON LEGISLATIVE DRAFTING. When Viscount Cave said he doubted "whether the Act meant two different things when it said 'promise or
acknowledgment' " whose "meaning" did he refer to? Parliament's? The draftsman of the Act? Why did the draftsman use both words if they mean the
same thing? Is it ever a good idea for a draftsman to use two words when one
will do? Does the word "acknowledgment" in s. 50 (1) above have a different
meaning from the "same word" in s. 51 (1) where it is coupled with "or
promise"?

NOTES. Part payment of a debt has always been regarded as equivalent to an
acknowledgment when made voluntarily by a debtor and without words or
other circumstances negativing the ordinary implication of acknowledgment
and promise to pay farther, and such payment may take the form of balancing
accounts between debtor and creditor or otherwise applying on the debt any
amount due by the creditor to the debtor, always providing the debtor assents
to the amount being so applied. See *Evans* v. *Davies* (1836), 4 A. & E. 840;
11 E.R. 1000 (payment of interest proved the obligation to pay the principal);
Turney v. *Dodwell* (1845), 3 E. & B. 136; 118 E.R. 1091 (part payment by
bill or note); *Guilbert* v. *Cummings*, [1929] 4 D.L.R. 705 (Man.) (part
payment by an agreed set-off.).

Where there are several debts owed by a debtor to a creditor, and the
debtor makes a payment without specifying on which debt the money is to be
applied the creditor may appropriate such payment to any or all statute-
barred debts, provided that the debtor has not expressly or impliedly appropriated the payment to any later or other debt. See *Wood* v. *Richmond*,
[1929] 2 D.L.R. 552 (Sask.); *Kaulbach* v. *Eichel*, [1930] 1 D.L.R. 983
(N.S.).

Such appropriation by the creditor will revive the balance of the debt, the
assent of the debtor to such appropriation being required to raise the implication of promise. *Ball* v. *Parker* (1877), 1 O.A.R. 593 at 604. It is possible
to have a payment made with the intention of being applied to all the separate
debts. In such case the statutory defence will be removed as to all. See *Wood*
v. *Richmond*, supra.

If a debtor makes a promise to pay a statute barred debt in part or in
instalments on what is the creditor suing? See *Earle* v. *Oliver* (1848), 2
Exch. 71; 154 E.R. 410 at 418.

What is the reason for refusing to allow a promise to pay a statute barred
tort liability, the same effect as a debt? See *Williston on Contracts*, students'
revised edition, secs. 186 and 188.

Suppose X makes a promissory note payable to A or order. A endorses
the note to B. After the statute has run, X writes A saying, I have not forgotten my note in your favour. I will pay it at once. May B sue X? See
Watson v. *Sample* (1899), 12 Man. L.R. 373 at 379; *Stamford*, etc. *Banking
Co.* v. *Smith*, [1892] 1 Q.B. 765. Would your answer be different according
to whether you viewed the promise, (1) as evidence negativing a presumption of
payment within six years; (2) as "reviving" the original cause of action; (3) as
constituting a new cause of action?

A owes B $500 but the statute has run against the debt. After the limitation period has expired A gives B a bill of exchange for $500. Has B a cause of action? On what? See *La Touche* v. *La Touche* (1865), 3 H. & C. 576; 159 E.R. 657; *Wright* v. *Wright* (1876), 6 O.P.R. 295. Compare a bill of exchange given to discharge an obligation unenforceable by reason of Statute of Frauds. *Kenzie* v. *Harper* (1908), 15 O.L.R. 582 and compare *Black* v. *Gesnet* (1847), 3 N.J.R. 157.

C. Subsequent Reliance

LLEWELLYN "WHAT PRICE CONTRACT? AN ESSAY IN PERSPECTIVE" (1931) 40 Yale L.J. 704, 741-44

[Reprinted by permission of the Yale Law Journal Company and Fred B. Rothman & Company from the *Yale Law Journal*.]

Neither causes nor processes of the development of the consideration concept are at all clear in detail. We do not know how the Germanic system of awarding what one may speak of as the advantage of proof to the apparently sounder side came to degenerate into the debt-defendant's power as of right to swear himself out of judgment. We do not know whether the fear of stout swearers or the growth of commercial transactions was the more vital factor in developing assumpsit; we know little if anything of the details of the latter pressure on the courts from, say, 1570 to 1620. We do not know in any clarity the process by which the case-misfeasance-tort root and the *quid-pro-quo* root out of debt were built together. What is clear, is the emergence of a current definition in terms of benefit to the promisor or detriment to the promisee as the agreed equivalent and inducing cause of the promise; a definition which purports both to show what is adequate and what is necessary to a successful action in assumpsit or its heirs. The current formulation has the merit of covering most cases, even if it does not cover all. Indeed it is obvious that as soon as the arbitrary but utterly necessary logical jump is made, of making mutual promises serve to support each other, the great bulk of business promises are comfortably cared for.

Four troublesome classes of cases remain. There are business promises such as "firm offers," understood to be good for a fixed time, but revoked before. They are frequent; they are and should be relied on. As to them our consideration doctrine is badly out of joint. Closely related in orthodox doctrine, less so in practice, is the second class; promises which call for acceptance by extended action (such as laying twenty miles of track), revoked while the work is in process. A third and hugely important class is that of either additional or modifying business promises made after an original deal has been agreed upon. Law and logic go astray whenever such dealings are regarded as truly comparable to new agreements. They are not. No business man regards them so. They are going-transaction adjustments, as different from agreement-formation as are corporate organization and corporate management; and the line of legal dealing with them which runs over waiver and estoppel is based on sound intuition. The fourth main trouble-making class has only a doctrinal connection with business; it lies chiefly in the field of family affairs; it includes the promise made and relied on, but which did not bargain for reliance, and in the case of promises to provide it laps over into the third party beneficiary problem. As to all of these classes but the first, a distinct but very uneven tendency is observable in the courts to strain by one dodge or another toward enforcement. That tendency is healthy. It may be expected to increase. It has already had some effects on orthodox doctrine, and may be expected to have more. Meanwhile the first class mentioned goes largely untouched.

When one attempts to estimate the net value of the consideration requirement the first step is to repeat that it does fit most normal cases in life, that it gives trouble only on the fringes. As a test of what promises *not* to enforce, it must be regarded as somewhat formalistic. The existence of bargain equivalency does indeed commonly evidence positively that the promise was deliberate—considered—meant. Such equivalency gives also fair ground for believing that *some* promise was in fact made; and thereby much reduces the danger from possible perjury, and even from misunderstanding. The giving of a bargain equivalent, be it by promise or by action, is furthermore an excellent objective indication not only of the creation of expectation in the promisee, but of the reasonableness of there being expectation, and of its being related to the promise. (And the size of the equivalent may help to "interpret" the expectation.) Yet it will be observed that the handing over of a signed promise in writing (which is *not* enough for enforcement) would go far in most circumstances to assure the same values; no lawyer, for example, can fail to be struck by the closeness with which exemptions from the requirement of writing under the statute of frauds are related to the presence of unambiguous consideration which is *substantially equivalent in fact* to the promise claimed. Nor is it apparent why in many cases deliberateness, due assurance that the promise was made and relied on, and properly so, might not all be evidenced by circumstances apart from either writing or consideration. The problem is acute only within the family. Outside, a writing might well be made a condition to "reasonableness" of any reliance; though very possibly, as with the statute of frauds on sales an exception might be needed for petty transactions. All in all, then, as a test for non-enforcement, our consideration requirement must be regarded as not yet wholly just to our needs.

As a positive test, a test for what promises *to* enforce, the same must be said. For here the requirement of the positive law runs in terms not of *factual* equivalency, but of *formal* equivalency under the bargain as stated. A consideration which in fact is largely, even wholly formal, may be enough; release of injury-claim for a dollar. This is well enough when the promise is one whose enforcement is in itself socially desirable: a charitable subscription, a promise to provide for a child on marriage, an option to buy land. And it is enforcement in such cases which has given foothold for the draftsmen in cases of a—socially—different character. But when the courts in such cases recognize in general language the adequacy of thoroughly formal consideration, they obscure the problem discussed above, as to government by contract; the same problem so clearly seen by the courts in usury and mortgage cases, and by the legislature in regulation of employment: that of discrepancy in bargaining power and semi-duress in fact. Though obscured, that problem recurs. It is therefore not surprising that the last quarter century has seen—in business cases—the incursion into the doctrine of consideration of a further doctrine of so-called "mutuality" whereby particular promises are matched off against each other, and some equivalency in fact (e.g. to buy if the other party has agreed to sell) frequently insisted on, even when formally adequate consideration is present. It is to be expected that this tendency will continue: and it is not unlikely that it will develop, as in the past, peculiarly to relieve the weaker bargainer. The lop-sidedness of bargain-result is thus taken as the mark of lop-sidedness of bargain-making. But the motivation being apparently not wholly conscious, the result has been (as so often during case-law growth) confusion in doctrine and uncertainty in outcome; and—natural enough in a business economy—a relief of smaller business men which finds little counterpart in the case of the laborer.

(i) *Charitable Subscriptions*

DALHOUSIE COLLEGE v. *BOUTILIER ESTATE*
Nova Scotia. Supreme Court of Canada. [1934] S.C.R. 642

CROCKET J. delivered the judgment of the court: This appeal concerns a claim which was filed in the Probate Court for the County of Halifax, Nova Scotia, in the year 1931, by the appellant College against the respondent Estate for $5,000, stated as having been "subscribed to Dalhousie Campaign Fund (1920)," and attested by an affidavit of the College Bursar, in which it was alleged that the stated amount was justly and truly owing to the College Corporation.

The subscription, upon which the claim was founded, was obtained from the deceased on June 4, 1970, in the course of a canvass which was being conducted by a committee, known as the Dalhousie College Campaign Committee, for the raising of a fund to increase the general resources and usefulness of the institution and was in the following terms:

"For the purpose of enabling Dalhousie College to maintain and improve the efficiency of its teaching, to construct new buildings and otherwise to keep pace with the growing need of its constituency and in consideration of the subscription of others, I promise to pay to the Treasurer of Dalhousie College the sum of Five Thousand Dollars, payment as follows:

Terms of payment as per letter from Mr. Boutilier.

A. 399.   Name Arthur Boutilier.

Date June 4th, 1920.

Make all cheques payable to the Treasurer of Dalhousie College."

So far as the record disclosed, the subscription was not accompanied or followed by any letter from the deceased as to the terms of payment. He died on October 29, 1928, without making any payment on account. It appears that some time after he signed the subscription form he met with severe financial reverses which prevented him from honouring his pledge. That he desired and hoped to be able to do so is evidenced by a brief letter addressed by him to the President of the University on April 12, 1926, in reply to a communication from the latter, calling his attention to the subscription and the fact that no payments had been made upon it. The deceased's letter, acknowledging receipt of the President's communication, states:

"In reply I desire to advise you that I have kept my promise to you in mind. As you are probably aware, since making my promise I suffered some rather severe reverses, but I expect before too long to be able to redeem my pledge."

The claim was contested in the Probate Court by the Estate on two grounds, viz.: that in the absence of any letter from the deceased as to terms of payment, the claimant could not recover; and that the claim was barred by the Statute of Limitations. Dr. A. Stanley MacKenzie, who had retired from the Presidency of the University after 20 years' service shortly before the trial, and others gave evidence before the Registrar of Probate. Basing himself apparently upon Dr. MacKenzie's statement that in consideration of the moneys subscribed in the campaign referred to, large sums of money were expended by the College on the objects mentioned in the subscription card, between the years 1920 and 1931, the Registrar decided that there was a good consideration for the deceased's subscription, citing *Sargent* v. *Nicholson* (1915), 25 D.L.R. 638, a decision of the Appeal Court of Manitoba, and *Y.M.C.A.* v. *Rankin* (1916), 27 D.L.R. 417, a decision of the Appeal Court of British Columbia, and that no supplementary letter was necessary to complete the agreement. He further held that the deceased's letter of April 12, 1926, constituted a sufficient acknowledgment to take the case out of the Statute of Limitations.

An appeal to the Judge of the County Court sitting as Judge of the Probate Court was dismissed, but on a further appeal to the Supreme Court of Nova Scotia *en banc*, this decision was reversed by the unanimous judgment of Chisholm, C.J., and Mellish, Graham, Caroll and Ross, JJ., on the ground that the subscription was a mere *nudum pactum*, and that nothing was shewn either by the document itself or by the evidence which imposed any binding contractual obligation upon the deceased in connection therewith. This, I take it, to be the gist of the reasons for the judgment of the Appeal Court as delivered by the learned Chief Justice, and embodies the whole problem with which we have now to deal.

There is, of course, no doubt that the deceased's subscription can be sustained as a binding promise only upon one basis, viz.: as a contract, supported by a good and sufficient consideration. The whole controversy between the parties is as to whether such a consideration is to be found, either in the subscription paper itself or in the circumstances as disclosed by the evidence.

So far as the signed subscription itself is concerned, it is contended in behalf of the appellant that it shews upon its face a good and sufficient consideration for the deceased's promise in its statement that it was given in consideration of the subscription of others. As to this, it is first to be observed that the statement of such a consideration in the subscription paper is insufficient to support the promise if, in point of law, the subscriptions of others could not provide a valid consideration therefor. I concur in the opinion of Chisholm, C.J., that the fact that others had signed separate subscription papers for the same common object or were expected so to do does not of itself constitute a legal consideration. Although there have been some cases in the United States in which a contrary opinion has been expressed, these decisions have been rejected as unsound in principle both by the Supreme Court of Massachusetts and the Court of Appeals of the State of New York. See *Cottage Street M. E. Church* v. *Kendall*, 121 Mass. 528; *Hamilton College* v. *Stewart*, (1848), 1 N.Y. Rep. 581; and *Albany Presbyterian Church* v. *Cooper*, (1889), 112 N.Y. Rep. 517. In the last mentioned case the defendant's intestate subscribed a paper with a number of others, by the terms of which they "in consideration of one dollar" to each of them paid "and of the agreements of each other" severally promised and agreed to and with the plaintiff's trustees to pay to said trustees the sums severally subscribed for the purpose of paying off a mortgage debt on the church edifice on the condition that the sum of $45,000 in the aggregate should be subscribed and paid in for such purpose within one year. The Court of Appeals held that it must reject the consideration recited in the subscription paper, the money consideration, because it had no basis in fact, and the mutual promise between the subscribers, because there was no privity of contract between the plaintiff church and the various subscribers.

A perusal of the reasons for judgment of the Appeal Court of Manitoba, as delivered by Cameron, J.A., in *Sargent* v. *Nicholson* already referred to, shews that the court also rejected the contention that it was a sufficient consideration that others were led to subscribe by the subscription of the defendant. In fact Cameron, J.A.'s opinion quotes with approval a passage from the opinion of Gray, C.J., in *Cottage Street M. E. Church* v. *Kendall*, that such a proposition appeared to the Massachusetts Supreme Court to be "inconsistent with elementary principles." The decision of the Appeal Court of British Columbia in *Y.M.C.A.* v. *Rankin* fully adopted the opinion of Cameron, J.A., in *Sargent* v. *Nicholson*, and is certainly no authority for the acceptance of other subscriptions as a binding consideration in such a case as the present one.

The doctrine of mutual promises was also put forward on the argument as a ground upon which the deceased's promise might be held to be binding. It was suggested that the statement in the subscription of the purpose for which it was made, viz.: "of enabling Dalhousie College to maintain and improve the efficiency of its teaching, to construct new buildings and otherwise to keep pace with the growing need of its constituency," constituted an implied request on the part of the deceased to apply the promised subscription to this object and that the acceptance by the College of his promise created a contract between them, the consideration for the promise of the deceased to pay the money being the promise of the College to apply it to the purpose stated.

I cannot think that any such construction can fairly be placed upon the subscription paper and its acceptance by the College. It certainly contains no express request to the College either "to maintain and improve the efficiency of its teaching" or "to construct new buildings and otherwise to keep pace with the growing need of its constituency," but simply states that the promise to pay the $5,000 is made for the purpose of enabling the College to do so, leaving it perfectly free to pursue what had always been its aims in whatever manner its Governors should choose. No statement is made as to the amount intended to be raised for all or any of the purposes stated. No buildings of any kind are described. The construction of new buildings is merely indicated as a means of the College keeping pace with the growing need of its constituency and apparently to be undertaken as and when the Governors should in their unfettered discretion decide the erection of any one or more buildings for any purpose was necessary or desirable.

It seems to me difficult to conceive that, had the deceased actually paid the promised money, he could have safely relied upon the mere acceptance of his own promise, couched in such vague and uncertain terms regarding its purpose, as the foundation of any action against the College Corporation.

So far as I can discover, there is no English or Canadian case in which it has been authoritatively decided that a reciprocal promise on the part of the promisee may be implied from the mere fact of the acceptance by the promisee of such a subscription paper from the hands of the promisor to do the thing for which the subscription is promised. There is no doubt, of course, that an express agreement by the promisee to do certain acts in return for a subscription is a sufficient consideration for the promise of the subscriber. There may, too, be circumstances proved by evidence, outside the subscription paper itself, from which such a reciprocal promise on the part of the promisee may well be implied, but I have not been able to find any English or Canadian case where it has actually been so decided in the absence of proof that the subscriber has himself either expressly requested the promisee to undertake some definite project or personally taken such a part in connection with the project enterprise that such a request might be inferred therefrom.

It is true that there are expressions in the judgments of the Manitoba Court of Appeal in *Sargent* v. *Nicholson* (1915), 25 D.L.R. 638, and of Wright J., of the Supreme Court of Ontario, in *Re Loblaw*, [1933] 4 D.L.R. 264; which seems to support the proposition that a request from the promisor to the promisee may be implied from the mere statement in the subscription paper of the object for which the subscription is promised and a reciprocal promise from the promisee to the promisor to carry out that purpose from the mere fact of the acceptance of the subscription, but an examination of both these judgments makes it clear that these expressions of opinion do not touch the real ground upon which either of the decisions proceeds.

There is no doubt either that some American courts have held that by acceptance of the subscription paper itself the promisee impliedly undertakes to carry out the purpose for which the subscription is made and treated this implied promise of the promisee as the consideration for the promise to pay. This view, however, has been rejected, as pointed out in 60 Corpus Juris, 959, on the ground that the promise implied in the acceptance involves no act advantageous to the subscriber or detrimental to the beneficiary, and hence does not involve a case of mutual promises and that the duty of the payee would arise from trusteeship rather than a contractual promise, citing *Albany Presbyterian Church* v. *Cooper*, above referred to. No suggestion of mutual promises was made in the last named case, notwithstanding that the subscription there involved was expressly stated to be for the single purpose of erecting a designated church building; neither was it made in the leading New York case of *Barnes* v. *Perine*, (1854), 2 Kernan's Rep. (12 N.Y. Appeals) 18, where the subscription was also stated to be for the erection of a specific church edifice.

As to finding the consideration for the subscription outside the subscription itself, the only evidence relied upon is that of Dr. MacKenzie that increased expenditures were made by the College for the purposes stated between the years 1920 and 1931 on the strength of the subscriptions obtained in the canvass of 1920. It is contended that this fact alone constituted a consideration for the subscription and made it binding. The decisions in *Sargent* v. *Nicholson; Y.M.C.A.* v. *Rankin;* and the judgment of Wright J., of the Supreme Court of Ontario, in *Re Loblaw*, adopting the two former decisions, are relied upon to sustain this proposition as well as some earlier Ontario cases and several American decisions.

There seems to be no doubt that the first three cases mentioned unqualifiedly support the proposition relied upon, as regards at least a subscription for a single distinct and definite object, such as the erection of a designated building, whether or not the expenditure would not have been made nor any liability incurred by the promisee *but for the promise* or not.

The earlier Ontario cases relied upon, however, do not appear to me to go that far. They all shew that there was either a direct personal interest on the part of the subscriber in the particular project undertaken or some personal participation in the action of the promisee as a result of which the expenditure or liability was incurred.

Regarding the American decisions, upon which *Sargent* v. *Nicholson* appears to have entirely proceeded—more particularly perhaps on the dictum of Gray C.J., in *Cottage Street M. E. Church* v. *Kendall* than any other—it may be pointed out that there are other American cases which shew that there must be something more than the mere expenditure of money or the incurring of liability by the promisee on the faith of the promise. *Hull* v. *Pearson* (1899), 56 N.Y. Sup. 518, a decision of the Appellate Division of the Supreme Court of New York, in which many of the American cases are reviewed, should perhaps be mentioned in this regard. One W. subscribed a certain sum for the work of the German department of a theological seminary. There was no consideration expressed in the memorandum, and there was no evidence of a request in the part of W. that the work should be continued, or of any expenditures on the part of the theological seminary in reliance on such request. Such department had been continued, but there was no evidence that it would not have been continued as it had been for a series of years but for the subscription. It was held that the subscription was without consideration and could not be enforced. Woodward J., in the course of his reasons, in which the full court concurred, said:

"It is true that there is evidence that the German department has been continued, but this does not meet the requirement. There is no evidence that it would not have been continued as it had been for a series of years if the subscription of Mr. Wild had not been made."

And further:

"He undoubtedly made the subscription for the purpose of aiding in promoting the work of the German department; but, in the absence of some act or word which clearly indicated that he accompanied his subscription by a request to do something which the corporation would not have done except for his subscription, there is no such request as would justify a constructive consideration in support of this promise."

These latter dicta seem to accord more with the English decisions, which give no countenance to the principle applied in *Sargent* v. *Nicholson* and *Y. M.C.A.* v. *Rankin* and in the earlier American cases, as is so pointedly illustrated by the judgments of Pearson J., in *In Re Hudson,* and Eve J., in *In Re Cory,* (1912), 29 T.L.R. 18. The head note in *In Re Hudson* states:

"A. verbally promised to give £20,000 to the Jubilee Fund of the Congregational Union, and also filled up and signed a blank form of promise not addressed to anyone, but headed 'Congregational Union of England and Wales Jubilee Fund,' whereby he promised to give £20,000 in five equal annual instalments of £4,000 each, for the liquidation of chapel debts. A. paid three instalments of £4,000 to the fund within three years from the date of his promise, and then died, leaving the remaining two instalments unpaid and unprovided for.

"The Congregational Union claimed £8,000 from A.'s executors, on the ground that they had been led by A.'s promise to contribute larger sums to churches than they would otherwise have done; that money had been given and promised by other persons in consequence of A.'s promise; that grants from the Jubilee Fund had been promised to cases recommended by

A.; and that churches to which promises had been made by the committee, and the committee themselves, had incurred liabilities in consequence of A.'s promise."

His Lordship held there was no consideration for the promise. "There really was, " he said, "in this matter, nothing whatever in the shape of a consideration which could form a contract between the parties."

And he added:

"I am bound to say that this is an attempt to turn a charity into something very different from a charity. I think it ought to fail, and I think it does fail. I do not know to what extent a contrary decision might open a new form of posthumous charity. Posthumous charity is already bad enough, and it is quite sufficiently protected by law without establishing a new principle which would extend the doctrine in its favour far more than it has been extended or ought to be extended."

In the *Cory* case a gift of 1,000 guineas was promised to a Y.M.C.A. Association for the purpose of building a memorial hall. The sum required was £150,000, of which £85,000 had been promised or was available. The committee in charge decided not to commit themselves until they saw that their efforts to raise the whole fund were likely to prove successful. The testator, whose estate it was sought to charge, promised the 1,000 guineas and subsequently the committee felt justified in entering into a building contract, which they alleged they were largely induced to enter into by the testator's promise. Eve J., held there was no contractual obligation between the parties and therefore no legal debt due from the estate.

Chisholm C.J., in the case at bar, said that without any want of deference to eminent judges who have held otherwise he felt impelled to follow the decisions in the English cases. I am of opinion that he was fully justified in so doing, rather than apply the principle contended for by the appellant in reliance upon the decision in *Sargent* v. *Nicholson* based, as the latter case is, upon the decisions of United States courts, which are not only in conflict with the English cases, but with decisions of the Court of Appeals of the State of New York, as I have, I think, shewn, and which have been subjected to very strong criticim by American legal authors, notably by Prof. Williston, as the learned Chief Justice of Nova Scotia has shewn in his exhaustive and, to my mind, very convincing judgment.

To hold otherwise would be to hold that a naked, voluntary promise may be converted into a binding legal contract by the subsequent action of the promisee alone without the consent, express or implied, of the promisor. There is no evidence here which in any way involves the deceased in the carrying out of the work for which the promised subscription was made other than the signing of the subscription paper itself.

I may add that, had I come to the opposite conclusion upon the legal question involved, I should have felt impelled, as Chisholm C.J., did, to seriously question the accuracy of the statement relied upon by the appellant that "this work was done and the increased expenditures were made on the strength of the subscriptions promised," if that statement was meant to refer to all the increased expenditures listed in the comparative statements produced by Dr. MacKenzie. The statement relied on does not profess to set out verbatim the language of the witness. The record of the evidence is apparently but a brief summary taken down by the Registrar. That the summary is inaccurate was shewn by the admission made on the argument before us that it was not $220,000 which was subscribed in all in 1920, but $2,200,000. The statement produced of expenditures on buildings, grounds and equipment since 1920 shews a grand total for the more than ten years of but $1,491,687—over $700,000 less than the aggregate of the 1920 campaign subscriptions—and this grand total includes over $400,000 for Shirriff Hall, which it is well known was the object of a special donation contributed by a wealthy lady, now deceased, as a memorial to her father. In the light of this correction it becomes quite as difficult to believe that the College Corporation, in doing "this work" and making "the increased expenditures" did so in reliance upon the deceased's subscription, as if the aggregate of the subscriptions had been but $220,000, as the Registrar took the figures down, and the Nova Scotia Supreme Court supposed, and the total expenditures $1,491,687. This evidence would assuredly seem to shut out all possibility of establishing a claim against the deceased's estate on any such ground as estoppel.

The appeal, I think, should be dismissed with costs.

QUESTION. Do you think the beneficiaries of the estate have a greater or lesser claim on the Boutilier money than the Dalhousie College?

C.A. WRIGHT, CASE COMMENT. 1935. 13 *Can. Bar Rev.* 108. [Comment on *Dalhousie College* decision.] ". . . While charity seems quite inconsistent with the bargain-theory of contracts, various attempts have been made to impose liability on a subscriber, either by the form in which the subscription card is drafted, or by a forced construction placed on such card viewed in the light of subsequent events. Courts who have done the latter, have evidently felt that the social desirability of enforcing such promises might compensate for any resulting strain on the accepted doctrines of consideration. . . .

"The Supreme Court of Canada in rejecting the argument not only brings Canadian doctrine back to the principle of the English cases, but overrules many decisions in Ontario and the Western Provinces which had proceeded on this line. In so doing, the Court was much influenced by Professor Williston's trenchant criticism of the 'promissory estoppel' doctrine as it had developed in the American Courts. It is not without interest that the American Law Institute Restatement of Contracts (for which Professor Williston was Reporter) has recently adopted as a statement of existing law, a section which supports the doctrine rejected in the present case. In so doing, however, the Restatement classifies the situations in which it applies as promises binding without consideration. Strange as this may sound to the common-law lawyer, it seems clear that there are such cases in our law. We usually cover such cases by some other form of words, however, and so do not always appreciate their inconsistency with the doctrine of consideration. In addition to the charitable subscription cases, there are other situations where, although no specific act is requested by a promisor, our courts have in effect followed the doctrine in question, and have found consideration merely because some detrimental action was taken in reliance upon a promise. The present case should draw attention to the fact that consideration exists only when certain definite acts are requested as the price of the promise. It would seem that if it is deemed desirable to enforce charitable subscriptions on the faith of which many public undertakings are begun, it would be comparatively simple to pass legislation on the subject. Particularly on the death of a promisor before payment such legislation would seem desirable, since the promisor would undoubtedly have fulfilled his promise had he lived, and in competition with other beneficiaries of the deceased's bounty, there seems no reason to reject the charity.

"Another method by which charitable subscriptions have been held binding is to imply a counter-promise to apply the money subscribed for the objects set out in the subscription card. The present decision would seem to deny the validity of such an approach on the ground that this 'duty of the payee would arise from trusteeship rather than a contractual promise.' On this view, even assuming such a promise, it would not furnish consideration as it would be merely a promise to perform an existing legal duty, and as such would furnish no detriment sufficient to support the subscription promise.

"If it is desired to turn promised 'charity' into a legal obligation, the magic device of a seal is always open to the collector. The fact that seals are practically never used would seem to support the opinion that it is not believed wise to let the subscriber think he is entering any binding obligation. If that is the impression sought to be created, there is no reason for courts to be astute in transmuting charity into a commercial transaction."

PUBLIC SUBSCRIPTIONS ACT
Nova Scotia. Revised Statutes. 1967. Chapter 257

1. Where any subscription list is opened and any subscription is made in aid of the erection of any road, bridge, place of worship, schoolhouse, or in aid of any other undertaking of public utility, or which is designated in the subscription list as, or appears therefrom to be, a public undertaking, and such undertaking is commenced, every person who has engaged by written subscription to contribute money, labour or other aid towards the undertaking, shall be held liable to perform such engagement, notwithstanding any apparent want of consideration in the agreement for the same.

2. (1) The following persons may require every person who has so subscribed to perform his engagement, that is to say

(a) where a public grant is made in aid of such undertaking, the commissioner or other person appointed to expend such grant;

(b) where no public grant is made, the person to whom the performance or superintendence of such undertaking has been entrusted, and

(c) the person who has engaged in, and is then carrying on, such undertaking.

(2) If any subscriber, after a written notice of at least one month, refuses or neglects to perform his engagement, he may be sued by such commissioner or other person in this section mentioned, or by the person to whom such subscription is payable.

(3) Nothing in this section shall be construed to bind or make liable the executors or administrators of, or the estate of, any subscriber, unless it expressly appears from the instrument subscribed by him that he intended that his estate should be liable by binding his executors or administrators.

3. All moneys or other aid so subscribed and recovered shall be applied and expended for the purpose for which the same would have been so subscribed, and for no other purpose whatever.

NOTE. The above statute was referred to by Chisholm C.J. in the *Dalhousie College* case, in the Nova Scotia Supreme Court. He said, "When the Legislature of Nova Scotia first passed—several years before confederation—the statute which is now R.S.N.S. 1923, c. 209, it is fair inference that then the opinion of this Province was that gratuitous promises could not be enforced. That is why the statute was passed." Do you agree? May the statute not have been merely declaratory of the common law?

Chisholm C.J. also said, "The statute . . . has clearly no application to a case like the present. It applies by its plain terms to public undertakings." Do you agree? Would a "school house" for which no public grant is made be included? Is a "place of worship" more or less a "public undertaking" than Dalhousie College? Does the word "public," which is used once in the title, twice in section 1 and once in section 2, have the same meaning each time it is used?

Compare section 2(3) with Dr. Wright's view about the desirability of legislation in the case of the death of a promisor since in competition with other beneficiaries there would seem to be no reason to reject the charity.

Would it be fair to infer that the Nova Scotia legislature declared the public policy of the province that charitable pledges should be enforceable? Should the Supreme Court of Canada then give effect to that policy? Prince Edward Island has an Act similar to the Nova Scotia Act. Was the Supreme Court of Canada justified in rejecting the American judicial views, the principle of two provincial statutes, and four Court of Appeal decisions?

Is it fair to argue that by using the expression "in consideration of the subscriptions of others" both the draftsman and the subscriber thought they were stating a binding promise just as much as if they had used a seal? Does the subscriber "understand" the seal better than he does the words about "consideration"? What does he intend?

How would you set up a pledge card that you wanted to be binding?

(ii) *Gratuitous Undertakings*

AMES, "THE HISTORY OF ASSUMPSIT." 1888. 2 *Harv. Law Rev.* 1: "The action against a bailee for negligent custody was looked upon . . . as a tort, and not as a contract. The immediate cause of the injury in the case of the bailee was, it is true, a nonfeasance, and not, as in the case of the surgeon or carpenter, a misfeasance. . . . The action against the bailee sounding in tort, consideration was no more an essential part of the count than it was in action against a surgeon . . . Oddly enough, the earliest attempts to charge bailees in assumpsit were made when the bailment was gratuitous. These attempts, just before and after 1600, were unsuccessful, because the plaintiff could not make out any consideration. The gratuitous bailment was of course not a benefit, but a burden to the defendant; and, on the other hand, it was not regarded as a detriment, but an advantage to the plaintiff. But in 1623 it was finally decided, not without a great straining, it must be conceded, of the doctrine of consideration, that a bailee might be charged in assumpsit on a gratuitous bailment." [See also Seavey, "Reliance on Gratuitous Promises" (1951), 64 *Harv. L.R.* 913.]

BAXTER v. *JONES*. 1903. 6 O.L.R. 360 (Ontario. Court of Appeal). The plaintiff asked the defendant, his fire insurance agent, through whom he was placing extra insurance on his mills and machinery, to notify the other companies who held his insurance. The defendant gratuitously agreed to do this but failed to carry out his promise. On a fire damage claim the other companies, not having been notified of the extra insurance, denied liability, but settled for $1000 less than they would have had to pay under the increased policies. This action was to recover the $1000. Held, for the plaintiff. MACLENNAN J.A.: ". . . Mr. Baxter says he went to [Mr. Jones] for this additional insurance just because his other risks were in his office, and, it is not contended that there was any consideration between the plaintiffs and the defendant in connection with the business. The only consideration in the matter was the premium which was paid to the company. As between the plaintiffs and defendant, therefore, the whole business was voluntary. It was contended that the procurement of the policy and the promise to notify the companies were one single transaction, and that having undertaken the business and performed it negligently, the defendant was responsible although there was no consideration for the contract: *Coggs* v. *Bernard* and *Elsee* v. *Gatward*." [Why should an action on the supposedly gratuitous promise of the defendant to notify the other companies be justified by the ancient law? Is it not a reasonable interpretation of the facts that the plaintiff agreed to buy insurance through the defendant agent at his request so that he would earn a commission on the premium? Then could not the one act be consideration for two promises, to procure and to notify?]

DE LA BERE v. *PEARSON, LIMITED*. [1908] 1 K.B. 280 (England. Court of Appeal). The defendants published a newspaper in which "readers . . . desiring financial advice in these columns" were invited to address their queries to the City Editor. The plaintiff, a regular reader (it is not reported that he was a purchaser or subscriber), wrote asking how best he could invest £800, and specifically requesting the name of a "good stock broker." The City Editor turned the letter over to an "outside stock broker" who persuaded the plaintiff to invest £1400 with him. No shares were bought, the money instead was appropriated to the stock broker's private affairs. He was an undischarged bankrupt. The City Editor knew that the broker was not on the Stock Exchange, but did not know of his bankruptcy although he could have found out. The publishers had done what they could to help several of their readers who had lost money to the broker. The plaintiff sued the defendant publishers for damages for breach of contract to exercise due care in giving financial advice to the plaintiff. The Lord Chief Justice held that the plaintiff was entitled to recover the £1400 sent by him to the broker for investment. The defendant appealed but the appeal was dismissed. On the question of consideration, nothing appears in the report of the argument. VAUGHAN WILLIAMS L.J.: "In the first place, I think there was a contract as between the plaintiff and the defendants. The defendants advertised, offering to give advice with reference to investments. The plaintiff, accepting that offer, asked for advice, and asked for the name of a good stock broker. The questions and answers were, if the defendants chose, to be inserted in their paper as published; such publication might obviously have a tendency to increase the sale of the defendants' paper. I think that this offer, when accepted, resulted in a contract for good consideration." [What was the bargained-for exchange?]

(iii) *Negligent Misstatement in Tort*

HEDLEY BYRNE & CO. LTD. v. *HELLER & PARTNERS LTD.*
[1964] A.C. 465 (H.L.)

The plaintiff, before advancing credit to a third party, asked the defendant banker for a credit report. The defendant replied: "for your private use and without responsibility on the part of this bank or its officials ... Re [third party]. Respectably constituted company, considered good for its ordinary business engagements. Your figures are larger than we are accustomed to see." In reliance on this report the plaintiff advanced credit and lost a large sum of money when the third party failed to honour its obligations. The House of Lords held that an action would lie for negligent misrepresentation causing financial loss, but in this particular case the defendant was protected by the opening sentence of its report.

LORD DEVLIN: The respondents [defendants] in this case cannot deny that they were performing a service. Their sheet anchor is that they were performing it gratuitously and therefore no liability for its performance can arise. My Lords, in my opinion this is not the law. A promise given without consideration to perform a service cannot be enforced as a contract by the promisee; but if the service is in fact performed and done negligently, the promisee can recover in an action in tort. This is the foundation of the liability of a gratuitous bailee. In the famous case of *Coggs* v. *Bernard*, (1703) 2 Ld.Raym. 909 where the defendant had charge of brandy belonging to the plaintiff and had spilt a quantity of it, there was a motion in arrest of judgment "for that it was not alleged in the declaration that the defendant was a common porter, nor averred that he had anything for his pains." The declaration was held to be good notwithstanding that there was not any consideration laid. Gould J. said: "The reason of the action is, the particular trust reposed in the defendant, to which he has concurred by his assumption, and in the executing which he has miscarried by his neglect." This proposition is not limited to the law of bailment. In *Skelton* v. *London & North Western Railway Co.* (1867) L.R. 2 C.P. 631, 636 Willes J. applied it generally to the law of negligence. He said: "Actionable negligence must consist in the breach of some duty ... if a person undertakes to perform a voluntary act, he is liable if he performs it improperly, but not if he neglects to perform it. Such is the result of the decision in the case of *Coggs* v. *Bernard*." Likewise in *Banbury* v. *Bank of Montreal,* [1918] A.C. 626, 654 where the bank had advised a customer on his investments, Lord Finlay L.C. said: "He is under no obligation to advise, but if he takes upon himself to do so, he will incur liability if he does so negligently."

The principle has been applied to cases where as a result of the negligence no damage was done to person or to property and the consequential loss was purely financial. In *Wilkinson* v. *Coverdale* 1 Esp. 75 the defendant undertook gratuitously to get a fire policy renewed for the plaintiff, but, in doing so, neglected formalities, the omission of which rendered the policy inoperative. It was held that an action would lie. In two similar cases the defendants succeeded on the ground that negligence was not proved in fact. Both cases were thus decided on the basis that in law an action would lie. In the first of them, *Shiells* v. *Blackburne,* 1 H.Bl. 158 the defendant had, acting voluntarily and without compensation, made an entry of the plaintiff's leather as wrought leather instead of dressed leather, with the result that the leather was seized. In *Dartnall* v. *Howard & Gibbs* (1825) 4 B. & C. 345 the defendants purchased an annuity for the plaintiff but on the personal security of two insolvent persons. The court, after verdict, arrested the judgment upon the ground that the defendants appeared to be gratuitous agents and that it was not averred that they had acted either with negligence or dishonesty.

Many cases could be cited in which the same result has been achieved by setting up some nominal consideration and suing in contract instead of in tort. In *Coggs* v. *Bernard* Holt C.J. put the obligation on both grounds. He said: ". . . secondly, it is objected, and there is no consideration to ground this promise upon, and therefore the undertaking is but nudum pactum. But to this I answer, that the owners trusting him with the goods is a sufficient consideration to oblige him to a careful management. Indeed, if the agreement had been executory, to carry these brandies from the one place to the other such a day, the defendant had not been bound to carry them. But this is a different case, for assumpsit does not only signify a future agreement, but in such a case as this, it signifies an actual entry upon the thing, and taking the trust upon himself. And if a man will do that, and miscarries in the performance of his trust, an action will lie against him for that, though nobody could have compelled him to do the thing."

De La Bere v. *Pearson Ltd.* is an example of a case of this sort decided on the ground that there was a sufficiency of consideration. The defendants advertised in their newspaper that their city editor would answer inquiries from readers of the paper desiring financial advice. The plaintiff asked for the name of a good stockbroker. The editor recommended the name of a person whom he knew to be an outside broker and whom he ought to have known, if he had made proper inquiries, to be an undischarged bankrupt. The plaintiff dealt with him and lost his money. The case being brought in contract, Vaughan Williams L.J. thought that there was sufficient consideration in the fact that the plaintiff consented to the publication of his question in the defendants' paper if the defendants so chose. For Barnes P. the consideration appears to have lain in the plaintiff addressing an inquiry as invited. In the same way when in *Everett* v. *Griffiths* the Court of Appeal was considering the liability of a doctor towards the person he was certifying, Scrutton L.J. said that the submission to treatment would be a good consideration.

My Lords, I have cited these instances so as to show that in one way or another the law has ensured that in this type of case a just result has been reached. But I think that today the result can and should be achieved by the application of the law of negligence and that it is unnecessary and undesirable to construct an artificial consideration. I agree with Sir Frederick Pollock's note on the case of *De La Bere* v. *Pearson Ltd.* where he said in *Contracts*, 13th ed., p. 140, that "the cause of action is better regarded as arising from default in the performance of a voluntary undertaking independent of contract."

My Lords, it is true that this principle of law has not yet been clearly applied to a case where the service which the defendant undertakes to perform is or includes the obtaining and imparting of information. But I cannot see why it should not be: and if it had not been thought erroneously that *Derry* v. *Peek* 14 App.Cas. 337 negatived any liability for negligent statements, I think that by now it probably would have been. It cannot matter whether the information consists of fact or of opinion or is a mixture of both, nor whether it was obtained as a result of special inquiries or comes direct from facts already in the defendant's possession or from his general store of professional knowledge. One cannot, as I have already endeavoured to show, distinguish in this respect between a duty to inquire and a duty to state.

I think, therefore, that there is ample authority to justify your Lordships in saying now that the categories of special relationships which may give rise to a duty to take care in word as well as in deed are not limited to contractual relationships or to relationships of fiduciary duty, but include also relationships which in the words of Lord Shaw in *Nocton* v. *Lord Ashburton* [1914] A.C. 932, 972 are "equivalent to contract," that is, where there is an assumption of responsibility in circumstances in which, but for the absence of consideration, there would be a contract. Where there is an express undertaking, an express warranty as distinct from mere representation, there can be little difficulty. The difficulty arises in discerning those cases in which the undertaking is to be implied. In this respect the absence of consideration is not irrelevant. Payment for information or advice is very good evidence that it is being relied upon and that the informer or adviser knows that it is. Where there is no consideration, it will be necessary to exercise greater care in distinguishing between social and professional relationships and between those which are of a contractual character and those which are not. It may often be material to consider whether the adviser is acting purely out of good nature or whether he is getting his reward in some indirect form. The service that a bank performs in giving a reference is not done simply out of a desire to assist commerce. It would discourage the customers of the bank if their deals fell through because the bank had refused to testify to their credit when it was good.

I have had the advantage of reading all the opinions prepared by your Lordships and of studying the terms which your Lordships have framed by way of definition of the sort of relationship which gives rise to a responsibility towards those who act upon information or advice and so creates a duty of care towards them. I do not understand any of your Lordships to hold that it is a responsibility imposed by law upon certain types of persons or in certain sorts of situations. It is a responsibility that is voluntarily accepted or undertaken, either generally where a general relationship, such as that of solicitor and client or banker and customer, is created, or specifically in relation to a particular transaction. In the present case the appellants were not, as in *Woods* v. *Martins Bank Ltd.* [1959] 1 Q.B. 55 the customers or potential customers of the bank. Responsibility can attach only to the single act, that is, the giving of the reference, and only if the doing of that act implied a voluntary undertaking to assume responsibility. This is a point of great importance because it is, as I understand it, the foundation for the ground on which in the end the House dismisses the appeal. I do not think it possible to formulate with exactitude all the conditions under which the law will in a specific case imply a voluntary undertaking any more than it is possible to formulate those in which the law will imply a contract. But in so far as your Lordships describe the circumstances in which an implication will ordinarily be drawn, I am prepared to adopt any one of your Lordships' statements as showing the general rule; and I pay the same respect to the statement by Denning L.J. in his dissenting judgment in *Candler* v. *Crane, Christmas & Co.* [1951] 2 K.B. 164 about the circumstances in which he says a duty to use care in making a statement exists.

I do not go further than this for two reasons. The first is that I have found in the speech of Lord Shaw in *Nocton* v. *Lord Ashburton* and in the idea of a relationship that is equivalent to contract all that is necessary to cover the situation that arises in this case. Mr. Gardiner does not claim to succeed unless he can establish that the reference was intended by the respondents to be communicated by the National Provincial Bank to some unnamed customer of theirs, whose identity was immaterial to the respondents, for that customer's use. All that was lacking was formal consideration. The case is well within the authorities I have already cited and of which *Wilkinson* v. *Coverdale* is the most apposite example.

I shall therefore content myself with the proposition that wherever there is a relationship equivalent to contract, there is a duty of care. Such a relationship may be either general or particular. Examples of a general relationship are those of solicitor and client and of banker and customer. For the former *Nocton* v. *Lord Ashburton* has long stood as the authority and for the latter there is the decision of Salmon J. in *Woods* v. *Martins Bank Ltd.* which I respectfully approve. There may well be others yet to be established. Where there is a general relationship of this sort, it is unnecessary to do more than prove its existence and the duty follows. Where, as in the present case, what is relied on is a particular relationship created ad hoc, it will be necessary to examine the particular facts to see whether there is an express or implied undertaking of responsibility.

I regard this proposition as an application of the general conception of proximity. Cases may arise in the future in which a new and wider proposition, quite independent of any notion of contract, will be needed. There may, for example, be cases in which a statement is not supplied for the use of any particular person, any more than in *Donoghue* v. *Stevenson* [1932] A.C. 562 the ginger beer was supplied for consumption by any particular person; and it will then be necessary to return to the general conception of proximity and to see whether there can be evolved from it, as was done in *Donoghue* v. *Stevenson*, a specific proposition to fit the case. When that has to be done, the speeches of your Lordships today as well as the judgment of Denning L.J. to which I have referred— and also, I may add, the proposition in the *American Restatement of the Law of Torts*, Vol. III, p. 122, para. 552, and the cases which exemplify it—will afford good guidance as to what ought to be said. I prefer to see what shape such cases take before committing myself to any formulation, for I bear in mind Lord Atkin's warning, which I have quoted, against placing unnecessary restrictions on the adaptability of English law. I have, I hope, made it clear that I take quite literally the dictum of Lord Macmillan, so often quoted from the same case, that "the categories of negligence are never closed." English law is wide enough to embrace any new category or proposition that exemplifies the principle of proximity.

I have another reason for caution. Since the essence of the matter in the present case and in others of the same type is the acceptance of responsibility, I should like to guard against the imposition of restrictive terms notwithstanding that the essential condition is fulfilled. If a defendant says to a plaintiff: "Let me do this for you; do not waste your money in employing a professional, I will do it for nothing and you can rely on me." I do not think he could escape liability simply because he belonged to no profession or calling, had no qualifications or special skill and did not hold himself out as having any. The relevance of these factors is to show the unlikelihood of a defendant in such circumstances assuming a legal responsibility, and as such they may often be decisive. But they are not theoretically conclusive and so cannot be the subject of definition. It would be unfortunate if they were. For it would mean that plaintiffs would seek to avoid the rigidity of the definition by bringing the action in contract as in *De La Bere* v. *Pearson Ltd.* and setting up something that would do for consideration. That, to my mind, would be an undesirable development in the law; and the best way of avoiding it is to settle the law so that the presence or absence of consideration makes no difference. . . .

(iv) *Promises to Convey Land*

CRABB v. *ARUN DISTRICT COUNCIL*
[1975] 3 W.L.R. 847 (C.A.)

LORD DENNING M.R.: This case cannot be properly understood without a map: but I will try to explain it as best I can. Near Bognor Regis there is a village called Pagham. There is a road there called Hook Lane running east and west. On the south side of that road there is an area of land called Windmill Park. In 1946 a Mr. Alford bought 5½ acres of it. It formed a big square field with its north side next to the road. Now you must imagine that big field divided into two parts by a line running from north to south, with two acres on the eastern side of the line and 3½ acres on the western side, and the two acres divided by a line horizontally into two halves, the front portion (1 acre) being next to the road and the back portion (1 acre) with no access to the road. Mr. Alford developed the two acres and left the other 3½ acres undeveloped. On these two acres Mr. Alford put two industrial buildings. On the front portion he erected offices and showrooms. On the back portion he erected a building for the manufacture of caravans. And he made a road on these two acres connecting the back portion to the front.

In 1962 Mr. Alford died. His executors decided to develop the remaining 3½ acres on the western side of the field. They obtained planning permission to erect dwelling houses on it. Under this proposal there was to be a new estate road made to give access from Hook Lane to the new housing estate. It was to be made on the 3½ acres but was to run alongside the boundary line between the 3½ acres and the two acres. It was to be called Mill Park Road. This road was to be to the advantage also of the buildings on the two-acre portion, because they could have access on to the near road. The proposal at that time was, however, that there should be only one access from the two acres on to the new road. This was to be at a point marked "A" in the front portion, about half-way up from Hook Lane. It was thought at that time that one access would be sufficient because the whole of the two acres were in one occupation. The vehicles from the back portion (where caravans were made) could go along their own existing road to the front portion (where the offices and showrooms were), and then out at point A. This was to be the only access to the two acres. The previous access (from a side lane) was to be closed.

Planning permission was given for this development. But the executors of Mr. Alford did not carry it out themselves. They sold the two acres to the plaintiff; and they sold the 3½ acres to the defendants, the Chichester

Rural District Council. The conveyances are of importance. By a conveyance dated September 1, 1965, the executors of Mr. Alford sold the whole of the two acres with the two industrial buildings to the plaintiff, and in the conveyance they agreed to erect a fence 5 ft. 6 in. high along the boundary line (save for the access gap at point A). They also granted him a right of access at point A to the proposed new road and a right of way along it to Hook Lane. By a conveyance dated December 8, 1966, the executors of Mr. Alford sold the 3½ acres to the defendants, but they expressly reserved the right (which they had already granted to the plaintiff) for the owner of the two acres to have access at point A to the proposed new road and a right of way along it to Hook Lane. In the same deed the defendants agreed to erect the fence 5 ft. 6 in. high along the boundary line (save for the access gap at point A).

So, on the conveyances the owners and occupiers of the two acres had a right of access at one point, namely, point A (halfway up the front portion). It was shown on the map as a gap about 20 feet wide; and from that point they had a right of way along the proposed new estate road, to get to Hook Lane. The defendants were to erect a close-boarded fence 5 ft. 6 in. high along the whole boundary between the two acres and the 3½ acres, except for the 20 feet gap at point A.

In 1967 the plaintiff had a new idea about his two acres. He thought it would be desirable to split up the two portions and sell them separately for separate use. The front portion (with the offices and showrooms) was clearly separated from the back portion (with the manufacturing). But, if they were split up, he would need another access. The access at point A would serve the front portion. But he would need another access at another point (to be called point B) so as to serve the back portion, together with a right of way along the new estate road from point B to Hook Lane.

Now, by this time the plaintiff had engaged as his architect Mr. Alford, who was the son of the original owner of the land. On June 22, 1967, Mr. Alford, as architect for the plaintiff, wrote this letter to the engineer of the defendant council:

"For the attention of Mr. Stonier:
Dear Sir . . . It would appear that Mr. Crabb may require two entrances off the new road, one to each of his two buildings. If you could let me know when you hope to get this fence line out I would be glad of the opportunity of meeting a representative of your department on the site so that these matters can be finally settled and the line of the fence agreed."

In pursuance of that letter there was a meeting on July 26, 1967, which was attended by the plaintiff and his architect, Mr. Alford, and by a representative of the defendants. There is no written note of what took place. Both the plaintiff and his architect, Mr. Alford, gave evidence about the meeting. But unfortunately the defendants gave no evidence about it. They undoubtedly had a representative there, but we do not know who it was. The engineer, Mr. Stonier, said that he himself was not present. The only other person who might have represented the defendants was a Mr. Queen. He was in Canada and not available to give evidence. But there is no doubt that they agreed the line of the fence which was to separate the plaintiff's land from the defendant's land. There is also no doubt that there was an agreement in principle that the plaintiff should have, not only the access at point A, but also an additional access at point B, so as to give access from the back portion of his land on to the new estate road. The plaintiff said that the defendant's representative made a firm commitment for a second access at B: but the judge said that the plaintiff was rather over sanguine. The judge preferred the evidence of Mr. Alford who was rather more cautious. Mr. Alford said: "I thought we had got final agreement in that there was to be access at point B, but I saw further processes beyond the meeting." He foresaw, no doubt, that there might have to be a document drawn up between the solicitors. Later on, in his evidence, Mr. Alford was asked whether there was to be any payment for this additional access. He said: "The normal anticipation at that time would be that some consideration would be demanded." But the defendants' representative did not ask for any payment. Mr. Alford said: "My strong feeling is we would not be asked to pay that consideration when talking to the defendants in 1967."

Summing up the evidence, as accepted by the judge, the result of the meeting on July 22, 1967, was that there was an agreement in principle that the plaintiff should have an additional access at point B to the land, because it was envisaged that he would sell his two acres of land in two portions: the front portion with access at point A to the new road, and the back portion with access at point B to the new road. But the judge found there was no definite assurance to that effect, and, even if there had been, it would not have been binding in the absence of either writing or consideration. In order to be binding, there would have to be the legal processes foreseen by Mr. Alford.

As it happened, no legal processes were gone through. The defendants made no formal grant to the plaintiff of any access at point B or any easement over the new road. But, nevertheless, the parties acted in the belief that he had or would be granted such a right. During the winter of 1967 the defendants erected a fence along the line of the agreed boundary, but they left gaps at point A with access to the front portion of the plaintiff's land at point B with access to the back portion. These two gaps were used by lorries which went in and out at points A and B as if they were exits and entrances. It was creating such a mess and disturbance of the plaintiff's land that there was a meeting on the site on January 31, 1968, at which the defendants agreed that they would undertake a tidying-up operation; and they did so.

On February 6, 1968, there was an important development. The defendants gave orders for gates to be constructed at points A and B, and they were in fact constructed. We have before us the contractors' account dated March 30, 1968. The contractors erected a fence 5 ft. 6 in. high all the way along the boundary: but they put gates in the fence at points A and B. At point A they erected a pair of oak close-boarded gates 18 ft. 0 ins. wide, 5 ft. 6 ins. high, complete with posts and fittings, at a cost of £117 5s. 6d. At point B they erected a similar pair 12 ft. 3 ins. wide and 5 ft. 6 ins. high, at a cost of £76 6s 0d. The gateposts were set firmly in concrete at points A and B, and were clearly intended to be permanent.

Some months later, in the autumn of 1968, the plaintiff agreed to sell the front portion of his land to a purchaser and assigned to the purchaser the right of access at point A. But, here is the important matter. In the conveyance of the front portion of October 4, 1968, the plaintiff did not reserve any right for himself (as the owner of the back portion) to go over the front portion so as to get out at point A. The plaintiff thought that he already had a right of access at point B (where gates had already ben erected) and so he did not need to reserve any right to get to point A. The judge found that: ". . . Mr. Crabb believed that he had an assurance by the council that he would have access at point B from the council's land and was content to rely on that assurance. He did not reserve any right of access over [the front portion] . . . Mr. Crabb would not have been prepared to proceed with the sale of [the front portion] to [the purchaser] without reserving access over it . . . if he had not believed . . . that he would have access over the council's land."

But then, in January 1969, there was a new development. The plaintiff put a padlock on the inside of the gate at point B. The defendants were incensed by this. But they did not say a word to the plaintiff. They went on to his land. They took down the gates at point B. They pulled them out of the concrete. They took them away and filled the gap with extra posts and a close-boarded fence to match the existing fence. In short, they shut up the access at point B. The judge said: "The council gave no notice to Mr. Crabb of its intention to take this step; it seems to me that it was a discourteous and high-handed act. . ."

It is that action, depriving the plaintiff of his access, which has led to all the trouble. The plaintiff sought to settle the matter by agreement. The defendants did not object to his having access at point B and an easement to serve the back portion of the land, but they wanted £3,000 for it. This was more than the plaintiff was willing to pay. So no agreement was reached. In consequence this back portion of land has been rendered sterile. The plaintiff has been unable to sell it or make use of it because it has no outlet anywhere.

In June 1971 the plaintiff brought this action claiming a right of access at point B and a right of way along the estate road. He had no such right by any deed or conveyance or written agreement. So, in strict law, on the conveyance, the defendants were entitled to their land, subject only to an easement at point A, but none at point B. To overcome this strict law, the plaintiff claimed a right of access at B on the ground of equitable estoppel, promissory or proprietary. The judge held that he could not avail himself of any estoppel. He said: "In the absence of a definite assurance by the representative of the council, no question of estoppel can arise, and that really concludes the action." The plaintiff appeals to this court.

When Mr. Millett, for the plaintiff, said that he put his case on an estoppel, it shook me a little: because it is commonly supposed that estoppel is not itself a cause of action. But that is because there are estoppels and estoppels. Some do give rise to a cause of action. Some do not. In the species of estoppel called proprietary estoppel, it does give rise to a cause of action. We had occasion to consider it a month ago in *Moorgate Mercantile Co. Ltd.* v. *Twitchings* [1975] 3 W.L.R. 286 where I said, at p. 297, that the effect of estoppel on the true owner may be that ". . . his own title to the property, be it land or goods, has been held to be limited or extinguished, and new rights and interests have been created therein. And this operates by reason of his conduct—what he has led the other to believe—even though he never intended it." The new rights and interests, so created by estoppel, in or over land, will be protected by the courts and in this way give rise to a cause of action.

This was pointed out in Spencer Bower and Turner, *Estoppel by Representation*, 2nd ed. (1966), pp. 279-282.

The basis of this proprietary estoppel—as indeed of promissory estoppel —is the interposition of equity. Equity comes in, true to form, to mitigate the rigours of strict law. The early cases did not speak of it as "estoppel." They spoke of it as "raising an equity." If I may expand what Lord Cairns L.C. said in *Hughes* v. *Metropolitan Railway Co.* (1877) 2 App. Cas. 439, 448: "it is the first principle upon which all courts of equity proceed," that it will prevent a person from insisting on his strict legal rights—whether arising under a contract, or on his title deeds, or by statute—when it would be inequitable for him to do so having regard to the dealings which have taken place between the parties.

What then are the dealings which will preclude him from insisting on his strict legal rights? If he makes a binding contract that he will not insist on the strict legal position, a court of equity will hold him to his contract. Short of a binding contract, if he makes a promise that he will not insist upon his strict legal rights—then, even though that promise may be unenforceable in point of law for want of consideration or want of writing—then, if he makes the promise knowing or intending that the other will act upon it, and he does act upon it, then again a court of equity will not allow him to go back on that promise: see *Central London Property Trust Ltd.* v. *High Trees House Ltd.* [1947] K.B 130 and *Charles Rickards Ltd.* v. *Oppenhaim* [1950] 1 K.B. 616, 623. Short of an actual promise, if he, by his words or conduct, so behaves as to lead another to believe that he will not insist on his strict legal rights—knowing or intending that the other will act on that belief—and he does so act, that again will raise an equity in favour of the other; and it is for a court of equity to say in what way the equity may be satisfied. The cases show that this equity does not depend on agreement but on words or conduct. In *Ramsden* v. *Dyson* (1866) L.R. 1 H.L. 129, 170 Lord Kingsdown spoke of a verbal agreement "or what amounts to the same thing, an expectation, created or encouraged." In *Birmingham and District Land Co.* v. *London and North Western Railway Co.* (1888) 40 Ch.D. 268, 277, Cotton L.J. said that ". . . what passed did not make a new agreement, but . . . what took place . . . raised an equity against him." And it was the Privy Council in *Plimmer* v. *Wellington Corporation* (1884) 9 App.Cas. 699, 713-714 who said that ". . . the court must look at the circumstances in each case to decide in what way the equity can be satisfied" giving instances.

Recent cases afford illustrations of the principle. In *Inwards* v. *Baker* [1965] 2 Q.B. 29 it was held that, despite the legal title being in the plaintiffs, the son had an equity to remain in the bungalow "as long as he desired to use it as his home." Danckwerts L.J. said, at p. 38: "equity protects him so that an injustice may not be perpetrated." In *E. R. Ives Investment Ltd.* v. *High* [1967] 2 Q.B. 379, it was held that Mr. High and his successors had an equity which could only be satisfied by allowing him to have a right of access over the yard, "so long as the block of flats has its foundations on his land." In *Siew Soon Wah* v. *Yong Tong Hong* [1973] A.C. 836, the Privy Council held that there was an "equity or equitable estoppel protecting the defendant in his occupation for 30 years." In *Bank Negara Indonesia* v. *Hoalim* [1973] 2 M.L.J. 3 the Privy Council held that, despite the fact that the defendant had no protection under the Rent Acts, he had an equity to remain "so long as he continued to practise his profession."

The question then is: were the circumstances here such as to raise an equity in favour of the plaintiff? True the defendants on the deeds had the title to their land, free of any access at point B. But they led the plaintiff to believe that he had or would be granted a right of access at point B. At the meeting of July 26, 1967, Mr. Alford and the plaintiff told the defendants' representative that the plaintiff intended to split the two acres into two portions and wanted to have an access at point B for the back portion; and the defendants' representative agreed that he should have this access. I do not think the defendants can avoid responsibility by saying that their representative had no authority to agree this. They entrusted him with the task of setting out the line of the fence and the gates, and they must be answerable for his conduct in the course of it: see *Attorney-General to the Prince of Wales* v. *Collom* [1916] 2 K.B. 193, 207; and *Moorgate Mercantile Co. Ltd.* v. *Twitchings* [1975] 3 W.L.R. 286, 298.

The judge found that there was "no definite assurance" by the defendants' representative, and "no firm commitment," but only an "agreement in principle," meaning I suppose that, as Mr. Alford said, there were "some further processes" to be gone through before it would become binding. But if there were any such processes in the mind of the parties, the subsequent conduct of the defendants was such as to dispense with them. The defendants actually put up the gates at point B at considerable expense. That certainly led the plaintiff to believe that they agreed that he should have the right of access through point B without more ado.

The judge also said that, to establish this equity or estoppel, the defendants must have known that the plaintiff was selling the front portion without reserving a right of access for the back portion. I do not think this was necessary. The defendants knew that the plaintiff *intended* to sell the two portions separately and that he would need an access at point B as well as point A. Seeing that they knew of his intention—and they did nothing to disabuse him but rather confirmed it by erecting gates at point B—it was their conduct which led him to act as he did: and this raises an equity in his favour against them.

In the circumstances it seems to me inequitable that the council should insist on their strict title as they did: and to take the highhanded action of pulling down the gates without a word of warning: and to demand of the plaintiff £3,000 as the price for the easement. If he had moved at once for an injunction in aid of his equity—to prevent them removing the gates—I think he should have been granted it. But he did not do so. He tried to negotiate terms, but these failing, the action has come for trial. And we have the question: in what way now should the equity be satisfied?

Here equity is displayed at its most flexible, see *Snell's Principles of Equity*, 27th ed. (1973), p. 568, and the illustrations there given. If the matter had been finally settled in 1967, I should have thought that, although nothing was said at the meeting in July 1967, nevertheless it would be quite reasonable for the defendants to ask the plaintiff to pay something for the access at point B, perhaps—and I am guessing—some hundreds of pounds. But, as Mr. Millett pointed out in the course of the argument, because of the defendants' conduct, the back land has been landlocked. It has been sterile and rendered useless for five or six years: and the plaintiff has been unable to deal with it during that time. This loss to him can be taken into account. And at the present time, it seems to me that, in order to satisfy the equity, the plaintiff should have the right of access at point B without paying anything for it.

I would, therefore, hold that the plaintiff, as the owner of the back portion, has a right of access at point B over the verge on to Mill Park Road and a right of way along that road to Hook Lane without paying compensation. I would allow the appeal and declare that he has an easement, accordingly.

Lawton and Scarman L.JJ. agreed.

HUBBS v. *BLACK*. 1918. 44 O.L.R. 545 (Ontario. Appellate Division). One Babcock purchased a cemetery plot for $10 and when his sister, Sarah Black, the defendant, expressed her intention to buy another for herself and her husband, Babcock said to her, "You need not buy a plot; I will give you and your man a burial in the plot." She replied: "If you give me a plot, I will put a tombstone there." Sarah Black bought a tombstone with her and her husband's names cut on it, and erected it on the plot. Babcock died and the plaintiff, William Hubbs, his nephew, brought this action to compel Sarah Black to refrain from further trespassing on the plot and to remove the body of her late husband from it. He had died six months before the action was commenced. Held, for the defendant.

RIDDELL J.: "Refraining from buying another plot is in itself sufficient consideration. . . . The tombstone bargain and purchase make the consideration perfect even if otherwise defective. . . . The second claim, the ghoulish demand that the corpse of the defendant's husband should be dug up and carried off the plot, of course falls with the first—not that the cold clay of the dead man has any rights, but that the defendant has the right to keep the body there until the end of time. It is reasonably certain that the plaintiff's ashes, if and when they are laid in the same plot, will not receive any pollution or injury from those of his dead uncle." [Query whether Babcock ever requested Sarah Black not to buy a plot, or to erect a tombstone. If he did not, what is the consideration for his promise? Sarah Black had been in "possession" of her part of the plot for fifteen years and Clute J. thought her possessory title was therefore valid.]

LORANGER v. *HAINES*. 1921. 50 O.L.R. 268 (Ontario. Appellate Division). Action by the purchaser for specific performance. At the trial MIDDLETON J. described the facts as follows: Loranger was a Detroit attorney; Haines was associated with him in promoting a patent. Haines bought a large parcel of land in Sandwich, Ontario. He intended to build a house on part and sell the rest. "While things were going well in the patent scheme, and millions seemed to be in sight, love and affection sprang up between these men, and Haines thought all that was necessary to secure him perfect happiness was that his friend Loranger should be ever near him, so he suggested that he would present him with a building site upon which a house might be built next his own. Loranger accepted, with some pretence of coy reluctance, and drafted an agreement in which, for 'consideration hereinafter mentioned,' Haines and his wife agreed to convey . . . . a parcel 84 feet in width by 182 feet in depth, to him." The agreement called for Loranger to build a "residence" on this parcel, to share in the cost of sewers, watermains and a roadway which would benefit Haines as well, and to give Haines first refusal if he should decide to sell. Loranger built, without any conveyance, a house costing $12,500, and spent $1,500 improving the land. "Things did not progress any too well in the patent paint company, and this hasty alliance has resulted in leisurely repentance. Haines now finds little pleasure in contemplating the coming and going of Loranger in his motor car from the mansion along the common drive. Loranger naturally wants his land. . . . Haines takes the position that the real consideration for his contemplated gift was the pleasure to be derived from proximity to his friend, and, this now turning out an apple of Sodom, he ought not to be compelled to consume it." Held, for the plaintiff. On appeal, affirmed. The things that Loranger undertook to do were a sufficient consideration. MEREDITH C.J.C.P.: "And quite apart from any question of contract, the defendant should assuredly be estopped from claiming title to and taking possession of the land upon which, not only with his knowledge, but at his request, the plaintiff has expended so much money—with the defendant's knowledge and before his eyes—on the faith of his promise to convey it to the plaintiff."

(v) *Estoppel*

SKIDMORE v. *BRADFORD* 1869. L.R. 8 Eq. 134. An uncle promised his nephew, Edward Bradford, that he would buy him a warehouse for £5,000. The uncle paid £1,000 and Edward Bradford entered into a contract to buy the warehouse. The uncle paid a further £500, but died before making any further payment. The estate was held liable to pay the balance. STUART V.C.: "If Edward Bradford were a mere volunteer there is no principle on which he would be entitled to come to this Court to have the testator's intended act of bounty completed. . . . But if on the faith of the testator's representation he has involved himself in any liability, or has incurred any obligation, he cannot be regarded as a volunteer, and if so, the testator's assets are liable to make good the representation on the faith of which the nephew has entered into this contract."

RE HUDSON 1885. 54 L.J. Ch. 811. COOKSON Q.C. in the argument: ". . . the testator signed a document by which he represented that the committee of the Jubilee Fund had £20,000 coming from him at their disposal, and relying on that document they have collected and expended money and incurred liabilities, and have in fact come under an obligation to provide £3,500 more than has come to their hands. The consideration for a contract need not consist of money; if a person suffers any detriment or inconvenience, that is sufficient consideration moving from him to support a contract by which another person comes under an obligation to him."

DAVEY Q.C.: "The argument is, that that which is a mere *nudum pactum* can be converted into a contract by something subsequently done by one of the parties. But that is not so. *Hammersly* v. *De Beil*, 12 Cl.&F. 45, [one of a group of cases relied on in *Skidmore* v. *Bradford*, supra] was for a time supposed to have established the rule that a man who changes his position in reliance on an expression of intention can insist upon effect being given to that expression of intention. But that idea is now exploded. If A represents to B that something is an existing fact, and B acts on the faith of that representation, A is bound: but that is not so where the representation is of an intention and not of a fact.

MADDISON v. *ALDERSON* 1883. 8 App.Cas. 467, 473. LORD SELBORNE: "I have always understood it to have been decided... that the doctrine of estoppel by representation is applicable only to representations as to some state of facts alleged to be at the time actually in existence, and not to promises *de futuro*, which, if binding at all, must be binding as contracts."

HUGHES v. METROPOLITAN RAILWAY CO.
(1877) 2 App.Cas. 439

By the terms of a lease, the landlord had the right to demand repairs on six months notice to the tenant. In October, the landlord gave the notice. In November and December the parties negotiated about the possibility of the tenant's buying the landlord's interest in the property. Had the negotiations been successful, there could, of course, have been no duty to repair at all. On December 31 the negotiations broke off, and in April the landlord asserted a right to forfeit the lease on the expiry of the six-month period from October. The House of Lords held that the landlord was not entitled to assert such a right.

LORD CAIRNS L.C.: "It is the first principle upon which all courts of equity proceed, that if parties who have entered into definite and distinct terms involving certain legal results—certain penalties or legal forfeiture—afterwards by their own act or with their own consent enter upon a course of negotiation which has the effect of leading one of the parties to suppose that the strict rights arising under the contract will not be enforced, or will be kept in suspense, or held in abeyance, the person who otherwise might have enforced those rights will not be allowed to enforce them where it would be inequitable having regard to the dealings which have then taken place between the parties."

CENTRAL LONDON PROPERTY TRUST LTD.
v. HIGH TREES HOUSE LTD.
[1947] K.B. 130

The plaintiffs leased a block of flats to the defendants, a wholly owned subsidiary, for 99 years from September 29, 1937, at a rent of £2500 a year. Only about one-third of the flats had been let by the outbreak of war in 1939 and on January 3, 1940, the plaintiffs agreed with the defendants to accept a reduced rent of £1250 a year "as from the commencement of the lease." In March of 1941 the affairs of the plaintiffs were handed over to a receiver, who after that managed the company. Only the reduced rent was paid until the receiver looked at the lease in September of 1945, when he claimed the whole amount for the quarter ending September 29, 1945, and arrears of £7916. The defendants did not pay and these "friendly proceedings" were commenced to recover £625 rent for each of the quarters ending September 29, 1945, and December 25, 1945. By early 1945 the flats were fully let.

DENNING J.: ... If I were to consider this matter without regard to recent developments in the law, there is no doubt that had the plaintiffs claimed it, they would have been entitled to recover ground rent at the rate of £2,500 a year from the beginning of the term, since the lease under which it was payable was a lease under seal which, according to the old common law, could not be varied by an agreement by parol (whether in writing or not), but only by deed. Equity, however stepped in, and said that if there has been a variation of a deed by a simple contract (which in the case of a lease required to be in writing would have to be evidenced by writing), the courts may give effect to it as is shown in *Berry* v. *Berry*, [1929] 2 K.B. 316. That equitable doctrine, however, could hardly apply in the present case because the variation here might be said to have been made without consideration. With regard to estoppel, the representation made in relation to reducing the rent, was not a representation of an existing fact. It was a representation, in effect, as to the future, namely, that payment of the rent would not be enforced at the full rate but only at the reduced rate. Such a representation would not give rise to an estoppel, because, as was said in *Jorden* v. *Money* (1854), 5 H.L.C. 185; 10 E.R. 868, a representation as to the future must be embodied as a contract or be nothing.

But what is the position in view of developments in the law in recent years? The law has not been standing still since *Jorden* v. *Money*. There has been a series of decisions over the last fifty years which, although they are said to be cases of estoppel are not really such. They are cases in which a promise was made which was intended to create legal relations and which, to the knowledge of the person making the promise, was going to be acted on by the person to whom it was made, and which was in fact so acted on. In such cases the courts have said that the promise must be honoured. The cases to which I particularly desire to refer are: *Fenner* v. *Blake*, [1900] 1 Q.B. 426, *In re Wickham* (1917), 34 T.L.R. 158 *Re William Porter & Co., Ld.*, [1937] 2 All E.R. 361 and *Buttery* v. *Pickard*, [1946] W.N. 25. As I have said they are not cases of estoppel in the strict sense. They are really promises—promises intended to be binding, intended to be acted on, and in fact acted in. *Jorden* v. *Money* can be distinguished, because there the promisor made it clear that she did not intend to be legally bound, whereas in the cases to which I refer the proper inference was that the promisor did intend to be bound. In each case the court held the promise to be binding on the party making it, even though under the old common law it might be difficult to find any consideration for it. The courts have not gone so far as to give a cause of action in damages for the breach of such a promise, but they have refused to allow the party making it to act inconsistently with it. It is in that sense, and that sense only, that such a promise gives rise to an estoppel. The decisions are a natural result of the fusion of law and equity: for the cases of *Hughes* v. *Metropolitan Ry. Co.* (1877), 2 App. Cas. 439, *Birmingham and District Land Co.* v. *London & North Western Ry. Co.* (1888), 40 Ch. D. 268 and *Salisbury (Marquess)* v. *Gilmore*, [1942] 2 K.B. 38, afford a sufficient basis for saying that a party would not be allowed in equity to go back on such a promise. In my opinion, the time has now come for the validity of such a promise to be recognized. The logical consequence, no doubt is that a promise to accept a smaller sum in discharge of a larger sum, if acted upon, is binding notwithstanding the absence of consideration: and if the fusion of law and equity leads to this result, so much the better. That aspect was not considered in *Foakes* v. *Beer* (1884), 9 App. Cas. 605. At this time of day however, when law and equity have been joined together for over seventy years, principles must be reconsidered in the light of their combined effect. It is to be noticed that in the Sixth Interim Report of the Law Revision Committee, pars. 35, 40, it is recommended that such a promise as that to which I have referred, should be enforceable in law even though no consideration for it has been given by the promisee. It seems to me that, to the extent I have mentioned, that result has now been achieved by the decisions of the courts.

I am satisfied that a promise such as that to which I have referred is binding and the only question remaining for my consideration is the scope of the promise in the present case. I am satisfied on all the evidence that the promise here was that the ground rent should be reduced to £1,250 a year as a temporary expedient while the block of flats was not fully, or substantially fully let, owing to the conditions prevailing. That means that the reduction in the rent applied throughout the years down to the end of 1944, but early in 1945 it is plain that the flats were fully let, and, indeed the rents received from them (many of them not being affected by the Rent Restrictions Acts), were increased beyond the figure at which it was originally contemplated that they would be let. At all events the rent from them must have been very considerable. I find that the conditions prevailing at the time when the reduction in rent was made, had completely passed away by the early months of 1945. I am satisfied that the promise was understood by all parties only to apply under the conditions prevailing at the time when it was made, namely, when the flats were only partially let, and that it did not extend any further than that. When the flats became fully let, early in 1945, the reduction ceased to apply.

In those circumstances, under the law as I hold it, it seems to me that rent is payable at the full rate for the quarters ending September 29 and December 25, 1945.

If the case had been one of estoppel, it might be said that in any event the estoppel would cease when the conditions to which the representation applied came to an end, or it also might be said that it would only come to an end on notice. In either case it is only a way of ascertaining what is the scope of the representation. I prefer to apply the principle that a promise intended to be binding, intended to be acted on and in fact acted on, is binding so far as its terms properly apply. Here it was binding as covering the period down to the early part of 1945, and as from that time full rent is payable.

I therefore give judgment for the plaintiff company for the amount claimed.

IMPERATOR REALTY CO., INC. v. TULL
New York. Court of Appeals. 1920. 127 N.E. 263

The parties to this action agreed in writing and under seal to exchange two parcels of land. The agreement was subject to the Statute of Frauds in force in the state of New York. On the day fixed for completion the defendant deliberately defaulted. In his defence he relied on a clause in the agreement to the effect that all requirements of the municipality of the city of New York be complied with by the seller. The plaintiff gave evidence which proved that after the making of the contract, the parties orally agreed that each would accept a deposit in a named Title Insurance Company to satisfy and discharge any municipal requirements of the other's parcel. The evidence showed that the plaintiff was, on the day for completion, ready and willing to convey, and although he could not convey free of municipal requirements, he was able and willing to deposit a sufficient amount of cash to free the property according to the oral agreement.

CARDOZO J.: . . . I think it is the law that, where contracts are subject to the statute, changes are governed by the same requirements of form as original provisions. . . . A recent decision of the House of Lords reviews the English precedents, and declares the rule anew: *Morris* v. *Baron & Co.*, [1918] A.C. 1. Oral promises are ineffective to make the contract, or any part of it, in the beginning. . . . Oral promises must also be ineffective to vary it thereafter. . . . Grant and consideration alike must find expression in a writing. . . .

A contract is the sum of its component terms. Any variation of the parts is a variation of the whole. The requirement that there shall be a writing extends to one term as to another. There can therefore be no contractual obligation when the requirement is not followed. This is not equivalent to saying that what is ineffective to create an obligation must be ineffective to discharge one. Duties imposed by law irrespective of contract may regulate the relations of parties after they have entered into a contract. There may be procurement or encouragement of a departure from literal performance which will forbid the assertion that the departure was a wrong. That principle will be found the solvent of many cases of apparent hardship. There may be an election which will preclude a forfeiture. There may be an acceptance of substituted performance, or an accord and satisfaction. . . . What there may not be, when the subject-matter is the sale of land, is an executory agreement, partly written and partly oral, to which, by force of the agreement and nothing else, the law will attach the attribute of contractual obligation.

The contract, therefore, stood unchanged. The defendant might have retracted his oral promise an hour after making it, and the plaintiff would have been helpless. He might have retracted a week before the closing, and, if a reasonable time remained within which to remove the violations, the plaintiff would still have been helpless. Retraction even at the very hour of closing might not have been too late if coupled with the offer of an extension which would neutralize the consequences of persuasion and reliance. . . .

The difficulty with the defendant's position is that he did none of these things. He had notified the plaintiff in substance that there was no need of haste in removing the violations, and that title would be accepted on deposit of adequate security for their removal in the future. He never revoked that notice. He gave no warning of a change of mind. He did not even attend the closing. He abandoned the contract, treated it as at an end, held himself absolved from all liability thereunder, because the plaintiff had acted in reliance on a consent which, even in the act of abandonment, he made no effort to recall.

I do not think we are driven by any requirement of the Statute of Frauds to sustain as lawful and effective this precipitate rescission, this attempt by an *ex post facto* revocation, after closing day had come and gone to put the plaintiff in the wrong. "He who prevents a thing from being done may not avail himself of the nonperformance, which he has, himself, occasioned, for the law says to him, in effect: "This is your own act, and, therefore, you are not damnified.' " *Dolan* v. *Rodgers*, 149 N.Y. 489, 491, 44 N.E. 167, quoting *West* v. *Blakeway*, 2 M. & Gr. 751. The principle is fundamental and unquestioned . . . *Mackay* v. *Dick*, 6 App. Cas. 251; *New Zealand Shipping Co.* v. *Societe des Ateliers, etc.*, 1919 A.C. 1, 5. Sometimes the resulting disability has been characterized as an estoppel, sometimes as a waiver. . . . We need not go into the question of the accuracy of the description. *Ewart on Estoppel*, pp. 15, 70; *Ewart on Waiver Distributed*, pp. 23, 143, 264. The truth is that we are facing a principle more nearly ultimate than either waiver or estoppel, one with roots in the yet larger principle that no one shall be permitted to found any claim upon his own inequity or take advantage of his own wrong. . . . The Statute of Frauds was not intended to offer an asylum of escape from that fundamental principle of justice. An apposite precedent is found in *Thomson* v. *Poor*, 147 N.Y. 402, 42 N.E. 13. In deciding that case, we put aside the question whether a contract within the Statute of Frauds could be changed by spoken words. We held that there was disability, or, as we styled it, estoppel, to take advantage of an omission induced by an unrevoked consent. A like principle is recognized even in the English courts, which have gone as far as those of any jurisdiction in the strict enforcement of the statute. They hold in effect that, until consent is acted on, either party may change his mind. After it has been acted on, it stands as an excuse for nonperformance. *Hickman* v. *Haynes*, L.R. 10 C.P. 598, 605; *Ogle* v. *Lord Vane*, 2 Q.B. 275; 2 I.B. 272, *Cuff* v. *Penn*, 1 Maule & S. 21; *Morris* v. *Baron & Co.* The defendant by his conduct has brought himself within the ambit of this principle. His words did not create a new bilateral contract. They lacked the written form prescribed by statute. They did not create a unilateral contract. Aside from the same defect in form, they did not purport to offer a promise for an act. They did, however, constitute the continuing expression of a state of mind, a readiness, a desire, persisting until revoked. A seller who agrees to change the wall paper of a room ought not to lose his contract if he fails to make the change through reliance on the statement of the buyer that new paper is unnecessary and that the old is satisfactory. The buyer may change his mind again and revert to his agreement. He may not summarily rescind because of the breach which he encouraged. That is what the defendant tried to do. When he stayed away from the closing and acted upon an election to treat the contract as rescinded, he put himself in the wrong.

[The opinion of Chase J. with whom Cardozo J. concurred is omitted. Hiscock C.J., Pound and Andrews JJ. also concurred. Collin and Crane JJ. dissented.]

COMBE v. COMBE
England. Court of Appeal. [1951] 1 All E.R. 767

ASQUITH L.J.: I will ask Denning, L.J., to deliver the first judgment.

DENNING L.J.: In this case a wife who has divorced her husband claims maintenance from him—not in the Divorce Court, but in the King's Bench on an agreement which is said to be embodied in letters. The parties were married in 1915. They separated in 1939. On Feb. 1, 1943, on the wife's petition, a decree *nisi* of divorce was pronounced. Shortly afterwards letters passed between the solicitors with regard to maintenance. On Feb. 9, 1943 (eight days after the decree *nisi*), the solicitor for the wife wrote to the solicitor for the husband:

"With regard to permanent maintenance, we understood that your client is prepared to make [the wife] an allowance of £100 per year free of income tax."

In answer, on Feb. 19, 1943, the husband's solicitors wrote:

The respondent has agreed to allow your client £100 per annum free of tax."

On Aug. 11, 1943, the decree was made absolute. On Aug. 26, 1943, the wife's solicitors wrote to the husband's solicitors, saying:

"Referring to your letter of Feb. 19 last, our client would like the £100 per annum agreed to be paid to her by your client to be remitted to us on her behalf quarterly. We shall be glad if you will kindly let us have a cheque for £25 for the first quarterly instalment and make arrangements for a similar remittance to us on Nov. 11, Feb. 11, May 11, and Aug. 11 in the future."

A reply did not come for nearly two months because the husband was away, and then he himself, on Oct. 18, 1943, wrote a letter which was passed on to the wife's solicitors:

". . . regarding the sum of £25 claimed on behalf of Mrs. Coombe . . . I would point out that whilst this is paid quarterly as from Aug. 11, 1943, the sum is not due till Nov. 11, 1943, as I can hardly be expected to pay this allowance in advance."

He never paid anything. The wife pressed him for payment, but she did not follow it up by an application to the divorce court. It is to be observed that she herself has an income of her own of between £700 and £800 a year, whereas her husband has only £650 a year. Eventually, after nearly seven years had passed since the decree absolute, she brought this action in the King's Bench Division on July 28, 1950, claiming £675 being arrears for six years and three quarters at £100 a year. Byrne, J., held that the first three quarterly instalments of £25 were barred by the Limitation Act, 1939, but he gave judgment for £600 in respect of the instalments which accrued within the six years before the action was brought. He held, on the authority of *Gaisberg* v. *Storr*, [1949] 2 All E.R. 411, that there was no consideration for the husband's promise to pay his wife £100 but, nevertheless, he held that the promise was enforceable on the principle stated in *Central London Property Trust, Ltd.* v. *Hightrees House, Ltd.* and *Robertson* v. *Minister of Pensions*, [1949] 2 All E.R. 767, because it was an unequivocal acceptance of liability, intended to be binding, intended to be acted on, and, in fact, acted on.

Much as I am inclined to favour the principle of the *Hightrees* case, it is important that it should not be stretched too far lest it should be endangered. It does not create new causes of action where none existed before. It only prevents a party from insisting on his strict legal rights when it would be unjust to allow him to do so, having regard to the dealings which have taken place between the parties. That is the way it was put in the case in the House of Lords which first stated the principle. . . . It is also implicit in all the modern cases in which the principle has been developed. Sometimes it is a plaintiff who is not allowed to insist on his strict legal rights. Thus, a creditor is not allowed to enforce a debt which he has deliberately agreed to waive if the debtor has carried on business or in some other way changed his position in reliance on the waiver. A landlord who has told his tenant that he can live in his cottage rent free for the rest of his life is not allowed to go back on it if the tenant stays in the house on that footing. Sometimes it is a defendant who is not allowed to insist on

his strict legal rights. His conduct may be such as to debar him from relying on some condition, denying some allegation, or taking some other
point in answer to the claim. Thus, a government department, who had
accepted a disease as due to war service, were not allowed afterwards to
say it was not, when the soldier, in reliance on the assurance, had abstained from getting further evidence about it: *Robertson* v. *Minister of
Pensions.* A buyer who had waived the contract date for delivery was not
allowed afterwards to set up the stipulated time as an answer to the seller.
A tenant who had encroached on an adjoining building, asserting that it
was comprised in the lease, was not allowed afterwards to say that it was
not included in the lease. A tenant who had lived in a house rent free by
permission of his landlord, thereby asserting that his original tenancy had
ended, was not afterwards allowed to say that his original tenancy continued. In none of these cases was the defendant sued on the promise,
assurance, or assertion as a cause of action in itself. He was sued for some
other cause, for example, a pension or a breach of contract, or possession,
and the promise, assurance, or assertion only played a supplementary role,
though, no doubt, an important one. That is, I think, its true function. It
may be part of a cause of action, but not a cause of action in itself. The
principle, as I understand it, is that where one party has, by his words or
conduct, made to the other a promise or assurance which was intended to
affect the legal relations between them and to be acted on accordingly,
then, once the other party has taken him at his word and acted on it, the
one who gave the promise or assurance cannot afterwards be allowed to
revert to the previous legal relations as if no such promise or assurance
had been made by him, but he must accept their legal relations subject to
the qualification which he himself has so introduced, even though it is not
supported in point of law by any consideration, but only by his word.

Seeing that the principle never stands alone as giving a cause of action
in itself, it can never do away with the necessity of consideration when
that is an essential part of the cause of action. The doctrine of consideration is too firmly fixed to be overthrown by a side-wind. Its ill effects have
been largely mitigated of late, but it still remains a cardinal necessity of
the formation of a contract, although not of its modification or discharge.
I fear that it was my failure to make this clear in *Central London Property
Trust, Ltd.* v. *Hightrees House, Ltd.*, which misled Byrne, J., in the
present case. He held that his wife could sue on the husband's promise as
a separate and independent cause of action by itself, although, as he held,
there was no consideration for it. That is not correct. The wife can only
enforce the promise if there was consideration for it. That is, therefore,
the real question in the case: Was there sufficient consideration to support the promise?

If it were suggested that, in return for the husband's promise, the wife
expressly or impliedly promised to forbear from applying to the court for
maintenance—that is, a promise, in return for a promise—there would
clearly be no consideration because the wife's promise would not be binding on her and, therefore, would be worth nothing. Notwithstanding her
promise, she could always apply to the divorce court for maintenance—
perhaps, only with leave—but nevertheless she could apply. No agreement by her could take away that right. There was, however, clearly no
promise by the wife, express or implied, to forbear from applying to the
court. All that happened was that she did, in fact, forbear—that is, she
did an act in return for a promise. Is that sufficient consideration? Uni-

lateral promises of this kind have long been enforced so long as the act of forbearance is done on the faith of the promise and at the request of the promisor, express or implied. The act done is then in itself sufficent consideration for the promise, even though it arises *ex post facto*, as Parker J., pointed out in *Wigan* v. *English and Scottish Law Life Assurance Assocn.*, [1909] 1 Ch. 291 at p. 298. If the findings of Byrne, J., are accepted, they are sufficient to bring this principle into play. His finding that the husband's promise was intended to be binding, intended to be acted upon, and was, in fact, acted on—although expressed to be a finding on the principle of the *Hightrees House* case—is equivalent to a finding that there was consideration within this long-settled rule, because it comes to the same thing expressed in different words: see *Oliver* v. *Davis.* My difficulty, however, is to accept the findings of Byrne, J., that the promise was "intended to be acted on." I cannot find any evidence of any intention by the husband that the wife should forbear from applying to the court for maintenance, or, in other words, any request by the husband, express or implied, that the wife should so forbear. He left her to apply, if she wished to do so. She did not do so, and I am not surprised, because it is very unlikely that the divorce court would have made any order in her favour, since she had a bigger income than her husband. Her forbearance was not intended by him, nor was it done at his request. It was, therefore, no consideration.

It may be that the wife has suffered some detriment because, after forbearing to apply to the court for seven years, she might not now get leave to apply. The court, however, is nowadays much more ready to give leave than it used to be; and I should have thought that, if the wife fell on hard times, she would still get leave. Assuming, however, that she has suffered some detriment by her forbearance, nevertheless, as the forbearance was not at the husband's request, it is no consideration.

The doctrine of consideration is sometimes said to work an injustice, but I see none in this case, nor was there any in . . . *Gaisberg* v. *Storr.* I do not think it would be right for this wife, who is better off than her husband, to take no action for six or seven years and then demand from him the whole £600. The truth is that in these maintenance cases the real remedy of the wife is, not by action in the King's Bench Division, but by application in the Divorce Court. I have always understood that no agreement for maintenance, which is made in the course of divorce proceedings prior to decree absolute, is valid unless it is sanctioned by the court—indeed, I said so in *Emanuel* v. *Emanuel*, [1945] 2 All E.R. 494. I know that such agreements are often made, but their only valid purpose is to serve as a basis for a consent application to the court. The reason why such agreements are invalid, unless approved, is because they are so apt to be collusive. Some wives are tempted to stipulate for extortionate maintenance as the price of giving their husbands their freedom. It is to remove this temptation that the sanction of the court is required. It would be a great pity if this salutory requirement could be evaded by taking action in the King's Bench Division. The Divorce Court can order the husband to pay whatever maintenance is just. Moreover, if justice so requires, it can make the order retrospective to decree absolute. That is the proper remedy of the wife here, and I do not think she has a right to any other. For these reasons I think the appeal should be allowed.

[The opinions of Asquith and Birkett L.JJ. are omitted.]

D. & C. BUILDERS, LTD. v. REES
[1965] 3 All E.R. 837 (C.A.)

LORD DENNING M.R.: D. & C. Builders, Ltd. ("the plaintiffs") are a little company. "D" stands for Mr. Donaldson, a decorator, "C" for Mr. Casey, a plumber. They are jobbing builders. The defendant, Mr. Rees, has a shop where he sells builders' materials.

In the spring of 1964 the defendant employed the plaintiffs to do work at his premises, 218, Brick Lane. The plaintiffs did the work and rendered accounts in May and June, which came to £746 13s. 1d. altogether. The defendant paid £250 on account. In addition the plaintiffs made an allowance of £14 off the bill. So in July, 1964, there was owing to the plaintiffs the sum of £482 13s. 1d. At this stage there was no dispute as to the work done. But the defendant did not pay.

On Aug. 31, 1964, the plaintiffs wrote asking the defendant to pay the remainder of the bill. He did not reply. On Oct. 19, 1964, they wrote again, pointing out that the "outstanding account of £480 is well overdue." Still the defendant did not reply. He did not write or telephone for more than three weeks. Then on Friday, Nov. 13, 1964, the defendant was ill with influenza. His wife telephoned the plaintiffs. She spoke to Mr. Casey. She began to make complaints about the work: and then said: "My husband will offer you £300 in settlement. That is all you'll get. It is to be in satisfaction." Mr. Casey said he would have to discuss it with Mr. Donaldson. The two of them talked it over. Their company was in desperate financial straits. If they did not have the £300, they would be in a state of bankruptcy. So they decided to accept the £300 and see what they could do about the rest afterwards. Thereupon Mr. Donaldson telephoned to the defendant's wife. He said to her: "£300 will not even clear our commitments on the job. We will accept £300 and give you a year to find the balance." She said: "No, we will never have enough money to pay the balance. £300 is better than nothing." He said: "We have no choice but to accept." She said: "Would you like the money by cash or by cheque. If it is cash, you can have it on Monday. If by cheque, you can have it tomorrow (Saturday)." On Saturday, Nov. 14, 1964, Mr. Casey went to collect the money. He took with him a receipt prepared on the company's paper with the simple words: "Received the sum of £300 from Mr. Rees." She gave him a cheque for £300 and asked for a receipt. She insisted that the words "in completion of the account" be added. Mr. Casey did as she asked. He added the words to the receipt. So she had the clean receipt: "Received the sum of £300 from Mr. Rees in completion of the account. Paid, M. Casey." Mr. Casey gave in evidence his reason for giving it: "If I did not have the £300 the company would have gone bankrupt. The only reason we took it was to save the company. She knew the position we were in."

The plaintiffs were so worried about their position that they went to their solicitors. Within a few days, on Nov. 23, 1964, the solicitors wrote complaining that the defendant had "extricated a receipt of some sort or other" from them. They said that they were treating the £300 as a payment on account. On Nov. 28, 1964, the defendant replied alleging bad workmanship. He also set up the receipt which Mr. Casey gave to his wife, adding: "I assure you she had no gun on her." The plaintiffs brought this action for the balance. The defendant set up a defence of bad workmanship and also that there was a binding settlement. The question of settlement was tried as a preliminary issue. The judge made these findings:

"I concluded that by the middle of August the sum due to the plaintiffs was ascertained and not then in dispute. I also concluded that there was no consideration to support the agreement of Nov. 13 and 14. It was a case of agreeing to take a lesser sum, when a larger sum was already due to the plaintiffs. It was not a case of agreeing to take a cheque for a smaller account instead of receiving cash for a larger account. The payment by cheque was an incidental arrangement."

The judge decided, therefore, the preliminary issue in favour of the plaintiffs. The defendant appeals to this court. He says that there was here an accord and satisfaction—an *accord* when the plaintiffs agreed, however reluctantly, to accept £300 in settlement of the account—and *satisfaction* when they accepted the cheque for £300 and it was duly honoured.

This case is of some consequence: for it is a daily occurrence that a merchant or tradesman, who is owed a sum of money, is asked to take less. The debtor says he is in difficulties. He offers a lesser sum in settlement, cash down. He says he cannot pay more. The creditor is considerate. He accepts the proffered sum and forgives him the rest of the debt. The question arises: is the settlement binding on the creditor? The answer is that, in point of law, the creditor is not bound by the settlement. He can the next day sue the debtor for the balance, and get judgment. The law was so stated in 1602 by Lord Coke in *Pinnel's Case*—and accepted in 1884 by the House of Lords in *Foakes* v. *Beer*.

Now, suppose that the debtor, instead of paying the lesser sum in cash, pays it by cheque. He makes out a cheque for the amount. The creditor accepts the cheque and cashes it. Is the position any different? I think not. No sensible distinction can be taken between payment of a lesser sum by cash and payment of it by cheque. The cheque, when given, is conditional payment. When honoured, it is actual payment. It is then just the same as cash. If a creditor is not bound when he receives payment by cash, he should not be bound when he receives payment by cheque. . . . In point of law payment of a lesser sum, whether by cash or by cheque, is no discharge of a greater sum.

This doctrine of the common law has come under heavy fire. It was ridiculed by Sir George Jessel M.R., in *Couldery* v. *Bartrum*. It was held to be mistaken by Lord Blackburn in *Foakes* v. *Beer*. It was condemned by the Law Revision Committee in their Sixth Interim Report (Cmnd. 5449), para. 20 and para. 22. But a remedy has been found. The harshness of the common law has been relieved. Equity has stretched out a merciful hand to help the debtor. The courts have invoked the broad principle stated by Lord Cairns L.C., in *Hughes* v. *Metropolitan Ry. Co.* (1877) 2 App. Cas. 439.

". . . it is the first principle upon which all courts of equity proceed if parties, who have entered into definite and distinct terms involving certain legal results . . . afterwards by their own act, or with their own consent, enter upon a course of negotiation which has the effect of leading one of the parties to suppose that *the strict rights arising under the contract will not be enforced*, or will be kept in suspense, or held in abeyance, that the person who otherwise might have enforced those rights *will not be allowed to enforce them where it would be inequitable, having regard to the dealings which have taken place between the parties.*" It is worth noticing that the principle may be applied, not only so as to suspend strict legal rights, but also so as to preclude the enforcement of them.

This principle has been applied to cases where a creditor agrees to accept a lesser sum in discharge of a greater. So much so that we can now say that, when a creditor and a debtor enter on a course of negotiation, which leads the debtor to suppose that, on payment of the lesser sum, the creditor will not enforce payment of the balance, and on the faith thereof the debtor pays the lesser sum and the creditor accepts it as satisfaction: then the creditor will not be allowed to enforce payment of the balance when it would be inequitable to do so. This was well illustrated during the last war. Tenants went away to escape the bombs and left their houses unoccupied. The landlords accepted a reduced rent for the time they were empty. It was held that the landlords could not afterwards turn round and sue for the balance: see *Central London Property Trust, Ltd.* v. *High Trees House, Ltd.* This caused at the time some eyebrows to be raised in high places. But they have been lowered since. The solution was so obviously just that no one could well gainsay it.

In applying this principle, however, we must note the qualification. The creditor is barred from his legal rights only when it would be *inequitable* for him to insist on them. Where there has been a *true accord*, under which the creditor voluntarily agrees to accept a lesser sum in satisfaction, and the debtor *acts on* that accord by paying the lesser sum and the creditor accepts it, then it is inequitable for the creditor afterwards to insist on the balance. But he is not bound unless there has been truly an accord between them.

In the present case, on the facts as found by the judge, it seems to me that there was no true accord. The debtor's wife held the creditor to ransom. The creditor was in need of money to meet his own commitments, and she knew it. When the creditor asked for payment of the £480 due to him, she said to him in effect: "We cannot pay you the £480. But we will pay you £300 if you will accept it in settlement. If you do not accept it on those terms, you will get nothing. £300 is better than nothing." She had no right to say any such thing. She could properly have said: "We cannot pay you more than £300. Please accept it on account." But she had no right to insist on his taking it in settlement. When she said: "We will pay you nothing unless you accept £300 in settlement," she was putting undue pressure on the creditor. She was making a threat to break the contract (by paying nothing) and she was doing it so as to compel the creditor to do what he was unwilling to do (to accept £300 in settlement): and she succeeded. He complied with her demand. That was on recent authority a case of intimidation. . . . In these circumstances there was no true accord so as to found a defence of accord and satisfaction. . . .There is also no equity in the defendant to warrant any departure from the due course of law. No person can insist on a settlement procured by intimidation.

In my opinion there is no reason in law or equity why the creditor should not enforce the full amount of the debt due to him. I would, therefore, dismiss this appeal.

JOHN BURROWS LTD. v. SUBSURFACE SURVEYS LTD.
(1968) 68 D.L.R. (2d) 354 (S.C.C.)

RITCHIE J.: This is an appeal from a judgment of the Appeal Division of the Supreme Court of New Brunswick (Bridges, C.J.N.B., dissenting) setting aside the judgment rendered at trial by Barry J., whereby he had awarded the appellant the sum of $42,000 together with interest of $420 as the amount due to it on what he found to be a valid promissory note made in its favour which was signed by the respondent company and endorsed by the respondent Whitcomb.

For some time prior to the events which gave rise to this action, John M. Burrows, the beneficial owner of all the shares in the capital stock of the appellant company, had been on friendly terms with the respondent, Whitcomb, with whom he appears to have been engaged in various business ventures, and on March 22, 1963, he became a party to an agreement whereby the appellant company (which then operated under the name of Subsurface Survey Limited), agreed to sell its assets to Mr. Whitcomb as of the close of business on January 31, 1963, for a total price of $127,274.43. Under the agreement $42,000 of the purchase price was "... to be secured by a promissory note made by the Purchaser and endorsed by an endorser acceptable to the Vendor payable to the Vendor within a period of ten years from the date of this Agreement, such promissory note to bear interest at the rate of 6% per annum with such interest being payable monthly and to provide for thirty days' notice by the Purchaser to the Vendor of any payments made on the principal thereof except the final payment payable on the date ten years from this Agreement." For the purpose of carrying out this transaction, Whitcomb caused the respondent company to be incorporated under the name of Subsurface Surveys Limited and the appellant agreed to accept a note signed by that company and endorsed by Whitcomb. In furtherance of this arrangement, the respondents executed the following document upon which this action is now brought:

Fredericton, N.B.

$42,000.00   March 28, 1963.

FOR VALUE RECEIVED Subsurface Surveys Ltd. promises to pay to John Burrows Ltd. or order at the Royal Bank of Canada the sum of forty-two Thousand Dollars ($42,000.00) in nine (9) years and ten (10) months from April 1st, 1963, together with interest at the rate of six per cent (6%) per annum from April 1st, 1963, payable monthly on the first day of May, 1963, and on the first day of each and every month thereafter until payment, provided that the maker may pay on account of principal from time to time the whole or any portion thereof upon giving thirty (30) days' notice of intention prior to such payment.

In default of payment of any interest payment or instalment for a period of ten (10) days after the same became due the whole amount payable under this note is to become immediately due.

SUBSURFACE SURVEYS LTD.

(Sgd.) "G. Murdoch Whitcomb"
President

(Sgd.) "G. Murdoch Whitcomb"
Endorser

The makers, endorsers, and guarantors hereof waive presentment for payment, notice of nonpayment, protest and notice of protest.

SUBSURFACE SURVEYS LTD.

(Sgd.) "G. Murdoch Whitcomb"
President

(Sgd.) "G. Murdoch Whitcomb"
Endorser.

On March 28th the respondent, Whitcomb, also executed an agreement with the appellant company wherein he is described as "the debtor" and the appellant is described as "the company", whereby he acknowledged that he had deposited 5,101 common shares of Subsurface Surveys Ltd. with John Burrows Limited "by way of pledge as security for payment of the said note", by which he clearly intended to refer to the document last hereinbefore recited. This agreement contains the following clause: "That on default being made by both Subsurface Surveys Ltd. and the Debtor in paying any principal or interest due at any time according to the terms of the said note the Company may forthwith cause the pledged shares to be transferred to the name of the Company on the share register of Subsurface Surveys Ltd. and the pledged shares shall thereupon become the absolute property of the Company."

So long as Burrows remained on friendly terms with the respondent Whitcomb the appellant company does not appear to have insisted on enforcing the letter of this agreement, and continuing indulgences were granted to the respondent with respect to the making of interest payments on the due dates so that by October 1, 1964, eleven payments had been accepted more than 10 days after they were due, but on November 23, 1964, there was a falling out between Burrows and Whitcomb and heated words were exchanged between them. On December 7th, the November 1st interest payment then being 36 days overdue, Burrows addressed a registered letter to both respondents in the following terms: "This letter will serve to inform you that, an interest payment due under the terms of the promissory note dated March 28, 1963 made by Subsurface Surveys Ltd. and endorsed by G. Murdoch Whitcomb being in default for more than 10 days, the whole amount payable under the note is now due.

"We hereby demand immediate payment of the principal amount of $42,000.00 and outstanding interest.

"If payment in full is not made by December 11, 1964, it is our intention to exercise our remedies under the agreement of March 28, 1963 between G. Murdoch Whitcomb and John Burrows Ltd."

The respondent Whitcomb's reaction to this demand was to tender the sum of $420, but things had gone too far and Mr. Burrows rejected the offer and made it plain that the matter would in future be handled by his solicitor. In due course, on January 14, 1965, this action was commenced whereby the appellant claimed against the respondents as maker and endorser of a promissory note, the sum of $42,000 by reason of the default made in the interest payments due for the months of October and November, 1964, together with interest to date.

The two defences raised by the respondents which form the subject of the appeal are:

(a) That the document referred to in paragraph 2 of the Statement of Claim is not a promissory note because it is not due at a fixed or determinable future time and is not for a sum certain as required by Section 176 (1) of the Bills of Exchange Act. . . . (and)

(c). . . (i) the Plaintiff is estopped from saying that the Defendants defaulted in the payment of such interest because by its conduct . . . it represented to the Defendants that late payment would be accepted without penalty of default which said representation was intended to affect the legal relations between the Plaintiff and the Defendants and which said representation was relied on and acted on by the Defendants.

As has been indicated, the appellant's action was originally framed as an action on a promissory note, but during the course of the trial, and at the suggestion of the learned trial Judge, the statement of claim was amended to include alternative claims for the principal amount of $42,000 as the balance due by the respondent company on the purchase price of the business and also as the balance due by both respondents on an account stated between them and the appellant. . . .

[The court then concluded that the document did constitute a promissory note.]

I am accordingly of opinion that the instrument in question was a promissory note, and there can be no doubt that the respondents were in default in their interest payments for more than 10 days after the same became due.

It remains to be considered whether the circumstances disclosed by the evidence were such as to justify the majority of the Court of Appeal in concluding that this was a case to which the defence of equitable estoppel or estoppel by representation applied.

Since the decision of the present Lord Denning in the case of *Central London Property Trust Ltd.* v. *High Trees House Ltd.*, [1947] K.B. 130, there has been a great deal of discussion, both academic and judicial, on the question of whether that decision extended the doctrine of estoppel beyond the limits which had been theretofore fixed, but in this Court in the case of *Conwest Exploration Co. Ltd. et al* v. *Letain*, 41 D.L.R. (2d) 198 at pp. 206-7, [1964] S.C.R. 20, Judson J., speaking for the majority of the Court, expressed the view that Lord Denning's statement had not done anything more than restate the principle expressed by Lord Cairns in *Hughes* v. *Metropolitan R. Co.* (1877), 2 App. Cas. 439 at p. 448, in the following terms:

". . . it is the first principle upon which all Courts of Equity proceed, that if parties who have entered into definite and distinct terms involving certain legal results—certain penalties or legal forfeiture—afterwards by their own act or with their own consent enter upon a course of negotiation which has the effect of leading one of the parties to suppose that the strict rights arising under the contract will not be enforced, or will be kept in suspense, or held in abeyance, the person who otherwise might have enforced those rights will not be allowed to enforce them where it would be inequitable having regard to the dealings which have thus taken place between the parties."

In the case of *Combe* v. *Combe*, (1951) 1 All E.R. 767, Lord Denning recognized the fact that some people had treated his decision in the *High Trees* case as having extended the principle stated by Lord Cairns and he was careful to restate the matter in the following terms [p. 770]:

"The principle, as I understand it, is that where one party has, by his words or conduct, made to the other a promise or assurance which was intended to affect the legal relations between them and to be acted on accordingly, then, once the other party has taken him at his word and acted on it, the one who gave the promise or assurance cannot afterwards be allowed to revert to the previous legal relations as if no such promise or assurance had been made by him, but he must accept their legal relations subject to the qualification which he himself has so introduced, even though it is not supported in point of law by any consideration, but only by his word."

It seems clear to me that this type of equitable defence can not be invoked unless there is some evidence that one of the parties entered into a course of negotiation which had the effect of leading the other to suppose that the strict rights under the contract would not be enforced, and I think that this implies that there must be evidence from which it can be inferred that the first party intended that the legal relations created by the contract would be altered as a result of the negotiations.

It is not enough to show that one party has taken advantage of indulgences granted to him by the other for if this were so in relation to commercial transactions, such as promissory notes, it would mean that the holders of such notes would be required to insist on the very letter being enforced in all cases for fear that any indulgences granted and acted upon could be translated into a waiver of their rights to enforce the contract according to its terms.

As Viscount Simonds said in *Tool Metal Mfg. Co.* v. *Tungsten Electric Co., Ltd.*, [1955] 2 All E.R. 657 at p. 660: ". . . the gist of the equity lies in the fact that one party has by his conduct led the other to alter his position. I lay stress on this, because I would not have it supposed, particularly in commercial transactions, that mere acts of indulgence are apt to create rights. . . ."

The learned trial judge dealt with the rule of estoppel by representation as applied to the circumstances of the present case in the following brief paragraphs:

"It is my opinion, however, that for such a rule to apply, the plaintiff must have known or should have known that his action or inaction was being acted upon by the defendant and that the defendant thereby changed his legal position. I do not believe that John Burrows ever gave any consideration to the fact that in accepting late payments of interest on the note, he was thereby leading Mr. Whitcomb—as an officer of the defendant corporation—into thinking that strict compliance would not be required at any time.

"It is a matter of regret that Mr. Burrows did not see fit to advise Mr. Whitcomb by letter or verbally of his intention to require strict adherence to the terms of the note; but be that as it may, it is my opinion that both defendants were always aware of the terms of P. 1 and knew that default in payment of interest exceeding 10 days could result in the plaintiff demanding full payment, as the plaintiff has now done."

Ritchie J.A., who did not agree with the learned trial judge's interpretation of the evidence, made the following observations in the course of his reasons for judgment [62 D.L.R. (2d) at p. 720]:

"By its conduct in accepting payments of interest after they were more than 10 days in default and, over a period of 16 months, not proceeding to enforce payment of the principal amount owing under P-1, the plaintiff gave the defendants a promise, or assurance, which it intended would affect the legal relations between them. Thereby, the plaintiff lulled the defendants into a false sense of security and misled them into the belief its strict rights to enforce immediate payment of the principal amount of $42,-000 would be held in abeyance or be suspended until they were informed otherwise. It was reasonable for the defendants so to interpret the plaintiff's conduct. As a result, the position of each defendant was prejudiced. In my respectful opinion, the evidence supports that conclusion."

With the greatest respect for the reasoning of the majority of the Court of Appeal, I prefer the interpretation placed on the evidence by the learned trial judge and by Bridges C.J.N.B., in his dissenting reasons for judgment where he said [p. 705]:

"For estoppel to apply, I think we must be satisfied that the conduct of Burrows amounted to a promise or assurance, intended to affect the legal relations of the parties to the extent that if an interest instalment became in default for 10 days the plaintiff would not claim the principal as due unless it had previously notified the defendants of its intention to do so or, if it had not so notified them, that notice would be given them the principal would be claimed if such instalment so in default were not paid. This is, I think, a great deal to infer."

I do not think that the evidence warrants the inference that the appellant entered into any negotiations with the respondents which had the effect of leading them to suppose that the appellant had agreed to disregard or hold in suspense or abeyance that part of the contract which provided that: ". . . on default being made by both Subsurface Surveys Ltd. and the Debtor in paying any principal or interest due at any time according to the terms of the said note the Company may forthwith cause the pledged shares to be transferred to the name of the Company on the share register of Subsurface Surveys Ltd. and the pledged shares shall thereupon become the absolute property of the Company." I am on the other hand of opinion that the behaviour of Mr. Burrows is much more consistent with his having granted friendly indulgences to an old associate while retaining his right to insist on the letter of the obligation, which he did when he and Whitcomb became estranged and when the respondents were in default in payment of an interest payment for a period of 36 days.

For all these reasons I would allow the appeal and restore the judgment of the learned trial Judge. The appellant is entitled to its costs both here and in the Appeal Division.

[Appeal allowed; trial judgment restored.]

WATSON v. *CANADA PERMANENT TRUST CO.* (1972) 27 D.L.R. (3d) 735 (B.C.S.C.). The plaintiff agreed with a company (Pan Arctic) that in certain circumstances, it should "keep the right to buy" certain shares. Subsequently the plaintiff sought to resile from his promise. Anderson J. held that there was no consideration, but nevertheless, that the plaintiff could not withdraw the promise: "He knew that Pan Arctic intended to act on his promise. Pan Arctic did act on the promise and the plaintiff cannot now repudiate that promise or act inconsistently with it. It should also be noted that Pan Arctic could have suffered great prejudice if the plaintiff were permitted to repudiate his promise. Accordingly, I would hold that the plaintiff could not withdraw his offer to sell." The British Columbia Court of Appeal affirmed the decision, but on the grounds that there was consideration in that Pan Arctic was bound, on the true construction of the document, to buy the shares.

UNIFORM COMMERCIAL CODE
American Law Institute, 1962

Section 2-209. Modification, Rescission and Waiver

(1) An agreement modifying a contract within this Article needs no consideration to be binding.

(2) A signed agreement which excludes modification or rescission except by a signed writing cannot be otherwise modified or rescinded, but except as between merchants such a requirement on a form supplied by the merchant must be separately signed by the other party.

(3) The requirements of the statute of frauds section of this article . . . must be satisfied if the contract as modified is within its provisions.

(4) Although an attempt at modification or rescission does not satisfy the requirements of subsection (2) or (3) it can operate as a waiver.

(5) A party who has made a waiver affecting an executory portion of the contract may retract the waiver by reasonable notification received by the other party that strict performance will be required of any term waived, unless the retraction would be unjust in view of a material change of position in reliance on the waiver.

COMMENT. . . . Purposes of Changes and New Matter.

1. This section seeks to protect and make effective all necessary and desirable modifications of sales contracts without regard to the technicalities which at present hamper such adjustments.

2. Subsection (1) provides that an agreement modifying a sales contract needs no consideration to be binding.

However, modifications made thereunder must meet the test of good faith imposed by this Act. The effective use of bad faith to escape performance on the original contract terms is barred, and the extortion of a "modification" without legitimate commercial reason is ineffective as a violation of the duty of good faith. Nor can a mere technical consideration support a modification made in bad faith. . . .

RESTATEMENT OF CONTRACTS (SECOND)
Tentative Draft 1964

90. A promise which the promisor should reasonably expect to induce action or forbearance on the part of the promisee or a third person is binding if injustice can be avoided only by enforcement of the promise. The remedy granted for breach may be limited as justice requires.

PROBLEM. A promises B $10,000 as a gift. B buys a car for $5,000. A revokes his promise. B's car is worth $4,000. What should be B's measure of recovery? Would it make any difference if A, instead of revoking the promise, had died leaving unpaid creditors and needy dependants?

4. UNILATERAL CONTRACTS

A "unilateral contract" is made by accepting an offer, not by a counter promise (which would create a "bilateral contract" of mutual promises) but by performing a requested overt act. The negotiation of a unilateral contract presents a number of problems, many arising in what are sometimes called the "reward cases." To whom is a reward offered? Must the offeree, whoever he may be, notify the offeror? If so, when? Does it matter that the offeror has or has not requested notice in his offer? Must the offeree know of the offer? Suppose that while A is out for a walk he is apprehended by a tired and lonesome dog whose collar identifies him as Fido, property of B, at a given address. A returns Fido to his owner's address and leaves him with an excited small son. Later A discovers that B had offered $50 for the return of the lost dog. Should A be heard to say he has a contractual right to the $50?

Perhaps the most tantalizing problem in unilateral contracts arises when the offeror wants to revoke. Oldster asks Youngster to look after him for the rest of his life and promises to leave Youngster $5,000 on his death. When he has enjoyed ten years of faithful service by Youngster and is on his death bed, Oldster announces that he revokes his offer. Note that the essential characteristic of the situation is that it is not bilateral. Oldster has not asked Youngster to commit himself with a promise to serve him for any length of time. Frequently in these cases the offeree is unwilling to commit himself. When should the state interfere to protect the interests of the parties, or of one of them? What interests ought to be protected?

WILLIAMS v. CARWARDINE
England. King's Bench. 1833. 4 B. & Ad. 621; 110 E.R. 590

At the trial before Park J., at the last Spring Assizes for the county of Hereford, the following appeared to be the facts of the case: One Walter Carwardine, the brother of the defendant, was seen on the evening of the 24th of March, 1831, at a public house at Hereford, and was not heard of again till his body was found on the 12th of April in the river Wye, about two miles from the city. An inquest was held on the body on the 13th of April and the following days till the 19th; and it appearing that the plaintiff was at a house with the deceased on the night he was supposed to have been murdered, she was examined before the magistrates but did not give them any information which led to the apprehension of the real offender. On the 25th of April the defendant caused a handbill to be published, stating that whoever would give such information as would lead to a discovery of the murderer of Walter Carwardine, should, on conviction receive a reward of £20; and any person concerned therein, or privy thereto (except the party who actually committed the offence), should be entitled to such reward, and every exertion used to procure a pardon; and it then added, that information was to be given, and application for the above reward was to be made, to William Carwardine, Holmer, near Hereford. Two persons were tried for the murder at the Summer Assizes, 1831, but acquitted. Soon after this the plaintiff was severely beaten and bruised by one Williams; and on the 23rd of August, 1831, believing she had not long to live, and to ease her conscience, she made a voluntary statement, containing information which led to the subsequent conviction of Williams. Upon this evidence it was contended, that as the plaintiff was not induced by the reward promised by the defendant to give evidence, the law would not imply a contract by the defendant to pay her the £20. The learned Judge was of opinion that the plaintiff, having given the information which led to the conviction of the murderer, had performed the condition on which the £20 was to become payable, and was therefore entitled to recover it; and he directed the jury to find a verdict for the plaintiff, but desired them to find specially whether she was induced to give the information by the offer of the promised reward. The jury found that she was not induced by the offer of the reward, but by other motives.

Curwood now moved for a new trial. There was no promise to pay the plaintiff the sum of £20. That promise could only be enforced in favor of persons who should have been induced to make disclosures by the promise of the reward. Here the jury found that the plaintiff was induced by other motives to give the information. They have, therefore, negatived any contract on the part of the defendant with the plaintiff.

DENMAN C.J.: The plaintiff, by having given information which led to the conviction of the murderer of Walter Carwardine, has brought herself within the terms of the advertisement, and therefore is entitled to recover.

LITTLEDALE J.: The advertisement amounts to a general promise to give a sum of money to any person who shall give information which might lead to the discovery of the offender. The plaintiff gave that information.

PARKE J.: There was a contract with any person who performed the condition mentioned in the advertisement.

PATTESON J.: I am of the same opinion. We cannot go into the plaintiff's motives.

[Rule refused. From the report of the trial in 5 C. & P. 574, it might appear from an admission of the defendant's counsel that the plaintiff knew of the offer at the time she gave the information. If she did not, could she be treated as a party to a contract? Could she have given the information in fulfilment of its condition?]

LOCKHART v. *BARNARD*. 1845. 14 M. & W. 674, 153 E.R. 646. The offer of a reward stated: ". . . Whoever will give such information as will lead to the immediate recovery of the above parcel, with its contents safe, if lost, or the early apprehension of the guilty parties if stolen, shall receive the above reward." POLLOCK C.B.: "Here the plaintiff communicates certain information to Cheshire, who, in return makes a communication to him; and then, deeming their joint knowledge sufficiently important to call for further inquiry, they jointly communicate it to Robinson and others, and he, as the agent of both, communicates it to a constable. I therefore think, that the finding of the jury, that the information which led to the detection of the felon was given, not by Lockhart alone, but by him jointly with Cheshire, and the entry of the verdict upon that finding, were perfectly right, and that no rule ought to be granted."

GIBBONS v. PROCTOR
England. Queen's Bench Division. 1891. 64 L.T. 594

DAY J.: This action is brought to recover a reward, which the defendant advertised as payable to the person who should prosecute to conviction the perpetrator of a certain crime. The facts are simple. The defendant published on the 29th May a handbill, in which he stated that he would give £25 to any person who should give information leading to the conviction of the offender in question, such information to be given to a superintendent of police of the name of Penn. The plaintiff is a police officer, and, in the early morning of the 29th May, the day of the afternoon of which the bill was published, communicated important information which led to the conviction of the offender to a comrade and fellow policeman called Coffin, telling Coffin, as his agent, to carry the information to the proper authority. Coffin, in accordance with the rules of the force, first informed his superior officer, Inspector Lennan, and Lennan sent on the information to Superintendent Penn. Both Coffin and Lennan were the agents of the plaintiff to carry on a message set going by him, and it reached Penn at a time when he had notice that the person sending him such information was entitled to the reward of £25. The condition was fulfilled after the publication of the handbill and the announcement therein contained of the defendant's offer of the reward to the informant.

[Lawrence J. agreed, and the non-suit was set aside and a verdict entered for £25.]

FITCH v. *SNEDAKER.* 1868. 38 N.Y. 248 (New York. Court of Appeals). The defendant offered a reward of $200 to any person or persons who would give such information as should lead to the apprehension and conviction of the person or persons guilty of the murder of a certain unknown female. The plaintiff gave information resulting in the arrest of the murderer before the plaintiff heard of the reward and in fact (as it appeared in the evidence at an earlier trial) before the reward was published. After he heard, he gave further information and testified at the trial, at which the murderer was convicted. The plaintiff claimed the reward, which was refused, and he brought this action. His evidence to show that his information led to the arrest was rejected because it was given before he knew of the reward. His evidence to show that his information and testimony led to a conviction was rejected because in order to claim the reward he had to show that he had brought about both the arrest and the conviction. Without his first evidence his second evidence was irrelevant. WOODRUFF J.: ". . . the first question is, Was there a contract between the parties?

"To the existence of a contract there must be mutual assent, or, in another form, offer and consent to the offer. The motive inducing consent may be immaterial, but the consent is vital. Without that there is no contract. How then can there be consent or assent to that of which the party has never heard? On the fifteenth day of October, 1859, the murderer, Fee, had, in consequence of information given by the plaintiffs, been apprehended and lodged in jail. But the plaintiffs did not, in giving that information, manifest any assent to the defendant's offer, nor act in any sense it reliance thereon; they did not know of its existence. The information was voluntary, and in every sense (material to this case) gratuitous. The offer could only operate upon the plaintiffs after they heard of it. It was prospective to those who will in the future give information."

THE CROWN v. CLARKE
West Australia. High Court of Australia. 1927. 40 C.L.R. 227

ISAACS A.C.J.: This is an appeal from the judgment of the Full Court of Western Australia. Evan Clarke proceeded, by petition of right under the *Crown Suits Act* 1898, to sue the Crown for £1,000 promised by proclamation for such information as should lead to the arrest and conviction of the person or persons who committed the murders of two police officers, Walsh and Pitman. . . . At the trial the Chief Justice gave judgment for the Crown. In the Full Court, by a majority, the judgment of McMillan C.J., the trial Judge, was reversed. In the result, two learned Judges thought the Crown should succeed while two others thought Clarke should succeed. . . .

The facts of this case, including inferences, are not, as I understand, in dispute. They amount to this: The information for which Clarke claims the reward was given by him when he was under arrest with Treffene on a charge of murder, and was given by him in circumstances which show that in giving the information he was not acting on or in pursuance of or in reliance upon or in return for the consideration contained in the proclamation, but exclusively in order to clear himself from a false charge of murder. In other words, he was acting with reference to a specific criminal charge against himself, and not with reference to a general request by the community for information against other persons. It is true that without his information and evidence no conviction was probable, but it is also abundantly clear that he was not acting for the sake of justice of from any impulse of conscience or because he was asked to do so, but simply and solely on his own initiative, to secure his own safety from the hand of the law and altogether irrespective of the proclamation. He has, in my opinion, neither a legal nor a moral claim to the reward. The learned Chief Justice held that Clarke never accepted or intended to accept the offer in the proclamation, and, unless the mere giving of the information without such intention amounted in law to an acceptance of the offer or to performance of the condition, there was neither "acceptance" nor "performance," and therefore there was no contract. I do not understand either of the learned Judges who formed the majority to controvert this. But they held that *Williams* v. *Carwardine* (1833), 110 E.R. 590, has stood so long that it should be regarded as accurate, and that, so regarded, it entitled the respondent to judgment. . . .

The controlling principle, then, is that to establish the *consensus* without which no true contract can exist, acceptance is as essential as offer, even in a case of the present class where the same act is at once sufficient for both acceptance and performance. But acceptance and performance of condition, as shown by the judicial reasoning quoted, involve that the person accepting and performing must act on the offer. . . .

Instances easily suggest themselves where precisely the same act done with reference to an offer would be performance of the condition, but done with reference to a totally distinct object would not be such a performance. An offer of £100 to any person who should swim a hundred yards in the harbour on the first day of the year, would be met by voluntarily performing the feat with reference to the offer, but would not in my opinion be satisfied by a person who was accidentally or maliciously thrown overboard on that date and swam the distance simply to save his life, without any thought of the offer. The offeror might or might not feel morally impelled to give the sum in such a case, but would be under no contractual obligation to do so. . . .

The appeal, . . . should, in my opinion, for the reasons stated, be allowed, and the judgment of McMillan C.J. restored.

[The opinion is considerably abbreviated. The opinions of Higgins and Starke JJ. are omitted.]

CARLILL v. CARBOLIC SMOKE BALL COMPANY
England. Court of Appeal. [1893] 1 Q.B. 256

The defendants, who were the proprietors and vendors of a medical preparation called "The Carbolic Smoke Ball", inserted in the Pall Mall Gazette of November 13th, 1891, and in other newspapers, the following advertisement:

"£100 reward will be paid by the Carbolic Smoke Ball Company to any person who contracts the increasing epidemic of influenza, colds, or any disease caused by taking cold, after having used the ball three times daily for two weeks according to the printed directions supplied with each ball. £1000 is deposited with the Alliance Bank, Regent Street, shewing our sincerity in the matter.

"During the last epidemic of influenza many thousand carbolic smoke balls were sold as preventives against this disease, and in no ascertained case was the disease contracted by those using carbolic smoke ball.

"One carbolic smoke ball will last a family several months, making it the cheapest remedy in the world at the price, 10s. post free. The ball can be refilled at a cost of 5s. Address, Carbolic Smoke Ball Company, 27, Princes Street, Hanover Square London."

The plaintiff, a lady, on the faith of this advertisement, bought one of the balls at a chemist's, and used it as directed three times a day, from November 20, 1891, to January 17, 1892, when she was attacked by influenza. Hawkins J. held that she was entitled to recover the £100. The defendants appealed.

LINDLEY L.J.: I will begin by referring to two points which were raised in the court below. I refer to them simply for the purpose of dismissing them. First, it is said no action will lie upon this contract because it is a policy. You have only to look at the advertisement to dismiss that suggestion. Then it is said that it is a bet. Hawkins J. came to the conclusion that nobody ever dreamt of a bet, and that the transaction had nothing whatever in common with a bet. I so entirely agree with him that I pass over this contention also as not worth serious attention.

Then, what is left? The first observation I will make is that we are not dealing with any inference of fact. We are dealing with an express promise to pay £100 in certain events. Read the advertisement how you will, and twist it about as you will, here is a distinct promise expressed in language which is perfectly unmistakable—"£100 reward will be paid by the Carbolic Smoke Ball Company to any person who contracts the influenza after having used the ball three times daily for two weeks according to the printed directions supplied with each ball."

We must first consider whether this was intended to be a promise at all, or whether it was a mere puff which meant nothing. Was it a mere puff? My answer to that question is No, and I base my answer upon this passage: "£1000 is deposited with the Alliance Bank, shewing our sincerity in the matter." Now, for what was that money deposited or that statement made except to negative the suggestion that this was a mere puff and meant nothing at all? The deposit is called in aid by the advertiser as proof of his sincerity in the matter—that is, the sincerity of his promise to pay this £100 in the event which he has specified. I say this for the purpose of giving point to the observation that we are not inferring a promise; there is the promise, as plain as words can make it.

Then it is contended that it is not binding. In the first place, it is said that it is not made with anybody in particular. Now that point is common to the words of this advertisement and to the words of all other advertisements offering rewards. They are offers to anybody who performs the conditions named in the advertisement, and anybody who does perform the conditions accepts the offer. In point of law this advertisement is an offer to pay £100 to anybody who will perform these conditions, and the performance of the conditions is the acceptance of the offer. That rests upon a string of authorities, the earliest of which is *Williams* v. *Carwardine* (1833), 110 E.R. 590, which has been followed by many other decisions upon advertisements offering rewards.

But then it is said, "Supposing that the performance of the conditions is an acceptance of the offer, that acceptance ought to have been notified." Unquestionably, as a general proposition, when an offer is made, it is necessary in order to make a binding contract, not only that it should be accepted, but that the acceptance should be notified. But is that so in cases of this kind? I apprehend that they are an exception to that rule, or, if not an exception, they are open to the observation that the notification of the acceptance need not precede the performance. This offer is a continuing offer. It was never revoked, and if notice of acceptance is required—which I doubt very much, for I rather think the true view is that which was expressed and explained by Lord Blackburn in the case of *Brogden* v. *Metropolitan Ry. Co.* (1877), 2 App. Cas. 666, 691—if notice of acceptance is required, the person who makes the offer gets the notice of acceptance contemporaneously with his notice of the performance of the condition. If he gets notice of the acceptance before his offer is revoked, that in principle is all you want. I, however, think that the true view, in a case of this kind, is that the person who makes the offer shews by his language and from the nature of the transaction that he does not expect and does not require notice of the acceptance apart from notice of the performance. . . .

It appears to me, therefore, that the defendants must perform their promise, and, if they have been so unwary as to expose themselves to a great many actions, so much the worse for them.

BOWEN L.J.: I am of the same opinion. . . .

It was said that there was no notification of the acceptance of the contract. One cannot doubt that, as an ordinary rule of law, an acceptance of an offer made ought to be notified to the person who makes the offer, in order that the two minds may come together. Unless this is done the two minds may be apart, and there is not that consensus which is necessary according to the English law—I say nothing about the laws of other countries—to make a contract. But there is this clear gloss to be made upon that doctrine, that as notification of acceptance is required for the benefit of the person who makes the offer, the person who makes the offer may dispense with notice to himself if he thinks it desirable to do so, and I suppose there can be no doubt that where a person in an offer made by him to another person, expressly or impliedly intimates a particular mode of acceptance as sufficient to make the bargain binding, it is only necessary for the other person to whom such offer is made to follow the indicated method of acceptance; and if the person making the offer, expressly or impliedly intimates in his offer that it will be sufficient to act on the proposal without communicating acceptance of it to himself, performance of the condition is a sufficient acceptance without notification.

That seems to me to be the principle which lies at the bottom of the acceptance cases, of which two instances are the well-known judgment of Mellish L.J. in *Harris' Case* (1872), 7 Ch.App. 587, and the very instructive judgment of Lord Blackburn in *Brogden* v. *Metropolitan Ry. Co.*, in which he appears to me to take exactly the line I have indicated.

Now, if that is the law how are we to find out whether the person who makes the offer does intimate that notification of acceptance will not be necessary in order to constitute a binding bargain? In many cases you look to the offer itself. In many cases you extract from the character of the transaction that notification is not required, and in the advertisement cases it seems to me to follow as an inference to be drawn from the transaction itself that a person is not to notify his acceptance of the offer before he performs the condition, but that if he performs the condition notification is dispensed with. It seems to me that from the point of view of common sense no other idea could be entertained. If I advertise to the world that my dog is lost, and that anybody who brings the dog to a particular place will be paid some money, are all the police or other persons whose business it is to find lost dogs to be expected to sit down and write me a note saying they have accepted my proposal? Why, of course, they at once look after the dog, and as soon as they have found the dog they have performed the condition. The essence of the transaction is that the dog should be found, and it is not necessary under such circumstances, as it seems to me, that in order to make the contract binding there should be any notification of acceptance. It follows from the nature of the thing that the performance of the condition is sufficient acceptance without notification of it, and a person who makes an offer in an advertisement of that kind makes an offer which must be read by the light of that common sense reflection. He does, therefore, in his offer impliedly indicate that he does not require notification of the acceptance of the offer.

[Appeal dismissed. Part of the opinions only are given and the concurring opinion of A.L. Smith L.J. is omitted.]

WOOD v. *LETRIK, LIMITED*, The Times, January 13, 1932. The defendants in an advertisement of their electric comb, stated: "What is your trouble? It is grey hair? In 10 days not a grey hair left. £500 guarantee." The plaintiff claimed he had bought a comb and used it as directed, the only result being that the comb scratched his head and made him feel uncomfortable. He sued for and recovered the £500. Rowlatt J. followed the *Carlill case*. Suppose that in either the *smoke-ball* or *comb case* the plaintiff had borrowed the smoke-ball or comb from a friend and had used it with disappointing results. Would you allow a recovery?

BISHOP v. *EATON*. 1894. 37 N.E. 665 (Massachusetts. Supreme Court). The defendant wrote the plaintiff, "If Harry needs more money, let him have it, or assist him to get it, and I will see that it is paid." The plaintiff endorsed a note for Harry for $200, and shortly after wrote to the defendant to this effect. The defendant denied receipt of the letter. The note was extended for one year, but the trial judge did not decide whether the defendant had agreed to the extension. If he hadn't he would be discharged. The plaintiff paid the note and the trial judge found for the plaintiff. The defendant appealed and a new trial was granted to establish whether he had consented to the extension. KNOWLTON J.: "We are of opinion that the plaintiff, after assisting Harry to get the money, did all that he was required to do when he reasonably sent the defendant the letter by mail informing him of what had been done. . . . Ordinarily there is no occasion to notify the offeror of the acceptance of such an offer, for the doing of the act is a sufficient acceptance, and the promisor knows that he is bound when he sees that action has been taken on the faith of his offer. But if the act is of such a kind that knowledge of it will not quickly come to the promisor, the promisee is bound to give him notice of his acceptance within a reasonable time after doing that which constitutes the acceptance.

In such a case it is implied in the offer that, to complete the contract, notice shall be given with due diligence, so that the promisor may know that a contract has been made. But where the promise is in consideration of an act to be done, it becomes binding upon the doing of the act so far that the promisee cannot be affected by a subsequent withdrawal of it, if within a reasonable time afterward he notifies the promisor. In accordance with these principles it has been held in cases like the present, where the guarantor would not know of himself, from the nature of the transaction, whether the offer has been accepted or not, that he is not bound without notice of the acceptance, reasonably given after the performance which constitutes the consideration."

GOLDTHORPE v. LOGAN
Ontario. Court of Appeal. [1943] 2 D.L.R. 519

LAIDLAW J.A. delivered the judgment of the Court: This is an appeal by the plaintiffs from a judgment of Hope J., dated April 10, 1942. The female appellant had some hairs on her face and wanted to have them removed. She saw advertisements published in a newspaper by the defendant Anne Graham Logan. She went to the place of business stated in the advertisement and consulted the defendant Kathleen Fitzpatrick, a registered nurse, who was an employee of the defendant Logan. She was told that her face could be definitely "cleared," that the hair could be removed permanently, and the result was guaranteed. She then submitted to a number of "treatments" by electrolysis for the purpose of removing the hairs but the result was not satisfactory. Hairs continued to grow on her face in the same way as before, and in spite of the efforts of the defendants to remedy the condition. . . .

There are three questions to be determined: (1) Was there any negligence on the part of the defendants which caused loss or damages to the plaintiffs? (2) Was there a contract between the defendant Logan and the plaintiff Pearl Elizabeth Goldthorpe? (3) If so, what is the result in law of a breach thereof on the part of that defendant? . . .

The plaintiffs, therefore, fail to establish liability of the defendants on the ground of negligence. But the alternative allegation to the effect that the defendant Logan is responsible in law by reason of a breach of contract made by or on her behalf with the female plaintiff requires careful consideration. The elements of a valid contract are well known, and it is only necessary to analyze the evidence to determine whether or not they exist in this case. I at once examined the advertisement published by the defendant Logan. It appears in two forms, but the portions relevant to the question now studied are the same. I excerpt the contents as follows: "Hairs . . . removed safely and permanently by Electrolysis. . . . No marks, No scars, Results Guaranteed. Anne Graham Logan . . . 140 Carlton St." What is the true nature and construction of this advertisement? It is a distinct communication by the defendant Logan to each and every member of the public. What intention did she possess and convey to such persons by the words she used? To ascertain that intention we may in this instance look at the surrounding circumstances. She was carrying on a business in which she appealed for public support and patronage. She required customers to buy services she desired to sell. She was a vendor seeking a purchaser. What she meant to say, and the sensible interpretation of her words is this: "If you will submit yourself to my treatment and pay me (certain charges) I undertake to remove hairs safely and permanently by electrolysis and I promise to obtain a satisfactory result." The effect in law of such a statement is to create an offer from the person by whom it is made to every person who is willing to accept the terms and conditions of it. It may perhaps, be suggested that this meaning and effect of the advertisement is strained and unfair. I think it is not. On the contrary, I read it in its plain meaning as the public would understand it. Moreover, after Mrs. Goldthorpe was persuaded by this public offer to attend at the defendant's place of business she was given further assurance that the hairs on her face could be successfully and permanently removed without stimulation, without risk, and without pain. The defendants again "guaranteed results." They did not ask for nor suggest any exemption, exception, or qualification of any kind, but on the contrary they made promises which were absolute and unlimited. They were reckless and rash without any regard whatever to the particular circumstances of the case. No physical examination of Mrs. Goldthorpe was required nor suggested. No inquiry was made for the purpose of disclosing any organic trouble or cause of the excessive hair. The defendants simply were content to take the risk of failure irrespective of any underlying causes of the unfortunate ailment, and they exposed themselves to just such an action as this. If the vendor's self-confidence had persuaded her into an excessive, extravagant promise, she cannot now escape a complaint from a credulous and distressed person to whom she gave assurance of future excellence and relief from her burden. The strong cannot disregard any undertaking binding in law, however lightly given, and the weak unfortunate person, however gullible, can be sure that the Courts of this country will not permit anyone to escape the responsibility arising from an enforceable promise. The words of Hawkins J., are fitting and applicable. He says: "Such advertisements do not appeal so much to the wise and thoughtful as to the credulous and weak portions of the community; and if the vendor of an article, whether it be medicine smoke or anything else. with a view to increase its sale and use, thinks fit publicly to promise to all who buy or use it that, to those who shall not find it as surely efficacious as it is represented by him to be he will pay a substantial sum of money, he must not be surprised if occasionally he is held to his promise:" *Carlill* v. *Carbolic Smoke Ball Co.,* [1893] 1 Q.B. 256.

I now consider whether there was acceptance in law of the offer made by the defendant. The offer was made to the public. Any member was free to lend oneself to the terms and conditions and assent thereto.

The female plaintiff accordingly accepted the offer, and her acceptance was communicated to the defendant Logan by her conduct. These parties had a common intention, and there was good consideration present. It was constituted by the detriment or inconvenience sustained by the female plaintiff. Her submission to the treatments, in accordance with advertisement, was a benefit sought by the advertiser. . . . I hold that there was an agreement made between the plaintiff, Pearl Elizabeth Goldthorpe and the defendant, Anne Graham Logan, and that such agreement is enforceable at law by the female plaintiff. . . .

[Appeal allowed in part.]

NOTE. The effect of the contractual analysis is that the defendant is made liable for the accuracy of her advertisement even though no negligence, in word or deed, was proved by the plaintiff. The use of contractual analysis to impose a strict liability in the interests of consumer protection is not uncommon.

SLOAN v. *UNION OIL COMPANY OF CANADA LTD.* [1955] 4
D.L.R. 664. (British Columbia Supreme Court). Sloan was employed as
credit manager of Union Oil when that Company was taken over by the
British American Oil Company Limited. While he was working with Union
Oil the Company announced a plan for "termination allowances." The
announcement of the plan ended with the words, "The Company reserves
the right to terminate or modify this Plan at any time." The plan had been
modified at least in 1945, 1944, and 1943, after the first announcement
put in evidence, in 1941. Sloan had been working for Union Oil for about
nineteen years when he began working for B.A. Oil in September, 1945,
after the takeover, and he later discovered that B.A. Oil had no termination allowance. He was told that B.A. Oil would regard unfavourably
any employee of theirs who tried to collect his termination allowance
from Union Oil. Sloan's lawyer advised him that he was entitled to so collect, but he took no steps until after he had left the service of B.A. Oil in
1950. He issued his writ at the last moment after very little negotiation,
but so as to come within the limitation period. Held, for the plaintiff.
WILSON J. found the announcements about termination allowances in
1945, just before the takeover, constituted "a promise that [the Union
Oil] would, if he continued in its employment until such time, short of
retirement age, as it should, without cause, dismiss him from its service,
pay him certain stated sums. The offer is clear. It is equally clear that
there was no verbal or written acceptance of the offer; no consideration
by way of a promise that he would so continue to serve. Therefore, if a
consideration moved from the plaintiff to the defendant, that consideration was not a promise but a performance, the doing of an act. For undoubtedly he did fulfil the terms of the defendant's offer, he did serve
them until dismissed, and it is this, and this only, that must be relied on
as consideration.

"Now he was, of course, already bound to serve them during his period
of employment and the consideration for that service was his salary. But
he was not bound to continue to serve them until he was dismissed. He
could, at any time, have quit his employment. By staying until he was
discharged he did something that was not required by his contract of employment and he says that his knowledge of the provision for a termination allowance was one of the factors which induced him to continue
his employment." WILSON J. referred to the *High Trees* and *Combe*
cases and remarked: "The promise or assurance here was not used, as in
the *High Trees* case, *supra*, to resist a claim but to enforce one. . . . I
think . . . that a majority of the Court [in the *Combe* case] would have
enforced the promise to pay £100 per year if it had been coupled with a
condition that the wife abstain from taking proceedings to collect alimony
and if the wife had so abstained. This, of course, apart from the other
point [that her agreement would have been unenforceable] which might
have defeated her claim. The interesting thing here is that Denning L.J.,
if I read him correctly, would have enforced the husband's promise on a
basis entirely unrelated to his judgment in the *High Trees House* case,
and on what he calls a long settled rule that a finding that there was a
promise intended to be binding, intended to be acted upon and in fact
acted upon is equivalent to a finding that there was consideration. . . . I
think that I must not rely on but distinguish the line of cases stemming
from the *High Trees House* judgment. . . . the doctrine stated [in that

case] is to be used as a shield but not a sword. Where a sword is required there must be consideration.

"But I think it is equally clear from *Combe* v. *Combe* . . . that, as stated by Denning L.J. the sword exists if the promise was in the nature of an offer, intended to be acted upon, and in fact acted upon. . . .

"It appears to me that *Combe* v. *Combe* brings latter day English law regarding consideration into a very near relationship with American law on the same subject. I propose to quote at some length from American authorities which seem to have anticipated the reasoning in *Combe* v. *Combe*, and have the added advantage of applying that reasoning to the relation of master and servant. I first cite this general statement from *Corbin on Contracts*, vol. 1, p. 221:

" 'There are cases in which an employer has promised a "bonus", some form of benefit in addition to agreed wages or salary, on condition that the employee or employees remain in service for a stated period. In such cases the offered promise is almost always so made as to make it unnecessary for the employee to give any notice of his assent. It is sufficient that he continues in the employment as requested. It is certain that after so continuing in performance, the employer cannot withdraw or repudiate his promise without liability either in damages or for a proportionate part of the bonus promised. A unilateral contract exists.' "

GRANT v. *PROVINCE OF NEW BRUNSWICK*
(1973) 35 D.L.R. (3d) 141 (N.B. App. Div.)

HUGHES C.J.N.B.: This is an appeal by the Province of New Brunswick (herein referred to as "the Province") from a judgment in the Queen's Bench Division directed against it in favour of the plaintiff for $4,800, being the value of 4,000 barrels of potatoes which the plaintiff alleged he sold to the Province in 1967 under a potato price stabilization programme, with costs to be taxed.

On this appeal as well as at trial, the Province contended that the evidence does not establish a contract between the parties and that consequently, the action should be dismissed. In the spring of 1967, there was in Canada a considerable surplus of potatoes produced in 1966 which could not be marketed. To stabilize the price of potatoes the Governor-General in Council passed Order in Council P.C. 1967-892 dated May 4, 1967, pursuant to the *Agricultural Stabilization Act*, 1957-58 (Can.), c. 22 [now R.S.C. 1970, c. A-9], designating potatoes as an agricultural commodity for the purpose of the Act and authorizing the Agricultural Stabilization Board to make payments to producers for potatoes grown in 1966, limited to deliveries of 1,000 barrels per producer, for use for starch manufacture and for other non-food uses approved by the Board. Programmes carried out under this Order in Council are referred to Program respectively. By a subsequent Order in Council the limitation of 1,000 barrels per producer was raised to 5,000 barrels.

These programmes were found inadequate to absorb the surplus potatoes in New Brunswick and an arrangement was entered into by the Minister of Agriculture for the Province with the Government of Canada to implement a potato price stabilization programme under which the Province undertook to purchase potatoes direct from growers resident in New Brunswick at the support price of $1.20 per barrel and to make payment for such potatoes direct to the producers. Under the programme purchases were limited to 5,000 barrels per producer including all potatoes sold under the Potato Starch Diversion Program and the Livestock Feed Diversion Program. The Agricultural Stabilization Board undertook as a term of the arrangement to pay the Province ½c per lb. for all potatoes purchased by the Province under the programme.

In entering into the arrangement with the Government of Canada neither the Minister of Agriculture nor the Government of the Province had statutory authority to do so and the cost of the programme was financed by special warrants. To implement the programme the Province appointed an administrator and established a committee consisting of potato farmers, officials of the Department of Agriculture and one representing the Agricultural Stabilization Board.

The committee's function was to process applications made by potato growers to ensure that the applicants were eligible and the potatoes offered for purchase qualified under the programme. In all, the Province received about 735 applications of which an estimated 700 were approved without question. Of the remaining 35, 25 were approved after the applicants satisfied the committee as to their eligibility. The remaining 10, of which the plaintiff was one, were refused the benefits of the programme.

The Province publicized the programme and prepared a form of application which was made available to growers who wished to dispose of their surplus potatoes by selling them to the Province. In the form, the grower was required to state his potato acreage, his 1966 production, the capacity of storage used by him, the number of acres which he rented in 1966, and the estimated quantity of potatoes which he offered for purchase, and the applicant was required to make a statutory declaration as to the truth of his statements. On the reverse side of the application there was printed certain general information relating to the programme which read as follows:

1. This program will have the effect of stabilizing the price of New Brunswick potatoes.
2. The support price is established at $1.20 per barrel (165 lbs.)— storage run. For the purpose of this program, 1 barrel = 4.08 cu. ft.
3. The Province will purchase potatoes at this support price and make payments directly to the grower. The Agricultural Stabilization Board will make a payment to the Province of one-half cent per pound on all potatoes so purchased.
4. The Minister of Agriculture for the Province of New Brunswick has designated that resident potato growers throughout the Province may apply.
5. Assistance will only be paid on potatoes actually grown by the applicant in 1966 and there will only be one eligible grower for each farm unit.
6. In all cases, applications will not be approved nor any payments authorized until an official inspector, appointed by the Minister, has certified that the quantity of potatoes offered is accurately stated and that the potatoes have broken down (if prior to June 15th) and been

disposed of in a manner satisfactory to the inspector. The percentage of No. 1's will be established by a Federal Inspector.

7. No consideration will be given to quantities below 50 barrels per grower.

8. The maximum amount eligible for assistance will be 5000 barrels per grower which will include all potatoes diverted through the Potato Starch Diversion and Livestock Feed Diversion Programs. The maximum allowed under the two diversion programs combined is 1000 barrels.

9. Growers are required to:
   (a) Utilize both the Starch Diversion and Livestock Feed Diversion Programs insofar as possible; and
   (b) Continue to sell on the market, all saleable potatoes at the highest possible market prices.

10. All applications must be filed in the office of the local District Agriculturist on or before June 30, 1967.

11. The program will be administered by a special committee appointed by the Minister and composed of representatives of both the potato producers and the Department of Agriculture.

12. Applicants attempting to falsify information with regard to this program will not be eligible for assistance.

13. All information and required forms can be obtained from the office of the District Agriculturist in each area or by writing to Peter C. Schousboe, Administrator of the Potato Price Stabilization Program, Department of Agriculture, Fredericton, N.B.

At the foot of the application there is a form to be completed by a federal Government inspector certifying the grade of potatoes offered for purchase and a certificate to be completed by a provincial inspector as to the grade and volume of the potatoes referred to in the application and stating there was evidence of excessive breakdown of the potatoes and that they had been disposed of in a manner satisfactory to the inspector. The certificate on the plaintiff's application was duly completed and signed by a federal Government inspector and by a provincial inspector.

After these certificates were completed and the potatoes disposed of, the plaintiff's application was placed by the administrator before the committee for its approval. Owing to certain information which came to its attention, the committee refused the plaintiff's application and the administrator wrote the plaintiff under date of October 5, 1967, stating, *inter alia*:

"The administration of this program is the responsibility of the Board appointed by the Minister of Agriculture and is subject to the guide lines and regulations established at the outset, through negotiation between the Federal Stabilization Board and the Province. One such regulation states that the potatoes offered must be the property of the applicant. Information received by the Board indicates that you do not qualify under this regulation.

I have been instructed by the Board to inform you that for this reason your application has not been approved. We cannot, therefore, pay any assistance on the potatoes offered in your application."

The plaintiff replied protesting he was in fact the owner of the potatoes offered. Later he appeared before the committee but was unable to satisfy its members that he owned the potatoes which he had offered. Later, he brought the present action claiming the price of 4,000 barrels of potatoes at $1.20 per barrel. At the trial he testified he owned the potatoes and his evidence was accepted by the learned trial Judge who directed that judgment be entered against the Province for the price claimed. On this appeal the Province did not challenge the trial Judge's finding that the plaintiff was the owner of the potatoes which he offered for purchase, but contended that payments made to applicants under the potato price stabilization programme constituted subsidies, the payment of which the applicant had no legal right to enforce.

Counsel for the plaintiff admitted that to succeed in the action the plaintiff must prove there was an offer to purchase or to sell made by one of the parties to the other and that the party to whom it was made accepted it. It is elementary that until an offer open for acceptance by a person to whom it is made has been accepted by him, no contract results.

If the plaintiff's application is to be construed as an offer by him to the Province of potatoes for purchase, I am unable to find anything in the evidence to establish that the Province accepted his offer since the administrator who must be taken to be the agent of the Province refused to approve the application by letter dated October 5, 1967, and nothing which occurred thereafter can be regarded as constituting an acceptance.

In his opening remarks at trial, counsel for the plaintiff stated that the plaintiff based his case on the acceptance by him of terms offered by the Province. I interpret this submission to mean that the plaintiff claims the Province made a general offer to all eligible potato producers resident in New Brunswick to purchase any potatoes grown by them in 1966, subject to the limitations and conditions specified in the general information on the reverse side of the application form which it had prepared and that the plaintiff, by offering his potatoes, having them measured and inspected, and by disposing of them in a manner satisfactory to the inspector appointed by the Province, had accepted the Province's offer. This is essentially the view taken by the trial Judge who interpreted the general information as an offer and not merely as a statement by the Province of its intention to purchase potatoes.

It may well be that the Province in publicizing the general information concerning its potato price stabilization programme intended merely to inform eligible potato growers resident in New Brunswick of a policy without any intention of making a binding offer which would obligate it to purchase all eligible potatoes offered by all eligible growers. In interpreting an offer the objective test should, I think, be applied. *Williston on Contracts*, 3rd ed., (1957), vol. 1, s. 94, contains the following statement at p. 339:

"It follows that the test of the true interpretation of an offer or acceptance is not what the party making it thought it meant or intended it to mean, but what a reasonable person in the position of the parties would have thought it meant."

It is to be observed that para. 3 of the general information does not expressly state that the Province will purchase all potatoes offered nor does para. 7 promise to approve applications and authorize payment when an inspector appointed by the Minister has certified the quantity of the potatoes is correctly stated and that the potatoes have broken down and been disposed of in a manner satisfactory to the inspector. It only states that the application will not be approved nor will payment be authorized until these things are done. There is, nevertheless, an implication in the general information that if and when these things have been done, payment will be authorized. Had the Province intended to reserve the right to select from whom it chose to purchase potatoes, it could have indicated there was a limit to the quantity or the value of the potatoes which it was prepared to purchase or it could have stated that the decision of the committee appointed to administer the programme was final or made it clear that the committee's approval was a condition to the right to payment.

I am not satisfied that the trial Judge erred in finding that the Province offered to purchase potatoes at the support price from all eligible growers resident in New Brunswick who offered their potatoes for purchase within the guide-lines set out in the information. Indeed, I accept the view that a reasonable person in the position of the plaintiff would be entitled to assume that if he complied with the conditions set out in the general information and disposed of his potatoes to the satisfaction of the inspector appointed by the Province, he was entitled to sell his potatoes to the Province and that the Province was legally bound to purchase and pay for them. I would accordingly affirm the decision of the trial Judge and dismiss the appeal with costs.

[Appeal dismissed.]

BEER v. *LEA*. 1912. O.W.N. 342 (Ontario. High Court). Lea gave a thirty day option to Doolittle to buy his land for a stipulated sum. The option was without consideration and called for payment of the sum within the thirty days. Doolittle interested Beer in the deal. On the last day of the option Doolittle arranged with Lea to meet him and Beer at a certain place and take up the option. Doolittle and Beer attended at the place and the court found Beer was prepared to make the cash payment. Lea, however, deliberately refrained from attending at the arranged meeting. Doolittle later telephoned Lea for an explanation and Lea thinking the time had expired, said he would have nothing further to do with it. MIDDLETON J.: "I think the plaintiff fails. I do not think there was an acceptance of the offer before it was withdrawn. . . . I think that the offer could only be accepted by a cash payment . . . and that this was a condition precedent to the existence of any contractual relationship. . . . Mr. Johnston very forcibly contends that Lea ought to be precluded from denying that there was an acceptance of the offer, because of his failure to attend at the place arranged. . . . I cannot follow this. There can be no contract unless there is an offer and an acceptance of that offer. If there is a contract, then either party may . . . by his conduct dispense with the fulfilment of the contract, according to its terms by the other, but so far as I can find, it has nowhere been suggested that one who has made an offer can dispense with an acceptance so as to create a contractual relationship."

ERRINGTON v. ERRINGTON
England. Court of Appeal. [1952] 1 All E.R. 149

DENNING L.J.: The facts are reasonably clear. In 1936 the father bought the house for his son and daughter-in-law to live in. The father put down £250 in cash and borrowed £500 from a building society on the security of the house, repayable with interest by instalments of 15s. a week. He took the house in his own name and made himself responsible for the instalments. The father told the daughter-in-law that the £250 was a present for them, but he left them to pay the building society instalments of 15s. a week themselves. He handed the building society book to the daughter-in-law and said to her: "Don't part with this book. The house will be your property when the mortgage is paid." He said that when he retired he would transfer it into their names. She has, in fact, paid the building society instalments regularly from that day to this with the result that much of the mortgage has been repaid, but there is a good deal yet to be paid. The rates on the house came to 10s. a week. The couple found that they could not pay those as well as the building society instalments so the father said he would pay them and he did so.

It is to be noted that the couple never bound themselves to pay the instalments to the building society, and I can see no reason why any such obligation should be implied. It is clear law that the court is not to imply a term unless it is necessary, and I do not see that it is necessary here. Ample content is given to the whole agreement by holding that the father promised that the house should belong to the couple as soon as they had paid off the mortgage. The parties did not discuss what was to happen if the couple failed to pay the instalments to the building society, but I should have thought it clear that, if they did fail to pay the instalments, the father would not be bound to transfer the house to them. The father's promise was a unilateral contract—a promise of the house in return for their act of paying the instalments. It could not be revoked by him once the couple entered on performance of the act, but it would cease to bind him if they left it incomplete and unperformed, which they have not done. If that was the position during the father's lifetime, so it must be after his death. If the daughter-in-law continues to pay all the building society instalments, the couple will be entitled to have the property transferred to them as soon as the mortgage is paid off, but if she does not do so, then the building society will claim the instalments from the father's estate and the estate will have to pay them. I cannot think that in those circumstances the estate would be bound to transfer the house to them, any more than the father himself would have been. . . .

In the present case it is clear that the father expressly promised the couple that the property should belong to them as soon as the mortgage was paid, and impliedly promised that, so long as they paid the instalments to the building society, they should be allowed to remain in possession. They were not purchasers because they never bound themselves to pay the instalments, but nevertheless they were in a position analogous to purchasers. They have acted on the promise and neither the father nor his widow, his successor in title, can eject them in disregard of it. The result is that, in my opinion, the appeal should be dismissed and no order for possession should be made. I come to this conclusion on a different ground from that reached by the learned judge, but it is always open to a respondent to support the judgment on any ground. If there is a dispute between the son and the daughter-in-law as to their respective rights in the house, that must be decided under s. 17 of the Married Women's Property Act, 1882. If the father's widow should cease to pay the rates, the actual occupier must pay them, because the father did not bind himself to pay them. He only did so out of paternal affection.

[The concurring opinions of Somervell and Hodson L.JJ. are omitted.]

DAWSON v. HELICOPTER EXPLORATION CO. LTD.
British Columbia. Supreme Court of Canada. [1955] 5 D.L.R. 404

Dawson, an American citizen, had been negotiating by mail with Kidd and Springer, in Vancouver, an arrangement to get at some mineral deposits at the head of Leduc River in British Columbia, in very rough country, which Dawson had discovered twenty years earlier. On January 13, 1951, Dawson wrote "A large mining company in Salt Lake is showing a definite interest. To protect my interest, it will be necessary for me to arrive at some definite arrangement soon." Springer replied on January 17, "I would be interested in making some arrangement next summer to finance you in staking claims for which we would give you an interest. I would suggest that we should pay for your time and expenses and carry you for a ten per cent non-assessable interest in the claims." Dawson replied on January 22. "Your proposition . . . appeals to me as being a fair one. . . ."

Thereafter Dawson was recalled to active duty in the United States Naval Reserve Engineering Corps, and sent to the Marshall Islands. Correspondence continued under rather difficult conditions, and on February 28 Dawson wrote, "As I informed you in a previous letter, your offer of a 10% non-assessable interest for relocating and finding these properties is acceptable to me, provided there is a definite arrangement to this effect in the near future." On March 5, Springer wrote, "I hereby agree that, if you take us in to the showings and we think they warrant staking, that we will stake the claims and give you a 10% non-assessable interest. The claims would be recorded in our name and we will have full discretion in dealing with them—you to get 10% of the vendor interest." Dawson replied on April 12, "If you will inform me, if and when you obtain a pilot for your copter, I will immediately take steps for a temporary release in order to be on hand." Dawson wrote again, on May 27, "Would like to know if your plans for further exploration work in the Unuk River area have become definite. . . . For me to get away from my present duties on a furlough it may be necessary for me to have several weeks notice."

On June 7, Springer wrote:

"Up to a little over a week ago it did not look as though we would be able to secure a pilot for our helicopter. However, we have a man now who we hope will be satisfactory.

"I was talking to Tom McQuillan, who is prospecting for us this year; he said he had been over your showings at the head of the Leduc River, and in his opinion it would be practically impossible to operate there, as the showings were in behind ice fields, which along with the extreme snow falls made it very doubtful if an economic operation could be carried on.

"We have also been delayed in getting away this year, due to pilot trouble, and have so much work lined up that I am doubtful whether we will have time to visit your showings, also I do not think we would be warranted in making the effort to get in there due to the unfavorable conditions. I must advise you therefore, not to depend on our making this trip, and suggest if you are still determined to go in, to make other arrangements."

Dawson did not reply. In 1952 he discovered that the Helicopter Company had made investigations and in 1953 arrangements were made for development by the company to which Springer had sold the claims in exchange for paid up stock. Dawson commenced this action in November, 1953, and his claim was dismissed by the trial Judge, who was affirmed by the British Columbia Court of Appeal.

RAND J.: . . . The substantial contention of the respondent is that any offer contained in the correspondence and in particular the letter of March 5th called for an acceptance not by promise but by performance of an act, the location of the claims by Dawson for the respondent. It is based upon the well-known conception which in its simplest form is illustrated by the case of a reward offered for some act to be done. To put it in other words, no intention was conveyed by Springer when he said "I hereby agree" that Dawson, if agreeable, should have replied "I hereby accept" or words to that effect: the offer called for and awaited only the act to be done and would remain revocable at any time until every element of that act had been completed.

The error in this reasoning is that such an offer contemplates acts to be performed by the person only to whom it is made and in respect of which the offeror remains passive, and that is not so here. What Dawson was to do was to proceed to the area with Springer or persons acting for him by means of the respondent's helicopter and to locate the showings. It was necessarily implied by Springer that he would participate in his own proposal. This involved his promise that he would do so, and that the answer to the proposal would be either a refusal or a promise on the part of Dawson to a like participation. The offer was unconditional but contemplated a performance subject to the condition that a pilot could be obtained by the respondent.

Dawson's answer of April 12th was, as I construe it, similarly an unqualified promissory acceptance, subject as to performance to his being able to obtain the necessary leave. It was the clear implication that Springer, controlling the means of making the trip, should fix the time and should notify Dawson accordingly. As the earlier letters show, Dawson was anxious to conclude some arrangement and if he could not make it with Springer he would seek it in other quarters.

Although in the circumstances, because the terms proposed involve such complementary action on the part of both parties as to put the implication beyond doubt, the precept is not required, this interpretation of the correspondence follows the tendency of Courts to treat offers as calling for bilateral rather than unilateral action when the language can be fairly so construed, in order that the transaction shall have such "business efficacy as both parties must have intended that at all events it should have": Bowen L.J. in The "Moorcock" (1889), 14 P.D. 64 at p. 68. In theory and as conceded by Mr. Guild, an offer in the unilateral sense can be revoked up to the last moment before complete performance. At such a consequence many Courts have balked; and it is in part that fact that has led to a promissory construction where that can be reasonably given. What is effectual is the real intention of both parties to close a business bargain on the strength of which they may, thereafter, plan their courses. . . .

ESTEY J.: . . . It is contended that the appellant's silence, after his receipt of the letter of June 7, 1951, until his interview in December, 1952, constitutes an abandonment of the contract. . . .

The letter of repudiation is dated June 7, 1951, and during the next month Kvale and McQuillan were taken into the area by helicopter. They were again taken into the area where, on August 2nd of that year, they staked a number of claims which were duly recorded. The record does not indicate when respondent changed its mind as indicated by Springer's remark to appellant at its office in December, 1952, but it is apparent that many of the difficulties emphasized in the letter of June 7th had either disappeared or been overcome by the following month. Upon this record it rather appears that the respondent concluded it could continue without assistance from the appellant and, therefore, wrote the letter of repudiation.

The respondent, in this letter of repudiation, set forth its reasons therefor which it would be difficult for the appellant, stationed as he was in the Marshall Islands, to effectively appraise. I do not think that under such circumstances a conclusion adverse to the appellant can be drawn from his failure to further press the respondent at that time. Immediately upon his return in December, 1950, he "wrote to the Mining Recorder at Prince Rupert" and apparently continued his examination to ascertain what had, in fact, taken place. He visited the premises in June and July, 1950, and relocated the three claims which he had found in 1931. When he had ascertained, at least in part, what had taken place, he made his position known to the respondent in December of 1952. Moreover, while silence may be evidence of repudiation, its weight must depend upon the circumstances and here I do not think his silence, coupled with the steps he took immediately upon his return from the Marshall Islands, sufficiently supports a conclusion that he, at any time, intended to abandon his rights under the contract.

Upon receipt of the letter of repudiation dated June 7, 1951, the appellant might have accepted it and forthwith claimed damages. Since, however, he did not accept it, the contract remained in force and binding upon both parties. It, therefore, remained the duty of the respondent, having obtained a pilot, to take the appellant into the area in August or September. Not only did the respondent not do so, but, notwithstanding the terms of its letter of repudiation, it, in fact, took Kvale and McQuillan into the area where they staked claims on behalf of the respondent. This conduct constituted a breach of its contract.

The appeal should be allowed with costs throughout and the matter referred back to the Supreme Court of British Columbia to determine the damages.

[Kerwin C.J. dissented. Cartwright J. concurred with Estey J. and Fauteux J. concurred with Rand J.]

RESTATEMENT OF CONTRACTS (SECOND), Tentative Draft, American Law Institute, 1964

24. Option Contracts.
An option contract is a promise which meets the requirements for the formation of a contract and limits the promisor's power to revoke an offer.
31. Invitation of Promise or Performance.
In case of doubt an offer is interpreted as inviting the offeree to accept either by promising to perform what the offeror requests or by rendering the performance, as the offeree chooses.
45. Option Contract created by Part Performance or Tender.
   (1) Where an offer invites an offeree to accept by rendering a performance and does not invite a promissory acceptance, an option contract is

created when the offeree begins the invited performance or tenders part of it.

(2) The offeror's duty of performance under any option contract so created is conditional on completion or tender of the invited performance in accordance with the terms of the offer.

63. Effect of Performance by Offeree where Offer invites either Performance or Promise.

(1) Where an offer invites an offeree to choose between acceptance by promise and acceptance by performance, the beginning of the invited performance or a tender of part of it is an acceptance by performance.

(2) Such an acceptance operates as a promise to render complete performance.

UNIFORM COMMERCIAL CODE
American Law Institute, 1962

2-206. Offer and Acceptance in Formation of Contract.

(1) Unless otherwise unambiguously indicated by the language or circumstances

(a) an offer to make a contract shall be construed as inviting acceptance in any manner and by any medium reasonable in the circumstances;

(b) an order or other offer to buy goods for prompt or current shipment shall be construed as inviting acceptance either by a prompt promise to ship or by the prompt or current shipment of conforming or non-conforming goods, but such a shipment of non-conforming goods does not constitute an acceptance if the seller seasonably notifies the buyer that the shipment is offered only as an accommodation to the buyer.

(2) Where the beginning of a requested performance is a reasonable mode of acceptance an offeror who is not notified of acceptance within a reasonable time may treat the offer as having lapsed before acceptance.

NOTE. There are problems in fitting together these sections of the Restatement and the Uniform Commercial Code. See Murray, "Contracts —A New Design for the Agreement Process" (1968), 53 Cornell L.R. 785.

CHAPTER 3

THIRD PARTY BENEFICIARIES

TWEDDLE v. ATKINSON
England. Queen's Bench, 1861. 1 B. & S. 393; 121 E.R. 762

The declaration stated that the plaintiff was the son of John Tweddle, deceased and before the making of the agreement hereafter mentioned, married the daughter of William Guy, deceased; and before the marriage the parents of the parties to the marriage orally promised to give the plaintiff a marriage portion; and after the marriage in order to give effect to their promises the parents entered into the following written agreement for the plaintiff's benefit:

"High Coniscliffe, July 11, 1855.
Memorandum of agreement made this day between William Guy, of, &c., of the one part, and John Tweddle, of, &c., of the other part. Whereas it is mutually agreed that the said William Guy shall and will pay the sum of £200 to William Tweddle, his son-in-law; and the said John Tweddle, father to the aforesaid William Tweddle, shall and will pay the sum of £100 to the said William Tweddle, each and severally the said sums on or before the 21st day of August, 1855. And it is hereby further agreed by the aforesaid William Guy and the said John Tweddle that the said William Tweddle has full power to sue the said parties in any court of law or equity for the aforesaid sum, hereby promised and specified."

The declaration further alleged that afterwards and before this suit, the plaintiff and his said wife, who is still living, ratified and assented to the said agreement, yet neither the said William Guy nor his executor has paid the promised sum of £200. Demurrer and joinder therein.

CROMPTON J.: It is admitted that the plaintiff cannot succeed unless this case is an exception to the modern and well-established doctrine of the action of assumpsit. At the time when the cases which have been cited were decided the action of assumpsit was treated as an action of trespass upon the case, and therefore in the nature of a tort; and the law was not settled, as it now is, that natural love and affection is not a sufficient consideration for a promise upon which an action may be maintained; nor was it settled that the promisee cannot bring an action unless the consideration for the promise moved from him. The modern cases have, in effect, overruled the old decisions; they show that the consideration must move from the party entitled to sue upon the contract. It would be a monstrous proposition to say that a person was a party to the contract for the purpose of suing upon it for his own advantage and not a party to it for the purpose of being sued. It is said that the father in the present case was agent for the son in making the contract, but that argument ought also to make the son liable upon it. I am prepared to overrule the old decisions, and to hold that, by reason of the principles which now govern the action of assumpsit, the present action is not maintainable.

[Judgment was given for the defendant. The concurring opinions of Wightman and Blackburn JJ. are omitted.]

DRIVE YOURSELF HIRE CO. LTD. v. STRUTT
[1954] 1 Q.B. 250, at 273-4.

DENNING L.J.: In 1861 . . . came the unfortunate case of *Tweddle* v.
Atkinson in which the Court of Queen's Bench departed from the law
as it had been understood for the previous 200 years and held, quite
generally, that no stranger could take advantage of a contract though
made for his benefit: and that was assumed, without argument, to be the
law by the House of Lords in *Dunlop Pneumatic Tyre Co. Ltd.* v. *Selfridge
& Co. Ltd.* I do not pause to consider whether this new rule was legiti-
mately introduced into the law. Incidentally, the courts of the United
States have not adopted this new rule. They have followed the original
common law, which is much more in accord with the needs of a civilised
society. So is the Scots law.

BESWICK v. BESWICK
[1966] 1 Ch. 549 (C.A.); [1968] A.C. 70 (H.L.)

LORD DENNING M.R.: Old Peter Beswick was a coal merchant in Eccles,
Lancashire. He had no business premises. All he had was a lorry, scales
and weights. He used to take the lorry to the yard of the National Coal
Board, where he bagged coal and took it round to his customers in the
neighbourhood. His nephew, John Joseph Beswick, helped him in the
business.

In March, 1962, old Peter Beswick and his wife were both over 70. He
had had his leg amputated and was not in good health. The nephew was
anxious to get hold of the business before the old man died. So they went
to a solicitor, Mr. Ashcroft, who drew up an agreement for them. The
business was to be transferred to the nephew: old Peter Beswick was to
be employed in it as a consultant for the rest of his life at £6 10s. a week.
After his death the nephew was to pay to his widow an annuity of £5 per
week, which was to come out of the business. The agreement was quite
short and I will read it in full:

"1. Peter Beswick to assign to John Joseph Beswick the goodwill, motor
lorry, scales, weights and other trade utensils of the business of a coal
merchant hitherto carried on by him in consideration of the transferee
employing the transferor as consultant to the said business for the remainder of the transferor's life at a weekly salary of £6 10s.   2. For the like
consideration the transferee, in the event of the death of the transferor,
to pay to the transferor's widow an annuity to be charged on the said
business at the rate of £5 per week.   3. The transferee not to sell the said
business in any way freed from his liability to the transferor, which
liability shall cease only on the death of the survivor of them the transferor
and his said widow.   4. The agreement between the parties to be deemed
for all purposes to have commenced to operate as from March 2, 1962.
5. The transferor to be free to devote only such time to the conduct of the
said business as he shall find convenient or shall at his own absolute
discretion decide.   6. For the consideration aforesaid the transferee to take
over the transferor's liability to the following creditors of the transferor:
George and Lydia Turner in the sum of £187, Joseph Beswick in the
sum of £250 or such lesser sums as shall be agreed with the said creditors
whether by compounding or otherwise."

After the agreement was signed, the nephew took over the business and
ran it. The old man seems to have found it difficult at first to adjust

to the new situation, but he settled down. The nephew paid him £6 10s. a week. But, as expected, he did not live long. He died on November 3, 1963, leaving his widow, who was 74 years of age and in failing health. The nephew paid her the first £5. But he then stopped paying her and has refused to pay her any more.

On June 30, 1964, the widow took out letters of administration to her husband's estate. On July 15, 1964, she brought an action against the nephew for the promised £5 a week. She sued in the capacity of administratrix of the estate of Peter Beswick, deceased, and in her personal capacity she claimed £175 arrears and a declaration. By amendment she claimed specific performance and the appointment of a receiver. The action came for hearing before the Vice-Chancellor of the County Palatine of Lancaster, who held that she had no right to enforce the agreement. He dismissed the action.

If the decision of the Vice-Chancellor truly represents the law of England, it would be deplorable. It would mean that the nephew could keep the business to himself, and at the same time repudiate his promise to pay the widow. Nothing could be more unjust. I am sure the Vice-Chancellor would have decided in favour of the widow if he had not felt himself bound by the decision of Wynn-Parry J. in *In re Miller's Agreement*, [1947] Ch. 615. That case is cited in the textbooks as if it were the last word on the subject: see Anson on Contracts, 22nd ed. (1964) p. 381; Cheshire and Fifoot on Contracts, 5th ed. (1960), p. 377. It is very like this case. So we must examine it with some care. In *In re Miller's Agreement* there were three partners. One of them had retired and transferred his interest to the other two. By a deed of covenant made by the three partners, the two continuing partners agreed to pay the retiring partner £5,000 a year during his life, and after his death to pay £1,000 a year to his three daughters during their lives. The two continuing partners also charged their interest in the firm with payment of those sums. The Revenue authorities claimed that estate duty was payable on the annuities payable to the daughters. That depended on whether the daughters had such an interest in property as would be protected in a court of law or equity. Wynn-Parry J. held that they had no such interest. "At common law," he said, "so far as the plaintiffs" (the daughters) "are concerned, the deed is res inter alios acta, and they have no right thereunder." As to section 56 of the Law of Property Act, 1925, "the section," he said, "has not the effect of creating rights, but only of assisting the protection of rights shown to exist." As to the charge: "The central function of a charge is to secure the performance of an obligation, and the charge is essentially ancillary." He concluded: "I cannot find . . . that the deed confers upon any of the daughters any right to sue . . .the payments, if and when made, will be no more than voluntary payments. . . ." He held, accordingly, that estate duty was not payable on the daughters' annuities.

I can understand the desire of the judge in that case to save the daughters from death duties, but I cannot subscribe to the way he did it. He was wrong in saying that the daughters had no enforceable interest. We have here the standard pattern of a contract for the benefit of a third person. A man has a business or other assets. He transfers them to another and, instead of taking cash, takes a promise by that other that he will pay an annuity or other sum to his widow or children. Can the transferee take the assets and reject the promise? I think not. In my opinion a contract such as this, for the benefit of widow and children, is binding. The party who makes the promise must honour it, unless he has some good reason why he should not do so. He may, for instance, be able to say that the contract should be rescinded as being induced by fraud or misrepresentation, or that it was varied or rescinded by agreement between the parties, before the widow or children knew about it and adopted it. But unless he has some good reason, he is bound. The executor of the dead man can sue to enforce it on behalf of the widow and children. The widow and children can join with the executor as plaintiffs in the action. If he refuses to sue they may sue in their own names joining him as a defendant. In this way they have a right which can be enforced. I will prove this by reference to the common law, reinforced by equity, and now by statute.

1. The Common Law

The common law on this subject was much considered in *Dutton* v. *Poole*, (1678) T. Raym. 302, in 1678. It was regarded at the time as a case of great consequence and is reported by no less than five of the old reporters. It was similar in principle to our present case. The facts were these: Sir Edward Poole owned timber trees in a wood in Oaksey Park, Wiltshire. He had several children, including his son and heir, Nevil, and a daughter Grizel. Sir Edward proposed to cut down the trees and sell them so as to raise portions for the younger children. The eldest son did not want him to do this, because he was the heir and would inherit the trees if they were left standing. There was a meeting between the father and mother and the eldest son. The son asked the father not to cut down the trees, and promised him that, if he did not cut them down, he would pay £1,000 to the daughter Grizel. In reliance on the promise, the father did not cut down any of the trees, and died. The eldest son inherited and had the benefit of them. The daughter Grizel (who had married Sir Ralph Dutton) claimed £1,000 from the eldest son. He refused to pay it to her.

The mother was the executrix of the father's estate. She could as executrix have sued to enforce the agreement. But she was the only person present when it was made, and if she brought the action, she would not be a competent witness. So the daughter and her husband themselves sued the eldest son for the £1,000. In that action the mother was a competent witness. She proved the agreement, and the plaintiffs obtained judgment for £1,000. The eldest son appealed to the Court of King's Bench sitting in banc. The case was argued twice. John Holt appeared for the eldest son. He said that the action ought to be brought by the father's executor for the benefit of the daughter; and not by the daughter herself, as she was "not privy to the promise nor consideration." Pollexsen appeared for the daughter. He said that the action was maintainable either by the party to whom the promise was made, or by the daughter. When the case was first argued, two of the four judges were disposed to accept Holt's argument and hold that the daughter could not sue. But at the second argument Scroggs C.J. with his three brethren all held that the daughter could sue, "for the son hath the benefit by having of the wood, and the daughter hath lost her portion by this means." The eldest son appealed to the Court of Exchequer Chamber, but the appeal was dismissed.

Two things appear from that case: First, it was accepted on all hands that the father's executrix could have sued for the benefit of the daughter.

Second, that in the special circumstances of that case (when a party could not give evidence), the daughter herself could sue on the contract although she was not a party to it. It was a decision of the Court of Exchequer Chamber and has never been overruled. It was approved by Lord Mansfield himself in 1776 who thought it so plain that "it is matter of surprise how a doubt could have arisen in that case." I know that in the 19th century some judges said that it was wrongly decided, but the criticsm is not merited. It would have been shocking if the daughter had been refused a remedy.

The case of *Tweddle* v. *Atkinson* is readily distinguishable. John Tweddle married Miss Guy. After the marriage the two fathers of the young couple made an agreement between themselves, the two fathers, to pay these sums: The husband's father promised to pay his son £100: the wife's father promised to pay his son-in-law £200: such payments to be made on or before August 21, 1855. Clearly the payments were to be mutual for the benefit of the young couple. Neither of the fathers made the promised payments: and afterwards both fathers died. Then the young husband sued the executor of his wife's father for the £200. The action failed for the very good reason that the husband's father had not done his part. He had not paid his promised £100. The son could not himself be sued for his father's failure to pay the £100: for he was no party to the contract. So he could not be allowed to sue his wife's father for the £200. Crompton J. said: "It would be a monstrous proposition to say that a person was a party to the contract for the purpose of suing upon it for his own advantage, and not a party to it for the purpose of being sued." But if the husband's father had paid his £100 and thus wholly performed his part, then the husband's father in his lifetime, or his executor after his death, could have sued the wife's father or his executor for the £200. As Wightman J. observed: "If the father of the plaintiff had paid the £100 which he promised, might not he have sued the father of the plaintiff's wife on his express promise?" To which the answer would undoubtedly be: "Yes, he could sue and recover the £200," but he would recover it not for his own benefit, or for the benefit of the estate, but for the benefit of the son.

Those two cases give the key at common law to the whole problem of contracts for the benefit of a third person. Although the third person cannot as a rule sue alone in his own name, nevertheless there is no difficulty whatever in the one contracting party suing the other party for breach of the promise. The third person should, therefore, bring the action in the name of the contracting party, just as an assignee used to do. Face to face with the contracting party, the defaulter has no defence. He is sued by one who has provided consideration and to whom he has given his promise to pay the third person. He has broken his promise and must pay damages. The defaulter sometimes seeks to say that the contracting party can only recover nominal damages because it is not he but the third person who has suffered the damage. The common law has never allowed the defaulter to escape by such a shifty means. It holds that the contracting party can recover the money which should have been paid to the third person. He can get judgment for the sum and issue a writ of fi. fa. or other machinery to enforce payment: but when he recovers it, he holds the proceeds for the benefit of the third person. He cannot retain the money himself because it belongs to the third person and not to him: see *In re Schebsman, Ex parte the Official Solicitor, the Trustee. Cargo*

Superintendents (London) Ltd. v. *Schebsman* [1944] Ch. 83. It is money had and received to the use of the third person. In *Robertson* v. *Wait*, (1853) 8 Exch. 299 Martin B. said: "If a person makes a contract whereby another obtains a benefit, why may not the former sue for it?" And in *Lloyd's* v. *Harper*, (1880) 16 Ch. D. 290, Lush L.J. said: "I consider it to be an established rule of law that where a contract is made with A for the benefit of B, A can sue on the contract for the benefit of B and recover all that B could have recovered if the contract had been made with B himself."

Such was the position at common law if the action was brought in the name of the contracting party by himself alone. But nowadays when joinder of parties is freely permissible, it is far better for the contracting party and the third person to join as co-plaintiffs. Judgment will be given for the plaintiffs for the amount: and on payment, it will go at once to the third person who is entitled to it.

2. *Equity*

Sometimes one of the contracting parties makes the contract on trust for the third person, in this sense, that from the very beginning the right to sue is vested in him as trustee for the third person as beneficiary. Such a contract is different from those we are considering. It cannot be rescinded or varied except with the consent of the third person beneficiary: see *In re Empress Engineering Co.*, (1880) 16 Ch. D 125. In such a case it is clearly established that the third person himself can sue in equity to enforce the contract: . . . but even so, he ought as a rule to join the trustee as a party. Here we have a case where there is admittedly no trust of the contractual right. Peter Beswick and his nephew might by agreement before his death have rescinded or varied the agreement, if they so wished. Nevertheless, although there is no trust, I do not think equity is powerless. It has in its hands the potent remedy of ordering a party specifically to perform his contract. If a party makes a promise to pay money to a third person, I see no reason why a court of equity should not order him to perform his promise. The action must be brought, of course, in the name of the other contracting party; but, that being done, there is no bar to a decree for specific performance being made. True it is for the payment of money, but a court of equity often decrees specific performance of a promise to pay money. It can enforce it by the appointment of a receiver, or other appropriate machinery. We have been referred to three cases where this has been done, although there was no trust. The first is *Keenan* v. *Handley*, (1864) 13 W.R. 930. Ellen Keenan was the mistress of Captain Handley. They lived as Mr. and Mrs. Coverdale and had a baby daughter called Lucy Coverdale. Captain Handley wrote this letter to Miss Keenan: "I will allow you £150 a year, to be continued to you while you live and to your child after your death, should she survive you." She and her daughter sued for specific performance. Kindersley V.-C. granted it. He ordered deeds to be executed for payment of the annuities, including the amounts to the daughter, although she was not a party to the agreement. The next case is *Peel* v. *Peel*, (1869) 17 W.R. 586, William Peel was in financial difficulty. His brother Edmund Peel agreed with his cousin, Sir Robert Peel, that Edmund would pay off William's debts and that Sir Robert would during his life pay William an annuity of £164 a year. Edmund paid off the debts but Sir Robert Peel did not

pay the amounts. Edmund Peel and William Peel sued for specific performance. James V.-C. granted it. He ordered Sir Robert to pay William
Peel £164 a year, although William was not a party to the agreement. The
third case is *Hohler* v. *Aston*, [1920] 2 Ch. 420, where Mrs. Aston agreed
with her nephew, Mr. Hohler, to make provision for her niece and her
husband, Mr. and Mrs. Rollo. Mrs. Aston died before doing so. Mr.
Hohler and Mr. and Mrs. Rollo sued the executors for specific performance. Sargant J. granted it. He said: "Mr. E. T. Hohler was entitled, and
is now entitled, to enforce for the benefit of the third parties, Mr. and Mrs.
Rollo, a contract made with Mrs. Aston for those third parties. The
third parties, of course, cannot themselves enforce a contract made for
their benefit, but the person with whom the contract is made is entitled
to enforce the contract."
  These cases in equity fit in exactly with the common law. The contracting party is entitled by himself alone, or jointly with the third person,
to have the contract performed according to its terms, and the court will
decree specific performance of it. . . .

  [Lord Denning then examined s. 56(1) of the Law of Property Act,
1925 (U.K.).]

4. *Conclusion*

  The general rule undoubtedly is that "no third person can sue, or be
sued, on a contract to which he is not a party": but at bottom that is
only a rule of procedure. It goes to the form of remedy, not to the underlying right. Where a contract is made for the benefit of a third person who
has a legitimate interest to enforce it, it can be enforced by the third
person in the name of the contracting party or jointly with him or, if he
refuses to join, by adding him as a defendant. In that sense, and it is a
very real sense, the third person has a right arising by way of contract.
He has an interest which will be protected by law. The observations to
the contrary in *In re Miller's Agreement* and *Green* v. *Russell* [1959] 2
Q.B. 226 are in my opinion erroneous. It is different when a third person
has no legitimate interest, as when he is seeking to enforce the maintenance
of prices to the public disadvantage, as in *Dunlop Pneumatic Tyre Co. Ltd.*
v. *Selfridge & Co. Ltd.*, [1915] A.C. 847: or when he is seeking to rely,
not on any right given to him by the contract, but on an exemption clause
seeking to exempt himself from his just liability. He cannot set up an
exemption clause in a contract to which he was not a party: see *Midland
Silicones Ltd.* v. *Scruttons Ltd.*, [1962] A.C. 446.
  The widow here sues in her capacity as executrix of her husband's
estate (and therefore as contracting party), and also in her personal
capacity (and therefore as a third person). This joint claim is clearly
good. She is entitled to an order for specific performance of the agreement,
by ordering the defendant to pay the arrears of £175, and the instalments of £5 a week as they fall due. The order for paying the arrears
of £175 is equivalent to a judgment for that sum and can be enforced by
fi. fa. or other appropriate machinery: see R.S.C. Ord. 42, r. 3. When
the money is recovered, it will go to the widow for her own benefit, and not
to her husband's estate. I would allow the appeal accordingly.
  [The nephew appealed to the House of Lords.]

LORD REID: My Lords, before 1962 the respondent's deceased husband carried on business as a coal merchant. By agreement of March 14, 1962, he assigned to his nephew, the appellant, the assets of the business and the appellant undertook first to pay him £6 10s. per week for the remainder of his life and then to pay to the respondent an annuity of £5 per week in the event of her husband's death. The husband died in November, 1963. Thereupon, the appellant made one payment of £5 to the respondent but he refused to make any further payment to her. The respondent now sues for £175 arrears of the annuity and for an order for specific performance of the continuing obligation to pay the annuity. The Vice-Chancellor of the County Palatine of Lancaster decided against the respondent but the Court of Appeal reversed this decision and, besides ordering payment of the arrears, ordered the appellant to pay to the respondent for the remainder of her life an annuity of £5 per week in accordance with the agreement.

It so happens that the respondent is administratrix of the estate of her deceased husband and she sues both in that capacity and in her personal capacity. So it is necessary to consider her rights in each capacity.

For clarity I think it best to begin by considering a simple case where, in consideration of a sale by A to B, B agrees to pay the price of £1,000 to a third party X. Then the first question appears to me to be whether the parties intended that X should receive the money simply as A's nominee so that he would hold the money for behoof of A and be accountable to him for it, or whether the parties intended that X should receive the money for his own behoof and be entitled to keep it. That appears to me to be a question of construction of the agreement read in light of all the circumstances which were known to the parties. There have been several decisions involving this question. I am not sure that any conflicts with the view which I have expressed: but if any does, . . . I would not agree with it. I think that *In re Schebsman* was rightly decided and that the reasoning of Uthwatt J. and the Court of Appeal supports what I have just said. In the present case I think it clear that the parties to the agreement intended that the respondent should receive the weekly sums of £5 in her own behoof and should not be accountable to her deceased husband's estate for them. Indeed the contrary was not argued.

Reverting to my simple example the next question appears to me to be: Where the intention was that X should keep the £1,000 as his own, what is the nature of B's obligation and who is entitled to enforce it? It was not argued that the law of England regards B's obligation as a nullity, and I have not observed in any of the authorities any suggestion that it would be a nullity. There may have been a time when the existence of a right depended on whether there was any means of enforcing it, but today the law would be sadly deficient if one found that, although there is a right, the law provides no means for enforcing it. So this obligation of B must be enforceable either by X or by A. I shall leave aside for the moment the question whether section 56 (1) of the Law of Property Act, 1925, has any application to such a case, and consider the position at common law.

Lord Denning's view, expressed in this case not for the first time, is that X could enforce this obligation. But the view more commonly held in recent times has been that such a contract confers no right on X and that X could not sue for the £1,000. Leading counsel for the respondent based his case on other grounds, and as I agree that the respondent succeeds on other grounds, this would not be an appropriate case in which to solve this question. It is true that a strong Law Revision Committee recommended so long ago as 1937 (Cmd. 5449): "That where a contract by its express terms purports to confer a benefit directly on a third party it shall be enforceable by the third party in his own name. . ."(p. 31). And, if one had to contemplate a further long period of Parliamentary procrastination, this House might find it necessary to deal with this matter. But if legislation is probable at any early date I would not deal with it in a case where that is not essential. So for the purposes of this case I shall proceed on the footing that the commonly accepted view is right.

What then is A's position? I assume that A has not made himself a trustee for X, because it was not argued in this appeal that any trust has been created. So, if X has no right, A can at any time grant a discharge to B or make some new contract with B. If there were a trust the position would be different. X would have an equitable right and A would be entitled and, indeed, bound to recover the money and account for it to X. And A would have no right to grant a discharge to B. If there is no trust and A wishes to enforce the obligation, how does he set about it? He cannot sue B for the £1,000 because under the contract the money is not payable to him, and, if the contract were performed according to its terms, he would never have any right to get the money. So he must seek to make B pay X.

The argument for the appellant is that A's only remedy is to sue B for damages for B's breach of contract in failing to pay the £1,000 to X. Then the appellant says that A can only recover nominal damages of 40s. because the fact that X has not received the money will generally cause no loss to A: he admits that there may be cases where A would suffer damage if X did not receive the money but says that the present is not such a case.

Applying what I have said to the circumstances of the present case, the respondent in her personal capacity has no right to sue, but she has a right as administratrix of her husband's estate to require the appellant to perform his obligation under the agreement. He has refused to do so and he maintains that the respondent's only right is to sue him for damages for breach of his contract. If that were so, I shall assume that he is right in maintaining that the administratrix could then only recover nominal damages because his breach of contract has caused no loss to the estate of her deceased husband.

If that were the only remedy available the result would be grossly unjust. It would mean that the appellant keeps the business which he bought and for which he has only paid a small part of the price which he agreed to pay. He would avoid paying the rest of the price, the annuity to the respondent, by paying a mere 40s. damages.

The respondent's first answer is that the common law has been radically altered by section 56 (1) of the Law of Property Act, 1925, and that that section entitles her to sue in her personal capacity and recover the benefit provided for her in the agreement although she was not a party to it. [After an examination of the history of the section, Lord Reid held that it did not have the wide meaning contended for by the widow and accepted by Lord Denning and the majority of the Court of Appeal.]

The respondent's second argument is that she is entitled in her capacity of administratrix of her deceased husband's estate to enforce the provision of the agreement for the benefit of herself in her personal capacity, and that a proper way of enforcing that provision is to order specific performance. That would produce a just result, and, unless there is some technical objection, I am of opinion that specific performance ought to be ordered. For the reasons given by your Lordships I would reject the arguments submitted for the appellant that specific performance is not a possible remedy in this case. I am therefore of opinion that the Court of Appeal reached a correct decision and that this appeal should be dismissed. [The other Lords agreed, in substance, with Lord Reid.]

DUNLOP PNEUMATIC TYRE CO. LTD. v. SELFRIDGE & CO. LTD.
England. House of Lords. [1915] A.C. 847

The facts of this case are shortly stated by Lord Sumner. There are two instances of sale and delivery complained of by Dunlop in this case. The steps in the Jameson transaction are as follows. Those in the other, the Strauss transaction are similar, and need not be analysed. On October 12, 1911, Messrs, Dew & Co., motor accessory factors, contracted with the appellants, the Dunlop Company, in terms of the latter's price maintenance agreement then current. By this contract Dew became bound, inter alia, to buy from the Dunlop Company motor tyres, covers, tubes, and sundries to the net value of £2000 before the expiration of September, 1912, and the appellants became bound, if the contract continued to subsist, as it did, to sell and deliver such goods up to that value, whenever reasonably required to do so.

On December 21, 1911, a Captain Jameson thought fit to ask the respondents, Selfridge's, who are described as wholesale and retail merchants, for their lowest price for a Dunlop motor tyre, grooved and non-skid, 815 by 105. Their answer was that, on receipt of his order, such a tyre would be procured and the price would be £5 18s. 2d., which was the appellants' list price, less 7½ per cent.

On January 1, 1912, Captain Jameson sent to the respondents an order for the tyre, and also the money for it, and on the same day the order was accepted, and delivery of the tyre was promised for the following day. In fact, on January 2 the respondents ordered this tyre from Dew by telephone. Dew, in turn, ordered it by telephone from the appellants; it was delivered by them to Dew, and they sent it to the respondents. These were the events of January 2. On the next day the respondents delivered it to Captain Jameson. Of course, the respondents did not mention Captain Jameson to Dew, nor did Dew mention the respondents to the appellants.

So far the respondents had signed no price maintenance agreement. They had been pressed to do so, and no doubt knew that the reason why they were being pressed by Dew was because the appellants, in turn, strictly required them to obtain these agreements from those of their customers to whom they sold. Within two or three days of January 3 they did sign such an agreement, dating it January 2, and delivering it to Dew, to whom it was addressed, a week or so afterwards. It is for breach of this agreement that the appellants sued.

The parties have been desirous of knowing their reciprocal rights and duties, if any, arising out of this agreement, and have accordingly raised two broad questions: (1.) Is there any agreement between these parties at all? (2.) If so, is there any consideration moving from the appellants to support it and make it bind the respondents to them? But for this there would have been a good deal to be said for the proposition that a bargain and sale, clearly complete before this agreement was signed or dated, could be no breach of it, and that the performance of that bargain by delivery of the goods after the price maintenance agreement was made could hardly be a ground for the grant of an injunction.

Phillimore J. gave judgment for the appellants for £10, the liquidated damages in respect of the two breaches, and granted an injunction restraining the respondents from selling Dunlop motor tyres, etc., below the appellants' current list prices.

The Court of Appeal reversed this decision and gave judgment for the respondents. They held that the contract of January 2 was not a contract between the appellants and the respondents at all, but was a contract between Dew and the respondents only, and that Dew were not legally competent at one and the same time to make a contract with the respondents by themselves as principals and as agents of the appellants. They therefore held that the action was not sustainable.

VISCOUNT HALDANE L.C.: My Lords, in my opinion this appeal ought to fail. . . .

My Lords, in the law of England certain principles are fundamental. One is that only a person who is a party to a contract can sue on it. Our law knows nothing of a jus quaesitum tertio arising by way of contract. Such a right may be conferred by way of property, as, for example, under a trust, but it cannot be conferred on a stranger to a contract as a right to enforce the contract in personam. A second principle is that if a person with whom a contract not under seal has been made is to be able to enforce it consideration must have been given by him to the promisor or to some other person at the promisor's request. These two principles are not recognized in the same fashion by the jurisprudence of certain continental countries or of Scotland, but here they are well established. A third proposition is that a principal not named in the contract may sue upon it if the promisee really contracted as his agent. But again, in order to entitle him so to sue, he must have given consideration either personally or through the promisee, acting as his agent in giving it.

My Lords, in the case before us, I am of opinion that the consideration, the allowance of what was in reality part of the discount of which Messrs. Dew, the promisees, were entitled as between themselves and the appellants, was to be given by Messrs. Dew on their own account, and was not in substance, any more than in form, an allowance made by the appellants. The case for the appellants is that they permitted and enabled Messrs. Dew, with the knowledge and by the desire of the respondents, to sell to the latter on the terms of the contract of January 2, 1912. But it appears to me that even if this is so the answer is conclusive. Messrs. Dew sold to the respondents goods which they had a title to obtain from the appellants independently of this contract. The consideration by way of discount under the contract of January 2 was to come wholly out of Messrs. Dew's pocket, and neither directly nor indirectly out of that of the appellants. If the appellants enabled them to sell to the respondents on the terms they did, this was not done as any part of the terms of the contract sued on.

No doubt it was provided as part of these terms that the appellants should acquire certain rights, but these rights appear on the face of the contract as jura quaesita tertio which the appellants could not enforce. Moreover, even if this difficulty can be got over by regarding the appellants as the principals of Messrs. Dew in stipulating for the rights in question, the only consideration disclosed by the contract is one given by Messrs. Dew, not as their agents, but as principals acting on their own account.

The conclusion to which I have come on the point as to consideration renders it unnecessary to decide the further question as to whether the appellants can claim that a bargain was made in this contract by Messrs. Dew as their agents; a bargain which, apart from the point as to consideration, they could therefore enforce. If it were necessary to express an opinion on this further question, a difficulty as to the position of Messrs. Dew would have to be considered. Two contracts—one by a man on his own account as principal, and another by the same man as agent—may be validly comprised in the same piece of paper. But they must be two contracts, and not one as here. I do not think that a man can treat one and the same contract as made by him in two capacities. He cannot be regarded as contracting for himself and for another uno flatu.

My Lords, the form of the contract which we have to interpret leaves the appellants in this dilemma, that, if they say that Messrs. Dew contracted on their behalf, they gave no consideration, and if they say they gave consideration in the shape of a permission to the respondents to buy, they must set up further stipulations, which are neither to be found in the contract sued upon nor are germane to it, but are really inconsistent with its structure. That contract has been reduced to writing, and it is in the writing that we must look for the whole of the terms made between the parties. These terms cannot, in my opinion, consistently with the settled principles of English law, be construed as giving to the appellants any enforceable rights as against the respondents.

I think that the judgment of the Court of Appeal was right, and I move that the appeal be dismissed with costs.

LORD DUNEDIN.: My Lords, I confess that this case is to my mind apt to nip any budding affection which one might have had for the doctrine of consideration. For the effect of that doctrine in the present case is to make it possible for a person to snap his fingers at a bargain deliberately made, a bargain not in itself unfair, and which the person seeking to enforce it has a legitimate interest to enforce. Notwithstanding these considerations I cannot say that I have ever had any doubt that the judgment of the Court of Appeal was right. . . .

That there are methods of framing a contract which will cause persons in the position of Selfridge to become bound, I do not doubt. But that has not been done in this instance; and as Dunlop's advisers must have known of the law of consideration, it is their affair that they have not so drawn the contract. . . .

[Opinions to the like effect were given by Lords Atkinson, Parker of Waddington, Sumner and Parmoor.]

THE SATANITA
England. Court of Appeal. [1895] P. 248

On July 5, 1894, the Valkyria and the Satanita were manoeuvring to get into position for starting for the fifty mile race at the Mudhook Yacht Club Regatta, when the Satanita ran into and sank the Valkyria.

The entry for the Satanita for the regatta was signed by the defendant, and contained the following clause: "I undertake that, while sailing under this entry, I will obey and be bound by the sailing rules of the Yacht Racing Association and the by-laws of the club."

The rules of the Yacht Racing Association, adopted by the club, provided among other things as follows:

Rule 24: ". . . If a yacht, in consequence of her neglect of any of these rules, shall foul another yacht . . . she shall forfeit all claim to the prize, and shall pay all damages."

The plaintiffs, in an action in personam in the Admiralty Division . . . alleged that by the terms of the entry and in consideration that the owner of the Valkyrie would race with the defendant under these rules, the defendant agreed that if the Satanita fouled the Valkyrie in consequence of her neglect of any of the rules, the Satanita would pay all damages. . . . The defendant denied that he had entered into such agreement as alleged. . . .

LORD ESHER M.R.: This is an action by the owner of a yacht against the owner of another yacht, and, although brought in the Admiralty Division, the contention really is that the yacht which is sued has broken the rules which by her consent governed her sailing in a regatta in which she was contesting for a prize.

The first question raised is whether, supposing her to have broken a rule, she can be sued for that breach of the rules by the owner of the competing yacht which has been damaged; in other words, was there any contract between the owners of those two yachts? Or it may be put thus: Did the owner of the yacht which is sued enter into obligation to the owner of the other yacht, that if his yacht broke the rules, and thereby injured the other yacht, he would pay damages? It seems to me clear that he did; and the way that he has undertaken that obligation is this. A certain number of gentlemen formed themselves into a committee and proposed to give prizes for matches sailed between yachts at a certain place on a certain day, and they promulgated certain rules, and said: "If you want to sail in any of our matches for our prizes, you cannot do so unless you submit yourselves to the conditions which we have thus laid down. And one of the conditions is, that if you do sail for one of such prizes you must enter into an obligation with the owners of the yachts who are competing, which they at the same time enter into similarly with you, that if by a breach of any of our rules you do damage or injury to the owner of a competing yacht, you shall be liable to make good the damage which you have so done." If that is so, then when they do sail, and not till then, that relation is immediately formed between the yacht owners. There are other conditions with regard to these matches which constitute a relation between each of the yacht owners who enters his yacht and sails it and the committee; but that does not in the least do away with what the yacht owner has undertaken, namely, to enter into a relation with the other yacht owners, that relation containing an obligation.

Here the defendant, the owner of the Satanita, entered into a relation with the plaintiff Lord Dunraven, when he sailed his yacht against Lord Dunraven's yacht, and that relation contained an obligation that if, by any breach of any of these rules, he did damage to the yacht of Lord Dunraven, he would have to pay the damages. . . .

[Only that part of the opinion is given that deals with the formation of the contract. Rigby and Lopes L.JJ. gave judgments to the same effect.

Rigby L.J. said, "To whom is the owner of that yacht to pay those damages? He cannot pay them to the club, nor do I think the club could recover them. The true and sensible construction is that he must pay the owner of the yacht fouled." The judgments were affirmed in the House of Lords *sub nomine Clarke* v. *Dunraven*, [1897] A.C. 59.]

MULHOLLAND v. MERRIAM
Ontario. Chancery. 1872. 19 Grant 288

STRONG V.C.: About the 6th of November, 1868, John Mulholland being possessed of a considerable amount in money and securities, the proceeds of the sale of his farm and also of some other property, executed an instrument in a very peculiar form. This document, which was prepared by Philip Green, a schoolmaster, residing in the neighbourhood of the defendant, may be thus described. The first part of it purports to be a bond by the defendant to John Mulholland in the penal sum of $400. What is declared to be the condition is as follows: John Mulholland purports thereby to assign to the defendant "all his estate real and personal, with notes and accounts, to the said William Merriam on condition that he pay his heirs in the manner following, namely," and then follows a direction to pay to each of the living children of John Mulholland except the defendant's wife $400, and the like sum to the children of two deceased daughters. It then contains the following clause: "The said William Merriam hereby becomes bound to pay the above mentioned sums to the parties herein named at the time of the decease of the said John Mulholland, or as soon after as can conveniently be done." A covenant on the part of Merriam to provide a maintenance for John Mulholland during the remainder of his life, completes the document.

This bond or agreement was executed by sealing by both John Mulholland and his son-in-law, the defendant, William Merriam.

The bill is filed by George B. Mulholland one of the sons of John Mulholland, to enforce payment of the $400, which by the instrument set forth was to be paid to him on his father's death, which took place in April, 1870. The defendant by his answer to the original bill alleges in paragraph 7 that he has "in all things fully performed the trusts and covenants in the said bond and agreement on his part to be performed."

At the hearing it was contended for the defendant, in the first place, that there was no jurisdiction; that no trust was created by the agreement, and that there was an absence of any privity, either at law or in equity, between the plaintiff and the defendant, the proper remedy of the instrument being an action at law, to be brought by the personal representative of John Mulholland. . . .

As to the first point raised by the defendant. I have had much doubt and difficulty, for it seemed to me at first that the bond could be considered in legal effect as nothing more than a personal covenant by Merriam the defendant with John Mulholland, and that consequently the only remedy on it could have been action at law by the personal representative of the latter. More mature consideration has led me to think I was wrong in my first impression both as to the proper construction of the instrument, and also as to the consequence which I thought would have attached, if that construction had been correct. . . .

[Strong V.C. then concluded that on the true construction of the document, Merriam was a trustee of the property conveyed to him, and so was bound to account to George, the beneficiary of that trust. The learned judge then went on to consider whether Merriam's promise could be enforced even if there were no trust of the property.]

I think there could be no doubt but that a personal representative of the testator recovering this money in an action at law would be considered as a trustee for the plaintiff, and, if so, it would, I think, follow that the plaintiff can maintain this suit. I quite agree that, in the naked case, where there is a covenant by one person with another to pay a sum of money to a stranger, or do any act for the benefit of a stranger who is not a party to the instrument or agreement, the person to whom the money is to be paid, or who is to be benefited, cannot sue either at law or in equity, inasmuch as there is no privity of contract. . . . There appears, it is true, to be an exception to this general rule recognized in some of the older cases, where it is laid down that the person to receive the benefit of the contract, though a stranger to it, may maintain an action upon it if he stand in such a relationship to the contracting party that it may be considered that the conract was made for his benefit, and in the very case of a contract made with a father to pay money to his son or daughter, it has been held upon this principle that the son or daughter might sue on the contract. . . . *Dutton* v. *Poole* (1678), 83 E.R. 523. . . .

This doctrine is not, however, now approved as regards courts of law, as appears from the late case of *Tweddle* v. *Atkinson* (1861), 121 E.R. 762. This, however, in my opinion, only goes to shew the applicability to a case like the present of a remedy in this Court proceeding on a doctrine which I will endeavour to point out. There can be no doubt, as I have already said, that this $400, if recovered in an action at law by a personal representative of John Mulholland, would not be assets in his hands to be distributed by him according to the *Statute of Distributions*, but would be impressed with a trust in equity in favor of the plaintiff. This *must* be so, for the only other alternative is, that it was in the power of the defendant entirely to defeat any or all of the gifts which the settlor made to his children, by compelling the personal representative to bring an action, the fruits of which would be free from any trust and liable to be distributed amongst the next of kin; which would of course, be absurd.

Then if the money, when recovered by the administrator, would be affected by a trust, it must also be, that the right of action which the personal representative has is also bound by a like trust; and, if this is so, there is the highest authority for saying that, even though the obligation of Merriam rests (as I have already determined it does not) merely on contract, and he should not be bound by any trust, yet, as the personal representative would be a trustee for the plaintiff, he and the plaintiff conjointly might maintain this bill. The authority which I refer to is the case of *Gregory* v. *Williams* (1817), 36 E.R. 224, decided by a very great Judge (Sir William Grant, M.R.), and it is approved by Mr. Spence, who, in his treatise, 2 *Equitable Jurisdiction*, 286, thus states both the case and the principle which it establishes: he says:

"There are instances where a third person has been expressly allowed to treat the party exacting the stipulation as his trustee, though such third person was a mere stranger to the parties. In the case of *Gregory* v. *Williams*, one Parker, who was in the possession of a farm belonging to the defendant Williams, was considerably indebted to Williams; he also owed a large debt to one Gregory. Parker, as Williams knew, was under apprehension that Gregory would arrest him; Williams, the landlord, and Parker, the tenant, entered into an agreement in writing, to which Gregory, the creditor, was neither party nor privy, to the following effect, namely: that, if Parker would make over to Williams all his stock and effects of every kind, he would pay the debt due to Gregory. Gregory subsequently was informed of this arrangement, and he and Parker filed their bill against Williams to enforce it. The stock and effects assigned to Williams by Parker had been sold at a loss; it was insisted by Williams that, if Gregory had any remedy, it was at law. Sir W. Grant considered it was at least doubtful whether Gregory could recover at law, for the engagement of Williams was not made directly to Gregory, but to Parker only, and the consideration was furnished by Parker only, for he alone did the act which constituted the consideration; Gregory was not a party to the contract; however, that learned Judge supported Gregory's right to sue in equity, saying 'Parker acts as his trustee, and Gregory may derive an equitable right through the medium of Parker's agreement, though it was at least questionable whether he could have maintained an action at law; it was like the case where a man promised the widow that, if she would allow his name to be joined with hers in the administration, he would make up the deficiency of the assets for the payment of the testator's debts; which promise was held to be binding in favour of the creditors, though they could not sue at law, as the promise was not made to them; so here, Gregory had a right to insist upon the benefit of the promise made to Parker to the extent of £900, which Parker represented to be the amount of the debt.' "

This case which never appears to have been overruled or even doubted, lays down a reasonable and convenient doctrine applying directly to the present case, and shewing that the plaintiff has an equitable right to enforce the contract (if it is nothing more than a contract) which the defendant entered into with John Mulholland. It is true that in the case of *Gregory* v. *Williams* the quasi trustee, Parker, was a co-plaintiff, and it may be said that a personal representative of the settlor John Mulholland ought to be a party here. But there is no such representative in existence, and if one was constituted it would only be for the express purpose of this suit since all the property of the intestate was made over by this assignment to the defendant, and there are now no assets to administer or debts to pay; and such an administrator would be a mere formal party as a trustee having not the slightest interest. I am therefore perfectly justified in directing as I do under the Consolidated Order 56, that the suit may proceed in the absence of any person representing the estate of John Mulholland.

Therefore in my judgment the suit is maintainable, *first* because the defendant is a trustee under the instrument of the 6th November, 1868, and the plaintiff is one of the *cestuis que trust*; *second*, even though the defendant be not a trustee, and is liable on contract only, the plaintiff has nevertheless an equitable right of suit on the authority of the case referred to. . . . .

LES AFFRETEURS REUNIS SOCIETE ANONYME v. *LEOPOLD WALFORD (LONDON) LIMITED*. [1919] A.C. 801 (England. House of Lords). LORD WRENBURY: ". . . We have here to do with a contract between two parties reserving a benefit to a third. The two parties are the shipowners and the charterers, the third party is the broker of one of them, who is to be remunerated in respect of a contract which is being made for the hire of a ship. The particular form of contract in question is of course prepared by, or is under the eyes of the broker who is negotiating the matter. It is sent to the principals for signature, and they sign it, and there is contained in it a clause which reserves a benefit to the broker. Under those circumstances an action is brought by the broker against the shipowner for the commission which is expressed to be payable to him under the contract between the shipowner and the charterer—a contract to which he himself, I agree, was not a party. By agreement between the parties the record is to be treated as if the charterer were joined as a plaintiff in the action. The case is one in which an action can be brought on behalf of a person to whom a benefit is reserved although he is not a party to it. That is the subject of the decision in *Robertson* v. *Wait*. Under those circumstances the shipowners, the defendants in the action, defend the action and in effect are here saying: "It is perfectly true that we attached our signature to this document; it is perfectly true that it contains in Article 29 this stipulation in favour of a third party; but that means nothing at all—that is not the bargain at all to which we were parties. The matter is governed by a certain custom.'

"My Lords, I feel myself in great difficulty in understanding a contention of that sort. It is said that in this particular business there exists a custom (and I will take it for the moment that the custom is proved) that in time charterparties broker's commission is payable out of hire earned and is not payable unless hire is earned. In this contract, however, there is a stipulation that the commission shall be on the estimated gross amount of hire on signing the charter ship lost or not lost. I find myself quite unable to understand how it can be set up that into a contract expressed in those terms there can be introduced a custom to an exactly contrary effect. Directly it is conceded that the broker, although not a party to the contract, can sue on the contract, inasmuch as he can sue by the charterer as trustee for him, it appears to me that the case really is over. I have only to read Article 29 and I find there an express stipulation—a stipulation which is accepted by the signature of the defendants, that this payment shall be made, and for that payment it appears to me that the defendants are liable. . . ."

NOTE ON THE TRUST CONCEPT. The courts, as the last cases show, sometimes invoke the notion of a "trust" to justify a remedy for the third party beneficiary excluded by *Tweddle* v. *Atkinson*. Trusts are generally the subject of a separate course in the law school curriculum. Meanwhile this short explanation may make the contract cases more intelligible. The explanation is so short, however, and so over simplified, as to be positively dangerous, and you may prefer to read Chapter 1 of Austin Scott, *The Law of Trusts*, which is generally acknowledged to be the modern classic.

You have already seen that, especially in conveyancing contracts, the equity courts will sometimes grant specific performance. The remedy is so available, in fact, that we speak of the purchaser having an equitable interest in the land. The vendor may have the legal title to the land, but since the court will compel him to convey it to the purchaser, that conveyance is anticipated, as it were, and the purchaser's existing interest is recognised. Thus, although the holder of the fee simple is said, sometimes, to have the largest bundle of rights in respect of the land that the law recognises, it may be that he holds very few, especially if, under a registry system, the agreement to convey can be registered so that the whole world will be deemed to know of its existence.

In such circumstances it might be said that the vendor holds the fee subject to the equity of the purchaser, who can, by action, compel him to hand over the title.

A somewhat similar relationship is recognised in the case of mortgages in most jurisdictions of Canada. The mortgagor, who owns real property in fee, pledges the title with the mortgagee to secure the repayment of money within some specified time, in which event the mortgagee to whom the mortgagor has conveyed the title, promises to reconvey. Again, equity would compel specific performance of the promise to reconvey. And again, the mortgagor has an equitable interest although the mortgagee has the legal title. Equity goes much further, in the mortgage cases, because the conveyance to the mortgagee may be subject only to a condition, rather than a promise to reconvey, and in either case, the equity courts would enforce the promise or the condition even after the time for its enforcement within the terms of the "mortgage contract" had passed. The mortgagor may redeem his title and has an "equity of redemption," not unlike the purchaser's "equity of specific performance," although the latter term is not used.

So in the case of a trust, the trustor, or settlor, the author of the trust, conveys the subject, or corpus, of the trust, usually land, to the trustee, who holds the legal title, but for the benefit of the *cestui que trust*, or beneficiary, who has an interest in the land that a court of equity would enforce against the trustee. Equity has long recognised this relationship, and elaborate rules have been built up, defining the duties of the trustee and the rights of the beneficiary. Some appreciation of the difficulty of safely attempting a short explanation of the trust concept can be had from this passage from Maitland's famous lectures on *Equity*, first published in 1910. After commenting on the difficulties of defining a "trust," he says, at p. 44:

"Where judges and text-writers fear to tread professors of law have to rush in. I should define a trust in some such way as the following—When a person has rights which he is bound to exercise on behalf of another or for the accomplishment of some particular purpose he is said to have those rights in trust for that other or for that purpose and he is called a trustee."

Maitland concedes that it is a "wide vague definition, but the best that I can make." He then proceeds to distinguish trusts from other devices of the law, including bailment. It may be helpful as well to look at Scott's attempt to distinguish trusts from contracts, which he presents at page 135 (Vol. 1) of the classic already mentioned.

Usually the subject matter of the trust is a piece of land, or other tangible property but this need not be so, and there is clearly no doubt that it can be a promise, and the promisee can be regarded as holding the right to enforce the promise in trust for the beneficiary of the promise. If the trust is irrevocable, which it would be taken to be if it were not expressly made revocable, then one striking difference from contract is the absence of that freedom with which the parties to contract can agree to alter their positions, or terminate their claims and duties altogether. This difference is perhaps one reason for hesitating, as the English courts seem prone to do, to "imply" a trust in what is rather obviously more like a contract relationship. In most cases neither party will have any such sophisticated and selfconscious intention about how his conduct should be classified, and any decision turning on "intention" is, at best, a judicial view of the "intent of the transaction," rather than of the intent of the parties.

YOUNG v. *CANADIAN NORTHERN RAILWAY CO.* [1931] A.C. 83 (Manitoba. Privy Council). Young was employed by the C.N.R. Company in 1920. He had no written agreement and, after signing an application for employment form, asked what wages he would receive. He was told he would receive the "going rate." There was then in existence a document describing itself as "Wage Agreement 4" the parties to which were, among others, the Company and "Division 4, Railway Employees' Department, American Federation of Labour." On June 13, 1927, Young was laid off although men junior to him were kept on. He contended that the Company was bound to him by the terms of "Wage Agreement 4" certain terms of which secured to him his seniority rights. He was not a member of the union, but it was admitted that as a general rule the Company applied the terms of the Agreement to all employees, irrespective of their membership in the union. Held, for the Company. LORD RUSSELL OF KILLOWEN: "[Wage Agreement No. 4] appears to their Lordships to be intended merely to operate as an agreement between a body of employers and a labour organization by which the employers undertake that as regards their workmen, certain rules beneficial to the workmen shall be observed. By itself it constitutes no contract between any individual employee and the company which employs him. If an employer refused to observe the rules, the effective sequel would be, not an action by any employee, not even an action by Division 4, against the employer for specific performance or damages, but the calling of a strike until the grievance was remedied."

THE LABOUR RELATIONS ACT
Ontario, Revised Statutes, 1970, Chapter 232

42. A collective agreement is, subject to and for the purposes of this Act, binding upon the employer and upon the trade union that is a party to the agreement whether or not the trade union is certified and upon the employees in the bargaining unit defined in the agreement.

RE SCHEBSMAN. [1943] 2 All E.R. 387 (England. High Court). UTHWATT J.: "I was referred to Professor Corbin's interesting article in The Law Quarterly Review, Vol. 46, on 'Contracts for the benefit of third persons' and have considered the cases to which he refers, but I am unable to see that they justify the conclusion at which he arrived that, in some cases of the class now under consideration, a fiction has been resorted to in order to raise a trust. The cases no doubt are hard to reconcile, but, to my mind, the explanation of them is that different minds may reach differing conclusions on the question whether the circumstances sufficiently show an intention to create a trust—and inferences as to intent may vary, as the cases on general charitable intent well show."

NOTE: The notion of a trust of a promise, which found favour in *Mulholland* v. *Merriam* and in the *Walford* case, is clearly capable of making great inroads on the rule denying an action to a third party beneficiary. For if the making of the promise in favour of the third party is in itself sufficient to create a trust, it is always open to a court to hold that the promise is enforceable at the suit of the third party. Even without the promisee's co-operation the third party could succeed, for once a trust is found a court will never allow the rights of a beneficiary to be defeated because of the recalcitrance of the trustee. It was indeed argued by Corbin in the article referred to by Uthwatt J. that the way was open, by means of the concept of trust of a promise, effectively to abolish the rule against third party beneficiaries. As is clear from the extract reproduced above, the suggestion has not been universally accepted.

NOTE. Insurance Legislation in all provinces creates significant exceptions to the rule against third party beneficiaries.

See, for example, Insurance Act R.S.O. 1970 c. 224, ss. 169, 208.

RE SCHEBSMAN
England. Court of Appeal. [1943] 2 All E.R. 768

Schebsman had been employed for some years by La Société Générale de Surveillance S.A., a Swiss Company, and its subsidiary, Cargo Superintendents (London), Ltd., an English company. Schebsman was a spendthrift with a short expectation of life. He was separated from his wife and daughter who were both dependent on him. The companies wanted to make an amicable separation with Schebsman and to that end the English company proposed to pay certain sums to him and after his death to his widow and daughter. Neither Mrs. Schebsman nor her daughter was connected with either company and neither was consulted in the negotiation. Provision was made for the wife and daughter as a "trump card" to get Schebsman to accept the arrangement. Schebsman quit his job on March 31, 1940, and executed the tripartite agreement with the two companies on September 20. He was adjudicated a bankrupt on March 5, 1942 and died on May 12, the same year. According to the agreement the sum now became payable to Mrs. Schebsman and if she died before a certain date, to her daughter.

Schebsman's trustee in bankruptcy claimed a declaration that all sums payable under the agreement formed part of the bankrupt estate. The widow, the daughter and the two companies were made parties to the action. The English company wanted to make payments in accordance with the contract. Uthwatt J. dismissed the motion.

LORD GREENE M.R.: . . . The first question which arises is whether or not Schebsman was a trustee for his wife and daughter of the benefit of the undertaking given by the English company in their favour. An examination of the decided cases does, it is true, show that the courts have on occasions adopted what may be called a liberal view on questions of this character. But in the present case, I cannot find in the contract anything to justify the conclusion that a trust was intended. It is not legitimate to import into the contract the idea of a trust when the parties have given no indication that such was their intention. To interpret this contract as creating a trust would, in my judgment, be to disregard the dividing line between the case of a trust and the simple case of a contract made between two persons for the benefit of a third. That dividing line exists, although it may not always be easy to determine where it is to be drawn. In the present case I find no difficulty. I will now turn to the other questions which arise.

At the outset of his address, counsel for the appellant suggested that the trustee in bankruptcy as claiming through Schebsman could claim all sums paid by the English company to Mrs. Schebsman or her daughter as money had and received to his use. As the discussion proceeded, this argument was abandoned by counsel for the appellant and rightly so. The transaction gave rise to no such privity between these ladies and Schebsman as would support a claim against them for money had and received. It was also conceded that at common law the English company is bound, as between itself and the trustee, to make payments to Mrs. Schebsman or her daughter in accordance with the contract: and that the trustee as claiming through Schebsman has no right at common law to require the company to pay these sums to himself. The contract was tripartite and its terms could only be varied by the consent of all three parties. Mrs. Schebsman and her daughter have, of course, no right to demand payment from the English company since they are not parties to the contract. When the company makes a payment to one of them it is, as between the company and the payee, a gratuitous payment made with the intention of passing the property in the money paid and this is sufficient to give to the payee at common law a good title to the money against the whole world. The question, what damages could be recovered by the representatives of Schebsman if the company were to break its contract has no bearing on anything, that we have to decide.

The argument of counsel for the appellant, as he developed it, rested entirely on equitable principles. It may be summarised as follows. Schebsman provided the whole of the consideration for the English company's undertaking to make the payments to his widow and daughter. These payments must, therefore, be regarded in the same light as voluntary gifts. In the case of a completed transfer of property by a man to his wife or daughter a presumption of advancement arises. But in the present case the transfer was not completed since Mrs. Schebsman and her daughter have no title to demand payment to themselves. It was, therefore, possible for Schebsman in his lifetime and for the trustee as his representative to intervene at any time and to assert as against Mrs. Schebsman and her daughter that any payments thereafter made to either of them would be held by the payee on behalf of the estate of Schebsman. The effect of such intervention, it was said, makes it impossible to treat any money in fact received thereafter by Mrs. Schebsman or her daughter as an advancement. If, notwithstanding the intervention, the company makes a payment to either of them, there will be a resulting trust for the trustee as representing Schebsman. As a corollary to this it was said that, in properly constituted proceedings, the English company can be compelled to make the covenanted payments direct to the trustee. The case, it was said, is analogous to that of an uncompleted gift or that of an imperfectly constituted trust. Mrs. Schebsman and her daughter are mere volunteers and equity will do nothing to assist them.

This argument is attractive, but, in my opinion, fallacious. It is important to bear in mind at the outset that, as between himself and the English company, Schebsman had no right to intervene and direct the company to make the payments to someone other than Mrs. Schebsman or her daughter. As between the three parties to the contract, its terms were that the payments should be made to Mrs. Schebsman and her daughter and made to them, clearly, for their own benefit. If, therefore, Schebsman in his lifetime had directed the company to make these payments to his executors, the company would have been entitled to ignore the direction. The proposition that, in properly constituted proceedings, the trustee could obtain direct payment to himself, depends for its validity upon the truth of the proposition that, as between himself and Mrs. Schebsman and her daughter the trustee is entitled to claim the money as his own. The former proposition cannot, therefore, be relied on in order to establish the latter proposition which must be made good, if at all, on its own merits. Indeed the former proposition relates to procedure only and means nothing more than that, if A is proposing to pay money to B which as between B and C belongs in equity to C, C can join A as a defendant in his action against B and thus procure payment by A direct to himself. It throws no light on the question which, for our purposes, is the relevant one, namely as between B and C, does the money belong in equity to C?

We must, therefore, consider the position as between Schebsman and his wife and daughter. I do not think that any help is obtained by considering the cases of uncompleted gifts or imperfectly constituted trusts. Indeed, these analogies seem to me to be misleading. If A instructs an agent to carry a present to B, the agent's authority is in its nature revocable and A can revoke his instructions at any time before the present is delivered. Similarly, if A is minded to create a trust in favour of B, a volunteer, and fails properly to constitute the trust, B has no remedy. But the present case is quite different. When he made the contract Schebsman did not constitute the English company his mandatory to transfer property of his own to his wife and daughter. Not only was the money in question never his property, but, once having made the contract, he had, as I have already pointed out, no right to call on the company to make the payment to his estate. In making the contract, he set in motion a piece of machinery which he had no power to stop by his own unilateral action save by releasing the company from the contract. Its operation would inevitably result in money reaching the hands of his widow and daughter assuming, as we must assume, that the English company would perform its contract. This, therefore, was no revocable mandate, nor was there any lack of completeness in the constitution of the machinery devised for securing these benefits for the widow and daughter. When he made the contract, Schebsman intended that his widow should receive those benefits for herself: it was part of the bargain between himself and the two companies that she should receive them: and he reserved to himself no right to call for payment to himself. The trustee could, presumably, release the company from its undertaking, but this would do no more than deprive the trustee of the right to sue for damages for its breach. The fact that such a release can be effected is no argument for saying that the trustee can claim the moneys as his own.

The question, therefore, is not will equity help the widow and daughter to retain the sums which will inevitably be paid to them, but will equity help the trustee in bankruptcy to recover them from the payees? I can find no principle which calls for an affirmative answer to this question. If it were otherwise, the result would be a curious one. Schebsman makes a contract intended to secure benefits to his wife and daughter after his death. It is true that they obtain no right to call for those benefits, but Schebsman with good reason trusts the company to make them. The company cannot avoid making them unless it is prepared to break its contract. In this confidence, let me assume, Schebsman makes his testamentary dispositions and dies with the satisfaction of knowing that the contract makes provision for his widow and daughter. It is said that his representative can abrogate his intention and call on his widow and daughter to pay over to his estate any sums they may receive and that equity will compel them to do so. In my opinion, no principle of equity requires this to be done.

It is, of course, true that Schebsman provided part of the consideration for which the English company gave its undertaking to make the payments. But he did so with the intention that the money paid should belong to the recipients beneficially, and in this sense the provision secured by the contract for the widow and daughter may perhaps be regarded as being an advancement to them. This was clearly his intention at the date of the contract. It is true that at that date and down to the date of his death all that Mrs. Schebsman and her daughter had was an expectancy, they had no legal rights whatever. But it was an expectancy that would necessarily mature into actual payment, subject always to the possibility that the three parties to the contract or their representatives might put an end to the contract by mutual consent and the possibility that Schebsman or his successors in title might release the company from its obligation. This being so, the advancement must, in my opinion, be regarded as completed when the contract was made since it was not in the power of Schebsman to change his mind and prevent it from becoming effective unless he could secure the agreement of both the other two parties to the contract or was prepared to release the company. I do not see how there can arise a resulting trust for Schebsman of money that was never his, the receipt of which by the payees he had no power by himself to prevent save by a release.

To say that there can be no effective advancement unless and until either the subject-matter reaches the hands of the person to be advanced or that person acquires a legal title to claim it, appears to me to be too narrow a proposition. I see no reason why in principle an advancement should not be regarded as complete and effective where the person desiring to make it sets in train for that purpose a process which it is out of his power to control by his own action. If the process is one which he can by his own action control as, for example, where he uses a mandatory to deliver the subject-matter of the advancement to the person whom he desires to benefit, the case is, of course, different. But where a person has done everything which the nature of the subject-matter permits to ensure that it will reach the object of his bounty and the nature of the transaction precludes the possibility of any subsequent intervention or change of mind on his part, the advancement must, in my opinion, be regarded as complete. In the present case the special nature of the transaction satisfies these tests. The circumstances that the three parties to the contract could put an end to it by mutual consent and that the company could be released are immaterial. They mean no more than that limited powers of revocation are provided. If, and only if, one or other of those powers is exercised can the intended advancement be prevented from taking effect. Cases of advancement made by such methods as these may be rare. But that is no reason for refusing to give effect to them when they occur.

There appears to me to be an additional reason why equity should not interfere. It is a fair inference from the form and substance of the contract that the two companies had themselves an interest in seeing that the widow and daughter of their employee should be provided for. The manner in which compensation should be provided for the loss by Schebsman of his employment was agreed between the three parties to the contract. The contract on its face could only mean that the sums payable to Mrs. Schebsman and her daughter are to be paid to them for their own benefit. How can Schebsman claim them for himself without breaking his contract? I do not see how he can, and, if this view be correct, it cannot be that, as between himself and the payees Schebsman can be heard to assert in a court of equity a claim the enforcement of which involves a breach of contract even when that contract is one to which Mrs. Schebsman and her daughter were not parties. . . .

[The appeal was dismissed with costs. The opinions of Luxmore and Du Parcq L.JJ. are omitted.]

JACKSON v. *HORIZON HOLIDAYS LTD.*
[1975] 3 All E.R. 92 (C.A.)

LORD DENNING M.R.: Mr. Jackson is a young man, in his mid-twenties. He has been very successful in his business. He is married with three small children. In November, 1970 there were twin boys of three years of age; and his wife had just had her third child. He had been working very hard. They determined to have a holiday in the sun. He decided on Ceylon. He enquired of Horizon Holidays Ltd. He made arrangements with their agent, a Mrs. Bremner, for a holiday at a hotel, the Pegasus Reef Hotel, Hendala Point, Ceylon. He wrote them a letter which shows that he wanted everything of the highest standard:

"With reference to our telephone conversation would you please confirm that you can arrange for my wife, myself and my two twin boys aged 3 years to stay for 28 days from 23rd January to stay at the Hotel Pegasus Reef, Hendala Point, Ceylon. Would you also arrange that the childrens room has an adjoining door to our room this is essential and is a condition of me booking this holiday. Would you please make sure that the balcony is facing the sea and would you also confirm the distance the hotel is from the sea. Would you confirm that the meals are four course with a choice of 3 or 4 dishes to each course. Could you confirm that there has been arrangements made that an English speaking Doctor would call on the Hotel if needed. Would you please make a clear answer to all these questions appreciating that you might have difficulties in answering some of these questions and not to send an evasive answer to any of these questions."

He spoke on the telephone to Mrs. Bremner. She led him to believe that the hotel would come up to his expectations. She wrote on the booking form: "Remarks Twins Room with connecting door essential. Total charge, £1,432." He sent it in and booked the holiday.

In the middle of January it was discovered that the Pegasus Reef Hotel would not be ready in time. So Horizon Holidays recommended a substitute. This was Brown's Beach Hotel. It was described in the advertisement as being "superbly situated right on the beach, with all facilities for an enjoyable holiday including mini-golf, excellent restaurant, cocktail lounge, swimming pool, beauty salon, hairdressers and gift shop . . . The bedrooms are well furnished and equipped in modern style. All rooms have private bath, shower, w.c., sea view and air-conditioning."

Mr. Jackson had some hesitation about this other hotel. But Horizon Holidays assured him that it would be up to his expectation. So Mr. Jackson accepted it. But Horizon Holidays reduced the charge. Instead of the price being the total sum of £1,434, now, because of the change of hotel, it would be £1,200. That included air travel to Ceylon and back and a holiday for four weeks. So they went there. The courier, Miss Redgrave, met them and took them to Brown's Beach Hotel. But they were greatly disappointed. Their room had not got a connecting door with the room for the children at all. The room for the children was mildewed— black with mildew, at the bottom. There was fungus growing on the walls. The toilet was stained. The shower was dirty. There was no bath. They could not let the children sleep in it. So for the first three days they had all the family in one room. The two children were put into one of the single beds and the two adults in the other single bed. After the first three days they were moved into what was said to be one of the best suites in the hotel. Even then, they had to put the children in to sleep in the sittingroom and the parents in the bedroom. There was dirty linen on the bed. There was no private bath but only a shower; no mini-golf course; no swimming pool, no beauty salon, no hairdressers' salon. Worst of all was the cooking. There was no choice of dishes. On some occasions, however, curry was served as an alternative to the main dish. They found the food very distasteful. It appeared to be cooked in coconut oil. There was a pervasive taste because of its manner of cooking. They were so uncomfortable at Brown's Hotel, that after a fortnight they moved to the Pegasus Reef Hotel. It appears that by that time it was nearing completion. But a lot of building work was still going on. At any rate, for the fortnight they were in the Pegasus Reef Hotel, where things were somewhat better than at Brown's Beach. They stayed out the four weeks and came home.

Soon after their return, Mr. Jackson wrote a letter setting out all his complaints from the beginning to the end. Then Mr. Jackson brought an action for damages in respect of the loss of his holiday for himself, his wife and the two small children. Horizon Holidays admitted liability. The contest was only on the amount of damages.

In *Jarvis* v. *Swans Tours Ltd.* [1973] Q.B. 233 it was held by this court that damages for the loss of a holiday may include not only the difference in value between what was promised and what was obtained, but also damages for mental distress, inconvenience, upset, disappointment and frustration caused by the loss of the holiday. The judge directed himself in accordance with the judgments in that case. He eventually awarded a sum of £1,100. Horizon Holidays Ltd. appeal. They say it was far too much. The judge did not divide up the £1,100. Counsel has made suggestions about it. Counsel for Horizon Holidays suggests that the judge gave £100 for diminution in value and £1,000 for the mental distress. But counsel for Mr. Jackson suggested that the judge gave £600 for the diminution in value and £500 for the mental distress. If I were inclined myself to speculate, I think the suggestion of counsel for Mr. Jackson may well be right. The judge took the cost of the holidays at £1,200. The family only had about half the value of it. Divide it by two and you get £600. Then add £500 for the mental distress.

On this question a point of law arises. The judge said that he could only consider the mental distress to Mr. Jackson himself, and that he could not consider the distress to his wife and children. He said: ". . . the damages are the Plaintiff's; that I can consider the effect upon his mind of his wife's discomfort, vexation and the like, although I cannot award a sum which represents her vexation."

Counsel for Mr. Jackson disputes that proposition. He submits that damages can be given not only for the leader of the party, in this case, Mr. Jackson's own distress, discomfort and vexation, but also for that of the rest of the party.

We have had an interesting discussion as to the legal position when one person makes a contract for the benefit of a party. In this case it was a husband making a contract for the benefit of himself, his wife and children. Other cases readily come to mind. A host makes a contract with a restaurant for a dinner for himself and his friends. The vicar makes a contract for a coach trip for the choir. In all these cases there is only one person who makes the contract. It is the husband, the host or the vicar, as the case may be. Sometimes he pays the whole price himself. Occasionally he may get a contribution from the others. But in any case it is he who makes the contract. It would be a fiction to say that the contract was made by all the family, or all the guests, or all the choir, and that he was only an agent for them. Take this very case. It would be absurd to say that the twins of three years old were parties to the contract or that the father was making the contract on their behalf as if they were principals. It would equally be a mistake to say that in any of these instances there was a trust. The transaction bears no resemblance to a trust. There was no trust fund and no trust property. No, the real truth is that in each instance, the father, the host or the vicar, was making a contract himself for the benefit of the whole party. In short, a contract by one for the benefit of third persons.

What is the position when such a contract is broken? At present the law says that the only one who can sue is the one who made the contract. None of the rest of the party can sue, even though the contract was made for their benefit. But when that one does sue, what damages can he recover? Is he limited to his own loss? Or can he recover for the others? Suppose the holiday firm puts the family into a hotel which is only half built and the visitors have to sleep on the floor? Or suppose the restaurant is fully booked and the guests have to go away, hungry and angry, having spent so much on fares to get there? Or suppose the coach leaves the choir stranded half-way and they have to hire cars to get home? None of them individually can sue. Only the father, the host or the vicar can sue. He can, of course, recover his own damages. But can he not recover for the others? I think he can. The case comes within the principle stated by Lush L.J. in *Lloyd's* v. *Harper* (1880) 16 Ch.D. 290, at 291: "...I consider it to be an established rule of law that where a contract is made with *A.* for the benefit of *B., A.* can sue on the contract for the benefit of *B.*, and recover all that *B.* could have recovered if the contract had been made with *B.* himself."

It has been suggested that Lush L.J. was thinking of a contract in which A was trustee for B. But I do not think so. He was a common lawyer speaking of the common law. His words were quoted with considerable approval by Lord Pearce in *Beswick* v. *Beswick.* I have myself often quoted them. I think they should be accepted as correct, at any rate so long as the law forbids the third persons themselves to sue for damages. It is the only way in which a just result can be achieved. Take the instance I have put. The guests ought to recover from the restaurant their wasted fares. The choir ought to recover the cost of hiring the taxis home. There is no one to recover for them except the one who made the contract for their benefit. He should be able to recover the expense to which they have been put, and pay it over to them. Once recovered, it will be money had and received to their use. (They might even, if desired, be joined as plaintiffs.) If he can recover for the expense, he should also be able to recover for the discomfort, vexation and upset which the whole party have suffered by reason of the breach of contract, recompensing them accordingly out of what he recovers.

Applying the principles to this case, I think that the figure of £1,100 was about right. It would, I think, have been excessive if it had been awarded only for the damage suffered by Mr. Jackson himself. But when extended to his wife and children, I do not think it is excessive. People look forward to a holiday. They expect the promises to be fulfilled. When it fails, they are greatly disappointed and upset. It is difficult to assess in terms of money; but it is the task of the judges to do the best they can. I see no reason to interfere with the total award of £1,100.

I would therefore dismiss this appeal.

ORR L.J.: I agree.

JAMES L.J.: In this case Mr. Jackson, as found by the judge on the evidence, was in need of a holiday at the end of 1970. He was able to afford a holiday for himself and his family. According to the form which he completed, which was the form of Horizon Holidays Ltd., he booked what was a family holiday. The wording of that form might in certain circumstances give rise to a contract in which the person signing the form is acting as his own principal and as agent for others. In the circumstances of this case, as indicated by Lord Denning M.R., it would be wholly unrealistic to regard this contract as other than one made by Mr. Jackson for a family holiday. The judge found that he did not get a family holiday. The costs were some £1,200. When he came back he felt no benefit. His evidence was to the effect that, without any exaggeration, he felt terrible. He said: "The only thing, I was pleased to be back, very pleased, but I had nothing at all from that holiday." For my part, on the issue of damages in this matter, I am quite content to say that £1,100 awarded was the right and proper figure in those circumstances. I would dismiss the appeal.

[Appeal dismissed. Leave to appeal to the House of Lords refused.]

MIDLAND SILICONES LTD. v. *SCRUTTONS LTD.* [1962] 2 W.L.R. 186 (England. House of Lords). Scruttons Ltd. were stevedores hired to handle a drum of silicone diffusion pump fluid from the ship to a lorry provided by the consignee, Midland Silicones Ltd. The stevedores were just lowering the drum on to the lorry when by their negligence it was dropped and some of the contents were lost. The loss was assessed at £593 12s. By virtue of the bill of lading between the shipper and the carrier, the carrier who moved the drum from New York to London was not to be liable for more than $500 (£179 1s.) in the event of damage. By virtue of the stevedoring contract between the carrier and Scruttons Ltd., Scruttons Ltd. agreed to be liable for damage while they were handling the drum, but they were entitled to "such protection as is afforded by the terms, conditions and exceptions of the bills of lading." By virtue of the sale of goods contract between the shipper and Midland the title in the drum passed from the shipper, or seller, to Midland while it was on board the ship, and thereafter Midland became subject to the same rights in respect of the drum as if the contract in the bill of lading had been made directly with Midland. There was no express contract between Midland and Scruttons Ltd. Diplock J. directed judgment for Midland for £593 12s. 2d. plus interest. The Court of Appeal dismissed an appeal. The House of Lords affirmed the Court of Appeal. On the question whether Scruttons Ltd., who had no contract with Midland, could take advantage of the clause in the bill of lading limiting the carrier's liability to $500, the House, with the exception of Lord Denning, who dissented, denied the protection on the ground that a third party cannot take advantage of a clause in a contract to which he is not a party. VISCOUNT SIMONDS: ". . . But, my Lords, all these contentions were but a prelude to one which, had your Lordships accepted it, would have been the foundation of a dramatic decision of this House. It was argued, if I understood the argument, that if A contracts with B to do something for the benefit of C, then C, though not a party to the contract, can sue A to enforce it. This is independent of whether C is A's undisclosed principal or a beneficiary under a trust of which A is trustee. It is sufficient that C is an 'interested person.' My Lords, if this is the law of England, then, subject always to the question of consideration, no doubt, if the carrier purports to contract for the benefit of the stevedore, the latter can enforce the contract. Whether that premiss is satisfied in this case is another matter, but, since the argument is advanced, it is right that I should deal with it. Learned counsel for the respondents met it, as they had successfully done in the courts below, by asserting a principle which is, I suppose, as well established as any in our law, a 'fundamental' principle, as Lord Haldane called it in *Dunlop Pneumatic Tyre Co. Ltd.* v. *Selfridge & Co. Ltd.*, [1915] A.C. 847, an 'elementary' principle, as it has been called times without number, that only a person who is a party to a contract can sue upon it. 'Our law,' said Lord Haldane, 'knows nothing of a jus quaesitum tertio arising by way of contract.' Learned counsel for the respondents claimed that this was the orthodox view and asked your Lordships to reject any proposition that impinged upon it. To that invitation I readily respond. For to me heterodoxy, or, as some might say, heresy, is not the more attractive because it is dignified by the name of reform. Nor will I easily be led by an undiscerning zeal for some abstract kind of justice to ignore our first duty, which is to administer justice according to law, the law which is established for us by Act of Parliament or the binding authority of precedent. The law is developed by the application of old principles to new circumstances. Therein lies its genius. Its reform by the abrogation of those principles is the task not of the courts of law but of Parliament. Therefore I reject the argument for the appellants under this head and invite your Lordships to say that certain statements which appear to support it in recent cases such as *Smith & Snipes Hall Farm* v. *River Douglas Catchment Board*, [1949] 2 K.B. 500, and *White* v. *John Warwick & Co. Ltd.*, [1953] 1 W.L.R. 1285, must be rejected. If the principle of jus quaesitum tertio is to be introduced into our law, it must be done by Parliament after a due consideration of its merits and demerits. I should not be prepared to give it my support without a greater knowledge than I at present possess of its operation in other systems of law. . . ." LORD DENNING: (dissenting) ". . . the question is: Did the owners of the goods impliedly authorize the carrier to employ stevedores on the terms that their liability should be limited to $500? I think they did. . . . The carrier simply passed on the self-same limitation as he himself had, and this must have been within his implied authority. It seems to me that when the owner of goods allows the person in possession of them to make a contract in regard to them, then he cannot go back on the terms of the contract, if they are such as he expressly or impliedly authorized to be made, even though he was no party to the contract and could not sue or be sued upon it. It is just the same as if he stood by and watched it being made. And his successor in title is in no better position. . . ." [Lord Reid pointed out that the House had been informed that questions of this kind frequently arise and that this action had been brought as a test case. How will the result affect the revision of the standard forms of the three contracts involved here?]

NOTE ON LEGAL METHOD. Compare Viscount Simonds' attitude toward judicial reform of the common law in the *Midland Silicone* case with his remarks in *Shaw* v. *Director of Public Prosecutions*, [1962] A.C. 220, where he had to decide whether to invent a new crime at common law, of corrupting public morals. Having said earlier in his judgment, at p. 267, that "I am no advocate of the right of the judges to create new criminal offences," he said, at p. 268, "When Lord Mansfield, speaking long after the Star Chamber had been abolished, said that the Court of King's Bench was the *custos morum* of the people and had the superintendency of offences *contra bonos mores*, he was asserting, as I now assert, that there is in that court a residual power, where no statute has yet intervened to supersede the common law, to superintend those offences which are prejudicial to the public welfare. Such occasions will be rare, for Parliament has not been slow to legislate when attention has been sufficiently aroused. But gaps remain and will always remain since no one can foresee every way in which the wickedness of man may disrupt the order of society. Let me take a single instance to which my noble and learned friend Lord Tucker refers. Let it be supposed that at some future, perhaps early, date homosexual practices between adult consenting males are no longer a crime. Would it not be an offence if even without obscenity, such practices were publicly advocated and encouraged by pamphlet and advertisement? Or must we wait until Parliament finds time to deal with such conduct? I say, my Lords, that if the common law is powerless in such an event, then we should no longer do her reverence. But I say that her hand is still powerful and that it is for Her Majesty's judges to play the part which Lord Mansfield pointed out to them."

QUESTION. Is the House of Lords better adapted to remould the law of contract or the criminal law in the delicate sphere of public morality? Contrast Lord Reid, in the *Shaw* case at p. 275: "Even if there is still a vestigial power of this kind it ought not, in my view, to be used unless there appears to be general agreement that the offence to which it is applied ought to be criminal if committed by an individual. Notoriously, there are wide differences of opinion today as to how far the law ought to punish immoral acts which are not done in the face of the public. Some think that the law already goes too far, some that it does not go far enough. Parliament is the proper place, and I am firmly of opinion the only proper place, to settle that. When there is sufficient support from public opinion, Parliament does not hesitate to intervene. Where Parliament fears to tread it is not for the courts to rush in."

Lord Reid also said, at p. 276, "I think that the following comments are as valid today as they were in 1824 '... I ... protest ... against arguing too strongly upon public policy—it is a very unruly horse, and when once you get astride it you never know where it will carry you. It may lead you from the sound law. It is never argued at all but when other points fail' (per Burrough J. in *Richardson* v. *Mellish* (1824). 2 Bing. 229, at p. 252)." Do you agree? Is there some rational basis for assigning some reforms to the legislature and some to the courts?

NEW ZEALAND SHIPPING CO. LTD. v. A. M. SATTERTHWAITE & CO. LTD.
[1975] A.C. 154 (P.C.)

LORD WILBERFORCE: The facts of this case are not in dispute. An expensive drilling machine was received on board the ship *Eurymedon* at Liverpool for transhipment to Wellington pursuant to the terms of a bill of lading no. 1262 dated June 5, 1964. The shipper was the maker of the drill, Ajax Machine Tool Co. Ltd. ("the consignor"). The bill of lading was issued by agents for the Federal Steam Navigation Co. Ltd. ("the carrier"). The consignee was A. M. Satterthwaite & Co. Ltd. of Christchurch, New Zealand ("the consignee"). For several years before 1964 the New Zealand Shipping Co. Ltd. ("the stevedore") had carried out 'all stevedoring work in Wellington in respect of the ships owned by the carrier, which was a wholly owned subsidiary of the stevedore. In addition to this stevedoring work the stevedore generally acted as agent for the carrier in New Zealand; and in such capacity as general agent (not in the course of their stevedoring functions) the stevedore received the bill of lading at Wellington on July 31, 1964. Clause 1 of the bill of lading, on the construction of which this case turns, was in the same terms as bills of lading usually issued by the stevedore and its associated companies in respect of ordinary cargo carried by their ships from the United Kingdom to New Zealand. The consignee became the holder of the bill of lading and owner of the drill prior to August 14, 1964. On that date the drill was damaged as a result of the stevedore's negligence during unloading.

At the foot of the first page of the bill of lading the following words were printed in small capitals: "In accepting this bill of lading the shipper, consignee and the owners of the goods, and the holders of this bill of lading agree to be bound by all of its conditions, exceptions and provisions whether written, printed or stamped on the front or back hereof." On the back of the bill of lading a number of clauses were printed in small type. It is only necessary to set out the following. The first and third paragraph of clause 1 provided:

"This bill of lading shall have effect (*a*) subject to the provisions of any legislation giving effect to the International Convention for the unification of certain rules relating to bills of lading dated Brussels, August 25, 1924, or to similar effect which is compulsorily applicable to the contract of carriage evidenced hereby and (*b*) where no such legislation is applicable as if the Carriage of Goods by Sea Act 1924, of Great Britain and the rules scheduled thereto applied hereto and were incorporated herein. Nothing herein contained shall be deemed to be a surrender by the carrier of any of his rights or immunities or an increase of any of his responsibilities or liabilities under the provisions of the said legislation or Act and rules (as the case may be) and the said provisions shall not (unless and to the extent that they are by law compulsorily applicable) apply to that portion of the contract evidenced by this bill of lading which relates to forwarding under clause 4 hereof. If anything herein contained be inconsistent with or repugnant to the said provisions, it shall to the extent of such inconsistency or repugnance and no further be null and void. . . .

"It is hereby expressly agreed that no servant or agent of the carrier (including every independent contractor from time to time employed by the carrier) shall in any circumstances whatsoever be under any liability whatsoever to the shipper, consignee or owner of the goods or to any holder of this bill of lading for any loss or damage or delay of whatsoever kind arising or resulting directly or indirectly from any act neglect or default on his part while acting in the course of or in connection with his employment and, without prejudice to the generality of the foregoing provisions in this clause, every exemption, limitation, condition and liberty herein contained and every right, exemption from liability, defence and immunity of whatsoever nature applicable to the carrier or to which the carrier is entitled hereunder shall also be available and shall extend to protect every such servant or agent of the carrier acting as aforesaid and for the purpose of all the foregoing provisions of this clause the carrier is or shall be deemed to be acting as agent or trustee on behalf of and for the benefit of all persons who are or might be his servants or agents from time to time (including independent contractors as aforesaid) and all such persons shall to this extent be or be deemed to be parties to the contract in or evidenced by this bill of lading."

Clause 11 provided:

"The carrier will not be accountable for goods of any description beyond £100 in respect of any one package or unit unless the value thereof shall have been stated in writing both on the broker's order which must be obtained before shipment and on the shipping note presented on shipment and extra freight agreed upon and paid and bills of lading signed with a declaration of the nature and value of the goods appearing thereon. When the value is declared and extra freight agreed as aforesaid the carrier's liability shall not exceed such value or pro rata on that basis in the event of partial loss or damage."

No declaration as to the nature and value of the goods having appeared in the bill of lading, and no extra freight having been agreed upon or paid, it was acknowledged by the consignee that the liability of the carrier was accordingly limited to £100 by the application of clause 11 of the bill of lading. Moreover, the incorporation in the bill of lading of the rules scheduled to the Carriage of Goods by Sea Act 1924 meant that the carrier and the ship were discharged from all liability in respect of damage to the drill unless suit was brought against them within one year after delivery. No action was commenced until April 1967, when the consignee sued the stevedore in negligence, claiming £880 the cost of repairing the damaged drill.

The question in the appeal is whether the stevedore can take the benefit of the time limitation provision. The starting point, in discussion of this question, is provided by the House of Lords decision in *Midland Silicones Ltd.* v. *Scruttons Ltd.* [1962] A.C. 446. There is no need to question or even to qualify that case in so far as it affirms the general proposition that a contract between two parties cannot be sued on by a third person even though the contract is expressed to be for his benefit. Nor is it necessary to disagree with anything which was said to the same effect in the Australian case of *Wilson* v. *Darling Island Stevedoring and Lighterage Co. Ltd.* (1956) 95 C.L.R. 43. Each of these cases was dealing with a simple case of a contract the benefit of which was sought to be taken by a third person not a party to it, and the emphatic pronouncements in the speeches and judgments were directed to this situation. But *Midland Silicones* left open the case where one of the parties contracts as agent for the third person: in particular Lord Reid's speech spelt out, in four propositions, the prerequisites for the validity of such an agency contract. There is of course nothing unique to this case in the conception of agency contracts: well known and common instances exist in the field of hire purchase, of bankers' commercial credits and other transactions. Lord Reid said, at p. 474:

"I can see a possibility of success of the agency argument if (first) the bill of lading makes it clear that the stevedore is intended to be protected by the provisions in it which limit liability, (secondly) the bill of lading makes it clear that the carrier, in addition to contracting for these provisions on his own behalf, is also contracting as agent for the stevedore that these provisions should apply to the stevedore, (thirdly) the carrier has authority from the stevedore to do that, or perhaps later ratification by the stevedore would suffice, and (fourthly) that any difficulties about consideration moving from the stevedore were overcome. And then to affect the consignee it would be necessary to show that the provisions of the Bills of Lading Act 1855 apply."

The question in this appeal is whether the contract satisfies these propositions.

Clause 1 of the bill of lading, whatever the defects in its drafting, is clear in its relevant terms. The carrier, on his own account, stipulates for certain exemptions and immunities: among these is that conferred by article III, rule 6, of the Hague Rules which discharges the carrier from all liability for loss or damage unless suit is brought within one year after delivery. In addition to these stipulations on his own account, the carrier as agent for, inter alios, independent contractors stipulates for the same exemptions.

Much was made of the fact that the carrier also contracts as agent for numerous other persons; the relevance of this argument is not apparent. It cannot be disputed that among such independent contractors, for whom, as agent, the carrier contracted, is the appellant company which habitually acts as stevedore in New Zealand by arrangement with the carrier and which is, moreover, the parent company of the carrier. The carrier was, indisputably, authorised by the appellant to contract as its agent for the purposes of clause 1. All of this is quite straightforward and was accepted by all the judges in New Zealand. The only question was, and is, the fourth question presented by Lord Reid, namely that of consideration.

It was on this point that the Court of Appeal differed from Beattie J., holding that it had not been shown that any consideration for the shipper's promise as to exemption moved from the promisee, i.e., the appellant company.

If the choice, and the antithesis, is between a gratuitous promise, and a promise for consideration, as it must be in the absence of a tertium quid, there can be little doubt which, in commercial reality, this is. The whole contract is of a commercial character, involving service on one side, rates of payment on the other, and qualifying stipulations as to both. The relations of all parties to each other are commercial relations entered into for business reasons of ultimate profit. To describe one set of promises, in this context, as gratuitous, or nudum pactum, seems paradoxical and is prima facie implausible. It is only the precise analysis of this complex of relations into the classical offer and acceptance, with identifiable consideration, that seems to present difficulty, but this same difficulty exists in many situations of daily life, e.g., sales at auction; supermarket purchases; boarding an omnibus; purchasing a train ticket; tenders for the supply of goods; offers of rewards; acceptance by post; warranties of authority by agents; manufacturers' guarantees; gratuitous bailments; bankers' commercial credits. These are all examples which show that English law, having committed itself to a rather technical and schematic doctrine of contract, in application takes a practical approach, often at the cost of forcing the facts to fit uneasily into the marked slots of offer, acceptance and consideration.

In their Lordship's opinion the present contract presents much less difficulty than many of those above referred to. It is one of carriage from Liverpool to Wellington. The carrier assumes an obligation to transport the goods and to discharge at the port of arrival. The goods are to be carried and discharged, so the transaction is inherently contractual. It is contemplated that a part of this contract, viz. discharge, may be performed by independent contractors—viz. the appellant. By clause 1 of the bill of lading the shipper agrees to exempt from liability the carrier, his servants and independent contractors in respect of the performance of this contract of carriage. Thus, if the carriage, including the discharge, is wholly carried out by the carrier, he is exempt. If part is carried out by him, and part by his servants, he and they are exempt. If part is carried out by him and part by an independent contractor, he and the independent contractor are exempt. The exemption is designed to cover the whole carriage from loading to discharge, by whomsoever it is performed: the performance attracts the exemption or immunity in favour of whoever the performer turns out to be. There is possibly more than one way of analysing this business transaction into the necessary components; that which their Lordships would accept is to say that the bill of lading brought into existence a bargain initially unilateral but capable of becoming mutual, between the shipper and the appellant, made through the carrier as agent. This became a full contract when the appellant performed services by discharging the goods. The performance of these services for the benefit of the shipper was the consideration for the agreement by the shipper that the appellant should have the benefit of the exemptions and limitations contained in the bill of lading. The conception of a "unilateral" contract of this kind was recognised in *Great Northern Railway Co.* v. *Witham* (1873) L. R. 9 C.P. 16 and is well established. This way of regarding the matter is very close to if not identical to that accepted by Beattie J. in the Supreme Court: he analysed the transaction as one of an offer open to acceptance by action such as was found in *Carlill* v. *Carbolic Smoke Ball Co.* [1893] 1 Q.B. 256. But whether one describes the shipper's promise to exempt as an offer to be accepted by performance or as a promise in exchange for an act seems in the present context to be a matter of semantics. The words of Bowen L.J. in *Carlill* v. *Carbolic Smoke Ball Co.* [1893] 1 Q.B. 256, 268: "why should not an offer be made to all the world which is to ripen into a contract with anybody who comes forward and performs the condition?" seem to bridge both conceptions: he certainly seems to draw no distinction between an offer which matures into a contract when accepted and a promise which matures into a contract after performance, and, though in some special contexts (such as in connection with the right to withdraw) some further refinement may be needed, either analysis may be equally valid. On the main point in the appeal, their Lordships are in substantial agreement with Beattie J.

The following points require mention. 1. In their Lordships' opinion, consideration may quite well be provided by the appellant, as suggested, even though (or if) it was already under an obligation to discharge to the carrier. (There is no direct evidence of the existence or nature of this obligation, but their Lordships are prepared to assume it.) An agreement to do an act which the promisor is under an existing obligation to a third party to do, may quite well amount to valid consideration and does so in the present case: the promisee obtains the benefit of a direct obligation which he can enforce. This proposition is illustrated and supported by

Scotson v. *Pegg* (1861) 6 H. & N. 295 which their Lordships consider to be good law.

2. The consignee is entitled to the benefit of, and is bound by, the stipulations in the bill of lading by his acceptance of it and request for delivery of the goods thereunder. This is shown by *Brandt* v. *Liverpool, Brazil and River Plate Steam Navigation Co. Ltd.* [1924] 1 K.B. 575 and a line of earlier cases. The Bills of Lading Act 1855, section 1 (in New Zealand the Mercantile Law Act 1908, section 13) gives partial statutory recognition to this rule, but, where the statute does not apply, as it may well not do in this case, the previously established law remains effective.

3. The appellant submitted, in the alternative, an argument that, quite apart from contract, exemptions from, or limitation of, liability in tort may be conferred by mere consent on the part of the party who may be injured. As their Lordships consider that the appellant ought to succeed in contract, they prefer to express no opinion upon this argument: to evaluate it requires elaborate discussion.

4. A clause very similar to the present was given effect by a United States District Court in *Carle & Montanari Inc.* v. *American Export Isbrandtsen Lines Inc.* [1968] 1 Lloyd's Rep. 260. The carrier in that case contracted, in an exemption clause, as agent, for, inter alios, all stevedores and other independent contractors, and although it is no doubt true that the law in the United States is more liberal than ours as regards third party contracts, their Lordships see no reason why the law of the Commonwealth should be more restrictive and technical as regards agency contracts. Commercial considerations should have the same force on both sides of the Pacific.

In the opinion of their Lordships, to give the appellant the benefit of the exemptions and limitations contained in the bill of lading is to give effect to the clear intentions of a commercial document, and can be given within existing principles. They see no reason to strain the law or the facts in order to defeat these intentions. It should not be overlooked that the effect of denying validity to the clause would be to encourage actions against servants, agents and independent contractors in order to get round exemptions (which are almost invariable and often compulsory) accepted by shippers against carriers, the existence, and presumed efficacy, of which is reflected in the rates of freight. They see no attraction in this consequence.

Their Lordships will humbly advise Her Majesty that the appeal be allowed and the judgment of Beattie J. restored. The respondent must pay the costs of the appeal and in the Court of Appeal.

[Viscount Dilhorne dissented.]

RESTATEMENT OF THE LAW OF CONTRACTS (SECOND)
American Law Institute. 1968 (Tentative Draft)

133. Intended and Incidental Beneficiaries.

(1) Unless otherwise agreed between promisor and promisee, a beneficiary of a promise is an intended beneficiary if recognition of a right to performance in the beneficiary is appropriate to effectuate the intention of the parties and either

    (a) the performance of the promise will satisfy an obligation of the promisee to pay money to the beneficiary; or

(b) the promisee manifests an intention to give the beneficiary the benefit of the promised performance.

(2) An incidental beneficiary is a beneficiary who is not an intended beneficiary.

135. Creation of Duty to Beneficiary.

A promise in a contract creates a duty in the promisor to any intended beneficiary to perform the promise, and the intended beneficiary may enforce the duty.

136. Overlapping Duties to Beneficiary and Promisee.

(1) A promise in a contract creates a duty in the promisor to the promisee to perform the promise even though there is also a similar duty to an intended beneficiary.

(2) Whole or partial satisfaction of the promisor's duty to the beneficiary satisfies to that extent the promisor's duty to the promisee.

137. Disclaimer by a Beneficiary.

A beneficiary who has not previously assented to the promise for his benefit may in a reasonable time after learning of its existence and terms render any duty to himself inoperative from the beginning by disclaimer.

138. Remedy of Specific Performance.

Where specific performance is otherwise an appropriate remedy, either the promisee or the beneficiary may maintain a suit for specific enforcement of a duty owed to an intended beneficiary.

140. Defences against the Beneficiary.

(1) A promise creates no duty to a beneficiary unless a contract is formed between the promisor and the promisee; and if a contract is voidable or unenforceable at the time of its formation the right of any beneficiary is subject to the infirmity.

(2) If a contract ceases to be binding in whole or in part because of impossibility, illegality, failure of a condition, or present or prospective failure of consideration, the right of any beneficiary is to that extent discharged or modified.

(3) Except as stated in Subsections (1) and (2) or as provided by the contract, the right of any beneficiary against the promisor is not subject to the promisor's defences or claims against the promisee or to the promisee's defences or claims against the beneficiary.

(4) A beneficiary's right against the promisor is subject to any defence or claim arising from his own conduct.

141. Remedies of Beneficiary of Promise to satisfy the Promisee's Duty; Reimbursement of Promisee.

(1) Where an intended beneficiary has an enforceable claim against the promisee, he can obtain a judgment or judgments against either the promisee or the promisor or both based on their respective duties to him. Satisfaction in whole or in part of either of these duties, or of a judgment thereon, satisfies to that extent the other duty or judgment, subject to the promisee's right of subrogation.

(2) To the extent that the claim of an intended beneficiary is satisfied from assets of the promisee, the promisee has a right of reimbursement

from the promisor, which may be enforced directly and also, if the beneficiary's claim is fully satisfied, by subrogation to the claim of the beneficiary against the promisor, and to any judgment thereon and to any security therefor.

142. Variation of a Duty to Beneficiary.

(1) Discharge or modification of a duty to an intended beneficiary by conduct of the promisee or by a subsequent agreement between promisor and promisee is ineffective if a term of the promise creating the duty so provides.

(2) In the absence of such a term, the promisor and promisee retain power to discharge or modify the duty by subsequent agreement.

(3) Such a power terminates when the beneficiary, before he receives notification of the discharge or modification, materially changes his position in justifiable reliance on the promise or brings suit on it or manifests assent to it in a manner invited or required by the promisor or promisee.

(4) If the promisee receives consideration for an attempted discharge or modification of the promisor's duty which is ineffective against the beneficiary, the beneficiary can assert a right to the consideration so received.

144. Mistake as to Duty to Beneficiary.

The effect of an erroneous belief of the promisor or promisee as to the existence or extent of a duty owed to an intended beneficiary is determined by the rules making contracts voidable for mistake.

147. Effect of a Promise of Incidental Benefit.

An incidental beneficiary acquires by virtue of the promise no right against the promisor or the promisee.

QUEBEC CIVIL CODE

1029. A party in like manner may stipulate for the benefit of a third person, when such is the condition of a contract which he makes for himself, or of a gift which he makes to another; and he who makes the stipulation cannot revoke it, if the third person have signified his assent to it.

PROBLEM. Able takes tickets for a voyage by himself and his wife on a ship owned by Baker. Mr. and Mrs. Able are both injured when the gangway is carelessly removed by one of the crew. On the face of the tickets is a clause which reads: "Neither Baker nor his servants shall be made liable for any injury whatsoever to the person of any passenger arising from the activities of Baker's servants, whether occasioned or caused by negligence or otherwise, and in this regard it is agreed that Baker contracts as agent for his servants." Advise Mr. and Mrs. Able.

See *Adler* v. *Dickson* [1955] 1 Q.B. 158, *Gore* v. *Van Der Lann* [1967] 2 Q.B. 31 *Cockerton* v. *Naviera Aznar S.A.* [1960] 2 Ll.R. 450, Odgers, *The Strange Case of Mrs. Gore* (1970) 86 L.Q.R. 69.

Chapter 4

ASSIGNMENT AND AGENCY

1. Note on Assignment

Contractual rights have long been treated as a species of property, and like other kinds of property, they have been bought and sold. The common law courts before the Judicature Act refused to recognize assignments, but the Courts of Equity did recognize and enforce them. In the case of contractual rights enforceable at law (choses in action) the Court of Equity, since it could not directly affect the decisions of the courts of law, achieved its end indirectly by permitting the assignee to bring his action in the name of the assignor, if necessary, enjoining the assignor from objecting. In the case of rights enforceable in equity (choses in equity) the assignee's right was directly enforceable by the Court of Equity.

The Judicature Act included a provision, now section 54(1) of the Ontario Conveyancing and Law of Property Act, and in force in all the common law provinces, but with variations in Saskatchewan and Manitoba, permitting assignments subject to certain restrictions. It was held in *Brandt's Sons & Co. v. Dunlop Rubber Co. Ltd.* [1905] A.C. 454 (H.L.) that the effect of the statute was not to impair the validity of the old equitable procedure. An assignment that fails to comply with the statute, therefore, may still be valid as an equitable assignment.

It is ironic that the establishment of free assignability coincided with the strengthening of the rule against third party beneficiaries (*Tweddle* v. *Atkinson,* supra). If A makes a promise to B, B can, in the next instant of time, assign the benefit of it to C, as a gift if he wishes. It seems odd to prevent A and B from agreeing to do the same thing directly, that is, to confer a direct benefit on C.

It will be noted that assignment under the statute is "subject to equities," that is, to defences that the debtor could have asserted against the assignor. The assignee of a debt, therefore, is generally in no better position than the assignor, even if he gives value for the debt in good faith without notice of the defences, and the debtor is generally no worse off by the assignment. This rule obviously limits the negotiability of debts; it is the assignee, and not the debtor, who takes the risk of the assignor's fraud or insolvency.

The commercial need for negotiability is met by the concept of the negotiable instrument defined by the Bills of Exchange Act (Canada) to mean a promissory note or a bill of exchange (including a cheque). The chief significance of a negotiable instrument is that the holder of one for value in good faith does *not* take "subject to equities," and so if a debt is embodied in a negotiable instrument and negotiated to a third party, it is generally the debtor, not the holder of the instrument, who takes the risk of the creditor's fraud or insolvency. This rule is subject to an important qualification in the case of consumer transactions.

THE CONVEYANCING AND LAW OF PROPERTY ACT
Ontario. Revised Statutes. 1970. c. 85

54. (1) Any absolute assignment, made on or after the 31st day of December, 1897, by writing under the hand of the assignor, not purporting to

be by way of charge only, of any debt or other legal chose in action of which express notice in writing has been given to the debtor, trustee or other person from whom the assignor would have been entitled to receive or claim such debt or chose in action is effectual in law, subject to all equities that would have been entitled to priority over the right of the assignee if this section had not been enacted, to pass and transfer the legal right to such debt or chose in action from the date of such notice, and all other remedies for the same, and the power to give a good discharge for the same without the concurrence of the assignor.

[This provision is substantially the same as sec. 25 (6) of the English Judicature Act of 1873, later s. 136 of the Law of Property Act.]

2. NOTE ON AGENCY

If A authorises B to act on his behalf, and B contracts on A's behalf with C, B is A's agent, and there is a contract between A and C. Such an arrangement creates three sets of relationship, those between A and B, B and C, and A and C.

The relationship between the principal and his agent is a contractual one, but no detailed attention is given to it here, though some of the cases elsewhere in the book arise out of agency relationships. The agent is generally held to owe his principal a special duty of trust that prevents him from profiting at his principal's expense.

The relationship between the agent and the third party is on the border line of contract, tort, and restitution. If a contract is formed between A and C, the agent, B, is ordinarily not personally liable, but there are a number of important exceptions to this rule, as where the agent undertakes to guarantee payment by the principal or where justice for some other reason requires the imposition of personal liability on the agent. If an agent claims to have authority that he does not in fact have and the principal in consequence is not liable to the third party, the agent can be held liable to the third party for what is called "breach of warranty of authority." Whether the basis of the warranty is contractual or tortious, the effect is to hold the agent to a guarantee that he has the authority he claims to have.

The relationship between principal and third party is the most interesting and significant aspect of agency, and the extract below from Seavey's article on the subject is a useful account.

SEAVEY, "THE RATIONALE OF AGENCY"
(1920) 29 Yale L.J. 859

[Reprinted by permission of the Yale Law Book Company and Fred B. Rothman & Company from the *Yale Law Journal*, vol. 29, pp. 860, 872-78, 880-86.]

Authority. This word is combined usually with the idea of representation and with delegation. It cannot be discarded since its long continued use has made it an essential part of our legal vocabulary. Unfortunately, however, it is used indiscriminately in two very different senses, e.g.: the power held by the agent, and the power coupled with the privilege of exercising it. Thus we have the qualifying and confusing words "real" and "apparent" added to it to explain that the principal may be bound by an act in excess of the agent's real authority if the act was within the scope of his apparent authority. This double use leads to inaccuracy and is unnecessary. Authority is from *auctoritas* meaning legal power, or power exercised in conformity to law. The confusion is due to using a word conveying a combination of elementary ideas, where one idea is to be expressed and where both are.

Using the single-idea word "power" to describe that which the agent holds, we escape confusion, and reserve "authority" for its proper and more limited use. "Power" has a definite meaning in law and its use is not limited to agency. It may be classified and analyzed. It is therefore both more exact and more helpful in connecting what are said to be the special rules of agency with the general body of the law. For present purposes, it may be said that a power is a legal ability by which a person may create, change, or extinguish legal relations.

"Authority" should be limited to its primitive meaning of a power which can be rightfully exercised, or a power which can be exercised without going beyond the privilege given to A by P. Thus the phrase given above would be paraphrased: a principal is bound where the agent acts in the exercise of his power, although without authority, i.e., although not privileged by his principal to exercise it. The existence and extent of the power is determined by public policy; authority is limited by the expression of the principal's will in accordance with the agreement with or direction to the agent. The agent always has both a power and an authority, the latter being sometimes identical with, sometimes smaller, but never larger, than the former. . . .

The Power

In the following discussion will be included cases of agency and also cases which resemble it only in externals, i.e. those situations where the law, operating upon the voluntary act of P, creates in A a power to affect the legal relations of P, this being created in order to prevent injustice. It will not include tort cases, being limited to those powers the exercise of which results in some form of contractual liability. These may be divided into two classes:

(*a*) *Powers, the exercise of which results in true contracts.* In this class is included all cases where the parties to be held, i.e., both principal and third party, intended or expressed an intention to create the specific agreement or an agreement of the sort made. Cases where the existence of the principal was unknown to the third party are excluded since the parties are as much a part of an agreement as the terms. Also excluded are certain cases where the agent exceeded his orders. For convenience, a further subdivision may be made:

(1) The powers originated by direct grant to the agent create what is usually called "real authority," so called, I presume, because the agent is privileged to exercise them in the performance of his fiduciary obligations. They are again subclassified into those created by "express authority" and those created by "implied authority," the latter referring to powers created by the conduct of the principal in connection with the usages and customs of the business of the locality.

That the existence of these powers is no departure from the operation of the ordinary principles relating to contracts is clear in most cases. If the principal has agreed to become a party to a particular contract and the agent obeys orders, there is an expressed consent conveyed as intended to the other party. Where the agent is given discretion as to the creation or terms of such contracts, there is a variation from the usual offer and acceptance situation where there is not the intervention of an agent. It is not true here that the contract is completed by the will of the principal alone, or that the agent is "a referee who settles the price," a mere "tetotum." The contract comes into existence through the independent will of the agent, for the latter is responsible for his acts and words so far as his status as an individual permits. But the contract does come into existence in accordance with the expressed will of the principal and there is no departure from the theory of contracts. Nor is there anything peculiar in "implied authority," which corresponds to contracts implied in fact. Actions have the same weight in expressing intentions as do words, and in neither agency nor contracts do we inquire what a party thinks; we interpret his words and acts. The power, therefore, includes all that the agent reasonably believes it contains and this is determined by custom, if there are no instructions to the contrary.

Where the existence, but not the name, of the principal is known, it might be thought that a true contract is not created. But in this case, T, the third person, by his agreement with A, the agent, shows his intention to contract with a person indicated by description and of course it is not necessary to know personally the other party to a contract. It is sufficient if he falls within the class intended to be dealt with. It may be objected that the agent is a party to the contract and that there is but one contract. It is true that in many cases the agent has been a successful plaintiff and an unsuccessful defendant. But those cases may be placed upon a number of different grounds—the form of the written agreement, a custom to hold the agent as guarantor, a right in the agent to sue created by his personal interest in the goods. In all of these cases there may be alternative or secondary agreements with the agent but these do not affect the existence of the intent to deal with the principal nor the reality of a consensual relationship with him. Of course if the third party chooses to deal exclusively with the agent, we have no question of agency, at least within the principles now discussed.

(2) The power created where the principal has led T to believe that a power existed in A. This refers, of course, to "ostensible authority" or the so-called "agency by estoppel." In this class of cases also, there is created a true contract. As has been pointed out, we may discard the use of the word estoppel as unnecessary, although doubtless the basis for liability is much the same as in estoppel. If P represents to T that A has authority to contract, the legal result is exactly the same as if A had authority to contract. Here A has a power to create contractual relations between P and T identical to those which would have been created by the same words spoken to A. It is objected that if A is not an agent, a misrepresentation that he is one will not make him one and, since, by hypothesis, there is no true agency, the obligation must rest upon estoppel. This is not, however, an accurate statement of the representation. In the statement by P that A is his agent, the only part material to T is that A has a power to create certain ascertainable contractual relations between P and T. This representation may be made, of course, by any action which indicates to a normal person that A has the particular power in question. This is indicated by conduct leading T to believe that A is a certain kind of an agent and that he has power to deal with the class of persons to which T belongs.

The situation is not different from that where P makes an offer personally to T. P's actual consent is unnecessary. The offer is made by the speaking of the words or the doing of an act with communication through authorized channels. With P's mental processes we are not concerned. In the case of agency the courts have used the language of estoppel, very largely because of the double use of the word "authority," a use which has led to phrasing indicating that the power is real only where it can be rightly exercised. That the contract is real, however, has never been questioned and therefore the power to make it must be real. If in these cases A purports to exercise the power, he has as against P, the rights and duties of an agent only where P's representations are such that A reasonably believed that P intended him to act as agent in the matter. But the existence of agency is not essential to the reality of the powers or of the contracts made by their exercise.

Entirely irrespective of this excursus upon estoppel, however, there are in these cases all the essentials of contracts and there is no divergence from general principles. But two points call for further notice.

The representation that another is an agent of a particular kind or has authority to do certain classes of acts, sweeps into the power conferred all acts that the customs and usages of the trade or locality have made usual. But, as Ewart points out, there would be no real contract created by such acts if T were not aware of the custom, since there would be no communication of P's holding out or offer, it being assumed that A is not authorized to make the representations as to the extent of his powers. Thus where there is a holding out to T that A is a particular kind of an agent and by the custom of the place such agents have authority to warrant, there is no holding out to T that A has this authority unless T knows the custom. In this, the situation differs from that where there is a direct grant of authority to A to warrant, for in this case A is authorized to state that he has such power.

The representation may be made in a great variety of ways, and so also the communication. T may receive his information individually or as one of a class. The communication may be by advertisements, by an office being kept open with signs indicating its character, or it may be through A himself. That "the authority of the agent cannot be proved by the agent's statement of it," is true; but there may be a power based upon statements which the principal has authorized the agent to make. If he so authorizes a statement, the fact that at the same time he instructs the agent not to exercise the power does not affect the rights of third persons who do not know of the instructions. This is the basis of the cases where an agent disobeys instructions and there are no elements of misrepresentation except in the agent's statements. Thus if P tells A to represent to buyers that he is P's horse selling agent and instructs him not to warrant, as is the custom, but also not to disclose this want of authority, A creates in himself a power to warrant by following the instructions. This is true whether A is a "general" or a "special" agent, since the power is created not by the agreement between P and A as to A's authority, but by the authorized statement of A that he is a horse selling agent. These "secret instructions" must be distinguished from the instructions considered later.

In much the same way where a principal intrusts goods to a selling agent, it is inferable as a fact that he causes the agent to represent that he has authority to sell the goods in the normal manner with the usual incidents of sale in the locality to which they are sent. Merely giving possession of goods to another is not a representation of ownership, even, perhaps, when they are sent to a place where such goods are commonly sold; but to intrust goods or the *indicia* of title to one for the purpose of sale or as security for a loan may be said to be equivalent to a representation that the agent has the usual power of sale. If this is such a representation, as most courts have considered it, the result is the same whether the goods were given to a "special" or to a "general" agent.

In all of these cases classified as containing powers resulting in true contracts, we find that either the act of the agent was rightful, i.e., he had authority, or there was a manifestation of assent given by the principal through some authorized channel to the third party. There can be no contract made by "holding out to the world" an agent as having a particular character or particular powers. In the absence of authority or representation, there is nothing to which the principal has expressed assent to the third person, and hence nothing to which the general rules of contract can be applied. This does not prevent, however, obligations arising the remedy for which lies in an action of assumpsit.

(b) In the second class of cases I have placed *powers, the exercise of which does not result in a contract, but which does create obligations enforceable in an action of assumpsit*. For further consideration, they may be divided into two groups: (1) where the existence of the principal is unknown and the agent acts in conformity to orders, and (2) where the agent acts contrary to orders and there is no element of representation of his authority by the principal to the third person. These are distinctive agency powers, existing only where all the elements of agency exist and seemingly created by the relationship. That they do exist canot be denied in view of the cases, and their existence prevents, if nothing else does, the conception that the agent is a sort of human machine conveying the assent of the principal to the third person. For in the case where the existence of the principal is undisclosed, the third person did not assent to the principal as a party to the contract, and in the second group of cases the principal never assented nor expressed assent to the contract as made. It is for this reason that it cannot be said that the resulting obligation is a true contract, there being no mutual assent, even by the use of the most violent presumptions.

In group (1) where the existence of the principal is unknown, the resulting obligations are accepted by the commentators as something like an excrescence. It may be that historically it can be explained only through the fiction of the identity of master and servant, or as the outcome of "a kind of common law equity, powerfully aided and extended by the fiction of the identity of principal and agent and the doctrine of reciprocity or mutuality of contractual obligations." Pollock says frankly that "the position of an undisclosed principal is an anomaly." Ames goes further. He charges the doctrine with the two sins of ignoring fundamental principles and of producing injustice. Of course if it ignores fundamental principles, we must expect that it will produce injustice, if we have faith in our principles. But I think that the doctrine is not as black or as peculiar as it is painted and that the case against it is somewhat overstated.

Of course it is a fiction, though not because of that an anomaly at common law, to designate as a contract that which is obviously not consensual. There is nothing necessarily inconsistent, however, in allowing an action of assumpsit either by or against the principal, based upon the agreement made by the agent. Accepting Lewis' theory as sound, that assumpsit lies against one who has caused the plaintiff to change his position for a stipulated reward, the technical objection against allowing suit by the third person fails. And the common law was accustomed to enforce promises made to another than the plaintiff. It created an obligation to pay when land was left upon a condition, and later created out of whole cloth, by the fiction of an implied promise, all those obligations now known as quasi-contractual. In the case of the undisclosed principal, the only fiction alleged is that of treating the principal as a party to the contract, and this fiction is not needed either to create rights in favor of or obligations against the principal. . . . A principal receives profits and controls the manner of making them. It is for this reason that his duty to exonerate is both personal and unlimited. Liability follows control and it is not unjust, therefore, to allow the third person to recover against one who is both the receiver of the profits and the *dominus* of the one making the contract. . . .

In group (2) where the agent acts contrary to instructions and there is no element of representation by the principal to the third person, the courts have created a power in the agent in certain cases:

1. Where the agent is intrusted with the management of a business or with a series of transactions, he has the powers usual to an agent of his class, and limitations sought to be placed upon it are ineffective unless brought to the attention of the third person dealing with the agent.

(a) Where the existence of the principal is unknown. This result has been severely criticized, but has been accepted without hesitation by a great majority of the courts.

(b) Where the existence of the principal is disclosed, the existence of this agency power has been denied, explicitly by many and implicitly by all who, admitting the soundness of the general rules of undisclosed principal, disagree with *Watteau* v. *Fenwick*. For if this case is correct, it must be because of a principle that an agent has a power, in certain cases, greater than his authority, although there has been no element of representation to the third person. That such a power does exist where the existence of the principal is disclosed as well as where it is not, is seen by an examination of the cases. As seen before, "a holding out to the world" is not a representation to the particular third person. Nor can there be a holding out to him that an agent has a power to contract in conformity to the customs of the trade or locality unless such third person knows of such customs. If, therefore, liability were placed upon grounds of representation, it should be a part of the case of a third person seeking to hold a principal where the agent had acted in accordance with the powers usually conferred upon such agents, but contrary to his individual orders, to show that he, the third person, knew of such holding out or knew of the customs. In fact the cases do not require this. It follows, therefore, that the power must be created by the relationship of principal and agent, and that the principal is not bound upon a theory that he assented or manifested any assent; he is bound because he is a principal.

This method of approach assists in solving the difficult question of what is meant by instructions. Where the power is based solely upon representations, the only instructions which do not affect third persons are those intended to be kept secret and those which are purely by way of advice. But, as pointed out by Mechem, there are many instructions not intended to be kept secret which affect the third person only if he is informed of them. For example, there is no reason to suppose that ordinarily a principal intends that an agent not authorized to warrant should keep this limitation secret. Yet in the case of a general agent, the principal would be held liable were a warranty such as is customary in the business to be given. In dealing with the situations coming within the class considered here, the principal's intent as to this concealment by the agent becomes immaterial; the third person is unaffected by any instructions not in conformity with the customs of the locality or business, unless he knew or should have known of the instructions.

2. Where the agent is intrusted with the management of a particular transaction, and is given neither the possession of goods, nor documents indicating a more extended authority, I have discovered no cases where a principal has been held liable for unauthorized acts. In making this distinction, I am aware that modern text writers and some courts are inclined either to cast aside or minimize the effect of the classification into general and special agents. But although the necessity for its application may be infrequent, the classification was made by the older judges and commentators and it plays an important part in the development of the law. It cannot be said that it is difficult to contrast a general agent with a special agent. Justice Strong, in *Butler* v. *Mapes*, has summed up the judicial attitude: "The purpose of [a special agency] is a single transaction, or a transaction with designated persons. . . . Authority to buy for a principal a single article of merchandise by one contract, or to buy several articles from a person named, is a special agency, but authority to make purchases from any persons with whom the agent may choose to deal, or to make an indefinite number of purchases, is a general agency."

There is considerable business sense in the classification, which in effect creates powers in proportion to the authority created in another and adopts a convenient rule of thumb for easy measurement. It must be borne in mind, of course, that a special agent may be given the most complete authority in dealing with the particular matter intrusted to him. If it is said in some cases that a special agent has "general powers," the meaning is that the agent has been given such authority in dealing in the particular transaction as a general agent normally has. It must be remembered also that there may be a representation by the principal that the agent has greater authority than that given him and that the power will be commensurate with the representation. Furthermore the instructions given a special agent may be intended to be kept secret, or may be merely advice, intended not to limit the agent's powers but to guide his discretion. In these cases the instructions do not limit his powers. Furthermore, the fact that the agent acted in bad faith and in fraud of the principal is immaterial, unless known to the third person, since the motive with which the act is done does not affect the exercise of the power.

Reasons for the creation of agency powers. Unless it is true that an agent's power may be greater than his authority in cases where there has ̖een no representation of authority, there would be no necessity to discuss the reasons for the liability of the principal. Assuming that such powers have been created by law, there must be some reasons of public policy which require their existence. It must be in the protection of some conceived interest of business that, except in the case of a special agent, one is prevented from creating powers limited to the express authority given. The employer's interests are fully protected only if he is allowed to create powers of any kind and limited in any manner so long as he does not affirmatively mislead others.

In the first place it is to be noted that the conception that interests can be protected only in certain defined ways is not limited to the law of agency or to powers. Only certain interests in land will be protected by the creation of easements; the desire of the parties to create an easement is not enough. So a statement of an intention to make an instrument negotiable will not make it such. A mortgagor cannot in advance cut off his equity of redemption. "The law will not permit the owner of an estate to grant it alternately to his heirs male and female." For one reason or another the law prevents the creation of extraordinary types of dealing, because conceived to be injurious to the individual or to the public. It is, therefore, not inconsistent with the custom of judicial decision to create powers in accordance with general customs, if there are affirmative reasons for so doing.

In all the cases where an agent exceeds his authority, one of two persons, both innocent, must suffer. Between these two classes of persons, we must select the class which, in the long run, should suffer. The reasons which have actuated the courts in placing the burden upon the employer may be grouped under three heads.

Trust reposed in the agent. It is said that there is no reason for preferring the third person for he has trusted the agent. True, he does trust, but not equally with, nor in the same way as does the principal. In the case where the principal is undisclosed, T trusts the solvency of the agent; where the principal is known, he trusts his truthfulness. In both cases A and T are adversary parties. On the other hand the principal trusts the truthfulness, the honesty, the loyalty and the discretion of the agent, for that is what A has agreed to give him. When the agency relationship has been established A and P are not adversary parties; the agent is a fiduciary and subject to the stringent rules created upon the hypothesis that the fiduciary exists only to benefit the *cestui*. There is a trusting with a power, as in the case of a trustee there is a trusting with a title. It is true that there is no general principle that a known trustee may bind the trust estate where he acts in excess of the authority given him but, in the absence of notice of the existence of a written authorization, he may create rights in favor of third persons by such act.

Control. Liability follows control and the principal has a power of control at all times. It is true that normally liability for unintended results comes only where there has been negligent conduct on the part of the one who is held. There are, however, extrahazardous uses where liability for injurious results is absolute. And one of the elements of such liability is that the use shall be both dangerous and novel. It is not introducing an incongruity to subject the principal to liability where he has attempted to create an unusual power which may be expected to cause injury to third persons dealing with reference to the usual business methods.

Business convenience. Agency is essentially commercial; generally there is neither time nor opportunity to examine the extent of the powers of the individual agent by tracing them to their source. They have to be classified and taken at a face value. The general agent must circulate more or less as does a negotiable instrument without hindering conditions. Because of this, an agent sent out habitually with powers limited in certain abnormal ways would be in a position to cause injury to third persons. In sending out an agent, the principal knows, or should know, that his vouchers will not be carefully looked to. And he knows that the agent will not be apt to mention a lack of authority, for this might often interfere with sales. He knows of the human qualities which, at times, will lead even a faithful agent to overstep his authority in the desire to make sales. It is said that the third party need not deal with the agent. But if business is to continue, agents must be dealt with and protection given as experience rather than logic dictates.

In reaching this result, the courts have had before them the more or less imperfect analogy of the liability of a master for the torts of his servant. In both cases, the courts cannot avoid the conclusion that it is good business sense to hold that where one employs and controls another in the performance of acts for the benefit of a business, that business ought to pay for the mistakes, negligence and errors of judgment of the one so employed. For this purpose, the general agent may be said to bear the same relation to the special agent that a servant bears to an independent contractor.

3. NOTE ON MERCANTILE AGENTS

An agent in possession of his principal's goods was thought to present something of a trap to third parties, who might be induced by the agent's possession to believe that he had the right to dispose of the goods. In this situation, the Factors Act provides that the third party is protected, even though the agent acts in defiance of the true owner's express instructions. To this extent the common law moves some way towards the maxim of French law "possession vaut titre"—that is towards protection of the third party, in contra-distinction to the general common law maxim "nemo dat quod non habet" (no one can give what he doesn't own), which tends to protect the true owner in such situations.

THE FACTORS ACT,
R.S.O. 1970, c. 156

1. (1) In this Act,

(a) "document of title" includes any bill of lading and warehouse receipt, as defined by The Mercantile Law Amendment Act, any warrant or order for the delivery of goods, and any other document used in the ordinary course of business as proof of the possession or control of goods, or authorizing or purporting to authorize, either by endorsement or delivery, the possessor of the document to transfer or receive goods thereby represented;

(b) "goods" includes wares and merchandise;

(c) "mercantile agent" means a mercantile agent having, in the customary course of his business as such agent, authority either to sell goods or to consign goods for the purpose of sale, or to buy goods, or to raise money on the security of goods;

(d) "pledge" includes any contract pledging or giving a lien or security on goods, whether in consideration of an original advance or of any further or continuing advance or of any pecuniary liability.

(2) A person shall be deemed to be in possession of goods or of the documents of title to goods where the goods or documents are in his actual custody or are held by any other person subject to his control or for him or on his behalf.

2. (1) Where a mercantile agent is, with the consent of the owner, in possession of goods or of the documents of title to goods any sale, pledge or other disposition of the goods made by him, when acting in the ordinary course of business of a mercantile agent, shall, subject to the provisions of this Act, be as valid as if he were expressly authorized by the owner of the goods to make the same; provided that the person taking under the disposition acts in good faith and has not at the time thereof

notice that the person making the disposition has not authority to make the same.

(2) Where a mercantile agent has, with the consent of the owner, been in possession of goods or of documents of title to goods, any sale, pledge or other disposition which would have been valid if the consent had continued, shall be valid notwithstanding the determination of the consent; provided that the person taking under the disposition acts in good faith and has not at the time thereof notice that the consent has been determined.

(3) Where a mercantile agent has obtained possession of any documents of title to goods by reason of his being or having been, with the consent of the owner, in possession of the goods represented thereby, or of any other documents of title to the goods, his possession of the first mentioned documents shall, for the purposes of this Act, be deemed to be with the consent of the owner.

(4) For the purposes of this Act the consent of the owner shall be presumed in the absence of evidence to the contrary.

3. A pledge by a mercantile agent of the documents of title to goods shall be deemed to be a pledge of the goods.

10. The provisions of this Act shall be construed in amplification and not in derogation of the powers exercisable by an agent independently of this Act.

4. NOTE ON BUYERS AND SELLERS IN POSSESSION

Another instance of protecting one who relies on the apparent ownership of goods signified by possession, is the case of the buyer or seller of goods left in possession of them with the true owner's consent.

THE SALE OF GOODS ACT
R.S.O. 1970, c. 421

25. (1) Where a person having sold goods continues or is in possession of the goods or of the documents of title to the goods, the delivery or transfer by that person, or by a mercantile agent acting for him, of the goods or documents of title under any sale, pledge, or other disposition thereof, to any person receiving the same in good faith and without notice of the previous sale, shall have the same effect as if the person making the delivery or transfer were expressly authorized by the owner of the goods to make the same.

(2) Where a person having bought or agreed to buy goods obtains, with the consent of the seller, possession of the goods or the documents of title to the goods, the delivery or transfer by that person, or by a mercantile agent acting for him, of the goods or documents of title, under any sale, pledge or other disposition thereof to any person receiving the same in good faith and without notice of any lien or other right of the original seller in respect of the goods, shall have the same effect as if the person making the delivery or transfer were a mercantile agent in possession of the goods or documents of title with the consent of the owner.

(3) In this section "mercantile agent" means a mercantile agent having, in the customary course of his business as such agent, authority either to sell goods or to consign goods for the purpose of sale, or to buy goods, or to raise money on the security of goods.

[This section was originally in the English Factors Act of 1889 as secs. 8-9.]

Note that where a transaction creates what is, in substance, a security interest in goods (for example, a conditional sale agreement, or a chattel mortgage, where interest in goods is retained in order to secure payment of a debt), the Personal Property Security Act R.S.O. 1970, c. 344 applies. In general, this Act requires registration by the secured party of his interest, and gives in return priority over subsequent purchasers from and creditors of the debtor.

CHAPTER 5

THIRD PARTIES AND MISTAKE
IN DEALINGS BETWEEN OTHERS

A problem that frequently confronts the courts in a variety of situations is which of two more-or-less innocent parties to favour, when one or both of them must suffer for the fraud of a third party. The problem arises in the assignment cases: a creditor assigns a debt to a *bona fide* purchaser, who pays full value for it; it then turns out that the debtor has a defence against the creditor; should he, or should he not be able to assert that defence against the assignee? Consider the problem of the mercantile agent who, contrary to his principal's instructions, disposes of goods to an innocent third party; should the principal, or should he not, be able to assert against the third party the agent's lack of authority? This chapter is concerned with two further situations in which a similar problem arises. The first is the case of mistaken identity. The owner of goods sells them to a rogue, mistakenly believing that the rogue is a wealthy and respectable citizen; the rogue promises to pay to the owner the price of the goods, takes the goods, sells them to an innocent third party, and disappears; should the original owner, or should he not, be able to recover the goods without compensation from the third party? The other case in this chapter is that of documents mistakenly signed. Here the rogue obtains a signature to a document by misrepresenting its nature; an innocent third party, relying on the signature then pays value to the rogue, who, as usual, disappears, or is insolvent. Should the signer, or should he not, be able to allege against the third party that his signature is void? These problems have not always been considered together, and it is hoped that the analogy drawn here will be found useful in analysing them.

1. MISTAKE OF IDENTITY

BOULTON v. JONES
England. Exchequer. 1857. 2 H. & N. 564; 157 E.R. 232

At the trial before the Assessor of the Court of Passage at Liverpool, it appeared that the plaintiff had been foreman and manager of one Brocklehurst, a pipe hose manufacturer, with whom the defendants had been in the habit of dealing, and with whom they had a running account. On the morning of the 13th of January, 1857, the plaintiff bought Brocklehurst's stock, fixtures, and business, and paid for them. In the afternoon of the same day, the defendant's servant brought a written order, addressed to Brocklehurst, for some leather hose. The goods were supplied by the plaintiff. The plaintiff's bookkeeper struck out the name of Brocklehurst and inserted the name of the plaintiff in the order. An invoice was afterwards sent in by the plaintiff to the defendants, who said they knew nothing of him. Upon these facts, the jury, under direction of the Assessor, found a verdict for the plaintiff, and leave was reserved to the defendants to move to enter a verdict for them.

POLLOCK C.B.: The point raised is, whether the facts proved did not show an intention on the part of the defendants to deal with Brocklehurst.

The plaintiff, who succeeded Brocklehurst in business, executed the order without any intimation of the change that had taken place, and brought this action to recover the price of the goods supplied. It is a rule of law, that if a person intends to contract with A, B cannot give himself any right under it. Here the order in writing was given to Brocklehurst. Possibly Brocklehurst might have adopted the act of the plaintiff in supplying the goods, and maintained an action for their price. But since the plaintiff has chosen to sue, the only course the defendants could take was to plead that there was no contract with him.

MARTIN B.: I am of the same opinion. This is not a case of principal and agent. If there was any contract at all, it was not with the plaintiff. If a man goes to a shop and makes a contract, intending it to be with one particular person, no other person can convert that into a contract with him.

BRAMWELL B.: The admitted facts are, that the defendants sent to a shop an order for goods, supposing they were dealing with Brocklehurst. The plaintiff, who supplied the goods, did not undeceive them. If the plaintiff were now at liberty to sue the defendants, they would be deprived of their right of set-off as against Brocklehurst. When a contract is made in which the personality of the contracting party is or may be of importance, as a contract with a man to write a book, or the like, or where there might be a set-off, no other person can interpose and adopt the contract. As to the difficulty that the defendants need not pay anybody, I do not see why they should, unless they have made a contract either express or implied. I decide the case on the ground that the defendants did not know that the plaintiff was the person who supplied the goods, and that allowing the plaintiff to treat the contract as made with him would be a prejudice to the defendants.

CHANNELL B.: In order to entitle the plaintiff to recover he must show that there was a contract with himself. The order was given to the plaintiff's predecessor in business. The plaintiff executes it without notifying to the defendants who it was who executed the order. When the invoice was delivered in the name of the plaintiff, it may be that the defendants were not in a situation to return the goods.

Rule absolute.

[From the Law Journal report (27 L.J. Ex. 117) it appears that the defendant had a set-off against Brocklehurst, and that the case was argued on that basis.]

CUNDY v. LINDSAY
England. House of Lords. 1878. 3 App. Cas. 459

In 1873, one Alfred Blenkarn hired a room at a corner house in Wood Street, Cheapside; it had two side windows opening into Wood Street, but though the entrance was from Little Love Lane it was by him constantly described as 37, Wood Street, Cheapside. His agreement for this room was signed "Alfred Blenkarn." The now respondents, Messrs. Lindsay & Co., were linen manufacturers carrying on their business in Belfast. In the latter part of 1873, Blenkarn wrote to the plaintiffs on the subject of a purchase from them of goods of their manufacture,—chiefly cambric handkerchiefs. His letters were written as from "37, Wood Street, Cheapside," where he pretended to have a warehouse, but in fact occupied only a room on the top floor, and that room, though looking into Wood Street on one side, could only be reached from the entrance in 5, Little Love Lane. The name signed to these letters was always signed without any initial as representing a Christian name, and was, besides, so written as to appear "Blenkiron & Co." There was a highly respectable firm of W. Blenkiron & Son, carrying on business in Wood Street,—but at number 123, Wood Street, and not at 37. Messrs. Lindsay, who knew the respectability of Blenkiron & Son, though not the number of the house where they carried on business, answered the letters, and sent the goods addressed to "Messrs. Blenkiron & Co., 37, Wood Street, Cheapside," where they were taken in at once. The invoices sent with the goods were always addressed in the same way. Blenkarn sold the goods, thus fraudulently obtained from Messrs. Lindsay, to different persons, and among the rest he sold 250 dozen of cambric handkerchiefs to the Messrs. Cundy, who were bona fide purchasers, and who resold them in the ordinary way of their trade. Payment not being made, an action was commenced in the Mayor's Court of London by Messrs. Lindsay, the junior partner of which firm, Mr. Thompson, made the ordinary affidavit of debt, as against Alfred Blenkarn, and therein named Alfred Blenkarn as the debtor. Blenkarn's fraud was soon discovered, and he was prosecuted at the Central Criminal Court, and convicted and sentenced. Messrs. Lindsay then brought an action against Messrs. Cundy for unlawful conversion of the handkerchiefs. The cause was tried before Mr. Justice Blackburn, who left it to the jury to consider whether Alfred Blenkarn with a fraudulent intent to induce the plaintiffs to give him the credit belonging to the good character of Blenkiron & Son, wrote the letters, and by fraud induced the plaintiffs to send the goods to 37, Wood Street,— were they the same goods as those bought by the defendants, and did the plaintiffs by the affidavit of debt intend, as a matter of fact, to adopt Alfred Blenkarn as their debtor. The first and second questions were answered in the affirmative, and the third in the negative. A verdict was taken for the defendants, with leave reserved to move to enter the verdict for the plaintiffs. On motion accordingly, the court, after argument, ordered the rule for entering judgment for the plaintiffs to be discharged, and directed judgment to be entered for the defendants. On appeal, this decision was reversed and judgment ordered to be entered for the plaintiffs, Messrs. Lindsay. This appeal was then brought.

LORD CAIRNS L.C.: My Lords, you have in this case to discharge a duty which is always a disagreeable one for any court, namely to determine as between two parties, both of whom are perfectly innocent, upon which of the two consequences of a fraud practised upon both of them must fall. My Lords, in discharging that duty your Lordships can do no more than apply, rigorously, the settled and well-known rules of law. Now, with regard to the title to personal property, the settled and well-known rules of law may, I take it, be thus expressed: by the law of our country the purchaser of a chattel takes the chattel, as a general rule, subject to what may turn out to be certain infirmities in the title. If he purchases the chattel in market overt, he obtains a title which is good against all the world; but if he does not purchase the chattel in market overt, and if it turns out that the chattel has been found by the person who professed to sell it, the purchaser will not obtain a title good as against the real owner. If it turns out that the chattel has been stolen by the person who has professed to sell it, the purchaser will not obtain a title. If it turns out that the chattel has come into the hands of the person who professed to sell it, by a *de facto* contract, that is to say, a contract which has purported to pass the property to him from the owner of the property, there the purchaser will obtain a good title, even although afterwards it should appear that there were circumstances connected with that contract, which would enable the original owner of the goods to reduce it, and to set it aside because these circumstances so enabling the original owner of the goods, or of the chattel, to reduce the contract and to set it aside, will not be allowed to interfere with a title for valuable consideration obtained by some third party during the interval while the contract remained unreduced.

My Lords, the question, therefore, in the present case, as your Lordships will observe, really becomes the very short and simple one which I am about to state. Was there any contract which, with regards to the goods in question in this case, had passed the property in the goods from Messrs. Lindsay to Alfred Blenkarn? If there was any contract passing that property, even although, as I have said, that contract might afterwards be open to a process of reduction upon the ground of fraud, still, in the meantime, Blenkarn might have conveyed a good title for valuable consideration to the present appellants.

Now, my Lords, there are two observations bearing upon the solution of that question which I desire to make. In the first place, if the property in the goods in question passed, it could only pass by way of contract; there is nothing else which could have passed the property. The second observation is this, your Lordships are not here embarrassed by any conflict of evidence, or any evidence whatever as to conversations or as to acts done; the whole history of the whole transaction lies upon paper. The principal parties concerned, the respondents and Blenkarn, never came in contact personally—everything that was done was done by writing. What has to be judged of, and what the jury in the present case had to judge of, was merely the conclusion to be derived from that writing, as applied to the admitted facts of the case.

Now, my Lords, discharging that duty and answering that inquiry, what the jurors have found is in substance this: it is not necessary to spell out the words, because the substance of it is beyond all doubt. They have found that by the form of the signatures to the letters which were written by Blenkarn, by the mode in which his letters and his applications to the respondents were made out, and by the way in which he left uncorrected the mode and form in which, in turn, he was addressed by the respondent; that by all those means he led, and intended to lead, the respondents to believe, and they did believe that the person with whom they were communicating was not Blenkarn, the dishonest and irresponsible man, but was a well known and solvent house of Blenkiron & Co., doing business in the same street. My Lords, those things are found as matters of fact, and they are placed beyond the range of dispute and controversy in the case.

If that is so, what is the consequence? It is that Blenkarn—the dishonest man, as I call him—was acting here just in the same way as if he had forged the signature of Blenkiron & Co., the respectable firm, to the application for goods, and as if, when, in return, the goods were forwarded and letters were sent, accompanying them, he had intercepted the goods and intercepted the letters, and had taken possession of the goods, and of the letters which were addressed to, and intended for, not himself, but the firm of Blenkiron & Co. Now, my Lords, stating that matter shortly in that way, I ask the question, how is it possible to imagine that in the state of things any contract could have arisen between the respondents and Blenkarn, the dishonest man? Of him they knew nothing, and of him they never thought. With him they never intended to deal. Their minds never, even for an instant of time, rested upon him, and as between him and them there was no consensus of mind which could lead to any agreement or any contract whatever. As between him and them there was merely the one side to a contract, where, in order to produce a contract, two sides would be required. With the firm of Blenkiron & Co., of course there was no contract, for as to them the matter was entirely unknown, and therefore the pretence of a contract was a failure.

The result, therefore, my Lords, is this, that your Lordships have not here to deal with one of those cases in which there is *de facto* a contract made which may afterwards be impeached and set aside, on the ground of fraud; but you have to deal with a case which ranges itself under a completely different chapter of law, the case namely in which the contract never comes into existence. My Lords, that being so, it is idle to talk of the property passing. The property remained, as it originally had been, the property of the respondents, and the title which was intended to be given to the appellants was a title which could not be given to them.

My Lords, I therefore move your Lordships, that this appeal be dismissed with costs, and the judgment of the Court of Appeal affirmed.

[Lords Hatherly and Penzance also gave reasons for dismissing the appeal. Lord Gordon concurred.]

KING'S NORTON METAL CO. LTD. v. EDRIDGE, MERRETT, & CO. LTD.
England. Court of Appeal. 1897. 14 T.L.R. 98

The action was brought to recover damages for the conversion of one ton of brass rivet wire. The plaintiffs were metal manufacturers at King's Norton, Worcestershire, and the defendants were metal merchants at Birmingham. It appeared that in 1896 the plaintiffs received a letter purporting to come from Hallam & Co., Soho Hackle Pin and Wire Works, Sheffield, at the head of which was a representation of a large factory with a number of chimneys, and in one corner was a printed statement that Hallam & Co. had depots and agencies at Belfast, Lille, and Ghent. The letter contained a request by Hallam & Co. for a quotation of prices for brass rivet wire. In reply, the plaintiffs quoted prices, and Hallam & Co. then by letter ordered some goods, which were sent off to them. These goods were never paid for. It turned out that a man named Wallis had adopted the name of Hallam & Co., and fraudently obtained goods by the above means, and that Wallis sold the goods to the defendants, who bought them bona fide, and with no notice of any defect of title in Wallis. It appeared that the plaintiffs had been paid for some goods previously ordered by Hallam & Co., by a cheque drawn by "Hallam and Co." The plaintiffs brought this action to recover damages for the conversion of these goods. At the trial, the learned judge non-suited the plaintiffs upon the ground that the property in the goods had passed to Wallis, who sold them to the defendants before the plaintiffs had disaffirmed the contract.

A. L. SMITH L.J. said the case was a plain one. The question was whether the plaintiffs, who had been cheated out of their goods by a rogue called Wallis, or the defendants were to bear the loss. The law seemed to him to be well settled. If a person induced by false pretences contracted with a rogue to sell goods to him and the goods were delivered the rogue could until the contract was disaffirmed give a good title to the goods to a bona fide purchaser for value. The facts here were that Wallis, for the purpose of cheating, set up in business as Hallam and Co., and got note-paper prepared for the purpose, and wrote to the plaintiffs representing that he was carrying on business as Hallam and Co. He got the goods in question and sold them to the defendants, who bought them bona fide for value. The question was, With whom, upon this evidence, which was all one way, did the plaintiffs contract to sell goods? Clearly with the writer of the letters. If it could have been shown that there was a separate entity called Hallam and Co. and another entity called Wallis then the case might have come within the decision in *Cundy* v. *Lindsay* (1878), 3 App. Cas. 459. In his opinion there was a contract by the plaintiffs with the person who wrote the letters, by which the property passed to him. There was only one entity, trading it might be under an *alias*, and there was a contract by which the property passed to him. Mr. Justice CAVE said that this was nothing more than a long firm fraud. Did any one ever hear of an attempt being made by a person who had delivered his goods to a long firm to get his goods back on the ground that he had made no contract with the long firm? The indictment against a long firm was always for obtaining the goods by false pretences, which presupposed the passing of the property. For these reasons there was no question to go to the jury, and the non-suit was right.

[Rigby and Collins L.JJ. delivered judgments to the same effect.]

PHILLIPS v. *BROOKS*. [1910] 2 K.B. 243 (England. High Court). On April 15, 1918, a man entered the plaintiff's shop and asked to see some pearls and some rings. He selected pearls at the price of £2550 and a ring at the price of £450. He produced a cheque book and wrote out a cheque for £3000. In signing it, he said: "You see who I am, I am Sir George Bullough," and he gave an address in St. James's Square. The plaintiff knew there was such a person as Sir George Bullough, and finding on reference to a directory that Sir George lived at the address mentioned, he said, "Would you like to take the articles with you?", to which the man replied: "You had better have the cheque cleared first, but I should like to take the ring, as it is my wife's birthday tomorrow," whereupon the plaintiff let him have the ring. The cheque was dishonoured, the person who gave it being in fact a fraudulent person named North, who was subsequently convicted of obtaining the ring by false pretences. In the meantime, namely on April 16, 1918, North, in the name of Firth, had pledged the ring with the defendants, pawnbrokers, who, bona fide and without notice, advanced £350 upon it. Held, for the defendants. HORRIDGE J.: "... I think the seller intended to contract with the person present, and there was no error as to the person with whom he contracted, although the plaintiff would not have made the contract if there had not been a fraudulent misrepresentation. ..."

INGRAM v. LITTLE
England. Court of Appeal. [1961] 1 Q.B. 31

The Misses Ingram advertised their car for sale for £725. A stranger calling himself Hutchinson came to the house on August 3, 1957, and after an examination of the car offered Miss Elsie Ingram £700 for it. The offer was refused. After some discussion he offered £717, which was accepted.

Hutchinson then took out his cheque book, but at this time Miss Elsie immediately told him that she was only willing to sell for cash, that she was not prepared to accept a cheque, and started to leave the room, Hutchinson then described himself as Mr. P. G. M. Hutchinson, with business interests at Guildford and as living at Stanstead House, Stanstead Road, Caterham. Miss Hilda Ingram, who was present, slipped out and checked in the area telephone directory at the local post office. Finding an entry for "Hutchinson, P. G. M., Stanstead House, Stanstead Road, Caterham 4665" Miss Hilda returned, reported this fact, and the Misses Ingram decided to take Hutchinson's cheque and the deal was concluded. Hutchinson disappeared with the car and has not been heard of since under that name. On August 6, 1957 a man calling himself Hardy sold the Ingram car to Reginald Little in Blackpool. Hardy, or Hutchinson, disappeared and has not been heard of since under either name. In December, 1957, Little sold the car to another dealer. The plaintiffs sued Little for the return of the car or damages for its conversion. Slade J. held that Hutchinson and Hardy were the same person, and that Little had bought in good faith, but he held that the plaintiffs' mistake as to the identity of the person with whom they were dealing prevented the formation of a contract. He gave judgment for the plaintiffs for £720, the agreed value of the car. The defendant appealed.

SELLERS L.J.: . . . The decision in the present case turns solely on whether "Hutchinson" entered into a contract which gave him a title to the car which would subsist until it was avoided on the undoubted fraud being discovered. . . .

It does not seem to me to matter whether the right view of the facts is, as the judge has held and as I would agree, that there was no concluded contract before the cheque was produced and before the vital fraudulent statements were made or that there was a concluded contract which "Hutchinson" at once repudiated by refusing to pay cash and that this repudiation was accepted by the plaintiffs and the transaction was then and there at an end. The property would not have passed until cash had been paid and it never was paid or intended to be paid.

Was there a contract of sale subsequently made which led to the plaintiffs taking "Hutchinson's" cheque and in exchange for it handing over the car and its log book?

The judgment held that there never was a concluded contract, applying, as I understand it, the elementary factors required by law to establish a contract.

The judge, treating the plaintiffs as the offerors and the rogue "Hutchinson" as the offeree, found that the plaintiffs in making their offer to sell the car not for cash but for a cheque (which in the circumstances of the Bank Holiday week-end could not be banked before the following Tuesday, August 6, 1957) were under the belief that they were dealing with, and therefore making their offer to, the honest P. G. M. Hutchinson of Caterham, whom they had reason to believe was a man of substance and standing.

"Hutchinson," the offeree, knew precisely what was in the minds of the two ladies for he had put it there and he knew that their offer was intended for P. G. M. Hutchinson of Caterham and that they were making no offer to and had no intention to contract with him, as he was. There was no offer which he "Hutchinson" could accept and, therefore, there was no contract.

The judge pointed out that the offer which the plaintiffs made was one which was capable of being accepted only by the honest P. G. M. Hutchinson of Caterham and was incapable of acceptance by "Hutchinson."

In all the circumstances of the present case I would accept the judge's findings. Indeed the conclusion so reached seems self-evident.

Is the conclusion to be held wrong in law? If it is, then, as I see it, it must be on the sole ground that as "Hutchinson" was present, albeit making fraudulent statements to induce the plaintiffs to part with their car to him in exchange for his worthless cheque and was successful in so doing, then a bargain must have been struck with him personally, however much he deceived the plaintiffs into thinking they were dealing with someone else.

Where two parties are negotiating together and there is no question of one or the other purporting to act as agent for another, and an agreement is reached, the normal and obvious conclusion would no doubt be that they are the contracting parties. A contrary finding would not be justified unless very clear evidence demanded it. The unfortunate position of the defendant in this case illustrates how third parties who deal in good faith with the fraudulent person may be prejudiced.

The mere presence of an individual cannot, however, be conclusive that an apparent bargain he may make is made with him. If he were disguised in appearance and in dress to represent someone else and the other party, deceived by the disguise, dealt with him on the basis that he was that person and would not have contracted had he known the truth then, it seems clear, there would be no contract established. If words are substituted for outward disguise so as to depict a different person from the one physically present, in what circumstances would the result be different?

Whether the person portrayed, by disguise or words, is known to the other party or not is important in considering whether the identity of the person is of any moment or whether it is a matter of indifference. If a man said his name was Brown when it was in fact Smith, and both were unknown to the other party, it would be difficult to say that there was any evidence that the contract was not made and intended to be made with the person present. In *King's Norton Metal Co. Ltd* v. *Edridge, Merrett & Co. Ltd.* (1897), 14 T.L.R. 98, one Wallis fraudulently described himself as Hallam & Co., making it appear a substantial firm with a large factory. The court held that the use of an assumed name by the buyer did not prevent a finding that the plaintiffs, the sellers of some brass rivet wire, had contracted with him.

But personal knowledge of the person fraudulently represented cannot, I think, be an essential feature. It might be a very strong factor but the qualities of a person not personally known might be no less strong. If a man misrepresented himself to be a Minister of the Crown or a stockbroker, confidence in the person so identified might arise although the individual so described was wholly unknown personally or by sight to the other party.

It would seem that there is an area of fact in cases of the type under consideration where a fraudulent person is present purporting to make a bargain with another and that the circumstances may justify a finding that, notwithstanding some fraud and deceit, the correct view may be that a bargain was struck with the person present, or on the other hand they may equally justify, as here, a finding the other way.

Some of the difficulties and perhaps confusion which have arisen in some of the cases do not, in my view, arise here.

If less had been said by the rogue, and if nothing had been done to confirm his statements by Miss Hilda Ingram, who communicated what she had learnt to Miss Elsie who was doing the main negotiation, the result might have been different, for the sellers' concern about the stability and standing of the buyer might not have been revealed and it might have been held that an offer in such circumstances was to the party present, whatever his true identity would be.

In *Phillips* v. *Brooks Ltd.* [1919] 2 K.B. 243, the rogue had apparently been in the shop some time inspecting the goods which were brought and displayed for sale to him without any regard to his identity—he was a "customer" only. The judgment of Horridge J. is, as I read it, based on a finding of fact that Phillips intended to deal with North as a customer. Viscount Haldane, in *Lake* v. *Simmons*, [1927] A.C. 487, has taken the view that the case could be explained on the ground that the fraudulent misrepresentation was not made until after the parties had agreed upon a sale.

That opinion has been criticised, mainly, I think, by academic writers, but if, as must be conceded, it is a possible view, and as *Phillips* v. *Brooks Ltd.* has stood for so long and is, as I think, a decision within an area of fact, I would not feel justified in saying it was wrong.

It is not an authority to establish that where an offer or acceptance is addressed to a person (although under a mistake as to his identity) who is present in person, then it must in all circumstances be treated as if actually addressed to him. I would regard the issue as a question of fact in each case depending on what was said and done and applying the elementary principles of offer and acceptance in the manner in which Slade J. directed himself.

The judgment quotes extensively from the article by Dr. Goodhart, the editor of the Law Quarterly Review, called "Mistake as to identity in the Law of Contract" (1941) 57 L.Q.R. 228, and I would join the judge in his expression of indebtedness to the author. Referring to *Phillips* v. *Brooks Ltd.* Dr. Goodhart asked "Did the shopkeeper believe that he was entering into a contract with Sir George Bullough and did North know this? If both answers are in the affirmative, then it is submitted that there was no contract."

I think there may be a doubt in that case whether both the answers should have been in the affirmative, but on the facts of the present case I feel no doubt and I would uphold the judge's views of no contract.

Dr. Goodhart might well be right when he said that "There is no branch of the law of contract which is more uncertain and difficult" than that involved in the present case, and I am conscious that our decision here will not have served to dispel the uncertainty. . . .

I am in agreement with the judge when he quotes, accepts and applies the following passage from Dr. Goodhart's article—"It is the interpretation of the promise which is the essential thing. This is usually based on the interpretation which a reasonable man, in the promisee's position, would place on it, but in those cases where the promisor knows that the promisee has placed a peculiar interpretation on his words, then this is the binding one. The English law is not concerned with the motives of the parties nor with the reasons which influenced their actions. For practical reasons it has limited itself to the simple questions: what did the promisor promise, and how should this be interpreted?"

Phillips v. *Brooks Ltd.* is the closest authority on which the defendant relies. Once that is distinguished on its facts, without going so far as to say it is wrong, authority leans strongly in favour of the judgment appealed from. . . .

DEVLIN L.J. (dissenting): . . . Before, therefore, I consider mistake, I shall inquire whether there is offer and acceptance in form. There is no doubt that H's offer was addressed to Miss Ingram and her acceptance apparently, addressed to him. But, it is argued, the acceptance was in reality addressed to P. G. M. Hutchinson, who was not the offeror, and, therefore, no contract was made. There can be no doubt upon the authorities that this argument must be settled by inquiring with whom Miss Ingram intended to contract: was it with the person to whom she was speaking or was it with the person whom he represented himself to be? . . . All that Miss Ingram or any other witness in her position can say is that she did in fact accept the offer made to her; and that, if she had not been tricked or deceived, she would not have accepted it.

Courts of law are not inexperienced in dealing with this sort of situation. They do so by means of presumptions. . . . Whether the court, when it acts in this way, is really ascertaining the intentions of the parties or whether it is simply providing a just solution of their difficulties is a theoretical question which I need not explore. . . .

In my judgment, the court cannot arrive at a satisfactory solution in the present case except by formulating a presumption and taking it at least as a starting point. The presumption that a person is intending to contract with the person to whom he is actually addressing the words of contract seems to me to be a simple and sensible one and supported by some good authority. . . .

I do not think it can be said that the presumption is conclusive, since there is at least one class of case in which it can be rebutted. If the person addressed is posing only as an agent it is plain that the party deceived has no thought of contracting with him but only with his supposed principal; if then there is no actual or ostensible authority, there can be no contract. *Hardman* v. *Booth* (1863), 1 H. & C. 803, is, I think, an example of this. Are there any other circumstances in which the presumption can be rebutted? It is not necessary to strain to find them, for we are here dealing only with offer and acceptance; contracts in which identity really matters may still be avoided on the ground of mistake. I am content to leave the question open, and do not propose to speculate on what other exceptions there may be to the general rule. What seems plain to me is that the presumption cannot in the present case be rebutted by piling up the evidence to show that Miss Ingram would never have contracted with H. unless she had thought him to be P. G. M. Hutchinson. That fact is conceded and, whether it is proved simpliciter or proved to the hilt, it does not go any further than to show that she was the victim of fraud. With great respect to the judge, the question that he propounded as the test is not calculated to show any more than that. He said: "Is it to be seriously suggested that they were willing to accept the cheque of the rogue other than in the belief, created by the rogue himself, that he, the rogue, was in fact the honest P. G. M. Hutchinson of the address in Caterham with the telephone number which they had verified?" In my judgment, there is everything to show that Miss Ingram would never have accepted H.'s offer if she had known the truth, but nothing to rebut the ordinary presumption that she was addressing her acceptance, in law as well as in fact, to the person to whom she was speaking. I think, therefore, that there was offer and acceptance in form.

On my view of the law, it, therefore, becomes necessary to consider next whether there has been a mistake that vitiates the contract. As both my brethren are of opinion that there has been no offer and acceptance, the result of this further inquiry cannot affect the decision in the present case or its ratio, and I shall, therefore, state my conclusion and my reasons for it as briefly as may be.

In my judgment there has been no such mistake. I shall assume without arguments what I take to be the widest view of mistake that is to be found in the authorities, and that is that a mistake avoids the contract if at the time it is made there exists some state of fact which, as assumed, is the basis of the contract and as it is in truth, frustrates its object. . . .

The fact that Miss Ingram refused to contract with H. until his supposed name and address had been "verified" goes to show that she regarded his identity as fundamental. In this she was misguided. She should have concerned herself with creditworthiness rather than with identity. The fact that H. gave P. G. M. Hutchinson's address in the directory was no proof that he was P. G. M. Hutchinson; and if he had been, that fact alone was no proof that his cheque would be met. Identity, therefore, did not really matter. Nevertheless, it may truly be said that to Miss Ingram, as she looked at it, it did. In my judgment, Miss Ingram's state of mind is immaterial to this question. When the law avoids a contract ab initio, it does so irrespective of the intentions or opinions or wishes of the parties themselves. . . . This rule applies in the case of mistake because the reason for the avoidance is the same, namely, that the consent is vitiated by nonagreement about essentials. It is for the court to determine what in the light of all the circumstances is to be deemed essential. In my judgment, in the present case H.'s identity was immaterial. His creditworthiness was not, but creditworthiness in relation to contract is not a basic fact; it is only a way of expressing the belief that each party normally holds that the other will honour his promise. . . .

There can be no doubt, as all this difference of opinion shows, that the dividing line between voidness and voidability, between fundamental mistake and incidental deceit, is a very fine one. That a fine and difficult distinction has to be drawn is not necessarily any reproach to the law. But need the rights of the parties in a case like this depend on such a distinction? The great virtue of the common law is that it sets out to solve legal problems by the application to them of principles which the ordinary man is expected to recognise as sensible and just; their application in any particular case may produce what seems to him a hard result, but as principles they should be within his understanding and merit his approval. But here, contrary to its habit, the common law, instead of looking for a principle that is simple and just, rests on theoretical distinctions. Why should the question whether the defendant should or should not pay the plaintiff damages for conversion depend upon voidness or voidability, and upon inferences to be drawn from a conversation in which the defendant took no part? The true spirit of the common law is to override theoretical distinctions when they stand in the way of doing practical justice. For the doing of justice, the relevant question in this sort of case is not whether the contract was void or voidable, but which of two innocent parties shall suffer for the fraud of a third. The plain answer is that the loss should be divided between them in such proportion as is just in all the circumstances. If it be pure misfortune, the loss should be borne equally; if the fault or imprudence of either party has caused or contributed to the loss, it should be borne by that party in the whole or in the greater part. In saying this, I am suggesting nothing novel, for this sort of observation has often been made. But it is only in comparatively recent times that the idea of giving to a court power to apportion loss has found a place in our law. I have in mind particularly the Law Reform Acts of 1935, 1943 and 1945, that dealt respectively with joint tortfeasors, frustrated contracts and contributory negligence. These statutes, which I believe to have worked satisfactorily, show a modern inclination towards a decision based on a just apportionment rather than one given in black or white according to the logic of the law. I believe it would be useful if Parliament were now to consider whether or not it is practicable by means of a similar act of law reform to provide for the victims of a fraud a better way of adjusting their mutual loss than that which has grown out of the common law.

[The judgment of Pearce L.J. is omitted. The appeal was dismissed but leave was granted to appeal to the House of Lords.]

LEWIS v. *AVERAY*
[1972] 1 Q.B. 198 (C.A.)

LORD DENNING M.R.: This is another case where one of two innocent persons has to suffer for the fraud of a third. It will no doubt interest students and find its place in the textbooks.

Mr. Lewis is a young man who is a post-graduate student of chemistry. He lives at Clifton near Bristol. He had an Austin Cooper "S" motor car. He decided to sell it. He put an advertisement in the newspaper offering it for £450. On May 8, 1969, in reply to the advertisement a man—I will simply call him the "rogue," for so he was—telephoned and asked if he could come and see the car. He did not give his name. He said he was speaking from Wales, in Glamorganshire. Mr. Lewis said he could come and see it. He came in the evening to Mr. Lewis's flat. Mr. Lewis showed him the car, which was parked outside. The rogue drove it and tested it. He said he liked it. They then went along to the flat of Mr. Lewis's fiancée, Miss Kershaw (they have since married). He told them he was Richard Green and talked much about the film world. He led both of them to believe that he was the well-known film actor, Richard Greene, who played Robin Hood in the "Robin Hood" series. They talked about the car. He asked to see the logbook. He was shown it and seemed satisfied. He said he would like to buy the car. They agreed a price of £450. The rogue wrote out a cheque for £450 on the Beckenham Branch of the Midland Bank. He signed it "R. A. Green." He wanted to take the car at once. But Mr. Lewis was not willing for him to have it until the cheque was cleared. To hold him off, Mr. Lewis said there were one or two small jobs he would like to do on the car before letting him have it, and that would give time for the cheque to be cleared. The rogue said. "Don't worry about those small jobs. I would like to take the car now." Mr. Lewis said: "Have you anything to prove that you are Mr. Richard Green?" The rogue thereupon brought out a special pass of admission to Pinewood Studios, which had an official stamp on it. It bore the name of Richard A. Green and the address, and also a photograph which was plainly the photograph of this man, who was the rogue.

On seeing this pass, Mr. Lewis was satisfied. He thought this man was really Mr. Richard Greene, the film actor. By that time it was 11 o'clock at night. Mr. Lewis took the cheque and let the rogue have the car and the logbook and the Ministry of Transport test certificate. Each wrote and signed a receipt evidencing the transaction. Mr. Lewis wrote:

"Received from
Richard A. Green, 59 Marsh Rd., Beckenham, Kent
the sum of £450 in return for Austin Cooper S Reg.
No. AHT 484B chassis No. CA257—549597
Keith Lewis."

The rogue wrote:
"Received logbook No. 771835 and M.O.T. for Mini-
Cooper S No. AHT 484B
R. A. Green."

Next day, May 9, 1969, Mr. Lewis put the cheque into the bank. A few days later the bank told him it was worthless. The rogue had stolen a cheque book and written this £450 on a stolen cheque.

Meanwhile, while the cheque was going through, the rogue sold the car to an innocent purchaser. He sold it to a young man called Mr. Averay. He was at the time under 21. He was a music student in London at the Royal College of Music. His parents live at Bromley. He was keen to buy a car. He put an advertisement in the "Exchange and Mart," seeking a car for £200. In answer he had a telephone call from the rogue. He said he was speaking from South Wales. He said that he was coming to London to sell a car. Mr. Averay arranged to meet him on May 11, 1969. The rogue came with the car. Young Mr. Averay liked it, but wanted to get the approval of his parents. They drove it to Bromley. The parents did approve. Young Mr. Averay agreed to buy it for £200. The rogue gave his name as Mr. Lewis. He handed over the car and logbook to young Mr. Averay. The logbook showed the owner as Mr. Lewis. In return Mr. Averay, in entire good faith, gave the rogue a cheque for £200. The rogue signed this receipt:

"Sale of Cooper S to A. J. Averay.
Received £200 for the Cooper S Registration No.
AHT 484B, the said car being my property absolutely,
there being no hire purchase charges outstanding or
other impediment to selling the car:
Keith Lewis
May 13, 1969."

A fortnight later, on May 29, 1969, Mr. Averay wanted the workshop manual for the car. So his father on his behalf wrote to the name and address of the seller as given in the logbook—that is, Mr. Lewis. Then, of course, the whole story came to light. The rogue had cashed the cheque and disappeared. The police have tried to trace him, but without success.

Now Mr. Lewis, the original owner of the car, sues young Mr. Averay. Mr. Lewis claims that the car is still his. He claims damages for conversion. The judge found in favour of Mr. Lewis and awarded damages of £330 for conversion.

The real question in the case is whether on May 8, 1969, there was a contract of sale under which the property in the car passed from Mr. Lewis to the rogue. If there was such a contract, then, even though it was voidable for fraud, nevertheless Mr. Averay would get a good title to the car. But if there was no contract of sale by Mr. Lewis to the rogue— either because there was, on the face of it, no agreement between the parties, or because any apparent agreement was a nullity and void ab initio for mistake, then no property would pass from Mr. Lewis to the rogue. Mr. Averay would not get a good title because the rogue had no property to pass to him.

There is no doubt that Mr. Lewis was mistaken as to the identity of the person who handed him the cheque. He thought that he was Richard Greene, a film actor of standing and worth: whereas in fact he was a rogue whose identity is quite unknown. It was under the influence of that mistake that Mr. Lewis let the rogue have the car. He would not have dreamed of letting him have it otherwise.

What is the effect of this mistake? There are two cases in our books which cannot, to my mind, be reconciled the one with the other. One of them is *Phillips* v. *Brooks Ltd.* [1919] 2 K.B. 243, where a jeweller had a ring for sale. The other is *Ingram* v. *Little* [1961] 1 Q.B. 31, where two ladies had a car for sale. In each case the story is very similar to the present. A plausible rogue comes along. The rogue says he likes the ring, or the car, as the case may be. He asks the price. The seller names it. The rogue says he is prepared to buy it at that price. He pulls out a cheque book. He writes, or prepares to write, a cheque for the price. The seller hesitates. He has never met this man before. He does not want to hand over the ring or the car not knowing whether the cheque will be met. The rogue notices the seller's hesitation. He is quick with his next move. He says to the jeweller, in *Phillips* v. *Brooks*: "I am Sir George Bullough of 11 St. James's Square"; or to the ladies in *Ingram* v. *Little* "I am P. G. M. Hutchinson of Stanstead House, Stanstead Road, Caterham"; or to the post-graduate student in the present case: "I am Richard Greene, the film actor of the Robin Hood series." Each seller checks up the information. The jeweller looks up the directory and finds there is a Sir George Bullough at 11 St. James's Square. The ladies check up too. They look at the telephone directory and find there is a "P. G. M. Hutchinson of Stanstead House, Stanstead Road, Caterham." The post-graduate student checks up too. He examines the official pass of the Pinewood Studios and finds that it is a pass for "Richard A. Green" to the Pinewood Studios with this man's photograph on it. In each case the seller feels that this is sufficient confirmation of the man's identity. So he accepts the cheque signed by the rogue and lets him have the ring, in the one case, and the car and logbook in the other two cases. The rogue goes off and sells the goods to a third person who buys them in entire good faith and pays the price to the rogue. The rogue disappears. The original seller presents the cheque. It is dishonoured. Who is entitled to the goods? The original seller? Or the ultimate buyer? The courts have given different answers. In *Phillips* v. *Brooks*, the ultimate buyer was held to be entitled to the ring. In *Ingram* v. *Little* the original seller was held to be entitled to the car. In the present case the deputy county court judge has held the original seller entitled.

It seems to me that the material facts in each case are quite indistinguishable the one from the other. In each case there was, to all outward appearance, a contract: but there was a mistake by the seller as to the identity of the buyer. This mistake was fundamental. In each case it led to the handing over of the goods. Without it the seller would not have parted with them.

This case therefore raises the question: What is the effect of a mistake by one party as to the identity of the other? It has sometimes been said that if a party makes a mistake as to the identity of the person with whom he is contracting there is no contract, or, if there is a contract, it is a nullity and void, so that no property can pass under it. This has been supported by a reference to the French jurist Pothier; but I have said before, and I repeat now, his statement is no part of English law. I know that it was quoted by Lord Haldane in *Lake* v. *Simmons* [1927] A.C. 487, 501, and, as such, misled Tucker J. in *Sowler* v. *Potter* [1940] 1 K.B. 271, into holding that a lease was void whereas it was really voidable. But Pothier's statement has given rise to such refinements that it is time it was dead and buried altogether.

For instance, in *Ingram* v. *Little* [1961] 1 Q.B. 31 the majority of the court suggested that the difference between *Phillips* v. *Brooks* [1919] 2 K.B. 243 and *Ingram* v. *Little* was that in *Phillips* v. *Brooks* the contract of sale was concluded (so as to pass the property to the rogue) before the rogue made the fraudulent misrepresentation: see [1961] 1 Q.B. 31, 51, 60: whereas in *Ingram* v. *Little* the rogue made the fraudulent misrepresentation before the contract was concluded. My own view is that in each case the property in the goods did not pass until the seller let the rogue have the goods.

Again it has been suggested that a mistake as to the identity of a person is one thing: and a mistake as to his attributes is another. A mistake as to identity, it is said, avoids a contract: whereas a mistake as to attributes does not. But this is a distinction without a difference. A man's very name is one of his attributes. It is also a key to his identity. If then, he gives a false name, is it a mistake as to his identity? or a mistake as to his attributes? These fine distinctions do no good to the law.

As I listened to the argument in this case, I felt it wrong that an innocent purchaser (who knew nothing of what passed between the seller and the rogue) should have his title depend on such refinements. After all, he has acted with complete circumspection and in entire good faith: whereas it was the seller who let the rogue have the goods and thus enabled him to commit the fraud. I do not, therefore, accept the theory that a mistake as to identity renders a contract void. I think the true principle is that which underlies the decision of this court in *King's Norton Metal Co. Ltd.* v. *Edridge Merrett & Co. Ltd.* (1897) 14 T.L.R. 98 and of Horridge J. in *Phillips* v. *Brooks* [1919] 2 K.B. 243, which has stood for these last 50 years. It is this: When two parties have come to a contract—or rather what appears, on the face of it, to be a contract—the fact that one party is mistaken as to the identity of the other does not mean that there is no contract, or that the contract is a nullity and void from the beginning. It only means that the contract is voidable, that is, liable to be set aside at the instance of the mistaken person, so long as he does so before third parties have in good faith acquired rights under it.

Applied to the cases such as the present, this principle is in full accord with the presumption stated by Pearce L.J. and also Devlin L.J. in *Ingram* v. *Little* [1961] 1 Q.B. 31, 61, 66. When a dealing is had between a seller like Mr. Lewis and a person who is actually there present before him, then the presumption in law is that there is a contract, even though there is a fraudulent impersonation by the buyer representing himself as a different man than he is. There is a contract made with the very person there, who is present in person. It is liable no doubt to be avoided for fraud, but it is still a good contract under which title will pass unless and until it is avoided. In support of that presumption, Devlin L.J. quoted, at p. 66, not only the English case of *Phillips* v. *Brooks*, but other cases in the United States where "the courts hold that if A appeared in person before B, impersonating C, an innocent purchaser from A gets the property in the goods against B." That seems to me to be right in principle in this country also.

In this case Mr. Lewis made a contract of sale with the very man, the rogue, who came to the flat. I say that he "made a contract" because in this regard we do not look into his intentions, or into his mind to know what he was thinking or into the mind of the rogue. We look to the outward appearances. On the face of the dealing. Mr. Lewis made a contract under which he sold the car to the rogue, delivered the car and the logbook to him, and took a cheque in return. The contract is evidenced by the receipts which were signed. It was, of course, induced by fraud. The rogue made false representations as to his identity. But it was still a contract, though voidable for fraud. It was a contract under which this property passed to the rogue, and in due course passed from the rogue to Mr. Averay, before the contract was avoided.

Though I very much regret that either of these good and reliable gentlemen should suffer, in my judgment it is Mr. Lewis who should do so. I think the appeal should be allowed and judgment entered for the defendant.

[Phillimore and Megaw L.J.J. agreed.]

2. DOCUMENTS MISTAKENLY SIGNED

FOSTER v. *MACKINNON*
England. Common Pleas. 1869. L.R. 4 C.P. 704

This was an action by an indorsee against an indorser on a bill of exchange for £3000. One Callow, who was called as a witness for the plaintiff, testified that the defendant, an elderly man, signed the note in his presence, he having taken the bill, as drawn and endorsed by one Cooper, to the defendant and asked him to sign it telling him it was a guarantee. The defendant had previously signed a guarantee for £3000 for Callow but no liability had resulted to him. Callow only showed the defendant the back of the paper; it was, however, in the ordinary shape of a bill of exchange, and bore a stamp, the impress of which was visible through the paper. The defendant wrote his signature right after Cooper's. Bovill C.J. at the trial told the jury that, if the endorsement was not the signature of the defendant, or if, being his signature, it was obtained upon a fraudulent representation that it was a guarantee, and the defendant signed it without knowing that it was a bill, and under the belief that it was a guarantee, and if the defendant was not guilty of any negligence in so signing the paper, he was entitled to the verdict. The jury found for the defendant. On a rule nisi for a new trial on grounds of misdirection and that the verdict was against the weight of evidence.

BYLES J. delivered the judgment of the Court: . . . The case presented by the defendant is, that he never made the contract declared on; that he never saw the face of the bill; that the purport of the contract was fraudulently mis-described to him; that, when he signed one thing, he was told and believed that he was signing another and an entirely different thing; and that his mind never went with his act.

It seems plain, on principle and on authority, that, if a blind man, or man who cannot read, or who for some reason (not implying negligence) forgot to read, has a written contract falsely read over to him, the reader misreading to such a degree that the written contract is of a nature altogether different from the contract pretended to be read from the paper which the blind or illiterate man afterwards signs; then, at least if there be no negligence, the signature so obtained is of no force. And it is invalid not merely on the ground of fraud, where fraud exists, but on the ground that the mind of the signer did not accompany the signature; in other words that he never intended to sign, and therefore in contemplation of law never did sign, the contract to which his name is appended.

The authorities appear to us to support this view of the law. In *Thoroughgood's Case* (1582), 2 Co. Rep. 9a; 76 E.R. 408, it was held that, if an illiterate man have a deed falsely read over to him, and he then seals and delivers the parchment; that parchment is nevertheless not his deed. In a note to *Thoroughgood's Case*, in Fraser's edition of *Coke's Reports*, it is suggested that the doctrine is not confined to the condition of an illiterate grantor; and a case in Keilway's *Reports*, 70, pl. 6, is cited in support of this observation. On reference to that case it appears that one of the judges did there observe that it made no difference whether the grantor were lettered or unlettered. That, however, was a case where the grantee himself was the defrauding party. But the position that, if a grantor or covenantor be deceived or misled as to the *actual contents* of the deed, the deed does not bind him, is supported by many authorities.... Accordingly, it has recently been decided in the Exchequer Chamber, that, if a deed be delivered, and a blank left therein be afterwards improperly filled up (at least if that be done without the grantor's negligence), it is not the deed of the grantor: *Swan v. North British Australasian Land Company* (1863), 2 H. & C. 175; 159 E.R. 73.

These cases apply to deeds; but the principle is equally applicable to other written contracts. Nevertheless, this principle, when applied to negotiable instruments, must be and is limited in its application. These instruments are not only assignable, but they form part of the currency of the country. A qualification of the general rule is necessary to protect innocent transferees for value. If, therefore, a man write his name across the back of a blank bill-stamp, and part with it, and the paper is afterwards improperly filled up, he is liable as indorser. If he write it across the face of the bill, he is liable as acceptor, when the instrument has once passed into the hands of an innocent indorsee for value before maturity, and liable to the extent of any sum which the stamp will cover.

In these cases, however, the party signing knows what he is doing; the indorser intended to indorse, and the acceptor intended to accept, a bill of exchange to be thereafter filled up, leaving the amount, the date, the maturity, and the other parties to the bill undetermined.

But, in the case now under consideration, the defendant, according to the evidence, if believed, and the finding of the jury, never intended to indorse a bill of exchange at all, but intended to sign a contract of an entirely different nature. It was not his design, and, if he were guilty of no negligence, it was not even his fault that the instrument he signed turned out to be a bill of exchange. It was as if he had written his name on a sheet of paper for the purpose of franking a letter, or in a lady's album, or on an order for admission to the Temple Church, or on the fly-leaf of a book, and there had already been, without his knowledge, a bill of exchange or a promissory note payable to order inscribed on the other side of the paper. To make the case clearer, suppose the bill or note on the other side of the paper in each of these cases to be written at a time subsequent to the signature, then the fraudulent misapplication of that genuine signature to a different purpose would have been a counterfeit alteration of a writing with intent to defraud, and would therefore have amounted to a forgery. In that case, the signer would not have been bound by his signature, for two reasons, first, that he never in fact signed the writing declared on, and, secondly, that he never intended to sign any such contract.

In the present case, the first reason does not apply, but the second reason does apply. The defendant never intended to sign that contract, or any such contract. He never intended to put his name to any instrument that then was or thereafter might become negotiable. He was deceived, not merely as to the legal effect, but as to the *actual contents* of the instrument.

We are not aware of any case in which the precise question now before us has arisen on bills of exchange or promissory notes, or been judicially discussed. . . . But, in *Putnam* v. *Sullivan*, an American case, reported in 4 Mass. 45, and cited in *Parsons on Bills*, vol. i, p. 111 n., a distinction is taken by Chief Justice Parsons between a case where an endorser intended to indorse such a note as he actually indorsed, being induced by fraud to indorse it, and a case where he intended to indorse a different note and for a different purpose. And the Court intimated an opinion that, even in such a case as that, a distinction might prevail and protect the indorsee.

The distinction in the case now under consideration is a much plainer one; for, on this branch of the rule, we are to assume that the indorser never intended to indorse at all, but to sign a contract of an entirely different nature.

For these reasons, we think the direction of the Lord Chief Justice was right.

[A new trial was granted because "the case should undergo further investigation."]

HOWATSON v. WEBB
England. Chancery Division. [1907] 1 Ch. 537

Webb was the managing clerk of one Hooper, a solicitor, who was engaged in building speculations near Edmonton, north of London, for the purposes of which Hooper had had various leases put in Webb's name as nominee for him. Some time after Webb had left Hooper's service, Hooper called him on the phone and asked him to come over and sign some deeds "transferring the Edmonton property." Webb went the same day and arrived about lunch time. Hooper seemed to be in a great hurry and asked Webb to sign and "Hurry up and come and join me at lunch." Webb asked ":What are the deeds?" to which Hooper replied, "They are just deeds transferring that property," presumably meaning the Edmonton property. Hooper then went out and Webb signed a number of deeds left open for signature on a table. One was a mortgage dated that day, June 2, 1899, between Webb and one Whitaker as mortgagee and contained Webb's covenant to pay the mortgagee £1000. During the next seven years Hooper paid the interest and £200 on principal. Webb was not called upon to pay any interest, but on February 2, 1906, the plaintiff, Miss Howatson, asked for payment of the principal. Miss Howatson took a transfer of the mortgage from Whitaker in October, 1902, and paid Whitaker, or possibly Hooper, as solicitor in the transaction, £800. Webb raised the defence of *non est factum*.

WARRINGTON J.: The question in this case is which of two innocent parties is to suffer for the roguery of a third party. . . . [After a careful review of *Foster* v. *Mackinnon* and some other cases, Warrington J. continued:]

What does the evidence in the present case shew? I may go so far in the defendant's favour as to say that Webb, having regard to his knowledge of Hooper, when Hooper said that the deeds were "deeds for transferring the Edmonton property" was justified in believing that they were deeds such as a nominee could be called upon to execute either in favour of a new nominee or for the purpose of putting an end to his own position of nominee, and certainly not a deed creating a mortgage to another person. But in my opinion that is not enough. He was told that they were deeds relating to the property to which they did in fact relate. His mind was therefore applied to the question of dealing with that property. The deeds did deal with that property. The misrepresentation was as to the contents of the deed, and not as to the character and class of the deed. He knew he was dealing with the class of deed with which in fact he was dealing, but did not ascertain its contents. The deed contained a covenant to pay. Under those circumstances I cannot say that the deed is absolutely void. It purported to be a transfer of the property, and it was a transfer of the property. If the plea of *non est factum* is to succeed the deed must be wholly, and not partly, void. If that plea is an answer in this case, I must hold it to be an answer in every case of misrepresentation. In my opinion the law does not go as far as that. The defence therefore fails. There must therefore be judgment for the plaintiff on the claim with costs. . . .

[The judgment of Warrington J., which has been drastically cut, was unanimously affirmed on appeal. [1908] 1 Ch. 1.]

CARLISLE AND CUMBERLAND BANKING CO. v. BRAGG
England. Court of Appeal. [1911] 1 K.B. 489

This was an action by the Bank on a written guarantee signed by Bragg in the following circumstances. Bragg and one Rigg had been drinking together. Rigg produced a paper, and asked Bragg to sign it; he didn't read it to Bragg, or tell him it was a guarantee. Rather he told him that it was a duplicate of a paper Bragg had signed the day before, which had got blurred in the rain. Bragg did not read the paper and testified later that he thought it was an insurance matter which he had previously signed. Rigg later forged the signature of an attesting witness and handed it to the Bank. Rigg owed the Bank the amount claimed from Bragg on the guarantee in this action. The jury were asked and answered: (1) Was the defendant induced to sign the guarantee by the fraud of Rigg? Yes. (2) Did the defendant know that the document which he signed was a guarantee? No. (3) Was the defendant negligent in signing the guarantee? Yes. (4) Was Rigg the agent of the bank? No. Pickford J. on these findings gave judgment for the defendant. The Bank appealed.

VAUGHAN WILLIAMS L.J.: In my opinion the judgment of Pickford J.

in this case was quite right. He held that the finding of negligence by the jury was immaterial, and he did so after discussing the case of *Foster* v. *Mackinnon* (1869), L.R. 4 C.P. 704, and coming to the conclusion that the doctrine there laid down as regards negligence really has reference to the particular case of a negotiable instrument, to an action on which the defence that the defendant was induced to sign the instrument by fraud and misrepresentation as to its nature is set up as against a bona fide holder for value. As I understand it, that doctrine is limited to negotiable instruments, and that was really the ground of the judgment of Pickford J. in this case. Now let me deal with the matter apart from any question of negotiable instruments. In this case the finding of the jury is that the signature of the defendant to this document was obtained by fraud. The jury were asked: "Was the defendant induced to sign the guarantee by fraud of Riggs?" They answered that he was. They then were asked: "Did the defendant know that the document which he signed was a guarantee?" They answered in the negative. It seems to me that on those findings alone the defendant would be entitled to say in respect of this guarantee that it was not, in contemplation of law, signed by him. His signature was obtained by fraud, and it is manifest on the evidence and findings of the jury, that he was not intending to sign any such document. What he was intending to sign was some document with reference to insurance. It appears to me that under the circumstances of this case the mere fact that the jury have found that there was negligence on the part of the defendant does not raise such an estoppel as prevents the defendant from setting up the defence that he never signed the guarantee and that his signature to the document was obtained from him by fraud; that he did not know of its nature, or intend to sign a document of that description. If the document in question had been not a guarantee, but a bill of exchange, and the question had arisen what was the position of a holder for value without notice of the fraud, the matter might have been different, because the law merchant, and now the statute law, puts persons who in such circumstances take bills of exchange and such like instruments in the position that they have to prove that they gave value for the bill or other like instrument honestly, but, if they prove that, it does not matter that it was originally procured by fraud.

The only other thing which I wish to say is on the question of negligence. I do not know whether the jury understood that there could be no material negligence unless there was a duty on the defendant towards the plaintiffs. Even if they did understand that, in my opinion, in the case of this instrument, the signature to which was obtained by fraud, and which was not a negotiable instrument, Pickford J. was right in saying that the finding of negligence was immaterial. I wish to add for myself that in my judgment there is no evidence whatsoever to shew that the proximate cause of the plaintiffs' advancing money on this document was the mere signature of it by the defendant. In my opinion, the proximate cause of the plaintiffs' making the advance was that Rigg fraudulently took the document to the bank, having fraudulently altered it by adding the forged signature of an attesting witness, and but for Rigg having done those things the plaintiffs would never have advanced the money at all. Under these circumstances I think that the appeal fails and must be dismissed.

[The concurring opinions of Buckley and Kennedy, L.JJ. are omitted. On the question of estoppel Buckley L.J. said, "On that question I agree that the existence of negligence may be relevant. . . . I do not think that there was in this case proof of any such negligence as would avail the plaintiffs as between themselves and the defendant. The defendant did not owe any duty to the plaintiffs, and the act of the defendant was not the act which involved the plaintiffs in loss. What involved the plaintiffs in loss was the act of Rigg. . . .]

PRUDENTIAL TRUST CO. LTD. v. CUGNET
Saskatchewan. Supreme Court of Canada. 1956. 5 D.L.R. 2d. 1

In January 1951 one Hunter visited Edmund Cugnet at his home in Weyburn where Cugnet was playing cards. He interrupted his game when Hunter told him he wanted to talk about his mineral rights in two quarter sections of land. They went into another room and Hunter then said he wanted an option to take petroleum leases on the expiration of existing leases given by Cugnet to Rio Bravo Oil Co. Ltd. and Bandy Lee in 1949. He offered to pay $32 on each quarter section for the option and $32 yearly rental when the option was exercised. After a short conversation Cugnet signed an "Assignment" which effectively transferred to the Prudential Trust Co. Ltd. an undivided one half interest in the petroleum in his land. He also granted to Prudential an exclusive option to take a petroleum and natural gas lease for 99 years. He also transferred to Prudential an undivided half interest in the mineral rights except coal. Later Prudential sent Cugnet a copy of the assignment and a cheque for $64. Cugnet didn't read either the documents he signed or the copy returned to him. In February Prudential registered a caveat against the land and in September Cugnet's solicitors wrote to Prudential requesting a return of the documents. In April 1952 Cugnet's son Raymond filed a caveat against the lands based on an agreement for sale between Edmund (vendor) and Raymond (purchaser) in 1945. This action was brought by Prudential to establish its rights under its caveat. Hunter had disappeared and was not called as a witness. He had acted as an agent of Amigo Petroleums Ltd., a company incorporated and owned by one Lamarr, who had agreed with Prudential that Prudential would hold its oil agreements in trust. Amigo's interests were later acquired by one Nickle and assigned by him to Canuck Freehold Royalties Ltd. Canuck also had an agreement with Prudential that it would hold Canuck's interests in trust. Prudential was, throughout, a "bare trustee." It was accepted that Canuck gave value for the assignment in good faith.

The trial Judge held that Cugnet never intended to complete the assignment and transfer and relied on Hunter's misrepresentation that the documents were an option only. He applied the principle of *non est factum*. The Court of Appeal dismissed an appeal but granted special leave to appeal to the Supreme Court of Canada.

LOCKE J.: . . . The question as to whether the respondents are entitled to rely upon the defence [of *non est factum*] is raised by the plea of estoppel by conduct in the reply to the statement of defence. The basis for the contention is that Edmund Cugnet having, by his conduct, enabled Hunter and his principals to sell what appeared on the face of it to be a half interest in the mineral rights to a purchaser for value acting in good faith, he cannot dispute the validity of the instruments as against the latter. The estoppel, it is said, arises by reason of the negligence of Edmund Cugnet. The question is the same as that referred to by Buckley L.J. in *Carlisle & Cumberland Banking Co. v. Bragg*, [1911] 1 K.B. 489. . . .

It is my opinion that the result of the authorities was correctly stated in the *Bragg* case. To say that a person may be estopped by careless conduct such as that in the present case, when the instrument is not negotiable, is to assert the existence of some duty on the part of the person owing to the public at large, or to other persons unknown to him who might suffer damage by acting upon the instrument on the footing that it is valid in the hands of the holder. I do not consider that the authorities support the view that there is any such general duty, the breach of which imposes a liability in negligence. . . . it is my opinion that the appeal should fail and be dismissed with costs.

CARTWRIGHT J. (dissenting): . . . Cugnet Senior was induced to sign this document by the fraudulent representation made to him by one Edward Hunter that it contained only the grant of an option. Cugnet Senior is literate, has had experience in buying and selling properties, has been successful, and, in his own words, has "lots of money." He signed the document without reading it. He does not suggest that anything was done to prevent him reading it but appears to have been anxious to return without delay to the game of cards which had been interrupted by Hunter's arrival. He had not met Hunter previously. Hunter took the document away with him but 2 or 3 weeks later Cugnet Senior received a copy of it together with a cheque for $64 the amount of the consideration which he had agreed to accept. He did not read this copy until some months later when his son, the respondent Raymond A. Cugnet, called his attention to its contents. In the meantime the copy had been hanging up on a spike in the kitchen at the home of Cugnet Senior. Prudential in taking the conveyance was acting as bare trustee for Amigo Petroleums Ltd. During February, 1951, the last-mentioned company transferred the one-half interest and the option to one Nickle who, in turn, transferred them for value to the appellant Canuck Freehold Royalties Ltd., hereinafter called "Canuck" for which Prudential holds as bare trustee. Canuck had no notice or knowledge of the fraud practised by Hunter. . . .

It is clear that Cugnet Senior knew that the deed which he was executing was one purporting to deal with the petroleum and natural gas under two correctly specified quarter-sections owned by him. On the assumption that a distinction can validly be drawn between the facts in *Howatson* v. *Webb*, [1907] 1 Ch. 537; [1908] 1 Ch. 1, and those in *Carlisle & Cumberland Banking Co.* v. *Bragg*, it is my view that on its facts the case at bar falls within the class of cases of which the former is an example.

If, however, it be assumed that the Courts below were right in holding that the document of January 26, 1951, was entirely different in nature from what Cugnet Senior believed it to be, it is my opinion that in signing and sealing the document without reading it he was guilty of such negligence that as between himself and Canuck, which gave valuable consideration on the strength of the deed which he had in fact signed and sealed, he must bear the loss.

The general principle was stated as follows by Lord Halsbury sitting in the Court of Appeal in *Henderson & Co.* v. *Williams*, [1895] 1 Q.B. 521 at pp. 528-9: "I think that it is not undesirable to refer to an American authority, which, I observe, was quoted in the case of *Kingsford* v. *Merry*, *Root* v. *French* in which, in the Supreme Court of New York, Savage C.J. makes observations which seem to me to be well worthy of consideration. Speaking of a bona fide purchaser who has purchased property from a fraudulent vendee and given value for it, he says: 'He is protected in doing so upon the principle just stated, that when one of two innocent persons must suffer from the fraud of a third, he shall suffer, who, by his indiscretion, has enabled such third person to commit the fraud. A contrary principle would endanger the security of commercial transactions, and destroy that confidence upon which what is called the usual course of trade materially rests.' "

In *Farquharson Bros. & Co.* v. *C. King & Co.*, [1902] A.C. 325 at pp. 331-2, Lord Halsbury L.C. presiding in the House of Lords reaffirmed the above passage and pointed out that in the case then before the House the Court of Appeal had fallen into error through disregarding the words "who, by his indiscretion."

A branch of the principle so stated is the rule that, generally speaking, a person who executes a document without taking the trouble to read it is liable on it and cannot plead that he mistook its contents, at all events, as against a person who acting in good faith in the ordinary course of business has changed his position in reliance on such document. But it is said that the plea of *non est factum* operates as an exception to this salutary rule. That this is so in the case of a blind or illiterate person may be taken to be established by *Thoroughgood's Case* (1583), 2 Co. Rep. 9a, 76 E.R. 408, but whether the exception extends to an educated person who is not blind is a question which was treated by Sir G. Mellish L.J. in *Hunter* v. *Walters* (1871), L.R. 7 Ch. 75, and by Warrington J. and the Court of Appeal in *Howatson* v. *Webb*, as being still open. . . .

An anxious consideration of all the authorities referred to by counsel and in the Courts below has brought me to the conclusion that, insofar as *Carlisle* v. *Bragg* decides that the rule that negligence excludes a plea of *non est factum* is limited to the case of negotiable instruments and does not extend to a deed such as the one before us, we should refuse to follow it. I do not read the judgment of Sir Lyman P. Duff C.J.C. in *Minchau* v. *Busse*, [1940] 2 D.L.R. 282, and particularly his reference at p. 294 to the judgment of Buckley L.J. as binding us to follow everything that was decided in *Carlisle* v. *Bragg*.

In my view the effect of the decisions prior to *Carlisle* v. *Bragg* is accurately summarized in Cheshire & Fifoot on Contract, 4th ed., pp. 206-7, as follows: "The rule before 1911 was that if A., the victim of the fraud of C., was guilty of negligence in executing a written instrument different in kind from that which he intended to execute, then he was estopped as against innocent transferees from denying the validity of the written contract."

That rule was, I think, laid down by Byles J. delivering the unanimous judgment of the Court in *Foster* v. *Mackinnon* (1869), L.R. 4 C.P. 704, as being applicable to all written contracts. It appears to me that the Court of Appeal in *Carlisle* v. *Bragg* misinterpreted the following passage in the judgment of Byles J. at p. 712:

"Nevertheless, this principle, when applied to negotiable instruments, must be and is limited in its application. These instruments are not only assignable, but they form part of the currency of the country. A qualification of the general rule is necessary to protect innocent transferees for value. If, therefore, a man write his name across the back of a blank bill-stamp, and part with it, and the paper is afterwards improperly filled up, he is liable as endorser. If he write it across the face of the bill, he is liable as acceptor, when the instrument has once passed into the hands of an innocent endorsee for value before maturity, and liable to the extent of any sum which the stamp will cover.

"In these cases, however, the party signing knows what he is doing: the endorser intended to endorse, and the acceptor intended to accept, a bill of exchange to be thereafter filled up, leaving the amount, the date, the maturity, and the other parties to the bill undetermined.

"But, in the case now under consideration, the defendant, according to the evidence, if believed, and the finding of the jury, never intended to endorse a bill of exchange at all, but intended to sign a contract of an entirely different nature. It was not his design, and, if he were guilty of no negligence, it was not even his fault that the instrument he signed turned out to be a bill of exchange."

This does not say that the rule, that the signer if guilty of negligence will be estopped from denying the validity of a document as against a purchaser for value in good faith, is confined to the case of negotiable instruments; but rather that a person who knows he is signing a negotiable instrument cannot deny its validity to a holder in due course although he was guilty of no negligence in affixing his signature.

It may be said that the term negligence is inappropriate because it presupposes a duty owed by Cugnet Senior to Canuck, but in the passages quoted the term is, I think, used as meaning that lack of reasonable care in statement which gives rise to an estoppel. As it was put by Sir William Anson in an article on *Carlisle & Cumberland Banking Co.* v. *Bragg* in 28 L.Q. Rev. 190 at p. 194: "And further, there seems some confusion between the negligence which creates a liability in tort, and the lack of reasonable care in statement which gives rise to an estoppel. Bragg might well have been precluded by carelessness from resisting the effect of his written words, though the Bank might not have been able to sue him for negligence."

On the facts in the case at bar it cannot be doubted that Cugnet Senior failed to exercise reasonable care in signing the document in question. He executed a deed which he knew dealt with the oil and gas under his property without reading it, relying on the statements as to its contents made by Hunter who was a stranger to him. It does not appear that anything was done to prevent his reading the document. He chose to sign it unread rather than to absent himself for a few more minutes from the game of cards. His conduct, in my opinion, precludes him from relying on the plea of *non est factum* as against Canuck which purchased relying on the deed, in good faith, for value, and without notice or knowledge of any circumstances affecting the validity of the deed.

The terms of the deed appear to me to be sufficiently clear and I think that the plea that it is void for uncertainty must be rejected.

In the result I would allow the appeal with costs throughout and direct that judgment be entered for the relief claimed in the amended statement of claim.

[The decision of Locke J. is severely cut. The concurring opinion of Nolan J., with whom Taschereau and Fauteux JJ. concurred, is omitted altogether. The appeal was dismissed.]

QUESTIONS. Should Cartwright J. not have concluded by ordering a new trial? Would evidence have been produced at this trial to show the extent to which Prudential was careless? Should "contributory negligence" (carelessness) be a defence, or should the responsibility be apportioned? Compare *Ingram* v. *Little* above.

SAUNDERS v. ANGLIA BUILDING SOCIETY
(*Gallie* v. *Lee*)
[1971] A.C. 1004 (H.L.)

LORD PEARSON: My Lords, this appeal raises questions of law as to the limits of the plea of non est factum, in a case where the person who signed the deed of assignment of a long lease of a house alleges that she was deceived by the assignee as to the nature and character of the deed, so that it was not her deed, and she relies on the plea not only against the assignee who is alleged to have deceived her but also against an innocent third party, the defendant building society, who afterwards in good faith and with no knowledge of any defect affecting her signature lent money to the assignee on the security of the house. There are also questions of fact on which two members at least of the Court of Appeal took different views from that of the learned trial judge.

In 1962 the plaintiff, Mrs. Gallie, was 78 years of age. She owned a long lease of a house, where she resided and earned her living by taking in lodgers. The ground rent was small, so that in broad effect she was the owner of the house. The only one of her relatives who frequently visited her was her nephew, Walter Parkin, aged about 40. He had a small garage at which he did motor repairing work. He had a friend and business associate, named William Robert Lee, whom she trusted, although in the event Lee proved to be untrustworthy.

The plaintiff told Parkin that she had made a will leaving her house to him. Later she handed over to him the deeds of her house thinking apparently that she was thereby transferring to him the ownership of the house or at any rate enabling him to raise money on the security of the house. She made it a condition that she would have the use of the house for the rest of her life. Parkin needed money for his business, and she wished to help him in this way. If a further step, such as the making of a deed of gift, was required, she would be willing to do this.

Parkin consulted with Lee. Parkin was in a difficulty. He had left his wife and three children, and for years had been living with another woman who had become known as "Mrs. Parkin." He was in arrear with maintenance payments to his wife, and he was afraid that if he became the owner of the house his wife might be able to force him to pay the maintenance. Lee needed money in order to purchase a house for himself and his family, as they were still living in his father's house. He saw the opportunity of raising money on the security of the plaintiff's house if he could become the owner of it. It was arranged, or at any rate proposed, between Parkin and Lee that the plaintiff should transfer the house to Parkin by deed of gift, and when she had done so Parkin should sell the house to Lee at a price of £2,000 or £2,500 (the evidence is not clear as to the amount of the proposed price) and Lee should raise money from a building society on the security of the house and should pay the price of £2,000 or £2,500 by making monthly payments to the woman known as "Mrs. Parkin." Lee consulted a firm of solicitors about the proposed transaction and was advised that a recent deed of gift on the title would be likely to deter a building society from lending money on the security of the house and that a direct sale by the plaintiff to Lee would be preferable. Accordingly, the solicitors drafted a deed of assignment of the house from the plaintiff to Lee at a stated price of £3,000. It may be that the conduct of the solicitors or their managing clerk fell below professional standards, but it is not necessary to investigate that aspect of the matter.

Lee and Parkin went to see the plaintiff. Lee had the deed, and he put it before the plaintiff for her to sign. The plaintiff had broken her spectacles and could not read effectively without them. She asked what the deed was, and Lee said, in the presence of Parkin and without any dissent from him, that the deed was "to do with the gift by deed to Wally for the house." The plaintiff, not having asked Parkin to read the deed to her or give his explanation of it, but assuming that Parkin and Lee knew what they were doing, and desiring to help Parkin in the way that he wished, signed the deed. Parkin witnessed the plaintiff's signature to the deed. The price of £3,000 was not paid or intended to be paid, so that in practical reality the assignment from the plaintiff to Lee was for no consideration. As between Lee and Parkin the intention was that £2,000 or £2,500 was to be made available in some way by Lee to Parkin: he might pay monthly instalments to the woman known as "Mrs. Parkin" or he might from time to time put money into the business of Parkin, in which Lee had some interest. It is not easy to gather from the evidence exactly what the arrangement was, and it probably was somewhat indefinite in its details, but I think that was the broad effect of it. If this arrangement, or something on these lines, had been duly carried out, the plaintiff's signature to the deed would have enabled Parkin through Lee to raise money on the security of the house in the way that Parkin considered most beneficial to himself.

Lee made to the defendant building society an application containing some false statements and supported it with a testimonial, drafted by him and signed by Parkin, also containing some false statements. The defendant building society, in response to the application, and in reliance on the title deeds including the plaintiff's assignment to Lee, and having no notice of any defect in the assignment or of anything unusual affecting it, and acting in complete good faith, lent £2,000 to Lee on the security of the house.

Then things went wrong. Lee failed to carry out his arrangement with Parkin. Lee was heavily indebted, and the sum which he had borrowed from the defendant building society was used up in paying his debts, and probably his other resources were insufficient to enable him to make any money available to Parkin. At any rate, he did not make the sum of £2,500 or £2,000 or any sum available to Parkin in any way. Thus, in the event, the plaintiff's execution of the deed of assignment did not bring any benefit to Parkin, although it would have done if his arrangement with Lee had been duly carried out by Lee.

The plaintiff commenced her action in July, 1964. By her amended statement of claim she claimed (1) against Lee a declaration that the assignment of the house to him was void, return of the title deeds or their value and damages for their detention, and damages for fraudulent misrepresentation, and (2) against the defendant building society a declaration that the assignment of the house to Lee was void, and the delivery up of the title deeds or their value and damages for their detention.

The plaintiff's evidence was, owing to her age and infirmity, taken on commission, so that the learned judge did not have the advantage of seeing and hearing her as she was giving her evidence. Evidence was given at the trial by Parkin, Lee and a witness named Hall who had been managing clerk of the solicitors concerned. The learned judge found that

Lee and Hall had told lies in the witness box and he could not rely on their evidence. As to Parkin, he found that he had told some lies in the witness box and that his evidence showed a high degree of confusion and inaccuracy, but nevertheless there were times in his evidence when he was saying simple things when the learned judge had the conviction that he was telling the truth. With regard to the plaintiff's evidence the learned judge said: "It is apparent from the transcript of that evidence first that she must have been a difficult witness, that her evidence is not very clear in a number of respects and in some respects it is contradictory."

He did, however, find as a fact that the plaintiff did not read the document, that Lee represented it to be a deed of gift to Parkin and that the plaintiff executed it in the belief that that was what it was. He also found as a fact that the plaintiff had no idea that the document took the form of an assignment on sale from her to Lee and that a sale or gift to him was something which she did not and would not for one moment have contemplated.

As at least two members of the Court of Appeal did not accept these findings of the learned judge, and I prefer their views to his (though undoubtedly these questions of fact are difficult), I will set out a few extracts from the plaintiff's evidence taken on commission, in order to show in outline what was the basis of their views:

"Q. Do you know that Mr. Parkin—that is Wally—gave the building society a testimonial about Mr. Lee so that he could get a mortgage on this house? Do you know that? A. I did not know what they were doing when they came to see me. I only said to my nephew—I didn't refer to Mr. Lee; I referred to my nephew, and I said to my nephew—'I don't mind helping you at all. I have helped you in the past and I will still help you as long as I can; but mind you are doing the right thing.' I have always trusted my nephew. Q. And if he told you a document was all right you believed him? A. I believe my nephew. I don't believe Mr. Lee. Q. And, of course, when your nephew and Mr. Lee came along with the document you thought it must be all right? A. I did. Q. And it was because your nephew was there that you were willing to sign it? A. Yes. . . . Q. Did you know that Mr. Lee stated that he would buy the house from Mr. Parkin? A. No, I did not know he was buying the house. I just thought he was having a loan on my house. Q. Mr. Lee was? A. Yes. But if my nephew had have come to me and said, 'Auntie, I am in difficulties,' I would have got him the money instead of bothering Mr. Lee. Q. But the money was to be borrowed on your deeds through Mr. Lee. Is that right? A. Yes. Q. And you were quite satisfied about that? A. Yes I done it to help my nephew with his business. . . . Q. Have you brought this action to help your nephew? A. I have, sir. . . . Q. Did it occur to you to ask Wally to read the document to you? A. I never thought of that, sir. Q. You thought it was all right. If Wally was there, it must be all right? A. I did."

The learned judge (1) made a declaration as against Lee that the alleged assignment of June 15, 1962, was void and of no effect, and directed an inquiry as to damages; (2) made a declaration in the same terms as against the defendant building society, and ordered them to deliver up the title deeds. There was no appeal by Lee. There was an appeal by the defendant building society, and it was allowed by the Court of Appeal.

The Master of the Rolls decided the case on a broad principle to which I will refer later.

Russell L.J. carefully examined the facts of the case and made two

comments on the plaintiff's evidence, and these were in effect his grounds
of decision. He said [1969] 2 Ch. 17, 40-41:

"The first is . . . it is inadequate to establish the minimum facts necessary
to establish the plea of non est factum, assuming that it would be sufficient
for that plea to show that the plaintiff was induced wholly by Lee's
falsehood to think that she was signing a deed of gift to Parkin whereas
she executed an assignment in terms for value to Lee. I think that the
plaintiff's evidence in this regard was unsatisfactory, and was inadequate
to discharge the burden of proof that is laid by law on this plea, which
requires strong and clear evidence for its discharge . . . At first sight, of
course, it is easy to see the difference between a voluntary assignment of
a leasehold property to A and an assignment for value of that property
to B. But what upon the plaintiff's own evidence was the essential character
of the document she was intending to execute? It was a document intended
by her to divest herself of her leasehold property by transferring it to
another, not as mere trustee for her, but so that the transferee should be
in a position to deal with the property and in particular by borrowing
money on the security of the property. Her evidence in my view makes
it plain that she understood that Lee and Parkin were jointly concerned
in a project of raising money on security of the property and this was her
intention. In those circumstances I do not consider that it is correct to
say that, for the purposes of the plea of non est factum, a transfer by her
to Lee is to be regarded as of a totally different character or nature from
a transfer to Parkin. The judge relied on the identity of the transferee
as constituting the essential nature or character of the instrument. In so
doing I think that he paid insufficient regard to what I may call the object
of the exercise. Suppose that Lee had carried through the arrangement
that Parkin had understood was made—had in fact paid Parkin. This would
have fulfilled the plaintiff's purpose in executing the document put before
her."

I respectfully agree with the reasoning of Russell L.J. and in particular
with the principle that importance should be attached to the "object of the
exercise," when dissimilar legal documents may have similar practical
effects. Another example of this will be found in *Mercantile Credit Co.
Ltd.* v. *Hamblin* [1965] 2 Q.B. 242, 267. In that case the defendant had
signed hire-purchase documents, and there was some evidence that she
intended to raise money by means of a mortgage of her car, and she had
pleaded non est factum. It became plain, however, that the object of the
proposed hire-purchase transaction was to produce the same practical effect
as a mortgage of the car would have produced (if it had been lawful).
She would sell the car through a dealer to a finance company, and take
it back from the finance company on hire purchase, with the result that
she would receive a lump sum down and would repay it with additions
by instalments over a period, so that she would for practical purposes be
in much the same position as if she had mortgaged the car. The plea of
non est factum failed.

I think Salmon L.J.'s view of the facts in the present case was consistent
with that of Russell L.J., but his main conclusion on the facts was this
[1969] 2 Ch. 17, 45:

"In the present case it seems plain from Mrs. Gallie's evidence, which was
given before an examiner and which we are, therefore, in just as good a
position to evaluate as was the judge, that Mrs. Gallie would have
executed the conveyance even if its true character and class and the nature

of the transaction had been properly explained to her and she had understood the explanation. Certainly she was not induced to sign by any false representation made to her by Lee."

In a later passage Salmon L.J. said, at p. 47: ". . . if Parkin had taken the trouble to explain the true nature of the document to her and told her that the solicitors had advised that it should be in that form and asked her to sign it, there can in my view be no real doubt but that she would have done so."

I think that conclusion of Salmon L.J. is probably right but there may be an element of doubt as to what the plaintiff would have done if she had been given a full explanation of the document. I would dismiss the appeal for the reasons given by Russell L.J. because they seem to me free from doubt.

In the judgments of the Court of Appeal in this case there was an elaborate and, if I may respectfully say so, illuminating and valuable discussion of the law relating to the plea of non est factum. It is not practicable in this opinion to examine what they have said at length and in detail, dealing with every point. It seems to me that the right course here is to examine the law on this subject with the aid of the judgments in the Court of Appeal and to endeavour to arrive at clear general propositions for the future on the basis of the earlier law which I think has become distorted in some respects.

I must, however, deal specifically with the broad principle stated by the Master of the Rolls as his conclusion from his investigation of the law, at pp. 36-37:

". . . whenever a man of full age and understanding, who can read and write, signs a legal document which is put before him for signature—by which I mean a document which, it is apparent on the face of it, is intended to have legal consequences—then, if he does not take the trouble to read it, but signs it as it is, relying on the word of another as to its character or contents or effect, he cannot be heard to say that it is not his document. By his conduct in signing it he has represented, to all those into whose hands it may come, that it is his document; and once they act upon it as being his document, he cannot go back on it, and say it was a nullity from the beginning."

In applying the principle to the present case, the Master of the Rolls said, at p. 37:

". . . Mrs. Gallie cannot in this case say that the deed of assignment was not her deed. She signed it without reading it, relying on the assurance of Lee that it was a deed of gift to Wally. It turned out to be a deed of assignment to Lee. But it was obviously a legal document. She signed it: and the building society advanced money on the faith of it being her document. She cannot now be allowed to disavow her signature."

There can be no doubt that this statement of principle by the Master of the Rolls is not only a clear and concise formulation but also a valuable guide to the right decision to be given by a court in any ordinary case. The danger of giving an undue extension to the plea of non est factum has been pointed out in a number of cases. For instance in *Muskham Finance Ltd.* v. *Howard* [1963] 1 Q.B. 904, 912 Donovan L.J. delivering the judgment of the court said:

"The plea of non est factum is a plea which must necessarily be kept within narrow limits. Much confusion and uncertainty would result in the field of contract and elsewhere if a man were permitted to try to disown his signature simply by asserting that he did not understand that which he had signed."

In *Hunter* v. *Walters* (1871) L.R. 7 Ch.App. 75, 87, Mellish L.J. said: "Now, in my opinion, it is still a doubtful question at law, on which I do not wish to give any decisive opinion, whether, if there be a false representation respecting the contents of a deed, a person who is an educated person, and who might, by very simple means, have satisfied himself as to what the contents of the deed really were, may not, by executing it negligently be estopped as between himself and a person who innocently acts upon the faith of the deed being valid, and who accepts an estate under it."

This passage was referred to by Farwell L.J. in *Howatson* v. *Webb* [1908] 1 Ch. 1, 3-4, where he said:

"I think myself that the question suggested, but not decided, by Mellish L.J. in that case will some day have to be determined, viz., whether the old cases on misrepresentation as to the contents of a deed were not based upon the illiterate character of the person to whom the deed was read over, and on the fact that an illiterate man was treated as being in the same position as a blind man: see *Thoroughgood's Case* and *Sheppard's Touchstone* p. 56; and whether at the present time an educated person, who is not blind, is not estopped from availing himself of the plea of non est factum against a person who innocently acts upon the faith of the deed being valid."

The principle stated by the Master of the Rolls can and should be applied so as to confine the scope of the plea of non est factum within narrow limits. It rightly prevents the plea from being successful in the normal case of a man who, however much he may have been misinformed about the nature of a deed or document, could easily have ascertained its true nature by reading it and has taken upon himself the risk of not reading it.

I think, however, that, unless the doctrine of non est factum, as it has been understood for at least a hundred years, is to be radically transformed, the statement of principle by the Master of the Rolls, taken just as it stands, is too absolute and rigid and needs some amplification and qualification. Doubts can be raised as to the meaning of the phrase "a man of full age and understanding, who can read and write." There are degrees of understanding and a person who is a great expert in some subjects may be like a child in relation to other subjects. Does the phrase refer to understanding of things in general, or does it refer to capacity for understanding (not necessarily in more than a general and elementary way) legal documents and property transactions and business transactions?

In my opinion, the plea of non est factum ought to be available in a proper case for the relief of a person who for permanent or temporary reasons (not limited to blindness or illiteracy) is not capable of both reading and sufficiently understanding the deed or other document to be signed. By "sufficiently understanding" I mean understanding at least to the point of detecting a fundamental difference between the actual document and the document as the signer had believed it to be. There must be a proper case for such relief. There would not be a proper case if (a) the signature of the document was brought about by negligence of the signer in failing to take precautions which he ought to have taken, or (b) the actual document was not fundamentally different from the document as the signer believed it to be. I will say something later about negligence and about fundamental difference.

In the present case the plaintiff was not at the material time a person who could read, because on the facts found she had broken her spectacles and could not effectively read without them. In any case her evidence (unless it was deliberately false, which has not been argued) shows that she had very little capacity for understanding legal documents and property transactions, and I do not think a reasonable jury would have found that she was negligent. In my opinion, it would not be right to dismiss the plaintiff's appeal on the ground that the principle stated by the Master of the Rolls is applicable to her case. I do not think it is.

The principle as stated is limited to a case in which it is apparent on the face of the document that it is intended to have legal consequences. That allows for possible success of the plea in a case such as *Lewis* v. *Clay* (1897) 67 L.J. Q.B. 224, where Clay had been induced to sign promissory notes by the cunning deception of a false friend, who caused him to believe that he was merely witnessing the friend's signature on several private and highly confidential documents, the material parts of which had been covered up.

I wish to reserve the question whether the plea of non est factum would ever be rightly successful in a case where (1) it is apparent on the face of the document that it is intended to have legal consequences; (2) the signer of the document is able to read and sufficiently understand the document; (3) the document is fundamentally different from what he supposes it to be; (4) he is induced to sign it without reading it. It seems unlikely that the plea ought ever to succeed in such a case, but it is inadvisable to rule out the wholly exceptional and unpredictable case.

I have said above that the statement of principle by the Master of the Rolls needs to be amplified and qualified unless the doctrine of non est factum, as it has been understood for at least a hundred years, is to be radically transformed. What is the doctrine, and should it be radically transformed?

As to the early history, the authorities referred to in the judgment of Byles J. in *Foster* v. *Mackinnon* (1869) L.R. 4 C.P. 704, 711-12 (and also referred to in *Holdsworth's History of English Law*, Vol. 8, pp. 50-51) were cited in the argument of this appeal. Having considered them I think they show that the law relating to the plea of non est factum remained in an undeveloped state until the judgment in *Foster* v. *Mackinnon*, and the modern development began with that judgment. It was the judgment of the court (Bovill C.J., Byles, Keating and Montague Smith JJ.) delivered by Byles J. He said, at p. 711:

"It seems plain, on principle and on authority, that, if a blind man, or a man who cannot read, or who for some reason (not implying negligence) forbears to read, has a written contract falsely read over to him, the reader misreading to such a degree that the written contract is of a nature altogether different from the contract pretended to be read from the paper which the blind or illiterate man afterwards signs; then, at least if there be no negligence, the signature so obtained is of no force. And it is invalid not merely on the ground of fraud, where fraud exists, but on the ground that the mind of the signer did not accompany the signature; in other words, that he never intended to sign, and therefore in contemplation of law never did sign, the contract to which his name is appended."

In my opinion, the essential features of the doctrine are contained in that passage and the doctrine does not need any radical transformation. A minor comment is that the phrase "who for some reason (not implying negligence) forbears to read" is (to use a currently fashionable word) too "permissive" in its tone. If a person forbears to read the document, he nearly always should be reckoned as negligent or otherwise debarred from succeeding on the plea of non est factum.

The passage which I have set out from Byles J.'s judgment, though I think it contains the essential features, was only a brief summary in a leading judgment, and there are further developments which need to be considered.

Ascertainment of the intention: I think the doctrine of non est factum inevitably involves applying the subjective rather than the objective test to ascertain the intention. It takes the intention which a man has in his own mind rather than the intention which he manifests to others (the intention which as reasonable men they would infer from his words and conduct).

There are, however, some cases in which the subjective test of intention can be applied so as to produce the same result as would be produced by the objective test. Suppose a man signs a deed without knowing or inquiring or having any positive belief or formed opinion, as to its nature or effect: he signs it because his solicitor or other trusted adviser advises him to do so. Then his intention is to sign the deed that is placed before him, whatever it may be or do. That is the intention in his own mind as well as the intention which by signing he manifests to others. Examples of this will be found in *Hunter* v. *Walters* (1871) 7 Ch.App. 75; *National Provincial Bank of England* v. *Jackson* (1886) 33 Ch.D. 1; *King* v. *Smith* [1900] 2 Ch. 425. In *King* v. *Smith*, Farwell J., at p. 430, cited and relied upon a passage in the judgment of Mellish L.J. in *Hunter* v. *Walters* (1817) L.R. 7 Ch.App. 75, 88, where he said:

"When a man knows that he is conveying or doing something with his estate, but does not ask what is the precise effect of the deed, because he is told it is a mere form, and has such confidence in his solicitor as to execute the deed in ignorance, then, in my opinion, a deed so executed, although it may be voidable upon the ground of fraud, is not a void deed."

Farwell J. said [1900] 2 Ch. 425, 430 that Mr. King "had absolute confidence in his solicitor, and executed any deed relating to his property that Eldred put before him."

I think this principle affords a solution to a problem that was raised in the course of the argument. Suppose that the very busy managing director of a large company has a pile of documents to be signed in a few minutes before his next meeting, and his secretary has arranged them for maximum speed with only the spaces for signature exposed, and he "signs them blind," as the saying is, not reading them or even looking at them. He may be exercising a wise economy of his time and energy. There is the possibility of some extraneous document, involving him in unexpected personal liability, having been fraudulently inserted in the pile, but this possibility is so improbable that a reasonable man would disregard it: *Bolton* v. *Stone* [1951] A.C. 850, 858. Such conduct is not negligence in any ordinary sense of the word. But the person who signs documents in this way ought to be held bound by them, and ought not to be entitled to avoid liability so as to shift the burden of loss on to an innocent third party. The whole object of having documents signed by him is that he makes them his documents and takes responsibility for them. He takes the chance of a fraudulent substitution. I think the right view of such a case is that the person who signs intends to sign the documents placed before him, whatever they may be, and so there is no basis on which he could successfully plead non est factum.

Negligence: It is clear that by the law as it was laid down in *Foster* v. *Mackinnon* (1869) L.R. 4 C.P. 704 a person who had signed a document differing fundamentally from what he believed it to be would be disentitled from successfully pleading non est factum if his signing of the document was due to his own negligence. The word "negligence" in this connection had no special, technical meaning. It meant carelessness, and in each case it was a question of fact for the jury to decide whether the person relying on the plea had been negligent or not. In *Foster* v. *Mackinnon* the Lord Chief Justice had told the jury that, if the indorsement was not the defendant's signature, or if, being his signature, it was obtained upon a fraudulent representation that it was a guarantee, and the defendant signed it without knowing that it was a bill, and under the belief that it was a guarantee and if the defendant was not guilty of any negligence in so signing the paper, the defendant was entitled to the verdict. On appeal this direction was held to be correct. In *Vorley* v. *Cooke* (1857) 1 Giffard 230, 236-237, Stuart V.-C. said: "It cannot be said that Cooke's conduct was careless or rash. He was deceived, as anyone with the ordinary amount of intelligence and caution would have been deceived, and he is therefore entitled to be relieved." Whatever may be thought of the merits of the decision in that case, this passage illustrates the simple approach to the question whether the signer of the deed had been negligent or not. Similarly, in *Lewis* v. *Clay* (1898) 67 L.J. Q.B. 224, 225, Lord Russell of Killowen C.J. left to the jury the question: "Was the defendant, in signing his name as he did, recklessly careless, and did he thereby enable Lord William Nevill to perpetrate the fraud?"

Unfortunately this simple and satisfactory view as to the meaning and effect of negligence in relation to the plea of non est factum became distorted in the case of *Carlisle and Cumberland Banking Co.* v. *Bragg* [1911] 1 K.B. 489. The defendant was induced to sign the document by fraud, and did not know that it was a guarantee, but thought that it was a mere proposal for insurance. The jury found that he had been negligent. Pickford J. considered that the finding of negligence was immaterial, and on appeal his view was upheld. Vaughan Williams L.J. said at p. 494:

"I do not know whether the jury understood that there could be no material negligence unless there was a duty on the defendant towards the plaintiffs. Even if they did understand that, in my opinion, in the case of this instrument, the signature to which was obtained by fraud, and which was not a negotiable instrument, Pickford J. was right in saying that the finding of negligence was immaterial. I wish to add for myself that in my judgment there is no evidence whatsoever to show that the proximate cause of the plaintiffs' advancing money on this document was the mere signature of it by the defendant. In my opinion, the proximate cause of the plaintiffs' making the advance was that Rigg fraudulently took the document to the bank, having fraudulently altered it by adding the forged signature of an attesting witness, and but for Rigg having done those things the plaintiffs would never have advanced the money at all."

The reasoning of the Court of Appeal in *Carlisle and Cumberland Banking Co.* v. *Bragg* has been criticised, for example, by Sir William Anson in the year 1912 in 28 *Law Quarterly Review*, at p. 190, and by Professor Guest in the year 1963 in 79 *Law Quarterly Review*, at p. 346.

Also doubts as to the correctness of the reasoning were expressed by Donovan L.J. delivering the judgment of the Court of Appeal in *Muskham Finance Ltd.* v. *Howard* [1963] 1 Q.B. 904, 913 and by Gavan Duffy J. in *Carlton and United Breweries Ltd.* v. *Elliott* [1960] V.R. 320. In my opinion *Carlisle and Cumberland Banking Co.* v. *Bragg* [1911] 1 K.B. 489 was wrong in the reasoning and the decision.

I think it is not right to say that in relation to the plea of non est factum, negligence operates by way of estoppel. The phrase "estoppel by negligence" tends, in this connection at any rate, to be misleading in several ways:

(1) The phrase is inaccurate in itself, as has been pointed out in *Spencer Bower and Turner on Estoppel by Representation,* 2nd ed. (1966), p. 69 and in the judgments of the Court of Appeal in this case. Estoppel in the normal sense of the word does not arise from negligence: it arises from a representation made by words or conduct.

(2) The phrase tends to bring in the technicalities of estoppel, and the requirement that the representation must be intended to be acted upon may cause difficulties.

(3) The phrase tends to bring in the technicalities of negligence as they have been developed in the tort of negligence. This is what happened in *Carlisle and Cumberland Banking Co.* v. *Bragg,* as shown by the passage cited above. The innocent third party who has paid or lent money on the faith of a negligently signed document should not have to prove the signer owed a duty to him, nor that the signer's negligence was the proximate cause of the money paid or lent.

(4) An estoppel must be pleaded and proved by the party relying on it. In relation to the plea of non est factum, this could put the burden of proof on the wrong party. The person who has signed the document knows with what knowledge or lack of knowledge and with what intention he signed the document, and how he was induced or came to sign it. He should have the burden of proving that his signature was not brought about by negligence on his part.

Salmon L.J. has said in his judgment in this case [1969] 2 Ch. 17, 48: "If, ... a person signs a document because he negligently failed to read it, I think he is precluded from relying on his own negligent act for the purpose of escaping from the ordinary consequences of his signature. In such circumstances he cannot succeed on a plea of non est factum. This is not in my view a true estoppel, but an illustration of the principle that no man may take advantage of his own wrong."

I agree.

The degree of difference required: The judgments in the older cases used a variety of expressions to signify the degree or kind of difference that, for the purposes of the plea of non est factum, must be shown to exist between the document as it was and the document as it was believed to be. More recently there has been a tendency to draw a firm distinction between (a) a difference in character or class, which is sufficient for the purposes of the plea, and (b) a difference only in contents, which is not sufficient. This distinction has been helpful in some cases, but, as the judgments of the Court of Appeal have shown, it would produce wrong results if it were applied as a rigid rule for all cases. In my opinion, one has to use a more general phrase, such as "fundamentally different" or "radically different" or "totally different."

I would dismiss the appeal.

LORD REID: My Lords, I am in general agreement with the speech of my noble and learned friend, Lord Pearson. In my opinion this appeal must fail however one states the law. The existing law seems to me to be in a state of some confusion. I do not think that it is possible to reconcile all the decisions, let alone all the reasons given for them. In view of some general observations made in the Court of Appeal I think that it is desirable to try to extract from the authorities the principles on which most of them are based. When we are trying to do that my experience has been that there are dangers in there being only one speech in this House. Then statements in it have often tended to be treated as definitions and it is not the function of a court or of this House to frame definitions; some latitude should be left for future developments. The true ratio of a decision generally appears more clearly from a comparison of two or more statements in different words which are intended to supplement each other.

The plea of non est factum obviously applies when the person sought to be held liable did not in fact sign the document. But at least since the sixteenth century it has also been held to apply in certain cases so as to enable a person who in fact signed a document to say that it is not his deed. Obviously any such extension must be kept within narrow limits if it is not to shake the confidence of those who habitually and rightly rely on signatures when there is no obvious reason to doubt their validity. Originally this extension appears to have been made in favour of those who were unable to read owing to blindness or illiteracy and who therefore had to trust someone to tell them what they were signing. I think that it must also apply in favour of those who are permanently or temporarily unable through no fault of their own to have without explanation any real understanding of the purport of a particular document, whether that be from defective education, illness or innate incapacity.

But that does not excuse them from taking such precautions as they reasonably can. The matter generally arises where an innocent third party has relied on a signed document in ignorance of the circumstances in which it was signed, and where he will suffer loss if the maker of the document is allowed to have it declared a nullity. So there must be a heavy burden of proof on the person who seeks to invoke this remedy. He must prove all the circumstances necessary to justify its being granted to him, and that necessarily involves his proving that he took all reasonable precautions in the circumstances. I do not say that the remedy can never be available to a man of full capacity. But that could only be in very exceptional circumstances; certainly not where his reason for not scrutinising the document before signing it was that he was too busy or too lazy. In general I do not think that he can be heard to say that he signed in reliance on someone he trusted. But, particularly when he was led to believe that the document which he signed was not one which affected his legal rights, there may be cases where this plea can properly be applied in favour of a man of full capacity.

The plea cannot be available to anyone who was content to sign without taking the trouble to try to find out at least the general effect of the document. Many people do frequently sign documents put before them for signature by their solicitor or other trusted advisers without making any enquiry as to their purpose or effect. But the essence of the plea non est factum is that the person signing believed that the document he signed had one character or one effect whereas in fact its character or effect was quite different. He could not have such a belief unless he had taken steps or been given information which gave him some grounds for his belief. The amount of information he must have and the sufficiency of the particularity of his belief must depend on the circumstances of each case. Further the plea cannot be available to a person whose mistake was really a mistake as to the legal effect of the document, whether that was his own mistake or that of his adviser. That has always been the law and in this branch of the law at least I see no reason for any change.

We find in many of the authorities statements that a man's deed is not his deed if his mind does not go with his pen. But that is far too wide. It would cover cases where the man had taken no precautions at all, and there was no ground for his belief that he was signing something different from that which in fact he signed. I think that it is the wrong approach to start from that wide statement and then whittle it down by excluding cases where the remedy will not be granted. It is for the person who seeks the remedy to show that he should have it.

Finally, there is the question to what extent or in what way must there be a difference between that which in fact he signed and that which he believed he was signing. In an endeavour to keep the plea within bounds there have been many attempts to lay down a dividing line. But any dividing line suggested has been difficult to apply in practice and has sometimes led to unreasonable results. In particular I do not think that the modern division between the character and the contents of a document is at all satisfactory. Some of the older authorities suggest a more flexible test so that one can take all factors into consideration. There was a period when here as elsewhere in the law hard and fast dividing lines were sought, but I think that experience has shown that often they do not produce certainty but do produce unreasonable results.

I think that in the older authorities difference in practical result was more important than difference in legal character. If a man thinks that he is signing a document which will cost him £10 and the actual document would cost him £1,000 it could not be right to deny him this remedy simply because the legal character of the two was the same. It is true that we must then deal with questions of degree but that is a familiar task for the courts and I would not expect it to give rise to a flood of litigation.

There must I think be a radical difference between what he signed and what he thought he was signing—or one could use the words 'fundamental' or 'serious' or 'very substantial.' But what amounts to a radical difference will depend on all the circumstances. If he thinks he is giving property to A whereas the document gives it to B the difference may often be of vital importance, but in the circumstances of the present case I do not think that it is. I think that it must be left to the courts to determine in each case in light of all the facts whether there was or was not a sufficiently great difference. The plea non est factum is in sense illogical when applied to a case where the man in fact signed the deed. But it is none the worse for that if applied in a reasonable way.

I would dismiss this appeal.

[Lord Hodson, Lord Wilberforce, and Viscount Dilhorne delivered concurring speeches.]

QUESTION. Is *Carlisle and Cumberland Banking Co.* v. *Bragg* good law in Canada?

CHAPTER 6

WRITTEN DOCUMENTS

1. Unsigned Documents (The Ticket Cases)

PARKER v. THE SOUTH EASTERN RAILWAY COMPANY
England. Court of Appeal. 1877. 2 C.P.D. 416

The plaintiff deposited a bag in a cloak-room at the defendants' railway station, paid the clerk 2d., and received a paper ticket, on one side of which were written a number and a date, and were printed notices as to when the office would be opened and closed, and the words "See Back." On the other side were printed several clauses relating to articles left by passengers, the last of which was, "The company will not be responsible for any package exceeding the value of £10." The plaintiff on the same day presented his ticket and demanded his bag, and the bag could not be found, and has not been since found. Parker claimed £24 10s. as the value of his bag. The company pleaded that they had accepted the goods on the condition that they would not be responsible for the value if it exceeded £10; and at the trial they relied on the words printed on the back of the ticket, and also on the fact that a notice to the same effect was printed and hung up in the cloak-room. The plaintiff gave evidence and denied that he had seen the notice, or read what was printed on the ticket. He admitted that he had often received such tickets and knew there was printed matter on them, but said that he did not know what it was. He said that he imagined the ticket to be a receipt for the money paid by him. Another case with very similar facts was tried at the same time.

Parker's case was tried at Westminster on the 27th of February, 1876, before Pollock B. The questions left by the judge to the jury were: 1. Did the plaintiff read or was he aware of the special condition upon which the articles were deposited? 2. Was the plaintiff, under the circumstances, under any obligation, in the exercise of reasonable and proper caution, to read or make himself aware of the condition?

The jury answered both questions in the negative, and the judge thereupon directed judgment to be entered for the plaintiff for the amount claimed, reserving leave to the defendants to move to enter judgment for them.

The defendants moved to enter judgment, and also obtained from the Common Pleas Division an order *nisi* for a new trial, on the ground of misdirection. The order was discharged, and the motion was refused by the Common Pleas Division. The Defendants appealed.

MELLISH L.J.: In this case we have to consider whether a person who deposits in the cloak-room of a railway company articles which are lost through the carelessness of the company's servants is prevented from recovering, by a condition on the back of the ticket, that the company would not be liable for the loss of goods exceeding the value of £10. It was argued on behalf of the railway company that the company's servants were only authorized to receive goods on behalf of the company upon the terms contained in the ticket. . . . I am of opinion that this objection cannot prevail. It is clear that the company's servants did not exceed the authority given them by the company. They did the exact thing they were authorized to do. They were authorized to receive articles on deposit as bailees on behalf of the company, charging 2d. for each article, and delivering a ticket properly filled up to the person leaving the article. This is exactly what they did in the present cases, and whatever may be the legal effect of what was done, the company must, in my opinion, be bound by it. The directors may have thought, and no doubt did think, that the delivering the ticket to the person depositing the article would be sufficient to make him bound by the conditions contained in the ticket, and if they were mistaken in that, the company must bear the consequence.

The question then is, whether the plaintiff was bound by the conditions contained in the ticket. In an ordinary case, where an action is brought on a written agreement which is signed by the defendant, the agreement is proved by proving his signature, and, in the absence of fraud, it is wholly immaterial that he has not read the agreement and does not know its contents. The parties may, however, reduce their agreement into writing, so that the writing constitutes the sole evidence of the agreement, without signing it; but in that case there must be evidence independently of the agreement itself to prove that the defendant has assented to it. In that case, also, if it is proved that the defendant has assented to the writing constituting the agreement between the parties, it is, in the absence of fraud, immaterial that the defendant had not read the agreement and did not know its contents. Now if in the course of making a contract one party delivers to another a paper containing writing, and the party receiving the paper knows that the paper contains conditions which the party delivering it intends to constitute the contract, I have no doubt that the party receiving the paper does, by receiving and keeping it, assent to the conditions contained in it, although he does not read them, and does not know what they are. I hold therefore that the case of *Harris* v. *Great Western Ry. Co.* (1876) 1 Q.B.D. 515, was rightly decided, because in that case the plaintiff admitted, on cross-examination, that he believed there were some conditions on the ticket. On the other hand, the case of *Henderson* v. *Stevenson* (1875), L.R. 2 Sc. & Div. 470, is a conclusive authority that if the person receiving the ticket does not know that there is any writing upon the back of the ticket, he is not bound by a condition printed on the back. The facts in the cases before us differ from those in both *Henderson* v. *Stevenson,* and *Harris* v. *Great Western Ry. Co.* because in both the cases which have been argued before us, though the plaintiffs admitted that they knew there was writing on the back of the ticket, they swore not only that they did not read it, but that they did not know or believe that the writing contained conditions, and we are to consider whether, under those circumstances, we can lay down as a matter of law either that the plaintiff is bound or that he is not bound by the conditions contained in the ticket, or whether his being bound depends on some question of fact to be determined by the jury, and if so, whether, in the present case, the right question was left to the jury.

Now, I am of opinion that we cannot lay down, as a matter of law, either that the plaintiff was bound or that he was not bound by the conditions printed on the ticket, from the mere fact that he knew there was writing on the ticket, but did not know that the writing contained conditions. I think there may be cases in which a paper containing writing is delivered by one party to another in the course of a business transaction, where it would be quite reasonable that the party receiving it should assume that the writing contained in it no condition, and should put it in his pocket unread. For instance, if a person driving through a turnpike gate received a ticket upon paying the toll, he might reasonably assume that the object of the ticket was that by producing it he might be free from paying toll at some other turnpike gate, and might put it in his pocket unread. On the other hand, if a person who ships goods to be carried on a voyage by sea receives a bill of lading signed by the master, he would plainly be bound by it, although afterwards in an action against the shipowner for the loss of the goods, he might swear that he had never read the bill of lading, and that he did not know that it contained the terms of the contract of carriage, and that the shipowner was protected by the exceptions contained in it. Now the reason why the person receiving the bill of lading would be bound seems to me to be that in the great majority of cases persons shipping goods do know that the bill of lading contains the terms of the contract of carriage; and the shipowner, or the master delivering the bill of lading, is entitled to assume that the person shipping goods has that knowledge. It is, however, quite possible to suppose that a person who is neither a man of business nor a lawyer might on some particular occasion ship goods without the least knowledge of what a bill of lading was, but in my opinion such person must bear the consequences of his own exceptional ignorance, it being plainly impossible that business could be carried on if every person who delivers a bill of lading had to stop to explain what a bill of lading was.

Now the question we have to consider is whether the railway company were entitled to assume that a person depositing luggage, and receiving a ticket in such a way that he could see that some writing was printed on it, would understand that the writing contained the conditions of contract, and this seems to me to depend upon whether people in general would in fact and naturally, draw that inference. The railway company, as it seems to me, must be entitled to make some assumptions respecting the person who deposits luggage with them: I think they are entitled to assume that he can read, and that he understands the English language, and that he pays such attention to what he is about as may be reasonably expected from a person in such a transaction as that of depositing luggage in a cloakroom. The railway company must, however, take mankind as they find them, and if what they do is sufficient to inform people in general that the ticket contains conditions, I think that a particular plaintiff ought not to be in a better position than other persons on account of his exceptional ignorance or stupidity or carelessness. But if what the railway company do is not sufficient to convey to the minds of people in general that the ticket contains conditions, then they have received goods on deposit without obtaining the consent of the persons depositing them to the conditions limiting their liability. I am of opinion, therefore, that the proper direction to leave to the jury in these cases is, that if the person receiving the ticket did not see or know that there was any writing on the ticket he is not bound by the conditions; that if he knew there was writing, and knew or believed that the writing contained conditions, then he is bound by the conditions; that if he knew there was writing on the ticket, but did not know or believe that the writing contained conditions, nevertheless he would be bound, if the delivering of the ticket to him in such a manner that he could see there was writing upon it, was, in the opinion of the jury, reasonable notice that the writing contained conditions.

I have lastly to consider whether the direction of the learned judge was correct, namely, "Was the plaintiff under the circumstances, under any obligation, in the exercise of reasonable and proper caution, to read and to make himself aware of the condition?" I think that this direction was not strictly accurate, and was calculated to mislead the jury. The plaintiff was certainly under no obligation to read the ticket, but was entitled to leave it unread if he pleased, and the question does not appear to me to direct the attention of the jury to the real question, namely, whether the railway company did what was reasonably sufficient to give the plaintiff notice of the condition.

On the whole, I am of opinion that there ought to be a new trial.

BRAMWELL L.J.: . . . Has not the giver of the paper a right to suppose that the receiver is content to deal on the terms in the paper? What more can be done? Must he say, "Read that?" As I have said, he does so in effect when he puts it into the other's hands. The truth is, people are content to take these things on trust. They know that there is a form which is always used—they are satisfied it is not unreasonable, because people do not usually put unreasonable terms into their contracts. If they did, then dealing would soon be stopped. Besides, unreasonable practices would be known. The very fact of not looking at the paper shews that this confidence exists. It is asked: What if there was some unreasonable condition, as for instance to forfeit £1000 if the goods were not removed in forty-eight hours? Would the depositors be bound? I might continue myself by asking: Would he be, if he were told "our conditions are on this ticket," and he did not read them. In my judgment, he would not be bound in either case. I think there is an implied understanding that there is no condition unreasonable to the knowledge of the party tendering the document and not insisting on its being read—no condition not relevant to the matter in hand. I am of opinion, therefore, that the plaintiffs, having notice of the printing, were in the same situation as though the porter had said, "Read that, it concerns the matter in hand": that if the plaintiffs did not read it, they were as much bound as if they had read it and had not objected.

The difficulty I feel as to what I have written is that it is too demonstrative. But, put in practical language, it is this: The defendants put into the hands of the plaintiff a paper with printed matter on it, which in all good sense and reason must be supposed to relate to the matter in hand. This printed matter the plaintiff sees, and must either read it, and object if he does not agree to it, or if he does read it and not object, or does not read it, he must be held to consent to its terms; therefore, on the facts, the judges should have directed verdicts for the defendants. . . .

[The opinion of Bramwell L.J. has been severely cut and the opinion of Baggallay L.J. omitted altogether. The Court ordered a new trial.]

LAMONT v. *CANADIAN TRANSFER CO. LTD.* 1909. 19 O.L.R. 291 (Ontario. Court of Appeal). The plaintiff having arrived in Toronto by steamer handed his baggage checks to his father-in-law in order that his trunks might be sent to his residence. The father-in-law gave the checks to a friend of his, one Horn, a customs officer, and asked him to have the trunks delivered. Horn took the checks and handed them, together with twenty-five cents, to Dunn, an agent of the Canadian Transfer Co., with instructions to send along the trunks. Dunn offered to do it without charge, but Horn refused, saying that he had been given the twenty-five cents. The agent then removed the steamer checks and replaced them by checks of the Can. Transfer Co. Fifteen minutes later Horn came back to Dunn and asked him for a receipt, which, without being read, was later passed on to the plaintiff, and not read by the latter until some ten days afterwards. On the face of the receipt, there was legibly printed a notice that the company should "not be liable for any loss or damage of any trunk for over $50." The trunk was either lost or stolen and the plaintiff sued the company for the value of his trunk, refusing to accept the $50 tendered by the defendants. Held, for the plaintiff. GARROW J.A.: ". . . the real question is, ought knowledge to be imputed to him under the circumstances? This is a pure question of fact, and, in my opinion, the reasonable inference is the other way. He had already made an unconditional contract after having been offered free cartage. He came back, not to get a new or different contract, but a mere receipt. That was what he asked for, and he might under the circumstances fairly and without negligence assume without reading it that he was merely getting what he had asked for and nothing more. If he had not come back no question could have been raised as to the defendants' liability, and the burden is of course upon them to shew that the new contract was substituted, with the plaintiff's consent, for the old, and in this they, in my opinion, fail. . . ."

CHAPELTON v. BARRY URBAN DISTRICT COUNCIL. [1940] 1 K.B. 532 (England (Wales). Court of Appeal). The plaintiff was injured when using a deck chair supplied for public use by the defendant Council. When he took the chair from the attendant he was handed a ticket. He glanced at it and slipped it into his pocket. He claimed to have no idea that there were conditions on it. In fact the ticket contained these words: "Available for 3 hours. Time expires where indicated by cut-off and should be retained and shown on request. The Council will not be made liable for any accident or damage arising from hire of chair." Near the pile of chairs was a notice: "Barry Urban District Council. Cold Knap. Hire of chairs 2d. per session of 3 hours. The public are respectfully requested to obtain tickets properly issued from the automatic punch in their presence from the Chair Attendants." The county court Judge found the damages to be £50 in addition to special damages, but held the plaintiff bound by the notice on the ticket. The Court of Appeal reversed him. SLESSER L.J.: "The very language of that 'respectful request' shows clearly, to my mind, that for the convenience of the local authority the public were asked to obtain from the chair attendants tickets, which were mere vouchers or receipts showing how long a person hiring a chair is entitled to use that chair. It is wrong, I think, to look at the circumstance that the plaintiff obtained his receipt at the same time as he took his chair as being in any way a modification of the contract which I have indicated. This was a general offer to the general public, and I think that it is right to say that one must take into account here that there was no reason why anybody taking one of these chairs should necessarily obtain a receipt at the moment he took his chair—and, indeed, the notice is inconsistent with that, because it 'respectfully requests' the public to obtain receipts for their money. It may be that somebody might sit in one of these chairs for one hour, or two hours, or, if the holiday resort was a very popular one, for a longer time, before the attendant came round for his money, or it may be that the attendant would not come to him at all for payment for the chair, in which case I take it that there would be an obligation upon the person who used the chair to search out the attendant, like a debtor searching for his creditor, in order to pay him the sum of 2d. for the use of the chair and to obtain a receipt for the 2d. paid.

"I think the learned county court judge has misunderstood the nature of this agreement. I do not think that the notice excluding liability was a term of the contract at all. . . . I think the object of the giving and the taking of this ticket was that the person taking it might have evidence at hand by which he could show that the obligation he was under to pay 2d. for the use of the chair for three hours had been duly discharged, and I think it is altogether inconsistent, in the absence of any qualification of liability in the notice put up near the pile of chairs, to attempt to read into it the qualification contended for. In my opinion, this ticket is no more than a receipt, and is quite different from a railway ticket which contains upon it the terms upon which a railway company agrees to carry the passenger."

OLLEY v. *MARLBOROUGH COURT LTD.* [1949] 1 K.B. 532 (C.A.) A man and his wife checked into a hotel, and paid a week's board and lodging in advance. They then went up to their room, where a notice was displayed as follows: "The proprietors will not hold themselves responsible for articles lost or stolen, unless handed to the manageress for safe custody in a sealed package and a receipt obtained." The wife's furs were stolen from her room because of the negligence of the hotel's servants, who gave the key to an unauthorised person. It was held by the majority of the court that the notice was seen by the plaintiffs too late for it to be a part of their contract with the hotel. DENNING L.J. said: "The first question is whether that notice formed part of the contract. Now people who rely on a contract to exempt themselves from their common law liability must prove that contract strictly. Not only must the terms of the contract be clearly proved, but also the intention to create legal relations— the intention to be legally bound—must also be clearly proved. The best way of proving it is by a written document signed by the party to be bound. Another way is by handing him before or at the time of the contract a written notice specifying its terms and making it clear to him that the contract is on those terms. A prominent public notice which is plain for him to see when he makes the contract or an express oral stipulation would, no doubt, have the same effect. But nothing short of one of these three ways will suffice. It has been held that mere notices put on receipts for money do not make a contract (see *Chapelton* v. *Barry Urban District Council*). So, also, in my opinion, notices put up in bedrooms do not of themselves make a contract. As a rule, the guest does not see them until after he has been accepted as a guest. The hotel company no doubt hope that the guest will be held bound by them, but the hope is vain unless they clearly show that he agreed to be bound by them, which is rarely the case."

J. SPURLING LTD. v. *BRADSHAW* [1956] 2 All E.R. 121. The plaintiffs were warehousemen, and the defendant, who had had previous dealings with the plaintiffs, delivered to them for storage eight barrels of orange juice. A few days later the plaintiffs sent to the defendant a document, called a landing account, acknowledging receipt of the goods, and referring to conditions on the back of the document. On the back, in small print, was included the following clause: "We will not in any circumstances . . . be liable for any loss, damage or detention howsoever, whensoever or wheresoever occasioned in respect of any goods entrusted to . . . us in the course of our business, even when such loss, damage or detention may have been occasioned by the negligence, wrongful act or default of ourselves or our servants or agents." When the defendant came to collect the barrels, they were found to be empty, and the defendant refused to pay the storage charges on the ground that the plaintiff had been negligent in storing the goods. The plaintiff brought an action, relying on the printed exemption clause. The Court held that the plaintiff could rely on the clause. DENNING L.J.: "This brings me to the question whether this clause was part of the contract. Counsel for the defendant urged us to hold that the plaintiffs did not do what was reasonably sufficient to give notice of the conditions within *Parker* v. *South Eastern Ry. Co.* I agree that the more unreasonable a clause is, the greater the notice which must be given of it. Some clauses which I have seen would need to be printed in red ink on the face of the document with a red hand pointing to it before the notice could be held to be sufficient. The clause in this case, however, in my judgment, does not call for such exceptional treatment, especially when it is construed, as it should be, subject to the proviso that it only applies when the warehouse-man is carrying out his contract and not when he is deviating from it or breaking it in a radical respect. So construed, the judge was, I think, entitled to find that sufficient notice was given. It is to be noticed that the landing account on its face told the defendant that the goods would be insured if he gave instructions; otherwise they were not insured. The invoice, on its face, told him they were warehoused "at owner's risk." The printed conditions, when read subject to the proviso which I have mentioned, added little or nothing to those explicit statements taken together. Next it was said that the landing account and invoice were issued after the goods had been received and could not therefore be part of the contract of bailment: but the defendant admitted that he had received many landing accounts before. True he had not troubled to read them. On receiving this account, he took no objection to it, left the goods there, and went on paying the warehouse rent for months afterwards. It seems to me that by the course of business and conduct of the parties, these conditions were part of the contract."

QUESTION. Is it relevant to ask who, as between plaintiff and defendant, could more efficiently insure against the loss of the goods?

McCUTCHEON v. DAVID MacBRAYNE LTD.

[1964] 1 All E.R. 430 (H.L.)

LORD DEVLIN: My Lords, when a person in the Isle of Islay wishes to send goods to the mainland he goes into the office of MacBrayne (the respondents) in Port Askaig which is conveniently combined with the local Post Office. There he is presented with a document headed "Conditions" containing three or four thousand words of small print divided into twenty-seven paragraphs. Beneath them there is a space for the sender's signature which he puts below his statement in quite legible print that he thereby agrees to ship on the conditions stated above. The appellant, Mr. McCutcheon, described the negotiations which preceded the making of this formidable contract in the following terms:

"Q.—Tell us about that document; how did you come to sign it? A.—

You just walk in the office and the document is filled up ready and all you have to do is to sign your name and go out. Q.—Did you ever read the conditions? A.—No. Q.—Did you know what was in them? A.—No."

There are many other passages in which the appellant and his brother-in-law, Mr. McSporran, endeavour more or less successfully to appease the forensic astonishment aroused by this statement. People shipping calves, the appellant said, (he was dealing with an occasion when he had shipped thirty-six calves), had not much time to give to the reading. Asked to deal with another occasion when he was unhampered by livestock, he said that people generally just tried to be in time for the boat's sailing; it would, he thought, take half a day to read and understand the conditions and then he would miss the boat. In another part of his evidence he went so far as to say that if everybody took time to read the document, "MacBrayne's office would be packed out the door." Mr. McSporran evidently thought the whole matter rather academic because, as he pointed out, there was no other way to send a car.

There came a day, Oct. 8, 1960, when one of the respondents' vessels was negligently sailed into a rock and sank. She had on board a car belonging to the appellant, which he had got Mr. McSporran to ship for him, and the car was a total loss. It would be a strangely generous set of conditions in which the persistent reader, after wading through the verbiage, could not find something to protect the carrier against "any loss . . . wheresoever or whensoever occurring"; and condition 19 by itself is enough to absolve the respondents several times over for all their negligence. It is conceded that if the form had been signed as usual, the appellant would have had no case. But by a stroke of ill luck for the respondents it was on this day of all days that they omitted to get Mr. McSporran to sign the conditions. What difference does that make? If it were possible for your lordships to escape from the world of make-believe, which the law has created, into the real world in which transactions of this sort are actually done, the answer would be short and simple. It should make no difference whatever. This sort of document is not meant to be read, still less to be understood. Its signature is in truth about as significant as a handshake that marks the formal conclusion of a bargain.

Your lordships were referred to the dictum of Blackburn J., in *Harris* v. *Great Western Ry. Co.* (1876) 1 Q.B.D. 515. The passage is as follows: "And it is clear law that where there is a writing, into which the terms of any agreement are reduced, the terms are to be regulated by that writing. And though one of the parties may not have read the writing, yet, in general, he is bound to the other by those terms; and that, I apprehend, is on the ground that, by assenting to the contract thus reduced to writing, he represents to the other side that he has made himself acquainted with the contents of that writing and assents to them, and so induces the other side to act upon that representation by entering into the contract with him, and is consequently precluded from denying that he did make himself acquainted with those terms. But then the preclusion only exists when the case is brought within the rule so carefully and accurately laid down by Parke B., in delivering the judgment of the Exchequer in *Freeman* v. *Cooke* (1848) 2 Exch. 654, that is, if he 'means his representation to be acted upon, and it is acted upon accordingly: or if, whatever a man's real intentions may be, he so conduct himself that a reasonable man would take the representation to be true, and believe that it was meant that he should act upon it, and did act upon it as true'." If the ordinary law of estoppel was applicable to this case, it might well be argued that the circumstances leave no room for any representation by the sender on which the carrier acted. I believe that any other member of the public in the appellant's place,—and this goes for lawyers as well as for laymen,—would have found himself compelled to give the same sort of answers as the appellant gave; and I doubt if any carrier who serves out documents of this type could honestly say that he acted in the belief that the recipient had "made himself acquainted with the contents". But Blackburn J. was dealing with an unsigned document, a cloakroom ticket. Unless your Lordships are to disapprove the decision of the Court of Appeal in *L'Estrange* v. *F. Graucob, Ltd.* [1934] 2 K.B. 394—and there has been no suggestion in this case that you should,—the law is clear, without any recourse to the doctrine of estoppel, that a signature to a contract is conclusive.

This is a matter that is relevant to the way in which the respondents put their case. They say that the previous dealings between themselves and the appellant, being always on the terms of their "risk note", as they call their written conditions, the contract between themselves and the appellant must be deemed to import the same conditions. In my opinion, the bare fact that there have been previous dealings between the parties does not assist the respondents at all. The fact that a man has made a contract in the same form ninety-nine times (let alone three or four times which are here alleged) will not of itself affect the hundredth contract, in which the form is not used. Previous dealings are relevant only if they prove knowledge of the terms, actual and not constructive, and assent to them. If a term is not expressed in a contract, there is only one other way in which it can come into it and that is by implication. No implication can be made against a party of a term which was unknown to him. If previous dealings show that a man knew of and agreed to a term on ninety-nine occasions, there is a basis for saying that it can be imported into the hundredth contract without an express statement. It may or may not be sufficient to justify the importation,—that depends on the circumstances; but at least by proving knowledge the essential beginning is made. Without knowledge there is nothing.

It is for the purpose of proving knowledge that the respondents rely on the dictum of Blackburn J. which I have cited. My lords, in spite of the great authority of Blackburn J., I think that this is a dictum which some day your lordships may have to examine more closely. It seems to me that when a party assents to a document forming the whole or a part of his contract, he is bound by the terms of the document, read or unread, signed or unsigned, simply because they are in the contract; and it is unnecessary, and possibly misleading, to say that he is bound by them because he represents to the other party that he has made himself acquainted with them. But if there be an estoppel of this sort, its effect is in my opinion limited to the contract in relation to which the representation is made; and it cannot (unless of course there be something else on which the estoppel is founded besides the mere receipt of the document) assist the other party in relation to other transactions. The respondents in the present case have quite failed to prove that the appellant made himself acquainted with the conditions that they had introduced into previous dealings. He is not estopped from saying that for good reasons or bad he signed the previous contracts without the slightest idea of what was in them. If that is so, previous dealings are no evidence of knowledge and so are of little or no use to the respondents in this case. I say "of little or no use" because the appellant did admit that he knew that there were some conditions, though he did not know what they were. He certainly did not know that they were conditions which exempted the respondents from liability for their own negligence, though, I suppose, if he had thought about them at all, he would have known that they probably exempted the respondents from the strict liability of a carrier. Most people know that carriers exact some conditions and it does not matter in this case whether the appellant's knowledge was general knowledge of this sort or was derived from previous dealings. Your lordships can therefore leave previous dealings out of it and ask yourselves simply what is the position of a man who, with that amount of general knowledge, apparently makes a contract into which no conditions are expressly inserted? The answer must surely be that either he does not make a contract at all because the parties are not ad idem or he makes the contract without the conditions. You cannot have a contract subject to uncommunicated conditions the terms of which are known only to one side.

It is at this point, I think, that their lordships in the Second Division fell into error. The Lord Justice-Clerk said: "It is, I think, well settled that, if A contracts with B for the carriage by B of A's goods, in the knowledge, gained through previous experience of similar transactions, that B carries goods subject to conditions, A is bound by these conditions under this later contract, if it is of a similar nature to those which have gone before, in the absence of agreement or information to the contrary. This applies even if A, knowing that there are conditions, does not take the trouble to ascertain precisely what these conditions are."

Similarly LORD MACKINTOSH said: "In these circumstances, I am of the opinion, following what I understand to be the law as laid down in *Parker* v. *South Eastern Ry. Co.* and particularly by Baggallay, L.J., that the [appellant], being aware by reason of his own previous experience, and of that of the agent who happened to be acting for him in the present transaction, that goods were carried on the [respondents'] vessels subject to certain conditions, and having been given no reason to think that these conditions were not still operative on Oct. 8, 1960, was bound by the conditions, although, as was proved to have been the case, he had never at any time acquainted himself with their purport."

My lords, I think, with great respect, that this is to introduce a new and fundamentally erroneous principle into the law of contract. There can be no conditions in any contract unless they are brought into it by expression, incorporation or implication. They are not brought into it simply because one party has inserted them into similar transactions in the past and has not given the other party any reason to think that he will not want to insert them again. The error is based, I think, on a misunderstanding of what are commonly called the ticket cases; I say this because the single authority cited for the proposition is one of the leading ticket cases, *Parker* v. *South Eastern Ry. Co.* The question in these cases is whether or not the passenger has accepted the ticket as a contractual document. If he knows that it contains conditions of some sort, he must know that it is meant to be contractual. If he accepts it as a contractual document, then prima facie (I am not dealing with questions of reasonable notice) he is bound by the conditions that are printed on it or incorporated in it by sufficient reference to some other document, whether he has inquired about them or not. That is all that Baggallay, L.J., is saying in *Parker* v. *South Eastern Ry. Co.* In the present case there is no contractual document at all. There is not so much as a peg on which to hang any terms that are not expressed in the contract nor a phrase which is capable of expansion. It is as if the appellant had been accepted as a passenger without being given a ticket at all. There is then no special contract and the contract is the ordinary one which the law imposes on carriers. As Baggallay, L.J., said "This clearly would be the nature of the contract if no ticket were delivered, as occasionally happens."

If a man is given a blank ticket without conditions or any reference to them, even if he knows in detail what the conditions usually exacted are, he is not, in the absence of any allegation of fraud or of that sort of mistake for which the law gives relief, bound by such conditions. It may seem a narrow and artificial line that divides a ticket that is blank on the back from one that says "For conditions see time-tables," or something of that sort, that has been held to be enough notice. I agree that it is an artificial line and one that has little relevance to every day conditions. It may be beyond your lordships' power to make the artificial line more natural: but at least you can see that it is drawn fairly for both sides, and that there is not one law for individuals and another for organizations that can issue printed documents. If the respondents had remembered to issue a risk note in this case, they would have invited your lordships to give a curt answer to any complaint by the appellant. He might say that the terms were unfair and unreasonable, that he had never voluntarily agreed to them, that it was impossible to read or understand them and that anyway, if he had tried to negotiate any change, the respondents would not have listened to him. The respondents would expect him to be told that he had made his contract and must abide by it. Now the boot is on the other foot. It is just as legitimate, but also just as vain, for the respondents to say that it was only a slip on their part, that it is unfair and unreasonable of the appellant to take advantage of it and that he knew perfectly well that they never carried goods except on conditions. The law must give the same answer: they must abide by the contract which they made. What is sauce for the goose is sauce for the gander. It will remain unpalatable sauce for both animals until the legislature, if the courts cannot do it, intervenes to secure that when contracts are made in circumstances in which there is no scope for free negotiation of the terms, they are made on terms that are clear, fair and reasonable and settled independently as such. That is what Parliament has done in the case of carriage of goods by rail and on the high seas.

I have now given my opinion on the main point in the case and the one on which the respondents succeeded below. On the other points on which the respondents failed below and which they put foward again as grounds for dismissing the claim, I have nothing to add to what your lordships have already said. In my opinion the appeal should be allowed.

THORNTON v. SHOE LANE PARKING LTD.
[1971] 2 Q.B. 163

LORD DENNING M.R.: In 1964 Mr. Thornton, the plaintiff, who was a free-lance trumpeter of the highest quality, had an engagement with the BBC at Farringdon Hall. He drove to the City in his motor car and went to park it at a multi-storey automatic car park. It had only been open a few months. He had never gone there before. There was a notice on the outside headed "Shoe Lane Parking." It gave the parking charges, 5s for two hours, 7s 6d for three hours, and so forth; and at the bottom: "ALL CARS PARKED AT OWNERS RISK." The plaintiff drove up to the entrance. There was not a man in attendance. There was a traffic light which showed red. As he drove in and got to the appropriate place, the traffic light turned green and a ticket was pushed out from the machine. The plaintiff took it. He drove on into the garage. The motor car was taken up by mechanical means to a floor above. The plaintiff left it there and went off to keep his appointment with the BBC. Three hours later he came back. He went to the office and paid the charge for the time that the car was there. His car was brought down from the upper floor. He went to put his belongings into the boot of the car; but unfortunately there was an accident. The plaintiff was severely injured. The judge has found it was half his own fault, but half the fault of Shoe Lane Parking Ltd. the defendants. The judge awarded him £3,637 6s 11d.

On this appeal the defendants do not contest the judge's findings about the accident. They acknowledge that they were at fault, but they claim that they are protected by some exempting conditions. They rely on the ticket which was issued to the plaintiff by the machine. They say that it was a contractual document and that it incorporated a condition which exempts them from liability to him. The ticket was headed 'Shoe Lane Parking.' Just below there was a 'box' in which was automatically recorded the time when the car went into the garage. There was a notice alongside: "Please present this ticket to cashier to claim your car." Just below the time, there was some small print in the left hand corner which said: "This ticket is issued subject to the conditions of issue as displayed on the premises." That is all.

The plaintiff says that he looked at the ticket to see the time on it, and put it in his pocket. He could see there was printing on the ticket, but he did not read it. He only read the time. He did not read the words which said that the ticket was issued subject to the conditions as displayed on the premises. If the plaintiff had read those words on the ticket and had looked round the premises to see where the conditions were displayed, he would have had to have driven his car on into the garage and walked round. Then he would have found, on a pillar opposite the ticket machine, a set of printed conditions in a panel. He would also have found, in the paying office (to be visited when coming back for the car) two more panels containing the printed conditions. If he had the time to read the conditions—it would take him a very considerable time—he would read this:

"CONDITIONS

The following are the conditions upon which alone motor vehicles are accepted for parking:

1. The customer agrees to pay the charges of [the defendants] . . .

2. The Customer is deemed to be fully insured at all times against all risks (including, without prejudice to the generality of the foregoing, fire, damage and theft, whether due to the negligence of others or not) and the [defendants] shall not be responsible or liable for any loss or misdelivery of or damage of whatever kind to the Customer's motor vehicle, or any articles carried therein or thereon or of or to any accessories carried thereon or therein *or injury to the Customer* or any other person *occurring when the Customer's motor vehicle is in the Parking Building howsoever that loss,*

misdelivery, damage or injury shall be caused; and it is agreed and understood that the Customer's motor vehicle is parked and permitted by the [defendants] to be parked in the Parking Building in accordance with this Licence entirely at the Customer's risk . . ."

There is a lot more. I have only read about one-tenth of the conditions. The important thing to notice is that the defendants seek by this condition to exempt themselves from liability, not only for damage to the car, but also for injury to the customer howsoever caused. The condition talks about insurance. It is well known that the customer is usually insured against damage to the car; but he is not insured against damage to himself. If the condition is incorporated into the contract of parking, it means that the plaintiff will be unable to recover any damages for his personal injuries which were caused by the negligence of the company.

We have been referred to the ticket cases of former times from *Parker* v. *South Eastern Ry. Co.* to *McCutcheon* v. *David MacBrayne Ltd.* They were concerned with railways, steamships and cloakrooms where booking clerks issued tickets to customers who took them away without reading them. In those cases the issue of the ticket was regarded as an *offer* by the company. If the customer took it and retained it without objection, his act was regarded as an *acceptance* of the offer: see *Watkins* v. *Rymill* and *Thompson* v. *London, Midland and Scottish Ry. Co.* These cases were based on the theory that the customer, on being handed the ticket, could refuse it and decline to enter into a contract on those terms. He could ask for his money back. That theory was, of course, a fiction. No customer in a thousand ever read the conditions. If he had stopped to do so, he would have missed the train or the boat.

None of those cases has any application to a ticket which is issued by an automatic machine. The customer pays his money and gets a ticket. He cannot refuse it. He cannot get his money back. He may protest to the machine, even swear at it; but it will remain unmoved. He is committed beyond recall. He was committed at the very moment when he put his money into the machine. The contract was concluded at that time. It can be translated into offer and acceptance in this way. The offer is made when the proprietor of the machine holds it out as being ready to receive the money. The acceptance takes place when the customer puts his money into the slot. The terms of the offer are contained in the notice placed on or near the machine stating what is offered for the money. The customer is bound by those terms as long as they are sufficiently brought to his notice beforehand, but not otherwise. He is not bound by the terms printed on the ticket if they differ from the notice, because the ticket comes too late. The contract has already been made: see *Olley* v. *Marlborough Court Ltd.* The ticket is no more than a voucher or receipt for the money that has been paid (as in the deckchair case, *Chapelton* v. *Barry Urban District Council*), on terms which have been offered and accepted before the ticket is issued. In the present case the offer was contained in the notice at the entrance giving the charges for garaging and saying 'at owners risk,' i.e. at the risk of the owner so far as damage to the car was concerned. The offer was accepted when the plaintiff drove up to the entrance and, by the movement of his car, turned the light from red to green, and the ticket was thrust at him. The contract was then concluded, and it could not be altered by any words printed on the ticket itself. In particular, it could not be altered so as to exempt the company from liability for personal injury due to their negligence.

Assuming, however, that an automatic machine is a booking clerk in disguise, so that the old fashioned ticket cases still apply to it, we then have to go back to the three questions put by Mellish L.J. in *Parker* v. *South Eastern Ry. Co.*, subject to this qualification: Mellish L.J. used the word 'conditions' in the plural, whereas it would be more apt to use the word 'condition' in the singular, as indeed Mellish L.J. himself did at the end of his judgment. After all, the only condition that matters for this purpose is the exempting condition. It is no use telling the customer that the ticket is issued subject to some "conditions" or other, without more; for he may reasonably regard "conditions" in general as merely regulatory, and not as taking away his rights, unless the exempting condition is drawn specifically to his attention. (Alternatively, if the plural 'conditions' is used, it would be better prefaced with the word "exempting," because the exempting conditions are the only conditions that matter for this purpose.) Telescoping the three questions, they come to this: the customer is bound by the exempting condition if he knows that the ticket is issued subject to it; or, if the company did what was reasonably sufficient to give him notice of it. Counsel for the defendants admitted here that the defendants did not do what was reasonably sufficient to give the plaintiff notice of the exempting condition. That admission was properly made. I do not pause to enquire whether the exempting condition is void for unreasonableness. All I say is that it is so wide and so destructive of rights that the court should not hold any man bound by it unless it is drawn to his attention in the most explicit way. It is an instance of what I had in mind in *J. Spurling Ltd.* v. *Bradshaw*. In order to give sufficient notice, it would need to be printed in red ink with a red hand pointing to it, or something equally startling.

However, although reasonable notice of it was not given, counsel for the defendants said that this case came within the second question propounded by Mellish L.J., namely that the plaintiff "knew or believed that the writing contained conditions." There was no finding to that effect. The burden was on the defendants to prove it, and they did not do so. Certainly there was no evidence that the plaintiff knew of this exempting condition. He is not, therefore, bound by it. Counsel for the defendants relied on a case in this court last year, *Mendelssohn* v. *Normand Ltd.* Mr. Mendelssohn parked his car in the Cumberland Garage at Marble Arch and was given a ticket which contained an exempting condition. There was no discussion as to whether the condition formed part of the contract. It was conceded that it did. That is shown by the report. Yet the garage company were not entitled to rely on the exempting condition for the reasons there given. That case does not touch the present, where the whole question is whether the exempting condition formed part of the contract. I do not think it did. The plaintiff did not know of the condition, and the defendants did not do what was reasonably sufficient to give him notice of it.

I do not think the defendants can escape liability by reason of the exempting condition. I would, therefore, dismiss the appeal.

[Megaw L.J. and Sir Gordon Wilmer delivered concurring judgments.]

BRITISH CRANE HIRE CORP. LTD. v. *IPSWICH PLANT HIRE LTD.* [1975] Q.B. 303 (C.A.)

Lord Denning M.R.: In June, 1970, a big earth-moving machine got stuck in the mud. It sank so far as to be out of sight. It cost much money to get it out. Who is to pay the cost?

The defendants, Ipswich Plant Hire Ltd., were doing drainage and other engineering works in the marshy land next the River Stour, near Cattawade Bridge in Essex. They are themselves in the hiring business, letting out cranes and so forth. But on this occasion they were doing the work themselves. They needed a dragline crane urgently. They got in touch with the plaintiffs, the British Crane Hire Corporation Ltd., and asked if they could hire a dragline crane. The plaintiffs responded quickly. They delivered it on Sunday, June 28, 1970. They let it on hire to the defendants, together with the driver, Mr. Humphrey. No doubt the driver remained the servant of the plaintiffs when he was driving the crane. The plaintiffs took it as far as they could by road. Then it was unloaded.

On the next day, Monday, June 29, 1970, the defendants' site agent, a Mr. Meadows, directed the driver the way to go across the marsh. When they got to a particularly bad patch, Mr. Meadows warned the driver that he ought to have "navimats," that is, sets of timber baulks which could be laid on the marsh and form a kind of roadway for the machine. The defendants ought to have supplied the "navimats," but they had not yet arrived. Mr. Meadows told the driver to wait for the "navimats." But the driver did not wait. He took his chance. He went on without "navimats." He got over that patch safely. Further on, there was another bad patch of marsh. The driver took his chance again. This time he fared worse. The dragline crane sank into the marsh. That was the "first mishap." They got it out after a good deal of work. There was no doubt that it was the fault of the driver, Mr. Humphrey, in not waiting for the "navimats." His negligence was the cause of that first mishap. His employers, the plaintiffs, must bear the cost of it.

On the next day, Tuesday, June 30, 1970, the "navimats" arrived. But there was a second mishap. On that day the dragline crane had to cross another bad patch. The driver, Mr. Humphrey, was this time using the "navimats." He had to make a turning movement or "spragging." He had just completed it when, in spite of the "navimats," this machine sank into the marsh. It went out of sight. Great efforts were needed to get it out. Heavy equipment was brought in. Eventually, at great expense, the machine was got out.

The question arises on the second mishap. Who is to bear the expense of recovering the machine from the marsh? The judge found that the sinking into the marsh was not the fault of the driver, Mr. Humphrey, but the fault of Mr. Meadows, the site agent of the defendants. The judge thought that Mr. Meadows ought to have directed the crane by a safer route across the marshy ground. On that account he held the defendants liable for the expense. That finding was challenged before us by Mr. McCowan for the defendants. He pointed out that the driver and the site agent had gone together over the ground and decided on this route. I was impressed by Mr. McCowan's submissions on this point. I doubt whether it would be right to hold the site agent guilty of negligence. It seems to me that this second mishap may have been a piece of bad luck which occurred without the fault of anyone. It was a hazard due to the nature of the marsh itself at that point.

But it does not follow that the plaintiffs fail on their claim. Even though the defendants were not negligent, nevertheless the plaintiffs say that the defendants are liable in contract for the costs of recovering the machine from the marsh. The plaintiffs say that the contract incorporated the conditions on a printed form under which the defendants are liable for the costs.

The judge found that the printed conditions were not incorporated into the contract. The plaintiffs appeal from that finding. The facts are these: the arrangements for the hire of the crane were all on the telephone. The plaintiffs agreed to let the defendants this crane. It was to be delivered on the Sunday. The hiring charges and transport charges were agreed. Nothing was said about conditions. There was nothing in writing. But soon after the crane was delivered, the plaintiffs, in accordance with their practice, sent forward a printed form to be signed by the hirer. It set out the order, the work to be done, and the hiring fee, and that it was subject to the conditions set out on the back of the form. The defendants would ordinarily have sent the form back signed: but this time they did not do so. The accident happened before they signed it. So they never did so. But the plaintiffs say that nevertheless, from the previous course of dealing, the conditions on the form govern the relationship between the parties. They rely on no. 6:

"Site conditions: The hirer shall take all reasonable precautions to ensure that the crane can safely be taken onto and kept upon or at the site and in particular to ensure that the ground is in a satisfactory condition to take the weight of the crane and/or its load. The hirer shall where necessary supply and lay timber or other suitable material for the crane to travel over and work upon and shall be responsible for the recovery of the crane from soft ground."

Also on no. 8: "The hirer shall be responsible for and indemnify the owner against . . . all expenses in connection with or arising out of the use of the plant." In support of the course of dealing, the plaintiffs relied on two previous transactions in which the defendants had hired cranes from the plaintiffs. One was February 20, 1969; and the other October 6, 1969. Each was on a printed form which set out the hiring of a crane, the price, the site, and so forth; and also setting out the conditions the same as those here. There were thus only two transactions many months before and they were not known to the defendants' manager who ordered this crane. In the circumstances I doubt whether those two would be sufficient to show a course of dealing.

In *Hollier* v. *Rambler Motors (A.M.C.) Ltd.* [1972] 2 Q.B. 71, 76, Salmon L.J. said he knew of no case "in which it has been decided or even argued that a term could be implied into an oral contract on the strength of a course of dealing (if it can be so called) which consisted at the most of three or four transactions over a period of five years." That was a case of a private individual who had had his car repaired by the defendants and had signed forms with conditions on three or four occasions. The plaintiff there was not of equal bargaining power with the garage company which repaired the car. The conditions were not incorporated.

But here the parties were both in the trade and were of equal bargaining power. Each was a firm of plant hirers who hired out plant. The defendants themselves knew that firms in the plant-hiring trade always imposed conditions in regard to the hiring of plant: and that their conditions were on much the same lines. The defendants' manager, Mr. Turner (who knew the crane), was asked about it. He agreed that he had seen these conditions or similar ones in regard to the hiring of plant. He said that most of them were, to one extent or another, variations of a form which he called "the Contractors' Plant Association form." The defendants themselves (when they let out cranes) used the conditions of that form. The conditions on the plaintiffs' form were in rather different words, but nevertheless to much the same effect. He was asked one or two further questions which I would like to read:

"(Q) If it was a matter of urgency, you would hire that machine out, and the conditions of hire would no doubt follow? (A) They would. (Q) Is it right that, by the very nature of your business, this is not something that happens just once a year, nor does it happen every day either, but it happens fairly regularly? (A) It does. (Q) You are well aware of the condition that it is the hirer's responsibility to make sure that soft ground is suitable for a vehicle or machine? (A) It is; it is also the owner's responsibility to see that the machine is operated competently."

Then the judge asked: "But it is the hirer's job to see what in relation to the ground? (A) That suitable timber was supplied for the machine to operate on in relation to soft ground." Then counsel asked: "And in fact it is the hirer's job to recover the crane from the soft ground, if it should go into it? (A) If the crane sank overnight of its own accord, I dare say it would be."

From that evidence it is clear that both parties knew quite well that conditions were habitually imposed by the supplier of these machines: and both parties knew the substance of those conditions. In particular that if the crane sank in soft ground it was the hirer's job to recover it: and that there was an indemnity clause. In these circumstances, I think the conditions on the form should be regarded as incorporated into the contract. I would not put it so much on the course of dealing, but rather on the common understanding which is to be derived from the conduct of the parties, namely, that the hiring was to be on the terms of the plaintiffs' usual conditions.

As Lord Reid said in *McCutcheon* v. *David Macbrayne Ltd.* [1964] 1 W.L.R. 125, 128 quoting from the Scottish textbook, *Gloag on Contract*, 2nd ed. (1929), p. 7: " 'The judicial task is not to discover the actual intentions of each party; it is to decide what each was reasonably entitled to conclude from the attitude of the other." It seems to me that, in view of the relationship of the parties, when the defendants requested his crane urgently and it was supplied at once—before the usual form was received —the plaintiffs were entitled to conclude that the defendants were accepting it on the terms of the plaintiffs' own printed conditions—which would follow in a day or two. It is just as if the plaintiffs had said: "We will supply it on our usual conditions," and the defendants said "Of course, that is quite understood."

Applying the conditions, it is quite clear that nos. 6 and 8 cover the second mishap. The defendants are liable for the cost of recovering the crane from the soft ground.

But, so far as the first mishap is concerned, neither condition 6 nor condition 8 (the indemnity clause) is wide enough to cover it: because that mishap was due to the negligence of their own driver. It requires very clear words to exempt a person from responsibility for his own negligence: see *Gillespie Bros. & Co. Ltd.* v. *Roy Bowles Transport Ltd.* [1973] Q.B. 400, 415. There are no such words here.

Even though the judge did not find that the conditions were incorporated, he held that there was an implied term that the hirer should return the chattel to the owner at the end of the hiring. Mr. McCowan pointed out that that implied term was not distinctly pleaded or relied upon. But, nevertheless, there is much to be said for it. When a machine is let out on hire for use on marshy land, and both parties know that it may sink into a marsh, then it seems to me that, if it sinks into the marsh, it is the hirer's job to recover it, so as to restore it to the owner at the end of the hiring. Take a motor car which is let out on hire, and by reason of a gale, or an icy road, it goes off the road into a ditch. It is the hirer's job to get it back on the road and restore it at the end of the hiring. Just as when he takes it on a long journey and falls ill a long distance away. It still is his duty to get it back and restore it to the owner at the end of the hiring. Of course, if it is lost or damaged and he can prove that it was not due to any fault on his part, he would not be liable. A bailee is not liable for loss or damage which he can prove occurred without any default on his part: but the return of the vehicle is different. It is the duty of the hirer to return the vehicle at the end of the hiring to the owner, and to pay the cost of doing so. Although he is not liable for loss or damage occurring without his fault, nevertheless he is liable to do what is reasonable to restore the property to the owner.

So, apart from the express conditions, it may well be, if it had been pleaded, that the plaintiffs could have recovered for the second mishap on an implied term. But, as it was not distinctly pleaded, I prefer to decide the case on the ground that conditions 6 and 8 formed part of the contract of hiring: and under them the plaintiffs are entitled to succeed in regard to mishap no. 2. I would affirm the decision of the judge, but on a different ground.

MEGAW L.J.: I agree.

SIR ERIC SACHS: With regard to the appeal, it is appropriate to start from the unchallenged finding that there was no negligence on the part of the plaintiffs' driver, Mr. Humphrey, and that by and large the finding of negligence on the part of Mr. Meadows, who was the defendants' site agent, cannot really be sustained. Accordingly, the position has to be approached upon the basis that this dragline sank without negligence on the part of either party.

What, then, was the position? Here we have two well established firms engaged in the business of letting out major equipment—cranes—used by large-scale contractors. One of the two parties, the defendants, on this occasion urgently required on a Friday that a dragline be delivered on Sunday for work on Monday on a marshy site. It was a 26-ton machine. It is well known that the use of great machines on marshy sites on which, if anything goes wrong, the machine may well sink in, involves risks, even if all concerned use reasonable care—risks that are higher than if those machines are used on normal ground, including soft surface ground. No one knew of that risk better than the defendants, who were aware of the site characteristics: and it was that risk which eventuated in this case—so that, with no one at fault, a 26-ton machine actually sank almost out of sight.

The business realities of the situation are plain. If the defendants had on Friday said to the plaintiffs, "Of course, if the machine sinks, you take that risk and pay the costs of recovery," the reply would have been: "That is nonsense, and you don't get the machine." Moreover, to hold that the plaintiffs did take the risk impliedly would be unrealistic and obviously contrary to the mythical officious bystander's views. But the matter goes further. Both sides knew, as Lord Denning M.R. has pointed out, that contracts of this type are normally subject to printed conditions, and Lord Denning M.R. has already cited the passages in the evidence of the defendants' manager Mr. Turner which are relevant to that fact. I would only add that this particular machine was worth something upwards of £10,000: and when the judge asked Mr. Turner "Have you ever let out £10,000 worth of machinery without attaching conditions?," the answer came: "We did not, no."

In those circumstances, how does the case stand as regards the terms of the contract? To avoid possible misunderstanding in relation to anything that may be contained in this judgment of mine, I would make it clear that nothing I am about to say, in relation either to the implied common law terms or to the express terms of the contract, is to be considered as having any relation to the position where the owner and the user are in wholly different walks of life, as in *Hollier* v. *Rambler Motors (A.M.C.) Ltd.* [1972] 2 Q.B. 71—where one, for instance, is an expert in a line of business and the other is not. Nor does anything I am about to say put any burden on the user of such a machine if the owner's servant—in this case the driver—causes damage by negligence; nor does anything I am about to say deal with the question of damage sustained by a chattel, as opposed to liability to return it, if it is intact or reasonably repairable.

The court's task, as has already been pointed out, is as stated by Lord Reid, "to decide what each was reasonably entitled to conclude from the attitude of the other." Taking first the relevant common law, this has been considerably canvassed in this court and was pronounced upon by the trial judge; and accordingly I agree with Lord Denning M.R. that it is right to say something about it. In my judgment, the trial judge went too far when he said that the defendants were under this obligation that they would return the machine to the plaintiffs at the end of the hiring. I would not be prepared to hold that the obligation of a bailee is absolute or can be stated in such plain wide terms. On the other hand, it does seem to me that someone who hires a chattel is under an obligation to return that article to the owner unless he shows good cause for not returning it. What is good cause must depend on the particular facts of the case and must involve questions of degree. In relation, for instance, to an ordinary passenger car, at one end of the scale would come a tyre puncture where there was a spare wheel aboard: such a puncture would be no excuse for leaving the car on the road. Similarly, if that car skidded without anyone's fault into a ditch, there would be no good cause to leave it there just because to get it out required £5 worth of services from a garage. On the other hand, if some great boulder descended on the vehicle and damaged it beyond repair, that might well be good cause for not returning it. As regards getting stuck in a snowdrift or a marsh, I would not think such a happening could normally constitute good cause.

In the present action, however, neither the pleadings (which had not been settled by Mr. Nelson), nor the evidence, nor the arguments at trial sufficiently raised the issue of the defendants' common law liability as a bailee for the case to be dealt with on that footing. Accordingly, I turn to consideration of the express terms of the transaction in this particular case. In my judgment, the responsibility was expressly placed on the user for the sinking of this machine into that marsh. Clauses 6 and 8 have already been recited by Lord Denning M.R. They do not impose on the user liability in cases where the owner's own servant was negligent; they are reasonable; and they are of a nature prevalent in the trade which normally contracts on the basis of such conditions. That was shown by the evidence and by reference to the conditions in a Contractors' Plant Association contract which, although expressed in a different way, yet had the same general tenor.

In all the circumstances, the plaintiffs were (to use Lord Reid's words) entitled to conclude that the defendants accepted the plaintiffs' conditions, at any rate if they were reasonable: and I have no doubt but that both parties contracted on the basis of these conditions. Accordingly, they apply to mishap no. 2 and they do not touch mishap no. 1 where the plaintiffs' own driver was negligent. I thus agree that the appeal should be dismissed, and so should the cross-appeal.

[Appeal and cross-appeal dismissed.]

2. PAROL EVIDENCE RULE

It is often said that the general rule is that a party who signs a contractual document is bound by its contents, even though he has not read the document, and even though the contents of the document may differ from the signer's understanding of the agreement. A statement often quoted is that of Scrutton L.J. in *L'Estrange* v. *Graucob* [1934] 2 K.B. 394 at 403. He said: "In cases in which the contract is contained in a railway ticket or other unsigned document, it is necessary to prove that an alleged party was aware, or ought to have been aware of its terms and conditions. These cases have no application when the document has been signed. When a document containing contractual terms is signed, then, in the absence of fraud, or, I will add, misrepresentation, the party signing it is bound, and it is wholly immaterial whether he has read the document or not." The following cases include a variety of techniques by which courts have managed to give relief to a party in spite of his signature to a contractual document.

Running through the cases are frequent references to the so-called "parol evidence rule," of which it has been said that it is not concerned especially with parol statements, that it is not a rule of evidence, and that it is not even a rule at all. Nevertheless references to it are so frequent that it cannot be ignored. A typical statement of the rule follows: "By the general rules of the common law, if there be a contract which has been reduced into writing, verbal evidence is not allowed to be given of what passed between the parties, either before the written instrument was made, or during the time that it was in a state of preparation, so as to add to, or subtract from, or in any manner to vary or qualify the written contract"; per Denman C.J. in *Goss* v. *Lord Nugent* (1833), 5 B. & Ad. 58.

PRENN v. SIMMONDS
[1971] 3 All E.R. 237 (H.L.)

LORD WILBERFORCE: My Lords, Dr. Simmonds's claim in this action is that under the terms of an agreement under seal dated 6th July 1960, he is entitled to acquire from Mr. Prenn, for a consideration of £6,000, a 4 per cent interest in the ordinary capital of a company controlled by Mr. Prenn called now Controls & Communications Ltd., but at the relevant date Radio & Television Trust Ltd. ("RTT"). This interest was worth at the date of the trial about £200,000. Mr. Prenn disputes the claim on the ground that a necessary condition set by the agreement has not been satisfied because less than £300,000 profits available for dividend on the ordinary stock of RTT over the relevant period has been earned. Dr. Simmonds maintains that the condition has been fulfilled. The dispute relates not to the figures, which are agreed, but to the definition of profits of RTT available for dividend on its ordinary stock. If this means the separate profits of RTT alone, the amount over the period fell just short of the target, by less than £10,000. If it means the consolidated profits of the group consisting of RTT and subsidiaries, the amount was largely exceeded. The small margin of deficiency, although capable of arousing sympathy for Dr. Simmonds, is not an argument for one or other side. A similar situation might arise on either interpretation and is inherent in the nature of "target" agreements.

The question is thus simply one of construction of the agreement and it should be capable of resolution shortly and cheaply. But Dr. Simmonds has claimed in the alternative that, if the agreement did not bear the meaning he contended for, it should be rectified so as to do so. This let in a mass of evidence, oral and documentary, as to the parties' intentions, which would not be admissible on construction, although (as I shall explain) counsel for Dr. Simmonds tried to bring some of it in on that issue. It also involved some issues of law. This part of the case overshadowed the rest, so that by far the greater part of the time spent both at first instance and in the Court of Appeal was concerned with it. In this House argument was heard first exclusively on the question of construction and, as your Lordships reached on it a conclusion in favour of Dr. Simmonds, no argument on rectification was heard. I now deal with this construction issue.

In order for the agreement of 6th July 1960 to be understood, it must be placed in its context. The time has long passed when agreements, even those under seal, were isolated from the matrix of facts in which they were set and interpreted purely on internal linguistic considerations. There is no need to appeal here to any modern, anti-literal, tendencies, for Lord Blackburn's well-known judgment in *River Wear Comrs.* v. *Adamson* (1877) 2 App.Cas. 743 at 763 provides ample warrant for a liberal approach. We must, as he said, enquire beyond the language and see what the circumstances were with reference to which the words were used, and the object, appearing from those circumstances, which the person using them had in view. Moreover, at any rate since 1859 (*Macdonald* v. *Longbottom* (1860) 1 E.&E. 977) it has been clear enough that evidence of mutually known facts may be admitted to identify the meaning of a descriptive term.

Counsel for Dr. Simmonds, however, contended for even greater extension of the court's interpretative power. They argued that later authorities have gone further and allow prior negotiations to be looked at in aid of the construction of a written document. In my opinion, they did not make good their contention. A modern authority in this House, which counsel for Dr. Simmonds invoked, is *Hvalfangerselskapet Polaris Aktieselskap* v. *Unilever Ltd.* (1933) 39 Com. Cas. 1 where it was necessary to interpret the words 'entire production'. There, as here, there was a claim for rectification in the alternative so that a great deal of evidence of matters prior to the contract was called. But the speeches give no support for a contention that negotiations leading up to the contract can be taken into account; at most they support the admission of evidence to establish a trade or technical meeting (not in question here) and, of course, they recognise the admissibility of evidence of surrounding circumstances. But they contain little to encourage, and much to discourage, evidence of negotiation or of the parties' subjective intentions.

I may refer to one other case to dispel the idea that English law is left behind in some island of literal interpretation. In *Utica City National Bank* v. *Gunn* (1918) 118 N.E. 607 the New York Court of Appeals followed precisely the English line. Cardozo J. in his judgment refers to "the genesis and aim of the transaction" citing Stephen's *Digest of the Law of Evidence*, and *Wigmore on Evidence*. Surrounding circumstances may, he says, "stamp upon a contract a popular or looser meaning" than the strict legal meaning, certainly when to follow the latter would make the transaction futile. "It is easier to give a new shade of meaning to a word than to give no meaning to a whole transaction." The whole judgment, as one may expect, combines classicism with intelligent realism.

So I think that Dr. Simmonds gains little support from authority. On principle, the matter is worth pursuing a little, because the present case illustrates very well the disadvantages and danger of departing from established doctrine and the virtue of the latter. There were prolonged negotiations between solicitors, with exchanges of draft clauses, ultimately emerging in cl. 2 of the agreement. The reason for not admitting evidence of these exchanges is not a technical one or even mainly one of convenience (although the attempt to admit it did greatly prolong the case and add to its expense). It is simply that such evidence is unhelpful. By the nature of things, where negotiations are difficult, the parties' positions, with each passing letter, are changing and until the final agreement, although converging, still divergent. It is only the final document which records a consensus. If the previous documents use different expressions, how does construction of those expressions, itself a doubtful process, help on the construction of the contractual words? If the same expressions are used, nothing is gained by looking back; indeed, something may be lost since the relevant surrounding circumstances may be different. And at this stage there is no consensus of the parties to appeal to. It may be said that previous documents may be looked at to explain the aims of the parties. In a limited sense this is true; the commercial, or business object, of the transaction, objectively ascertained, may be a surrounding fact. Cardozo J. thought so in the *Utica Bank* case. And if it can be shown that one interpretation completely frustrates that object, to the extent of rendering the contract futile, that may be a strong argument for an alternative interpretation, if that can reasonably be found. But beyond that it may be difficult to go; it may be a matter of degree, or of judgment, how far one interpretation, or another, gives effect to a common intention; the parties, indeed, may be pursuing that intention with differing emphasis, and hoping to achieve it to an extent which may differ, and in different ways. The words used may, and often do, represent a formula which mean different things to each side, yet may be accepted because that is the only way to get "agreement" and in the hope that disputes will not arise. The only course then can be to try to ascertain the "natural" meaning. Far more, and indeed totally, dangerous is it to admit evidence of one party's objective—even if this is known to the other party. However strongly pursued this may be, the other party may only be willing to give it partial recognition, and in a world of give and take, men often have to be satisfied with less than they want. So, again, it would be a matter of speculation how far the common intention was that the particular objective should be realised. In the present case, Lord Denning M.R. seems to have taken into account Dr. Simmonds's anxiety (as testified by a witness) to protect himself against unilateral decisions by Mr. Prenn; and an argument pressed on us was that, if Mr. Prenn's interpretation (i.e. that only the holding company's profits were relevant) was correct, Dr. Simmonds would, in this matter on which he felt so anxious, in some respect at least, be completely in Mr. Prenn's hands, for Mr. Prenn could decide just how much, or how little, of the subsidiaries' profits were to be passed to the holding company. I cannot see how any of this can be admissible because, I repeat, I cannot see how it is helpful. Given the fact of Dr. Simmonds's anxiety, the whole question is how far does the agreement meet it; how can we know, except by interpreting the agreement, how far Mr. Prenn was willing to meet him or how far Dr. Simmonds decided to take what he could get? Even the argument that Mr. Prenn's interpretation would put Dr. Simmonds in his hands, although apparently attractive, I find to be dangerous; a man in Dr. Simmonds's position—a professional man— entering into relations with the source of finance and benefits to come, might decide, in his own interest, that if he could not get all the protection he wanted, the risk of partial protection was one to accept; that Mr. Prenn had to be trusted to act fairly. To say that the clause had this result is not to say that it was futile or frustratory: it is to say that a better clause could, with hindsight, in Dr. Simmonds's interest have been drawn. But the court cannot construct such a clause out of the material given.

In my opinion, then, evidence of negotiations, or of the parties' intentions, and a fortiori of Dr. Simmonds's intentions, ought not to be received, and evidence should be restricted to evidence of the factual background known to the parties at or before the date of the contract, including evidence of the "genesis" and objectively the "aim" of the transaction.

As to the circumstances, and the object of the parties, there is no controversy in the present case. The agreement itself, on its face, almost supplies enough, without the necessity to supplement it by outside evidence. But some expansion, from undisputed facts, makes for clearer understanding and I include a reference to these in what follows.

In the year (1959) before the making of the contract, RTT was controlled by Crompton Parkinson Ltd., a large public electrical engineering company. RTT itself did not trade, but had a wholly-owned trading subsidiary, Airmec Ltd., which employed Dr. Simmonds as managing director and as its leading technician. The structure of RTT was such that Crompton Parkinson held 94 per cent of its ordinary capital, and the whole of an issue of redeemable preference stock; the amount required to redeem it being £294,716 (there were also some capital certificates but I need not refer to this complication). Mr. Prenn desired to secure the services of Dr. Simmonds in his group of companies and decided to do so by purchasing, from Crompton Parkinson, RTT together, of course, with its subsidiary, Airmec, which in turn would bring with it Dr. Simmonds's services. So in July-August, 1959 an agreement was reached by which Mr. Prenn agreed to buy the 94 per cent of the ordinary capital and the preference stock. For this he paid £160,000 in cash. The balance, £294,716, was to be paid by four equal instalments on 19th August 1960, 1961, 1962 and 1963. The agreement provided that any money applied by RTT in redeeming preference stock was to go in reduction of the balance of the purchase price; and it was no doubt in Mr. Prenn's prima facie interest that the preference stock should be redeemed out of profits of RTT so as to avoid his having to find cash from his own resources.

The critical sale agreement between Mr. Prenn and Dr. Simmonds was dated 6th July 1960, after a period of negotiation. Its connection with the Crompton Parkinson agreement is manifest, both from the recital of the latter in it, and from the coincidence of the critical date in cl. 2 with the date—19th August 1963—stated in the Crompton Parkinson agreement as the terminal date for payment. A reading of the agreement shows that it was intended to secure for Dr. Simmonds the provision of an interest in the equity of RTT and that this was to be conditional on Dr. Simmonds remaining with RTT long enough to ensure that the Crompton Parkinson debt was paid off out of profits of RTT and on RTT in fact earning enough to enable the debts to be paid. Thus cl. 3 of the agreement provided for the sale to go off if Dr. Simmonds left RTT before the terminal date either voluntarily or through dismissal for gross misconduct. In order to make good this description of the agreement, I must set out a number of its provisions. After stating the parties there are recitals and definitions:

"WHEREAS:

A. In this agreement the following words and expressions shall have the meanings set opposite them:

R.T.T.:   Radio and Television Trust Limited . . .

Ordinary Stock Units: The Ordinary stock units of 6d. each in the capital of R.T.T. . . .

The Contract: The contract created by exchange of letters dated 21st July 1959 from Mr. Prenn to K. R. Cork as agent for C.P. and 29th July 1959 from C.P. to Mr. Prenn as varied by a Memorandum in writing dated 19th August 1959 being a contract for the purchase by Mr. Prenn of the interest of C.P. in R.T.T. and which includes 356,944 Preference Stock Units remaining in the hands of C.P. Under the terms of this contract as varied there is an obligation on the part of Mr. Prenn to pay the sum of £294,716, being the balance of the purchase money by ur equal instalments on 19th August in 1960, 1961, 1962 and 1963 respectively.

B. Under the Contract any money received by C.P. from R.T.T. for any of the said 356,944 Preference Stock Units redeemed after 19th August 1959 is to be applied by C.P. in or towards payment of the balance of the said purchase money . . ."

Then the operative part:

"1. (a) [Provided for a payment by Mr. Prenn to Dr. Simmonds of £6,600.] (b) [Provided for the sale to Dr. Simmonds of shares in RTT.] (c) [Provided for sale of further shares to Dr. Simmonds.]

2. The provisions of Clause 1 hereof shall not take effect unless and until any one of the following conditions has been satisfied:

(a) The said sum of £294,716 has been paid or satisfied in full on or before the due dates for payment thereof under the Contract out of monies provided by R.T.T. redeeming its Preference Stock Units out of its profits which would otherwise be available for dividend or

(b) The aggregate profits of R.T.T. earned during the four years ending

19th August 1963 and available for dividend on the Ordinary Stock. Units for the time being issued whether declared or not shall have amounted to £300,000 after payment or provision for income tax and profits tax PROVIDED ALWAYS that the conditions of this sub-paragraph (*b*) shall only apply if the Preference Stock Units or any of them are redeemed otherwise than out of the profits of R.T.T. which would otherwise be available for dividend or the terms of payment of the said balance of the purchase price under the Contract or any part thereof shall be re-arranged or all or any part of the said sum of £294,716 shall be satisfied from any other source

3. The provisions of clause 1 shall not take effect if at any time before 20th August 1963 Dr. Simmonds ceases to be employed by R.T.T. either directly or through any of its subsidiaries by reason of his own act or is dismissed for gross misconduct and at the time of such termination neither of the conditions in clause 2 shall have been fulfilled."

Clauses 4 and 5 contained other consequential provisions.

What, then, with this background, is the meaning of cl. 2? Its purpose is plain. Paragraph (*a*) provides that Dr. Simmonds is not to get his shares unless the outstanding debt to Crompton Parkinson has been repaid by means of redemption of preference stock out of profits of RTT. But this might not be fair to Dr. Simmonds, for Mr. Prenn, under his agreement with Crompton Parkinson, was not obliged to redeem the preference stock, or, if he did, might not use RTT's profits to do so. So para (*b*) is evidently designed to protect Dr. Simmonds against these possibilities. There are three alternative events which might bring it into operation, stated under the proviso. If any of these happened, Dr. Simmonds was to get his shares if the aggregate profits of RTT earned over the four years ending 19th August 1963 and available for dividend on the ordinary stock units whether declared or not should have amounted to £300,000 after payment or provision for income tax and profits tax. All of this was in the nature of an inducement to Dr. Simmonds, to procure whose expert services was a main object of the Crompton Parkinson purchase, and who was the mainspring of the profit earning activities of RTT through Airmec, to ensure that enough profits were earned to match the £294,716 which, on this hypothesis, was to be paid by Mr. Prenn, otherwise than out of RTT's profits, to Crompton Parkinson.

What profits, then, are contemplated by this clause? The profits of the RTT group, including Airmec, or only such separate profits as reach RTT as holding company? This is the whole question in the case.

As a final preliminary matter, before answering this question, it is necessary to state a few more matters of fact which must have been present to the minds of both parties. First, it must have been known to those businessmen, at least in general terms, that under the Companies Act 1948 there had to be placed before the shareholders of RTT in general meeting a consolidated profit and loss account giving a true and fair view of the profits of RTT and its subsidiaries combined just as if it was an account of a single company. No doubt there would also be separate profit and loss accounts of each individual company, including RTT itself, but I have no hesitation in asserting that both under the scheme of the Act and in accepted business practice, the significant document is the consolidated account which alone would show whether the enterprise represented by the group was making profit or not.

Secondly, as one would expect, accounts in this form had been prepared by RTT. There are among the documents consolidated profit and loss accounts of RTT and subsidiaries for the year ended 31st March 1958, the fifteen months ended 30th June 1959, the nine months ended 31st March 1960, the three relevant periods immediately before the agreement. Each of these shows the consolidated profit on trading (i.e. of the group), the dividend paid (i.e. on the preference and ordinary capital of RTT) and the balance on profit and loss account (of RTT and the subsidiaries). Thirdly, there are minutes showing how the decisions as to dividends (on RTT capital) out of the profits (of the group) were made. Minutes of 11th August 1959 and 10th June 1960 show, as one would expect, that these were made by the board of the holding company, which then instructed the subsidiaries to declare the appropriate amount by way of dividend, in favour of the holding company.

In the light of this, the meaning of cl. 2 of the agreement seems to me clear. The references to "profits" in para (a) and in para (b) can only, in my opinion, be to the consolidated profits of the group consisting of RTT and its subsidiaries. It is only these profits which could provide an incentive to Dr. Simmonds to remain and work with the group and which could be a measure of his success. On the other hand, no purpose can be discerned why the reference should be to the separate profits of RTT, which in fact means such part of the group profits as the board of that company, effectively Mr. Prenn, decided to pass up to the parent company.

Linguistically, the arguments point decidedly the same way. The reference to profits "earned," and that to income and profits tax, point strongly to consolidated profits. The use of the words "R.T.T." even coupled with the definition appears to me perfectly neutral, since other usages of "R.T.T." in the agreement (definition of 'the Contract' and cl. 3) dispel any idea that the draftsman had in mind any segregation of RTT (qua parent) from the rest of its group. The reference (in para (b)) to profits "available for dividend on the Ordinary Stock Units," so far from pointing towards the limited construction, points, for me, the other way. For both commercially and on the established accounting practice, all profits of the group are available for these dividends. It is true that a large part of the profits was ploughed back into the business of the subsidiaries, and that both parties must have contemplated that this would be done, but this is not to the point. To say so is to confuse the earning of profits with their appropriation; all profits earned are available for dividend; what is done with them is a matter of choice which rests with those who control the company. Even if they decided to "plough them back" they still remain "available for dividend," so long as they remain in the balance sheet as "balance on profit and loss account."

One other argument I must mention. It is based on para (a). The reference there to profits otherwise available for dividend must, it is said, be to profits of the holding company, because it is only out of them that preference stock can be redeemed. This is said to be borne out by s. 58 of the Companies Act 1948, which requires that redeemable preference shares can only be redeemed out of "profits available for dividend" (or by a new issue). The use of these same words in para (a) is argued to show that only separate profits of RTT can be meant. In my opinion, this argument is fallacious. Paragraph (a) can just as well be referring to group profits; in a real sense (since RTT does not trade) its preference stock can only be redeemed by profits earned by the group. Admittedly, before redemption can occur, they have to be passed up to RTT (holding) by way of dividend on the subsidiaries; but they are still group profits. The only difference between para (*a*) and para (*b*) is that in the one case a "passing up" operation is presupposed, in the other not. But the "profits" are the same—group profits. The use of the words "available for dividend" in s. 58 proves nothing, since that section is not concerned with any particular type of company or with any distinction between parent and subsidiary. It is simply, in effect, saying that redeemable preference shares must be redeemed out of profits, not out of capital. What those profits are, in the case of a group, must be decided on arguments outside the section.

To sum up, Mr. Prenn's construction does not fit in any way the aim of the agreement, or correspond with commercial good sense, nor is it, even linguistically, acceptable. The converse of each of these propositions applies to Dr. Simmonds's interpretation. I would accept it. It follows, in consequence, that the alternative claim for rectification does not arise.

LONGLEY v. BARBRICK
Nova Scotia. Supreme Court. 1962. 36 D.L.R. (2d) 672

COFFIN J.: This is an action for the foreclosure of a mortgage and for deficiency judgment.

The basic documents on which the claim is founded are as follows:

(1) A mortgage dated January 23, 1959, made by Beatrice Barbrick, the defendant herein, as mortgagor, to United Realties Limited, as mortgagee. The consideration set forth in the mortgage is $5,000 and the proviso stipulates that the mortgage shall be void on the payment of this sum with interest at 8% per annum calculated half-yearly not in advance, as well after as before maturity, in 8 years from the date thereof by monthly instalments of $70.40 each including principal and interest on the first day of each and every month commencing on March 1, 1959, to and including January 1, 1966, and the balance of said principal sum and interest on February 1, 1966.

(2) An agreement made January 23, 1959, between the same parties, reciting the mortgage, and also reciting that the actual sum of money advanced to Beatrice Barbrick by United Realties was $2,500. This agreement followed the above recitals by acknowledging that the difference between the $5,000 and the $2,500 was being given by Beatrice Barbrick to United Realties Ltd. as a bonus in consideration of its granting the loan.

(3) Assignment of mortgage dated April 30, 1959, from United Realties Ltd. to the plaintiff Charles F. Longley. This document recited the mortgage and undertook that the principal sum $4,924.53 together with interest at the rate of 8% on April 1, 1959, was then owing and unpaid.

These then are the main documents to be considered. There are other exhibits to which reference will be made. But the case itself depends on the right of the plaintiff to enforce the original mortgage and the collateral agreement as assigned by the last-mentioned assignment of mortgage.

At this point I am going to refer in some detail to the facts from which the dispute in the case in question arose.

The defendant Beatrice Barbrick described how she originally purchased the property involved in 1946. She had been in the Army from 1942 to

November, 1945, retiring as a Lance-Corporal, after which she worked at nursing homes and from 1949 to 1958 or 1959 served in the Polio Clinic.

She had saved some money and this she invested in her house. When questioned as to the background of the mortgage she said that as she needed some money she made inquiries as a result of which she called "Town & Country" at Halifax and talked to "a Mr. John Hickey". He later came out to see her and she informed him that she needed $2,500, to which, according to her evidence, he replied, "I think that can be arranged without any trouble but I'll have to see the Manager". He later called Miss Barbrick and said that the manager agreed to let her have $2,500 at 8% for 96 months.

In two or three days she was instructed to go to a lawyer's office in the Roy Building, which she did, and when she actually entered his office, she was accompanied by a Mrs. Drysdale. Mrs. Drysdale held the existing mortgage on her property and, among other things, the loan which the defendant was seeking was to pay this mortgage.

Miss Barbrick continued in her evidence to say that the lawyer gave Mrs. Drysdale a paper to sign which she supposed was a receipt. Mrs. Drysdale then obtained her cheque and went straight out. He then said to Miss Barbrick " 'Sit down' and 'You sign here for your money,' which was 600 and some dollars. I don't remember the exact amount of the cheque". The defendant then received her cheque, which she understood was the $2,500 less Mrs. Drysdale's account and less certain legal fees.

Miss Barbrick insisted that the mortgage had not been read to her before she signed it. As to the collateral agreement, this, too, she said was not read to her nor explained to her. She did not get a copy of it at the time but it was mailed to her subsequently. . . .

Some evidence as to the actual execution of the mortgage and the agreement was given by the solicitor, in whose office the documents were signed by the defendant. He said that on instructions from United Realties Ltd. he had prepared a mortgage and contacted Miss Barbrick, who came to his office and went through the documents. He also said that there was a mortgage and a collateral agreement. As to whether she asked any questions or he explained anything to her, his answer was, "It's very difficult. I know what my usual practice was—not only the mortgage but also the collateral agreement to the mortgagors. In my own mind I felt they understood what they were signing in this type of mortgage". On cross-examination he was asked by Mr. Jackson if he remembered explaining the mortgage to Miss Barbrick and he replied—"No. I can't recall this particular transaction. As you will note from the date on the document it took place some time ago and I've done several since then. Q. The same would apply to the collateral agreement, I suppose? A. That is correct." In all fairness to the solicitor I am in agreement with the suggestion of the defendant's counsel that the solicitor understood that all details had been thoroughly discussed with the defendant before she ever reached his office. It was, in fact, to Town & Country Real Estate Limited that she was looking for guidance.

At the time the mortgage was assigned to the plaintiff Mr. Longley, apparently only two payments had been made, and there was a balance owing at that time of $4,924.53. The amount paid by Mr. Longley for this mortgage was $3,170. . . .

The defendant pleaded *non est factum* and something should be said of the authorities on that point. . . .

I accept the evidence of the defendant on the facts leading up to the execution of the relevant documents in this case. I find as a fact that Town & Country Real Estate Ltd. undertook to arrange for her a mortgage of $2,500 at 8% for 96 months and that she understood it was for such a mortgage that she signed the application of January 16, 1959.

I also find that the mortgage and collateral agreement were not fully read and explained to her by the solicitor who drew up the documents, when she was in his office. I have already discussed the reasons for this and it is my view that if Town & Country Real Estate Ltd. had given a detailed explanation of this proposal in advance and instructed the defendant to have independent advice before the documents were signed, the whole unfortunate situation could have been avoided.

Having found these facts, it is my view that the bonus of $2,500 is . . . void under the plea of *non est factum* because she was so misled as to the contents of the documents that her "mind did not go with her signature". . . .

Mr. Longley's evidence was that he made no inquiries about the security when he took the assignment (and there is no affirmative evidence to contradict him on this point) but he has his remedies against the original mortgagee under the terms of the assignment of mortgage.

The mortgage will be amended and the principal sum reduced from $5,000 to $2,500 with an appropriate reduction in interest charges, resulting in a mortgage bearing the same date as that now under dispute, but securing the principal sum of $2,500 only and interest at 8%. The instalments will be reduced accordingly.

The defendant is entitled to a rectification of the said mortgage and to an accounting showing the correct balance now owing on the basis of the mortgage as so amended.

The defendant will have the costs of this action and as she has succeeded substantially on her counterclaim, the costs of the counterclaim.

[Coffin J. also held that "the bonus of $2,500 is bad as a bonus on the ground that it is unfair and unconscionable within the prohibitions enunciated by *G. & C. Kreglinger* v. *New Patagonia Meat & Cold Storage Co.*, [1914] A.C. 25." This part of the opinion is omitted.]

NOTE. The ordinary rule is that the assignee of a chose in action is bound by all defences available against the assignor. On this basis, Longley, even though he took the assignment of the mortgage in good faith, would only be in as good a position as the assignor, Town & Country Real Estate. In Ontario, however, s. 7 of the Conveyancing and Law of Property Act creates an exception to the general rule. That section provides: "A receipt for consideration money or other consideration in the body of a conveyance or endorsed thereon is, in favour of a subsequent purchaser not having notice that the money or other consideration thereby acknowledged to be received was not in fact paid or given wholly or in part, sufficient evidence of the payment of the whole amount thereof." By the definition section, a conveyance includes a mortgage, and a purchaser includes the assignee of a mortgage.

COLLINS v. *FOREST HILL INVESTMENT CORP. LTD.* (1967) 63 D.L.R. 492. (Ont. Co. Ct.) WILLMOTT Co. Ct. J.: "It is true that in *Longley* v. *Barbrick* . . ., Coffin J. made a finding of *non est factum* in respect of a mortgage providing for a 100 per cent bonus. Coffin J. seems to regard a mortgage involving a bonus as different in nature and character from a mortgage without a bonus. Such a distinction appears, with respect, to be too fine to be a valid foundation for a finding of *non est factum*, and the decision seems to be contrary to principle and the weight of authority." Note that relief may often be available in cases like *Longley* v. *Barbrick* under the Unconscionable Transactions Relief Act, chapter 7, *infra*. What is the effect of s. 5 of that Act?

FARAH v. BARKI
Ontario. Supreme Court of Canada. [1955] 2 D.L.R. 657

On March 8, 1951, Barki wrote out and signed a document stating "I hereby declare having sold today to Mr. Bryan Farah 650 shares of Joy Heat and Equipment Company for the price of $6500. payable by Mr. Farah on the 15th of December 1951." Farah read over and signed the document but in an action by Barki on the alleged contract Farah testified that while he read the document he did not appreciate that he was personally becoming the purchaser of the shares. He thought, as Barki had previously proposed to him, that the shares were to be transferred to him and that he should act for Barki in controlling the company and carry out a sale of the shares to one Joy, if that should prove possible. Farah had introduced Barki to Joy, who carried on the furnace business and he and Barki incorporated the company. Joy was given 350 shares at a par value of $10 and continued to manage the business. Barki invested $6,500, for which he got 650 shares. The company did very poorly. Arrangements were proposed, but which fell through, for the sale of Barki's shares to Joy. It was at this stage that Barki made the proposal to Farah on which he relied. The trial judge accepted Farah's evidence and dismissed the action and remarked that the contract looked to him very much like a "smart trick" by which Barki endeavoured to recompense himself for a bad investment. The Ontario Court of Appeal allowed an appeal and concluded that the trial judge had made no finding of fraud. Farah appealed to the Supreme Court.

KELLOCK J. [after discussing the facts and evidence]: ... In these circumstances, I think the finding of the learned trial Judge is to be interpreted as a finding of fraudulent misrepresentation on the part of the respondent as to the nature of the document which he asked the appellant to sign, and which he trusted he would sign, as he did, under the influence of the previous discussion without appreciating the real nature of the document, understanding that it was to be followed by a more formal document. The question therefore arises as to whether or not in such circumstances the appellant can successfully resist an action upon the document.

Winfield in his 13th edition of *Pollock on Contracts* at p. 384, quotes the language of Lord Chelmsford in *Wythes* v. *Labouchere* (1858), 3 De G. & J. 593 at p. 601, 44 E.R. 1397, namely: "It may be said generally that a man of business who executes 'an instrument of a short and intelligible description cannot be permitted to allege that he executed it in blind ignorance of its real character'."

Winfield goes on to state that: "Strictly this may be an *inference of fact* rather than a rule of law; but under such conditions the inference is irresistible."

This puts the point too rigidly. As stated by Farwell J. in *May* v. *Platt*, [1900] 1 Ch. 616 at p. 623, fraud "unravels everything". The cases, however, such as that presently before the Court, in which a man may escape from a short and clear document, which he admits reading before signing, must be few. But that is not impossible. . . .

In *Blay* v. *Pollard*, [1930] 1 K.B. 628, where fraud was not pleaded, Scrutton L.J., in the course of his judgment, said at p. 633: "As a general rule mistake as to the legal effect of what you are signing, when you have read the document, does not avail. . . . It would be very dangerous to allow a man over the age of legal infancy to escape from the legal effect of a document he has, after reading it, signed, in the absence of an express misrepresentation by the other party of that legal effect."

The learned Lord Justice continued, however, quoting from *Fry on Specific Performance* as follows: " 'It equally follows that the mistake of one party to a contract can never be a ground for compulsory rectification, so as to impose on the second party the erroneous conception of the first. The error of the plaintiff alone may, however, where (but, it is conceived, only where) there has been fraud or conduct equivalent to fraud on the part of the defendant, be a ground for putting the defendant to elect between having the transaction annulled altogether or submitting to the rectification of the deed in accordance with the plaintiff's intention'. . . This rests on unilateral mistake in one party, fraud or conduct equivalent to fraud in the other party.". . .

[The opinions of Kerwin C.J.C. and Rand J. also allowing the appeal are omitted. Cartwright and Fauteux JJ. concurred with Kellock J.]

ROYAL BANK OF CANADA v. HALE
British Columbia. Supreme Court. 1961. 30 D.L.R. (2d) 138

In February 1958 the Royal Bank at Kitimat lent ABC Sheet Metal and Plumbing Ltd. $25,000, taking as security five notes for $5,000 each, an assignment of ABC's book debts, and personal guarantees from Hale and his three brothers for the aggregate sum of $25,000. The guarantees signed by the brothers were on the Royal Bank's standard form, which contained the guarantors' promise to guarantee payment, not only of the $25,000 but "of all debts and liabilities, present or future, direct or indirect, absolute or contingent, matured or not, at any time owing by ABC . . . to the bank." The form also stated (Para. 13) that it covered "all agreements between the parties relative to this guarantee . . ." and that "none of the parties shall be bound by any representation . . . which is not embodied herein." At that time the brothers knew that ABC owed nearly $20,000 to companies in which they were interested, and that these debts had been assigned by the companies to the Bank back in 1955. The Bank claimed in this action on the guarantees not only the balance owing on ABC's loan (the direct debt) but on the assignments (the indirect debts) as well. The trial also embraced four other actions arising in almost identical circumstances where the Hale brothers guaranteed a loan by the Bank to Prince George Heating and Sheet Metal Ltd. In their defence the Hale brothers pleaded that there was mutual mistake or, a unilateral mistake in that they were induced by the Bank to believe that the guarantees applied only to the direct debts. The evidence of the background of the transactions was admitted over the Bank's objection, and showed among other things that in 1957 the Hale brothers had given similar guarantees for $20,000 for ABC and when the loan was repaid the guarantee form was given back, although at that time the indirect debts of 1955 had been assigned to the Bank to the knowledge of its Vancouver officials, but not to the knowledge of the Kitimat manager. In connection with the Prince George guarantees, A. W. Hale had written when returning the guarantee form to the Prince George branch manager, that "it was our understanding that we were personally guaranteeing the loan only." In his reply to this letter the manager did not comment one way or the other on the extent of the personal guarantee.

MUNROE J.: . . . In the circumstances of this case . . . I hold that the evidence tendered by the defendants in support of their pleadings is admissible. How else could the Court determine whether or not any mistake had occurred? . . .

While it is clear beyond any doubt that the defendants and all the representatives of the plaintiff with whom they negotiated did not contemplate, far less intend, that the guarantees were taken and delivered for any purpose beyond the known purpose of securing the bank loans, nevertheless, the intention of the plaintiff corporation, as distinguished from the state of mind of its officials, must be determined from the terms of the document, and not otherwise. Since the guarantee form is not so limited in its terms, I cannot hold that the plaintiff was mistaken as to its legal effect, and the defence of mutual mistake therefore fails.

There remains for consideration the major defence raised on behalf of the defendants, namely, that the guarantees ought not to be enforced *vis-à-vis* the indirect debt because of a unilateral mistake (on the part of the defendants) as to the legal effect of the guarantee, which mistake was induced by the (innocent) misrepresentation of the plaintiff and that it would be inequitable to enforce the guarantees in the manner contended for by the plaintiff.

In my view, the guarantees, in their literal and plain meaning, appear to render the defendants liable to the plaintiffs for the indirect debts herein claimed unless the defence of unilateral mistake should prevail, even though the plaintiff has rarely if ever before sought to enforce such liability. I have no hesitation in finding, upon the evidence, that the defendants when they executed the guarantees, were mistaken in their belief that they were thereby guaranteeing only the bank loans, and not the indirect debt. Then, were the defendants so misled by the words, acts or conduct of the plaintiff's officials? The answer to that question can best be ascertained by a consideration of the evidence and a review of the business dealings between the parties, which dealings began in 1955 when a loan was obtained from the plaintiff for $250,000 for a company in which the defendants were interested and interlocking guarantees given by several companies for $500,000; the 1957 loan to ABC at Kitimat when guarantees of the defendants were given for the same amount as the loans; the return and discharge of that guarantee (which the plaintiff now claims was a vital asset) when the loan was repaid, some 2 years after the assignments of book debts which created the liability which the plaintiff says now exists: the fact that when the current loans were being negotiated, none of the plaintiff's officials nor any of the defendants ever thought about such indirect liability: the fact that all the persons concerned intended that the guarantees were given and accepted in order to provide adequate security only for the loans and not to secure any obligation arising out of the assignment of book debts; the fact that the guarantees contain no specific reference to said pre-existing indirect liability; the significant fact that the guarantees are for amounts identical to the bank loans; the fact that the only consideration received by the defendants for the giving of the guarantees was the loan of the monies to the companies; the covering letter of June 9, 1958, enclosing the guarantee in which the defendant A. W. Hale showed defendants' understanding or misunderstanding when he said, in part: "It was our understanding that we were personally guaranteeing the loan only"; the plaintiff manager's reply of June 10, 1958, wherein no reference is made to that statement; all of these circumstances, when taken together, lead to the irresistible inference and I find that, if the plaintiff's present inter-pretation of the guarantees is correct, it (the plaintiff) induced the defend-ants to think otherwise, and thereby misled them, and knew or ought reasonably to have known that that was so.

It is clear from the evidence that all the plaintiff's officials with whom the defendants negotiated, and the defendants, knew and understood that the real purpose of the guarantees was to guarantee only the bank loans, and had the parties been left to their own resources to prepare an appropri-ate document to set out their common intention, I have no doubt that they would, if properly advised, have prepared a document under which the defendants would have guaranteed the bank loans and nothing more. . . .

In reaching my conclusions, I have not been unmindful of the need of the Courts to restrict the plea of mistake within narrow limits because of the dangerous confusion that would ensue if a man were able to disown his signature merely by proving that he misunderstood the contents or effect of a document. But there is ample authority, founded in good sense, that the Courts will relieve a person of his contract where a misunderstanding as to its true effect was induced, even though innocently, by the other party and where injustice would be done if performance were to be enforced. . . . And once it is shown that the misrepresentation was an inducing cause, it is no answer to suggest or prove that other considerations co-existed and co-operated with the misrepresentation in producing the result. See 23 Hals., 2nd ed., pp. 50-1.

In my view, the defendants, by signing the guarantees in question in these actions, intended to enter into a transaction fundamentally different than that which they actually signed, insofar as the guarantees purport to create liability beyond the bank loans, and that it would be not only inequitable but unconscionable not to relieve them from liability for the indirect obli-gations sued upon herein, which liability arose by reason of a unilateral mistake on the part of the defendants, induced by the plaintiff, to be inferred from their previous dealings.

The plaintiff submits that para. 13 of the guarantee, above quoted, is conclusive against the defendants and relies upon *Spelchan* v. *Long et al.* (1956), 2 D.L.R. (2d) 707, but in that case it was held that there were no misrepresentations as to the contents of the contract, and it is distinguish-able also in several other respects. Paragraph 13 does not purport to say that the guarantor shall be precluded from equitable relief for any inducing misrepresentation, and if it did, it would be ineffective for that purpose. I hold that para. 13 of the guarantee is not a bar to the relief claimed herein by the defendants and in so doing I adopt the views expressed by Denning L.J., in *Curtis* v. *Chemical Cleaning & Dyeing Co.*, [1951] 1 K.B. at pp. 808 *et seq.* and also in *Neuchatel Asphalte Co.* v. *Barnett*, [1957] 1 All E.R. 362, wherein he stated, in the latter case, at p. 365:

"It is a well settled rule of construction that, if one party puts forward a printed form of words for signature by the other and it is afterwards found that those words are inconsistent with the main object and intention of the transaction as disclosed by the terms specially agreed, then the court will limit or reject the printed words so as to ensure that the main object of the transaction is achieved. . . . We do not allow printed forms to be made a trap for the unwary." . . .

[At the opening of the trial the defendants amended their defence and paid into Court the full balance remaining due upon the loan to ABC and to Prince George, and denied liability on the indirect debts. In the result, there was an order for payment out to the plaintiff's solicitor of the moneys paid into Court and all the actions were dismissed.]

CURTIS v. *CHEMICAL CLEANING AND DYEING CO., LTD.* [1951] 1 All E.R. 631 (England. Court of Appeal). The defendants are cleaners and dyers. The plaintiff took a white satin wedding dress to them for cleaning. When the dress was returned it was found that there was a stain on it which had not been there when it was left for cleaning. The trial judge found that the stain was caused by the defendant's negligence. The defendants relied on a receipt which the plaintiff signed. The receipt set out her name and address and a description of the dress and in the bottom right hand corner under the amount to be charged, was printed: "This or these articles is accepted on condition that the company is not liable for any damage howsoever arising, or delay." The plaintiff was told she had to sign the document because she had to accept responsibility for damage to the beads and sequins on the dress. The trial judge awarded damages at £32 10s. The defendants appealed. The Court of Appeal dismissed the appeal. DENNING L.J.: "If the party affected signs a written document, knowing it to be a contract which governs the relations between him and the other party, his signature is irrefragable evidence of his assent to the whole contract, including the exempting clauses, unless the signature is shown to be obtained by fraud or misrepresentation. . . . What is a sufficient misrepresentation for this purpose? . . . In my opinion, any behaviour by words or conduct is sufficient to be a misrepresentation if it is such as to mislead the other party about the existence or extent of the exemption. If it conveys a false impression, that is enough. If the false impression is created knowingly, it is a fraudulent misrepresentation; if it is created unwittingly, it is an innocent misrepresentation. But either is sufficient to disentitle the creator of it to the benefit of the exemption. . . . In those circumstances, by failing to draw attention to the width of the exemption clause, the assistant created the false impression that the exemption related to the beads and sequins only, and that it did not extend to the material of which the dress was made. It was done perfectly innocently, but, nevertheless, a false impression was created. It was probably not sufficiently precise and unambiguous, to create an estoppel . . . but, nevertheless, it was a sufficient misrepresentation to disentitle the cleaners from relying on the exemption, except in regard to the beads and sequins. . . .

"The second point made by counsel for the defendant was that, even if there was an innocent misrepresentation, the plaintiff cannot, in point of law, avoid the terms of the contract. He said that an innocent misrepresentation gives no right to damages but only to rescission, that rescission was not possible because the contract was executed, and that in any case rescission was of no use to the plaintiff, because, once rescission has taken place, there would be no contract to sue upon. That is an attractive argument, but I do not think it is right. One answer to it is that an executed contract can in a proper case be rescinded for innocent misrepresentation;

and if the present contract was rescinded, the plaintiff could sue in tort for negligence, because any task undertaken must be done carefully."

QUESTION: If the "receipt" signed in the *Curtis* case had carried the words "None of our agents or employees has any authority to alter, vary or qualify in any way these terms and conditions" would the case have been decided differently?

HAWRISH v. BANK OF MONTREAL
(1969) 2 D.L.R. (3d) 60 (S.C.C.)

The judgment of the Court was delivered by JUDSON J.: This action was brought by the Bank of Montreal against Andrew Hawrish, a solicitor in Saskatoon, on a guarantee which the solicitor had signed for the indebtedness and liability of a newly formed company, Crescent Dairies Limited. This company had been formed for the purpose of buying the assets of Waldheim Dairies Limited, a cheese factory in which Hawrish had an interest.

By January, 1959, the line of credit granted by the bank to the new company was almost exhausted. The bank then asked Hawrish for a guarantee, which he signed on January 30, 1959. The guarantee was on the bank's usual form and stated that it was to be a continuing guarantee and to cover existing as well as future indebtedness of the company up to the amount of $6,000.

The defence was that when he signed the guarantee, Hawrish had an oral assurance from the assistant manager of the branch that the guarantee was to cover only existing indebtedness and that he would be released from his guarantee when the bank obtained a joint guarantee from the directors of the company. The bank did obtain a joint guarantee from the directors on July 22, 1959, for the sum of $10,000. Another joint guarantee for the same amount was signed by the directors on March 22, 1960. Between the dates of these two last-mentioned guarantees there had been some changes in the directorate.

Hawrish was never a director or officer of the new company but at the time when the action was commenced, he was a shareholder and he was interested in the vendor company. At all times the new company was indebted to the vendor company in an amount between $10,000 and $15,000. Hawrish says that he did not read the guarantee before signing. On February 20, 1961, Crescent Dairies Ltd., whose overdraft was at that time $8,000, became insolvent. The bank then brought its action against Hawrish for the full amount of his guarantee—$6,000.

The trial Judge dismissed the bank's action. He accepted the guarantor's evidence of what was said before the guarantee was signed and held that parol evidence was admissible on the ground that it was a condition of signing the guarantee that the appellant would be released as soon as a joint guarantee was obtained from the directors. He relied upon *Standard Bank v. McCrossan*, 55 D.L.R. 238. . . . The Court of Appeal . . . reversed this decision and gave judgment for the bank. In their view the parol evidence was not admissible and the problem was not the same as that in *Standard Bank v. McCrossan*. Hall J.A., corrrectly stated the *ratio* of the *Standard Bank* case in the following paragraph of his reasons [p. 373]: "In my opinion the learned trial judge erred in holding that the respondent was able to establish such condition by parol evidence. The condition found, if indeed it is one, was not similar to that which existed in *Standard Bank* v. *McCrossan, supra,* in that it did not operate merely as a suspension or delay of the written agreement. It may be permissible to prove by extraneous evidence an oral agreement which operates as a suspension only."

The relevant provisions of this guarantee may be summarized as follows:

(a)   It guarantees the present and future debts and liabilities of the customer (Crescent Dairies Ltd.) up to the sum of $6,000.

(b)   It is a continuing guarantee and secures the ultimate balance owing by the customer.

(c)   The guarantor may determine at any time his further liability under the guarantee by notice in writing to the bank. The liability of the guarantor continues until determined by such notice.

(d)   The guarantor acknowledges that no representations have been made to him on behalf of the bank; that the liability of the guarantor is embraced in the guarantee; that the guarantee has nothing to do with any other guarantee; and that the guarantor intends the guarantee to be binding whether any other guarantee or security is given to the bank or not.

The argument before us was confined to two submissions of error contained in the reasons of the Court of Appeal:

(a)   that the contemporaneous oral agreement found by the trial Judge neither varied nor contradicted the terms of the written guarantee but simply provided by an independent agreement a manner in which the liability of the appellant would be terminated; and

(b)   that oral evidence proving the making of such agreement, the consideration for which was the signing of the guarantee, was admissible.

I cannot accept these submissions. In my opinion, there was no error in the reasons of the Court of Appeal. This guarantee was to be immediately effective. According to the oral evidence it was to terminate as to all liability, present or future, when the new guarantees were obtained from the directors. But the document itself states that it was to be a continuing guarantee for all present and future liabilities and could only be terminated by notice in writing, and then only as to future liabilities incurred by the customer after the giving of the notice. The oral evidence is also in plain contradiction of the terms of para. (d) of my summary above made. There is nothing in this case to permit the introduction of the principle in *Pym* v. *Campbell* (1856), 6 El. & Bl. 370, 119 E.R. 903, which holds that the parol evidence rule does not prevent a defendant from showing that a document formally complete and signed as a contract, was in fact only an escrow.

The appellant further submitted that the parol evidence was admissible on the ground that it established an oral agreement which was independent of and collateral to the main contract.

In the last half of the 19th century a group of English decisions, of which *Lindley* v. *Lacey* (1864), 17 C.B. (N.S.) 578, 144 E.R. 232; *Morgan* v. *Griffith* (1871), L.R. 6 Ex. 70, and *Erskine* v. *Adeane* (1873), L.R. 8 Ch. 764, are representative, established that where there was parol evidence of a distinct collateral agreement which did not contradict nor was inconsistent with the written instrument, it was admissible. These were cases between landlord and tenant in which parol evidence of stipulations as to repairs and other incidental matters and as to keeping down game and dealing with game was held to be admissible although the written leases were silent on these points. These were held to be independent agreements which were not required to be in writing and which were not in any way inconsistent with or contradictory of the written agreement.

The principle formulated in these cases was applied in *Byers* v. *McMillan* (1887), 15 S.C.R. 194. In this case Byers, a woodcutter, agreed in writing with one Andrew to cut and deliver 500 cords of wood from certain lands. The agreement contained no provision for security in the event that Byers was not paid upon making delivery. However, before he signed, it was orally agreed that Byers was to have a lien on the wood for the amount to which he would be entitled for his work and labour. Byers was not paid and eventually sold the wood. The respondents, the McMillans, in whom the contract was vested as a result of various assignments, brought an action of replevin. It was held by a majority of this Court that they could not succeed on the ground that the parol evidence of the oral agreement in respect of the lien was admissible. Strong J., with whom the other members of the majority agreed, said at pp. 202-3:

"*Erskine* v. *Adeane*, 8 Ch. App. 764; *Morgan* v. *Griffith*, L.R. 6 Ex. 70; *Lindley* v. *Lacey*, 17 C.B. (N.S.) 578, afford illustrations of the rule in question by the terms of which any agreement collateral or supplementary to the written agreement may be established by parol evidence, provided it is one which as an independent agreement could be made without writing, and that it is not in any way inconsistent with or contradictory of the written agreement. . . .

"These cases (particularly *Erskine* v. *Adeane* which was a judgment of the Court of Appeal) appear to be all stronger decisions than that which the appellant calls upon us to make in the present case, for it is difficult to see how an agreement, that one·who in writing had undertaken by his labor to produce a chattel which is to become the property of another shall have a lien on such product for the money to be paid as the reward of his labor, in any way derogates from the contemporaneous or prior writing. By such a stipulation no term or provision of the writing is varied or in the slightest degree infringed upon; both agreements can well stand together; the writing provides for the performance of the contract, and the consideration to be paid for it, and the parol agreement merely adds something respecting security for the payment of the price to these terms."

In *Heilbut, Symons & Co.* v. *Buckleton*, [1913] A.C. 30 at p. 47, a case having to do with the existence of a warranty in a contract for the sale of shares, there is comment on the existence of the doctrine and a note of caution as to its application:

"It is evident, both on principle and on authority, that there may be a contract the consideration for which is the making of some other contract. "If you will make such and such a contract I will give you one hundred pounds," is in every sense of the word a complete legal contract. It is collateral to the main contract, but each has an independent existence, and they do not differ in respect of their possessing to the full the character and status of a contract. But such collateral contracts must from their very nature be rare. The effect of a collateral contract such as that which I have instanced would be to increase the consideration of the main contract by 100*l*., and the more natural and usual way of carrying this out would be by so modifying the main contract and not by executing a concurrent and collateral contract. Such collateral contracts, the sole effect of which is to vary or add to the terms of the principal contract, are therefore viewed with suspicion, by the law. They must be proved strictly. Not only the terms of such contracts but the existence of an animus contrahendi on the part of all the parties to them must be clearly shewn. Any laxity on these points would enable parties to escape from the full performance of the obligations of contracts unquestionably entered into by them and more especially would have the effect of lessening the authority of written contracts by making it possible to vary them by suggesting the existence of verbal collateral agreements relating to the same subject-matter."

Bearing in mind these remarks to the effect that there must be a clear intention to create a binding agreement, I am not convinced that the evidence in this case indicates clearly the existence of such intention. Indeed, I am disposed to agree with what the Court of Appeal said on this point. However, this is not in issue in this appeal. My opinion is that the appellant's argument fails on the ground that the collateral agreement allowing for the discharge of the appellant cannot stand as it clearly contradicts the terms of the guarantee bond which state that it is a continuing guarantee.

The appellant has relied upon *Byers* v. *McMillan*. But upon my interpretation that the terms of the two contracts conflict, this case is really against him as it is there stated by Strong J., that a collateral agreement cannot be established where it is inconsistent with or contradicts the written agreement. To the same effect is the unanimous judgment of the High Court of Australia in *Hoyt's Proprietary Ltd.* v. *Spencer* (1919), 27 C.L.R. 133, which rejected the argument that a collateral contract which contradicted the written agreement could stand with it. Knox C.J., said at p. 139: "A distinct collateral agreement, whether oral or in writing, and whether prior to or contemporaneous with the main agreement, is valid and enforceable even though the main agreement be in writing, provided the two may consistently stand together so that the provisions of the main agreement remain in full force and effect notwithstanding the collateral agreement. This proposition is illustrated by the decisions in *Lindley* v. *Lacey* (17 C.B. (N.S.), 578), *Erskine* v. *Adeane* (L.R. 8 Ch. 756), *De Lassalle* v. *Guildford* ([1901] 2 K.B., 215) and other cases."
I would dismiss the appeal with costs.
[Appeal dismissed.]

MORGAN v. GRIFFITH
England. Exchequer. 1871. L.R. 6 Ex. 70

The plaintiff became tenant of the defendant on Michaelmas Day, 1867, on oral terms that included the signing of a lease. The plaintiff found the land was overrun with rabbits and when the lease was presented for signature he refused to sign unless the rabbits were destroyed. The defendant later promised to destroy them when the plaintiff threatened to quit. At Michaelmas, 1868, the lease was again tendered. The plaintiff refused to sign it, but the defendant repeated his promise. The plaintiff then asked to have the promise incorporated in the lease, which the defendant refused, although he repeated his promise. The plaintiff signed. The lease contained the plaintiff's promise that he would not hunt or destroy game, but preserve it and allow the defendant and his friends to hunt. The rabbits were not destroyed and the plaintiff quit at Michaelmas, 1870. He then brought this action. The defendant pleaded the parol evidence rule, but the trial judge admitted the oral evidence of his promise, and the plaintiff got a verdict. The defendant appealed this ruling of the judge.

KELLY C.B.: All that is possible has been said on behalf of the defendant, but it has failed to convince me. I think the verbal agreement was entirely collateral to the lease, and was founded on a good consideration. The plaintiff, unless the promise to destroy the rabbits had been given, would not have signed the lease, and a court of equity would not have compelled him to do so, or only on the terms of the defendant performing his undertaking. The decision of the county court judge must therefore be affirmed.

[Pigott B., who was of the same opinion, observed that the "verbal agreement" did not appear to contain any terms which conflicted with the written document.]

ANGELL v. DUKE
England. Queen's Bench. 1875. 32 L.T.R. 320

At the trial before Blackburn J., at the London Sittings after Hilary Term, it was proved that the defendant had let the house and furniture to the plaintiff by a written agreement dated the 24th March, 1873, and evidence was tendered of a promise alleged to have been made by the defendant before that date to put more furniture into the house, and to change some of that which was already in it. It was also alleged that there was a promise to the same effect made after the date of the written agreement.

The learned judge rejected evidence of the earlier promise, and ruled that the agreement was conclusive as to all that referred to taking the house and the furniture, and that the plaintiff could not recover upon any prior agreement made during the negotiation and not put into the written record of the agreement, and refused leave to move. He also held, that if the above ruling was right, the plaintiff could not show a fresh consideration, and ruled that there was no subsequent consideration and nonsuited the plaintiff.

COCKBURN C.J.: I am of opinion that there should be no rule. To allow the plaintiff to recover in this action would be to allow a parol agreement to conflict with a written agreement afterwards entered into. I agree with the cases which have been cited to this extent, that there may be instances of collateral parol agreements which would be admissible, but this is not the case here: something passes between the parties during the course of the negotiations but afterwards the plaintiff enters into a written agreement to take the house and the furniture in the house, which is specified. Having once executed that, without making the terms of the alleged parol agreement a part of it, he cannot afterwards set up the parol agreement.

[The opinions of Blackburn, Field and Mellor JJ. are omitted.]

NOTE. The view of Cockburn C.J. in *Angell* v. *Duke* at the trial may be contrasted with his views when, at an earlier stage in the same proceedings, it was argued on a demurrer that the *Statute of Frauds* barred the action as disclosed in the declaration. Cockburn C.J. there said [L.R. 10 Q.B. 174 at p. 127] "... We must see what the true history of the transaction is, and, of course, the sequence of events. ... The agreement for a transfer of the interest in land or the house is posterior. ... The other is something antecedent and collateral to that contract, that is, a separate agreement entered into in order to induce the intended tenant to accept the tenancy." It is difficult to tell from the reports whether the facts proven at the trial differed materially from the allegations in the declaration, which said, in part, "the plaintiff ... objected to become tenant ... upon the ground that the ... premises were then in imperfect order and repair and insufficiently furnished . . . and the defendant then, in order thereby to induce the [plaintiff] to become . . . tenant . . . verbally promised the plaintiff that he, the defendant, would . . . do such work and repairs and send such additional furniture. . . ."

PYM v. CAMPBELL
England. King's Bench. 1856. 6 E. & B. 370; 119 E.R. 903

Campbell proposed to purchase Pym's invention and arranged a meeting at which Pym, Campbell and two engineers, Fergusson and Abernethie were to attend, and the engineers were to inspect and approve the invention. Pym arrived late and after the engineers had left. It was agreed that since the parties were together if the engineers could be found the sale might be arranged. Fergusson was found and approved, but Abernethie could not be found, but Campbell drew up a paper which both he and Pym signed and it was agreed that if later Abernethie approved the invention the paper should be an agreement and if he did not it should not be one. Abernethie did not approve.

The Lord Chief Justice told the jury that, if they were satisfied that, before the paper was signed, it was agreed amongst them all that it should not operate as an agreement until Abernethie approved of the invention, they should find for the defendant on the pleas denying the agreement. Verdict for the defendant.

Thomas Serjt., in the ensuing term obtained a rule nisi for a new trial on the ground of misdirection.

ERLE J.: I think that this rule ought to be discharged. The point made is that this is a written agreement, absolute on the face of it, and that evidence was admitted to shew it was conditional: and if that had been so it would have been wrong. But I am of opinion that the evidence shewed that in fact there was never any agreement at all. The production of a paper purporting to be an agreement by a party, with his signature attached, affords a strong presumption that it is his written agreement; and, if in fact he did sign the paper *animo contrahendi*, the terms contained in it are conclusive, and cannot be varied by parol evidence: but in the present case the defence begins one step earlier: the parties met and expressly stated to each other that, though for convenience they would then sign the memorandum of the terms, yet they were not to sign it as an agreement until Abernethie was consulted. I grant the risk that such a defence may be set up without ground; and I agree that a jury should therefore always look on such a defence with suspicion: but, if it be proved that in fact the paper was signed with the express intention that it should not be an agreement, the other party cannot fix it as an agreement upon those so signing. The distinction in point of law is that evidence to vary the terms of an agreement in writing is not admissible, but evidence to shew that there is not an agreement at all is admissible.

[The opinions of Lord Campbell C.J. and Crompton J. to the like effect, are omitted.]

ALAMPI v. SWARTZ
(1964) 43 D.L.R. (2d) 11 (Ont. C.A.)

McGILLIVRAY J.A. delivered the judgment of the Court: This is an appeal by the plaintiff from the judgment of Ferguson J. [38 D.L.R. (2d)

300, [1963] 2 O.R. 11], dismissing the plaintiff's action upon a lease in writing for damages for failure to give her complete possession of certain premises and from the further award to the defendants of the sum of $360 by way of counterclaim.

The premises in question bear the number 934 Bloor St. West and comprise two stores with two small rooms behind, an apartment above, a basement below and a double garage at the back. The defendants had purchased all of these premises in October, 1959, under an agreement of purchase and sale. By the agreement the vendor Klenck was to remain in possession of the west store at a rental of $75 per month until March 31, 1961. At some date subsequent to the above purchase a nephew of the plaintiff, one Oliva, noticing that the east store was for rent consulted an Italian real estate agent named Aloi, on the plaintiff's behalf, about it and Aloi sent his man with Oliva to examine the premises. Oliva was shown through both stores but not through the apartment above them as it was occupied, so Oliva was told, by a crippled lady who was not to be disturbed. Following this negotiations as to renting occurred and were completed at the agent's office in the presence of the defendant Frank Swartz, the plaintiff, the agent and Oliva. An agreement was reached at that time whereby there were to be two leases, one of which would permit the plaintiff to occupy the east store forthwith on July 1, 1960, the other lease, hereinafter described, was to take effect some nine months later when Klenck would have vacated the west store. Aloi, the agent, was asked to draw the leases and refused but referred the defendant to a lawyer by name of Sukornyk. The defendant, Frank Swartz, then attended with Aloi at Sukornyk's office and two leases were drawn.

The first lease for the east half of 934 Bloor St. West was to run from July 1, 1960, to March 31, 1961, at a rental of $130 per month. This was to cover the eastern store premises which the plaintiff intended to use and did subsequently use as a fish store, plus a portion of the rooms at the back with use of the basement. The door to the apartment stairs was on the west side of the building and it was not indicated at this stage that the plaintiff would have any interest in the apartment.

The second lease which specifies rental of $270 per month (subsequently to increase to $280 per month) was to commence April 1, 1961 (the day following the expiry date of the first lease), and run to June 30, 1970, purports to convey the property "municipally known as the whole of 934 Bloor St. West." There is only one 934 Bloor St. West, although subsequent to their purchase of the property the defendants put up 934½ Bloor St. West over the apartment door contrary to the municipal by-laws. There is no suggestion that this number was up prior to the execution of the lease.

The plaintiff's position is that the whole of 934 Bloor St. West was what she was contracting for and that the words in the lease meant precisely what they said. The defendants asserted that only the two stores were covered by the description in the second lease and, in the alternative, claim that they, the defendants, were unilaterally mistaken; and that by reason of the mistake they are entitled to have the lease rescinded.

The defendant Frank Swartz testified that his son pointed out to him a few days after the second lease was signed that it would include the apartment and garage and Klenck, the tenant of the west store, testified that he had told Swartz shortly after the lease was executed that all parts of the premises were included and, if it was his intention only to rent the two stores, he should do something about it. Notwithstanding this the defendants, though claiming to have communicated with the lawyer who drew the lease, did nothing and the plaintiff was allowed to go into possession of the east store and spend a substantial sum on plumbing, flooring, et cetera, and no question was raised till some nine months later when possession under the new lease was to be taken and the plaintiff's nephew demanded keys for the premises. At that time the defendants refused to hand over the keys to the apartment upon the ground that it was not included in the lease. The plaintiff refused, under the circumstances, to occupy the west store though she continued in possession of the east store and paid rent therefor which was accepted without prejudice by the defendants.

The agent Aloi stated that he considered when completing the transactions that he had been acting for the defendants and Frank Swartz testified that he had paid the agent for his services. The agent's testimony was that the apartment was specifically discussed in the course of the negotiations and that the agreement reached was not for the stores alone but for the complete premises.

The learned trial Judge heard evidence as to the meaning of the descriptive words in the lease and also evidence regarding events preceding the signing of the lease directed to establishing the contention of the defendants that it was not the intention of the parties that more than the two store properties should be included. After commenting on the effect of such evidence he made the following finding [p. 306 D.L.R., p. 17 O.R.]: "The question for decision is one of fact only. I think that the parties were in agreement when the leases were executed, and when the two leases are read together, there is no difficulty in explaining any latent ambiguity in the second lease. . . . In this view of the case I am not concerned with the problem of rectification." [i.e., the trial Judge accepted the defendant's evidence that the intention of both parties was to include only the stores and not the apartment, and he held that the second lease could, and did, express that intention.] He thereupon found, as the plaintiff had not gone into possession of both stores, that she was in breach of the lease and accordingly he dismissed the plaintiff's action and allowed the counterclaim.

The main grounds of appeal from the finding are that the trial Judge:

(1) erred in admitting parol evidence to vary a written unambiguous contract;

(2) erred in failing to apply the principle that the defendants had to establish beyond a reasonable doubt that the lease was intended to mean other than what the plain words of the lease stated;

(3) erred in failing to hold that the defendants were estopped from alleging any latent ambiguity in the lease in view of their admitted knowledge and conduct;

(4) erred, if there was an ambiguity, in failing to apply the *contra proferentes* rule to the interpretation of the lease.

The rule as to the admissibility of parol evidence in connection with written contracts is well settled, namely, that where there is no ambiguity in the words of a contract, no explanation contrary to the words is to be allowed.

As a consequence where no ambiguity exists as to the terms expressed, the terms themselves as they appear in the instrument provide the only test as to the intention of the parties. The rule is applied both in the administration of law and of equity though in cases where in a Court of equity an extraordinary remedy, such as specific performance, or correction of a document in writing, is sought and a defendant pleads mistake parol evidence of extrinsic circumstances indicating the intention of the parties may be heard. Except in such last-mentioned instances parol evidence is not to be admitted to vary the words of the written document. It is, however, admitted for the purpose of explaining terms of the contract and to prove the facts upon which the interpretation of the written document depends and so is admissible to establish the validity of the document or the identity of the parties, to explain technical terms or commercial usage, and in all other places where the admission of such evidence is necessary to enable the Court to construe the document before it: *Shore* v. *Wilson* (1842), 9 Cl. & Fin. 355 at p. 565, 8 E.R. 450.

Pursuant to the above principle where it is necessary to do so, evidence to ascertain and identify property referred to in a document is admissible so long as it does not contradict a clear description of the property; and so has been admitted to identify properties bearing descriptions such as "the farm," "the mill property," "my house," "Mr. O's House," or property described as being in a particular parish or place.

Evidence so admitted does not offend against the general rule. It may not contradict a term in the contract but, as has been said, is adduced to assign definite meaning to the terms used or to relate them to the proper subject-matter. If, however, after such evidence has been led it then appears that the term under construction is ambiguous and capable of more than one meaning evidence of a different class may be admitted, namely evidence of intention. Such an ambiguity, a "latent ambiguity," because not apparent upon the face of the writing, demands evidence of intention to establish whether there was an agreement at all, or if the parties intended a particular one of alternate meanings to prevail. Such latent ambiguities have arisen where it was found that two railway stations bore the name of the one mentioned in the contract (*Robinson* v. *Great Western R. Co.* (1866), 35 L.J.C.P. 123) or where an agreement was made for a lease of premises "as per plan agreed upon" and it appeared that two plans had been inspected (*Hodges* v. *Horsfall* (1829), 1 Russ. & My. 116, 39 E.R. 45).

In the present instance the property demised by the lease was described as "that messuage and tenement situate, lying and being in the City of Toronto and in the County of York and being municipally known as the whole of 934 Bloor St. West." Evidence was properly adduced to establish what property was comprised in this description. The assessment rolls for the City of Toronto for each of the years 1959 and 1960 were produced. In each the property known as 934 Bloor St. West appeared as comprising both stores and the apartment above them. No evidence was adduced to indicate any other municipal record bearing a different meaning. In addition the defendant Frank Swartz testified that it was pointed out to him by his son immediately following execution of the lease that no part of these premises was excluded from its terms and the tenant Klenck had also testified that he had pointed out to Swartz, at about the same time, that such was the situation. It thus appears, not only from the municipal record but from the interpretation by laymen who saw the lease, that the literal meaning of the descriptive words was clear. Indeed the trial Judge has made no finding that this was not the literal meaning. He has found, however, that it was the intention of the parties that the descriptions should be construed as applying only to the store parts of the premises and as a consequence that is what the words of the description meant. This decision he arrived at upon certain extrinsic evidence of events which preceded the signing of the lease which evidence was introduced to indicate the intention of the parties to the lease. This evidence under proper circumstances was admissible as relating to the alternate defence plea of unilateral mistake but as has been pointed out such extrinsic evidence, if admitted, may only be considered where some latent ambiguity in the terms of the lease has first been established. It appears to have been upon the ground of the existence of such a latent ambiguity that the trial Judge felt free in this instance to use such extrinsic evidence to interpret the contract. With all deference I am satisfied that in so doing he erred for I am unable to find anything resembling a latent ambiguity in that part of the evidence properly adduced to indicate the meaning of the descriptive words. The extrinsic evidence could not be used to establish the latent ambiguity. It could only be used after the latent ambiguity had been first established and this was not done. In construing written documents a primary rule of construction is that words must be given their ordinary and grammatical meaning. Evidence having been adduced in this case which clearly established that meaning and no ambiguity having been established, it must be held that the evidence as to intention was wrongly given consideration on this issue.

I consider now a further submission made to this Court by the defendants that, should they fail on the first issue, as they have, the Court should, in view of the finding by the trial Judge as to intention, give effect to the alternate defence of unilateral mistake: the substance of this submission being that the trial Judge has found in effect that the plaintiff was aware of an error in the description and by remaining silent allowed the defendants to subscribe to something different to that which was intended.

To succeed on a plea of unilateral mistake the defendant must establish:
(1) that a mistake occurred;
(2) that there was fraud or the equivalent of fraud on the plaintiff's part in that she knew or must be taken to have known when the agreement was executed that the defendant misunderstood its significance and that she did nothing to enlighten the defendant: *Blay* v. *Pollard & Morris*, [1930] 1 K.B. 628; *Farah* v. *Barki*, [1955] 2 D.L.R. 657, [1955] S.C.R. 107.

It is hardly necessary to add that an allegation of fraud should be pleaded. In *May* v. *Platt*, [1900] 1 Ch. 616 (followed in *Blay* v. *Pollard, supra*), Farwell J., states at p. 623:

"In my judgment, in order to get rescission after conveyance, the allegations would have had to be very different. I have always understood the law to be that in order to obtain rectification there must be a mistake common to both parties, and if the mistake is only unilateral, there must be fraud or misrepresentation amounting to fraud. It is true that Lord Romilly in *Harris* v. *Pepperell*, L.R. 5 Eq. 1 and *Garrard* v. *Frankel*, 30 Beav. 445 and perhaps Bacon V.-C. in *Paget* v. *Marshall*, 28 Ch. D. 255, appear to have shrunk from stigmatising the defendants' conduct in terms as fraud, but they treated it as equivalent to fraud, and in my opinion would have had no jurisdiction to grant the relief that they did in the absence of fraud. Rescission after conveyance of land can only be obtained on the ground of unfair dealing: see *Brownlie* v. *Campbell*, (1880) 5 App. Cas. 937, per Lord Selborne; *Soper* v. *Arnold*, 37 Ch. D. 102, per Cotton L.J. It is only necessary to say this in the present case, in consequence of the defendant's argument. If it were a case of fraud, which unravels everything, there would be no difficulty in looking into the evidence to see how the contract was induced, as well as how it was carried out. But in the absence of fraud, of which there is no suggestion, I cannot see how the evidence could be admitted for any purpose whatever."

In the present case there is no allegation of fraud and no indication in the pleadings that fraud is suggested. Even, however, were an amendment to the pleadings to be allowed I am of the opinion that the evidence falls short of establishing the equivalent of fraud on the plaintiff's part. There were, of course, no actual representations made by the plaintiff, fraudulent or otherwise, but, if proved to the Court's satisfaction that the plaintiff was aware of an error on the defendants' part and by her silence she deliberately allowed them to be misled, the Court might treat such silence as the equivalent of fraud and grant relief. Such knowledge on the plaintiff's part has not been established. Indeed positive evidence to the contrary is to be found in the testimony of those, other than Frank Swartz, who were present when the lease was negotiated as all state that discussions regarding the apartment occurred at that time and it was intended that it should be included. The circumstances considered by the trial Judge as opposed to this were stated to be:

(1) *"The effect of the plaintiff obtaining the possession of the whole building for $270 per month would have the effect of letting the plaintiff into possession of the apartment free of rent."* [p. 304 D.L.R., p. 15 O.R.]

With deference the evidence does not support this opinion. Prior to June 16, 1960, the rent which the defendants had been receiving for the stores, plus apartment, plus garage was $287 per month out of which they were paying approximately $27 per month (spread over the year) for heating, giving a net return of $260 per month; and the witness Klaiman, a real estate agent, called by the defendants, not by the plaintiff, testified that the rental value of apartment and stores would be about $202. None of these figures would indicate that the net return to the defendants under the new lease of $270 per month increasing to $280 would be much, if any, less than they had been receiving, or could get, for the garage and stores when the lease was made. Indeed the figures would indicate that the return to the defendants might be greater.

(2) *Neither the plaintiff nor her nephew examined the upstairs apartment prior to making the lease.*

Her nephew's evidence, already stated, was that he sought to do so but was told that a crippled person occupying the apartment was not to be disturbed. Some confirmation for this statement was to be found in testimony by that woman's son that his mother, who occupied the apartment as of that date, was old and crippled.

(3) *The fact that the lease provided that the lessor was to pay one-half the heating charges led to an inference that the lessor was to have partial occupancy of the premises.*

The evidence on this point was that there had been substantial argument regarding these charges when the lease was negotiated and that this compromise was the result. The plaintiff paid no heating charges at all when occupying the east store and the agreement as it appears in the new lease could readily have been a compromise as it was stated to be.

(4) *"When the leases are read together it seems to me that 'whole' is the 'whole' of that which is the 'half'."* [p. 306 D.L.R., p. 17 O.R.]

This referred to the lease for the east store which had run from June 16, 1960, to March 1, 1961, and which was described as for "the east half of

934 Bloor Street West." There can be no question that the wording referred to in this lease, taken with that of the new lease, might bear the
interpretation given it in the above quotation. It is, however, far from conclusive. The first lease did not stipulate, for instance, that it was not to
include the east half of the apartment above the store but neither did it
stipulate that it was to include use of the cellar which in effect it did. The
entrance to the apartment was on the west half and had the lease been for
the west half the apartment might well have been mentioned if it were intended that it should be included or otherwise. In the east half such was
not the case and there was not the same necessity to refer to it. Nor can
undue weight be given to the description in the first lease as Sukornyk who
drew both leases was unaware of the existence of the apartment. These
factors indicate the limited significance to be derived from the wording of
the first lease.

The degree of proof required of the defendant in these circumstances is
high. In an action for rectification of a written agreement Duff J., in *The
"M. F. Whalen"* v. *Point Anne Quarries Ltd.* (1921), 63 D.L.R. 545 at
pp. 567-8, 63 S.C.R. 109 at pp. 125-6 [affd [1923] 1 D.L.R. 45], stated
it to be as follows:

" . . . where the parties have finally reduced their agreement to writing,
a writing, that is to say which is intended to be the record of the agreement between them, it was not at common law competent to either of them
to resort to previous negotiations or contemporary conversations or other
matters for the purpose of varying or adding to its terms as expressed in the
writing . . . In commercial affairs it is of great importance that such documents should be regarded as final and on this principle the Courts have
uniformly acted recognizing that the very purpose of expressing agreements
in writing is to reduce the terms of them to permanent form and to preclude subsequent disputes as to such terms. . . .

"Where one of the parties denies the alleged variation the parol evidence
of the other party is not sufficient to entitle the Court to act. Such parol
evidence must be adequately supported by documentary evidence and by
considerations arising from the conduct of the parties satisfying the Court
beyond reasonable doubt that the party resisting rectification did in truth
enter into the agreement alleged. It is not sufficient that there should be a
mere preponderance of probability, the case must be proved to a demonstration in the only sense in which in a Court of law an issue of fact can
be established to a demonstration, that is to say, the evidence must be so
satisfactory as to leave no room for such doubt."

In the present instance where rescission is sought and fraud or its equivalent must be demonstrated the degree of proof required is at least as high
as that stated by Duff J., to be necessary where rectification is sought. In my
opinion the evidence referred to falls short of establishing that either the
plaintiff or her agent was aware when the document was produced for their
signatures that the lands covered by the lease agreement were intended by
the defendants to comprise anything less than the description in the lease
called for. The defendants cannot succeed on this plea of unilateral mistake.

There is an added reason for refusing this appeal. If it was not the intention of the defendants that the description should cover the whole of
the premises as stated it was by their negligence, or that of their agents,
that it so appeared in the lease. In addition they clearly understood its full
significance within a day after execution of the document but failed to take
any action to notify the plaintiff or to procure its correction. Instead they

permitted the plaintiff to expend money upon part of the premises under the impression, derived from the lease, that she was later to be put in possession of the whole. These circumstances, amounting to estoppel, are in themselves sufficient to cause the Court to refuse relief in this case.

I turn then to the question of the plaintiff's damages. For obvious reasons no assessment of her damages was made at trial and it is convenient that this Court should now assess them. The trial Judge found that, from the time of the date of the new lease, the plaintiff occupied the east store under the new lease. Such being the case her claim is properly framed as upon a breach of contract for quiet enjoyment of the whole of the premises. She thus becomes entitled for a stipulated period to the value to her of the portion of the premises to which she was not given possession less the contractual rent which she was obligated to pay. It was her intention to operate a grocery business in the westerly store and evidence was led to establish her loss of profits resulting from failure to secure possession. The evidence on this point was most unsatisfactory. A witness by the name of Taylor, a real estate and business broker, testified as to what he considerd the value to the owner of the west store would be. He estimated it at $200 per month. This witness had at one time worked as a clerk for Dominion Stores, had at a later period run a variety store of his own, and had for some seven years operated a real estate business. He testified that he specialized chiefly in properties in the east end of the city. He could recall no particular instance where he had dealt with a store lease west of Yonge Street and it was demonstrated that he had but a hazy knowledge of the area surrounding 934 Bloor St. West (he did not know if 934 Bloor St. West was east or west of Bathurst Street) and his testimony as to what a grocery store of this type should earn was not based upon any particular similar store elsewhere. Nor was any information forthcoming that the plaintiff had ever run a grocery business or knew anything about it and her possibility of success or failure in the new venture, keeping in mind her rudimentary knowledge of English, could not be evaluated. The evidence as to contingent loss is thus unreliable and the damages by way of loss of profits remote. Davis J.A., in *Re Schulte-United Ltd., Liggett Co.* v. *The Trustee*, [1934] 4 D.L.R. 51 at pp. 57-8, [1934] O.R. 453 at p. 462, 15 C.B.R. 520 at p. 528, indicates the weight to be given such evidence. He said:

"I agree with the statement of law laid down by Audette J., in the Exchequer Court in *The King* v. *Goldstein*, [1924] Ex. C.R. 56, at p. 60:

'It seems that the question of the loss of estimated profits as a mode of arriving at the compensation for the value of this unexpired term, can no more be considered, than can be considered by the expropriating party the probable loss a lessee might make, and claim a set off therefor. The question of the loss of profits *per se* is too remote. It is personal to the individual. Through the ability, skill, sagacity and wisdom of one individual large profits might be realized in a business; while another person dealing with a similar and even the same business, but wanting in those qualities, would bring the business into the Bankruptcy Court.

No allowances can be made for loss of profits *qua* estimated profits.' "

The premises withheld from possession had, however, a certain rental value which was established by the evidence. At the time of the execution of the lease here in question the west store was rented for $75, the apartment for $105 and the garage for $7, a total of $187 per month. When Klenck, the occupant of the west store left, it remained vacant for a period of three and a half months. It was then rented for $100 per month but the lessee gave up his lease because of the smell from the fish store operated by the plaintiff on the east side. The defendants again, at that time, sought without success to rent the west store and eventually, rather than have it vacant, occupied it themselves. The smell from the fish store also made it difficult to rent the apartment for as much as before and the rental from it at the time of trial was but $90 per month. The rental value of that part of the premises not surrendered may thus be said to range from $187 to $197 per month and the return from the whole building on such a basis would be:

Rent for east store	$130		
Rent for balance of premises	$187	to	$197
Net return	$317	to	$327 per month

For this the plaintiff was called upon by her lease to pay $270 per month plus one-half the cost of heating estimated at $12 per month. This would involve an outlay by the plaintiff of approximately $282 per month which, when subtracted from the calculated net return of $317, *supra*, would indicate that the plaintiff's loss has been $35 per month; or when subtracted from a net return of $327, a loss of $45 per month. In the light of these figures an assessment of her loss at $40 per month would appear to be reasonable and I would give judgment on that basis. As it is to be assumed that the defendants will not continue to withhold full possession after the date hereof the plaintiff's damages are assessed at $40 per month from April 1, 1961 to January 31, 1964, a total of 34 months, without prejudice to the plaintiff's right to sue for damages of a similar nature should she be further deprived of complete possession of the premises described in the lease.

For the reasons stated I would allow this appeal with costs. I would direct that the judgment below be set aside and that judgment be entered for the plaintiff for $1,360 with costs and that the counterclaim be dismissed without costs.

[Appeal allowed.]

CORBIN ON CONTRACTS § 542, (one-volume edition p. 515)

Of course, an otherwise "plain" meaning should not be disturbed by the proof of irrelevant circumstances or of those having only a remote bearing or inconsequential weight. But until a court knows the circumstances it can not properly say that they have no probative value. It seems highly probable that when a court says that it will enforce a contract in accordance with the "plain and clear" meaning of its words, the relevant surrounding circumstances have in fact been proved and have been carefully weighed; the losing party has merely urged the drawing of inferences therefrom that the court is unwilling to draw. It is a very commonly reported statement that words are to be given "their plain, ordinary, and popular meaning"; but this is always limited by adding some such clause as the following: "in the absence of relevant evidence indicating that the words were used with a different meaning." If there is in fact a "plain, ordinary, and popular" meaning of words used by the parties, that fact is evidential that the parties used them with that meaning. It is fully overcome, however, as soon as the court is convinced that one of the parties used and understood the words in a different sense and that the other party had reason to know it.

There are, indeed, a good many cases holding that the words of a writing are too "plain and clear" to justify the admission of parol evidence as to their interpretation. In other cases, it is said that such testimony is admissible only when the words of the writing are themselves "ambiguous." Such statements assume a uniformity and certainty in the meaning of language that do not in fact exist; they should be subjected to constant attack and disapproval. In many cases it is said that such testimony is offered in order to "contradict" the writing; but the existence of such "contradiction" can be determined only after the writing has been interpreted. It is easy to jump to a conclusion; and it is easy to dispose of testimony that is not believed by saying that it is "not admissible."

LONG v. SMITH
Ontario. Divisional Court. 1911. 23 O.L.R. 121

Smith agreed on Saturday to buy a piano from Long for $575. The first price quoted was $650, but when Smith returned with his wife for a second look, the price was reduced. Neither Smith nor his wife knew anything about pianos and when Smith wanted to bring an expert on Monday to advise him Long insisted that if he did the price would have to go back to $650. The parties then reached what Smith, who was evidently a foreigner, called a "wordable understanding" that if he afterwards found that he had been overcharged, or that the piano was unsatisfactory, Smith could return it and get back his $10, or exchange the piano for another. When Smith wanted this oral agreement added to the printed form of the contract of sale, Long said he could not alter it but that his word could be relied on. The printed form provided that it was the whole agreement. Smith had the piano for two or three weeks during which time he had it valued by an expert at $400. The piano was returned but Long would not accept it. Smith then left it on the sidewalk and Long took it in and kept it in "storage." The county court Judge dismissed Long's action for $565. Long appealed.

BOYD C. delivered the judgment of the Court.: . . . The legal objection is that it is not competent to give oral testimony *dehors* the terms of the writing, because it is there printed at the bottom, "This contract contains the whole agreement between myself and William Long" (the plaintiff). This form of expression is referable to the fact that the printed form is intended for the use of local agents, and provided that such persons are "not to make any promises, verbal or otherwise, outside of the agreement, or in any way to alter the same."

The present contract was made direct with Mr. Long, the principal, who, of course, could modify the printed form. The evidence now given goes to shew that the writing does not contain the whole agreement. There was a condition or promise entered into, upon the faith of which the contract was signed, which is not expressed therein. This assertion as to the whole being in writing cannot be used as an instrument of fraud; the plaintiff cannot ignore the means by which he obtained the contract sued upon, falsify his own undertaking, and, by the help of the Court, fasten an unqualified engagement on the defendant. The whole purchase was to be nullified if it turned out as a fact that there had been a gross overcharge. And such appears to be now the actual situation.

Then, apart from this shackle upon the truth, it is argued that it is contrary to the rule of evidence and the decisions of the Courts to allow oral testimony to be given which is inconsistent with or repugnant to the terms of the written instrument. No little difficulty and confusion has arisen in the application of this rule to the varying transactions of business life, which is not lessened by the discordant opinions of the Judges. But, without trying to reconcile differences, there is a well-marked line of cases establishing this doctrine, that evidence may be given of a prior or a contemporaneous oral agreement which constitutes a condition upon which the performance of the written agreement is to depend. The oral evidence may be such as to affect the performance of the written agreement by shewing that it is not to be operative till the condition is complied with. The enforcement of the contract may be suspended or arrested till the stipulation orally agreed on has been satisfied. Here there was to be in substance and in essence no bargain if the piano was not worth the price stated in the writing. At the outset, and before the signing of the contract, the defendant was practically prevented from getting correct information as to the value from a competent person, but it was left for him to satisfy himself on that point forthwith thereafter. Ten dollars he had paid, but there was no intention of paying any more till he was satisfied as to the truth of the representation as to value. . . .

Contract or no contract depended upon this test, whether the piano was or was not overcharged; that was a question of fact and one to be settled as a matter initiatory or precedent. The meaning of the transaction was that, though the writing was signed and $10 paid, yet, if it was found that there had been an overcharge, the $10 was to be returned, the piano taken back, and the contract at an end. This contemplated speedy action; and action was taken forthwith by the purchaser, and the result made known to the seller, and the piano was returned.

The purchaser was inveigled into signing the contract by the representation of the real value of the piano and the accompanying promise. The representation proving untrue, the failure to fulfil the promise introduces the element of deception and fraud on the part of the seller. This suggests another aspect of the case upon which this decision in favour of the defendant may be supported. The evidence here may very well support the finding that there was a deceitful representation as to the fair and reasonable value of the piano—a matter well known to the seller, but not to the purchaser—and the prudence of the purchaser laid asleep by the promise. Though this be not in writing nor mentioned in the written evidence of the contract, it may be relied upon to protect the purchaser when sued for the price. . . . In brief, this contract was induced by material representations which were untrue to the knowledge of the plaintiff, and he has no *locus standi* to enforce a contract so obtained.

Wemple v. *Knopf*, 15 Minn. 440, cited by Mr. Raney, is distinguishable. In that case the parol evidence was offered to shew that, though the obligation in writing was complete and imported an absolute engagement, yet it was subject to be defeated by subsequent revocation on the part of the defendant. That was in defeasance of the obligation already contracted, and so was repugnant to the writing. But here all the circumstances shew that the obligation was not to arise if the piano was not, at the time, of the value represented. The defendant did not agree to purchase a piano only worth in reality $400 for the expressed price of $575.

The judgment should be affirmed with costs.

FERLAND v. KEITH
(1958) 15 D.L.R. (2d) 472 (Ont. C.A.)

MCGILLIVRAY J.A. delivered the judgment of the Court: This is an appeal by Lindley Motors (Hamilton) Ltd., one of the third parties, from the judgment in favour of the defendant in the third party proceedings herein. The judgment dated February 21, 1958 is in favour of the defendant against the third parties for $1,800.35, together with the costs of the third party proceedings, the costs which the defendant was ordered to pay the plaintiff under the judgment in the main action, and the defendant's costs as between solicitor and client of defending the main action. No appeal was taken by the third party, Bowerbank.

The third party proceedings were tried by Moorhouse J. with a jury at Toronto.

In the main action the plaintiff sued the defendant as owner and driver of a motor vehicle following a highway accident and recovered judgment for $1,800.35 and costs. The defendant will be referred to hereafter as the respondent and Lindley Motors (Hamilton) Ltd. as the appellant.

The basis of the claim for relief over by the respondent against the appellant was for breach of contract or in the alternative for breach of duty as agent, in that the appellant when the vehicle in question was sold by it, had contracted with the respondent to insure the vehicle for public liability and property damage (P.L. and P.D.) and had failed to do so. The claim against the third party Bowerbank was based upon the same transaction and was for breach of duty as agent.

The appellant was engaged in Hamilton in the business of selling new and used cars and the third party, Bowerbank, was his salesman and the person who sold the motor car to the respondent.

The sale was made on May 12, 1956. The respondent whose name by birth was Alexander Keith but who sometimes used the surname of his stepfather and called himself Alexander Keith Russell, was an infant at the time and his stepfather, Thomas Russell, accompanied him to make the purchase. The latter's purpose in so doing was because he understood it was necessary for him to sign for the unpaid purchase-price and insurance, and because he believed he would be personally liable for any damage caused by the vehicle and so wished to be sure that it was adequately covered for public liability and property damage before any deal was negotiated.

The negotiations with respect to the purchase were carried on with the third party Bowerbank, an employee of the appellant, upon the appellant's premises. A suitable car was selected and Bowerbank started to make out papers which he stated to the purchaser included the cost of the insurance. When asked what that meant, he stated that it only covered collision damage. Mr. Russell replied, "Well what does that mean?" and was informed it meant for damages to his own car only. The salesman was then told that on no account would they take the car unless it was covered for public liability and property damage as well. The salesman said at first that he could not get that coverage. He did not say why; but when told that the deal was off without it he said, "Well we can get it. There is no telling how much it will cost as the boy is under age." He said he would get it fully insured through the same company. The respondent then agreed to take the car and agreed that the cost of the additional insurance would be added to the price. The salesman thereupon secured another insurance application form and both insurance forms were signed in blank by the respondent.

The amount of coverage for P.L. and P.D. damage for which the policy was to be written was never stated. Mr. Russell simply said that they wanted "good, strong coverage" and Bowerbank undertook to secure it.

It was the respondent's intention to take the car with him to Camp Borden where he was stationed. To get it within the camp area it was necessary for him to produce evidence that the car was covered for P.L. and P.D. The respondent asked Bowerbank when the insurance would become effective and was told "the car is covered from the moment it leaves the lot." The respondent then requested that he be given some proof to furnish the authorities at Camp Borden that the car was covered whereupon Bowerbank furnished him with a letter upon the appellant's stationery to the effect that the car was covered for P.L. and P.D. This letter was turned in to the guardhouse at Camp Borden and a daily pass was issued as well as a sticker for the windshield. The pass was produced at trial but evidence was given that the authorities at Borden had destroyed the letter along with other accumulated papers. It was never denied, however, that such a letter was given.

A written contract had been completed in which the sale price of the car was stated to be $1,320 but in which the above provisions as to insurance were not included. Five days after purchase of the car the respondent's mother attended at the finance company and paid off all that was said to be owing. To do so she was required to pay and did pay $1,583. No evidence was given as to what the additional charge of $263 was intended to cover.

Due, no doubt, to the fact that the respondent was moved from place to place he never received any insurance policy. He asked his mother to inquire as to why no policy or policies had been received. She did so and received a copy of a policy on the Saturday before August 7th which was the day of the accident. She did not read the policy but put it in a drawer to give it to her son. The original policy finally arrived several weeks after the accident with postmarks indicating that it had been at many places prior to arriving at its destination. The policy was for fire, theft and collision only and the premium for two years was stated to be $248.

At the trial of the action the evidence given by the respondent and his witnesses was never denied. Though both third parties were represented by the same counsel, Bowerbank did not go into the witness box and only one witness was called for the defence. He was Raymond Walter Lindley, Vice-President and Sales Manager of the appellant. His evidence in chief was that he heard no discussion of insurance when Mr. Bowerbank brought the order into his office. On cross-examination he changed this to say that he had never had any discussion of insurance with the respondent but had discussed fire, theft and collision insurance with Bowerbank and had noted on the respondent's copy of the written contract that such coverage existed.

Certain questions were put to the jury and answered as follows: "1. Did the defendants agree to obtain insurance for public liability and property damage in respect of the motor vehicle sold to Alexander Keith? Answer:

Yes. 2. If your answer to question one is yes, was it a condition of the sale of such vehicle that such insurance would be obtained by the defendants? Answer: Yes." On these questions the trial Judge entered judgment in the terms already stated.

At the trial a sale agreement was filed for the amount of the sale $1,320, and terms of payment were stated to be 3 payments of $55 per month and 21 payments of $68 per month. This document immediately above the signature contained the following clause: "The above and the terms (and the relevant warranty, if any) on the back hereof shall comprise the entire agreement affecting this purchase and no other agreement, understanding, representation, condition or warranty either expressed or implied by law or otherwise is a part of this transaction, any such agreement, understanding, representation, condition or warranty being hereby expressly excluded."

The grounds of appeal were as follows:

1. In view of the terms of the clause of the agreement quoted above, the learned trial Judge erred in admitting evidence that the third parties had agreed to obtain P.L. and P.D. insurance.

2. Even if admitted, the learned trial Judge should have held, having regard to the written contract, that it was not open to him to put to the jury the question whether the third parties had agreed to obtain such insurance.

3. There being no agreement as to the amount of coverage, there could be no meeting of the minds of the parties on this point and so no contract upon which action could be based.

4. If it be considered that the agreement to obtain the specific insurance mentioned was independent of the contract of the sale then there was no consideration for such agreement.

5. No evidence was adduced by the respondent to show that Bowerbank had actual or ostensible authority to make the contract alleged.

It is abundantly clear from the facts stated nor is it denied that a promise to secure insurance for P.L. and P.D. was a prerequisite to any contract being entered into for the sale of the car in this case and the jury has so found.

Counsel for the appellant at the hearing on appeal stated that the written contract on which he based this appeal was for payment of $1,320 for the car plus $248 for collision insurance, fire and theft. This was not evident upon the evidence but I accept it here. This, of course, is precisely the contract that was presented to the respondent in the first place and which he refused to accept unless some arrangements were made to provide cover for P.L. and P.D. insurance. Before he would accept the contract offered him it was necessary that an additional contract be arranged between the parties, and that is exactly what occurred. In my opinion, this latter contract was wholly a collateral one given the respondent in consideration of his agreement to execute the agreement for purchase originally offered him, and it is upon this collateral contract that this action is brought.

It was argued on appeal that the jury, having answered a question put them as to whether the agreement to furnish P.L. and P.D. was a condition of the sale, and having answered "Yes," it should follow that as a "condition" it can only refer to and must be a part of the written contract. It is difficult at this stage to see how the jury, never having been charged regarding the meaning of a "condition" or of a "collateral agreement," could be thinking of the word "condition" in a technical sense; far more likely, it would seem, its members considered that they were applying themselves to the question of whether the written agreement comprised the complete contract or contracts—a proper matter for determination by a jury. Moreover when the definition of the word itself is sought Murray's New English Dictionary gives it as "something demanded or required as a prerequisite to the granting or performance of something else." This definition seems broad enough to cover either a separate preceding agreement or a clause to be included in the written agreement itself. I do not consider that the circumstances justify giving effect to the appellant's contention on this point.

Were I of the opinion however that the finding of the jury indicated a contrary intention I should have no hesitancy about varying the jury's findings to say that this was an agreement independent of the written contract.

Having reached the conclusion that this is a collateral oral agreement, evidence as to the nature of the oral agreement was properly admitted, and it is unnecessary to consider the effect of the clause in the written agreement cited above, which limited any claims as to agreements, conditions, etc. other than those set out therein; but were it necessary to do so, I would feel that this case comes squarely within the words of Boyd C., in *Long* v. *Smith* (1911), 23 O.L.R. 121 at p. 127, a decision of a Divisional Court in which it was stated: "The evidence now given goes to shew that the writing does not contain the whole agreement. There was a condition or promise entered into, upon the faith of which the contract was signed, which is not expressed therein. This assertion as to the whole being in writing cannot be used as an instrument of fraud; the plaintiff cannot ignore the means by which he obtained the contract sued upon, falsify his own undertaking, and, by the help of the Court, fasten an unqualified engagement upon the defendant. . . . Then, apart from this shackle upon the truth, it is argued that it is contrary to the rule of evidence and the decisions of the Courts to allow oral testimony to be given which is inconsistent with or repugnant to the terms of the written instrument. No little difficulty and confusion has arisen in the application of this rule to the varying transactions of business life, which is not lessened by the discordant opinions of the Judges. But, without trying to reconcile differences, there is a well-marked line of cases establishing this doctrine, that evidence may be given of a prior or a contemporaneous oral agreement which constitutes a condition upon which the performance of the written agreement is to depend."

Oral evidence as to the written contract might be admitted here in any event upon another ground. There is an ambiguity apparent in the written contract in the discrepancy between the purchase-price of the car and the amount required to be paid. As stated above, this was said by counsel to be accounted for by the amount to be paid for collision insurance, of which there was no mention in the contract. The ambiguity is a patent ambiguity. Where patent ambiguities are concerned, evidence is not generally admissible as to what either party intended by any of the written terms; but it has been held that evidence of the conduct of the parties may be admitted to explain such ambiguity—(*Cooke* v. *Anderson & Anderson*, [1945] 2 D.L.R. 698 at p. 707); and, when evidence of conduct is considered in this case, it appears that a letter was given and received stating that the insurance stipulated for had been effected. This, on the authority of the above case and the other authorities mentioned therein would be sufficient to admit the oral evidence adduced at the trial of this action.

[McGillivray J.A. also rejected arguments that the promise to obtain insurance was unenforceable because the amount of coverage had not been agreed, and because there was no consideration for it. The appeal was dismissed.]

CITY AND WESTMINSTER PROPERTIES (1934) *LTD.* v. *MUDD* [1959] 1 Ch. 129. To the knowledge of his landlord, a tenant had for years used the back part of his shop for living and sleeping, despite a prohibition of such use in his lease. A new lease was drawn up containing a covenant by the tenant to use the premises for "showrooms, workrooms and offices only," but the landlord orally assured the tenant that he could continue to live on the premises, and on the strength of that assurance the tenant signed the lease. Now the landlord brings an action for forfeiture of the lease on the ground that the tenant is living on the premises in breach of his covenant. Harman J. held that the oral promise prevailed over the writing. He said: "If the defendant's evidence is to be accepted, as I hold it is, it is a case of a promise made to him before the execution of the lease that, if he would execute it in the form put before him, the landlord would not seek to enforce against him personally the covenant about using the property as a shop only. The defendant says that it was in reliance on this promise that he executed the lease and entered on the onerous obligations contained in it. He says, moreover, that but for the promise made he would not have executed the lease, but would have moved to other premises available to him at the time. If these be the facts, there was a clear contract acted upon by the defendant to his detriment and from which the plaintiffs cannot be allowed to resile. . . .

The plea that this was a mere licence retractable at the plaintiffs' will does not bear examination. The promise was that so long as the defendant personally was tenant, so long would the landlords forbear to exercise the rights which they would have if he signed the lease. He did sign the lease on this promise and is therefore entitled to rely on it so long as he is personally in occupation of the shop."

NOTE. It is interesting to consider this case in connexion with the *High Trees* case in chapter 2. What would have been the tenant's remedy in the *Mudd* case if the landlord's assurance had been given after the lease had been executed?

There are many other cases in which an oral statement has been accepted even in flat contradiction of a written contractual document. See, for example, *Couchman* v. *Hill* [1947] K.B. 554, *Webster* v. *Higgin* [1948] 2 All E.R. 127, *Harling* v. *Eddy* [1951] 2 K.B. 739. See also K.W. Wedderburn, *Collateral Contracts*, [1959] Camb. L.J. 58.

In *Francis* v. *Trans Canada Trailer Sales Ltd.* (1969) 6 D.L.R. (3d) 705 (Sask. C.A.) the plaintiff purchased a used trailer from the defendants. Before the plaintiff agreed to buy, the defendants orally told him that the trailer had only been used three months and carried the same warranty as a new trailer. However, the printed document later signed by the plaintiff contained a clause of a familiar kind excluding all "representations, warranties or conditions, expressed or implied, statutory or otherwise." Woods J.A., giving the judgment of the Court of Appeal, held that the oral statement of the defendants constituted a warranty collateral to the written agreement, and, he said: "Where, as here, the collateral agreement is consideration for the entering into the written agreement, the exclusionary clause cannot prevail against it."

MENDELSSOHN v. NORMAND LTD.
[1969] 3 W.L.R. 139 (C.A.)

LORD DENNING M.R.: On January 25, 1967, Mr. Mendelssohn and his wife and friends were about to go on a holiday to the continent. They were going to have lunch at the Cumberland Hotel at Marble Arch. Mr. Mendelssohn drove the car into the Cumberland Garage. It was a Rolls Royce car with a distinguished number HON 1. It was not his car but his friend's car. Mr. Mendelssohn drove the car up the ramp to the first floor into the open space. He stopped the car and got out. There was luggage on the back seat. One piece was a suitcase containing jewellery and other valuables. It was covered up by a rug. Mr. Mendelssohn was about to lock up the car when an attendant came up to him. I will give Mr. Mendelssohn's own account of what took place. He says: "I took my key out of the ignition and was just going to lock the door when the attendant came up and said: 'You are not allowed to lock your car.' I explained to him about the luggage and that we were just going across for lunch. I explained to him that the luggage was rather valuable and that I would not be long. He then said: 'Sorry, but those are the rules and I cannot allow you to lock it.' So I gave him the keys into his hand and told him as soon as he had moved the car to lock it up. This he agreed to do."

The attendant gave Mr. Mendelssohn a ticket for the car. Mr. Mendelssohn went off to lunch. After an hour Mr. Mendelssohn came back. He paid his fee at the reception desk and went up to his car. It had been moved a few yards but there was no attendant there at that moment. Mr. Mendelssohn found that the driver's door was unlocked. The key was in the ignition. The rug appeared to be just in the same position on the back seat. He got in. At that moment a different attendant came up and took the ticket. Mr. Mendelssohn drove the car on various errands: but between six and seven o'clock that evening he found that the suitcase was missing. He went back to the garage. Enquiries were made. It was never found. Mr. Mendelssohn was satisfied that it had been taken whilst the car was in the garage. He sued the garage company, Normand Ltd., for £200 as compensation for the loss of this suitcase. The judge held that the suitcase had been stolen from the car when the door was left unlocked. He concluded that it was stolen by one of the attendants at the garage, and in all probability by the man who had received this car on the first floor. The garage company are, therefore, liable for the loss of the suitcase unless they can bring themselves within the exempting conditions. That is clear from *Morris v. C. W. Martin & Sons Ltd.* [1966] 1 Q.B. 716. The only question for us is whether the garage company are protected by the conditions.

There are two conditions here to be considered. First, a condition on a notice displayed at the reception desk. This could not be seen by a driver when he brought his car into the garage, but only when he came back to collect it. He might see it when he went to the reception desk to pay the charge. In the window there was a notice saying in large letters: "Customer's Property. Important Notice" and then in smaller letters a condition exempting the company from loss of or damage to a vehicle or its contents. Mr. Mendelssohn had been to the reception desk many times before. He may have seen the notice, but he had never read it. Such a notice is not imported into the contract unless it is brought home to the party so prominently that he must be taken to have known of it and agreed to it, see *Olley* v. *Marlborough Court Ltd.* [1949] 1 K.B. 532, and *McCutcheon* v. *David Macbrayne Ltd.* [1964] 1 W.L.R. 125, 124, by Lord Devlin. That was not so here. The garage company did not prove that Mr. Mendelssohn knew of the terms of this notice or that he agreed to it. They cannot, therefore, rely upon it.

Secondly, there was a condition on the ticket. The attendant gave Mr. Mendelssohn a ticket with printed conditions on it. Mr. Mendelssohn had been to this garage a hundred times and he had always been given a ticket with the selfsame wording. Every time he had put it into his pocket and produced it when he came back for the car. He may not have read it. But that does not matter. It was plainly a contractual document: and, as he accepted it without objection, he must be taken to have agreed to it. That appears from *J. Spurling Ltd.* v. *Bradshaw* [1956] 1 W.L.R. 461, 467. As Lord Devlin said in *McCutcheon* v. *David Macbrayne Ltd.* at p. 134: "when a party assents to a document forming the whole or a part of his contract, he is bound by the terms of the document, read or unread, signed or unsigned, simply because they are in the contract." The conditions on that ticket were, therefore, part of the contract.

The ticket on the face said: "Cumberland Garage . . . FOR TERMS OF GARAGE SEE OVER." On the back there is the heading: "Conditions on which vehicles are accepted": and then follow the conditions. "(1) The garage proprietors will not accept responsibility for any loss or damage sustained by the vehicle its accessories or contents however caused. . . ." I need not mention the others except (6): "No variation of these conditions will bind the garage proprietors unless made in writing signed by their duly authorised manager."

The judge held that the condition (1) on the ticket was ambiguous. He took the words: ". . .any loss or damage sustained by the vehicle its accessories or contents however caused," and he said: "These words seem to me to be inept applied to this case as I cannot envisage loss 'sustained by' the contents of the vehicle." On that ground he held that the defendants could not rely on the condition. I agree that the condition is ambiguous. The ambiguity is due, no doubt, to a printer's error. By mistake the printers missed out the little word "of." The condition should have read: "will not accept responsibility for any loss *of*, or damage sustained by, the vehicle its accessories or contents however caused." The omission of the word "of" means that the condition is ambiguous. It has a wider meaning, which I can best express by inserting brackets: "any loss (or damage sustained by the vehicle its accessories or contents) however caused"—so that it means any loss of anything however caused. It has also a narrower meaning by inserting the word "of" so that it reads: "any loss *of*, or damage sustained by the vehicle its accessories or contents howsoever caused": so that it covers loss of the contents however caused. The ambiguity affords good reason for adopting the narrower meaning; but not for throwing over the condition altogether. Even the narrower meaning is enough to exempt the garage company. Prima facie the company can rely on it.

I cannot agree, therefore, with the ground on which the judge based his decision. But the case does not end there. The plaintiff has put in a cross-notice. He seeks to support the judgment on other grounds. He relies on the conversation which Mr. Mendelssohn had with the attendant. The man promised to lock up the car. In other words, he promised to see that the contents were safe. He did not do so. Instead he left the car unlocked. It was probably he who took the suitcase himself. What is the effect of such a promise? It was not within the *actual* authority of the attendant to give it but it was within his *ostensible* authority. He was there to receive cars on behalf of the garage company. He had apparent authority to make a statement relating to its custody. Such a statement is binding on the company. It takes priority over any printed condition. There are many cases in the books when a man has made, by word of mouth, a promise or a representation of fact, on which the other party acts by entering into the contract. In all such cases the man is not allowed to repudiate his representation by reference to a printed condition, see *Couchman* v. *Hill* [1947] 1 K.B. 554; *Curtis* v. *Chemical Cleaning and Dyeing Co.* [1951] 1 K.B. 805; and *Harling* v. *Eddy* [1951] 2 K.B. 739; nor is he allowed to go back on his promise by reliance on a written clause, see *City and Westminster Properties* (1934) *Ltd.* v. *Mudd* [1959] Ch. 129, 145 by Harman J. The reason is because the oral promise or representation has a decisive influence on the transaction— it is the very thing which induces the other to contract—and it would be most unjust to allow the maker to go back on it. The printed condition is rejected because it is repugnant to the express oral promise or representation. As Devlin J. said in *Firestone Tyre and Rubber Co. Ltd.* v. *Vokins & Co. Ltd.* [1951] 1 Lloyd's Rep. 32, 39: "It is illusory to say: 'We promise to do a thing, but we are not liable if we do not do it'." To avoid this illusion, the law gives the oral promise priority over the printed clause.

There is a second ground too. It derives from the deviation cases. If a man promises to keep a thing in a named place, but instead keeps it in another place, he cannot rely on an exemption clause, see *Gibaud* v. *Great Eastern Railway Co.* [1921] 2 K.B. 426. That doctrine has been extended to cases where a man promises to perform his contract in a certain way and instead performs it in an entirely different way. He too cannot rely on an exemption clause: because it is construed as applying only when he is carrying out his contract in the stipulated way and not when he is breaking it in a fundamental respect. Those cases still stand and are in no way diminished in authority by *Suisse Atlantique Société d'Armement Maritime S.A.* v. *N.V. Rotterdamsche Kolen Centrale* [1967] 1 A.C. 361. It was there said to be all a matter of construction. So here, the garage company agreed to keep this Rolls Royce car locked up; instead they left it unlocked and whilst unlocked their servant stole the suitcase. This was so entirely different a way of carrying out the contract that the exemption clause cannot be construed as extending to it.

On both these grounds, I think that the garage company cannot rely on the exemption condition. I would dismiss the appeal.

[Edmund Davies and Phillmore L.JJ. agreed.]

JAQUES v. *LLOYD D. GEORGE & PARTNERS, LTD.*
[1968] 1 W.L.R. 625 (C.A.)

LORD DENNING M.R.: Mr. Jaques, the plaintiff, was the proprietor of a café business at 195 Chingford Road, Walthamstow. He had a lease which had seven years to run. But he was advised by his doctor that he ought to give up the business. So he put it into the hands of two estate agents for sale in the middle of 1965. They had not found a purchaser by October, 1965. Then a Mr. Higgins went along to see Mr. Jaques. He was a representative of another firm of estate agents called Lloyd D. George & Partners Ltd., the defendants. He told Mr. Jaques that he had heard that he was wanting to sell the business, and he would like to assist him. Mr. Jaques told him that the price he would like to get was £2,950. Mr. Higgins went away. He came back again on November 28, 1965, and said: "I have found a prospective purchaser; he will pay £2,500." Mr. Jaques replied: "I am willing to sell for £2,500 if it is a cash price." Mr. Higgins said: "Yes, it will be a cash price." He added: "If we find a suitable purchaser and the sale goes through, you will pay us £250." Then Mr. Higgins produced a printed form of particulars of sale. He wrote down the details of the business and he asked Mr. Jaques to sign the form. There were conditions on the form. Mr. Higgins said: "You realise we are sole agents." Mr. Jaques said: "No, it is already in the hands of two agents." Thereupon Mr. Higgins struck out one of the clauses in the form. Mr. Jaques signed the form with the remaining clauses in it. Mr. Higgins did not explain them to Mr. Jaques. He went away, taking the form with him. He did not leave a copy with Mr. Jaques. Unbeknown to Mr. Jaques the form contained these important clauses: "I hereby instruct you to use your best endeavours to sell the above in accordance with the terms appearing below." Then this term: "(3) Should you be instrumental in introducing a person willing to sign a document capable of becoming a contract to purchase at a price, which at any stage of the negotiations has been agreed by me, I agree to pay you a commission of £250 or 7½ per cent. of the selling price, whichever is the greater."

A few days later, on December 3, 1965, Mr. Higgins brought along the prospective purchaser, a Mr. Sullivan and his wife. Mr. Jaques did not think much of them. They were not suitable people to run a café. He told Mr. Higgins so. Mr. Higgins said: "What do you want to bloody-well worry about? As long as you get your money you can hop it." Mr. Higgins produced a printed form of contract of sale. Under it Mr. Jaques was to sell the business to Mr. Sullivan for £2,500. Mr. Sullivan was to pay a deposit of £250 to Mr. Higgins' firm as selling agents for the vendors. There was also this: "This agreement is subject to the landlord under the said lease granting his licence to assign and the purchaser hereby agrees to supply satisfactory references for this purpose." Mr. Jaques and Mr. Sullivan signed the form. Mr. Higgins got them both to instruct the same solicitor. He said: "If you take our solicitor, we can get the deal through quickly." So the one firm of solicitors acted for the vendor, the purchaser and the agents.

Mr. Sullivan paid his deposit of £250 to the agents and gave the names of four references. The solicitors took up the references but they were far from satisfactory. In consequence the landlord refused to grant a licence to assign, on the simple ground that the purchaser, Mr. Sullivan, was not a suitable person to buy the business. So the sale fell through. Mr. Jaques told the agents to release the deposit to Mr. Sullivan. The agents gave the retort direct: "Not bloody likely." They claimed that they were entitled to commission, £250, equal to the amount of the deposit, although the sale had never gone through.

So the parties went to law. In the first place the purchaser, Mr. Sullivan, issued proceedings against the vendor, Mr. Jaques, and the agents, claiming back his deposit of £250. On December 21, 1966, the county court judge gave judgment against Mr. Jaques for £250 and costs. He held that the agents had received the deposit as agents for the vendor, and that the vendor had to pay it back to the purchaser, although he had not received a penny of it himself.

Naturally enough, Mr. Jaques then turned round on the agents and said: "You received this £250 as my agents. Pay it back to me as money had and received." The agents had no answer, but at the doors of the county court they put in a counterclaim for commission. They said that on the terms of their printed form they were entitled to £250 commission which wiped out the deposit.

The judge held that the agents were entitled to stick to the £250, although they had done nothing to deserve it. He said: "I have the greatest sympathy for the plaintiff, but I am driven to decide against him." He referred to a dictum of Upjohn L.J. in *Ackroyd & Sons* v. *Hasan* and asked himself: Does the clause cover the event which has happened? As it did, he held that the agents were entitled to their commission. Mr. Jaques appeals to this court.

We have had many cases on commission claimed by estate agents. The common understanding of mankind is that commission is only payable by the vendor when the property is sold. It is payable out of the purchase-money. But some agents have sought, by their printed form, to get commission even though the property has not been sold or the purchase-money received. At first it was "when a binding contract is signed." Next it was if they introduce a person "ready, able and willing to purchase." Then they missed out "able" and wanted commission if they only got a "prospective" purchaser or a "willing" purchaser who was unable to purchase. Now we have got to the widest clause that I have yet seen. "Should you be instrumental in introducing a person willing to sign a document capable of becoming a contract to purchase." Can an estate agent insert such a clause and get away with it? I think not.

I regard this clause as wholly unreasonable and totally uncertain. Suppose a man signed a piece of paper which had just got on it the address of the premises and the price. That could be said to be "a document capable of becoming a contract," even though there was not an offer contained in it. So also if a man signed a document which was expressly "subject to contract": or even signed a blank form with all the blanks to be filled in. It might be said to be "a document capable of becoming a contract." Even if the man was quite unable to complete, he might still be a person "willing" to sign. So we are faced with the question in this case: To what extent can estate agents go in putting a form before vendors to sign?

The principles which in my opinion are applicable are these: When an estate agent is employed to find a purchaser for a business or a house, the ordinary understanding of mankind is that the commission is payable out of the purchase price when the matter is concluded. If the agent seeks to depart from that ordinary and well-understood term, then he must make it perfectly plain to his client. He must bring it home to him such as to make sure he agrees to it. When his representative produces a printed form and puts it before the client to sign, he should explain its effect to him, making it clear that it goes beyond the usual understanding in these matters. In the absence of such explanation, a client is entitled to assume that the form contains nothing unreasonable or oppressive. If he does not read it

and the form is found afterwards to contain a term which is wholly unreasonable and totally uncertain, as this is, then the estate agent cannot
enforce it against the innocent vendor. Applying this principle, I think
that the clause in this case was wholly unreasonable and totally uncertain.
It can and should be rejected leaving the agent to his commission on the
usual basis, namely if the sale goes through, he gets his commission. . . .

Another principle is that an estate agent cannot rely on the printed
form when his representative misrepresents the content or effect of it.
In *Dennis Reed Ltd.* v. *Goody* [1950] 2 K.B. 277, the representative
said it was "merely a routine matter" when he asked the seller to sign.
In the present case he said: "If we find a suitable purchaser and the deal
goes through, you pay £250." That is equivalent to a representation that
the usual terms apply. It was a misrepresentation of the effect of the
document. No person can hold another to a printed form which has been
induced by misrepresentation, albeit an innocent misrepresentation. I well
remember Scrutton L.J. in *L'Estrange* v. *F. Graucob Ltd.* saying with
emphasis: "in the absence of fraud . . . or, *I will add, misrepresentation*,
the party signing it is bound."

Applying this other principle, I think that the agent misrepresented the
effect of the document, and for this reason it can and should be avoided,
leaving the agent to claim for commission on the usual basis. It was said
that this misrepresentation was not pleaded. True enough. But the claim
for commission was not inserted until the last moment. And I see no reason
why, in answer to it, Mr. Jaques should not put forward the misrepresentation, especially as Mr. Higgins did not go into the witness box to say
anything to the contrary. . . .

I would, therefore, allow this appeal. Mr. Jaques is entitled to the £250
deposit paid to the agents. The counterclaim of the agents for commission
should be dismissed.

I may add that Mr. Jaques did not claim in this action the costs which
he had had to pay in the action brought against him by Mr. Sullivan.
He might perhaps have recovered it . . . but it would have to be raised as a
claim for breach of duty by the agent in not handing over the deposit when
told to. It is too late to raise it now in this action. . . .

I would, therefore, allow the appeal and hold that Mr. Jaques is entitled
to judgment for the £250.

[Edmund Davies L.J. and Cairns J. agreed in the result, but for
different reasons. Edmund Davies L.J. thought that the clause in dispute
clearly covered this case, and that its possible uncertainty in other
situations could not avail the plaintiff here. But he thought that the
plaintiff was entitled to succeed on the basis of misrepresentation by
the defendant. Cairns J. refused to consider the misrepresentation argument because it had not been pleaded, but he agreed with Lord Denning
that the clause was too uncertain to be enforceable. Neither judgment
referred to Lord Denning's wider dicta on unreasonableness and oppression.]

NOTE. In consumer transactions within the scope of the Ontario Business
Practices Act, oral evidence is admissible to prove an "unfair practice." See
chapter 7, below. In British Columbia section 27 of the Trade Practices Act
has the effect of abolishing the parol evidence rule for transactions within the
scope of the Act. In the United Kingdom a Law Commission Working Paper
(No. 70, 1976) recommends total abolition of the rule.

3. RECTIFICATION

U.S.A. v. *MOTOR TRUCKS, LIMITED*
Ontario. Privy Council. [1924] A.C. 196

By contract dated May 18, 1918, the respondent company contracted to machine high-explosive shells for the appellant Government; the contract provided for cancellation by notice in the event of anticipated termination of the war, and for payments to be made to the respondents thereupon. The payments were to include reimbursement for the cost of buildings, plant, etc., which the respondents had to add to their facilities for the purpose of carrying out the contract. Notice to terminate the contract was given in November 1918, and the parties thereupon negotiated as to the sum to be paid to the respondents. Ultimately a sum of $1,653,115 was agreed, which included $376,496, being the full amount which the respondents claimed in respect of land and buildings. After deducting from the above total a large sum which had been advanced by the appellant Government to the respondents, together with interest thereon, it was agreed that $637,812 was due to the respondents.

The parties accordingly entered into a formal contract dated October 7, 1919, but not actually signed until November 8. The contract provided that it should supersede the original contract of May 18, 1918, which was thereby terminated, and that the appellant Government should pay to the respondents the sum of $637,812 in full settlement for work and goods delivered and expenses incurred under the original contract; it further provided as follows: "(4) Title to all property specified in Schedule A, hereto annexed and made a part hereof, shall vest in the United States immediately upon execution of this agreement."

The land and buildings were not included in the schedule.

The agreed sum was paid on November 10, 1919, but the respondents subsequently denied the right of the appellant Government to possession of the land and buildings.

The appellant Government brought an action against the respondents in the Supreme Court of Ontario, claiming rectification of the schedule by the inclusion of the land and buildings, and specific performance of the contract as so rectified; alternatively they claimed repayment of the sum paid in respect of the land and buildings.

The trial judge (Kelly J.) found that the intention was that the land and buildings should become the property of the appellant Government. He ordered and declared that the respondents were trustees of the land and buildings for such person as the appellant Government might direct, with rectification of the schedule, the respondents to convey the land accordingly.

On appeal to the Appellate Division the judgement of Kelly J. was reversed and the action dismissed, Meredith C.J. dissenting. The judgments of the majority of the Court were based mainly upon the conclusions of fact.

THE EARL OF BIRKENHEAD: . . . The question which requires the decision of the Board is whether or not it was the intention of the parties that the land and buildings, which had been paid for as claimed without deduction, should be inserted in schedule A and whether, if so, they were omitted therefrom by mutual mistake, so that rectification of an incomplete schedule should be ordered, or whether on the true interpretation of the intentions of the parties the respondents were entitled to receive all that they had expended upon acquiring the land and erecting the building, and, being so compensated, to retain both as their own.

The answer to these questions can only be found by reference to some legal considerations which their Lordships will hereinafter examine. If the parties intended that the lands and buildings should be included in schedule A, so that the omission in the instrument was accidental, rectification ought undoubtedly to be decreed. The Board, therefore, finds it necessary to examine the actions and the words of the parties at the relevant periods. And in enforcing the conclusions which will hereafter be stated their Lordships think it right to make it plain that they have entirely ignored the memorandum of the minutes of the meeting on October 7, 1919. In the opinion of the Board the terms of this memorandum were not admissible and should not have been admitted as evidence.

Their Lordships have reached the conclusion that both the appellants and the respondents intended that the land and buildings should be included in schedule A. That the appellants so intended has not been seriously disputed; and upon this point the Board entertains no doubt. Their Lordships, after giving careful attention to the matter, are no less confident that the respondents clearly understood that the award contemplated the transfer as owners to the United States of the land and buildings for which under its terms that Government had paid the respondents complete and generous compensation. . . .

It remains, therefore, to consider what view in fact and in law must be taken of the respondents' remaining contention that their agreement to part with the ownership of the lands and buildings (in which is implicit their agreement to insert them in the schedule) was produced by an error as to their legal rights under the original contract. Whether they possessed any such rights as those supposed under that contract it is not necessary to consider, for the trial judge found as a fact that those who represented the company were not at any single relevant moment forgetful of any right whatsoever which they may have possessed under that agreement. And their Lordships, so far from quarrelling with this finding, most expressly accept and approve it. Nothing need be added in parting with this contention, except that in all the circumstances it required considerable hardihood to conceive and put it forward.

But even if the company's officials had made a mistake—in the circumstances wholly incredible—such a mistake could not in law have produced any effect upon the rights of the parties. For it is not contended, and could not be, that the mistake was shared by the appellants; and unilateral error, which in such a case as the present would hardly be distinguishable from carelessness, does not afford to the respondents any ground of defence in proceedings such as these.

It was further suggested that the present action involved an attempt to enforce a parol contract inconsistently with the principle of the Statute of Frauds. It is however, well settled by a series of familiar authorities that the Statute of Frauds is not allowed by any Court administering the doctrines of equity to become an instrument for enabling sharp practice to be committed. And indeed the power of the Court to rectify mutual mistake implies that this power may be exercised notwithstanding that the true agreement of the parties has not been expressed in writing. Nor does the rule make any inroad upon another principle, that the plaintiff must show first that there was an actually concluded agreement antecedent to the instrument which is sought to be rectified; and secondly, that such agreement has been inaccurately represented in the instrument. When this is proved either party may claim, in spite of the Statute of Frauds, that the instrument on which the other insists does not represent the real agreement. The statute, in fact, only provides that no agreement not in writing and not duly signed shall be sued on; but when the written instrument is rectified there is a writing which satisfies the statute, the jurisdiction of the Court to rectify being outside the prohibition of the statute.

The respondents, however, advance still a further point of law. They contend that a plaintiff was not allowed to sue in the old Court of Chancery for the specific performance of a contract with a parol variation. There seems no reason on principle why a court of Equity should not at one and the same time reform and enforce a contract; the matter, however, has been much discussed in the Court, and the balance of distinguished authority not unequally maintained. But the difficulty, which was almost entirely technical, has been, in the view of the Board, removed by the provisions of the Judicature Act, 1873, s. 24, which are reproduced in s. 16 of the Judicature Act of the Province of Ontario, ch. 56 of the Revised Statutes of 1914. This section provides that the Court, which is to administer equity as well as law, is to grant, either absolutely or on such reasonable terms and conditions as it shall deem best, all such remedies as any of the parties may appear to be entitled to in respect of any and every legal and equitable claim properly brought forward by them in such cause or matter, so that, as far as possible, all matters so in controversy between the parties may be completely and finally determined, and all multiplicity of legal proceedings discouraged.

The analogous provisions of the English Judicature Act are stated by Sir Edward Fry in his book on *Specific Performance*, 5th ed., para. 816. The learned author holds (and the Board agrees with him) that the controversy between the Chancery judges has now become obsolete, inasmuch as since the Judicature Act the Court can entertain an action in which combined relief will be given simultaneously for the reformation of a contract, and for the specific performance of the reformed contract.

Despite some differences in subsequent decisions, in which the principles of s. 24 of the Judicature Act have not been sufficiently considered, it has been held by P. O. Lawrence J., and by the Court of Appeal in the very recent case of *Craddock Brothers* v. *Hunt*, [1922] 2 Ch. 809, that the principle as laid down by Sir Edward Fry must now prevail.

Their Lordships are of the same opinion, and conclude that under this head no difficulty confronts the appellants in the present case.

The board has thought it proper to consider the matters raised in this appeal with some particularity, partly because of the importance of the case, and partly out of respect for the learned judges who took a different view in the Appellate Division. But on analysis the issue has proved to be extremely simple. Both parties intended the lands and buildings to be included in the schedule. These were inadvertently omitted. Rectification must follow unless some exceptional ground for excluding this remedy is advanced. The respondents have attempted only to show that they agreed to the schedule in its intended form by reason of an error as to their existing legal rights. This contention has been rightly negatived on the facts, and would, in any event, be irrelevant in law.

Their Lordships will, therefore, humbly advise His Majesty that this appeal should be allowed, the judgment of the Appellate Division of the Supreme Court set aside with costs, and the judgment of Kelly J. restored. The respondents will pay the costs of the appeal.

BERCOVICI v. PALMER
(1966) 59 D.L.R. (2d) 513 (Sask. C.A.)

APPEAL from a judgment of MacPherson J., *infra*, ordering rectification of a written agreement for the sale of land.

The judgment appealed from was in part as follows:

MACPHERSON J.: The plaintiff claims rectification of an agreement in writing. The defendant counterclaims for rectification in another respect.

The plaintiff and her late husband for many years carried on two retail businesses at Regina Beach, a resort where the businesses were open only in the summer. In July, 1958, a few months after her husband's death, the plaintiff realized she could not carry them on and decided to sell.

She agreed to sell to the defendant for $24,000 to be paid on terms which do not concern the issues before me. The plaintiff took over the businesses on July 26, 1958, and on July 28, 1958, the parties and the defendant's husband, who negotiated the deal, went to the office of the plaintiff's solicitor to put it in writing. The solicitor was on holiday but one of his partners took instructions and prepared a brief memorandum which the parties and the defendant's husband then and there signed.

The defendant then instructed her own solicitor and correspondence ensued between him and the plaintiff's solicitor on his return. On August 21, 1958, a formal agreement was signed.

This litigation arises from the fact that there is included in the recitals of the agreement of August 21st a parcel of land which the plaintiff says was there in error and which the defendant says was always part of the deal.

The parcel is not contiguous with any other land concerned and is occupied by a summer cottage known as Rob Roy. It is legally described as "Lot 6 in Block 33, Lakeview, Regina Beach, etc." It was then owned by the plaintiff. The store premises agreed to be sold are described as "Lot 1 in Block 33A, Lakeview, Regina Beach, etc." Blocks 33 and 33A are distinct. The agreement mentions, in addition to the store property, "Lot 6 in Block 33A, Lakeview, Regina Beach, etc." The plaintiff never has owned Lot 6 in Block 33A.

Thus the plaintiff seeks rectification to delete reference to Lot 6 altogether and the defendant seeks rectification to correct the description from Block 33A to Block 33.

[His Lordship considered the applicable law and continued:]

On the evidence I am satisfied beyond any fair and reasonable doubt that the property Rob Roy was not intended by either of the parties to be included in their transaction. If it is Rob Roy which is described in the agreement as Lot 6, etc., it got in it by some inexplicable error on the part of the plaintiff's solicitor and its inclusion went unnoticed until late in 1963 by all parties and their solicitors.

The facts which so satisfy me are best listed:

The defendant and her husband were interested in buying the business interests of the plaintiff in Regina Beach, that is the store and the lease on the pavilion. There was no relationship between these businesses and Rob Roy cottage.

Rob Roy was never mentioned by any of the parties in any of their negotiations or in the memorandum of July 28, 1958, even by inference, and their solicitors were never instructed to include it.

The purchase price was calculated without Rob Roy being in the mind of either party.

I do not accept Mr. Palmer's statement that in a quarrel between him and the plaintiff concerning certain stock invoices within a week of the takeover, that the plaintiff said: "Now I will not include Rob Roy." If this were true he should have instructed his wife's solicitor to ensure it was included, if, in fact, the parties so intended. Furthermore, he did not check the final agreement or attend the signing of it only because he was not, by then, on speaking terms with the plaintiff.

From the date of the takeover, July, 1958, until October, 1963, the defendant did not demand possession of Rob Roy or its keys or its rent although she and her husband, who was the business head of the family, knew of its existence and location and must have known it was occupied. Neither said that they had even gone to look at it after the transaction.

Similarly the defendant never paid taxes or sought to insure Rob Roy. The fire policies assigned by the plaintiff were checked fully after a fire in August, 1961.

The defendant and her husband were not shy of quarreling with the plaintiff. In fact disagreement started within a few days of the first memorandum and continued for over five years. This disagreement was in relation to liability for certain invoices totalling, the defendant said, between $1,000 and $1,500. Why would they overlook an asset worth twice as much? The plaintiff sold Rob Roy in 1960 for $2,700.

The letter from the defendant's solicitor to the plaintiff's solicitor of August 6, 1958, refers to "both properties," *i.e.*, the store and the pavilion. If Rob Roy were intended to be included one would think he would use a term indicating more than two.

The agreement of August 21, 1958, lists contents of all buildings except Rob Roy.

The plaintiff in my view did nothing before or after the agreement in question inconsistent with the position she now takes, that Rob Roy was not included. Her failure to observe that Rob Roy was in the agreement was satisfactorily explained by her lack of knowledge of lot numbers and her reliance on her solicitor who had acted for her and her late husband for many years. I found her quite believable.

There will therefore be an order for rectification of the agreement between the parties dated August 21, 1958, deleting therefrom the second paragraph of the recitals, that is, all reference to Lot 6. The plaintiff shall have her costs.

The counterclaim is dismissed with costs to the plaintiff.

[The defendant appealed to the Court of Appeal.]

The judgment of the Court was delivered by CULLITON C.J.S.: This is an appeal from the judgment of MacPherson, J., *supra*, in which he ordered rectification of a written agreement for sale made between the respondent as vendor and the appellant as purchaser. The learned trial Judge held that Lot 6, Block 33A, was included in the written agreement by mutual mistake and contrary to the real agreement between the parties and ordered that reference thereto be deleted from the written agreement. From this judgment the appellant has appealed.

The principles to be followed by the Court in an action for rectification have been clearly stated in numerous judicial decisions. Duff J. (as he then was), in delivering one of the judgments of the Supreme Court of Canada in *Hart* v. *Boutilier* (1916), 56 D.L.R. 620 at p. 630, said: "The power of rectification must be used with great caution; and only after the Court has been satisfied by evidence which leaves no "fair and reasonable doubt"

(*Fowler* v. *Fowler* (1859), 4 DeG. & J. 250, at 264, 45 E.R. 97), that the deed impeached does not embody the final intention of the parties. This evidence must make it clear that the alleged intention to which the plaintiff asks that the deed be made to conform, continued concurrently in the minds of all the parties down to the time of its execution; and the plaintiff must succeed in shewing also the precise form in which the instrument will express this intention."

He again repeated these principles in *The M. F. Whalen* v. *Point Anne Quarries, Ltd.* (1921), 63 D.L.R. 545 at p. 568, 63 S.C.R. 109 [affd [1923] 1 D.L.R. 45, 39 T.L.R. 37] when he stated: "First it must be shewn not only that the agreement as stated in the writing, the agreement in this case to tow barges, was not the whole of the agreement between the parties and it must further be shewn that the parties did agree upon something which did not appear in the writing, in this case to tow barges plus scows and that the agreement, that is to say the intention to contract in this sense continued concurrently in the minds of both parties down to the time the document went into operation."

The same principles have been followed by the English Court of Appeal. In *Frederick E. Rose (London), Ltd.* v. *Wm. H. Pim, Jr. & Co. Ltd.,* [1953] 2 All E.R. 739 at p. 747, Denning L.J., said: "Rectification is concerned with contracts and documents, not with intentions. In order to get rectification, it is necessary to show that the parties were in complete agreement on the terms of their contract, but by an error wrote them down wrongly."

It is clear from the judgment of the learned trial Judge that in the disposition of the case he directed himself in accordance with the foregoing principles. It is equally clear that there was evidence upon which he could properly make the findings of fact upon which he founded the order for rectification. Such findings were in part based upon his determination of the credibility of the witnesses and there are no circumstances that would warrant this Court in reversing the same: *Prudential Trust Co. Ltd. and Can. Williston Minerals Ltd.* v. *Forseth and Forseth*, 21 D.L.R. (2d) 587, [1960] S.C.R. 210.

Learned counsel contended that in an action for rectification the only evidence that can be considered is the evidence of what took place prior to the execution of the written document and that in the instant case the learned trial Judge erred in law in considering the conduct of the parties subsequent to that time. In support of this argument learned counsel relied upon the judgments in *Lovell and Christmas, Ltd.* v. *Wall* (1911), 104 L.T. 85; *Earl of Bradford* v. *Earl of Romney* (1862), 30 Beav. 431, 54 E.R. 956, and *Brown* v. *Hillar*, [1951] 4 D.L.R. 383, [1951] O.R. 634. With all deference I must say that I do not think the judgments in these cases advance the appellant's argument. In each case there is reiterated the established principle that subsequent declarations of the parties are not admissible for the purpose of construing a written contract. In this case the learned trial Judge was not faced with the question of construction but with the question of rectification.

In *The M. F. Whalen* v. *Point Anne Quarries Ltd., supra,* Duff J. (as he then was), at p. 568 said: "Where one of the parties denies the alleged variation the parol evidence of the other party is not sufficient to entitle the Court to act. Such parol evidence must be adequately supported by documentary evidence *and by considerations arising from the conduct of the parties* satisfying the Court beyond reasonable doubt that the party resisting rectification did in truth enter into the agreement alleged. It is not sufficient that there should be a mere preponderance of probability, the case must be proved to a demonstration in the only sense in which in a Court of law an issue of fact can be established to a demonstration, that is to say, the evidence must be so satisfactory as to leave no room for such doubt. *Hart* v. *Boutilier* (1916), 56 D.L.R. 620, at p. 630; *Fowler* v. *Fowler* (1859), 4 De G. and J. 250 at p. 264, 45 E.R. 97; *Clarke* v. *Joselin* (1888), 16 O.R. 68 at p. 78." (The italics are mine.)

In *Hart* v. *Boutilier, supra,* it is obvious that Duff J. gave effect to considerations arising from the conduct of the parties for at p. 636 he said: "The respondent's subsequent conduct is not less difficult to understand." In the same case Idington J., makes it clear that in an action for rectification reliance may be placed upon considerations arising from the conduct of the parties. At p. 630 he stated: "The conduct of the parties and the outstanding features and nature of the transaction must in such cases often be relied upon as a better guide than what either may merely swear to."

The case of *Smith* v. *Hemeon,* [1953] 4 D.L.R. 157, was an action for rectification. MacDonald J., in the application of the principles propounded in *Hart* v. *Boutilier, supra,* at p. 161 had this to say: "Here there is no evidence other than the testimony of the plaintiff; for the defendant neither took the stand nor introduced any evidence. In such a case as this one must make up his mind definitely as to the credibility of the plaintiff as a witness, remembering that the issue is not merely as to the plaintiff's intention, but also as to the defendant's. Whilst a plaintiff cannot testify as to the intention of the defendant as such, his testimony may well make clear what the subject of the transaction was. In this case the plaintiff has satisfied me that the negotiations between the parties and the oral agreement they reached related to the Red Lot and to it alone. *Very germane to such a case is consideration of the subsequent conduct of the parties:* cf. *Hart* v. *Boutilier, supra; Armstrong* v. *Wright* (1930), 2 M.P.R. 309, and *Belding* v. *McRae* (1947), 20 M.P.R. 325." (The italics are mine.) With the views so expressed by MacDonald J., I am in complete agreement.

There was, as would be expected, a denial by the appellant of the evidence given by the respondent, as to what was the real contract between the parties. The learned trial Judge, in satisfying himself beyond any reasonable doubt that the appellant did in truth enter into the agreement as alleged by the respondent, looked to certain documentary evidence and to the consideration arising from the conduct of the parties. This he was entitled to do. In my opinion the learned trial Judge properly stated and applied the law and as his findings of fact cannot be disturbed, the appeal will be dismissed with costs.

[Appeal dismissed; judgment for plaintiff.]

JOSCELYNE v. NISSEN
[1970] 1 All E.R. 1213 (C.A.)

RUSSELL L.J.: The judgment which I am about to read is the judgment of the court. This is an unhappy dispute between father and daughter which has led to an investigation into differing expressions of judicial views on what is required before a contractual instrument may be rectified by the court.

The father (with the mother) were living as tenants of a house called

Martindale in Enfield. He carried on from there and from an office at the nearest railway station a car hire business both self-drive and chauffeur driven, the cars being garaged at Martindale. In 1960, he was given notice to quit. The daughter and the husband lived in a house belonging to the husband also in Enfield. To help her parents in their difficulty the daughter bought Martindale with the help of a mortgage, let the husband's house furnished to pay off the mortgage instalments, and moved to Martindale. The father and mother lived in the ground floor, the daughter and husband on the first floor. Each floor had its own kitchen and bathroom facilities. The daughter helped with the car hire business to some extent. In 1963 the mother was seriously ill with two strokes, returning from hospital in January, 1964, unable to look after herself. The father even with the aid of a home help had to devote much of his time to looking after her, his business was suffering as a result, and he felt that he could not really carry on. Because of this he and the daughter discussed a scheme by which she should take over the business, a scheme that culminated in the signing by them of an agreement on 18th June 1964.

For the present purposes it is sufficient to say that it was found by the county court judge that at an early stage it was made clear between them in conversation that if the business and its assets were, as proposed, made over to the daughter she should in return pay him a weekly pension to supplement his old age pension and in addition pay the expenses in connection with Martindale attributable to the parents' part of the house, and that these expenses should include the gas, electricity and coal bills and also the cost of the necessary home help. It is not before this court disputed that it was expressly agreed and intended that these particular items should be paid for by the daughter as such expenses and that they negotiated on that footing: it is not disputed that the father and the daughter continued in this expressed accord thereafter and when they signed the agreement still intended that it should provide for such payment. It is however argued for the daughter that the contract signed did not on its true construction provide for payment of these matters and that since there was here no complete concluded contract antecedent to the written agreement then in point of law the remedy of rectification is not available to the father.

The various steps leading to the signing of the agreement need not be detailed, since they do not touch on the particular matters. The agreement signed was in the following form. It was made between the father and the daughter and stated:

"Whereby it is agreed as follows: 1 [The daughter] shall be deemed to have taken over from [the father] the business of a car hire proprietor hitherto carried on by [the father] under the style of Station Hire from "Martindale" Stanley Road, Enfield aforesaid under the style of "Station Cars" as from the first day of May One thousand nine hundred and sixty-three. 2 [The daughter] shall be deemed to have taken over all the assets and liabilities of the business of self-drive and chauffeur driven car hire carried on under the style and from the premises aforesaid as from the first day of May One thousand nine hundred and sixty-three. 3 [The daughter] shall indemnify [the father] and his estate and effects from any claims or payment made in respect of the liabilities of the said business including all past or future claims in respect of income tax and/or surtax arising in respect of the business. 4 In consideration of the transfer of the assets of the self-drive and chauffeur driven portion of the said business [the daughter] shall pay by way of a pension to [the father] (such pension to be payable for the life of [the father] or the duration of the business) the sum of Three pounds ten shillings per week. 5 [The father] shall be permitted to have the use of any of the cars of the business when not needed for business work and to carry out driving work for [the daughter] subject to payment to him of one fifth of the charge made to each customer. 6 [The daughter] shall discharge all expenses in connection with the whole premises "Martindale" Stanley Road Enfield aforesaid and shall indemnify [the father] from and against any claim arising in respect of the same. 7 [The daughter] shall permit [the father] during his life to have the uncontrolled right to reside at and occupy the ground floor of "Martindale" Stanley Road Enfield aforesaid or such other property as may be agreed upon in writing free of all rent and outgoings of every kind in any event. 8 [The daughter] shall be entitled to at least three annual weeks holiday in each year. 9 [The father] shall be entitled to at least three weeks annual holiday in each year. 10 [The daughter] hereby agrees with [the father] that she will not at any time sell the whole or any part of the said business without [the father] receiving one half of the said moneys or otherwise deal with the same or take in a partner without the consent of [the father] which consent may be arbitrarily withheld by [the father] without assigning any reason therefor."

For a time all went well under the agreement, the daughter paying the gas, coal and electricity bills attributable to the ground floor and also the weekly cost of the home help, in addition to the pension of £3 10s weekly, but of course taking the profits of the business. (There were separate gas meters for the two floors, but the ground floor electricity meter carried the electricity for the garage while we were told that the first floor electricity meter carried the current for the ground floor immersion heater.) Trouble then arose because of incursions on the ground floor of drivers and customers of the business. It was suggested that the parents move upstairs and the daughter and the husband downstairs, in variation of the agreement. The parents refused because of the mother's difficulty in movement. The father went away for a holiday and on his return found that the mother and all their belongings had been moved upstairs behind his back. The fat was in the fire, proceedings started in the county court, and the status quo was restored as a result of interlocutory proceedings. However the daughter was no doubt then advised that the language of the agreement did not require her to pay for the items that we have mentioned and she stopped doing so. (As indicated, she necessarily continued to pay for the parents' immersion heater; the father necessarily paid for the garage electricity; though who was the gainer by this is not known.)

The father to meet this new attitude amended his particulars of claim to raise this point either as a matter of construction or by way of rectification. The county court judge decided against the father on construction but in his favour on rectification. A cross-appeal by the father on the question of construction was not pursued. The relevant facts on the question of rectification we have already stated.

For the daughter it is argued that the law is that the father cannot get rectification of the written instrument save to accord with a complete antecedent concluded oral contract with the daughter, and, as was found by the judge, there was none. For the father it is argued that if in the course of negotiation a firm accord has been expressly reached on a particular term of the proposed contract, and both parties continue minded that the contract should contain appropriate language to embrace that term, it matters not that the accord was not part of a complete antecedent concluded oral contract.

The point of law has a curious judicial history, involving apparently the disappearance from professional sight of the case in the Court of Appeal of *Lovell and Christmas Ltd.* v. *Wall* (1911) 104 L.T. 85 until its existence was recognised in the judgment of Denning L.J. in *Frederick E. Rose (London) Ltd.* v. *Wm. H. Pim Junr. & Co. Ltd.* [1953] 2 Q.B. 450 apart from a passing reference by Eve J., who had been the trial judge in the *Lovell and Christmas* case.

It is convenient to start with the case of *Mackenzie* v. *Coulson*, (1869) L.R. 8 Eq. 368, a decision of Sir W. M. James V.-C. There a policy of insurance was in terms in accordance with the wishes of the assured and the insurers sought rectification based on an insurance slip which is not a contract; the facts are a little complicated but it would seem that the insurers sought to impute to the assured an intention (and mistake) based on knowledge of a junior clerk of an agent of the assured of the contents of the slip. We should have thought this a difficult proposition to sustain. In deciding against rectification Sir W. M. James V.-C. used this language (1869) L.R. 8 Eq. at 375:

"Courts of Equity do not rectify contracts: they may and do rectify instruments purporting to have been made in pursuance of the terms of contracts. But it is always necessary for a Plaintiff to show that there was an actual concluded contract antecedent to the instrument which is sought to be rectified; and that such contract is inaccurately represented in the instrument. In this instance there never was any contract other than this policy which the Plaintiffs have so signed . . . It is impossible for this Court to rescind or alter a contract with reference to the terms of the negotiation which preceded it." This statement of the law supports the daughter's contention.

We turn next to the lost cause of *Lovell and Christmas Ltd.* v. *Wall* in this court. A covenant not to be concerned in the business of a provision merchant was held not broken by manufacturing and selling margarine, and it was further held that here was no case for rectification so as to provide that the covenantor should not compete with the business of the covenantee, company or its subsidiaries. We do not think that it is necessary to examine closely the facts of the case, save to say that we do not think that the facts demonstrated that such a firm accord on the relevant term had been reached in the course of negotiation as even on the father's argument is required. There is no doubt however that general statements of the law as contended for by the daughter were firmly made, albeit obiter, and made in the face of the argument that is now put forward by the father. Sir Herbert Cozens-Hardy M.R. said (1911) 104 L.T. at 88:

"The essence of rectification is to bring the document which was expressed and intended to be in pursuance of a prior agreement into harmony with that prior agreement. Indeed, it may be regarded as a branch of the doctrine of specific performance. It presupposes a prior contract, and it requires proof that, by common mistake, the final completed instrument as executed fails to give proper effect to the prior contract."

He had in the course of argument said: "Surely rectification ought to be looked upon as a branch of specific performance subject to an exception in the case of voluntary settlements."

Fletcher Moulton L.J. said:

"Rectification can only come where there is a case of contract. And, as James V.-C. put it so well in the case which has been cited of *Mackenzie* v. *Coulson*, the law does not make new contracts for parties. All it does is to rectify an incorrect expression in writing of the contract that was made. And, to my mind, it is not only clear law, but it is absolutely necessary logic, that there cannot be a rectification unless there has been a pre-existing contract which has been inaptly expressed. The consequence is that if you have to ascertain whether there was or was not a pre-existing contract, for that purpose you must look at what happened before the contract was entered into. It is a very great mistake to think that that can lightly be done unless you can prove the existing contract. If the completed contract is badly expressed, all the "communings beforehand," whether you have gone into them or not, have to be rejected by the court in deciding the nature of the instrument."

Buckley L.J. expressed himself somewhat differently:

"In ordering rectification the court does not rectify contracts, but what it rectifies is the erroneous expression of contracts in documents. For rectification it is not enough to set about to find out what one or even both of the parties to the contract intended. What you have got to find out is what intention was communicated by one side to the other, and with what common intention and common agreement they made their bargain."

Next to be considered are obiter dicta at first instance of Younger and Romer JJ. In *Faraday* v. *Tamworth Union* (1916) 86 L.J. Ch. 436 at 438, the former expressed the provisional opinion that even had there been mutual mistake the contract could not have been rectified since the Union could not contract except under seal. In *W. Higgins Ltd.* v. *Northampton Corpn.* [1927] 1 Ch. 128, at 136 (in which there was on the facts no mutual mistake) Romer J. said this:

"But where, as here, there is no precedent contract between the parties, I cannot see that I have any jurisdiction to make a different contract between the parties from the only one which exists, merely because I come to the conclusion that both parties previously to making that contract had intended to make a different one. There is a passage in a judgment of Younger J.'s which was cited to me which supports the view that I have expressed. It is only a dictum, because in that particular case he was able to set aside a contract entered into under a mistake of one party, inasmuch as the mistake had been contributed to or induced by, although innocently, the acts of the defendants; but he did say in the course of his judgment that, had there been a mutual mistake, he did not see how he could have rectified the contract."

Romer J. then quoted from the judgment of Younger J. with approval and disapproved a decision of Grantham J. in *McCartney* v. *Brighton Corpn.* (1904) The Times, 20th May which might have been in the opposite sense. In *Schofield* v. *W. C. Clough & Co.* [1913] 2 K.B. 103 at 105 Sir Herbert Cozens-Hardy M.R. quoted in argument from the judgment in *Mackenzie* v. *Coulson* but did not curiously enough mention his own opinion to the same effect in *Lovell and Christmas Ltd.* v. *Wall*. In *Craddock Bros.* v. *Hunt* [1923] 2 Ch. 136, at 159, we find an obiter dictum of Warrington L.J.·

"The jurisdiction of Courts of equity in this respect is to bring the written document executed in pursuance of an antecedent agreement into conformity with that agreement. The conditions to its exercise are that there must be an antecedent contract and the common intention of embodying or giving effect to the whole of that contract by the writing, and there must be clear evidence that the document by common mistake failed to embody such contract and either contained provisions not agreed upon or omitted something that was agreed upon, or otherwise departed from its terms."

The same view is indicated, again obiter, by the Judicial Committee of the Privy Council in *United States of America* v. *Motor Trucks Ltd.* where it was said:

"Nor does the rule make any inroad upon another principle, that the plaintiff must show first that there was an actually concluded agreement antecedent to the instrument which is sought to be rectified; and secondly, that such agreement has been inaccurately represented in the instrument."

In the train of this undoubtedly formidable array of judicial opinion comes the judgment of Clauson J. in *Shipley Urban District Council* v. *Bradford Corpn.* This was again obiter, since the case was decided on the construction of the instrument in question; but the case was very fully argued and the arguments very fully considered in a reserved judgment. (This case went to appeal and was argued both on construction and rectification; but this court dismissed the appeal on construction and expressed no opinion on rectification). This was also a case in which the parties could only contract under seal. The absence of reference to *Lovell and Christmas Ltd.* v. *Wall* suggests that it had found no place in current textbooks, which appear to have been fully combed by counsel, though not the English and Empire Digest. Clauson J. after reviewing the authorities, many of which do not appear to have been cited in the *Lovell and Christmas* case, said:

"Notwithstanding these authorities, counsel for the Corporation argued, as I understood them, that the jurisdiction of the Court to rectify a document is limited to the case where it is possible to prove that before the execution of the document there was in existence a legally enforceable agreement, whether oral or written (or possibly an agreement which would be legally enforceable but for some statutory provision requiring special formalities) in terms which the document was intended to record, but failed by mutual mistake to record. They argued, and in my view correctly, that, in view of the inability, which the plaintiffs admitted, of the Council and the Corporation to bind themselves to such an agreement as that in dispute otherwise than under seal, it was impossible to predicate that there was any agreement between the Council and the Corporation except that constituted by the sealed document. They drew the conclusion (which, indeed, appears to me to be, on their premises, inevitable) that the Court could not rectify an agreement between two such bodies as the Council and the Corporation even on the clearest evidence that the document, even by the merest copying slip, failed to record what all parties intended it to record. Even as regards such bodies as the Council and the Corporation this would seem to be rather startling; but it will be observed—and counsel for the defendants did not shrink from accepting this conclusion—that in the case of ordinary individuals, an instrument, on this theory, cannot be rectified except on proof of a previously existing legally binding document, proof which, in the case of most written contracts (though not, of course, as a rule in the case of conveyances) is not usually available, simply because negotiation has not, even where intentions have been found to coincide, crystallized into contract, until the moment of executing the written contract. It must be conceded that, whether or not it is difficult to reconcile the defendants' argument with principle and with the long and ancient line of authorities which I have summarized above, there is some justification to be found in the books for their contention. It is to be remembered that many, perhaps even most, rectification cases deal with the reforming of a final instrument, such as a conveyance or a settlement, so as to accord with a previous instrument, such as a contract for sale or articles for a settlement, and that the high standard of mutual mistake which the Court requires—Thurlow L.C. in *Shelburne (Countess Dowager)* v. *Earl of Inchiquin* (1784) 1 Bro. C.C. 338 at 341 even used the phrase 'irrefragable' —makes cases where mutual mistake can be proved, in the absence of any previous written instrument, very rare, and that where, in the absence of any previous instrument, mutual mistake can be clearly proved, the matter may very often be put right out of Court, without litigation. It would thus not be surprising to find that, in cases where the exact point was not material, language may be used in general terms, in relation to cases of rectification by reference to a previous written instrument, which is not strictly accurate in reference to a case where rectification proceeds on proof of mutual mistake in recording the concurrent intention of the parties at the moment of execution of the instrument which it is sought to rectify. [He then referred to the judgment in *Mackenzie* v. *Coulson* and continued:] The language of the Vice-Chancellor was, if I may respectfully say so, perfectly accurate in reference to the cases which he obviously had in mind, where mutual mistake is sought to be established by reference to the terms of a previous contract. His words, however, apart from their context, have, there is no doubt, found their way into works of no little authority in such a form as to suggest, as, indeed, the defendants' counsel argued, that the jurisdiction of the Court cannot be exercised, even in cases of clear mutual mistake, in the attempt to embody in the instrument the concurrent intention of the parties existing at the moment of the execution of the instrument, unless a previously existing contract can be proved. It is sufficient for me to say that, had it been necessary for me to decide the point, I should not have felt justified in accepting this interpretation of the Vice-Chancellor's language as correct."

He then referred to other dicta that we have mentioned indicating that he was unable to accept them as correct.

Next we have *Crane* v. *Hegeman-Harris Co. Inc.* [1939] 1 All E.R. 664, [1971] 3 All E.R. 245-8, n., decided by Simonds J. The facts need not be set out. Simonds J. said:

"Before I consider the facts and come to a conclusion whether the defendants are right in their contention, it is necessary to say a few words upon the principles which must guide me in this matter. I am clear that I must follow the decision of Clauson J. as he then was, in *Shipley Urban District Council* v. *Bradford Corpn.* [1936] Ch. 375, the point of which is that, in order that this court may exercise its jurisdiction to rectify a written instrument, it is not necessary to find a concluded and binding contract between the parties antecedent to the agreement which it is sought to rectify. The judge held, and I respectfully concur with his reasoning and his conclusion, that it is sufficient to find a common continuing intention in regard to a particular provision or aspect of the agreement. If one finds that, in regard to a particular point, the parties were in agreement up to the moment when they executed their formal instrument, and the formal instrument does not conform with that common agreement, then this court has jurisdiction to rectify, although it may be that there was, until the formal instrument was executed, no concluded and binding contract between the parties. That is what the judge decided, and, as I say, with his reasoning I wholly concur, and I can add nothing to his authority in the matter, except that I would say that, if it were not so, it would be a strange thing, for the result would be that two parties binding themselves by a mistake to which each had equally contributed, by an instrument which did not express their real intention, would yet be bound by it. That is a state of affairs which I hold is not the law, and, until a higher court tells me it is the law, I shall continue to exercise the jurisdiction which Clauson J., as I think rightly, held might be entertained by this court. Secondly. I want to say this upon the principle of the jurisdiction. It is a jurisdiction which is to be exercised only upon convincing proof that the concluded instrument does not represent the common intention of the parties. That is particularly the case where one finds prolonged negotiations between the parties eventually assuming the shape of a formal instrument in which they have been advised by their respective skilled legal advisers. The assumption is very strong in such a case that the instrument does represent their real intention, and it must be only upon proof which Lord Eldon, I think, in a somewhat picturesque phrase described as 'irrefragable' that the court can act. I would rather, I think, say that the court can only act if it is satisfied beyond all reasonable doubt that the instrument does not represent their common intention, and is further satisfied as to what their common intention was. For let it be clear that it is not sufficient to show that the written instrument does not represent their common intention unless positively also one can show what their common intention was. It is in the light of those principles that I must examine the facts of this somewhat complicated case."

It is we think probable that the eminent counsel concerned in the case did not really dispute that Clauson J.'s opinion represented the law on the relevant point; it does not appear from the judgment that they did, and very many more cases would have been cited had they done so. Equally in the Court of Appeal [1939] 4 All E.R. 68, Sir Wilfrid Greene M.R. said:

"Two arguments on behalf of the present appellant were before Simonds J., and these arguments are before us. They were these. First, that upon the facts of the case no case for rectification had been made out: secondly, that the matter in question, namely, the issue between the parties as to whether or not the agreement ought to be rectified was a matter which fell within the terms of the arbitration submission, which could have been raised before the arbitrator, and ought to have been raised before him, and could not be raised after he had issued his award and was *functus officio* . . . Simonds J., in a judgment of conspicuous clarity, rejected the appellant's argument on both points. He found that the facts brought to his mind that high degree of conviction which unquestionably is to be insisted upon in rectification cases."

Sir Wilfrid Greene M.R. continued:

"The case is no doubt one of importance to the parties and for that reason I have thought proper to put in my own language my reasons for saying that this appeal should be dismissed, but I might have been content to say that the judgment of Simonds J., both on law and on fact, is one with which I am in entire agreement."

Clauson and Goddard L.JJ. agreed. In referring particularly to the judge's rejection of the argument on rectification, in our view Sir Wilfrid Greene M.R. was referring in fact to his rejection of argument on the facts, not the law. Accordingly, we have in *Crane* v. *Hegeman-Harris Co. Inc.* in both courts an acceptance of the law on rectification as not requiring a complete antecedent concluded contract, in a case in which the decision must have been otherwise if such an antecedent contract was essential to rectification. But it seems to us that the contrary was not really argued, and we leave aside for the moment whether in those circumstances the principles of precedent require us to be bound by this case on the relevant point.

Next we refer to the horsebeans case in this court, *Frederick E. Rose* v. *Wm. H. Pim Junr. & Co. Ltd.* [1953] 2 Q.B. 450. That was a case in which there was nothing that could be described as an outward expression between the parties of an accord on what was to be involved in a term of a proposed agreement. It turned out that locked separately in the breast of each party was the misapprehension that the word 'horsebeans' meant another commodity, but as we understand the case there was no communication between them to the effect that when they should speak of horsebeans that was to be their private label for the other commodity. The decision in our judgment does not assert or reinstate the view that an antecedent complete concluded contract is required for rectification: it only shows that prior accord on a term or the meaning of a phrase to be used must outwardly have been expressed or communicated between the parties. Denning L.J. said:

"It is not necessary that all the formalities of the contract should have been executed so as to make it enforceable at law: see *Shipley Urban District Council* v. *Bradford Corpn.*; but, formalities apart, there must have been a concluded contract. There is a passage in *Crane* v. *Hegeman-Harris Co. Inc.* which suggests that a continuing common intention alone will suffice, but I am clearly of opinion that a continuing common intention is not sufficient unless it has found expression in outward agreement. There could be no certainty at all in business transactions if a party who had entered into a firm contract could afterwards turn round and claim to have it rectified on the ground that the parties intended something different. He is allowed to prove, if he can, that they *agreed something different*: see *Lovell and Christmas* v. *Wall*, per Lord Cozens-Hardy M.R., and per Buckley L.J.; but not that they intended something different."

Insofar as this passage might be taken to suggest that an antecedent complete concluded contract is necessary it would be in conflict with the views of both courts in *Crane* v. *Hegeman-Harris*, and is not supported by the other judgments. Insofar as it speaks of agreement in the more general sense of an outwardly expressed accord of minds it does no more than assent to the argument of counsel for the defendants on the true width of the views of Simonds J.

We conclude this review of authority with a few other cases to which our attention was drawn. In *Earl* v. *Hector Whaling Ltd.* [1961] 1 Ll.R. 459 at 470 Harman L.J. said:

"As to the facts, it does not appear to me that there ever was an oral agreement. There was a common intention, and that is enough. In spite of Lord Justice Denning's observations in *Frederick E. Rose (London) Ltd.* v. *William H. Pim Junr. & Co. Ltd.*, I think that Mr. Justice Clauson's original decision in *Shipley Urban District Council* v. *Bradford Corporation*, (as followed by Mr. Justice Simonds (as he then was)) in *Crane*

v. *Hegeman-Harris Company, Inc.*, that you do not need a prior contract, but a prior common intention, is right; and here, as it seems to me, both parties always intended that there should be a written agreement, and they came to a common intention as to what that written agreement was to be, or thought they did; and if the evidence satisfied one that that common intention did not appear in the written document, then you would have a case for rectification."

We do not take Pearce L.J. to suggest the contrary view.

Lastly reference was made to a decision of Megaw J. shortly noted (so far) in *London Weekend Television Ltd.* v. *Paris and Griffith* (1969) 113 Sol. Jo. 222. He expressed the view that the propositions of Simonds J. in *Crane's* case were binding as a result of their express approval by this court. He then used this phrase, according to the report, a phrase which if correct covers the present case:

"Where two persons agreed expressly with one another what was the meaning of a particular phrase but did not record their definition in the contract itself, if one of the parties sought to enforce the agreement on the basis of some other meaning, he could be prevented by an action for rectification."

In our judgment the law is as expounded by Simonds J. in *Crane's* case, with the qualification that some outward expression of accord is required. We do not wish to attempt to state in any different phrases that with which we entirely agree, except to say that it is in our view better to use only the phrase "convincing proof" without echoing an old fashioned word such as "irrefragable" and without importing from the criminal law the phrase "beyond all reasonable doubt." Remembering always the strong burden of proof that lies on the shoulders of those seeking rectification, and that the requisite accord and continuance of accord of intention may be the more difficult to establish if a complete antecedent concluded contract be not shown, it would be a sorry state of affairs if when that burden is discharged a party to a written contract could, on discovery that the written language chosen for the document did not on its true construction reflect the accord of the parties on a particular point, take advantage of the fact.

The contention in law for the daughter would, we apprehend, involve this proposition, that if all the important terms of an agreement were set out in correspondence with clarity, but expressly "subject to contract," and the contract by a slip of the copyist unnoticed by either party, departed from what had been "agreed," there could not be rectification. We have been puzzled by the suggestion of Sir Herbert Cozens-Hardy M.R. in the *Lovell and Christmas* case that rectification should be regarded as a branch of the doctrine of specific performance; we do not see any necessary connection, more particularly since rectification is available in the case of voluntary settlements. In our judgment the view of Simonds J. and this court on the point were correct and on the facts found by the county court judge the father established a claim to rectification. It is not necessary therefore to decide whether we were bound in any event by the decision of this court in *Crane's* case, notwithstanding that (in our view) the contrary was not argued, the particular point of law being in fact essential to the dismissal of the appeal. This question of precedent was discussed at some length in this court in *Morelle Ltd.* v. *Wakeling* [1955] 2 Q.B. 379 and as at present advised it would appear to us that it may well not be right to say that the decision in *Crane's* case was made per incuriam: we refer in particular to the judgment of the full court in *Morelle's* case, though we are not completely content on this point. This court is not omniscient in the law, nor are counsel, however eminent. We work under great pressure from the lists, and whilst not always ready to accept a concession on a point of law from the Bar it is not infrequent to do so, and moreover on a point essential to the decision of the appeal, without further investigation. We are attracted by a suggestion that the conceded point of law should be open to argument in another case, provided it is made plain that that should not be made the basis for the further suggestion that, where an argument, though put forward, had been only weakly or inexpertly put forward, the point of law should similarly be open; for much uncertainty could thus be undesirably introduced.

We wish to stress that this is a case of rectification based on antecedent expressed accord on a point adhered to in intention by the parties to the subsequent written contract: we were in no way concerned with arguments as to collateral terms of a contract.

The actual order of the county court judge would appear to have rectified the wrong clause in the agreement, and to have omitted the reference, in the accepted evidence of the father, to payment of expenses being made out of the business. Counsel were able to agree the proper form of order. The order will accordingly be varied so as to provide that in lieu of rectification of cl. 7 of the contract thereby ordered, cl. 6 shall be rectified so as to read:

"[The daughter] shall until she sells the business and out of the proceeds of the business discharge [the father's] expenses in respect of gas, coal, electricity and home help incurred by him while occupying 'Martindale' . . . aforesaid or such property as may be agreed upon in pursuance of clause 7 hereof and shall indemnify [the father] from and against any claim arising in respect of the same."

We would add that we very much hope that the father and the daughter will now be able to return to a proper familial relationship after their differences, which will have given them the distinction, if such it be, of being enshrined in the law reports. So the result is that the appeal is dismissed. The cross-appeal was not pursued.

[Appeal dismissed.]

PAGET v. MARSHALL
(1884) 28 Ch. D. 255

BACON V.C.: The case before me is in a very narrow compass. The Plaintiff had taken the lease of a site from the *Goldsmiths' Company* upon a contract to build upon it a very valuable and commodious structure. He did so, and his plans are in evidence; it is quite clear what his intention was. He built two separate ground-floor tenements, Nos. 49 and 50, to be let to two separate tenants. He kept a third, No. 48, including ground and first floors, intending to occupy it himself, and the fourth part, that coloured blue on the model, he had to let when the negotiation commenced with the Defendant. So that the subject in dispute is beyond all question. The two shops, Nos. 49 and 50, were separate and distinct things—as separate as if they had been in some other street—and the third, No. 48, was equally separate and distinct—built by the Plaintiff for his own occupation, and for carrying on his own business, and constructed so that those objects might be conviently performed by him. To that end he built on the ground floor of No. 48 a staircase communicating with the first floor of No. 48, and he partitioned off the first floor of No. 48, so that in its turn it became just as distinct a building—just as distinct a tenement—as Nos. 49 and 50, and the purpose was distinct. Then, the part coloured blue (which included the whole first floor of the block except that of No. 48, and all the upper floors without any exception) being still available, and the Plaintiff willing to let it, he constructed a staircase which led from the street past the first floor of No. 48, and landed upon the blue part, I will call it, that is sufficient description,—no communication whatever either in fact being made, or according to the evidence ever intended to be made, between the ground or first floor of No. 48 and the part coloured blue. That was the state of things when these parties met to negotiate. The partition which effectually severed the first floor of No. 48 from the part coloured blue, had been completely settled and arranged. The Defendant on his first visit looked over all that was then to let, ascertained what the Plaintiff meant to let, saw the first floor over No. 48, said that it would make a very handsome warehouse, but knew at the same time that it was not to be let, because, to use his own expression in his own evidence, the Plaintiff told him "we mean to use that for ourselves." That is the evidence which the Defendant has given on this occasion. He says that he was satisfied to some extent with what he looked at, and desired to acquire it, but he must have a packing-room. He could not mean the first floor, that which he said was a magnificent warehouse could not be a packing-room, it could not in the nature of things; and he does not say that that was in his mind, still he insists more than once on the necessity of having a packing-room. I am mentioning these facts in order to ascertain, as it is my duty to do, what I must take to be proved to have been the intention of the parties when they entered into the negotiation. He asks for a packing-room. The brother goes with him down into a cellar—a cellar under No. 48, in the basement of No. 48— they look about there, and the brother comes in and says, "You cannot have it." No wonder, because there can be no access to it but from the floor of No. 48, and that went off.

Now, it would be impossible for me to connect, and there was a very faint attempt made to connect, the necessity which was present in the Defendant's mind to have a packing-room, with the magnificent first floor, which he now says he had in his mind when he was present. The statement about putting up the inscription by no means encourages any such notion. The Defendant desired to advertise to the public by means of a large inscription on the front of that which was to be his the trade which he was carrying on. He wished also to have a similar inscription over No. 48. That was resisted. It was the subject of discussion between them; the reason it was resisted was explained to him: "If we granted you that, it would look as if you were carrying on your business in our warehouse;" but they said that, in order to accommodate him they would be willing to insert a tablet, containing his name and business, provided it did not interfere with the architectural decorations of No. 48. These facts are beyond all question. Both parties are agreed. Then the Plaintiff writes a letter in which he offers to let, among other things, the first floor of No. 48. This is answered very readily by the Defendant, who accepts the offer. Instructions are sent to the solicitors, instructions consisting only of this letter. Mr. Marten made a point that the Plaintiff, in his pleadings, said they had no other instructions. They must have had some other instructions. I should read the word "other" used by him in the pleadings as meaning no different instructions, no variation in form or otherwise from the words that appear in the letter. Then the lease is prepared and executed in accordance with the letter, including the first floor of No. 48.

Under these circumstances, the facts being as I have stated, am I, because the lease has been executed under seal, demising to the Defendant that which the Plaintiff never meant to let him have, that which the Defendant says he knew at one time the Plaintiff intended to keep for himself, that which he has never claimed at any period prior to the letter—am I to say that the agreement is to be held to be irrevocable? It would be against every principle that regulates the law relating to mistakes, and it would be directly at variance with the proved facts in this case. On the evidence, it looks like a common mistake. The Defendant, it is true, says in his defence, that he took it on the faith that the first floor of No. 48 was intentionally included in the letter of the 13th of November, 1883. Certainly he never said so until it is said in the defence, which I am looking at now; but he has not said so in his evidence. He has never said that he intended to take that. The argument addressed to me has been this:—"The separation of No. 48 and the blue, is effected solely by means of a brick-on-end partition; and that is easily removed." People building brick-on-end partitions do not mean them to be easily removed, unless there is some purpose to remove them, and here, using the Defendant's own evidence on this occasion, at that time the partition was effectually finished, and the Defendant knew that the Plaintiff intended to reserve it for his own use in his own business. The law being such as I have said, it is not necessary to say anything about how easily you can make holes in a partition, and how you can knock down a partition; you can pull down the front of a house with equal ease if you have proper appliances and proper workmen to do it. The way it is forced on my attention is the reason why the partition was first made, why it was found to be in existence when the Defendant first inspected it, why he knew from that time as well as he knows now that it was never the intention of the Plaintiff that he should have that "magnificent" room which formed one of two rooms which constituted the business place intended by the Plaintiff for his own use, and to which the access was made by one staircase communicating with nothing but the upper room.

But without being certain, as I cannot be certain on the facts before me, whether the mistake was what is called a common mistake—that is, such a common mistake as would induce the Court to strike out of a marriage settlement a provision or limitation—that there was to some extent a common mistake I must in charity and justice to the Defendant believe, because I cannot impute to him the intention of taking advantage of any incorrect expression in this letter. He may have persuaded himself that the letter was right; but if there was not a common mistake it is plain and palpable that the Plaintiff was mistaken, and that he had no intention of letting his own shop, which he had built and carefully constructed for his own purposes.

Upon that ground, therefore, I must say that the contract ought to be annulled. I think it would be right and just and perfectly consistent with other decisions that the Defendant should have an opportunity of choosing whether he will submit, as the Plaintiff asks that he should submit, to have the lease rectified by excluding from it the first floor of No. 48, whether he will choose to take his lease with that rectification, or whether he will choose to throw up the thing entirely, because the object of the Court is, as far as it can, to put the parties into the position in which they would have been if the mistake had not happened. Therefore I give the Defendant an opportunity of saying whether he will or will not submit to rectification. If he does not, then I shall declare that the agreement is annulled. Then we shall have to settle the terms on which it should be annulled. The Plaintiff does not object, if the agreement is annulled, to pay the Defendant any reasonable expenses to which he may have been put by reason of the Plaintiff's mistake; but it must be limited to that. I should like, if it be convenient for counsel or for the parties, to have an answer to the proposition I have made, in order that that may be fully before the persons whom it interests. I may say that I can find no reason for a reduction of the rent. I listened attentively to what Sir John Ellis said, and to what Mr. Farmer said, and I cannot but think that the rent of £500, if the lease is rectified, ought not, with any show of justice, to suffer any reduction.

Marten for the Defendant, agreed to strike out the first floor of No. 48 from the lease; the lease in other respects standing as it was executed.

BACON V.C.: Then the decree will be, the Defendant electing to have rectification instead of cancellation of the lease, let the lease be rectified by omitting from it all mention of the first floor of No. 48. Then as to the costs of the action, the Plaintiff is not entitled to costs, because he has made a mistake, and the Defendant ought not to have any costs, because his opposition to the Plaintiff's demand has been unreasonable, unjust, and unlawful.

NOTE. Compare the approach of the Court to a somewhat similar problem in *Alampi* v. *Swartz*, supra. *Paget* v. *Marshall* was followed in *Devald* v. *Zigeuner* (1958) 16 D.L.R. (2d) 285 (Ont. H.C.). In *Riverlate Properties Ltd.* v. *Paul* [1974] 3 W.L.R. 564, the English Court of Appeal held that rectification is only available if the party seeking to enforce the document shares the other's mistake, or if, knowing of the mistake, he deliberately keeps silent in order to take advantage of it. The optional remedy was disapproved. See Comment, (1975) 53 Can. Bar Rev. 340.

PROBLEM. You are assisting in the drafting of a new Contracts Code. It is to take the form of statutory text, with each section followed by an official comment explaining the purpose and effect of the text. Draft the section or sections (with official comment) on the effect of written documents on contractual relationships.

CHAPTER 7

PROTECTION OF WEAKER PARTIES

1. INFANTS

REX v. *RASH*
Ontario. Court of Appeal. 1923. 53 O.L.R. 245

ROSE J.: The question as put in the stated case is, whether the magistrate was right as a matter of law in holding that a person under the age of 21 years can be convicted of the offence of removing, concealing, or disposing of any of his property, with intent to defraud his creditors (the *Criminal Code*, sec. 417 (a)). To that question, put in that broad way, the answer is: "Yes: an infant, in some circumstances, can incur debts of certain kinds, and can have creditors; and if he disposes of his property with intent to defraud those creditors he can be convicted." But upon the whole case it is apparent that the question intended to be submitted for the opinion of the Court is a much narrower question than the one formally put. It is, in effect: "Are persons who have supplied goods to an infant trader for the purposes of his trade, and who have not been paid, 'creditors' within the meaning of sec. 417?" That is the question which was argued and which must be answered.

If a similar question arose in England, where the *Infants' Relief Act, 1874*, is in force, the answer would have to be in the negative, for the Act makes void all contracts entered into by infants, after the passing of the Act, for goods supplied (other than contracts for necessaries): and, as was admitted in *Regina* v. *Wilson* (1879), 5 Q.B.D. 28, by counsel for the prosecution, it cannot be contended that, since the passing of the Act, the contracts of an infant for goods supplied in the way of trade are valid or result in debts, or that the persons who supply such goods are creditors capable of being defrauded. But in Ontario there is no statute corresponding to the *Infants' Relief Act*, and what has to be ascertained is the relationship created, at common law, by a contract made between an infant trader and those who supply him with the goods in which he deals.

At common law, certain contracts made by infants are void, in the strict sense, and incapable of ratification: see *Beam* v. *Beatty* (1902), 3 O.L.R. 345; 4 O.L.R. 554; *Phillips* v. *Greater Ottawa Development Co.* (1916), 38 O.L.R. 315.

Others are usually described as valid. Such are contracts for necessaries, although, considering the fact that the person who supplies necessaries recovers, not the agreed price, but the value, probably confusion would have been avoided if it had been recognised that, as pointed out by Fletcher Moulton L.J., in *Nash* v. *Inman*, [1908] 2 K.B. 1, an infant, like a lunatic, is incapable of making a contract of purchase in the strict sense of the words; that, if a man satisfies the needs of an infant or lunatic by supplying to him necessaries, the law will imply an obligation to repay him for the services so rendered, and will enforce that obligation against the estate of the infant or lunatic; that consequently the basis of the action is hardly contract—the obligation arises *re* and not *consensu*.

Contracts of a third (and this the largest) class may be avoided or enforced at the option of the infant: *Bruce* v. *Warwick* (1815), 6 Taunt. 118; 128 E.R. 978, "The law so far protects him, as to give him an opportunity to consider it when he comes of age: and it is good or voidable at his election:" *Holt* v. *Ward Clarencieux* (1732), 2 Str. 937; 93 E.R. 954. These contracts are usually described as voidable. Contracts, such as are here in question, by which the infant undertakes to pay for goods supplied to him for use in trade are of this class, and what has to be determined is the precise meaning of the word "voidable" as applied to them— is it correct to say quite generally, as in Halsbury's *Laws of England*, vol. 17, p. 64, note (1), that "voidable means valid until repudiated, not invalid until confirmed;" or ought it to be said, as in *Anson on Contracts*, 15th ed., p. 186, that an infant's "voidable" contracts must be divided under two heads, (a) those which are valid and binding on the infant until disaffirmed, and (b) those which are not binding until ratified after majority? If such a division as is suggested by Anson is justified, there is no doubt that contracts such as we have to deal with in this case will fall into the author's class (b); and that it is justified, will, I think, appear when there are considered, first, some of the cases which have arisen out of contracts by an infant for the purchase of goods (other than necessaries) or out of other contracts which would clearly be in class (b), if there is such a class, and secondly, some of the cases that are usually cited in support of the broad general proposition that voidable means valid until repudiated. . . . [A long discussion of cases is omitted.]

My conclusion accords with that reached, in a civil case, by the Supreme Court of Mississippi in *Edmunds* v. *Mister* (1881), 58 Miss. 765 (cited in 27 Corpus. Juris., p. 476). There, soon after attaining his majority, a man who, while an infant, had contracted debts (I use the expression in the popular sense) conveyed his property to his daughter for life with reversion to himself, the conveyance being without consideration, and with the avowed intention of defeating "creditors"—although, as the grantor said, he was unwilling to plead infancy and intended to pay his debts. The Court held that the conveyance was valid, because the holders of the demands for goods furnished during the grantor's minority were not creditors. . . . For these reasons, my answer to the question submitted is in the negative.

[The concurring opinions of Mulock C.J. Ex., and Kelly, Masten and Orde JJ. are omitted. See MASTEN J. at p. 253: "If an adult contracts with an infant, the infant can enforce the contract though the adult cannot. This was decided by the Court of King's Bench in 1813 . . . and has ever since been accepted as the law. Such a right of action by the infant predicates and necessitates as its foundation, an existing valid contract."]

NOTE. Compare the following statements: Middleton J. in *Re Sovereign Bank* (1915), 35 O.L.R. 448 at 453: "No doubt in ordinary cases, an infant is called upon to repudiate within a reasonable time after attaining majority." Garrow J.A. at p. 456: "An infant may by contract become the holder of shares in a bank. The legal effect of such a contract is the same as that of other voidable contracts of an infant, namely, that it is valid until repudiated. See *Edwards* v. *Carter*, [1893] A.C. 360: And, the repudiation must, to be effective, take place within a reasonable time after full age is reached." It will be noticed however that the Court is here dealing with a situation of the kind described by Anson as one "when an infant acquired an interest in permanent property to which obligations attach, etc."

For a criticism of this twofold division see *Williston on Contracts*, rev. ed., secs. 231-9.

SALE OF GOODS ACT
Ontario. Revised Statutes. 1970. Chapter 421

3. (1) Capacity to buy and sell is regulated by the general law concerning capacity to contract, and to transfer and acquire property; provided that where necessaries are sold and delivered to an infant or minor or to a person who by reason of mental incapacity or drunkenness is incompetent to contract, he must pay a reasonable price therefor.

(2) Necessaries in this section mean goods suitable to the conditions in life of such infant or minor or other person, and to his actual requirements at the time of the sale and delivery.

INFANTS ACT
British Columbia. Revised Statutes. 1960. Chapter 193

2. All contracts, whether by specialty or by simple contract, entered into by infants for the repayment of money lent or to be lent, or for goods supplied or to be supplied (other than contracts for necessaries), and all accounts stated with infants, shall be absolutely void: Provided always that this enactment shall not invalidate any contract into which an infant may, by an existing or future Statute, or by the rules of the common law or equity, enter, except such as now by law are voidable. [37 & 38 Vict., c. 62, s. 1.]

3. No action shall be brought whereby to charge any person upon any promise made after full age to pay any debt contracted during infancy, or upon any ratification made after full age of any promise or contract made during infancy, whether there shall or shall not be any new consideration for such promise or ratification after full age. [37 & 38 Vict., c. 62, s. 2.]

4. Where a minor over the age of sixteen years, who has no parent or legal guardian, or who does not reside with his parent or guardian, enters into an engagement, written or verbal, to perform any service or work, he shall be liable upon the same, and shall have the benefit thereof, as if he had been of legal age, and the provisions of the last two preceding sections shall not apply to such engagement.

NASH v. *INMAN*
England. Court of Appeal. [1908] 2 K.B. 1

The action was brought by specially indorsed writ by a tailor carrying on business in Saville Row, London, for £145 10s. 3d. for clothes supplied to the defendant while an undergraduate at Cambridge University between October 29, 1902, and June 16, 1903. The defendant was an infant at the time of the sale and delivery of the goods. He had been at school at Uppingham, and in October, 1902, he went up as a freshman to Trinity College, Cambridge. He was the son of an architect of good position, who had a town house at Hampstead, and a country establishment called Wade Court, near Havant. The clothes supplied to the defendant included, among other things, eleven fancy waistcoats at two guineas each, or £1 15s. for cash. Upon an application for judgment under Order xiv., the defendant set up the plea of infancy, and the action was adjourned into Court and was tried before Ridley J. and a special jury. At the trial the plaintiff claimed only £122 19s. 6d., the cash price of the goods, in lieu of £145 10s. 3d., the credit price. The only witness called on behalf of the plaintiff was a traveller in his employ, who stated that he went to Cambridge and other places to solicit orders for the plaintiff, and that, hearing that the defendant was spending money freely and was likely to be a good customer, he called upon him personally at his lodgings in Cambridge and obtained the first order for clothes; and he gave evidence as to the goods supplied, and stated that they were charged for at the usual prices.

Counsel for the defendant thereupon submitted that, subject to his formally proving infancy, which was not admitted, there was no evidence to go to the jury, and he called the defendant's father, who proved the date of the defendant's birth, and then went on to state that he was satisfied that his son on going to the university was amply supplied with proper clothes according to his position; and he gave particulars of his outfit. The learned judge then held that there was no evidence to go to the jury that the goods were necessaries, and directed judgment to be entered for the defendant.

The plaintiff applied for judgment or a new trial, on the ground that the judge himself had decided the issues of fact instead of leaving them to the jury.

Cozens-Hardy M.R.: This case is undoubtedly one of difficulty and also, I think, one of importance. It is an action by a tailor against Mr. Inman, who was at the date of the transactions in question an infant. There under Order xiv., and the action was adjourned into Court, and came on for trial before Ridley J. and a special jury. In substance the position is this: The plaintiff sues the defendant for goods sold and delivered. The defendant pleads infancy at the date of the sale, and his plea is proved. What is the consequence of that? The consequence of that is that the *Infants' Relief Act, 1874*, becomes applicable. Under that Act all contracts for goods supplied are absolutely void, the only exception being contracts for necessaries. Then s. 2 of the *Sale of Goods Act, 1893*, provides as follows: "Capacity to buy and sell is regulated by the general law concerning capacity to contract, and to transfer and acquire property." That, of course, includes the Act of 1874. Then follows this proviso: "Provided that where necessaries are sold and delivered to an infant, or minor, or to a person who by reason of mental incapacity or drunkenness is incompetent to contract, he must pay a reasonable price therefor." The section then defines necessaries as follows: "Necessaries in this section mean goods suitable to the condition in life of such infant or minor or other person, and to his actual requirements at the time of the sale and delivery." What is the effect of that? The plaintiff sues for goods sold and delivered. The defendant pleads infancy. The plaintiff must then reply, "The goods sold were necessaries within the meaning of the definition in s. 2 of the *Sale of Goods Act, 1893*." It is not sufficient, in my view, for him to say, "I have discharged the onus which rests upon me if I simply shew that the goods supplied were suitable to the condition in life of the infant at the time."

There is another branch of the definition which cannot be disregarded. Having shewn that the goods were suitable to the condition in life of the infant, he must then go on to shew that they were suitable to his actual requirement at the time of the sale and delivery. Unless he establishes that fact, either by evidence adduced by himself or by cross-examination of the defendant's witnesses, as the case may be, in my opinion he has not discharged the burden which the law imposes upon him. Our attention has been called by Mr. McCardie, in his very able and learned argument, to a number of authorities going back for a very long period, which he said established that the burden on a plaintiff who supplied goods to an infant was simply to shew that the goods were of a class which might be necessaries, having regard to the position in life of the defendant and his family, and that, unless the judge withdrew the case from the jury on the ground that the articles in question could not be necessaries, it was for the jury to find as a matter of fact, Aye or No, were these articles necessaries? It had never, he said, been the law that the plaintiff was required to go into the question, which might present great difficulties, of whether or not the goods were actually required by the defendant at the date of the sale, or, in other words, to say what was the state of the defendant's wardrobe at the time when the goods were ordered.

I think there is very great force up to a certain point in that argument. But it must be remembered that the law on this subject has been developed and altered in the course of the last century. It was until quite recently doubted whether it was even admissible to prove that the infant was supplied with goods of the class—being goods which might properly be necessary—at the date when the contract was made, so that he really did not want any more. It was not until the decision of the Divisional Court in *Barnes* v. *Toye*, 13 Q.B.D. 410, in 1884, overruling the direction given by A.L. Smith J., that it could be said to be at all established that that was even admissible evidence unless you went further and proved that the plaintiff knew he was sufficiently supplied. The point arose again in *Johnstone* v. *Marks* (1887), 19 Q.B.D. 509, before what was no doubt a Divisional Court, but it was composed of three members of the Court of Appeal, Lord Esher M.R., Lindley L.J., and Lopes L.J. In that case the county court judge had rejected evidence to prove that the defendant was sufficiently supplied with clothes at the time of the sale. Lord Esher said: "I am of opinion that the evidence was improperly rejected. It lies upon the plaintiff to prove, not that the goods supplied belong to the class of necessaries as distinguished from that of luxuries, but that the goods supplied when supplied were necessaries to the infant. The circumstance that the infant was sufficiently supplied at the time of the additional supply is obviously material to this issue, as well as fatal to the contention of the plaintiff with respect to it." Lindley L.J. said: "If an infant can be made liable for articles which may be necessaries without proof that they are necessaries, there is an end to the protection which the law gives him. If he has enough of such articles, more cannot possibly be necessary to him." Although it may be true that the language which I have just read from the judgments of Lord Esher and Lindley L.J. goes further than was absolutely necessary for the decision of the case, that language is perfectly clear and unambiguous, and seems to me to be logically involved in the definition of necessaries,

After those two decisions there was passed in the year 1893 an Act of Parliament which defines, in a manner that admits of no doubt, what are those necessaries for which, and for which alone, an infant can be made liable on assumpsit, and that definition in terms includes the second element which Lord Esher and Lindley L.J. said was involved in the term "necessaries," and the burden of proving which, they said, rested on the plaintiff. That being so, how does the matter stand? The plaintiff called evidence to prove the delivery of the goods. It is not of course contended, and it could not be contended, that the infant would be liable for the credit price or for the cash price of the goods, because by the terms of the statute he is only liable for a reasonable price, but that is a subsidiary point. There being no pleadings, the infancy of the defendant was not admitted, and the father was called to prove the date of his son's birth. There was no cross-examination as to that, and the infancy is not disputed. Then he went on to give evidence, which was quite clear and explicit and was not shaken in cross-examination, that the infant, who was an undergraduate at Cambridge, and had just gone up to the university when these goods were supplied, was in fact supplied with clothes suitable and necessary and proper for his condition in life, and for his position as an undergraduate of Trinity College, Cambridge.

The learned judge ruled as a matter of law that there was no evidence fit to be submitted to the jury that these articles, or any of them, were necessaries within the meaning of the statutory definition, and, thinking as I do that there was no evidence in support of that which was a necessary issue, I cannot say that the learned judge was wrong in the view which he took. We have scarcely heard any suggestion that there was even a scintilla of evidence to support that which is an affirmative issue, that the goods were suitable to the requirements of the infant. Nay more, I think, if the matter had been left to the jury, and the jury had found that they were suitable to the requirements of the infant at that time, and application had been made for a new trial, it would have been the duty of this Court to grant a new trial on the ground that there was no evidence to support the verdict, and that it was perverse. Under these circumstances it seems to me that this appeal fails, and that there is no ground for interfering with the judgment which was entered for the defendant.

FLETCHER MOULTON L.J.: I am of the same opinion. I think that the difficulty and at the same time the suggestion of hardship to the plaintiff in such a case as this disappear when one considers what is the true basis of an action against an infant for necessaries. It is usually spoken of as a case of enforcing a contract against the infant, but I agree with the view expressed by the Court in *Rhodes* v. *Rhodes* (1890), 44 Ch. D. 94, in the parallel case of a claim for necessaries against a lunatic, that this language is somewhat unfortunate. An infant, like a lunatic, is incapable of making a contract of purchase in the strict sense of the words; but if a man satisfied the needs of the infant or lunatic by supplying to him necessaries, the law will imply an obligation to repay him for the services rendered, and will enforce that obligation against the estate of the infant or lunatic. The consequence is that the basis of the action is hardly contract. Its real foundation is an obligation which the law imposes on the infant to make a fair payment in respect of needs satisfied. In other words the obligation arises *re* and not *consensu*. I do not mean that this nicety of legal phraseology has been adhered to. The common and convenient phrase is that an infant is liable for goods sold and delivered provided that they are necessaries, and there is no objection to that phraseology so long as its true meaning is understood. But the treatment of such actions by the Courts of Common Law has been in accordance with that principle I have referred to. That the articles were necessaries had to be alleged and proved by the plaintiff as part of his case, and the sum he recovered was based on a *quantum meruit*. If he claimed anything beyond this he failed, and it did not help him that he could prove that the prices were agreed prices. All this is very ancient law, and is confirmed by the provisions of s. 2 of the *Sale of Goods Act, 1893*—an Act which was intended to codify the existing law. That section expressly provides that the consequence of necessaries sold and delivered to an infant is that he must pay a reasonable price therefor.

The Sale of Goods Act, 1893, gives a statutory definition of what are necessaries in a legal sense, which entirely removes any doubt, if any doubt previously existed, as to what that word in legal phraseology means. . . . Hence, if an action is brought by one who claims to enforce against an infant such an obligation, it is obvious that the plaintiff in order to prove his case must shew that the goods supplied come within this definition. That a plaintiff has to make out his case is, I should have thought, the first lesson that any one studying English law would learn; and the elaborate argument of Mr. McCardie that if you look at the authorities in the past, going back nearly a hundred years, you will find cases in which particular defendants might have taken a higher standpoint and insisted upon a right which they did not insist on does not appear to me to touch the plain and obvious conclusion that in order to succeed in the action the plaintiff must shew that he has supplied necessaries. That is to say, the plaintiff has to shew, first, that the goods were suitable to the condition in life of the infant; and secondly, that they were suitable to his actual requirements at the time—or, in other words, that the infant had not at the time an adequate supply from other sources. There is authority to show that this was the case even before the Act of 1893. In *Johnstone* v. *Marks* this doctrine is laid down with the greatest clearness, and the *ratio decidendi* of that case applies equally to cases since that Act. Therefore there is no doubt whatever that in order to succeed in an action for goods sold and delivered to an infant the plaintiff must shew that they satisfy both the conditions I have mentioned. Everything which is necessary to bring them within s. 2 it is for him to prove.

Passing on from general principles, let me take the facts of the present case. In my opinion they raise no point whatever as to the duty of the judge as contrasted with the duty of the jury arising from the peculiar character of the action. We have only to follow the lines of the law consistently administered by this Court for many more years than I can think of, an example of which as applied to the case of the supply of necessaries to an infant is given by the decision of the Court of Exchequer Chamber in the case of *Ryder* v. *Wombwell* (1868), L.R. 4 Ex. 32. Questions of law are for the judge; questions of fact are for the jury, but, as the Court there laid down, the particular question of fact in issue in such a case, like all other questions of fact, ought not to be left to the jury by the judge unless there is evidence upon which they could reasonably find in the affirmative. The issue in that case was whether certain articles were suitable to the condition in life of the defendant, the infant, and the Court of Exchequer Chamber thought that no jury could reasonably find that those articles were suitable to the condition of that defendant, and therefore they said that the judge—not by reason of any peculiar rule applicable to actions of this kind, but in the discharge of his regular duties in all cases of trial by a jury—ought not to have left the question to the jury because there was no evidence on which they could reasonably find for the plaintiff. We have before us a similar case, in which the issue is not only whether the articles in question were suitable to the defendant's condition in life, but whether they were suitable to his actual requirements at the time of the sale and delivery; and how does the evidence stand? The evidence for the plaintiff shewed that one of his travellers, hearing that a freshman at Trinity College was spending money pretty liberally, called on him to get an order for clothes, and sold him within nine months goods which at cash prices came to over £120, including an extravagant number of waistcoats and other articles of clothing, and that is all that the plaintiff proved. The defendant's father proved the infancy, and then proved that the defendant had an adequate supply of clothes, and stated what they were. That evidence was uncontradicted. Not only was it not contradicted by any other evidence, but there was no cross-examination tending to shake the credit of the witness, against whose character and means of knowledge nothing could be said. On that uncontradicted evidence the judge came to the conclusion, to use the language of the Court in *Ryder* v. *Wombwell*, that there was no evidence on which the jury might properly find that these goods were necessary to the actual requirements of the infant at the time of sale and delivery, and therefore, in accordance with the duty of the judge in all cases of trial by jury, he withdrew the case from the jury and directed judgment to be entered for the defendant. In my opinion he was justified by the practice of the Court in so doing, and this appeal must be dismissed.

[The concurring opinion of Buckley L.J. is omitted.]

2. FORFEITURES

SHATILLA v. *FEINSTEIN*
Saskatchewan. Court of Appeal. [1923] 3 D.L.R. 1035

Feinstein carried on business as a wholesale drygoods merchant in Saskatoon and on April 16, 1920, sold his business to Shatilla on the express understanding that Feinstein and his brother, who were most active in the business, would not compete within the corporate limits of Saskatoon for five years. They agreed to pay $10,000 on breach of the covenant recoverable on each and every such breach as liquidated damages and not as a penalty. During 1921 Feinstein became a shareholder and director of Harley Henry Ltd. who engaged in the wholesale drygoods business. Shatilla sued to recover on the covenant. The trial judge held the covenant to be a penalty and unenforceable, but he also held that there had been a breach and directed a reference to ascertain actual damages. The plaintiff appealed on the ground, among others not here material, that the covenant was valid as a genuine pre-estimate of liquidated damages.

MARTIN J.A. delivered the judgment of the Court: . . . The main question to be determined is, whether or not the sum fixed by the covenant is a penalty, or whether it is recoverable by way of liquidated damages. When the damages which may arise out of the breach of a contract are in their nature uncertain, the law permits the parties to agree beforehand as to the amount to be paid in case of breach. Whether such an agreement has been made by the parties or not, or whether the sum agreed upon is a penalty, must depend upon the circumstances of each case. If the sum fixed is in excess of any actual damage which can possibly arise from the breach of the contract, the sum fixed as damage is not considered to be a *bonâ fide* pre-estimate of the damage. The same principle is applied when the payment of a larger sum is stipulated in the event of the breach of a covenant to pay a smaller sum. In the case of a contract containing a single stipulation which, if broken at all, can be broken once only—such as a covenant not to reveal a trade secret—when the parties have agreed to the amount which shall be paid in case of breach and referred to such sum as liquidated damages, there would appear to be no reason, on the authorities, why the Court should not treat such sum as liquidated damages. If, however, the covenant is one which is capable of being broken more than once, such as an agreement not to solicit the customers of a firm, or an agreement not to sell certain specified articles below a certain price, the question is a more difficult one. In such a case, however, the damage in the case of each breach is of the same kind, and the fact that such damage may vary in amount for each breach has not been held by the Courts to raise a presumption that the sum agreed upon is a penalty, particularly where the parties have agreed to the sum as liquidated damages. This, I think, is a fair deduction from the decision in the House of Lords in *Dunlop Pneumatic Tyre Co. Ltd.* v. *New Garage and Motor Co.*, [1915] A.C. 79.

In cases, however, where it is agreed to pay a fixed sum on the breach of a number of stipulations of various degrees of importance, a presumption is said to be raised against the sum so fixed being treated as liquidated damages, even though the parties have referred to it as such; that is, there is a presumption against the parties having pre-estimated the damages. The damage likely to accrue from breaches of various kinds in such a case is different in kind and amount, and a separate estimate in the case of each breach would be necessary. Such a presumption may, however, be rebutted if it is shown on the face of the agreement, or on the evidence, that the parties have taken into consideration the different amounts of damages that might occur, and had actually arrived at an amount which was considered proper under all the circumstances. Even then, however, the amount fixed must not be extravagant or unreasonable.

In *Elphinstone* v. *Monkland Iron & Coal Co.* (1886), 11 App. Cas. 332, the facts were that the lessees of land had been granted the privilege of placing slag from blast furnaces on land let to them, and covenanted to restore the land at a certain date. Provision was made that failing performance the lessees should pay the lessors "at the rate of £100 per Imperial acre for all ground not so restored, together with legal interest thereon, from and after the date when the operations should have been completed until paid." It was held that the sum, although it was described in one part of the agreement as "the penalty therein stipulated," was not a penalty but estimated or stipulated damages. Lord Watson, at pp. 342-3, said:—

"When a single lump sum is made payable by way of compensation, on the occurrence of one or more or all of several events, some of which may occasion serious and others but trifling damage, the presumption is that the parties intended the sum to be penal, and subject to modification. The payments stipulated in article 12 are not of that character; they are made proportionate to the extent to which the respondent company may fail to implement their obligations, and they are to bear interest from the date of the failure. I can find neither principle nor authority for holding that payments so adjusted by the contracting parties with reference to the actual amount of damage ought to be regarded as penalties.". . .

In *Clydebank Engineering & Shipbuilding Co.,* v. *Don Jose Castaneda,* [1904] A.C. 6, the shipbuilding company contracted for the construction of four vessels of war for the Spanish Government, each of which was to be completed at a certain date. In the event of non-completion they were to pay £500 for each ship for every week's delay. The contract entered into contained the following clause:—"The contractors undertake that the said vessel shall be finished, complete and ready for sea, the first vessels in six and three-quarter months, and the second in seven and three-quarter months from signing of this contract and accompanying specifications and plans." And also:—"The penalty for later delivery shall be at the rate of £500 per week for each vessel not delivered by the contractors in contract time."

It appeared from the evidence that the sum to be paid on breach of delivery was suggested by the contracting company itself, and this fact must have had some influence on the decision of the Court. It was held that the sum stipulated was liquidated damage, and not a penalty. . . .

In *Webster* v. *Bosanquet*, [1912] A.C. 394, the plaintiff and defendant carried on business as partners in exporting and selling Ceylon tea. The partnership was dissolved, and an agreement was entered into which contained the following provisions at p. 396:—

"And the said Bosanquet shall not be at liberty to sell during the period aforesaid [10 years] the whole or any part of the tea crops of the Marawilla and or Palamcotta estates to any person other than the said Webster without first offering to the said Webster the option of buying the same, so long as Webster shall pay to Bosanquet the yearly payment of 75*l*; and if the said Bosanquet shall fail, neglect, or refuse to sell the whole or any part of the crop of the Marawilla and or Palamcotta estates as hereinbefore provided to the said Webster, he shall pay to Webster the sum of 500*l* as liquidated damages and not as a penalty."

It was held by Privy Council that the claim was recoverable by way of liquidated damages. Lord Mersey, at pp. 397-8, said:

"The cases in which the Courts have had to consider whether a stipulated payment in respect of the breach of a contract should be regarded as liquidated damages fixing once for all the sum to be paid, or merely as a penalty covering the damages though not assessing them, are innumerable and perhaps difficult to reconcile. But it is unnecessary to examine them, for their effect is sufficiently and very clearly stated in the *Clydebank* case. From that case it appears that, whatever be the expression used in the contract in describing the payment, the question must always be whether the construction contended for renders the agreement unconscionable and extravagant and one which no court ought to allow to be enforced."

And again at pp. 398-9:—"It was suggested in the course of the argument that to treat the £500 as liquidated damages might involve such extravagant consequences as to render the agreement absurd, for the sum might be claimed in respect of every pound of tea sold in breach of the stipulation. Their Lordships, however, are of the opinion that the stipulation is not capable of such an interpretation. The parties to the agreement were merchants using language in the sense which it is used in their trade. When they speak of 'a part of a crop' they are not contemplating packets which might be sold over a grocer's counter, but parcels such as were in fact sold in the present case."

In *Dunlop Pneumatic Tyre Co.* v. *New Garage*, [1915] A.C. 79, the defendants had agreed not to sell the plaintiffs' goods at prices less than those set out in the price list of the plaintiffs and not to sell to certain persons whom the plaintiffs did not desire to supply, and to pay £5 for each and every article sold in breach of the agreement "as and by way of liqui-dated damages and not as a penalty." It was held that the stipulation was to be construed as one for liquidated damages. . . .

The covenant in the present case covers a number of matters which would constitute breach of it. It provides that the defendant shall not "carry on or be engaged in or take part in or be in any way interested in the business of wholesale drygoods, etc." This, the main portion of the covenant, is further described by words preceding it: "directly or indirectly, either as principal or agent or as director or manager of a company, or as a servant in any capacity." There could be many breaches of this covenant, some of which would be very important, others of a less important and even trivial character. For instance, if the defendant had engaged as a clerk with some one carrying on a similar business, or if he purchased a small amount of stock in a similar business, it could scarcely be said that such action would cause serious damage to the plaintiffs, nor that it would constitute an important breach of the agreement; certainly it would seem "extravagant and unconscionable" that for either one of such breaches he should pay damages amounting to $10,000. On the other hand, if he ac-tually went into business in partnership with some one or carried on a com-peting business on his own account, or became manager of a company carrying on a similar business, or purchased a large interest in a similar concern carrying on business as a company and became a director of such company, such breach as would be of an important character and might conceivably cause serious damage to the plaintiffs. I think the law as laid down by Lord Watson in the *Elphinstone case, supra,* is applicable to the facts of this case, and that it must be held that the covenant provides a pen-alty which the Court will not enforce. The covenant provides for the pay-ment of a lump sum upon the occurrence of any one of a number of things differing in importance, and some of them trivial in character, and where a sum is stipulated to be paid as liquidated damages, and is payable not on the happening of a single event but of one or more of a number of events, some of which might result in inconsiderable damage, the Court may de-cline to construe the words "liquidated damages" according to their ordi-nary meaning and may treat such a sum as a penalty. Lord Dunedin, in the *Dunlop* case, [1915] A.C. at p. 89, considers that if there are various breaches to which an indiscriminate sum is applied, "then the strength of the chain must be taken to be its weakest link," and if it can be seen clearly that the loss in one particular breach could never amount to the sum stated then the conclusion that the sum is a penalty may be reached. I think this statement of the law is peculiarly applicable to the facts of the present case. . . .

PROBLEM. Draft a clause for Shatilla that would have achieved his object.

HOWE v. SMITH
England. Court of Appeal. 1884. 27 Ch.D. 89

FRY L.J.: . . . On the 24th of March, 1881, the Defendant and Plaintiff entered into an agreement in writing, by which the Defendant agreed to sell and the purchaser agreed to buy certain real estate for £12,500, of which £500 was in the contract stated to have been paid on the signing of the agreement as a deposit and in part payment of the purchase-money. The contract provided for the payment of the balance on the 24th of April,

1881, and it further provided by the 8th condition that if the purchaser should fail to comply with the agreement the vendor should be at liberty to resell the premises, and the deficiency on such second sale thereof, with all expenses attending the same, should be made good by the defaulter and be recoverable as liquidated damages.

The Plaintiff, the purchaser, did not pay the balance of his purchase-money on the day stipulated, and he has been guilty of such delay and neglect in completing that, according to our judgment already expressed, he has lost all right to the specific performance of the contract in equity.

The question then arises which has been argued before us, . . . whether or not the Plaintiff is entitled to recover the £500 paid on the signing of the contract.

The £500 was paid, in the words of the contract, as "a deposit and in part payment of the purchase-money." What is the meaning of this expression? The authorities seem to leave the matter in some doubt. . . .

These authorities appear to afford no certain light to answer the inquiry whether, in the absence of express stipulation, money paid as a deposit on the signing of a contract can be recovered by the payer if he has made such default in performance of his part as to have lost all right to performance by the other party to the contract or damages for his own non-performance.

Money paid as a deposit must, I conceive, be paid on some terms implied or expressed. In this case no terms are expressed, and we must therefore inquire what terms are to be implied. The terms most naturally to be implied appear to me in the case of money paid on the signing of a contract to be that in the event of the contract being performed it shall be brought into account, but if the contract is not performed by the payer it shall remain the property of the payee. It is not merely a part payment, but is then also an earnest to bind the bargain so entered into, and creates by the fear of its forfeiture a motive in the payer to perform the rest of the contract.

The practice of giving something to signify the conclusion of the contract, sometimes a sum of money, sometimes a ring or other object, to be repaid or redelivered on the completion of the contract, appears to be one of the great antiquity and very general prevalence. It may not be unimportant to observe as evidence of this antiquity that our own word "earnest" has been supposed to flow from a Phoenician source. . . .

Taking these early authorities into consideration, I think we may conclude that the deposit in the present case is the earnest or *arrha* of our earlier writers; that the expression used in the present contract that the money is paid "as a deposit and in part payment of the purchase-money," relates to the two alternatives, and declares that in the event of the purchaser making default the money is to be forfeited, and that in the event of the purchase being completed the sum is to be taken in part payment.

Such being my view of the nature of the deposit, it appears to me to be clear that the purchaser lost all right to recover it if he has lost both his right to specific performance in equity and his right to sue for damages for its non-performance at law. . . .

In a word, the purchaser has, in my opinion, been guilty of such delay, whether measured by the rules of law or equity, as deprives him of his right to specific performance, and of his right to maintain an action for damages—and under these circumstances I hold that the purchaser has no right to recover his deposit. . . .

[The opinions of Cotton and Bowen L.JJ. are omitted and that of Fry L.J. has been severely cut.]

STOCKLOSER v. JOHNSON
[1954] 1 Q.B. 476 (C.A.)

The plaintiff agreed to buy certain plant and machinery from the defendant. The price was payable in instalments, and the agreement provided that in case of default by the purchaser, the vendor was entitled (after giving notice) to retake possession of the machinery and to retain all payments made by the purchaser. The purchaser did default, and now claims the return of the instalments paid.

DENNING L.J.: There was acute contest as to the proper legal principles to apply in this case. On the one hand [counsel for the plaintiff] urged us to hold that the buyer was entitled to recover the instalments at law. He said that the forfeiture clause should be ignored as it was of a penal character; and once it was ignored it meant that the buyer was left with a simple right to repayment of his money . . . subject only to a cross-claim for damages. In asking us to ignore the forfeiture clause, [counsel for the plaintiff] relied on the familiar tests which are used to distinguish between penalties and liquidated damages . . . . There is, I think, a plain distinction between penalty cases, strictly so called, and cases like the present. It is this: when one party seeks to exact a penalty from the other, he is seeking to exact payment of an extravagant sum either by action at law or by appropriating to himself moneys belonging to [the other party]. The claimant invariably relies, like Shylock, on the letter of the contract to support his demand, but the courts decline to give him their aid because they will not assist him in an act of oppression. . . .

In the present case, however, the seller is not seeking to exact a penalty. He only wants to keep money which already belongs to him. The money was handed to him in part payment of the purchase price, and, as soon as it was paid, it belonged to him absolutely. He did not obtain it by extortion or oppression or anything of that sort, and there is an express clause—a forfeiture clause, if you please—permitting him to keep it. It is not the case of a seller seeking to enforce a penalty, but a buyer seeking restitution of money paid. If the buyer is to recover it, he must, I think, have recourse to somewhat different principles from those applicable to penalties, strictly so called.

On the other hand, [counsel for the defendant] urged us to hold that the buyer could only recover the money if he was able and willing to perform the contract, and for this purpose he ought to pay or offer to pay the instalments which were in arrears and be willing to pay the future instalments as they became due; . . . I think that this contention goes too far in the opposite direction. If the buyer was seeking to re-establish the contract, he would of course have to pay up the arrears and to show himself willing to perform the contract in the future, just as a lessee, who has suffered a forfeiture, has to do when he seeks to re-establish the lease. So also if the buyer were seeking specific performance he would have to show himself able and willing to perform his part. But the buyer's object here is not to re-establish the contract. It is to get his money back, and to do this I do not think that it is necessary to go so far as to show that he is ready and willing to perform the contract.

I reject, therefore, the arguments of counsel at each extreme. It seems to me that the cases show the law to be this: (1) *When there is no forfeiture clause.* If money is handed over in part payment of the purchase price, and then the buyer makes default as to the balance, then so long as the seller keeps the contract open and available for performance, the buyer cannot recover the money; but once the seller rescinds the contract or treats it as at an end owing to the buyer's default, then the buyer is entitled to recover his money by action at law subject to a cross-claim by the seller for damages: ... (2) *But when there is a forfeiture clause or the money is expressly paid as a deposit (which is equivalent to a forfeiture clause)*, then the buyer who is in default cannot recover the money at law at all. He may, however, have a remedy in equity, for, despite the express stipulation in the contract, equity can relieve the buyer from forfeiture of the money and order the seller to repay it on such terms as the court thinks fit. ...

The difficulty is to know what are the circumstances which give rise to this equity. ... Two things are necessary: first, the forfeiture clause must be of a penal nature, in this sense, that the sum forfeited must be out of all proportion to the damage, and, secondly, it must be unconscionable for the seller to retain the money. ...

In the course of the argument before us Somervell L.J. put an illustration which shows the necessity for this equity even though the buyer is not ready and willing to perform the contract. Suppose a buyer has agreed to buy a necklace by instalments, and the contract provides that, on default in payment of any one instalment, the seller is entitled to rescind the contract and forfeit the instalments already paid. The buyer pays 90 per cent of the price but fails to pay the last instalment. He is not able to perform the contract because he simply cannot find the money. The seller thereupon rescinds the contract and retakes the necklace and resells it at a higher price. Surely equity will relieve the buyer against forfeiture of the money on such terms as may be just.

Again, suppose that a vendor of property, in lieu of the usual 10 per cent deposit, stipulates for an initial payment of 50 per cent of the price as a deposit and part payment; and later, when the purchaser fails to complete, the vendor resells the property at a profit and in addition claims to forfeit the 50 per cent deposit. Surely the court will relieve against the forfeiture. The vendor cannot forestall this equity by describing an extravagant sum as a deposit, any more than he can recover a penalty by calling it liquidated damages. ...

[In the end, Denning L.J. concluded that in this particular case it was not unconscionable for the vendor to retain the money. Somervell and Romer L.JJ. agreed in the result, but Romer L.J. expressly dissented from Denning L.J.'s view of the power of the court to relieve against forfeiture. He thought that the powers of the court ought to be considerably narrower.]

GISVOLD v. *HILL*. 1963. 37 D.L.R. (2d) 606 (British Columbia. Supreme Court). The plaintiffs agreed to sell a house to the defendants and in a *standard form* of real estate contract acknowledged receipt of one dollar "being deposit on account of proposed purchase price" of $17,500. The balance of the purchase price was to be paid on closing. At that time the defendants failed to pay. Three months later the plaintiffs sold the house for $17,900 but the higher price actually netted a lower return to the plaintiffs since they had to pay a salesman's commission of $700 which meant that they received only $17,200, a loss of $300. The court would have allowed the $300 as damages but for a clause in the agreement which provided, "It is understood that time shall be of the essence hereof, and unless the balance of the cash payment is paid and a formal agreement entered into within the time mentioned to pay the balance, the owner may (at his option) cancel this agreement, and in such event the amount paid by the purchaser shall be absolutely forfeited to the owner as liquidated damages." Held, the one dollar deposit was liquidated damages fixed "in advance of the breach and the plaintiffs are bound thereby regardless of the actual damage." AIKINS J.: ". . . Regardless of whether or not in appropriate circumstances a sum of money stated to be liquidated damages and which is disproportionately small in relation to the probable loss may be regarded as a penalty, and relief given to the party to whom the sum is to be paid by allowing him to recover his actual loss, and I do not purport to decide this question, the circumstances of the present case are not in my opinion such as to justify any such relief being given. In the present case the parties entered into a binding agreement to sell and purchase. The parties agreed to a deposit of one dollar. It was stipulated that time should be of the essence. The plaintiffs and the defendants agreed that if the defendants did not make the payment they agreed to make on the agreed date then the plaintiffs would have the right to cancel the agreement and in such event that the deposit would be forfeited as liquidated damages. The Interim Agreement was dated the 16th of March and the cash payment of the balance was to be made on the 25th day of the same month. This is a comparatively short period, nine days only, and I cannot conceive that the parties, if they had directed their minds consciously to the question of what loss the plaintiffs might suffer if the purchase price was not paid at the end of the nine day period, would have come to the conclusion that the value of the house would fluctuate in any substantial amount over such a short time, and that there might be substantial damages. In these circumstances, on the plaintiffs exercising their right, given to them by the agreement, of electing to cancel and retain the house and forfeit the deposit, I do not think it can be said that the forfeiture of the deposit of $1.00 as liquidated damages is unreasonable. It is also an important circumstance of this case that the plaintiffs on default by the defendants were not left in the position that the only thing they could do was forfeit the one dollar deposit. The plaintiffs had an election, they did not have to accept the one dollar, they could, if they had seen fit to do so, have sued to enforce the agreement. In these circumstances the plaintiffs must be held to their bargain. The plaintiffs' action is accordingly dismissed with costs."

[The full report indicates that the plaintiffs signed the standard form in the space for the signature of the vendor's agent and they may not have fully understood the nature of the document they were signing.]

3. CLAUSES EXCLUDING LIABILITY

Many of the cases in previous chapters have been concerned with clauses designed to exclude or limit the liability of one party. Such clauses, variously called excluding, exclusion, exclusionary, exempting, exemption, exception and disclaimer clauses are particularly common in standard form contracts, and particularly where one party has superior bargaining power. Dean Havighurst, in *The Nature of Private Contract*, has described the thought that lies behind the insertion of such clauses. He wrote: "A business that deals with many customers or suppliers or employees or holders of dealer franchises or tenants does not ordinarily find it feasible to conduct a thorough investigation in each case of character and emotional stability. Furthermore, if the dealing is expected to extend over a long period, character and emotional stability, unexceptionable at the time, may later suffer deterioration. It is far simpler to require adhesion to a contract that commits the business legally to a performance far less than it expects to render, to hedge promises about with conditions that it does not expect to insist upon, unless the other party proves to be evil or unstable. If carefully prepared, the contract, supplemented by verbal assurances, may yield the advantage of raising the expectations necessary to induce the desired performance and at the same time insulate against legal liability.

Such a course cannot always be characterized as sharp dealing. These are not harsh terms imposed in every instance by reason of superior bargaining power. The business may be quite competitive. But informed, intelligent and well-balanced people are not as a rule too much concerned about the extent of the legal pressure available in the event of dispute. In deciding with whom they will deal they are apt to take more account of the attractiveness of other terms and of the company's reputation for fair dealing.

For the business enterprise, then, good judgment prompts elimination, as far as possible, of the legal hazard. If a few are constrained to deal elsewhere because the proposition is not attractive from a legal standpoint, they are probably the litigious-minded people and their loss is good riddance.

I have several wealthy neighbours who apparently are obsessed with worry about burglars. They have great iron fences surrounding their properties and fierce dogs. When the fierce dogs bark behind the iron fences, the evil person bent upon intrusion tends to be dissuaded. For the business enterprise, possessed of assets and obsessed with worry about evil litigants, the contract of adhesion is a great iron fence. The business may not have fierce dogs, but it has lawyers— lawyers who keep the fences in repair and lawyers who make appropriate noises when prospective litigants approach. The evil person bent upon a lawsuit tends to be dissuaded.

However, as you readily see, there is here a problem. The iron fence that excludes the bad man also excludes the good. And a man who sincerely believes that his claim is just may sometimes be regarded by the enterpriser as evil. The contract of adhesion, though conceived in a worthy cause, has the effect of depriving every adherent of a day in court.

The question is: To what extent is this deprivation of public concern?"

CANADIAN-DOMINION LEASING CORP. LTD. v. SUBURBAN SUPERDRUG LTD.
(1966) 56 D.L.R. (2d) 43 (Alta. App. Div.)

The judgment of the Court was delivered by KANE J.A.: This is an appeal from the judgment of Gardiner D.C.J., dismissing with costs the appellant's claim for arrears of rent under an agreement in writing dated November 23, 1962, whereby the appellant leased a Berg Selector to the respondent for a term of 5 years in consideration of the respondent agreeing to pay rent of $48.99 every 3 months during the term; and for interest on the arrears.

The appellant is engaged in the business of leasing commercial and industrial equipment to commercial and industrial stores. The respondent carries on a general drug-store business at Edmonton.

In November, 1962, and it would appear on the 7th of that month, one Nye, a representative of W. H. Galaugher & Associates Ltd., called upon Sam Hardin, the president of the respondent. He wished to interest Hardin in a Berg Selector unit. Mr. Hardin stated he would like to see the selector in operation and Nye had one outside Hardin's store in his parked automobile. He brought the selector into the store and demonstrated it to Hardin.

This unit is a motion type showcase designed for the display for sale of small items of jewellery and small giftware. It works on a chain driven motor operated arrangement on an automatic principle with a series of trays revolving. The automatic principle of it is that it revolves, stops each 10 seconds, then runs again for a few seconds and stops again, and so on, so each tray in turn becomes visible through a window to a prospective customer as he stands in front of the machine. Mr. Hardin stated that "The idea is a gimmick type idea" to attract attention and present the largest amount of this type of merchandise in the smallest amount of floor space. The unit is 30 ins. in width.

Mr. Hardin testified he leased the selector because it opened a new avenue of sales, that he was particularly struck with the motion of the selector and the small amount of floor space it required.

Following the demonstration on November 7th, the respondent signed certain documents which Nye had with him to the knowledge and consent of the appellant.

Under one of these, the respondent requested the appellant to purchase from the Galaugher company one Berg Selector and agreed upon acceptance of this request by the appellant to lease the selector from the appellant. Under another such document the respondent as lessee executed a lease of the selector from the appellant as lessor. The lease was for a term of 5 years on a monthly rental of $16.33. The respondent delivered to Nye four cheques, each payable to the appellant in the amount of $48.99 dated respectively November 7, 1962, February 7th, May 7th and August 7th, 1963, covering the first year's rental. The selector was then left with the respondent on November 7th.

The lease I have referred to is a one sheet document. On the front under the heading "Terms and Conditions of Lease" appear paragraphs numbered 1 to 4. Under para. 4 appear the following words: "See reverse side for additional terms and conditions which are part of this lease." Under those words appear the further sentence, "The undersigned agree to all the terms and conditions set forth above *and on the reverse side hereof*, and in witness thereof hereby execute this lease."

The documents bear date as to execution by the respondent of November 7, 1962, and of execution by the appellant, November 23, 1962. Such execution was made at the bottom of the front of the sheet. On the reverse side of this sheet there are printed cls. 5 to 24 inclusive.

About 5 or 6 days after November 7th, the motor stopped running and accordingly the selector stopped operating automatically. The respondent was able to operate the selector manually for a few days; then it stopped working completely. The respondent wrote the Galaugher company immediately. It did not communicate with the appellant. The Galaugher company sent an electrical contractor, Mr. Souch, who replaced the motor with another at no cost to the respondent. The unit then operated for about 2 or 3 weeks: then it broke down. Mr. Hardin was not sure whether after the second breakdown Mr. Souch, whom he called, replaced or fixed the motor. He thought it was replaced. In any event, whether it was replaced or repaired, the selector then operated for about 3 or 4 weeks when it broke down again. Hardin then had the selector put in the basement of the store. He testified that he wrote to the Galaugher company, told it that he could not make the selector operate and informed it that Mr. Souch was of the opinion the motor was not suitable for the job. He further stated that he asked the Galaugher company to remove it or to let him know where he could send it. He testified that the selector worked "really good" for about 6 weeks altogether, but when it did not operate it was a detriment in that it took up 30 ins. of floor space, serving no other purpose than a counter top.

The four cheques above mentioned were duly paid although the selector only operated for a very short time. The respondent refused to pay any further amounts. The appellant then commenced this action claiming $783.84 as balance of rental and interest at the rate of 2% per month on unpaid rentals. The trial Judge found that the selector was far from being reasonably fit and suitable for the purpose for which it was intended and that in fact it had to be completely discarded by the respondent. He dismissed the appellant's action and directed that after payment of the amount owing to the respondent under the judgment (this would be the taxed costs), the appellant might have the selector.

The appellant contends there was no evidence before the trial Judge from which he could reasonably find that the selector was not reasonably fit and suitable for its purposes.

It was also contended on behalf of the appellant that the trial Judge was in error in holding there was an implied warranty that the selector was reasonably fit for the purpose for which it was hired because,

(a) this implied warranty was never intended to apply to a person in the position of the respondent; it not being an owner in possession of the selector;

(b) the appellant was not in the position of an owner in possession but relied on the respondent's selection of the chattel to be hired.

The appellant refers to para. 2 of the lease which reads as follows:

"2. SELECTION OF EQUIPMENT. Lessee has requested the equipment of the type and quantity specified above and has selected the supplier named above. Lessor agrees to order such equipment from said supplier but shall not be liable for performance of this lease or damages if for any reason the supplier delays or fails to fill the order. Lessee shall accept such equipment if delivered in good repair and hereby authorizes lessor to insert the serial numbers of each item of equipment so delivered. Any delay in delivery shall not affect the validity of this lease."

(c) The respondent should not be permitted to raise defects in the selector at this time.

The appellant refers to para. 12 of the lease which reads as follows:

"12. NOTICE OF DEFECTS: Unless lessee gives lessor written notice of each defect or other proper objection to an item of equipment within five (5) business days after receipt thereof it shall be conclusively presumed as between lessee and lessor that the item of equipment was delivered in good repair and that lessee accepts it as an item of equipment described in this lease."

(d) The combined effect of paras. 12 and 18 of the lease are sufficient to exclude the implied warranty.

Paragraph 12 has been set out above. Paragraph 18 reads as follows: "18. ENTIRE AGREEMENT. This instrument constitutes the entire agreement between lessor and lessee. No agent or employee of the supplier is authorized to bind lessor to this lease, to waive or alter any term or condition printed herein or add any provision hereto. Except as provided in paragraph 3 hereof a provision may be added hereto or a provision hereof may be altered or varied only by a writing signed and made part hereof by an authorized officer of lessor. Waiver by lessor of any provision hereof in one instance shall not constitute a waiver as to any other instance."

(e) The effect of para. 4 of the lease is sufficient in itself to exclude an implied warranty.

Paragraph 4 reads as follows:

"4. WARRANTIES. Lessor makes no representations or warranty (express, implied, statutory or otherwise) as to any matter whatsoever, including without limitation, the condition of the equipment, its merchantability or its fitness for any particular purpose. Lessor agrees that to the extent permitted by law any representation or warranty by the manufacturer or supplier of the equipment is for the benefit of both lessee and lessor and may be enforced jointly or separately."

In my view, the appellant in the circumstances of this case cannot rely on the exemption clauses in the lease.

The respondent was entitled to receive a selector capable of self-propulsion for, at the very least, a reasonable time. What it received was a selector which within a matter of just a few days ceased to operate by self-propulsion because the motor was defective. When that motor was replaced the selector operated for only another short period. When the second motor was either replaced or repaired, the selector operated for another very short period of time. After this third breakdown, the selector was put into the basement of the respondent's store. It was of no use to the respondent for the purposes for which he had agreed to rent it.

Karsales (Harrow), Ltd. v. *Wallis,* [1956] 2 All E.R. 866, was a case in which the defendant had inspected a Buick automobile, found it to be in good condition, and entered into a hire-purchase agreement. The car was left by the seller outside the defendant's garage at night. When the defendant inspected it the following morning, he found it to be in deplorable condition and incapable of self-propulsion. It was held by the Court of Appeal that the car delivered was not the car contracted to be taken and that there was a fundamental breach of contract which disentitled the plaintiff from relying on the exception clause in the contract, which clause read as follows:

"3(g) No condition or warranty that the vehicle is roadworthy or as to its age, condition or fitness for any purpose is given by the owner or implied herein."

In the *Karsales* case, Denning L.J. (now Lord Denning), said (at pp. 868-69):

"The law about exempting clauses, however, has been much developed in recent years, at any rate about printed exempting clauses, which so often pass unread. Notwithstanding earlier cases which might suggest the contrary, it is now settled that exempting clauses of this kind, no matter how widely they are expressed, only avail the party when he is carrying out his contract in its essential respects. He is not allowed to use them as a cover for misconduct or indifference or to enable him to turn a blind eye to his obligations. They do not avail him when he is guilty of a breach which goes to the root of the contract. It is necessary to look at the contract apart from the exempting clauses and see what are the terms, express or implied, which impose an obligation on the party. If he has been guilty of a breach of those obligations in a respect which goes to the very root of the contract, he cannot rely on the exempting clauses."

In the same case Parker L.J. (now Lord Chief Justice), said (at p. 871):

"Accordingly, Mutual Finance, Ltd., and their assignees, the plaintiffs, said (in effect) that it does not matter what is delivered so long as it bears the appellation of a "Buick" car as described in the agreement, and that the hirer is bound to take it. In my judgment, however extensive the exception clause may be, it has no application if there has been a breach of a fundamental term."

Parker L.J., further stated (at p. 871): "Applying that to the facts of this case, it seems to me that the vehicle delivered in effect is not properly described (as the agreement describes it) as a motor vehicle, "Buick", giving the chassis and engine number. By that I am not saying that every defect in a car which renders it for the moment unusable on the road amounts to a breach of a fundamental term; but where, as here, a vehicle is delivered incapable of self-propulsion except after a complete overhaul and in the condition referred to by my Lord, it seems to me that it is abundantly clear that there was a breach of a fundamental term and that accordingly the exceptions in cl. 3(g) do not apply."

In *Astley Industrial Trust, Ltd.* v. *Grimley*, [1963] 2 All E.R. 33, it was held that a finance company which had let on hire-purchase a Bedford tipper, was in the circumstances under an obligation as to the fitness of the tipping lorry, such obligation being that it was a lorry of the make specified, and a tipper, and a motor vehicle capable of self-propulsion along a road and of receiving and carrying materials. It was also held that no breach of the fundamental terms and implied conditions had been proved. The contract under consideration contained a provision as follows:

"3. The hirer's acceptance of delivery of the vehicle shall be conclusive that he has examined the vehicle and found the same to be complete and in good order and condition and in every way satisfactory to him. Except where it is implied by the Hire-Purchase Acts, 1938 and 1954 the [finance company] give no warranty as to the state or quality of the vehicle, and, save as aforesaid, any warranty as to description, repair, quality or fitness for any purpose is hereby excluded."

In his judgment Pearson L.J. (now Lord Pearson), said (p. 44): "In my view the finance company are not entitled to say that they had no obligation at all under the agreement as to the fitness of the vehicle for the first defendant's purpose. They were letting on hire to him a Bedford tipper, and it had to be a Bedford tipper, i.e. a lorry of that make, and a tipper. It had to be an automobile, capable of self-propulsion along a road, and it had to be capable of receiving and carrying and tipping loads of materials. The condition or fundamental term is to be implied in this case, as it was in the *Karsales* case and in the *Apps* case [*Yeoman Credit Ltd.* v. *Apps*, [1961] 2 All E.R. 281]."

In the same case Upjohn L.J., who agreed with the judgment of Pearson L.J., said, speaking of implied conditions, warranties or stipulations relating to hiring, whether simple hire or hire-purchase (at p. 46): "First, there is an implied stipulation that the vehicle hired corresponds with the description of the vehicle contracted to be hired, or to put it in another way, the lender must lend that which he contracts to lend and not something which is essentially different. Thus, as my Lord has pointed out, a tipping lorry plainly hired for use as such must be capable of self-propulsion to a reasonable degree and must have a rear compartment capable of being mechanically tipped.

This implied stipulation is a fundamental implied term and breach of it at once gives the hirer the right, if he desires to do so, to treat the contract as repudiated. Furthermore, being a fundamental term the lender cannot by clauses of exclusion or exception, however widely phrased, exclude liability for this fundamental term for the simple reason that the law will not permit one of the contracting parties to escape liability for failure to deliver that which he has contracted to lend by delivery of something which is essentially different. The question whether or not the motor vehicle delivered complies with this fundamental obligation of the lender is very largely a question of fact and degree and must depend on the circumstances of each case."

A very helpful article appears in Cheshire and Fifoot, *Law of Contract*, 6th ed. In the introductory paragraph of that article at pp. 116-17 the authors state: "In a number of cases, now extending over many years, judges have ruled from time to time that no exempting clause, however wide, may protect a party who has broken the basic duties created by the very nature and character of the contract. A variety of language has been used to describe this over-riding consideration. The words "fundamental term" are, perhaps, most often on judicial lips. But this phrase, in so far as it suggests that the courts are only adding a further term to those already expressed or implied in the contract, is misleading. The essential assumption is that the party at fault has done more than break a term of the contract, however important this may be: he has failed to satisfy the very purpose for which the contract was designed and he may no longer rely on one of its component parts. If this were not the essence of the doctrine, it could not be used, as it is, to cancel an exemption clause in whatever language it may be drafted. A more appropriate title, it is therefore suggested, is 'the doctrine of the fundamental obligation.' "

With respect, I agree with Bastin J. (*Schmidt* v. *International Harvester Co. of Canada Ltd.* (1962), 38 W.W.R. 180 at p. 183), when he said that to invoke the principle of the *Karsales* case there must be proved a breach of contract of a flagrant nature.

The respondent by its pleadings did not allege a breach going to the root of the contract unless para. 6 which reads as follows: "6. The defendant denies that it has failed to pay any monies legally owing for rental of a Berg Selector or otherwise," can be treated as such an allegation.

However, the issue was in fact fought out even though not pleaded and, as pointed out by O'Connor C.J.A., delivering the judgment of the Court in *McPhail and McPhail* v. *Richards and Pitcairn* (1953), 12 W.W.R. (N.S.) 433 at p. 437, generally speaking, the practice now is that the pleadings may be taken as amended to follow the course of the trial. Reference may also be made to *Jones & Lyttle, Ltd.* v. *Mackie,* [1917] 3 W.W.R. 1021 (reversed on other grounds in the Supreme Court of Canada, 52 D.L.R. 685, 59 S.C.R. 668, [1918] 2 W.W.R. 82); *Berge* v. *Grew* [1928] 1 D.L.R. 361 at pp. 364-5, 23 A.L.R. 281 [1927] 3 W.W.R. 811.

In the present case in my view the appellant cannot rely on the exemption clauses in the lease.

The respondent was entitled to receive under the lease agreement a selector capable of self-propulsion for at least a reasonable period of time. This he did not receive.

In the circumstances there was such a breach of the fundamental obligation as to disentitle the appellant to succeed in its claim.

I would dismiss the appeal with costs.

[Appeal dismissed; judgment for defendant.]

SUISSE ATLANTIQUE SOCIETE D'ARMEMENT MARITIME S.A. v. N.V. ROTTERDAMSCHE KOLEN CENTRALE
[1966] 2 All E.R. 69 (H.L.)

LORD REID: My Lords, I am satisfied that, for the reasons given by your lordships, the appeal could not succeed on any of the grounds submitted to the Court of Appeal and to your lordships at the first hearing of this appeal. But at the end of his opening address, counsel for the appellants put forward a new contention based on there having been a fundamental breach of contract by the respondents. Normally this House would not permit a new question of that character to be argued; but this is a Consultative Case Stated by arbitrators, and the appellants could still raise such a new question before the arbitrators. So, in order to avoid delay and expense, your lordships adjourned the hearing on terms as to costs and ordered the parties to lodge supplementary cases dealing with this new contention. I only intend to deal with the new question argued at the second hearing.

The case arises out of a charterparty for two years' consecutive voyages made on Dec. 21, 1956, between the appellants, the owners, and the respondents, the charterers. After a dispute, the parties made a further agreement on Oct. 8, 1957, to perform the charterparty for the remainder of the two year period. The purpose of the charterparty was that, on each voyage, the vessel should proceed in ballast to an Atlantic port in the United States and there load coal to be carried to a port in the Netherlands. During this remaining part of the two years the vessel made only eight voyages and she spent some 380 days in ports of loading or discharge. There was provision for payment of demurrage with wide exceptions of causes of delay beyond the control of the charterer; but the respondents have admitted liability to pay demurrage for some 150 days. The complaint of the appellants is that, by reason of the failure of the respondents to perform their contractual obligations to load and discharge within the lay days, the appellants have been deprived of the freight which would have been earned on the additional voyages which would have been performed had there not been this delay for which the respondents are responsible. They claim that six or nine more voyages would have been performed within the period if the respondents had fulfilled their obligations, and they estimate their loss from that cause at $875,000, or alternatively $580,000. The respondents' answer is that the appellants are only entitled to demurrage at the agreed rate of $1,000 per day and they have paid some $150,000 as demurrage.

The new contention submitted by the appellants is that the breaches of contract which caused these delays amounted to fundamental breach or breach going to the root of the contract, so that, at some time during the currency of the agreement, the appellants would have been entitled to treat the breaches as a repudiation, to terminate or rescind the contract and to claim damages at common law. It is, I think, clear that, if they did have that right, they must be held to have elected not to treat the breaches as repudiatory; but they argue that, nevertheless, the fact that there was a fundamental breach prevents the respondents from relying on the demurrage clause as limiting their responsibility. So the first question must be whether these delays can be regarded as involving fundamental breach. If so, it is for the arbitrators, at least in the first instance, to decide whether there was fundamental breach. The respondents deny that these breaches are capable of being regarded as amounting to fundamental breach. General use of the term "fundamental breach" is of recent origin, and I can find nothing to indicate that it means either more or less than the well known type of breach which entitles the innocent party to treat it as repudiatory and to rescind the contract. The appellants allege that the respondents caused these delays deliberately (i.e., with the wilful intention of limiting the number of contractual voyages). They do not allege fraud or bad faith. This allegation would appear to cover a case where the charterers decided that it would pay them better to delay loading and discharge and pay the resulting demurrage at the relatively low agreed rate, rather than load and discharge more speedily and then have to buy more coal and pay the relatively high agreed freight on the additional voyages which would then be possible. If facts of that kind could be proved, I think that it would be open to the arbitrators to find that the respondents had committed a fundamental or repudiatory breach. One way of looking at the matter would be to ask whether the party in breach has by his breach produced a situation fundamentally different from anything which the parties could as reasonable men have contemplated when the contract was made. Then one would have to ask not only what had already happened but also what was likely to happen in future. And there the fact that the breach was deliberate might be of great importance.

If fundamental breach is established, the next question is what effect, if any, that has on the applicability of other terms of the contract. This question has often arisen with regard to clauses excluding liability, in whole or in part, of the party in breach. I do not think that there is generally much difficulty where the innocent party has elected to treat the breach as a repudiation, bring the contract to an end and sue for damages. Then the whole contract has ceased to exist, including the exclusion clause, and I do not see how that clause can then be used to exclude an action for loss which will be suffered by the innocent party after it has ceased to exist, such as loss of the profit which would have accrued if the contract had run its full term. But that is not the situation in the present case, where, in my view, the appellants elected that the contract should continue in force. Where the contract has been affirmed by the innocent party, at first sight the position is simple. You must either affirm the whole contract or rescind the whole contract; you cannot approbate and reprobate by affirming part of it and disaffirming the rest—that would be making a new contract. So the clause excluding liability must continue to apply. But that is too simple, and there is authority for two quite different ways of holding that, in spite of affirmation of the contract as a whole by the innocent party, the guilty party may not be entitled to rely on a clause in it. One way depends on construction of the clause. The other way depends on the existence of a rule of substantive law.

As a matter of construction, it may appear that the terms of the exclusion clause are not wide enough to cover the kind of breach which has been committed. Such clauses must be construed strictly and, if ambiguous, the narrower meaning will be taken. Or it may appear that the terms of the clause are so wide that they cannot be applied literally; that may be because this would lead to an absurdity, or because it would defeat the main object of the contract or perhaps for other reasons. And where some limit must be read into the clause, it is generally reasonable to draw the line at fundamental breaches. There is no reason why a contract should not make a provision for events which the parties do not have in contemplation or even which are unforeseeable, if sufficiently clear words are used; but if some limitation has to be read in, it seems reasonable to suppose that neither party had in contemplation a breach which goes to the root of the contract. Then the true analysis seems to me to be that the whole contract, including the clause excluding liability, does survive after election to affirm it, but that that does not avail the party in breach. The exclusion clause does not change its meaning; as a matter of construction it never did apply and does not after election apply to this type of breach, and, therefore, is no answer to an action brought in respect of this type of breach. But applying a strict construction to these clauses is not sufficient to exclude them in all cases of fundamental breach. It cannot be said as a matter of law that the resources of the English language are so limited that it is impossible to devise an exclusion clause which will apply to at least some cases of fundamental breach without being so widely drawn that it can be cut down on any ground by applying ordinary principles of construction. So, if there is to be a universal rule that, no matter how the exclusion clause is expressed, it will not apply to protect a party in fundamental breach, any such rule must be a substantive rule of law nullifying any agreement to the contrary and to that extent restricting the general principle of English law that parties are free to contract as they may see fit.

There is recent authority for the existence of such a rule of law, but I cannot find support for it in the older authorities. Most of them arose out of deviation from the contractual voyage or similar breaches of contracts of carriage by land. Any deviation has always been regarded as a breach going to the root of the contract, and it was held in these earlier cases that, if the consignor's goods were lost after there had been a deviation, the shipowner could not rely on clauses excluding or limiting his liability. The reasons given for this varied, but I do not think that it is useful now to examine them in detail because it was made clear in the speeches in this House in *Hain S.S. Co. Ltd.* v. *Tate & Lyle, Ltd.* [1936] 2 All E.R. 597 that there is no special rule applicable to deviation cases; the ordinary principles of the law of contract must be applied. The special feature of these cases is that the consignor's goods were lost before he knew of the deviation and, therefore, before he had any opportunity to elect whether or not to treat it as bringing the contract to an end. When he learns of the deviation and of the subsequent loss of his goods, there is hardly room for any election, but the fact that he sues for their value could be treated as an election to terminate the contract by reason of and immediately after the deviation. Among the reasons given in the earlier cases I do not find any reliance on any rule of law that a party guilty of a breach going to the root of the contract can never rely on clauses excluding his liability. And I do not think that the decision in *Tate & Lyle's* case assists us. There, the owners of the goods had known of the deviation and had elected to waive it before the goods were lost. The breach was not a continuing breach and it did not cause the loss of the goods. In this case, the breach, if it was a fundamental breach, was a continuing breach and it did cause the loss of which the appellants complain.

I think that *Smeaton Hanscomb & Co., Ltd.* v. *Sassoon I. Setty, Son & Co. (No. 1)* [1953] 2 All E.R. 1471 can be regarded as the first of the series of recent cases dealing with fundamental breach. There the question was whether a claim by the buyer was barred by a clause in the contract "Any claim must be made within fourteen days from the final discharge of the goods . . ." Devlin J., said: "It is, no doubt, a principle of construction that exceptions are to be construed as not being applicable for the protection of those for whose benefit they are inserted if the beneficiary has committed a breach of a fundamental term of the contract, and that a clause requiring the claim to be brought within a specified period is to be regarded as an exception for this purpose. . .I do not think that what is a fundamental term has ever been closely defined. It must be something, I think, narrower than a condition of the contract, for it would be limiting the exceptions too much to say that they applied only to breaches of warranty. It is, I think, something which underlies the whole contract so that, if it is not complied with, the performance becomes something totally different from that which the contract contemplates."

It is true that Devlin J., says that he is applying a principle of construction, but I think that he is really applying a substantive rule of law. He does not reach his conclusion by construing the clause in its context; there is no statement of any reason why the apparently general terms of this particular clause must be cut down or limited so as to make it only applicable to claims in respect of breaches which do not go to the root of the contract or which are not breaches of fundamental terms. And it does not appear to me to be obvious that some canon of construction would require a limitation of the apparently general terms of this clause.

The next case is *Karsales (Harrow), Ltd.* v. *Wallis* [1956] 2 All E.R. 866. There the contract provided that "No condition or warranty that the vehicle is roadworthy or as to its age, condition or fitness for any purpose is given by the owner or implied herein."

Denning L.J., said: "Notwithstanding earlier cases which might suggest the contrary, it is now settled that exemption clauses of this kind, no matter how widely they are expressed, only avail the party when he is carrying out his contract in its essential respects. He is not allowed to use them as a cover for misconduct or indifference or to enable him to turn a blind eye to his obligations. They do not avail him when he is guilty of a breach which goes to the root of the contract."

And Parker L.J., said "In my judgment, however extensive the exception clause may be, it has no application if there has been a breach of a fundamental term."

This is a clear statement of a rule of law. If it is right, it would be irrelevant that, on its true construction, an exempting clause must be held to be intended to apply to the breach in question, and that it is not so wide in its terms that as a matter of construction in its context its applicability must be limited. It must mean that the law does not permit contracting out of common law liability for a fundamental breach. I think that I should go on to examine the rest of the series of recent cases, but, under the present practice of the Court of Appeal with regard to the binding character of any of its own decisions, it was hardly to be expected that this statement of the law would not be followed. I should add that I cannot deduce from the authorities cited in *Karsales (Harrow), Ltd.* v. *Wallis* that the proposition stated in the judgments could be regarded as in any way settled law. . . .

In *U.G.S. Finance, Ltd.* v. *National Mortgage Bank of Greece and National Bank of Greece, S.A.* (1964) 1 Lloyd's Rep. 446, the question related to a condition to the effect that interest coupons were forfeited if not presented within six years. Lord Denning, M.R., repeated in substance what he had said in *Karsales (Harrow), Ltd.* v. *Wallis*, and added:

"The doctrine does not depend on the customer electing to disaffirm the contract. Usually he has no option open to him. The contract has been broken irretrievably before he gets to know of it, and the only course for him is to sue for the breach. So the point does not very often arise. But even if he does get to know of it, in time to affirm or disaffirm, he can still treat the contract as in being, and sue for the breach (without being defeated by the exemption clause) provided always that the breach itself is continuing to operate and cause damage to him."

A different view was expressed by Pearson L.J.: "As to the question of 'fundamental breach', I think there is a rule of construction that normally an exception or exclusion clause or similar provision in a contract should be construed as not applying to a situation created by a fundamental breach of the contract. This is not an independent rule of law imposed by the court on the parties willy-nilly in disregard of their contractual intention. On the contrary it is a rule of construction based on the presumed intention of the contracting parties. It involves the implication of a term to give to the contract that business efficacy which the parties as reasonable men must have intended it to have. This rule of construction is not new in principle but it has become prominent in recent years in consequence of the tendency to have standard forms of contract containing exceptions clauses drawn in extravagantly wide terms, which would produce absurd results if applied literally."

If this new rule of law is to be adopted, how far does it go? In its simplest form it would be that a party is not permitted to contract out of common law liability for a fundamental breach. If that were right, then a demurrage clause could not stand as limiting liability for loss resulting from a fundamental breach; and the same would apply to any clause providing for liquidated damages. I do not suppose that anyone has intended that this rule should go quite so far as that; but I would find it difficult to say just where the line would have to be drawn. In my view, no such rule of law ought to be adopted. I do not take that view merely because any such rule is new or because it goes beyond what can be done by developing or adapting existing principles. Courts have often introduced new rules when, in their view, they were required by public policy. In former times, when Parliament seldom amended the common law, that could hardly have been avoided. There are recent examples although, for reasons which I gave in *Shaw* v. *Director of Public Prosecutions* [1962] A.C. 220 I think that this power ought now to be used sparingly. But my main reason is that this rule would not be a satisfactory solution of the problem which undoubtedly exists.

Exemption clauses differ greatly in many respects. Probably the most objectionable are found in the complex standard conditions which are now so common. In the ordinary way the customer has no time to read them, and, if he did read them, he would probably not understand them. If he did understand and object to any of them, he would generally be told that he could take it or leave it. If he then went to another supplier, the result would be the same. Freedom to contract must surely imply some choice or room for bargaining. At the other extreme is the case where parties are bargaining on terms of equality and a stringent exemption clause is accepted for a quid pro quo or other good reason; but this rule appears to treat all cases alike. There is no indication in the recent cases that the courts are to consider whether the exemption is fair in all the circumstances or is harsh and unconscionable, or whether it was freely agreed by the customer. It does not seem to me to be satisfactory that the decision must always go one way if, e.g., defects in a car or other goods are just sufficient to make the breach of contract a fundamental breach, but must always go the other way if the defects fall just short of that. This is a complex problem which intimately affects millions of people, and it appears to me that its solution should be left to Parliament. If your lordships reject this new rule, there will certainly be a need for urgent legislative action but that is not beyond reasonable expectation.

I have no doubt that exemption clauses should be construed strictly, and I think that this case must be decided by considering whether there is any ground for adopting any but the natural meaning of the demurrage clause. Having provided for the calculation of the laydays and for extension of the laydays when delays are caused by various events for which the charterer is not responsible, cl. 3 of the charterparty continues:

"If longer detained, charterer to pay $1,000 U.S. currency payable in the same manner as the freight per running day (or pro rata for part thereof) demurrage. If sooner dispatched, vessel to pay charterer or his agents $500 U.S. currency per day (or pro rata for part thereof) dispatch money for lay time saved."

It is impossible to hold that these words are not wide enough to apply to the circumstances of the present case, whether or not there was fundamental breach. So the only question is whether there is any reason for limiting their scope. The authorities are against the appellants, but, even putting them aside, I can find no such reason. The appellants chose to agree to what they now say was an inadequate sum for demurrage, but that does not appear to me to affect the construction of this clause. Even if one assumes that the $1,000 per day was inadequate and was known to both parties to be inadequate when the contract was made, I do not think that it can be said that giving to the clause its natural meaning could lead to an absurdity or could defeat the main object of the contract or could for any other reason justify cutting down its scope. If there was a fundamental breach, the appellants elected that the contract should continue, and they did so in the knowledge that this clause would continue. On the whole matter I am of opinion that this appeal fails.

[The other Law Lords agreed in dismissing the appeal.]

NOTE. The doctrine of fundamental breach seems to have survived the *Suisse Atlantique* case. In *Harbutt's Plasticine Ltd.* v. *Wayne Tank and Pump Co. Ltd.* [1970] 1 All E.R. 225 the defendants supplied pipe for use in the plaintiff's factory. The pipe was quite unsuitable for the purpose, and, as a result, a fire occurred which destroyed the plaintiff's factory. The plaintiffs brought an action for this loss, and the defendants sought to rely on a clause excluding liability for such loss. The Court of Appeal (Lord Denning M.R., Widgery and Cross L.JJ.) held that the exemption clause was ineffective because the defendants had committed a fundamental breach of the contract. Lord Denning said that where a fundamental breach "puts an end" to the contract (as he held that the breach did in this case) it follows that the party in breach cannot rely on the exemption clause. According to Lord Denning, only where the fundamental breach is of such a nature as to leave the contract open to be performed, and, in addition, the innocent party elects to affirm the contract, does it become a matter of construction whether or not the exemption clause applies in the particular circumstances. One may ask how the result in *Harbutt's Plasticine* fits with Lord Reid's criteria of freedom and fairness. One may ask too about the effect of the decision on insurance practices; though the action was brought in the plaintiffs' name, the party really interested in the success of the action was the plaintiffs' insurer. The defendants may or may not have been insured against the liability imposed on them.

Lord Denning indicates that only in rather narrow circumstances does it become a question of construction whether the exemption clause applies, and the tenor of his judgment suggests that he would not incline in construing such clauses to favour the party seeking to rely on them. The line between a rule of construction and a rule of law can be a narrow one, as Lord Reid said, and as is suggested by some of the Canadian cases decided after *Suisse Atlantique*, despite the Supreme Court of Canada's approval of that case in *B.G. Linton Construction Ltd.* v. *Canadian National Railway Co.* (1974) 49 D.L.R. (3d) 548.

R. G. McLEAN LTD. v. CANADIAN VICKERS LTD.
[1971] 1 O.R. 207 (Ont. C.A.)

ARNUP J.A.: This is an appeal by the defendants from the judgment of Wilson J., dated February 18, 1969. There were originally cross-actions between the parties, with a counterclaim in one of the actions, but the issues were the same in each action and they were consolidated. For convenience I will herein refer to R. G. McLean Limited throughout as "plaintiff" and the two defendants collectively as "the defendant." After the transactions giving rise to the issues in this action, Canadian Vickers Limited sold its "George Mann Division" to the defendant R. W. Crabtree & Sons (Canada) Limited, and whatever may be the rights of the latter company as against Canadian Vickers Ltd., the matter was argued before this Court as if the two defendants were one and I do not propose to refer again to R. W. Crabtree & Sons (Canada) Ltd.

The action arises from the sale by the defendant to the plaintiff of a two-colour press. The plaintiff had previously purchased from the Mann company a two-colour press and, after considerable discussion between the parties, it was decided that the plaintiff should purchase a second press as identical as possible to the first one, with the idea of running them in tandem. By using both presses it would be possible to print two-colour material using one press and an additional two colours using the other, and thereby turn out a finished product in four colours. The parties entered into a written contract dated September 30, 1964, covering the sale by the defendant to the plaintiff of the second press at a price of $75,850, plus applicable taxes, with an adjustment in the price dependent upon the rate of exchange. The agreement was expressed to be "subject to the conditions of sale of goods attached hereto. . . ."

It contemplated that a conditional sales agreement would subsequently be executed and, in pursuance of this, such an agreement dated August 18, 1965, was entered into. That contract contained the following provision:

"9. There are no representations, warranties, collateral agreements, conditions, express or implied, statutory or otherwise with respect to the machine or this agreement or affecting the rights of the parties other than as specifically contained herein and other than those contained in paragraphs numbered 12 and 13 of the Vendor's standard conditions of sale, a copy of which is attached hereto."

It is common ground that, of the "standard conditions of sale" referred to in both agreements, cl. 12 is the most important. This clause reads as follows:

"12.   Warranty
(a) Subject to fair and proper use we undertake to repair or replace all parts of our manufacture which shall, during the twelve month's immediately following the date on which the goods are despatched, be found to be defective due either to faulty workmanship or the use of defective material.
(b) In any such case you shall (unless otherwise arranged) despatch within fourteen days the part or parts alleged to be defective and our Works free and carriage paid together with a full report thereon. Should it be found that the defect is due to faulty workmanship or defective materials we will repair or replace the part or parts and return them to you carriage paid. Any customs dues or import charges payable however in connection with the repaired or replacement part shall be to your account. We shall not be responsible for dismantling or reassembly or any charges in connection therewith.
(c) In the case of goods supplied but not manufactured by us our sole responsibility shall be to give to you the same warranty as given to us by our Sub-contractor provided that we are not called upon to bear any liability or expense greater than the amount recovered from our Sub-contractor.
(d) If items or materials are supplied by you to us fo machining or for further work to be performed upon them or for incorporation in goods of our supply, our liability in the event of any part of our work on such items or materials being faulty, shall be limited to the rectification of such work.
(e) This condition No. 12 is in substitution for and excludes all express conditions warranties or liabilities of any kind relating to the goods sold whether as to fitness or otherwise and whether arising under the Sale of Goods Act, 1893 or other statute or in tort or by implication of law or otherwise. In no event shall we be liable for any direct or indirect loss or damage (whether special, consequential or otherwise) or any other claims except as provided for in these conditions.
(f) The above warranty shall not apply to second-hand goods and shall not be valid in cases where repairs or alterations have been carried out without our sanction."

The learned trial Judge correctly found on the evidence [[1969] 2 O.R. 249 at p. 251; 5 D.L.R. (3d) 100 at p. 102] that "the new press was expected to turn out the highest quality offset lithographic printing. Anything less was not within the contemplation of the buyer or seller." Following the installation of the new press in the plaintiff's premises in Toronto, a long series of difficulties ensued. Some of these were capable of being repaired and were minor in nature, and were, in fact, repaired by the defendant or by the plaintiff itself. Problems continued, however, throughout the fall of 1965 and the early winter of 1966. Representatives of the defendant were sent out from England to try to locate the source of the trouble. Many things were tried but in the end it became obvious to the defendant that, whatever the trouble was, it could not be pinpointed and they were unable to fix it.

It was at this point (which was shortly before March 30, 1966) that the defendant finally offered to take back the press and to refund the payments made by the plaintiff. The plaintiff refused this suggestion, pointing out that it had already incurred more than $36,000 in expenses and direct losses. The offer, however, was not conditional upon the plaintiff agreeing to forego any claim for damages. This becomes significant in considering the question of damages, which I shall deal with later.

The learned trial Judge, after considering the totality of the defects, both those which had been fixed and those which could not either be found or fixed, concluded [at p. 253 O.R., p. 104 D.L.R.] that the machine had "never operated as anticipated by both the vendor and purchaser on any proper commercial basis for the production of very high quality lithographing offset prints, in spite of genuine and sincere efforts made by employees of the vendor and purchaser working together to produce the desired results." While he does not in terms make a finding that the defects in their totality were such as to constitute a "fundamental breach of contract" on the part of the defendant, it is clear that such was his intention; he considered in detail and quoted at length from the leading cases on the subject and concluded [at p. 260 O.R., p. 111 D.L.R.] ". . . the failure to supply a press which would do the quality of printing contemplated by both parties to the contract when it was made was of so serious a nature in this case that for commercial purposes there was a breach of condition which the plaintiff has treated as a breach of warranty."

It is not necessary for us to determine whether the finding of a "fundamental breach" is a finding of fact, with which this Court could interfere only if satisfied that the learned trial Judge was "clearly wrong," because after reviewing the evidence we are of the opinion that the evidence justifies the conclusion reached by the trial Judge. In short, the machine simply did not do the job which it had been purchased to do and could not be made to do it by all efforts of both parties.

A finding that a "fundamental breach" of contract had taken place does not by any means end the inquiry necessary to determine the rights of the parties. The next question is: assuming a fundamental breach had occurred, what were the rights of the plaintiff? The law on the subject of "fundamental breach" was reviewed in each of the judgments in the House of Lords in *Suisse Atlantique Société D'Armement Maritime S.A.* v. *N.V. Rotterdamsche Kolen Centrale*, [1967] 1 A.C. 361. Not all of the learned law Lords expressed the matter in the same way, and undoubtedly difficulties will arise in future cases in endeavouring to apply to particular circumstances the various statements and principles there enunciated. However, it is clear from that case that, when a fundamental breach has occurred, and the innocent party has learned of it, he then has a right to accept the repudiation evidenced by the acts which constitute the fundamental breach, to treat the contract as at an end and to sue the other party to the contract for such damages as he may have sustained. It was conceded before us that in that event "the damages are at large," and this is undoubtedly so.

It is clear to us that the plaintiff in this case did not accept the repudiation and treat the contract as at an end. On the contrary, it continued to insist that the defendant make further efforts to try to repair the defective machine, and, when the defendant finally threatened to institute proceedings for replevin under its conditional sales contract, by reason of the failure of the plaintiff to make the instalment payments required by that contract, the plaintiff through its solicitor denied the right of the defendant to institute such proceedings, stated that it (the plaintiff) was "not in default of its contract" and asserted that it would claim damages against the defendant flowing out of any attempt to repossess the machine.

The judgments in the *Suisse Atlantique* case, *supra*, further make it clear that, if the innocent party does not accept the repudiation, then the contract continues in force and the problem becomes one of construction of the contract itself. Most of the cases, as this one does, involve a consideration of an "exclusion clause," as clauses such as cl. 12, quoted above, have been termed. Notwithstanding some earlier judgments which seemed to hold that such an exclusion clause, by application of a rule of substantive law, should be treated as nullified where there had been a fundamental breach of the contract, the House of Lords came to the conclusion that where the repudiation has not been accepted by the innocent party, all of the clauses of the contract, including the "exclusion clause" must be considered. However, as it was put by Lord Reid in the *Suisse Atlantique* case, *supra*, at p. 398, it may be possible to construe the exclusion clause as never having been intended to apply to a situation that neither party had in contemplation, *i.e.*, a breach so fundamental as to go to the root of the contract.

Turning therefore to the construction of the entire contract, including the exclusion clause, and endeavouring to ascertain the intention of the parties from the words they have used, and bearing in mind that we must try to give business efficacy to what the parties have stated they intended, I ask myself: did these parties contemplate that, if there were defects in the machine attributable to defective parts or faulty workmanship, the defendant was to be liable to the extent indicated in cl. 12(a), but, if the machine was so defective as to be quite incapable of performing the function which both parties contemplated it should perform, the defendant was to be under no liability at all? This latter alternative is the contention advanced on behalf of the defendant as to the appropriate meaning of the concluding sentence of subcl. (e) of cl. 12.

Notwithstanding the broad language of subcl. (e), I am unable to construe it in the way contended for. Such a construction would, for all practical purposes, render nugatory the prime contractual obligations of the defendant. It would make those ostensible obligations what Lord Wilberforce called "a mere declaration of intention": *Suisse Atlantique*, *supra*, at p. 432. In short, cl. 12 does not exclude liability for a fundamental breach of contract resulting in performance totally different from what the parties had in contemplation. The clause can be given business efficacy if its operation is limited to identifiable defects due to faulty workmanship or use of defective material, which defects can be rectified, and which do not prevent performance of the contract as contemplated by the parties.

I therefore conclude, on the issue of liability, that there was a fundamental breach of the contract by the defendant; that the plaintiff did not, as it might have done, treat the contract as ended and sue for damages; that, construing the contract as a whole, the plaintiff is not precluded from asserting a cause of action for breach of warranty, which cause of action it is compelled to assert, notwithstanding that the breach was in law a breach of condition. In the circumstances of this case, the plaintiff was obliged to treat, and did treat, the breach of condition as a breach of warranty. . . .

[The appeal was allowed in part on the question of damages.]

HENNINGSEN v. BLOOMFIELD MOTORS
161 A. (2d) 69 (S.C.N.J., 1960)

The plaintiff was injured by a defect in a new car purchased by her husband. She sued the dealer and the manufacturer, who both sought to rely on a clause in the contract of sale excluding all liability for defects except a limited obligation to replace defective parts.

FRANCIS J.: . . . Judicial notice may be taken of the fact that automobile manufacturers, including Chrysler Corporation, undertake large scale advertising programs over television, radio, in newspapers, magazines and all media of communication in order to persuade the public to buy their products. As has been observed above, a number of jurisdictions, conscious of modern marketing practices, have declared that when a manufacturer engages in advertising in order to bring his goods and their quality to the attention of the public and thus to create consumer demand, the representations made constitute an express warranty running directly to a buyer who purchases in reliance thereon. The fact that the sale is consummated with an independent dealer does not obviate that warranty. . . .

In view of the cases in various jurisdictions suggesting the conclusion which we have now reached with respect to the implied warranty of merchantability, it becomes apparent that manufacturers who enter into promotional activities to stimulate consumer buying may incur warranty obligations of either or both the express or implied character. These developments in the law inevitably suggest the inference that the form of express warranty made part of the Henningsen purchase contract was devised for general use in the automobile industry as a possible means of avoiding the consequences of the growing judicial acceptance of the thesis that the described express or implied warranties run directly to the consumer.

In the light of these matters, what effect should be given to the express warranty in question which seeks to limit the manufacturer's liability to replacement of defective parts, and which disclaims all other warranties, express or implied? In assessing its significance we must keep in mind the general principle that, in the absence of fraud, one who does not choose to read a contract before signing it, cannot later relieve himself of its burdens. . . .And in applying that principle, the basic tenet of freedom of competent parties to contract is a factor of importance. But in the framework of modern commercial life and business practices, such rules cannot be applied on a strict, doctrinal basis. The conflicting interests of the buyer and seller must be evaluated realistically and justly, giving due weight to the social policy evinced by the Uniform Sales Act, the progressive decisions of the courts engaged in administering it, the mass production methods of manufacture and distribution to the public, and the bargaining position occupied by the ordinary consumer in such an economy. This history of the law shows that legal doctrines, as first expounded, often prove to be inadequate under the impact of later experience. In such case, the need for justice has stimulated the necessary qualifications or adjustments. . . .

In these times, an automobile is almost as much a servant of convenience for the ordinary person as a household utensil. For a multitude of other persons it is a necessity. Crowded highways and filled parking lots are a commonplace of our existence. There is no need to look any farther than the daily newspaper to be convinced that when an automobile is defective, it has great potentiality for harm.

No one spoke more graphically on this subject than Justice Cardozo in the landmark case of *MacPherson* v. *Buick Motor Co.*, 217 N.Y. 382, 111 N.E. 1050, (Ct.App.1916): "Beyond all question, the nature of an automobile gives warning of probable danger if its construction is defective. This automobile was designed to go 50 miles per hour. Unless its wheels were sound and strong, injury was almost certain. It was as much a thing of danger as a defective engine for a railroad. . . . The dealer was indeed the one person of whom it might be said with some approach to certainty that by him the car would not be used. . . . Precedents drawn from the days of travel by stagecoach do not fit the conditions of travel to-day. The principle that the danger must be imminent does not change, but the things subject to the principle do change. They are whatever the needs of life in a developing civilization require them to be."

In the 44 years that have intervened since that utterance, the average car has been constructed for almost double the speed mentioned; 60 miles per hour is permitted on our parkways. The number of automobiles in use has multiplied many times and the hazard to the user and the public has increased proportionately. The Legislature has intervened in the public interest, not only to regulate the manner of operation on the highway but also to require periodic inspection of motor vehicles and to impose a duty on manufacturers to adopt certain safety devices and methods in their construction. . . . It is apparent that the public has an interest not only in the safe manufacture of automobiles, but also, as shown by the Sales Act, in protecting the rights and remedies of purchasers, so far as it can be accomplished consistently with our system of free enterprise. In a society such as ours, where the automobile is a common and necessary adjunct of daily life, and where its use is so fraught with danger to the driver, passengers and the public, the manufacturer is under a special obligation in connection with the construction, promotion and sale of his cars. Consequently, the courts must examine purchase agreements closely to see if consumer and public interests are treated fairly.

What influence should these circumstances have on the restrictive effect of Chrysler's express warranty in the framework of the purchase contract? As we have said, warranties originated in the law to safeguard the buyer and not to limit the liability of the seller or manufacturer. It seems obvious in this instance that the motive was to avoid the warranty obligations which are normally incidental to such sales. The language gave little and withdrew much. In return for the delusive remedy of replacement of defective parts at the factory, the buyer is said to have accepted the exclusion of the maker's liability for personal injuries arising from the breach of the warranty, and to have agreed to the elimination of any other express or implied warranty. An instinctively felt sense of justice cries out against such a sharp bargain. But does the doctrine that a person is bound by his signed agreement, in the absence of fraud, stand in the way of any relief?

In the modern consideration of problems such as this, Corbin suggests that practically all judges are "chancellors" and cannot fail to be influenced by any equitable doctrines that are available. And he opines that "there is sufficient flexibility in the concepts of fraud, duress, misrepresentation and undue influence, not to mention differences in economic bargaining power" to enable the courts to avoid enforcement of unconscionable provisions in long printed standardized contracts. 1 Corbin on Contracts (1950) §128, p. 188. Freedom of contract is not such an immutable doctrine as to admit of no qualification in the area in which we are concerned. As Chief Justice Hughes said in his dissent in *Morehead* v. *People of State of New York ex rel. Tipaldo*, 298 U.S. 587, 627, 56 S. Ct. 918, 930, 80 L.Ed. 1347, 1364 (1936): "We have had frequent occasion to consider the limitations on liberty of contract. While it is highly important to preserve that liberty from arbitrary and capricious interference, it is also necessary to prevent its abuse, as otherwise it could be used to override all public interests and thus in the end destroy the very freedom of opportunity which it is designed to safeguard."

That sentiment was echoed by Justice Frankfurter in his dissent in *United States* v. *Bethlehem Steel Corp.*, 315 U.S. 289, 326, 62 S. Ct. 581, 599, 86 L.Ed. 855, 876 (1942): "It is said that familiar principles would be outraged if Bethlehem were denied recovery on these contracts. But is there any principle which is more familiar or more firmly embedded in the history of Anglo-American law than the basic doctrine that the courts will not permit themselves to be used as instruments of inequity and injustice? Does any principle in our law have more universal application than the doctrine that courts will not enforce transactions in which the relative positions of the parties are such that one has unconscionably taken advantage of the necessities of the other?

These principles are not foreign to the law of contracts. Fraud and physical duress are not the only grounds upon which courts refuse to enforce contracts. The law is not so primitive that it sanctions every injustice except brute force and downright fraud. More specifically, the courts generally refuse to lend themselves to the enforcement of a 'bargain' in which one party has unjustly taken advantage of the economic necessities of the other."

The traditional contract is the result of free bargaining of parties who are brought together by the play of the market, and who meet each other on a footing of approximate economic equality. In such a society there is no danger that freedom of contract will be a threat to the social order as a whole. But in present-day commercial life the standardized mass contract has appeared. It is used primarily by enterprises with strong bargaining power and position. "The weaker party, in need of the goods or services, is frequently not in a position to shop around for better terms, either because the author of the standard contract has a monopoly (natural or artificial) or because all competitors use the same clauses. His contractual intention is but a subjection more or less voluntary to terms dictated by the stronger party, terms whose consequences are often understood in a vague way, if at all." Kessler, "Contracts of Adhesion—Some Thoughts About Freedom of Contract," 43 Colum. L. Rev. 629, 632 (1943); Ehrenzweig, "Adhesion Contracts in the Conflict of Laws," 53 Colum. L. Rev. 1072, 1075, 1089 (1953). Such standarized contracts have been described as those in which one predominant party will dictate its law to an undetermined multiple rather than to an individual. They are said to resemble a law rather than a meeting of the minds. . . .

Vold, in the recent revision of his *Law of Sales* (2d ed. 1959) at page 447, wrote of this type of contract and its effect upon the ordinary buyer:

"In recent times the marketing process has been getting more highly organized than ever before. Business units have been expanding on a scale never before known. The standardized contract with its broad disclaimer clauses is drawn by legal advisers of sellers widely organized in trade associations. It is encountered on every hand. Extreme inequality of bargaining between buyer and seller in this respect is now often conspicuous. Many buyers no longer have any real choice in the matter. They must often accept what they can get though accompanied by broad disclaimers. The terms of these disclaimers deprive them of all substantial protection with regard to the quality of the goods. In effect, this is by force of contract between very unequal parties. It throws the risk of defective articles on the most dependent party. He has the least individual power to avoid the presence of defects. He also has the least individual ability to bear their disastrous consequences."

The warranty before us is a standardized form designed for mass use. It is imposed upon the automobile consumer. He takes it or leaves it, and he must take it to buy an automobile. No bargaining is engaged in with respect to it. In fact, the dealer through whom it comes to the buyer is without authority to alter it; his function is ministerial—simply to deliver it. The form warranty is not only standard with Chrysler but, as mentioned above, it is the uniform warranty of the Automobile Manufacturers Association. Members of the Association are: General Motors, Inc., Ford, Chrysler, Studebaker-Packard, American Motors, (Rambler), Willys Motors, Checker Motors Corp., and International Harvester Company. Automobile Facts and Figures (1958 Ed., Automobile Manufacturers Association) 69. Of these companies, the "Big Three" (General Motors, Ford, and Chrysler) represented 93.5% of the passenger-car production for 1958 and the independents 6.5%. Standard & Poor (Industrial Surveys, Autos, Basic Analysis, June 25, 1959) 4109. And for the same year the *"Big Three"* had 86.72% of the total passenger vehicle registrations. *Automotive News*, 1959 Almanac (Slocum Publishing Co., Inc.) p. 25.

The gross inequality of bargaining position occupied by the consumer in the automobile industry is thus apparent. There is no competition among the car makers in the area of the express warranty. Where can the buyer go to negotiate for better protection? Such control and limitation of his remedies are inimical to the public welfare and, at the very least, call for great care by the courts to avoid injustice through application of strict common-law principles of freedom of contract. Because there is no competition among the motor vehicle manufacturers with respect to the scope of protection guaranteed to the buyer, there is no incentive on their part to stimulate good will in that field of public relations. Thus, there is lacking a factor existing in more competitive fields, one which tends to guarantee the safe construction of the article sold. Since all competitors operate in the same way, the urge to be careful is not so pressing. See "Warranties of Kind and Quality," 57 Yale L. J. 1389, 1400 (1948).

Although the courts, with few exceptions, have been most sensitive to problems presented by contracts resulting from gross disparity in buyer-seller bargaining positions, they have not articulated a general principle condemning, as opposed to public policy, the imposition on the buyer of a skeleton warranty as a means of limiting the responsibility of the manufacturer. They have endeavored thus far to avoid a drastic departure from age-old tenets of freedom of contract by adopting doctrines of strict construction, and notice and knowledgeable assent by the buyer to the attempted exculpation of the seller. . . .Accordingly to be found in the cases are statements that disclaimers and the consequent limitation of liability will not be given effect if "unfairly procured," . . . if not brought to the buyer's attention and he was not made understandingly aware of it, . . . or if not clear and explicit, . . . [A detailed discussion of some of these cases is omitted.]

It is undisputed that the president of the dealer with whom Henningsen dealt did not specifically call attention to the warranty on the back of the purchase order. The form and the arrangement of its face, as described above, certainly would cause the minds of reasonable men to differ as to whether notice of a yielding of basic rights stemming from the relationship with the manufacturer was adequately given. The words "warranty" or "limited warranty" did not even appear in the fine print above the place for signature, and a jury might well find that the type of print itself was such as to promote lack of attention rather than sharp scrutiny. The inference from the facts is that Chrysler placed the method of communicating its warranty to the purchaser in the hands of the dealer. If either one or both of them wished to make certain that Henningsen became aware of that agreement and its purported implications, neither the form of the document nor the method of expressing the precise nature of the obligation intended to be assumed would have presented any difficulty.

But there is more than this. Assuming that a jury might find that the fine print referred to reasonably served the objective of directing a buyer's attention to the warranty on the reverse side, and, therefore, that he should be charged with awareness of its language, can it be said that an ordinary layman would realize what he was relinquishing in return for what he was being granted? Under the law, breach of warranty against defective parts or workmanship which caused personal injuries would entitle a buyer to damages even if due care were used in the manufacturing process. Because of the great potential for harm if the vehicle was defective, that right is the most important and fundamental one arising from the relationship. Difficulties so frequently encountered in establishing negligence in manufacture in the ordinary case make this manifest. . . . Any ordinary layman of reasonable intelligence, looking at the phraseology, might well conclude that Chrysler was agreeing to replace defective parts and perhaps replace anything that went wrong because of defective workmanship during the first 90 days or 4,000 miles of operation, but that he would not be entitled to a new car. It is not unreasonable to believe that the entire scheme being conveyed was a proposed remedy for physical deficiencies in the car. *In the context* of this warranty, only the abandonment of all sense of justice would permit us to hold that, as a matter of law, the phrase "its obligation under this warranty being limited to making good at its factory any part or parts thereof" signifies to an ordinary reasonable person that he is relinquishing any personal injury claim that might flow from the use of a defective automobile. Such claims are nowhere mentioned. The draftsmanship is reflective of the care and skill of the Automobile Manufacturers Association in undertaking to avoid warranty obligations without drawing too much attention to its effort in that regard. No one can doubt that if the will to do so were present, the ability to inform the buying public of the intention to disclaim liability for injury claims arising from breach of warranty would present no problem.

In this connection, attention is drawn to the Plymouth Owner Certificate mentioned earlier. Obviously, Chrysler is aware of it because the New

Car Preparation Service Guide sent from the factory to the dealer directs that it be given to the purchaser. That certificate contains a paragraph called "Explanation of Warranty." Its entire tenor relates to replacement of defective parts. There is nothing about it to stimulate the idea that the intention of the warranty is to exclude personal injury claims. . . .

The task of the judiciary is to administer the spirit as well as the letter of the law. On issues such as the present one, part of that burden is to protect the ordinary man against the loss of important rights through what, in effect, is the unilateral act of the manufacturer. The status of the automobile industry is unique. Manufacturers are few in number and strong in bargaining position. In the matter of warranties on the sale of their products, the Automotive Manufacturers Association has enabled them to present a united front. From the standpoint of the purchaser, there can be no arms length negotiating on the subject. Because his capacity for bargaining is so grossly unequal, the inexorable conclusion which follows is that he is not permitted to bargain at all. He must take or leave the automobile on the warranty terms dictated by the maker. He cannot turn to a competitor for better security.

Public policy is a term not easily defined. Its significance varies as the habits and needs of a people may vary. It is not static and the field of application is an ever increasing one. A contract, or a particular provision therein, valid in one era may be wholly opposed to the public policy of another. . . . Courts keep in mind the principle that the best interests of society demand that persons should not be unnecessarily restricted in their freedom to contract. But they do not hesitate to declare void as against public policy contractual provisions which clearly tend to the injury of the public in some way. . . .

Public policy at a given time finds expression in the Constitution, the statutory law and in judicial decisions. In the area of sale of goods, the legislative will has imposed an implied warranty of merchantability as a general incident of sale of an automobile by description. The warranty does not depend upon the affirmative intention of the parties. It is a child of the law; it annexes itself to the contract because of the very nature of the transaction. . . . The judicial process has recognized a right to recover damages for personal injuries arising from a breach of that warranty. The disclaimer of the implied warranty and exclusion of all obligations except those specifically assumed by the express warranty signify a studied effort to frustrate that protection. True, the Sales Act authorizes agreements between buyer and seller qualifying the warranty obligations. But quite obviously the Legislature contemplated lawful stipulations (which are determined by the circumstances of a particular case) arrived at freely by parties of relatively equal bargaining strength. The lawmakers did not authorize the automobile manufacturer to use its grossly disproportionate bargaining power to relieve itself from liability and to impose on the ordinary buyer, who in effect has no real freedom of choice, the grave danger of injury to himself and others that attends the sale of such a dangerous instrumentality as a defectively made automobile. In the framework of this case, illuminated as it is by the facts and the many decisions noted, we are of the opinion that Chrysler's attempted disclaimer of an implied warranty of merchantability and of the obligations arising therefrom is so inimical to the public good as to compel an adjudication of its invalidity.

NOTE. (1965) 81 Law Quarterly Review 34

The Israeli Law of Standard Contracts, 1964, empowers the court to invalidate certain conditions, not approved by a Special Tribunal, included in a contract for the supply of goods or the rendering of services, if such conditions were fixed beforehand by the supplier of goods or services for use in many contracts with persons not designated at the time when the said conditions were originally formulated.

Article 14 of the said Law provides, that if a court in legal proceedings between the supplier and receiver of goods or services (who is called "the receiver") finds that a restrictive condition contained in a standard contract, in the light of the provisions of the contract and of all surrounding circumstances, is oppressive for the receiver or affords an unfair advantage for the supplier likely to be oppressive for the receiver, the court may hold the said condition in whole or in part to be invalid, and may order the return of what the receiver paid by virtue of the said condition.

Restrictive conditions are defined as follows:

(1) Conditions which exclude or limit the liability of the supplier towards the receiver, where such liability would arise either by virtue of a contract or statute, but for the existence of the restrictive condition.

(2) Conditions which entitle the supplier to cancel or change the conditions of a contract or to delay its execution in his sole discretion, or to bring about otherwise the termination of the contract or of rights arising from it, unless such termination depends on the fact that the receiver broke the contract or depends on circumstances independent of the supplier.

(3) Conditions which permit the receiver to exercise a right arising out of the contract only after having obtained the consent of the supplier or of someone else on the latter's behalf.

(4) Conditions which force the receiver to deal with the supplier in matters not directly connected with the object of the contract or restrict the liberty of the receiver to deal in such a matter with a third party.

(5) A condition which forms a waiver declared beforehand on the part of the receiver in regard to rights which would arise out of the contract, but for the existence of such a waiver.

(6) A condition which empowers the supplier or somebody else on his behalf to act in the name of the receiver in order to realise a right of the supplier towards the receiver.

(7) A condition which establishes that the books or other documents made by the supplier or on his behalf should be binding upon the receiver or imposes otherwise upon the receiver the burden of proof in regard to matters where such burden of proof would not exist, but for the said condition.

(8) A condition which makes the right of the receiver to obtain relief in legal proceedings dependent upon the fulfilment of a condition precedent or limits the said right by fixing a time-bar or otherwise. A submission to arbitration is however valid.

(9) A submission to arbitration if the supplier has a greater influence than the receiver upon the appointment of the arbitrator or in regard to the fixing of the place where the arbitration is to take place, or a condition which entitles the supplier in his sole discretion to select a court for the decision of a dispute.

The Law provides that if one of the said conditions has been invalidated by the court this does not necessarily entail the invalidity of the other conditions contained in the contract.

The Law applies also to cases in which the state is the supplier.

The new statute does not apply to conditions which were fixed and confirmed by legislation or are contained in international conventions to which the State of Israel is a party, or to contracts between an Israeli corporate body confirmed as such by the Government, and between a foreign supplier and the statute does not apply to conditions which are more favourable for the receiver.

The statute does not repeal any provision contained in any other law, which entitles the receiver to other legal remedies.

Every supplier has the possibility of submitting a draft contract to a special tribunal for approval and if such approval is given the courts are not entitled to question the validity of restrictive conditions thus approved by the tribunal. Against the decision of the tribunal appeals lie to the Supreme Court of Israel, which may be filed either by the supplier or by the Attorney-General.

An approval given by the tribunal remains in force for five years, or for a shorter period, if thus determined by the tribunal. If the tribunal refuses to approve a restrictive condition the same is invalid.

4. Unconscionability

MARSHALL v. CANADA PERMANENT TRUST CO.
(1968) 69 D.L.R. (2d) 260 (Alta. S.C.)

KIRBY J.: This is an action for specific performance of an agreement for sale of land.

On January 30, 1967, the plaintiff offered to purchase the S.E. ¼ of section 27, and the N.W. ¼ of section 26, both in township 38, range 14, west of the 4th meridian, from the defendant for the sum of $7,000 cash, payable immediately upon execution of a transfer by the vendor. The offer was accepted by the owner of these lands, John A. Walsh, on the same date. Both the offer and acceptance are in writing. Cash in the sum of $100 was paid by the purchaser to the vendor. At the time the document was executed, Walsh was a patient at Bow View Rest Home, Calgary.

The plaintiff, in relating the circumstances under which the transaction was made, testified that having tried wihout success to purchase farm lands from Walsh's brother in the same general area, and on hearing that John Walsh might sell his half-section of land, he went to see him at the rest home and asked him if he wanted to sell his farm near Castor. He stated that Walsh said that he did wish to sell for cash, and felt that he should get between $7,000 and $8,000; that Walsh pointed out that the land was under a lease; that he offered $7,000 cash and would take over the lease. He stated that through an employee of the rest home he was put in touch with Canada Permanent Mortgage Company, who in turn referred him to a solicitor who drew up the offer to purchase and acceptance. The solicitor, he said, showed him a copy of the lease. He related that he returned to the home on Monday, January 30th, with the offer to purchase, which was signed by him and Walsh in the presence of a witness—a member of the staff, and gave him a cheque for $100, which Walsh signed and instructed him to give to his solicitor for deposit in the main branch of the Bank of Montreal, which he did. On February 22nd, he received a letter from a firm of solicitors, informing him that they were acting in this matter, did not intend to deliver a transfer, and were in the process of applying for appointment of a committee for Walsh.

On February 24th, agents for the solicitor for the plaintiff sent a prepared transfer of the lands from Walsh to the plaintiff, together with a certified cheque for $7,000, to the solicitors for Walsh. On March 11th, the cheque was returned with a letter declining to deliver a transfer to the lands in question.

On March 30th, Canada Permanent Trust Company was appointed a committee for the estate of John A Walsh, pursuant to the provisions of the *Mentally Incapacitated Persons Act*, 1955 (Alta.), c. 3.

The defendant seeks a declaration of rescission of the memorandum of agreement on the grounds that the consideration which the plaintiff proposed to pay to Walsh for the lands in question, was grossly inadequate, that the agreement entered into between the plaintiff and Walsh was not fair and reasonable, and that the plaintiff took advantage of Walsh by reason of the inequality of their positions. In the alternative to specific performance the plaintiff claims damages.

Simply stated, the ground on which the defendant seeks to have the agreement rescinded is that the transaction was unconscionable. In *Knupp* v. *Bell* (1966), 58 D.L.R. (2d) 466 [affd 67 D.L.R. (2d) 256], in considering the equitable jurisdiction of the Court to set aside unconscionable transactions, MacPherson, J. (Saskatchewan Court of Queen's Bench), refers to an article by Bradley E. Crawford in the *Canadian Bar Review*, vol. 44, No. 1 (March, 1966), p. 142, entitled "Restitution—Unconscionable Transaction—Undue Advantage Taken of Inequality Between Parties," which he accepts as a fair statement of the law in this matter. The author says at p. 143:

"The jurisdiction of equity is to set aside bargains contracted by persons under [undue] influence is well known. But what is referred to here is something distinct from that. It is also technically distinct from the simple refusal of the courts to grant specific performance where the contract has been obtained by sharp practice. In the cases now under discussion the courts intervene to rescind the contract whenever it appears that one of the parties was incapable of adequately protecting his interests and the other has made some immoderate gain at his expense. If the bargain is fair the fact that the parties were not equally vigilant of their interest is immaterial. Likewise if one was not preyed upon by the other, an improvident or even grossly inadequate consideration is no ground upon which to set aside a contract freely entered into. It is the combination of inequality and improvidence which alone may invoke this jurisdiction. Then the onus is placed upon the party seeking to uphold the contract to show that his conduct throughout was scrupulously considerate of the other's interests."

Applying this law, the learned Justice held that where a senile woman of no business experience and who was very easily led was induced to sell her lands to a neighbour at the grossly inadequate price of $35 per acre without taking independent advice from competent members of her family, no binding obligation was created. Hence, no action for specific performance would lie to enforce the contract.

In the *Bar Review* article, reference is made to the judgment in *Waters* v. *Donnelly* (1884), 9 O.R. 391, in which Boyd, C., said at p. 401:

"There is an important decision in 1876, by Sir Edward Sullivan then M.R., and now Lord Chancellor of Ireland, which was affirmed by the

Court of Appeal and in which he thus defines the law applicable to this case: 'I take the law of the Court to be, that if two persons, no matter whether a confidential relationship exists between them or not, stand in such a relation to each other that one can take an undue advantage of the other, whether by reason of distress, or recklessness, or wildness, or want of care, and when the facts shew that one party has taken undue advantage of the other by reason of the circumstances I have mentioned, a transaction resting upon such unconscionable dealing will not be allowed to stand; and there are several cases which shew, even where no confidential relationship exists, that where parties were not on equal terms, the party who gets a benefit cannot hold it without proving that everything has been right and fair and reasonable on his part:' *Slator* v. *Nolan*, Ir. R. 11 Eq. 386.

"The method of investigation is to determine first whether the parties were on equal terms, if not, and the transaction is one of purchase, and any matters requiring explanation arise, then it lies on the purchaser to shew affirmatively that the price given was the value."

The Chancellor referred to *Baker* v. *Monk* (1864), 4 De G.J. & S. 386, 46 E.R. 968, in which Turner, L.J., referred to *Evans* v. *Llewellin* (1787), 1 Cox 333, 29 E.R. 1191, in laying down the principle on which the Court acts in cases of purchase, that though there was no actual fraud, it is something like fraud for an undue advantage was taken of the vendor's situation, and then proceeded to eliminate moral fraud on the part of the purchaser, but said that it is enough if the parties are not on equal terms, that an improvident contract has been entered into, in order to invoke the protection of the Court. The Chancellor then alluded to the doctrine elucidated by Lord Selborne, L.C., in *Earl of Aylesford* v. *Morris* (1873), L.R. 8 Ch. 484, that if the parties met under such circumstances as in the particular transaction to give the stronger party dominion over the weaker, then the principle is applied of requiring the one who gets the benefit to prove that the transaction was fair, just and reasonable.

Applying these principles, the Court affirmed a decision rescinding an agreement for the exchange of land and chattels which had been held to be improvident, the plaintiff having been found to be ignorant, wanting skill in business, and comparatively an imbecile of intellect, and the transaction, one into which he would not have entered had he been properly advised and protected.

On the basis of these principles, in this case, the plaintiff's claim for specific performance must fail, and the defendant is entitled to rescission, if it is established:

(1) That Walsh was incapable of protecting his interests;

(2) That it was an improvident transaction for Walsh.

With respect to (1), it is not material whether Marshall was aware of Walsh's incapacity; with respect to (2), the onus rests with the plaintiff to show that the price given for the land corresponded to its fair value.

Was Walsh incapable of protecting his interests?

Marshall, 52 years of age, described himself as a farmer, merchant, auctioneer. It was quite evident that he was an alert, intelligent businessman.

The rest home records indicate Walsh to have been 68 years of age at the time of his admission to the home on June 14, 1966. Dr. Mortis, the house physician for the rest home, referring to the medical records of the home with respect to Walsh, testified that the symptoms reflected in these records were typical of brain damage due to hardening of the arteries: that Walsh had been from the time of his admission, given different forms of medication, some, sedative in nature; that Walsh had a minor stroke on December 14, 1966, and that following such a stroke, ability to think, to rationalize, to speak, gets progressively worse. He expressed the opinion that after the stroke Walsh was definitely not capable of transacting business, and that while it was not surprising that he could read a document, he could not relate to the past or future.

On the basis of this medical evidence, I am satisfied, and find, that Walsh was incapable of protecting his interests at the time the memorandum of agreement was entered into.

Was it an improvident transaction for Walsh?

Marshall testified that although he saw Walsh's brother after the transaction, the latter did not refer to the transaction as being unfair. With respect to the land, he gave evidence to the effect that the N.W. $\frac{1}{4}$ of section 26 had only 90 acres under cultivation, which was in stubble, the rest being coulee, had no utilities, no buildings, and fences which were non-existent to very poor; that it was thick with weeds and had been over-farmed. As to the S.E. $\frac{1}{4}$ of section 27, he said the land was poor, that it had no buildings or utilities, and was only partially fenced. He testified that he had made an offer that year to Walsh's brother Lloyd, of $20,000 for three quarter-sections of land a half mile distant from the John Walsh farm, all of which was in summer fallow, having a home, barn, electric power, well and propane, pig fence and corrals. The improvements, he said, were worth $10,000. He felt that the balance of $10,000 for the three quarter-sections was comparable to his offer of $7,000 for the half-section belonging to John Walsh. He produced a copy of a transfer of the S.E. $\frac{1}{4}$ of section 26, in the same township and range, dated February 20, 1959, which had been sold for a consideration of $2,000, and a copy of a transfer of three quarter-sections of section 6, in township 39, and the same range, dated October 27, 1958, in which the land was sold for $7,500. He estimated the cost of putting in a crop to be $16 per acre, and the average yield in the Castor area being 12 bushels per acre it would realize approximately $18 per acre. He felt that this supported his belief that he had paid a fair price for the land.

Photographs were produced showing the growing crops on this land, taken in September, 1967. They indicate a very low yield, and that the land was infested with wild oats and thistle.

Marshall admitted that he had been offered $75 per acre for his own land, $5\frac{1}{2}$ miles distant; that he had not discussed other land values with Walsh, and had not suggested to Walsh that he get independent advice.

F. C. Hunt, a real estate agent, who has carried on that business at Castor for some 20 years, gave evidence with respect to land transactions in the Castor area effected through him in 1967. One quarter-section, six to eight miles distant from the Walsh farm, sold for $8,000; this land, he said, was not as well located as the Walsh land. Three quarter-sections, five to six miles west of the Walsh farm, he said he had sold for $50 an acre; this farm had 205 acres under cultivation, and had a home and power, with some parts of it coulee, comparable to the Walsh farm. He also, in the same year, sold a half-section eight miles distant from the Walsh farm, for $17,000, a half of which was under cultivation, and which he said was not quite as good as the Walsh farm. In 1964 he sold a whole section, one to two miles east of the Walsh farm, for $30,000. This farm, he said, had fair improvements, but the land was no better than that of the Walsh farm. He estimated the Walsh farm to be worth $50 an acre on the basis of the subsisting one year lease to a tenant he did not consider a good farmer. This, he said, would adversely effect the value of the land. With respect to the Lloyd Walsh farm, he placed a value of $50 an acre on the land without the buildings.

Evidence was given by Lawrence Dunkle, the farmer who leased the Walsh farm. He testified that in July, 1966, he had visited Walsh in the rest home and had offered him $14,000 to $15,000 for the half-section, that in October he had offered $15,000. He stated he would still pay $14,000 to $15,000 for it.

Evidence of other recent sales of comparable land in the district is a proper basis for determining the value of land: *Re Calgary Power Ltd.* v. *Big Lake Farming Co. Ltd.* (1963), 37 D.L.R. (2d) 265, 41 W.W.R. 124.

The evidence of Hunt as to the values of comparable land in the same general area in 1967 must be taken as more realistic than that of comparable land in the same general area sold in 1958 and 1959. The offer made by Dunkle to Walsh in 1967 for this half-section is in line with Hunt's valuation of this land at $50 per acre. On the basis of this evidence I am satisfied, and find, that the price agreed upon by Walsh was considerably less than the actual value of this land, and it therefore was an improvident transaction for him.

By virtue of the authorities cited above, the defendant is entitled to rescission of the agreement, and it is ordered accordingly. The caveat and certificate of *lis pendens* will forthwith be withdrawn. The plaintiff has not established that he has suffered, or is entitled to any damage by reason of the non-performance of the agreement.

There was nothing in the conduct of Walsh on the two occasions when Marshall visited him in the rest home, and consummated this transaction, as related by him in his evidence, to suggest that Walsh, was suffering from mental incapacity. This is supported by the evidence of the receptionist at the home, who witnessed the signatures to the offer and acceptance. The house physician testified that Walsh, by the nature of his disability, could give the impression of reasonable understanding, even though he was not capable of transacting business. An officer of Canada Permanent Trust Company accepted instructions from Walsh for his last will and testament, and pursuant to these instructions a will was prepared by the trust company and executed by Walsh in the presence of a trust officer of the company, on January 12, 1967. Dr. Mortis gave as his opinion, that he doubted whether Walsh could have understood the will at the time of its execution. He testified that he was not consulted by the trust company as to Walsh's competence to make a will, and was not consulted as to his mental capacity until March, 1967.

Since Walsh's mental capacity was not evident to the trust officer in the early part of January, one who could be expected to be observant and cautious in matters of this kind, and was not evident to the receptionist, who witnessed his signature, it is reasonable to conclude that it was not evident to Marshall when the transaction was effected. For this reason there will be no costs.

[Action dismissed.]

MUNDINGER v. MUNDINGER
(1968) 3 D.L.R. (3d) 338 (Ont. C.A.)

The judgment of the Court was delivered orally by SCHROEDER, J.A.: This is an appeal from a judgment pronounced by Hartt, J., on September 5, 1967, whereby he dismissed the plaintiff's action against her husband for alimony; for an order declaring that a certain separation agreement entered into between the parties on June 9, 1965, was null and void and should be set aside on the ground that the plaintiff was induced to execute it through the husband's fraud and threats and by reason of duress and undue influence, at a time when, to his knowledge, she was suffering from a serious nervous breakdown and was not in a mentally competent condition to appreciate the nature and quality of her act; and further dismissing the plaintiff's claim for an order declaring null and void a certain conveyance by the wife to the husband of property known and described for municipal purposes as 23 Oriole Gardens in the City of Toronto, and a conveyance by the wife to the husband of her interest in a 50-acre parcel of land in the Township of Uxbridge in the County of Ontario both of which properties had been registered in the names of the spouses as joint tenants.

The parties were married on April 5, 1939, and resided throughout their married life in the City of Toronto. There were three children of the marriage who are now of age and married. The wife complained of many acts of cruelty on the part of the husband during their married life and more particularly of his conduct to her towards the end of the period of cohabitation. Her principal complaint was as to an intimate and adulterous relationship between the husband and one Doris Johnson, which he stubbornly continued notwithstanding his wife's emphatic objections. She alleged that her husband's maltreatment had caused her to have a nervous breakdown. She became so depressed in this unhappy state of affairs that while under the care of her family physician who was administering tranquilizers to her she took an overdose of those drugs and became so dangerously ill that she was confined to the hospital on April 26, 1965, where she remained until May 14, 1968.

During her confinement in the hospital the husband demanded a separation. This ill-timed and inconsiderate request was a severe shock to the appellant which aggravated the condition of tension and anxiety under which she was then labouring. Shortly after her return from the hospital the husband presented and asked her to sign a separation agreement which had been prepared by his solicitor, which provided, *inter alia*, that in consideration of $5,000 she was to relinquish all rights to support and maintenance, was to convey to her husband her undivided one-half interest in the Oriole Gardens property the equity value of which was said to be $20,000, and to convey her one-half interest in the farm property near Uxbridge, which was said to have a value of approximately $40,000. Although she was advised by the respondent that she did not require a solicitor she heeded the advice of a friend and consulted Mr. Bowden McLean, a solicitor, who wrote a letter dated June 1, 1965, to Messrs. Rowland and Givertz, the respondents solicitors, expressing his client's dissatisfaction with the agreement and stating the terms which would be acceptable to her.

When the husband was apprised of the terms so proposed he flew into a violent rage and a quarrel ensued, in the course of which he addressed his wife in an abominable manner and adopted a very threatening attitude towards her. He stated that he had a solicitor who could look after their affairs and it was not necessary that she be separately advised. On or about June 9, 1965, the defendant redrafted the agreement as previously prepared by his solicitors in the same terms but substituting for the sum of $5,000 to be paid to the wife, the sum of $10,000. In the result the appellant was induced to telephone Mr. McLean, to advise him that she had settled her affairs with her husband and that he should submit his account for services rendered.

The defendant is the president of the Mundinger Company Limited and related enterprises which engages in the merchandising of musical instruments and provides musical instruction. For many years following the marriage the wife took an active part in the business as an officer and employee of the company and more especially in the teaching activity. In 1952 or 1953 the said Doris Johnson entered the service of the company and almost immediately thereafter replaced the wife not only in the conduct of the company's affairs but apparently, also, in the husband's affections. The learned Judge found that the continued association between the defendant and Mrs. Johnson on a personal basis "was such that the defendant well knew that it was injurious to the health of the plaintiff". "On this ground alone", he stated, "I would have found that the plaintiff, Mrs. Mundinger, was entitled to alimony." He held, however, that the separation agreement signed by the wife was a bar to her cause of action. He stated: "I have given to the evidence prolonged and anxious consideration, and I have come to the conclusion that on the evidence before me, and having in mind the onus of proof that a case had not been made out." He found on the evidence of one Jack Souter and Dr. Caroline Hobbs, a resident intern at St. Michael's Hospital, that the wife was mentally capable of entering into these transactions, disregarding almost entirely the evidence of her family physician who had treated her for many years and of Dr. Fischer, an eminent psychiatrist under whose care she had been for several years prior to the dates with which we are concerned. Both of these medical witnesses, who were familiar with the unhappy situation in which this unfortunate plaintiff was involved, testified that, in their opinion, she was not in a mental condition to exercise proper judgment in matters affecting her property rights and temporal welfare. The evidence of the witnesses Souter and Givertz, the solicitor, was based on their observation of the appellant during the short period when she executed the separation agreement and deeds respectively. The young resident intern formed no settled opinion as to the mental capacity of the appellant to transact business of such a nature and, in any event, her testimony upon this point was quite inconclusive. There was no proper ground for preferring it to the evidence of her general physician and Dr. Fischer.

With deference to the learned Judge's view we are all of the opinion that he arrived at his decision in this case under the belief that despite the circumstances disclosed in evidence the onus of proof lay throughout on the plaintiff. The transactions in question are unconscionable and improvident on their very face as the learned Judge suggested. The plaintiff, now 52 years of age, has devoted the most important years of her life to her husband and their three children. She was influenced by her husband when suffering from the effects of a serious nervous breakdown, while under the influence of tranquillizers and other forms of sedation prescribed for her condition and doubtless also while affected by brandy which was liberally provided by the husband for reasons best known to himself, to surrender all rights to future support and maintenance and to part with a valuable interest in two pieces of real estate for the paltry consideration of $10,000. Her condition was such that it can clearly be asserted that her husband was in a position of dominance and control over her of which he took full advantage by exercising undue influence upon her to carry off this improvident and nefarious transaction.

The governing principle applicable here was laid down by this Court in the oft-cited case of *Vanzant* v. *Coates* (1917), 40 O.L.R. 556, 39 D.L.R. 485. It was there held that the equitable rule is that if the donor is in a situation in which he is not a free agent and is not equal to protecting himself, a Court of Equity will protect him, not against his own folly or carelessness, but against his being taken advantage of by those in a position to do so because of their position. In that case the circumstances were the advanced age of the donor, her infirmity, her dependence on the donee; the position of influence occupied by the donee, her acts in procuring the drawing and execution of the deed; and the consequent complete change of a well-understood and defined purpose in reference to the disposition of the donor's property. It was held that in those circumstances the onus was on the plaintiff to prove by satisfactory evidence that the gift was a voluntary and deliberate act by a person mentally competent to know, and who did know, the nature and effect of the deed, and that it was not the result of undue influence. That onus had not been discharged; and it was therefore held to be unnecessary for the defendant to prove affirmatively that the influence possessed by the plaintiff had been unduly exercised.

The principle enunciated in *Vanzant* v. *Coates, supra*, has been consistently followed and applied by the Courts of this Province and the other common law Provinces of Canada. The effect of the relevant decisions was neatly stated by Professor Bradley E. Crawford in a commentary written by him and appearing in 44 *Canadian Bar Review* 142 (1966) at p. 143, from which I quote the following extract:

"If the bargain is fair the fact that the parties were not equally vigilant of their interest is immaterial. Likewise if one was not preyed upon by the other, an improvident or even grossly inadequate consideration is no ground upon which to set aside a contract freely entered into. It is the combination of inequality and improvidence which alone may invoke this jurisdiction. Then the onus is placed upon the party seeking to uphold the contract to show that his conduct throughout was scrupulously considerate of the other's interests."

This correctly sets forth the effect of the decisions bearing upon this and like problems and I adopt it as an accurate statement of the law. On the evidence in the present case there was that combination of inequality and improvidence which justifies the Court in saying that the defendant has failed to discharge the onus which, in the circumstances, was cast upon him.

The appeal is allowed with costs. The separation agreement shall be declared null and void and set aside. The deed of the farm property shall likewise be declared null and void and be set aside. There shall be a declaration that the wife is entitled to alimony for a sum to be determined on a reference to the Master for that purpose which shall be payable from the date of the commencement of the action. There shall also be a reference to the Master with respect to the residential property at Oriole Gardens which has been sold by the defendant and to fix the proportion of the proceeds thereof payable to the appellant. Counsel stated that since the conveyance of the farm property to the husband he has expended certain monies in the making of improvements thereto. On the reference to the Master there shall also be an inquiry as to the extent of these improvements and their value, the wife to be allowed occupation rent for the period during which she was excluded from enjoyment of the property. The sum of $10,000 paid by the husband to the wife will, of course, be taken into account by the Master in determining what is due to the appellant. The appellant shall have the costs of the trial, the costs of the appeal and the costs of the reference on a solicitor-and-client basis. Appeal allowed.

LLOYDS BANK LIMITED v. BUNDY
[1975] 1 Q.B. 326

LORD DENNING M.R.: Broadchalke is one of the most pleasing villages in England. Old Herbert Bundy, the defendant, was a farmer there. His home was at Yew Tree Farm. It went back for 300 years. His family had been there for generations. It was his only asset. But he did a very foolish thing. He mortgaged it to the bank. Up to the very hilt. Not to borrow money for himself, but for the sake of his son. Now the bank have come down on him. They have foreclosed. They want to get him out of Yew Tree Farm and to sell it. They have brought this action against him for possession. Going out means ruin for him. He was granted legal aid. His lawyers put in a defence. They said that, when he executed the charge to the bank he did not know what he was doing: or at any rate that the circumstances were such that he ought not to be bound by it. At the trial his plight was plain. The judge was sorry for him. He said he was a "poor old gentleman." He was so obviously incapacitated that the judge admitted his proof in evidence. He had a heart attack in the witness-box. Yet the judge felt he could do nothing for him. There is nothing, he said, "which takes this out of the vast range of commercial transactions." He ordered Herbert Bundy to give up possession of Yew Tree Farm to the bank. Now there is an appeal to this court. The ground is that the circumstances were so exceptional that Herbert Bundy should not be held bound.

Herbert Bundy had only one son, Michael Bundy. He had great faith in him. They were both customers of Lloyds Bank Ltd., the plaintiff, at the Salisbury branch. They had been customers for many years. The son formed a company called M.J.B. Plant Hire Ltd. It hired out earth-moving machinery and so forth. The company banked at Lloyds too at the same branch.

In 1961 the son's company was in difficulties. The father on September 19, 1966, guaranteed the company's overdraft for £1,500 and charged Yew Tree Farm to the bank to secure the £1,500. Afterwards the son's company got further into difficulties. The overdraft ran into thousands. In May 1969 the assistant bank manager, Mr. Bennett, told the son the bank must have further security. The son said his father would give it. So Mr. Bennett and the son went together to see the father. Mr. Bennett produced the papers. He suggested that the father should sign a further guarantee for £5,000 and to execute a further charge for £6,000. The father said that he would help his son as far as he possibly could. Mr. Bennett did not ask the father to sign the papers there and then. He left them with the father so that he could consider them overnight and take advice on them. The father showed them to his solicitor, Mr. Trethowan, who lived in the same village. The solicitor told the father that £5,000 was the utmost that he could sink in his son's affairs. The house was worth about £10,000 and this was half his assets. On that advice the father on May 27, 1969, did execute the further guarantee and the charge, and Mr. Bennett witnessed it. So at the end of May, 1969 the father had charged the house to secure £7,500.

During the next six months the affairs of the son and his company went from bad to worse. The bank had granted the son's company an overdraft up to a limit of £10,000, but this was not enough to meet the outgoings. The son's company drew cheques which the bank returned unpaid. The bank were anxious. By this time Mr. Bennett had left to go to another branch. He was succeeded by a new assistant manager, Mr. Head. In November 1969 Mr. Head saw the son and told him that the account was unsatisfactory and that he considered that the company might have to cease operations. The son suggested that the difficulty was only temporary and that his father would be prepared to provide further money if necessary.

On December 17, 1969, there came the occasion which, in the judge's words, was "important and disastrous" for the father. The son took Mr. Head to see his father. Mr. Head had never met the father before. This was his first visit. He went prepared. He took with him a form of guarantee and a form of charge filled in with the father's name ready for signature. There was a family gathering. The father and mother were there. The son and the son's wife. Mr. Head said that the bank had given serious thought as to whether they could continue to support the son's company. But that the bank were prepared to do so in this way: (i) the bank would continue to allow the company to draw money on overdraft up to the existing level of £10,000, but the bank would require the company to pay 10 per cent of its incomings into a separate account. So that 10 per cent would not go to reduce the overdraft. Mr. Head said that this would have the effect "of reducing the level of borrowing." In other words, the bank was cutting down the overdraft. (ii) The bank would require the father to give a guarantee of the company's account in a sum of £11,000 and to give the bank a further charge on the house of £3,500, so as to bring the total charge to £11,000. The house was only worth about £10,000, so this charge for £11,000 would sweep up all that the father had.

On hearing the proposal, the father said that Michael was his only son and that he was 100 per cent behind him. Mr. Head produced the forms that had already been filled in. The father signed them and Mr. Head witnessed them there and then. On this occasion, Mr. Head, unlike Mr. Bennett did not leave the forms with the father: nor did the father have any independent advice.

It is important to notice the state of mind of Mr. Head and of the father. Mr. Head said in evidence:

"Defendant asked me what in my opinion the company was doing wrong and company's position. I told him. I did not explain the company's affairs very fully as I had only just taken over the account. . . . Michael said that company had a number of bad debts. I was not entirely satisfied with this. I thought the trouble was more deep seated. . . . It did not occur to me that there was any conflict of interest. I thought there was no conflict of interest. I would think the defendant relied on me implicitly to advise him about the transaction as bank manager. . . . I knew he had no other assets except Yew Tree Cottage."

The father said in evidence: "I always thought Head was genuine. I have always trusted him. . . . No discussion how business was doing that I can remember. I simply sat back and did what they said." The solicitor, Mr. Trethowan, said of the father: "He is straightforward. Agrees with anyone. . . . I doubt if he understood all that Head explained to him."

So the father signed the papers. Mr. Head witnessed them and took them away. The father had charged the whole of his remaining asset, leaving himself with nothing. The son and his company gained a respite. But only for a short time. Five months later, in May 1970, a receiving order was made against the son. Thereupon the bank stopped all overdraft facilities for the company. It ceased to trade. The father's solicitor, Mr. Trethowan, at once went to see Mr. Head. He said he was concerned that the father had signed the guarantee.

In due course the bank insisted on the sale of the house. In December 1971 they agreed to sell it for £9,500 with vacant possession. The family were very disappointed with this figure. It was, they said, worth much more. Estate agents were called to say so. But the judge held it was a valid sale and that the bank could take all the proceeds. The sale has not been completed because Herbert Bundy is still in possession. The bank have brought these proceedings to evict Herbert Bundy.

Now let me say at once that in the vast majority of cases a customer who signs a bank guarantee or a charge cannot get out of it. No bargain will be upset which is the result of the ordinary interplay of forces. There are many hard cases which are caught by this rule. Take the case of a poor man who is homeless. He agrees to pay a high rent to a landlord just to get a roof over his head. The common law will not interfere. It is left to Parliament. Next take the case of a borrower in urgent need of money. He borrows it from the bank at high interest and it is guaranteed by a friend. The guarantor gives his bond and gets nothing in return. The common law will not interfere. Parliament has intervened to prevent moneylenders charging excessive interest. But it has never interfered with banks.

Yet there are exceptions to this general rule. There are cases in our books in which the courts will set aside a contract, or a transfer of property, when the parties have not met on equal terms—when the one is so strong in bargaining power and the other so weak—that, as a matter of common fairness, it is not right that the strong should be allowed to push the weak to the wall. Hitherto those exceptional cases have been treated each as a separate category in itself. But I think the time has come when we should seek to find a principle to unite them. I put on one side contracts or transactions which are voidable for fraud or misrepresentation or mistake. All those are governed by settled principles. I go only to those where there has been inequality of bargaining power, such as to merit the intervention of the court.

The first category is that of "duress of goods." A typical case is when a man is in a strong bargaining position by being in possession of the goods of another by virtue of a legal right, such as by way of pawn or pledge or taken in distress. The owner is in a weak position because he is in urgent need of the goods. The stronger demands of the weaker more than is justly due: and he pays it in order to get the goods. Such a transaction is voidable. He can recover the excess: see *Astley* v. *Reynolds* (1731) 2 Stra. 915 and *Green* v. *Duckett* (1883) 11 Q.B.D. 275. To which may be added the cases of "colore officii," where a man is in a strong bargaining position by virtue of his official position or public profession. He relies upon it so as to gain from the weaker—who is urgently in need—more than is justly due: see *Pigott's* case cited by Lord Kenyon C.J. in *Cartwright* v. *Rowley* (1799) 2 Esp. 723, 723-724; *Parker* v. *Bristol and Exeter Railway Co.* (1851) 6 Exch. 702 and *Steele* v. *Williams* (1853) 8 Exch. 625. In such cases the stronger may make his claim in good faith honestly believing that he is entitled to make his demand. He may not be guilty of any fraud or misrepresentation. The inequality of bargaining power—the strength of the one versus the urgent need of the other—renders the transaction voidable and the money paid to be recovered back: see *Maskell* v. *Horner* [1915] 3 K.B. 106.

The second category is that of the "unconscionable transaction." A man is so placed as to be in need of special care and protection and yet his weakness is exploited by another far stronger than himself so as to get his property at a gross undervalue. The typical case is that of the "expectant heir." But it applies to all cases where a man comes into property, or is expected to come into it—and then being in urgent need—another gives him ready cash for it, greatly below its true worth, and so gets the property transferred to him: see *Evans* v. *Llewellin* (1787) 1 Cox 333. Even though there be no evidence of fraud or misrepresentation, nevertheless the transaction will be set aside: see *Fry* v. *Lane* (1888) 40 Ch.D. 312, 322 where Kay J. said: "The result of the decisions is that where a purchase is made from a poor and ignorant man at a considerable undervalue, *the vendor having no independent advice*, a court of equity will set aside the transaction." This second category is said to extend to all cases where an unfair advantage has been gained by an unconscientious use of power by a stronger party against a weaker: see the cases cited in *Halsbury's Laws of England*, 3rd ed., vol. 17 (1956), p. 682 and, in Canada, *Morrison* v. *Coast Finance Ltd.* (1965) 55 D.L.R. (2d) 710 and *Knupp* v. *Bell* (1968) 67 D.L.R. (2d) 256. The third category is that of "undue influence" usually so called. These are divided into two classes as stated by Cotton L.J. in *Allcard* v. *Skinner* (1887) 36 Ch.D. 145, 171. The first are those where the stronger has been guilty of some fraud or wrongful act—expressly so as to gain some gift or advantage from the weaker. The second are those where the stronger has not been guilty of any wrongful act, but has, through the relationship which existed between him and the weaker, gained some gift or advantage for himself. Sometimes the relationship is such as to raise a presumption of undue influence, such as parent over child, solicitor over client, doctor over patient, spiritual adviser over follower. At other times a relationship of confidence must be proved to exist. But to all of them the general principle obtains which was stated by Lord Chelmsford L.C. in *Tate* v. *Williamson* (1866) 2 Ch.App. 55, 61:

"Wherever two persons stand in such a relation that, while it continues, confidence is necessarily reposed by one, and the influence which naturally grows out of that confidence is possessed by the other, and this confidence is abused, or the influence is exerted to obtain an advantage at the expense of the confiding party, the person so availing himself of his position will not be permitted to retain the advantage, although the transaction could not have been impeached if no such confidential relation had existed."

Such a case was *Tufton* v. *Sperni* [1952] 2 T.L.R. 516.

The fourth category is that of "undue pressure." The most apposite of that is *Williams* v. *Bayley* (1866) L.R. 1 H.L. 200, where a son forged his father's name to a promissory note and, by means of it, raised money from the bank of which they were both customers. The bank said to the father, in effect: "Take your choice—give us security for your son's debt. If you do take that on yourself, then it will all go smoothly: if you do not, we shall be bound to exercise pressure." Thereupon the father charged his property to the bank with payment of the note. The House of Lords held that the charge was invalid because of undue pressure exerted by the bank. Lord Westbury said, at pp. 218-219:

"A contract to give security for the debt of another, which is a contract without consideration, is above all things, a contract that should be based upon the free and voluntary agency of the individual who enters into it."

Other instances of undue pressure are where one party stipulates for an unfair advantage to which the other has no option but to submit. As where an employer—the stronger party—has employed a builder—the weaker party—to do work for him. When the builder asked for payment of sums properly due (so as to pay his workmen) the employer refused to pay unless he was given some added advantage. Stuart V.-C. said: "Where an agreement, hard and inequitable in itself, has been exacted under circumstances of pressure on the part of the person who exacts it, this court will set it aside": see *Ormes* v. *Beadel* (1860) 2 Giff. 166, 174 (reversed on another ground, 2 De G.F. & J. 333) and *D. & C. Builders Ltd.* v. *Rees* [1966] 2 Q.B. 617, 625.

The fifth category is that of salvage agreements. When a vessel is in danger of sinking and seeks help, the rescuer is in a strong bargaining position. The vessel in distress is in urgent need. The parties cannot be truly said to be on equal terms. The Court of Admiralty have always recognised that fact. The "fundamental rule" is "if the parties have made an agreement, the court will enforce it, unless it be manifestly unfair and unjust; but if it be manifestly unfair and unjust, the court will disregard it and decree what is fair and just." See *Akerblom* v. *Price* (1881) 7 Q.B.D. 129, 133, *per* Brett L.J., applied in a striking case *The Port Caledonia and The Anna* [1903] P. 184, when the rescuer refused to help with a rope unless he was paid £1,000.

Gathering all together, I would suggest that through all these instances there runs a single thread. They rest on "inequality of bargaining power." By virtue of it, the English law gives relief to one who, without independent advice, enters into a contract upon terms which are very unfair or transfers property for a consideration which is grossly inadequate, when his bargaining power is grievously impaired by reason of his own needs or desires, or by his own ignorance or infirmity, coupled with undue influences or pressures brought to bear on him by or for the benefit of the other. When I use the word "undue" I do not mean to suggest that the principle depends on proof of any wrongdoing. The one who stipulates for an unfair advantage may be moved solely by his own self-interest, unconscious of the distress he is bringing to the other. I have also avoided any reference to the will of the one being "dominated" or "overcome" by the other. One who is in extreme need may knowingly consent to a most improvident bargain, solely to relieve the straits in which he finds himself. Again, I do not mean to suggest that every transaction is saved by independent advice. But the absence of it may be fatal. With these explanations, I hope this principle will be found to reconcile the cases. Applying it to the present case, I would notice these points:

(1) The consideration moving from the bank was grossly inadequate. The son's company was in serious difficulty. The overdraft was at its limit of £10,000. The bank considered that its existing security was insufficient. In order to get further security, it asked the father to charge the house— his sole asset—to the uttermost. It was worth £10,000. The charge was for £11,000. That was for the benefit of the bank. But not at all for the benefit of the father, or indeed for the company. The bank did not promise to continue the overdraft or to increase it. On the contrary, it required the overdraft to be reduced. All that the company gained was a short respite from impending doom.

(2) The relationship between the bank and the father was one of trust and confidence. The bank knew that the father relied on it implicitly to advise him about the transaction. The father trusted the bank. This gave the bank much influence on the father. Yet the bank failed in that trust. It allowed the father to charge the house to his ruin.

(3) The relationship between the father and the son was one where the father's natural affection had much influence on him. He would naturally desire to accede to his son's request. He trusted his son.

(4) There was a conflict of interest between the bank and the father. Yet the bank did not realise it. Nor did it suggest that the father should get independent advice. If the father had gone to his solicitor—or to any man of business—there is no doubt that any one of them would say: "You must not enter into this transaction. You are giving up your house, your sole remaining asset, for no benefit to you. The company is in such a parlous state that you must not do it."

These considerations seem to me to bring this case within the principles I have stated. But, in case that principle is wrong. I would also say that the case falls within the category of undue influence of the second class stated by Cotton L.J. in *Allcard* v. *Skinner*, 36 Ch.D. 145, 171. I have no doubt that the assistant bank manager acted in the utmost good faith and was straightforward and genuine. Indeed the father said so. But beyond doubt he was acting in the interests of the bank—to get further security for a bad debt. There was such a relationship of trust and confidence between them that the bank ought not to have swept up his sole remaining asset into its hands—for nothing—without his having independent advice. I would therefore allow this appeal.

[Cairns L.J. and Sir Eric Sachs agreed in the result but on the ground mentioned in the last paragraph. The document executed on Dec. 17 was set aside.]

McKENZIE v. BANK OF MONTREAL
(1975) 55 D.L.R. (3d) 641 (Ont. H.C.) affd. C.A. 12 O.R. (2d) 719

STARK J.: The plaintiff is a middle-aged widow living in Queenston. The defendant Vernon Lawrence was an intimate friend and companion of the plaintiff. The remaining defendants consist of the Bank of Montreal and several servants and agents of the bank. The plaintiff seeks damages on several different grounds against the defendants, but several of these grounds were found to be no longer applicable and were abandoned by the plaintiff during the course of these proceedings. In the result, the plaintiff seeks damages against the defendants in respect of two important matters: firstly, she claims damages for the wrongful seizure and detention of her motor-car for a period of three months; secondly, she claims that the defendant, the Bank of Montreal, through its officers William H. O'Brien and Carl C. Warwick, with the connivance and assistance of Vernon Lawrence, unlawfully coerced and forced the plaintiff into executing a mortgage in favour of the Bank of Montreal in the amount of $16,013.33, mortgaging her farm lands and premises to secure the indebtedness of Vernon Lawrence to the Bank of Montreal.

The circumstances giving rise to this action were sad and most unfortunate for the plaintiff. The chief cause of the sad events that followed arose from the plaintiff's companionship with Vernon Lawrence, who as it turned out, deceived both her and the Bank of Montreal. The plaintiff met the defendant Vernon Lawrence some 10 years before the hearing of this action. At that time Lawrence was a car salesman and Mrs. McKenzie was looking for a new car. A strong friendship developed between the two and when, in 1964, Mrs. McKenzie's mother died, and then in 1967 she lost her father, she became very upset over these bereavements. He father's estate was settled in the fall of 1967 and she became the beneficiary of some $17,000. She talked over her future plans with Lawrence and at Christmas time in 1967 he asked her to marry him and he presented her with an engagement ring. No date was ever set for a wedding and in fact no wedding ever occurred. She described Lawrence as being very gentlemanly, very kind, courteous, well-dressed, polite and quiet-spoken. He told her he had been raised on a farm and that he would like to get back to farming. She herself was employed and still is employed as a private secretary to an official of the Bright's Wine Company. Together, the two of them started looking for a farm property and finally found one which they jointly purchased, chiefly, but not entirely, with her money and which they planned to operate as a fruit farm which would eventually become the marital homestead. She regarded this farm as essentially her own property and said she had no thought of giving him a one-half share. As it turned out, when the time for closing came, there was a shortage of funds to complete the purchase and this shortage was made up by Lawrence borrowing the necessary balance, and placing a new and larger mortgage upon the property. At any rate, she quite understood that the property was being taken in joint tenancy and the arrangement was that she would continue at her job, that her aunt would reside with the two of them on the farm and attend to the household duties and that Lawrence would grow and harvest the fruit, operate the farm as a going concern and keep up the necessary mortgage and tax payments.

By 1968 the farm was getting into operation. Lawrence hired outside help, but much of the costs entailed in acquiring additional farm machinery, in paying fruit pickers and in the costs of repairing and plumbing were met by her. In the early stages Lawrence appears to have been receiving moneys from time to time from the crops and he told her that he was using the proceeds for additional farm equipment and for paying wages. A small amount of the proceeds did find its way into her hands. From time to time Lawrence appears to have engaged in different pursuits. During these years, in addition to working on the farm, he appears to have been employed partly as a car salesman, and then later in the operation of a used car lot. It was only at a much later time that she realized that she was not receiving all her mail and that Lawrence was not in fact looking after mortgage payments and that numerous debts were being incurred.

It is apparent that up until the middle of May, 1970, and probably even later than that date, the plaintiff had complete faith and trust in Lawrence and seemed to have willingly complied with whatever he wished her to do.

It was in 1969 that Mrs. McKenzie's motor-car was badly damaged in an accident. At first she intended to have the car repaired, but on the advice of her constant companion, she was persuaded to obtain a new car. Lawrence told her he could make a good deal. He told her that the car salesman might wheel and deal with her, and that he knew the tricks of the trade. She said that she could not afford a new car. But he told her not to worry, that he would see to getting the money and pay up the difference. He told her that the hotel where he had once worked as manager still owed him some money; and accordingly, adopting his recommendation, she purchased a 1969 Cougar convertible car, half the cost of which was provided by the turning-in of her former vehicle. It appears from the evidence that the cash required to pay the balance was obtained by Lawrence from the Bank of Montreal, with whom he had now become a regular customer. The motor-car was always considered to be the property of Mrs. McKenzie and from the outset was duly registered in her name and at all times it remained registered in her name. However, unknown to Mrs. McKenzie, by a document dated February 10, 1969, Vernon Lawrence, who by this time was becoming more and more personally indebted to the Bank of Montreal, granted a chattel mortgage covering Mrs. McKenzie's vehicle, as well as a second car which he owned himself to provide security to the bank. In this document he of course covenanted that he was the sole owner of the property therein described. The description of Mrs. McKenzie's car was correct, except in one particular, namely, that the serial number incorrectly appeared containing the number "4," instead of the letter "H." No inquiry was made at this time by the Bank of Montreal as to the ownership of the car, except to check with the used car agency which had sold the car and to obtain the serial number, which serial number turned out to be incorrect.

It should be noted that Jean McKenzie was not a customer of the Bank of Montreal, and appears to have been completely unaware of Lawrence's various transactions with the bank. The bank, on the other hand, appears to have been completely taken in by Lawrence's affable and suave appearance and by the various statements of assets which he filed, which statements as it turned out were in many parts quite untrue. For example, in these statements he represented that he was the owner of the farm property and placed a very high valuation upon it. It should also be noted that early in 1970 the bank did have a search made of the farm property and did ascertain that the property was being held in joint tenancy.

By this time, the bank became increasingly concerned over Lawrence's failure to meet payments on notes as they fell due and it was determined to adopt sterner measures. On March 2, 1970, the plaintiff Jean McKenzie, who was at her usual place of employment, was distressed to observe that a tow-truck was removing her Cougar convertible from the parking lot. She complained immediately to the manager of the towing company, a James Essex, one of the defendants in this action. He advised her to talk to the bailiff Harold Smith, another defendant. She did so and then communicated with William H. O'Brien, manager of the local Bank of Montreal. According to Mrs. McKenzie he told her that she could not have the car back because Lawrence owed them money. When she threatened to call the police, she claimed that the manager told her that if she called the police, he too would have to call the police and have Lawrence picked up and arrested for fraud. In her evidence, she said:

"I was very upset and emotional. I thought I'd better talk to Mr. Lawrence. I didn't want to get him in trouble. When I did talk to Lawrence he said it was a misunderstanding and that he would get my car back."

Some time elapsed and then according to her testimony she called O'Brien again. When she was asked the question "Were your suspicions aroused?," her answer was: "He was very charming and he kept talking to me and I believed him. He has always been kind and helpful to me."

The next event to be noted is that on April 7, 1970, the bank signed a default judgment against Lawrence in the sum of $16,013.33 and costs. There is no evidence that Mrs. McKenzie knew of this.

Finally, according to her evidence, on the evening of May 28, 1970, Lawrence told her that the two of them would have to go to the bank to sign a release and that they would have to sign over one-half of the fruit crops for that season, if she wished the return of her car. This she agreed to, but when Lawrence met her the next day, he introduced a new factor. According to her he said that he owed the bank $2,000 and that would have to be paid before the car would be returned to her. Accordingly, the two of them then went to Mrs. McKenzie's credit union and she borrowed $2,000 on her own account and took from Lawrence a promise that he would repay this amount to the credit of her account. That afternoon Mrs. McKenzie left work shortly before 5:00 p.m. Lawrence picked her up and they went to the Bank of Montreal. They met Mr. O'Brien the manager, who was just leaving and who turned them over to Mr. Warwick, the credit manager, who according to her, said very little, just "that there were a few formalities and papers to sign." She said, "Warwick had a bunch of papers before him and flipped them up and over." At this point the witness demonstrated how Warwick with his right finger showed her where to sign. She continued, "I couldn't see the whole of the page. No mention was made to me of what I was signing. I didn't read them. I thought all banks could be trusted." She was asked, "Was there any discussion about a mortgage?," and answered, "There was no mention of a mortgage made at the bank." What in fact she signed, as appears from the exhibits, was a "Mortgage as Additional Security" between Vernon Lawrence and Jean McKenzie and the bank, reciting an indebtedness of some $16,000. This mortgage was dated May 5, 1970, and describes by metes and bounds the farm property. It appears to have been executed under seal, was duly witnessed and the customary affidavit completed by the witness, and affidavits as to age also duly completed by Vernon Lawrence and Jean McKenzie. However, Mrs. McKenzie contends that the only witness present was Mr. Warwick and that no one was present to administer any oaths. She also signed documents assigning all the fruit crops to the bank, directed to the company to whom they usually sold the crops, although she said it had been her clear understanding that half only of the crops was to be assigned. She admits that she asked no questions and was given no explanations. She stated that the entire attendance took only five to 10 minutes, and this is pretty well admitted by Mr. Warwick, who thinks, however, it was more like 10 to 15 minutes. She appears to have appended her signature to the various papers at least eight or nine times in all and after this was completed and the cheque for $2,000 was handed over, she in turn received the keys to her car. Later on, she discovered some slight damage had been done to her car while it was out of her possession, and while the appraisal of this damage was only done at a very recent date, I find as a fact that it approximated $50 in amount.

In addition to the setting aside of this mortgage on the lands, which she claims is invalid, she did ask originally for the cancellation of the assignment relating to the fruit crops. However, this assignment bore no fruit because Lawrence was already indebted to the assignee in amounts exceeding the value of the fruit. It is clear also in my mind that her claim for the return of the $2,000 which she paid to the bank cannot be allowed. She was under no misapprehension or confusion as to the making of this payment, which she clearly did quite voluntarily and without complaint.

The only other facts arising from the evidence which need be mentioned are that the bank officials do not dispute the fact that there was no long discussion or explanation of the documents to Mrs. McKenzie, since she never asked for any explanation. Their evidence stressed that she seemed quite willing to sign the documents and it did not occur to any of them that she should be advised to seek independent consultation. It was clear from the evidence that the proposed deal had been arranged beforehand with the bank and with Lawrence and that the documents had been prepared well in advance; and that the bank assumed that Mrs. McKenzie was quite willing to sign the various papers, since she made no protest and had accompanied Lawrence to the bank for that purpose.

The plaintiff contends that long before May 29, 1970, when the mortgage in favour of the bank was executed against the farm property, the bank officials must have been aware of the untrustworthiness and of the deceit of Vernon Lawrence. In that connection, the following dates are of special significance. On January 20, 1970, a title search of the farm property was instituted by the bank, which disclosed that Jean McKenzie was one of the registered owners. This appears from ex. 46.

Exhibit 65 indicates that a search made by the Bank of Montreal on January 20, 1970, revealed the joint ownership of the farm property, but only four days before that time, namely, on January 16, 1970, Vernon Lawrence had tendered a personal financial statement to the bank, in which he claimed that he was the owner of the real estate, that its value was $75,000 and that the farm equipment alone was worth $9,500. Previous financial statements had also revealed over-valuation of assets as well as wrongful claims to ownership. Again, by April 7, 1970, the Bank of Montreal had signed a default judgment against Vernon Lawrence for a sum in excess of $16,000 and costs. It is of some significance also that the mortgage of the farm lands which Vernon Lawrence and Jean McKenzie executed on May 29, 1970, actually bears the date as having been made on May 5, 1970, by which time, as the exhibits show, the bank had learned that the registration of the motor-car had at all times been in the name of Jean McKenzie alone. By this time the bank also knew that not only were their loans to Lawrence long overdue, but they had also learned by this time that payments on prior encumbrances of the mortgaged property had also fallen badly into arrears. Thus, it is the plaintiff's contention that armed with all this knowledge, and being fully aware of the complete untrustworthiness of their customer, who had deceived both the bank and Mrs. McKenzie, all this information imposed a duty upon the bank to make sure that Mrs. McKenzie fully understood and comprehended the nature of the obligations she was being asked to assume on May 29, 1970, at her first and only attendance at the bank. It is the plaintiff's contention that the bank used the possession of her motor-car, which they had wrongfully seized, as a lever to induce her to sign the various documents, including the assignment of the fruit crops and the mortgage given by way of collateral on the farm property. The plaintiff contends that she was told to sign the papers as a matter of formality only and that this constituted a misrepresentation to her. In effect, she is saying that the Bank of Montreal and Vernon Lawrence conspired together to involve her improperly in his personal debts, at a time when the bank was greatly concerned over a heavy financial loss which they might have to take, and which they were anxious to avoid at all costs.

The paramount question then appears to me to be simply this: is there a duty upon the bank under the circumstances which I have outlined, not only to avoid any deception of a third person who is a stranger to them, but to make sure that that third person is not deceived or deluded in any way, and that no undue pressure is brought to bear? By way of additional facts, it is only necessary to point out that with the consent of all parties, the farm property was duly sold and the proceeds are lying in Court awaiting the outcome of this proceeding.

Upon consideration of the lengthy evidence in this case, it appears clear to me that the plaintiff at the time of the completion of the documents on May 29, 1970, must herself, to at least some extent, have been aware of the deceits and dishonest practices of the defendant Lawrence. Her emotional attraction to this man overruled her appreciation of his deficiences, and she seems to have been so much under his influence that she was quite prepared to sign whatever documents he produced. It is true that she was a mature and responsible woman, who had on more than one occasion in the past, dealt with real estate and executed mortgages. Even on her own evidence there was no misrepresentation made to her by any bank official, other than her evidence, not seriously contradicted, that the signing of the papers was a formality only. It is true also that there was no suggestion by her that the bank failed to answer her inquiries. Indeed, she chose to make no inquiries, and simply signed the documents as they were presented to her. She was relying still upon the promises that Lawrence made to her, and even after these events took place, Lawrence remained with her at the farm and with her consent for many weeks. Through the incident of the car seizure, and the plaintiff's subsequent telephone conversations, and of course through whatever conversations the bank officials must have had with Lawrence, the bank knew of the close relationship between the two persons. Was the bank entitled to assume that the plaintiff was acting upon Lawrence's advice, and that she was content to do so? It must be remembered also that by this time the bank had a judgment in execution against Lawrence, and part of the arrangement with Lawrence was that if the various documents were executed and the moneys paid, forbearance in proceeding with seizures would be shown, so that Lawrence could get his crops in. To an extent, this would have benefited the plaintiff as well. But the bank, knowing all of this, and knowing Lawrence's precarious financial condition, with un-satisfied judgments against him and with full knowledge of his untrust-worthiness, did not apparently deem it necessary or advisable to take any steps to ensure that the plaintiff appreciated the full extent of what she was doing.

With the knowledge that the bank possessed, there was surely some duty resting upon the bank, either to require that she obtain independent advice or at the least to ensure that full disclosure be made to her of Lawrence's heavy debts with the bank, of his failure to keep up mortgage payments and taxes on the farm, and therefore of the unlikelihood that the farming venture could ever succeed. These explanations were never attempted, on the bank's own admission; and in any event, could never have been delivered in the few minutes allotted for the signing of the necessary papers.

It must be remembered that the only thought uppermost in the plain-tiff's mind and the only purpose in her attendance at the bank, was the recovery of her motor-car. Her keys were handed over to her only after all the papers had been signed; and this withholding of her car placed the bank in a very strong and unfair bargaining position.

Thus, this case falls within the category of the many cases cited by the plaintiff. Such a case, for example, as *Vanzant* v. *Coates* (1917), 40 O.L.R. 556, 39 D.L.R. 485, a decision of the Ontario Court of Appeal. There, at p. 560 O.L.R., p. 488 D.L.R., Ferguson J.A., speaking for the Court, refers to the rule of equity laid down in *Parfitt* v. *Lawless* (1872), L.R. 2 P. & D. 462: ". . . that if a gift made to one who holds a position of influence be attacked by him who is the subject of that influence the Courts of Equity cast upon the former the burden of proving that the transaction was fairly conducted as between strangers; that the weaker was not unduly impressed by the natural influence of the stronger":

Of this rule, at p. 561 O.L.R., p. 489 D.L.R., the learned Judge says: "But the rule is not, I think, confined to well-known legal or family relationships, but extends to circumstances, as well as to persons, and to any transaction in which it is shewn that the person benefited has in-fluence or is in a position to exercise influence over the other party."

Again, at the same page: "The underlying equitable rule seems to be, that if the party is in a situation in which he is not a free agent, and is not equal to protecting himself, a Court of Equity will protect him, not against his own folly or carelessness, but against his being taken advantage of by those in a position to do so, because of their position."

The leading authority of *Nocton* v. *Ashburton* (*Lord*) (1914), 83 L.J. Ch. 784, places very high the duty of persons who are acting in con-fidential relationships. There the House of Lords recognized the doctrine of obligation to exercise care by persons in particular situations, who are doing acts which may injure the property or persons of others. At p. 790, the Lord Chancellor used this language: "Although liability for negli-gence in word has in material respects been developed in our law differently from liability for negligence in act, it is none the less true that a man may come under a special duty to exercise care in giving informa-tion or advice."

It appears to me that in the case at bar, under the peculiar facts of the case, the bank was under a special duty to the plaintiff not to dismiss the matter as a mere formality but to provide the plaintiff with the necessary information or advice, or to see that she obtained it. Had the bank not been personally interested in the result, the advice would have been quite different.

In the case of *Waters* v. *Donnelly* (1884), 9 O.R. 391 at p. 401, Chancellor Boyd quoted with approval and adopted the following language from the case of *Slator* v. *Nolan* (1876), Ir.R. 11 Eq. 386:

"I take the law of the Court to be, that if two persons, no matter whether a confidential relationship exists between them or not, stand in such a relation to each other that one can take an undue advantage of the other, whether by reason of distress, or recklessness, or wildness, or want of care, and when the facts shew that one party has taken undue advantage of the other by reason of the circumstances I have mentioned, a transaction resting upon such unconscionable dealing will not be allowed to stand; and there are several cases which shew, even where no confidential relationship exists, that where parties were not on equal terms, the party who gets a benefit cannot hold it without proving that everything has been right and fair and reasonable on his part."

Particularly in point is the recent decision of *Lloyds Bank Ltd.* v. *Bundy*, [1974] 3 All E.R. 757. It is true that in that case, the defendant Bundy was a customer of the bank and in the case at bar the plaintiff was not. But the principles enunciated in that case are applicable here. Special circumstances existed there, which imposed a duty of fiduciary care upon the bank; and in the case at bar, the special circumstances which I have outlined, placed a similar duty upon the bank. Whether the case at hand be regarded as one of misrepresentation, in that the signing of the documents was much more than a mere formality, or whether the bank used the pressure of the possession of the motor-car to obtain a benefit for itself, it would be strange indeed if the Courts could find no relief. As Lord Denning put it in the *Lloyds Bank* case at p. 763:

"There are cases in our books in which the courts will set aside a contract, or a transfer of property, when the parties have not met on equal terms, when the one is so strong in bargaining power and the other so weak that, as a matter of common fairness, it is not right that the strong should be allowed to push the weak to the wall. Hitherto those exceptional cases have been treated each as a separate category in itself. But I think the time has come when we should seek to find a principle to unite them. I put on one side contracts or transactions which are voidable for fraud or misrepresentation or mistake. All those are governed by settled principles. I go only to those where there has been inequality of bargaining power, such as to merit the intervention of the court."

Lord Denning then divides into four the various categories of such cases, into any one of which it appears to me the case at bar might fall. He says the first category is that of "duress of goods." At p. 763:

"A typical case is when a man is in a strong bargaining position by being in possession of the goods of another by virtue of a legal right, such as, by way of pawn or pledge or taken in distress. The owner is in a weak position because he is in urgent need of the goods."

At p. 764 he writes: "This second category is said to extend to all cases where an unfair advantage has been gained by an unconscientious use of power by a stronger party against a weaker."

The third category he mentions is that of "undue influence"; and under this category he cites the general principle as laid down by Lord Chelmsford in *Tate* v. *Williamson* (1866), 2 Ch. App. 55 at p. 61:

"Wherever the persons stand in such a relation that, while it continues, confidence is necessarily reposed by one, and the influence which naturally grows out of that confidence is possessed by the other, and this confidence is abused, or the influence is exerted to obtain an advantage at the expense of the confiding party, the person so availing himself of his position will not be permitted to retain the advantage, although the transaction could not have been impeached if no such confidential relation had existed."

The fourth category discussed by Lord Denning is that of "undue pressure." Here Lord Denning adopts the language of Lord Westbury in the case of *Williams* v. *Bayley* (1866), L.R. 1 H.L. 200: "A contract to give security for the debt of another, which is a contract without consideration, is, above all things, a contract that should be based upon the free and voluntary agency of the individual who enters into it."

In the case at hand the plaintiff was being asked to give a contract providing security for the debts of Lawrence, and the only real consideration for the contract was the return to her of her car which had been wrongfully seized.

Finally, Lord Denning deals with a fifth category which is not applicable here. Then, at p. 765, he continues:

"Gathering all together, I would suggest that through all these instances there runs a single thread. They rest on "inequality of bargaining power." By virtue of it, the English law gives relief to one who, without independent advice, enters into a contract on terms which are very unfair or transfers property for a consideration which is grossly inadequate, when his bargaining power is grievously impaired by reason of his own needs or desires, or by his own ignorance or infirmity, coupled with undue influences or pressures brought to bear on him by or for the benefit of the other. When I use the word "undue" I do not mean to suggest that the principle depends on proof of any wrongdoing. The one who stipulates for an unfair advantage may be moved solely by his own self-interest, unconscious of the distress he is bringing to the other. I have also avoided any reference to the will of the one being "dominated" or "overcome" by the other. One who is in extreme need may knowingly consent to a most improvident bargain, solely to relieve the straits in which he finds himself. Again, I do not mean to suggest that every transaction is saved by independent advice. But the absence of it may be fatal."

Of course, the bank officials were acting in the interests of the bank; they were anxious to obtain valuable security for a bad debt. Ordinarily they would have had no special duty towards the plaintiff who was not their customer; but their special knowledge of Lawrence's affairs and of his crooked dealings fixed them with an obligation towards the plaintiff to ensure that the plaintiff in mortgaging her farm was really doing what she wished to do and with full knowledge of the probable consequences.

I find therefore that the mortgage signed by the plaintiff cannot be allowed to stand, at least in so far as she is concerned. In my view, her default judgment against Lawrence as to her sole ownership of the farm, is not binding against the bank. Consequently, being a joint tenant of the farm by registration, she is entitled to one-half of the proceeds, plus interest, of the amount presently standing in Court.

I turn now to the seizure of the plaintiff's motor-car. This was wrongful on the part of the defendant and its servants and agents, since any proper investigation of its title would have disclosed that the registration and ownership of the car from the time of its purchase and continuously thereafter, was always in the plaintiff's name. Moreover, even after being informed of their error, the bank continued in possession for a period of some three months. The car was seized without any prior notification to her, and her first knowledge of the seizure was when she observed it being removed from the office premises where she worked. She was embarrassed and mortified; and for the three months that followed was without use of her car and with the necessity of explaining its absence to her friends. Even when the bank did learn of its error, it would not release the car until the cash payment of $2,000 was made by the plaintiff. I consider that she is entitled to damages which I assess at $2,000, being both general and exemplary or punitive damages, covering the loss of use of her car, and covering also the damages for the embarrassment as well as the inconvenience to which she was made subject and covering also any physical injury to the vehicle.

Accordingly, the plaintiff is entitled to recover these sums from the defendants, together with her costs of these proceedings which should be taxed on the Supreme Court scale.

Judgment for the plaintiff therefore in the amount of one-half the amount of the moneys presently standing in Court, together with interest, plus judgment for the sum of $2,000, and the costs of these proceedings.

[Judgment for plaintiff.]

MACAULAY v. A. SCHROEDER MUSIC PUBLISHING CO. LTD.
[1974] 1 W.L.R. 1308 (H.L.)

A song writer, aged 21 and unknown, entered into an agreement with music publishers in their "standard form" whereby the publishers engaged his exclusive services during the term of the agreement. By clause 1 the agreement was, subject as thereinafter provided, to remain in force for five years. By clause 3 (a) the song writer assigned to the publishers the full copyright for the whole world in all his musical compositions during the term. Clauses 5 to 8 dealt with the song writer's remuneration, which was to be by royalties on works published. By clause 9 (a) if the total royalties during the term exceeded £5,000 the agreement was automatically extended for a further five years. By clause 9 (b) the publishers could determine the agreement at any time by one month's written notice. No such right was given to the song writer. By clause 16 (a) the publishers had the right to assign the agreement. By clause 16 (b) the song writer agreed not to assign his rights under the agreement without the publishers' prior written consent. The song writer brought an action claiming, inter alia, a declaration that the agreement was contrary to public policy and void. Plowman J. so held and made the declaration sought, and his judgment was affirmed by the Court of Appeal.

The publishers appealed to the House of Lords.

LORD DIPLOCK: My Lords, the contract under consideration in this appeal is one whereby the respondent accepted restrictions upon the way in which he would exploit his earning power as a song writer for the next ten years. Because this can be classified as a contract in restraint of trade the restrictions that the respondent accepted fell within one of those limited categories of contractual promises in respect of which the courts still retain the power to relieve the promisor of his legal duty to fulfil them. In order to determine whether this case is one in which that power ought to be exercised, what your Lordships have in fact been doing has been to assess the relative bargaining power of the publisher and the song writer at the time the contract was made and to decide whether the publisher had used his superior bargaining power to exact from the song writer promises that were unfairly onerous to him. Your Lordships have not been concerned to inquire whether the public have in fact been deprived of the fruit of the song writer's talents by reason of the restrictions, nor to assess the likelihood that they would be so deprived in the future if the contract were permitted to run its full course.

It is, in my view, salutary to acknowledge that in refusing to enforce provisions of a contract whereby one party agrees for the benefit of the other party to exploit or to refrain from exploiting his own earning power, the public policy which the court is implementing is not some 19th-century economic theory about the benefit to the general public of freedom of trade, but the protection of those whose bargaining power is weak against being forced by those whose bargaining power is stronger to enter into bargains that are unconscionable. Under the influence of Bentham and of laissez-faire the courts in the 19th century abandoned the practice of applying the public policy against unconscionable bargains to contracts generally, as they had formerly done to any contract considered to be usurious; but the policy survived in its application to penalty clauses and to relief against forfeiture and also to the special category of contracts in restraints of trade. If one looks at the reasoning of 19th-century judges in cases about contracts in restraint of trade one finds lip service paid to current economic theories, but if one looks at what they said in the light of what they did, one finds that they struck down a bargain if they thought it was unconscionable as between the parties to it and upheld it if they thought that it was not.

So I would hold that the question to be answered as respects a contract in restraint of trade of the kind with which this appeal is concerned is: "Was the bargain fair?" The test of fairness is, no doubt, whether the restrictions are both reasonably necessary for the protection of the legitimate interests of the promisee and commensurate with the benefits secured to the promisor under the contract. For the purpose of this test all the provisions of the contract must be taken into consideration.

My Lords, the provisions of the contract have already been sufficiently stated by my noble and learned friend, Lord Reid. I agree with his analysis of them and with his conclusion that the contract is unenforceable. It does not satisfy the test of fairness as I have endeavoured to state it. I will accordingly content myself with adding some observations directed to the argument that because the contract was in a "standard form" in common use between music publishers and song writers the restraints that it imposes upon the song writer's liberty to exploit his talents must be presumed to be fair and reasonable.

Standard forms of contracts are of two kinds. The first, of very ancient origin, are those which set out the terms upon which mercantile transactions of common occurrence are to be carried out. Examples are bills of lading, charterparties, policies of insurance, contracts of sale in the commodity markets. The standard clauses in these contracts have been settled over the years by negotiation by representatives of the commercial interests involved and have been widely adopted because experience has shown that they facilitate the conduct of trade. Contracts of these kinds affect not only the actual parties to them but also others who may have a commercial interest in the transactions to which they relate, as buyers or sellers, charterers or shipowners, insurers or bankers. If fairness or reasonableness were relevant to their enforceability the fact that they are widely used by parties whose bargaining power is fairly matched would raise a strong presumption that their terms are fair and reasonable.

The same presumption, however, does not apply to the other kind of standard form of contract. This is of comparatively modern origin. It is the result of the concentration of particular kinds of business in relatively few hands. The ticket cases in the 19th century provide what are probably the first examples. The terms of this kind of standard form of contract have not been the subject of negotiation between the parties to it, or approved by any organisation representing the interests of the weaker party. They have been dictated by that party whose bargaining power, either exercised alone or in conjunction with others providing similar goods or services, enables him to say: "If you want these goods or services at all, these are the only terms on which they are obtainable. Take it or leave it."

To be in a position to adopt this attitude towards a party desirous of entering into a contract to obtain goods or services provides a classic instance of superior bargaining power. It is not without significance that on the evidence in the present case music publishers in negotiating with song writers whose success has been already established do not insist upon adhering to a contract in the standard form they offered to the respondent. The fact that the appellants' bargaining power vis-à-vis the respondent was strong enough to enable them to adopt this take-it-or-leave-it attitude raises no presumption that they used it to drive an unconscionable bargain with him, but in the field of restraint of trade it calls for vigilance on the part of the court to see that they did not.

PRIDMORE v. CALVERT
(1975) 54 D.L.R. (3d) 133 (B.C.S.C.)

The plaintiff was injured in a motor accident by the defendant's negligence. The defendant relied on a release signed by the plaintiff.

Toy J: The final question for determination has given me the greatest concern. The plaintiff was attended by an insurance adjuster within 48 hours of the accident. After signing a statement disclosing the circumstances of the accident, the plaintiff then signed a release of all her claims in favour of the defendants and their insurers. The defendants' counsel has pleaded and relied on that release as a complete defence to the plaintiff's claims.

Although the plaintiff's version of the signing of the release—or releases—is in many respects uncertain and vague, and in some instances she professed not to remember, I ascribe her lack of recollection to her state of mind and general condition at that time. The insurance adjuster gave his evidence in an admirably frank fashion, and I am prepared to accept his evidence as accurate and truthful.

In coming to the conclusion that I have, I have relied on a recent judgment of my brother Anderson J., in *Towers* v. *Affleck*, [1974] 1 W.W.R. 714. Anderson J. at p. 717 said: ". . . the true question to be determined here is whether the parties were on such unequal footing, in all the circumstances, that it would be inequitable to hold the plaintiff to her bargain." He said further, at pp. 719-20:

"I have reached the conclusion that on the whole of the evidence the plaintiff has proved by a preponderance of evidence that the parties were on such an unequal footing that it would be unfair and inequitable to hold her to the terms of the agreement which she signed. Having reached the conclusion that the defendant was in a dominant position, it becomes necessary to consider whether the settlement was fair and reasonable. I have asked myself the question whether any practising lawyer would have approved the settlement. The answer is in the negative.

"While the Court will not lightly set aside settlement agreements, the Court will set aside contracts and bargains of an improvident character made by poor and ignorant persons acting without independent advice unless the other party discharges the onus on him to show that the transaction is fair and reasonable: see *Whittet* v. *Bush* (1888), 40 Ch.D. 312. While there is no evidence of poverty or financial distress in this case, I think that one of the major factors in the *Whittet* case was that the purchaser's solicitors acted for all parties and that the vendors did not receive any independent advice. *An experienced insurance adjuster plays the same role as a practising solicitor.*" (Italics my own).

In my view, the plaintiff should not be bound by the release that she signed for the reasons which I will detail shortly, but which in my judgment are supported by facts of greater weight than those relied on by my brother Anderson, in *Towers* v. *Affleck, supra*:

1. The plaintiff is a woman of limited intelligence. I do not mean that in a disparaging sense, but she told me that she started her training as a practical nurse at age 15. There was no evidence of any later academic training.

2. The plaintiff had worked throughout her married life as a practical nurse and in 1971 her husband died. The plaintiff had no close personal friends to whom she turned for advice or counselling of a confidential nature.

3. At the material time she sought no legal advice nor any lay advice concerning the signing of the release.

4. There was no evidence to suggest that the plaintiff had any business acumen at all, much less any knowledge of "releases."

5. The defendants' adjuster courteously arranged for an interview with the plaintiff at her home where she was recuperating on the second day after the accident.

6. The plaintiff's poor physical condition was apparent to the defendant's adjuster, who observed that the plaintiff was taking pills, that she was suffering from headaches, that she was in pain, and when walking, she did so in a guarded fashion.

7. The defendants' adjuster know that the plaintiff was unable to work and was under a doctor's care.

8. The defendants' adjuster, without having examined the scene of the accident, without having solicited the plaintiff's doctor's opinion, or even having interviewed the defendant driver, was prepared to assess the claim and settle it "on the spot" at his first meeting with the plaintiff. There was a second release executed by the plaintiff two days later which is the operative release, but I do not attach great significance to that fact, as for all realistic purposes, the plaintiff was in the same condition and position of reliance on the adjuster on the second day as she was on the first. The release being one I was not familiar with in form, I now reproduce that document in full:

"AGREEMENT AND RELEASE

For and In Consideration of the payment of the sum of Three Hundred & Thirty One Dollars, the receipt of which is hereby acknowledged, and of the promise of payment to the undersigned of benefits in accordance with the Schedule of Benefits set forth below, by the Company accepting this Agreement,

SCHEDULE OF BENEFITS

(1) To pay all reasonable and necessary expenses incurred for medical, dental or surgical treatment, ambulance, hospital, professional nursing services and prosthetic devices, furnished to the named beneficiary within 180 days of the date of this Agreement, as a result of the accident described herein, provided that such expenses are not paid or payable by any collateral source and do not exceed $2,000; and

(2) To pay $17.66 (payable monthly) for each day within 180 days of the date of this Agreement that said beneficiary is continuously and necessarily disabled and confined indoors under the care of a licensed physician other than himself, due to the bodily injury incurred because of the accident described herein; provided that the total of said per diem payments shall not exceed $2,000;

and, provided the total amount payable hereunder for this release, plus said expense payments, plus said per diem payments, shall not exceed the limit of liability for bodily injury to one person provided by the policy of insurance applicable to the releasee named herein, the undersigned hereby releases and forever discharges Thomas Calvert and Innes Calvert, the Insurance Company accepting this Agreement, and any and all other persons, firms or corporations liable or who might be claimed to be liable, from any and all claims, demands, damages, actions, causes of action or suits of any kind or nature whatsoever, and particularly on account of all injuries, known and unknown, both to person and property, which have resulted or may in the future develop because of bodily injuries sustained by Sheila Pridmore as a result of an accident which occurred on or about the 28 day of August 1972 at or near Kingsway & East 10th Avenue, Vancouver, B.C. It is also agreed and understood that this settlement is the compromise of a doubtful and disputed claim, that the payment is not to be construed as an admission of liability on the part of the persons, firms, and corporations hereby released, by whom liability is expressly denied. This Agreement and Release contains the entire agreement between the parties hereto, and the terms of this instrument are contractual and not a mere recital. It is further agreed that all parties to this instrument have carefully read the contents thereof and the signatures below are the voluntary and free act of each.

In Witness whereof I have hereunto set my hand(s) and seal(s) this 1 day of September, 1972.

IN PRESENCE OF

                                        (signed) "Sheila Pridmore" (SEAL)
                                                                    (SEAL)

                              Accepted By:
     x State Farm Mutual Automobile Insurance Company
        State Farm Fire and Casualty Company
        State Farm County Mutual Insurance Company of Texas
        State Farm General Insurance Company
     62-026-410   By (signed) "Ken Haughton"

Claim Number   Authorized Representative
                8449 Main St.   321-254
                   Address   Telephone No."

9. The stated consideration of $331.40 which the plaintiff received "on the spot" on September 1, 1972, was calculated by the adjuster on August 30th as follows:

—For out-of-pocket expenses, such as torn
    clothing, damaged wig, etc. $131.40
—Extra $200.00

The adjuster asked the plaintiff how much she wanted for her "injuries" and she apparently asked the adjuster's opinion. He volunteered the figure of $200. That amount, one could only conclude as being in satisfaction of the plaintiff's whole general damage claim, except her actual loss of earnings, providing they did not exceed 180 days.

10. The adjuster computed the plaintiff's monthly income and broke it down to a daily wage loss claim and arrived at the figure of $17.66 per day. That amount the plaintiff was to receive in addition to medical expenses not otherwise covered and the above-mentioned sum of $331.40.

11. The adjuster was a man experienced in his work, and, before me, acknowledged that he had three interests to serve: one, his employer, the insurer; two, the defendants, namely, the insured persons; and three, the plaintiff, because she was, in any event, entitled to receive no-fault benefits of $50 per week for as long as she was off work up to a maximum of 108 weeks. I pause here to note that of the $17.66 daily benefit to be paid, as calculated by the adjuster, the plaintiff was entitled as of right to receive $7.15 as a result of her entitlement to no-fault benefits. I find that at the times the plaintiff was solicited to sign the two releases, she was not advised of her right to claim no-fault benefits of $50 per week and postpone her claims for general damages and out-of-pocket expenses until she had effected a complete recovery.

12. I further find that with respect to the $200 extra paid to her as referred to in para. 9 above, that she advanced no such claim herself, but was induced by the adjuster to advance such a claim. It is accordingly my opinion that the figure selected by the adjuster of $200 was not one that could properly be construed as a fair and reasonable estimate for the plaintiff's pain and suffering or loss of amenities, but one deliberately designed by the defendants' insurers to foreclose the possibility of a future claim by the plaintiff from anything in excess of 180 days of loss of income and her no-fault benefits. The defendants' adjuster and counsel on the defendants' behalf at trial sought to justify the adjuster's conduct by relating that the plaintiff had told the adjuster that her doctor had said she would probably be back to work in a couple or three weeks. If that estimate was entitled to be acted upon, the $200 figure for loss of amenities and pain and suffering might be construed as reasonable. But if the agreement and release form ran its full course of $2,000 or a 180 days off work, could a figure of $200 be justified to compensate a person for suffering, or continued suffering in the manner that the defendants' adjuster observed when he attended at the plaintiff's residence?

13. The defendants' adjuster further conceded, with admirable candor that he did not explain the harshness of the release to the plaintiff.

Would any lawyer purporting to advise the plaintiff as to her rights have advised her to accept such a settlement? Posing the question that Anderson J., did in *Towers* v. *Affleck* brings quickly to mind numerous reasons why a complete settlement and release under the conditions which existed on both August 30, and September 1, 1972, should not have been made, only a few of which I will mention:

(a) The attending doctor's concurrence to settle should have been considered.

(b) Lawyers, and adjusters, exposure to these matters militates against a quick "on the spot" settlement.

(c) Without a firm, if not written, medical opinion, no settlement should have been made.

(d) A doctor's first opinion, or prognosis, many times have been shown to be inaccurate and the majority of them are quick to concede the point.

(e) The pain, headaches and general demeanour of the plaintiff, witnessed by the defendants' adjuster on the second and fourth days after the accident, should have been sufficient for any person purporting to give her independent advice to counsel her against signing such a serious document.

Accordingly, the plaintiff has satisfied me, on the balance of probabilities, that she was on such an unequal footing with respect to the defendants and their representatives, that in all the circumstances, it would be inequitable to hold her to the bargain that was made. There will accordingly be judgment for the plaintiff for general damages, special damages and allowing deductions as previously detailed, for the net amount of $20,995.11.

[Judgment for paintiff.]

PROBLEM. Able asks his neighbour, Baker, whether he is willing to sell his house. Baker agrees to sell the house and suggests a price of $50,000. Baker is 75 years old, but perfectly alert and sane to all appearances; nevertheless, to avoid any suggestion of sharp practice, Able suggests that Baker should take independent advice; Baker is insulted at the implied reflection on his business acumen, and insists on his competence to handle his own affairs. Able therefore agrees (in writing) to purchase the house for $50,000; "$10,000 cash, balance first mortgage; date of closing and terms of mortgage to be agreed." Baker then discovers that the house is worth $75,000, and he concludes that his business acumen is not what it was. Can he avoid the sale?

5. CONSUMER PROTECTION

SALE OF GOODS ACT
R.S.O. 1970 c. 421

13. In a contract of sale, unless the circumstances of the contract are such as to show a different intention, there is,

(a) an implied condition on the part of the seller than in the case of a sale he has a right to sell the goods, and that in the case of an agreement to sell he will have a right to sell the goods at the time when the property is to pass;

(b) an implied warranty that the buyer will have and enjoy quiet possession of the goods; and (*c*) an implied warranty that the goods will be free from any charge or encumbrance in favour of any third party, not declared or known to the buyer before or at the time when the contract is made.

14. Where there is a contract for the sale of goods by description, there is an implied condition that the goods will correspond with the description, and, if the sale is by sample as well as by description, it is not sufficient that the bulk of the goods corresponds with the sample if the goods do not also correspond with the description.

15. Subject to this Act and any statute in that behalf, there is no implied warranty or condition as to the quality or fitness for any particular purpose of goods supplied under a contract of sale, except as follows:

1. Where the buyer, expressly or by implication, makes known to the seller the particular purpose for which the goods are required so as to show that the buyer relies on the seller's skill or judgment, and the goods are of a description that it is in the course of the seller's business to supply (whether he is the manufacturer or not), there is an implied condition that the goods will be reasonably fit for such purpose, but in the case of a contract for the sale of a specified article under its patent or other trade name there is no implied condition as to its fitness for any particular purpose.

2. Where goods are bought by description from a seller who deals in goods of that description (whether he is the manufacturer or not), there is an implied condition that the goods will be of merchantable quality, but if the buyer has examined the goods, there is no implied condition as regards defects that such examination ought to have revealed.

3. An implied warranty or condition as to quality or fitness for a particular purpose may be annexed by the usage of trade.

4. An express warranty or condition does not negative a warranty or condition implied by this Act unless inconsistent therewith.

53. Where any right, duty or liability would arise under a contract of sale by implication of law, it may be negatived or varied by express agreement or by the course of dealing between the parties, or by usage, if the usage is such as to bind both parties to the contract.

CONSUMER PROTECTION ACT
R.S.O. 1970 c. 50

PART II

EXECUTORY CONTRACTS

30. This Part applies to executory contracts for the sale of goods or services where the purchase price, excluding the cost of borrowing, exceeds $50.

31. (1) Every executory contract, other than an executory contract under an agreement for variable credit, shall be in writing and shall contain,

(*a*) the name and address of the seller and the buyer;

(*b*) a description of the goods or services sufficient to identify them with certainty;

(*c*) the itemized price of the goods or services and a detailed statement of the terms of payment;

(*d*) where credit is extended, a statement of any security for payment under the contract, including the particulars of any negotiable instrument, conditional sale agreement, chattel mortgage or any other security;

(*e*) where credit is extended, the statement required to be furished by section 36;

(*f*) any warranty or guarantee applying to the goods or services and, where there is no warranty or guarantee, a statement to this effect; and

(*g*) any other matter required by the regulations.

(2) An executory contract is not binding on the buyer unless the contract is made in accordance with this Part and the regulations and is signed by the parties, and a duplicate original copy thereof is in the possession of each of the parties thereto.

(3) Where the amount to be paid by a buyer under an executory contract is determined after an allowance for a trade-in and is stated in the contract to be subject to adjustment after the existence or amount of liens against the trade-in is ascertained or confirmed, the statement of the terms of payment and the statement of the cost of credit shall be based upon the amount as determined upon the information provided by the buyer but, upon any subsequent adjustment, the percentage rate by which the cost of borrowing is expressed, the total number of instalments required to pay the total indebtedness or the price shown in the contract shall not be changed.

32. Where a trade-in is delivered or money is paid, whether by way of deposit or otherwise, on account of the proposed purchase of goods or services but no binding contract is entered into in respect of the goods and no delivery of the goods or any part thereof has been made to the buyer or no performance of the services has been made, the seller shall upon the request of the buyer return such trade-in or refund in full the moneys so paid, as the case may be.

33. (1) Where a seller solicits, negotiates or arranges for the signing by a buyer of an executory contract at a place other than the seller's permanent place of business, the buyer may rescind the contract by delivering a notice of rescission in writing to the seller within two days after the duplicate original copy of the contract first comes into the possession of the buyer, and the buyer is not liable for any damages in respect of such rescission.

(2) Where a buyer rescinds a contract under subsection 1,

(*a*) The buyer shall immediately return any goods received under the contract and the seller shall bear the expense of the return, not exceeding the expense of returning the goods from the place where the buyer received their delivery; and

(*b*) the seller shall return any moneys received or realized in respect of the contract, whether from the buyer or any other person, and shall return any trade-in received under the contract.

(3) Where part of the consideration for the sale of goods is a trade-in, the title to the trade-in does not pass to the seller until the two-day period mentioned in subsection 1 has expired without rescission of the contract.

(4) A notice of rescission may be delivered personally or sent by registered mail addressed to the person to whom delivery is required to be made

at the address shown in the contract, and delivery by registered mail shall be deemed to have been made at the time of mailing.

34. Any provision in any executory contract or in any security agreement incidental thereto under which the seller may acquire title to, possession of or any rights in any goods of the buyer, other than the goods passing to the buyer under the contract, is not enforceable.

35. (1) Where a buyer under an executory contract has paid two-thirds or more of the purchase price of the goods as fixed by the contract, any provision in the contract, or in any security agreement incidental thereto, under which the seller may retake possession of or resell the goods upon default in payment by the buyer is not enforceable except by leave of a judge of a county or district court.

(2) Upon an application for leave under subsection 1, the judge may, in his absolute discretion, grant or refuse leave or grant leave upon such terms and conditions as he considers advisable.

44. This Act applies notwithstanding any agreement or waiver to the contrary.

44a. (1) In this section, "consumer sale" means a contract for the sale of goods made in the ordinary course of business to a purchaser for his consumption or use, but does not include a sale,

    (a) to a purchaser for resale;

    (b) to a purchaser whose purchase is in the course of carrying on business;

    (c) to an association of individuals, a partnership or a corporation;

    (d) by a trustee in bankruptcy, a receiver, a liquidator or a person acting under the order of a court.

(2) The implied conditions and warranties applying to the sale of goods by virtue of *The Sale of Goods Act* apply to goods sold by a consumer sale and any written term or acknowledgment, whether part of the contract of sale or not, that purports to negative or vary any of such implied conditions and warranties is void and, if a term of a contract, is severable therefrom, and such term or acknowledgment shall not be evidence of circumstances showing an intent that any of the implied conditions and warranties are not to apply.

45. The rights of a buyer or borrower under this Act are in addition to any rights of the buyer or borrower under any other Act, or by the operation of law, and nothing in this Act shall be construed to derogate from such rights.

[Note: ss. 44-5 are in part IV of the Act.]

CONSUMER PRODUCTS WARRANTIES BILL (Ont.), 1976 (Bill 110)

NOTE: The Bill was given first reading in 1976. It is expected to be reintroduced in 1977 with substantial changes. [1979: not yet reintroduced.]

1. (1) In this Act,

    (a) "consumer" means a natural person who is the owner or has the right to possess and use a consumer product, but does not include a natural person, partnership or association of individuals acting in the course of carrying on business;

    (b) "consumer product" means a chattel personal including a chattel that becomes a fixture but not including a food, drink, medicine, cosmetic, clothing or a chose in action;

(c) "express warranty" means an affirmation of fact or promise relating to the quality, condition, quantity, performance of efficacy of a consumer product or relating to its use and maintenance where the tendency of such affirmation is to induce the buyer to purchase the consumer product;

(d) "implied warranty" means a warranty provided for by this Act to be an implied warranty;

(e) "manufacturer," when used in relation to a consumer product, means,

(i) a person who manufactures or assembles the consumer product,

(ii) a person who describes or holds himself out to the public as the manufacturer of the consumer product,

(iii) a person under whose brand name the consumer product is offered for sale,

(iv) where the consumer product is imported into Canada and there is no manufacturer as defined in subclause i, ii, or iii in Canada, the person who imported the consumer product,

and more than one person may be manufacturers of the same consumer product;

(f) "retail buyer" means a consumer who buys a consumer product from a retail seller;

(g) "retail seller" means a seller who engages in the business of selling consumer products to consumers;

(h) "sale" means the transfer of the right to possess and use a consumer product and includes the transfer of possession or right to possession under an agreement to sell or conditional sale agreement or under a lease with an option to purchase or a lease for more than one year and "sell" and other forms of the verb have a corresponding meaning;

(i) "seller" means a person who sells a consumer product to a consumer and includes a retail seller;

(j) "warranty" means an express or implied warranty.

(2) This Act does not apply in respect of a consumer product purchased by the consumer thereof for a consideration that is less than $25.

(3) Sections 12 to 16 and sections 51, 52 and 53 of *The Sale of Goods Act* do not apply in respect of the sale of consumer products.

2. There is an implied warranty by the seller of a consumer product to the consumer to whom the consumer product is sold,

(a) that the seller has a right to sell the consumer product;

(b) that the consumer will have and enjoy quiet possession of the consumer product; and

(c) that the consumer product is free from any charge or encumbrance not declared or known to the consumer before or at the time the sale is made.

3. (1) Where there is a sale of a consumer product to a retail buyer by description formulated by the retail buyer, there is an implied warranty by the retail seller that the consumer product conforms to the description.

(2) Where there is a sale of a consumer product to a retail buyer,

    (*a*) by sample;

    (*b*) by description formulated by the retail seller; or

    (*c*) by description made by a person other than the retail seller,

there is an implied warranty,

    (*d*) by the retail seller in a case to which clause *a* or *b* applies; or

    (*e*) by the manufacturer and retail seller jointly in a case to which clause *c* applies,

to the retail buyer that the consumer product corresponds to the description or sample.

(3) For the purposes of subsection 2, the description of a consumer product includes description by advertisement or by label or associated with the product orally or in writing.

(4) For the purposes of subsection 2, where a sale is by sample as well as description, it is not sufficient that the consumer product corresponds with the sample if the consumer product does not also correspond with the description.

4. There is an implied warranty by the manufacturer and retail seller jointly to the consumer of a consumer product that,

    (*a*) the consumer product and its components will perform for a reasonable length of time, having regard to the price and all surrounding circumstances;

    (*b*) the consumer product is in such an actual state that a buyer fully acquainted with the facts and therefore knowing what hidden defects exist would buy it for all purposes for which the consumer product is normally used without abatement of the price obtainable for such consumer product if in a reasonably sound state or without special terms unless,

        (i) the retail seller or manufacturer has disclosed to the retail buyer defects in the consumer product or that the consumer products are not suitable for all purposes for which they are normally used, or

        (ii) the defect should have been apparent to the consumer where he has examined the consumer product prior to purchase, or

        (iii) it is common knowledge among consumers that the particular consumer products are not suitable for all such purposes.

5. There is an implied warranty by the manufacturer and retail seller jointly to the consumer of a consumer product that spare parts and reasonable repair facilities will be available for a reasonable period of time.

6. (1) There is an implied warranty by the retail seller to the retail buyer of a consumer product that the consumer product is reasonably fit for the particular purpose for which it is required, unless the circumstances are such as to show that the retail buyer did not rely, or that it was unreasonable for the retail buyer to rely, on the retail seller's skill and judgment.

(2) For the purposes of this section, a particular purpose for which the consumer product is required includes not only an unusual or special purpose but also a normal or usual purpose.

7. (1) An express warranty made by a retail seller in connection with the sale of a consumer product to a retail buyer.

    (*a*) if made in writing or published or broadcast, is an express war-

ranty by the retail seller to the consumer of the consumer product;
(*b*) if not made in writing or published or broadcast, is an express
warranty by the retail seller to the retail buyer of the consumer product.

(2) An express warranty made in writing or published or broadcast by
a person other than a retail seller in connection with the sale of a consumer
product to a retail buyer is a warranty by the retail seller and the manufacturer, jointly, to the consumer of the consumer product.

(3) An express warranty does not negative an implied warranty.

(4) For the purposes of this section, "made in writing or published or
broadcast" means,
(*a*) made in writing and accompanying the product, whether on
the package or separately, or handed to the buyer in the process of
completing the sale;
(*b*) made in writing and distributed or displayed to the general
public, whether by advertisement, sign display or other means;
(*c*) made by television or radio broadcast to the general public,
and the person who causes the affirmation to be printed, distributed, displayed, published or broadcast shall be deemed to be the person who
makes the affirmation.

8. (1) Any term or acknowledgment whether written or otherwise
and whether part of the agreement of sale or not, that purports to negative, exclude, restrict or diminish any warranty under this Act or the
availability or scope of any remedy otherwise available for the breach
thereof is void and of no effect and, if a term of a contract, is severable
therefrom, and such term or acknowledgment shall not be evidence of circumstances showing an intent that any of such warranties are not to apply.

(2) No person shall include in a written agreement any thing that purports to be a term or acknowledgment that is void and of no effect under
subsection 1.

(3) Any act or representation by an employee or agent of a retail seller
or manufacturer having apparent authority shall be deemed to be an act or
representation of the retail seller or manufacturer.

9. (1) Where a warranty is given by this Act to a consumer, the person
by whom the warranty is given owes a duty to the consumer to perform
the warranty and is liable to the consumer in damages for any breach
thereof or, where the warranty is given in connection with a contract of
sale between them, to rescission of the contract, or both.

(2) In the trial of an issue under subsection 1, oral evidence respecting
the facts necessary to establish an implied or express warranty is admissible notwithstanding that there is a written agreement and notwithstanding that the evidence pertains to a representation or undertaking that
is or is not provided for in the agreement.

(3) The measure of damages for breach of warranty is the estimated
loss directly and naturally resulting in the ordinary course of events
from the breach of warranty.

(4) No action shall be brought under subsection 1 after the expiration
of two years from the time the breach of warranty is first alleged.

10. (1) Where by this Act the retail seller and manufacturer give a
warranty jointly, the retail seller and all manufacturers of the consumer
product are jointly and severally liable under section 9 but as between
themselves, in the absence of any contract, express or implied, each is
liable to make contribution and indemnify each other in the degree in

which they are respectively found to be responsible for the creation of the circumstances leading to the creation of the warranty and its breach.

(2) Where a claim for damages under section 9 is settled, for the purposes of an action for contribution or indemnity in respect of the amount paid under the settlement, the person settling shall satisfy the court that the amount of the settlement was reasonable, and in the event that the court finds the amount of the settlement was excessive it may fix the amount at which the claim should have been settled.

(3) Where the right of contribution or indemnity under this section is disclaimed or restricted by the terms of an agreement and it appears to the court that the disclaimer or restriction is unreasonable or unfair for the reason that the person against whom the disclaimer or restriction is imposed has no means to avoid liability or for any other reason, the court may declare the term void and of no effect, and the term shall be deemed to be severable from the agreement for the purpose.

BUSINESS PRACTICES ACT
S.O. 1974, c. 131

1. In this Act,

> (b) "consumer" means a natural person but does not include a natural person, partnership or association of individuals acting in the course of carrying on business;
>
> (c) "consumer representation" means a representation, statement, offer, request or proposal,
>
>> (i) made respecting or with a view to the supplying of goods or services, or both, to a consumer, or
>>
>> (ii) made for the purpose of or with a view to receiving consideration for goods or services, or both, supplied or purporting to have been supplied to a consumer;

2. For the purposes of this Act, the following shall be deemed to be unfair practices,

> (a) a false, misleading or deceptive consumer representation including, but without limiting the generality of the foregoing,
>
>> (i) a representation that the goods or services have sponsorship, approval, performance characteristics, accessories, uses, ingredients, benefits or quantities they do not have,
>>
>> (ii) a representation that the person who is to supply the goods or services has sponsorship, approval, status, affiliation or connection he does not have,
>>
>> (iii) a representation that the goods are of a particular standard, quality, grade, style or model, if they are not,
>>
>> (iv) a representation that the goods are new, or unused, if they are not or are reconditioned or reclaimed, provided that the reasonable use of goods to enable the seller to service, prepare, test and deliver the goods for the purpose of sale shall not be deemed to make the goods used for the purposes of this subclause,
>>
>> (v) a representation that the goods have been used to an extent that is materially different from the fact,
>>
>> (vi) a representation that the goods or services are available for a reason that does not exist,
>>
>> (vii) a representation that the goods or services have been sup-

plied in accordance with a previous representation, if they have not,

(viii) a representation that the goods or services or any part thereof are available to the consumer when the person making the representation knows or ought to know they will not be supplied,

(ix) a representation that a service, part, replacement or repair is needed, if it is not,

(x) a representation that a specific price advantage exists, if it does not,

(xi) a representation that misrepresents the authority of a salesman, representative, employee or agent to negotiate the final terms of the proposed transaction,

(xii) a representation that the proposed transaction involves or does not involve rights, remedies or obligations if the representation is false or misleading,

(xiii) a representation using exaggeration, innuendo or ambiguity as to a material fact or failing to state a material fact if such use or failure deceives or tends to deceive,

(xiv) a representation that misrepresents the purpose or intent of any solicitation of or any communication with a consumer;

(b) an unconscionable consumer representation made in respect of a particular transaction and in determining whether or not a consumer representation is unconscionable there may be taken into account that the person making the representation or his employer or principal knows or ought to know,

(i) that the consumer is not reasonably able to protect his interests because of his physical infirmity, ignorance, illiteracy, inability to understand the language of an agreement or similar factors,

(ii) that the price grossly exceeds the price at which similar goods or services are readily available to like consumers,

(iii) that the consumer is unable to receive a substantial benefit from the subject-matter of the consumer representation,

(iv) that there is no reasonable probability of payment of the obligation in full by the consumer,

(v) that the proposed transaction in excessively one-sided in favour of someone other than the consumer,

(vi) that the terms or conditions of the proposed transaction are so adverse to the consumer as to be inequitable,

(vii) that he is making a misleading statement of opinion on which the consumer is likely to rely to his detriment,

(viii) that he is subjecting the consumer to undue pressure to enter into the transaction;

(c) such other consumer representations under clause a as are prescribed by the regulations made in accordance with section 16.

3. (1) No person shall engage in an unfair practice.

(2) A person who performs one act referred to in section 2 shall be deemed to be engaging in an unfair practice.

4. (1) Subject to subsection 2, any agreement, whether written, oral or implied, entered into by a consumer after a consumer representation that is an unfair practice and that induced the consumer to enter into the agreement,

(a) may be rescinded by the consumer and the consumer is entitled to any remedy therefor that is at law available, including damages; or

(*b*) where rescission is not possible because restitution is no longer possible, or because rescission would deprive a third party of a right in the subject-matter of the agreement that he has acquired in good faith and for value, the consumer is entitled to recover the amount by which the amount paid under the agreement exceeds the fair value of the goods or services received under the agreement or damages, or both.

(2) Where the unfair practice referred to in subsection 1 comes within clause *b* of section 2, the court may award exemplary or punitive damages.

(3) Each person who makes the consumer representation referred to in subsection 1 is liable jointly and severally with the person who entered into the agreement with the consumer for any amount that the consumer is entitled to under subsections 1 and 2.

(4) Notwithstanding subsection 2 of section 42*a* of *The Consumer Protection Act*, the liability of an assignee of an agreement under subsection 1 or of any right to payment thereunder is limited to the amount paid to the assignee under the agreement.

(5) A remedy conferred by subsection 1 may be claimed by the giving of notice of the claim by the consumer in writing to each other party to the agreement within six months after the agreement is entered into.

(6) A notice under subsection 5 may be delivered personally or sent by registered mail addressed to the person to whom delivery is required to be made, and delivery by registered mail shall be deemed to have been made at the time of mailing.

(7) In the trial of an issue under subsection 1, oral evidence respecting an unfair practice is admissible notwithstanding that there is a written agreement and notwithstanding that the evidence pertains to a representation of a term, condition or undertaking that is or is not provided for in the agreement.

(8) This section applies notwithstanding any agreement or waiver to the contrary.

(9) Subsection 3 does not apply to a person who, on behalf of another person, prints, publishes, distributes, broadcasts or telecasts a representation or an advertisement that he accepts in good faith for printing, publishing, distributing, broadcasting or telecasting in the ordinary course of his business.

[Note: There is a restricted statutory definition of "services."]

THE UNCONSCIONABLE TRANSACTIONS RELIEF ACT
R.S.O. 1970, c. 472

1. In this Act,

(a) "cost" of the loan means the whole cost to the debtor of money lent and includes interest, discount, subscription, premium, dues, bonus, commission, brokerage fees and charges, but not actual lawful and necessary disbursements made to a registrar of deeds, a master or local master of titles, a clerk of a county or district court, a sheriff or a treasurer of a municipality;

(c) "creditor" includes the person advancing money lent and the assignee of any claim arising or security given in respect of money lent.

(d) "debtor" means a person to whom or on whose account money lent is advanced and includes every surety and endorser or other person liable for the repayment of money lent or upon any agreement or collateral or other security given in respect thereof;

(e) "money lent" includes money advanced on account of any person in any transaction that, whatever its form may be, is substantially one of money-lending or securing the repayment of money so advanced and includes and has always included a mortgage within the meaning of *The Mortgages Act.*

2. Where, in respect of money lent, the court finds that, having regard to the risk and to all the circumstances, the cost of the loan is excessive and that the transaction is harsh and unconscionable, the court may,

(a) re-open the transaction and take an account between the creditor and the debtor;

(b) notwithstanding any statement or settlement of account or any agreement purporting to close previous dealings and create a new obligation, re-open any account already taken and relieve the debtor from payment of any sum in excess of the sum adjudged by the court to be fairly due in respect of the principal and the cost of the loan;

(c) order the creditor to re-pay any such excess if the same has been paid or allowed on account by the debtor;

(d) set aside either wholly or in part or revise or alter any security given or agreement made in respect of the money lent, and, if the creditor has parted with the security, order him to indemnify the debtor.

3. The powers conferred by section 2 may be exercised,

(a) in an action or proceeding by a creditor for the recovery of money lent;

(b) in an action or proceeding by the debtor notwithstanding any provision or agreement to the contrary, and notwithstanding that the time for repayment of the loan or any instalment thereof has not arrived;

(c) in an action or proceeding in which the amount due or to become due in respect of money lent is in question.

4. (1) In addition to any right that a debtor may have under this or any other Act or otherwise in respect of money lent, he may apply for relief under this Act to a judge of the county or district court of the county or district in which he resides, and the judge on the application may exercise any of the powers of the court under section 2.

5. Nothing in this Act affects the rights of a *bona fide* assignee or holder for value without notice, or derogates from the existing powers or jurisdiction of any court.

THE UNIFORM COMMERCIAL CODE

Section 2-302. Unconscionable Contract or Clause

(1) If the court as a matter of law finds the contract or any clause of the contract to have been unconscionable at the time it was made the court may refuse to enforce the contract, or it may enforce the remainder of the

contract without the unconscionable clause, or it may so limit the application of any unconscionable clause as to avoid any unconscionable result.

(2) When it is claimed or appears to the court that the contract or any clause thereof may be unconscionable the parties shall be afforded a reasonable opportunity to present evidence as to its commercial setting, purpose and effect to aid the court in making the determination.

Comment . . . The principle is one of the prevention of oppression and unfair surprise . . . and not of disturbance of allocation of risks because of superior bargaining power.

SUPPLY OF GOODS (IMPLIED TERMS) ACT 1973 (U.K.) amending the SALE OF GOODS ACT, 1893 (U.K.)

NOTE. Section 14 of the U.K. Act corresponds to section 15 of the Ontario Act and s. 55 corresponds to s. 53.

4. For section 55 of the principal Act (exclusion of implied terms and conditions) there shall be substituted the following section:

55. (1) Where any right, duty or liability would arise under a contract of sale of goods by implication of law, it may be negatived or varied by express agreement, or by the course of dealing between the parties, or by usage if the usage is such as to bind both parties to the contract, but the foregoing provision shall have effect subject to the following provisions of this section.

(2) An express condition or warranty does not negative a condition or warranty implied by this Act unless inconsistent therewith.

(3) In the case of a contract of sale of goods, any term of that or any other contract exempting from all or any of the provisions of section 12 of this Act shall be void.

(4) In the case of a contract of sale of goods, any term of that or any other contract exempting from all or any of the provisions of section 13, 14 or 15 of this Act shall be void in the case of a consumer sale and shall, in any other case, not be enforceable to the extent that it is shown that it would not be fair or reasonable to allow reliance on the term.

(5) In determining for the purposes of subsection (4) above whether or not reliance on any such term would be fair or reasonable regard shall be had to all the circumstances of the case and in particular to the following matters—

(a) the strength of the bargaining positions of the seller and buyer relative to each other, taking into account, among other things, the availability of suitable alternative products and sources of supply;

(b) whether the buyer received an inducement to agree to the term or in accepting it had an opportunity of buying the goods or suitable alternatives without it from any source of supply;

(c) whether the buyer knew or ought reasonably to have known of the existence and extent of the term (having regard, among other things, to any custom of the trade and any previous course of dealing between the parties);

(d) where the term exempts from all or any of the provisions of section 13, 14 or 15 of this Act if some condition is not complied with, whether it was reasonable at the time of the contract to expect that compliance with that condition would be practicable;

(*e*) whether the goods were manufactured, processed, or adapted to the special order of the buyer.

(6) Subsection (5) above shall not prevent the court from holding, in accordance with any rule of law, that a term which purports to exclude or restrict any of the provisions of section 13, 14 or 15 of this Act is not a term of the contract.

(7) In this section "consumer sale" means a sale of goods (other than a sale by auction or by competitive tender) by a seller in the course of a business where the goods—

(*a*) are of a type ordinarily bought for private use or consumption; and

(*b*) are sold to a person who does not buy or hold himself out as buying them in the course of a business.

(8) The onus of proving that a sale falls to be treated for the purposes of this section as not being a consumer sale shall lie on the party so contending.

(9) Any reference in this section to a term exempting from all or any of the provisions of any section of this Act is a reference to a term which purports to exclude or restrict, or has the effect of excluding or restricting, the operation of all or any of the provisions of that section, or the exercise of a right conferred by any provision of that section, or any liability of the seller for breach of a condition or warranty implied by any provision of that section.

(10) It is hereby declared that any reference in this section to a term of a contract includes a reference to a term which although not contained in a contract is incorporated in the contract by another term of the contract.

PROBLEM. Able advertises electric appliances at "rock bottom prices." His practice is to buy appliances from various manufacturers and to sell them under his own name. Baker and Charlie, two customers, come into Able's shop. Baker is buying a vacuum cleaner for his resort hotel for use in the hotel and in Baker's own cottage next door. Charlie is buying a vacuum cleaner as a gift for his wife. Able demonstrates the operation of a machine, expatiating on its efficiency, rugged construction, and low price. Baker and Charlie ask about warranties. Able explains that at his new low prices there are no warranties, and that the customer gets the best value for money if he does not pay for the administration of a scheme of warranties. Baker and Charlie both agree to buy a vacuum cleaner. Able produces two copies of a document headed "sale agreement" and covered with fine print which Baker and Charlie sign without reading. Baker and Charlie pay the price ($100) and take delivery of the vacuum cleaners. These break down after a few days' use. It turns out that the machines were defectively designed by the manufacturer, Dog Vacuums Ltd., the motors being of the wrong type for such machines and tending to burn out after a few hours' use. Able denies responsibility and points out that the document signed by Baker and Charlie contains the following:

"Neither Able nor the manufacturer makes any representation of any sort as to the suitability or fitness of the goods for any particular purpose, and undertakes no obligation whatever as to their quality or condition. Without limiting the generality of the foregoing the parties hereby expressly agree to exclude all warranties, representations and conditions, express or implied, statutory or common law, whether or not part of this agreement or of any collateral agreement, express or implied."

Baker has the motor of his machine replaced at his own expense only to find that the replaceable paper bags, without which the machine cannot be used, are unobtainable.

1. Advise Baker and Charlie.

2. Assuming that the dispute with Baker and Charlie has been settled, advise Able on the drafting of contractual documents for future use.

3. Draft a speech in the legislature outlining any reforms that you may consider desirable (or explaining why none is needed) as a result of your conclusions on the present state of the law in (1), above.

CHAPTER 8

PUBLIC POLICY

This chapter exposes part of the "inarticulate major premise" said to underlie every judicial decision. Here are illustrations of the cases where the common law courts conceive of their task as the weighing of conflicting social policies. The cases reported bristle with problems and they hardly need any introduction in a preliminary note. It is sufficient to remind you that by no means all the classes of case where an otherwise sufficient contract has been held to be illegal because it is against "public policy" are illustrated. A few cases have been selected, instead, to bring out the difficulty of applying social concepts to complex economic and commercial situations in a law court; to show how some contracts abuse the administration of justice; and above all, to enquire into the difficult problem of logic, justice and experience: what effect ought to be given to an illegal contract?

Obviously the traditional English attitude toward public policy in the law is most unsympathetic, as the following judicial observations make clear. Yet can a legal system ignore both consciously and unconsciously the policy problems in the law? If it cannot, is it more desirable that these questions remain undiscussed in open court or is it, as Thorson P. said in another connection in *The Queen* v. *Supertest Petroleum Corp. Ltd.*, [1954] 3 D.L.R. 245, 250, quoting Joseph H. Choate, "only on the anvil of discussion that the spark of truth can be struck out"?

The "paramount public policy," that is, the policy that the courts usually assume without discussion, is well expressed by Jessel M.R., in *Printing & Numerical Registering Co.* v. *Sampson* (1875), L.R. 19 Eq. 462, 465: ". . . if there is one thing which more than another public policy requires it is that men of full age and competent understanding shall have the utmost liberty of contracting and that their contracts when entered into freely and voluntarily shall be held sacred and shall be enforced by Courts of justice." It is against this background that the following cases should be studied.

EGERTON v. *BROWNLOW*. 1853. 4 H.L.C. 1; 10 E.R. 359. PARKE B.: "It is the province of the judge to expound the law only; the written from the statutes, the unwritten or common law from the decisions of our predecessors and of our existing Courts, from text writers of acknowledged authority, and upon the principles to be clearly deduced from them by sound reason and just inference; not to speculate upon what is best, in his opinion, for the advantage of the community. Some of these decisions may have no doubt been founded upon the prevailing and just opinions of the public good; for instance, the illegality of covenants in restraint of marriage or trade. They have become part of the recognized law, and we are therefore bound by them, but we think we are not thereby authorised to establish as law everything which we may think for the public good, and prohibit everything which we think otherwise." (E.R. p. 409.) POLLOCK L.C.B.: "My Lords, it may be that Judges are no better able to discern what is for the public good than other experienced and enlightened members of the community; but that is no reason for their refusing to entertain the question, and declining to decide upon it." (E.R. p. 419.)

NOTE. Lord Wright, in *Fender* v. *St. John-Mildmay*, [1938] A.C. 1, at p. 42, said, "[It] is, I think, clear that this dictum of Pollock C.B. and certain observations in *Egerton* v. *Brownlow* to a similar effect cannot be regarded as fixing the modern law, which in my opinion is as stated by Parke B." Why is it that two centuries ago judges could develop ideas of "public policy" but today the subject is closed? Compare *Williston on Contracts*, 1937, rev. ed., sec. 1629, who "respectfully doubts," as inconsistent with the history of our law, the dictum of Lord Halsbury in *Janson* v. *Driefontein Consolidated Mines, Ltd.*, [1902] A.C. 484, 491, "I deny that any court can 'invent a new public policy'." Williston cites in support the following cases, as instances where the courts have made new applications of the doctrines: *Wilson* v. *Carnley*, [1908] 1 K.B. 729; *Neville* v. *Dominion of Canada News Company Ltd.*, [1915] 3 K.B. 556; *Horwood* v. *Millar's Timber and Trading Co.*, [1917] 1 K.B. 305. Although *Fender* v. *Mildmay* is cited in *Williston* he does not refer to the general observations quoted above. Is the assumption that the heads of policy are closed an assumption that the court is not concerned with public policy; that it is a matter that must be left to the legislatures? Despite the dicta in *Fender* v. *Mildmay* is there any possibility of conflict within a judge's mind as he struggles with twentieth century problems using nineteenth century and earlier tools?

See also *Corbin on Contracts*, sec. 1375, footnote 10, where he describes Baron Parke's statement as "conservative."

An American view was expressed in *Henningsen* v. *Bloomfield Motors*, 32 N.J. 358, 121 A.2d 69 (S.C.N.J., 1960). The court was dealing with a contract for the sale of an automobile, certain clauses of which severely limited the right of the buyer to recover for damage caused by any defects in the automobile. The court said: "Public policy is a term not easily defined. Its significance varies as the habits and needs of a people may vary. It is not static and the field of application is an ever increasing one. A contract or a particular provision therein, valid in one era, may be totally opposed to the public policy of another."

GORDON v. FERGUSON
Nova Scotia. Supreme Court *en banc*. 1961. 30 D.L.R. (2d) 420

Dr. Gordon employed Dr. Ferguson in his practice as a physician and surgeon in the town of Dartmouth which is located across the harbour from the city of Halifax and connected by the MacDonald Bridge. Over ninety per cent of Dr. Gordon's patients resided in Dartmouth and a "negligible number" resided in Halifax although Dr. Gordon and his staff used Halifax hospitals. One of the terms of the employment provided: "8 The Employee shall not, on the termination for any cause whatever of his employment herein, engage in the practice of medicine and/or surgery similar to that now carried on by the Employer, or engage to work for any person, firm or association of medical practitioners in the vicinity within the Town of Dartmouth . . . and a radius of twenty miles from the boundaries thereof, for a period of five years from the time the employment under this agreement ceases." Dr. Gordon lawfully terminated the agreement and gave the required one month's notice on December 5, 1960 and Dr. Ferguson worked with Dr. Gordon until January 5, 1961 when he opened a practice on his own in Dartmouth. Dr. Gordon then took action for an injunction to restrain the breach of Clause 8 of the agreement. Parker J. dismissed the action. Dr. Gordon appealed.

MacDonald J.: ... The appellant contended before us that the trial Judge was in error: 1. in refusing to uphold the validity of the restrictive covenant in cl. 8 or to sever therefrom, and to enforce, such part thereof as was valid. ...

I come now to the first contention which briefly engaged the time of the Court. The topic of cl. 8 of the Agreement set out above is the restriction of the activities of the employer subsequent to the termination of the Agreement, and it is clear that such a covenant—as between master and servant—must be kept distinct from authorities which have reference to the sale of a business or goodwill.

The clause prohibits certain types of activity in a local area for a specified period of time. The clause involves a restraint of trade and is presumed to be void as contrary to public policy but will be upheld if found to be reasonable having regard to the legitimate interests of the parties and also of the public. It can only be viewed as reasonable in the first sense if it is directed to the protection of the covenantee's proprietary interest in his business—and is no wider than is reasonably necessary for that purpose. (*See Herbert Morris Ltd. v. Saxelby*, [1961] 1 A.C. 688 at p. 710). The employer is entitled to covenant against misuse of trade secrets of which knowledge will be acquired in his service and against the unfair invasion of his trade connection, *i.e.*, to prevent customers, clients or patients from being enticed away from him by a servant who has acquired knowledge of them or influence over them in the course of his service. (See *Cheshire & Fifoot on Contracts*, 5th ed., p. 316.)

Accordingly it is always essential to consider the nature and extent of the business of the employer and the character of the work done for the employer during the service (*Mason v. Provident Clothing & Supply Co.*, [1913] A.C. 724 at p. 742; *British Reinforced Concrete Engineering Co. v. Schelff*, [1921] 2 Ch. 563; *Pellow v. Ivey* (1933), 49 T.L.R. 422) The importance of this consideration is that: "A restraint is not valid unless the nature of the employment is such that customers will either learn to rely upon the skill or judgment of the servant or will deal with him directly and personally to the virtual exclusion of the master, with the result that he will probably gain their custom if he sets up business on his own account": *Cheshire & Fifoot*, p. 317; *Routh v. Jones*, [1947] 1 All E.R. 179 at p. 181 (affirmed) [1947] 1 All E.R. 758.

It cannot be denied that the mutual relationship herein involved was such as to give the employer a great practical interest in seeking to curtail the future activities of his professional employee. The only question is whether the restriction he imposed thereon was reasonably necessary in kind (*i.e.*, the professional activities sought to be curtailed), in area and in duration or whether it went beyond the legitimate bounds of self-protection.

The genus of prohibited activity was limited "to the practice of medicine and/or surgery similar to that carried on by the employer," which in fact embraced the general practice of medicine and minor surgery.

The trial Judge inferentially held that the covenant was reasonable as regards the parties and the public in respect of the kind of practice and the kind of work done by the employee as he invalidated the covenant on the express grounds that the restriction was unreasonable in point of area, and he could not substitute a more limited area. It is to be noted, however, that the matter of reasonableness of a restraint in this class of case is a question of law for the Court. The appellant in his notice of appeal purports to exclude from this appeal various "findings" of the trial Judge stated therein. In my view this does not preclude review of any ground otherwise relevant to the determination of the question of law as to whether the covenant was valid or invalid.

One of such grounds in my opinion is that the restriction (in so far as it prohibits the practice of medicine of the kind specified) has the effect of preventing the employee from professional dealings with prospective patients in the area in question without any limitation as to whether they had or had not any previous connection with the practice of the employer or had or had not been brought into contact with the employee in the course of his services. In this sense I think that the prohibition against the practice of medicine, etc. was excessive in that it precludes the employee from dealing with persons unconnected with the practice of the employer before or during the currency of the Agreement, including persons who have moved into the area in question since the termination of the Agreement. This is a clear ground of invalidity. (See *New Method Cleaners & Launderers Ltd.* v. *Hartley*, [1939], 1 D.L.R. 711, 46 Man. R. 414, and cases cited therein; *cf. M. & S. Drapers* v. *Reynolds*, [1957] 1 W.L.R. 9, where a covenant was held unreasonable for the converse reason that it extended to many activities connected with the servant prior to his employment.) The root idea which permits restriction of the future activities of an employee as reasonable between the parties has been well illustrated by Evershed, J.:

"Where the circumstances are such that the servant has, by virtue of his engagement, been put in the position . . . of acquiring a special or intimate knowledge of the affairs of the customers, clients or patients of his master's business or of means of influence over them, there exists a subject-matter of contract, a proprietary interest or goodwill in the matter which is entitled to protection, since otherwise the master would be exposed to *unfair competition* on the part of his former servant—*competition flowing* not so much from the personal skill of the assistant as *from the intimacies and knowledge of the master's business acquired by the servant from the circumstances of his employment*": (*Routh* v. *Jones*, [1947] 1 All E.R. 179 at p. 181 (affirmed, *ibid.*, p. 758)).

But that idea does not extend to protection against competition *per se* or to protection against matters unrelated to the service.

This inclusiveness of the ban on subsequent practice is of particular significance in this case when taken in conjunction with the width of the area (and its growing population) and the length of time to which the ban relates. Moreover, it is a factor which cannot be cured under the doctrine of severance; for its limitation would require the addition of a comprehensive proviso to the covenant.

In this Court the appellant contended (1) that the covenant was reasonable, particularly in terms of geographical area (as well as time), and (2) that if too wide in area, the provisions relating thereto could be severed.

Construed, as it must be, by reference to the ordinary rules of contractual construction (*Gare's Covenants in Restraint of Trade*, 1935, pp. 120-5; *Batt on Master & Servant*, 4th ed., pp. 114-5) the covenant related to the area formed by the then Town of Dartmouth and 20 miles from the boundaries thereof, a description which clearly embraces the City of Halifax and some of its environs. It was said that Halifax was not intended to be included; but this is by no means clear, for though the bulk of the employer's practice related to persons in and about the town, it did involve tending to patients hospitalized in Halifax. In any event, I know of no way of excluding Halifax from the area of the covenant by way of construction as distinguished from severance.

It has been suggested that the same excision can be accomplished by the admission of counsel for the plaintiff, at the trial and on the appeal, that he abandoned any claim to an injunction in respect of Halifax. It is my view, however, that once the question of the legality of cl. 8 was put in issue, the question fell to be considered on the basis of the clause as written; and that no voluntary contraction of its physical coverage can avail to save it if the clause is invalid, *cf. Mills et al.* v. *Gill* [1952], D.L.R. 27 at pp. 41-2, O.R. 257 at pp. 271-2, 16 C.P.R. 46 at pp. 61-2, for a similar gesture; and *Allen Mfg. Co.* v. *Murphy* (1911), 23 O.L.R. 467 at p. 475, in which the Court rejected the submission—where the stated area was the Dominion of Canada—that as the injunction was limited to the City of Toronto, the agreement should be upheld to that extent—and answered that "to do so would, in effect, be making a new covenant, not that to which the parties agreed".

As to the first contention, it is clear in my view that the covenant, properly construed, is invalid for the reason indicated above and because it purports to apply to an area excessive in extent.

Upon the modern authorities there appears to me to be adequate reason for holding that the area in question is also unreasonable in extent, even if its application to the area 20 miles to the west of Dartmouth (*i.e.*, in and about Halifax) could be excluded.

The appellant placed much reliance on *Mills et al.* v. *Gill, supra,* wherein McLennan J., upheld a covenant between a Medical Clinic and a staff physician restricting the latter from practising medicine *within the corporate limits of Oshawa and 5 miles thereof* for 5 years. The evidence established, however, that the practice of the Clinic was drawn from an area comprising Oshawa and *a radius of 25 miles therefrom*—so there could be no objection to the more restricted area prohibited by the contract. In *Lock* v. *Nelson & Harvey Ltd.* (1959), 22 D.L.R. (2d) 298, 33 C.P.R. 138, the area of exclusion was wider in appearance than in fact. There the trial Judge upheld a covenant between a customs-brokerage firm and its branch manager at Huntingdon, a port of entry, restricting the latter from engaging in a similar business *within a radius of 30 miles from Huntingdon* for 2 years; but it appears that the reference to 30 miles was designed to exclude him merely from transacting business at two nearby ports of entry where the company had branches—so that in effect the restriction was simply as to doing business at Huntingdon.

The second has reference to the so-called doctrine of severance and resolves itself into the question whether the excess of geographical area can be carved out of the area indicated so as to limit the operation of the covenant to the Town of Dartmouth (as it stood on May 1, 1959) and surrounding territory marked out by a radius of less than 20 miles.

In pursuing this topic regard must be had to the fact that though area and duration are factors in the total view, each must also be considered in relation to the other (*Fitch* v. *Dowes*, [1921] 2 A.C. 158 at p. 163).

The topic of the Severability of Covenants in restraint of trade is one of great confusion, a study of which yields only a few conclusions:

1. That in appropriate instances where a covenant (between master and servant) taken as a whole is unreasonable, it may be made enforceable or a matter of construction by severing from it that part of it which is bad

(*cf. Pauge* v. *Gauvin*, [1954] S.C.R. 15). Whether this can be done or not depends upon very technical considerations, such as whether it constitutes one entire or indivisible covenant or a series of several and independent covenants, or whether it is in such a form as to admit the excision of a word or phrase without other alteration, and so as not to change the substance of the remainder. (See generally Gare, *supra*, c. 5; Cheshire & Fifoot, *supra*, pp. 326-9; Batt, *supra*, pp. 110-14.) There is, indeed, no sure test for the proper determination of such questions; but there is a general caution against carving out of void covenants the maximum which the employer validly could have inserted, and some clue to the exercise of severance is afforded by the authoritative opinion of Younger L.J., in *Attwood* v. *Lamont*, [1920] 3 K.B. 571 at pp. 592-6.

2. That it is seldom that any previous case is a controlling guide to decision of an instant case because of the inevitable differences in the covenants concerned.

3. (In my view) that such guidance as there may be—in a matter so largely one of public policy—is to be sought in the Canadian rather than in the English decisions as more likely to reflect what is adapted to our conditions.

Reference has been had in argument to various Canadian cases involving the questions of severance, particularly in relation to the area of restraint in contracts of service; but it is enough to discuss a few of the more significant ones:

Hall v. *More*, [1928] 1 D.L.R. 1028, 39 B.C.R. 346—a decision of the British Columbia Court of Appeal—concerned the validity of a term in an agreement between physicians engaged to render services to miners and providing that upon its termination the defendant would not for 5 years practise medicine in *the City of Nanaimo or within the radius of 20 miles therefrom*. It was held that the restriction as to space was unreasonable, particularly as restricting the exercise of the healing art in sparsely settled areas outside the city; but that as it was reasonable as to one of the areas embraced in the contract (the city) and so described as to be severable, the restriction should be confined to *the City of Nanaimo*. This is a clear case of severance as to area.

New Method Cleaners & Launderers Ltd. v. *Hartley*, [1939] 1 D.L.R. 711, 46 Man. R. 414, was a decision of the Manitoba Court of Appeal holding that a covenant by a laundry delivery man, whose route was confined to the City of Winnipeg, wherein he agreed not to solicit business from any of the employer's customers *within the Province* for 1 year, was invalid, *inter alia*, as being excessive as to area. An interim injunction having been granted restraining the laundry man from soliciting *within the City of Winnipeg*, the Court held that this was not a permissible severance of the covenant "but the substitution for it of a new covenant in which an area limited to the City of Winnipeg . . . took the place of the geographical limits of the Province." (p. 715) *Hall* v. *More*, *supra*, was distinguished on the ground that the severability present in that case was absent from the covenant in question. (*Cf. Can. Fur Auction Sales* v. *Nealy*, (1954) 62 Man. R. 148.)

In *George Weston Ltd.* v. *Baird* (1916), 31 D.L.R. 730, 37 O.L.R. 514, the Appellate Division of Ontario held invalid, as unreasonable as to space, a covenant by a cake salesman (or pedlar) not to solicit orders etc. in the City of Toronto. In holding that the covenant was not such as enabled severance to be made, reference was made to the judicial reluctance to exercise the power of severance and refusal to do so where the valid are not clearly severable from the invalid restrictions; Lennox, J., saying "The Court should not be asked to devise or frame an *ex post facto* contract." (p. 738 D.L.R., p. 527 O.L.R.)

R. C. Young Ins. Ltd. v. *Bricknell*, [1955], 5 D.L.R. 487, O.W.N. 638, 23 C.P.R. 73, is a recent decision of the Court of Appeal of Ontario. The immediate question was as to the validity of a covenant whereby an employee of the company covenanted not to carry on or be interested *in the business of an insurance agent* within the City of Niagara Falls and four other named localities for 3 years. The company was acting as a general insurance agent but there was no evidence that it engaged in every kind of insurance. The Court of Appeal unanimously held the covenant invalid on the ground that it prohibited the employee from carrying on the business of insurance agent without any limitation as to the kinds of business, and therefore extended to the carrying on of types of business which the company did not carry on. Though it is uncertain whether any question of severance arose, the judgment went on to say (p. 491 D.L.R., p. 639 O.W.N., pp. 74-5 C.P.R.):

"We think that it is improper in construing an agreement of the kind in question, to add or subtract from the plain language used by the parties in defining their rights. Either the clause is good or it is bad in law. If the effect of it goes beyond what is reasonably necessary for the protection of the employer, it is bad ... the question is not whether the covenantee could make a valid agreement but whether the agreement actually made is valid, and *if the covenant is invalid in part, the entire covenant fails.*"

It is not necessary here to espouse the view that severance is not permissible in appropriate cases; but I can find nothing in the decisions to sanction its application to the present case so as to limit the territorial area of prohibition stated. However described, the plain intention was to enjoin the employee from competing with the employer in a defined area and it is equally plain that the employer's patients, though mainly resident in the Town of Dartmouth, were also drawn from a region of uncertain extent lying to the north, south and east of the town. The radius of 20 miles from the boundaries of the town may be an inexact description of the area of the employer's practice. Nonetheless, it was so described in plain words; and words which in my view require that cl. 8 be viewed as an indivisible covenant, and not merely an agglomeration of independent and several covenants, and therefore one admitting of no curtailment of the area of the prohibited activity by way of severance. The first contention therefore fails.

PATTERSON J.: ... Fifty years ago when travel was largely by horse and buggy the restriction of 20 miles would undoubtedly have been excessive; in fact unreasonable from the standpoint of the public. Perhaps the same could be said of 25 years ago. I think that whether 20 miles is now reasonable or not there must be taken into consideration the rapid and convenient communications of today. I am trying to think what would have happened had the defendant carried out his contract and set up his office just outside the 20 miles limit. It seems to me that his former patients in Dartmouth, their families and those who had heard of his good reputation and thus had confidence in him would prefer him. Would this distance of 20 miles present such an inconvenience to them that they would prefer going to a strange doctor? The inconvenience was slight, a motor drive of 20 miles with a time consuming element both ways of less than an hour. And this when we know that hundreds every day are on our highways on much longer journeys with not even an idle excuse. The convenience of modern travel is in no way better illustrated than by the well-known fact that thousands of employees in Nova Scotia drive daily to their work at a distance of more than 20 miles. . . .

[The part of the opinion dealing with the second and third contentions is omitted. MacQuarrie and Currie JJ. concurred with MacDonald J. The dissenting opinion of Patterson J. with whom Bissett J. concurred, is largely omitted. The judgment was affirmed by the Supreme Court of Canada, [1962] S.C.R. vii: appeal dismissed with costs.]

PEARCE v. *BROOKS*
England. Exchequer Chamber. 1866. L.R. 1 Ex. 213

The plaintiffs sold on a hire purchase agreement to the defendant a new miniature brougham, the defendant to pay £50 down and in case the brougham was returned before a second instalment was paid, fifteen guineas was to be forfeited as well as the £50 and any damage to the vehicle was to be paid for. The defendant returned the brougham before the second instalment was paid, and it was damaged. This action was brought to recover either the fifteen guineas or the amount of the damage. It was objected that to the knowledge of the plaintiffs the defendant was a prostitute and wanted the brougham "to assist her in carrying on her immoral vocation." The jury found the carriage was used by the defendant as part of her display, to attract men, and that the plaintiffs knew it was supplied to be used for that purpose. Bramwell B. at the trial directed a verdict for the defendant and the plaintiffs, pursuant to leave, obtained a rule nisi for a verdict for the fifteen guineas. It was argued that there was no evidence that the plaintiffs knew the purpose for which the brougham was to be used and that it had not been proved that the plaintiffs expected to be paid out of the receipts of the defendant's prostitution. On the first point, Bramwell B. said, in the course of the argument: "At the trial I was first disposed to think that there was no evidence on this point, and I put it to the jury, that, in some sense, everything which is supplied to a prostitute is supplied to her to enable her to carry on her trade, as, for instance, shoes sold to a street-walker; and that the things supplied must be not merely such as would be necessary or useful for ordinary purposes, and might be also applied to an immoral one; but they must be such as would under the circumstances not be required, except with that view. The jury, by the mode in which they answered the question showed that they appreciated the distinction; and on reflection I think they were entitled to draw the inference which they did. They were entitled to bring their knowledge of the world to bear upon the facts proved. The inference that a prostitute (who swore that she could not read writing) required an ornamental brougham for the purposes of her calling, was as natural a one as that a medical man would want a brougham for the purpose of visiting his patients; and the knowledge of the defendant's condition being brought home to the plaintiffs, the jury were entitled to ascribe to them also the knowledge of her purpose."

POLLOCK C.B.: We are all of the opinion that this rule must be discharged. I do not think it is necessary to enter into the subject at large after what has fallen from the bench in the course of the argument, further than to say that . . . I have always considered it as settled by law that any person who contributes to the performance of an illegal act by supplying a thing with the knowledge that it is going to be used for that purpose, cannot recover the price of the thing so supplied. If, to create that incapacity, it was ever considered necessary that the price should be bargained or expected to be paid out of the fruits of the illegal act (which I do not stop to examine), that proposition has been overruled . . . and has now ceased to be the law. Nor can any distinction be made between an illegal and an immoral purpose; the rule which is applicable to the matter is, *ex turpi causa non oritur actio*, and whether it is an immoral or an illegal purpose in which the plaintiff has participated, it comes equally within the terms of the maxim, and the effect is the same; no cause of action can arise out of either the one or the other. The rule of the law was well settled in *Cannan v. Bryce*, (1819), 3 B. & A. 179; 106 E.R. 628, that was a case which at time it was decided, I, in common with many other lawyers in Westminster Hall, was at first disposed to regard with surprise. But the learned judge (then Sir Charles Abbott) who decided it, though not distinguished as an advocate, nor at first eminent as a judge, was one than whom few have adorned the bench with clearer views, or more accurate minds, or have produced more beneficial results in the law. The judgment in that case was, I believe, emphatically *his* judgment; it was assented to by all the members of the Court of King's Bench, and is now the law of the land. If, therefore, this article was furnished to the defendant for the purpose of enabling her to make a display favourable to her immoral purposes, the plaintiffs can derive no cause of action from the bargain. I cannot go with Mr. Chambers in thinking that everything must be found by a jury in such a case with that accuracy from which ordinary decency would recoil. For criminal law it is sometimes necessary that details of a revolting character should be found distinctly, and minutely, but for civil purposes it is not necessary. If evidence is given which is sufficient to satisfy the jury of the fact of the immoral purpose, and of the plaintiff's knowledge of it, and that the article was required and furnished to facilitate that object, it is sufficient, although the facts are not expressed with such plainness as would offend the sense of decency. I agree with my brother Bramwell that the verdict was right and that the rule must be discharged. Rule discharged.

[The concurring opinions of Martin, Pigott, and Bramwell BB., are omitted.]

The following rhyme is taken from Fletcher and Russell, *Crustula Juris*, 38:

I'll tell you the story of naughty Miss Brooks,
As I find it set forth in the Exchequer books.
Her infamous business the better to ply,
It seemed to her good to invest in a fly

Or a brougham, the book calls it, which I take to be,
Some kind of a carriage for one, two or three,
Or more likely for two, since I find it avowed
That while two is good company three is a crowd.

Well, this awful Miss Brooks drove her brougham over London,
And many I trow, the poor wretch that she undone,

For the brougham, don't you see, was so constant in action,
That the good jurors said 'twas her greatest attraction.

And that was the reason why sporty old Bram,
And Pollock et al. say they don't care a damn,
If the price was to come from her vile occupation
Or from money she got in some honest vocation,

The plaintiffs well knew when they sold the caleche
And let her get off without paying the cash,
That the thing was desired, as the jurymen say,
As the principal part of the lady's display.

So McKinnel and Robinson, Cannon and Brice,
And this Pearce and Brooks case make it strong as a vice,
If the purpose illegal should be, or immoral,
The Court will not help you to settle the quarrel.

CLARK v. *HAGAR*. 1893. 22 S.C.R. 510. The plaintiff had sold a house
to one J. who was to the knowledge of the plaintiff a prostitute. J. had
given a mortgage for part of the purchase and had later conveyed her
equity of redemption to the defendant. This action was brought for foreclosure and the defendant alleged that the consideration for the execution
of the mortgage was illegal and immoral and that therefore the mortgage
was of no effect. GWYNNE J.: "All contracts entered into between a plaintiff and defendant and all instruments executed for the purpose of passing
property from the former to the latter, with the intent and for the purpose,
operating in the mind of the transferor, that the property transferred shall
be applied by the transferee in the accomplishment of a purpose which is
in contravention of the principles of the common law or the provisions of
a statute, are void and incapable of being enforced by either of the parties
against the other upon the illegality being made to appear in due form of
law in an action upon the contract or instrument, and that an instrument
executed by the transferee for the purpose of securing to the transferor payment of the consideration money for the property so transferred is in like
manner void and incapable of being enforced by the transferor against the
transferee upon the illegality being made to appear in like manner.

"Knowledge in the mind of the transferor that the transferee intended
to apply the property when transferred to him to an illegal purpose will not
avoid a contract between the parties or an instrument which transfers the
property from the one to the other unless, having regard to the particular
nature of the property transferred, and to the condition in life and occupation of the person to whom it is transferred, a just inference can be
drawn from the facts in evidence that the property was so transferred with
the intent and for the purpose, operating in the mind of the transferor, that
the property when transferred should be applied by the transferee to the
illegal purpose alleged in the plea.

"Applying these principles to the present case I am of opinion, for all
the reasons above stated, that the appellant has wholly failed in establishing that the deed executed by the plaintiff to the appellant's grantor, and
which constitutes the consideration for the execution of the mortgage sued
upon and the root of the appellant's title to the premises mortgaged, is
void. If the contention of the appellant should prevail I cannot see that it

would be possible for any of these unfortunate creatures who lead a life similar to that led by the appellant's grantor to enter into any contract with any person knowing her character for the purchase in fee of a house to shelter her or for the purchase of any of the necessaries of life, and the golden rule laid down in *Pearce* v. *Brooks* upon which case the appellant so much relied would be utterly ignored and set at naught namely—that it is necessary in cases like the present to distinguish between such things as, while being necessary or useful for the ordinary purpose of life, may also be applied to an immoral purpose, and those which are such as under the circumstances in evidence would appear not to be required except for an immoral purpose. No such principle has yet been laid down, or is sanctioned, by any of the decided cases, and there is not in my opinion any principle of law or of public morals or of Christian morality which could sanction the affirmation of such a principle."

HOLMAN v. JOHNSON
England. King's Bench. 1775. 1 Cowp. 341; 98 E.R. 1120

Assumpsit for goods sold and delivered: Plea *non assumpsit*, and verdict for the plaintiff. Upon a rule to show cause why a new trial should not be granted, Lord Mansfield reported the case, which was shortly this: The plaintiff, who was resident at and inhabitant of Dunkirk, together with his partner, a native of that place, sold and delivered a quantity of tea, for the price of which the action was brought, to the order of the defendant, knowing it was intended to be smuggled by him into England; they had, however, no concern in the smuggling scheme itself, but merely sold this tea to him, as they would have done to any other person in the common and ordinary course of their trade.

LORD MANSFIELD: There can be no doubt that every action tried here must be tried by the law of England; but the law of England says that in a variety of circumstances, with regard to contracts legally made abroad, the laws of the country where the cause of action arose shall govern. There are a great many cases which every country says shall be determined by the laws of foreign countries where they arise. But I do not see how the principles on which that doctrine obtains are applicable to the present case. For no country ever takes notice of the revenue laws of another.

The objection that a contract is immoral or illegal as between plaintiff and defendant, sounds at all times very ill in the mouth of the defendant. It is not for his sake, however, that the objection is ever allowed; but it is founded in general principles of policy, which the defendant has the advantage of, contrary to the real justice as between him and the plaintiff, by accident, if I may so say. The principle of public policy is this: *Ex dolo malo non oritur actio.* No court will lend its aid to a man who founds his cause upon an immoral or illegal act. If from the plaintiff's own stating or otherwise, the cause of action appears to arise *ex turpi causa,* or the transgression of a positive law in this country, there the court says he has no right to be assisted. It is upon that ground the court goes; not for the sake of the defendant, but because they will not lend their aid to such a plaintiff. So if the plaintiff and defendant were to change sides, and the defendant was to bring his action against the plaintiff, the latter would then have the advantage of it; for where both are *equally* in fault, *potior est conditio defendentis.*

The question therefore is, whether in this case the plaintiff's demand is founded upon the ground of any immoral act or contract, or upon the ground of his being guilty of anything which is prohibited by a positive law of this country. An immoral contract it certainly is not; for the revenue laws themselves, as well as the offences against them, are all *positivi juris*. What, then, is the contract of the plaintiff? It is this: being a resident and inhabitant of Dunkirk, together with his partner, who was born there, he sells a quantity of tea to the defendant, and delivers it at Dunkirk to the defendant's order, to be paid for in ready money there, or by bills drawn personally upon him in England. This is an action brought merely for the goods sold and delivered at Dunkirk. Where, then, or in what respect is the plaintiff guilty of any crime? Is there any law of England transgressed by a person making a complete sale of a parcel of goods at Dunkirk, and giving credit for them? The contract is complete, and nothing is left to be done. The seller, indeed, knows what the buyer is going to do with the goods, but he has no concern in the transaction itself. It is not a bargain to be paid in case the vendee should succeed in landing the goods; but the interest of the vendor is totally at an end, and his contract complete by the delivery of the goods at Dunkirk.

To what a dangerous extent would this go if it were to be held a crime. If contraband clothes are bought in France, and brought home hither, or if glass bought abroad, which ought to pay a great duty, is run into England, shall the French tailor or the glass manufacturer stand to the risk or loss attending their being run into England? Clearly not. Debt follows the person, and may be recovered in England, let the contract of debt be made where it will; and the law allows a fiction for the sake of expediting the remedy. Therefore, I am clearly of the opinion that the vendors of these goods are not guilty of any offence, nor have they transgressed against the provisions of any act of Parliament. . . .

The gist of the whole turns upon this, that the conclusive delivery was at Dunkirk. If the defendant had bespoke the tea at Dunkirk to be sent to England at a certain price; and the plaintiff had undertaken to send it into England, or had any concern in the running it into England, he would have been an offender against the laws of this country. But upon the facts of the case, from the first to the last, he clearly had offended against no law of England. Therefore, let the rule for a new trial be discharged.

[The three other judges concurred.]

NOTE. The dictum that the revenue laws of another country are not noticed cannot now be deemed consistent with the general policy of the law. By virtue of international comity any contract having for its object the violation of the laws of another state would undoubtedly not be enforced. See *Pollock on Contracts*. 13th ed., pp. 302-4.

COMPARATIVE LAW NOTE. The following Reuters' dispatch appeared in the Toronto *Globe and Mail* on August 25, 1962, from Chikwawa, Nyasaland:

A "crocodile man" who agreed to murder a girl for 90 shillings and was not paid the full amount took legal action in a native authority court—and was awarded 50 shillings.

An African named Ellard told the court here that in 1959 another African named Odrick asked him to kill the girl, apparently because he suspected her of witchcraft. Odrick told the court he chose Ellard because he could "appear as a crocodile at any time."

Ellard said he donned the head and skin of a crocodile, swam down the Shire River to where the girl was getting water, and pulled her in.

He said he stabbed her and broke her arms, then dragged her to the bank and left her body mutilated as if by a crocodile. Her death subsequently was attributed to misadventure.

Ellard said Odrick paid him only 10 shillings and promised to pay the balance later. The court ordered Odrick to pay 50 shillings into court in settlement and gave him a receipt.

Police now are holding both men for questioning in the death and a spokesman said charges are being drawn up.

A legal authority said that a native authority court deals with cases involving African native law and customs, minor criminal cases and civil cases affecting natives. It has no power over major offenses, such as murder, and was within its right to decide what was a civil matter—in this case non-payment of debt.

ALEXANDER v. RAYSON
England. Court of Appeal. [1936] 1 K.B. 169

Mrs. Rayson leased a flat in Piccadilly from Mr. Alexander in 1929, at a rent of £1200 a year. The arrangement was set out in two documents, one a lease which also provided for certain services, the other an agreement which provided for practically the same services and in addition for the supply and maintenance of a frigidaire. Both documents were dated October 29, 1929, and the lease provided for an annual rent of £450 payable quarterly, and the agreement for £750 also payable quarterly. Mrs. Rayson, thinking Mr. Alexander had failed to supply some of the services, on September 29, 1934, refused to pay the quarterly instalment, although she tendered the £112 10s. due under the lease, which Mr. Alexander refused. He then brought this action. In her defence Mrs. Rayson alleged that there was no consideration for the £750 and in any case Mr. Alexander had not performed his obligations and had thereby repudiated the lease and agreement. Later, she amended her pleadings to add the defence of illegality, alleging that the enforcement of the *agreement* would be contrary to public policy "in that its execution was obtained by the plaintiff for the purposes of defrauding the Westminster City Council by deceiving them as to the true rateable value of the said premises and by inducing them to believe that the true rent received by the plaintiff in respect of the said premises was £450 and by concealing from them the terms of the said agreement." Testimony was offered that the flat had been assessed at £720 gross and £597 net, but Mr. Alexander had represented to the Assessment Committee that the rent of £450 was his only income from the property and the assessment was reduced to £270, until later, the Committee having itself discovered the existence of the agreement from Mrs. Rayson, the £720 gross and £579 net assessments were restored. The trial was interrupted to contest whether, if the testimony were accepted, it afforded a defence. Du Parcq J. held that it did not, and Mrs. Rayson appealed. On the question of consideration the Court of Appeal in a judgment prepared by Romer L.J. held for the plaintiff. On the question of illegality:

ROMER L.J.: . . . The second issue raises a question of much greater difficulty.

It is settled law that an agreement to do an act that is illegal or immoral or contrary to public policy, or to do any act for a consideration that is illegal, immoral, or contrary to public policy, is unlawful, and, therefore, void. But it often happens that an agreement which, in itself, is not unlawful is made with the intention of both or one of the parties to make use of the subject-matter for an unlawful purpose—that is to say, a purpose that is illegal, immoral, or contrary to public policy. The most common instance of this is an agreement for the sale or letting of an object where the agreement is unobjectionable on the face of it, but where the intention of both or one of the parties is that the object shall be used by the purchaser or hirer for an unlawful purpose. In such a case any party to the agreement who had the unlawful intention is precluded from suing on it. *Ex turpi causa non oritur actio*. The action does not lie because the Court will not lend its help to such a plaintiff. Many instances of this are to be found in the books. . . .

[In] all these cases the plaintiff was endeavouring to enforce by action an agreement, or a clause in an agreement, which was tainted by the unlawful intention of the plaintiff, or the unlawful intention of the defendant known to the plaintiff, with regard to the purposes for which the subject-matter of the agreement was to be used. To such an action the maxim *ex turpi causa non oritur actio* applies.

But the maxim does not require, nor does the language of it suggest, that a completely executed transfer of property, or of an interest in property, made in pursuance of such an agreement must be regarded as being invalid. This is laid down in clear terms in the well-known case of *Feret* v. *Hill* (1854), 15 C.B. 207; E.R. 400. In that case A procured B to grant him a lease of premises by means of a false representation that he intended to carry on a certain lawful trade therein. Having obtained possession, A converted the place into a brothel, whereupon B forcibly expelled him. It was held that A might maintain ejectment, the fraudulent misrepresentation and the subsequent illegal use of the premises not being sufficient at law to avoid the lease. As the lease had been obtained by fraudulent misrepresentation it could have been set aside in equity and, since the Judicature Act, in any division of the High Court. With that aspect of the matter we are not now concerned. The importance of the case lies in the fact that the lease was held to be a valid one notwithstanding the intention of A to use the demised premises for an unlawful purpose. On this question Mr. Justice Maule expressed himself as follows, at 224: "The plaintiff is not calling upon the Court to enforce any agreement at all. The agreement was an agreement on the part of the defendant to demise certain premises to the plaintiff for a given term. When the instrument was executed, and possession was given under it, it received its full effect; no aid of a Court of Justice was required to enforce it. This action of ejectment is brought, not for the purpose of enforcing the agreement, but the plaintiff asks the Court to afford him a remedy against one who has extruded him from a lawful possession. . . ."

This distinction between an action brought to enforce an unlawful agreement and one brought to assert a right of property already acquired under such an agreement is further illustrated by the case of *Taylor* v. *Chester* (1869), L.R. 4 Q.B. 309. The defendant in that case was the keeper of a brothel and as such had supplied wine and supper to the plaintiff "for the purpose of being consumed there by the plaintiff and divers prostitutes in a debauch there to incite them to riotous, disorderly, and immoral conduct." When the debauch was over there followed, in due course, the reckoning. Being unable or unwilling to pay it at once, the plaintiff deposited with the defendant the half of a £50 note as security. He subsequently repented of his action and instituted proceedings against the defendant for the purpose of obtaining the return of the half banknote. It was held that he was not entitled to recover. The property in the half note had passed to the defendant and, in spite of the illegality of the agreement under which it had passed, the defendant was entitled to keep it. . . .

Much to the same effect is the case of *Gordon* v. *Chief Commissioner of Metropolitan Police*, [1910] 2 K.B. 1080. The money which the plaintiff was claiming in that action had been earned by him in carrying on an illegal business. But the money had become his property and he was held entitled to recover it. He was not asking the Court to enforce any illegal contract or to grant relief dependent in any way on any illegal transaction on his part, but solely on the unjustifiable detention of his money by the defendant.

In view of these various authorities it seems plain that if the plaintiff had let the flat to the defendant to be used by her for an illegal purpose he could not have successfully sued her for the rent, but the leasehold interest in the flat purporting to be granted by the lease would nevertheless have been legally vested in her. The result would have been that the defendant would be entitled to remain in possession of the flat without payment of rent until and unless the plaintiff could eject her without having to rely on the lease or agreement. . . .

In the present case the defendant does not, as a matter of fact, desire to remain in possession of the flat. She is, and has for some time been, anxious to leave it. But, if the plaintiff has by his conduct placed himself in the same position in law as though he had let the flat with the intention of its being used for an illegal purpose, he has no one but himself to thank for any loss which he may suffer in consequence.

That brings us to the real crux of this case. Has the plaintiff placed himself in that position? In the cases to which we have referred there was an intention to use the subject-matter of the agreement for an unlawful purpose. In the present case, on the other hand, the plaintiff's intention was merely to make use of the lease and agreement—that is, the documents themselves—for an unlawful purpose. Does that make any difference? In our opinion, it does not. It seems to us, and it is here that we respectfully disagree with Mr. Justice du Parcq, that the principles applicable to the two cases are identical. That this is so seems to be established by the decision of this Court in *Scott* v. *Brown, Doering, McNab and Co.*, [1892] 2 Q.B. 724. In that case the plaintiff brought an action against some stockbrokers, through whom he had purchased shares in a projected company, to obtain rescission of the purchase contract and repayment of the purchase money on the ground that the defendants, while acting as the plaintiff's brokers, had delivered their own shares to him instead of purchasing them on the Stock Exchange. At the trial it appeared from the plaintiff's own evidence that the money sought to be recovered had been paid by the plaintiff in pursuance of an agreement between him and one of the defendants by which such defendant was, with the money, to purchase on the Stock Exchange a number of shares in the company at a premium with the sole object of inducing the public to believe that there was a real market for the shares and that they were at a real premium. The object, in other words, was "to rig the market." It was held by this Court applying the principle of *ex turpi causa non oritur actio*, that the action was based on an illegal contract and that the money could not be recovered. It will be observed that there was no intention on the part of the plaintiff in that case to use the shares in an unlawful way. The intention was merely to make use of the existence of the share contract in order to defraud the public by inducing them to believe that it recorded a genuine transaction. In delivering judgment Lord Justice Lindley, as he then was, said (at p. 729): "The plaintiff's purchase was an actual purchase, not a sham purchase; that is true, but it is also true that the sole object of the purchase was to cheat and mislead the public. Under these circumstances the plaintiff must look elsewhere than to a Court of justice for such assistance as he may require against the persons he employed to assist him in his fraud, if the claim to such assistance is based on his illegal contract. Any rights which he may have irrespective of his illegal contract will, of course, be recognized and enforced. But his illegal contract confers no rights on him: see *Pearce* v. *Brooks*." It was the transaction of purchase on the market at a particular price, and not the thing purchased, of which an illegal use was to be made. So in the present case it was the formulation of the transaction in a particular way by means of the lease and agreement, and not the subject-matter of the transaction, of which an illegal use was to be made. In one sense, no doubt, it may be said that the plaintiff intended to use only the lease for an unlawful purpose, and not to use, but to conceal the agreement. In reality there was only one transaction between the parties. The splitting of it up into two documents was a device essential for the success of the plaintiff's fraud and both documents must be regarded as equally fraudulent in purpose.

For these reasons we are of opinion that the plaintiff is not entitled to seek the assistance of a Court of justice in enforcing either the lease or the agreement. Mr. Justice du Parcq (who came to a different conclusion) considered that the present case was much the same as one in which a party to an agreement enters into it with the intention of altering it at a later date and using the document so altered for his own fraudulent purposes. "I cannot think," said the learned Judge, "that if a man says 'when I have got this agreement I am going by forgery to alter it,' he is thereby precluded from getting his rights against the other party to the agreement under the agreement in fact made." He thought that in such a case it was something altogether too remote from the contract itself to say that the contract was illegal. In that we respectfully agree with him. But, with all deference, it seems to us that the case he supposed is fundamentally different from the case now before us. In the former case the document is a harmless one, and can only be rendered dangerous by a subsequent act. We see no reason why, before the commission of that act, the document should not be used for an innocent purpose. The intention was mental only and no overt step in carrying out the fraudulent intention was taken in the transaction itself. In the present case, however, the documents themselves were dangerous in the sense that they could be and were intended to be used for a fraudulent purpose, without alteration; and the splitting of the transaction into two documents was an overt step in carrying out the fraud. We cannot think that the plaintiff is entitled to bring these documents into a Court of justice and ask the Court to assist him in carrying them into effect.

The plaintiff's counsel contended that this view is inconsistent with the decision in *In re Thomas, Jaquess* v. *Thomas*, [1894] 1 Q.B. 747. But there is no such inconsistency. In that case one Jaquess had handed over money to Thomas, who was a solicitor, to be used by Thomas in conducting certain litigation. Jaquess subsequently sought to obtain from Thomas an account of the money so handed over to him and a taxation of his bill of costs. Thomas sought to resist the claim on the ground that the money in question had been subscribed by various persons under a champertous, and therefore illegal, agreement. It is not surprising that he failed in his defence, for apart altogether from the fact that Thomas was an officer of the Court—a fact on which the Court commented with some vigour—Thomas could not justify misappropriating the money of Jaquess merely because it had come to Jaquess from a tainted source. Nor, of course, was Jaquess in any way asking the Court to enforce the champertous agreement. In these respects the case is not unlike that of *Gordon* v. *Chief Commissioner of Metropolitan Police.*

Counsel for the plaintiff further contended that inasmuch as the plaintiff had failed in his attempted fraud, and therefore could no longer use the documents for an illegal purpose, he was now entitled to sue on them. The law, it was said, would allow the plaintiff a *locus poenitentiae.* So perhaps, it would have done, had the plaintiff repented before attempting to carry his fraud into effect: see *Taylor* v. *Bowers* (1876), 1 Q.B.D. 291. But, as it is, the plaintiff's repentance came too late—namely, after he had been found out. Where the illegal purpose has been wholly or partly performed the law allows no *locus poenitentiae.* . . . . It will not be any the readier to do so when the repentance, as in the present case, is merely due to the frustration by others of the plaintiff's fraudulent purpose.

In our opinion, the appeal with regard to the second issue must be allowed and the order directing payment by the defendant of the costs of that issue should be discharged. It is true that this issue (being the issue raised in paragraph 2a of the defence) goes only to the validity of the agreement. But this, in our opinion, is immaterial. The moment that the attention of the Court is drawn to the illegality attending the execution of the lease it is bound to take notice of it, whether such illegality be pleaded or not. It had not been pleaded in the case of *Scott* v. *Brown, Doering, McNab and Co.* See, too, the observations of Lord Justice Vaughan Williams in *Gordon* v. *Chief Commissioner of Metropolitan Police.*

If, therefore, when the trial is resumed before Mr. Justice du Parcq the plaintiff should fail to disprove the charge of fraud made against him, his action, as far as it is based on the lease and the agreement, should be dismissed. It will, however, apparently still be open to the plaintiff to ask for leave to amend his statement of claim by alleging an oral agreement and claiming relief based on it. His application for this purpose was ordered by Mr. Justice du Parcq to stand over until after the hearing of this appeal. But we do not intend to suggest that if and when the application is made it should be granted. It should be added that the defendant seems not unwilling to pay the rent accrued due under the lease. Should she do so the plaintiff is, of course, entitled to retain it. But if he seeks the assistance of the Court to recover it such assistance must be refused. . . .

[Appeal allowed; action to be further heard.]

NOTE. The foregoing cases provide examples of some kinds of agreements that the courts have declined to enforce on grounds of public policy. These are contracts in restraint of trade (*Gordon* v. *Ferguson*), contracts to defraud the revenue (*Alexander* v. *Rayson*), and sexually immoral contracts (*Pearce* v. *Brooks*). Other agreements of which the courts have similarly refused enforcement include contracts to commit a crime or a tort, contracts prejudicial to public safety, contracts prejudicial to the administration of justice or designed to oust the jurisdiction of the court, contracts to promote corruption in public life, and contracts prejudicial to the status of marriage. Whether the courts will enlarge this somewhat miscellaneous collection seems to be a moot point.

Many of the most difficult and interesting problems arise when an agreement, or its performance, involves in some way a breach of statute or other regulation. In a highly regulated society, there is hardly any area of modern life that is not affected by regulations of one sort or another. The difficult question is how should the courts treat an agreement that seems to involve the contravention of some regulation. The following cases are concerned with this question.

KINGSHOT v. BRUNSKILL
Ontario. Court of Appeal. [1953] O.W.N. 133

ROACH J.A. delivered the judgment of the Court: The facts of this case are simple but it raises an important question under *The Farm Products Grades and Sales Act*, R.S.O. 1950, c. 130, and the regulations passed thereunder.

The plaintiff operates a fruit and market garden on 34 acres of land in the county of Peel. On that land he has a small apple orchard. He is not a large producer of apples and his main income is derived from the operation of greenhouses. In the fall of 1950 he had harvested his apple crop and the apples were stored on his premises. Among these apples were 846 bushels of Spy and Delicious apples. They were in bushel baskets. No effort had been made by him to grade or sort them, although there was no mixture of the two varieties in any basket. In harvesting the apples the plaintiff had taken the empty baskets and marked some of them "Fancy Delicious" and the others of them "Fancy Grade Spies." It was stated in evidence that the usual practice is to mark the baskets or hampers with the name and quality of the variety which the producer intends, after grading, that those hampers shall contain. The hampers were then sent out to the orchard and the apples were picked from the tree and placed in the appropriate hampers. The plaintiff had no intention of offering those apples for sale to the public until they were first graded in compliance with the regulations passed under the Act.

The defendant resides on land about one mile from the plaintiff's premises. His main business is the growing and marketing of apples and purchasing apples from other apple growers, grading them and marketing them.

On 14th December the defendant came to the plaintiff's premises and inquired whether or not the plaintiff would sell his Spy apples. The plaintiff replied that he would not sell the Delicious and Spies separately and that if he sold them he wanted to sell the whole lot. It was apparent to the defendant that the apples had not been graded. After some preliminary discussion, the defendant entered into a contract with the plaintiff to purchase the apples at $1.10 per bushel and paid the plaintiff a deposit of $25. As the learned trial judge said in his reasons there was no warranty, express or implied. The defendant inspected the apples and simply bought what he saw in the premises where they were stored. Under the terms of the contract it was the defendant's obligation to remove the apples. From time to time he removed quantities of them to his own premises, graded them and sold them. By April, 1951 there were still some hampers of apples which the defendant had not yet removed. The plaintiff requested the defendant to remove them because he needed the space, and when the defendant delayed removing them the plaintiff sent them over to the defendant's premises. During the course of the removal by the defendant he paid the plaintiff on account the further sum of $200. When the last of the apples had been delivered by the plaintiff to the defendant, the defendant called an inspector appointed under the regulations and the inspector marked the last consignment of delivery with a detention order, as he was permitted to do under the regulations. Notice of that detention order was given to the plaintiff. The defendant, alleging that of the total quantity of apples received by him there were certain defective apples, computed the balance that he owed to the plaintiff and sent him a cheque for $619.80, being the amount which the defendant considered represented the balance owing by him. This cheque was marked "in full payment for apples." This cheque was not accepted by the plaintiff but was returned to the defendant. The plaintiff thereupon sued the defendant for the sum of $719.60, which sum was made up of $705.60, being the balance owing for the apples, plus $14.00 being the value of hampers which the defendant had not returned to the plaintiff.

The defendant pleaded that the apples had not been graded, packed or marked in accordance with *The Farm Products Grades and Sales Act* and the regulations passed thereunder and in particular, regulation 3 (a), (c), (d), (f) and (g), and that the sale of the apples was thereby prohibited by statute and illegal. The learned trial judge gave effect to that plea and it is with some regret that I feel myself constrained to agree with that decision.

Section 2(1) of the statute authorizes the Minister of Agriculture, subject to the approval of the Lieutenant-Governor in Council, to make certain regulations respecting farm products as defined in the statute. Farm products as there defined include fruit. The regulations that the Minister may make as aforesaid include regulations,

"(a) establishing grades and classes for any farm product;

"(b) providing for the inspection, grading, packages and packing, marketing, handling, shipping, transporting, advertising, purchasing and selling of farm products within Ontario."

Pursuant to the authority contained in the statute, regulations were made and they are known as Regulations 87 (1 C.R.O. 1950, p. 431). Regulation 3 thereof provides in part as follows:

"No person shall pack, transport, ship, advertise, sell, offer for sale or have in possession for sale any produce.

"(a) unless the produce has been graded, packed and marked in accordance with the provisions of the Act and these regulations;

"(b) which is below the minimum grade for the produce but this provision shall not apply to produce for an establishment [establishment is defined in Regulation 1 as including any plant, factory or premises where produce is canned, preserved or otherwise processed];

"(c) where the faced or shown surface falsely represents the contents;

"(d) in a package unless the package is properly filled and packed;

"(f) in a package which has been previously marked unless the marks are completely removed;

"(g) which is so immature or so diseased or otherwise affected as to be unfit for human consumption."

By s. 8 of the statute every person who contravenes any of the provisions of the Act or the regulations is guilty of an offence and liable on summary conviction to the penalties therein set out.

It must be concluded that the main object of the statute and the regulations passed thereunder is the protection of the public. The penalty authorized by the statute is imposed wholly for the protection of the public. Therefore, if the sale here in question was forbidden by the regulations, then it was illegal and notwithstanding that the defendant resold the apples after having graded them and made a profit thereby, the plaintiff cannot recover in an action for the price of those apples. Reference may be made to *Anderson, Limited* v. *Daniel*, [1924] 1 K.B. 138, and *Little* v. *Poole* (1829), 9 B. & C. 192.

I have looked in vain for any provision in the regulations that would exempt the plaintiff in the circumstances of this case from their application. It is not difficult to conceive a case in which a farmer who has a small orchard on his farm may have neither the manpower nor the equipment necessary to grade and pack the product of his orchard, in accordance with the regulations. His neighbour, with a much larger orchard and specializing in the growing of fruit, has the necessary help and equipment for the grading and packing of the produce not only of his own orchard but of others in the neighbourhood. It would seem not unreasonable that the first of those two farmers should be permitted to sell his whole crop of fruit to the second of those two farmers, who, having the necessary help and equipment, could grade it and pack it in accordance with the regulations before offering it for sale to the public. The regulations, however, do not appear to provide for such a case. There is no provision in the regulations that would exempt the first of those two farmers in that hypothetical case from compliance with the regulations. The Court cannot read into the regulations exemptions which might appear to the Court to be justifiable in a given set of circumstances.

For these reasons the appeal must be dismissed with costs.

QUESTION ON LEGAL METHOD. The Court's interpretation of the Act and regulations is obviously possible. Is it a necessary one?

PICBELL LTD. v. PICKFORD & BLACK LTD.
Nova Scotia. Supreme Court *en banc.* [1951] 2 D.L.R. 119

ILSLEY C.J.: The plaintiff's action is for a declaration that a certain agreement between the plaintiff and the defendant dated March 30, 1946, is a valid and subsisting agreement, for specific performance by the defendant of the agreement, for payment of the sum of $7,500 alleged to be due and payable by the defendant to the plaintiff for hire or use of the steamship "Dufferin Bell" for the period April 10, 1950, to May 10, 1950, under the terms of the said agreement and for such further and other relief as to the Court shall seem meet.

The agreement is set out in full in para. 4 of the statement of claim. It provided that the plaintiff would purchase one 4,700-ton Park Steamship, probably the "Dufferin Park" (also or later called the "Dufferin Bell") from the Park Steamships Ltd., that on acquisition of this steamship the plaintiff would charter it to the defendant for the period of 84 months (subject to an abbreviation of this period in circumstances which have not developed) and that the defendant would pay the plaintiff $12.500 per month during the term of the charter, the first of such payments to be made one month after the date of delivery of the steamship. Provision was however made in the agreement for downward adjustments in the rate of hire and the statement of claim alleges that the rate of hire was so adjusted downward to $7,500 a month, apparently after this action was brought but before delivery of the statement of claim.

The ship came alongside her loading berth for the following voyage on April 10, 1946, and was operated by the defendant Company until April 15, 1950, when the defendant for the first time notified the plaintiff that the agreement of March 30, 1946, was a nullity. The defendant paid the plaintiff $12,500 a month during the 4 years it operated the ship.

On these facts and the others set out in the agreement and supplementary agreement "re setting down for hearing," this Court is asked to answer the following question:

"Whether or not by reason of the matters and things set out in paragraph 11 of the Defence herein, or otherwise, the charter by the Plaintiff to the Defendant of the steamship 'Dufferin Bell' purporting to be evidenced by and purporting to be made pursuant to the paper writing set out in paragraph 4 of the Statement of Claim herein is or was illegal, null and void and of no effect either in whole or in part."

The ground on which the defendant argues that the charter was illegal, null and void is that it was made in contravention of s. 9 of Order in Council P.C. 6785 [76 Can. Gaz. 718], being sch. A of the agreement re setting down for hearing. This section is as follows:

"9. All persons or parties, agencies, organizations or associations proposing to charter any vessel exceeding 150 tons gross register, not being classified by the Department of Fisheries as a fishing vessel, shall submit in advance full particulars, including rates and conditions of charter hire, to the Director for approval on behalf of the Board; and no such charter as aforesaid shall be made without such approval."

It may not be irrelevant to recall that during March and April of 1946, price control and the control of charges for services were still prevalent throughout the whole or nearly the whole of the Canadian economy. . . .

If, then, there was no approval, what becomes of the charter? P.C. 6785 had the same effect as a statute. . . .

The result is clear: the making of the charter was prohibited—and prohibited for public purposes and in the public interest. Must the Court then refuse to render assistance in enforcing it? Is it null and void as an illegal contract? Many cases were cited in support of the proposition that if a contract may be performed either in a lawful or in an unlawful way and if a party in the performance of his part of the contract without the knowledge of the other party elects to perform it in an unlawful way, he cannot be heard to allege his own wrong. It was contended on behalf of the plaintiff that the contract made on March 30th for a charter which was made on April 10th could have been performed in a lawful way, that it was the charterer's duty to submit the particulars to the Director of Shipping and obtain approval thereof and that it cannot be heard to allege its own wrong in not doing so. However, the question submitted to this Court is not as to the illegality of the agreement of March 30th; it is as to the illegality of the charter. The class of cases applicable to the determination of this question is that relating not to unlawful performance, but to prohibited contracts. This was a prohibited contract. It is unnecessary to decide whose obligation it was under s. 9 to submit the particulars in advance. The concluding words of the section prohibited both parties and each party from making the charter unless the particulars had been submitted and approval obtained.

I am therefore of opinion that there was an illegal act on the plaintiff's part as well as on the defendant's part in making this charter without prior approval. However excusable it may have been in the popular sense, I think it was illegal for the plaintiff to make itself a party to this charter, whether it had *mens rea* or not. The prohibition contained in s. 9 was for public purposes and for the benefit of the public. Section 9 prohibited both parties from entering into a charter unless one of them had submitted particulars in advance and obtained approval. If neither had, both violated the section when they made the charter and became subject to the penalties set out in s. 10. . . .

If, then, the charter was illegal, was it also void? I am of opinion that it was. In *Cope* v. *Rowlands* (1836), 2 M. & W. 149 at p. 157, 150 E.R. 707, Parke B. said the following: "It is perfectly settled, that where the contract which the plaintiff seeks to enforce, be it express or implied, is expressly or by implication forbidden by the common or statute law, no court will lend its assistance to give it effect. It is equally clear that a contract is void if prohibited by a statute, though the statute inflicts a penalty only, because such a penalty implies a prohibition." Many other cases are to the like effect.

It is argued on behalf of the plaintiff, however, that the defendant having continued to hold and operate the ship after P.C. 6785 was repealed on December 31, 1946, cannot now repudiate the agreement on the ground of illegality, that having approbated the agreement in this way, the defendant is precluded from raising the question of illegality. As the Court may of its own motion raise this question, if the defendant does not do so, any such preclusion of the defendant would not help the plaintiff. And it is hardly germane to the question before the Court to consider whether the defendant is not precluded from disputing his status as a charterer under a charter of some kind. Some cases use the word "preclude" as applicable to a situation where a person disputes his status as a shareholder after a winding-up; *Re Acme Products Ltd.*, [1932] 4 D.L.R. 330 at p. 332, 40 Man. R. 444. But the real basis for deciding that persons who acquired their shares under void contracts of purchase are in some circumstances nevertheless shareholders is that they have agreed to become such by subsequent independent binding agreements resulting from their conduct: *Re Home Ass'ce Co.*, (1950) 4 D.L.R. 145 . . . The question whether the defendant is precluded from disputing his status as charterer under the charter in question is merely another way of stating the question as to whether there was a binding agreement by conduct made after December 31, 1946, reaffirming the charter. And that question is not before the Court. Whether an independent agreement from the defendant's conduct in keeping and operating the ship after December 31, 1946, and paying the agreed rate of charter hire to the plaintiff for over 3 years, can be spelled out is not for this Court to determine on the question submitted. Nor of course are the terms of that agreement, if any. It may very well be that the passage cited by Estey J. in the *Home Ass'ce Case* from *Re London & Northern Ins. Corp.* (1869), L.R. 4 Ch. 682 at p. 688 would apply: " 'All those acts were,

however, done in conformity with, and in pursuance of, this void transaction; and there was no evidence of any separate agreement on the part
of Colonel Stace and Mr. Worth.' "

Whether a new agreement arose after December 31, 1946, or not—a
question on which I am not called upon to express an opinion—I am quite
clear that if a contract is void at its inception because it is prohibited by
statute, the repeal of the prohibitory statute will not validate that contract.
Pollock on Contracts, 13th ed., p. 361 seems to suggest the contrary by the
following language: "Perhaps the parties might be entitled to the benefit of
a subsequent change in the law if their actual intention in making the contract was not unlawful." This tentative suggestion has no clear case support
that I can find and in my opinion is inconsistent with the nature of a contract which is illegal and void by reason of statutory prohibition. . . .

The answer to the question is therefore as follows: The charter by the
plaintiff to the defendant of the steamship "Dufferin Bell" purporting to
be evidenced by and purporting to be made pursuant to the paper writing
set out in para. 4 of the statement of claim herein is and was illegal, null
and void and of no effect either in whole or in part.

MACDONALD J.: . . . There can be little doubt that the combined effect
of the prohibition in s. 9 against making an unapproved charter and the
penalty provided in s. 10 for doing so was to render utterly void a charter
made in contravention thereof; notwithstanding the absence of a declaration in the Order in Council that a charter so made would be void. . . .

It may be necessary to stress the fact that in law the contract was not
merely unlawful or unenforceable but void; for it has been argued that as
the Order in Council which it contravened was revoked as of December
31, 1946, it became valid thereupon and therefrom. . . .

If the decisions had not made it so abundantly clear that the making
of such a charter in contravention of such a prohibition as that contained
in s. 9 is an act devoid of legal effect, I should have sought some ground
for holding that upon its repeal a Court should not refrain from giving due
present-effect to it. Some precedents for such an attitude could indeed be
found in recent United States decisions in relation to the repeal of usury
laws and of prohibitory liquor legislation: cf. *Williston on Contracts*, ss.
1683 and 1758; and note in 50 Har. L. Rev., p. 834.

Such an attempt might well have been based on the desirability of maintaining the effectiveness of private bargaining so far as possible, and a conclusion of present-validity reached if the contract were merely unlawful or
unenforceable. The state of the law is such, however, that the charter herein cannot be regarded merely as having passed through a limbo of suspended animation or eclipse into the broad uplands of awakening validity;
for it was void on its making and therefore never was in law a charter. The
very fact of making the charter having been forbidden, the legal result is
that no such charter was made, in the sense that it had any status as a
legal fact at the time, or could gain such status as an enforceable contract
upon the repeal of the prohibition which its making contravened. There is
accordingly nothing in existence which may be revived by such repeal; and
in any case there is no applicable doctrine providing for the revival of *void*
contracts: *Williston on Contracts*, s. 1758; 31 Hals., 2nd ed., p. 557;
Dever v. *Corcoran* (1856), 8 N.B.R. 338; and compare the *Interpretation
Act*, s. 19 (1) (a) and (b).

Whether or not there has sprung from the ashes of illegality a new and enforceable contract like unto the invalid charter in its terms is a question which, fortunately, I do not have to answer.

Judgment accordingly.

[Hall, Parker and Currie JJ., concur with Ilsley C.J.]

QUESTIONS ON LEGAL METHOD. Is the argument that the contract is void on its making not begging the question? How does a "contract" become "void"? Is it not open to a court to decide that certain objective conduct should not be recognized by the state for a certain period or for certain purposes, and yet to decide that later it should be recognized for a different period and for different purposes? Is it possible to distinguish completely between the conduct of the parties and the "legal" effects to be attributed to the conduct?

If, as the Court intends, the charter is illegal and void from the beginning, what is the offence for which the penalty is provided? Did the Governor in Council intend to make it an offence to enter into a "void charter"? It was not, apparently, an offence to carry out the terms of the "void charter."

Compare section 26 (1) of *The Planning Act,* R.S.O. 1960, c. 296, which authorizes a council of a municipality to designate an area as an area of subdivisional control, "and thereafter no person shall convey land in the area by way of a deed or transfer on any sale, or enter into an agreement of sale and purchase of land in the area. . . ." Is an agreement entered into in contravention of this provision "void"? See *Queensway Construction Limited and Frances Truman* v. *Trusteel Corporation (Canada) Limited* (1961), 28 D.L.R. (2d) 480, holding that for certain purposes and in certain conditions legal effect would be given to the agreement. See also section 26 (8), which provides a penalty of $500 for contravention of subdivision control. Is a deed contravening the section "void"? Can the question of illegality be properly answered without a full understanding of the purpose of the Act?

See *The Planning Act Amendment Act,* S.O., 1960-61, c. 76, which repeals section 26 and enacts a new section 26 expressly providing that "an agreement, conveyance . . . made in contravention of this section . . . does not create or convey any interest in land, but this section does not affect an agreement entered into, subject to the express condition contained therein that such agreement is to be effective only if the provisions of this section are complied with." The subsection providing for a penalty was not reenacted. See notes, (1959), 37 *Canadian Bar Review* 636 and (1961), 39 *ibid.* 461.

ST. JOHN SHIPPING CORP. v. JOSEPH RANK, LTD.
[1957] 1 Q.B. 267

DEVLIN J.: The continued depreciation of the pound is beginning to take effect on the criminal law. A maximum fine which at the time when Parliament fixed it would have been regarded as a sharp disincentive (if the word was then in use) may now prove to be little or no deterrent. In 1932 Parliament enacted the Merchant Shipping (Safety and Loadline Conventions) Act, 1932, which, inter alia, by sections 44 and 57, made it an offence to load a ship so that her loadline was submerged. The temptation to overload a freighter and so to submerge her marks is, of course, that the more she carries the more she will earn for the same expenditure on the voyage. So Parliament, when prescribing a fine as the punishment for an offence against section 44 related it to the earning capacity of the ship. The maximum fine was not to exceed the court's estimate of the extent to which the earning capacity of the ship was, or would have been, increased by reason of the submersion; and was also not to exceed £100 for every inch or fraction of an inch by which the loadline was submerged. I suppose that in 1932 £100 was considered an outside figure of earning capacity per inch, but freights now are very different from what they were then.

When the master of the plaintiffs' ship *St. John* was prosecuted at Birkenhead under the Act and, on November 28, 1955, found to have overloaded his ship by more than 11 inches, he was fined the maximum of £1,200; but the amount of cargo by which the ship was overloaded was 427 tons and the extra freight earned was £2,295. So the ship came very well out of this situation; and she and other ships will doubtless continue to come very well out of similar situations until the Act of 1932 is amended.

I can see that it is a situation that must cause some concern to cargo owners whose property is at risk. The ship was carrying a cargo of about 10,000 tons of grain from Mobile, Alabama, U.S.A., to Birkenhead. The defendants held a bill of lading for about 3,500 tons of this quantity on which the freight due was nearly £19,000. The defendants, apparently in association with the charterers, decided that some additional punishment should be inflicted on the plaintiffs, and that it should take the form of withholding the £2,295 extra freight. The defendants have withheld £2,000, for which sum they are being sued in this action; and another cargo owner has withheld £295 and is being sued for it in an action that depends on this one.

This is the explanation of how this dispute has arisen. But I, of course, have not got to decide whether the defendants are morally justified in trying to make good deficiencies in the criminal law; nor is any justification of that sort put forward in the case. The defendants' case in law is that since the plaintiffs performed the contract of carriage, evidenced by the bill of lading, in such a way as to infringe the Act of 1932, they committed an illegality which prevents them from enforcing the contract at all; the defendants say they were not obliged to pay any freight, and so cannot be sued for the unpaid balance. If this is right, and if all the consignees had exerted to the full their legal powers, the effective penalty for the plaintiffs' misdeed would have been the loss of the whole freight of more than £50,000.

I do not, of course, regard an offence against the Act of 1932 as a trivial matter, particularly if it is committed deliberately, and if the safety of lives at sea is involved. It is an offence for which the master of a British ship (the plaintiffs' ship was registered in Panama) could be imprisoned. The agreed statement of facts, on which this case is being tried, does not say that the overloading in the U.S.A. was deliberate; for the purposes of the defendants' argument that finding is not required. But there is material in the agreed case which would make such a finding not at all improbable. The vessel was not overloaded when she left her loading port on November 2, 1955; she had then three-eighths of an inch to spare. But it seems plain that she was not then sufficiently bunkered to take her across the Atlantic. On November 5 she called at Port Everglades, Florida, for bunkers, and the 600 tons which she then took on caused her loadline to become submerged by about 10 inches. It is hard to believe that that fact was not appreciated at the time. As she went across the Atlantic her load was, of course, lightened by the consumption of bunkers, but, on the other hand, she passed into the winter zone and the net result was that when she arrived in the Mersey her loadline, as I have said, was submerged by more than 11 inches.

It is a misfortune for the defendants that the legal weapon which they are wielding is so much more potent than it need be to achieve their purpose. Believing, rightly or wrongly, that the plaintiffs have deliberately committed a serious infraction of the Act and one which has placed their property in jeopardy, the defendants wish to do no more than to take the profit out of the plaintiffs' dealing. But the principle which they invoke for this purpose cares not at all for the element of deliberation or for the gravity of the infraction, and does not adjust the penalty to the profits unjustifiably earned. The defendants cannot succeed unless they claim the right to retain the whole freight and to keep it whether the offence was accidental or deliberate, serious or trivial. The application of this principle to a case such as this is bound to lead to startling results. Mr. Wilmers does not seek to avert his gaze from the wide consequences. A shipowner who accidentally overloads by a fraction of an inch will not be able to recover from any of the shippers or consignees a penny of the freight. There are numerous other illegalities which a ship might commit in the course of the voyage which would have the same effect; Mr. Roskill has referred me by way of example to section 24 of the Merchant Shipping (Safety Conventions) Act, 1949, which makes it an offence to send a ship to sea laden with grain if all necessary and reasonable precautions have not been taken to prevent the grain from shifting. He has referred me also to the detailed regulations for the carriage of timber—similar in character to regulations under the Factories Acts—which must be complied with if an offence is not to be committed under section 61 of the Act of 1932. If Mr. Wilmers is right, the consequences to shipowners of a breach of the Act of 1932 would be as serious as if owners of factories were unable to recover from their customers the cost of any articles manufactured in a factory which did not in all respects comply with the Acts. Carriers by land are in no better position; again Mr. Wilmers does not shrink from saying that the owner of a lorry could not recover against the consignees the cost of goods transported in it if in the course of the journey it was driven a mile an hour over its permitted speed. If this is really the law, it is very unenterprising of cargo owners and consignees to wait until a criminal conviction has been secured before denying their liabilities. A service of trained observers on all our main roads would soon pay for itself. An effective patrol of the high seas would probably prove too expensive, but the maintenance of a corps of vigilantes in all principal ports would be well worth while when one considers that the smallest infringement of the statute or a regulation made thereunder would relieve all the cargo owners on the ship from all liability for freight.

Of course, as Mr. Wilmers says, one must not be deterred from enunciating the correct principle of law because it may have startling or even calamitous results. But I confess I approach the investigation of a legal proposition which has results of this character with a prejudice in favour of the idea that there may be a flaw in the argument somewhere.

Mr. Wilmers puts his case under three main heads. In the first place he submits that, notwithstanding that the contract of carriage between the parties was legal when made, the plaintiffs have performed it in an illegal manner by carrying the goods in a ship which was overloaded in violation of the statute. He submits as a general proposition that a person who performs a legal contract in an illegal manner cannot sue upon it, and he relies upon a line of authorities of which *Anderson Ltd.* v. *Daniel*, [1924] 1 K.B. 138 is probably the best known. He referred particularly to the formulation of the principle by Atkin L.J. in the following passage: "The question of illegality in a contract generally arises in connexion with its formation, but it may also arise, as it does here, in connexion with its performance. In the former case, where the parties have agreed to something which is prohibited by Act of Parliament, it is indisputable that the contract is unenforceable by either party. And I think that it is equally unenforceable by the offending party where the illegality arises from the fact that the mode of performance adopted by the party performing it is in violation of some statute, even though the contract as agreed upon between the parties was capable of being performed in a perfectly legal manner."

As an alternative to this general proposition and as a modification of it, Mr. Wilmers submits that a plaintiff cannot recover if, in the course of carrying out a legal contract made with a person of a class which it is the policy of a particular statute to protect, he commits a violation of that statute.

Secondly, he relies upon the well-known principle. . . . that a plaintiff cannot recover money if in order to establish his claim to it, he has to disclose that he committed an illegal act. These plaintiffs, he submits, cannot obtain their freight unless they prove that they carried the goods safely to their destination, and they cannot prove that without disclosing that they carried them illegally in an overloaded ship.

Thirdly, he relies upon the principle that a person cannot enforce rights which result to him from his own crime. He submits that the criminal offence committed in this case secured to the plaintiffs a larger freight than they would have earned if they had kept within the law. A part of the freight claimed in this case is therefore a benefit resulting from the crime and in such circumstances the plaintiff cannot recover any part of it.

I am satisfied that Mr. Wilmers's chief argument is based on a misconception of the principle applied in *Anderson Ltd.* v. *Daniel*, which I have already cited. In order to expose that misconception I must state briefly how that principle fits in with other principles relating to illegal contracts. There are two general principles. The first is that a contract which is entered into with the object of committing an illegal act is unenforceable. The application of this principle depends upon proof of the intent, at the time the contract was made, to break the law; if the intent is mutual the contract is not enforceable at all, and, if unilateral, it is unenforceable at the suit of the party who is proved to have it. This principle is not involved here. Whether or not the overloading was deliberate when it was done, there is no proof that it was contemplated when the contract of carriage was made. The second principle is that the court will not enforce a contract which is expressly or impliedly prohibited by statute. If the contract is of this class it does not matter what the intent of the parties is; if the statute prohibits the contract, it is unenforceable whether the parties meant to break the law or not. A significant distinction between the two classes is this. In the former class you have only to look and see what acts the statute prohibits; it does not matter whether or not it prohibits a contract; if a contract is deliberately made to do a prohibited act, that contract will be unenforceable. In the latter class, you have to consider not what acts the statute prohibits, but what contracts it prohibits; but you are not concerned at all with the intent of the parties; if the parties enter into a prohibited contract, that contract is unenforceable.;

The principle enunciated by Atkin L.J. and cited above is an offshoot of the second principle that a prohibited contract will not be enforced. If the prohibited contract is an express one, it falls directly within the principle. It must likewise fall within it if the contract is implied. If, for example, an unlicensed broker sues for work and labour, it does not matter that no express contract is alleged and that the claim is based solely on the performance of the contract, that is to say, the work and labour done; it is as much unenforceable as an express contract made to fit the work done. The same reasoning must be applied to a contract which, though legal in form, is performed unlawfully. Jenkins L.J. in his illuminating judgment in *B. and B. Viennese Fashions* v. *Losane*, [1952] 1 All E.R. 909, has shown how illogical it would be if the law were otherwise. In that case the regulations required that the seller of utility goods should furnish to the buyer an invoice containing certain particulars. The plaintiff made a contract of sale for non-utility goods, to which the regulations did not apply; but he purported to perform it by delivering to the buyer without objection utility garments to which the regulations did apply; and he did not furnish the invoice. If the court enforced his claim for the price of the garments, it would have, in effect, been enforcing a contract for the supply of utility garments without furnishing an invoice, which, had it originally been made in that form, would have been prohibited. But whether it is the terms of the contract or the performance of it that is called in question, the test is just the same: is the contract, as made or as performed, a contract that is prohibited by the statute?

Mr. Wilmers's proposition ignores this test. On a superficial reading of *Anderson Ltd.* v. *Daniel* and the cases that followed and preceded it, judges may appear to be saying that it does not matter that the contract is itself legal, if something illegal is done under it. But that is an unconsidered interpretation of the cases. When fully considered, it is plain that they do not proceed upon the basis that in the course of performing a legal contract an illegality was committed; but on the narrower basis that the way in which the contract was performed turned it into the sort of contract that was prohibited by the statute.

All the cases which Mr. Wilmers cited in support of his submission show, I think, that this is the true basis. Some of the earlier cases on which he relied—those in which the principle was first being formulated—show this most clearly; and I take as an example of them *Cope* v. *Rowlands* (1836) 2 M. & W. 149. In that case the plaintiff brought an action for work and labour done by him as a broker and the plea was that he was not duly licensed to act as a stockbroker pursuant to the statute. The statute imposed a penalty on any unlicensed person acting as a broker. Parke B. (the italics below are those in the report) declared the law to be as follows: "It is perfectly settled, that where the contract which the plaintiff seeks to enforce, be it express or implied, is expressly or by implication forbidden by the common or statute law, no court will lend its assistance to give it effect. It is equally clear that a contract is void if prohibited by a statute, though the statute inflicts a penalty only, because such a penalty implies a prohibition. . . And it may be safely laid down, notwithstanding some dicta apparently to the contrary, that if *the contract* be rendered illegal, it can make no difference, in point of law, whether the statute which makes it so has in view the protection of the revenue, or any other object. The sole question is, whether the statute *means to prohibit the contract?*" After considering the language of the Act Parke B. went on to say that the language "shows clearly that the legislature had in view, as *one* object, the benefit and security of the public in those important transactions which are negotiated by brokers. The clause, therefore, which imposes a penalty, must be taken . . . to imply a prohibition of all unadmitted persons to act as brokers, and consequently to prohibit, by necessary inference, all contracts which such persons make for compensation to themselves for so acting; and this is the contract on which this action is . . . brought."

Now this language—and the same sort of language is used in all the cases—shows that the question always is whether the statute meant to prohibit the contract which is sued upon. One of the tests commonly used, and frequently mentioned in the later cases, in order to ascertain the true meaning of the statute, is to inquire whether or not the object of the statute was to protect the public or a class of persons, that is, to protect the public from claims for services by unqualified persons or to protect licensed persons from competition. Mr. Wilmers (while saying that, if necessary, he would submit that the Act of 1932 was passed, inter alia, to protect those who had property at sea) was unable to explain the relevance of this consideration to his view of the law. If in considering the effect of the statute the only inquiry that you have to make is whether an act is illegal, it cannot matter for whose benefit the statute was passed; the fact that the statute makes the act illegal is of itself enough. But if you are considering whether a contract not expressly prohibited by the Act is impliedly prohibited, such considerations are relevant in order to determine the scope of the statute.

This, then, is the principle which I think is to be derived from the class of cases which Mr. Wilmers cited. Not unnaturally, he cited those cases in which the result at least was consistent with the proposition for which he was contending. Had he cited these cases in which the claim succeeded because the statute was held not to imply a prohibition of any contract, he would, I think, have seen the fallacy in his argument. For that submits the point to the crucial test. The plaintiff does an illegal act, being one prohibited by the statute, but he does it in performance of a legal contract, since the statute is construed as prohibiting the act merely and not prohibiting the contract under which it is done. If in such a case it had been held that it did not matter whether the contract was legal or not since the mode of performing it was illegal, Mr. Wilmers's argument would be well supported. But in fact the contrary has been held. I take as an example of cases of this type, *Wetherell* v. *Jones* (1832) 3 B. & Ad. 221. The plaintiff sued for the price of spirits sold and delivered. A statute of George IV provided that no spirits should be sent out of stock without a permit. The court held that the permit obtained by the plaintiff was irregular because of his own fault and that he was therefore guilty of a violation of the law, but that the statute did not prohibit the contract. Tenterden C.J. stated the law as follows: "Where a contract which a plaintiff seeks to enforce is expressly, or by implication, forbidden by the statute or common law, no court will lend its assistance to give it effect: and there are numerous cases in the books where an action on the contract has failed, because either the consideration for the promise or the act to be done was illegal, as being against the express provisions of the law, or contrary to justice, morality, and sound policy. But where the consideration and the matter to be performed are both legal, we are not aware that a plaintiff has ever been precluded from recovering by an infringement of the law, not contemplated by the contract, in the performance of something to be done on his part."

The last sentence in this judgment is a clear and decisive statement of the law; it is directly contrary to the contention which Mr. Wilmers advances, which I therefore reject both on principle and on authority.

So Mr. Wilmers's wider proposition fails. Mr. Roskill is right in his submission that the determining factor is the true effect and meaning of the statute, and I turn therefore to consider Mr. Wilmers's alternative proposition that the contract evidenced by the bill of lading is one that is made illegal by the Act of 1932. I have already indicated the basis of this argument, namely, that the statute being one which according to its preamble is passed to give effect to a convention "for promoting the safety of life and property at sea," it is therefore passed for the benefit of cargo owners among others. That this is an important consideration is certainly established by the authorities. But I follow the view of Parke B. in *Cope* v. *Rowlands*, which I have already cited, that it is one only of the tests. The fundamental question is whether the statute means to prohibit the contract. The statute is to be construed in the ordinary way; one must have regard to all relevant considerations and no single consideration, however important, is conclusive.

Two questions are involved. The first—and the one which hitherto has usually settled the matter—is: does the statute mean to prohibit contracts at all? But if this be answered in the affirmative, then one must ask: does this contract belong to the class which the statute intends to prohibit? For example, a person is forbidden by statute from using an unlicensed vehicle on the highway. If one asks oneself whether there is in such an enactment an implied prohibition of all contracts for the use of unlicensed vehicles, the answer may well be that there is, and that contracts of hire would be unenforceable. But if one asks oneself whether there is an implied prohibition of contracts for the carriage of goods by unlicensed vehicles or for the repairing of unlicensed vehicles or for the garaging of unlicensed vehicles, the answer may well be different. The answer might be that collateral contracts of this sort are not within the ambit of the statute.

The relevant section of the Act of 1932, section 44, provides that the ship "shall not be so loaded as to submerge" the appropriate loadline. It may be that a contract for the loading of the ship which necessarily has this effect would be unenforceable. It might be, for example, that the contract for bunkering at Port Everglades which had the effect of submerging the loadline, if governed by English law, would have been unenforceable. But an implied prohibition of contracts of loading does not necessarily extend to contracts for the carriage of goods by improperly loaded vessels. Of course, if the parties knowingly agree to ship goods by an overloaded vessel, such a contract would be illegal; but its illegality does not depend on whether it is impliedly prohibited by the statute, since it falls within the first of the two general heads of illegality I noted above where there is an intent to break the law. The way to test the question whether a particular class of contract is prohibited by the statute is to test it in relation to a contract made in ignorance of its effect.

In my judgment, contracts for the carriage of goods are not within the ambit of this statute at all. A court should not hold that any contract or class of contracts is prohibited by statute unless there is a clear implication, or "necessary inference," as Parke B. put it, that the statute so intended. If a contract has as its whole object the doing of the very act which the statute prohibits, it can be argued that you can hardly make sense of a statute which forbids an act and yet permits to be made a contract to do it; that is a clear implication. But unless you get a clear implication of that sort, I think that a court ought to be very slow to hold that a statute intends to interfere with the rights and remedies given by the ordinary law of contract. Caution in this respect is, I think, especially necessary in these times when so much of commercial life is governed by regulations of one sort or another, which may easily be broken without wicked intent. Persons who deliberately set out to break the law cannot expect to be aided in a court of justice, but it is a different matter when the law is unwittingly broken. To nullify a bargain in such circumstances frequently means that in a case—perhaps of such triviality that no authority would have felt it worth while to prosecute—a seller, because he cannot enforce his civil rights, may forfeit a sum vastly in excess of any penalty that a criminal court would impose; and the sum forfeited will not go into the public purse but into the pockets of someone who is lucky enough to pick up the windfall or astute enough to have contrived to get it. It is questionable how far this contributes to public morality. In *Vita Food Products Inc.* v. *Unus Shipping Co.*, [1939] A.C. 237, Lord Wright said: "Nor must it be forgotten that the rule by which contracts not expressly forbidden by statute or declared to be void are in proper cases nullified for disobedience to a statute is a rule of public policy only, and public policy understood in a wider sense may at times be better served by refusing to nullify a bargain save on serious and sufficient grounds." It may be questionable also whether public policy is well served by driving from the seat of judgment everyone who has been guilty of a minor transgression. Commercial men who have unwittingly offended against one of a multiplicity of regulations may nevertheless feel that they have not thereby forfeited all right to justice, and may go elsewhere for it if courts of law will not give it to them. In the last resort they will, if necessary, set up their own machinery for dealing with their own disputes in the way that those whom the law puts beyond the pale, such as gamblers, have done. I have said enough, and perhaps more than enough, to show how important it is that the courts should be slow to imply the statutory prohibition of contracts, and should do so only when the implication is quite clear. I have felt justified in saying as much because, to any judge who sits in what is called the Commercial Court, it must be a matter of special concern. This court was instituted more than half a century ago so that it might solve the disputes of commercial men in a way which they understood and appreciated, and it is a particular misfortune for it if it has to deny that service to any except those who are clearly undeserving of it.

I think also that it is proper, in determining the scope of the statute, to have regard to the consequences I have already described and to the inconveniences and injury to maritime business which would follow from upholding the defendants' contention in this case. In the light of all these considerations I should not be prepared to treat this statute as nullifying contracts for the carriage of goods unless I found myself clearly compelled by authority to do so. I can find no such authority in the cases which Mr. Wilmers has cited, nor even any analogous cases in which the law has been stretched as far. Of course, the construction of each Act depends upon its own terms, but I can find no authority in which any Act has been given anything like so wide an effect as Mr. Wilmers wants the Act of 1932 to be given. In the statutes to which the principle has been applied, what was prohibited was a contract which had at its centre—indeed often filling the whole space within its circumference—the prohibited act; contracts for the sale of prohibited goods, contracts for the sale of goods without accompanying documents when the statute specifically said there must be accompanying documents; contracts for work and labour done by persons who were prohibited from doing the whole of the work and labour for which they demanded recompense. It is going a long way further to say that contracts which depend for their performance upon the use of an instrument which has been treated in a forbidden way should also be forbidden. In the only case I have seen where the contention appeared to go as far as that the claim failed. The relevant facts in *Smith* v. *Mawhood* (1845) 14 M. & W. 452, appear sufficiently from the judgment of Alderson B., where he also dealt with the contention: "But here the legislature has merely said, that where a party carries on the trade or business of a dealer in or seller of tobacco, he shall be liable to a certain penalty, if the house in which he carries on the business shall not have his name, etc., painted on it, in letters publicly visible and legible, and at least an inch long, and so forth. He is liable to the penalty, therefore, by carrying on the trade in a house in which these requisites are not complied with; and there is no addition to his criminality if he makes fifty contracts for the *sale* of tobacco in such a house. It seems to me, therefore, that there is nothing in the Act of Parliament to prohibit every act of sale, but that its only effect is to impose a penalty, for the purpose of the revenue, on the carrying on of the trade without complying with its requisites."

A contract for the sale of tobacco was therefore not to be considered void merely because the premises in which the tobacco was sold did not comply with the law. So it might be said that a contract for carriage of goods is not to be considered void merely because the ship in which they are carried does not comply with the law. But I recognize that each case must be determined by reference to the relevant statute and not by comparison with other cases. I reach my conclusion—in the words of Lord Wright in *Vita Food Products Inc.* v. *Unus Shipping Co.*—on "the true construction of the statute, having regard to its scope and its purpose and to the inconvenience which would follow from any other conclusion."

In view of the importance of this question, I have thought it right to determine it upon general grounds rather than upon the particular wording of section 44. But I must note that Mr. Roskill also particularly relies upon the wording of subsection (2) of that section. This subsection, to which I have already referred, is the one which says that the fine is to be such "as the court thinks fit to impose having regard to the extent to which the earning capacity of the ship was, or would have been, increased by reason of the submersion." Mr. Roskill submits that this shows that the statute contemplated that, notwithstanding the breach of it, there would be an "'earning capacity" and, therefore, that contracts for the payment of freight must be intended to remain alive. . . .

I turn now to Mr. Wilmers's second point. He submitted that the plaintiffs could not succeed in a claim for freight without disclosing that they had committed an illegality in the course of the voyage; or, put another way, that part of the consideration for the payment of freight was the safe carriage of the goods, and therefore they must show that they carried the goods safely. In the passage I have quoted from the judgment in *Wetherell* v. *Jones*, Tenterden C.J. carefully distinguished between an infringement of the law in the performance of the contract and a case where "the consideration and the matter to be performed" were illegal. There is a distinction there—of the sort I have just been considering—between a contract which has as its object the doing of the very act forbidden by the statute, and a contract whose performance involves an illegality only incidentally. It may be, therefore, that the second point is the first point looked at from another angle. However that may be, there is no doubt that if the plaintiffs cannot succeed in their claim for freight without showing that they carried the goods in an overloaded ship, they must fail.

But, in my judgment, the plaintiffs need show no more in order to recover their freight than that they delivered to the defendants the goods they received in the same good order and condition as that in which they received them. Indeed, they are entitled to recover their freight without deduction (but subject to counterclaim) if the goods they delivered were substantially the same as when loaded: see *Scrutton on Charterparties*, 16th ed., p. 391. art. 144. It may be true that it is a term of the contract of carriage that the goods should be carried safely. Article III of the Hague Rules provides, for example, in rule 2, "that the carrier shall properly and carefully load, handle, stow, carry, keep, care for and discharge the goods carried." But no one has ever heard of a claim for freight being supported by a string of witnesses describing the loading, handling, stowing, keeping, caring for and discharging the goods. The truth is that if the goods have been delivered safely, it must follow that they have been carried safely. If, therefore, they are proved to have been delivered undamaged, the shipowner need prove no more. The law is that they shall be carried safely—not that they should not be exposed to danger on the voyage. If the plaintiffs had to prove that they were not exposed to danger on the voyage, then no doubt they would also have to prove that the ship complied with all the safety regulations affecting her; but in the claim for freight they need only prove safe delivery. This point fails.

On Mr. Wilmers's third point I take the law from the dictum in *Beresford* v. *Royal Insurance Co. Ltd.*, [1937] 2 K.B. 197, that was adopted and applied by Lord Atkin: "no system of jurisprudence can with reason include amongst the rights which it enforces rights directly resulting to the person asserting them from the crime of that person." I observe in the first place that in the Court of Appeal in the same case Lord Wright doubted whether this principle applied to all statutory offences. His doubt was referred to by Denning L.J. in *Marles* v. *Philip Trant & Sons*, which I have already cited. The distinction is much to the point here. The Act of 1932 imposes a penalty which is itself designed to deprive the offender of the benfits of his crime. It would be a curious thing if the operation could be performed twice—once by the criminal law and then again by the civil. It would be curious, too, if in a case in which the magistrates had thought fit to impose only a nominal fine, their decision could, in effect, be overridden in a civil action. But the question whether the rule applies to statutory offences is an important one which I do not wish to decide in the present case. The dicta of Lord Wright and Denning L.J. suggest that there are cases where its application would be morally unjustifiable; but it is not clear that they go as far as saying that the application would not be justified in law. I prefer, therefore, to deal with Mr. Wilmers's submission in another way.

The rights which cannot be enforced must be those "directly resulting" from the crime. That means, I think, that for a right to money or to property to be unenforceable the property or money must be identifiable as something to which, but for the crime, the plaintiff would have had no right or title. That cannot be said in this case. The amount of the profit which the plaintiffs made from the crime, that is to say, the amount of freight which, but for the overloading, they could not have earned on this voyage, was, as I have said £2,295. The quantity of cargo consigned to the defendants was approximately 35 per cent of the whole and, therefore, even if it were permissible to treat the benefit as being divisible pro rata over the whole of the cargo, the amount embodied in the claim against the defendants, would not be more than 35 per cent. of £2,300. That would not justify the withholding of £2,000. The fact is that the defendants and another cargo owner have between them withheld money, not on a basis that is proportionate to the claim against them, but so as to wipe out the improper profit on the whole of the cargo. I do not, however, think that the defendants' position would be any better if they had deducted no more than the sum attributable to their freight on a pro rata basis. There is no warrant under the principle for a pro rata division; it would be just as reasonable to say that the excess freight should be deemed to attach entirely to the last 427 tons loaded, leaving the freight claim on all the rest unaffected. But in truth there is no warrant for any particular form of division. The fact is that in this type of case no claim or part of a claim for freight can be clearly identified as being the excess illegally earned.

In *Beresford* v. *Royal Insurance Co. Ltd.* the court dismissed the claim of a personal representative who claimed on policies of life insurance which had matured owing to the assured committing suicide in circumstances that amounted to a crime. Mr. Wilmers submitted that the only benefit which the assured or his estate derived from the claim was the acceleration of the policies and that notwithstanding that some of the policies had been in force for a considerable time and therefore, I suppose, had a surrender value before the suicide was committed, the plaintiff was not allowed to recover anything. So in the present case, he submits, the commission of the crime defeats the whole claim to freight notwithstanding that the earning of the greater part of it was irrespective of the crime.

The comparison does not seem to me to be just. In *Beresford* v. *Royal Insurance Co. Ltd.*, but for the crime committed by the assured, no part of the policy moneys could have been claimed in that form, that is to say, as money repayable on the happening of the event insured against, or at that time. That does not necessarily mean that, so far as public policy was concerned, the plaintiff could recover nothing. If the plaintiff, for example, had sued for the return of premiums, assuming the contract permitted it, I have not been referred to any observation in the case which would suggest that an action in that form would fail on the grounds of public policy. The claim which the court was considering under the policy depended entirely upon proof of death and the death was a crime. In the present case the right to claim freight from the defendants was not brought into existence by a crime; the crime affected only the total amount of freight earned by the ship.

The result is that there must be judgment for the plaintiffs for £2,000. But the defendants will not have fought the action altogether in vain if it brings to the attention of the competent authorities the fact that section 44 of the Act of 1932 is out of date and ought to be amended. I have already noted that for a similar offence a British master can be imprisoned and it must be very galling for those concerned to see a foreign master do the same thing without the law providing any effective deterrent.

[Judgment for plaintiffs.]

ARCHBOLDS (FREIGHTAGE), LTD. v. SPANGLETT, LTD.
[1961] 1 Q.B. 374 (C.A.)

The defendants were furniture manufacturers in London and owned a number of vans with "C" licences under the Road and Rail Traffic Act, 1933, which enabled them to carry their own goods, but did not allow them to carry for reward the goods of others. The plaintiffs were carriers with offices in London and Leeds, and their vehicles had "A" licences under the Act, which enabled them to carry the goods of others for reward. The plaintiffs' London office, as a result of a telephone conversation with some unidentified persons from the defendants' office, believed that the defendants' vehicle had "A" licences, and employed the defendants to carry a part of a load for them on the defendants' van which was taking some of their (the defendants') furniture from London to Leeds.

The defendants' driver, having delivered those goods, spoke on the telephone to the traffic manager of the plaintiffs' office at Leeds to see if he could obtain a load for his empty van from Leeds to London, and said that he had just carried goods from the plaintiffs' London office to Leeds. The traffic manager replied that he had a load, which was in fact 200 cases of whisky, but he made no inquiries from the driver as to whether he had an "A" licence. The defendants' van was duly loaded with the whisky, which was stolen on the way to the London docks owing to the driver's negligence.

On a claim by the plaintiffs for damages for the loss of the whisky, the defendants pleaded the illegality of the contract, in that their van did not have an "A" licence as required by the Act of 1933. . . .

DEVLIN L.J.: The effect of illegality upon a contract may be threefold. If at the time of making the contract there is an intent to perform it in an unlawful way, the contract, although it remains alive, is unenforceable at the suit of the party having that intent; if the intent is held in common, it is not enforceable at all. Another effect of illegality is to prevent a plaintiff from recovering under a contract if in order to prove his rights under it he has to rely upon his own illegal act; he may not do that even though he can show that at the time of making the contract he had no intent to break the law and that at the time of performance he did not know that what he was doing was illegal. The third effect of illegality is to avoid the contract ab initio and that arises if the making of the contract is expressly or impliedly prohibited by statute or is otherwise contrary to public policy.

The defendants do not seek to bring this case under either of the first two heads. They cannot themselves enforce the contract because they intended to perform it unlawfully with a van that they knew was not properly licensed for the purpose: but that does not prevent the plaintiffs, who had no such intent and were not privy to it, from enforcing the contract. Nor can it be said that the plaintiffs committed any illegal act. To load a vehicle is not to use it on the road, which is what is forbidden;

no doubt loading would be enough to constitute aiding and abetting if the plaintiffs knew of the defendants' purpose, but they did not.

So what the defendants say is that the contract is prohibited by the Road and Rail Traffic Act, 1933, s.1. In order to see whether the contract falls within the prohibition it is necessary to ascertain the exact terms of the contract and the exact terms of the prohibition. For reasons which I shall explain later, I shall begin by ascertaining the latter. Section 1 of the Act provides that no person shall use a goods vehicle on a road for the carriage of goods for hire or reward except under a licence. Section 2 provides for various classes of licences, "A," "B" and "C." It is agreed that the carriage of the goods which were the subject-matter of this contract required an "A" licence. The fact that the van had a "C" licence does not therefore help one way or the other; and it is admitted that the defendants' use of this van for the carriage of these goods was prohibited. As I have noted, the plaintiffs are not to be treated as using the van because they supplied the load. Section 1(3) provides that the driver of the vehicle or, if he is an agent or servant, his principal, shall be deemed to be the person by whom the vehicle is being used.

The statute does not expressly prohibit the making of any contract. The question is therefore whether a prohibition arises as a matter of necessary implication. It follows from the decision of this court in *Nash* v. *Stevenson Transport Ltd.*, [1936] 2 K.B. 128, that a contract for the use of unlicensed vehicles is prohibited. In that case the plaintiff held "A" licences which the defendant wanted to purchase. But the Act of 1933 provides that licences may not be transferred or assigned, and it was therefore agreed that the defendant should run the vehicles in the plaintiff's name so that they might obtain the benefit of his licences. It was held by the court that that was an illegal agreement because the defendant was the person who was using the vehicles and the plaintiff the person who was licensed to use them; thus the user was not the licensee. In the present case there was no contract for the use of the vehicle.

On the other hand, it does not follow that because it is an offence for one party to enter into a contract, the contract itself is void. In *In re Mahmoud and Ispahani*, [1921] 1 K.B. 716 Scrutton L.J. said: "In *Bloxsome* v. *Williams*, (1824) 3 B. & C. 232, the position was that the defendant, a horse dealer, was prohibited from trading on Sunday, but there was nothing illegal in another person making a contract with a horse dealer, except that if he knew that the person with whom he was dealing was a horse dealer and was guilty of breaking the law he might be aiding and abetting him to break the law. But merely to make a contract with a horse dealer, without knowing he was a horse dealer, was not illegal."

The general considerations which arise on this question were examined at length in *St. John Shipping Company* v. *Joseph Rank Ltd.* and Pearce L.J. has set them out so clearly in his judgment in this case that I need add little to them. Fundamentally they are the same as those that arise on the construction of every statute; one must have regard to the language used and to the scope and purpose of the statute. I think that the purpose of this statute is sufficiently served by the penalties prescribed for the offender; the avoidance of the contract would cause grave inconvenience and injury to innocent members of the public without furthering the object of the statute. Moreover, the value of the relief given to the wrongdoer if he could escape what would otherwise have been his legal obligation might, as it would in this case, greatly outweigh the punishment that could be imposed upon him, and thus undo the penal effect of the statute.

I conclude, therefore, that this contract was not illegal for the reason that the statute does not prohibit the making of a contract for the carriage of goods in unlicensed vehicles and this contract belongs to this class. I am able, therefore, to arrive at my judgment without an examination of the exact terms of the contract. It would have been natural to have begun by looking at the contract; I have not done so because it is doubtful whether the state of the pleadings permits a thorough examination. But as Mr. Karmel's argument before us turned upon its terms, I think that I should deal with them.

The defendants contend that this was a contract of carriage by a specified vehicle, namely, the van SXY902 then being driven by Randall. The plaintiffs agree that it was contemplated that the van SXY902 should be used for the contract but dispute that the contract was so limited. The words used in the contract were "a covered van" and the plaintiffs submit, and the judge has so held, that "it was open to the defendants to carry the goods in any vehicle they liked."

I have reached no final conclusion on this point. Assuming, as for the purpose of this argument I do, that the statute prohibits every contract for the carriage of goods in an unlicensed vehicle, I do not think that the question whether this contract falls within the statute depends on whether it was limited to the use of the vehicle SXY902. According to the defendants' argument, the significance of the point lies in the fact that they have to accept the burden of proving that there was no way in which they could have performed the contract legally. If only the one van could have been used under the contract, they claim to have discharged that burden; otherwise they concede that they cannot prove that they could not, if they had tried, have got hold of some other licensed van. In my judgment, this is not the decisive test.

It is a familiar principle of law that if a contract can be performed in one of two ways, that is, legally or illegally, it is not an illegal contract, though it may be unenforceable at the suit of a party who chooses to perform it illegally. That statement of the law is meaningful if the contract is one which is by its terms open to two modes of performance; otherwise it is meaningless. Almost any contract—certainly any contract for the carriage of goods by road—can be performed illegally; any contract of carriage by road can be performed illegally simply by exceeding the appropriate speed limit. The error in the defendants' argument, I think, is that they are looking at the facts which determine their capacity to perform and not at the terms of the contract. Suppose that the contract were for a vehicle with an "A" licence, or—what is substantially the same thing—for a specified vehicle warranted as holding an "A" licence. That would not be an illegal contract for it would be a contract for the use of a licensed vehicle and not an unlicensed one. If those were the express terms of the contract, it would not be made illegal because all the carrier's vehicles, or the specified vehicles as the case might be, had "C" licences. The most that that could show would be that the carrier might well be unable to perform his contract. Or suppose that the contract were for any "A" vehicle owned by the defendant and the defendant had a fleet of five "A" vehicles and five "C" vehicles. That would be a legal contract and it would not be made illegal because, at the time when it was made, it was physically impossible for the defendant to get any of his "A" vehicles to the loading place in time. If the contract is for a specified vehicle with an "A" licence, loading to begin within a week, it is not illegal because when the contract was made the vehicle had no "A" licence; one might be obtained in time and the court will not decide the question of legality by inquiring whether an "A" licence could or could not have been obtained for it within the week. So in this case it is irrelevant to say that the van SXY902 had in fact not got an "A" licence and could not conceivably have got one in time. The error in the defendants' argument is that they assume that because the parties were contracting about a specified vehicle and because that specified vehicle had in fact (a fact known to one party and not to the other) only a "C" licence, therefore they were contracting about a vehicle with a "C" licence. It is the terms of the contract that matter; the surrounding facts are irrelevant, save in so far as being known to both parties, they throw light on the meaning and effect of the contract. The question is not whether the vehicle was in fact properly licensed but whether it was expressly or by implication in the contract described or warranted as properly licensed. If it was so described or warranted, then the legal position is, not that the contract could only be performed by a violation of the law, but that unless it could be performed legally, it could not be performed at all. The fact that, as in this case, it may be known to one of the parties at the time of making the contract that he cannot perform it legally and therefore that it will inevitably be broken, does not make the contract itself illegal.

So the correct line of inquiry into the terms of the contract in this case should have been not as to whether it provided for performance by a specified vehicle or by any vehicle that the defendants chose to nominate, but as to whether the defendants warranted or agreed that the vehicle which was to do the work, whether a specified vehicle or any other, was legally fit for the service which it had to undertake, that is, that it had an "A" licence.

I think there is much to be said for the argument that in a case of this sort there is, unless the circumstances exclude it, an implied warranty that the van is properly licensed for the service for which it is required. It would be unreasonable to expect a man when he is getting into a taxi-cab to ask for an express warranty from the driver that his cab is licensed; the answer, if it took any intelligible form at all, would be to the effect that it would not be on the streets if it were not. The same applies to a person who delivers goods for carriage by a particular vehicle; he cannot be expected to examine the road licence to see if it is in order. But the issue of warranty was not raised in the pleadings or at the trial and so I think it is preferable to decide this case on the broad ground which Pearce L.J. has adopted and with which, for the reasons I have given, I agree.

There are many pitfalls in this branch of the law. If, for example, Mr. Field had observed that the van had a "C" licence and said nothing, he might be said to have accepted a mode of performance different from that contracted for and so varied the contract and turned it into an illegal one: see *St. John Shipping Corporation* v. *Joseph Rank Ltd.* where that sort of point was considered. Or, to take another example, if a statute prohibits the sale of goods to an alien, a warranty by the buyer that he is not an alien will not save the contract. That is because the terms of the prohibition expressly forbid a sale to an alien; consequently, the question to be asked in order to see whether the contract comes within the prohibition is whether the buyer is in fact an alien, not whether he represented himself as one. *In re Mahmoud* is that sort of case. The statute forbade the buying and selling of certain goods between unlicensed persons. The buyer falsely represented himself as having a licence. It is not said that he so warranted but, if he had, it could have made no difference. Once the fact was established that he was an unlicensed person the contract was brought within the category of those that were prohibited. *Strongman* v. *Sincock*, [1955] 2 Q.B. 525, exemplifies another sort of difficulty. It was an action brought by a builder against a building owner to recover the price of building work done. The statute forbade the execution of building operations without a licence. The building owner expressly undertook to obtain the necessary licence and failed to do so; and it was held that the builder could not recover. The builder, I dare say, might have contended that, having regard to the undertaking, the contract he made was for licensed operations and therefore legal. But unfortunately he had himself performed it illegally by building without a licence and he could not recover without relying on his illegal act because he was suing for money for work done. The undertaking might make the contract legal but not the operations. All these cases are distinguishable from the present one, where the contract is not within the prohibition and the plaintiffs themselves committed no illegal act and did not aid or abet the defendants. Apart from the pleading point, it might not matter if the last two cases were not distinguishable, since the plaintiffs could obtain damages for breach of the warranty as in *Strongman* v. *Sincock*.

[Appeal dismissed with costs.]

ASHMORE, BENSON, PEASE & CO. LTD. v. *A. V. DAWSON LTD.*
[1973] 1 W.L.R. 828 (C.A.)

LORD DENNING M.R.: In February, 1967 a big piece of engineering equipment called a tube bank was being carried from Stockton-on-Tees to Hull where it was to be shipped to Poland. It was very heavy. It weighed 25 tons. It was loaded on an articulated lorry. Halfway to Hull that lorry with its load tipped over. Damage was done to the load. It cost £2,225 to repair. The manufacturers claim damages from the hauliers. In answer the hauliers plead that the load was too heavy for the vehicle: and that the contract of carriage, or the performance of it, was illegal.

The relevant regulations are the Motor Vehicles (Construction and Use) Regulations 1966 (S.I. 1966 No. 1288). They were made by virtue of the Road Traffic Act 1960, section 64. Subsection (2) of section 64 says: "... it shall not be lawful to use on a road a motor vehicle or trailer which does not comply with any such regulations as aforesaid ..."

In the present case the vehicle was an articulated vehicle with a tractor and trailer. Under regulation 73 (2) the maximum weight laden was specified as 30 tons. Now the unladen weight of the vehicle was 10 tons. This load (consisting of the tube bank) was 25 tons. So the total weight laden was 35 tons. So it was five tons over the regulation weight. Furthermore, the tube bank was top heavy. It had fittings on the top which made its centre of gravity high. Not only was it in breach of the regulations, but it was a dangerous and unsafe load to be carried on this vehicle along the roads of England. The evidence showed clearly that the only vehicle suitable for this load was a "low loader," which is underslung so that it can take heavier weights and bigger loads. So the expedition was certainly illegal.

I turn now to consider the contract of carriage. The makers of the tube bank were Ashmore, Benson, Pease & Co. Ltd. of Stockton-on-Tees. Their transport manager was a Mr. Bulmer. His assistant was Mr. Jones. Two of these tube banks were to be sent from the works at Stockton-on-Tees to the port of Hull. Mr. Bulmer told Mr. Jones to arrange for the carriage of the two tube banks and to give the work to A. V. Dawson Ltd. That was a small firm in which the principals were Mr. Arthur Vernon Dawson, the father, and Mr. Maurice Dawson, the son. This firm had 10 articulated vehicles. The biggest of them was only a 30 tonner. They had no low loaders. They had worked for Ashmores for several years. Mr. Jones knew the whole of their fleet well; and Mr. Bulmer had known it for some six months. On getting the instructions, Mr. Jones telephoned Dawsons and spoke to Mr. Maurice Dawson, the son. He suggested that Maurice Dawson should come up and see the nature of the load. Maurice Dawson did so. The weight of it was shown plainly on the plate and on each tube bank and on the case. It was "25 tons." It was arranged that Dawsons should take the loads. The price was arranged: it was £55 for the trip for each of the two articulated vehicles. If it had been on low loaders (which Dawsons had not got), the price would have been £85 or more for each: but here it was £55. Later that day Dawsons sent two of their drivers with the articulated vehicles to get the two loads. The tube banks were loaded on to the trailers. Mr. Bulmer was there for a short time. He saw them loaded, and so did Mr. Jones. The tube banks were firmly secured in by chains.

Early next morning the two drivers came and set off on the journey for Hull. When they were about half-way there, the leading vehicle toppled over. It was driven by Mr. Harvey, the best and most experienced driver that Dawsons had. Mr. Harvey was asked the cause: "What do you say caused your lorry to topple over?" He answered: "The camber in the road to the left plus the weight of the load, plus the height of the load." The judge found that Mr. Harvey made an error of judgment. But that was not the real cause of the toppling over. The real cause was the overweight. The articulated lorry was a most unsuitable vehicle on which to carry it. The whole transaction was illegal, being in breach of the regulations.

Assuming, however, that Mr. Harvey was negligent, the question is whether the illegality prevents Ashmores from suing for that negligence. This depends on whether the contract itself was unlawful, or its performance was unlawful.

The first question is whether the contract of carriage, when made, was lawful or not. The judge found that it was lawful, because it could have been lawfully performed. He cited *Waugh* v. *Morris* (1873) L.R. 8 Q.B. 202, 208, and said:

"I find that this contract was concluded between Jones on behalf of the plaintiffs and Maurice Dawson on behalf of the defendants. I find that Jones was relying on Maurice Dawson and his company to carry out the contract, a contract which could perfectly easily be carried out lawfully, and that he relied on the defendants to do so. It was not a term of the contract that it should be carried on any particular lorry. The contract was concluded at a time when Mr. Jones was asking Mr. Maurice Dawson to look at the load and say that he could carry it for the sum offered."

I am not altogether satisfied with that finding. Mr. Jones admitted that he knew a little about motor vehicle construction and the regulations. He was asked by Mr. Ross-Munro: "You knew, for example, that there were specific loads for articulated lorries, didn't you?" And he said: "I would say yes." I would have thought that Mr. Jones, being in the business, would have known that the lorries which Dawsons were going to provide could not lawfully carry these loads.

Although I have these misgivings, I am prepared to accept the judge's finding that the contract was lawful when it was made. But then the question arises: was it lawful in its performance? The judge's attention does not seem to have been drawn to this point. Yet there are authorities which show that illegality in the performance of a contract may disable a person from suing on it, if he participated in the illegality. This was pointed out by Atkin L.J. in *Anderson Ltd.* v. *Daniel* [1924] 1 K.B. 138, 149 in a passage which was quoted by Devlin J. in *St. John Shipping Corporation* v. *Joseph Rank Ltd.* [1957] 1 Q.B. 267, 282:

"The question of illegality in a contract generally arises in connection with its formation, but it may also arise, as it does here, in connection with its performance. In the former case, where the parties have agreed to do something which is prohibited by Act of Parliament, it is indisputable that the contract is unenforceable by either party. And I think that it is equally unenforceable by the offending party where the illegality arises from the fact that the mode of performance adopted by the party performing it is in violation of some statute, even though the contract as agreed upon between the parties was capable of being performed in a perfectly legal manner."

That passage was further approved by Jenkins L.J. in *B. and B. Viennese Fashions* v. *Losane* [1952] 1 All E.R. 909, 913, where he said: "that illegality in the performance of a contract may avoid it although the contract was not illegal ab initio."

In this case the parties entered into the performance of the contract when Dawson's driver took the articulated vehicle (the 30-tonner) up to Ashmore's works to pick up this load. Mr. Bulmer, the transport manager, came along and saw it. Mr. Jones, his assistant, was there. Both saw this 25-ton tube bank being loaded on to the articulated lorry. Mr. Bulmer must have known that this was illegal: and Mr. Bulmer's knowledge would affect Ashmores. Mr. Jones was asked: "Mr. Bulmer would know the specific loads for articulated lorries, would he not? (A.) Like the back of his hand, yes." Then as to these particular lorries, Mr. Jones was asked: "Mr. Bulmer would have had all the knowledge in the world and would have known what weight these lorries were permitted to carry but you didn't know?" "Well," said Mr. Jones, "I would say he would have a good idea what they would carry, yes."

Now Mr. Bulmer was not called to give evidence. The reason was because he left the employment of Ashmores some years ago and had gone to Zambia. But he had given a statement in which he had said: "Identical loads to the one in question have been carried on similar vehicles belonging to G. Stiller (Haulage) Ltd., Middleton St. George, Darlington, completely without incident."

On that evidence I think that Mr. Bulmer must have known that those articulated lorries of Dawsons were only permitted to carry 20 tons. Nevertheless, realising that 25 tons was too heavy—much too heavy—for them, he was content to let them carry the loads because it had happened before without trouble. He was getting the transport done cheaper too by £30 saved on each trip by each load. Not only did Mr. Bulmer know of the illegality. He participated in it by sanctioning the loading of the vehicle with a load in excess of the regulations. That participation in the illegal performance of the contract debars Ashmores from suing Dawsons on it or suing Dawsons for negligence. I know that Dawsons were parties to the illegality. They knew, as well as Mr. Bulmer, that the load was overweight in breach of the regulations. But in such a situation as this, the defendants are in a better position. In pari delicto, potior est conditio defendentis. I would therefore allow the appeal and enter judgment for the defendants.

KIRIRI COTTON CO. LTD. v.
RANCHHODDAS KESHAVJI DEWANI.
[1960] A.C. 192 (J.C.P.C., on appeal from the
Court of Appeal for Eastern Africa.)

The facts were simple. The plaintiff came to Kampala in March, 1953, and looked for somewhere to live. At the end of May, 1953, he took a flat in Salisbury Road, but he had to pay 10,000 shillings premium. He now said that that premium was illegal because it was in contravention of the Rent Restriction Ordinance, and he claimed the return of it.

The oral evidence was so short that it could be set out in full. Only the plaintiff gave evidence. He said:

"I came to Kampala, Uganda, in 1953—March. I lived with a brother for 1½ months. I took a flat but I had to pay key money. I was searching for some time.

I got a flat at Kololo but after 2-3 days I had to leave as I had trouble with a co-tenant. Then I got in touch with C. B. Patel, after having difficulty. I borrowed 10,000/- from the company as my brother was a director."

Cross-examination: "I paid the money by borrowing the money."

It was apparent from that evidence, as the trial judge said, that during the negotiations for the flat the plaintiff was at a disadvantage. He was having difficulty in obtaining accommodation—and he only got the flat by paying a premium of 10,000 shillings, which he borrowed for the purpose. He took it under a sublease dated September 17, 1953. This was prepared by lawyers. It contained provisions whereby the defendant company, in consideration of the sum of 10,000/- paid by the plaintiff by way of premium, subleased to him Flat No. 1 on the first floor for residence only, having three rooms, one kitchen, one bathroom and one lavatory. The term was seven years and one day from May 31, 1953. The rent was 300/- a month payable monthly in advance. And there were several covenants on either side.

The Rent Restriction Ordinance, 1949, of Uganda, provided by section

3(2): "Any person whether the owner of the property or not who in consideration of the letting or subletting of a dwelling-house ... to a person asks for, solicits or receives any sum of money other than rent ... shall be guilty of an offence and liable to a fine not exceeding Shs. 10,000 or imprisonment for a period not exceeding six months or to both such fine and imprisonment. ..."

The judgment of their Lordships was delivered by LORD DENNING, who stated the facts set out above, and continued: Their Lordships desire to point out at once that neither party thought they were doing anything illegal. The lease was for more than seven years and it was thought that, on a lease for that length of time, there was nothing wrong in asking for a premium or receiving it.

This was an easy mistake to make, as will be seen if one reads section 3(1) and (2) of the Rent Restriction Ordinance:

"3. (1) No owner or lessee of a dwelling-house or premises shall let or sublet such dwelling-house or premises at a rent which exceeds the standard rent.

(2) Any person whether the owner of the property or not who in consideration of the letting or subletting of a dwelling-house or premises to a person asks for, solicits or receives any sum of money other than rent or any thing of value whether such asking, soliciting or receiving is made before or after the grant of a tenancy shall be guilty of an offence and liable to a fine not exceeding Shs. 10,000 or imprisonment for a period not exceeding six months or to both such fine and imprisonment:

Provided that a person acting bona fide as an agent for either party to an intended tenancy agreement shall be entitled to a reasonable commission for his services:

"And provided further that nothing in this section shall be deemed to make unlawful the charging of a purchase price or premium on the sale, grant, assignment or renewal of a long lease of premises where the term or unexpired term is seven years or more."

Anyone reading the last proviso to that section—without more—might well think that a premium could be charged on the lease of this flat for seven years and one day. He would readily assume that the word "premises" included a flat. But he would be wrong. For if he took pains to look back to the definition section 2, he would find that in this Ordinance, the word "premises" refers only to business premises and not to residential flats at all. And so this proviso does not apply to this flat—because by the very terms of the sublease it was let "for residence only." Their Lordships ought perhaps to set out the material words of the definition clause which produces this result—it says that " 'dwelling-house' means any building or part of a building let for human habitation as a separate dwelling" and " 'premises' means any building or part of a building let for business, trade or professional purpose or for the public service."

It was owing to the failure of the lawyers to refer to those definitions—or at any rate to appreciate the importance of them—that the mistake arose.

Their Lordships also think it right to point out that there was no evidence to show whether the premium of 10,000/– was extortionate or not. Their Lordships were told that no standard rent had been fixed for this flat because it was a new flat. It is obvious that if the standard rent were to be fixed at, say, 450/– a month for seven years, there would be nothing extortionate in a premium of 10,000/– down and a rent of 300/– a month thereafter: for it would come in the long run to much about the same.

Nevertheless, no matter whether the mistake was excusable or inexcusable, or the premium fair or extortionate, the fact remains that the landlord received a premium contrary to the provisions of the Ordinance: and the question is whether the tenant can recover it back—remembering always that there is nothing in the Uganda Ordinance, comparable to the English Acts, enabling a premium to be recovered back.

This omission in the Ordinance was considered to be decisive by the Court of Appeal for Eastern Africa in a case a few years ago. . . . The court was then differently constituted from what it is now. The judges argued in this wise: "We do not know the reason, but the Uganda legislature in its wisdom has included in the Ordinance no provision comparable to section 8(2) of the Rent Restriction Act of 1920. . . . Without this statutory right of recovery, the giver of the illegal premium is left in the position of one who, although he himself has committed no substantive offence, has aided and abetted the commission of an offence by another. In these circumstances he could not go to a civil court with clean hands, and the principle stated by Lord Ellenborough in *Langton* v. *Hughes*, (1813) 1 M. & S. 593, would have application: 'What is done in contravention of an Act of Parliament, cannot be made the subject-matter of an action.' "

In considering the validity of this reasoning, their Lordships would point out that the observation of Lord Ellenborough was made in a case where a party was seeking the aid of the court in order positively to enforce an illegal contract. It should be confined to cases of that description. His observation has no application to cases such as the present, where a party is seeking to recover money paid or property transferred under an illegal transaction. In such cases the general principle was stated by Littledale J. in *Hastelow* v. *Jackson*, (1828) 8 B. & C. 221, "If two parties enter into an illegal contract, and money is paid upon it by one to the other, that may be recovered back before the execution of the contract, but not afterwards." In accordance with this principle, so long as the illegal transaction has not been fully executed and carried out, the courts have in many cases shown themselves ready to entertain a suit for recovery of the money paid or property transferred. These were cases in which it appeared to the court that, even though the transaction was illegal, nevertheless it was better to allow the plaintiff to resile from it before it was completed, and to award restitution to him rather than to allow the defendant to remain in possession of his illegal gains . . . But so soon as the illegal transaction has been fully executed and carried out the courts will not entertain a suit for recovery. . . . unless it appears that the parties were not in pari delicto. . . .

It is clear that in the present case the illegal transaction was fully executed and carried out. The money was paid. The lease was granted. It was and still is vested in the plaintiff. In order to recover the premium, therefore, the plaintiff must show that he was not in pari delicto with the defendant. That was, indeed, the way he put his claim in the pleadings. After setting out the lease, the payment of the premium and the entry into occupation, the statement of claim proceeded simply to say: "By virtue of the provisions of subsection (2) of section 3 of the Rent Restriction Ordinance, the receipt of the said sum of Shs. 10,000 by the defendant from the plaintiff . . . was illegal but the plaintiff is entitled to recover the same since he (the plaintiff) was not in pari delicto with the defendant.

The plaintiff claims the sum of Shs. 10,000 as money received by the defendant for the use of the plaintiff."

The issue thus becomes: Was the plaintiff in pari delicto with the defendant? Mr. Elwyn Jones, for the appellant, said they were both in pari delicto. The payment was, he said, made voluntarily, under no mistake of fact, and without any extortion, oppression or imposition, and could not be recovered back. True, it was paid under a mistake of law, but that was a mistake common to them both. They were both equally supposed to know the law. They both equally mistook it and were thus in pari delicto. . . .

Their Lordships cannot accept this argument. It is not correct to say that everyone is presumed to know the law. The true proposition is that no man can excuse himself from doing his duty by saying that he did not know the law on the matter. Ignorantia juris neminem excusat. Nor is it correct to say that money paid under a mistake of law can never be recovered back. The true proposition is that money paid under a mistake of law, by itself and without more, cannot be recovered back. . . . If there is something more in addition to a mistake of law—if there is something in the defendant's conduct which shows that, of the two of them, he is the one primarily responsible for the mistake—then it may be recovered back. Thus, if as between the two of them the duty of observing the law is placed on the shoulders of the one rather than the other—it being imposed on him specially for the protection of the other —then they are not in pari delicto and the money can be recovered back; . . . Likewise, if the responsibility for the mistake lies more on the one than the other—because he has misled the other when he ought to know better—then again they are not in pari delicto and the money can be recovered back; . . . These propositions are in full accord with the principles laid down by Lord Mansfield relating to the action for money had and received. Their Lordships have in mind particularly. . . . his celebrated judgment. . . . on May 19, 1760, in *Moses* v. *Macferlan*, 2 Burr. 1005, when he sat in banco. Their Lordships were referred to some cases 30 or 40 years ago where disparaging remarks were made about the action for money had and received: but their Lordships venture to suggest that these were made under a misunderstanding of its origin. It is not an action on contract or imputed contract. If it were none such could be imputed here, as their Lordships readily agree. It is simply an action for restitution of money which the defendant has received but which the law says he ought to return to the plaintiff. This was explained by Lord Wright in *Fibrosa Spolka Akcyjna* v. *Fairbairn Lawson Combe Barbour Ltd.*, [1943] A.C. 32. All the particular heads of money had and received, such as money paid under a mistake of fact, paid under a consideration that has wholly failed, money paid by one who is not in pari delicto with the defendant, are only instances where the law says the money ought to be returned.

In applying these principles to the present case, the most important thing to observe is that the Rent Restriction Ordinance was intended to protect tenants from being exploited by landlords in days of housing shortage. One of the obvious ways in which a landlord can exploit the housing shortage is by demanding from the tenant "key-money." Section

3(2) of the Rent Restriction Ordinance was enacted so as to protect tenants from exploitation of that kind. This is apparent from the fact that the penalty is imposed only on the landlord or his agent and not upon the tenant. It is imposed on the person who "asks for, solicits or receives any sum of money," but not on the person who submits to the demand and pays the money. It may be that the tenant who pays money is an accomplice or an aider and abettor . . . but he can hardly be said to be in pari delicto with the landlord. The duty of observing the law if firmly placed by the Ordinance on the shoulders of the landlord for the protection of the tenant: and if the law is broken, the landlord must take the primary responsibility. Whether it be a rich tenant who pays a premium as a bribe in order to "jump the queue," or a poor tenant who is at his wit's end to find accommodation, neither is so much to blame as the landlord who is using his property rights so as to exploit those in need of a roof over their heads.

Seeing then that the parties are not in pari delicto, the tenant is entitled to recover the premium by the common law: and it is not necessary to find a remedy given by the Ordinance, either expressly or by implication. The omission of a statutory remedy does not, in cases of this kind, exclude the remedy by money had and received. That is amply shown by the numerous cases to which their Lordships were referred, such as those arising under the statutes against usury, lotteries and gaming, in which there was no remedy given by the statute but nevertheless it was held that an action lay for money had and received. . . .

Their Lordships find themselves in full agreement with the judgment of the High Court of Uganda and of the Court of Appeal for Eastern Africa, and will humbly advise Her Majesty that this appeal should be dismissed. The appellant must pay the costs.

MISTRY AMAR SINGH v. SERWANO WOFUNIRA KULUBYA.
[1964] A.C. 142 (J.C.P.C., on appeal from the Court of Appeal for Eastern Africa)

The respondent, an African, who was the registered proprietor of certain "mailo" lands, purported by three agreements to lease the lands to the appellant, an Indian, but the consents of the Governor and the Lukiko to the transactions were not obtained as required by section 2(d) of the Buganda Possession of Land Law, c. 25 of 1957 Revision, and section 2 of the Uganda Land Transfer Ordinance, c. 114 of the 1951 Revision, the result of the omission being that under the above statutes both the respondent and the appellant had contravened the law and committed punishable offences. On a claim by the respondent, based on his registered ownership of the lands—his claim for rent and mesne profits having been abandoned—to possession and eviction of the appellant, the latter pleaded that the agreements by which the lands were leased were illegal in the absence of the necessary consents and that the respondent could not file an action on them. The respondent acknowledged that the transactions were illegal.

The judgement of their Lordships was delivered by LORD MORRIS OF BORTH-Y-GEST, who stated the facts set out above and continued: In the judgments of the Court of Appeal it was pointed out (rightly as their Lordships think) that a rejection of the plaintiff's claim would have the result that the defendant, a non-African, would be entitled to remain permanently in possession of African land, to the exclusion of the registered African owner, and without payment of any nature whatsoever.

Although, as has been seen, the plaintiff set out in his plaint that he had entered into agreements to lease the plots of land to the defendant, his right to claim possession did not depend upon those agreements. His claim was in the end based independently of those agreements. Though the plaintiff did in his plaint claim mesne profits and damages, he later abandoned those claims and at the trial he made no claim for rent or for mesne profits. He was able to rest his claim upon his registered ownership of the property. The defendant did not have and could not show any right to the property. In view of the terms of the legislative provisions he could not assert that he had acquired any leasehold interest. For the same reason the defendant could not assert that he had any right to occupy. As a non-African he had no right without the consent in writing of the Governor to occupy or enter into possession of the land or to make any contract to take the land on lease. Quite irrespective of the circumstance that the plaintiff by giving certain notices to quit had purported to withdraw any permission to occupy, the defendant was not and never had been in lawful occupation.

The defendant, for his part, could not point to or rely upon the illegal agreements as justifying any right or claim to remain in possession, and without doing so he could not defeat the plaintiff's claim to possession. In so far as the plaintiff may have thought that in the circumstances it was reasonable to give the defendant notices to quit he could give such notices without their being related to or dependent upon the unlawful agreements. Because the agreements were unlawful no leasehold interest vested in the defendant. He had no right to hold over or to hold from year to year. His occupation of the land was contrary to law.

Their Lordships consider, therefore, that the plaintiff's right to possession was in no way based upon the purported agreements. It was the defendant who might have needed to rely upon them because had they been valid and permissible agreements the defendant would have contended that the tenancies would have needed for their termination longer periods of notice than those contained in the notices to quit that were given. As it was, the contention of the defendant (based on paragraph 3 of the defence) was that the plaintiff was disabled from suing because he had been a party to illegal agreements. It was quite correct as set out in that paragraph of the defence that the plaintiff had been a party to illegal agreements. At the time of the trial, however, he was not basing his claim "on the said agreements." Indeed, he could have presented his claim (if it were limited to a claim for possession) without being under any necessity of setting out the unlawful agreements in his plaint. He required no aid from the illegal transactions in order to establish his case. ... It was sufficient for him to show that he was the registered proprietor of the plots of land and that the defendant, who was a non-African, was in occupation without possessing the consent in writing of the Governor for such occupation and accordingly had no right to occupy. It is true that the plaintiff referred to the purported agreements to which he had been a party and that he repudiated them and acknowledged that they were illegal. It was, however, in spite of and not because of those illegal agreements that he was entitled to possession. Though the plaintiff had offended by being a party to the illegal and ineffective agreements their Lordships do not consider that considerations of public policy demanded the failure of his claim for possession: on the contrary, such considerations pointed to the necessity of upholding it in order to eject a non-African who was in unlawful occupation. Their Lordships agree with Forbes V.-P. "that it would be contrary to public policy for the courts to refuse to assist an African to eject a non-African in illegal occupation of the former's land, even though the African may have committed an illegal act in permitting the non-African to enter on the land." This their Lordships consider is in line with the decision of the Court of Appeal in *Bowmakers Ltd. v. Barnet Instruments Ltd.*, [1945] K.B. 65, in which case du Parcq L.J., delivering the judgment of the court, said: Prima facie, a man is entitled to his own property, and it is not a general principle of our law (as was suggested) that when one man's goods have got into another's possession in consequence of some unlawful dealings between them, the true owner can never be allowed to recover those goods by an action. The necessity of such a principle to the interests and advancement of public policy is certainly not obvious. The suggestion that it exists is not, in our opinion, supported by authority."

In his judgment in *Scott v. Brown, Doering, McNab & Co.*, [1892] 2 Q.B. 724, Lindley L.J. thus expressed a well-established principle of law: "Ex turpi causa non oritur actio. This old and well-known legal maxim is founded in good sense, and expresses a clear and well-recognised legal principle, which is not confined to indictable offences. No court ought to enforce an illegal contract or allow itself to be made the instrument of enforcing obligations alleged to arise out of a contract or transaction which is illegal, if the illegality is duly brought to the notice of the court, and if the person invoking the aid of the court is himself implicated in the illegality. It matters not whether the defendant has pleaded the illegality or whether he has not. If the evidence adduced by the plaintiff proves the illegality the court ought not to assist him." Lindley L.J. added: "Any rights which he may have irrespective of his illegal contract will, of course, be recognised and enforced." A. L. Smith L.J. said: "If a plaintiff cannot maintain his cause of action without shewing, as part of such cause of action, that he has been guilty of illegality, then the courts will not assist him in his cause of action."

In the earlier case of *Taylor v. Chester* (1869) L.R. 4 Q.B. 309, it was said: "The true test for determining whether or not the plaintiff and the defendant were in pari delicto, is by considering whether the plaintiff could make out his case otherwise than through the medium and by the aid of the illegal transaction to which he was himself a party." In that case it became impossible for the plaintiff to recover except through the medium and by the aid of an illegal transaction to which he was himself a party. He was therefore defeated by the principle which is expressed in the maxim "in pari delicto potior est conditio possidentis." That was a case, therefore, where a plaintiff was forced, in order to support his claim, to plead the illegality of a contract. The case was referred to in the judgment of the Court of Appeal in *Bowmakers Ltd. v. Barnet Instruments Ltd.*, where it was said: "In our opinion, a man's right to possess his own chattels will as a general rule be enforced against one who, without any claim of right, is detaining them, or has converted them to his own use, even though it may appear either from the pleadings, or in the course of a trial, that the chattels in question came into the defendant's possession by reason of an illegal contract between himself and the plaintiff, provided that the plaintiff does not seek, and is not forced, either to found his claim on the illegal contract or to plead its illegality in order to support his claim."

For these reasons their Lordships consider that the plaintiff was neither obliged to found his claim on the illegal agreements into which he entered nor, in order to support his claim, to plead or to depend upon the agreements. He was not therefore, "in pari delicto" with the defendant.

This conclusion is reinforced when the scope and purpose of the legislative provisions are considered. Their Lordships agree with the view expressed in the Court of Appeal that the legislation was intended to be for the benefit of Africans as a class. In a case in 1957 the Court of Appeal for Eastern Africa recognised that the object of the Land Transfer Ordinance is to protect Africans by regulating any transfer of mailo land and by controlling (as a matter of public policy) the sale of mailo land to non-Africans. . . . Section 2 of the Land Transfer Ordinance positively prohibits occupation by a non-African unless the consent in writing of the Governor has been given. A non-African who commits a breach of the provisions of the Ordinance becomes guilty of an offence. The circumstance that under the Possession of Land Law an owner of "mailo" land also commits an offence if, without the approval in writing of the Governor and the Lukiko, he permits "one who is not of the Protectorate" to lease, occupy or use such land does not alter the fact that the purpose of the legislation is to protect Africans and to preserve African land for use by Africans. In this case the plaintiff, in spite of what was set out in his pleadings and in spite of the claims which the pleadings at first contained, did not at the trial in any way rely upon or seek to enforce the unlawful agreements though he had himself made it known that he had entered into them. That, however, did not make him "in pari delicto" with the defendant. He was a member of the protected class.

In his judgment in *Browning* v. *Morris*, (1778) 2 Cowp. 790, Lord Mansfield said: "But, where contracts or transactions are prohibited by positive statutes, for the sake of protecting one set of men from another set of men; the one, from their situation and condition, being liable to be oppressed or imposed upon by the other; there, the parties are not in pari delicto; and in furtherance of those statutes, the person injured, after the transaction is finished and completed, may bring his action and defeat the contract." So in *Kearley* v. *Thomson*, (1890) 24 Q.B.D. 742, Fry L.J. referred to the case of oppressor and oppressed " . . . in which case usually the oppressed party may recover the money back from the oppressor. In that class of cases the delictum is not par, and therefore the maxim does not apply. Again, there are other illegalities which arise where a statute has been intended to protect a class of persons, and the person seeking to recover is a member of the protected class. Instances of that description are familiar in the case of contracts void for usury under the old statutes, and other instances are to be found in the books under other statutes, which are, I believe, now repealed, such as those directed against lottery keepers. In these cases of oppressor and oppressed, or of a class protected by statute, the one may recover from the other, notwithstanding that both have been parties to the illegal contract."

Their Lordships agree with the conclusions which were reached in the Court of Appeal and accordingly will humbly advise Her Majesty that the appeal should be dismissed. The appellant must pay the costs of the appeal.

[Appeal dismissed.]

RISK, "RECENT DEVELOPMENTS IN CONTRACTS"
(Special Lectures of the Law Society of Upper Canada, 1966)

The inquiry into purposes of statutes is obviously not a simple, mechanical task; the courts often have scope and an obligation to reason and to elaborate meaning. Is this not particularly true of illegality problems? In most situations the statutes are not at all concerned with contracts; they are concerned, for example, with the loading of ships, or licensing trucks or electricians. To speak of an implied prohibition is usually to invoke an intention which simply did not exist. Perhaps a more accurate approach would be to ask whether the statutory expression of attitudes and purposes, whatever may have been its primary concern, demands as well that the consequences of illegality be imposed on an agreement. Considering the gravity of the consequences and the difficulty business-men have in avoiding tripping in our tangled garden of regulation, I suggest that the answer ought not often to be affirmative.

Several recent cases have raised the interesting possibility of avoiding some of the consequences of illegality through an action on a warranty or collateral promise. The first is *Strongman* (1945), *Ltd.* v. *Sincock.*, [1955] 2 Q.B. 525. There, the agreement was for renovations to buildings. A licence to do the work was required; the owner, an architect, assured the builder that he would obtain the licence, and did not. The agreement was illegal, and therefore the builder could not enforce the promise to pay. He recovered the same amount for breach of an undertaking by the owner that he would obtain the licence. In *Archbolds* v. *Spanglett* Devlin, L.J. assumed for the purpose of argument that an agreement for carrying goods in an unlicensed truck was illegal and stated: "There is much to be said for the argument that in a case of this sort there is, unless the circumstances exclude it, an implied warranty that the van is properly licensed for the service for which it is required."

The future of this possibility of implied promises is difficult to predict. The courts may balk, fearing that somehow illegality will eventually be swallowed entirely. Nevertheless, perhaps an implication of a promise that an illegal agreement is legal would make sense where the responsibility for the illegality can reasonably be attributed to one party only, where the other has acted in good faith, and where the purpose of the statute giving rise to the illegality does not also deny the implication. The implication would be a fairy story told to rescue someone who had acted in good faith, but this is probably a good cause for which to tell fairy stories.

Next, the problem of the violation of a statutory prohibition or requirement associated with or during performance. Consider the plight of the owner of a driving school who makes a claim for payment for instruction, and is met with these defences, all based on mythical statutes: the school was not licensed, a statement setting out the terms of the agreement was not given to the pupil before the instruction began, and parts of the lessons were given on streets in a park area forbidden to commercial use. The statutes do not deal specifically with private agreements. He will probably fail, if for no other reason than that the lack of a licence makes the agreement illegal. This defense is included to indicate the difference between the agreement and performance.

Assume he had a licence, and the agreement for instruction was originally legal. What are the consequences, if any, of the subsequent violations? I think the most useful approach is simply to ask whether the purpose of the requirement or prohibition ought, upon violation, to lead to a denial of his claim. Driving in the restricted park area probably ought not to have any effect; none of the possible purposes for forbidding commercial vehicles seems to have any bearing on the agreement for instruction. The failure to deliver the statement is a more difficult question. What are the purposes of the requirement? To protect pupils? If so, from what? From some abuse with which the claim for payment is associated? These seem to me to be the proper questions. I hesitate to offer answers, for I do not know the purposes of these mythical statutes, but I do suggest that the issue is probably a difficult one.

Assume the claim fails. There is considerable authority for the proposition that the agreement is illegal, that is, although legal at the time of creation, it is rendered illegal by the subsequent violation during performance. There is also authority for the proposition that it is because the agreement is illegal that the claim fails. If so, would a claim by the pupil for damages for inadequate instruction also fail? Probably not, but the reasoning supporting this result would have considerable difficulty avoiding schizophrenia faced with the general principle that neither party can enforce an illegal agreement. I suggest that a distinction can and should be made between the agreement and its performance. If the purpose of the requirement or prohibition violated during performance leads to denying the claim, that alone should be sufficient ground for the result. This analysis can lay claim to recent support and, perhaps, to the merit of simplicity.

DAWSON AND PALMER, *CASES ON RESTITUTION*, 1018 (2nd ed. 1958)

The decisions on restitution in connection with illegality leave much to be desired. The maxim that the law will not aid a party to an illegal transaction is certainly not universally observed, but it is observed too often, without enough account taken of the seriousness of the illegality, the nature of the plaintiff's participation, the individual injustice of the enrichment, and whether a judgment depriving the defendant of that enrichment will subvert the policies underlying the rules of law that make the transaction illegal.

DAVIDSON & CO. LTD. v. *McLEERY* (1969) 6 D.L.R. (3d) 331 (B.C.S.C.)

GREGORY J.: This is an action by a firm of stockbrokers against a client for what is, in effect, the balance of a trading account in respect of the sale and purchase of securities over a period long enough that both the *Securities Act*, 1962 (B.C.), c. 55, and the *Securities Act*, 1967 (B.C.), c. 45, apply. However, in the view I take of the case it is unnecessary to consider which transactions came within which Act because the provisions I find it necessary to consider are virtually identical except for the numbering of the sections. Where I refer to a section by number I will use the number in the 1967 Act.

Although a number of defences were raised on the pleading and relied on in argument, the only one I regard as meritorious enough to consider is that the plaintiff's claim arises through its unlawful act in permitting the defendant's trading to be put through one Frank Head, a "salesman in training" or "sales trainee" employed by the plaintiff brokers who was, to the knowledge of the plaintiff, not licensed under the *Securities Act, 1967* and that the plaintiff's breach of the *Securities Act, 1967* renders its claim unenforceable. This defence, in my judgment, *if valid*, applies equally to the $9,045 and interest claimed on a promissory note made by the defendant in favour of the plaintiff and to the $2,519.43 claimed in respect of an open account, because the consideration for the note arose by reason of the defendant's trades through Head, the plaintiff's unlicensed sales trainee, no less than did the amount claimed in respect of the open account: See *Skale* v. *Becker*, [1927] 1 D.L.R. 723, 59 O.L.R. 651.

The only evidence I "heard" was the reading in from examinations for discovery, of the defendant by counsel for the plaintiff and of Douglas Gordon, an officer of plaintiff company, by counsel for the defendant. There was some conflict in the evidence, and I do not have the advantage trial judges normally have of basing a finding of the reliability of the testimony of a witness in part on his observation of the witness's demeanour in giving his evidence in open Court. Making matters more difficult for me in deciding the facts is that each counsel made the mistake of reading in evidence harmful to his own case and/or helpful to his opponent's.

I direct my attention first to the allegation that the plaintiff's claim arises through its unlawful act in permitting the defendant's trading to be put through by an unlicensed salesman. Section 7(1) (*c*) provides that:

7(1) No person shall,
  (*c*) act as a salesman of or on behalf of a person or company in connection with a trade in a security by the person or company unless he is registered as a salesman of the person or company and the person or company is registered as a broker....

Mr. Gordon's evidence was that Head and another unlicensed sales trainee " . . . were allowed to take orders: they were not allowed to solicit orders." Asked what he meant by "take orders" he replied "If clients came in and were potential clients for the house, for them they were allowed to take the orders." Head was paid on what Gordon called a "bonus arrangement" the main factor considered with respect to the bonus (which was paid once a month) being " . . . the number of clients that he introduced to the house." He also testified that the number of sales effected by the clients would have " . . . an indirect bearing on (the bonus)." Asked what he meant by his use of the word "indirect," Gordon testified that "the other factors . . . we considered in bonusing [were] the length of time that he put in the office, how he was developing as a potential salesman and how he was progressing with his I.D.A. course."

I do not believe that I can accept Gordon's evidence as being entirely truthful. The remuneration paid by the plaintiff to Head varied so greatly that I think the inescapable conclusion is that the remuneration was based chiefly on sales. In July, 1966, Head's total remuneration was $342.50; in August it was $1,388.25; in September $518.75 and in October $1,319.45. It was not until September, 1966, that Head even enrolled in the I.D.A. course and, as far as the evidence indicated, Head began to work for the plaintiff only in June or July so it appears evident to me that if the progress a sales trainee was making with his I.D.A. course and the length of time that he put in in the office had anything at all to do with his remuneration, these were very minor factors indeed in comparison with the amount of business he produced for the plaintiff brokers.

I conclude from Gordon's uncontradicted evidence (that sales trainees were allowed to take orders but not allowed to solicit orders) that Gordon *thought* that this was neither prohibited by nor an offence under s. 7(1) (c) of the *Securities Act, 1967*: on the other hand I can think of no greater inducement to a sales trainee to disobey the instructions not to solicit orders than to pay the trainee chiefly on the basis of the volume of orders he secured.

There was no evidence led to suggest that Head's handling of orders from the defendant was supervised by any licensed salesman, and on the evidence before me I see no escape from the conclusion that the plaintiff, in breach of the *Securities Act, 1967*, knowingly and willingly allowed an unlicensed employee to trade in securities. (I specifically refrain from expressing any opinion whether or not it would constitute a violation of the *Securities Act, 1967*, for a licensed broker to permit an unlicensed sales trainee to accept orders under the direct supervision of and handled by a licensed salesman, particularly if the trainee were paid a fixed salary). So much for the "unlawful conduct" on the part of the plaintiff upon which the defence is based and I turn my attention to the defendant.

I have no hesitation in finding on the evidence that the defendant knew that Head was unlicensed. Neither Head nor the plaintiff failed faithfully to carry out the defendant's orders to buy and sell securities, to make proper charges and to render prompt and accurate accounts both of security trades and of the financial position between the plaintiff and defendant as a result of the trades. It is clear therefore that the defendant, whose purchases and sales were made on the basis of his own judgment and accurately carried out, can level no greater criticism at the plaintiff than that the plaintiff was in breach of the *Securities Act, 1967*, by allowing Head to do what the defendant wanted him to do.

This, however, is not the whole story as far as the defendant is concerned because it is clear that he and Head were conspiring with one another to defraud the plaintiff, specifically by allowing the defendant, without any knowledge of any one in the plaintiff's office except Head himself, to trade under the names of four persons, thereby obtaining a line of credit which both Head and the defendant knew the defendant could not get if he were doing all the trading in his own name. If the plaintiff is not entitled to recover because it violated the *Securities Act, 1967*, the defendant will have succeeded in defrauding the plaintiff despite the facts that the plaintiff's violation of the statute was known to and fully concurred in by the defendant and that the defendant suffered no loss or damage whatever thereby.

Counsel for the defendant relied on a number of authorities in support of the defendant's position. One line of cases had to do with the right of a real estate agent to recover commission when the salesman was not licensed according to statute. For example, *Commercial Life Ass'ce Co. v. Drever*, [1948] 2 D.L.R. 241, [1948] S.C.R. 306, a decision of the Supreme Court of Canada and in particular to a paragraph in the judgment of Locke J., at p. 246: "It is unfortunate that the services of the respondent [real estate agent], which were an effective cause of the sale, should go unrewarded but, as stated by Lord Mansfield in *Holman v. Johnson* (1775), 1 Cowp. 341 at p. 343, 98 E.R. 1120: "The objection, that a contract is immoral or illegal as between plaintiff and defendant, sounds at all times very ill in the mouth of the defendant. It is not for his sake, however, that the objection is ever allowed; but it is founded in general principles of policy, which the defendant has the advantage of, contrary to the real justice, as between him and the plaintiff, by accident, if I may say so. The principle of public policy is this; ex dolo malo non oritur actio. No Court will lend its aid to a man who founds his cause of action upon an immoral or an illegal act."

While this passage, taken out of context, supports the defendant's position in the case at bar, it must be read in light of the specific statutory provision in the Alberta *Real Estate Agents' Licensing Act* quoted at p. 244: "No person shall be entitled to recover any compensation for any act done in contravention of the provisions of this Act, or to be reimbursed for any expenditure incurred by him in or in connection with the doing of any such act."

A similar statutory provision is found in the *Real Estate Act*, R.S.B.C. 1960, c. 330, and in my judgment takes away much of the force of the defendant's argument in so far as it depended upon *Marriette Agencies Ltd.* v. *Georgia Gulf Estates Ltd.* (1964), 44 D.L.R. (2d) 242, 47 W.W.R. 89, a decision of Wootton, J., of this Court and likewise, in respect of the Saskatchewan *Real Estate Agents' Licensing Act*, the case of *Prince Albert Properties & Land Sales Ltd.* v. *Kushneryk*, [1955] 5 D.L.R. 458, 16 W.W.R. 567.

Quite apart however from the fact that the Real Estate Acts of the several Provinces of Canada seem to contain a specific provision that an unlicensed agent or a licensed agent whose salesman is unlicensed is disentitled to recover a commission, it must be borne in mind that in the case at bar the action is not for the plaintiff's brokerage fees on the defendant's trades but rather for the balance of a trading account owing the plaintiff as a result of securities bought and sold through the plaintiff.

In my judgment the strongest case the defendant's counsel cited in support of his client's position was a decision of the Ontario High Court, *Maschinenfabrik Seydelman K-G* v. *Presswood Bros. Ltd.*, 47 D.L.R. (2d) 214, [1965] 1 O.R. 177, in which Hughes J., held that an action by the plaintiff to recover the purchase price of certain electrical machinery sold to the defendant was void and unenforceable because the plaintiff had failed to comply with a regulation under the Ontario *Power Commission Act* requiring the equipment to be approved before sale, ending up with the result that the defendant got the equipment (which incidentally was subsequently approved) without having to pay for it. This case, while not binding upon me, caused me a good deal of concern until I dug a little deeper than counsel had done into the law and found that the decision of Hughes J. had been reversed by the Ontario Court of Appeal: 53 D.L.R. (2d) 224, [1966] 1 O.R. 316.

Counsel for the defendant also relied on *Montreal Trust Co. et al.* v. *C.N.R. Co.*, [1939] 3 D.L.R. 497, [1939] A.C. 613, 50 C.R.T.C. 1, a decision of the Privy Council. The [D.L.R.] headnote reads as follows: "A lease whereby a railway company director through a nominee leases a residence to the company for its president's use falls within the provision of s. 121 of the Railway Act. R.S.C. 1927, c. 170, prohibiting a director from being interested in any contract with the company, and such a lease is "for his own use and benefit" within the meaning of such provision notwithstanding that the director only acted at the company's request, derived no profit from the transaction, and that the president had an option to purchase the premises for the price paid by the director. The effect of s. 121 was not merely to avoid the director's interest in the prohibited contract but to render it null and void. Hence a claim for rent must be dismissed."

The [D.L.R.] report also contains an editorial note which I think sums up the defendant's position better than I did earlier on in these reasons. The editorial note reads: "It is settled law that a contract prohibited by statute for the protection of the public is illegal and unenforceable. Most of the cases arising under the rule relate to ascertaining whether a contract is impliedly prohibited by statute. Where a penalty is imposed for the doing of an act and it is determined that *one* of the statute's objects is the protection of the public and not merely of the revenue, the act will be deemed prohibited by the statute and illegal."

I do not believe that in any of the cases cited by counsel, not all of which I have referred to, is there any authority for the proposition he asserts on behalf of the defendant which, as I (rather bluntly) put it at p. 335 of these reasons, that because the plaintiff violated the *Securities Act, 1967*, the defendant should succeed in his conspiracy to defraud the plaintiff despite the facts that the plaintiff's breach of the statute was known to and fully concurred in by the defendant and that the defendant suffered no loss or damage whatever thereby.

If this were an action simply to recover brokerage I think, on the authorities, I would have no alternative than to dismiss the action. But as the action is brought for the balance owing the plaintiff on a trading account I believe that I can both follow the authorities binding on me and do justice. If I cannot do both then at least I will try to do justice, and I will not permit the defendant to succeed in his effort to defraud the plaintiff on the mere basis the plaintiff violated a provision of the *Securities Act, 1967*.

There will be judgment for the plaintiff for $12,550.84, interest on $9,045 at 8% per annum from August 6, 1968, to the date judgment is entered and costs.

I direct the District Registrar of the Court to send a copy of my reasons for judgment to the Attorney-General for his consideration of criminal proceedings against the defendant and Head and a copy to the British Columbia Securities Commission for its consideration of the conduct of the plaintiff, not merely because the plaintiff violated the provisions of the *Securities Act, 1967*, but also to give the Commission an opportunity to clarify (or to give the Commission an opportunity to recommend to the Attorney-General that he introduce legislation to clarify) what, if anything, an unlicensed sales trainee should be allowed to do in respect of trading in securities.

PROBLEM. Statute provides that "every dealer in used motor vehicles, before he enters into a contract to sell a used motor vehicle, shall give to the purchaser a certificate of mechanical fitness. . . ."

Able, a dealer in used motor vehicles, sells a used car to Baker without providing the statutory certificate. Can Able sue Baker for the agreed price, or the return of the car? Can Baker counter-claim for injuries caused by the fact that the car, in breach of contract, was defective?

CHAPTER 9

PERFORMANCE AND BREACH

Non-performance of a contractual obligation may not only give rise to an action for damages, or specific enforcement, but also may have the effect of excusing the party not in breach from his obligations. The following cases deal with this effect.

BOONE v. *EYRE*
England. King's Bench 1777. 1 H. Bl. 273, note; 126 E.R. 160, note (a)

Covenant in a deed whereby the plaintiff conveyed to the defendant the equity of redemption of a plantation in the West Indies, together with the stock of negroes upon it, in consideration of £500 and an annuity of £160 per annum for his life; and covenanted that he had a good title to the plantation, and was lawfully possessed of the negroes, and that the defendant should quietly enjoy. The defendant covenanted that, the plaintiff well and truly performing all and everything therein contained on his part to be performed, he the defendant would pay the annuity. The breach assigned was the non-payment of the annuity. Plea: that the plaintiff was not at the time of making the deed legally possessed of the negroes on the plantation, and so had not a good title to convey.

To which there was a general demurrer.

LORD MANSFIELD: The distinction is very clear, where mutual covenants go to the whole of the consideration of both sides, they are mutual conditions, the one precedent to the other. But where they go only to a part, where a breach may be paid for in damages, there the defendant has a remedy on his covenant, and shall not plead it as a condition precedent. If this plea were to be allowed any one negro not being the property of the plaintiff would bar the action.

[Judgment for the plaintiff.]

QUESTIONS. As the report of the pleadings is written, is the defendant's covenant subject to an express condition? If so, why does Lord Mansfield set out a test for implying a condition?

DUKE OF ST. ALBAN'S v. *SHORE*
England. Exchequer Chamber. 1789. 1 H. Bl. 270; 126 E.R. 158

Debt for £500 the penalty of articles of agreement.

The declaration stated the agreement to have been made between the plaintiff and the defendant on the 30th of March, 1787, by which the defendant was to purchase of the plaintiff a certain farm land with the appurtenances, together with an acre and half of boggy land, at the price of £2594 which was to be paid at Lady-Day then next. . . . Plea: " . . . that after the making of the said agreement, and before Lady-Day then next following, to wit, on the 20th of March A.D. 1788, the said duke cut down divers . . . the said trees . . . whereby the said duke disabled himself from performing . . . for which reason, he the said William declined and refused to carry the said articles into execution on his part, as he lawfully might, &c."

LORD LOUGHBOROUGH delivered the judgment of the Court: It is clear in this case, that unless the plaintiff has done all that was incumbent on him to do, in order to create a performance by the defendant, (if I may use the expression,) he is not entitled to maintain the action. If he has not set forth a sufficient title, judgment must be against him whatever the plea is, and if the plea be a good bar, the same consequence must follow. It was argued on the part of the plaintiff, that the agreement respecting the trees was not a condition precedent, and therefore a breach of that agreement could not be pleaded in bar of the action. In support of this argument the case of *Boone* v. *Eyre* was cited; but in that case, though the Court of King's Bench held the plea insufficient, yet they laid down a clear and well founded distinction, that where a covenant went to the whole of the consideration on both sides, there it was a condition precedent; but where it did not go to the whole, but only to a part, there it was not a condition precedent, and each party must resort to his separate remedy; and for this plain and obvious reason, because the damages might be unequal. . . . We found our opinion on the present case, on the ground of the distinction in *Boone* v. *Eyre*, which we think a fair and sound one. Then the question is, whether the covenant of the plaintiff goes to the whole consideration of that which was to be done by the defendant? Now the duke clearly covenanted to convey an estate to the defendant, in which all the timber growing on the estate was necessarily included. The timber was not disjoined from the estate by the separate valuation of it. It was expressly agreed that all trees, &c. which then were upon any of the estates should be valued. But it is not to be permitted to a party contracting to convey land which includes the timber, by his own act to change the nature of it between the time of entering into the contract and that of performing it. There may be cases where the timber growing on an estate is the chief inducement to a purchase of that estate. But it is not necessary to inquire whether it be the chief inducement to a purchase or not; for if it may be in any sort of a consideration to the party purchasing to have the timber, the party selling ought not to be permitted to alter the estate by cutting down any of it. This is not an action of covenant where one party has performed his part, but is brought for a penalty on the other party refusing to execute a contract. But to entitle the party bringing the action to a penalty, he ought punctually, exactly, and literally, to complete his part. We are therefore of opinion that the plea is a good bar to the action, and on this we give our judgment . . . [for the defendant.]

GRAVES v. LEGG
England. Exchequer. 1854. 9 Exch. 709; 156 E.R. 304

The defendants agreed to buy 300 to 350 bales of wool of fair average quality from the plaintiff to be shipped from Odessa with all despatch to Liverpool, Hull or London, "subject to . . . the names of the vessels to be declared as soon as the wool was shipped." Afterwards 333 bales of wool of the prescribed quality were shipped on the "Science" to Liverpool in safe and good condition. The defendants refused to take the wool because the plaintiff had failed to declare the name of the vessel as soon as he had promised, and as a result the defendants lost the market, which had since declined. Demurrer.

PARKE B. delivered the judgment of the Court: The question . . . is, whether the provision, that the names of the vessels should be declared as soon as the wools were shipped, was a condition precedent to the defendants' obligation to accept and pay for the wools according to the contract stated in the declaration, and under the circumstances stated in the plea.

This contract, we think, is to be construed with reference to some of those circumstances. It is stated in the plea, that the wool was bought, with the knowledge of both parties, for the purpose of re-selling it in the course of the defendants' business; that it is an article of fluctuating value, and not saleable until the names of the vessels in which it was shipped should have been declared according to the contract.

The declaration having averred, according to the 57th section of the *Common Law Procedure Act*, the performance of conditions precedent generally, the defendant proceeds in this plea to specify this condition of declaring the names of the vessels, as one on the breach of which he insists. The loss which he avers to have sustained by that breach is immaterial. The only question is whether the performance of the agreement was a condition precedent or not to the defendant's contract to accept and pay for the goods.

In the numerous cases on the subject, in which it has been laid down that the general rule is, to construe covenants and agreements to be dependent or independent according to the intent and meaning of the parties to be collected from the instrument, and of course to the circumstances legally admissible in evidence with reference to which it is to be construed, one particular rule well acknowledged is, that where a covenant or agreement goes to part of the consideration on both sides, and may be compensated in damages, it is an independent covenant or contract. . . . [The] reason . . . besides the inequality of damages, seems to be, that where a person has received part of the consideration for which he entered into the agreement, it would be unjust, that, because he had not the whole, he should therefore be permitted to enjoy that part without either payment or doing anything for it. Therefore the law obliges him to perform the agreement on his part, leaving him to his remedy to recover any damage he may have sustained in not having received the whole consideration. . . . [It] must appear upon the record that the consideration was executed in part. . . . When that appears, it is no longer competent for the defendant to insist upon the non-performance of that which was originally a condition precedent; and this is more correctly expressed, than to say it was not a condition precedent at all.

In this case, if the stipulation, that the names of the vessels should be stated as soon as the wools were shipped, was originally a condition precedent, it is so still. No other benefit was taken under the contract itself, as the consideration for the promise to pay the money, than the shipment and delivery of the goods by the named vessels; nor was any subsequently received by the acceptance of the goods or any part thereof. After such acceptance, the defendants would have been bound to pay the price, or the residue of it, and could not have insisted on the neglect to name in due time, but, if there had been any such neglect, would nevertheless have had their remedy for the damages by cross action on the contract to declare the names. In the state of things on this record, the simple question is, whether this contract was originally a condition precedent or not. Looking at the nature of the contract; and the great importance of it to the object with which the contract was entered into with the knowledge of both parties, we think it was a condition precedent, quite as much, indeed as the shipping of the goods at Odessa with all dispatch after the end of August. And with respect to the shipment itself, Mr. Blackburn [one of the Counsel] did not venture to contend that the performance of the plaintiff's contract in that respect was not a condition precedent.

The defendants, therefore, have a right to object to fulfill the contract on their part, as the plaintiff did not fulfill his, though they could no longer object to the plaintiff's non-performance, had they afterwards taken any benefit under the contract.

[Judgment for the defendants.]

KINGSTON v. PRESTON
England. King's Bench. 1773. 2 Douglas, 689; 99 E.R. 437
(in argument in *Jones* v. *Barkley*)

This was an action of debt for non-performance of covenants contained in certain articles of agreement between the plaintiff and the defendant. The declaration stated: That, by articles made the 24th of March, 1770, the plaintiff, for the considerations thereinafter mentioned, covenanted with the defendant to serve him for one year and a quarter next ensuing, as a covenant servant, in his trade of a silk-mercer, at £200 a year, and, in consideration of the premises the defendant covenanted that, at the end of the year and a quarter, he would give up his business of a mercer to the plaintiff, and a nephew of the defendant or some other person to be nominated by the defendant, and give up to them his stock in trade, at a fair valuation; and that, between the young traders, deeds of partnership should be executed for fourteen years, and from and immediately after the execution of the said deeds the defendant would permit the said young traders to carry on the said business in the defendant's house.

Then the declaration stated a covenant by the plaintiff, that he would accept the business and stock-in-trade, at a fair valuation, with the defendant's nephew, or such other person, &c., and execute such deeds of partnership, and, further, that the plaintiff should and would, at and before the sealing and delivery of the deeds, cause and procure good and sufficient security to be given to the defendant, to be approved of by the defendant, for the payment of £250 monthly to the defendant, in lieu of a moiety of the monthly produce of the stock in trade, until the value of the stock should be reduced to £4000. Then the plaintiff averred that he had performed and been ready to perform his covenants, and assigned for breach on the part of the defendant, that he had refused to surrender and give up his business at the end of the said year and a quarter.

The defendant pleaded: 1. That the plaintiff did not offer sufficient security; and, 2, that he did not give sufficient security for the payment of the £250, &c.

And the plaintiff demurred generally to both pleas.

LORD MANSFIELD, in delivering the judgment of the Court, expressed himself to the following effect: There are three kinds of covenants: 1. Such as are called mutual and independent, where either party may recover damages from the other for the injury he may have received by a breach of the covenants in his favor, and where it is no excuse for the defendant to allege a breach of the covenants on the part of the plaintiff. 2. There are covenants which are conditions and dependent, in which the performance of one depends on the prior performance of another, and therefore, till this prior condition is performed, the other party is not liable to an action on his covenant. 3. There is also a third sort of covenants, which are mutual conditions to be performed at the same time; and in these, if one party was ready and offered to perform his part, and the other neglected or refused to perform his, he who was ready and offered has fulfilled his engagement, and may maintain an action for the default of the other though it is not certain that either is obliged to do the first act. His Lordship then proceeded to say, that the dependence or independence of covenants was to be collected from the evident sense and meaning of the parties, and that, however transposed they might be in the deed, their precedency must depend on the order of time in which the intent of the transaction requires their performance. That, in the case before the Court, it would be the greatest injustice if the plaintiff should prevail. The essence of the agreement was, that the defendant should not trust to the personal security of the plaintiff, but, before he delivered up his stock and business, should have good security for the payment of the money. The giving such security, therefore, must necessarily be a condition precedent. Judgment was accordingly given for the defendant, because the part to be performed by the plaintiff was clearly a condition precedent.

RULES OF PRACTICE
Ontario. Supreme Court. 1960

148. Any condition precedent, the performance or occurrence of which is intended to be contested, shall be distinctly specified in his pleading by the party relying thereon, and an averment of the performance or occurrence of all conditions precedent necessary for the case by the plaintiff or defendant shall be implied in his pleading.

McDONALD v. *MURRAY* (1885) 11 O.A.R. 101 (Ont. C.A.) PATTERSON J.A.: ... "When people bargain together, whether it is to barter one piece of property for another, or to exchange property for money, each party ordinarily expects to receive what he bargains for when he parts with what he is to give. If the intention is that either of them is to part with his property, and take his chance of the other afterwards performing his part, or paying damages for his default, it is not the ordinary transaction of sale or exchange, and when it is intended we may reasonably expect to find some express declaration of that intention."

CEHAVE N.V. v. *BREMER HANDELGESELLSCHAFT M.B.H.*
[1976] Q.B. 44 (C.A.)

LORD DENNING M.R.: In 1970, the sellers, a German company, agreed to sell to the buyers, a Dutch company, 12,000 metric tons of U.S. citrus pulp pellets. Those pellets are a by-product of oranges. The juice is extracted and tinned. The orange rinds are dried and made into pellets. The pellets are used as an ingredient in making cattle food.

In September 1970, there were two contracts of sale, each for 6,000 metric tons, delivery in bulk be made by six instalments of 1,000 tons each over the first six months of 1971. Under the first contract of September 24, the price was $73.50 per metric ton. Under the second contract of September 28, the price was $73.75. In each case c.i.f. Rotterdam. Each contract incorporated the terms issued by the Cattle Food Trade Association, form 100, for shipment of feeding stuffs in bulk "Talequale c.i.f. terms." That form contained two sentences material to this dispute in clause no. 7: "Shipment to be made in good condition . . . each shipment shall be considered a separate contract."

The first three or four shipments were quite satisfactory. This case is concerned with a shipment made early in May 1971. It was by the German vessel the *Hansa Nord*. She took on about 3,400 metric tons of citrus pulp pellets at Port Manatee in Florida. Four bills of lading were issued. They were appropriated by the sellers as follows: two were for 1,000 tons each on the second contract. One for 1,000 tons and one for 419.856 tons on the first contract. But there was no physical appropriation of the cargo as between the two contracts.

On May 14 the buyers paid the price and got the shipping documents. The *Hansa Nord* arrived in Rotterdam on Friday, May 21, and started unloading on Saturday, May 22. It was finished by May 25. The cargo was discharged into lighters. The out-turn weights were:

Ex-hold no. 1 . . . 1,260 metric tons.
Ex-hold no. 2 . . . 2,053 metric tons.

It is to be noticed that by this time the market price had fallen greatly. The contract price for these 3,400 tons was (when converted into sterling) about £100,000. But the market price on May 24 in Rotterdam was, for sound goods, only £86,000. This may give an explanation of subsequent happenings.

The cargo ex no. 2 hold (2,053 tons) was in good condition. But some of the cargo ex no. 1 hold (1,260 tons) was found to be damaged. On May 24 the buyers rejected the whole cargo (both no. 2 and no. 1 holds) on the ground that it was not shipped in good condition and they claimed repayment of the purchase price of £100,000. On the next day the sellers refused, saying that the goods were shipped in good condition: and that the damage must have occurred at sea and that the buyers ought to lodge their claim with the insurers.

So there it was. The goods were in the lighters with both sellers and buyers disclaiming ownership. Now comes an astonishing sequence of events. There was a Mr. Baas in Rotterdam who was an importer of feeding products (including citrus pulp pellets). On May 29, 1971, if not before, he inspected the cargo in the lighters. On June 1, 1971, the lighter owners applied ex parte to the Rotterdam County Court, the Commercial Court I expect, asking it to authorise a sale of the goods. They applied by their lawyer, a Mr. Driessen. The sellers were not told of this application. But the buyers were. They were represented by the same lawyer as the lighter owners, Mr. Driessen. On the same day this court granted the application and authorised the sale. It appointed agents to make the sale. The agents approached Mr. Baas. They did not approach any other possible bidders. They sold the whole cargo to Mr. Baas (out of both no. 2 and no. 1 holds) for a sum equivalent to £33,720. The expenses of sale were deducted, leaving the net proceeds at £29,903. These were paid into a Dutch bank "to the order of whom it may concern." On the self-same day, Mr. Baas sold the whole cargo to the buyers (i.e., the original buyers under the two contracts) at the same price and upon the same terms as he had himself bought them from the agents of the court. The board of appeal found: "as a fair inference from the evidence . . . that the buyers and Mr. Baas intended that he (Baas) should acquire the cargo for their (the buyers') benefit, or on their behalf . . ."

Having bought the whole cargo from Mr. Baas, the buyers transported it in the same way as they would have done if it had never suffered any damage. They took the lighters by canal to their plant at Veghel, a journey of some 60 miles. The buyers then used the entire cargo to manufacture cattle food at their processing plant at Veghel. They used it in the self-same way as they would sound goods except that they used "smaller percentages in their compound feeds than would be normal with sound goods." This difference in manufacture did not cause them any loss. At any rate, there is no finding that it did. And it was surely for them to prove it.

The upshot of it all was, therefore, that the buyers took the whole cargo and used all of it for their business just as if they had never rejected it save for the smaller percentages. So the ubiquitous Mr. Baas had helped them greatly. They paid only £33,720 for it instead of the contract price of £100,000. The board of appeal of the trade association felt it necessary to make this comment:

"We wish to record that we are not satisfied that we have been presented with a full account of how the goods were disposed of in Rotterdam after rejection by the buyers. The witnesses produced by the buyers gave contradictory evidence on this question, as well as on other less vital issues."

That is a devastating comment. The buyers must have known the truth. But they did not tell it to the board of appeal. At any rate, not the whole truth.

Nevertheless, despite that devastating comment, the board of appeal made their award in favour of the buyers. They ordered the sellers to repay to the buyers the £100,000 with interest, and directed the proceeds of sale (£29,903) to be repaid to the sellers. So the buyers have got the entire cargo and used it for their cattle food, but instead of paying £100,000 for it, they have only paid them £30,000. The judge has upheld this award [1974] 2 Lloyd's Rep. 216, 227. The sellers appeal to this court. They recognise that they may have to pay something by way of damages for the damaged goods, but they deny that the buyers had any right to reject the whole cargo.

The board of appeal found a breach of the express clause "Shipped in good condition." They said: ". . . on the balance of probability, not all the goods in hold no. 1 were shipped in good condition as required by the contract, nor on balance of probability were they reasonably fit to be carried on the contemplated voyage."

The board of appeal also found a breach of the implied condition as to merchantability contained in section 14 (2) of the Sale of Goods Act 1893. They said:

"The goods in hold 1 were 'merchantable' on arrival in Rotterdam in a commercial sense, though at a lower price than would be paid for sound goods: we find and hold, however, that they were not 'of merchantable quality' within the meaning of the phrase when used in the Sale of Goods Act 1893."

The board of appeal did not find a breach of the implied condition of fitness contained in section 14 (1) of the Act. They found all the elements about reliance and so forth, but they did not find that the goods were unfit. They could hardly have found them unfit, seeing that they were in fact used for that purpose.

"Shipped in good condition"

The judge held that, in contracts for the sale of goods, a stipulation

must either be a "condition" or a "warranty" and that there could be
no tertium quid. Accepting that distinction, he held that this stipulation
"shipped in good condition" was a "condition" and not a "warranty"
[1974] 2 Lloyd's Rep. 216,225; so that, for any breach of it by the
seller, the buyer was entitled to treat the contract as repudiated.

Those decisions by the judge are so important that they deserve careful
consideration.

The general law apart from the sale of goods

For the last 300 or 400 years the courts have had to grapple with this
problem: in what circumstances can a party, who is in breach himself of
a stipulation of the contract, call upon the other side to perform his part
or sue him for non-performance? At one time the solution was thought
to depend on the nature of the stipulation itself, and not on the extent of
the breach or its consequences. Under the old forms of pleading, a plaintiff had to aver and prove that he had performed all conditions precedent
or that he was ready and willing to perform them. The question, therefore, was whether the stipulation (which he had broken) was a condition
precedent or not: or, in the terminology of the 18th century, whether it
was an *independent* covenant (the breach of which did not debar him
from suing the other side), or a *dependent* covenant (the breach of which
did debar the plaintiff because the performance by the other was *dependent* on the plaintiff performing his). This distinction was well stated by
Serjeant Williams in his notes to *Pordage* v. *Cole* (1669) 1 Wms. Saund.
319, 320b:

"... where there are several covenants, promises or agreements, which
are *independent* of each other, one party may bring an action against the
other for a breach of his covenants, etc. without averring a performance
of the covenants, etc. on his, the plaintiff's part; and it is no excuse for
the defendant to allege in his plea a breach of the covenants, etc. on
the part of the plaintiff; ... But where the covenants, etc. are *dependent*,
it is necessary for the plaintiff to aver and prove a performance of the
covenants, etc. on his part, to entitle himself to an action for the breach
of the covenants on the part of the defendant ..."

Although that division was treated as exhaustive, nevertheless, when
the courts came to apply it, they had regard to the extent of the breach.
This was done by Lord Mansfield in 1777 in the great case of *Boone* v.
Eyre (Note) (1777) 1 Hy.Bl. 273, of which there was no satisfactory record
until Lord Kenyon in 1796 produced a manuscript note of it: see *Campbell*
v. *Jones* (1796) 6 Term Rep. 570, 573 and *Glazebrook* v. *Woodrow* (1799)
8 Term Rep. 366, 373. It is summarised in the notes to *Cutter* v. *Powell*
(1795) 6 Term Rep. 320 (*Smith's Leading Cases*, 13th ed. (1929), vol.
2, pp. 16-17). The plaintiff conveyed to the defendant a plantation in
the West Indies, together with the stock of negroes on it, in consideration
of £500 down and an annuity of £100 a year, and covenanted that he
had a good title to the plantation and was lawfully possessed of the negroes.
Some time later the defendant discovered that the plaintiff had no title to
the negroes and stopped paying the annuity. The court held that the defendant was liable to pay the annuity. He could not escape simply because the plaintiff had not "a title to a few negroes." His remedy was to
bring a cross-action for damages. It would be different "if the plaintiff
had no title at all to the plantation itself" (see 8 Term Rep. 366, 374): for
then the plaintiff could not have recovered the annuity. In the language of

those times, if the breach went to the whole consideration, the covenant was considered to be a condition precedent and the defendant could plead the breach in bar of the action: but if the breach went "only to a part, where a breach may be paid for in damages, there the defendant has a remedy on his covenant, and shall not plead it as a condition precedent." (1 Hy.Bl. 273n.)

In short, if the breach went to the root of the matter, the stipulation was to be considered a condition precedent: but if the breach did not go to the root, the stipulation was considered to be an independent covenant which could be compensated for in damages: see *Davidson* v. *Gwynne* (1810) 12 East 381, 389, *per* Lord Ellenborough C.J.; *Ellen* v. *Topp* (1851) 6 Exch. 424, 441; and *Graves* v. *Legg* (1854) 9 Exch. 709, 716.

Apart from those cases of "breach going to the root," the courts at the same time were developing the doctrine of "anticipatory breach." When one party, before the day when he is obliged to perform his part, declares in advance that he will not perform it when the day comes, or by his conduct evinces an intention not to perform it, the other may elect to treat his declaration or conduct as a breach going to the root of the matter and to treat himself as discharged from further performance: see *Hochster* v. *De la Tour* (1853) 2 E. & B. 678. By his prior declaration or conduct, the guilty party is said to repudiate the contract. The word "repudiation" should be confined to those cases of an *anticipatory* breach, but it is also used in connection with cases of an *actual* breach going to the root of the contract: see *Heyman* v. *Darwins Ltd.* [1942] A.C. 356, 378-379 by Lord Wright. All of them were gathered together by Lord Blackburn in his famous speech in *Mersey Steel and Iron Co. Ltd.* v. *Naylor, Benzon & Co.* (1884) 9 App.Cas. 434, 443-444:

"The rule of law, as I always understood it, is that where there is a contract in which there are two parties, each side having to do something (it is so laid down in the notes to *Pordage* v. *Cole*, 1 Wms. Saund. 319, 320) if you see that the failure to perform one part of it goes to the root of the contract, goes to the foundation of the whole, it is a good defence to say, 'I am not going on to perform my part of it when that which is the root of the whole and the substantial consideration for my performance is defeated by your misconduct.' . . . I repeatedly asked Mr. Cohen whether or not he could find any authority which justified him in saying that every breach of a contract . . . must be considered to go to the root of the contract, and he produced no such authority. There are many cases in which the breach may do so; it depends upon the construction of the contract."

Those last words are clearly a reference to a "condition" strictly so called, in which any breach entitled the other to be discharged from further performance. But the earlier words are quite general. They refer to all terms other than conditions strictly so called.

The Sale of Goods Act

Such was the state of the law when the Sale of Goods Act 1893 was passed on February 20, 1894. I have studied the then current edition of *Benjamin, Sale of Personal Property*, 4th ed. (1888), and the little books which Judge Chalmers wrote before (1890) and after the Act (*Chalmers' Sale of Goods Act*, 1893, 1st ed. (1894)), and the proceedings in Parliament. These show that until the year 1893 there was much confusion in the use of the words "condition" and "warranty." But that confusion was removed by the Act itself and by the judgment of Bowen L.J. in

Bentsen v. *Taylor, Sons & Co.* [1893] 2 Q.B. 274, 280. Thenceforward those words were used by lawyers as terms of art. The difference between them was that if the promisor broke a *condition* in any respect, however slight, it gave the other party a right to be quit of his obligations and to sue for damages: unless he by his conduct waived the condition, in which case he was bound to perform his future obligations but could sue for the damage he had suffered. If the promisor broke a *warranty* in any respect, however serious, the other party was not quit of his future obligations. He had to perform them. His only remedy was to sue for damages: see *The Mihalis Angelos* [1971] 1 Q.B. 164, 193 and *Wickman Machine Tool Sales Ltd.* v. *L. Schuler A.G.* [1972] 1 W.L.R. 840, 851.

Now that division was not exhaustive. It left out of account the vast majority of stipulations which were neither "conditions" nor "warranties" strictly so called: but were intermediate stipulations, the effect of which depended on the breach. The cases about these stipulations were legion. They stretched continuously from *Boone* v. *Eyre (Note)*, 1 Hy.Bl. 273, in 1777 to *Mersey Steel and Iron Co. Ltd.* v. *Naylor, Benzon & Co.* (1884) 9 App.Cas. 434. I cannot believe that Parliament in 1893 intended to give the go-by to all these cases: or to say that they did not apply to the sale of goods. Those cases expressed the rules of the common law. They were preserved by section 61 (2) of the Act of 1893, which said: "The rules of the common law, including the law merchant, save in so far as they are inconsistent with the express provisions of this Act . . . shall continue to apply to contracts for the sale of goods." There was nothing in the Act inconsistent with those cases. So they continued to apply.

In 1962 in the *Hongkong Fir Shipping Co. Ltd.* v. *Kawasaki Kisen Kaisha Ltd.* [1962] 2 Q.B. 26, the Court of Appeal drew attention to this vast body of case law. They showed that, besides conditions and warranties, strictly so called, there are many stipulations of which the effect depends on this: if the breach goes to the root of the contract, the other party is entitled to treat himself as discharged: but if it does not go to the root, he is not. In my opinion, the principle embodied in these cases applies to contracts for the sale of goods just as to all other contracts.

The task of the court can be stated simply in the way in which Upjohn L.J. stated it at p. 64. First, see whether the stipulation, on its true construction, is a condition strictly so called, that is, a stipulation such that, for any breach of it, the other party is entitled to treat himself as discharged. Second, if it is not such a condition, then look to the extent of the actual breach which has taken place. If it is such as to go to the root of the contract, the other party is entitled to treat himself as discharged: but, otherwise, not. To this may be added an anticipatory breach. If the one party, before the day on which he is due to perform his part, shows by his words or conduct that he will not perform it in a vital respect when the day comes, the other party is entitled to treat himself as discharged.

"Shipped in good condition"

This brings me back to the particular stipulation in this case: "Shipped in good condition." Was this a condition strictly so called, so that *any* breach of it entitled the buyer to reject the goods? Or was it an intermediate stipulation, so that the buyer cannot reject unless the breach is so serious as to go to the root of the contract?

If there was any previous authority holding it to be a *condition* strictly so called, we should abide by it, just as we did with the clause "expected ready to load": see *Finnish Government (Ministry of Food)* v. *H. Ford & Co. Ltd.* (1921) 6 Ll.L.Rep. 188; *The Mihalis Angelos* [1971] 1 Q.B. 164. But, there is no such authority with the clause "shipped in good condition." I regard this clause as comparable to a clause as to quality, such as "fair average quality." If a small portion of the goods sold was a little below that standard, it would be met by commercial men by an allowance off the price. The buyer would have no right to reject the whole lot unless the divergence was serious and substantial: see *Biggin & Co. Ltd.* v. *Permanite Ltd.* [1951] 1 K.B. 422, 439, *per* Devlin J. and *Christopher Hill Ltd.* v. *Ashington Piggeries Ltd.* [1972] A.C. 441, 511, *per* Lord Diplock. That is shown in this very case by clause 5 in form no. 100 which contains percentages of contamination, below which there is a price allowance, and above which there is a right in the buyer to reject. Likewise with the clause "shipped in good condition." If a small portion of the whole cargo was not in good condition and arrived a little unsound, it should be met by a price allowance. The buyers should not have a right to reject the whole cargo unless it was serious and substantial. This is borne out by the difficulty which often arises (as in this case) on a c.i.f. contract as to whether the damage was done before shipment or took place after shipment: for in the latter case the buyer would have no claim against the seller but would be left to his claim against the insurers. So, as matter of good sense, the buyer should be bound to accept the goods and not reject them unless there is a serious and substantial breach, fairly attributable to the seller.

In my opinion, therefore, the term "shipped in good condition" was not a condition strictly so called: nor was it a warranty strictly so called. It was one of those intermediate stipulations which gives no right to reject unless the breach goes to the root of the contract.

On the facts stated by the board of appeal, I do not think the buyer was entitled to reject these instalments of the contract. The board only said that "not all the goods in hold no. 1 were shipped in good condition." That does not say how many were bad. In any case, their condition cannot have been very bad, seeing that all of them were in fact used for the intended purpose. The breach did not go to the root of the contract. The buyer is entitled to damages, but not to rejection.

"Merchantable"

The board of appeal made this finding: "The goods in hold 1 were 'merchantable' on arrival at Rotterdam in a commercial sense, though at a lower price than would be paid for sound goods; we find and hold, however, that they were not 'of merchantable quality' within the meaning of the phrase when used in the Sale of Goods Act 1893."

The board of appeal were not lawyers: but they had a legal adviser. And I am afraid that in reaching that finding they were not advised correctly. The statute uses the words "merchantable quality" in a commercial sense. The board should, therefore, have applied it in the commercial sense. They should not have been persuaded to give it some other "statutory sense."

Now we were taken through many of the definitions which have been given by judges of "merchantable quality," particularly that of Dixon J. in *Australian Knitting Mills Ltd.* v. *Grant* (1933) 50 C.L.R. 387, 418; of Lord Wright in *Cammell Laird & Co. Ltd.* v. *Manganese Bronze and Brass Co. Ltd.* [1934] A.C. 402, 430, as amended by Lord Reid in *Hardwick Game Farm* v. *Suffolk Agricultural Poultry Producers Association* [1969] 2 A.C. 31, 77 and by Lord Guest in *B. S. Brown & Son Ltd.* v. *Craiks Ltd.* [1970] 1 W.L.R. 752, 758. But, as Lord Reid pointed out in that case, at p. 754: ". . . judicial observations can never be regarded as complete definitions: they must be read in light of the facts and issues raised in the particular case. I do not think it is possible to frame, except in the vaguest terms, a definition of 'merchantable quality' which can apply to every kind of case."

For myself, I think the definition in the latest statute is the best that has yet been devised. It is contained in section 7 (2) of the Supply of Goods (Implied Terms) Act 1973. The statute itself only applies to contracts made after May 18, 1973. But the definition seems to me appropriate for contracts made before it. It runs as follows:

"Goods of any kind are of merchantable quality within the meaning of this Act if they are as fit for the purpose or purposes for which goods of that kind are commonly bought as it is reasonable to expect having regard to any description applied to them, the price (if relevant) and all other relevant circumstances; and any reference in this Act to unmerchantable goods shall be construed accordingly."

In applying that definition, it is as well to remember that, by the statute, we are dealing with an implied *condition*, strictly so called, and not a warranty. For any breach of it, therefore, the buyer is entitled to *reject* the goods: or, alternatively, if he chooses to accept them or has accepted them, he has a remedy in damages. In these circumstances, I should have thought a fair way of testing merchantability would be to ask a commercial man: was the breach such that the buyer should be able to reject the goods? In answering that question the commercial man would have regard to the various matters mentioned in the new statutory definition. He would, of course, have regard to the purpose for which goods of that kind are commonly bought. If a buyer buys "waste silk" and it is of no use for the purpose of "waste silk," he can reject it: see *Gardiner* v. *Gray* (1815) 4 Camp. 144. If he buys dates for food and they are of no use for food, he can reject them: see *Asfar & Co.* v. *Blundell* [1896] 1 Q.B. 123, 127. But if he buys groundnuts for cattlefood, and they can reasonably be used for cattlefood, he may not be able to reject them, even though they are not suitable for poultry; see *Hardwick Game Farm* v. *Suffolk Agricultural Poultry Producers Association* [1969] 2 A.C. 31. The commercial man would also, of course, have regard to the description applied to them. If motor horns are sold, expressly or impliedly, as "new" and then the buyer finds that they are dented and scratched, he ought to be able to reject them: see *Jackson* v. *Rotax Motor and Cycle Co.* [1910] 2 K.B. 937. If they are sold as "second hand" or "shop soiled," then he must take them as they are: see *Bartlett* v. *Sidney Marcus Ltd.* [1965] 1 W.L.R. 1013; unless there is something radically wrong with them. He would also have regard to the price. If they are sold at the market price, the buyer would expect them to be of good quality and condition; and, if they were not, he would be able to reject them: see *Jones* v. *Just* (1868) L.R. 3 Q.B. 197 (much better reported in 9 B. & S. 141); and *B. S. Brown & Son Ltd.* v. *Craiks Ltd.* [1970] 1 W.L.R. 752, 754-755, per Lord Reid: but, if they are sold at a "cut" price or "bargain" price, or a lower price, he would have to put up with something less. He would not be entitled to reject them simply because they were not perfect. The commercial man would also have regard to any other relevant circumstances. If there was a clause, express or implied, which would give the buyer an allowance off the price for the particular shortcomings, such that a commercial man would say: "The buyer is entitled to a price allowance but not to reject them"—again the goods would be of merchantable quality. The buyer would be entitled to an allowance or damages in lieu, but not entitled to reject the lot.

Our present case comes within that last illustration. These citrus pulp pellets were bought for cattle food. That was the purpose for which such pellets are commonly bought. They were as fit for that purpose as it was reasonable to expect. That is shown by the fact that they were actually used for that purpose. Some of them arrived damaged, but not to such an extent that the buyer was entitled to reject the cargo in both holds, or either of them. That damage was such as to entitle the buyer to an allowance off the price for breach of the clause "shipped in good condition": but not such as to entitle him to reject the lot on the ground that it was not of "merchantable quality." That is, I think, what the board of appeal meant when they found that the goods were "merchantable" on arrival at Rotterdam in a commercial sense, though at a lower price than would be paid for sound goods. In short, the buyers are entitled to an allowance or damages for the damaged goods, but not entitled to reject the lot. This makes commercial good sense. It often happens that the market price falls between the making of the contract and the time for delivery. In such a situation, it is not fair that a buyer should be allowed to reject a whole consignment of goods just because a small quantity are not up to the contract quality or condition. The proper remedy is a price allowance and not complete rejection. I feel sure that is what the board of appeal thought in this case. They only found otherwise because they thought the law constrained them to do so. Their instinct was right. Having found that in a commercial sense the goods were merchantable, there was no breach of section 14 (2).

Damages

In my opinion, therefore, the buyers were not entitled to reject the goods. They are, however, entitled to damages for the difference in value between the damaged goods and sound goods on arrival at Rotterdam. The case must be remitted to the board for this to be determined.

I would allow the appeal, accordingly.

ORMROD L.J.: . . . We have all been brought up since our student days to ask the question in the form: "Is this stipulation a condition or a warranty?" But before the Sale of Goods Act 1893 was passed the question was whether the buyer was bound to accept the goods. The answer depended, to use modern language, on whether the stipulation "went to the root of the contract," although it was differently phrased, e.g., "the buyer was entitled to get what he bargained for" or "the seller had failed to perform an essential term of the contract." The words "condition" and "warranty" were used in various senses in different cases but the distinction depended largely on the old rules of pleading. Section 11 (1) (b) of the Act was clearly intended to remove this confusion of terminology but the essential dichotomy was not affected; it was and is, between the right to reject or the right to damages. The modern form of the question tends to put the cart before the horse and to obscure the issue.

If one asks oneself the question in the form, "Did the parties intend that the buyer should be entitled to reject the goods if they were not shipped in good condition?" the answer must be that it depends on the nature and effects of the breach. This is directly in line with Diplock L.J.'s approach in the *Hongkong Fir Shipping Co.* case [1962] 2 Q.B. 26, 69-70, not surprisingly, since there can be very little difference in principle between whether the ship is seaworthy and whether goods are in good condition. There is obviously a strong case for applying the general principle of the *Hongkong Fir Shipping Co.* case to contracts for the sale of goods. The question remains, however, and it is the kernel of Mr. Hallgarten's submission, whether it is open to the court to do so. The parties themselves, of course, can do it by express agreement as, indeed, they have done in the present case in relation to quality. Clause 5 provides that breach of the terms as to quality shall entitle the buyer to an allowance but that if the goods contain over 5 per cent of sand or in excess of .005 per cent of castor seed husk, the buyer may reject the parcel. If it can be done expressly, it can be done by implication, unless it is in some way prohibited. Mr. Hallgarten argues that section 11 (1) (*b*) compels the court to choose between condition and warranty. I do not think that the subsection was intended to have any prohibitory effect. It is essentially a definition, defining "condition" and "warranty" in terms of remedies. Nor is the classification absolutely rigid, for it provides that a buyer may treat a condition as a warranty if he wishes, by accepting the goods. It does not, however, envisage the possibility that a breach of warranty might go to the root of the contract, and so, in certain circumstances, entitle the buyer to treat the contract as repudiated. But the law has developed since the Act was passed. It is now accepted as a general principle since the *Hongkong Fir Shipping Co.* case [1962] 2 Q.B. 26 that it is the events resulting from the breach, rather than the breach itself, which may destroy the consideration for the buyer's promise and so enable him to treat the contract as repudiated.

PANOUTSOS v. *RAYMOND HADLEY*
CORPORATION OF NEW YORK
England. Court of Appeal. [1917] 2 K.B. 473

By a contract in writing made in London and dated September 27, 1915, which was made on the printed form of the "London Flour Trade Association. American Flour Contract," the Raymond Hadley Corporation of New York (herein called the sellers), who had also a place of business in London, sold to Panoutsos (herein called the buyer) 4000 tons of flour to be despatched from the Atlantic seaboard by steamer or steamers to Greece as per bills of lading dated not later than November 7, 1915; "each shipment shall be deemed a separate contract"; and there was this clause written into the contract: "Cash against documents in New York. Payment by confirmed bankers' credit." Any dispute arising out of the contract was to be referred to arbitration according to the printed rules indorsed thereon.

On October 16 the National Bank of Commerce of New York wrote to the sellers in New York stating that they had been requested to open a credit in favour of the sellers for about $270,000 in respect of the shipment of 4,000 tons of flour shipped up to November 7, 1915, and adding:

"In advising you that this credit has been opened we are acting merely as agent for our foreign correspondents and cannot assume any responsibility for its continuance." This letter showed that the credit was not irrevocable and therefore was not a "confirmed bankers' credit." The sellers, however, on October 21 and again on October 27, 28, 29, and 30 made shipments of flour in part fulfilment of the contract, for which they were duly paid by the New York bank in pursuance of the credit in exchange for shipping documents. Meanwhile on October 27, the sellers took exception to the credit as not being irrevocable. On November 15 they requested the buyer to extend the time for the shipment of the balance of the flour from November 7 to November 30, and to this the buyer agreed. On November 25 the sellers notified the buyer that the balance of their contract was cancelled on the ground (so far as material) that the buyer had failed to perform the condition as to "payment by confirmed bankers' credit." The buyer refused to accept the cancellation, and the dispute was referred to arbitration. The arbitrators found that the credit was not a confirmed bankers' credit within the meaning of the contract, but that the sellers took no exception to it at the time it was opened.

Before the arbitrators the sellers contended that the buyer had failed to comply with the conditions of the contract, as he had failed to open a credit at New York, which would be irrevocable until November 30; and that the fact that they had made shipments without insisting on this condition did not release the buyer in respect of subsequent shipments, especially having regard to the term of the contract that "each shipment shall be deemed a separate contract." The buyer contended that the sellers had accepted as satisfactory the credit which has been opened, and, having made a shipment under it, had waived any possible objection to it and could not repudiate their obligation to ship the balance of the flour, or could not do so without giving due notice to him so as to enable him to remove any valid objection and furnish such a credit as would satisfy them.

The arbitrators awarded that the sellers were in default in not shipping the balance of the flour in accordance with the contract, and that they should pay a certain sum as damages.

The question for the opinion of the Court was whether or not upon the above facts there was any evidence upon which the arbitrators could properly find that the sellers had waived the term in the contract that payment should be by confirmed bankers' credit.

If the Court should be of opinion that the question should be answered in the affirmative, then the award was to stand; if in the negative, then the award was to be in favour of the sellers.

Bailhache J. held that when the sellers knew that the credit was not in order, and yet proceeded to act upon it as if it was in order, they must be taken to have waived the informality so long as they chose to act upon that credit, but that they were not bound to act upon it to the end merely because they acted upon it at first and waived the informality up to a point. In his opinion the sellers could at any time insist upon the credit being put in order, but if they desired to cancel the contract because the credit upon which they had acted was not in order they must give reasonable notice to the buyer of their intention to do so; which they had not done. He therefore confirmed the award. The sellers appealed.

VISCOUNT READING C.J.: . . . The question put to the Court is "whether or not upon the above findings of fact"—to which must now be added "coupled with our findings of fact" — "there was any evidence upon which the arbitrators could properly find that the sellers had waived the term in the contract that payment should be by confirmed bankers' credit." It was therefore admitted that there was no confirmed bankers' credit, but the buyer contended that there had been a waiver of that condition of the contract. In answer to that the sellers said that there had been no such waiver, and if there had been a waiver that they were entitled at any time to insist upon the condition being performed. The buyer replied that no doubt the sellers were entitled to insist upon the performance of the condition, but that, having waived its performance hitherto, they must give reasonable notice to the buyer of their intention to insist upon its performance in the future so as to give him an opportunity of putting the credit right. Bailhache J. held that the sellers must be taken to have waived the performance of the condition, that the buyer was entitled to reasonable notice, and that such notice had not in fact been given. He therefore answered the question in favour of the buyer.

In my opinion the learned judge was right. It is open to a party to a contract to waive a condition which is inserted for his benefit. If the sellers chose to ship without the safeguard of a confirmed bankers' credit, they were entitled to do so, and the buyer performed his part of the contract by paying for the goods shipped, though there was no confirmed bankers' credit, inasmuch as that condition had been waived. If at a later stage the sellers wished to avail themselves of the condition precedent, in my opinion there was nothing in the facts to prevent them from demanding the performance of the condition if they had given reasonable notice to the buyer that they would not ship unless there was a confirmed bankers' credit. If they had done that and the buyer had failed to comply with the condition, the buyer would have been in default, and the sellers would have been entitled to cancel the contract without being subject to any claim by the buyer for damages.

In *Bentsen* v. *Taylor, Sons & Co.,* [1893] 2 Q.B. 283, Bowen L.J. stated the law as to waiver thus: "Did the defendants by their acts or conduct lead the plaintiff reasonably to suppose that they did not intend to treat the contract for the future as at an end, on account of the failure to perform the condition precedent?" Reading sellers for defendants and buyer for plaintiff in that passage, it applies exactly to the present case. The sellers did lead the buyer to think so, and when they intended to change that position it was incumbent on them to give reasonable notice of that intention to the buyer so as to enable him to comply with the condition which up to that time had been waived.

The case of *In re Tyrer & Co. and Hessler & Co.,* 6 Com. Cas. 143; 7 Com. Cas. 166 was cited as an authority for the proposition that the moment the sellers chose to avail themselves of the failure to perform the condition precedent they could put an end to the contract without giving the buyer an opportunity of remedying the default which had hitherto been waived. That case is not an authority for that proposition. It shows that, where there are stipulated times in a charterparty for payment of the hire of a ship and a power to withdraw the ship if the payment is not made at the stipulated time, the mere fact that there has been default in payment at one or more stipulated times, of which advantage has not been taken, does not entitle the party in default at a subsequent time to a notice so as to enable him to comply with the condition before the right to withdraw arises. That is a totally different case from the present. I cannot find any authority to support the proposition that, when one party has led another to believe that he may continue in a certain course of conduct without any risk of the contract being cancelled, the first-mentioned party can cancel the contract without giving any notice to the other so as to enable the latter to comply with the requirement of the contract. It seems to me to follow from the observations of Bowen L.J. in *Bentsen* v. *Taylor, Sons & Co.* that there must be reasonable notice given to the buyer before the sellers can take advantage of the failure to provide a confirmed bankers' credit. That is the decision of Bailhache J.

The only question which remains is whether reasonable notice has been given. We have more material before us than Bailhache J. had when he came to the conclusion that no reasonable notice had been given. I am not prepared to draw the inference of fact that reasonable notice had been given before the sellers cancelled the contract. If notice had been given on October 27, and on November 25 the sellers had cancelled the contract, I should have thought that that would have been ample notice to enable the buyer to provide the confirmed credit in New York. But I cannot find any such notice on the part of the sellers of their intention to insist upon the performance of the condition. . . .

The result is that the decision of Bailhache J. is right, and the appeal must be dismissed.

[Lord Cozens-Hardy M.R. and Scrutton L.J. agreed.]

TURNEY AND TURNEY v. *ZHILKA.* 1959. 18 D.L.R. (2d) 497 (Ontario. Supreme Court of Canada). A contract for the sale of "all and singular the land and not buildings situate on the East side of the 5th Line west in the township of Toronto and known as 60 acres or more having frontage of about 2046 feet on 5th Line more or less, by a depth of about . . . feet, more or less (lot boundaries about as fenced), being part of west ½ lot 5 Con 5 west" contained a condition, "Providing the property can be annexed to the Village of Streetsville and a plan is approved by the Village Council for subdivision." The vendor only owned 62.37 acres, but he thought he had 65 acres and that he could retain five acres around his buildings. The purchaser claimed 60.87 acres, leaving the vendor 1.5 acres. The Village of Streetsville did not annex the property. An action for specific performance by the purchaser, was dismissed. As to the defence of non-compliance with the *Statute of Frauds*, the Court held that there was not only lack of sufficient certainty of description, "but the evidence makes it quite clear that the parties never reached any agreement, oral or written, on the quantity or description of the land to be retained or the land to be conveyed." The purchaser was willing to waive the annexation condition. On this point, JUDSON J.: "The date for the completion of the sale is fixed with reference to the performance of this condition—'60 days after plans are approved'. Neither party to the contract undertakes to fulfil this condition, and neither party reserves a power of waiver. The purchaser made some enquiries of the village council but the evidence indicates that he made little or no progress and received little encouragement and that the prospects of annexation were very remote. After the trouble arose over the quantity and description of the land, the purchaser purported to waive this condition on the ground that it was solely for his benefit and was severable, and sued immediately for specific performance without reference to the condition and the time for performance fixed by the condition. The learned trial Judge found that the condition was one introduced for the sole benefit of the purchaser and that he could waive it. . . .

"But here there is no right to be waived. The obligations under the contract, on both sides, depend upon a future uncertain event, the happening of which depends entirely on the will of a third party—the village council. This is a true condition precedent—an external condition upon which the existence of the obligation depends. Until the event occurs there is no right to performance on either side. The parties have not promised that it will occur. In the absence of such a promise there can be no breach of contract until the event does occur. The purchaser now seeks to make the vendor liable on his promise to convey in spite of the non-performance of the condition and this to suit his own convenience only. This is not a case of renunciation or relinquishment of a right but rather an attempt by one party, without the consent of the other, to write a new contract. Waiver has often been referred to as a troublesome and uncertain term in the law but it does at least presuppose the existence of a right to be relinquished."

BARNETT v. HARRISON
(1975) 57 D.L.R. (3d) 225 (S. C. C.)

DICKSON J.: "The rule in *Turney and Turney* v. *Zhilka* has been in effect since 1959, and has been applied many times. In the interests of certainty and predictability in the law, the rule should endure unless compelling reason for change be shown. If in any case the parties agree that the rule should not apply, that can be readily written into the agreement."

DAKIN & CO., LIMITED v. LEE
England. King's Bench Division. [1916] 1 K.B. 566 (Div. Ct.)

The plaintiffs were builders. The action was brought to recover the sum of £352 4s. 4d., the balance of the price of certain repairs carried out by the plaintiffs at the defendant's house, 37 Wimbledon Park Road, Wandsworth. Part of the claim related to work contained in a specification which by a verbal contract the parties had agreed should be done for £264. The balance of the claim was for extras and additional work. The only question raised on the appeal related to the claim in respect of the contract work.

The defence was that the work referred to in the specification had not been completed, and the official referee found as a fact that the contract had not been fulfilled in the three following instances: (1) A letter from the plaintiffs which accompanied the specification stated that the concrete which was to be placed under a part of one of the side walls of the house, which was to be underpinned, was to be of the depth of 4 feet. Only 2 feet of concrete was placed there. (2) Columns of hollow iron, 5 inches in diameter were to be used for the support of a certain bay window. The columns supplied were of solid iron 4 inches in diameter. (3) The joists over the bay window were to be cleated at the angles and bolted to caps and to each other. This was not done. The defendant had resumed her occupation of the house after the plaintiffs' workmen had left, and after receiving the plaintiffs' account she offered to settle the whole claim by a payment of £250 in addition to a sum of £50 which she had already paid.

The official referee held that the plaintiffs had not performed their contract, in that the defendant had been given something different from, and less strong and secure than, what she was entitled to have under the contract, and that the plaintiffs were therefore not entitled to recover any part of the contract price or any sum in respect of the contract work. The official referee disallowed the claim for extras, but allowed a sum of £70 for the additional work, which was less than the sums paid before action and paid into Court, and the official referee therefore entered judgment for the defendant. The plaintiffs appealed.

SANKEY J.: . . . I do not think that the official referee took the correct view of either the law or the facts. In my opinion the law applicable to cases of this sort is as follows. Where a builder has supplied work and labour for the erection or repair of a house under a lump sum contract, but has departed from the terms of the contract, he is entitled to recover for his services, unless (1) the work that he had done has been of no benefit to the owner; (2) the work he has done is entirely different from the work which he has contracted to do; or (3) he has abandoned the work and left it unfinished.

As to the first case, namely, where the work as done is of no benefit to the owner, the authority is *Farnsworth* v. *Garrard* (1807), 1 Camp. 38; 170 E.R. 867. An illustration of the second case, where the work done is entirely different from the work which the builder contracted to do, may be found, I think, in the case of *Forman & Co. Proprietary* v. *Ship Liddlesdale*, [1900] A.C. 190, 201. The gist of the decision is given where Lord Hobhouse says: "It is also made clear that the substitution of iron for steel not only added to the weight and to the expenses, but altered the structure of the vessel—to her advantage, as the plaintiffs contend, but as the defendant says, causing a rigidity in her framework which is a source of danger to her. That is a matter on which opinions vary; but there is no dispute that the alteration is not consistent with the plaintiffs' obligation to restore the vessel to her original condition prior to the accident."

Another illustration of the same class of case, namely, where the work done is entirely different from the work contracted to be done, may be found in the observations of Day J. in *London School Board* v. *Wall*, Hudson's *Building Contracts*, 3rd ed., vol. 2, p. 165. A similar rule applies in the sale of goods, where the plaintiff cannot recover if he supplies an article entirely different from that which he has contracted to supply.

With regard to the third case, namely, where the builder has abandoned the work or left the house or the repairs unfinished, the authority is *Sumpter* v. *Hedges*, [1898] 1 Q.B. 673. There the plaintiff had abandoned the work and left it incomplete. Mr. Cassels in the course of his argument put by way of illustration the case of a builder who, having contracted to build a 10 foot wall, built a wall of 2 feet only, and he contended that in that case the builder could not recover. In my opinion that would come into the third category of cases which I have mentioned; the builder would be held not to have finished the work and to have abandoned it. . . .

But then it is said that the first contract, not having been performed, has gone, and that there is no evidence of any new contract by the defendant to pay for the work that was actually done. She says that no promise to pay for that work can be implied from the fact that the defendant occupied the house because the work was carried out on the employer's land, and therefore could not be rejected. I think there is a fallacy underlying that argument. I do not think that the contract can be said to have gone where the house has been substantially completed or the repairs have been substantially carried out, though not entirely in the manner provided for by the contract. The true view and the true method of ascertaining the amount due to the plaintiff in such a case is, I think, that given by Parke B. in the case of *Thornton* v. *Place* (1832), 1 Moo. & R. 218; 174 E.R. 74 at p. 75, where he says: "What the plaintiff is entitled to recover is the price agreed upon in the specification, subject to a deduction; and the measure of that deduction is the sum which it would take to alter the work so as to make it correspond with the specification." Where repairs have been substantially completed, or a house has been substantially erected, in accordance with the contract I find no difficulty in holding either that the contract has been performed, or that there is an implied request by the defendant to do the work and an implied promise to pay. I cannot hold that, where a builder has done ninety-nine hundredths of the work according to the contract and the remaining one hundredth in a different way, the building owner is not obliged to pay for any part of the work done. The present case, in my view, is an example of that. Unfortunately, we have not the advantage of hearing exactly what the learned referee said when he gave his judgment, but I am satisfied that there was no finding by him that the work done by the plaintiffs was of no benefit to the defendant, or that it was entirely different from that which the plaintiffs contracted to do, and there is no finding that they either abandoned the work or left the repairs unfinished. I do not think there is any evidence—certainly our attention has not been drawn to it—to show that the contract has not been substantially completed, and I do not think that because there was a slight variation in the depth of the concrete, a very insignificant variation in the columns, and a still more insignificant variation in the beams by their not being cleated, it is possible to say that the repairs have not been substantially done.

Under these circumstances, I think the judgment of the learned official referee was wrong, and that this appeal ought to be allowed.

[The defendant appealed and the Court of Appeal dismissed the appeal. Ridley J. also gave an opinion in the Divisional Court.]

JACOB & YOUNGS, INC. v. *KENT*
New York. Court of Appeal. 1921. 230 N.Y. 239; 129 N.E. 889

CARDOZO J.: The plaintiff built a country residence for the defendant at a cost of upwards of $77,000, and now sues to recover a balance of $3,483.46, remaining unpaid. The work of construction ceased in June, 1914, and the defendant then began to occupy the dwelling. There was no complaint of defective performance until March, 1915. One of the specifications for the plumbing works provides that "all wrought-iron pipe must be well galvanized, lap welded pipe of the grade known as 'standard pipe' of Reading manufacture."

The defendant learned in March, 1915, that some of the pipe, instead of being made in Reading, was the product of other factories. The plaintiff was accordingly directed by the architect to do the work anew. The plumbing was then encased within the walls except in a few places where it had to be exposed. Obedience to the order meant more than the substitution of other pipe. It meant the demolition at great expense of substantial parts of the completed structure. The plaintiff left the work untouched, and asked for a certificate that the final payment was due. Refusal of the certificate was followed by this suit.

The evidence sustains a finding that the omission of the prescribed brand of pipe was neither fraudulent nor willful. It was the result of the oversight and inattention of the plaintiff's subcontractor. Reading pipe is distinguished from Cohoes pipe and other brands only by the name of the manufacturer stamped upon it at intervals of between six and seven feet. Even the defendant's architect, though he inspected the pipe upon arrival, failed to notice the discrepancy. The plaintiff tried to show that the brands installed, though made by other manufacturers, were the same in quality, in appearance, in market value and in cost as the brand stated in the contract—that they were indeed the same thing, though manufactured in another place. The evidence was excluded, and a verdict directed for the defendant. The Appellate Division reversed, and granted a new trial.

We think the evidence, if admitted, would have supplied some basis for the inference that the defect was insignificant in its relation to the project. The courts never say that one who makes a contract fills the measure of his duty by less than full performance. They do say, however, that an omission, both trivial and innocent, will sometimes be atoned for by allowance of the resulting damage, and will not always be the breach of a condition to be followed by a forfeiture. . . The distinction is akin to that between dependent and independent promises, or between promises and conditions. . . . Some promises are so plainly independent that they can never by fair construction be conditions of one another. . . . Others are so plainly dependent that they must always be conditions. Others, though dependent and thus conditions when there is departure in point of substance, will be viewed as independent and collateral when the departure is insignificant. . . . Considerations partly of justice and partly of presumable intention are to tell us whether this or that promise shall be placed in one class or in another. The simple and the uniform will call for different remedies from the multifarious and the intricate. The margin of departure within the range of normal expectation upon a sale of common chattels will vary from the margin to be expected upon a contract for the construction of a mansion or a "skyscraper." There will be harshness sometimes and oppression in the implication of a condition when the thing upon which labor has been expended is incapable of surrender because united to the land, and equity and reason in the implication of a like condition when the subject-matter, if defective, is in shape to be returned. From the conclusion that promises may not be treated as dependent to the extent of their uttermost minutiae without a sacrifice of justice, the progress is a short one to the conclusion that they may not be so treated without a perversion of intention. Intention not otherwise revealed may be presumed to hold in contemplation the reasonable and probable. If something else is in view, it must not be left to implication. There will be no assumption of a purpose to visit venial faults with oppressive retribution.

Those who think more of symmetry and logic in the development of legal rules than of practical adaptation to the attainment of a just result will be troubled by a classification where the lines are so wavering and blurred. Something, doubtless, may be said on the score of consistency and certainty in favor of a stricter standard. The courts have balanced such considerations against those of equity and fairness, and found the latter to be the weightier. The decisions in this state commit us to the liberal view, which is making its way, nowadays, in jurisdictions slow to welcome it. *Dakin & Co.* v. *Lee*, [1916] 1 K.B. 566. Where the line is to be drawn between the important and the trivial cannot be settled by a formula. "In the nature of the case precise boundaries are impossible." 2 *Williston on Contracts*, p. 841. The same omission may take on one aspect or another according to its setting. Substitution of equivalents may not have the same significance in fields of art on the one side and in those of mere utility on the other. Nowhere will change be tolerated, however, if it is so dominant or pervasive as in any real or substantial measure to frustrate the purpose of the contract. . . . There is no general license to install whatever, in the builder's judgment, may be regarded as "just as good." . . . The question is one of degree, to be answered, if there is doubt, by the triers of the facts, . . . and, if the inferences are certain, by the judges of the law. . . .

We must weigh the purpose to be served, the desire to be gratified, the excuse for deviation from the letter, the cruelty of enforced adherence. Then only can we tell whether literal fulfillment is to be implied by law as a condition. This is not to say that the parties are not free by apt and certain words to effectuate a purpose that performance of every term shall be a condition of recovery. That question is not here. This is merely to say that the law will be slow to impute the purpose, in the silence of the parties, where the significance of the default is grievously out of proportion to the oppression of the forfeiture. The willful transgressor must accept the penalty of his transgression. . . . For him there is no occasion to mitigate the rigor of implied conditions. The transgressor whose default is unintentional and trivial may hope for mercy if he will offer atonement for his wrong.

In the circumstances of this case, we think the measure of the allowance is not the cost of replacement, which would be great, but the difference in value, which would be either nominal or nothing. Some of the exposed sections might perhaps have been replaced at moderate expense. The defendant did not limit his demand to them, but treated the plumbing as a unit to be corrected from cellar to roof. In point of fact, the plaintiff never reached the stage at which evidence of the extent of the allowance became necessary. The trial court had excluded evidence that the defect was unsubstantial, and in view of that ruling there was no occasion for the plaintiff to go farther with an offer of proof. We think, however, that the offer, if it had been made, would not of necessity have been defective because directed to difference in value. It is true that in most cases the cost of replacement is the measure. The owner is entitled to the money which will permit him to complete, unless the cost of completion is grossly and unfairly out of proportion to the good to be attained. When that is true, the measure is the difference in value. Specifications call, let us say, for a foundation built of granite quarried in Vermont. On the completion of the building, the owner learns that through the blunder of a subcontractor part of the foundation has been built of the same quality quarried in New Hampshire. The measure of allowance is not the cost of reconstruction. "There may be omissions of that which could not afterwards be supplied exactly as called for by the contract without taking down the building to its foundations, and at the same time the omission may not affect the value of the building for use or otherwise, except so slightly as to be hardly appreciable." . . . The rule that gives a remedy in cases of substantial performance with compensation for defects of trivial or inappreciable importance, has been developed by the courts as an instrument of justice. The measure of the allowance must be shaped to the same end.

The order should be affirmed, and judgment absolute directed in favour of the plaintiff upon the stipulation, with costs in all courts.

McLAUGHLIN J.: I dissent. The plaintiff did not perform its contract. Its failure to do so was either intentional or due to gross neglect which, under the uncontradicted facts, amounted to the same thing, nor did it make any proof of the cost of compliance, where compliance was possible. . . .

No explanation was given why pipe called for by the contract was not used, nor was any effort made to show what it would cost to remove the pipe of other manufacturers and install that of the Reading Manufacturing Company. The defendant had a right to contract for what he wanted. He had a right before making payment to get what the contract called for. It is no answer to say that the pipe put in was just as good as that made by the Reading Manufacturing Company, or that the difference in value between such pipe and the pipe made by the Reading Manufacturing Company would be either "nominal or nothing." Defendant contracted for pipe made by the Reading Manufacturing Company. What his reason was for requiring this kind of pipe is of no importance. He wanted that and was entitled to it. It may have been a mere whim on his part, but even so, he had a right to the kind of pipe, regardless of whether some other kind, according to the opinion of the contractor or experts, would have been "just as good, better, or done just as well." He agreed to pay only upon condition that the pipe installed were made by that company and he ought not to be compelled to pay unless that condition be performed. . . . The rule, therefore, of substantial performance, with damages for unsubstantial omissions, has no application. . . .

NOTE. Dean Havighurst, in his casebook, asks: How do you explain the absence of any issue arising from the refusal of the architect to give a certificate? Why did the owner refuse to make the final payment? Because he did not get Reading pipe? How did the pipe get into the litigation?

RESTATEMENT OF THE LAW OF CONTRACTS (SECOND)

266. In determining whether a failure to perform . . . is material, the following circumstances are significant.

    (a) The extent to which the injured party will be deprived of the benefit which he reasonably expected;

    (b) The extent to which the injured party can be adequately compensated for that part of the benefit of which he will be deprived;

    (c) The extent to which the party failing to perform . . . will suffer forfeiture;

    (d) The likelihood that the party failing to perform . . . will cure his failure, taking account of all the circumstances including any reasonable assurances;

    (e) The extent to which the behavior of the party failing to perform . . . comports with standards of good faith and fair dealing.

QUESTIONS. Dean Havighurst invites, in his casebook on Contracts, a comparison of the language of the predecessor of s. 266 with the sentence beginning "We must weigh the purpose to be served . . . etc." in Cardozo J.'s judgment in *Jacob and Youngs* v. *Kent,* above. Which do you prefer?

Why did the Institute not simply state rules? Why "significant" or persuasive "circumstances" rather than binding rules?

BIGHAM v. BRAKE
Ontario. Divisional Court. 1927. 32 O.W.N. 271

ORDE J.A., in a written judgment, said that the contract in question upon this appeal required the plaintiff to build for the defendant a concrete brick foundation and wall and three piers, the work to be in compliance with a by-law of the City of Toronto, regulating the erection and providing for safety of buildings, for a lump sum of $400. For work of this character the by-law clearly required the use of cement mortar, which is declared to mean mortar made with Portland cement and clean, sharp sand, in the proportion of one part of cement to not more than three parts of sand, the addition of hydrated lime to the amount of not more than 10 per cent. of the amount of the cement being permitted. The plaintiff did not even attempt to conform to this by-law, but prepared a mortar composed almost wholly of lime and sand with a small quantity of cement, amounting approximately to about three parts of cement to five parts of lime and forty-two parts of sand.

It was contended that but for the damage done by frost, for which the Assistant Master held the defendant and not the plaintiff responsible, the work done by the plaintiff would have been as good as if he had complied with the by-law. This is to some extent mere speculation. The evidence disclosed, and the Assistant Master finds, that the mortar used by the plaintiff was deficient in quality even as lime mortar. It is probable that but for the frost the wall might have stood and perhaps served the purpose for which it was intended, but it could hardly have been as good and safe a wall as if built according to the contract.

The plaintiff relies upon *H. Dakin & Co. Ltd.* v. *Lee,* [1916] 1 K.B. 566, and *House Repair and Service Co. Ltd.* v. *Miller* (1921), 49 O.L.R. 205, and contends that there was here a substantial compliance with the contract entitling him to recover the contract price, or in any case the value of the work done. That contention cannot prevail here. Whether or not a particular case comes within the principle enunciated in the *Dakin* case must be largely a question of fact. Here it is fairly evident that what was done has proved of no value to the defendant, and is so substantially different from what was contracted for as to bring the case within two of the exceptions stated in the head-note to the *Dakin* case.

The appeal should be dismissed.

[Latchford C.J. and Smith J.A. agreed with Middleton J.A., who said, in part: "Contractors and builders should understand that they cannot recover upon a contract unless they comply with its terms, and that the *Dakin* case does not decide that a contractor or builder may substitute something more convenient for him or less expensive and then demand payment, upon the theory that it is 'just as good' or 'almost as good,' and treat the case as one calling for some abatement in the contract price.]

SUMPTER v. *HEDGES*
England. Court of Appeal. [1898] 1 Q.B. 673

The action was for work done and materials provided. The plaintiff, a builder, had contracted with the defendant to build upon the defendant's land two houses and stables for the sum of £565. The plaintiff did part of the work, amounting in value to about £333, and had received payment of part of the price. He then informed the defendant that he had no money, and could not go on with the work. The learned judge found that he had abandoned the contract. The defendant thereupon finished the buildings on his own account, using for that purpose certain building materials which the plaintiff had left on the ground. The judge gave judgment for the plaintiff for the value of the materials so used, but allowed him nothing in respect of the work which he had done upon the buildings.

A. L. SMITH L.J.: . . . In this case the plaintiff, a builder, entered into a contract to build two houses and stables on the defendant's land for a lump sum. When the buildings were still in an unfinished state the plaintiff informed the defendant that he had no money, and was not going on with the work any more. The learned judge has found as a fact that he abandoned the contract. Under such circumstances, what is a building owner to do? He cannot keep the buildings on his land in an unfinished state for ever. The law is that, where there is a contract to do work for a lump sum, until the work is completed the price of it cannot be recovered. Therefore the plaintiff could not recover on the original contract. It is suggested however that the plaintiff was entitled to recover for the work he did on a quantum meruit. But, in order that that may be so, there must be evidence of a fresh contract to pay for the work already done. With regard to that, the case of *Munro* v. *Butt* (1858), 8 E. & B. 738: 120 E.R. 275, appears to be exactly in point. That case decides that, unless the building owner does something from which a new contract can be inferred to pay for the work already done, the plaintiff in such a case as this cannot recover on a quantum meruit. In the case of *Lysaght* v. *Pearson* (not reported except in Times Newspaper of March 3, 1879), to which we have been referred, the case of *Munro* v. *Butt* does not appear to have been referred to. There the plaintiff had contracted to erect on the defendant's land two corrugated iron roofs. When he had completed one of them, he does not seem to have said that he abandoned the contract, but merely that he would not go on unless the defendant paid him for what he had already done. The defendant thereupon proceeded to erect for himself the second roof. The Court of Appeal held that there was in that case something from which a new contract might be inferred to pay for the work done by the plaintiff. That is not this case. In the case of *Whitaker* v. *Dunn* (1887), 3 Times L.R. 602, there was a contract to erect a laundry on defendant's land, and the laundry erected was not in accordance with the contract, but the official referee held that the plaintiff could recover on a quantum meruit. The case came before a Divisional Court, consisting of Lord Coleridge C.J. and myself, and we said that the decision in *Munro* v. *Butt* applied, and there being no circumstances to justify an inference of a fresh contract the plaintiff must fail. My brother Collins thinks that that case went to the Court of Appeal, and that he argued it there, and the Court affirmed the decision of the Queen's Bench Division. I think the appeal must be dismissed.

COLLINS L.J.: . . . I agree. I think the case is really concluded by the finding of the learned judge to the effect that the plaintiff had abandoned the contract. If the plaintiff had merely broken his contract in some way so as not to give the defendant the right to treat him as having abandoned the contract, and the defendant had then proceeded to finish the work himself, the plaintiff might perhaps have been entitled to sue on a quantum meruit on the ground that the defendant had taken the benefit of the work done. But that is not the present case. There are cases in which, though the plaintiff has abandoned the performance of a contract, it is possible for him to raise the inference of a new contract to pay for the work done on a quantum meruit from the defendant's having taken the benefit of that work, but, in order that that may be done, the circumstances must be such as to give an option to the defendant to take or not to take the benefit of the work done. It is only where the circumstances are such as to give that option that there is any evidence on which to ground the inference of a new contract. Where, as in the case of work done on land, the circumstances are such as to give the defendant no option whether he will take the benefit of the work or not, then one must look to other facts than the mere taking the benefit of the work in order to ground the inference of a new contract. In this case I see no other facts on which such an inference can be founded. The mere fact that a defendant is in possession of what he cannot help keeping, or even has done work upon it, affords no ground for such an inference. He is not bound to keep unfinished a building which in an incomplete state would be a nuisance on his land. I am therefore of opinion that the plaintiff was not entitled to recover for the work which he had done. I feel clear that the case of *Whitaker* v. *Dunn* to which reference has been made, was the case which as counsel I argued in the Court of Appeal, and in which the Court dismissed the appeal on the ground that the case was concluded by *Munro* v. *Butt*.

[The appeal was dismissed. The opinion of Chitty L.J. to the same effect is omitted.]

THE SALE OF GOODS ACT
Ontario. Revised Statutes. 1970. Chapter 421

30. (2) Where there is a contract for the sale of goods to be delivered by stated instalments that are to be separately paid for and the seller makes defective deliveries in respect of one or more instalments or the buyer neglects or refuses to take delivery of or pay for one or more instalments, it is a question in each case depending on the terms of the contract and the circumstances of the case whether the breach of contract is a repudiation of the whole contract or whether it is a severable breach giving rise to a claim for compensation but not to a right to treat the whole contract as repudiated.

MAPLE FLOCK COMPANY, LTD. v. UNIVERSAL FURNITURE PRODUCTS (WEMBLEY), LTD.
England. Court of Appeal. [1934] 1 K.B. 148

LORD HEWART C.J. The judgment which I am about to read is the judgment of the whole Court.

The appellant company are manufacturers of rag flock, and the respondents are manufacturers of furniture and bedding for which they use such flock. The action was brought by the appellants for breach by the respondents of a contract in writing, dated March 14, 1932, for the sale by the appellants to the respondents of 100 tons of black lindsey flock at £15 2s. 6d. per ton, to be delivered in three loads per week as required. It was further stipulated that there should be a written guarantee that all flock supplied under the contract should conform to the Government standard. The load was 1½ tons or 60 bags. The Government standard was that required under the *Rag Flock Act, 1911*, which had been fixed by regulation under the Act at not more than 30 parts of chlorine in 100,000 parts of flock. The Act made it a penal offence punishable by fine for any person (inter alia) to sell or have in his possession for sale or use or to use flock not conforming to that standard. A person charged under the Act might, however, if he could prove that he bought it from some one resident in the United Kingdom under a warranty that it complied with the Government standard, and that he had taken reasonable steps to ascertain and did in fact believe in the accuracy of the warranty, bring the seller before the Court by information and transfer the burden of the offence to him.

The appellant company duly gave a written guarantee as required by the contract and deliveries were at once commenced and continued of 1½ tons each. The sixteenth of these deliveries was made on April 28, 1932, and, according to the respondent's evidence, was duly accepted and the stuff put into use; a further delivery was made on April 29, 1932, and another on May 2, 1932. On that latter date the respondents notified the appellants that a sample drawn from the delivery of April 28, 1932, had been analysed and showed a contamination of 250 parts of chlorine, instead of the maximum allowed by law of 30 parts. The respondents thereupon claimed to rescind the contract; the appellants protested, and some negotiations took place, during which two more deliveries were tendered and taken, each of 1½ tons. Eventually the respondents adhered to their claim that they were entitled to rescind, and the writ was issued by the appellants claiming damages on the ground that the refusal of the respondents to take further deliveries was wrongful.

No complaint is made in respect of the 15 deliveries made before April 28, 1932, or in respect of the four deliveries made after that date. The respondents made no claim for damages in respect of the delivery said to be defective, because it had all been used before the report was received on the sample. The learned Judge finds that the sample was taken in the usual way—namely, one handful drawn from one bag of the 60 bags which constituted the delivery, and he held that the respondents were entitled, applying the ordinary rules of probability, to say that such must be the condition of the whole or substantially the whole of that delivery of 1½ tons. On the other hand the appellants produced analyses of the flock they had in store from time to time, including an analysis dated April 29, 1932, all of which showed percentages of chlorine well below the Government maximum, though they could not identify any sample as drawn from the flock actually delivered to the respondents. In their evidence they described the process of manufacture by washing which they used. The learned Judge finds that it would be quite wrong to make any general criticism at all of the way in which the appellants conducted their business; he was very favourably impressed, he said, by the evidence of Mr. Jebb, who gave evidence for them; he seemed to the Judge a careful, scrupulous and honourable man. Mr. Jebb could give no explanation of so gross a degree of contamination and was disposed to think some mistake had been made as to the sample. The learned Judge, however, finding that the sample must be taken as a fair test of the delivery, held that the defendants, as prudent traders, could properly say to themselves, in regard to the defective delivery, "it might happen again." He nowhere finds that it was a reasonable inference that it would happen again. His conclusion appears to us to be that there was a mere possibility, not a reasonable probability, that it would happen again. On the contrary, he finds that the occurrence was a very extraordinary thing. We think that on the evidence, and the findings of the learned judge, the true inference of fact is that there was no reasonable probability of any such improper delivery being repeated under the contract.

The decision of this case depends on the true construction and application of s. 31, sub-s. 2, of the *Sale of Goods Act, 1893*, which is in [substantially the language of the Ontario Act reproduced above]. That sub-section was based on decisions before the Act, and has been the subject of decisions since the Act. A contract for the sale of goods by instalments is a single contract, not a complex of as many contracts as there are instalments under it. The law might have been determined in the sense that any breach of condition in respect of any one or more instalments would entitle the party aggrieved to claim that the contract has been repudiated as a whole; or on the other hand the law as established might have been that any breach, however serious, in respect of one or more instalments should not have consequences extending beyond the particular instalment or instalments or affecting the contract as a whole. The sub-section, however which deals equally with breaches either by the buyer or the seller, requires the Court to decide on the merits of the particular case what effect, if any, the breach or breaches should have on the contract as a whole.

The language of the Act is substantially based on the language used by Lord Selborne L.C. in *Mersey Steel and Iron Co.* v. *Naylor, Benzon & Co.* (1884), 9 App. Cas. 434, where he said: "I am content to take the rule as stated by Lord Coleridge in *Freeth* v. *Burr* (1874), L.R. 9 C.P. 208, which is in substance, as I understand it, that you must look at the actual circumstances of the case in order to see whether the one party to the contract is relieved from its future performance by the conduct of the other; you must examine what the conduct is, so as to see whether it amounts to a renunciation, to an absolute refusal to perform the contract, such as would amount to a rescission if he had the power to rescind, and whether the other party may accept it as a reason for not performing his part." In *Freeth* v. *Burr*, Lord Coleridge C.J. stated the true question to be: "Whether the acts and conduct of the party evince an intention no longer to be bound by the contract." These were both cases of breach by the buyer in not making punctual payment, and in each case it was clear that the buyer had some justification for the course he took. The case of breach by the seller in making defective deliveries may raise different questions. Lord Selborne in the passage above quoted did not refer to any question of intention, but said that what is to be examined is the conduct of the party. Lord Coleridge in *Freeth* v. *Burr*, citing *Hoare* v. *Rennie* (1859), 5 H. & N. 19; 157 E.R. 1083, on the question of a seller's breach, states thus one aspect of the rule: "Where by the non-delivery of part of the thing contracted for the whole object of the contract is frustrated, the party making default renounces on his part all the obligations of the contract." In other words, the true test will generally be, not the subjective mental state of the defaulting party, but the objective test of the relation in fact of the default to the whole purpose of the contract.

Since the Act, the sub-section has been discussed by a Divisional Court in *Millars' Karri and Jarrah Company* (1902) v. *Weddel, Turner & Co.*

(1909), 14 Com. Cas. 25, where the contract being for 1100 pieces of timber, the first instalment of 750 pieces was rejected by the buyers; an arbitrator awarded "that the said shipment was, and is, so far from complying with the requirements of the said contract as to entitle the buyers to repudiate and to rescind the whole contract and to refuse to accept the said shipment and all further shipments under the said contract." The Court upheld the award. Bigham J. thus stated what in his opinion was the true test, "Thus, if the breach is of such a kind, or takes place in such circumstances as reasonably to lead to the inference that similar breaches will be committed in relation to subsequent deliveries, the whole contract may there and then be regarded as repudiated and may be rescinded. If, for instance, a buyer fails to pay for one delivery in such circumstances as to lead to the inference that he will not be able to pay for subsequent deliveries; or if a seller delivers goods differing from the requirements of the contract, and does so in such circumstances as to lead to the inference that he cannot, or will not, deliver any other kind of goods in the future, the other contracting party will be under no obligation to wait to see what may happen; he can at once cancel the contract and rid himself of the difficulty." Walton J. concurred.

This ruling was more recently applied in *Robert A. Munroe & Co.* v. *Meyer*, [1930] 2 K.B. 312, where under a contract for the sale of 1500 tons of bone meal, 611 tons were delivered which were seriously adulterated. The sellers were middlemen, who relied on their suppliers, the manufacturers, for correct delivery: when the buyers discovered that the deliveries did not conform to the contract they claimed that they were entitled to treat the whole contract as repudiated by the sellers. It was held that they were right in so claiming, on the ground that "in such a case as this, where there is a persistent breach, deliberate so far as the manufacturers are concerned, continuing for nearly one-half of the total contract quantity, the buyer, if he ascertains in time what the position is, ought to be entitled to say that he will not take the risk of having put upon him further deliveries of this character." [1930] 2 K.B. 331, per Wright J. On the other hand in *Taylor* v. *Oakes Roncoroni & Co.* [1922], 27 Com. Cas. 261, Greer J., as he then was, and the Court of Appeal, declined to hold that the buyers were entitled to refuse to go on with the contract, but held that the breach was a severable breach, as it was a case "where the instalment delivered failed in a slight but appreciable degree to come up to the standard required by the contract description."

With the help of these authorities we deduce that the main tests to be considered in applying the sub-section to the present case are, first, the ratio quantitatively which the breach bears to the contract as a whole, and secondly the degree of probability or improbability that such a breach will be repeated. On the first point, the delivery complained of amounts to no more than $1\frac{1}{2}$ tons out of a contract for 100 tons. On the second point, our conclusion is that the chance of the breach being repeated is practically negligible. We assume that the sample found defective fairly represents the bulk; but bearing in mind the judge's finding that the breach was extraordinary and that the appellant's business was carefully conducted, bearing in mind also that the appellants were warned, and bearing in mind that the delivery complained of was an isolated instance out of 20 satisfactory deliveries actually made both before and after the instalment objected to, we hold that it cannot reasonably be inferred that similar breaches would occur in regard to subsequent deliveries. Indeed, we do not understand that the learned judge came to any different conclusion. He seems, however, to have decided against the appellants on a third and separate ground, that is, that a delivery not satisfying the Government requirements would or might lead to the respondents being prosecuted under the Act. Though we think he exaggerates the likelihood of the respondents in such a case being held responsible, we do not wish to under-rate the gravity to the respondents of their being even prosecuted. But we cannot follow the judge's reasoning that the bare possibility, however remote, of this happening would justify the respondents in rescinding in this case. There may indeed be such cases, as also cases where the consequences of a single breach of contract may be so serious as to involve a frustration of the contract and justify rescission, or furthermore, the contract might contain an express condition that a breach would justify rescission, in which case effect would be given to such a condition by the Court. But none of these circumstances can be predicated of this case. We think the deciding factor here is the extreme improbability of the breach being repeated, and on that ground, and on the isolated and limited character of the breach complained of, there was, in our judgment, no sufficient justification to entitle the respondents to refuse further deliveries as they did.

The appeal must accordingly be allowed and judgment entered for the appellants, with costs here and below, for damages for their breach of contract in refusing further deliveries.

BETTINI v. GYE
England. Queen's Bench Division. 1876. 1 Q.B.D. 183

The defendant was the director of the Royal Italian Opera in Covent Garden, London and the plaintiff was a professional singer who agreed with the defendant as follows (in an English translation from the French):

1. Mr. Bettini undertakes to fill the part of prime tenor assoluto in the theatres, halls, and drawing-rooms, both public and private, in Great Britain and in Ireland, during the period of his engagement with Mr. Gye.

2. This engagement shall begin on the 30th of March, 1875, and shall terminate on the 13th of July, 1875.

3. The salary of Mr. Bettini shall be £150 per month, to be paid monthly.

4. Mr. Bettini shall sing in concerts as well as in operas, but he shall not sing anywhere out of the theatre in the United Kingdom of Great Britain and Ireland, from the 1st of January to the 31st of December, 1875, without the written permission of Mr. Gye, except at a distance of more than fifty miles from London, and out of the season of the theatre.

5. Mr. Gye shall furnish the costumes to Mr. Bettini for his characters, according to the ordinary usage of theatres.

6. Mr. Bettini will conform to the ordinary rules of the theatre in case of sickness, fire, rehearsals, &c.

7. Mr. Bettini agrees to be in London without fail at least six days before the commencement of his engagement, for the purpose of rehearsals.

8. In case Mr. Gye shall require the services of Mr. Bettini at a distance of more than ten miles from London, he shall pay his travelling expenses.

9. Mr. Bettini shall not be obliged to sing more than four times a week in opera. Mr. Bettini, in order to assist the direction of Mr. Gye, will sing, upon the request of Mr. Gye, in the same characters in which he has already sung, and in other characters of equal position. In case of the sick-

ness of other artists, Mr. Bettini agrees to replace them in their characters of first tenor assoluto.

10. Mr. Gye shall have the right to prolong the period limited above upon the same conditions, provided that the period does not go beyond the end of the month of August.

The plaintiff was prevented by temporary illness from being in London before March 28, although the agreement required him to be there "without fail" by March 24. The defendant terminated the agreement on the ground that the plaintiff was late in arrival and had given no notice of his inability to be in London for the purpose of rehearsals. The case was argued on a demurrer to the plea of the plaintiff's late arrival.

BLACKBURN J. delivered the judgment of the Court: In this case the parties have entered into an agreement in writing, which is set out on the record.

The Court must ascertain the intention of the parties, as is said by Parke B., in delivering the judgment of the Court in *Graves* v. *Legg* (1854), 156 E.R. 304, "To be collected from the instrument and the circumstances legally admissible in evidence with reference to which it is to be construed." He adds: "One particular rule well acknowledged is, that where a covenant or agreement goes to part of the consideration on both sides, and may be compensated in damages, it is an independent covenant or contract." There was no averment of any special circumstances existing in this case, with reference to which the agreement was made, but the Court must look at the general nature of such an agreement. By the 7th paragraph of the agreement, "Mr. Bettini agrees to be in London, without fail at least six days before the commencement of his engagement for the purpose of rehearsals." The engagement was to begin on the 30th of March, 1875. It is admitted on the record that the plaintiff did not arrive in London till the 28th of March, which is less than six days before the 30th, and therefore it is clear that he has not fulfilled his part of the contract.

The question raised by the demurrer is, not whether the plaintiff has any excuse for failing to fulfil this part of his contract, which may prevent his being liable in damages for not doing so, but whether his failure to do so justified the defendant in refusing to proceed with the engagement, and fulfil his, the defendant's part. And the answer to that question depends on whether this part of the contract is a condition precedent to the defendant's liability or only an independent agreement, a breach of which will not justify a repudiation of the contract, but will only be a cause of action for a compensation in damages. . . .

We think the answer to this question depends on the true construction of the contract taken as a whole.

Parties may think some matter, apparently of very little importance, essential; and if they sufficiently express an intention to make the literal fulfilment of such a thing a condition precedent, it will be one; or they may think that the performance of some matter, apparently of essential importance and prima facie a condition precedent, is not really vital, and may be compensated for in damages, and if they sufficiently expressed such an intention, it will not be a condition precedent.

In this case, if to the 7th paragraph of the agreement there had been added words to this effect: "And if Mr. Bettini is not there at the stipulated time, Mr. Gye may refuse to proceed further with the agreement"; or if, on the other hand, it had been said, "And if not there, Mr. Gye may postpone the commencement of Mr. Bettini's engagement for as many days as Mr. Bettini makes default, and he shall forfeit twice his salary for that time," there could have been no question raised in the case. But there is no such declaration of the intention of the parties either way. And in the absence of such an express declaration, we think that we are to look to the whole contract, and applying the rule stated by Parke B. to be acknowledged, see whether the particular stipulation goes to the root of the matter, so that a failure to perform it would render the performance of the rest of the contract by the plaintiff a thing different in substance from what the defendant has stipulated for; or whether it merely partially affects it and may be compensated for in damages. Accordingly as it is one or the other, we think it must be taken to be or not to be intended to be a condition precedent.

If the plaintiff's engagement had been only to sing in operas at the theatre, it might very well be that previous attendance at rehearsals with the actors in company with whom he was to perform was essential. And if the engagement had been only for a few performances, or for a short time, it would afford a strong argument that attendance for the purpose of rehearsals during the six days immediately before the commencement of the engagement was a vital part of the agreement. But we find, on looking to the agreement, that the plaintiff was to sing in theatres, halls, and drawing rooms, both public and private, from the 30th of March to the 13th of July, 1875, and that he was to sing in concerts as well as in operas, and was not to sing anywhere out of the theatre in Great Britain or Ireland from the 1st of January to the 31st of December, 1875, without the written permission of the defendant, except at a distance of more than fifty miles from London.

The plaintiff, therefore, has, in consequence of this agreement, been deprived of the power of earning anything in London from the 1st of January to the 30th of March; and though the defendant has, perhaps, not received any benefit from this, so as to preclude him from any longer treating as a condition precedent what had originally been one, we think this at least affords a strong argument for saying that subsequent stipulations are not intended to be conditions precedent, unless the nature of the thing strongly shows they must be so.

And, as far as we can see, the failure to attend at rehearsals during the six days immediately before the 30th of March could only affect the theatrical performances and, perhaps, the singing in duets or concerted pieces during the first week or fortnight of this engagement, which is to sing in theatres, halls, and drawing-rooms, and concerts, for fifteen weeks.

We think, therefore, that it does not go to the root of the matter so as to require us to consider it a condition precedent.

The defendant must, therefore, we think, seek redress by a cross-claim for damages.

Judgment must be given for the plaintiff.

QUESTIONS. Is this decision consistent with *Kingston* v. *Preston*, above? If the defendant cross-claimed for damages, as suggested, would the plaintiff have any defence in the fact that his absence was caused by illness? See *Poussard* v. *Spiers and Pond*. If the plaintiff's absence had been caused by some capricious delay on his part, would it have affected the decision in the case?

POUSSARD v. SPIERS and POND
England. Queen's Bench Division. 1876. 1 Q.B.D. 410

BLACKBURN J.: This was an action for the dismissal of the plaintiff's wife from a theatrical engagement. On the trial before my brother Field it appeared that the defendants, Messrs. Spiers & Pond, had taken the Criterion Theatre, and were about to bring out a French opera, which was to be produced simultaneously in London and Paris. Their manager, Mr. Hingston, by their authority, made a contract with the plaintiff's wife, which was reduced to writing in the following letter:

Criterion Theatre, Oct. 16th, 1874.

To Madame Poussard.

On behalf of Messrs. Spiers & Pond I engage you to sing and play at the Criterion Theatre on the following terms:

You to play the part of Friquette in Lecocq's opera Les Pres Saint Gervais, commencing on or about the 14th of November next, at a weekly salary of eleven pounds (£11) and to continue on at that sum for a period of three months, providing the opera shall run for that period. Then, at the expiration of the said three months, I shall be at liberty to re-engage you at my option, on terms then to be arranged, and not to exceed fourteen pounds per week for another period of three months. Dresses and tights requisite for the part to be provided by the management, and the engagement to be subject to the ordinary rules and regulations of the theatre.

E. P. Hingston, Manager.

Ratified:

Spiers & Pond

Madame Poussard, 46 Gunter Grove, Chelsea.

The first performance of the piece was announced for Saturday, the 28th of November. No objection was raised on either side as to this delay, and Madame Poussard attended rehearsals, and such attendance, though not expressed in the written engagement, was an implied part of it. Owing to delays on the part of the composer, the music of the latter part of the piece was not in the hands of the defendants till a few days before that announced for the production of the piece, and the latter and final rehearsals did not take place till the week on the Saturday of which the performance was announced. Madame Poussard was unfortunately taken ill, and though she struggled to attend the rehearsals, she was obliged on Monday, the 23rd of November, to leave the rehearsal, go home and go to bed, and call in medical attendance. In the course of the next day or two an interview took place between the plaintiff and Mr. Leonard (Madame Poussard's medical attendant) and Mrs. Liston, who was the defendant's stage manager, in reference to Madame Poussard's ability to attend and undertake her part, and there was a conflict of testimony as to what took place. According to the defendant's version, Mrs. Liston requested to know as soon as possible what was the prospect of Madame Poussard's recovery, as it would be very difficult on such short notice to obtain a substitute; and that in the result the plaintiff wrote stating that his wife's health was such that she could not play on the Saturday night, and that Mrs. Liston had better, therefore engage a young lady to play the part; and this, if believed to be accurate, amounted to a rescission of the contract. According to the evidence of the plaintiff and the doctor, Mrs. Liston told them that Madame Poussard was to take care of herself and not come out till quite well, as she, Mrs. Liston, had procured, or would procure, a temporary substitute; and Madame Poussard could resume her place as soon as she was well. This, it was contended by the plaintiff, amounted to a waiver by the defendants of a breach of the condition precedent, if there was one.

The jury found that the plaintiff did not rescind the contract, and that Mrs. Liston, if she did waive the condition precedent (as to which they were not agreed), had no authority from the defendants so to do.

These findings, if they stand, dispose of those two questions.

There was no substantial conflict as to what was in fact done by Mrs. Liston. Upon learning, on the Wednesday (the 25th of November), the possibility that Madame Poussard might be prevented by illness from fulfilling her engagement, she sent to a theatrical agent to inquire what artistes of position were disengaged, and learning that Miss Lewis had no engagement till the 25th of December, she made a provisional arrangement with her, by which Miss Lewis undertook to study the part and be ready on Saturday to take the part, in case Madame Poussard was not then recovered so far as to be ready to perform. If it should turn out that this labour was thrown away, Miss Lewis was to have a douceur for her trouble. If Miss Lewis was called on to perform, she was to be engaged at £15 a week up to the 25th of December, if the piece ran so long. Madame Poussard continued in bed and ill, and unable to attend either the subsequent rehearsals or the first night of the performance on the Saturday, and Miss Lewis's engagement became absolute, and she performed the part on Saturday, Monday, Tuesday, Wednesday, and up to the close of her engagement, the 25th of December. The piece proved a success, and in fact ran for more than three months.

On Thursday, the 4th of December, Madame Poussard, having recovered, offered to take her place, but was refused, and for this refusal the action was brought.

On the 21st of January Madame Poussard left England.

My brother Field, at the trial, expressed his opinion that the failure of Madame Poussard to be ready to perform, under the circumstances, went so much to the root of the consideration as to discharge the defendants, and that he should therefore enter judgment for the defendants; but he asked the jury five questions.

The first three related to the supposed rescission and waiver. The other questions were in writing and were: 4. Whether the non-attendance on the night of the opening was of such material consequence to the defendants as to entitle them to rescind the contract? To which the jury said, "No." And, 5. Was it of such consequence as to render reasonable for the defendants to employ another artiste, and whether the engagement of Miss Lewis, as made, was reasonable? To which the jury said, "Yes." Lastly, he left the question of damages, which the jury assessed at £83.

On these answers he reserved leave to the plaintiff to move to enter judgment for £83.

A cross rule was obtained on the ground that the verdict was against evidence and that the damages were excessive.

We think that, from the nature of the engagement to take a leading, and, indeed, the principal, female part (for the prima donna sang her part in male costume as the Prince de Conti) in a new opera which (as appears from the terms of the engagement) it was known might run for a longer or shorter time, and so be a profitable or losing concern to the defendants, we can, without the aid of the jury, see that it must have been of great importance to the defendants that the piece should start well, and consequently that the failure of the plaintiff's wife to be able to perform on the opening and early performances was a very serious detriment to them.

This inability having been occasioned by sickness was not any breach of contract by the plaintiff, and no action can lie against him for the failure thus occasioned. But the damage to the defendants and the consequent failure of consideration is just as great as if it had been occasioned by the plaintiff's fault, instead of by his wife's misfortune. The analogy is complete between this case and that of a charter-party in the ordinary terms, where the ship is to proceed in ballast (the act of God, &c., excepted) to a port, and there load a cargo. If the delay is occasioned by excepted perils, the ship owner is excused. But if it is so great as to go to the root of the matter, it frees the charterer from his obligation to furnish a cargo; see per Bramwell B., delivering the judgment of the majority of the Court of Exchequer Chamber in *Jackson* v. *Union Marine Insurance Co.* (1874), L.R. 10 C.P. 125 at p. 141.

And we think that the question, whether the failure of a skilled and capable artiste to perform in a new piece through serious illness is so important as to go to the root of the consideration, must to some extent depend on the evidence; and is a mixed question of law and fact. Theoretically, the facts should be left to and found separately by the jury, it being for the judge or the Court to say whether they, being so found, show a breach of a condition precedent or not. But this course is often (if not generally) impracticable; and if we can see that the proper facts have been found, we should act on these without regard to the form of the questions.

Now, in the present case, we must consider what were the courses open to the defendants under the circumstances. They might, it was said on the argument before us (though not on the trial), have postponed the bringing out of the piece till the recovery of Madame Poussard, and if her illness had been a temporary hoarseness incapacitating her from singing on the Saturday, but sure to be removed by the Monday, that might have been a proper course to pursue. But the illness here was a serious one, of uncertain duration, and if the plaintiff had at the trial suggested that this was the proper course, it would, no doubt, have been shown that it would have been a ruinous course; and that it would have been much better to have abandoned the piece altogether than to have postponed it from day to day for an uncertain time, during which the theatre would have been a heavy loss.

The remaining alternatives were to employ a temporary substitute until such time as the plaintiff's wife should recover; and if a temporary substitute capable of performing the part adequately could have been obtained upon such a precarious engagement on any reasonable terms, that would have been a right course to pursue; but if no substitute capable of performing the part adequately could be obtained, except on the terms that she should be permanently engaged at higher pay than the plaintiff's wife, in our opinion it follows, as a matter of law, that the failure on the plaintiff's part went to the root of the matter and discharged the defendants.

We think, therefore, that the fifth question put to the jury, and answered by them in favour of the defendants, does find all the facts necessary to enable us to decide as a matter of law that the defendants are discharged.

The fourth question is, no doubt, found by the jury for the plaintiff; but

698 MILNER'S CASES AND MATERIALS ON CONTRACTS

we think in finding it they must have made a mistake in law as to what was a sufficient failure of consideration to set the defendants at liberty, which was not a question for them.

This view taken by us renders it unnecessary to decide anything on the cross-rule for a new trial.

The motion must be refused with costs.

QUESTIONS. Was illness a material factor in this case? Why can no action lie against M. Poussard for the failure occasioned by Madame Poussard's illness? Is there not a breach of the promise to sing? What terms must the court imply in this contract in order that Madame Poussard be excused? What reason in policy is there for such implied terms?

ROBINSON v. DAVISON
England. Exchequer. 1871. 40 L.J. Exch. 172

In December, 1869, the plaintiff, a professor of music, agreed with the defendant's wife (a pianist of great renown in her profession under the name of Arabella Goddard), that for a certain fee she should provide a vocalist and a pianoforte, and herself play on the pianoforte, at a concert to be given by the plaintiff at Brigg on the evening of the 14th of January, 1870. In pursuance of this agreement the plaintiff incurred expenses in preparing for the concert. About 9 a.m. on the 14th of Jan., the plaintiff received at Brigg a letter from the defendant's wife, posted in London on the afternoon of the 13th, in which she told him that a sudden attack of illness would prevent her from fulfilling her engagement on the 14th, and enclosed her doctor's certificate to that effect. The plaintiff therefore incurred further expenses in despatching mounted messengers to warn people not to come, and taking other steps to put off the concert. It was proved that the illness was such as to make it dangerous to life for the defendant's wife to go to Brigg or attempt to play, and that she knew this about midday on the 13th. The plaintiff's counsel admitted, both at nisi prius and on this argument, that if any illness could excuse non-performance of the contract, the illness of the defendant's wife was sufficient to do so, but denied that anything short of death could do so. . . .

At the trial Brett J. ruled that it was an implied term of the contract that if the defendant's wife was so ill as to make it unreasonable to expect her to go to Brigg and play, she would be excused, and the defendant would not be liable.

[Plaintiff's counsel obtained a rule nisi for a new trial.]

KELLY C.B.: This is a contract not merely for personal service, but for a service which can be performed by one person only, and the question is whether illness, which prevents that person from performing the contract, is a lawful and sufficient excuse? I think it is. In *Hall* v. *Wright* (1859), 120 E.R. 695 Pollock C.B. laid down the law very clearly, and though he was in the minority there, yet very correctly as I think. "Now it must be conceded on all hands that there are contracts to which the law implies exceptions and conditions which are not expressed. All the contracts for personal services which can be performed only during the lifetime of the party contracting are subject to the implied condition that he shall be alive to perform them; and should he die, his executor is not liable to an action for the breach of contract occasioned by his death. So, a contract by an author to write a book within a reasonable time, or by a painter to paint a picture within a reasonable time, would, in my judgment, be deemed subject to the condition that, if the author became insane or the painter paralytic, and so incapable of performing the contract by the act of God, he would not be liable personally in damages, any more than his executors would be if he had been prevented by death."

If so, that law is applicable to this case. This is a contract—not indeed by an artist to paint—but by an artist of another description, to play the piano at a certain time and place. Now, the principle laid down in *Taylor v. Caldwell* (1863), 122 E.R. 309, *Boast v. Firth* (1868), L.R. 4 C.P. 1, and the other cases referred to is the same, namely, that where the service is of this kind—personal to the contracting party—paralysis or blindness or any disability or incapacity, whatever be its nature, which arises from the act of God and falls on the contracting party, excuses him from the performance of his contract. . . .

[Kelly C.B. than discussed *Taylor v. Caldwell*, which he was prepared to regard as a direct authority.]

BRAMWELL B.: . . . The main question is this: It being admitted that the lady was not fit to perform her contract, and that it was dangerous for her either to go down to the place or to play, and that if there she was not well enough to play efficiently—is it not—I do not say an implied condition —but is it not a part of the bargain between the parties, as much so as if stated in black and white, that under these circumstances she shall be excused? Nay, further, that she shall not be at liberty to play? Because this tells both ways. If she had gone down, being unable to play efficiently, and had insisted on playing and receiving the fee, the plaintiff would have had a right to say and with reason, "No, you shan't play, and I shan't pay you."

But it is said that this is engrafting a condition on an express contract. That was the fallacy in some Judges among the majority in *Hall v. Wright* first to suppose the contract and then say "You must not imply a condition that is not properly in it," the whole question being what was the contract? I retain the opinion I expressed there in unabated strength, and I think the reasons of that opinion are applicable here. That opinion is that where the contract is for personal services, which you cannot do by deputy, and which your executors cannot do for you if you die, and you are without intentional default incapacitated either in body or mind from performance, then you are excused by virtue of the original terms of the bargain.

Of course if any one chooses to say in black and white, "I agree to play absolutely, on such a day, and not to die in the meantime, or if I die or fall ill, to pay damages," that is a possible contract, and if so drawn out would be—play or pay. But what is the contract? Perhaps only one hundredth part of the things in the mind of the parties is expressed. But are we not to suppose there were many other things left unexpressed, which they would have a right to insist on? To suppose that the parties made such a contract as that the lady was to play in any event, and whether able to do so with safety or not, is utterly irrational, and unless there were much more cogent evidence of it, I think they did not make such a contract. . . .

CLEASBY B.: . . . This is a contract to perform as a pianist, and one which requires the exercise of the highest faculties of the art, the greatest skill and the most exquisite taste, and if not well done it is not done at all. It is, moreover, to be done by one person only. The contract is based on the assumption which both parties make of the continuance of life, and sufficient health to perform the contract. Both parties make the assumption; both are equally guilty of the imprudence and folly, if there be any, of making such a contract; and not one more than the other. This is the foundation of the contract; if the foundation fails, everything fails. As soon as the act of God has caused· an incapacity to do the thing contracted for, the whole falls to the ground.

This is very well expressed in *Boast* v. *Firth,* which was a case of service as an apprentice, and therefore most like this. Brett J. there said: "It has been argued with much force that the covenant is absolute and unconditional, and therefore that, though the apprentice was prevented by the act of God from performing the stipulated services, still the defendant is bound to pay damages. If the first proposition could be sustained, the second, I apprehend, would follow. But the first is denied on the part of the defendant. It is said that where the contract is for personal services, and both parties must have known and contemplated, at the time of entering into it, that the performance of the services was dependent on the servant's continuing in a condition of health to make it possible for him to render them, and a disability arises from the act of God, the non-performance of the contract is excused; and that this is a contract of that nature. I agree with both these propositions." The contract here is of that nature.

[Rule discharged.]

NOTE. The death of an employer is usually held to terminate the liability to employ on the same grounds, *Farrow* v. *Wilson* (1869), L.R. 4 C.P. 744, but this is not necessarily so, if the contract did not call for the personal co-operation of the deceased. *Phillips* v. *Alhambra Palace Co.,* [1901] 1 K.B. 59.

CUTTER v. POWELL
England. King's Bench. 1795. 6 T.R. 320; 101 E.R. 573

To assumpsit for work and labour done by the intestate Cutter, the defendant pleaded the general issue. And at the trial at Lancaster the jury found a verdict for the plaintiff for £31 10s. subject to the opinion of this court on the following case.

The defendant being at Jamaica subscribed and delivered to T. Cutter the intestate a note, whereof the following is a copy: "Ten days after the ship Governor Parry, myself master, arrives at Liverpool, I promise to pay to Mr. T. Cutter the sum of thirty guineas, provided he proceeds, continues and does his duty as second mate in the said ship from hence to the port of Liverpool. Kingston, July 31st, 1793." The ship Governor Parry sailed from Kingston on the 2nd of August, 1793, and arrived in the port of Liverpool on the 9th of October following. T. Cutter went on board the ship on the 31st of July, 1793, and sailed in her on the 2nd day of August, and proceeded, continued and did his duty as second mate in her from Kingston until his death, which happened on the 20th of September following, and before the ship's arrival in the port of Liverpool. The usual wages of a second mate of a ship on such a voyage, when shipped by the month out and home is four pounds per month; but when seamen are shipped by the run from Jamaica to England, a gross sum is usually given. The usual length of a voyage from Jamaica to Liverpool is about eight weeks.

ASHURST J.: We cannot collect that there is any custom prevailing among merchants on these contracts; and therefore we have nothing to guide us but the terms of the contract itself. This is a written contract, and it speaks for itself. And as it is entire, and as the defendant's promise depends on a condition precedent to be performed by the other party, the condition must be performed before the other party is entitled to receive anything under it. It has been argued however that the plaintiff may now recover on a quantum meruit: but she has no right to desert the agreement; for wherever there is an express contract the parties must be guided by it; and one party cannot relinquish or abide by it as it may suit his advantage. Here the intestate was by the terms of his contract to perform a given duty before he could call upon the defendant to pay him anything; it was a condition precedent, without performing which the defendant is not liable. And that seems to me to conclude the question: the intestate did not perform the contract on his part; he was not indeed to blame for not doing it; but still as this was a condition precedent, and as he did not perform it, his representative is not entitled to recover.

Postea to the defendant: Unless some other information relative to the usage in cases of this kind should be laid before the Court before the end of this term: but the case was not mentioned again.

[The opinions of Lord Kenyon C.J. and Grose and Lawrence JJ. are omitted.]

NOTE. The rights of seamen in circumstances like those in *Cutter* v. *Powell* are now governed by the *Canada Shipping Act*, R.S.C., 1970, c. S-9. See especially ss. 197-206.

STUBBS v. *HOLYWELL RAILWAY COMPANY*. 1867. L.R. 2 Ex. 311 (England. Exchequer). Stubbs was appointed consulting engineer to the defendants, to complete the construction of certain works. The work was to be completed in fifteen months from Dec. 5th, and Stubbs was to be paid £500 as his salary, in five equal quarterly instalments. Stubbs worked one quarter and was paid in March £100. He worked for two more quarters, and part of the fourth quarter when he died. His administrator sued for £200. MARTIN B.: "Suppose a man enters into a contract to do a certain piece of work for a certain sum, then if he die before he completes it, he can recover nothing, not even if before his death he had done nine-tenths of it. For the contract was for the whole work, and not for nine-tenths of it. But suppose that the contract is for performance of a certain piece of work for a certain sum, to be paid at the rate, say of £50 a month, then the person employed earns £50 at the end of each successive month. It is true that if, after doing a portion of the work, he refused to do the rest, he might not be able to recover, because he could not prove that he was ready and willing to perform his part of the contract. But such a case as the present has no analogy with that of a refusal by the person employed to continue performance. The contract, no doubt, is ended by the death of Stubbs, but only in this sense, that the act of God has made further performance impossible. . . . No vested right of action is taken away by death. The contract is at an end, but it is not rescinded, for rescission is the act of two parties, not of one."

THE APPORTIONMENT ACT
Ontario. Revised Statutes. 1970. Chapter 23

3. All rents, annuities, dividends, and other periodical payments in the

nature of income, whether reserved or made payable under an instrument in writing or otherwise, shall, like interest on money lent, be considered as accruing from day to day, and are apportionable in respect of time accordingly.

CHAPTER 10

MISTAKE

1. MISREPRESENTATIONS

Commonly, statements are made that induce the making of a contract. When such statements turn out to be false, the courts have had considerable difficulty in determining whether or not relief should be given, and, if so, to what extent. The House of Lords held in 1889 (*Derry* v. *Peek*, 14 App. Cas. 337) that no action for the tort of deceit would lie unless the statement complained of was made recklessly or with actual knowledge of its falsity. The classification of a representation as a term of the contract was one route to relief. The first cases below are concerned with this classification.

In 1964, the House of Lords held that an action will lie for damages caused by a negligent statement (*Hedley Byrne* v. *Heller* [1964] A.C. 465), thereby opening another possible route to relief. Further, the Courts of Equity before the Judicature Act granted relief for misrepresentation in the form of rescission (but not damages.) See *Redgrave* v. *Hurd* and the cases following it, below.

HEILBUT, SYMONS & CO. v. *BUCKLETON*
England. House of Lords. [1913] A.C. 30

LORD MOULTON: My Lords, in this action the plaintiff sought relief in damages against the defendants in respect of two contracts whereby the defendants undertook to procure for the plaintiff, and the plaintiff undertook to accept, the allotment of 5000 and 1000 shares in a company called the Filisola Rubber and Produce Estates, Limited. The claim for such relief was mainly based on the allegation that the plaintiff had been induced to enter into these contracts by the false and fraudulent representation of the defendants that the said company was a rubber company. This was the sole ground for relief which was put forward by the plaintiff in the proceedings before action and in the indorsement on the writ; but in the statement of claim an alternative claim for damages was included, based on the breach of an alleged warranty given by the defendants that the company was a rubber company.

At the trial the substantial case which was sought to be made on behalf of the plaintiff had reference solely to the alleged false and fraudulent representation. Evidence was given by the plaintiff and not challenged by the defendants, as to a conversation which took place over the telephone between the plaintiff and Mr. Johnston, a representative of the defendants, in which undoubtedly Mr. Johnston stated that the company was a rubber company. The making of the alleged representation was therefore not in issue, and the whole of the evidence on both sides was directed to the issue whether such representation was false, and whether, if so, it was fraudulently made. No evidence was given upon the issue of a warranty having been given by the defendants that the company was a rubber company other than so far as the proof of the conversation above referred to may have amounted to such evidence.

In answer to questions put to them by the judge, the jury found (1) that the company could not properly be described as a rubber company; (2)

that the defendants did not fraudulently represent, but that (3) they did warrant that it was a rubber company. Against the second of these findings there is no appeal, so that the only questions before us are as to whether the first and third of these findings can stand.

The alleged warranty rested entirely upon the following evidence. The plaintiff got a friend to ring up on the telephone Mr. Johnston (a representative of the defendants, for whose acts they accepted the full responsibility) to tell him that the plaintiff wished to speak to him. The plaintiff's evidence continues thus: "I went to the telephone and I said 'Is that you, Johnston?' He said, 'Yes.' I said 'I understand that you are bringing out a rubber company' and he said 'We are.' "

The material part of the evidence ends here. The further conversation related to the soundness of the company, but no claim for relief is based on what then passed either by way of fraudulent representation or warranty.

The plaintiff then asked if he could have some shares. Mr. Johnston said he thought he could let him have 5000 at a premium of 1s. 3d., which the plaintiff expressed himself ready to take, but no bargain was then concluded. On the next day, however, Mr. Johnston accepted in writing the offer of the plaintiff as to taking 5000 shares. Later on the plaintiff applied to Mr. Johnston for a further 1000 shares and obtained them at a somewhat higher premium. In each case the terms of the contract were reduced to writing by Mr. Johnston, acting for the defendants, and sent to the plaintiff. The contracts were not contracts of sale of the shares of the company (which had not then been issued), but contracts whereby the defendants (who were underwriters of the shares in the forthcoming issue) undertook to procure for the plaintiff the allotment of the shares on his applying for them. There is, of course, no conflict as to the actual terms of these contracts, which appear from the letters. They were acted upon by the plaintiff, who duly applied for and received the allotments of 5000 and 1000 shares of the company, such allotments having been procured by the defendants by the exercise of their rights as underwriters. The plaintiff parted with some of his shares but retained the remainder, and it is in respect of these latter that the damages are claimed in this action. [The trial Judge allowed damages at £406 5s. and the Court of Appeal affirmed the judgment.]

There is no controversy between the parties as to certain points of fact and of law. It is not contested that the only company referred to was the Filisola Rubber and Produce Estates, Limited, or that the reply of Mr. Johnston to the plaintiff's question over the telephone was a representation by the defendants that the company was "a rubber company," whatever may be the meaning of that phrase; nor is there any controversy as to the legal nature of that which the plaintiff must establish. He must shew a warranty, i.e., a contract collateral to the main contract to take the shares, whereby the defendants in consideration of the plaintiff taking the shares promised that the company itself was a rubber company. The question in issue is whether there was any evidence that such a contract was made between the parties.

It is evident, both on principle and on authority, that there may be a contract the consideration for which is the making of some other contract. "If you will make such and such a contract I will give you one hundred pounds," is in every sense of the word a complete legal contract. It is collateral to the main contract, but each has an independent existence, and they do not differ in respect of their possessing to the full the character and status of a contract. But such collateral contracts must from their very nature be rare. The effect of a collateral contract such as that which I have instanced would be to increase the consideration of the main contract by £100, and the more natural and usual way of carrying this out would be by so modifying the main contract and not by executing a concurrent and collateral contract. Such collateral contracts, the sole effect of which is to vary or add to the terms of the principal contract, are therefore viewed with suspicion by the law. They must be proved strictly. Not only the terms of such contracts but the existence of an *animus contrahendi* on the part of all the parties to them must be clearly shewn. Any laxity on these points would enable parties to escape from the full performance of the obligations of contracts unquestionably entered into by them, and more especially would have the effect of lessening the authority of written contracts by making it possible to vary them by suggesting the existence of verbal agreements relating to the same subject-matter.

There is in the present case an entire absence of any evidence to support the existence of such a collateral contract. The statement of Mr. Johnston in answer to plaintiff's question was beyond controversy a mere statement of fact, for it was in reply to a question for information and nothing more. No doubt it was a representation as to fact, and indeed it was the actual representation upon which the main case of the plaintiff rested. It was this representation which he alleged to have been false and fraudulent and which he alleged induced him to enter into the contracts and take the shares. There is no suggestion throughout the whole of his evidence that he regarded it as anything but a representation. Neither the plaintiff nor the defendants were asked any question or gave any evidence tending to shew the existence of any *animus contrahendi* other than as regards the main contracts. The whole case for the existence of a collateral contract therefore rests on the mere fact that the statement was made as to the character of the company, and if this is to be treated as evidence sufficient to establish the existence of a collateral contract of the kind alleged the same result must follow with regard to any other statement relating to the subject-matter of a contract made by a contracting party prior to its execution. This would negative entirely the firmly established rule that an innocent representation gives no right to damages. It would amount to saying that the making of any representation prior to a contract relating to its subject-matter is sufficient to establish the existence of a collateral contract that the statement is true and therefore to give a right to damages if such should not be the case.

In the history of English law we find many attempts to make persons responsible in damages by reason of innocent misrepresentation, and at times it has seemed as though the attempts would succeed. On the Chancery side of the Court the decisions favouring this view usually took the form of extending the scope of the action for deceit. There was a tendency to recognize the existence of what was sometimes called "legal fraud," i.e., that the making of an incorrect statement of fact without reasonable grounds, or of one which was inconsistent with information which the person had received or had the means of obtaining, entailed the same legal consequences as making it fraudulently. Such a doctrine would make a man liable for forgetfulness or mistake or even for honestly interpreting the facts known to him or drawing conclusions from them in a way which the Court did not think to be legally warranted. The high water mark of these decisions is to be found in the judgment by the Court of Appeal in the case of *Peek* v. *Derry* (1887), 37 Ch. D. 541, when they laid down that where a defendant has made a mis-statement of fact and the Court is of opinion that he had no reasonable grounds for believing that it was true he may be made liable in an action of deceit if it has materially tended to induce the plaintiff to do an act by which he has incurred damage. But on appeal to your Lordships' House this decision was unanimously reversed, and it was definitely laid down that, in order to establish a cause of action sounding in damages for misrepresentation, the statement must be fraudulent or, what is equivalent thereto, must be made recklessly, not caring whether it be true or not. The opinions pronounced in your Lordships' House in that case shew that both in substance and in form the decision was, and was intended to be, a reaffirmation of the old common law doctrine that actual fraud was essential to an action for deceit, and it finally settled the law that an innocent misrepresentation gives no right of action sounding in damages.

On the Common Law side of the Court the attempts to make a person liable for an innocent misrepresentation have usually taken the form of attempts to extend the doctrine of warranty beyond its just limits and to find that a warranty existed in cases where there was nothing more than an innocent misrepresentation. The present case is, in my opinion, an instance of this. But in respect of the question of the existence of a warranty the Courts have had the advantage of an admirable enunciation of the true principle of law which was made in very early days by Holt C.J. with respect to the contract of sale. He says [*c.* 1690]: "An affirmation at the time of the sale is a warranty, provided it appear on evidence to be so intended." So far as decisions are concerned, this has, on the whole, been consistently followed in the Courts of Common Law. But from time to time there have been dicta inconsistent with it which have, unfortunately, found their way into textbooks and have given rise to confusion and uncertainty in this branch of the law. For example, one often sees quoted the dictum of Bayley J. in *Cave* v. *Coleman* 3 Man. & Ry. 2, where, in respect of a representation made verbally during the sale of a horse, he says that "being made in the course of dealing, and before the bargain was complete, it amounted to a warranty"—a proposition that is far too sweeping and cannot be supported. A still more serious deviation from the correct principle is to be found in a passage in the judgment of the Court of Appeal in *De Lassalle* v. *Guildford*, [1901] 2 K.B. 215, at p. 221, which was cited to us in the argument in the present case. In discussing the question whether a representation amounts to a warranty or not the judgment says: "In determining whether it was so intended, a decisive test is whether the vendor assumes to assert a fact of which the buyer is ignorant, or merely states an opinion or judgment upon a matter of which the vendor has no special knowledge, and on which the buyer may be expected also to have an opinion and to exercise his judgment."

With all deference to the authority of the Court that decided that case, the proposition which it thus formulates cannot be supported. It is clear that the Court did not intend to depart from the law laid down by Holt C.J. and cited above, for in the same judgment that dictum is referred to and accepted as a correct statement of the law. It is, therefore, evident that the use of the phrase "decisive test" cannot be defended. Otherwise it would be the duty of a judge to direct a jury that if a vendor states a fact of which the buyer is ignorant, they must, as a matter of law, find the existence of a warranty, whether or not the totality of the evidence shows that the parties intended the affirmation to form part of the contract; and this would be inconsistent with the law as laid down by Holt C.J. It may well be that the features thus referred to in the judgment of the Court of Appeal in that case may be criteria of value in guiding a jury in coming to a decision whether or not a warranty was intended; but they cannot be said to furnish decisive tests, because it cannot be said as a matter of law that the presence or absence of those features is conclusive of the intention of the parties. The intention of the parties can only be deduced from the totality of the evidence, and no secondary principle of such a kind can be universally true.

It is, my Lords, of the greatest importance, in my opinion, that this House should maintain in its full integrity the principle that a person is not liable in damages for an innocent misrepresentation, no matter in what way or under what form the attack is made. In the present case the statement was made in answer to an inquiry for information. There is nothing which can by any possibility be taken as evidence of an intention on the part of either or both of the parties that there should be a contractual liability in respect of the statement. It is a representation as to a specific thing and nothing more. The judge, therefore, ought not to have left the question of warranty to the jury, and if, as a matter of prudence, he did so in order to obtain their opinion in case of appeal, he ought then to have entered judgment for the defendants notwithstanding the verdict.

It will, of course, be evident that I have been dealing only with warranty or representation relating to a specific thing. This is wholly distinct from the question which arises when goods are sold by description and their answering to that description becomes a condition of the contract. It is, in my opinion, a failure to recognize that in the present case the parties were referring (as is evident by the written contracts) to one specific thing only that led Farwell L.J. to come to a different conclusion from that to which your Lordships ought, in my opinion, to come in this appeal.

[Order of the Court of Appeal reversed and judgment entered for the appellants. Viscount Haldane L.C. and Lord Atkinson also gave reasons for allowing the appeal.]

QUESTIONS. If the defendant had sold his own shares to the plaintiff under the circumstances set out in the principal case, could the plaintiff have claimed "rescission" of the contract? If the representation had been held to be a "term" of the contract, would your answer differ?

NOTE. Heilbut, Symonds v. *Buckleton* was severely criticised by the American scholar, Williston, in *Representation and Warranty in Sales* (1914) 27 Harv. L.R. 1. Williston's view was that a misrepresentation inducing a sale ought always to give the deceived buyer a remedy, even though the representation was innocent, and no intention to contract could be spelled out. Williston was the draftsman of the Uniform Sales Act, and so it is not surprising to find that the definition of warranty in that Act includes: "Any affirmation of fact or any promise by the seller relating to the goods ... if the natural tendency of such affirmation or promise is to induce the buyer to purchase the goods, and if the buyer purchases the goods relying thereon." The Uniform Sales Act is now superseded by the Uniform Commercial Code. Section 2-313 of the Code provides:

"(1) Express warranties by the seller are created as follows:

(a) Any affirmation of fact or promise made by the seller to the buyer which relates to the goods and becomes part of the basis of the bargain creates an express warranty that the goods shall conform to the affirmation or promise. . . .

(2) It is not necessary to the creation of an express warranty that the seller use formal words such as 'warrant' or 'guarantee' or that he have a specific intention to make a warranty, but an affirmation merely of the value of the goods or a statement purporting to be merely the seller's opinion or commendation of the goods does not create a warranty."

SCHAWEL v. READE
[1913] 2 I.R. 81 (H.L.)

LORD MACNAGHTEN: My Lords—This case has been a rather prolonged one, but I think it lies within a very narrow compass. The question relates to the soundness of a horse. An Austrian gentleman, of some position, was buying horses for the Austrian Government. He bought a horse from Mr. Reade. The horse was not fit for the purposes for which he bought it. His allegation was that he had a warranty, either express or implied. He desired to return the horse to Mr. Reade. Mr. Reade would not have it back; it was put up for sale, and sold for a small price, and he brought this action and recovered as damages the price which he paid for the horse.

My Lords, the question really is, was there a warranty either express or implied? I leave out the question of fraud, because it has been dealt with, and disposed of. Now, what Mr. Schawel says himself is this. He is asked to tell the jury:—"What happened when you were at the defendant's place on the afternoon of March 22nd?" (A.) "The horses were pulled out; I think there were four. Two were sent away at once, for I did not care for them. We looked at the remaining two, 'Mallow Man' and a chestnut horse. A little later I said I did not want the chestnut. The chestnut was sent away and 'Mallow Man' was left there alone." (Q.) "Tell the jury what you said to the defendant, and what the defendant said to you." (A.) "When this horse stood there, I walked up to him, and looked at him. Mr. Reade said, 'You need not look for anything; the horse is perfectly sound. If there was anything the matter with the horse, I should tell you.' That was all." My Lords, I must say, speaking for myself, that is about as plain a warranty of the soundness of the horse as could be given.

Then, my Lords, after three days' trial, the jury evidently being very much in favour of the plaintiff, and not altogether believing the defendant, the summing up was very short. The Lord Chief Justice seems to have been desirous in the first instance to clear away the question of fraud, in order that no implication of fraud might rest upon Mr. Reade: possibly he had forgotten what he had said, and he was not intentionally telling stories. There was some question as regards the form of the question to be left to the jury, and, although it does not so appear from the shorthand notes submitted to the House, it seems to be admitted that the ultimate form of the question that was to be left to the jury was settled before the Lord Chief Justice's charge. The Lord Chief Justice says that he would deal with the question very shortly, and he disposes of the question of fraud—at least he says he should hesitate before he charged fraud against the defendant, and he adds: "That is no direction in point of law; it is merely an observation for you to go upon if you wish. I do not force my observations upon you." Then he says: "There are two other questions that will make Mr.

Reade responsible if they are established against him. The first question you have to try is: Did the defendant, at the time of the sale, represent to the plaintiff, in order that the plaintiff might purchase the horse, that the horse was fit for stud purposes? That is plain enough. Did he make any representation to him that the horse was fit for stud purposes, as sound? If you believe Schawel, he did." Then His Lordship goes on a little lower down, "It is really a question of credit." Then again he says: "First look around and see what you think you ought to believe. Mr. Schawel says he walked up to the horse and looked at him, and that Mr. Reade said, 'You need not look for anything; the horse is perfectly sound. If there was anything the matter with the horse, I should tell you.' You heard all that. Did he invent that?" Then he goes on: "This is the question for you—Did the defendant at the time of the sale represent to the plaintiff that the horse was sound? The defendant wanted to sell the horse. Did the plaintiff act on the defendant's representation in the sale of the horse? Did he cease examining the horse? He looked at his height, but he did not examine his eyes. We can all throw our eyes over a horse, but we do not examine him like a vet. It is for you to say whether you will answer that first question, Yes or No. Was the horse fit for stud purposes? You heard all that." I think there is no question about that now.

Then coming to the actual form of the questions, the first question—and this is really the material question—is, "Did the defendant at the time of the sale represent to the plaintiff, in order that the plaintiff might purchase the horse, that the horse was fit for stud purposes, and did the plaintiff act upon that representation in the purchase of the horse?" Now, the word "warranty" does not appear in that question, but that seems to me to contain all the elements of warranty. The real question put to the jury was—and I think that both parties were agreed upon that—Did the defendant warrant the horse or not? Taking what he said there, if the jury believed it, as unquestionably they did—and the Chief Justice said he believed every word that Mr. Schawel said—was that a warranty express or implied? In my opinion, my Lords, it is a clear and express warranty. It was done for the purpose of the sale, and the plaintiff acted upon it; that was put to the jury, and they so found.

I am therefore of opinion that the learned Judges of the Court of Appeal were wrong in reversing the order of the Divisional Court; and I move your Lordships that the appeal should be allowed, and the order of the Divisional Court should be restored with costs.

LORD ATKINSON: My Lords, I concur.

I think it is perfectly clear that of the three questions left to the jury, question No. 1, does not deal with fraud at all. The only other issue in the case was warranty. It would appear to me that the Lord Chief Justice, unfortunately as it now appears, was induced, on the solicitation or on the objection of Mr. Serjeant Moriarty, to change the bare question which he proposed to leave to the jury, namely, Is this a warranty? into the form in which he left it; but what he meant to do was to embody in this question, which he actually left to the jury, the different elements which constitute and create a warranty.

Now, the jury have found that the representation was made, that is, that the defendant said to the plaintiff, "You need not look at the horse; he is perfectly sound. If he was not, I should have told you." They have also found that the plaintiff relied upon that, and ceased his examination;

and they have found that that statement was made for the purpose of the sale. If one takes that last expression, "for the purpose of the sale," and looks back to the summing up of the learned Lord Chief Justice, I think it is perfectly plain that the jury must have understood that that was part of the transaction, and meant to be the basis of the sale. If that was the intention of the man who made the statement, and if the person to whom it was addressed acted upon it, then that constitutes a warranty. A statement is made, it is acted upon, and it is made by the person who makes it for the purpose of the sale, that is, with the intention of bringing about the sale. I do not know what other ingredient is necessary to create a warranty, and, therefore, I think in effect, though not in form, the jury have found that there was a warranty; and that they must have understood the main points in the controversy is evident. The case, to a great degree, I think, if not entirely, went upon the question as to which of the two accounts was true—whether the account of the plaintiff was true, or whether the account of the defendant was true, and it seems to have been conducted really upon the assumption that that question would determine the whole action. I therefore, concur with the opinion that my noble and learned friend has expressed, that the judgment of the Court of Appeal was erroneous; that the judgment of the Divisional Court was right, and that the judgment of the Court of Appeal should be reversed, and that of the Divisional Court restored.

LORD MOULTON: My Lords, I concur.

I am of opinion that, by their answer to the first question, the jury have found an express warranty that the horse was sound. I do not think, nor do I believe, it would be contended that as an abstract question the elements which constitute a warranty are accurately set forth in the form of the first question so as to be applicable to every case. But if you apply the terms of that question to the facts of the present case, it seems to me that the finding is an express and thoroughly justified finding of an express warranty in the most absolute form.

As the noble and learned Lord who has last addressed the House has pointed out, the contest between the parties at the end was practically a contest as to which of two tales should be believed. The plaintiff had given his account of what was said, and the defendant had given his account; and I think there is no doubt whatever that by their verdict the jury showed that they accepted the plaintiff's account. Now, if they did, there was no alternative but they must find that the representation was that which the plaintiff had said it was; and therefore, I read to myself this answer of the jury to the first question in connexion with the actual representation, and I find that they say that the defendant at the time of the sale said to the plaintiff, "You need not look for anything; the horse is perfectly sound. If there was anything the matter with the horse, I should tell you"—that he said that in order that the plaintiff might purchase the horse, and that the plaintiff acted upon that representation, and desisted from his personal examination of that horse. That is what in this case the answer to the question put by the Lord Chief Justice amounts to.

Now, it would be impossible, in my mind, to have a clearer example of an express warranty where the word "warrant" was not used. The essence of such warranty is that it becomes plain by the words, and the action, of the parties that it is intended that in the purchase the responsibility of the soundness shall rest upon the vendor; and how in the world could a vendor more clearly indicate that he is prepared and intends to take upon himself the responsibility of the soundness than by saying, "You need not look at that horse, because it is perfectly sound," and sees that the purchaser thereupon desists from his immediate independent examination?

My Lords, it seems to me, as found by the jury in their answer to the first question, we have clearly and unmistakably all the elements of an express warranty; and on this ground I concur in the motion that is before the House, that the order of the Court of Appeal should be discharged, and the order of the Court below restored.

ESSO PETROLEUM CO. LTD. v. MARDON
[1976] 2 W.L.R. 583 (C.A.)

LORD DENNING M.R.: "This is," said the judge, "a tragic story of wasted endeavour and financial disaster." It is a long story starting as long ago as 1961, and finishing in 1967. Since then eight years have been spent in litigation.

In 1961 Esso Petroleum wanted an outlet for their petrol in Southport. They found a vacant site which was very suitable. It was on Eastbank Street, one of the busiest streets of the town. It had already got outline planning permission for a filling station. Esso thought of putting in a bid for the site. But before doing so, they made calculations to see if it would be a paying proposition. They made a careful forecast of the "estimated annual consumption" of petrol. This was the yardstick by which they measured the worth of a filling station. They called it the "e.a.c." In this case they estimated that the throughput of petrol would reach 200,000 gallons a year by the second year after development. This would accrue to their benefit by sales of petrol. In addition, they would get a substantial rental from a tenant. On May 25, 1961, the Esso local representatives recommended the go ahead. They gave the figures, and said: "We feel most strongly that this does genuinely represent a first-class opportunity of gaining representation in the centre of Southport." On that recommendation Esso bought the site and proceeded to erect a service station.

But then something happened which falsified all their calculations. Esso had thought that they could have the forecourt and pumps fronting on to the busy main street. But the Southport Corporation, who were the planning authority, refused to allow this. They insisted that the station should be built "back to front." So that only the showroom fronted on to the main street. The forecourt and pumps were at the back of the site and only accessible by side streets. They could not be seen from the main street. Esso had no choice but to comply with these planning requirements. They built the station "back to front." It was finished early in 1963.

Now at this point Esso made an error which the judge described as a "fatal error." They did not revise their original estimate which they had made in 1961. They still assessed the e.a.c. (estimated annual consumption) of petrol at 200,000 gallons. Whereas they should have made a reappraisal in the light of the building being now "back to front." This adversely affected the site's potential: because passing traffic could not see the station. It would reduce the throughput greatly. The judge found that this "fatal error" was due to want of care on the part of Esso. There can be no doubt about it.

It was under the influence of this "fatal error" that Esso sought to find a tenant for the service station. They found an excellent man, Mr. Philip Lionel Mardon. He was seen by Esso's local manager, Mr. Leitch. Now Mr. Leitch had had 40 years' experience in the petrol trade. It was on his calculations and recommendations that Esso had bought this site and developed it. At the decisive interview Mr. Leitch was accompanied by the new area manager, Mr. Allen. I will give what took place in the words of the judge:

"Mr. Mardon was told that Esso estimated that the throughput of the Eastbank Street site, in its third year of operation, would amount to 200,000 gallons a year. I also find that Mr. Mardon then indicated that he thought 100,000 to 150,000 gallons would be a more realistic estimate, but he was convinced by the far greater expertise of, particularly, Mr. Leitch. Mr. Allen is a far younger man and, although on his appointment as manager for the area I am satisfied he made his own observations as to the potentiality of the Eastbank Street site, in the result he accepted Mr. Leitch's estimate. Mr. Mardon, having indicated that he thought that a lower figure would be a more realistic estimate, had his doubts quelled by the experience and the estimate furnished by Mr. Leitch, and it was for that reason, I am satisfied, because of what he was told about the estimated throughput in the third year, that he then proceeded to negotiate for and obtain the grant of a three-year tenancy at a rent of £2,500 a year for the first two years, rising to £3,000 yearly in the last year."

To the judge's summary, I would only add a few questions and answers by Mr. Allen in evidence:

"Q. Now we know that the person who originally put forward this estimated 200,000 gallons forecast was Mr. Leitch? A. Yes. Q. Would somebody have checked Mr. Leitch's figures before they reached you? A. Oh, very much so. . . . Q. You have told my Lord that you accept that, at that interview . . . you might have said that Eastbank was capable of achieving a throughput of 200,000 gallons after the second complete year? A. Yes. Q. Would that have been your honest opinion at the time? A. Most certainly."

All the dealings were based on that estimate of a throughput of 200,000 gallons. It was on that estimate that Esso developed the site at a cost of £40,000: and that the tenant agreed to pay a rent of £2,500, rising to £3,000. A few answers by Mr. Allen will show this:

"Q. Would you agree that the potential throughput of a station is an important factor in assessing what rent to charge a tenant? A. Yes. . . . Q. The rent would be substantially higher if your estimate was one of 200,000 gallons than if your estimate was one of 100,000 gallons? A. Generally speaking, that is right. . . . Q. You would be able to command a higher rent if the throughput was 200,000 than if it was 100,000? A. Had it been an estimated throughput of 100,000 gallons, they [Esso] would not have bought it in the first place."

Having induced Mr. Mardon to accept, Mr. Leitch and Mr. Allen sent this telegram to their head office: "We have interviewed a Mr. Philip Lionel Mardon for tenancy and find him excellent in all respects. We recommend strongly that he be granted tenancy." So a tenancy was granted to Mr. Mardon. It was dated April 10, 1963, and was for three years at a rent of £2,500 for the first two years, and £3,000 for the third year. It required him to keep open all day every day of the week, including Sunday. It forbade him to assign or underlet.

On the next day Mr. Mardon went into occupation of the service station and did everything that could be desired of him. He was an extremely good tenant and he tried every method to increase the sales and profitability of the service station. Esso freely acknowledge this.

But the throughput was most disappointing. It never got anywhere near the 200,000 gallons. Mr. Mardon put all his available capital into it. It was over £6,000. He raised an overdraft with the bank and used it in the business. He put all his work and endeavour into it. No one could have done more to make it a success. Yet when the accounts were taken for the first 15 months, the throughput was only 78,000 gallons. After paying all outgoings, such as rent, wages and so forth, there was a net loss of £5,800. The position was so serious that Mr. Mardon felt he could not continue. On July 17, 1964, he wrote to Mr. Allen: "I reluctantly give notice to quit forthwith. This is an endeavour to salvage as much as I can in lieu of inevitable bankruptcy." Mr. Allen did not reply in writing, but saw Mr. Mardon. As a result he put in a written report to his superiors recommending that Mr. Mardon's rent should be reduced to £1,000 a year, plus a surcharge according to the amount of petrol sold. Mr. Allen telexed to his superiors on several occasions pressing for a decision. It culminated in a telex he sent on August 28, 1964: "Unless we hear soon the tenant is likely to resign and we will have difficulty in replacing this man with a tenant of the same high standard." This brought results. On September 1, 1964, a new tenancy agreement was made in writing. It granted Mr. Mardon a tenancy for one year certain and thereafter determinable on three months' notice. The rent was reduced to £1,000 a year, and a surcharge of 1d. to 2d. a gallon, according to the amount sold.

Again Mr. Mardon tried hard to make a success of the service station: but again he failed. It was not his fault. The site was simply not good enough to have a throughput of more than 60,000 or 70,000 gallons. He lost more and more money over it. In order to help him, Esso tried to get another site for him—a "cream" site—so that he could run the two sites in conjunction to offset his losses. But they never found him one. Eventually on January 1, 1966, he wrote to Esso appealing to them to find a solution. He consulted solicitors who wrote on his behalf. But Esso did nothing to help. Quite the contrary. They insisted on the petrol being paid for every day on delivery. On August 28, 1966 (by some mistake or misunderstanding while Mr. Mardon was away), they came and drained his tanks of petrol and cut off his supplies. That put him out of business as a petrol station. He carried on as best he could with odd jobs for customers, like washing cars. Esso had no pity for him. On December 1, 1966, they issued a writ against him claiming possession and £1,133 13s. 9d. for petrol supplied. This defeated him. On March 7, 1967, he gave up the site. He had tried for four years to make a success of it. It was all wasted endeavour. He had lost all his capital and had incurred a large overdraft. It was a financial disaster.

Such being the facts, I turn to consider the law. It is founded on the representation that the estimated throughput of the service station was 200,000 gallons. No claim can be brought under the Misrepresentation Act 1967, because that Act did not come into force until April 22, 1967: whereas the representation was made in April 1963. So the claim is put in two ways. First, that the representation was a collateral warranty.

Second, that it was a negligent misrepresentation. I will take them in order.

Collateral Warranty

Ever since *Heilbut, Symons & Co.* v. *Buckleton* [1913] A.C. 30, we have had to contend with the law as laid down by the House of Lords that an innocent misrepresentation gives no right to damages. In order to escape from that rule, the pleader used to allege—I often did it myself—that the misrepresentation was fraudulent, or alternatively a collateral warranty. At the trial we nearly always succeeded on collateral warranty. We had to reckon, of course, with the dictum of Lord Moulton, at p. 47, that "such collateral contracts must from their very nature be rare." But more often than not the court elevated the innocent misrepresentation into a collateral warranty: and thereby did justice—in advance of the Misrepresentation Act 1967. I remember scores of cases of that kind, especially on the sale of a business. A representation as to the profits that had been made in the past was invariably held to be a warranty. Besides that experience, there have been many cases since I have sat in this court where we have readily held a representation—which induces a person to enter into a contract—to be a warranty sounding in damages. I summarised them in *Dick Bentley Productions Ltd.* v. *Harold Smith (Motors) Ltd.* [1965] 1 W.L.R. 623, 627, when I said:

"Looking at the cases once more, as we have done so often, it seems to me that if a representation is made in the course of dealings for a contract for the very purpose of inducing the other party to act upon it, and actually inducing him to act upon it, by entering into the contract, that is prima facie ground for inferring that it was intended as a warranty. It is not necessary to speak of it as being collateral. Suffice it that it was intended to be acted upon and was in fact acted on."

Mr. Ross-Munro, retaliated, however, by citing *Bisset* v. *Wilkinson* [1927] A.C. 177, where the Privy Council said that a statement by a New Zealand farmer that an area of land "would carry 2,000 sheep" was only an expression of opinion. He submitted that the forecast here of 200,000 gallons was an expression of opinion and not a statement of fact: and that it could not be interpreted as a warranty or promise.

Now I would quite agree with Mr. Ross-Munro that it was not a warranty—in this sense—that it did not *guarantee* that the throughput *would be* 200,000 gallons. But, nevertheless, it was a forecast made by a party—Esso—who had special knowledge and skill. It was the yardstick (the e.a.c.) by which they measured the worth of a filling station. They knew the facts. They knew the traffic in the town. They knew the throughput of comparable stations. They had much experience and expertise at their disposal. They were in a much better position than Mr. Mardon to make a forecast. It seems to me that if such a person makes a forecast, intending that the other should act upon it—and he does act upon it, it can well be interpreted as a warranty that the forecast is sound and reliable in the sense that they made it with reasonable care and skill. It is just as if Esso said to Mr. Mardon: "Our forecast of throughput is 200,000 gallons. You can rely upon it as being a sound forecast of what the service station should do. The rent is calculated on that footing." If the forecast turned out to be an unsound forecast such as no person of skill or experience should have made, there is a breach of warranty. Just as there is a breach of warranty when a forecast is made—"expected to load" by a certain date—if the maker has no reasonable grounds for it: see *Samuel Sanday and Co.* v. *Keighley, Maxted and Co.* (1922) 27 Com.Cas. 296; or bunkers "expected 600/700 tons": see *Efploia Shipping Corporation Ltd.* v. *Canadian Transport Co. Ltd.* (*The Pantanassa*) [1958] 2 Lloyd's Rep. 449, 455-457 by Diplock J. It is very different from the New Zealand case where the land had never been used as a sheep farm and both parties were equally able to form an opinion as to its carrying capacity: see particularly *Bisset* v. *Wilkinson* [1927] A.C. 177, 183-184.

In the present case it seems to me that there was a warranty that the forecast was sound, that is, Esso made it with reasonable care and skill. That warranty was broken. Most negligently Esso made a "fatal error" in the forecast they stated to Mr. Mardon, and on which he took the tenancy. For this they are liable in damages. The judge, however, declined to find a warranty. So I must go further.

Negligent misrepresentation

Assuming that there was no warranty, the question arises whether Esso are liable for negligent misstatement under the doctrine of *Hedley Byrne & Co. Ltd.* v. *Heller & Partners Ltd.* [1964] A.C. 465. It has been suggested that *Hedley Byrne* cannot be used so as to impose liability for negligent pre-contractual statements: and that, in a pre-contract situation, the remedy (at any rate before the Act of 1967) was only in warranty or nothing. Thus in *Hedley Byrne* itself Lord Reid said, at p. 483: "Where there is a contract there is no difficulty as regards the contracting parties: the question is whether there is a warranty." And in *Oleificio Zucchi S.P.A.* v. *Northern Sales Ltd.* [1965] 2 Lloyd's Rep. 496, 519, McNair J. said: ". . . as at present advised, I consider the submission advanced by the buyers, that the ruling in [*Hedley Byrne* [1964] A.C. 465] applies as between contracting parties, is without foundation."

As against these, I took a different view in *McInerny* v. *Lloyds Bank Ltd.* [1974] 1 Lloyd's Rep. 246, 253 when I said: ". . . if one person, by a negligent misstatement, induces another to enter into a contract—with himself or with a third person—he may be liable in damages."

In arguing this point, Mr. Ross-Munro took his stand in this way. He submitted that when the negotiations between two parties resulted in a contract between them, their rights and duties were governed by the law of contract and not by the law of tort. There was, therefore, no place in their relationship for *Hedley Byrne* [1964] A.C. 465, which was solely on liability in tort. He relied particularly on *Clark* v. *Kirby-Smith* [1964] Ch. 506 where Plowman J. held that the liability of a solicitor for negligence was a liability in contract and not in tort, following the observations of Sir Wilfrid Greene M.R. in *Groom* v. *Crocker* [1939] 1 K.B. 194, 206. Mr. Ross-Munro might also have cited *Bagot* v. *Stevens Scanlan & Co. Ltd.* [1966] 1 Q.B. 197, about an architect; and other cases too. But I venture to suggest that those cases are in conflict with other decisions of high authority which were not cited in them. These decisions show that, in the case of a professional man, the duty to use reasonable care arises not only in contract, but is also imposed by the law apart from contract, and is therefore actionable in tort. It is comparable to the duty of reasonable care which is owed by a master to his servant, or vice versa. It can be put either in contract or in tort: see *Lister* v. *Romford Ice and Cold Storage Co. Ltd.* [1957] A.C. 555, 587 by Lord Radcliffe and *Matthews* v. *Kuwait*

Bechtel Corporation [1959] 2 Q.B. 57. The position was stated by Tindal C.J., delivering the judgment of the Court of Exchequer Chamber in *Boorman* v. *Brown* (1842) 3 Q.B. 511, 525-526:

"That there is a large class of cases in which the foundation of the action springs out of privity of contract between the parties, but in which, nevertheless, the remedy for the breach, or non-performance, is indifferently either assumpsit or case upon tort, is not disputed. Such are actions against attorneys, surgeons, and other professional men, for want of competent skill or proper care in the service they undertake to render: ... The principle in all these cases would seem to be that the contract creates a duty, and the neglect to perform that duty, or the nonfeasance, is a ground of action upon a tort."

That decision was affirmed in the House of Lords in (1844) 11 Cl. & Fin. 1, when Lord Campbell, giving the one speech, said, at p. 44: "... wherever there is a contract, and something to be done in the course of the employment which is the subject of that contract, if there is a breach of a duty in the course of that employment, the plaintiff may either recover in tort or in contract."

To this there is to be added the high authority of Viscount Haldane L.C., in *Nocton* v. *Lord Ashburton* [1914] A.C. 932, 956: "... the solicitor contracts with his client to be skilful and careful. For failure to perform his obligation he may be made liable at law in contract or even in tort, for negligence in breach of a duty imposed on him."

That seems to me right. A professional man may give advice under a contract for reward; or without a contract, in pursuance of a voluntary assumption of responsibility, gratuitously without reward. In either case he is under one and the same duty to use reasonable care: see *Cassidy* v. *Ministry of Health* [1951] 2 K.B. 343, 359-360. In the one case it is by reason of a term implied by law. In the other, it is by reason of a duty imposed by law. For a breach of that duty he is liable in damages: and those damages should be, and are, the same, whether he is sued in contract or in tort.

It follows that I cannot accept Mr. Ross-Munro's proposition. It seems to me that *Hedley Byrne & Co. Ltd.* v. *Heller & Partners Ltd.* [1964] A.C. 465, properly understood, covers this particular proposition: if a man, who has or professes to have special knowledge or skill, makes a representation by virtue thereof to another—be it advice, information or opinion—with the intention of inducing him to enter into a contract with him, he is under a duty to use reasonable care to see that the representation is correct, and that the advice, information or opinion is reliable. If he negligently gives unsound advice or misleading information or expresses an erroneous opinion, and thereby induces the other side to enter into a contract with him, he is liable in damages. This proposition is in line with what I said in *Candler* v. *Crane, Christmas & Co.* [1951] 2 K.B. 164, 179-180, which was approved by the majority of the Privy Council in *Mutual Life and Citizens' Assurance Co. Ltd.* v. *Evatt* [1971] A.C. 793. And the judges of the Commonwealth have shown themselves quite ready to apply *Hedley Byrne* [1964] A.C. 465, between contracting parties; see in *Sealand of the Pacific Ltd.* v. *Ocean Cement Ltd.* (1973) 33 D.L.R. (3d) 625; and New Zealand *Capital Motors Ltd.* v. *Beecham* [1975] 1 N.Z.L.R. 576.

Applying this principle, it is plain that Esso professed to have—and did in fact have—special knowledge or skill in estimating the throughput of a filling station. They made the representation—they forecast a throughput of 200,000 gallons—intending to induce Mr. Mardon to enter into a tenancy on the faith of it. They made it negligently. It was a "fatal error." And thereby induced Mr. Mardon to enter into a contract of tenancy that was disastrous to him. For this misrepresentation they are liable in damages.

The measure of damages

Mr. Mardon is not to be compensated here for "loss of a bargain." He was given no bargain that the throughput *would* amount to 200,000 gallons a year. He is only to be compensated for having been induced to enter into a contract which turned out to be disastrous for him. Whether it be called breach of warranty or negligent misrepresentation, its effect was *not* to warrant the throughput, but only to induce him to enter the contract. So the damages in either case are to be measured by the loss he suffered. Just as in *Doyle* v. *Olby (Ironmongers) Ltd.* [1969] 2 Q.B. 158, 167 he can say: "... I would not have entered into this contract at all but for your representation. Owing to it, I have lost all the capital I put into it. I also incurred a large overdraft. I have spent four years of my life in wasted endeavour without reward: and it will take me some time to re-establish myself."

For all such loss he is entitled to recover damages. It is to be measured in a similar way as the loss due to a personal injury. You should look into the future so as to forecast what would have been likely to happen if he had never entered into this contract: and contrast it with his position as it is now as a result of entering into it. The future is necessarily problematical and can only be a rough-and-ready estimate. But it must be done in assessing the loss.

[Ormrod and Shaw L.JJ. agreed.]

REDGRAVE v. HURD
England. Court of Appeal. 1881. 20 Ch.D. 1

The plaintiff, a solicitor, advertised for "a partner, an efficient lawyer and advocate about forty, who would not object to purchase advertiser's suburban residence." After two interviews with the defendant in which the plaintiff represented that his business brought in £300 to £400 a year, the plaintiff and defendant met to settle the terms of the partnership and the plaintiff produced three summaries of business done in 1877, 1878 and 1879. The gross receipts amounted to less than £200 a year. When he asked how the difference of income was made up the defendant was shown some papers which represented other business. The defendant did not inspect these papers but Fry J. concluded that they showed business amounting to about £5 a year. The defendant wished the written agreement to set out that the £1600 was for the purchase of both the house and the partnership but the plaintiff refused, and the agreement did not refer to the practice. The agreement was signed on March 2, 1880, and the defendant agreed to pay £1600 for the house. He paid £100 on deposit and on April 17, was let into possession. Finding the law practice was "utterly worthless" he gave up possession and refused to complete the purchase.

The plaintiff brought this action for specific performance. The defendant denied liability because he had been induced into making the agreements by the plaintiff's false representations about the law practice made for that purpose. He counterclaimed for "rescission," the return of his deposit, and damages for his loss in moving his family. Fry J. gave judgment for the plaintiff and dismissed the counterclaim. He said, in part: "If he had intended to rely upon that parol representation . . . having the materials before him he would have made some inquiry into it."

JESSEL M.R.: As regards the defendant's counterclaim, we consider that it fails so far as damages are concerned, because he has not pleaded knowledge on the part of the plaintiff that the allégations made by the plaintiff were untrue, nor has he pleaded the allegations themselves in sufficient detail to found an action for deceit. It only remains to consider the claim of the plaintiff for specific performance, and so much of the counterclaim of the defendant as asks to have the contract rescinded.

Before going into the details of the case I wish to say something about my view of the law applicable to it, because in the text-books, and even in some observations of noble Lords in the House of Lords, there are remarks which I think, according to the course of modern decisions, are not well founded, and do not accurately state the law. As regards the rescission of a contract, there was no doubt a difference between the rules of Courts of Equity and the rules of Courts of Common Law—a difference which of course has now disappeared by the operation of the Judicature Act, which makes the rules of equity prevail. According to the decisions of the Courts of Equity it was not necessary, in order to set aside a contract obtained by material false representation, to prove that the party who obtained it knew at the time when the representation was made that it was false. It was put in two ways, either of which was sufficient. One way of putting the case was, "A man is not to be allowed to get a benefit from a statement which he now admits to be false. He is not to be allowed to say, for the purpose of civil jurisdiction, that when he made it he did not know it to be false; he ought to have found that out before he made it." The other way of putting it was this: "Even assuming that moral fraud must be shewn in order to set aside a contract, you have it where a man, having obtained a beneficial contract by a statement which he now knows to be false, insists upon keeping that contract. To do so is a moral delinquency: no man ought to seek to take advantage of his own false statements." The rule in equity was settled, and it does not matter on which of the two grounds it was rested. As regards the rule of Common Law there is no doubt it was not quite so wide. There were, indeed, cases in which, even at Common Law, a contract could be rescinded for misrepresentation, although it could not be shewn that the person making it knew the representation to be false. They are variously stated, but I think, according to the later decisions, the statement must have been made recklessly and without care, whether it was true or false, and not with the belief that it was true. But, as I have said, the doctrine in equity was settled beyond controversy, and it is enough to refer to the judgment of Lord Cairns in the *Reese River Silver Mining Company* v. *Smith*, Law Rep. 4 H.L. 64, in which he lays it down in the way which I have stated.

There is another proposition of law of very great importance which I think it is necessary for me to state, because, with great deference to the very learned Judge from whom this appeal comes, I think it is not quite accurately stated in his judgment. If a man is induced to enter into a contract by a false representation it is not a sufficient answer to him to say, "If you had used due diligence you would have found out that the statement was untrue. You had the means afforded you of discovering its falsity, and did not choose to avail yourself of them." I take it to be a settled doctrine of equity not only as regards specific performance but also as regards rescission, that this is not an answer unless there is such delay as constitutes a defence under the Statute of Limitations. That, of course, is quite a different thing. Under the statute delay deprives a man of his right to rescind on the ground of fraud, and the only question to be considered is from what time the delay is to be reckoned. It has been decided, and the rule was adopted by the statute, that the delay counts from the time when by due diligence the fraud might have been discovered. Nothing can be plainer, I take it, on the authorities in equity than that the effect of false representation is not got rid of on the ground that the person to whom it was made has been guilty of negligence. . . .

As regards the facts of this case, I agree with conclusions of Mr. Justice Fry on every point but one, and my failure to agree with him in that one is the cause of my concurring in reversing his decision. What he finds in effect is that the defendant Hurd was induced to enter into the contract by a material misrepresentation made to him by the plaintiff Redgrave, but he comes to the conclusion that either he did not finally rely upon that representation, or that if he did rely upon it he made an inquiry which, although ineffectual and made, as he says, carelessly and inefficiently, bound him in a Court of Equity, and prevented him from saying that he relied on the representation. . . .

[The Master of the Rolls then examined the evidence, with particular regard to the fact that the defendant asked for the papers showing the amount of business and was referred to some papers in the plaintiff's office, and continued.]

Then that being so the learned Judge came to the conclusion either that the defendant did not rely on the statement, or that if he did rely upon it he had shewn such negligence as to deprive him of his title to relief from this Court. As I have already said, the latter proposition is in my opinion not founded in law, and the former part is not founded in fact; I think also it is not founded in law, for when a person makes a material representation to another to induce him to enter into a contract, and the other enters into that contract, it is not sufficient to say that the party to whom the representation is made does not prove that he entered into the contract, relying upon the representation. If it is a material representation calculated to induce him to enter into contract, it is an inference of law that he was induced by the representation to enter into it, and in order to take away his title to be relieved from the contract on the ground that the representation was untrue, it must be shewn either that he had knowledge of the facts contrary to the representation, or that he stated in terms, or shewed clearly by his conduct, that he did not rely on the representation. If you tell a man, "You may enter into partnership with me, my business is bringing in between £300 and £400 a year," the man who makes that representation must know that it is a material inducement to the other to enter into the partnership, and you cannot investigate as to whether it was more or less probable that the inducement would operate on the mind of the party to whom the representation was made. Where you have neither evidence that he knew the facts to shew that the statement was untrue, or that he said or did anything to shew that he did not actually rely upon the statement, the inference remains that he did so rely, and the statement being a material statement, its being untrue is a sufficient ground for rescinding the contract. . . .

[The opinions of Baggallay and Lush L.JJ. who concurred in allowing the appeal are omitted.]

NEWBIGGING v. ADAM
England. Court of Appeal. 1886. 34 Ch.D. 582

The plaintiff was induced by the misrepresentation of the defendants as to the adequacy of some machinery to contribute £10,024 2s. 7d. to a partnership to which he was admitted. The business proved unsuccessful and this action was brought to dissolve the partnership and for, amongst other claims, an order that the defendants repay the plaintiff £9,279 6s. 1d. and indemnify him against all liabilities to which he had or might become liable in the partnership name. It was so ordered and the defendants appealed on the ground that this order amounted to damages for innocent misrepresentation.

BOWEN L.J.: ... If we turn to the question of misrepresentation, damages cannot be obtained at law for misrepresentation which is not fraudulent, and you cannot, as it seems to me, give in equity any indemnity which corresponds with damages. If the mass of authority there is upon the subject were gone through I think it would be found that there is not so much difference as is generally supposed between the view taken at common law and the view taken in equity as to misrepresentation. At common law it has always been considered that misrepresentations which strike at the root of the contract are sufficient to avoid the contract on the ground explained in *Kennedy* v. *Panama, New Zealand, and Australian Royal Mail Company* (1867), L.R. 2 Q.B. 580; but when you come to misrepresentation it seems to me to be this, and nothing more, that he is entitled to have the contract rescinded, and is entitled accordingly to all the incidents and consequences of such rescission. It is said that the injured party is entitled to be replaced in *statu quo*. It seems to me that when you are dealing with innocent misrepresentation you must understand that proposition that he is to be placed *in statu quo* with this limitation—that he is not to be replaced in exactly the same position in all respects, otherwise he would be entitled to recover damages, but is to be replaced in his position so far as regards the rights and obligations which have been created by the contract into which he has been induced to enter. That seems to me to be the true doctrine, and I think it is put in the neatest way in *Redgrave* v. *Hurd* (1881), 20 Ch. D. 14 [After considering that case and quoting a passage from Jessel M.R.'s judgment, Bowen L.J. continued:] With great respect for the shadow and memory of that great name I cannot help saying that this is not a perfect exposition of what the common law was, but, so far as the rule of equity goes, I must assume that the Master of the Rolls spoke with full knowledge of the equity authorities, and he treats the relief as being the giving back by the party who made the misrepresentation of the advantages he obtained by the contract.

Now those advantages may be of two kinds. He may get an advantage in the shape of an actual benefit, as when he receives money; he may also get an advantage if the party with whom he contracts assumes some burthen in consideration of the contract. In such a case it seems to me that complete rescission would not be effected unless the misrepresenting party not only hands back the benefits which he has himself received—but also re-assumes the burthen which under the contract the injured person has taken upon himself. Speaking only for myself I should not like to lay down the proposition that a person is to be restored to the position which he held before the misrepresentation was made, nor that the person injured must be indemnified against loss which arises out of the contract, unless you place upon the words "out of the contract" the limited and special meaning which I have endeavoured to shadow forth. Loss arising out of the contract is a term which would be too wide. It would embrace damages at common law, because damages at common law are only given upon the supposition that they are damages which would naturally and reasonably follow from the injury done. I think *Redgrave* v. *Hurd* shews that it would be too wide, because in that case the Court excluded from the relief which was given the damages which had been sustained by the plaintiff in removing his business, and other similar items. There ought, as it appears to me, to be a giving back and a taking back on both sides, including the giving back and taking back of the obligations which the contract has created, as well as the giving back and taking back of the advantages. . . .

I have not found any case which carries the doctrine further, and it is not necessary to carry it further in order to support the order now appealed from. A part of the contract between the Plaintiff and *Adam & Co.* was that the Plaintiff should become and continue for five years partner in a new firm and bring in £10,000. By this very contract he was to pledge his credit with his partners in the new firm for the business transactions of the new firm. It was a burthen of liability imposed on him by the very contract. It seems to me that the £9000 odd, and, indeed, all the moneys brought in by him or expended by him for the new firm up to the £10,000, were part of the actual moneys which he undertook by the true contract with *Adam & Co.* to pay. Of course he ought to be indemnified as regards that. I think, also, applying the same doctrine, he ought to be indemnified against all the liabilities of the firm, because they were liabilities which under the contract he was bound to take upon himself. . . .

[The decisions of Cotton and Fry L.JJ. concurring in dismissing the appeal are omitted.]

REDICAN v. *NESBITT*
Canada. Supreme Court. [1924] S.C.R. 135

The defendants entered into a contract to purchase a leasehold property from the plaintiff represented by one Wing, her agent. In due course an assignment of lease executed by the plaintiff and assented to by the landlord (the City of Toronto) was delivered to the defendants' solicitor with the keys of the property, the cheque of one of the defendants for the purchase money being simultaneously handed to the plaintiff's solicitor. The defendants also took an assignment of insurance and paid some arrears of taxes. On inspecting the property two days later—which is said to have been their first opportunity of doing so—they discovered, as they allege, that it had been misrepresented to them by Wing in several particulars, which they claim are of such importance that, had they known the truth in regard to them, they would not have purchased. On learning of these matters they stopped payment of the cheque given for the purchase money having first notified the vendor's husband that that would be done. An action by the vendor was at once begun for the sum of $2,969.84 being the balance of account owing under an offer to purchase by the defendants from the plaintiff and accepted by her.

The defendants by way of counter-claim asked for rescission. The action was tried by a jury. The questions submitted and the answers returned by the jury are as follows:

1. (a) Did Mrs. Nesbitt's agent, Wing, knowingly, make any untrue

statements as to the house or its contents for the purpose of deceiving the defendants in any material way and inducing them to make the offer to purchase? No.

(b) Did they make the offer relying upon such statements? Refer to question 1 (a).

2. If you find there were any such statements, what were they? We find that there is no evidence that such statements were made knowingly.

3. Did Wing make any untrue statement without knowing they were untrue but relying upon which defendants signed, and without having such statements they would not have signed their offer to purchase? Yes.

4. If so, what were such innocent misrepresentations? (a) That the house was lighted electrically. (b) That there were five bedrooms.

Upon these answers the trial judge entered judgment for the plaintiff. This judgment was affirmed by the Appellate Division of the Supreme Court of Ontario. The defendants appealed to the Supreme Court of Canada.

ANGLIN J.: . . . That this is not an action on the cheque referred to in the amendment of the special indorsement allowed at the trial, as the plaintiff now seeks to maintain, is made clear by the facts that the claim and the judgment are not against the maker of the cheque alone, but are against her and her co-purchaser jointly. The amendment made at the trial should not therefore be regarded as having changed the cause of action as originally stated. It merely added an allegation facilitating proof of the amount of the plaintiff's claim as a sum liquidated. The action remained one for money due and owing upon the contract.

It is, however, equally clear that it is in no sense the equitable action for specific performance. The plaintiff asserted a purely common law claim for payment of a sum of money due under a contract, perfectly valid, *Rutherford* v. *Acton-Adams*, [1915] A.C. 866, 868, subject to any defence to which such a claim is open. He did not require the aid of a court of equity to be relieved of the leasehold with its burdens; the defendants by taking the conveyance had assumed them. For the recovery of the purchase money the common law remedy was adequate and there was no ground for the plaintiff invoking the interference of a court of equity. It follows that the defendants will not necessarily succeed by establishing a case which would have disentitled the plaintiff to specific performance in a court of equity. That remedy is so distinctly discretionary that the court may withhold it although a case for rescission has not been made out.

But innocent misrepresentation, such as will support a demand for rescission in equity, though unavailing at common law, will serve as a good equitable defence to a claim for payment under the contract as well as afford ground for a counter-claim for rescission. Rescission is, of course, destructive of the basis of the plaintiff's claim; the right to rescission when established is an effective defence. But whether misrepresentation is set up by way of equitable defence or as the basis of a counter-claim for rescission, the burden on the defendant is the same. If the case made by him would not warrant a decree for rescission it will not avail as a defence to the claim for payment. In preferring this defence a defendant assumes the role of actor and a plea which, if established, would defeat a counter-claim for rescission is equally effective by way of reply to the defence of misrepresentation if set up by the plaintiff. . . .

In the present case the defendants plead misrepresentation as a ground both of defence and of counter-claim. They assert that it was fraudulent and, alternatively, that if innocent it was so material as to afford ground for rescission.

The jury negatived fraud and on this branch of the case, if they are not entitled to have the action dismissed on the other, the defendants ask for a new trial on the ground of misdirection and refusal by the learned trial judge to submit an essential element of it to the jury. I defer dealing with that aspect of the appeal.

The jury found that innocent misrepresentations inducing the contract had been made by the plaintiff's agent, and upon them the defendants maintain they are entitled to rescission. The trial judge rejected this claim on the ground that the contract for sale had been fully executed by the delivery of the deed and the acceptance of the cheque in payment, and that rescission of a contract after execution cannot be had for mere innocent misrepresentation unless it be such as renders the subject of sale different in substance from what was contracted for. . . . The suggestion that the property differed so completely in substance from what the defendants intended to acquire that there was a failure of consideration is not borne out by the facts. Neither is there any foundation for a suggestion of mutual mistake as a basis for rescission. *Debenham* v. *Sawbridge* [1901] 2 Ch. 98, 109. The trial judge regarded the handing over of the cheque as absolute payment and as a completion of the contract by the defendants just as the delivery of the conveyance and possession constituted completion on the part of the plaintiff.

In the Appellate Divisional Court this judgment was sustained, the late Sir W. R. Meredith C.J.O. giving the judgment of the majority of the court, on the ground that the contract became "executed" upon delivery and acceptance of the conveyance, whether the giving and taking of the cheque should or should not be regarded as payment of the purchase money.

Although Mr. Pollock in his treatise on the *Law of Contracts* (9th ed. p. 593) would seem to imply the existence of some doubt as to the doctrine enunciated in Lord Campbell's dictum in *Wilde* v. *Gibson* (1848), 1 H.L. Cas. 605; 9 E.R. 897 at p. 909, that "where the conveyance has been executed . . . a Court of Equity will set aside the conveyance only on the ground of fraud," pointing out that it has not been uniformly followed (see *Fry on Specific Performance*, 9th ed., p. 312), it is too well established to admit of controversy, assuming that his Lordship meant where the contract had been fully carried out. . . .

But on the question when a contract will, for the purpose of this rule, be deemed to have ceased to be "executory" and to have become "executed" the authorities are not so clear. I have not found any reported case in which it has been determined whether or not after delivery and acceptance of the conveyance and taking of possession a contract of sale remains "executory" until actual payment of the purchase money then due; nor indeed have I found any authority in which the contrary has been categorically determined. In many of the cases it is broadly stated, as it was by Lord Campbell, that after conveyance rescission will not be granted for innocent misrepresentation. But, on examination of the facts in such cases, it is clear either that payment of the purchase money had been made or as in the case of a contract for a lease, that all that the plaintiff seeking rescission was required by the contract to do had been done. . . .

[Anglin J. then quoted from a number of text writers and concluded:]
The foundation of the rule that an executed contract will not be rescinded

for innocent misrepresentation appears to be somewhat obscure. In *Angel v. Jay*, [1911] 1 K.B. 666, 671, Darling J. states, apparently without disapproval, the contention of counsel that "the foundation of the doctrine" is that "when property has passed the persons concerned cannot be placed in the same position as they were in before the estate became vested." In numerous cases the vesting of the property has been referred to as a serious obstacle to rescission. In other cases the supersession of the contract for sale by the executed conveyance accepted by the purchaser and the resultant restriction of his rights to those assured by the latter instrument appears to be the ground upon which rescission of the contract after acceptance of conveyance is refused. So far does the court go in maintaining this doctrine that, where under a court sale the purchase money was still in court, the purchaser who had accepted the title and taken his conveyance was refused relief in respect of subsequently discovered incumbrances.

In the case now before us it is probably unnecessary to determine the effect on the right of a purchaser to rescission of his acceptance of a conveyance and taking of possession without making payment. What might have been a formidable obstacle to the granting of rescission to the defendants was suggested by the trial judge, namely, the inability of the court to compel the landlord's assent to a re-assignment of the leasehold to the plaintiff. The effect of the acceptance of the conveyance assented to by the lessor and of the taking of possession of the property by the defendants may have been to give to the lessor rights against them as tenants the relinquishment of which the court could not exact.

Although the execution of the contract does not afford an answer to a claim for rescission in cases of fraudulent misrepresentation, inability to effect *restitutio in integrum,* unless that has become impossible owing to action of the wrong-doer, will ordinarily preclude rescission. *Kerr on Fraud* (5th ed.) 387-90. *A fortiori* is this the case where innocent misrepresentation only is relied upon. . . .

But I strongly incline to the view that while the acceptance of the cheque as payment was in this sense conditional that, if it should be dishonoured, the right to sue for the money due under the contract would revive, the transaction was, nevertheless, intended to be closed and the contract completely executed so far as the purchasers were concerned by their taking of the deed and the keys and handing over the cheque. They had obtained the full consideration for which they contracted and, if the vendor saw fit to accept the cheque they tendered in payment in lieu of cash, they should not be heard to say that the contract had not been fully executed. I cannot think that the vendor's right to have the contract treated as executed and completed can be defeated by the fact that she took a cheque as the equivalent of a cash payment, and still less by the accident that the cheque was not presented for payment during the two days which intervened between the closing of the sale and the stopping of payment. Bearing in mind the well established custom of solicitors with regard to the closing of sales of real estate, when delivery of conveyance and possession was given and accepted and a cheque (then good) for the purchase money was tendered and taken, what was performed was what the parties intended should be done when they contracted.

Without, therefore, necessarily affirming the position taken in the judgment of the majority of the learned judges of the Appellate Divisional Court, I am of the opinion that, under all the circumstances of this case, the contract for sale was executed and that, according to a well settled rule in equity, rescission for innocent misrepresentation is not an available remedy for the defendants.

I am clearly of the opinion, however, that a new trial must be directed because the issue of fraud was not properly presented to the jury. In substance the learned trial judge charged that, in order to establish fraud, the defendants must show that Wing actually knew his representations were false. He did not tell the jury that the representations would be fraudulent if they were false and were made without belief in their truth, or recklessly, careless whether they were true or false. . . . The attention of the trial judge was thus pointedly drawn to the feature of fraudulent misrepresentation which his question did not cover. Counsel expressly asked that it should be covered. The learned judge distinctly stated his view that intention to deceive was essential and impliedly that a false statement made with reckless carelessness as to its truth or falsehood would not be fraudulent. He declined to amend the questions as suggested, stating that he had "covered" the case.

Counsel is not obliged to quarrel with the judge or to press an objection *ad nauseam*. Having stated his position and his request for the submission of a proper question having been refused Mr. Grant had, I think, sufficiently discharged his duty and was not called upon to renew the same objection at the close of the charge. The learned judge had definitely expressed his purpose to adhere to an adverse view of the law. . . .

[Appeal allowed with costs and a new trial granted. Davies C.J. concurred with Anglin J. The opinions of Idington, Duff and Mignault JJ. are omitted. While Idington J. agreed in the result he also went beyond the grounds taken by the rest of the Court in that he appeared willing to grant rescission even though the contract was executed on the apparent ground that the misrepresentation led to an "error *in substantialibus*." "I think a difference of a few acres, is no more important than the four rooms instead of five as misrepresented and electric light in this case to the appellants."]

COLE v. *POPE*. 1898. 29 S.C.R. 291 (British Columbia. Supreme Court of Canada). In June, 1896, the appellant and others had taken up a gold mining claim known as the "Eldorado" in the neighbourhood of Rossland, B.C., of which the appellant represented himself to be the owner of an undivided half. The respondent, believing and relying entirely upon the appellant's representation as to ownership, purchased the undivided half of "Eldorado" for $5,250, which he paid in cash. It shortly appeared that the "Eldorado" claim was almost wholly within a prior claim, the "Mascot," and the balance was in fact included in other claims. The respondent therefore got nothing for his $5,250. Both parties dealt upon the mistaken belief that the "Eldorado" was an actually existing mining right. The respondent brought this action to have the contract rescinded and to obtain repayment of the $5,250. The trial judge dismissed the action. The full court reversed him. The Supreme Court of Canada dismissed the appeal. STRONG C.J.: "The learned trial judge considered the respondent's right to rescission dependent entirely on the misrepresentation, and held that in the present state of the law an executed contract—and especially an executed contract for the sale of an interest in land—will not be rescinded for mere innocent misrepresentation. . . . I conclude therefore in favour of the proposition that mere innocent representation will not warrant the rescission of an executed contract for the sale of an interest in land.

"There is, however, another principle which I think may be invoked in the respondent's favour and which is quite open to him on the pleadings and evidence before us.

"It has been determined by several authorities and is well established law that where by the mutual mistake of the parties to a contract of sale the subject of the sale turns out to be non-existent or is already the property of the purchaser, both parties having fallen into error merely, and there being no fraud or deceit in the case, the purchaser who has paid his purchase money and taken a conveyance will be relieved and the contract rescinded by a Court of Equity. In such a case where there is a complete failure of consideration as in the present case it would be unjust and unconscientious that the vendor should retain money paid to him for a supposed consideration which has utterly failed."

MacKENZIE v. *ROYAL BANK OF CANADA.* [1934] A.C. 468 (Ontario. Privy Council). An action *in forma pauperis* by Mrs. Mac-Kenzie, to set aside a contract of guarantee with a pledge of shares worth about $10,000 on the grounds of undue influence by her husband and innocent misrepresentation by her husband's bank. She lost on the first ground but she established that she had been induced to part with her securities and to guarantee the debts of her husband's business by a misrepresentation. In 1913 she had hypothecated the shares with the Bank to assist the company then just formed by her husband. During the war the company prospered and in 1918 the shares were released to her. By 1920, however, the company was in difficulties, and on December 31, Mrs. MacKenzie again hypothecated her shares, making them "general and continuing collateral security for payment of the present and future indebtedness and liability of MacKenzie Ld." In May of 1921 the company went into bankruptcy and after the Bank realized its security for the company's debt, there ceased to be any "indebtedness and liability of MacKenzie Ld." to which the pledged shares could attach. In November a new company, MacKenzie Manufacturing Company, Ld. was formed. The Bank sold to Mr. MacKenzie the assets of the old company for $125,000, MacKenzie sold them to the new company for the same price, the Bank advanced the price to the company and took the assets as security for the loss, putting the Bank in much the same relation to the new company as it had been to the old. Mr. MacKenzie and the Bank's manager then asked Mrs. MacKenzie to pledge her shares once again to the Bank and they assured her that her shares were still bound under the hypothecation of December 31, 1920 and that this new guarantee was her only hope of getting them back. After she had signed she was given a form to be taken to a lawyer and signed by him, intimating that he had given her independent advice, and that she fully understood the transaction. Her lawyer signed the document as a matter of form, saying that he had given her no advice for he knew nothing about the new company. LORD ATKIN: "If it had been incumbent upon the bank to prove that the lady had had independent advice, their Lordships would have had the greatest difficulty in coming to the conclusion that the bank had discharged the onus. Independent advice to be of any value must be given before the transaction, for the question is as to the will of the party at the time of entering into the disputed transaction. Advice given after the event when the supposed contracting party is already bound is given under entirely different circumstances, with a different position presented to the minds both of the adviser and his client. It is unnecessary, however, to emphasize this point, for their Lordships are not able to take the view that the transaction was one in respect of which there was an onus upon the bank to prove that the plaintiff had independent advice. . . . But their Lordships have come to the conclusion that the contract cannot be allowed to stand for another reason. A contract of guarantee, like any other contract, is liable to be avoided if induced by material misrepresentation of an existing fact, even if made innocently. In this case it is unnecessary to decide whether contracts of guarantee belong to the special class where, even at common law, such an innocent misrepresentation would afford a defence to an action on the contract. The evidence conclusively establishes a misrepresentation by the bank that the plaintiff's shares were still bound to the bank with the necessary inference, whether expressed or not, and their Lordships accept the plaintiff's evidence that it was expressed, that the shares were already lost, and that the guarantee of the new company offered the only means of salving them. It does not seem to admit of doubt that such a misrepresentation made as to the plaintiff's private rights and depending upon transactions in bankruptcy, of the full nature of which she had not been informed, was a representation of fact. That it was material is beyond discussion. It consequently follows that the plaintiff was at all times, on ascertaining the true position, entitled to avoid the contract and recover her securities. There were subsequent renewals of the guarantee before the plaintiff was advised of the true facts, but counsel for the bank very properly conceded that they would be in the same position as the original guarantee. There is no difficulty as to restitutio in integrum. The mere fact that the party making the representation has treated the contract as binding and has acted on it does not preclude relief. Nor can it be said that the plaintiff received anything under the contract which she is unable to restore."

O'FLAHERTY v. *McKINLEY*
Newfoundland. Court of Appeal. [1953] 2 D.L.R. 514

DUNFIELD J.: The plaintiff in this case, a young lady who had not owned a car before, bought a second-hand Hillman sedan in April, 1950, from the defendant, who is an automobile dealer and garageman. She says she wanted and asked for a 1950 model. He and his staff told her it was a 1950 Hillman, which had gone 4,000 odd miles; that is admitted. She was charged $1325, so far as the defendant was concerned.

The defendant says that the previous owner, who traded the car to him against a Standard "Vanguard" car, for which defendant is agent, told him and his staff it was a 1950 Hillman, and they accepted that statement. It appears that in 1949 Hillman redesigned their car. As often happens in a new design, it had some shortcomings, and these were made good in the 1950 model; but the changes were mostly internal, and the 1949 and 1950 cars were externally very much alike, and would not be readily distinguishable except by their own agents. The previous owner, who was in the witness-box, denies that he represented the car to be a 1950 model; but the plaintiff's counsel accepts the defence position that there was innocent misrepresentation only. The plaintiff asks for rescission of the contract of sale and the return of her money including certain collateral expenditures.

The transaction was not clean-cut. Plaintiff paid down $675. She also signed documents in connection with the finance of the car involving a concern called the Industrial Acceptance Corp. The practical effect of these is as follows: The buyer borrows and the seller gets from the Corporation the balance of the purchase-money, viz., $650. The documents purport to transfer the title to the car and the debt to the Corporation pending payment off by instalments. The Corporation goes on to collect from the buyer by instalments of $47 a month a total sum exceeding $650 by a good deal. The corporation insures the car against collision, theft and fire. There is a provision in the agreement that if the purchaser dies the instalments come to an end. I was struck by the benevolence of this; but I am told by counsel that the Corporation also insures the life of the purchaser for a sufficient period. I note that a blank on the front of the form contains the typewritten statement that the car is a 1950 model, but a clause in small print on the back says that a statement as to year-model is not to affect the situation whether true or not. This appears objectionable, as few read these small type paragraphs; though one can quite see that the finance corporation does not want to take responsibility for any such technical point.

In fact, the plaintiff has paid off the finance corporation since this action began, so it is not necessary to add it as a party, as was suggested when the action first came in; and the action has now been pleaded and fought on the same basis as if it had been a direct sale without the intervention of the finance corporation. We are therefore spared from having to consider the effect of these transactions. It may be that the apparent assignment could be held to be in fact a mortgage to the finance corporation, or a mortgage to the vendor assigned to the corporation.

However, the plaintiff claims a total payment of $1,580.14 with rescission of the contract of sale. The difference, $255.14, between $1,325 and $1,580.14 is made up of [registration, insurance, repairs, taxes and carrying charges].

The defendant counterclaims for $158.53, an unpaid bill for repairs and maintenance done for the plaintiff.

The plaintiff, who was a novice driver, and her two brothers, also novices, drove the car about 7,000 miles during the summer of 1950. In early September 1950 the plaintiff happened to call at Adelaide Motors Ltd., who are agents for the Hillman, and happened to remark that the car was a 1950 model, and was then told that it was a 1949 model. She forthwith saw her solicitors and instructed them to write repudiating the contract of sale. The car was not run after that. It was, however, kept out of doors in the plaintiff's yard, she not having a garage, during the past winter. Defendant says he offered to house the car in his garage for the winter without prejudice to the rights of either party, but that this offer was refused. Fortunately it was not a hard winter; but nevertheless a winter in the open is not desirable.

Mr. Furlong, K.C., for the defendant, takes the position that rescission cannot be granted unless the parties can be restored substantially to their original positions, which is not possible, because the car has done 7,000 miles and been subjected to a winter's exposure. But as to this, a dealer in the witness-box remarked that mileage on a second-hand car was not very serious until it began to get up to 15,000 miles. This car has now done about 11,700 miles. Again, it is a known fact that a good many people keep cars in the open during the winter, and most people keep them in unheated garages. There is evidence that plaintiff's brother started the engine now and then to keep the battery alive. I hear nothing about the battery freezing.

It happens that two Courts of Appeal in Canada have dealt with similar cases. In *Addison* v. *Ottawa Auto & Taxi Co.*, (1913), 16 D.L.R. 318, the Ontario Court of Appeal affirming Boyd C., at first instance, dealt with these facts. Plaintiff purchased a car from defendants on the representation that it was a new one. Actually it had been sold, used a few months, involved in an accident, and rebuilt and renovated at a cost of $500. Plaintiff was ignorant of an alleged trade custom to call rebuilt cars "new" cars. What she wanted and thought she was getting was a car that had not been sold to or driven by anybody. She was a complete novice as to cars. She took the car and used it from September until the 3rd of the following May, but repudiated the sale promptly on discovering "the deception which had been practised on her." Defendant put up the same plea as in this case; that it would be unfair for him to have to take it back after the use she had made of it. The Court of Appeal, however, Meredith C.J.O., Maclaren, Magee and Hodgins JJ.A., affirmed the judgment of Boyd C. and dismissed the appeal. Meredith C.J.O. [16 D.L.R. at p. 324] quotes Rigby L.J. in *Lagunas Nitrate Co.* v. *Lagunas Syndicate*, [1899] 2 Ch. 392 at p. 457, where he says: " 'The obligation of the vendors to take back the property in a deteriorated condition is not imposed by way of punishment for wrongdoing, whether fraudulent or not, but because on equitable principles it is thought more fair that they should be compelled to accept compensation than that they should go off with the full [benefit] of their wrongdoing. Properly speaking it is not now in the discretion of the Court to say whether compensation ought to be taken or not. If substantially compensation can be made, rescission with compensation is *ex debito justitiae.*' "

Again Meredith C.J.O. says (p. 325): "The Chancellor allowed as compensation for any deterioration in the car and for the use of it by the respondent the amount of the interest on the purchase-money, to which she would have been entitled, and we cannot see that, under all the circumstances, the allowance is not a reasonable one."

That of course was a case verging on fraud, though Boyd C. suggests that the vendor may have felt justified in treating the car as a new car.

Again in *Gearhart* v. *Kraatz* (1918), 40 D.L.R. 26, 11 S.L.R. 106, the Saskatchewan Appellate Division (Haultain C.J.S., Newlands, Lamont and Elwood JJ.A.) dealt with a case relating to the sale of mules. These animals were sold on a representation that they were of a certain age; they were used for some months; it was discovered that they were very much older than was represented; and the sale was repudiated. Lamont J.A. states the law as to deterioration as follows (pp. 29-30):

"The rule is that where the representee has lost or destroyed the subject matter of the contract, or so dealt with it as to produce an entire alteration in its physical, commercial or legal character, quality or substance, as distinct from mere depreciation, decay or deterioration in the ordinary course of events, the representee is not entitled to his rescission. 20 Hals. 750-51. . . .

"Assuming, therefore, the representation was not fraudulent, it was material; it was false and induced the contract, and the defendant is entitled to have it rescinded."

A well-made car ought to be able to go, with proper maintenance, 50,000 to 100,000 miles; therefore it seems to me that the mere increase of the mileage from 4,700 to 11,700 does not substantially alter the character of the vehicle. It is still a young car.

But I consider also that the representation as to the year-model of a car

is very material. A car is not just a car. One make may be better than
another, and a car of one year of a certain maker very different in its satis-
faction-giving qualities from a car of the same maker of another year.
Evidence in this case indicates that the 1950 Hillman is a much better car
than the 1949 Hillman in respect of its internal structure, regardless of the
similarity in appearance; and it may command a better price on resale. A
contract to supply a 1950 model cannot be considered to be satisfied by the
supply of a 1949 model. I think there is what is called an *error in substantialibus.* . . .

I think the contract must be avoided, and that the plaintiff must have
her money, namely, $1,325, back forthwith; without interest, following
the Ontario Court of Appeal in the *Addison* case; and that the car must be
immediately returned to the defendant. But as to the subsidiary claims of
the plaintiff, for registration, insurance, repairs, tax, and the additional
sums paid by her to the finance company, these are not directly connected
with the misrepresentation; she would have had to pay such charges as
these if it had been a 1950 car and not a 1949 car. And on looking over
the bill for repairs and maintenance, after excluding the cost of repairing
small damages which she or her brothers did to the car, I cannot see that
there is any excessive cost; to my mind she paid or is charged no more than
anyone might expect to pay for the maintenance of a second-hand car in
good condition running 7,000 miles. Nor has any effort been made to
prove the allegation that the defendant's repair or maintenance charges
are excessive. The defendant must therefore have judgment for the full
amount of his counter-claim on the repair and maintenance bill.

Let judgment be entered accordingly, with costs to plaintiff on the claim
and to defendant on the counter-claim, the payment into Court not covering the counter-claim in full.

WINTER J. (dissenting): . . . The action was based upon innocent misrepresentation, the statement of the defendant that the car was a 1950
model. But it is clear that the statement was made in the course of a transaction which resulted in a very simple contract, a contract of sale, and that
it was embodied in the contract as a term thereof. . . .

Once the buyer has definitely accepted the goods, he is taken to have
elected to rely upon any claim he may have for damages if any condition is
afterwards proved to have been broken. (I am assuming what cannot be
doubted in both cases, that the representation was a condition and not a
mere warranty). It is too late for him to claim to repudiate the contract
and return the goods. At a certain critical time, before he finally accepts
the goods or notifies the seller to that effect, he is given an election, a choice
between two courses of action. He is supposed to envisage the possibility
of the seller failing to carry out all his promises and any loss he may himself suffer as a result. He can, if he wish, rely entirely upon his right in that
case to recover the loss. And so he may accept the goods there and then
and leave it at that. In a pecuniary sense, in theory at least, he will not
suffer. Or he may think it preferable to reject the goods altogether if they are
not what they should be under the contract. For this purpose he is allowed
a reasonable time in which to satisfy himself on that point, and that is usually done by an examination of the goods. What is a reasonable time
depends upon the facts and the contract; in the case of unascertained goods
it is usually appreciably longer than where the goods are specific. It follows
that if the reasonable time passes and he does nothing, he is taken to have

accepted the goods. He has made his election. He cannot have it both ways.

Applying all this to the present case and to *Leaf* v. *International Galleries* [1950] 1 All E.R. 693, which I purposely include because I can see no essential difference between them, it is abundantly clear that in both instances the buyer kept the goods for a much longer time than could be considered reasonable before seeking any redress. In actual fact, neither buyer made any examination at all. Both clearly elected to follow the former of the two courses of action I have mentioned. Both chose to rely entirely upon what the seller had said and both afterwards complained, it seems to me, most illogically, that the seller was unreliable and that they should be granted the election over again. . . .

I think a distinction must be made between two very different things, though I have never seen it made in any reported case. It is one thing for a buyer to make a genuine inspection of goods, or inquiries about them, with a view to satisfying himself that they are what he wants, and quite another to make up his mind whether he will choose rejection or damages as a remedy if he should need one. It is the latter, as I see it, that the Act contemplates when it speaks of a reasonable time, not the former; or at least, the latter must always be there. The striking feature that I see in both this case and *Leaf* v. *International Galleries* is that they are cases of the latter. Both buyers made up their minds not to examine at all, and both learned the truth quite accidentally. In my view both made the election as to the remedy within a very short time after delivery, if not at that very moment. . . .

I have to add one other observation. It might be argued that, if my view of the case is correct, the plaintiff is without remedy altogether; that, again as in *Leaf* v. *International Galleries*, she chose to limit her claim to rescission. I think that that view would be most unfair and in any case is not the true one. The original statement of claim was confused and it was doubtful whether it claimed rescission or damages. It was later amended to make it clear that rescission was in fact claimed. I think that, if there is any doubt whether damages are claimed in the alternative, the Court has power even now to amend the pleadings to make that clear also. There can be no doubt whatever, on the facts, that the plaintiff is entitled to damages.

[Walsh C.J. also gave reasons for dismissing the appeal.]

LEAF v. *INTERNATIONAL GALLERIES*. [1950] 1 All E.R. 693 (England. Court of Appeal). In an action for rescission of a contract for the sale of a painting in 1944, for £85, it was established that the painting had been innocently misrepresented by the defendant Galleries as a painting by Constable of Salisbury Cathedral. In 1949 the plaintiff tried to sell the painting and learned that it was not a Constable and was really worth very little. Held, for the defendant Galleries. DENNING L.J.: "I agree that on a contract for the sale of goods an innocent material misrepresentation may, in a proper case, be a ground for rescission even after the contract has been executed. . . . Although rescission may in some cases be a proper remedy, it is to be remembered that an innocent misrepresentation is much less potent than a breach of condition; and a claim to rescission for innocent misrepresentation must at any rate be barred when a right to reject for breach of condition is barred. A condition is a term of the contract of a most material character, and if a claim to reject on that account is barred, it seems to me a fortiori that a claim to rescission on the ground of innocent misrepresentation is also barred.

"So, assuming that a contract for the sale of goods may be rescinded in a proper case for innocent misrepresentation, the claim is barred in this case for the self-same reason as a right to reject is barred. The buyer has accepted the picture. He had ample opportunity for examination in the first few days after he had bought it. Then was the time to see if the condition or representation was fulfilled. Yet he has kept it all this time. Five years have elapsed without any notice of rejection. In my judgment he cannot now claim to rescind. His only claim, if any, as the county judge said, was one for damages, which he has not made in this action. In my judgment, therefore, the appeal should be dismissed."

SHANKLIN PIER LTD. v. DETEL PRODUCTS LTD.
[1951] 2 K.B. 854

The plaintiffs were the owners of a pier at Shanklin, in the Isle of Wight, which, during the war, was partly demolished and allowed to fall into disrepair. On July 22, 1946, they entered into a contract with contractors to have the necessary repairs effected and to have the whole pier repainted with two coats of bitumastic or bituminous paint. Under this contract the plaintiffs had, however, the right to vary the specification.

On July 22, 1946, the South Coast director of the defendant company, as a result of an inquiry by the plaintiffs, went to Shanklin with the object of obtaining for his company the contract for the repainting or for the materials for the repainting of the pier. He there saw the managing director of the plaintiff company, and later also the plaintiff's architect, and told them that certain paint manufactured by the defendants and known as D.M.U. would be suitable for the work. He showed a pamphlet to the architect which stated that two coats of D.M.U. applied to a clean metal surface would keep the underwater surface, top sides, and wind and water line of a ship free from corrosion for over four years. He told the architect that the paint was not subject to creep, suggested that two coats should be used on the pier as a protective coat, and promised him that it should have a life of at least seven to ten years.

On the faith of those statements the plaintiffs caused the specification in their contract with the contractors to be amended by the substitution of two coats of D.M.U. That paint was bought by the contractors from the defendants and applied to the pier, but it proved to be unsatisfactory and lasted only about three months.

The plaintiffs, by their statement of claim, now claimed against the defendants that, in consideration of the plaintiffs' specifying that the contractors should use for repainting the pier two coats of a paint known as D.M.U., manufactured by the defendants, the defendants warranted that the D.M.U. paint would be suitable for repainting the pier, would give a surface impervious to dampness, would prevent corrosion and the creeping of rust, and would have a life of from seven to ten years. The plaintiffs further alleged that, in reliance on that warranty, they duly specified that the contractors should use D.M.U. paint for repainting the pier in lieu of the bituminous paint originally specified; that the contractors bought quantities of the paint from the defendants and used it on the pier; and that, contrary to the warranty, the paint was not suitable for repainting the pier or for the protection of the pier from damp or corrosion or rust, and its life was of a very short duration, with the result that the plaintiffs were put to extra expense amounting to £4,127.

McNAIR J.: This case raises an interesting and comparatively novel question whether or not an enforceable warranty can arise as between parties other than parties to the main contract for the sale of the article in respect of which the warranty is alleged to have been given. [His Lordship stated the facts set out above and continued:]

The defence, stated broadly, is that no warranty such as is alleged in the statement of claim was ever given and that, if given, it would give rise to no cause of action between these parties. Accordingly, the first question which I have to determine is whether any such warranty was ever given. [His Lordship reviewed the evidence about the negotiations which led to the acceptance by the plaintiffs of two coats of D.M.U. in substitution for the paint originally specified, and continued:]

In the result, I am satisfied that, if a direct contract of purchase and sale of the D.M.U. had then been made between the plaintiffs and the defendants, the correct conclusion on the facts would have been that the defendants gave to the plaintiffs the warranties substantially in the form alleged in the statement of claim. In reaching this conclusion, I adopt the principles stated by Holt C.J., in *Crosse* v. *Gardner* (1689) 1 Show. 68 and *Medina* v. *Stoughton* (1700) 1 Ld. Raym. 593 that an affirmation at the time of sale is a warranty, provided it appear on evidence to have been so intended.

Counsel for the defendants submitted that in law a warranty could give rise to no enforceable cause of action except between the same parties as the parties to the main contract in relation to which the warranty was given. In principle this submission seems to me to be unsound. If, as is elementary, the consideration for the warranty in the usual case is the entering into of the main contract in relation to which the warranty is given, I see no reason why there may not be an enforceable warranty between A and B supported by the consideration that B should cause C to enter into a contract with A or that B should do some other act for the benefit of A.

Counsel for the defendants, however, relied upon the decision of the Court of Appeal in *Drury* v. *Victor Buckland Ltd.* [1941] 1 All E.R. 269, and particularly upon the judgment of Scott L.J. In that case the plaintiff, who had been approached by an agent of the defendants, dealers in refrigerating machines, agreed to purchase such a machine, but, being unable or unwilling to pay forthwith the whole of the purchase price, the deal was put through by the defendants' selling the machine to a finance company, who in turn entered into a hire-purchase agreement with the plaintiff, under which she eventually, when the whole of the hire-purchase instalments had been paid, acquired title to the machine. The machine proving unsatisfactory, the plaintiff sued the defendants, claiming damages for breach of the implied warranty or condition under s. 14, sub-s. 1, of the Sale of Goods Act, 1893.

The claim failed, Scott L.J., saying: "It was a sale by the Buckland Company [the defendants] to the hire-purchase company. The property passed to them on the terms that they [the defendants] would get paid by the hire-purchase company. Therefore, the claim against them [the defendants] for damages for breach of warranty is a cause of action unsupported by any contract of sale which would carry it." This judgment can readily be understood in relation to its subject-matter, namely, an implied statutory condition or warranty arising out of a contract of sale, and one can well understand it being said that, as there was no contract of sale between the plaintiff and the defendants, no such implied warranty or condition could arise between them; but I do not read it as affording any support for the wider proposition for which counsel for the defendants contended.

The same view of the effect of this judgment as I have indicated was, I think, taken by Jones J., in *Brown* v. *Sheen and Richmond Car Sales Ltd.* [1950] 1 All E.R. 1102, a case in which the judge entered judgment against a motor car dealer on an express rail warranty given in relation to the purchase of a car, the transaction, as in *Drury's* case, being carried through with the assistance of a finance company. It was here sought to distinguish *Brown's* case on the ground that in the statement of facts in the report in All England Law Reports it was stated that "the plaintiff agreed to buy" the motor car from the defendants, but the pleadings in *Brown's* case which I have examined, lend no support for suggesting that in that case there was in any legal sense any agreement to sell between the plaintiff and the defendants.

Accordingly, in my judgment the plaintiffs are entitled to recover against the defendants for breach of the express warranties alleged.

[Judgment for the plaintiffs.]

ANDREWS v. *HOPKINSON*
[1957] 1 Q.B. 229

The plaintiff, being minded to buy a car, visited the premises of a dealer in second-hand cars and was shown by the sales manager a 1934 saloon car which had been in his possession for about a week. The manager said: "It's a good little bus. I would stake my life on it. You will have no trouble with it." The price was agreed and it was arranged that the plaintiff should pay a deposit and that the balance should be payable on hire-purchase terms. On the following day an agreement was signed to sell the car to a finance company and a hire-purchase agreement was executed in the usual form between the finance company and the plaintiff. The dealer had no reason to anticipate that the plaintiff would have the car examined by a competent mechanic before taking it on the road or would himself examine it. A week after the transaction the plaintiff was injured when his car came into collision with a truck owing to failure of the drag-link joint of the steering which was not safe or fit for use on the highway. The defective condition of the joint was of long standing and, though probably not discoverable by an ordinary owner-driver, could have been simply discovered by any competent mechanic, and a motor dealer should have appreciated that in such a car this joint was one of the most likely places to find excessive and dangerous wear.

McNair J., reading his judgment, stated the facts . . . and continued: On the evidence given before me I am satisfied (1) that the defective condition of the drag-link joint was the cause of the accident; (2) that this condition was of long standing; (3) that at the time when the plaintiff took delivery of the car it was, by reason of these defects, not in good condition and safe and fit for use on a public highway; (4) that this defective condition could have been discovered by any competent mechanic (though probably not by a ordinary owner-driver) without stripping down the steering mechanism, by the simple and recognized method of manually pulling upon the ball pin after jacking up the car for examination; (5) that any motor dealer ought to appreciate that in the case of an old car such as the car in question, one of the most likely places to find excessive and dangerous wear affecting the roadworthiness is in the steering mechanism, and particularly in the drag-link joint where such joint forms part of the steering mechanism; (6) that the defendant had no reason to anticipate that the plaintiff would himself have the car examined by a competent mechanic before taking it on the road, or would himself examine it.

As a result of this accident the car was wrecked and the plaintiff suffered serious injuries involving the fracture of three ribs and a fracture of the left wrist. Happily the fractures united well and there was no residual disability. He was off work for seven or eight weeks. The special damages have been agreed at £245 5s. 6d. and I assess the general damages at the sum of £400.

In these circumstances the plaintiff brings his action against the defendant, basing his claim upon three grounds. He first claims that in the circumstances which I have narrated the defendant warranted that the car was in good condition and reasonably safe and fit for use on the public highway; that he acted on this warranty, and that damage was caused by breach of that warranty. Secondly, he claims that the collision was caused by the negligence of the defendant, particularly by the negligence set out in paragraph 6 of the statement of claim, that the defendant knew, or ought to have known, the said car was defective and therefore dangerous and unfit for use on a highway, and that the defendant failed to take any or sufficient steps to remedy this defect to ensure the car was reasonably safe and fit to use on a public highway; failed to warn the plaintiff that the car was defective and dangerous and unfit to be used on a public highway. Thirdly, by way of amendment made at a late stage of the hearing, the plaintiff relied on the implied warranty similar to that implied in certain cases of sale of goods under section 14 (1) of the Sale of Goods Act, 1893. [Section 15 of the Ontario Act.]

As to breach of warranty, in the first place it is clear that in law the relationship between the plaintiff and the defendant was not a relationship of seller and purchaser. The hire-purchase transaction evidenced in the documents was a reality and cannot be treated as a mere colourable transaction . . .

Secondly, I am satisfied (1) applying the principle stated by Holt J. in *Crosse* v. *Gardner* (1689) 1 Shaw. 69 and *Medina* v. *Stoughton,* (1700) 1 Ld. Raym. 593, that if the transaction between the plaintiff and defendant had been in law a sale, the words deposed to by the plaintiff as being the words used by Mr. Hopkinson, junior, could properly be held to be words of warranty, i.e., an affirmation made at the time of sale intended to be a warranty; (2) that the words amounted at least to a warranty that the car was in good condition and reasonably safe and fit for use on a public highway; and (3) that the plaintiff acted upon this warranty in the sense that without it he would not have accepted delivery of the car or entered into the hire-purchase agreement.

On these findings I adopt the reasoning of Jones J. in *Brown* v. *Sheen and Richmond Car Sales Ltd.,* [1950] 1 All E.R. 1102 and follow my own decision in *Shanklin Pier Ltd.* v. *Detel Products Ltd.,* where I set out at some length the reasons that led me to the conclusion (as they do in this case) that there may be an enforceable warranty between A, the intended purchaser of a car, and B, the motor dealer, supported by the consideration that B should cause the hire-purchase finance company to enter into a hire-purchase agreement with A, the intended purchaser.

It was rather faintly argued that even on these findings the defendant would only be liable for the difference in value between the car as delivered and the car as warranted. Though this, no doubt, may be the prima facie measure of damages in an ordinary case of breach of warranty in the sale of goods, I feel no doubt at all that on the facts of this case the whole of the damages can fairly be considered as loss directly and naturally resulting in the ordinary course of events from the breach of warranty and so recoverable as damages for breach. I hold, accordingly, that as damages for breach of warranty the plaintiff is entitled to judgment for £645 5s. 6d.

[McNair J. also found for the plaintiff on the independent ground of negligence, and suggested (without deciding) that he might also succeed for breach of implied warranty.]

MISREPRESENTATION ACT 1967
1967 CHAPTER 7 (U.K.)

1. Where a person has entered into a contract after a misrepresentation

   (a) the misrepresentation has become a term of the contract; or
   (b) the contract has been performed;

or both, then, if otherwise he would be entitled to rescind the contract without alleging fraud, he shall be so entitled, subject to the provisions of this Act, notwithstanding the matters mentioned in paragraphs (a) and (b) of this section.

2. (1) Where a person has entered into a contract after a misrepresentation has been made to him by another party thereto and as a result thereof he has suffered loss, then, if the person making the misrepresentation would be liable to damages in respect thereof had the misrepresentation been made fraudulently, that person shall be so liable notwithstanding that the misrepresentation was not made fraudulently, unless he proves that he had reasonable ground to believe and did believe up to the time the contract was made that the facts represented were true.

(2) Where a person has entered into a contract after a misrepresentation has been made to him otherwise than fraudulently, and he would be entitled, by reason of the misrepresentation, to rescind the contract, then, if it is claimed, in any proceedings arising out of the contract, that the contract ought to be or has been rescinded, the court or arbitrator may declare the contract subsisting and award damages in lieu of rescission, if of opinion that it would be equitable to do so, having regard to the nature of the misrepresentation and the loss that would be caused by it if the contract were upheld, as well as to the loss that rescission would cause to the other party.

(3) Damages may be awarded against a person under subsection (2) of this section whether or not he is liable to damages under subsection (1) thereof, but where he is so liable any award under the said subsection (2) shall be taken into account in assessing his liability under the said subsection (1).

3. If any agreement (whether made before or after the commencement of this Act) contains a provision which would exclude or restrict—

   (a) any liability to which a party to a contract may be subject by reason of any misrepresentation made by him before the contract was made; or

(b) any remedy available to another party to the contract by reason of such a misrepresentation;

that provision shall be of no effect except to the extent (if any) that, in any proceedings arising out of the contract, the court or arbitrator may allow reliance on it as being fair and reasonable in the circumstances of the case.

4. (1) In paragraph (c) of section 11(1) of the Sale of Goods Act 1893 (condition to be treated as warranty where the buyer has accepted the goods or where the property in specific goods has passed) the words "or where the contract is for specific goods, the property in which has passed to the buyer" shall be omitted.

(2) In section 35 of that Act (acceptance) before the words "when the goods have been delivered to him, and he does any act in relation to them which is inconsistent with the ownership of the seller" there shall be inserted the words "(except where section 34 of this Act otherwise provides)."

5. Nothing in this Act shall apply in relation to any misrepresentation or contract of sale which is made before the commencement of this Act.

NOTE. The Act is not in force in any Canadian jurisdiction. For a detailed criticism of its provisions, see Atiyah and Treitel, "Misrepresentation Act," 1967 (1967) 30 Mod. L.R. 369.

NOTE ON ADVERTISING. Advertising methods common to us today have their origins in the last century, and the cases on misrepresentation are part of the common law background of the subject. Besides these cases you may recall the *Carlill* case, above, p. 410, in which the offeror was conceded a right to "puff" in his offer. The modern problems include a curious distortion of grammar that results in a kind of double talk. The following illustration will suffice.

Under the title "More Canadians are gulled by advertisers than any other brand" Strowan Robertson, in the magazine *Canadian Art* (September October 1962, p. 347), objects to the advertising slogan, "More Canadians use Colgates' than any other tooth paste." He asks how many Canadians believe that the advertiser has said, "Canadians use Colgates' more than any other tooth paste." Such a claim would, Robertson thinks, "require proof," but he adds that no such claim was made. Let us suppose that the Canadians do believe the advertiser said one thing, and that, grammatically interpreted, he said another. Let us suppose too, that the advertiser knew that he would be taken to mean what "Canadians believe" he meant rather than literally what he said. Should the advertiser's claim then "require proof"? Does it require proof? Who can require it? Is it a misrepresentation?

Professor I. A. Richards points out in his essay "The Future of the Humanities in General Education" in his *Speculative Instruments* (1955) another and greater danger presented by the irresponsible advertiser: the danger of trivialization. He illustrates with a wartime advertisement showing a man drinking beer in comfort surrounded by newspapers with disaster headlines. The caption read, "In a world of strife/There is peace in beer/In these bewildering times, where can a man turn to replenish the wells of his courage ... to repair the walls of his faith." Would it be cricket to hold the advertiser responsible, not for what he says, grammatically interpreted, but for what he believes his audience believes, in the hope that this responsibility may also counter the trivialization?

RANGER v. *HERBERT A. WATTS (QUEBEC) LTD.* (1970) 10 D.L.R. (3d) 395 (Ont. H.C.) The defendants were manufacturers of cigarettes, who advertised that those finding "cash certificates" in cigarette packages would win the amount of money indicated on the certificate. The plaintiff found a certificate for $10,000 in a package of cigarettes he had purchased. On the certificate it was indicated that the holder would be required to answer a time-limited skill-testing question. The defendants' representative telephoned the plaintiff and asked him to solve an arithmetical problem; the plaintiff was upset at the time, had lost his glasses, and was therefore unable to write down the figures. He was unable to give the correct answer, and the defendants refused to pay the money. Haines J. held that there was a contract between the parties, one of the terms of which was that the test would be fairly administered with advance notice and an attempt to ensure that the claimant was in a reasonable state to undergo the test. The learned judge found that the test had not been fairly administered, and he awarded $10,000 for breach of contract. He also said: "It seems to me the time has arrived for an examination of our law upon the obligation of manufacturers and vendors of products to implement their undertaking given in the news media by nation-wide advertising. By such means they stimulate reliance upon the safety and quality of their products; and in order to stimulate sales offer a host of prizes. To allow a producer to evade the fair implication of his advertising is to permit him to reap a rich harvest of profit without obligation to the purchaser. . . . By newspaper, radio, and television every home has become the display window of the manufacturer, and the stand of every pitchman. By extraordinary skill the printed and spoken word together with the accompanying art form and drama have become an alluring and attractive means of representation of quality and confidence. Honesty in advertising is a concept worthy of re-examination."

COMBINES INVESTIGATION ACT
Statutes of Canada 1976, c. C-23

s.36 (1) No person shall, for the purpose of promoting directly or indirectly the supply or use of a product or for the purpose of promoting directly or indirectly, any business interest, by any means whatever, make a representation to the public that is false or misleading in a material respect. . . .

(5) Any person who violates subsection (1) is guilty of an offence and is liable (a) on conviction on indictment, to a fine in the discretion of the court or to imprisonment for five years or to both; or (b) on summary conviction, to a fine of twenty-five thousand dollars or to imprisonment for one year or to both.

31.1 (1) Any person who has suffered loss or damage as a result of conduct that is contrary to any provision of Part V [Section 36 is in Part V] . . . may, in any court of competent jurisdiction, sue for and recover from the person who engaged in the conduct . . . an amount equal to the loss or damage proved to have been suffered by him. . .

NOTE. See also Business Practices Act (Ont.), chapter 7, *supra.*

PROBLEM. Able advertises a hair dye as "safe and gentle to the mildest skin."

Baker buys some from Charlie, a retailer, and contracts dermatitis from its use. Inside the package is a sheet of paper headed "Directions for use." At the bottom is printed "Able is not responsible for any injuries." Can Baker sue Able?

2. MISTAKE AS TO CONTRACTUAL TERMS

The cases in this section raise some aspects of the problem of mistake on the part of one or both of the parties which one party asserts as evidence that they are not in true agreement, that a valid bargain has not been struck, that a promise has not been made. In this section, these complexities are increased by the addition of an element of direct ambiguity in the dealings: mistake as to the terms agreed upon. See chapter 6, above, especially section 3.

HOBBS v. ESQUIMALT & NANAIMO RAILWAY COMPANY
British Columbia. Supreme Court of Canada. 1899. 29 S.C.R. 450

Hobbs paid the Railway Company $120 on account of the purchase of a quarter section of land at three dollars an acre, payment to be made over three years. The receipt described the land without reservation and was signed by John Trutch, Land Commissioner for the Railway. The Company claimed that Mr. Trutch had no authority to convey the minerals and three years later offered a conveyance with minerals reserved. Hobbs asked for specific performance. The trial Judge refused it but declared that Hobbs was entitled to a conveyance with the reservation or to repayment of the purchase money with interest and compensation for improvements. The Court of Appeal denied him the option of repayment.

TASCHEREAU J. (dissenting): I would dismiss this appeal. The reason given in the courts below against the appellant's right to specific performance are, in my opinion, unanswerable. There has been no contract between this company and Hobbs. The company thought they were selling the land without the minerals. Hobbs thought he was buying the land with the minerals. So that the company did not sell what Hobbs thought he was buying, and Hobbs did not buy what the company thought they were selling. Therefore, there was no contract between them. Hobbs would not have bought it if he had known that the company were selling only surface rights, and the company would not have sold if they had thought that Hobbs intended to buy the land with the minerals. The ratification by the company stands upon no better ground. It was nothing but ratification of a sale without the minerals.

The rule that any one dealing with another has the right to believe that this other one means what he says, or says what he means, is one that cannot be gainsaid. But it has no application here. Assuming that the agent sold the land with the minerals, he did what he had not the power to do. However, he did not do it.

I would dismiss the appeal with costs.

KING J.: The facts are stated in the judgment of the late Chief Justice Davie before whom the case was tried.

It is found by him that Mr. Trutch acted beyond the scope of his authority in agreeing to a sale of the land without reservation of the minerals, but that the contract so made was rectified [ratified] by the company. He, however, was of opinion that, in so ratifying it, the company were under a mistake as to its legal effect, and upon this ground he declined to compel performance but left the plaintiff to his common law remedy for breach of contract.

A first question is as to whether there was, by reason of the alleged mistake, a contract at all. . . .

Here the parties were *ad idem* as to the terms of the contract. It was expressed in perfectly unambiguous language in the offer of the plaintiff and in the acceptance of defendants; and the alleged difference is in a wholly esoteric meaning which one of them gives to the plain words.

Then the legal right existing (as held by the Court below) is it a case (as also held by it) where a court will leave the party aggrieved by a breach to his common law remedy? As already mentioned *Stewart* v. *Kennedy* (1895), 15 App. Cas. 75, is not a case relating to the effect of mistake upon the exercise of the equitable jurisdiction of English Courts of Equity, but English authorities having been referred to, the jurisprudence is thus summarized by Lord Macnaghton (p. 105):

"It cannot be disputed that the Court of Chancery had refused specific performance in cases of mistake when the mistake has been on one side only, and even when the mistake on the part of the defendant resisting specific performance, has not been induced or contributed to by any act or omission on the part of the plaintiff. But I do not think it is going too far to say that in all those cases—certainly in all that have occurred in recent times—the court has thought rightly or wrongly that the circumstances of the particular case under consideration were such that (to use a well known phrase) it would be 'highly unreasonable' to enforce the agreement specifically."

In *Tamplin* v. *James* (1880), 15 Ch. D. 215, James L.J. says:

"If a man will not take reasonable care to ascertain what he is buying he must take the consequences. It is not enough for a purchaser to swear: 'I thought the farm sold contained twelve fields which I knew, and I find it does not include them all,' or 'I thought it contained 100 acres and it only contains 80.' It would open the door to fraud if such a defence was to be allowed. Perhaps some of the cases on this subject go too far (i.e. in the direction of allowing such defence) but for the most part the cases where a defendant has escaped on the ground of a mistake not contributed to by the plaintiff have been cases where a hardship amounting to injustice would have been inflicted upon him by holding him to his bargain and it was unreasonable to hold him to it."

Hence it may be, as stated in *Fry on Specific Performance*, that the court considers with more favour as a defence the allegation of mistake in an agent than in a principal.

The alleged mistake is given in the evidence of Mr. Dunsmuir, the vice-president of the company. Speaking of the contract entered into by Mr. Trutch, he says:

"It only sold the surface. That is, we term it land in our office. We do not say surface right, we say land, land minus the minerals."

It is evident, then, that we may put Mr. Trutch aside, and treat the case on this point as if the company, upon an application by plaintiff for purchase of 160 acres of land, had entered into an agreement to sell the land in the identical words used by Mr. Trutch. In effect they say:

"We agreed to sell the land, but this means land reserving the minerals."

It may well be that in the administration of their varied business a loose but convenient form of speech may have been used in the office, but it is not stated that it was supposed to be a correct one, and it appears incredible that a company, a large part of whose business is that of a land company could reasonably suppose that in dealings with third persons for the sale of land, the word "land" means land with reservation of minerals. Mr. Trutch does not say that he misconceived the meaning of the word. His impression was that he had verbally notified the plaintiff that the minerals were to be reserved, and if he had done so the plaintiff would be precluded from obtaining the specific performance he seeks; but it has been found that notice was not given. The form of the company conveyances expressly reserving the minerals show that they were aware how to effect such object. The alleged mistake was therefore an unreasonable and careless one, and in view of the fact that the plaintiff went into possession under the contract, I do not think that it can be said to be unconscionable or highly unreasonable to enforce the specific performance of the contract.

[Appeal allowed with costs. Gwynne, Sedgwick and Girouard JJ. concurred, Gwynne J. with written reasons. In the Appendix of Privy Council Appeals in 31 S.C.R. a note indicates that the appeal was dismissed upon settlement between the parties.]

RAFFLES v. *WICHELHAUS*
England. Exchequer. 1864. 2 H. & C. 906; 159 E.R. 375

It was ageed at Liverpool that the plaintiff should sell to the defendants 125 bales of Surat cotton, guaranteed middling fair merchant's Dhollerah, to arrive ex "Peerless" from Bombay; and that the cotton should be taken from the quay, and that the defendants would pay the plaintiff at the rate of 17s. ¼d. per pound after the arrival of the goods in England. The goods did arrive by the "Peerless" but the defendants refused to accept the goods or pay the plaintiff for them. It was pleaded that the ship mentioned in the agreement was meant by the defendants to be the ship called the "Peerless" that sailed from Bombay in October; and that the plaintiff was only ready and willing and offered to deliver to the defendants cotton which arrived by another and different ship, which was also called the "Peerless," and which sailed from Bombay in December. Demurrer and joinder therein.

Milward, in support of the demurrer. The contract was for the sale of a number of bales of cotton of a particular description, which the plaintiff was ready to deliver. It is immaterial by what ship the cotton was to arrive, so that it was a ship called the "Peerless." The words "to arrive ex 'Peerless' " only meant that, if the vessel is lost on the voyage, the contract is to be at an end. [Pollock C.B. It would be a question for the jury whether both parties meant the same ship called the "Peerless."] That would be so if the contract was for the sale of a ship called the "Peerless," but it is for the sale of cotton on board a ship of that name. [Pollock C.B. The defendant only bought that cotton which was to arrive by a particular ship. It may as well be said that, if there is a contract for the purchase of certain goods in warehouse A., that is satisfied by the delivery of goods of the same description in warehouse B.] In that case there would be goods in both warehouses; here it does not appear that the plaintiff had any goods on board the other "Peerless." [Martin B. It is imposing on the defendant a contract different from that which he entered into. Pollock C.B. It is like a contract for the purchase of wine coming from a particular estate in France or Spain, where there are two estates of that name.] The defendant has no right to contradict by parol evidence a written contract good upon the face of it. He does not impute misrepresentation or fraud, but only says that he fancied the ship was a different one. Intention is of no avail, unless stated at the time of the contract. [Pollock C.B. One vessel sailed in October and the other in December.] The time of sailings is no part of the contract.

Mellish (Cohen with him), in support of the plea. There is nothing on the face of the contract to show that any particular ship called the "Peerless" was meant; but the moment it appears that two ships called the "Peerless" were about to sail from Bombay, there is a latent ambiguity, and parol evidence may be given for the purpose of showing that the defendant meant one "Peerless" and the plaintiff another. That being so, there was no *consensus ad idem*, and therefore no binding contract. [He was then stopped by the Court.]

PER CURIAM: There must be judgment for the defendants.

QUESTIONS. A offers to sell goods to B ex "Peerless" from Bombay. B accepts. There are two ships "Peerless." What is the situation if

(1) A knows or has reason to know this fact, but B does not know, or have reason to know;

(2) B knows or has reason to know of it, but A does not;

(3) Both know or have reason to know of it;

(4) Neither of them knows or has reason to know it at the time of communication?

FALCK v. *WILLIAMS.* [1900] A.C. 176 (New South Wales. Privy Council). After a protracted negotiation dealing with three different proposals: a Barcelona charter for the ship "Semiramis," an offer of a Liverpool charter, and a Fiji charter, the appellant telegraphed a code message, "Shale Copyright Semiramis Begloom Escorte Sultana Brilliant Argentina Bronchil." Decoded this meant, "Shale. Your rate is too low, impossible to work business at your figures. Semiramis. Have closed in accordance with your order. Confirm. Two Ports Fiji Islands, Sultana, Brilliant, Argentina. Keep a good look-out for business for this vessel and wire us when anything good offers." The appellant said the first two words dealt with both the Barcelona charter and the Liverpool proposal, and the next three words dealt with the "Semiramis." The respondent said that the first two words referred to the Liverpool proposal, the second two to the Barcelona charter, and that Escorte was to be read with what followed. Held, for the respondent. LORD MACNAGHTEN: "Indeed, the whole controversy when the matter is thrashed out seems to be narrowed down to this question—'Is the word "estcorte" to be read with what has gone before or with what follows?' In their Lordships' opinion there is no conclusive reason pointing one way or the other. The fault lay with the appellant's agent. If he had spent a few more shillings on his message, if he had even arranged the words he used more carefully, if he had only put the word 'estcorte' before the word 'begloom' instead of after it, there would have been no difficulty. It is not for their Lordships to determine what is the true construction of Buch's telegram. It was the duty of the appellant as plaintiff to make out that the construction which he put upon it was the true one. In that he must fail if the message was ambiguous, as their Lordships hold it to be. If the respondent had been maintaining his construction as plaintiff he would equally have failed."

HENKEL v. PAPE
England. Exchequer. 1870. L.R. 6 Ex. 7

Declaration for goods bargained and sold, and for goods sold and delivered.

Pleas, first, except as to £7 never indebted; and, secondly, as to £7, payment into Court. The plaintiffs accepted the money paid into Court, and joined issue on the first plea.

The plaintiffs are gun manufacturers in London and Birmingham, and the defendant is a gun-maker at Newcastle-upon-Tyne. On the 4th of June, 1870, the plaintiffs received from the defendant the following letter: "Send sample Snider, with sword-bayonet, forward immediately. I can fix an order for fifty, I think, and it may lead to many large orders. Can you do them at 34s. net cash on delivery, so as to secure the order? I shall have to cut very fine, and several will be in for it." In reply the plaintiffs wrote: "We have forwarded you this day sample Snider, with sword-bayonet. We cannot possibly do them for less than 35s. net cash." With this letter the sample was sent. On the 7th of June the plaintiffs received the following telegram purporting to come from the defendant: "Send by mail immediately *the* Snider rifles same as pattern. Must be here in the morning. Ship sails then." The plaintiffs on receipt of this communication sent fifty rifles to the defendant. On the 9th of June they received the following letter from him. "I am surprised that you sent fifty instead of three rifles. The telegram was to send three." In fact, the clerk who sent the telegraph message had by mistake telegraphed the word "the" instead of "three." The defendant had written "three," and not "the," on the message paper. Under these circumstances the plaintiffs insisted on the defendant accepting the fifty rifles sent, but the defendant declined to take more than three. This action was then brought. The defendant paid a sum into court sufficient to cover the price of three rifles and their carriage. He denied his liability as to the residue of the plaintiffs' claim, contending that he could not be made responsible for the mistake of the telegraph clerk.

The cause was tried before Blackburn J., at the Surrey Summer Assizes, 1870, when a verdict was directed for the defendant, with leave to move to enter a verdict for the plaintiffs for the invoice price of the remaining forty-seven rifles.

H. Thompson Chitty moved accordingly: The telegraph clerk was the defendant's agent to transmit the message, and the defendant is responsible for the mistake in the transmission. *Chitty on Contracts,* 6th ed., p. 197. There is no privity between the plaintiffs and the telegraph clerk, nor can they proceed against the Post-office, his employers: *Playford* v. *United Kingdom Telegraph Company,* L.P. 4 Q.B. 706. Their right remedy is against the defendant. Suppose in a letter written by himself he had made the mistake, he would clearly have been liable; and in the transmission of each particular message the telegraph clerk is the agent of the sender. Upon the sender therefore must rest the responsibility of any error committed by the agent in the course of his employment.

KELLY C.B.: We are of opinion that in this case there should be no rule. The question is whether the defendant has entered into a contract to purchase fifty rifles, and there is no doubt he might have bound himself either by letter or a telegraphic message. But the Post-office authorities are only agents to transmit messages in the terms in which the senders deliver them.

They have no authority to do more. Now in this case the evidence is that the defendant agreed to take three rifles, and three only, and he authorized the telegraph clerk to send a message to that and to no other effect. That being so, there was no contract between the plaintiffs and defendant for the purchase of fifty rifles. The defendant cannot be made responsible because the telegraph clerk made a mistake in the transmission of the message. There was no contract between the parties such as the plaintiffs rely on. The verdict therefore ought to stand.

[Bramwell, Piggott, and Cleasby, BB. concurred. Rule refused.]

DICKSON v. *REUTER'S TELEGRAM CO., LTD.* 1872. 2 C.P.D. 62 (England. Common Pleas). In this case the plaintiff received a telegram not intended for him, and claimed damages from the defendant Company amounting to £2600 representing losses on barley shipped by mistake in reliance on the message. Held, for the defendant. There was no contractual relationship between the plaintiff recipient of the telegram and the telegraph company, and a telegraph company is not supposed to have guaranteed towards all mankind the accuracy and care of their servants in all parts of the globe wherever they deliver a message. Nor is a telegraph company liable for innocent misrepresentations. [As to liability of a telegraph company to the sender, both for negligence and in contract, see *Kinghorne* v. *The Montreal Telegraph Co.* noted on p. 10.]

QUESTIONS. Suppose A writes an offer to buy sixty rifles which B accepts. A intended to write six. Is there a contract? A dictates a letter to his stenographer offering to buy six rifles. The stenographer takes it down as sixty. A signs the letter without reading it over. B accepts. Is there a contract? A, after dictating, tells his stenographer to sign the letter and mail it, and B accepts. Is there a contract? In *Henkel* v. *Pape* was there a contract for three rifles? Suppose the plaintiff were unwilling to sell three at the price quoted. Was any offer for three communicated to him?

SMITH v. HUGHES
England. Queen's Bench. 1871. L.R. 6 Q.B. 597

The plaintiff, a farmer, took a sample of some oats to Hughes, the manager of the defendant, who was an owner and trainer of horses. The plaintiff claimed to have said "I have some good oats for sale" and when Hughes replied "I am always a buyer of good oats," offered forty to fifty quarters at 35s. a quarter, Hughes took away a sample, and later wrote to say that he would take the oats at 34s. and the plaintiff sent him sixteen quarters, which Hughes complained were *new* oats. The plaintiff admitted they were and denied that he had any old oats. Hughes claimed that he had replied to the plaintiff, "I am always a buyer of good *old* oats," and that the plaintiff had replied, "I have some good old oats for sale." Hughes insisted that the plaintiff take the oats back. At the trial the Judge put two questions to the jury for their consideration: Was the word "old" used by the plaintiff or the defendant? If so, they must find for the defendant. If the word "old" was not used, were they of the opinion that the plaintiff believed that Hughes believed, or was under the impression, that he was contracting for the purchase of old oats? If so, they must find for the defendant. Otherwise, for the plaintiff. The jury did not answer the question specifically, but found a verdict for the defendant. On appeal the question was whether the direction was correct.

COCKBURN C.J.: . . . It is to be regretted that the jury were not required to give specific answers to the questions so left to them. For, it is quite possible that their verdict may have been given for the defendant on the first ground; in which case there could, I think, be no doubt as to the propriety of the judge's direction; whereas now, as it is possible that the verdict of the jury—or at all events of some of them—may have proceeded on the second ground, we are called upon to consider and decide whether the ruling of the learned judge with reference to the second question was right.

For this purpose we must assume that nothing was said on the subject of the defendant's manager desiring to buy old oats, nor of the oats having been said to be old; while on the other hand, we must assume that the defendant's manager believed the oats to be old oats, and that the plaintiff was conscious of the existence of such belief, but did nothing, directly or indirectly, to bring it about, simply offering his oats and exhibiting his sample, remaining perfectly passive as to what was passing in the mind of the other party. The question is whether, under such circumstances, the passive acquiescence of the seller in the self-deception of the buyer will entitle the latter to avoid the contract. I am of opinion that it will not. . . .

I take the true rule to be, that where a specific article is offered for sale, without express warranty, or without circumstances from which the law will imply a warranty—as where, for instance, an article is ordered for a specific purpose—and the buyer has full opportunity of inspecting and forming his own judgment, if he chooses to act on his own judgment, the rule *caveat emptor* applies. If he gets the article he contracted to buy, and that article corresponds with what it was sold as, he gets all he is entitled to, and is bound by the contract. Here the defendant agreed to buy a specific parcel of oats. The oats were what they were sold as, namely, good oats according to the sample. The buyer persuaded himself they were old oats, when they were not so; but the seller neither said nor did anything to contribute to his deception. He has himself to blame. The question is not what a man of scrupulous morality or nice honour would do under such circumstances. The case put of the purchase of an estate, in which there is a mine under the surface, but the fact is unknown to the seller, is one in which a man of tender conscience or high honour would be unwilling to take advantage of the ignorance of the seller; but there can be no doubt that the contract for the sale of the estate would be binding. . . .

Now, in this case, there was plainly no legal obligation in the plaintiff in the first instance to state whether the oats were new or old. He offered them for sale according to the sample, as he had a perfect right to do, and gave the buyer the fullest opportunity of inspecting the sample, which, practically, was equivalent to an inspection of the oats themselves. What, then, was there to create any trust or confidence between the parties, so as to make it incumbent on the plaintiff to communicate the fact that the oats were not, as the defendant assumed them to be, old oats? If, indeed, the buyer, instead of acting on his own opinion, had asked the question whether the oats were old or new or had said anything which intimated his understanding that the seller was selling the oats as old oats, the case would have been wholly different; or even if he had said anything which shewed that he was not acting on his own inspection and judgment, but assumed as the foundation of the contract that the oats were old, the silence of the seller, as a means of misleading him, might have amounted to a fraudulent concealment, such as would have entitled the buyer to avoid the contract. Here, however, nothing of the sort occurs. The buyer in no way refers to the seller, but acts entirely on his own judgment. . . .

In the case before us it must be taken that, as the defendant, on a portion of the oats being delivered, was able by inspection to ascertain that they were new oats, his manager might, by due inspection of the sample, have arrived at the same result. The case is, therefore, one of the sale and purchase of a specific article after inspection by the buyer. Under these circumstances the rule *caveat emptor* clearly applies; more especially as this cannot be put as a case of latent defect, but simply one in which the seller did not make known to the buyer a circumstance affecting the quality of the thing sold. The oats in question were in no sense defective, on the contrary they were good oats, and all that can be said is that they had not acquired the quality which greater age would have given them. There is not, so far as I am aware, any authority for the position that a vendor who submits the subject-matter of sale to the inspection of the vendee, is bound to state circumstances which may tend to detract from the estimate which the buyer may injudiciously have formed of its value. Even the civil law, and the foreign law, founded upon it, which require that the seller shall answer for latent defects, have never gone the length of saying that, so long as the thing sold answers to the description under which it is sold, the seller is bound to disabuse the buyer as to any exaggerated estimate of its value.

It only remains to deal with an argument which was pressed upon us, that the defendent in the present case intended to buy old oats, and the plaintiff to sell new, so that the two minds were not *ad idem*; and that consequently there was no contract. This argument proceeds on the fallacy of confounding what was merely a motive operating on the buyer to induce him to buy with one of the essential conditions of the contract. Both parties were agreed as to the sale and purchase of this particular parcel of oats. The defendant believed the oats to be old, and was thus induced to agree to buy them, but he omitted to make their age a condition of the contract. All that can be said is, that the two minds were not *ad idem* as to the age of the oats; they certainly were *ad idem* as to the sale and purchase of them. Suppose a person to buy a horse without warranty, believing him to be sound, and the horse turns out unsound could it be contended that it would be open to him to say that, as he had intended to buy a sound horse, and the seller to sell him an unsound one, the contract was void, because the seller must have known from the price the buyer was willing to give, or from his general habits as a buyer of horses, that he thought the horse was sound? The cases are exactly parallel.

The result is that, in my opinion, the learned judge of the county court was wrong in leaving the second question to the jury, and that, consequently, the case must go down to a new trial.

BLACKBURN J.: . . . The jury were directed that, if they believed the word "old" was used, they should find for the defendant—and this was right; for if that was the case it is obvious that neither did the defendant intend to enter into a contract on the plaintiff's terms, that is, to buy his parcel of oats without any stipulation as to their quality; nor could the plaintiff have been led to believe he was intending to do so.

But the second direction raises the difficulty. I think that, if from that direction the jury would understand that they were first to consider whether they were satisfied that the defendant intended to buy this parcel of oats on the terms that it was part of his contract with the plaintiff that they were old oats, so as to have the warranty of the plaintiff to that effect, they were properly told that, if that was so, the defendant could not be bound to a contract without any warranty unless the plaintiff was misled. But I doubt whether the direction would bring to the minds of the jury the distinction between agreeing to take the oats under the belief that they were old, and agreeing to take the oats under the belief that the plaintiff contracted that they were old.

The difference is the same as that between buying a horse believed to be sound, and buying one believed to be warranted sound; but I doubt if it was made obvious to the jury, and I doubt this the more because I do not see much evidence to justify a finding for the defendant on this latter ground if the word "old" was not used. There may have been more evidence than is stated in the case; and the demeanour of the witnesses may have strengthened the impression produced by the evidence there was; but it does not seem a very satisfactory verdict if it proceeded on this latter ground. I agree, therefore, in the result that there should be a new trial.

HANNEN J.: . . . If, therefore, in the present case, the plaintiff knew that the defendant, in dealing with him for oats, did so on the assumption that the plaintiff was contracting to sell him old oats, he was aware that the defendant apprehended the contract in a different sense to that in which he meant it, and he is thereby deprived of the right to insist that the defendant shall be bound by that which was only the apparent, and not the real bargain.

This was the question which the learned judge intended to leave to the jury; as I have already said, I do not think it was incorrect in its terms, but I think that it was likely to be misunderstood by the jury. The jury was asked, "whether they were of opinion, on the whole of the evidence, that the plaintiff believed the defendant to believe, or to be under the impression that he was contracting for the purchase of old oats? If so, there would be a verdict for the defendant." The jury may have understood this to mean that, if the plaintiff believed the defendant to believe that he was buying old oats, the defendant would be entitled to the verdict, but a belief on the part of the plaintiff that the defendant was making a contract to buy the oats, of which he offered him a sample, under a mistaken belief that they were old, would not relieve the defendant from liability unless his mistaken belief were induced by some misrepresentation of the plaintiff, or concealment by him of the fact which it became his duty to communicate. In order to relieve the defendant it was necessary that the jury should find not merely that the plaintiff believed the defendant to believe that he was buying old oats, but that he believed the defendant to believe that he, the plaintiff, was contracting to sell old oats.

I am the more disposed to think that the jury did not understand the question in this last sense because I can find very little, if any, evidence to support a finding upon it in favour of the defendant. It may be assumed that the defendant believed the oats were old, and it may be suspected that the plaintiff thought he so believed, but the only evidence from which it can be inferred that the plaintiff believed that the defendant thought that the plaintiff was making it a term of the contract that the oats were old is that the defendant was a trainer, and that trainers, as a rule, use old oats and that the price given was high for new oats, and more than a prudent man would have given.

Having regard to the admitted fact that the defendant bought the oats after two days' detention of the sample, I think that the evidence was not sufficient to justify the jury in answering the question put to them in the defendant's favour, if they rightly understood it; and I therefore think there should be a new trial.

BELL v. *LEVER BROTHERS, LTD.* [1932] A.C. 161 (England. House of Lords). LORD ATKIN: "The Court [in *Smith* v. *Hughes*] ordered a new trial. It is not quite clear whether they considered that if the defendant's contention was correct, the parties were not *ad idem* or there was a contractual condition that the oats were old oats. In either case the defendant would succeed in defaulting the claim.

"In these cases I am inclined to think that the true analysis is that there is a contract, but that the one party is not able to supply the very thing whether goods or services that the other party contracted to take; and therefore the contract is unenforceable by the one if executory, while if executed the other can recover money paid on the ground of failure of consideration."

QUESTIONS. Suppose that A writes B. "I offer to sell you my horse for $100." B, knowing that A intends to offer to sell his cow, and not his horse, and knowing that "horse" is an error, replies, "I accept." Is there any contract for a horse or a cow? Suppose that A, on learning of his error, now wants to hold B to take the horse, has he the right?

LONDON COUNTY COUNCIL v. *HENRY BOOT & SONS LTD.* [1959] 1 W.L.R. 1069 (H.L.) The plaintiffs (respondents) were building contractors who had entered into an agreement with the London County Council for the construction of apartment buildings. The parties executed a standard form contract which included a clause providing for increased payment to the contractors in the event of increases in the "rates of wages" paid out by the contractors. There existed a scheme, designed to ensure that workman would have a proper holiday even if they changed jobs, whereby an employer contributed regularly to the cost of the employee's annual holiday by buying "holiday stamps" for him. The dispute in this case was on the question of whether an increase in the cost of the holiday stamps was an increase in the "rates of wages" so as to entitle the contractor to increased payment for the work. It so happened that before executing the contract the parties had foreseen the problem, and the Council had expressed its view that the clause would not cover an increase in the cost of the stamps, whereas the plaintiffs, through their trade association had expressed the contrary view. The parties reached no conclusion, and executed the contract as printed. It was argued that there was no completed agreement, since the parties differed on the terms to which each thought he was agreeing. The House of Lords rejected that argument, holding that there was a binding agreement which they interpreted in favour of the Council.

LORD DENNING: ... I may add, perhaps, a word on the correspondence which took place before the contract was executed. The London County Council there made it clear that they did not regard holiday credits as coming within the rise-and-fall clause; but the builders' association took a different view. Neither side inserted any words in the contract so as to clear up the difference between them. They left the rise-and-fall clause as it was. It was suggested that on this account there was no consensus ad idem; Your Lordships rejected this suggestion without wishing to hear further argument upon it. There was, to all outward appearances, agreement by the parties on the one thing that really mattered—on the terms that should bind them. In case of difference as to the meaning of those terms, it was for the court to determine it. It does not matter what the parties, in their innermost states of mind, thought the terms meant. They may each have meant different things. But still the contract is binding according to its terms—as interpreted by the court.

In my opinion, on the true interpretation of clause 23A, holidays credits do not come within it.

A. ROBERTS & CO. LTD. v. LEICESTERSHIRE COUNTY COUNCIL

[1961] 1 Ch. 555. The plaintiffs, who were building contractors, submitted a tender for the construction of a school for the defendant Council. By the terms of the tender, the work was to be completed in eighteen months. The defendants accepted the plaintiffs' tender, but sent to them for execution a document which allowed a period of thirty months for completion of the work, the date for completion being one year later than that in the plaintiffs' tender. The plaintiffs executed the document without noticing the discrepancy, which was evidently to the advantage of the Council. On discovering the discrepancy, the plaintiffs sued for rectification of the contract so that it should conform with the date submitted in the tender. It was clear that the Council never intended to agree to anything except the thirty month period, and that the plaintiffs never intended to agree to anything except the shorter period. But Pennycuick J. ordered rectification on the ground that the Council knew of the plaintiffs' understanding, and could not therefore be allowed to insist on different terms.

For a comment on this case and the *Boot* case, see Atiyah, "Judicial Techniques and the English Law of Contract" (1968), 2 Ottawa L.R. 337.

See also chapter 6, *supra*.

PROBLEM 1. Able has two race horses for sale by auction, "Pegasus" worth $10,000, described in the auction catalogue as "lot 1," and "Glanders" worth $500 and described as "lot 2." By mistake the sale numbers attached to the horses' hips are interchanged and "Glanders" is led in as "lot 1" and knocked down to Baker for $8,000. "Pegasus" is knocked down as "lot 2" to Charlie for $500. Baker and Charlie pay the prices and take delivery respectively of "Glanders" and "Pegasus." The mistake comes to light the next day. What is the legal position of the three parties? See *Diamond* v. *B.C. Thoroughbred Breeders' Society* (1965), 52 D.L.R. (2d) 146.

PROBLEM 2. (a) Able agreed to sell, and Baker to buy a house at "300 Spadina" for $50,000. Able's house was at 300 Spadina Avenue, but Baker mistakenly assumed that it was at 300 Spadina Road and had inspected the outside of that house. Able's house is worth $25,000; 300 Spadina Road is worth

$75,000. Able brings an action for specific performance, and Baker counter-claims for damages.

(b) The house was accurately described in the document as 300 Spadina Avenue, but Baker mistakenly thought it was the house at 300 Spadina Road. During the course of negotiations Baker had said that he was pleased that the new subway would be so close. The new subway is close to 300 Spadina Road but not to 300 Spadina Avenue. Able wondered at the time what Baker meant but then dismissed the matter from his mind.

3. MISTAKE IN ASSUMPTIONS

This section is concerned with the problems that arise when the parties are agreed on the same terms, but the motive that induced one party to enter into the agreement later turns out to have been based on a false assumption. This is the case where a party buys a valueless stone believing it to be a diamond, or where one buys a piece of land believing it to contain a gold mine. The problem is closely connected with the problem of relief against unjust enrichment, for the man who sells a cheap stone for the price of a diamond is clearly enriched if the money has actually changed hands; even if the price is not yet paid when the mistake comes to light, the problem may still usefully be regarded as one of enrichment, for if the court will enforce the seller's rights against the buyer, the seller surely has obtained some-thing of value from the buyer, namely, a right of action against him. See the remarks of Bowen L.J. in *Newbigging* v. *Adam, supra.* By classifying the problem as one of enrichment, however, one is no nearer a solution. For life is full of enrichments, and indeed, of mistakes, and the unanswered question is when, if at all, should a court of Justice step in to restore an enrichment caused by an agreement entered into on a false assumption. On the whole question see Palmer, *Mistake and Unjust Enrichment*, Ohio State University Press, 1962.

BELL v. LEVER BROTHERS, LTD.
England. House of Lords. [1932] A.C. 161

Lever Brothers, Ltd., holding practically all the stock of the Niger Com-pany, Limited, entered into an agreement with Bell in 1926 by which the latter was to be employed by Lever Brothers for five years at £8,000 a year, and to act as chairman of the Niger Company. In 1929, in view of the amalgamation of the Niger Company with other companies, Lever Brothers entered into an agreement with Bell on March 19, to pay him £30,000 in satisfaction of all Bell's claims against them. The money was paid and the employment terminated.

Later in the year, Lever Brothers discovered that Bell had been, in 1927, dealing in, and making profits on his own account amounting to perhaps £1,000, in the same materials that the Niger Company dealt in, and had not disclosed these secret profits.

Lever Brothers thereupon brought action claiming the return of the £30,000 paid under the agreement of 1929, alleging fraudulent misrepre-sentation, and breach of the former employment contracts.

At the trial before Wright J. the jury denied that the agreement of 1929 was induced by fraud, but found that Bell had committed a breach of the employment contract by undertaking the private dealings, and that Lever Brothers were entitled to terminate the employment contract by reason of such breach, and would have terminated such contract had the facts been known. They further found that Lever Brothers did not know of the private dealings in 1929 and would not have entered into the agreement of March 19, 1929, had such facts been known to them.

On these findings Wright J. gave judgment for the plaintiffs, Lever Brothers, stating that the agreement was based on a mutual mistake, which, in the language of *Kennedy* v. *Panama Royal Mail Co.* (1867), L.R. 2 Q.B. 580, went "to the substance . . . or root of the matter." The mistake was the existence of the previous service agreement. Bell appealed.

In the Court of Appeal, Scrutton L.J., said, in part: ". . . In my opinion, on the facts of the present case the defendants were under an obligation, before and at the time of their negotiation of the contracts to terminate their services to disclose their dealings in breach of their contracts, and the contracts to terminate can be avoided by this non-disclosure. Wright J.'s ground of decision, with which I agree, is sufficient to support his judgment, but I think it could also be supported on the ground of failure to disclose material facts.

"I only desire to add that, in my view, the case of *Kennedy* v. *Panama etc. Co.* so far as it decides that an innocent misrepresentation, though material, is not a ground for rescission unless it is also fundamental, is no longer law, in view of the fusion of common law and equity by the Judicature Acts, the rule of equity prevailing. Also I reserve liberty to consider the decision in *Seddon* v. *North Eastern Salt Co.*, [1905] 1 Ch. 326, so far as it decides that executed contracts cannot be rescinded for innocent and material misrepresentation. The appeal must be dismissed with costs." Lawrence and Greer L.JJ. agreed with Scrutton L.J. So Bell appealed again. In the House of Lords, Lords Atkin, Blanesburgh and Thankerton gave reason for allowing the appeal. Viscount Hailsham and Lord Warrington of Clyffe dissented, taking the view that, in the words of Lord Warrington, "the erroneous assumption on the part of both parties to the agreement that the service contracts were undeterminable except by agreement was of such a fundamental character as to constitute an underlying assumption without which the parties would not have made the contract."

LORD ATKIN: . . . Two points present themselves for decision. Was the agreement of March 19, 1929, void of reason of a mutual mistake of Mr. D'Arcy Cooper and Mr. Bell?

Could the agreement of March 19, 1929, be avoided by reason of the failure of Mr. Bell to disclose his misconduct in regard to the cocoa dealings?

My Lords, the rules of law dealing with the effect of mistake on contract appear to be established with reasonable clearness. If mistake operates at all it operates so as to negative or in some cases nullify consent. The parties may be mistaken in the identity of the contracting parties, or in the existence of the subject-matter of the contract at the date of the contract, or in the quality of the subject-matter of the contract. These mistakes may be by one party, or by both, and the legal effect may depend upon the class of mistake above mentioned. Thus a mistaken belief by A. that he is contracting with B., whereas in fact he is contracting with C., will negative consent where it is clear that the intention of A. was to contract only with B. So the agreement of A. and B. to purchase a specific article is void if in fact the article had perished before the date of sale. In this case, though the parties in fact were agreed about the subject-matter, yet· a consent to transfer or take delivery of something not existent is deemed useless, [and] the consent is nullified. As codified in the Sale of Goods Act the contract is expressed to be void if the seller was in ignorance of the destruction of the specific chattel. I apprehend that if the seller with knowledge that a chattel was destroyed purported to sell it to a purchaser, the latter might sue for damages for non-delivery though the former could not sue for non-acceptance, but I know of no case where a seller has so committed himself. This is a case where mutual mistake certainly and unilateral mistake by the seller of goods will prevent a contract from arising. Corresponding to mistake as to the existence of the subject-matter is mistake as to title in cases where, unknown to the parties, the buyer is already the owner of that which the seller purports to sell to him. The parties intended to effectuate a transfer of ownership: such a transfer is impossible: the stipulation is *naturali ratione inutilis*. This is the case of *Cooper* v. *Phibbs* (1867), L.R. 2 H.L. 149 where A. agreed to take a lease of a fishery from B., though contrary to the belief of both parties at the time A. was tenant for life of the fishery and B. appears to have had no title at all. To such a case Lord Westbury applied the principle that if parties contract under a mutual mistake and misapprehension as to their relative and respective rights the result is that the agreement is liable to be set aside as having proceeded upon a common mistake. Applied to the context the statement is only subject to the criticism that the agreement would appear to be void rather than voidable. Applied to mistake as to rights generally it would appear to be too wide. Even where the vendor has no title, though both parties think he has, the correct view would appear to be that there is a contract: but that the vendor has either committed a breach of the stipulation as to title, or is not able to perform his contract. The contract is unenforceable by him but is not void.

Mistake as to quality of the thing contracted for raises more difficult questions. In such a case a mistake will not affect assent unless it is the mistake of both parties, and is as to the existence of some quality which makes the thing without the quality essentially different from the thing as it was believed to be. Of course it may appear that the parties contracted that the article should possess the quality which one or other or both mistakenly believed it to possess. But in such a case there is a contract and the inquiry is a different one, being whether the contract as to quality amounts to a condition or a warranty, a different branch of the law. The principles to be applied are to be found in two cases which as far as my knowledge goes, have always been treated as authoritative expositions of the law. The first is *Kennedy* v. *Panama Royal Mail Co.*

In that case the plaintiff had applied for shares in the defendant company on the faith of a prospectus which stated falsely but innocently that the company had a binding contract with the Government of New Zealand for the carriage of mails. On discovering the true facts the plaintiff brought an action for the recovery of the sums he had paid on calls. The defendant brought a cross action for further calls. . . .

The Court came to the conclusion in that case that, though there was a misapprehension as to that which was a material part of the motive inducing the applicant to ask for the shares, it did not prevent the shares from being in substance those he applied for.

The next case is *Smith* v. *Hughes* (1871), L.R. 6 Q.B. 597, the well known case as to new and old oats. . . .

In these cases I am inclined to think that the true analysis is that there is a contract, but that the one party is not able to supply the very thing whether goods or services that the other party contracted to take; and therefore the contract is unenforceable by the one if executory, while if executed the other can recover back money paid on the ground of failure of the consideration.

We are now in a position to apply to the facts of this case the law as to mistake as far as it has been stated. It is essential on this part of the discussion to keep in mind the finding of the jury acquitting the defendants of fraudulent misrepresentation or concealment in procuring the agreements in question. Grave injustice may be done to the defendants and confusion introduced into the legal conclusion, unless it is quite clear that in considering mistake in this case no suggestion of fraud is admissible and cannot strictly be regarded by the judge who has to determine the legal issues raised. The agreement which is said to be void is the agreement contained in the letter of March 19, 1929, that Bell would retire from the Board of the Niger Company and its subsidiaries, and that in consideration of his doing so Levers would pay him as compensation for the termination of his agreements and consequent loss of office the sum of £30,000 in full satisfaction and discharge of all claims and demands of any kind against Lever Brothers, the Niger Company or its subsidiaries. The agreement, which as part of the contract was terminated, had been broken so that it could be repudiated. Is an agreement to terminate a broken contract different in kind from an agreement to terminate an unbroken contract, assuming that the breach has given the one party the right to declare the contract at an end? I feel the weight of the plaintiffs' contention that a contract immediately determinable is a different thing from a contract for an unexpired term, and that the difference in kind can be illustrated by the immense price of release from the longer contract as compared with the shorter. And I agree that an agreement to take an assignment of a lease for five years is not the same thing as to take an assignment of a lease for three years, still less a term for a few months. But, on the whole, I have come to the conclusion that it would be wrong to decide that an agreement to terminate a definite specified contract is void if it turns out that the agreement had already been broken and could have been terminated otherwise. The contract released is the identical contract in both cases, and the party paying for release gets exactly what he bargains for. It seems immaterial that he could have got the same result in another way, or that if he had known the true facts he would not have entered into the bargain. A buys B's horse; he thinks the horse is sound and he pays the price of a sound horse; he would certainly not have bought the horse if he had known as the fact is that the horse is unsound. If B has made no representation as to soundness and has not contracted that the horse is sound, A is bound and cannot recover back the price. A buys a picture from B; both A and B believe it to be the work of an old master, and a high price is paid. It turns out to be a modern copy. A has no remedy in the absence of representation or warranty. A agrees to take on lease or to buy from B an unfurnished dwelling-house. The house is in fact uninhabitable. A would never have entered into the bargain if he had known the fact. A has no remedy, and the position is the same whether B knew the facts or not, so long as he made no representation or gave no warranty. A buys a roadside garage business from B abutting on a public thoroughfare; unknown to A, but known to B, it has already been decided to construct a bypass road which will divert substantially the whole of the traffic from passing A's garage. Again A has no remedy. All these cases involve hardship on A and benefit B, as most people would say, unjustly. They can be supported on the ground that it is of paramount importance that contracts should be observed, and that if parties honestly comply with the essentials of the formation of contracts—i.e., agree in the same terms on the same subject-matter—they are bound, and must rely on the stipulations of the contract for protection from the effect of facts unknown to them.

This brings the discussion to the alternative mode of expressing the result of a mutual mistake. It is said that in such a case as the present there is to be implied a stipulation in the contract that a condition of its efficacy is that the facts should be as understood by both parties—namely, that the contract could not be terminated till the end of the current term. The question of the existence of conditions, express or implied, is obviously one that affects not the formation of contract, but the investigation of the terms of the contract when made. A condition derives its efficacy from the consent of the parties, express or implied. They have agreed, but on what terms. One term may be that unless the facts are or are not of a particular nature, or unless an event has or has not happened, the contract is not to take effect. With regard to future facts such a condition is obviously contractual. Till the event occurs the parties are bound. Thus the condition (the exact terms of which need not here be investigated) that is generally accepted as underlying the principle of the frustration cases is contractual, an implied condition. Sir John Simon formulated for the assistance of your Lordships a proposition which should be recorded: "Whenever it is to be inferred from the terms of a contract or its surrounding circumstances that the consensus has been reached upon the basis of a particular contractual assumption, and that assumption is not true, the contract is avoided: i.e., it is void ab initio if the assumption is of present fact and it ceases to bind if the assumption is of future fact."

I think few would demur to this statement but its value depends upon the meaning of "a contractual assumption," and also upon the true meaning to be attached to "basis," a metaphor which may mislead. When used expressly in contracts, for instance, in policies of insurance, which state that the truth of the statements in the proposal is to be the basis of the contract of insurance, the meaning is clear. The truth of the statements is made a condition of the contract, which failing, the contract is void unless the condition is waived. The proposition does not amount to more than this that, if the contract expressly or impliedly contains a term that a particular assumption is a condition of the contract, the contract is avoided if the assumption is not true. But we have not advanced far on the inquiry how to ascertain whether the contract does contain such a condition. Various words are to be found to define the state of things which make a condition. "In the contemplation of both parties fundamental to the continued validity of the contract," "a foundation essential to its existence," "a fundamental reason for making it," are phrases found in the important judgment of Scrutton L.J. in the present case. The first two phrases appear to me to be unexceptionable. They cover the case of a contract to serve in a particular place, the existence of which is fundamental to the service, or to procure the services of a professional vocalist, whose continued health is essential to performance. But "a fundamental reason for making a contract" may, with respect, be misleading. The reason of one party only is presumably not intended, but in the cases I have suggested above, of the sale of a horse or of a picture, it might be said that the fundamental reason for making the contract was the belief of both parties that the horse was sound or the picture an old master, yet in neither case would the condition as I think exist. Nothing is more dangerous than to allow oneself liberty to construct for the parties contracts which they have not in terms made by importing implications which would appear to make the contract more business-like or more just. The implications to be made are to be no more than are "necessary" for giving business efficacy to the transaction, and it appears to me that, both as to existing facts and future facts, a condition would not be implied unless the new state of facts makes the contract something different in kind from the contract in the original state of facts. Thus, in *Krell* v. *Henry*, [1903] 2 K.B. 740, Vaughan Williams L.J. finds that the subject of the contract was "rooms to view the procession": the postponement, therefore, made the rooms not rooms to view the procession. This also is the test finally chosen by Lord Sumner in *Bank Line* v. *Arthur Capel & Co.*, [1919] A.C. 435, agreeing with Lord Dunedin in *Metropolitan Water Board* v. *Dick Kerr*, [1918] A.C. 119, where, dealing with the criterion for determining the effect of interruption in "frustrating" a contract, he says: "An interruption may be so long as to destroy the identity of the work or service, when resumed, with the work or service when interrupted." We therefore get a common standard for mutual mistake and implied conditions whether as to existing or as to future facts. Does the state of the new facts destroy the identity of the subject-matter as it was in the original state of facts? To apply the principle to the infinite combinations of facts that arise in actual experience will continue to be difficult, but if this case results in establishing order into what has been a somewhat confused and difficult branch of the law it will have served a useful purpose.

I have already stated my reasons for deciding that in the present case the identity of the subject-matter was not destroyed by the mutual mistake, if any, and need not repeat them.

It now becomes necessary to deal with the second point of the plaintiffs —namely, that the contract of March 19, 1929, could be avoided by them in consequence of the non-disclosure by Bell of his misconduct as to the cocoa dealings. Fraudulent concealment has been negatived by the jury; this claim is based upon the contention that Bell owed a duty to Levers to disclose his misconduct, and that in default of disclosure the contract was voidable. Ordinarily the failure to disclose a material fact which might influence the mind of a prudent contractor does not give the right to avoid the contract. The principle of caveat emptor applies outside contracts of sale. There are certain contracts expressed by the law to be contracts of the utmost good faith, where material facts must be disclosed; if not, the contract is voidable. Apart from the special fiduciary relationships, contracts for partnership and contracts of insurance are the leading instances. In such cases the duty does not arise out of contract; the duty of a person proposing an insurance arises before a contract is made, so of an intending partner. Unless this contract can be brought within this limited category of contracts *uberrimae fidei* it appears to me that this ground of defence must fail. I see nothing to differentiate this agreement from the ordinary contract of service; and I am aware of no authority which places contracts of service within the limited category I have mentioned. It seems to me clear that master and men negotiating for an agreement of services are as unfettered as in any other negotiation. Nor can I find anything in the relation-of master and servant, when established, that places agreements between them within the protected category.

It is said that there is a contractual duty of the servant to disclose his past faults. I agree that the duty in the servant to protect his master's property may involve the duty to report a fellow servant whom he knows to be wrongfully dealing with that property. The servant owes a duty not to steal, but, having stolen, is there superadded a duty to confess that he has stolen? I am satisfied that to imply such a duty would be a departure from the well established usage of mankind and would be to create obligations entirely outside the normal contemplation of the parties concerned. If a man agrees to raise his butler's wages, must the butler disclose that two years ago he received a secret commission from the wine merchant; and if the master discovers it, can he, without dismissal or after the servant has left, avoid the agreement for the increase in salary and recover back the extra wages paid? If he gives his cook a month's wages in lieu of notice can he, on discovering that the cook has been pilfering the tea and sugar, claim the return of the month's wages? I think not. He takes the risk; if he wishes to protect himself he can question his servant, and will then be protected by the truth or otherwise of the answers.

I agree with the view expressed by Avory J. in *Healy* v. *Société Anonyme Française Rubastic*, [1917] 1 K.B. 946, on this point. It will be noticed that Bell was not a director of Levers, and, with respect, I cannot accept the view of Greer L.J. that if he was in fiduciary relationship to the Niger Company he was in a similar fiduciary relationship to the share-holders, or to the particular shareholders (Levers) who held 99 per cent of the shares. Nor do I think that it is alleged or proved that in making the agreement of March 19, 1929, Levers were acting as agents for the Niger Company. In the matter of the release of the service contract and the pay-ment of £30,000 they were acting quite plainly for themselves as principals. It follows that on this ground also the claim fails.

The result is that in the present case servants unfaithful in some of their work retain large compensation which some will think they do not deserve. Nevertheless it is of greater importance that well established principles of contract should be maintained than that a particular hardship should be redressed; and I see no way of giving relief to the plaintiffs in the present circumstances except by confiding to the Courts loose powers of introducing terms into contracts which would only serve to introduce doubt and con-fusion where certainty is essential.

I think therefore that this appeal should be allowed; and I agree with the order to be proposed by my noble and learned friend, Lord Blanesburgh.

SOLLE v. BUTCHER
[1950] 1 K.B. 671

The plaintiff rented from the defendant an apartment, and took a lease at £250 a year for seven years. Both parties believed that the apartment was not governed by rent control legislation, and that £250 was a legal rent. In fact the apartment was controlled by the Rent Acts, and the maximum rent chargeable was £140 a year. But £250 was a fair rent, and by comply-ing with certain formalities before the execution of the lease, the landlord could have charged that amount. The plaintiff now claims to be entitled to a five-year lease at £140.

DENNING L J. . . . It is clear that here there was a contract. The parties agreed in the same terms on the same subject-matter. It is true that the landlord was under a mistake which was to him fundamental: he would not for one moment have considered letting the flat for seven years if it meant that he could only charge £140 a year for it. He made the fundamental mistake of believing that the rent he could charge was not tied down to a controlled rent; but, whether it was his own mistake or a mistake common to both him and the tenant, it is not a ground for saying that the lease was from the beginning a nullity. Any other view would lead to remarkable results, for it would mean that, in the many cases where the parties mistakenly think a house is outside the Rent Restriction Acts when it is really within them, the tenancy would be a nullity, and the tenant would have to go; with the result that the tenants would not dare seek to have their rents reduced to the permitted amounts lest they should be turned out.

Let me next consider mistakes which render a contract voidable, that is, liable to be set aside on some equitable ground. Whilst presupposing that a contract was good at law, or at any rate not void, the court of equity would often relieve a party from the consequences of his own mistake, so long as it could do so without injustice to third parties. The court, it was said had power to set aside the contract whenever it was of opinion that it was unconscientious for the other party to avail himself of the legal advantage which he had obtained. . . .

The court had, of course, to define what it considered to be unconscientious, but in this respect equity has shown a progressive development. It is now clear that a contract will be set aside if the mistake of the one party has been induced by a material misrepresentation of the other, even though it was not fraudulent or fundamental; or if one party, knowing that the other is mistaken about the terms of an offer, or the identity of the person by whom it is made, lets him remain under his delusion and concludes a contract on the mistaken terms instead of pointing out the mistake. That is, I venture to think, the ground on which the defendant in *Smith* v. *Hughes* would be exempted nowadays, and on which, according to the view by Blackburn J. of the facts, the contract in *Lindsay* v. *Cundy*, was voidable and not void; . . .

A contract is also liable in equity to be set aside if the parties were under a common misapprehension either as to facts or as to their relative and respective rights, provided that the misapprehension was fundamental and that the party seeking to set it aside was not himself at fault. . . .

Bell v. *Lever Brothers, Ltd.* . . . was treated in the House of Lords as a case at law depending on whether the contract was a nullity or not. If it had been considered on equitable grounds, the result might have been different.

[Judgment was given for the defendant on terms that the plaintiff must elect between rescission and payment of the full rent.]

NOTE. Denning L.J.'s approach has not been without its critics. See, for example, W. E. D. Davies, *Mistake in Equity*, (1969) 3 Manitoba Law Journal, 82.: [The references are to *Bell* v. *Lever Bros.*, and *Solle* v. *Butcher*.] "It is submitted that it is clear from this judgment that, in the opinion of Lord Atkin, mistake either renders a contract void ab initio or else has no effect at all, and that there is no room for an intermediate type of mistake which renders a contract voidable in equity, for all the hypothetical examples given by Lord Atkin are examples of contracts which, according to Lord Denning's view, would be voidable in equity, yet Lord Atkin clearly states that in such cases the mistaken party *has no remedy at all*; indeed *Bell* v. *Lever Bros.* itself is a classical example of a contract which would, under Lord Denning's doctrine, be voidable in equity. Professor A. G. Guest has suggested that "in view of the very narrow scope of mistake at common law, there is considerable force in the argument that the Court should be allowed a residuary discretion to impose such a solution as justice demands," and Lord Atkin himself admitted that the rule which he expounded could cause hardship, but it is submitted that the cure proposed by Lord Denning is worse than the disease and that Lord Denning's doctrine is objectionable not only because it is flatly contrary to authority, but because it represents Palm Tree Justice in its purest and most objectionable form. According to Lord Denning's doctrine a contract will be set aside if it is unjust in all the circumstances to enforce it and the party seeking to set it aside has not been at fault. But who is to say what is "unjust in all the circumstances" or what constitutes "fault"? Under Lord Denning's doctrine equity would vary not only with the length of the chancellor's foot, but with the feet of every judge in the land. The concept of "what is just and fair" may be all very appealing to a judge on the Olympian heights of the bench or to an academic lawyer in the cloistered confines of a university, but for the practising solicitor in his office, trying to advise his client with at least a reasonable degree of certainty, it can make life impossible. As Lord Atkin said, it is of the utmost importance that contracts should be observed, and it is also of the utmost importance that people should be able to plan their affairs secure in the knowledge that if they follow their solicitor's advice the courts will uphold their transactions: if certainty in the law is important to solicitors, it is even more important to the business men who are their clients."

SCOTT v. *COULSON*
[1903] 2 Ch. 249

The plaintiff agreed to sell to the defendant an insurance policy on the life of a man called A. T. Death. Both parties then assumed that Death was living, and the price agreed to be paid by the defendant was £460, slightly more than the cash surrender value. Actually Death was dead, so that the policy was worth £777, its face value. The contract was executed by assignment of the policy, at which time the purchaser had some reason to suspect the truth. When the vendor later discovered the truth, he brought an action to set aside the sale.

VAUGHAN WILLIAMS L.J.: On the facts of this case, if one takes those which were found by the learned judge in his judgment, I do not see what room there is for argument on any question of law. If we are to take it that it was common ground that, at the date of the contract for the sale of this policy, both the parties to the contract supposed the assured to be alive, it is true that both parties entered into this contract upon the basis of a common affirmative belief that the assured was alive; but as it turned out that this was a common mistake, the contract was one which cannot be enforced. This is so at law; and the plaintiffs do not require to have recourse to equity to rescind the contract, if the basis which both parties recognized as the basis is not true. Having regard to the evidence, it seems to be clear that the learned judge came to a right conclusion. If it had turned out that the vendors or their agent had requested Coulson to find out whether the assured was dead or alive, and Coulson had come back and said he could not find out, I should have said that, apart from argument, it would have been almost impossible to arrive at the conclusion that both parties had entered into the contract upon the basis that the assured was alive. But it turns out that no such inquiry was requested to be made. The only inquiry requested to be made was that contained in Coulson's letter of March 15, 1902, in which he requested inquiry to be made about the assured. Therefore the inference cannot arise which, if it had arisen, would have been fatal to the plaintiffs' contention that this contract was entered into upon the basis that the assured was still alive. If one gets rid of that, what is there left? We have before us the conditions of the proposed sale which were before both parties, in which it certainly seems to be assumed that the assured was still alive.

All I say with regard to the matter is that the material date all through is the date of the contract. If at that date a good contract was entered into, I cannot conceive that it could be rescinded. But it turns out that it was a contract entered into under a common mistake existing at the date of it, and therefore it follows that an assignment executed in pursuance of such a contract cannot be supported.

The learned judge has arrived at a right conclusion, and this appeal must therefore be dismissed, with costs.

ROMER L.J.: I agree that this appeal must be dismissed. Upon the facts of the case it appears to me that the learned judge came to the right conclusion, namely, that the contract entered into between the parties to the sale and purchase of this policy rested upon the basis of the assured being still alive. It turns out that, before the matter was concluded by assignment to the defendants, the fact upon which the contract was based was not the fact. The defendant Coulson must be taken to have known that the basis upon which the contract had been entered into, and the common belief upon which both parties had acted, did not exist. That was a circumstance which went to the root of the matter, and rendered it improper to insist upon the completion of the contract. What did Coulson do when he received the information leading him to the knowledge or belief that the assured was dead? 'Did he do what he ought to have done—tell the plaintiffs? Not at all. He allowed the plaintiffs to go on under the old belief, and to execute the assignment on the footing that the old basis continued and that the defendants were entitled to an assignment. I need scarcely say that that was wholly unjustifiable from a legal point of view, and also from an equitable point of view, and none the less so because the defendants apparently thought they were justified in taking the assignment.

Such a transaction cannot be allowed to stand, and therefore this appeal must be dismissed.

COZENS-HARDY L.J.: I agree. I think the case was argued by Mr. Clerke in the only possible way it could be put on behalf of the defendants. Having regard to the facts as found by the learned judge, it appears to me to be quite plain that at the date of the contract there was a common mistake, both parties being under the belief that the assured was alive.

It would be quite shocking to say that the defendants have rendered the contract absolute simply by having obtained from the vendors an assignment after one of the defendants, Coulson, had full notice that the basis on which the contract has been entered into had had no existence. Under such circumstances it is impossible that the defendants can be allowed to derive any benefit from the assignment.

The appeal must, therefore, be dismissed with costs.

HYRSKY v. SMITH
(1969) 5 D.L.R. (3d) 385 (Ont. H.C.)

LIEFF J.: The evidence in this case and the agreed statement of facts submitted by counsel indicate the following chronology of events.

In May, 1959, the defendant vendor and the plaintiffs entered into an agreement of purchase and sale of certain lands for the consideration of $4,700 to be paid on the basis of $60 per month with interest charged at the rate of 6%. The plaintiffs did not search the title of the said lands, nor did they instruct their solicitor to do so. A deed of conveyance was executed by the defendant on December 17, 1962, and was registered in the Registry Office for the Registry Division of Algoma on January 16, 1963, as Instrument T-52260, and is filed as ex. 1 in these proceedings. It is agreed that this deed expressly sets out the mutual intention of the parties and by the wording in that deed the parties understood that the northern-most boundary of the lands was to measure 1000 ft. Although a survey of the lands which was procured prior to the execution of the deed revealed a northern boundary of only 877.2 ft., both parties have agreed that where there exists a discrepancy as between the survey and the deed, the latter was to govern as indicative of the intention of the parties.

The problem which confronts the Court here concerns the northerly portion of the lands, bearing dimensions 76 ft. by 1000 ft. In October, 1966, almost four years after the registration of the deed, it was learned that the vendor had no clear title to this part of the property purchased by the plaintiffs. It was in fact owned by a third party who subsequently built upon this northerly 76 ft. Consequently, it is now apparent that the title to the land purported to be conveyed by Instrument T-52260 is defective in that the defendant had no title to the north portion of the land, being 76 ft. by 1000 ft. Instead of a conveyance of land possessing a breadth of 160 ft. as was the intention of the parties, the defendant actually conveyed a parcel of land possessing a breadth of 84 ft. The plaintiffs, accordingly, have now claimed rescission of the deed and repayment of the sum of $5,387.57 together with interest.

The purchasers bought the property for investment purposes and revealed this to the vendor prior to taking the deed. The purchasers wished to subdivide this vacant land into some 17 building lots but they did not relate this specific purpose to the vendor. The principal portion of the land which was actually conveyed to the plaintiffs has remained in the same state, both physically and with respect to title as it had been at the time of the conveyance in 1963. There are, however, arrears of taxes owing for the years 1967 and 1968.

The oft-quoted classic statement as to whether a party is entitled to the remedy of rescission after the conveyance has been completed is attributable to Duff J. (as he then was), in the case of *Redican* v. *Nesbitt*, 25 O.W.N. 448, [1924] S.C.R. 135 at pp. 144-47, [1924] 1 D.L.R. 536 at pp. 541-44 as follows:

"The principle appears to be that, save in exceptional cases to which reference will be made, the maxim *caveat emptor* applies, and that the purchaser, if he wishes to protect himself in respect of the absence of title or defect in the title or in the quantity or quality of the estate, must do so by covenants in the conveyance. . . . The rule does not apply where there is error *in substantialibus,* where, for example, it turns out that the vendee has purchased his own property; nor does it apply where the transaction has been brought about by the fraud of the vendor. . . .

"The ratio of the rule being that the purchaser can and ought to protect himself except in the two cases mentioned by covenants in the conveyance, one naturally expects to find that the execution of the conveyance, the acceptance of it by the purchaser, and the vesting of the estate in him are in themselves sufficient to bring the rule into play. . . .

"The whole point is: At what stage does *caveat emptor* apply?

"The vendee may rely after completion upon warranty, contractual condition, error *in substantialibus,* or fraud. Once the conveyance is settled and the estate has passed, it seems a reasonable application of the rule to hold that as to warranty or contractual condition resort must be had to the deed unless there has been a stipulation at an earlier stage which was not to be superseded by the deed, as in the case of a contract for compensation. . . . Representation which is not fraudulent, and does not give rise to error *in substantialibus,* could only operate after completion as creating a contractual condition or a warranty. Finality and certainty in business affairs seem to require that as a rule, when there is a formal conveyance, such a condition or warranty should be therein expressed, and that the acceptance of the conveyance by the vendee as finally vesting the property in him is the act which for this purpose marks the transition from contract *in fieri* to contract executed; and this appears to fit in with the general reasoning of the authorities."

It is apparent that in the case at bar, the facts do not support nor do the plaintiffs base their claim for rescission on any contractual condition outside of the deed, or on an allegation of fraud. The success or failure of their claim turns upon whether there had been an error *in substantialibus* or whether there had been a breach of an express condition or warranty in the deed of conveyance.

As to what constitutes an error *in substantialibus* no authority appears to have given a definitive answer. The earlier cases have used the phrase, "total failure of consideration" rather than "error in *substantialibus*" and counsel for the defendant has urged that the latter phrase has the same restricted meaning as the former. Plaintiffs' counsel, on the other hand, submitted that the more recently used phrase is broader in scope than the earlier exception and in fact includes a "total failure of consideration."

The Roman doctrine of *error in substantia* rendered contracts void where there existed mistakes as to quality which related to the substance of the subject-matter of the contract. In *Kennedy* v. *Panama, etc. Royal Mail Co.* (1867), L.R. 2 Q.B. 580, Blackburn J., considered the origin of this doctrine and summarized the principle at pp. 587-88 as follows:

"The principle is well illustrated in the civil law, as stated in the Digest, lib. 18, tit. 4. De Contrahendâ Emptione, leges, 9, 10, 11. There,— after laying down the general rule, that where the parties are not at one as to the subject of the contract there is no agreement, and that this applies where the parties have misapprehended each other as to the corpus, as where an absent slave was sold and the buyer thought he was buying Pamphilus and the vendor thought he was selling Stichus, and pronouncing the judgment that in such a case there was no bargain because there was 'error in corpore,' the framers of the digest moot the point thus: 'Inde quaeritur, si in ipso corpore non erretur, sed in substantia error sit, ut, puta, si acetum pro vino veneat, aes pro auro, vel plumbum pro argento vel quid aliud argento simile: an emptio et venditio sit'; and the answers given by the great jurists quoted are to the effect, that if there be misapprehension as to the substance of the thing there is no contract; but if it be only a difference in some quality or accident, even though the misapprehension may have been the actuating motive to the purchaser, yet the contract remains binding. Paulus says: 'Si aes pro auro veneat, non valet, aliter at que si aurum quidem fuerit, deterius autem quam emptor existimarit: tunc enim emptio valet.' Ulpianus, in the eleventh law, puts an example as to the sale of a slave very similar to that of the unsound horse in *Street* v. *Blay,* 2 B. & Ad. 456. And, as we apprehend, the principle of our law is the same as that of the civil law; and the difficulty, in every case is to determine whether the mistake or misapprehension is as to the substance of the whole consideration, going, as it were, to the root of the matter, or only to some point, even though a material point, an error as to which does not affect the substance of the whole consideration."

Consequently, for a contract to be rescinded for mutual mistake, the mistake must go to the root of the contract. In order to constitute an error *in substantialibus*, there must be a mutual fundamental mistake as to the quality of the subject-matter. The application of this principle must, of course, turn upon the facts of each individual case. A practical statement of the test which governs the applicability of the doctrine of fundamental mutual mistake which gives rise to an error *in substantialibus* was put forth by G. H. Treitel in his work, *The Law of Contract,* 2nd ed., p. 179, as follows:

"A thing has many qualities. A car may be black, old, fast and so forth. For any particular purpose one or more of these qualities may be uppermost in the minds of the persons dealing with the thing. Some particular quality may be so important in the minds of the parties that they actually use that quality to *identify* the thing. If the thing lacks that quality, it is suggested that the parties have made a fundamental mistake, even though they have not mistaken one thing for another, or made a mistake as to the existence of the thing. A practical test for deciding this question is to imagine that one can ask the parties, immediately after they made the contract, what the subject-matter of the contract was. If, in spite of the mistake, they would give the right answer the contract is valid at law."

Having regard to these principles, has the common mistake of the parties as to the quantity of land being conveyed resulted in an error *in substantialibus*? In the case of *De Clerval* v. *Jones* (1908), 8 W.L.R. 300, the purchaser of land brought an action against the vendor as a result of a mutual mistake by the parties resulting in a substantial deficiency in acreage. The parties were under the mistaken belief that the block of land contained 160.86 acres whereas in fact it contained only 97 acres. Beck J., thought that the circumstances warranted rescission and he had this to say at pp. 306-7:

"Where there is a mutual mistake, going not necessarily to an essential but to a material, substantial, and important element of the contract, it seems to me that the Court will ordinarily order rescission, even though the contract has been completely executed, if it can do so on equitable terms.

"In the present case I am satisfied that both the plaintiff and Riley, the defendant's agent, were convinced that the land in question comprised approximately at least 160 acres (i.e., they were mutually mistaken as to the quantity), and that, had the plaintiff been aware of the actual deficiency, he would not have entered into the contract. I think that the deficiency being so great it is so material, substantial, and important that the plaintiff is entitled to relief. It is not, however, a case for specific performance; nor, in view of the decision of the Supreme Court of Canada in *Penrose* v. *Knight,* Cassel's Digest, p. 777, can I order payment of a sum by way of compensation. I think justice will be best achieved by ordering that the contract be rescinded, the defendant re-paying to the plaintiff within a limited time, which I will fix on the settlement of the minutes of judgment, the amount he has received on account of purchase money, with interest, together with the value of the permanent improvements made by the plaintiff (these sums to be ascertained by the clerk of the Court), with the option, however, to the defendant of paying to the plaintiff, by way of compensation for the deficiency, the sum of $504, being the price of 63 acres at $8 per acre."

There is a similar deficiency as to quantity of land in the instant case and there often can be a fine line between quantity and quality. If the mistake as to quantity is so substantial so that in essence it changes the quality of the subject-matter, then a proper case for rescission may exist. In the case at bar, the deficiency approximated one-half of the land purchased and the remnant was unsuitable as a consequence for the purpose for which the purchasers bought the property. I think that on this basis, there can be little doubt that the mistake was so fundamental that the quality and the very identity of the parcel of land which was the subject-matter of the sale had undergone a significant transformation. I believe that if the minds of the parties, upon completion of the sale, had been directed to answer the question, "What was the subject-matter of the agreement?" they would have responded by stating not just a block of land but a parcel of land bearing the specific dimensions set out in the deed.

Counsel for the defendant vendor, however, had urged that the circumstance does not amount to a "total failure of consideration" which he submits is the proper test of an error *in substantialibus*. But what is meant by a "total failure of consideration"? Most of the cases in which Courts have permitted rescission by reason of a total failure of consideration have been situations where the purchaser and vendor of land mistakenly entered into a transaction whereby the purchaser bought land which had all along been his own property, or have been situations analogous thereto: *Bingham* v. *Bingham* (1748), 1 Ves. Sen. 126, 27 E.R. 934; *Cooper* v. *Phibbs* (1867), L.R. 2 H.L. 149.

In an Australian case, *Svanosio* v. *McNamara* (1956), 96 C.L.R. 186, referred to by counsel for the defendant, the plaintiff purchased a hotel and its liquor licence. After the conveyance, the purchaser learned that some of the rooms of the hotel (approximately one-third of the hotel) were situate on adjoining Crown land and he accordingly claimed rescission of the agreement on the ground of common mistake. It was held by the High Court of Australia, on appeal, that only a total failure of consideration could justify rescission and that there could be no rescission for this partial failure of consideration. The Court stated at p. 209: "There are *dicta* in the cases that relief can be given after the contract has been completed where there is a common mistake upon a material point although there is only a partial failure of consideration. . . . But the proper principle appears to be that, in the case of a completed contract of sale, rescission is only possible on the ground of common mistake where, contrary to the belief of the parties, there is nothing to contract about as in *Bingham* v. *Bingham* (1748), 1 Ves. Sen. 126 and *Cooper* v. *Phibbs* (1867), L.R. 2 H.L. 149."

There is little doubt that the cases which have allowed rescission because of a "total failure of consideration" have been limited to only those where there existed a situation, in the words of Cheshire and Fifoot in their text on *The Law of Contract*, 6th ed., p. 187, of *res sua* or *res extincta*. I prefer to think, however, that this aspect of the law in Ontario has broadened in scope with the use of the phrase, "error *in substantialibus*" to include not only the aforesaid restricted examples of a total failure of consideration but also what may be said to be a virtual failure of consideration. In fact, Dixon C.J., and Fullagar J., in the *Svanosio* case, *supra,* at least pay lip service to this possible extension of the principle at pp. 198-9, although it is not reflected in the decision: "Other statements of the general rule extend the scope of the exception beyond cases of fraud, using various expressions, the general effect of which is, we think, correctly stated by saying that there must be a total failure of consideration or what amounts practically to a total failure of consideration."

I am inclined to believe that the phrase "error *in substantialibus*" used by the Courts today carries the meaning enunciated earlier in these reasons and that is: In equity, a contract is subject to rescission if the parties suffered from a common fundamental misapprehension as to the facts which went to the very root of the contract: *Grist* v. *Bailey*, [1966] 2 All E.R. 875.

In the case at bar, there were no words of qualification such as "more or less" accompanying the description of the lands in the agreement of purchase and sale and there is a considerable disparity between the quantity of land actually conveyed and the quantity described by the defendant in the deed. Having regard to the fact that this difference amounts to almost one-half of the lands described in the deed, and having regard to the fact that, to the knowledge of the vendor, the purchaser intended to use these lands for investment purposes, the conclusion is inescapable that there existed a common fundamental mistake as to the very quality of the subject-matter of the contract which can be equated to an error *in substantialibus*.

In arriving at this conclusion, I am aware of the policy consideration implicit in the doctrine of *caveat emptor*, as enunciated by Grove J., in *Clare* v. *Lamb* (1875), L.R. 10 C.P. 334 at pp. 338-39, as follows: "In the case of the purchase of an interest in land, the person who sells places at the disposal of the buyer such title-deeds as he possesses and under which he claims. The purchaser has full opportunity for investigating the title of the vendor, and when he takes a conveyance he is assumed to have done so. Considerable inconvenience might result if this were not the rule. Conveyancers may agree upon the title, and, long after the conveyance has been executed, the whole transaction completed, and the proceeds disbursed, the seller might be called upon to return the purchase-money, by reason of some defect of which he had no notice at the time." To the same effect, see *Allen* v. *Richardson* (1879), 13 Ch. D. 524 at p. 539, and *Joliffe* v. *Baker* (1883), 11 Q.B.D. 255 at p. 265. It is true that under our present-day system of conveyancing, the purchaser has ample opportunity to inquire and to inspect before he is compelled to close the transaction and it may be said that execution of the conveyance can be looked upon as a declaration that he is satisfied with the outcome of his investigation. However that may be and notwithstanding the need for certainty and permanence in the law of conveyancing, these policy considerations must yield to the desirability of doing equity where there has been an error *in substantialibus*. For the reasons given above, the plaintiff is entitled to some remedy.

Having found that there was an error *in substantialibus* it becomes unnecessary to consider the second branch of the plaintiffs' case and that is whether there has been a breach of a condition or warranty stated in the deed. None the less I feel compelled to put forth a few brief remarks. The conveyance was made pursuant to the Short Forms of Conveyances Act, R.S.O. 1960, c. 372, and contained the usual covenants regarding the right to convey, the right of the purchaser to quiet possession free from all encumbrances, and the covenant that the vendor has done no act to encumber the lands. Covenants for title may be either absolute or qualified. The former consists of covenants warranting against all defects in title by whomsoever created which may be discovered. In contrast, qualified covenants for title are limited in effect and only relate to title defects arising from acts or omissions of the vendor himself and any of his predecessors in title subsequent to the last conveyance of the land for valuable consideration. Cases such as *Thackeray* v. *Wood* (1865), 6 B. & S. 766, 122 E.R. 1376, and *Amar Singh* v. *Mitchell*, 30 D.L.R. 719 [1917] 1 W.W.R. 201, indicate that qualified covenants for title do not mean that the vendor covenants that he has title but only that he has done nothing himself to cause the defect in title. Covenants under the Short Forms of Conveyancing Act are only qualified covenants for title. This seems to be the case because if an agreement of purchase and sale does not set out the form of deed to be given by the vendor, the purchaser can only request a deed in the statutory form. By such covenants the grantor merely covenants that he has in himself the power to grant notwithstanding anything he may have done. In the instant case, the defect in title cannot be attributed to any act of the vendor and consequently there has been no breach of any covenant in the deed.

Only the question of remedy remains. I do not think that this is a proper case for rectification of the deed. McRuer C.J.H.C., set out the prerequisites of this remedy in *Devald* v. *Zigeuner*, [1958] O.W.N. 381 at pp. 382-83, 16 D.L.R. (2d) 285 at p. 290, as follows:

"In *Cheshire & Fifoot, Contracts*, 4th ed., p. 185, the essentials for rectification on the basis of mutual mistake were set out as follows:—

1. The relief was not granted unless a complete agreement was reached prior to the written instrument which it is sought to rectify.

2. Both parties must have intended that the exact terms of the alleged prior contract should be reduced to writing, and the intention must have continued unchanged up to the time when the instrument was executed.

3. Clear evidence of a mistake common to both parties must be adduced, and the burden of proving this lay on the party who alleged that the instrument ought to be altered.

4. The sole purpose of equity's intervention was to cure literal faults and thus to prevent the intention of the parties already clearly revealed in their prior agreement, from being nullified by their failure to express it accurately in the subsequent document."

Also see the judgment of Culliton C.J.S., in *Bercovici* v. *Palmer* (1966), 59 D.L.R. (2d) 513, 58 W.W.R. 111, in which may be found a careful review of the principles applicable to rectification. The deed cannot now be made to conform with the common intention of the parties. No question of a mere literal fault in the deed exists. There has been an error *in substantialibus* by both parties and equity will permit in this case nothing less than rescission of the deed. Moreover, having regard to the circumstances, I do not think there were laches on the plaintiffs' part so as to disentitle them to relief.

In the result, therefore, judgment should go on behalf of the plaintiffs rescinding the deed in question. The plaintiffs are also entitled to repayment of $5,387.57 which sum comprises payments made by the plaintiffs of $5,154.77, of $207.40 for taxes, and of $25.40 for legal fees; and also interest at 6% on all moneys expended by the plaintiffs.

The matter of costs caused me some concern because had the plaintiffs searched the title as a prudent purchaser should have done, all of this litigation would never have arisen. For this reason and because the case is somewhat unique, I exercise my discretion and make no order as to costs.

[Judgment for plaintiffs.]

SHERWOOD v. WALKER
(1887) 66 Mich. 568, 33 N. W. 919, (Mich. S.C.)

MORSE J.: Replevin for a cow. Suit commenced in justice's court. Judgment for plaintiff. Appealed to circuit court of Wayne county, and verdict and judgment for plaintiff in that court. The defendants bring error, and set out 25 assignments of the same.

The main controversy depends upon the construction of a contract for the sale of the cow. The plaintiff claims that the title passed, and bases his action upon such claim. The defendants contend that the contract was executory, and by its terms no title to the animal was acquired by plaintiff.

The defendants reside at Detroit, but are in business at Walkerville, Ontario, and have a farm at Greenfield, in Wayne county, upon which were some blooded cattle supposed to be barren as breeders. The Walkers are importers and breeders of polled Angus cattle.

The plaintiff is a banker living at Plymouth, in Wayne county. He called upon the defendants at Walkerville for the purchase of some of their stock, but found none there that suited him. Meeting one of the defendants afterwards, he was informed that they had a few head upon this Greenfield farm. He was asked to go out and look at them, with the statement at the time that they were probably barren, and would not breed.

May 5, 1886, plaintiff went out to Greenfield and saw the cattle. A few days thereafter, he called upon one of the defendants with the view of purchasing a cow, known as "Rose 2d of Aberlone." After considerable talk, it was agreed that defendants would telephone Sherwood at his home in Plymouth in reference to the price. The second morning after this talk he was called up by telephone, and the terms of the sale were finally agreed upon. He was to pay five and one-half cents per pound, live weight, fifty pounds shrinkage. He was asked how he intended to take the cow home, and replied that he might ship her from King's cattle-yard. He requested defendants to confirm the sale in writing, which they did by sending him the following letter:

"WALKERVILLE, May 15, 1886.

T. C. SHERWOOD,
President, etc.,—

Dear Sir: We confirm sale to you of the cow Rose 2d of Aberlone, lot 56 of our catalogue, at five and a half cents per pound, less fifty pounds shrink. We inclose herewith order on Mr. Graham for the cow. You might leave check with him, or mail to us here, as you prefer.

Yours truly,

HIRAM WALKER & SONS."

The order upon Graham inclosed in the letter reads as follows:

"WALKERVILLE, May 15, 1886.

George Graham: You will please deliver at King's cattle-yard to Mr. T. C. Sherwood, Plymouth, the cow Rose 2d of Aberlone, lot 56 of our catalogue. Send halter with cow, and have her weighed.

Yours truly,

HIRAM WALKER & SONS."

On the twenty-first of the same month the plaintiff went to defendants' farm at Greenfield, and presented the order and letter to Graham, who informed him that the defendants had instructed him not to deliver the cow. Soon after, the plaintiff tendered to Hiram Walker, one of the defendants, $80, and demanded the cow. Walker refused to take the money or deliver the cow. The plaintiff then instituted this suit.

After he had secured possession of the cow under the writ of replevin, the plaintiff caused her to be weighed by the constable who served the writ, at a place other than King's cattle-yard. She weighed 1,420 pounds.

When the plaintiff, upon the trial in the circuit court, had submitted his proofs showing the above transaction, defendants moved to strike out and exclude the testimony from the case, for the reason that it was irrelevant, and did not tend to show that the title to the cow passed, and that it showed that the contract of sale was merely executory. The court refused the motion, and an exception was taken.

The defendants then introduced evidence tending to show that at the time of the alleged sale it was believed by both the plaintiff and themselves that the cow was barren and would not breed: that she cost $850, and if not barren would be worth from $750 to $1,000; that after the date of the letter, and the order to Graham, the defendants were informed by said Graham that in his judgment the cow was with calf, and therefore they instructed him not to deliver her to plaintiff, and on the twentieth of May, 1886, telegraphed to the plaintiff what Graham thought about the cow being with calf, and that consequently they could not sell her. The cow had a calf in the month of October following.

[The Court then upheld an instruction pursuant to which the jury had found that title had passed to plaintiff. The Sale of Goods Act, s.19, provides that where there is a sale of specific goods the property usually passes to the buyer when the contract is made.]

It appears from the record that both parties supposed this cow was barren and would not breed, and she was sold by the pound for an insignificant sum as compared with her real value if a breeder. She was evidently sold and purchased on the relation of her value for beef, unless the plaintiff had learned of her true condition, and concealed such knowledge from the defendants. Before the plaintiff secured possession of the animal, the defendants learned that she was with calf, and therefore of great value, and undertook to rescind the sale by refusing to deliver her. The question arises whether they had a right to do so.

The circuit judge ruled that this fact did not avoid the sale, and it made no difference whether she was barren or not. I am of the opinion that the court erred in this holding. I know that this is a close question, and the dividing line between the adjudicated cases is not easily discerned. But it must be considered as well settled that a party who has given an apparent consent to a contract of sale may refuse to execute it, or he may avoid it after it has been completed, if the assent was founded, or the contract made, upon the mistake of a material fact,—such as the subject-matter of the sale, the price, or some collateral fact materially inducing the agreement; and this can be done when the mistake is mutual. 1 Benj. Sales, § §605, 606; Leake, Cont. 339; Story, Sales (4th ed.), § §148, 377. See, also, *Cutts* v. *Guild,* 57 N.Y. 229; *Harvey* v. *Harris,* 112 Mass. 32; *Gardner* v. *Lane,* 9 Allen, 492; S.C. 12 Allen, 44; *Hutchmacher* v. *Harris' Adm'rs,* 38 Penn. St. 491; *Byers* v. *Chapin,* 28 Ohio St. 300; *Gibson* v. *Pelkie,* 37 Mich. 380, and cases cited; *Allen* v. *Hammond,* 11 Pet. 63, 71.

If there is a difference or misapprehension as to the substance of the thing bargained for, if the thing actually delivered or received is different in substance from the thing bargained for and intended to be sold, then there is no contract; but if it be only a difference in some quality or accident, even though the mistake may have been the actuating motive to the purchaser or seller, or both of them, yet the contract remains binding. "The difficulty in every case is to determine whether the mistake or mis-apprehension is as to the substance of the whole contract, going, as it were, to the root of the matter, or only to some point, even though a material point, an error as to which does not affect the substance of the whole consideration." *Kennedy* v. *Panama, etc., Mail Co.,* L.R. 2 Q.B. 580, 588.

It has been held, in accordance with the principles above stated, that where a horse is bought under the belief that he is sound, and both vendor and vendee honestly believe him to be sound, the purchaser must stand by his bargain, and pay the full price, unless there was a warranty.

It seems to me, however, in the case made by this record, that the mistake or misapprehension of the parties went to the whole substance of the agreement. If the cow was a breeder, she was worth at least $750; if barren, she was worth not over $80. The parties would not have made the contract of sale except upon the understanding and belief that she was incapable of breeding, and of no use as a cow. It is true she is now the identical animal that they thought her to be when the contract was made; there is no mistake as to the identity of the creature. Yet the mistake was not of the mere quality of the animal, but went to the very nature of the thing. A barren cow is substantially a different creature than a breeding one. There is as much difference between them for all purposes of use as there is between an ox and a cow that is capable of breeding and giving milk. If the mutual mistake had simply related to the fact whether she was with calf or not for one season, then it might have been a good sale; but the mistake affected the character of the animal for all time, and for her present and ultimate use. She was not in fact the animal, or the kind of animal, the defendants intended to sell or the plaintiff to buy. She was not a barren cow, and, if this fact had been known, there would have been no contract. The mistake affected the substance of the whole consideration, and it must be considered that there was no contract to sell or sale of the cow as she actually was. The thing sold and bought had in fact no ex-istence. She was sold as a beef creature would be sold; she is in fact a breeding cow, and a valuable one.

The court should have instructed the jury that if they found that the cow was sold, or contracted to be sold, upon the understanding of both parties that she was barren, and useless for the purpose of breeding, and that in fact she was not barren, but capable of breeding, then the defendants had a right to rescind, and to refuse to deliver, and the verdict should be in their favor.

The judgment of the court below must be reversed, and a new trial granted, with costs of this Court to defendants.

[Campbell C.J., and Champlin J., concurred.]

SHERWOOD J. (dissenting): I do not concur in the opinion given by my brethren in this case. I think the judgments before the justice and at the circuit were right.

I agree with my Brother Morse that the contract made was not within the statute of frauds, and that payment for the property was not a condition precedent to the passing of the title from the defendants to the plaintiff. And I further agree with him that the plaintiff was entitled to a delivery of the property to him when the suit was brought, unless there was a mistake made which would invalidate the contract; and I can find no such mistake.

There is no pretense that there was any fraud or concealment in the case, and an intimation or insinuation that such a thing might have existed on the part of either of the parties would undoubtedly be a greater surprise to them than anything else that has occurred in their dealings or in the case.

As has already been stated by my brethren, the record shows that the plaintiff is a banker, and farmer as well, carrying on a farm, and raising the best breeds of stock, and lived in Plymouth, in the county of Wayne, 23 miles from Detroit; that the defendants lived in Detroit, and were also dealers in stock of the higher grades; that they had a farm at Walkerville, in Canada, and also one in Greenfield, in said county of Wayne, and upon these farms the defendants kept their stock. The Greenfield farm was about 15 miles from the plaintiff's.

In the spring of 1886 the plaintiff, learning that the defendants had some "polled Angus cattle" for sale, was desirous of purchasing some of that breed, and, meeting the defendants, or some of them, at Walkerville, inquired about them, and was informed that they had none at Walkerville, "but had a few head left on their farm in Greenfield, and they asked the plaintiff to go and see them, stating that in all probability they were sterile and would not breed." In accordance with said request, the plaintiff, on the fifth day of May, went out and looked at the defendants' cattle at Greenfield, and found one called "Rose 2d," which he wished to purchase, and the terms were finally agreed upon at five and one-half cents per pound, live weight, 50 pounds to be deducted for shrinkage. The sale was in writing, and the defendants gave an order to the plaintiff directing the man in charge of the Greenfield farm to deliver the cow to plaintiff. This was done on the fifteenth of May. On the twenty-first of May plaintiff went to get his cow, and the defendants refused to let him have her; claiming at the time that the man in charge at the farm thought the cow was with calf, and, if such was the case, they would not sell her for the price agreed upon.

The record further shows that the defendants, when they sold the cow, believed the cow was not with calf, and barren; that from what the plaintiff had been told by defendants (for it does not appear he had any other knowledge or facts from which he could form an opinion) he believed the cow was farrow, but still thought she could be made to breed.

The foregoing shows the entire interview and treaty between the parties as to the sterility and qualities of the cow sold to the plaintiff. The cow had a calf in the month of October.

There is no question but that the defendants sold the cow representing her of the breed and quality they believed the cow to be, and that the purchaser so understood it. And the buyer purchased her believing her to be of the breed represented by the sellers, and possessing all the qualities stated, and even more. He believed she would breed. There is no pretense that the plaintiff bought the cow for beef, and there is nothing in the record indicating that he would have bought her at all only that he thought she might be made to breed. Under the foregoing facts,—and these are all that are contained in the record material to the contract,—it is held that because it turned out that the plaintiff was more correct in his judgment as to one quality of the cow than the defendants, and a quality, too, which could not by any possibility be positively known at the time by either party to exist, the contract may be annulled by the defendants at their pleasure. I know of no law, and have not been referred to any, which will justify any such holding, and I think the circuit judge was right in his construction of the contract between the parties.

It is claimed that a mutual mistake of a material fact was made by the parties when the contract of sale was made. There was no warranty in the case of the quality of the animal. When a mistaken fact is relied upon as ground for rescinding, such fact must not only exist at the time the contract is made, but must have been known to one or both of the parties. Where there is no warranty, there can be no mistake of fact when no such fact exists, or, if in existence, neither party knew of it, or could know of it; and that is precisely this case. If the owner of a Hambletonian horse had speeded him, and was only able to make him go a mile in three minutes, and should sell him to another, believing that was his greatest speed, for $300, when the purchaser believed he could go much faster, and made the purchase for that sum, and a few days thereafter, under more favorable circumstances, the horse was driven a mile in 2 min. 16 sec., and was found to be worth $20,000, I hardly think it would be held, either at law or in equity, by any one, that the seller in such case could rescind the contract. The same legal principles apply in each case.

In this case neither party knew the actual quality and condition of this cow at the time of the sale. The defendants say, or rather said, to the plaintiff, 'they had a few head left on their farm in Greenfield, and asked plaintiff to go and see them, stating to plaintiff that in all probability they were sterile and would not breed.' Plaintiff did go as requested, and found there three cows, including the one purchased, with a bull. The cow had been exposed, but neither knew she was with calf or whether she would breed. The defendants thought she would not, but the plaintiff says that he thought she could be made to breed, but believed she was not with calf. The defendants sold the cow for what they believed her to be, and the plaintiff bought her as he believed she was, after the statements made by the defendants. No conditions whatever were attached to the terms of sale by either party. It was in fact as absolute as it could well be made, and I know of no precedent as authority by which this Court can alter the contract thus made by these parties in writing, and interpolate in it a condition by which, if the *defendants should be mistaken in their belief that the cow was barren,* she should be returned to them, and their contract should be annulled.

It is not the duty of courts to destroy contracts when called upon to enforce them, after they have been legally made. There was no mistake of any such material fact by either of the parties in the case as would license the vendors to rescind. There was no difference between the parties, nor misapprehension, as to the substance of the thing bargained for, which was a cow supposed to be barren by one party, and believed not to be by the other. As to the quality of the animal, subsequently developed, both parties were equally ignorant, and as to this each party took his chances. If this were not the law, there would be no safety in purchasing this kind of stock.

. . . In this case, if either party had superior knowledge as to the qualities of this animal to the other, certainly the defendants had such advantage.

I understand the law to be well settled that "there is no breach of any implied confidence that one party will not profit by his superior knowledge as to facts and circumstances" equally within the knowledge of both, because neither party reposes in any such confidence unless it be specially tendered or required, and that a general sale does not imply warranty of any quality, or the absence of any; and if the seller represents to the purchaser what he himself believes as to the qualities of an animal, and the purchaser buys relying upon his own judgment as to such qualities, there is no warranty in the case, and neither has a cause of action against the other if he finds himself to have been mistaken in judgment.

ABERLONE, ROSE OF

Being an Entry for an Index

(An epic poem by the late Professor Brainerd Currie)

With cross-references to *Sherwood* v. *Walker,* 66 Mich. 568, 33 N.W. 919, 11 Am. St. 531 (1887), and to the *Christabel* of Mr. Samuel Taylor Coleridge—not to mention Mr. Ogden Nash, in a tight spot.

'Tis the middle of night on the Greenfield farm
And the creatures are huddled to keep them from harm.
   Ah me!—Ah moo!
Respectively their quidsome balm
How mournfully they chew!
And one there is who stands apart
With hanging head and heavy heart.
Have pity on her sore distress,
This norm of bovine loveliness.
Her gentle limbs, her hornless brow
Proclaim no ordinary cow:
Fair as a pasture sweet with hay
Mown in the very month of May!
Nay, fairer yet! And yet more fair!
She stands alone, the short black hair
Heaving sometimes on her breast,
Shunned and despised by all the rest.
If one should ask her why she doth grieve
She would answer sadly, "I can't conceive."

Her shame is a weary weight like stone
For Rose the Second of Aberlone.

Her sire is of a noble line.
Of most aristocratic kine:
Angus of Aberdeen, black and polled;
Their name is proud and their get pure gold.
Their procreation hath won renown,
But Rose the Second hath let them down.
Her forebears have labored for bitter meed,
For Rose is barren and will not breed.
Now the gate that is strait and the way that is narrow
Call for a cow to forego being farrow.
In a cow one condones a trifle of loose
Morality if she will just reproduce.
The stars in their courses deliver us
From the cow that is non-frugiferous!
If a heifer aspires to a niche on high
She must certainly plan to fructify,
And when she reaches puberty
Must concentrate on uberty.
No honor is there for the boss of that ilk
That produceth no young and giveth no milk;
And this is the reason her kith make moan
For Rose the Second of Aberlone. . . .

'Tis the middle of night before the exam,
And there's nothing to eat but a cold bit of ham.
                    Ah me!—Ah moo!
Mark how the eager students cram,
What coffee black they brew!

A dismal specter haunts this wake—
The law of mutual mistake;
And even the reluctant drone
Must cope with Rose of Aberlone.
She rules the cases, she stalks the page
Even in this atomic age.
In radioactive tracts of land,
In hardly collectible notes of hand,
In fiddles of dubious pedigree,
In releases of liability,
In zoning rules unknown to lessors,
In weird conceits of law professors,
In printers' bids and ailing kings,
In all mutations and sorts of things,
In many a hypothetical
With characters alphabetical,
In many a subtle and sly disguise
There lurks the ghost of her sad brown eyes.
That she will turn up in some set of facts is
Almost as certain as death and taxes:
For students of law must still atone
For the shame of Rose of Aberlone.

MAGEE v. PENNINE INSURANCE CO.
[1969] 2 W.L.R. 1278 (C.A.)

LORD DENNING M.R.: In 1961 Mr. Thomas Magee, senior, the plaintiff, aged 58, acquired an Austin car. He signed a proposal form for insurance. In it he said that the car belonged to him. He was asked to give details of his driving licence "and of all other persons who to your present knowledge will drive." These were the details he gave:

(1) "Thomas Magee"—that is himself—"provisional licence aged 58."

(2) "John Magee"—that is his elder son— "Police mobile driver, aged 35." He had an annual licence.

(3) "John J. Magee"—that is his younger son—"joiner, aged 18— provisional licence."

Mr. Magee signed this declaration: "I . . . do hereby declare that the car described is and shall be kept in good condition and that the answers above given are in every respect true and correct and I . . . hereby agree that this declaration shall be the basis of the contract of insurance between the company and myself . . . ." Those details were not written in by Mr. Magee himself. They were written in by Mr. Atkinson at the garage where he got the car. The details unfortunately were completely wrong. Mr. Thomas Magee had never driven a car himself. He had never had a licence, not even a provisional one. He was getting the car really for his son of 18 to drive. And we all know that a young man of 18 has to pay a much higher insurance than a man of 25 or over. This company said they would not have insured a young man of 18.

The judge found that Mr. Thomas Magee, the father, had not been fraudulent. He did not himself fill in the details. They were filled in by Mr. Atkinson, the man at the garage. And then Mr. Thomas Magee signed them. It was Mr. Atkinson who made some mistake or other. But there it was. A misrepresentation was made and on the faith of it being true, the insurance company granted an insurance policy to Mr. Magee.

Thereafter the policy was renewed each year and the premiums were paid. In 1964 that car was replaced by another. The policy was renewed for the new car without anything further being said about the drivers or the ownership. The company assumed, no doubt, that the same details applied.

On April 25, 1965, there was an accident. The younger son, John Magee, was driving the new car at 4 o'clock in the morning. He ran into a shop window. The plate glass was smashed and the car was a complete wreck. The father, Mr. Thomas Magee, put in a claim form, in which he said that the car was £600 in value. That was clearly wrong because the price new was only £547 the year before. The insurers thereupon got their engineer to look at it. On May 12, 1965, the broker wrote to Mr. Thomas Magee a letter, in which he said: ". . . We have today been advised by your insurers that their engineer considers your vehicle is damaged beyond repair. The engineer considers that the pre-accident market value of the vehicle was £410 and they are therefore prepared to offer you this amount, less the £25 accidental damage excess in settlement of your claim. We should be pleased to receive your confirmation that this is acceptable. . . ." There was no written acceptance, but it was accepted by word of mouth. That seemed to be a concluded agreement whereby the company agreed to pay £385.

But within the next few days the insurance company made further inquiries. One of their representatives saw Mr. Magee and took a statement from him. Then the truth was discovered. Mr. Magee did not drive at all. He had never had a driving licence, not even a provisional one. He said that the car was never his property but was his son's car: and that it was his son, the younger son, who had driven the car and was the only person who had ever driven it. On discovering those facts, the insurance company said they were not liable on the insurance policy.

They had been induced to grant it, they said, by the misrepresentations in the original proposal form; and also by reason of non-disclosure of material facts, namely, that the son aged 18 was normally to be the driver.

Mr. Magee brought an action in the county court in which he claimed the £385. He said it was payable under the insurance policy, or, alternatively, on an agreement of compromise contained in the letter of May 12.

The judge rejected the claim on the policy itself, because the insurance was induced by misrepresentation. He found that the company were entitled to repudiate the policy because of the inaccuracy of Mr. Magee's answers. That finding was not challenged in this court. Mr. Taylor, on behalf of Mr. Magee, admitted that he could not claim on the policy.

But the judge upheld the claim on the letter of May 12. He said it was a binding contract of compromise. I am not so sure about this. It might be said to be a mere quantification of the account which should be paid in case the insurance company were liable: and that it did not preclude them from afterwards contesting liability. But, on the whole, I do not think we should regard it as a mere quantification. The letter contains the important words: "in settlement of your claim," which import that it is to be settled without further controversy. In short, it bears the stamp of an agreement of compromise. The consideration for it was the ascertainment of a sum which was previously unascertained.

But then comes the next point. Accepting that the agreement to pay £385 was an agreement of compromise. Is it vitiated by mistake? The insurance company were clearly under a mistake. They thought that the policy was good and binding. They did not know, at the time of that letter, that there had been misrepresentations in the proposal form. If Mr. Magee knew of their mistake—if he knew that the policy was bad—he certainly could not take advantage of the agreement to pay £385. He would be "snapping at an offer which he knew was made under a mistake": and no man is allowed to get away with that. But I prefer to assume that Mr. Magee was innocent. I think we should take it that both parties were under a common mistake. Both parties thought that the policy was good and binding. The letter of March 12, 1968, was written on the assumption that the policy was good whereas it was in truth voidable.

What is the effect in law of this common mistake? Mr. Taylor said that the agreement to pay £385 was good, despite this common mistake. He relied much on *Bell* v. *Lever Brothers, Ltd.* [1932] A.C. 161, and its similarity to the present case. He submitted that, inasmuch as the mistake there did not vitiate that contract, the mistake here should not vitiate this one. I do not propose today to go through the speeches in that case. They have given enough trouble to commentators already. I would say simply this: A common mistake, even on a most fundamental matter, does not make a contract void at law: but it makes it voidable in equity. I analysed the cases in *Solle* v. *Butcher* [1950] 1 K.B. 671, and I would repeat what I said there, at p. 693: "A contract is also liable in equity to be set aside if the parties were under a common misapprehension either as to facts or as to their relative and respective rights, provided that the misapprehension was fundamental and that the party seeking to set it aside was not himself at fault." Applying that principle here, it is clear that, when the insurance company and Mr. Magee made this agreement to pay £385, they were both under a common mistake which was fundamental to the whole agreement. Both thought that Mr. Magee was entitled to claim under the policy of insurance, whereas he was not so entitled. That common mistake does not make the agreement to pay £385 a nullity, but it makes it liable to be set aside in equity.

This brings me to a question which has caused me much difficulty. Is this a case in which we ought to set the agreement aside in equity? I have hesitated on this point, but I cannot shut my eyes to the fact that Mr. Magee had no valid claim on the insurance policy: and, if he had no claim on the policy, it is not equitable that he should have a good claim on the agreement to pay £385, seeing that it was made under a fundamental mistake. It is not fair to hold the insurance company to an agreement which they would not have dreamt of making if they had not been under a mistake. I would, therefore, uphold the appeal and give judgment for the insurance company.

[Fenton Atkinson L.J. agreed. Winn L.J. dissented.]

PROBLEM 1. A, in quoting orally for the supply of glass to B, a building contractor, miscalculates the amount of glass required by misplacing a decimal point and quotes a price of $2,000, about one-third of the proper price. B, knowing that the price is extraordinarily low, asks A to confirm the quotation in writing, and A does so. B calculates his own tender for the whole building on the basis of the figure of $2,000 for the glass, and B's tender is successful. B then places an order for the glass, but A refuses to supply. See *Imperial Glass Ltd.* v. *Consolidated Supplies Ltd.* (1960) 22 D.L.R. (2d) 759 (B.C.C.A.)

PROBLEM 2. Able agrees to lease to Baker for 5 years a highway service station for $1,000 a month.

(1) A by-law has been passed prohibiting the use of the land as a service station; neither party knows of the by-law.

(2) As in (1) but Able knows of the by-law.

(3) The by-law is passed after the lease has run for a month.

(4) Would it make any difference in (3) if either party, or both parties, foresaw the possibility of the enactment of such a by-law? What if a reasonable man would have foreseen it?

(5) Would it make any difference in (3) if the rent were based in part on Baker's sales of gasoline (e.g., $900 plus 1% of profits)?

CHAPTER 11

UNEXPECTED CHANGES IN CIRCUMSTANCES

The cases on mistake in assumptions were concerned with agreements entered into on the basis of a false assumption about past or existing circumstances. This chapter is concerned with false assumptions about future events. In many respects the problems are similar. In these cases too the question for the court is often the same: When is it just to restore a benefit where subsequent unexpected events have caused an agreement to enrich one party at the expense of the other?

The cases in this chapter are usually classified under the label of Impossibility of Performance or Frustration or both. Since it is quite clear that a person may promise the impossible and a court may award damages on his inevitable breach of his promise, impossibility is not always a defence. Moreover, what is legally "Impossible" is sometimes capable of performance if, say, the performer goes to inordinate expense. During the Second World War it was commonly said that "the impossible only takes a little longer." The label is therefore a bit misleading. Nor is Frustration an entirely satisfactory single label.

The cases in the first section are intended to raise the first problem: when ought changed or unforeseen circumstances to provide some defence?

The cases in the second section raise the question of compensation for partial benefits conferred and relief for partial losses sustained.

1. RELAXATION OF THE RULE OF ABSOLUTE PROMISES

TAYLOR v. *CALDWELL*
England. Queen's Bench. 1863. 3 B. & S. 826; 122 E.R. 309

BLACKBURN J. delivered the judgment of the Court: In this case the plaintiffs and the defendants had, on the 27th May, 1861, entered into a contract by which the defendants agreed to let the plaintiffs have the use of The Surrey Gardens and Music Hall on four days then to come viz., the 17th June, 15 July, 5th August, and 19th August, for the purpose of giving a series of four grand concerts, and day and night fetes at the Gardens and Hall on those days respectively; and the plaintiffs agreed to take the Gardens and Hall on those days, and pay £100 for each day.

The parties inaccurately called this a "letting" and the money to be paid a "rent"; but the whole agreement is such as to shew that the defendants were to retain the possession of the Hall and Gardens so that there was to be no demise of them, and that the contract was merely to give the plaintiffs the use of them on those days. Nothing however, in our opinion, depends on this. The agreement then proceeds to set out various stipulations between the parties as to what each was to supply for these concerts and entertainments, and as to the manner in which they should be carried on. The effect of the whole is to shew that the existence of the Music Hall in the Surrey Garden in a state fit for a concert was essential for the fulfilment of the contract,—such entertainment as the parties contemplated in their agreements could not be given without it.

After the making of the agreement, and before the first day on which a concert was to be given, the Hall was destroyed by fire. This destruction, we must take it on the evidence, was without the fault of either party, and was so complete that in consequence the concerts could not be given as intended. And the question we have to decide is whether, under these circumstances, the loss which the plaintiffs have sustained is to fall upon the defendants. The parties when framing their agreement evidently had not present to their minds the possibility of such a disaster, and have made no express stipulation with reference to it, so that the answer to the question must depend upon the general rules of law applicable to such a contract.

There seems no doubt that where there is a positive contract to do a thing, not in itself unlawful, the contractor must perform it or pay damages for not doing it, although in consequence of unforeseen accidents the performance of his contract has become unexpectedly burthensome or even impossible. The law is so laid down in 1 Roll. Abr. 450, Condition (G), and in the note (2) to *Walton* (1673), 2 Wms. Saund. 421 a. 6th ed.; 85 E.R. 1234, and is recognised as the general rule by all the judges in the much discussed case of *Hall* v. *Wright* (1859), 120 E.R. 695. But this rule is only applicable when the contract is positive and absolute, and not subject to any condition either express or implied; and there are authorities which, as we think, establish the principle that where, from the nature of the contract, it appears that the parties must from the beginning have known that it could not be fulfilled unless when the time for the fulfilment of the contract arrived some particular specified thing continued to exist, so that, when entering into the contract, they must have contemplated such continuing existence as the foundation of what was to be done; there, in the absence of any express or implied warranty that the thing shall exist, the contract is not to be construed as a positive contract, but as subject to an implied condition that the parties shall be excused in case, before breach, performance becomes impossible from the perishing of the thing without default of the contractor.

There seems little doubt that this implication tends to further the great object of making the legal construction such as to fulfil the intention of those who entered into the contract. For in the course of affairs men in making such contracts in general would, if it were brought to their minds, say that there should be such a condition.

Accordingly, in the Civil law, such an exception is implied [in some obligations]. . . .

Although the Civil law is not of itself authority in an English Court, it affords great assistance in investigating the principles on which the law is grounded. And it seems to us that the common law authorities established that in such a contract the same condition of the continued existence of the thing is implied by English law.

There is a class of contracts in which a person binds himself to do something which requires to be performed by him in person; and such promises, e.g. promises to marry, or promises to serve for a certain time, are never in practice qualified by an express exception of the death of the party; and therefore in such cases the contract is in terms broken if the promisor dies before fulfilment. Yet it was very early determined that, if the performance is personal, the executors are not liable; *Hyde* v. *The Dean of Windsor* (1597), Cro. Eliz. 552; 78 E.R. 798. See 2 *Wms. Exors.*

1560, 5th ed. where a very apt illustration is given. "Thus," says the learned author, "if an author undertakes to compose a work, and dies before completing it, his executors are discharged from this contract: for the undertaking is merely personal in its nature, and, by the intervention of the contractor's death, has become impossible to be performed." For this he cites a dictum of Lord Lyndhurst in *Marshall* v. *Broadhurst* 1 Tyr. 348, 349, and a case mentioned by Patteson J. in *Wenworth* v. *Cock* (1839), 10 A. & E. 42; 113 E.R. 17 at p. 18. In *Hall* v. *Wright,* Crompton J., in his judgment, puts another case. "Where a contract depends upon personal skill, and the act of God renders it impossible, as, for instance, in the case of a painter employed to paint a picture who is struck blind, it may be that the performance might be excused."

It seems that in those cases the only ground on which the parties or their executors can be excused from the consequences of the breach of the contract is, that from the nature of the contract there is an implied condition of the continued existence of the life of the contractor, and perhaps, in the case of the painter of his eyesight. In the instances just given, the person, the continued existence of whose life is necessary to the fulfilment of the contract, is himself the contractor, but that does not seem in itself to be necessary to the application of the principle; as is illustrated by the following example. In the ordinary form of an apprentice deed the apprentice binds himself in unqualified terms to "serve until the full end and term of seven years to be fully complete and ended," during which term it is covenanted that the apprentice his master "faithfully shall serve," and the father of the apprentice in equally unqualified terms binds himself for the performance by the apprentice of all and every covenant on his part. (See the form, 2 Chitty on Pleading, 370, 7th ed. by Greening.) It is undeniable that if the apprentice dies within the seven years, the covenant of the father that he shall perform his covenant to serve for seven years is not fulfilled, yet surely it cannot be that an action would lie against the father? Yet the only reason why it would not is that he is excused because of the apprentice's death.

These are instances where the implied condition is of the life of a human being, but there are others in which the same implication is made as to the continued existence of a thing. For example, where a contract of sale is made amounting to a bargain and sale, transferring presently the property in specific chattels, which are to be delivered by the vendor at a future day; there, if the chattels, without the fault of the vendor, perish in the interval, the purchaser must pay the price and the vendor is excused from performing his contract to deliver, which has thus become impossible.

That this is the rule of the English law is established by the case of *Rugg* v. *Minett* (1809), 11 East, 210; 103 E.R. 985, where the article that perished before delivery was turpentine, and it was decided that the vendor was bound to refund the price of all those lots in which the property had not passed; but was entitled to retain without deduction the price of those lots in which the property had passed, though they were not delivered, and though in the conditions of sale, which are set out in the report, there was no express qualification of the promise to deliver on payment. It seems in that case rather to have been taken for granted than decided that the destruction of the thing sold before delivery excused the vendor from fulfilling his contract to deliver on payment.

This also is the rule in the Civil law, and it is worth noticing that Pothier, in his celebrated *Traité du Contrat de Vente* (see Part 4, 307, &c; and

Part 2, Ch. 1, sect. 1, art. 4, 1), treats this as merely an example of the more general rule that every obligation *de certo corpore* is extinguished when the thing ceases to exist. See *Blackburn on the Contract of Sale,* 173.

The same principle seems to be involved in the decision of *Sparrow* v. *Sowgate* (1625), W. Jones, 29; 82 E.R. 16, where, to an action of debt on an obligation by bail, conditioned for the payment of the debt or the render of the debtor, it was held a good plea that before any default in rendering him the principal debtor died. It is true that was the case of a bond with a condition, and a distinction is sometimes made in this respect between a condition and a contract. But this observation does not apply to *Williams* v. *Lloyd* (1629), W. Jones, 179, 82 E.R. 95. In that case the count, which was in assumpsit, alleged that the plaintiff had delivered a horse to the defendant, who promised to redeliver it on request. Breach, that though requested to redeliver the horse he refused. Plea, that the horse was sick and died, and the plaintiff made the request after its death; and on demurrer it was held a good plea, as the bailee was discharged from his promise by the death of the horse without default or negligence on the part of the defendant. "Let it be admitted," says the Court, "that he promised to deliver it on request, if the horse die before, that is become impossible by the act of God, so the party shall be discharged, as much as if an obligation were made conditioned to deliver the horse on request, and he died before it." And Jones, adds the report, cited 22 Ass. 41, in which it was held that a ferryman who had promised to carry a horse safe across the ferry was held chargeable for the drowning of the animal, only because he had overloaded the boat, and it was agreed that notwithstanding the promise no action would have lain had there been no neglect or default on his part.

It may, we think, be safely asserted to be now English law, that in all contracts of loan of chattels or bailments, if the performance of the promise of the borrower or bailee to return the things lent or bailed becomes impossible because it has perished, this impossibility (if not arising from the fault of the borrower or bailee from some risk which he has taken upon himself) excuses the borrower or bailee from the performance of his promise to redeliver the chattel.

The great case of *Coggs* v. *Bernard* (1703), 1 Smith's L.C. 171, 5th ed., 2 L. Raym. 909; 92 E.R. 107, is now the leading case on the law of bailments, and Lord Holt, in that case, referred so much to the Civil law that it might perhaps be thought that this principle was there derived direct from the civilians, and was not generally applicable in English law except in the case of bailments; but the case of *Williams* v. *Lloyd,* above cited, shews that the same law had been already adopted by the English law as early as *The Book of Assizes.* The principle seems to us to be that, in contracts in which the performance depends on the continued existence of a given person or thing, a condition is implied that the impossibility of performance arising from the perishing of the person or thing shall excuse the performance.

In none of these cases is the promise in words other than positive, nor is there any express stipulation that the destruction of the person or thing shall excuse the performance; but that excuse is by law implied, because from the nature of the contract it is apparent that the parties contracted on the basis of the continued existence of the particular person or chattel. In the present case, looking at the whole contract, we find that the parties contracted on the basis of the continued existence of the Music Hall at the time when the concerts were to be given; that being essential to their performance.

We think, therefore, that the Music Hall having ceased to exist, without fault of either party, both parties are excused, the plaintiffs from taking the Gardens and paying the money, the defendants from performing their promise to give the use of the Hall and Gardens and other things. Consequently the rule must be absolute to enter the verdict for the defendants.

QUESTIONS. Why is it necessary to imply a condition to excuse the plaintiff? Is that part of the decision an *obiter dictum*? Has the plaintiff not suffered a "total failure of consideration"?

NOTE. Is the condition one implied from the facts or one implied by law? From the vantage point of having read the cases in Chapter 9, do you think it is possible to draw any sharp distinction between a condition implied in fact and one implied in law? Do you think any useful purpose is served by drawing the distinction anyway?

Perhaps the greatest insight into the problem may be had from a study of Fuller, *Basic Contract Law*, pp. 666-70. Professor Fuller develops the notion of "tacit assumptions." He says, in part:

"In *Taylor* v. *Caldwell* the court says that when framing their agreement the parties 'had not present to their minds the possibility' of a disaster affecting the Music Hall, and concludes that the parties 'must have contemplated' the 'continuing existence' of the Hall 'as the foundation' of their agreement.

"Is there a contradiction here? The court seems to say that the parties did not think of the possibility of the Hall's burning and therefore assumed it would not burn. But how can the parties assume that no fire will occur, when the possibility of a fire was never present to their minds? If this possibility was not present to their minds, would it not be more accurate to say that they assumed nothing about a fire, either that it would or would not occur?

"The difficulty here does not lie in any dispute about psychological fact, but in the inappropriateness of the language ordinarily used to describe certain elementary psychological truths. Words like 'intention,' 'assumption,' 'expectation' and 'understanding' all seem to imply a *conscious* state involving an awareness of alternatives and a deliberate choice among them. It is, however, plain that there is a psychological state which can be described as 'tacit assumption' that does not involve a consciousness of alternatives. The absent-minded professor stepping from his office into the hall as he reads a book 'assumes' that the floor of the hall will be there to receive him. His conduct is conditioned and directed by this assumption, even though the possibility that the floor has been removed does not 'occur' to him, that is, is not present in his conscious mental processes.

"...Underlying questions of this sort, and indeed, underlying much of contract law generally, are certain basic problems of psychology that have never been satisfactorily solved. We speak constantly of things that were 'intended' or 'assumed' without having a clear conception of the psychological processes involved in 'intending' and 'assuming.' The lawyer or judge who turns to psychology for help in dealing with these problems is likely to be disappointed.

"...In spite of hopeful beginnings promising a more comprehensive psychological treatment of human behaviour, for the time being the only methods available for dealing with problems like that raised by *Taylor* v. *Caldwell* are essentially those resting on intuition and introspection. We 'just know' that the burning of a music hall violates a tacit assumption of the parties who executed a contract for hiring it; we 'just know' that a two per cent increase in the price of beans does not violate a tacit assumption underlying a contract to deliver a ton of beans for a fixed price. . . ."

PARADINE v. JANE
England. King's Bench. 1647. Aleyn 26; 82 E.R. 897

In debt the plaintiff declares upon a lease for years rendering rent at the four usual feasts; and for rent behind for three years, ending at the Feast of the Annunciation, 21 Car. brings his action; the defendant pleads, that a certain German prince, by name Prince Rupert, an alien born, enemy to the King and kingdom, had invaded the realm with an hostile army of men; and with the same force did enter upon the defendant's possession, and him expelled, and held out of possession from the 19th of July 18 Car. till the Feast of Annunciation, 21 Car. whereby he could not take the profits; whereupon the plaintiff demurred, and the plea was resolved insufficient. . . .

It was resolved, that the matter of the plea was insufficient; for though the whole army had been alien enemies, yet he ought to pay his rent. And this difference was taken, that where the law creates a duty or charge, and the party is disabled to perform it without any default in him, and hath no remedy over, then the law will excuse him. As in the case of waste, if a house be destroyed by tempest, or by enemies, the lessee is excused. Dyer, 33.a. Inst. 53. d. 283 c. 12 H.4.6. so of an escape. Co. 4.84.b. 33 H. 6.1. So in 9 E.3. 16, a *supersedeas* was awarded to the justices, that they should not proceed in a *cessavit* upon a cesser during the war, but when the party by his own contract creates a duty or charge upon himself, he is bound to make it good, if he may, notwithstanding any accident by inevitable necessity, because he might have provided against it by his contract. And therefore if the lessee covenant to repair a house, though it be burnt by lightning, or thrown down by enemies, yet he ought to repair it. Dyer 33.3; 40 E. III.6.h. Now the rent is a duty created by the parties upon the reservation, and had there been a covenant to pay it, there had been no question but the lessee must have made it good, notwithstanding the interruption by enemies, for the law would not protect him beyond his own agreement, no more than in the case of reparations; this reservation then being a covenant in law, and whereupon an action of covenant hath been maintained (as Roll said) it is all one as if there had been an actual covenant. Another reason was added, that as the lessee is to have the advantage of casual profits so he must run the hazard of casual losses, and not lay the whole burthen of them upon his lessor; and Dyer 56.6. was cited for this purpose, that though the land be surrounded, or gained by the sea, or made barren by wildfire, yet the lessor shall have his whole rent: and judgment was given for the plaintiff.

CAPITAL QUALITY HOMES LTD. v. COLWYN CONSTRUCTION LTD.
(1975) 9 O.R. (2d) 617 (Ont. C.A.)

EVANS J.A.: The defendant Colwyn Construction Limited appeals from the judgment of the Honourable Mr. Justice Keith granting the plaintiff recovery from the defendant of the sum of $13,980 being the return of a deposit paid by the plaintiff pursuant to an agreement for sale between the parties relative to certain undeveloped land in the City of Windsor.

The trial proceeded on an agreed statement of facts which was presented orally to the Court by counsel and which may be briefly summarized as follows: Under an agreement dated January 5, 1969, the plaintiff, purchaser, agreed to purchase from the defendant, vendor, 26 building lots each comprising parts of lots within a registered plan of subdivision. The date fixed for closing was July 30, 1970. Both parties were aware that the purchaser was buying building lots for the purpose of erecting a home on each lot with the intention of selling the several homes by way of separate conveyances. Under the terms of the agreement it was entitled to a conveyance of a building lot upon payment of $6,000 and, upon full payment, to 26 separate deeds of conveyance each representing one building lot. It is agreed that no demand for any conveyance was made prior to the date of closing.

When the sale agreement was executed the designated land was not within an area of subdivision control and not subject to any restriction limiting the right to convey. On June 27, 1970, certain amendments [1970, c. 72, s. 1] to the *Planning Act*, R.S.O. 1960, c. 296, came into effect whereby these lands came under the provisions of what is now s. 29 of the *Planning Act*, R.S.O. 1970, c. 349, which in certain circumstances restricts an owner's right to convey and makes necessary the obtaining of a consent from the relevant committee of adjustment designated in the amending legislation. In the absence of such consent no interest in part of a lot within a registered plan of subdivision can be conveyed.

The vendor was accordingly precluded from conveying the 26 building lots in 26 separate deeds without proper consents and while a conveyance to the purchaser of all lots in one deed may have been permissible, the purchaser in any event would be unable to reconvey individual building lots to prospective home buyers as it had intended without complying with the restrictive provisions of the new legislation.

This substantial change in the law, prohibiting and restricting conveyancing of the lands, 33 days prior to the anticipated closing date, resulted in some discussion between the parties relative to possible postponement of the closing date in order to devise some method of circumventing the restrictions to which the lands were now subject. No arrangement was made to extend closing. On the agreed date of closing the purchaser insisted that the vendor deliver conveyances for each individual building lot with the consents necessary to effectually transfer the lots. The vendor insisted that it was the responsibility of the purchaser to obtain the necessary consents. On the closing date the balance of the agreed purchase price was tendered by the solicitors for the purchaser but no conveyances were forthcoming in the mode contemplated by the agreement. It is common ground that the purchaser would not withdraw its demand for 26 individual conveyances with consents attached and that the vendor did not provide such conveyances. Following failure to close on the agreed date, the purchaser contended that the vendor was in default and on August 5, 1970, repudiated the agreement and made demand upon the vendor for the return of the balance of the deposit.

Although the statement of facts agreed to by counsel does not state that the relatively short period of time, 33 days, between the effective date of the amending legislation and the stipulated closing date made impossible the obtaining of the necessary consents, the argument indicated that such was the understanding and I have accordingly assumed that the time factor was so limited that the parties were in agreement that it would have been impossible to process the applications for consents prior to the closing date.

The trial Judge stated in his reasons [1973] 3 O.R. 651 at p. 655, 37 D.L.R. (3d) 671 at p. 675, that he did not consider it necessary to deal with the "theory of commercial frustration" which was argued before him and proceeded to found his judgment on the narrow ground "that the vendor could not deliver separate and effective conveyances for each building lot as it was required to do under the express terms of the agreement without having first secured the consent required under the *Planning Act*." He went on to hold that the vendor was not justified in its default and that the purchaser was entitled to repudiate the contract and recover its deposit.

Accordingly, I propose to deal with this appeal on the basis of the argument advanced before us, *i.e.*, on the doctrine of frustration and its applicability to contracts involving the sale and purchase of land.

However, before proceeding I wish to advert to a recent case to which counsel has not referred. While it does not deal specifically with the doctrine of frustration the factual situation is almost identical to the case under appeal, although the ground upon which it was defended is dissimilar. I refer to the judgment of Osler J., in *Innes et al.* v. *Van de Weerdhof*, [1970] 2 O.R. 334, 10 D.L.R. (3d) 722, in which an agreement for the sale of land was entered into on September 14, 1967, and a deposit of $1,000 paid. A closing date was set and later extended to March 1, 1968, on condition that a further sum of $3,000 be paid and that time remain of the essence. After the time allowed for requisitions had passed the purchaser became aware that the land was subject to a subdivision control by-law which became effective February 1, 1968, that is, some months after the agreement was signed. There was also a breach of an existing zoning by-law. It became apparent that a committee of adjustment consent as required by the subdivision control by-law would not be available by the extended closing date. The purchaser made tender but refused the conveyance without the consent and because of the zoning breach. The purchaser sought the return of his deposit and the vendor resisted payment. The latter argued that neither the zoning by-law nor the subdivision control by-law were properly raised as requisitions within the time allowed by the agreement and the purchasers, as the result of their failure, were obligated to accept whatever the vendor could give, no matter how deficient the vendor's title might be in respect of either matter. Osler J., followed a long line of authorities which distinguished matters which go to the root of title and those which do not. The zoning by-law did not go to the root of title and was considered to have been waived while the subdivision control by-law did go to the root of title and could be raised at any time prior to closing. In the absence of the requisite consent at the date of closing, with time being of the essence of the transaction, the purchaser was entitled to insist upon his right to reject the conveyance without the consent and rescind the agreement. He went on to hold that the effect of the by-law was to bring about a complete failure of consideration and directed the deposit to be returned to the purchaser.

Turning now to the argument advanced on the appeal, the appellant, vendor, submitted that the supervening legislation which restricted transfer of the lots was a burden falling upon the purchaser. The argument was that upon execution of an agreement for the sale of land the purchaser became the equitable owner of the lands and any amending legislation which affected either zoning or alienation of land was a burden to be assumed by the purchaser. Accordingly, the purchaser was in error in attempting to repudiate the agreement and could not recover the deposit paid.

The respondent, purchaser, took the position that the effect of the new legislation was to make impossible the fulfilment of the terms of the contract; that there was a failure of consideration and that equity would not force the purchaser to take something fundamentally different from that for which it had bargained.

The vendor also argued that the obligation to obtain the consent of the committee of adjustment rested upon the purchaser. I do not agree. Unless otherwise provided in the agreement of sale the vendor is required to convey a marketable title in fee simple. There was no provision in the instant agreement which would permit the vendor to escape from that normal obligation.

That default alone was sufficient to entitle the purchaser to the return of its deposit.

The issues for determination, as I apprehend them, are:

(1) Does the doctrine of impossibility of performance of a contract, *i.e.*, frustration, have any application when the contract is for the purchase and sale of land?

(2) Assuming that frustration is applicable to agreements for sale of land, does the factual situation in this case permit the doctrine to be invoked?

(3) Assuming that (1) and (2) are both answered in the affirmative what results flow therefrom?

In order to show the birth and development of the doctrine of frustration it is necessary to recall that the common law exacted strict performance of contractual obligations. A promise demanded performance and if performance became impossible, not matter what the reason, the defaulting party was liable in damages. *Paradine* v. *Jane*, (1647), Aleyn 26, 82 E.R. 897, restated the principle and it is alleged that the justification for imposing such onerous obligations was that if contracting parties voluntarily entered into absolute and unconditional agreements they cannot complain if their lack of foresight in failing to provide against all contingencies created hardships to them.

English Courts, prior to *Taylor et al.* v. *Caldwell et al.*, (1863), 3 B. & S. 826, 122 E.R. 309, followed the rule that impossibility of performance of a contract did not relieve the party unable to perform from liability in damages. Subsequently, that rigid rule was relaxed and contracts were held to be terminated and the parties discharged when the events which denied fulfilment of the contract were caused by some circumstance beyond the control of the contracting parties. In *Taylor et al.* v. *Caldwell, supra*, the subject-matter of the contract was destroyed before the date upon which performance was required. Blackburn J., held that when a music-hall which was rented for the purpose of holding concerts, was accidentally destroyed by fire prior to the concerts being held, the owner was discharged from his contract and not liable in damages. The common law doctrine of contract was uncompromising in its insistence on performance and if a party could not actually perform an act because some event made it physically impossible, then specific performance could not be ordered but the party failing would be liable in damages for non-performance. The breakthrough by Blackburn J. was accomplished by holding that a contract is not to be construed as absolute if the contracting parties from the beginning must have known that its fulfilment depended upon the continued existence of some peculiar thing and therefore must have realized that his continuing existence was the foundation of the bargain. He held that the contract is "subject to an implied condition that the parties shall be excused in case, before breach, performance becomes impossible from the perishing of the thing without default of the contractor." He implied a term or condition into the contract. The doctrine of impossibility of performance or as it is now generally called, the doctrine of frustration, developed rapidly, particularly in commercial contracts and English Courts sought to do justice by holding that a contract was discharged when some catastrophic event occurred, the result of which was to destroy the very basis of the contract.

Krell v. *Henry*, [1903] 2 K.B. 740 (C.A.), dealt with a hire of premises to view a coronation subsequently cancelled and the Court held that the view of the coronation procession was the foundation of the contract and the non-happening of it prevented the performance of the contract. *Marshall* v. *Glanvill et al.*, [1917] 2 K.B. 87, was concerned with a contract of employment and the liability of the employee to compulsory military service was held to determine the contract.

In all these commercial contract cases in which the principle is referred to as "frustration of the adventure" the Court has implied into the contract a term or condition because the contract itself does not provide for the supervening act which produces the frustration. Lord Sumner in *Cheong Yne Steamship Co. Ltd.* v. *Hirji Mulji et al.*, [1926] 1 W.W.R. 917, [1926] A.C. 497, referred to the doctrine of frustration as "a device by which the rules as to absolute contracts can be reconciled with a special exception which justice demands." The legal effect of the frustration of a contract does not depend upon the intention of the parties, or their opinions or even knowledge as to the event that has brought about the frustration, but upon its occurrence in such circumstances as to show it to be inconsistent with the further prosecution of the adventure. On the contrary, it seems that when the event occurs, the meaning of the contract must be taken to be, not what the parties did intend (for they had neither thought nor intention regarding it) but that which the parties, as fair and reasonable men, would presumably have agreed upon if, having such possibility in view, they had made express provision as to their several rights and liabilities in the event of its occurrence: *Dahl* v. *Nelson et al.*, (1880), 6 App. Cas. 38.

The supervening event must be something beyond the control of the parties and must result in a significant change in the original obligation assumed by them. The theory of the implied term has been replaced by the more realistic view that the Court imposes upon the parties the just and reasonable solution that the new situation demands.

Lord Radcliffe in *Davis Contractors Ltd.* v. *Fareham Urban District Council*, [1956] A.C. 696 at pp. 728-9, stated:

"So perhaps it would be simpler to say at the outset that frustration occurs whenever the law recognizes that without default of either party a contractual obligation has become incapable of being performed because the circumstances in which performance is called for would render it a thing radically different from that which was undertaken by the contract. Non haec in foedera veni. It was not this that I promised to do."

The development of the doctrine briefly referred to above is traced with considerable detail in Cheshire & Fifoot, *Law of Contracts*, 7th ed. (1969), at p. 506, and following. The *Law Reform (Frustrated Contracts) Act*, 1943 (U.K.), c. 40, defined the position of the parties in England when a contract is discharged by frustration and set out those particular contracts to which the Act did not apply.

The controversial question that is still undecided by the House of Lords is whether the doctrine of frustration can be applied to a lease of land. Cases involving the destruction of a chattel, the subject of the contract, as in *Howell* v. *Coupland* (1876), 1 Q.B.D. 258, or the destruction of a music-hall, the existence of which was the foundation of the contract as in *Taylor et al.* v. *Caldwell et al.*, *supra*, or those cases in which the performance of the contract has become illegal because of some supervening legislation are to be distinguished from land leases which are considered to be more than contracts, since they create estates in land which give rise to proprietary rights in addition to purely personal rights as found in all commercial contracts. In the development of the modern law of contracts an increasingly wider conception of the doctrine of frustration as a ground of discharge of commercial contracts came into operation but the English Courts have consistently held that the doctrine of frustration has no application when the contract creates an estate in land.

In *Cricklewood Property & Investment Trust, Ltd.* v. *Leighton's Investment Trust, Ltd.*, [1945] A.C. 221, Lord Russell of Killowen and Lord Goddard held to the view that the doctrine of frustration cannot apply to a demise of real property. Viscount Simon L.C., and Lord Wright took the position that the doctrine is modern and flexible and ought not to be restricted by an arbitrary formula. Lord Porter expressed no opinion on the question. The case involved a building lease for a term of 99 years. The war of 1939 broke out and restrictions imposed by the Government made it impossible for the building to be proceeded with at that time. The Court unanimously held that the doctrine, even if it were capable of application to a lease, did not apply as the compulsory suspension of building did not strike at the root of the transaction since the lease had 90 years to run from the date the restriction was imposed and therefore the interruption in performance was likely to last only for a small fraction of the term.

In *Cricklewood Property & Investment Trust Ltd.*, v. *Leighton's Investment Trust, Ltd.*, *supra*, the trial Judge would have held the contract to be discharged, had he not been convinced that there was clear authority that the doctrine of frustration could not be applied to a demise of real property. The Court of Appeal affirmed his judgment on the ground that frustration was not applicable. It was only when the case was considered in the House of Lords that some doubt was cast upon the earlier cases which had come to be regarded as authoritative. Viscount Simon L.C. defined "frustration" as [at p. 228.]

" . . . the premature determination of an agreement between parties, lawfully entered into and in course of operation at the time of its premature determination, owing to the occurrence of an intervening event or change of circumstances so fundamental as to be regarded by the law both as striking at the root of the agreement, and as entirely beyond what was contemplated by the parties when they entered into the agreement."

He was of the opinion that the doctrine could apply to a lease of land although he considered that the instances in which it could be successfully invoked were very rare. He stated that the Court of Appeal was in error in concluding that the authorities held that a lease cannot in any circumstances be ended by frustration.

In *Matthey* v. *Curling*, [1922] 2 A.C. 180, Atkin L.J., in a dissenting judgment in the Court of Appeal, at p. 183, observed at pp. 199-200:

". . . it does not appear to me conclusive against the application to a lease of the doctrine of frustration that the lease, in addition to containing contractual terms, grants a term of years. Seeing that the instrument as a rule expressly provides for the lease being determined at the option of the lessor upon the happening of certain specified events, I see no logical absurdity in implying a term that it shall be determined absolutely on the happening of other events—namely, those which in an ordinary contract work a frustration."

Lord Simon adopted the above passage as exactly expressing his view. Lord Wright agreed with Lord Simon and pointed out that the doctrine of frustration is not subject to being constricted by an arbitrary formula.

In *Hillingdon Estates Co.* v. *Stonefield Estates, Ltd.*, [1952] 1 All E.R. 853, [1952] Ch. 627, a contract for the sale of land was involved. The contract was executed in 1938 and the lands were intended to be used for a building development. In 1948, some 10 years after the contract was entered into, the County Council expropriated the lands. The purchasers, to whom no conveyance of the legal estate had yet been made, brought action claiming that the foundation of the contract was the development of the land, that development had been frustrated by the expropriation and that therefore the contract was extinguished. The vendors counterclaimed for specific performance of the contract. Vaisey J. dismissed the action and granted specific performance. He pointed out that the expropriation raised no obstacle to the conveyance of the legal estate and held that the contract, far from being frustrated, could and should be carried out and stated at p. 856: "The complete absence of authority does rather suggest to my mind that the doctrine of frustration does not operate normally in the case of contracts for the sale of land." The learned Judge referred to the long delay involved and balanced the vendor's right to payment of the purchase price against the purchaser's right to receive the expropriation compensation. This case was criticized by Professor Laskin, now Laskin C.J.C., in *Special Lectures, Law Society of Upper Canada* (1960), p. 400, who pointed out that specific performance was not available since the vendor was unable to give title on closing.

Vaisey J. seemed to be of the view that the purchasers were no worse off than they would have been if they had completed their contract before the compulsory taking occurred. In his opinion if they had not delayed completion of the contract the property would have been transferred to the purchasers from whom it would then have been expropriated. The result is that one is left in some doubt whether the long delay in completion of the contract and also the fact that a substantial part of the payment sought to be recovered represented interest may have had some bearing upon the decision since these factors affected the equities between the parties. For these reasons I believe the case can be distinguished.

There can be no frustration if the supervening event results from the voluntary act of one of the parties or if the possibility of such event arising during the term of the agreement was contemplated by the parties and provided for in the agreement. In the instant case the planning legislation which supervened was not contemplated by the parties, not provided for in the agreement and not brought about through a voluntary act of either party. The factor remaining to be considered is whether the effect of the planning legislation is of such a nature that the law would consider the fundamental character of the agreement to have been so altered as to no longer reflect the original basis of the agreement. In my opinion the legislation destroyed the very foundation of the agreement. The purchaser was purchasing 26 separate building lots upon which it proposed to build houses for resale involving a reconveyance in each instance. This purpose was known to the vendor. The lack of ability to do so creates a situation not within the contemplation of the parties when they entered into the agreement. I believe that all the factors necessary to constitute impossibility of performance have been established and that the doctrine of frustration can be invoked to terminate the agreement.

The doctrine of frustration has been applied to commercial contracts since *Taylor et al.* v. *Caldwell et al., supra.* In *Cricklewood* v. *Leighton's, supra,* Viscount Simon L.C., and Lord Wright held against the accepted view that leases were outside the doctrine since a lease in addition to being a contract creates an estate in the land demised for the period of the agreed term. I adopt the reasoning of Viscount Simon L.C. and his conclusion that there is no binding authority precluding the application of the doctrine of frustration to contracts involving the lease of lands. I am also in accord with his observations that the doctrine is flexible and ought not to be restricted by any arbitrary formula. I see no reason why the doctrine cannot be logically extended to contracts involving the purchase and sale of land. If the supervening event makes the contract incapable of fulfilment as contemplated by the parties, then it appears to me illogical and unreasonable to contend that the fundamental object of the contract can be effected because the equitable interest in the land has passed to the purchaser.

The problem has been dealt with in Canadian Courts with varying results. Middleton J.A. in *Goulding* v. *Rabinovitch*, (1927), 60 O.L.R. 607, [1927] 3 D.L.R. 820, held that a supervening expropriation frustrated an option contract but denied recovery of the option deposit. He adopted [at pp. 609-10 O.L.R., p. 821 D.L.R.] the reasoning of Lord Alverstone C.J. in *Blakely* v. *Muller & Co. et al.*, (1903), 88 L.T. 90, that: " ' . . . each party must rest in the position in which he is found to be when the event occurs which makes the contract impossible of performance . . .' " [see *Civil Service Cooperative Society, Ltd.* v. *General Steam Navigation Co.*, [1903] 2 K.B. 756 at pp. 760-1 (footnote)]. The *Frustrated Contracts Act*, R.S.O. 1970, c. 185, would no doubt be invoked today to provide for recovery of the deposit.

The British Columbia Court of Appeal distinguished *Goulding* v. *Rabinovitch* in *Cahan* v. *Fraser*, [1951] 4 D.L.R. 112, 3 W.W.R. (N.S.) 665, and allowed recovery of the deposit when an option to purchase a home was frustrated by reason of a flood which made inspection of the premises impossible.

Counsel referred to *Danforth Heights Ltd.* v. *McDermid Bros.*, (1922),

52 O.L.R. 412, [1923] 4 D.L.R. 757, where the Court of Appeal discussed the effect of a municipal by-law declaring certain lands "residential" upon an agreement, made prior to the passing of the by-law, to purchase property for commercial purposes situated within the prohibited area and whether the land which the vendors were able to convey was so essentially different in character from the lands which the parties believed themselves to be contracting for that specific performance ought not to be required of the purchasers. While the appeal was decided on other grounds Sutherland J., was of the view that if the facts supported the conclusion the land being purchased for a specific purpose to the knowledge of the parties could not be used for such purpose because of the by-law that there was a failure of consideration and specific performance should not be required of the purchaser. Masten J. was of a similar opinion while Rose J. was of the opinion that the factual situation did not warrant the finding of the trial Judge that the land was essentially different in character from that which the purchaser agreed to purchase. I do not consider this decision to be of much assistance since two other members of the Court did not comment on this aspect of the argument.

The vendor submitted that the amendment did not affect the "vested rights" of the parties to the agreement and in support relied upon *Township of Nepean* v. *Leikin*, [1971] 1 O.R. 567, 16 D.L.R. (3d) 113. That case involved a dispute between the township and the vendor of a block of and in excess of 10 acres with respect to payment of 5% of the value of the land as a condition to the granting of a consent by the committee of adjustment of the township. The facts are that a sale of land had been negotiated and a formal agreement executed, but the deal was not closed when the *Planning Act* was amended so as to make the conveyance of the land which, prior to the amendment, had been exempt now subject to approval by the committee of adjustment. The vendor obtained the consent and a conveyance was duly registered by the purchaser. The question for determination was the effect to be given to the repeal of s. 26 (1) (*c*) which came into force subsequent to execution of the agreement for sale but prior to the date of actual transfer.

Section 26 (1) of the *Planning Act*, prior to the amendment which became effective on May 3, 1968 [1968, c. 96, s. 2], provided as follows:

26 (1) The council of a municipality may by by-law designate any area within the municipality as an area of subdivision control and thereafter no person shall convey land in the area by way of a deed or transfer on any sale, or mortgage or charge land in the area, or enter into an agreement of sale and purchase of land in the area or enter into any agreement that has the effect of granting the use of or right in land in the area directly or by entitlement to renewal for a period of twenty-one years or more unless . . .

> (*c*) the land is ten acres or more in area and each parcel of land remaining in the grantor, mortgagor or vendor abutting on the land conveyed or otherwise dealt with is also ten acres or more in area; or . . .
>
> (*e*) the consent,
>> (i) of the committee of adjustment of the municipality under subsection 2*a* of section 32*b* . . .
>>
>> is given to convey, mortgage, charge or enter into an agreement with respect to the land.

The amendment deleted the exemption previously applicable to lots of 10 acres or more and made a consent necessary. Speaking for the Court I held that the vendor's obligation to convey existed prior to the amendment and that by virtue of s. 14 (1) (c) of the *Interpretation Act*, R.S.O. 1960, c. 191 [now R.S.O. 1970, c. 225], which reads:

14 (1) Where an Act is repealed or where a regulation is revoked, the repeal or revocation does not, except as in this Act otherwise provided . . .

(c) affect any right, privilege, obligation or liability acquired, accrued, accruing or incurred under the Act, regulation or thing so repealed or revoked;

that obligation was not affected unless the repealing legislation stated in unequivocal language that it was to be given retroactive effect. I was of the opinion that the amendment was not to be viewed retrospectively and that a consent was not required and therefore the township was not entitled to succeed.

In my view the present case is distinguishable from *Township of Nepean* v. *Leikin, supra*. In the latter the Court was concerned with the repeal or amendment of existing legislation which did not have retrospective effect while in the case under review the new legislation contained in s. 26 (4) dealt for the first time with conveyances of part lots within a plan of subdivision and absolutely prohibited conveyances of part lots without a consent from the appropriate authority. The *Interpretation Act* cannot be invoked here as the *Planning Act* was not repealed but a new provision was added which was made applicable to a conveyance of part of any lot within a plan of subdivision whether registered before or after the effective date of the new provision. I do not consider *Township of Nepean* v. *Leikin* to be applicable to the present factual situation.

I adopt the reasoning of Lord Simon in *Cricklewood* v. *Leighton's, supra*, and accept his conclusion that there is no binding authority in England precluding the application of the doctrine of frustration to contracts involving a lease of land. I believe the situation to be the same in Ontario and I am unable to distinguish any difference between leases of land and agreements for the sale of land, so far as the application of the doctrine is concerned. Each is more than a simple contract. In the former an estate in land is created while in the latter an equitable estate arises. There does not appear to be any logical reason or binding legal authority which would prohibit the extension of the doctrine to contracts involving land.

If the factual situation is such that there is a clear "frustration of the common venture" then the contract, whether it is a contract for the sale of land or otherwise, is at an end and the parties are discharged from further performance and the adjustment of the rights and liabilities of the parties are left to be determined under the *Frustrated Contracts Act*. In my opinion, on the facts of this case, the contract was frustrated; the doctrine was applicable and should be invoked with the result that both parties are discharged from performance of the contract and the purchaser is entitled to recover the full amount paid as it is not claimed that the vendor incurred any expenses in connection with the performance of the contract, prior to frustration, which would entitle it to retain a portion of the money paid as provided for in s. 3 (2) of the *Frustrated Contracts Act*. Accordingly, the vendor must refund to the purchaser the balance of the deposit money, that is, $13,980.

The judgment below is affirmed and the appeal is dismissed with costs.

[Appeal dismissed.]

HOWELL v. COUPLAND
England. Queen's Bench Division, 1876. 1 Q.B.D. 258

The plaintiff is a potato merchant at Holbeach, Lincolnshire, and the defendant a farmer at Whaplode in the same county.

In 1872 the defendant, at the proper season, and in the due course of husbandry, appropriated between eighty and ninety acres of land for the growth of potatoes,—sixty-eight acres at Whaplode, and about twenty at Holbeach.

In March of the same year the plaintiff and the defendant entered into the following contract: "A memorandum of agreement, made this . . . day of . . . , 1872, between Robert Coupland, of Whaplode, and John Howell, of Holbeach, whereby Robert Coupland agrees to sell, and the said John Howell agrees to purchase, 200 tons of regent potatoes grown on land belonging to the said Robert Coupland in Whaplode, at and after the rate of £3 10s. 6d. per ton, to be riddled on 1⅝ in. riddle, and delivered at Holbeach railway station, good and marketable ware, during the months of September or October, as the said John Howell may direct, and, under his direction, the purchaser to find riddles. It is further agreed between the said Robert Coupland and the said John Howell that the said potatoes shall be paid for when and as they are taken away."

At the time of making the contract, out of the sixty-eight acres in Whaplode twenty-five were actually sown with potatoes, and the remaining forty-three acres were ready for sowing. The forty-three acres were afterwards sown in due course, and the whole sixty-eight acres together were amply sufficient, in an ordinary season and in the ordinary course of cultivation, to produce a much larger quantity than two hundred tons, the land producing, on an average, seven tons to the acre.

In July and August, without any fault on the part of the defendant, a disease, which no skill or care on the part of the defendant could have prevented attacked the crop and caused it to fail; and when the time for taking it up arrived, the whole marketable produce of the crop of the lands of the defendant, both in Whaplode and Holbeach together, amounted to no more than 79 tons 8 cwt., and this quantity the defendant delivered to the plaintiff. The rest of the crop had perished from the disease.

If the defendant had had other land to plant with potatoes at the time when the disease was discovered, which in fact he had not, it would have been too late to sow it.

The present action was brought to recover damages for the non-delivery of the residue of the two hundred tons. The verdict at the trial was entered for £432 5s., but a rule was obtained to enter the verdict for the defendant, on the ground that he was not liable to deliver the ungrown potatoes. It was made absolute by the Court of Queen's Bench. The plaintiff appealed.

LORD COLERIDGE C.J.: I am of opinion that the judgment ought to be affirmed. [The Lord Chief Justice read the contract and facts.] The Court of Queen's Bench held that, under these circumstances, the principle of *Taylor* v. *Caldwell* (1863), 122 E.R. 309, and *Appleby* v. *Myers* (1867), L.R. 2 C.P. 651, applied, and the defendant was excused from the performance of his contract. The true ground, as it seems to me, on which the contract should be interpreted, and which is the ground on which, I believe, the Court of Queen's Bench proceeded, is that by the simple and obvious construction of the agreement, both parties understood and agreed that there should be a condition implied that before the time for the performance of the contract the potatoes should be, or should have been in existence, and should still be existing when the time came for the performance. They had been in existence, and had been destroyed by causes over which the defendant, the contractor, had no control, and it became impossible for him to perform his contract; and, according to the condition which the parties had understood should be in the contract, he was excused from the performance. It was not an absolute contract of delivery under all circumstances, but a contract to deliver so many potatoes, of a particular kind, grown on a specific place, if deliverable from that place. On the facts the condition did arise and the performance was excused. I am, therefore, of opinion that the judgment of the Queen's Bench should be affirmed.

MELLISH L.J.: I am of the same opinion. The words of the contract are clear: the defendant "agrees to sell two hundred tons of regent potatoes grown on land belonging to him in Whaplode." That is, potatoes which shall be grown in Whaplode. They are to be grown there, and delivered to the plaintiff provided they are grown there. Is not that a condition,—so that, according to the cases on which the Court of Queen's Bench acted, if the thing perishes before the time for performance, the vendor is excused from performance by the delivery of the thing contracted for? No doubt there is a distinction in the present case, that the potatoes, the things contracted for, were not in existence at the time the contract was entered into. But can that make any real difference in principle? Suppose the potatoes had been full grown at the time of the contract, and afterwards the disease had come and destroyed them; according to the authorities it is clear that the performance would have been excused; and I cannot think it makes any difference that the potatoes were not then in existence. This is not like the case of a contract to deliver so many goods of a particular kind, where no specific goods are to be sold. Here there was an agreement to sell and buy two hundred tons out of a crop to be grown on specific land, so that it is an agreement to sell what will be and may be called specific things; therefore neither party is liable if the performance becomes impossible. The language of this contract is much easier to imply a condition from than in most former cases where it has been held to be implied.

CLEASBY B.: I am of the same opinion. I put my decision, not so much on the ground that the defendant was excused by the act of God rendering the performance impossible, as upon the terms of the contract itself. This is not like a contract where the parties have agreed to deliver a cargo of grain at Odessa or any other port by a given time, in which case the parties are bound by the contract, although its performance has become impossible by *vis major*. Here there was not an absolute contract to deliver two hundred tons of potatoes in September and October, but two hundred tons of potatoes grown on particular land. Not two hundred tons of potatoes simply, but two hundred tons of potatoes grown on particular land. The crop on this particular land has failed, and there is nothing to which the promise can apply. If the crop had existed at the time of the contract, and had afterwards failed, there can be no doubt that the principle of the decided cases would apply and the defendant would be excused; and I cannot see any difference in principle from the fact that the crop had not been sown at the date of the contract.

[James and Baggallay L.JJ. also delivered judgments agreeing that the appeal be dismissed.]

QUESTION. If the defendant had refused to deliver the 79 tons 8 cwt. of potatoes to the plaintiff in the *Howell* case, could the plaintiff have recovered damages to that extent?

SNIPES MOUNTAIN CO. v. BENZ BROS. & CO.
Washington. Supreme Court. 1931. 298 P. 714

PARKER J.: The plaintiff, Snipes Mountain Company, seeks reformation of a written contract for the sale of one hundred tons of potatoes by it to the defendant, Benz Bros. & Co., and recovery of an unpaid balance claimed to be due upon the agreed purchase price of sixty-four tons of the potatoes delivered under the contract. The reformation sought is to have the written contract show that the potatoes contracted to be sold were only potatoes growing upon certain specified land, to the end that the plaintiff will be entitled to recover for the potatoes grown upon that land, all of them having been delivered under the sale contract, though amounting only to sixty-four tons. The defendant resists the plaintiff's claims of reformation and recovery, and by cross-complaint claims damages from the plaintiff for its failure to deliver thirty-six tons of the potatoes. The cause, being of equitable cognizance, proceeded to trial in the superior court for Yakima county, sitting without a jury, and resulted in a decree awarding to the plaintiff reformation of the contract and recovery as prayed for, and, in effect, denying the defendant's claim of damages. From this disposition of the case in the superior court, the defendant has appealed to this court.

The contract, as partly printed and partly written, insofar as need be here noticed, reads as follows: . . .

"We hereby confirm purchase from you of One Hundred tons Yakima Netted Gem Potatoes, graded 75% U.S. No. 1 Grade and 25% U.S. No. 2 grade, packed in new branded bags, even weight 100 lbs. each, and screened at car door, at $25.00 per ton, sacked, f. o. b. Nass or Granger, Wash. For Delivery not before Oct. 10th, 1929, when mature and for delivery not later than Nov. 1st, 1929. Receipt is hereby acknowledged of cash payment of Five Hundred and no/100 Dollars ($500.00). Balance to be paid on delivery. . . ."

During the negotiations leading up to the signing of the written contract, two members of the defendant's firm visited the growing crop of potatoes on the plaintiff's land, knowing that was all the potatoes being grown by the plaintiff during the season of 1929. The potatoes were then found to be in promising condition, having matured to the extent that they were then from about the size of a walnut to about the size of a hen's egg. Those participating in the negotiations were then well convinced that the crop would yield considerably more than one hundred tons, and then so expressed themselves. The evidence shows practically conclusively that all who conducted the negotiations and participated in the execution of the contract contemplated that it was a contract for the sale and purchase of one hundred tons of those particular potatoes, and no others; and that, in so far as the written contract failed to expressly so provide, there occurred a mutual mistake of the parties in its preparation. The contract was by the decree reformed by inserting therein between the words "potatoes" and "graded" the words "grown during the year 1929 on the following described premises: [Here follows a description of the land, being the land on which the members of the defendant's firm saw and examined the growing potatoes.]" We are of the opinion that the evidence well supports the reformation portion of the decree.

Was the plaintiff absolved from liability for its failure to deliver to the defendant the whole of the one hundred tons of potatoes as contracted for? The evidence renders it plain that the failure of the crop to yield one hundred tons or more was not in the least the fault of the plaintiff. The small yield, less than half the normal yield, was wholly the result of a partial crop failure from natural causes. The plaintiff harvested and delivered to the defendant the whole of the crop, constituting sixty-four tons of potatoes. To that extent the contract was strictly performed by the plaintiff. The applicable law, we think, is well stated in general terms in a note in 12 A. L. R. 1288 by the editors, as follow: "Whether or not a contract for the sale of produce to be delivered at a certain future date contemplates that it shall be grown on a particular tract of land, so that a failure of the crop on that land will excuse non-delivery, is often a close question of construction of the particular contract. The rule appears to be that if the parties contemplate a sale of the crop, or a certain part of the crop, of a particular tract of land, and by reason of a drought or other fortuitous event, without the fault of the promisor, the crop of that land fails or is destroyed, non-performance is to that extent excused; the contract, in the absence of an express provision controlling the matter, being considered as subject to an implied condition in this regard. . . ." Our decision in *Robinson Co.* v. *McClaine*, 98 Wash. 322, 167 P. 912, and authorities therein noticed, are in harmony with this view of the law. We are of the opinion that the failure of the crop to produce more than sixty-four tons of potatoes absolved the plaintiff from liability for its failure to deliver to the defendant any additional potatoes, and that therefore the plaintiff is entitled to recover from the defendant the unpaid portion of the purchase price of the sixty-four tons of potatoes delivered; and that the defendant is not entitled to damages as claimed by it.

The judgment is affirmed.

[Tolman C.J., and Holcomb, Mitchell, and Main JJ., concur.]

PARRISH & HEIMBECKER LTD. v. *GOODING LUMBER LTD.*
(1968) 67 D.L.R. (2d) 495 (Ont. C.A.), affd., S.C.C., [1968] S.C.R. viii

MacKay J.A. (orally): This is an appeal by the defendant from a judgment awarding damages to the plaintiff for breach of contracts for the delivery of certain quantities of corn. The plaintiffs are dealers in grain. The defendant ordinarily is engaged in the trucking and lumber business and has a number of trucks. His place of operation or headquarters is Parkhill, Ontario. In that district one Sanderson, an employee of the plaintiff, had been buying corn from a farmer by the name of Willemse. Willemse suggested to Sanderson that he would prefer to deal through the defendant in the sale of his corn. Sanderson thereupon got in touch with the defendant Gooding and as a result of an oral agreement, certain written documents, which have been filed as ex. 1 in the action, were entered into by the parties. They are headed "Confirmation," addressed to Gooding Lumber Company Limited, Parkhill, and one of them is as follows:

Confirmation

Parrish &
Heimbecker

43 Scott Street
Toronto 1, Ont.
Nov. 8th, 1965.

Gooding Lumber Ltd.,
Parkhill, Ontario
We confirm purchase from you as follows:
25 loads each about 23 tons #2 C E Yellow
K D Corn 47.93 per ton Del'd Owen Sound
Shipping instructions: As available — Nov. —
Dec.
1 load to C. W. Beattie
24 loads to Great Lakes Elevator Ltd.

There are a number of other similar orders, some providing for delivery to Hanover, some to one other location, but the orders are all in the same form.

It was the intention of Gooding to purchase the corn from three district farmers. It developed that because of weather conditions the farmers were unable to harvest all of their corn and only part of the orders for corn, which had been accepted by Gooding, were delivered. The plaintiff thereupon brought action for damages for failure to deliver. The confirmation orders to which I have referred contained at the bottom thereof the following clause: "If the above is not correct, please wire or phone us immediately; failure to do this is understood as acceptance to these terms. Subject to strikes, embargoes, etc. or other conditions beyond our control."

The learned trial Judge found as a fact that because of weather conditions there was no corn in the immediate vicinity of Parkhill available for the defendant to purchase to fill the balance of these contracts. The area referred to by the trial Judge was an area of within 10 to 20 miles of Parkhill. There was evidence that corn was available in other areas of the Province that the defendant could have purchased to fulfil the contracts.

I am in agreement with the conclusions of the learned trial Judge that these were contracts in writing and that they cannot be varied by any oral understanding. The submission of counsel for the defendant is that he says Sanderson learned at some time or knew who the farmers were from whom Gooding intended to purchase the corn and that by reason of this knowledge the provision in the orders in relation to strikes, embargoes or other conditions beyond their control applied and the corn not being available from these three farmers, there was frustration of the contract. Like the trial Judge, I am unable to accede to this proposition for the reasons I have briefly stated, that is that it was not part of the contract that the corn was to be purchased from any particular source. Sanderson, the agent of the plaintiff, said he did not know two of the farmers and that in making the contracts with the defendant he was not concerned as to from whom the defendant was to purchase the corn and that so far as he was concerned, the defendant could have obtained the corn from any source.

In our view, having regard to the wording of the contracts, it is immaterial that the plaintiff's agent Sanderson may have known of the defendant's intention to purchase the corn from particular sources. Therefore, for the reasons given by the learned trial Judge and accepting his findings, the appeal will be dismissed with costs.

[Kelly J.A. concurs with MacKay J.A.]

LASKIN J.A. (orally) (dissenting): I cannot agree that these contracts should be viewed in the absolute terms in which the majority has treated them. I think it is clear that the original attitude of the common law that a contract duty is absolute has been considerably modified over the past one hundred years as we have come to recognize that mutual assumptions by parties that underlie their commercial relations cannot be ignored, and that, in the enforcement of a contract, allowance must be made if a failure of those assumptions supervenes, without fault of the contracting parties, after the contract has been made.

In this particular case, the contracts in question originated in oral discussions initiated by the representative of the plaintiff. They consist of written confirmations of the oral arrangements, these being sent by the plaintiff to the defendant and countersigned by the latter. I see nothing in the written documents, all of which are in common form, that in any way precludes the reliance by the defendant on what to me was a common understanding on which the contracts between them were made. The defendant is not in any professional or business sense a grainbroker. It is a lumber company engaged also in trucking, and this the plaintiff knew. When the plaintiff's representative approached the president of the defendant company, the conversation between them indicated that the corn, which was the subject-matter of their relations, would be coming from three farmers in particular or at the most from the Parkhill area and its environs which the trial Judge himself put at a 10 to 20 mile radius from Parkhill.

It is also material to the basis on which these contracts were concluded that the price to be paid by the defendant for the corn obtainable from the farmers was a price fixed by the plaintiff and the plaintiff also fixed the trucking charge that would be paid to the defendant for the transportation of the corn to the specified destinations set out in the written confirmations. It seems to me, therefore, that in the circumstances it would be changing the fundamental character of the contract to require the defendant who, for all practical purposes, was in a factoring position as between the plaintiff and the farmers in the area, to obtain the grain from some other area and at the same time insist that it accept payment on the basis of a price and trucking arrangement which contemplated that the grain would come from the area about which the representatives of the parties had reached an understanding.

I do not think that it is an answer to the defence proposed by the defendant that the plaintiff would have been prepared to receive grain from any source so long as it fulfilled the specifications of the contract. This, with great respect, does not meet the principle upon which I put my judgment. The question is whether the defendant is entitled to be excused from performance if grain is not available from the specified area for a reason not attributable to any fault on his part. It is undoubted that it was impossible to harvest the grain in order to meet the contract delivery dates. I do not say that the contracts themselves necessarily terminated when performance at the required time proved impossible, and I am prepared to assume that the plaintiff could have kept the contract alive and required the defendant to perform at a later time when it would be possible to harvest corn from the particular area. However, the plaintiff did not put his case on this basis but rather sued on the basis of the failure of the defendant to meet the contract delivery dates according to their specific terms.

In my view, the foundation on which the arrangements between the parties proceeded collapsed. Accordingly, the defendant had a valid excuse for non-delivery.

I would, therefore, have allowed the appeal, set aside the judgment below and dismissed the plaintiff's action with costs, both at the trial and in this Court, to the defendant.

[Appeal dismissed.]

H. R. & S. SAINSBURY LTD. v. STREET
[1972] 3 All E.R. 1127 (Q.B.)

MACKENNA J.: In this case the plaintiff buyers, H. R. & S. Sainsbury Ltd., claim damages against the defendant seller, Mr. D. J. Street, under an alleged contract for the sale of "about 275 tons" of feed barley for delivery in August and September, 1970. The defendant denies the contract. He alleges in the alternative that if he agreed to sell it was a condition precedent of his obligation to deliver that he should in 1970 harvest a crop of at least that tonnage on his farm at East Knoyle in Wiltshire, that he did not harvest such a crop but a smaller one of only 140 tons, and that his failure to harvest the larger crop excused him from the obligation to deliver any barley, even the smaller tonnage. He admittedly delivered none. The plaintiffs concede that he harvested only the smaller tonnage and further concede that they are not entitled to recover damages for his failure to deliver barley which he did not harvest, but assert that they are entitled to recover damages for his failure to deliver the 140 tons actually harvested. It is agreed that if they are entitled to recover any damages these should be computed at the rate of £7.50 per ton.

Thus there are two questions which I must decide: (i) did the defendant agree to sell "about 275 tons" of feed barley to the plaintiffs? If he did, (ii) was he under any obligation to deliver the 140 tons which he actually harvested?

I shall now state my findings of fact which I base mainly on the evidence of Mr. Davis, the plaintiffs' agent. Where the defendant's evidence differs from that of Mr. Davis, I reject the defendant's.

The plaintiffs are corn merchants carrying on business at Trowbridge and Calne. They buy corn from farmers like the defendant and sell them seed and fertilisers.

In 1968 the defendant bought part of Summerleaze Farm at East Knoyle and together with his wife leased the remainder. The farm was 395 acres of which 182 were arable. The land was in poor condition when the defendant began to farm and his first crop of barley, grown on the 182 acres, and harvested in the summer of 1968, yielded about 140 tons of which he sold 110 to the plaintiffs in four lots, each on the National Association of Corn and Agricultural Merchants form of Contract Note for Home Grown Grain. I am told that the terms of this note have been agreed between the merchants on the one side and the National Farmers Union on the other. 1969 produced a better harvest, 290 tons or so, possibly because the defendant had improved the land and by this means increased the yield. He sold 260 tons to the plaintiffs in six lots, five of them of 50 tons each made in 1969 and the sixth of 10 tons made on 5th June 1970. Each of these contracts was on the standard form. The first five were signed by Mr. Cullen, Mr. Davis's predecessor as the plaintiff's representative in that part of Wiltshire where the defendant had his farm. The sixth was signed by Mr. Davis.

In early June, 1970 Mr. Davis and a Mr. Brakespeare together visited the defendant at his farm. Mr. Davis had just entered the plaintiffs' employment and the purpose of the visit was to introduce him to the defendant who was by now a good customer of his employers. The defendant had bad tidings for the new agent. He told him either that he was going to give up farming or going to sell Summerleaze Farm—Mr. Davis thinks that he said the former, the defendant that he said the latter —and that it was unlikely there would be much for Mr. Davis to sell him. He added that he would be interested to sell the outcome of his 1970 harvest which was barley again and that he would like Mr. Davis to quote him a price for it. Mr. Davis answered that he would discuss the price with his grain director, Mr. Beaven. Mr. Davis has no recollection of any discussion of the contract of 5th June for delivery of 10 tons of barley in mid-July 1970, which must have been of the 1969 crop. Possibly this contract had been negotiated by Mr. Cullen before his retirement and was merely signed by Mr. Davis. Nothing turns on this.

Mr. Davis got Mr. Beaven's authority to offer the defendant £20 a ton for the 1970 crop and on 1st July, 1970 Mr. Davis visited the defendant for the second time. The visit had been preceded by a telephone conversation but Mr. Davis is uncertain whether the price of £20 a ton was mentioned on the telephone or whether the defendant was merely told that Mr. Davis would be calling on him. When he arrived at the farm on 1st July Mr. Davis told the defendant that he had discussed the price with Mr. Beaven and was authorised by him to offer £20 a ton for collection at harvest time. Collection at that time was necessary as the defendant was then intending to leave the farm at Michaelmas. For the same reason it was the intention of both parties that the defendant should sell the plaintiffs the whole of his crop. Agreements for the sale of feed barley are always expressed in tons, whether because that is the kind of sale for which the standard form is adapted, or because the merchants like to fix an upper limit to their liability, or for some other reason, I do not know. So, in Mr. Davis's words to me: "We had to estimate approximately what the total tonnage would be." In making the estimate they took a figure of 30 cwt per acre and at first applied it to a round figure of 200 acres. Mr. Davis, who had his pad of contract notes with him, had begun to write opposite the printed words "Quantity about" the figure of 300 tons, when it was decided between them that that figure would be too high for the real acreage which was not 200 but 182. So Mr. Davis crossed out what he had begun to write and wrote instead "275 tons." My note of this part of Mr. Davis's evidence is in these words: "So it was agreed, allowing for slightly less acreage, that the figure we would arrange to buy was 275 tons. We were expecting to buy the total outcome ⌐ the harvest."

I have noted the reason he gave for taking 30 cwt as the figure per acre: "30 cwt is the average figure one would expect from the farm. One or other of us would have mentioned it and the other would have accepted it." The figure was taken without any examination of the actual crop or any consideration of its history to date, which was known to the defendant although not to Mr. Davis. For reasons which I shall state presently there was no solid ground for expecting in July that the defendant's crop would yield as much as 30 cwt an acre when it came to be harvested in mid-

August. Here I should add that the printed conditions on the back of the form provide that when the word "about" is used with reference to quantity this shall mean 5 per cent over or under the quantity stated.

Mr. Davis also wrote in the date, the defendant's name and address, a description of the goods, the agreed price per cwt, and the permitted moisture precentage. Having done so, he gave the top copy to the defendant and kept the carbon copies for the plaintiffs' use. It is more usual for agents to post the farmer his copy of the contract, and Mr. Cullen had always done so. On his return to the office Mr. Davis filled in the parts of the form relating to the manner of delivery, which was to be bulk and not sacks, the time of delivery, which was to be August to September, and the terms of payment which were to be monthly. These matters had been agreed between them at the farm.

The harvesting of the crop began in mid-August and went on until the beginning of September. The yield was poor, 140 tons only. Mr. Key, an expert called by the defendant, basing himself very largely on information he was given by the defendant, explained why, in his view, the figure was so low. I shall summarise his reasons: (i) a determined effort which the defendant had made in the autumn of 1969 to eliminate couch grass, a common and troublesome weed in cornfields, of which there was a lot at Summerleaze, had been defeated. Wet weather had followed the chisel ploughing, which was the method used to eliminate the weed, and this had made it difficult to kill it. (ii) January, February and March had been exceptionally wet months and the bad weather had delayed the sowing. It should have been finished by March. It began only in April. 100 acres had been sown in April when wet weather stopped work for another week. When sowing was resumed it was found impossible to make a seed bed. The drill of the combine corn drill, which was being used to make the seed bed, became clogged up. Instead of being inserted in holes made by the drill, the seed now had to be broadcast on the surface of the land as if it were a fertiliser. (iii) After the seed is sown warmth and rain are needed for growth. May and June are critical months. July is an important month. In 1970 May, June and July, taken together, were exceptionally dry months. The average figures of rainfall in this district for five years compared with the figures for 1970 are as follows:

	5 years	1970
May	3.852	1.00
June	2.266	1.61
July	2.696	2.87

(iv) The seed used by the defendant was uncertified. It was his own seed from the previous year's crop, untreated and unscreened. (v) The artificial manure used by the defendant contained none of the nitrogen which was needed to help the growth of the crop. (vi) Even if the conditions had been favourable Mr. Key would have thought an estimate of 30 cwt optimistic for the defendant's land. Part of it is on Oxford clay which Mr. Key considers unsuitable for corn. Part of it is on greensand which is less good than chalk. The average figure for Wiltshire, which is largely a chalk county, is only 28.6 cwt per acre.

Generally the harvest had not been a good one, and for this reason and because of an expected shortage of maize in the United States which would increase the demand for barley, the price of barley was rising daily.

By the end of August it had risen to £23 or £24. Late in that month Mr. Davis paid the defendant a visit to enquire about a date for collection. The defendant said that he was not yet ready to deliver. He was having trouble with his drier because the replacement of a broken part was being delayed. He added that the harvest had not come anywhere near his earlier expectations and that he now expected it to be about 180 tons. He did not suggest that he was under no obligation to deliver his tonnage, either because he had not made a contract or because his contract did not bind him to deliver the reduced tonnage. He promised to get in touch with the plaintiffs' office at Trowbridge on the following Monday. He did not do so. On 4th September Mr. Beaven, the grain director, wrote to him: "With reference to our contract for 275 tons of Grinding Barley purchased from you on the 1st July by our Mr. Davis, contract No. 1729, would you please let us know when we can start collection and oblige."

He did not answer this letter. Shortly after receiving it, tempted by the higher market price, he decided to sell his barley to other merchants. He was put in touch through a friend with Kent and Fleet Ltd., merchants carrying on business near Salisbury, and Mr. Pratt of that company telephoned to him on 8th September. He agreed in this telephone conversation to sell the larger part of his barley to them for £27 a ton. Deliveries began the next day. By 21st September he had delivered 96 tons 4 cwt and on 12th October he delivered another 10 tons 14 cwt, almost 107 tons in all. He said that he kept back between 30 and 35 tons for himself. He had not yet succeeded in selling his farm and thought that he might need this tonnage as winter feed for his calves. He in fact sold another 25 tons 2 cwt 2 quarters in March, 1971 to Wiltshire Farmers Ltd., at a price of £29.25.

In the meantime, on 16th September, the plaintiffs had succeeded in contacting the defendant. Mr. Harman, an assistant of Mr. Beaven's, spoke to the defendant on the telephone. He said that his company would like to start collecting the barley they had bought from him, and could the defendant say when it would be available. The defendant replied to the effect that they could not have it at that price and that anyway he had sold it. Mr. Harman passed the receiver to Mr. Beaven who continued the conversation. Mr. Beaven told him that if he sold the barley away from them he, Mr. Beaven, would take the appropriate action.

A letter of the same date from the plaintiffs to the defendant confirmed this conversation. It pointed out that they had bought 275 tons of barley from him on 1st July at £20, that he had told them on the telephone that he had now sold this barley elsewhere, that he was therefore defaulting on the contract, and that unless they heard from him by midday on 18th September they would buy this quantity of barley against him. They did not hear from him, and they bought barley through brokers in Bristol, 250 tons on 18th September and another 50 tons on 21st September. In each case the seller was another merchant and the price was £30 a ton. Some letters were written to the defendant which he did not answer. The matter was put by the plaintiffs in their solicitors' hands. They wrote to the defendant who replied on 12th October. There had been a gross misunderstanding, he wrote; he had not sold any corn to the plaintiffs.

Evidence was given by Mr. Thompson, the grain manager of Wiltshire Farmers Ltd., about his company's practice when a farmer is unable to make a full delivery of the contracted tonnage. They would expect him to let them have the whole of his yield which they would accept even though the price had fallen. They would do nothing about the shortfall if it had not been his fault. Where the sale was to be of the produce of so many acres, or of a particular crop, they would convert the acres into tons, using a factor of 30 cwt an acre.

As I have stated at the beginning of this judgment, the plaintiffs are willing to accept as correct the defendant's figure of 140 tons or so as his yield of barley, and have agreed with him that the damages for the failure to deliver this quantity, if they are recoverable, shall be assessed at £7.50 per ton. They have also abandoned their claim to recover damages for the difference between the contract figure of about 275 tons and the tonnage actually produced.

I am now able to answer the two questions stated at the beginning of my judgment. As to the first, I find that there was a contract between the plaintiffs and the defendant for the purchase of 275 tons of feed barley (5 per cent more or less) to be grown by the defendant on his farm at East Knoyle, that the contract was partly oral and partly in writing, that so far as it was in writing it is contained in the copy of the contract note given by the plaintiffs' agent to the defendant on 1st July 1970, and that the oral terms are those which were afterwards added in ink by the plaintiffs' agent on the retained carbon copies.

As to the second, I am prepared to assume, consistently with the plaintiffs' abandonment of their claim for damages for the tonnage not in fact produced, that it was an implied condition of the contract that if the defendant, through no fault of his, failed to produce the stipulated tonnage of his growing crop, he should not be required to pay damages. It seems a very reasonable condition, considering the risks of agriculture and the fact that the crop was at the contract date still growing. But a condition that he need not deliver any if, through some misfortune, he could not deliver the whole is a very different one, and in my opinion so unreasonable that I would not imply it unless compelled to do so by authority. The way in which the parties chose the more or less conventional figure of 30 cwt per acre as the estimated yield of the crop is, I think, an additional reason in this case against the implication. If they had intended that a failure to achieve this optimistic tonnage would mean the end of the contract for both of them, they would have gone about the business of estimating yield in a much more cautious manner. Counsel for the defendant argued that it was reasonable that the defendant should be freed of all his obligations under the contract if without his fault he failed to produce the whole tonnage. 275 tons (5 per cent more or less) set an upper limit to the quantity which the plaintiffs could be compelled to take. It was reasonable, he said, that there should be a lower limit to the amount which the defendant could be compelled to deliver. In a year when the defendant's yield was high market prices would probably be low and it would be a benefit to the plaintiffs not to be required to take more than an agreed tonnage at the contract price fixed in advance. In a year when the yield was low, as in the present case, it would be a benefit to the defendant if he were free to disregard his contract and to sell his crop to some other buyer at the higher market price. The contract should, if possible, be construed as giving him this freedom. I am not persuaded by the argument. The upper limit of 275 tons might in the circumstances of a particular case be beneficial to both parties. But even if it could be beneficial only to the buyer that is no reason for implying a term that the same figure shall serve as a lower limit to the seller's obligation to deliver, so that his failure to reach that figure, if blameless, would release him from the contract.

I must now consider the three authorities which counsel for the defendant put before me in support of his argument. The first was *Howell* v. *Coupland*, a decision of the Court of Queen's Bench, upheld by the Court of Appeal. This is the headnote in the report of the decision of the Court of Queen's Bench:

"Plaintiff and defendant entered into an agreement in March, whereby defendant agreed to sell and plaintiff to purchase '200 tons of regent potatoes grown on land belonging to defendant in W., at rate of 3*l*. 10*s*. 6*d*. per ton, to be delivered in September or October, and paid for as taken away.' In March defendant had sixty-eight acres ready for potatoes, which were sown, and were amply sufficient to grow more than 200 tons in an average year; but in August the potato blight appeared and the crop failed, so that the [defendant] was able to deliver only 80 tons. The plaintiff having brought an action for the non-delivery of the other 120 tons:—
Held, that the contract was for a portion of a specific crop, and was within the principle of *Taylor* v. *Caldwell*, and the contract must be taken to be subject to the implied condition that the parties shall be excused, if, before breach, performance becomes impossible from the perishing of the thing without default in the contractor."

Blackburn J. gave his reasons for the decision:

"The principle of *Taylor* v. *Caldwell*, which was followed in *Appleby* v. *Myers*, (1867) L.R. 2 C.P. 651 in the Exchequer Chamber, at all events, decides that where there is a contract with respect to a particular thing, and that thing cannot be delivered owing to it perishing without any default in the seller, the delivery is excused. Of course, if the perishing were owing to any default of the seller, that would be quite another thing. But here the crop failed entirely owing to the blight, which no skill, care, or diligence of the defendant could prevent . . . But the contract was for 200 tons of a particular crop in particular fields, and therefore there was an implied term in the contract that each party should be free if the crop perished. The property and risk had clearly not been transferred under the terms of this contract, so that the consequence of the failure of the crop is, that the bargain is off so far as the 120 tons are concerned."

It is clear from the statement of the facts in the headnote that the case raised no question about the seller's obligation to deliver the potatoes which he had in fact produced, and clear from the last sentence quoted from the judgment of Blackburn J. that it gives no support to the view that the bargain was off both as to the 120 tons and the 80. There is nothing in the judgments of the Court of Appeal which touches this question.

After the decision of *Howell* v. *Coupland* the Sale of Goods Act 1893 was passed. Its relevant provisions are contained in the following sections:

"5 . . . (2) There may be a contract for the sale of goods, the acquisition of which by the seller depends upon a contingency which may or may not happen . . .

6. Where there is a contract for the sale of specific goods, and the goods without the knowledge of the seller have perished at the time when the contract is made, the contract is void.

7. Where there is an agreement to sell specific goods, and subsequently

the goods, without any fault on the part of the seller or buyer, perish before the risk passes to the buyer, the agreement is thereby avoided . . .

61 . . . (2) The rules of the common law, including the law merchant, save in so far as they are inconsistent with the express provisions of this Act, and in particular the rules relating to the law of principal and agent and the effect of fraud, misrepresentation, duress or coercion, mistake, or other invalidating cause, shall continue to apply to contracts for the sale of goods."

The rule in *Howell* v. *Coupland* is, I think, preserved by s. 5 (2). If I am wrong in that view, because the growing of a crop cannot be considered the 'acquisition' of goods within the meaning of that section, then it is preserved by s. 61 (2). I do not think it is preserved by ss. 6 or 7. These sections are, in my opinion, dealing with goods existing, and a crop not yet grown does not answer either description. I quote a passage from the judgment of Atkin L.J. in *Re Wait*, which was the next case cited by counsel for the defendant:

"The case of *Howell* v. *Coupland* would now be covered either by s. 5, sub-s. 2, of the Code or, as is suggested by the learned authors of the last two editions of Benjamin on Sale . . . by s. 61, sub-s. 2, of the Code."

The decision in *Wait's* case, [1927] 1 Ch. 606 does not touch the question which I have to decide, and I pass from it to the third case cited by counsel for the defendant, *Barrow, Lane & Ballard Ltd.* v. *Phillip Phillips & Co. Ltd.*, [1929] 1 K.B. 574, a decision of Wright J. in which he applied s. 6 of the Sale of Goods Act 1893 to the following facts. The plaintiffs had sold the defendants goods described as "700 bags marked E.C.P. and known as Lot 7 of Chinese ground nuts in shell then lying at the National Wharves in London." Unknown to either party there were not 700 bags then lying at the wharves but only 591, as the wharfingers or their servants had abstracted 109. The contract of sale was made on 11th October 1927. On 12th October the sellers gave the buyers a delivery order for the 700 bags and the buyers gave bills of exchange for the price. Between 11th October and 6th December more bags were abstracted, but there were still just enough to meet two delivery orders totalling 150 bags sent by the sellers to the warehouse on 6th or 7th December. All the rest had gone. The sellers sued the buyers on the bills for the price of 591 bags. The buyers admitted liability for the 150 actually delivered but disputed liability for the balance. The buyers won. The following passage gives the reason for the decision:

"Does the case come within s. 6 of the Sale of Goods Act, so that it would be the same as if the whole parcel had ceased to exist? In my judgment it does. The contract here was for a parcel of 700 bags, and at the time when it was made there were only 591 bags. A contract for a parcel of 700 bags is something different from a contract for 591 bags, and the position appears to me to be in no way different from what it would have been if the whole 700 bags had ceased to exist. The result is that the parties were contracting about something which, at the date of the contract, without the knowledge or fault of either party, did not exist. To compel the buyer in those circumstances to take 591 bags would be to compel him to take something which he had not contracted to take, and would in my judgment be unjust."

If there had been no misfortune the sellers could not have compelled the buyers to take 591 bags in lieu of 700. That was not the buyers' contract. Their obligation was to take 700 bags and nothing less. Section 6 should not be so construed as to oblige them to take the lesser quantity. There are two steps in this reasoning. First there is the construction of the contract, which is held not to impose any obligation on the buyers to accept less than 700 bags. The second step is the construction of s. 6. Neither part of the decision compels me to decide the present case in favour of the defendant. Because the contract in that case did not oblige the buyers to accept less than 700 bags is no reason why the implied condition in this case, which excuses the defendant from making full delivery, should be construed as excusing him from delivering the lesser quantity in fact produced if the plaintiffs were willing to accept it. The meaning of s. 6 cannot affect the present case.

A passage in *Benjamin on Sale* (7th ed. (1931), 156-7) is relevant:

"It was not decided in *Howell* v. *Coupland* whether the seller might have refused delivery of the 80 tons which he in fact delivered. Blackburn J. and Quain J. seemed to have thought that he was liable to deliver what he could . . . On the other hand, in *Lovatt* v. *Hamilton*, (1839) 5 M. & W. 639, where goods were sold "to arrive" by a particular ship, and only a small part arrived in that ship, the Court of Exchequer held that the buyers were not entitled to it, as the contract was entire for the whole quantity . . . But this was a case of condition precedent; and it is arguable that, as the seller's excuse under s. 7 is a privilege operating by way of condition subsequent . . . he should not be entitled to excuse himself to an extent more than is necessary. The question is one of the presumed intention of the parties. Where the subject-matter of the sale is such an indivisible whole as a number of volumes forming one work, the intention would doubtless be that the seller should be wholly discharged. The case of a mere quantity of specific goods is not so clear."

I have four comments to make on this passage: (1) I would distinguish *Lovatt* v. *Hamilton*, on the language of the contract which provided for the sale of "50 tons of palm oil, to arrive per Mansfield, at 32*l*. per ton . . . In case of non-arrival, or the vessels not having so much in after delivery of former contracts, this contract to be void." The ship had only 7 tons in after delivery of former contracts. It was held that the buyers were not entitled to these 7 tons. The case is, I think, distinguishable. It is one thing to hold that where a contract provides that it shall be void in a certain case, this means that it shall be wholly inoperative, which is the decision in *Lovatt's* case. It is another to hold that the failure of an implied condition must always operate to discharge the whole contract, which I am in effect asked to hold.

(2) I have already expressed the view that s. 7 of the Sale of Goods Act 1893 is not the relevant section in a case like *Howell* v. *Coupland*. The excuse is given to the seller either by a condition of the kind referred to in s. 5 (2) of the Sale of Goods Act 1893 or by one implied under some provision of the common law preserved by s. 61 (2).

(3) The condition which excuses the defendant can be cast either in the form of a condition precedent to the existence of an obligation to deliver, or in the form of a condition subsequent to the existence of such an obligation determining the same, without affecting the substance of the matter. "He shall be under an obligation to deliver in the future if he produces . . ." would be in form a condition precedent. "He is under an obligation to deliver in the future but that obligation shall be discharged if he does not produce . . ." would be in form a condition subsequent. The

difference is a matter of words, not of substance: see *Williston on Sales.* For this reason I should not wish to rest anything, in this case at least, on the distinction between the two kinds of condition.

(4) What is said in this passage about the presumed intention of the parties seems to me very relevant in determining what condition shall be implied. It should be a condition which will give effect to the presumed intention of reasonable men. In the case which the writer supposes it would be unreasonable to compel the buyer to accept delivery of the odd volume. This difficulty could be met in one of two ways, either by implying a condition in cases of that kind that the contract shall be wholly discharged, or by implying a condition in such cases, or indeed in all cases when the seller is excused, that the buyer shall have an option of accepting part delivery. The United States Sales Act cited in *Williston on Sales* (3rd ed. 1948, vol. 1, pp. 16-18, para. 8) expressly allows the buyer, in case of deterioration or partial destruction of the subject-matter of a sale or contract to sell, to require such performance as remains possible.

So much for the authorities, which do not, I think, oblige me to decide this case in the defendant's favour. Therefore my judgment will be for the plaintiffs for £1,050.

[Judgment for the plaintiffs.]

KRELL v. HENRY
England. Court of Appeal. [1903] 2 K.B. 740

The plaintiff, Paul Krell, sued the defendant, C. S. Henry, for £50, being the balance of a sum of £75 for which the defendant had agreed to hire a flat at 56A Pall Mall on the days of June 26 and 27, for the purpose of viewing the processions to be held in connection with the coronation of His Majesty. The defendant denied his liability, and counterclaimed for the return of the sum of £25, which had been paid as a deposit, on the ground that, the procession not having taken place owing to the serious illness of the King, there had been a total failure of consideration for the contract entered into by him.

Darling J. held that there was an implied condition in the contract that the procession should take place, and gave judgment for the defendant on the claim and counter-claim. The plaintiff appealed. The defendant on the appeal abandoned his counter-claim for £25.

VAUGHAN WILLIAMS L.J.: The real question in this case is the extent of the application in English law of the principle of the Roman law which has been adopted and acted on in many English decisions, and notably in the case of *Taylor* v. *Caldwell* (1863), 122 E.R. 309. That case at least makes it clear that "where, from the nature of the contract, it appears that the parties must from the beginning have known that it could not be fulfilled unless, when the time for the fulfilment of the contract arrived, some particular specified thing continued to exist, so that when entering into the contract they must have contemplated such continued existence as the foundation of what was to be done; there, in the absence of any express or implied warranty that the thing shall exist, the contract is not to be considered a positive contract, but as subject to an implied condition that the parties shall be excused in case, before breach, performance becomes impossible from the perishing of the thing without default of the contractor."

Thus far it is clear that the principle of the Roman law has been introduced into the English law. The doubt in the present case arises as to how far this principle extends. The Roman law dealt with obligations *de certo corpore*. Whatever may have been the limits of the Roman law, the case of *Nickoll* v. *Ashton,* [1901] 2 K.B. 126, makes it plain that the English law applies the principle not only to cases where the performance of the contract becomes impossible by the cessation of existence of the thing which is the subject-matter of the contract, but also to cases where the event which renders the contract incapable of performance is the cessation or non-existence of an express condition or state of things, going to the root of the contract, and essential to its performance. It is said, on the one side, that the specified thing, state of things, or condition the continued existence of which is necessary for the fulfilment of the contract, so that the parties entering into the contract must have contemplated the continued existence of that thing, condition, or state of things as the foundation of what was to be done under the contract, is limited to things which are either the subject-matter of the contract or a condition or state of things, present or anticipated, which is expressly mentioned in the contract.

But, on the other side, it is said that the condition or state of things need not be expressly specified, but that it is sufficient if that condition or state of things clearly appears by extrinsic evidence to have been assumed by the parties to be the foundation or basis of the contract, and the event which causes the impossibility is of such a character that it cannot reasonably be supposed to have been in the contemplation of the contracting parties when the contract was made. In such a case the contracting parties will not be held bound by the general words which, though large enough to include, were not used with reference to a possibility of a particular event rendering performance of the contract impossible.

I do not think that the principle of the civil law as introduced into the English law is limited to cases in which the event causing the impossibility of performance is the destruction or non-existence of some thing which is the subject-matter of the contract or of some condition or state of things expressly specified as a condition of it. I think that you first have to ascertain, not necessarily from the terms of the contract, but, if required, from necessary inferences, drawn from surrounding circumstances recognised by both contracting parties, what is the substance of the contract, and then to ask the question whether that substantial contract needs for its foundation the assumption of the existence of a particular state of things. If it does, this will limit the operation of the general words, and in such case, if the contract becomes impossible of performance by reason of the non-existence of the state of things assumed by both contracting parties as the foundation of the contract, there will be no breach of the contract thus limited.

Now what are the facts of the present case? The contract is contained in two letters of June 20 which passed between the defendant and the plaintiff's agent, Mr. Cecil Bisgood. These letters do not mention the coronation, but speak merely of the taking of Mr. Krell's chambers, or, rather, of the use of them, in the daytime of June 26 and 27, for the sum of £75, £25 then paid, balance £50 to be paid on the 24th. But the affidavits, which by agreement between the parties are to be taken as stating the facts of the case, shew that the plaintiff exhibited on his premises, third floor, 56A Pall Mall, an announcement to the effect that windows to view the Royal coronation procession were to be let, and that the defendant was induced by that announcement to apply to the housekeeper on the premises, who said that the owner was willing to let the suite of rooms for the purpose of seeing the Royal procession for both days, but not nights, of June 26 and 27. In my judgment the use of the rooms was let and taken for the purpose of seeing the Royal procession. It was not a demise of the rooms, or even an agreement to let and take the rooms. It is a licence to use rooms for a particular purpose and none other. And in my judgment the taking place of these processions on the days proclaimed along the proclaimed route which passed 56A Pall Mall, was regarded by both contracting parties as the foundation of the contract; and I think that it cannot reasonably be supposed to have been in the contemplation of the contracting parties, when the contract was made, that the coronation would not be held on the proclaimed days, or the processions not take place on those days along the proclaimed route; and I think that the words imposing on the defendant the obligation to accept and pay for the use of the rooms for the named days, although general and unconditional, were not used with reference to the possibility of the particular contingency which afterwards occurred.

It was suggested in the course of the argument that if the occurrence, on the proclaimed days, of the coronation and the procession in this case were the foundation of the contract, and if the general words are thereby limited or qualified, so that in the event of the non-occurrence of the coronation and procession along the proclaimed route they would discharge both parties from further performance of the contract, it would follow that if a cabman was engaged to take some one to Epsom on Derby Day at a suitable enhanced price for such a journey, say £10, both parties to the contract would be discharged in the contingency of the race at Epsom for some reason becoming impossible; but I do not think this follows, for I do not think that in the cab case the happening of the race would be the foundation of the contract. No doubt the purpose of the engager would be to go to see the Derby, and the price would be proportionately high; but the cab had no special qualifications for the purpose which led to the selection of the cab for this particular occasion. Any other cab would have done as well. Moreover, I think that, under the cab contract, the hirer even if the race went off, could have said, "Drive me to Epsom; I will pay you the agreed sum; you have nothing to do with the purpose for which I hired the cab," and that if the cabman refused he would have been guilty of a breach of contract, there being nothing to qualify his promise to drive the hirer to Epsom on a particular day.

Whereas in the case of the coronation, there is not merely the purpose of the hirer to see the coronation procession, but it is the coronation procession and the relative position of the rooms which is the basis of the contract as much for the lessor as the hirer; and I think that if the King, before the coronation day and after the contract, had died, the hirer could not have insisted on having the rooms on the days named. It could not in the cab case be reasonably said that seeing the Derby race was the foundation of the contract, as it was of the licence in this case. Whereas in the present case, where the rooms were offered and taken, by reason of their peculiar suitability from the position of the rooms for a view of the coronation procession, surely the view of the coronation procession was the foundation of the contract, which is a very different thing from the purpose of the man who engaged the cab—namely, to see the race—being held to be the foundation of the contract.

Each must be judged by its own circumstances. In each case one must ask oneself, first, what, having regard to all the circumstances, was the foundation of the contract? Secondly, was the performance of the contract prevented? Thirdly, was the event which prevented the performance of the contract of such a character that it cannot reasonably be said to have been in the contemplation of the parties at the date of the contract? If all these questions are answered in the affirmative (as I think they should be in this case), I think both parties are discharged from further performance of the contract. I think that the coronation procession was the foundation of this contract, and that the non-happening of it prevented the performance of the contract; and, secondly, I think that the non-happening of the procession, to use the words of Sir James Hannen in *Baily* v. *De Crespigny*, (1869), L.R. 4 Q.B. 180, was an event "of such a character that it cannot reasonably be supposed to have been in the contemplation of the contracting parties when the contract was made, and that they are not to be held bound by general words which, though large enough to include, were not used with reference to the possibility of the particular contingency which afterwards happened."

The test seems to be whether the event which causes the impossibility was or might have been anticipated and guarded against. It seems difficult to say, in a case where both parties anticipate the happening of an event, which anticipation is the foundation of the contract, that either party must be taken to have anticipated, and ought to have guarded against, the event which prevented the performance of the contract. In both *Jackson* v. *Union Marine Insurance Co.*, (1873), L.R. 8 C.P. 572; 10 C.P. 125, and *Nickoll* v. *Ashton* the parties might have anticipated as a possibility that perils of the sea might delay the ship and frustrate the commercial venture; in the former case the carriage of the goods to effect which the charterparty was entered into; in the latter case the sale of the goods which were to be shipped on the steamship which was delayed. But the Court held in the former case that the basis of the contract was that the ship would arrive in time to carry out the contemplated commercial venture, and in the latter that the steamship would arrive in time for the loading of the goods the subject of the sale.

I wish to observe that cases of this sort are very different from cases where a contract or warranty or representation is implied, such as was implied in *The Moorcock*, (1889), 14 P.D. 64, and refused to be implied in *Hamblyn* v. *Wood*, [1891] 2 Q.B. 488. But *The Moorcock* is of importance in the present case as shewing that whatever is the suggested implication—be it condition, as in this case, or warranty or representation—one must, in judging whether the implication ought to be made, look not only at the words of the contract, but also at the surrounding facts and the knowledge of the parties of those facts. There seems to me to be ample authority for this proposition. Thus in *Jackson* v. *Union Marine Insurance Co.*, in the Common Pleas, the question whether the object of the voyage had been frustrated by the delay of the ship was left as a question of fact to the jury, although there was nothing in the charter-party defining the time within which the charterers were to supply the cargo of iron rails for San Francisco, and nothing on the face of the charter-party to indicate the importance of time in the venture; and that was a case in which, as Bramwell B. points out in his judgment at p. 148 in 10 C.P., *Taylor* v. *Caldwell* was a strong authority to support the conclusion arrived at in the judgment—that the ship not arriving in time for the voyage contemplated, but at such time as to frustrate the commercial venture, was not only a breach of the contract but discharged the charterer, though he had such an excuse that no action would lie.

And, again, in *Harris* v. *Dreesman*, (1854), 23 L.J. (Ex.) 210, the vessel had to be loaded, as no particular time was mentioned, within a reasonable time; and, in judging of a reasonable time, the Court approved of evidence being given that the defendants, the charterers, to the knowledge of the plaintiff, had no control over the colliery from which both parties knew that the coal was to come; and that, although all that was said in the charter-party was that the vessel should proceed to Spital Tongue's Spout (the spout of the Spital Tongue's Colliery), and there take on board from the freighters a full and complete cargo of coals, and five tons of coke, and although there was no evidence to prove any custom in the port as to loading vessels in turn.

Again it was held in *Mumford* v. *Gething*, (1859), 7 C.B. (N.S.) 305; 141 E.R. 834, that, in construing a written contract of service under which A was to enter the employ of B, oral evidence is admissible to shew in what capacity A was to serve B. . . . The rule seems to be that which is laid down in *Taylor on Evidence*, vol. ii, s. 1028: "It may be laid down as a broad and distinct rule of law that extrinsic evidence of every material fact which will enable the Court to ascertain the nature and qualities of the subject-matter of the instrument, or, in other words, to identify the persons and things to which the instrument refers, must of necessity be received." And Lord Campbell in his judgment says: "I am of opinion that, when there is a contract for the sale of a specific subject-matter, oral evidence may be received, for the purpose of shewing what the subject-matter was, of every fact within the knowledge of the parties before and at the time of the contract." See per Campbell C.J., *Macdonald* v. *Longbottom*, (1859), 1 E. & E. 977; 120 E.R. 1177 at p. 1179. It seems to me that the language of Willes J. in *Lloyd* v. *Guibert*, (1865), 35 L.J. (Q.B.) 74, 75, points in the same direction.

I myself am clearly of opinion that in this case, where we have to ask ourselves whether the object of the contract was frustrated by the non-happening of the coronation and its procession on the days proclaimed, parol evidence is admissible to shew that the subject of the contract was rooms to view the coronation procession, and was so to the knowledge of both parties. When once this is established, I see no difficulty whatever in the case. It is not essential to the application of the principle of *Taylor* v. *Caldwell* that the direct subject of the contract should perish or fail to be in existence at the date of the performance of the contract. It is sufficient if a state of things or condition expressed in the contract and essential to its performance perishes or fails to be in existence at that time. In the present case the condition which fails and prevents the achievement of that which was, in the contemplation of both parties, the foundation of the contract, is not expressly mentioned either as a condition of the contract or the purpose of it; but I think for the reasons which I have given that the principle of *Taylor* v. *Caldwell* ought to be applied.

This disposes of the plaintiff's claim for £50 unpaid balance of the price agreed to be paid for the use of the rooms. The defendant at one time set up a cross-claim for the return of the £25 he paid at the date of contract. As that claim is now withdrawn it is unnecessary to say anything about it. I have only to add that the facts of this case do not bring it within the principle laid down in *Stubbs* v. *Holywell Ry. Co.* (1867),

L.R. Ex. 311; that in the case of contracts falling directly within the rule of *Taylor* v. *Caldwell* the subsequent impossibility does not affect rights already acquired, because the defendant had the whole of June 24 to pay the balance, and the public announcement that the coronation and processions would not take place on the proclaimed days was made early on the morning of the 24th, and no cause of action could accrue till the end of that day. I think this appeal ought to be dismissed.

[The concurring opinions of Romer L.J. and Stirling L.J. are omitted.]

HERNE BAY STEAM BOAT CO. v. *HUTTON.* [1903] 2 K.B. 683 (England. Court of Appeal). The defendant who had agreed to charter a boat in order to take passengers to see the royal naval review at Spithead, was held not excused by the King's illness which caused the review to be cancelled. While it might have been the defendant's purpose so to use the boat, such purpose was not contemplated by both parties as the foundation of the contract. ROMER L.J.: ... "the object was a matter with which the defendant, as hirer of the ship, was alone concerned."

TSAKIROGLOU & CO. LTD. v. *NOBLEE THORL G.M.B.H.*
England. House of Lords. [1962] A.C. 93

The respondents agreed on October 4, 1956, to buy 300 tons of Sudanese groundnuts from the appellants for shipment from Port Sudan to Hamburg during November or December. On October 29 the British and French forces began military operations against Egypt to protect the Suez Canal. The Canal was blocked to navigation from November 2 until April 9, 1957. The usual route for such a shipment was via the Canal and the appellants refused to ship the nuts, although it was feasible to have shipped them via the Cape of Good Hope during November and December. The Cape route is 11,137 miles. The Canal route is 4,386 miles. Freight surcharges were imposed, first of 25%, as from November 10, and then of 100% as from December 13. The rate was £7 10s. per ton. The market price of Sudanese nuts in Hamburg was about £68 15s. per ton between January 1 and 13, 1957.

The case was heard by an umpire under arbitration proceedings who awarded £5,625 as damages, to the respondents. The board of appeal of the Incorporated Oil Seed Association upheld the award and Diplock J. on a stated case upheld the award. His decision was affirmed by the Court of Appeal. Clause 6 of the I.O.S.A. standard form contract provided that "in case of ... war ... and in all cases of force majeure preventing the shipment within the time fixed ... the period allowed ... shall be extended by not exceeding two months. After that, if the case of force majeure be still operating, the contract shall be cancelled." It was unanimously agreed that clause 6 did not relieve the defendants: there was no "war" and the "shipment" was not prevented via the Cape.

VISCOUNT SIMONDS: ... I come then to the main issue and, as usual, I find two questions interlocked: (1) What does the contract mean? In other words, is there an implied term that the goods shall be carried by a particular route? (2) Is the contract frustrated?

It is convenient to examine the first question first, though the answer may be inconclusive. For it appears to me that it does not automatically follow that, because one term of a contract, for example, that the goods shall be carried by a particular route, becomes impossible of performance, the whole contract is thereby abrogated. Nor does it follow, because as a matter of construction a term cannot be implied, that the contract may not be frustrated by events. In the instant case, for example, the impossibility of the route via Suez, if that were assumed to be the implied contractual obligation, would not necessarily spell the frustration of the contract.

It is put in the forefront of the appellants' case that the contract was a contract for the shipment of goods via Suez. This contention can only prevail if a term is implied, for the contract does not say so. To say that that is nevertheless its meaning is to say in other words that the term must be implied. For this I see no ground. It has been rejected by the learned trial judge and each of the members of the Court of Appeal. . . .

I turn now to what was the main argument for the appellants: that the contract was frustrated by the closure of the Canal from November 2, 1956, till April 1957. Were it not for the decision of McNair J. in *Green's* case, [1959] 1 Q.B. 131, I should not have thought this contention arguable and I must say with the greatest respect to that learned judge that I cannot think he has given full weight to the decisions old and new of this House upon the doctrine of frustration. He correctly held upon the authority of *Reardon Smith Line Ltd.* v. *Black Sea and Baltic General Insurance Co. Ltd.*, [1939] A.C. 562, that "where a contract, expressly or by necessary implication, provides that performance, or a particular part of the performance, is to be carried out in a customary manner, the performance must be carried out in a manner which is customary at the time when the performance is called for." But he concluded that the continued availability of the Suez route was a fundamental assumption at the time when the contract was made and that to impose upon the sellers the obligation to ship by an emergency route via the Cape would be to impose upon them a fundamentally different obligation which neither party could at the time when the contract was performed have dreamed that the sellers would be required to perform. Your Lordships will observe how similar this line of argument is to that which supports the implication of a term that the route should be via Suez and no other. I can see no justification for it. We are concerned with a c.i.f. contract for the sale of goods, not a contract of affreightment, though part of the sellers' obligation will be to procure a contract of affreightment. There is no evidence that the buyers attached any importance to the route. They were content that the nuts should be shipped at any date in November or December. There was no evidence, and I suppose could not be, that the nuts would deteriorate as the result of a longer voyage and a double crossing of the Equator, nor any evidence that the market was seasonable. In a word, there was no evidence that the buyers cared by what route or, within reasonable limits, when the nuts arrived. What, then, of the sellers? I recall the well-known passage in the speech of Lord Atkinson in *Johnson* v. *Taylor Bros. & Co. Ltd.*, [1920] A.C. 144, where he states the obligations of the vendor of goods under a c.i.f. contract, and ask which of these obligations is (to use McNair J.'s word) "fundamentally" altered by a change of route. Clearly the contract of affreightment will be different and so may be the terms of insurance. In both these respects the sellers may be put to greater cost: their profit may be reduced or even disappear. But it hardly needs reasserting that an increase of expense is not a ground of frustration: see *Larrinaga & Co. Ltd.* v. *Société Franco-Américaine des Phosphates de Medulla, Paris* (1922), 38 T.L.R. 739.

Nothing else remains to justify the view that the nature of the contract was "fundamentally" altered. That is the word used by Viscount Simon in *British Movietonews Ltd.* v. *London and District Cinemas Ltd.*, [1952] A.C. 166, at p. 185, and by my noble and learned friend Lord Reid in *Davis Contractors Ltd.* v. *Fareham Urban District Council*, [1956] A.C. 696, at p. 723. In the latter case my noble and learned friend Lord Radcliffe used the expression "radically different" and I think that the two expressions mean the same thing, as perhaps do other adverbs which have been used in this context. Whatever expression is used, I venture to say what I have said myself before and others more authoritatively have said before me: that the doctrine of frustration must be applied within very narrow limits. In my opinion this case falls far short of satisfying the necessary conditions. Reluctant as I am to differ from a judge so experienced in commercial law as McNair J., I am glad to find that my view is shared by Ashworth J. and all the members of the Court of Appeal.

Upon this part of the case I have not thought it necessary to deal with Pearson J.'s decision in *Société Franco Tunisienne d'Armement* v. *Sidermar S. P.A.*, [1961] 2 Q.B. 278. There the question was whether a charterparty was frustrated by the blocking of the Suez Canal. The learned judge held that it was, but was at pains to point out that the position was very different in a contract for the sale of goods. Upon that point I agree with him and need not discuss the matter further.

I come finally to a question which has given me some trouble. I refer to the sixth finding in the special case which I have already fully set out. It will be remembered that the vital words were "not commercially or fundamentally different." Diplock J., regarding this as a finding of fact, thought that the case was thereby concluded. I cannot regard this as a correct decision. It is a question of law whether a contract has been frustrated and it is commonly said that frustration occurs when conditions arise which are fundamentally different from those contemplated by the parties. But it does not follow from the use by the arbitrator of the word "fundamentally" in describing the difference between the actual and the contemplated conditions that the court is precluded from forming its own judgment whether or not a contract has been frustrated. It is of great value to the court to know that lay arbitrators with special knowledge do or do not regard the new circumstances as so different from those contemplated that they think "fundamental" an appropriate word to use. But the value is evidential only. It has not the sanctity of a finding of fact. I do not say that an arbitrator should be debarred from the use of the word "fundamental" or "radical" or any other word which he thinks apt to give emphasis to his view. But if he does so he must not be taken indirectly to determine the question of law which the court must decide.

In my opinion, the appeal should be dismissed with costs.

LORD RADCLIFFE: . . . This contract was a sale of goods, which involved dispatching the goods from Port Sudan to Hamburg; but, of course, the transport was not the whole but only one of the incidents of the contract, in which particular incident neither vendors nor buyers were directly implicated. There was nothing to prevent the vendors from dispatching the goods as contracted, unless they were impliedly bound as a term of the contract to use no other route than that of the Suez Canal. I do not see why that term should be implied and, if it is not implied, the true question seems to me to be, since shipment was due to be made by some route during November/December, whether it was a reasonable action for a mercantile man to perform his contract by putting the goods on board a ship going round the Cape of Good Hope and obtaining a bill of lading on this basis. A man may habitually leave his house by the front door to keep his appointments; but, if the front door is stuck, he would hardly be excused for not leaving by the back. The question, therefore, is what is the reasonable mercantile method of performing the contract at a time when the Suez Canal is closed, not at a time when it is open. To such a question the test of "the usual and customary route" is ex hypothesi inapplicable.

On the facts found by the special case I think that the answer is inevitable. The voyage would be a much longer one in terms of miles; but length reflects itself in such matters as time of arrival, condition of goods, increase of freight rates. A change of route may, moreover, augment the sheer hazard of the transport. There is nothing in the circumstances of the commercial adventure represented by the appellants' contract which suggests that these changes would have been material. Time was plainly elastic. Not only did the vendors have the option of choosing any date within a two-month period for shipment, but also there was a wide margin within which there might be variations of the speed capacity of the carrying vessel or vessels selected. There was no stipulated date for arrival at Hamburg. Nothing appears to suggest that the Cape voyage would be prejudicial to the condition of the goods or would involve special packing or stowing, nor does there seem to have been any seasonal market to be considered. With all these facts before them, as well as the measure of freight surcharge that would fall to the vendors' account, the board of appeal made their finding that performance by shipping on the Cape route was not "commercially or fundamentally different" from shipping via the Suez Canal. We have no material which would make it possible for us to differ from that conclusion.

It has been a matter of debate whether this finding ought to be treated as a finding of fact, by which a court would be bound, or as a holding of law, which as such, would be open to review. It was treated as the first by the learned trial judge: it was treated more as the second by the Court of Appeal whose view of it was, I think, that, while of the utmost relevance for the determination of the final issue of the case, it did not bind the court so as to dictate what it should decide. So far as the distinction can be made between law and fact, I agree with the Court of Appeal. I regard it as a mixed question of fact and law whether transport via the Cape of Good Hope was so materially different from transport via the Suez Canal that it was not within the range of the c.i.f. contract or, alternatively, was so radically different that it left that contract frustrated. The ultimate conclusion is a conclusion of law, but in a case of this sort that conclusion is almost completely determined by what is ascertained as to mercantile usage and the understanding of mercantile men.

I do not believe that in this, as in many other branches of commercial law, it is possible to analyse very precisely where law begins and facts end. That is because in this field legal obligations and legal rights are largely founded upon usage and practice, which themselves are established as matters of fact. Many things which are now regarded as settled principles of law originated in nothing more than common mercantile practice, and the existence and terms of this practice have been vouched sometimes by questions put to and answered by special juries, sometimes by the findings and views of commercial arbitrators and sometimes by the bare statements of the judges, founded upon their experience at the Bar or on the Bench. It would be difficult, for instance, to separate the judgments on commercial law delivered by three such masters as Lord Esher, Scrutton L.J. and Lord Sumner from their personal acquaintance with mercantile usages and their translation of the one into the terms of the other.

I do not think, therefore, that it is right to be very analytical in distinguishing between questions of law and questions of fact in matters of this kind. Since Lord Mansfield's day commercial law has been ascertained by a co-operative exchange between judge and jury, and now that arbitrators have taken the place of juries I do not think that we can start all over again with an absolute distinction between the respective spheres of judge and arbitrator. Generally speaking, I do not think that a finding in the form which we have here can ever be conclusive on the legal issue. When all necessary facts have been found it remains a question of law for the court what on the true construction of the contract are the obligations imposed or whether, having regard to the terms of the contract and the surrounding circumstances, any particular term is to be implied. But, when the implication of terms depends essentially upon what is customary or usual or accepted practice, it is inevitable that the findings of fact, whatever they may be, go virtually the whole way towards determining the legal result.

The finding in this case is perhaps unusual in that it does not speak for any usage or practice of trade—ex hypothesi, there was no established usage once the Suez Canal was blocked—but rather for the view of mercantile men as to the significance of adopting the alternative route. It is a summary way of stating that a voyage by that route would not involve any elements of difference that would be regarded as material by persons familiar with the trade. It would be contrary to common sense that a court, which cannot uninstructed assess the commercial significance of, say, a surcharge of £7 10s. per ton for freight in a c.i.f. contract of this kind, should not pay careful attention to such a view from such a source; just as it would be, I think, contrary to principle that a court should regard a view so expressed as finally conclusive of the legal issue.

I must add that I do not think that such a finding is altogether satisfactory for the purposes of a special case. It is in essence a summary of the commercial significance of several separate aspects of the Cape route as contrasted with the Suez Canal route, and it is embarrassing for a court which has to answer the question raised by the case to have before it only the summary and not the arbitrator's findings upon the individual aspects which make up the conclusion. I can see that, if this form came into general use, a court might feel obliged to send back the case containing it for further and more explicit findings. It would have been better if the special case had identified the several aspects of difference, length, time, cost, risk, etc., which, as it is, the court is left to infer, and had made with regard to them, both separately and together, the finding that was clearly intended, that they were not significant from the mercantile point of view.

I agree with the opinions already expressed by my noble and learned friends who have preceded me, that the exception clause, clause 6 of the contract, does not apply.

I would dismiss the appeal.

[The opinions of Lords Reid, Hodson, and Guest dismissing the appeal are omitted.]

DAVIS CONTRACTORS LTD. v. FAREHAM URBAN DISTRICT COUNCIL
England. House of Lords. [1956] A.C. 696

Davis tendered for the construction of seventy-eight houses within a period of eight months, at Gudgeheath Lane, Fareham, for £92,425. In a letter dated March 18, 1946 (ref. RL/JEM) accompanying the tender, Davis said, "Our tender is subject to adequate supplies of material and labour being available as and when required to carry out the work within the time specified." The agreement which was later signed by Davis contained only one reference to the letter. Appendix I to the agreement was headed "Materials and goods to be purchased directly by the contractor in respect of which variation of the contract sum is desired in accordance with clause 68B of the conditions of the contract." Under this heading Davis wrote, "As terms of letter attached dated March 18, 1946, reference RL/JEM." In later negotiations Davis actually supplied a detailed schedule of prices which was intended to constitute the appendix I schedule. The tender was made a part of the agreement. The contract took twenty-two months to complete, the delay being caused chiefly by the lack of skilled labour. With extras, the payments by Fareham amounted to £94,424. Davis claimed in this action that the contract price was inapplicable owing to the delay, and asked to be paid a total of £115,233 on a quantum meruit basis. The arbitrator awarded damages amounting to £17,258, but the Court of Appeal held that the letter was not incorporated into the contract and the contract was not frustrated. Davis then appealed to the House of Lords. The appeal was dismissed. Only the question of frustration is dealt with in the following excerpt.

LORD RADCLIFFE: . . . But, in my opinion, full weight ought to be given to the requirement that the parties "must have made" their bargains on the particular footing. Frustration is not to be lightly invoked as the dissolvent of a contract.

Lord Loreburn ascribes the dissolution to an implied term of the contract that was actually made. This approach is in line with the tendency of English courts to refer all the consequences of a contract to the will of those who made it. But there is something of a logical difficulty in seeing how the parties could even impliedly have provided for something which ex hypothesi they neither expected nor foresaw; and the ascription of frustration to an implied term of the contract has been criticized as obscuring the true action of the court which consists in applying an objective rule of the law of contract to the contractual obligations that the parties have imposed upon themselves. So long as each theory produces the same result as the other, as normally it does, it matters little which theory is avowed (see *British Movietonews Ltd.* v. *London and District Cinemas Ltd.,* [1952] A.C. 166, at p. 184, *per* Viscount Simon). But it may still be of some importance to recall that, if the matter is to be approached by way of implied term, the solution of any particular case is not to be found by inquiring what the parties themselves would have agreed on had they been, as they were not, forewarned. It is not merely that no one can answer that hypothetical question: it is also that the decision must be given "irrespective of the individuals concerned, their temperaments and failings, their interest and circumstances" (*Hirji Mulji* v. *Cheong Yue Steamship Co.*

Ltd., [1926] A.C. 497, at p. 510). The legal effect of frustration "does not depend on their intention or their opinions, or even knowledge, as to the event." On the contrary, it seems that when the event occurs "the meaning of the contract must be taken to be, not what the parties did intend (for they had neither thought nor intention regarding it), but that which the parties, as fair and reasonable men, would presumably have agreed upon if, having such possibility in view, they had made express provision as to their several rights and liabilities in the event of its occurrence" (*Dahl* v. *Nelson* (1881), 6 App. Cas. 38, *per* Lord Watson).

By this time it might seem that the parties themselves have become so far disembodied spirits that their actual persons should be allowed to rest in peace. In their place there rises the figure of the fair and reasonable man. And the spokesman of the fair and reasonable man, who represents after all no more than the anthropomorphic conception of justice, is and must be the court itself. So perhaps it would be simpler to say at the outset that frustration occurs whenever the law recognizes that without default of either party a contractual obligation has become incapable of being performed because the circumstances in which performance is called for would render it a thing radically different from that which was undertaken by the contract. Non haec in foedera veni. It was not this that I promised to do.

There is, however, no uncertainty as to the materials upon which the court must proceed. "The data for decision are, on the one hand, the terms and construction of the contract, read in the light of the then existing circumstances, and on the other hand the events which have occurred" (*Denny, Mott & Dickson Ltd.* v. *James B. Fraser & Co. Ltd.*, [1944] A.C. 265, at p. 274, *per* Lord Wright). In the nature of things there is often no room for any elaborate inquiry. The court must act upon a general impression of what its rule requires. It is for that reason that special importance is necessarily attached to the occurrence of any unexpected event that, as it were, changes the face of things. But, even so, it is not hardship or inconvenience or material loss itself which calls the principle of frustration into play. There must be as well such a change in the significance of the obligation that the thing undertaken would, if performed, be a different thing from that contracted for.

I am bound to say that, if this is the law, the appellants' case seems to me a long way from a case of frustration. Here is a building contract entered into by a housing authority and a big firm of contractors in all the uncertainties of the post-war world. Work was begun shortly before the formal contract was executed and continued, with impediments and minor stoppages but without actual interruption, until the 78 houses contracted for had all been built. After the work had been in progress for a time the appellants raised the claim, which they repeated more than once, that they ought to be paid a larger sum for their work than the contract allowed; but the respondents refused to admit the claim and, so far as appears, no conclusive action was taken by either side which would make the conduct of one or the other a determining element in the case.

That is not in any obvious sense a frustrated contract. But the appellants' argument, which certainly found favour with the arbitrator, is that at some stage before completion the original contract was dissolved because it became incapable of being performed according to its true significance and its place was taken by a new arrangement under which they were entitled to be paid, not the contract sum, but a fair price on quantum meruit for the work that they carried out during the 22 months that elapsed between commencement and completion. The contract, it is said, was an eight months' contract, as indeed it was. Through no fault of the parties it turned out that it took 22 months to do the work contracted for. The main reason for this was that, whereas both parties had expected that adequate supplies of labour and material would be available to allow for completion in eight months, the supplies that were in fact available were much less than adequate for the purpose. Hence, it is said, the basis or the footing of the contract was removed before the work was completed; or, slightly altering the metaphor, the footing of the contract was so changed by the circumstances that the expected supplies were not available that the contract built upon that footing became void. These are the findings which the arbitrator has recorded in his supplemental award.

In my view, these are in substance conclusions of law, and I do not think that they are good law. All that anyone, arbitrator or court, can do is to study the contract in the light of the circumstances that prevailed at the time when it was made and, having done so, to relate it to the circumstances that are said to have brought about its frustration. It may be a finding of fact that at the time of making the contract both parties anticipated that adequate supplies of labour and material would be available to enable the contract to be completed in the stipulated time. I doubt whether it is, but even if it is, it is no more than to say that when one party stipulated for completion in eight months, and the other party undertook it, each assumed that what was promised could be satisfactorily performed. That is a statement of the obvious that could be made with regard to most contracts. I think that a good deal more than that is needed to form a "basis" for the principle of frustration.

The justice of the arbitrator's conclusion depends upon the weight to be given to the fact that this was a contract for specified work to be completed in a fixed time at a price determined by those conditions. I think that his view was that, if without default on either side the contract period was substantially extended, that circumstance itself rendered the fixed price so unfair to the contractor that he ought not to be held to his original price. I have much sympathy with the contractor, but, in my opinion, if that sort of consideration were to be sufficient to establish a case of frustration, there would be an untold range of contractual obligations rendered uncertain and, possibly, unenforceable.

Two things seem to me to prevent the application of the principle of frustration to this case. One is that the cause of the delay was not any new state of things which the parties could not reasonably be thought to have foreseen. On the contrary, the possibility of enough labour and materials not being available was before their eyes and could have been the subject of special contractual stipulation. It was not made so. The other thing is that, though timely completion was no doubt important to both sides, it is not right to treat the possibility of delay as having the same significance for each. The owner draws up his conditions in detail, specifies the time within which he requires completion, protects himself both by a penalty clause for time exceeded and by calling for the deposit of a guarantee bond and offers a certain measure of security to a contractor by his escalator clause with regard to wages and prices. In the light of these conditions the contractor makes his tender, and the tender must necessarily take into account the margin of profit that he hopes to obtain upon his adventure and in that any appropriate allowance for the obvious risks of delay. To my mind, it is useless to pretend that the contractor is not at risk if delay does occur, even serious delay. And I think it a misuse of legal terms to call in frustration to get him out of his unfortunate predicament. . . .

[The decisions of Viscount Simonds and Lords Morton of Henryton, Reid, and Somervell of Harrow, dismissing the appeal, are omitted.]

2. RELIEF ON TERMS: RESTITUTION AND RELIANCE

APPLEBY v. *MYERS*
England. Exchequer Chamber. 1867. L.R. 2 C.P. 651

This was an action brought to recover £419 for work done and materials provided by the plaintiffs, engineers, for the defendant, under the circumstances hereinafter mentioned. The following case was stated, by consent, without pleadings, for the opinion of the Court:

On the 30th of March, 1865, the plaintiffs entered into an agreement with the defendant, which was headed, "Specification and estimate of engine, boiler, lifts, etc., for B. Meyers, Esq., Southwark Street. Messrs. Tillott & Chamberland, architects, 30th March, 1865." This contract contained ten distinct parts or divisions, viz. 1. boiler; 2. engine; 3. shafting; 4. lifts; 5. shafting; 6. drying-room; 7. copper pans; 8. tanks; 9. pump; 10. steamboxes; under each of which headings were particular descriptions of the work to be done in connection with each respectively, and the prices to be charged for the same; and the document concluded with these words:

"We offer to make and erect the whole of the machinery of the best materials and workmanship of their respective kinds, and to put it to work, for the sum above named respectively, and to keep the whole in order, under fair wear and tear, for two years from the date of completion. All brickwork, carpenters' and masons' work, and materials, are to be provided for us; but the drawings and general instructions required for them to work to will be provided by us, subject to the architects' approval.

(signed) Appleby Brothers."

The total cost of the above works, if they had been completed under the contract, would have amounted to £459.

On the 4th of July, 1865, a fire accidentally broke out on the premises of the defendant in Southwark Street, which entirely destroyed the premises and the works which then had been erected by the plaintiffs in part performance of the contract. At the time of the fire the works contracted for had not been completed.

At the time of the fire, portions of the items Nos. 1 to 8 were erected and fixed, and some of the materials for the others were on the premises.

The defendant had not completed the carpenters' and masons' work. The tank had been erected by the plaintiffs, and was used by the defendant by taking water therefrom for the purpose of his business; but the other apparatus connected with it, as specified in No. 8 was not complete. The plaintiff's workmen were still engaged in continuing the erection and completion of the same at the time of the fire.

The premises were the property of the defendant, in his occupation, and under his entire control. The plaintiffs had access to them only for the purpose of performing their contract.

The question for the opinion of the Court was, whether, under the above circumstances, the plaintiffs were entitled to recover the whole or any portion of the contract price.

The Court of Common Pleas gave judgment for the plaintiffs for an amount equal to the value of the work and materials actually done and provided by them under the agreement. The defendants appealed to the Court of Exchequer Chamber.

BLACKBURN J. delivered the judgment of the Court: This case was partly argued before us at the last sittings; and the argument was resumed and completed at the present sittings.

Having had the advantage of hearing the very able argument of Mr. Holl and Mr. Hannen, and having during the interval had the opportunity of considering the judgment of the Court below, there is no reason that we should further delay expressing the opinion at which we have all arrived, which is, that the judgment of the Court below is wrong and ought to be reversed.

The whole question depends upon the true construction of the contract between the parties. We agree with the Court below in thinking that it sufficiently appears that the work which the plaintiffs agreed to perform could not be performed unless the defendant's premises continued in a fit state to enable the plaintiffs to perform the work on them; and we agree with them in thinking that, if by any default on the part of the defendant, his premises were rendered unfit to receive the work, the plaintiffs would have had the option to sue the defendant for this default, or to treat the contract as rescinded, and sue on a quantum meruit. But we do not agree with them in thinking that there was an absolute promise or warranty by the defendant that the premises should at all events continue so fit. We think that where, as in the present case the premises are destroyed without fault on either side, it is a misfortune equally affecting both parties; excusing both from further performance of the contract, but giving a cause of action to neither.

Then it was argued before us, that, inasmuch as this was a contract of that nature which would in pleading be described as a contract for work, labour, and materials, and not as one of bargain and sale, the labour and materials necessarily became the property of the defendant as soon as they were at his risk. We think that, as to a great part at least of the work done in this case, the materials had not become the property of the defendant; for, we think that the plaintiffs, who were to complete the whole for a fixed sum, and keep it in repair two years, would have had a perfect right, if they thought that a portion of the engine which they had put up was too slight, to change it and substitute another in their opinion better calculated to keep in good repair during the two years, and without consulting or asking the leave of the defendant. But, even on the supposition that the materials had become unalterably fixed to the defendant's premises, we do not think that, under such a contract as this, the plaintiffs could recover anything unless the whole work was completed. It is quite true that materials worked by one into the property of another become part of that property. This is equally true, whether it be fixed or movable property. Bricks built into a wall become part of the house; thread stitched into a coat which is under repair, or planks and nails and pitch worked into a ship, under repair, become part of the coat or the ship; and therefore, generally, and in the absence of something to shew a contrary intention, the bricklayer or tailor, or shipwright, is to be paid for the work and materials he has done and provided, although the whole work is not complete. It is not material whether in such a case the non-completion is because the shipwright did not choose to go on with the work, as was the case in *Roberts* v. *Havelock* (1832), 3 B. & Ad. 404; 110 E.R. 145, or because in consequence of a fire he could not go on with it, as in *Menetone* v. *Athawes* (1764), 3 Burr. 1592; 97 E.R. 998. But, though this is the prima facie contract between those who enter into contracts for doing work and supplying materials, there is nothing to render it either illegal or absurd in the workman to agree to complete the whole, and be paid when the whole is complete, and not till then: and we think that the plaintiffs in the present case had entered into such a contract. Had the accidental fire left the defendant's premises untouched, and only injured a part of the work which the plaintiffs had already done, we apprehend that it is clear the plaintiffs under such a contract as the present must have done that part over again, in order to fulfil their contract to complete the whole and "put it to work for the sums above named respectively." As it is, they are, according to the principle laid down in *Taylor* v. *Caldwell* (1863), 122 E.R. 309, excused from completing the work; but they are not therefore entitled to any compensation for what they have done, but which has, without any fault of the defendant, perished. The case is in principle like that of a shipowner who has been excused from the performance of his contract to carry goods to their destination, because his ship has been disabled by one of the excepted perils, but who is not therefore entitled to any payment on account of the part-performance of the voyage, unless there is something to justify the conclusion that there has been a fresh contract to pay freight pro rata.

On the argument, much reference was made to the Civil Law. The opinions of the great lawyers collected in the Digest afford us very great assistance in tracing out any question of doubtful principle; but they do not bind us: and we think that, on the principles of English law laid down ... the plaintiffs, having contracted to do an entire work for a specific sum, can recover nothing unless the work be done, or it can be shewn that it was the defendant's fault that the work was incomplete, or that there is something to justify the conclusion that the parties have entered into a fresh contract. . . .

KING v. *LOW*. 1901. 3 O.L.R. 234 (Ontario. Court of Appeal). The defendants agreed to build a house on an island in the St. Lawrence for one George F. Benson at a price of $4,450. The plaintiffs were plumbing sub-contractors who agreed with the defendants to install the plumbing for $500. When $488 worth of plumbing work had been completed the house was destroyed by fire and the defendants refused to pay the plaintiffs anything on account of their work. Boyd C. at a jury trial, said, "The evidence shews substantial completion (to within $12), and the omission to do the greater part of the work arose from delays to be charged against the contractors rather than the plaintiffs." He was reversed on appeal. ARMOUR C.J.O.: "The plaintiffs did not bring this action for the contract price, alleging that they had substantially completed their contract; but admitted that they had not completed their contract, and brought it for the value of the work done by them." *Appleby* v. *Myers* was cited.

GOULDING v. *RABINOVITCH*. 1927. 60 O.L.R. 607 (Ontario. Court of Appeal). On February 25, 1926, Rabinovitch gave Goulding a 60-day option to purchase land for $68,000. Goulding paid $1,000 for the option. On March 12 the C.N.R. commenced proceedings to expropriate the land. Goulding claimed the return of the $1,000. Lennox J. held that the contract was frustrated and Goulding could recover on a total failure of consideration. Rabinovitch appealed. MIDDLETON J.A.: "I agree with the findings of the learned trial Judge, but not with his legal conclusion. . . . Without the fault of either party, by the action of the railway company, the completion of the contract became impossible. But there was by no means a total failure of consideration. The plaintiff had the benefit of the option for the period between the making of the option-contract and the registration of the plan, and during the same period the defendant's hands were tied—he could not sell the land. In the end he had to accept from the railway company a sum considerably below the price named in the contract. Each will lose money; each must bear his own misfortune."

FONG v. *KERWIN.* [1929] 3 D.L.R. 612 (Ontario. Court of Appeal). Kerwin agreed to lease his premises to Fong to be used as a laundry and to make the necessary changes (at a cost of some $800), but only if Fong would give him four months' rent in advance. Fong advanced the money, went into possession and put his name on the door. Kerwin got a building permit and commenced the renovations. Kerwin and Fong together applied for a laundry licence, but were told it could not be issued until the tubs were in and "everything installed." All was proceeding well until a petition presented by the neighbours against a laundry at the place was heeded and the licence refused. RIDDELL J.A.: "No doubt, the intention was that the premises should be used as a laundry; and the question whether the defendant can insist upon the lease does not arise here—the whole question being whether when the money was paid as a term of the lease being entered into at all, it can be recovered back. To ask that question is to answer it—the money was paid as a consideration for the defendant making the necessary changes and entering into the lease, for whatever it was worth; I can find no semblance of foundation for the proposition that it was paid for a consideration that has failed, and in my view it would be grossly unjust to compel the defendant to pay back the money received as a condition precedent to his making the expenditures he was required to make, and leave him out the money so expended by him."

FIBROSA SPOLKA AKCYJNA v. FAIRBAIRN LAWSON COMBE BARBOUR LTD.
England. House of Lords. [1943] A.C. 32

The respondents were a limited company carrying on at Leeds the business of manufacturing textile machinery, and by a contract in writing dated July 12, 1939, the respondents agreed to supply the appellants, a Polish company, of Vilna, with certain flax-hackling machines as therein specified and described, at a lump sum price of £4,800. The machines were of a special kind. The place of erection of the machinery was not mentioned in the contract, but it was agreed that it was the intention of the parties that it was to be erected at Vilna. By the terms of the contract, delivery was to be in three to four months from the settlement of final details. The machines were to be packed and delivered by the respondents c.i.f. Gdynia, the services of a skilled monteur to superintend erection were to be provided by the respondents and included in the price, and payment was to be made by cheque on London, one-third of the price (£1600) with the balance (£3200) against shipping documents. By clause 7 of the conditions of sale attached to the contract: "... Should dispatch be hindered or delayed by your instructions, or lack of instructions, or by any cause whatsoever beyond our reasonable control including strikes, lock-outs, war, fire, accidents ... a reasonable extension of time shall be granted. ..." By clause 10 provisions were made for dispatch and possible storage pending dispatch.

On July 18, 1939, the appellants paid to the respondents £1000 on account of the initial payment of £1600 due under the contract. On September 1, 1939, Germany invaded Poland and on September 3, Great Britain declared war on Germany. On September 7, the appellants' agents in England wrote to the respondents: "Owing to the outbreak of hostilities, it is now quite evident that the delivery of the hackling machines on order for Poland cannot take place. Under the circumstances we shall be obliged if you will kindly arrange to return our initial payment of £1000 at your early convenience." To this request, the respondents replied on the next day refusing to return the sum and stating that "considerable work had been done upon these machines and we cannot consent to the return of this payment. After the war the matter can be reconsidered." There was further correspondence between the parties or their agents which failed to produce agreement, and on May 1, 1940, the appellants issued a writ and by their statement of claim alleged that the respondents had broken the contract by refusing to deliver the machines, while the appellants "are and have at all material times been ready and willing to take delivery of the said machinery and pay for the same." The prayer of the claim was (a) for damages for breach of contract, (b) for specific performance or, alternatively, return of the £1000 with interest, and (c) for further or other relief. The substantial defence of the respondents was that the contract had been frustrated by the German occupation of Gdynia in September, 1939, and that in these circumstances the appellants had no right to the return of the £1000. Tucker J. dismissed the action on March 7, 1941, and the Court of Appeal affirmed his decision on May 15, 1941. The appellants appealed to the House of Lords.

VISCOUNT SIMON L.C.: My Lords, this is the appeal of a Polish company who were plaintiffs in the action against the decision of the Court of Appeal composed of MacKinnon and Luxmoore L.JJ. and Stable J., affirming the judgment of Tucker J. at the trial in favour of the respondents. After the Court of Appeal's judgment and before the appeal came to be argued at your Lordships' bar, the town of Vilna, where the appellants had carried on its business, and indeed the whole of Poland, under the laws of which state the appellants were incorporated, were occupied by our enemy, Germany. The question might, therefore, arise whether the appellants should now be debarred from prosecuting its appeal. ... To obviate any difficulty on this head, the appellants, at the suggestion of the House, applied to the Board of Trade, and the department gave to the appellants' solicitors a licence to proceed with the appeal, notwithstanding that their clients might be in the position of an alien enemy. The House was content to let the case proceed on this basis. ... If, as the result of the decision of the House, any payment becomes due to the appellants, and if they were in the position of alien enemies within the meaning of the

Trading with the Enemy Act, 1939, the payment would be regulated by the Act.

Before passing to the main question involved in the appeal, I must mention another contention of the appellants which was based on clause 7 of the conditions of sale attached to the contract. This clause contained the provision that "should dispatch be hindered or delayed by . . . any cause beyond our reasonable control including . . . war . . . a reasonable extension of time shall be granted." The appellants argued that there could be no frustration by reason of the war which broke out during the currency of the contract because this contingency was expressly provided for in clause 7, and, therefore, there was no room for an implied term such as has often been regarded as a suitable way in which to express and apply the doctrine of frustration. I entirely agree with the Court of Appeal that in the circumstances of the present case this is a bad point. The ambit of the express condition is limited to delay in respect of which "a reasonable extension of time" might be granted. That might mean a minor delay as distinguished from a prolonged and indefinite interruption of prompt contractual performance which the present war manifestly brings about. A similar argument was unsuccessfully urged in *Bank Line, Ltd.* v. *Arthur Capel & Co.,* [1919] A.C. 435, and in other cases, a recent instance of which is *W . . Tatem, Ltd.* v. *Gamboa,* [1939] 1 K.B. 132. The principle is that where supervening events, not due to the default of either party, render the performance of a contract indefinitely impossible, and there is no undertaking to be bound in any event, frustration ensues, even though the parties may have expressly provided for the case of a limited interruption. As MacKinnon L.J. points out, the unsoundness of the contrary view is implicit in *Jackson* v. *Union Marine Insurance Co., Ltd.* (1874), L.R. 10 C.P. 125, for the charterparty in that case contained an exception of perils of the sea, but none the less the contract was held to have been terminated and the adventure to have been frustrated by the long delay due to the stranding of the ship. The situation arising from the outbreak of the present war, so far as this country, Germany and Poland are concerned, makes applicable Lush J.'s well-known observation in *Geipel* v. *Smith* (1872), L.R. 7 Q.B. 404, 414: "A state of war" (in that case the Franco-German war of 1870) "must be presumed to be likely to continue so long and so to disturb the commerce of merchants as to defeat and destroy the object of a commercial adventure like this." There is a further reason for saying that this contention of the appellants must fail, namely, that, while this country is at war with Germany and Germany is occupying Gdynia, a British subject such as the respondents could not lawfully make arrangements to deliver c.i.f. Gdynia, and, therefore, the contract could not be further performed because of supervening illegality. A provision providing for a reasonable extension of time if dispatch is delayed by war cannot have any application when the circumstances of the war make dispatch illegal. . . .

Mr. Linton Thorp, in conducting the argument for the appellants before us, admitted that, if the point with which I have already dealt was decided against him, the only other issue to be determined was whether, when this contract became frustrated, the appellants could, in the circumstances of the present case, claim back from the respondents the £1000 which they had paid when placing the order. As to this, MacKinnon L.J., in delivering the judgment of the Court of Appeal said: "Tucker J. held that having regard to the principle laid down in *Chandler* v. *Webster* [1904] 1 K.B.

493, and other like cases, this claim must fail. We think he was right, and, further, that that principle must equally bind this court to reject the claim. Whether the principle can be overruled is a matter that can only concern the House of Lords." This alleged principle is to the effect that where a contract has been frustrated by such a supervening event as releases from further performances, "the loss lies where it falls," with the result that sums paid or rights accrued before that event are not to be surrendered, but all obligations falling due for performance after that event are discharged. This proposition, whether right or wrong, first appears, not in *Chandler* v. *Webster* but in *Blakely* v. *Muller & Co.* [1903] 2 K.B. 670n., decided in January, 1903, by a Divisional Court, which was also a case arising out of the abandonment of the coronation procession owing to King Edward VII's sudden illness. In that case, Channell J. said: "If the money was payable on some day subsequent to the abandonment of the procession, I do not think it could have been sued for. If, however, it was payable prior to the abandonment of the procession, the position would be the same as if it had been actually paid and could not be recovered back, and could be sued for. . . . It is impossible to import a condition into a contract which the parties could have imported and have not done so. All that can be said is that, when the procession was abandoned, the contract was off, not that anything done under the contract was void. The loss must remain where it was at the time of the abandonment. It is like the case of a charterparty where the freight is payable in advance, and the voyage is not completed, and the freight, therefore, not earned. Where the non-completion arose through impossibility of performance, the freight could not be recovered back." In *Civil Service Co-operative Society Ltd.*, v. *General Steam Navigation Co.* [1903] 2 K.B. 756., which was decided in the Court of Appeal in October, 1903, Lord Halsbury L.C. expressed entire concurrence with this passage in the judgment of Channell J. Lord Alverston C.J., who was a party to both these decisions, took the same view.

If we are to approach this problem anew, it must be premised that the first matter to be considered is always the terms of the particular contract. If, for example, the contract is "divisible" in the sense that a sum is to be paid over in respect of completion of a defined portion of the work, it may well be that the sum is not returnable if completion of the whole work is frustrated. If the contract itself on its true construction stipulates for a particular result which is to follow in regard to money already paid, should frustration afterwards occur, this governs the matter. The ancient and firmly established rule that freight paid in advance is not returned if the completion of the voyage is frustrated . . . should, I think, be regarded as a stipulation introduced into such contracts by custom, and not as the result of applying some abstract principle.

And so, a fortiori, if there is a stipulation that the prepayment is "out and out." To take an example, not from commerce, but from sport, the cricket spectator who pays for admission to see a match cannot recover the entrance money on the ground that rain has prevented play if, expressly or by proper implication, the bargain with him is that no money will be returned. Inasmuch as the effect of frustration may be explained as arising from an implied term: see *Joseph Constantine Steamship Line, Ltd.* v. *Imperial Smelting Corporation, Ltd.*, [1942] A.C. 154, it is tempting to speculate whether a further term could be implied as to what was to happen, in the event of frustration, to money already paid, but, if the parties were assumed to have discussed the point when entering into the contract, they could not be supposed to have agreed on a simple formula which would be fair in all circumstances, and all that could be said is that, in the absence of such agreement, the law must decide. The question now to be determined is whether, in the absence of a term in the contract dealing with the matter, the rule which is commonly called the rule in *Chandler* v. *Webster* should be affirmed.

This supposed rule has been constantly applied in a great variety of cases which have since arisen—and necessarily so, because the rule had been laid down in plain terms by the Court of Appeal in England in 1904, and the present appeal provides the first occasion on which it can be effectively challenged. A very different rule prevails in Scotland, as was made plain by the decision of this House in *Cantiare San Rocco S.A.* v. *Clyde Shipbuilding and Engineering Co., Ltd.*, [1924] A.C. 226. In that case the Earl of Birkenhead was careful to reserve the question whether *Chandler* v. *Webster* and the other English cases on the point were rightly decided, saying: "The question is as to the law of Scotland, and I desire to say nothing which may in any way fetter opinion if those authorities hereafter come to be reviewed by this House, for none of them is binding upon your Lordships." Similarly in the same case, Viscount Finlay observed that it would be out of place on that occasion to enter into the question dealt with in *Chandler* v. *Webster*, adding: The principle of English law was re-stated with great clearness by Lord Parmoor in the case of *French Marine* v. *Compagnie Napolitaine d'Eclairage et de Chauffage par le Gaz*, [1921] 2 A.C. 494, 523. This statement forms no part of the judgment of the House of Lords in that case, but there is no doubt that the principle has been repeatedly acted on in the Court of Appeal." Lord Dunedin in the *Cantiare San Rocco* case referred to the different angle of approach from which an English or a Scottish judge would look at the question, and thought that the cause was to be found in the reluctance of the English law to order the repayment of money once paid. But he added: "I do not enlarge on the topic, for I am not at all concerned to criticize English law. . . . For the purpose of this case, it is sufficient to say, as I unhesitatingly do, that *Chandler* v. *Webster*, if it had been tried in Scotland, would have been decided the other way." Lord Dunedin's restraint was not imitated by Lord Shaw whose pronouncement included a vigorous denunciation of the proposition that the loss lies where it falls as amounting to a maxim which "works well enough among tricksters, gamblers and thieves." The learned Lord asserted that this was part of the law of England (presumably meaning that it had been so laid down by the English Court of Appeal), but patriotically rejoiced that it had never been part of the law of Scotland.

Mr. Valentine Holmes, in his able argument for the respondents, asked us to consider whether this House would be justified in disturbing a view of the law which has prevailed for nearly forty years, which has been so frequently affirmed, which has been constantly applied in working out the rights of the parties to commercial contracts, and which, moreover at any rate furnishes a simple rule against the effect of which the parties to a contract can, if they so desire, expressly provide. These are weighty considerations, but I do not think they ought to prevail in the circumstances of this case over our primary duty of doing our utmost to secure that the law on this important matter is correctly expounded and applied. If the view which has hitherto prevailed in this matter is found to be based on a misapprehension of legal principles, it is of great importance that these principles should be correctly defined, for, if not, there is a danger that the error may spread in other directions, and a portion of our law be erected on a false foundation. Moreover, though the so-called rule in *Chandler* v. *Webster* is nearly forty years old, it has not escaped much unfavourable criticism. My noble and learned friend Lord Atkin when sitting in the Court of Appeal as Atkin L.J., in *Russkoe Obschestvo d'lia Izgstovlenia Snariadov I' voennick Pripassov* v. *John Stirk & Sons, Ltd.*, (1922), 10 Ll. L. Rep. 214, doubted whether any two business people in the world would ever make a contract which embodied such a doctrine as *Chandler* v. *Webster* laid down, and in the present case the Court of Appeal, while bound by previous authority, hinted a hope that this House might be able to substitute a "more civilized rule". I think, therefore, that we ought to regard ourselves as at liberty to examine the challenged proposition freely, and to lay down what we regard as the true doctrine in English law without being hampered by a course of practice based on previous decisions in the Court of Appeal.

The locus classicus for the view which has hitherto prevailed is to be found in the judgment of Collins M.R. in *Chandler* v. *Webster*. It was not a considered judgment, but it is hardly necessary to say that I approach this pronouncement of the then Master of the Rolls with all the respect due to so distinguished a common lawyer. When his judgment is studied, however, one cannot but be impressed by the circumstance that he regarded the proposition that money in such cases could not be recovered back as flowing from the decision in *Taylor* v. *Caldwell*, (1863), 122 E.R. 309. *Taylor* v. *Caldwell*, however, was not a case in which any question arose whether money could be recovered back, for there had been no payment in advance, and there is nothing in the judgment of Blackburn J., which, at any rate in terms, affirms the general proposition that "the loss lies where it falls." The application by Collins M.R. of *Taylor* v. *Caldwell* to the actual problem with which he had to deal in *Chandler* v. *Webster* deserves close examination. He said: "The plaintiff contends that he is entitled to recover the money which he has paid on the ground that there has been a total failure of consideration. He says that the condition on which he paid the money was that the procession should take place, and that, as it did not take place, there has been a total failure of consideration. That contention does no doubt raise a question of some difficulty, and one which has perplexed the courts to a considerable extent in several cases. The principle on which it has been dealt with is that which was applied in *Taylor* v. *Caldwell*—namely, that where from causes outside the volition of the parties, something which was the basis of, or essential to the fulfilment of, the contract has become impossible, so that, from the time when the fact of that impossibility has been ascertained, the contract can no further be performed by either party, it remains a perfectly good contract up to that point, and everything previously done in pursuance of it must be treated as rightly done, but the parties are both discharged from further performance of it. If the effect were that the contract were wiped out altogether, no doubt the result would be that money paid under it would have to be repaid as on a failure of consideration. But that is not the effect of the doctrine; it only releases the parties from further performance of the contract. Therefore the doctrine of failure of consideration does not apply."

It appears to me that the reasoning in this crucial passage is open to two criticisms:

(a) The claim of a party, who has paid money under a contract, to get the money back, on the ground that the consideration for which he paid it has totally failed, is not based on any provision contained in the contract, but arises because, in the circumstances that have happened, the law gives a remedy in quasi-contract to the party who has not got that for which he bargained. It is a claim to recover money to which the defendant has no further right because in the circumstances that have developed the money must be regarded as received to the plaintiff's use. It is true that the effect of frustration is that, while the contract can no further be performed, "it remains a perfectly good contract up to that point, and everything previously done in pursuance of it must be treated as rightly done," but it by no means follows that the situation existing at the moment of frustration is one which leaves the party that has paid money and has not received the stipulated consideration without any remedy. To claim the return of money paid on the ground of total failure of consideration is not to vary the terms of the contract in any way. The claim arises not because the right to be repaid is one of the stipulated conditions of the contract, but because, in the circumstances that have happened, the law gives the remedy. It is the failure to distinguish between (1) the action of assumpsit for money had and received in a case where the consideration has wholly failed, and (2) an action on the contract itself, which explains the mistake which I think has been made in applying English law to this subject-matter. Thus, in *Blakely* v. *Muller & Co.*, [1903] 2 K.B. 760, Lord Alverstone C.J. said "I agree that *Taylor* v. *Caldwell* applies, but the consequence of that decision is that neither party here could have sued on the contract in respect of anything which was to be done under it after the procession had been abandoned." That is true enough, but it does not follow that because the plaintiff cannot sue "on the contract" he cannot sue dehors the contract for the recovery of a payment in respect of which consideration has failed. In the same case, Wills J. relied on *Appleby* v. *Myers*, (1867), L.R. 2 C.P. 651, where a contract was made for the erection by A. of machinery on the premises of B., to be paid for on completion. There was no prepayment and in the course of the work the premises were destroyed by fire. It was held that both parties were excused from further performance, and that no liability accrued on either side, but the liability referred to was liability under the contract, and the learned judge seems to have thought that no action to recover money in such circumstances as the present could be conceived of unless there was a term of the contract, express or implied, which so provided. Once it is realized that the action to recover money for a consideration that has wholly failed rests, not on a contractual bargain between the parties, but as Lord Sumner said in *Sinclair* v. *Brougham*, [1914] A.C. 398, 452., "upon a notional or imputed promise to repay," or (if it is preferred to omit reference to a fictitious promise) upon an obligation to repay arising from the circumstances, the difficulty in the way of holding that a prepayment made under a contract which has been frustrated can be recovered back appears to me to disappear.

(b) There is, no doubt, a distinction between cases in which a contract is "wiped out altogether," e.g., because it is void as being illegal from the start or as being due to fraud which the innocent party has elected to treat as avoiding the contract, and cases in which intervening impossibility "only releases the parties from further performance of the contract." But does the distinction between these two classes of case justify the deduction of Collins M.R. that "the doctrine of failure of consideration does not apply" where the contract remains a perfectly good contract up to the date of frustration? This conclusion seems to be derived from the view that, if the contract remains good and valid up to the moment of frustration, money which has already been paid under it cannot be regarded as having been paid for a consideration which has wholly failed. The party that has paid the money has had the advantage, whatever it may be worth, of the promise of the other party. That is true, but it is necessary to draw a distinction. In English law, an enforceable contract may be formed by an exchange of a promise for a promise, or by the exchange of a promise for an act—I am excluding contracts under seal—and thus, in the law relating to the formation of contract, the promise to do a thing may often be the consideration, but when one is considering the law of failure of consideration and of the quasi-contractual right to recover money on that ground, it is, generally speaking, not the promise which is referred to as the consideration, but the performance of the promise. The money was paid to secure performance and, if performance fails the inducement which brought about the payment is not fulfilled.

If this were not so, there could never be any recovery of money, for failure of consideration, by the payer of the money in return for a promise of future performance, yet there are endless examples which show that money can be recovered, as for a complete failure of consideration, in cases where the promise was given but could not be fulfilled: see the notes in Bullen and Leake's *Precedents of Pleading*, 9th ed., p. 263. In this connexion the decision in *Rugg* v. *Minett*, (1809), 11 East, 210; 103 E.R. 985, is instructive. There the plaintiff had bought at auction a number of casks of oil. The contents of each cask were to be made up after the auction by the seller to the prescribed quantity so that the property in a cask did not pass to the plaintiff until this had been done. The plaintiff paid in advance a sum of money on account of his purchases generally, but a fire occurred after some of the casks had been filled up, while the others had not. The plaintiff's action was to recover the money he had paid as money received by the defendants to the use of the plaintiffs. The Court of King's Bench ruled that this cause of action succeeded in respect of the casks which at the time of the fire had not been filled up to the prescribed quantity. A simple illustration of the same result is an agreement to buy a horse, the price to be paid down, but the horse not to be delivered and the property not to pass until the horse had been shod. If the horse dies before the shoeing, the price can unquestionably be recovered as for a total failure of consideration, notwithstanding that the promise to deliver was given. This is the case of a contract de certo corpore where the certum corpus perishes after the contract is made, but, as Vaughan Williams L.J.'s judgment in *Krell* v. *Henry*, [1903] 2 K.B. 740, explained, the same doctrine applies "to cases where the event which renders the contract incapable of performance is the cessation or non-existence of an express condition or state of things, going to the root of the contract, and essential to its performance." I can see no valid reason why the right to recover prepaid money should not equally arise on frustration arising from supervening circumstances as it arises on frustration from destruction of a particular subject-matter. The conclusion is that the rule in *Chandler* v. *Webster* is wrong, and that the appellants can recover their £1000.

While this result obviates the harshness with which the previous view in some instances treated the party who had made a prepayment, it cannot be regarded as dealing fairly between the parties in all cases, and must sometimes have the result of leaving the recipient who has to return the money at a grave disadvantage. He may have incurred expenses in connexion with the partial carrying out of the contract which are equivalent, or more than equivalent, to the money which he prudently stipulated should be prepaid, but which he now has to return for reasons which are no fault of his. He may have to repay the money, though he has executed almost the whole of the contractual work, which will be left on his hands. These results follow from the fact that the English common law does not undertake to apportion a prepaid sum in such circumstances—contrast the provision, now contained in s. 40 of the *Partnership Act, 1890*, for apportioning a premium if a partnership is prematurely dissolved. It must be for the legislature to decide whether provisions should be made for an equitable apportionment of prepaid moneys which have to be returned by the recipient in view of the frustration of the contract in respect of which they were paid. I move that the appeal be allowed, and that judgment be entered for the appellants.

[The opinions (allowing the appeal) of Lords Atkin, Russell of Killowen, Macmillan, Wright, Roche, and Porter are omitted.]

NOTE. The facts of *Chandler* v. *Webster* are stated briefly by Lord Atkin as follows:

"In that case the plaintiff had hired a room to view the coronation procession on Thursday, June 26, 1902. On June 10 he wrote to the defendant: 'I beg to confirm my purchase of the first floor room of the Electric Lighting Board at 7 Pall Mall to view the procession on Thursday, June 26, for the sum of £141 15s., which amount is now due. I shall be obliged if you will take the room on sale, and I authorize you to sell separate seats in the room, for which I will erect a stand.' It became the subject of controversy whether, in view of certain other terms arranged between the parties the whole sum became due before the procession became impossible, but the courts decided, as was clearly the case, that it did so become due. It may be noted that the defendant had nothing to do under the contract but allow the plaintiff the use of the room. On June 19 the plaintiff paid the defendant £100 on account of the price of the room, but had not paid the balance at the time the procession was abandoned. The plaintiff claimed the return of the £100 on a total failure of consideration, the defendant counter-claimed for the balance of £41 15s." The plaintiff's claim failed, and the defendant's counter-claim succeeded.

NOTE ON RESTITUTION. On the general theory of the English law of restitution, or unjust enrichment, or quasi-contract, Lord Wright said in the *Fibrosa* case.:

"It is clear that any civilized system of law is bound to provide remedies for cases of what has been called unjust enrichment or unjust benefit, that is to prevent a man from retaining the money of or some benefit derived from another which it is against conscience that he should keep. Such remedies in English law are generally different from remedies in contract or in tort, and are now recognized to fall within a third category of the common law which has been called quasi-contract or restitution. The root idea was stated by three Lords of Appeal. Lord Shaw, Lord Sumner and Lord Carson, in *R. E. Jones, Ltd.* v. *Waring & Gillow, Ltd.* [1926] A.C. 670, 696, which dealt with a particular species of the category, namely, money paid under a mistake of fact. . . ."

After quoting from *Moses* v. *Macferlan* Lord Wright continued:

"Lord Mansfield does not say that the law implies a promise. The law implies a debt or obligation which is a different thing. In fact, he denies that there is a contract; the obligation is as efficacious as if it were upon a contract. The obligation is a creation of the law, just as much as an obligation in tort. The obligation belongs to a third class, distinct from either contract or tort, though it resembles contract rather than tort. This statement of Lord Mansfield has been the basis of the modern law of quasi-contract, notwithstanding the criticisms which have been launched against it. Like all large generalizations, it has needed and received qualification in practice. There is, for instance, the qualification that an action for money had and received does not lie for money paid under an erroneous judgment or for moneys paid under an illegal or excessive distress. The law has provided other remedies as being more convenient. The standard of what is against conscience in this context has become more or less canalized or defined, but in substance the juristic concept remains as Lord Mansfield left it.

"The gist of the action is a debt or obligation implied, or, more accurately, imposed, by law in much the same way as the law enforces as a debt the obligation to pay a statutory or customary impost. This is important because some confusion seems to have arisen though perhaps only in recent times when the true nature of the forms of action have become obscured by want of user. . . .

"Lord Atkin in the *United Australia* case [1941] A.C. 1, 29, after instancing the case of the blackmailer, says: 'The man has my money which I have not delivered to him with any real intention of passing to him the property. I sue him because he has the actual property taken.' He adds: 'These fantastic resemblances of contracts invented in order to meet requirements of the law as to forms of action which have now disappeared should not in these days be allowed to affect actual rights.' Yet the ghosts of the forms of action have been allowed at times to intrude in the ways of the living and impede vital functions of the law. Thus in *Sinclair* v. *Brougham*, 1914 A.C. 398, 452, Lord Sumner stated that "all these causes of action [sc. for money had and received] are common species of the genus assumpsit. All now rest, and long have rested, upon a notional or imputed promise to repay.' This observation, which was not necessary for the decision of the case, obviously does not mean that there is an actual promise of the party. The phrase 'notional or implied promise' is only a way of describing a debt or obligation arising by construction of law. The claim for money had and received always rested on a debt or obligation which the law implied or more accurately imposed, whether the procedure actually in vogue at any time was debt or account or indebitatus assumpsit. Even the fictitious assumpsit disappeared after the Act of 1852. I prefer Lord Sumner's explanation of the cause of action in *Jones's* case. This agrees with the words of Lord Atkin which I have just quoted, yet serious legal writers have seemed to say that these words of that great judge in *Sinclair* v. *Brougham* closed the door to any theory of unjust enrichment in English law. I do not understand why or how. It would indeed be a reductio ad absurdum of the doctrine of precedents. In fact, the common law still employs the action for money had and received as a practical and useful, if not complete or ideally perfect, instrument to prevent unjust enrichment, aided by the various methods of technical equity which are also available, as they were found to be in *Sinclair* v. *Brougham*."

Compare Denning J. in *Nelson* v. *Larholt*, [1948] 1 K.B. 339, at p. 343:

"The rightful owner can recover the amount from anyone who takes the money with notice, subject, of course, to the limitation that he cannot recover twice over. This principle has been evolved by the courts of law and equity side by side. In equity it took the form of an action to follow moneys impressed with an express trust, or with a constructive trust owing to a fiduciary relationship. In law it took the form of an action for money had and received or damages for conversion of a cheque. It is no longer appropriate, however, to draw a distinction between law and equity. Principles have now to be stated in the light of their combined effect. Nor is it necessary to canvass the niceties of the old forms of action. Remedies now depend on the substance of the right, not on whether they can be fitted into a particular framework. The right here is not peculiar to equity or contract or tort, but falls naturally within the important category of cases where the court orders restitution, if the justice of the case so requires."

And contrast Lord Porter in *Reading* v. *Attorney-General* in the House of Lords, [1951] A.C. 507, at p. 513-14.

THE FRUSTRATED CONTRACTS ACT
R.S.O. 1970 Chapter 185

1. In this Act,
    (a) "contract" includes a contract to which the Crown is a party;
    (b) "court" means the court or arbitrator by or before whom a matter falls to be determined;
    (c) "discharged" means relieved from further performance of the contract.
2. (1) This Act applies to any contract that is governed by the law of Ontario whether it was made before or after the 1st day of June, 1949, that after the 1st day of June, 1949, has become impossible of performance or been otherwise frustrated and the parties to which for that reason have been discharged.
    (2) This Act does not apply,
    (a) to a charterparty or a contract for the carriage of goods by sea, except a time charterparty or a charterparty by way of demise;
    (b) to a contract of insurance; or
    (c) to a contract for the sale of specific goods where the goods, without the knowledge of the seller, have perished at the time the contract was made, or where the goods, without any fault on the part of the seller or buyer, perished before the risk passed to the buyer.
3. (1) The sums paid or payable to a party in pursuance of a contract before the parties were discharged,
    (a) in the case of sums paid, are recoverable from him as money received by him for the use of the party by whom the sums were paid; and
    (b) in the case of sums payable, cease to be payable.
    (2) If, before the parties were discharged, the party to whom the sums were paid or payable incurred expenses in connection with the performance of the contract, the court, if it considers it just to do so having regard to all the circumstances, may allow him to retain or to recover, as the case may be, the whole or any part of the sums paid or payable not exceeding the amount of the expenses, and, without restricting the generality of the foregoing, the court, in estimating the amount of the expenses, may include such sum as appears to be reasonable in respect of overhead

expenses and in respect of any work or services performed personally by the party incurring the expenses.

(3) If, before the parties were discharged, any of them has, by reason of anything done by any other party in connection with the performance of the contract, obtained a valuable benefit other than a payment of money, the court, if it considers it just to do so having regard to all the circumstances, may allow the other party to recover from the party benefitted the whole or any part of the value of the benefit.

(4) Where a party has assumed an obligation under the contract in consideration of the conferring of a benefit by any other party to the contract upon any other person, whether a party to the contract or not, the court, if it considers it just to do so having regard to all the circumstances, may, for the purposes of subsection 3, treat any benefit so conferred as a benefit obtained by the party who has assumed the obligation.

(5) In considering whether any sum ought to be recovered or retained under this section by a party to the contract, the court shall not take into account any sum that, by reason of the circumstances giving rise to the frustration of the contract, has become payable to that party under any contract of insurance unless there was an obligation to insure imposed by an express term of the frustrated contract or by or under any enactment.

(6) Where the contract contains a provision that upon the true construction of the contract is intended to have effect in the event of circumstances that operate, or but for the provision would operate, to frustrate the contract, or is intended to have effect whether such circumstances arise or not, the court shall give effect to the provision and shall give effect to this section only to such extent, if any, as appears to the court to be consistent with the provision.

(7) Where it appears to the court that a part of the contract can be severed properly from the remainder of the contract, being a part wholly performed before the parties were discharged, or so performed except for the payment in respect of that part of the contract of sums that are or can be ascertained under the contract, the court shall treat that part of the contract as if it were a separate contract that had not been frustrated and shall treat this section as applicable only to the remainder of the contract.

[This Act is modelled on that prepared by the Conference of Commissioners on Uniformity of Legislation in Canada (see their 1948 Proceedings) and that in turn is based on *The Law Reform (Frustrated Contracts) Act, 1943* of the United Kingdom, Williams, *Law Reform (Frustrated Contracts) Act, 1943* is a valuable monograph on the history of the Act and the changes it introduced.]

CHAPTER 12

THE STATUTE OF FRAUDS

The Statute of Frauds was originally passed in 1677 as 29 Car. II, c. 3. Its long title was "An Act for prevention of Frauds and Perjuries" and its preamble indicated that it was aimed at the "prevention of many fraudulent practices which are commonly endeavoured to be upheld by perjury, and subordination of perjury." It has since been adopted in virtually all commonwealth and American common law jurisdictions, with or without some modification. In a sense it can be thought of as part of the common law, and in this sense it is not a typical statute. Nevertheless it is a statute and its interpretation over nearly three hundred years has produced some surprising results. An adequate account of the Statute of Frauds would "fill a book": *Corbin on Contracts* devotes 793 pages (a whole volume) to it, and *Williston on Contracts* (3rd ed.), 599 pages. The original version contained some twenty-five sections but only sections 4 and 17 which latter section is now in the Sale of Goods Act, are of chief concern to the student of contract law. These sections are set out in modern form below. In 1677 contract law was regarded as a minor branch of the law of property and most of the sections dealt with what is now covered in law school courses in real property or land law. In this short account an attempt has been made to present a general, but, it is hoped, an accurate picture of the present status of the Statute. Because it appears rather indiscriminately throughout the law of contracts, and if examined case by case might take up too much time, the highlights are set out in the form of text notes. All that has been attempted is an introduction to some very difficult problems of statutory interpretation.

THE STATUTE OF FRAUDS
Ontario. Revised Statutes. 1970, c. 444

4. No action shall be brought
> [1] whereby to charge any executor or administrator upon any special promise to answer damages out of his own estate, or
> [2] whereby to charge any person upon any special promise to answer for the debt, default or miscarriage of any other person, or
> [3] to charge any person upon any agreement made upon consideration of marriage, or
> [4] upon any contract or sale of lands, tenements or hereditaments, or any interest in or concerning them, or
> [5] upon any agreement that is not to be performed within the space of one year from the making thereof,

unless the agreement upon which the action is brought, or some memorandum or note thereof is in writing and signed by the party to be charged therewith or some person thereunto by him lawfully authorized.

[The paragraphing and numbering have been introduced for convenience in reading and for reference.]

6. No special promise made by a person to answer for the debt, default or miscarriage of another person, being in writing and signed by the party to be charged therewith, or by some other person by him thereunto law-

fully authorized, shall be deemed invalid to support an action or other proceeding to charge the person by whom the promise was made by reason only that the consideration for the promise does not appear in writing, or by necessary inference from a written document.

8. No action shall be brought whereby to charge a person upon or by reason of a representation or assurance made or given concerning or relating to the character, conduct, credit, ability, trade or dealings of any other person, to the intent or purpose that such other person may obtain money, goods or credit thereupon, unless the representation or assurance is made by a writing signed by the party to be charged therewith.

THE SALE OF GOODS ACT
Ontario. Revised Statutes. 1970, c. 421

5. (1) A contract for the sale of any goods of the value of $40 or upwards shall not be enforceable by action unless the buyer shall accept part of the goods so sold, and actually receive the same, or give something in earnest to bind the contract or in part payment, or unless some note or memorandum in writing of the contract is made and signed by the party to be charged or his agent in that behalf.

(2) This section shall apply to every such contract, notwithstanding that the goods may be intended to be delivered at some future time, or may not at the time of such contract be actually made, procured, or provided, or fit or ready for delivery, or some act may be requisite for the making or completing thereof, or rendering the same fit for delivery.

(3) There is an acceptance of goods within the meaning of this section when the buyer does any act in relation to the goods which recognizes a pre-existing contract of sale, whether there be an acceptance in performance of the contract or not.

HISTORICAL NOTE. To appreciate the Statute it is necessary to understand something of its historical background, which is briefly set out in Plucknett, *A Concise History of the Common Law* (5th ed., 1956) 55-6. Shortly stated, there were two principal conditions commonplace then that are now completely changed. In 1677 a party to a contract was an incompetent witness. It was not until the latter half of the 19th century that we conceded that despite his interest in the outcome of a case a party might, under oath, and subject to cross-examination, tell the truth, or something like the truth. Moreover, the jury was then free to act on its own knowledge, or supposed knowledge, and it was not subject to judicial review. (See Bushel's Case (1670), Vaughan 135; 124 E.R. 1006, and Plucknett, *op. cit.* p. 131.) Rather the jury was subject to a form of penal correction known as "attainder." Now, however, parties may and almost always do testify, the judge directs the jury and may non-suit the plaintiff, and a court of appeal may upset a verdict as being against the weight of evidence and order a new trial. These procedural reforms have to a large extent removed the necessity for the Statute of Frauds, but except in two jurisdictions, it seems to be still with us. (On the whole subject of the Statute of Frauds, see Fuller, *Basic Contract Law*, Ch. 9, pp. 940-81. This short treatment is one of the most helpful available.)

THE CONTRACTS LISTED IN THE STATUTE. The odd collection of contracts included in the statute could only be understood with a full knowledge of the social conditions and economic thought of the 17th century, if then. (For a full discussion, see 6 Holdsworth, *History of English Law*, pp. 379-97, and an illustrated article: Hening, "The Original Drafts of the Statute of Frauds (29 Car. II c. 3) and Their Authors" (1913), 61 *U. of Pa. L. Rev.* 283.) It is not clear whether the purpose of the Statute was or is to prevent frauds and perjuries by guaranteeing the certainty of evidence, or to secure evidence of the deliberation of the parties, or both, and there seems today to be little reason for the selection that has persisted through almost 300 years. Consider the curious results illustrated in the following cases:

M orally hired S to work for him for fourteen months as proofreader at a monthly salary. Two weeks after the contract was made S was fired. Although both parties doubtless still retained clear recollections of the agreement, writing was just as necessary as if the contract had been broken during the thirteenth month.

B orally promised O on May 1, 1976, to erect a three storey country house according to plans and specifications, the work to be completed by October 31, 1976. O orally promised B to pay him in monthly installments as the work progressed. On June 1 B defaulted. The contract is not within the statute.

Clause [1] needs no separate consideration from clause [2]. It would appear to qualify under clause [2] as a case of a promise to answer for the debt or default of another person, the other person being the deceased. There are very few cases under clause [1] and it can be disregarded in this short exposition of the general principles of the Statute and the surprising interpretation placed on it by the courts.

Clause [2] is usually called the "guarantee" or "suretyship" section. It has generated a very considerable body of litigation and it can hardly be regarded as an example of clear drafting. The first word suggests that not every promise to answer for the debt, default or miscarriage of another person comes within the statute and must therefore be in writing. Only "special" promises are referred to in both clause [1] and [2]. No one seems to attach any significance to the word, and its presence may now be ignored. This and other peculiarities in the Statute lead us to believe that it may have been drafted by persons who were not as careful of their words as they might have been. Hence it may very well be that the words "debt, default or miscarriage" all refer to the same thing. Just as even today draftsmen will use unnecessary pairs of words where one will do, as, for instance, "null and void", so the draftsman of 1677 may have had but one idea and a plethora of words. It is, however, easy to imagine different meanings here. "Debt" was, of course, in 1677 a term of art. But "default" was not, nor was "miscarriage." If default, however, could be limited to a failure to perform a contract duty that was not a debt, there would remain the whole range of tort liabilities of "another person" that one might promise to answer for. In *Kirkham* v. *Martin*, (1819), 2 B. & Ald. 613; 106 E.R. 490, the defendant had promised orally to answer for the tortious conduct of his son, who had killed the plaintiff's horse. The defendant pleaded the Statute of Frauds (most jurisdictions require that the Statute be pleaded if it is to be relied on, unlike most "law," which is not pleaded). The plaintiff argued that the Statute of Frauds only applied to debt, but the Court, with a sympathy for the Statute that was unusual even in 1819, held that the word "miscarriage" comprehended "that species of wrongful act for the consequences of which the law would make the party civilly responsible."

A more significant interpretation of clause [2], this time, more as one might expect, narrowing the meaning of the words, "answer for," is to be found in *Lakeman* v. *Mountstephen* (1874), L.R. 7 H.I., 17.

Mountstephen was a contractor who had been putting in a sewer for the town Brixham, and the Board of Health asked him to purchase pipes to connect the sewer to certain houses, whose inhabitants seemed unwilling to spend the money for the connection. The Board had power to connect the pipes itself and charge the inhabitants, but Mountstephen hesitated to take on the contract. Lakeman was Chairman of the Board, and asked Mountstephen what his objection was. Mountstephen replied, "None of you or the board will order the work, or become responsible for the payment." Lakeman then said, "Go on, Mountstephen, and do the work, and I will see you paid." Mountstephen did the work, but the Board refused to pay him because, as they said, they had not ordered it. Mountstephen then sued Lakeman on his "promise." Lakeman took the position that the Board was primarily liable, he had orally "specially promised" to answer for the Board's default, and the Statute protected him. It was held, for the plaintiff, that Lakeman had, by his words, made himself primarily liable. The Statute didn't apply because there wasn't any "other person" involved, Lakeman had promised to pay in any event. Query whether Lakeman in fact intended to be liable except in the unlikely case, as he probably thought, that the Board would not order and pay for the work. If so, he only intended to be a guarantor, or surety; that is, he only intended to pay if the Board, the real primary debtor, did not. This kind of case is sometimes labelled an "indemnity" case, but like most labels, it is dangerous to apply loosely. The intent of the transaction should be clearly exposed before the transaction is labelled anything. Since the intent has to be determined with imperfect hindsight, the Court may have a good deal of choice in determining the outcome.

In *Eastwood* v. *Kenyon* (referred to on page 294, on another point) Sarah Sutcliffe's husband, the defendant, had promised the plaintiff, who owed Blackburn money advanced to help pay Sarah's expenses, that he would pay Blackburn. Apart from the consideration question, the Court held that the defendant's promise to the plaintiff to pay the plaintiff's debt to Blackburn was not within the Statute, Lord Denman said, "If the promise had been made to Blackburn, doubtless the Statute would have applied: it would then have been strictly a promise to answer for the debt of another; . . . we are of opinion that the Statute applies only to promises made to the person to whom another is answerable." (113 E.R. 482, at p. 485.) One interpretation of clause [2] has produced what might be called the primary purpose rule. The purpose referred to is that of the contracting parties, not of the Statute. Where one purpose of the contract may be that one party should become a surety for the debt of another, but it is clear that the same party has another, supposedly more important purpose that is not within the Statute, the Statute has been held not to apply. Two cases will show the basis of the rule.

(1) An importer of linseed sold some to a first buyer, who in turn sold it to a second buyer. The first buyer had not paid for his purchase and the importer could claim a lien on the linseed, but the second buyer wanted the linseed immediately and promised to pay what was owing to the importer if he would release the linseed at once. This promise was made with the object of freeing the linseed from the importer's lien which he held until he was paid by the buyer. If the first buyer paid the importer no

doubt the second buyer would be discharged of his promise. The second buyer's promise was held not to be within the Statute and therefore was enforceable although oral. See *Fitzgerald* v. *Dressler* (1859), 7 C.B.N.S. 374; 141 E.R. 861. In fact the second buyer escaped liability on another ground, the promise was made on his behalf by a sixteen year old clerk who had not told the second buyer about it. Williams J. said, "At the time the promise was made the defendant was substantially the owner of the linseed in question, which was subject to the lien of the original vendors for the contract price. The effect of the promise was neither more nor less than this, to get rid of the encumbrance, or, in other words, to buy off the plaintiff's lien.

These exceptions, where an object of the contract is to free property in which the promisor has an interest, are sometimes called the "property cases."

(2) A stock broker orally agreed with a person who was not in the Stock Exchange that the outsider would introduce customers to the stock broker and the stock broker would share half of his profits from business introduced, and the outsider would contribute one half of any losses suffered by the stock broker as a result of such business. The two were not partners. If the stock broker sued the outsider for his contribution toward a loss suffered, and the outsider pleaded the Statute, it is likely that he would not be protected. See *Sutton & Co.* v. *Grey*, [1894] 1 Q.B. 285. Relying on *Couturier* v. *Hastie*, (1852), 8 Ex. 40; 155 E.R. 1250, the Court of Appeal held in a very similar situation that the outsider is like a "del credere" agent, who not only procures purchasers, but who guarantees the purchasers' credit for an extra commission. "The contract is not a guarantee with regard to a matter in which the defendant has no interest except by virtue of the guarantee, it is an indemnity with regard to a transaction in which the defendant has an interest equally with the plaintiffs." These exceptions, where the promisor has an interest beyond the guarantee, where he selects purchasers with greater care, or, as in *Grey's* case, he is almost a partner, have been called the "del credere" cases.

These propositions were reviewed in *Harburg India Rubber Comb Co.* v. *Martin*, (1902) 1 K.B. 778. In that case the plaintiffs were judgment creditors of an English company called the Crowdus Accumulator Syndicate Limited of which the defendant was a director and large shareholder. The plaintiffs were proceeding on their judgment when the defendant orally promised the plaintiff's agent that he would endorse two bills of exchange if the agent would discontinue the proceedings. On the faith of this promise the proceedings were stopped. The defendant failed to endorse the bills, and the plaintiffs commenced this action on the oral promise. The defendant pleaded the Statute and the plaintiffs argued that the transaction came within the exceptions. Mathew J. at the trial agreed and gave the judgment for the plaintiffs. The Court of Appeal reversed Mathew J. and regarded the transaction as one of guarantee only. Vaughan Williams L.J. said, in part:

". . . Our attention has been called to a great number of cases in which the Court has treated various transactions, as being outside s. 4. Most of the earlier cases were what I may call 'property cases'. They were cases in which either the person who made the promise had property which he wished to relieve from liability, or there was property which he wished to acquire. It is not necessary for me to go through those cases, but I cannot agree that the present case comes within any of that class. The defendant's promise was not, as it seems to me, either a new contract of purchase, or a new contract for the release of any property which either was his or in which he had an interest.

"Our attention was next called to the exception which has been established by what I may call the 'del credere cases,' beginning with *Couturier* v. *Hastie*, and coming down to *Sutton & Co.* v. *Grey*. It has been said, and I think truly, that these cases are of a different species from property cases. I say of a different species, not of a different genus, because I think there is a wider genus, which can be plainly and simply defined, within which both of these species fall. So far as I can see, the authorities have left us with a general rule, which I will attempt to define presently, and each of these two classes of cases falls within that general rule. In each of them I think, the form of the promise given by the promisor has never been held to be conclusive of the matter. He may, or he may not, promise in terms to answer for the debt of another; but, whether he does so or not, it is the substance, not the form, which is regarded.

"Before leaving these instances I wish to mention one other class, which I do not treat as an exception from s. 4, but which, I think, does not come within the section at all. I mean the cases which have been spoken of as 'indemnity cases'. Of course in one sense all guarantees, whether they come within s. 4 or not, are contracts of indemnity. But the difference between those indemnities which come within the section and those which do not is very shortly thus expressed in the notes to *Forth* v. *Stanton*, 1 Williams' *Notes to Saunders*, ed. 1871, p. 234; 'These cases establish that the statute applies only to promises made to the person to whom another is already or is to become answerable.' . . .

"In my judgment, the circumstances of the present case shew plainly that there was a guarantee of the payment of a debt for which the syndicate was primarily liable, and not an original promise by the defendant to keep the plaintiffs indemnified. In my judgment, a contract of indemnity does not come within s. 4, but I think there is nothing to justify us in holding that in the present case the contract is a contract of indemnity. In my opinion, it is a contract of guarantee—'a promise to answer for the debt of another.'

"I will now go back to those cases which, so far as the words of the contract are concerned, might come within s. 4, but which have been held not to come within it because of the object of the contract. Whether you look at the 'property cases' or at the 'del credere cases,' it seems to me that in each of them the conclusion arrived at really was that the contract in question did not fall within the section because of the object of the contract. In each of those cases there was in truth a main contract—a larger contract—and the obligation to pay the debt of another was merely an incident of the larger contract. As I understand those cases, it is not a question of motive—it is a question of object. You must find what it was that the parties were in fact dealing about. What was the subject-matter of the contract? If the subject-matter of the contract was the purchase of property— the relief of property from a liability, the getting rid of encumbrances, the securing greater diligence in the performance of the duty of a factor, or the introduction of business into a stockbroker's office—in all those cases there was a larger matter which was the object of the contract. That being the object of the contract, the mere fact that as an incident to it—not as the immediate object, but indirectly—the debt of another to a third person will be paid, does not bring the case within the section. This definition or rule for ascertaining the kind of cases outside the section covers both 'property cases' and 'del credere cases'.

"Can we then in the present case find any larger contract? I cannot. It seems to me plain upon the evidence that the only matter which was present to the mind of the defendant, and was presented by him to Mr. Winter, was this: 'Will you forbear for a time? Will you give the syndicate, which I believe has a future before it, an opportunity of turning round? I believe that if it has that opportunity, it will do well and will be able to pay you. And to induce you thus to forbear I will give you bills which shall secure the payment at specified periods of the judgment debt, in case the syndicate does not pay you itself.' That, I think is the true effect of the conversation, and it seems to me that was the whole of the contract, and there was neither a purchase nor a del credere arrangement, nor anything else beyond that bargain. And the mere fact that the defendant had, as he seems to have done, financed the syndicate to a large extent, and that that was his motive for thus coming forward and bargaining for forbearance, cannot make any difference in the object of the contract. That might have been the motive which induced him to make himself answerable for the debt of the syndicate, but it was not the object of the contract. The object was simply to obtain the forbearance of the creditors in respect of the debt.

"It was suggested that the true definition of cases which do not come within s. 4 should be, not those in which the obligation to pay the debt of another is an incident of a larger contract, but those in which the main object is to secure the promisor's own personal interest. But, I think, if such a definition were adopted, there would be nothing left to come within s. 4, because in every case there must be a consideration for which the promisor bargains to come to him from the promisee. That is as true of mere forbearance as of anything else. If the contract is that the promisor will be answerable for the debt due to the promisee if he will forbear, if the main object is to obtain that forbearance, and the promisor wishes to obtain it, that would be sufficient to take the case out of the statute. In my opinion so to hold would be simply to repeal s. 4. . . ."

For a collection of the cases dealing generally with guarantees see Falconbridge "Annotation on Guarantees and the Statute of Frauds," 55 D.L.R. 1.

Clause [3]. This clause, which brings within the Statute "any agreement made upon consideration of marriage", calls for only a brief comment. It might, on a hasty reading, appear to make every engagement to marry a matter requiring writing. In such cases, however, the consideration is not *marriage*, but the mutual *promise to marry*. The common cases are those where one lover promises the other to convey property in consideration of the marriage, or where a parent promises to convey property to a son or daughter on his or her forthcoming marriage. Oddly enough, an agreement between parents of a loving couple that each will convey property to his respective child on marriage is not within the Statute because, again, the consideration is the mutual promise. See *Philpott* v. *Wallett* (1682), 3 Levinz 65; 83 E.R. 579, *Harrison* v. *Cage* (1698), 1 Ld. Raymond 386; 91 E.R. 1156, and *Tweddle* v. *Atkinson* (1861), 1 B. & S. 393; 121 E.R. 762.

Clause [4]. This clause, which is rather oddly, and probably accidentally, worded, brings within the Statute practically every land transaction. It speaks of "any contract *or* sale of lands . . . ," but there seems to be common agreement that the draftsman intended to say "any contract *for* the sale of lands. . . ." The expression "contract of lands" is not usual English, and "sale of lands" is quite a different thing from a contract, with which section 4 is mostly concerned, and other parts of the Statute deal in some detail with the "sale" of land.

In one area the contract for the sale of land may be of particular interest to students of contract law, rather than conveyancing, or real estate transactions, by whatever name the course on contracts for the sale of land may be called. When trees are cut from land and sold, there may be conversion of the "realty" into "personalty," and similarly, when gas or oil is sold after being extracted from land, it may be "personalty." Depending on where the transformation takes place, a contract for newly cut timber, or timber to be cut, may come within the Statute or not. See *Tilbury Town Gas Co. Ltd* v. *Maple Leaf Oil & Gas Co. Ltd.* (1915), 35 D.L.R. 4 (P.C.) 186 at p. 204, and *King* v. *Freeman*, [1942] O.R. 561 (neither case involved the Statute).

Clause [5]: "any agreement that is not to be performed within the space of one year from the making thereof." Presumably the purpose of clause [5] is to bring into the protection of the Statute contracts which from their terms may be the subject of litigation long after the parties (who couldn't testify anyway) and witnesses might have forgotten the terms. But if that was its purpose it seems to have been much broader than need be, and like so many statutory reforms, to have caught cases probably never intended by the reformers. The critical time, usually, is not how long a period there was between the making and the performing of the contract, but between its making or breaking, and the time it comes up for trial, for that is when the witnesses' memories will be tested.

The first problem case is the one where the contract itself is silent about its duration. (It will be convenient here to deal with illustrations drawn from employment contracts, and many cases are to be found in this area, but the language is broad enough to catch any kind of contract that runs over a year in performance, so do not be misled by the limits of the illustrations.) If M hires S for an indeterminate time, is the contract within the Statute? If S is a healthy young man, it may be that the parties contemplated years of service. Is the test of contemplation, or "intention" of the parties, sufficient? Suppose S in fact quits two months later? Is the test of what in fact happened sufficient? Does it leave the parties themselves with sufficient guide? Should the parties have to wait, in all such cases, to see what happens?

The test usually applied is a simpler one. The court asks what could have happened. Is performance within a year possible? If so, the oral contract is enforceable. If not, the oral contract is unenforceable. *Adams* v. *Union Cinemas, Ltd.*, [1939] 3 All E.R. 136 is a case of this type. Adams was employed as a controller of theatres by the defendant, who had suggested that he might be employed for a two year period in this post, and Adams so claimed in his reaction for wrongful dismissal. The evidence established, however, that no final agreement had been reached on this point, and that the contract was one for general hiring with no time specified. If the oral contract for two years had been proved Adams would have been caught by the Statute. Lord Justice MacKinnon commented on the odd result: ". . . the plaintiff and his advisers, perhaps by inadvertence or by too sanguine an expectation, thought the defendants would not be so ungentlemanly as to plead the Statute." And Du Parcq L.J. said, "I must confess that I should be very sorry to have to explain the facts of this case and the im-

portance of the legal issues in this case to an intelligent foreigner, because I can imagine his asking; 'Why is it that counsel for the defendants was apparently much more anxious even than counsel for the plaintiff to show that his client had entered into an agreement to employ the plaintiff for a longer time and at a larger salary? Is it because of undue generosity on their part, or how is it to be explained?' I can imagine that, when one had to tell him that the reason was that, if only the defendants could satisfy the court that they had given their word to the plaintiff that they would employ him for two years, then the court would at once decide that, in the circumstances, they need not pay him a penny and they were not bound to employ him, the intelligent foreigner would find a little difficulty in understanding the explanation."

Once it was established that Adams had only a contract of indefinite duration, despite the fact that both parties had obviously contemplated a two year period although it was understood that Adams would not go on working as a controller without clear written agreement, the court applied the test of what "might be."

If the test then is, what could have happened, does death, which can always happen, mean that every oral contract not to be performed within the space of one year is enforceable notwithstanding the Statute because it could be so performed by one party dying? Perhaps the easiest answer is that a contract for a fixed period is not performed if the party dies before the fixed period is up. The party is excused for his non-performance, but legally speaking, he is not regarded as having performed. Nor is it necessary to regard a contract for an indefinite term as "performed" by death. On the other hand, a contract to perform for the rest of a party's life; for example, an appointment for life, even of a healthy young man, is fully performed if he works for six months and then is killed in a highway accident. He has done all he promised to do. The oral promises are enforceable. But see *Ste. Marie* v. *Ste. Marie*, [1929] 4 D.L.R. 1076, to the contrary, citing *Davey* v. *Shannon*, (1879), 4 Ex.D. 81, which was, however, disapproved of by the Court of Appeal in *McGregor* v. *McGregor*, (1888), 21 Q.B.D. 424.

If the test is, what could have happened, the case of a two year oral contract with an express provision that either party could terminate the contract by giving the other six months notice, would clearly be one where the contract could be performed in six months, certainly in less than twelve months. *Hanau* v. *Ehrlich*, [1912] A.C. 39, is such a case. You may find the Court of Appeal decisions, reported in [1911] 2 K.B. 1056, more interesting than those in the House of Lords. A. T. Lawrence L.J. said, "As in this case the employment of the plaintiff was for a period of two years, it could not be performed by either within one year. I do not think the existence of the power to give notice affects the contractual period for performance. Its exercise terminates the obligation further to perform but the exercise of this power, though contained in the contract, is not the same thing as the performance of the contract. The words 'not to be performed' in the statute apply to the obligations undertaken by each party towards the other. Giving notice is the exercise of a right; performance is the fulfilment of a duty. This view is certainly more in accordance with the express object of the Statute of Frauds than the construction contended for by the plaintiff." The plaintiff had contended that the agreement amounted to an agreement for an indefinite period within a maximum of two years, that the Statute did not apply, and that the contract was enforceable.

Do you agree with the literal analysis of A. T. Lawrence L.J. and his view that the object of the Statute was to prevent enforcement of this well proven contract? Is there a difference between the "object of the Statute" and a literal reading of some of its words?

Fletcher Moulton L.J. was less satisfied with the result. He remarked: "If I were free . . . I should say that beyond all question it might possibly be performed within the year . . . It is impossible to predicate the period of the performance of this contract is more than a year. Moreover, supposing the notice to be given, then six months after that date the contract is wholly performed. There is no ghostly survival of the contract for the remainder of the two years; the contract is wholly performed when the notice has expired. I have, therefore, no hesitation in saying that, if I were free to use my own intellect . . . I should certainly allow this appeal . . . But I am bound by the authorities, and agree that this appeal must be dismissed." Buckley L.J. said on this question of the authorities, "It is now two centuries too late to ascertain the meaning of s. 4 by applying one's own mind independently to the interpretation of its language. Our task is a much more humble one; it is to see how that section has been expounded in decisions and how the decisions apply to the present case." This reluctant obeisance to authority by two members of the Court of Appeal probably encouraged the appeal to the House of Lords, who, however, affirmed the lower court. Lord Atkinson said, "Where the language of a statute is ambiguous and one finds that a particular construction has been put upon it by a number of authorities, extending over a very great length of time, it would be unwise and wrong to adopt a different construction."

Why should Lord Atkinson think it would be "unwise"? Is he supposing that someone relies on the "number of authorities"? Who relies on them? The courts? Lawyers? Business men? The general public, that is, contracting parties?

Another surprising interpretation is to be found in *Donellan* v. *Read*, (1832), 3 B. & Ad. 899; 110 E.R. 330, which held that where the duty of one party to a contract is to be performed within a year, the fact that the duty of the other party clearly cannot be performed within the year does not bring the contract within the protection of the Statute. In *Donellan* v. *Read* an oral promise was given to pay an increased rent of £5 a year for the remaining years of a lease, in exchange for £50 worth of improvements in the house. The improvements were carried out between August and November in 1827 at an expense of £55. The defendant paid the increased rent for one quarter, at Christmas time 1827, but refused to pay it thereafter. Littledale J. thought it wrong that one party, having enjoyed the whole of the other party's performance, could ignore his own promise. *Donellan* v. *Read* has been much criticised. See *Williston on Contracts*, 3rd ed., sec. 504, where the various authorities are collected. In *Boydell* v. *Drummond*, (1809), 11 East 142; 103 E.R. 958, Bayley J. said "I cannot say that a contract is *performed* when a great part of it remains *un*-performed within the year, or in other words, that *part performance is performance*. The mischief meant to be prevented by the statute was the leaving to memory the terms of a contract for longer than a year. The persons might die who were to prove it, or they might lose their faithful recollection of the terms of it." The exception is sometimes justified on the distinction between an action brought on "any special promise" in clauses [1] and [2], and an action brought on "any agreement" in clause [5], the idea being that the bilateral character of the "agreement" is gone once one party has completely performed and only a unilateral "promise" remains as the subject of an action.

One final permutation remains to be considered. Suppose that an oral contract calls for a performance by one party for a specific period of three years, and the other party's performance is for an indefinite time. One might expect a combination of *Adams* v. *Union Cinemas, Ltd., supra*, and *Donellan* v. *Read* to result in a holding that the Statute does not apply. This situation is essentially what confronted the Court in *Reeve* v. *Jennings*, [1910] 2 K.B. 522. Reeve employed Jennings in his dairy business on an indefinite hiring, so that Reeve's obligations to pay Jennings and to keep him in his employ could be performed within a year. Jennings, on the other hand, agreed that he would not compete in the dairy business for three years after quitting or being discharged. The original agreement was in writing, but its extension was oral. Jennings left about two years after the oral extension of the agreement and immediately entered into business on his own. The Court was faced with a nice choice of policies, since it presumably didn't wholly like either restraint of trade clauses or the Statute. The county court judge who tried the case held that the oral extension did not come within the Statute and enforced the contract. The appeal was allowed. Bray J. said, ". . . I must hold that this contract was within the statute. As regards one side it was clearly not to be performed within the year, as regards the other side it could be, *but it was not the intention of the parties that it should be performed within the year.* I think that this case does not come within the exception laid down in *Donellan* v. *Read* and the appeal must, therefore, be allowed." (Italics added)

A commonly recurring question is raised where a contract is entered into on Monday, to start on Tuesday, and run for a year. In *Smith* v. *Gold Coast and Ashanti Explorers, Ltd.*, [1903] 1 K.B. 285, 838, Lord Alverstone, C.J., said, "I think that these cases shew that a contract for a year's service to commence on the day after the day on which the contract was made is not an agreement which is not to be performed within the space of one year from the making thereof, within the meaning of section 4." Compare *Dollar* v. *Parkington* (1901), 84 L.J. 470 (*contra*). In *Britain* v. *Rossiter*, (1899), 11 Q.B.D. 123, an oral contract made on Saturday, April 21, for a year's employment to begin on Monday, April 23, was held to come within the Statute and so be unenforceable.

The Sale of Goods Act. In the original section, which appeared as section 17 of the Statute, the words "shall not be enforceable" were "no contract . . . shall be allowed to be good."

The peculiarities of this section may be left to the more specialized courses of Commercial Law or Sales, but two features are worth noting briefly. The first is the fact that the limit of money has not changed in nominal amount since 1677, when the original section set the limit at £10. Today's value would be closer, probably, to $1000, but only in some American jurisdictions has there been any recognition of the changing value of currency. The most common limit in the United States is $500. In all likelihood the $500 limit is much closer in principle to the original £10 than $40, or $30, which is the lowest figure in any Statute of Frauds in Canada. It is obvious that the original section 17 was aimed at very substantial sales only.

The other remarkable feature about the sale of goods section is the presence of alternatives to the note or memorandum, in the form of part payment, the handing over of some earnest, or delivery, acceptance and actual receipt of the goods. No such alternative is given in section 4 clause [4], dealing with contracts for sale of land, but the Chancery Courts have, in this area, taken certain liberties with the Statute and have developed a somewhat similar rule. See below in the Note on Part Performance and *Deglman* v. *Guaranty Trust Company of Canada and Constantineau*, p. 309. See also p. 59.

THE MEMORANDUM OR NOTE. One of the most interesting interpretation problems arises from the words "some memorandum or note." It was clear that a formal contract, or even a simple contract wholly reduced to writing but not under seal, was not required although quite acceptable. What was a "note"? In *Bailey* v. *Sweeting* (1861), 9 C.B.N.S. 843; 142 E.R. 332, the dispute was over a sale of "chimney glasses" and the "note" which was held sufficient read as follows:

"Cheltenham, December 3, 1859.

Gentlemen,—In reply to your letter of the 1st instant, I beg to say that the only parcel of goods, selected for ready money was the chimney-glasses, amounting to £38 10s. 6d., which goods I have never received, and have long since declined to have for reasons made known to you at the time; with regard to the other items, viz., £11 4s. 9d., £14 13s., and £13 13s., for goods had subsequently (less cases returned), those goods are, I believe, subject to the usual discount of £5 per cent, and I am quite ready to remit you cash for these parcels at once, and on receipt of your reply to this letter will instruct a friend to call on you and settle accordingly.

I am yours,

Geo. Sweeting."

In effect the "note" was a repudiation of the contract! In a modern English case, *Farr, Smith & Co.*, v. *Messers, Ltd*. [1928] 1 K.B. 397, a statement of defence setting out the terms of a contract and signed by the defendant's counsel was accepted as sufficient when the action by the original plaintiff was dropped and recommenced by a corporate plaintiff.

The "note" apparently need not even be a communication between the plaintiff and defendant. A letter to the defendant's agent, setting out or referring to the written terms and signed by the defendant has been held sufficient. See *Gibson* v. *Holland* (1865), L.R. 1 C.P. 1. In that case Erle C.J. went so far as to prefer such a "note." He said: "Indeed one would incline to think that a statement by the party to his own agent would be the more satisfactory evidence of the two."

The note need not be a contemporaneous record of the agreement. In rather unusual circumstances, in *Farr, Smith & Co.* v. *Messers Ltd.*, [1928] 1 K.B. 397, a statement of defence in an earlier action on the same contract was successfully used as the note. Counsel for the defence as agent of the defendant, had signed the defence, which contained the terms of the agreement!

Since many contracts are "unilateral" in form, and the offer is likely to be the only writing of the terms, it is not surprising that the written offer, when accepted by performance of the requested act, is regarded as a sufficient note. See *Reuss* v. *Picksley*, (1866), L.R. 1 Ex. 342. Willes J. said: "Now all that was signed here was not a formal agreement but a proposal on one side, and there was an assent to that proposal on the other. All difficulty as to the terms of the proposal is out of the case. It contained the names of the parties and all the terms by reference to the letter of the 8th

September, which must be taken to be recited in the letter of the 9th. The only question is, whether it is sufficient to satisfy the statute that the party charged should sign what he proposes as an agreement, and that the other party should afterwards assent without writing to the proposal? As to this it is clear, both on reasoning and authority, that the proposal so signed and assented to, does become a memorandum or note of an agreement within the 4th section of the statute.

"It has been urged upon us that this conclusion will lead to fraud and perjury, and to the very mischiefs the statute was passed to prevent. We do not concur in that view, because no one will be able to enforce an agreement of the sort we are now discussing, without proving that he did or was ready to do his part to entitle him to performance on the part of the other contracting party."

Apart from the form the document takes, one might suppose that at least the parties must be reasonably identified. In *Vandenbergh* v. *Spooner*, (1866), L.R. 1 Ex. 316, although Martin B. was "not well satisfied" about the meaning of the "note," Bramwell B. said for the whole court: "The document was signed by the defendant, and was in the following terms: 'D. Spooner agrees to buy the whole of the lots of marble purchased by Mr. Vandenbergh, now lying at the Lyme Cobb, a 1s. per foot.' Can the essentials of the contract be collected from this document by means of a fair construction or reasonable intendment? We have come to the conclusion that they cannot, inasmuch as the seller's name as seller is not mentioned in it, but occurs only as part of the description of the goods."

Evidence was also given to the effect that, after the defendant had signed this document, he wrote out what he alleged to be a copy of it, which at his request the plaintiff, supposing it to be a genuine copy, signed. This was in the following words: "Mr. J. Vandenbergh agrees to sell to W. D. Spooner the several lots of marble purchased by him, now lying at Lyme, at 1s. the cubic foot, and a bill at one month. (Signed) Julius Vandenbergh." The jury however were of the opinion that the first document stated the contract actually made.

Compare *Newell* v. *Radford*, (1867), L.R. 3 C.P. 52, where the defendant's agent solicited an order from the plaintiff and entered in the plaintiff's book: "Mr. Newell, 32 sacks culasses at 39s., 280 lbs., to wait orders. June 8. John Williams." Boville C.J. said: "In this case it is not disputed that the signature of the agent Williams would be sufficient to bind the defendant, but it is contended that the written memorandum does not sufficiently show which of the parties was the buyer. At first sight this indeed might not appear quite clear, except to a man in the trade; but it has always been held that you may prove what the parties would have understood to be the meaning of the words used in the memorandum, and that for this purpose parol evidence of the surrounding circumstances is admissible: . . . In this case it was shown that the plaintiff was a baker, and that the defendant was a dealer in flour which the plaintiff would require for his trade; and looking at the nature of the entry in relation to those facts, I think there can be no reasonable doubt that it was a sale from the defendant to the plaintiff. If however there were any doubt, looking at the entry alone, it is set at rest by the two letters which passed between the plaintiff and defendant, which sufficiently identify the contract, and in which the relative positions of the parties as buyer and seller is distinctly stated."

Although it is essential that the memorandum disclose both the contracting parties with sufficient certainty of identification it may be possible that the parties are described, rather than named, and if the description is sufficiently definite viewed in the light of surrounding circumstances the memorandum will be good. For example "if the vendor is described in the contract as 'proprietor,' 'owner,' 'mortgagee,' or the like, the description is sufficient although he is not named; but if he is described as 'vendor' or as 'client' or 'friend' of a named agent, that is not sufficient; the reasons given being, in the language of Lord Cairns, that the former description 'is a statement of matter of fact as to which there can be perfect certainty, and none of the dangers struck at by the Statute of Frauds can arise;' the reason against the latter descripion being that in order to find out who is vendor, client, or friend you must go into evidence on which there might possibly be a conflict." (Kay J. in *Jarrett* v. *Hunter*, (1886), 4 Ch.D. 182, 184). Hence, if a memorandum is signed by an agent "on behalf of the vendor" it will be held insufficient. *Potter* v. *Duffield* (1874), L.R. 18 Eq. 4. But if A signs "on behalf of the proprietors" the memorandum is good. *Rossiter* v. *Miller*, (1878), 3 App.Cas. 1124. As to situations in which an agent signs as one of the contracting parties, though acting for an undisclosed principal, see Jessel M.R. in *Commins* v. *Scott*, (1875), L.R. 20 Eq. 11 at p. 15: "There can be no doubt that if a written contract is made in this form, A.B. agrees to sell Blackacre to C.D. for £1000, then E.F., the principal of A.B., can sue G.H., the principal of C.D., on that contract." See also *Filby* v. *Hounsell*, [1896] 2 Ch. 737.

A "note" or "memorandum" would obviously be of little help if the terms were not set out, and Grose J. said as much in *Wain* v. *Warlter* (1803), 5 East 10; 102 E.R. 972. "What is required to be in writing, therefore, is the 'agreement' (not the promise, as mentioned in the first part of the clause), or some note or memorandum of the agreement. Now the 'agreement' is that which is to show what each party is to do or perform, and by which both parties are to be bound; and this is required to be in writing. If it were only necessary to show what one of them was to do, it would be sufficient to state the promise made by the defendant who was to be charged upon it. But if we were to adopt this construction it would be the means of letting in those very frauds and perjuries which it was the object of the statute to prevent. For without the parol evidence the defendant cannot be charged upon the written contract for want of a consideration in law to support it. The effect of the parol evidence then is to make him liable: and thus he would be charged with the debt of another by parol testimony, when the statute was passed with the very intent of avoiding such a charge, by requiring that the 'agreement,' by which must be understood the 'whole agreement,' should be in writing."

Wain v. *Warlters* was an action on a promise to pay the debt of another in the "note" of which no consideration is mentioned. The case must now be considered in the light of section 6 of the Statute of Frauds. What effect has the statutory change upon the "principle" upon which *Wain* v. *Warlters* was decided? How do you determine the *ratio decidendi* of a case of interpretation?

Some rather interesting doubts can be raised by speculating on the reason the draftsman referred to a "special promise" in Clauses [1] and [2], an "agreement" in Clauses [3] and [5] and a "contract" in Clause [4] and yet requires the "agreement" to be in writing.

A nice distinction is taken in *Hoadly* v. *McLaine*, (1834), 10 Bing.

482; 131 E.R. 982, where a rather common type of situation was dealt with. The plaintiff agreed in writing to build a "new, fashionable, and handsome landaulet with the following appointments" (which were set out in detail). No price was specified, but the plaintiff claimed £480 which the defendant refused to pay and to which he pleaded the statute. A "great number of coachmakers... proved that the landaulet was of such exquisite workmanship, and so highly ornamented, as to be cheap at the price demanded." The jury awarded £200 damages. In reply to the defence of the statute, i.e., that the price or consideration was not in writing, it was argued that the undertaking was only to pay on a "quantum meruit," and no price could be stated in the note because none has been agreed. The "note" was held sufficient. Tindal C.J. said:

"What is implied by law is as strong to bind the parties as if it were under their hand. This is a contract in which the parties are silent as to price, and therefore leave it to the law to ascertain what the commodity contracted for is reasonably worth.

"It has been contended, that this would open a door for perjury, and let in the mischief which the statute of frauds proposes to exclude. But I cannot agree in that proposition; for it does not appear that any specific price was agreed on; and if it had appeared that such was the case, this note would not have been evidence of such a bargain, as the case of *Elmore* v. *Kingscote*, (1826), 5 B. & C. 583; 108 E.R. 217, expressly decides.

"Thus the law stands on the note or memorandum of May, 1832. But we may look at all the writings to see what the contract was; and here, from the defendant's letter of April, 1833, it appears that, after he had seen the carriage, he desired the plaintiff to send in his *bill*. He must have known whether he had contracted for a stipulated price or not; and it may therefore he inferred, from this letter, that he knew he was to pay the reasonable charge when the article was made up."

The "note" must be "signed by the party to be charged," that is, by the defendant (or his agent). If he signs but the plaintiff does not, only one of them would be bound, notwithstanding the "logic" of the mutuality doctrine. Of course, once the plaintiff is in court, he would presumably be required to perform his side of the bargain so far at least as it was a condition precedent to the defendant's liability. But what constitutes a signature? Apparently now a sales slip from a department store would be regarded as signed, if the slip has the name of the business printed on it. See *Evans* v. *Hoare*, [1892] 1 Q.B. 593, where Denman J. said:

"This was an action for wrongful dismissal. The plaintiff entered the defendant's services as a ledger clerk at £80 a year; the salary was twice raised £10 a year until it reached £100. On February 19, 1890, the plaintiff signed an agreement as follows:

"5, Campbell Terrace, Cannhill Road,
Leytonstone, Feb. 19, 1890.

Messrs. Hoare, Marr & Co., 26, 29 Budge Row,
London, E.C.

Gentlemen,—In consideration of your advancing my salary to the sum of £130 per annum, I hereby agree to continue my engagement in your office for three years, from and commencing January 1, 1890, at a salary at the rate of £130 per annum aforesaid, payable monthly as hitherto.

Yours obediently,
George E. Evans."

"If this agreement was within s. 4 of the Statute of Frauds, the judgment was justified. The learned judge gave judgment for the defendants on the ground that the document was not signed within that section. This decison would be right unless the words 'Messrs. Hoare, Marr & Co.,' at the commencement, can, under the circumstances, be held to be 'a signature by a person authorized thereunto by the defendants.' In fact, the document was drawn up by one Harding, who was authorized by the defendants to draw it up and take it, in its present shape in all other respects, for the plaintiff's signature. It appears to me that the case falls within the principle of the decisions cited in favour of the plaintiff, especially *Schneider* v. *Norris* (1814), 2 M. & S. 286; 105 E.R. 388. In the present case it is impossible to doubt that the word 'your,' twice used in the written document, refers to the defendants, whose name and address is given in full at the head of the document. Nor can I doubt that both Harding and the defendants intended that this document, when signed by Evans, should be the final memorandum of the contract binding upon the defendants as well as the plaintiff."

In *Cohen* v. *Roche*, [1927] 1 K.B. 169 a printed page from the catalogue of an auction sale was allowed as a signature when pasted into the auctioneer's book.

Perhaps the most indefensible of the interpretative glosses on the Statute is the notion that it is permissible to link up two separate documents, neither of which is sufficient in itself, by parol evidence. The extreme case is *Pearce* v. *Gardner*, [1897] 1 Q.B. 688. There the only memorandum or note tendered in evidence by the plaintiff was a letter addressed to "Dear Sir" and containing the terms signed by the defendant. The plaintiff testified that the letter had been received in an envelope addressed to him, but he did not produce the envelope. In allowing the letter as a "note," Lord Esher M.R. said,

"The great struggle was as to whether in that state of things the letter and the envelope can be taken together to constitute the memorandum required. No case has been cited deciding this point either way so that we have now to determine the matter. I adopt the suggestion made in Dart on Vendors and Purchasers, at p. 253 of the 6th edition, which is as follows: 'In the case of a letter, if the name of the party to whom it is addressed appear in an indorsed direction, or be written at the foot of the letter, no difficulty on the above point can arise: if an envelope be used the name may often not appear in the letter; but the Court, it is conceived would receive evidence connecting the envelope with the enclosure." The common sense of the matter seems to me to be that the envelope and the letter within it were sent together and may be taken together; so that the effect is the same as if the name of the plaintiff had been written at the foot or endorsed on the letter."

See also *Oliver* v. *Hunting*, (1890), 44 Ch.D. 205. Kekewich J.: "The elementary proposition about which there is no doubt is this,—the memorandum to be signed by the party sought to be charged, so as to bring a particular case within the Statute of Frauds, need not be on one piece of paper, nor need it be a complete document, signed by the party at one and the same time. It may be contained in two or more pieces of paper, but they must be so connected that you can read them together, so as to form one memorandum of the contract between the parties. Directly you get beyond that, you get into difficulty. One can illustrate that in a simple manner. An intending purchaser accepts an offer made by a proposing vendor thus: 'In reply to your letter of the 14th instant." Can one annex to that reply the letter of the 14th instant? Surely one cannot, without inquiring what letter it is; unless the purchaser has, with unusual prudence, completed the reference by saying, 'In reply to your letter of the 14th instant, a copy of which is on the other side.' In the absence of any such complete evidence as that, one must inquire what the letter of the 14th instant was, because *non constat*, it may have been a reference to any one of half a dozen different letters; and so, from that very simple illustration, one can go through a large variety of more complex ones. It is not for me to say that the old rule was better or worse than the present rule.... I take the old rule from the original edition of Lord Blackburn, *On the Contract of Sale*; ... 'If the contents of the signed paper themselves make reference to the others, so as to show by internal evidence that the papers refer to each other, they may all be taken together as one memorandum in writing [as in the case which I have mentioned of a letter referring to a previous letter, of which the copy is annexed]: but if it is necessary, in order to connect them, to give evidence of the intention of the parties that they should be connected, shown by circumstances not apparent on the face of the writings, the memorandum is not all in writing, for it consists partly of the contents of the writings and partly of the expression of an intention to unite them, and that expression is not in writing.'

"The old case of *Boydell* v. *Drummond*, (1809), 11 East, 142; 103 E.R. 958 ... might be consistent with that rule; but certainly of late a different rule has been introduced, and it is a rule, to say the least, consistent with the convenience of mankind, because if you were to exclude parol evidence to explain such a doubtful reference as 'the letter of the 14th instant,' or it might be simply 'your letter,' the result might in a large number of cases be gross injustice. Now I take it to be quite settled that in a case of that kind you may give parol evidence to show what the document referred to was. I take it that you may go further than that, and if you find a reference to something, which may be a conversation, or may be a written document, you may give evidence to show whether it was a conversation or a written document; and, having proved that it was a written document, you may put that written document in evidence, and so connect it with the one already admitted or proved.... The illustration [Bramwell L.J. in *Long* v. *Millar*, (1878), 4 C.P.D. 450] gives is this (at p. 454). Suppose that A writes to B, saying that he will give £1000 for B's estate, and at the same time states the terms in detail, and suppose that B simply writes back in return, "I accept your offer." In that case there may be an identification of the documents by parol evidence, and it may be shown that the offer alluded to by B is that made by A, without infringing the Statute of Frauds, sec. 4, which requires a note or memorandum in writing. If that is sound, which I take it to be, according to other cases, and according to the convictions of Judges in older cases which are introduced into the old law, it is difficult, perhaps, to say where parol evidence is to stop; but substantially it never stops short of this, that whenever parol evidence is required to connect two written documents together, then that parol evidence is admissible. You are entitled to rely upon a written document, which requires explanation. Perhaps the real principle upon which that is based is, that you are always entitled in regarding the construction and meaning of a written document to inquire into the circumstances under which it was written, not in order to find an interpretation by the writer of the language, but to ascertain from the surrounding facts and circumstances, with reference to what, and with what intent, it must have been written. I think myself that must be the principle on which parol evidence of this kind is admitted. Turning to the case before me, I find a letter of the 12th of September, 1888, written by the defendant to Mrs. Oliver, and in that he says: 'I beg to acknowledge receipt of check, value £375 on account of the purchase-money for the Fletton Manor House estate, for which I thank you.' I have two things here perfectly clear, that there is a property called Fletton Manor House estate, which constitutes the subject of a purchase, and, therefore, the subject of a sale, I have also that £375 is part of the purchase-money for that house: but, beyond that I have no terms of a contract. I am entitled to consider the circumstances under which the letter was written, in order to give any meaning that I properly can to it—not to add terms to it, but to find out what the meaning necessarily must be, having regard to the facts and circumstances—and, having got the evidence which I have in this case, the conclusion is inevitable that it refers to a previous memorandum of terms of agreement under which Mrs. Oliver becomes the purchaser of this particular property for the price of £2,375, on account of which the check for £375 was sent. Having got that evidence in, having got the connection between the two documents, I have then enough to enable me to read the two documents together, and, reading them together, I have a distinct memorandum of contract, specifying all the terms, the second one supplying what the first one omitted to give, namely, singularly enough, the property which was intended to be purchased and sold. That being so, the objection that there is no memorandum within the Statute of Frauds fails."

Compare *Thomson* v. *McInnes*, (1911), 12 Comm. L.R. 563, where the High Court of Australia held that the use of the word "purchase-money" in a receipt signed by the vendor could not refer to another document. Griffith C.J. said: "It is sufficient if the note signed by the party to be charged refers to some other document in such a manner as to incorporate it with the document signed, so that they can be read together. That has been settled for a long time. But the whole contract must be shown by the writing. The reference, therefore, in the document signed must be to some other document as such, and not merely to some transaction or event in the course of which another document may or may not have been written. . . . Whether there is a reference or not depends, first of all upon the construction of the document which is signed. You must, first of all, find some words in that document which are capable of being construed as referring to a document and not to a transaction or event. If there are words capable of such a construction, then, and not before, the question arises as to their meaning . . . in *Long* v. *Millar* the words "the purchase" used in a receipt were held to mean a written document. . . . In all the cases it was held that the word in question meant a written document. Kekewich J. in *Oliver* v. *Hunting* suggested that this was the old rule, and that there was now a new rule. With the greatest respect for that learned judge I do not agree with him. The rule has always been the same. Some judges may have been more liberal in their application of the rule than others, or may have taken a more liberal view of the words to be construed. The rule is thus stated by Baggallay L.J. in *Long* v. *Millar*: 'The true principle is that there must exist a writing to which the document signed by the party to be charged can refer, but that this document may be identified by verbal evidence! I think it unfortunate that any doubt should be entertained as to that doctrine. It is as well settled as any doctrine relating to contracts.' "

NOTE. The Courts of Equity early developed a doctrine known as "part performance" whereby a buyer of land who has substantially relied on as oral contract of sale might enforce the contract notwithstanding the absence of a signed writing. There were two basic strands to the doctrine, first that it was inequitable for the vendor to take advantage of the Statute after the purchaser's reliance, and second, that the acts of reliance offered substitute proof of the making of the contract alleged which the court might accept in lieu of the statutory writing. It is unclear whether the doctrine applies to contracts other than for the sale of land.

DEGLMAN v. *GUARANTY TRUST CO. OF CANADA AND CONSTANTINEAU*
Ontario. Supreme Court of Canada. [1954] 3 D.L.R. 785

RAND J.: In this appeal the narrow question is raised as to the nature of part performance which will enable the Court to order specific performance of a contract relating to lands unenforceable at law by reason of s. 4 of the *Statute of Frauds*, R.S.O. 1950, c. 371. The respondent Constantineau claims the benefit of such a contract and the appellant represents the next-of-kin other than the respondent of the deceased, Laura Brunet, who resist it.

The respondent was the nephew of the deceased. Both lived in Ottawa. When he was about 20 years of age, and while attending a technical school, for 6 months of the school year 1934-35 he lived with his aunt at No. 550 Besserer St. Both that and the house on the adjoining lot, No. 548, were owned by the aunt and it was during this time that she is claimed to have agreed that if the nephew would be good to her and do such services for her as she might from time to time request during her lifetime she would make adequate provision for him in her will, and in particular that she would leave to him the premises at No. 548. While staying with her the nephew did the chores around both houses which, except for an apartment used by his aunt, were occupied by tenants. When the term ended he returned to the home of his mother on another street. In the autumn of that year he worked on the national highway in the northern part of Ontario. In the spring of 1936 he took a job on the railway at a point outside of Ottawa and at the end of that year, returning to Ottawa, he obtained a position with the city police force. In 1941 he married. At no time did he live at the house No. 548 or, apart from the 6 months, at the house No. 550.

The performance consisted of taking his aunt about in her own or his automobile on trips to Montreal and elsewhere, and on pleasure drives, of doing odd jobs about the two houses, and of various accommodations such as errands and minor services for her personal needs. . . . These circumstances, Spence J. at trial and the Court of Appeal [[1953] O.W.N. 665], finding a contract, have held to be sufficient grounds for disregarding the prohibition of the statute.

The leading case on this question is *Maddison* v. *Alderson* (1883), 8 App. Cas. 467. The facts there were much stronger than those before us. The plaintiff, giving up all prospects of any other course of life, had spent over 20 years as housekeeper of the intestate until his death without wages on the strength of his promise to leave her the manor on which they lived. A defectively executed will made her a beneficiary to the extent of a life interest in all his property, real and personal. The House of Lords held that, assuming a contract, there had been no such part performance as would answer s. 4.

The Lord Chancellor, Earl of Selborne, states the principle in these words [p. 475]: "All the acts done must be referred to the actual contract, which is the measure and test of their legal and equitable character and consequences."

At p. 479, referring to the rule that payment of the purchase-price is not sufficient, he says: "The best explanation of it seems to be, that the payment of money is an equivocal act, not (in itself) until the connection is established by parol testimony, indicative of a contract concerning land. . . . All the authorities shew that the acts relied upon as part performance must be unequivocally, and in their own nature, referable to some such agreement as that alleged."

Lord O'Hagan, at p. 485, uses this language: "It must be unequivocal. It must have relation to the one agreement relied upon, and to no other. It must be such, in Lord Hardwicke's words, Amb. 587, 'as could be done with no other view or design than to perform that agreement.' "

At p. 489 Lord Blackburn, speaking of the delivery of possession as removing the bar of the statute, says: "This is, I think in effect to construe the 4th section of the Statute of Frauds as if it contained these words, 'or unless possession of the land shall be given and accepted.' Notwithstanding the very high authority of those who have decided those cases, I should not hesitate if it was res integra in refusing to interpolate such words, or put such a construction on the statute."

I am quite unable to distinguish that authority from the matter before us. Here, as there, the acts of performance by themselves are wholly neutral and have no more relation to a contract connected with premises No. 548 than with those of No. 550 or than to mere expectation that his aunt would requite his solicitude in her will, or that they were given gratuitously or on terms that the time and outlays would be compensated in money. In relation to specific performance, strict pleading would seem to require a demonstrated connection between the acts of performance and a dealing with the land before evidence of the terms of any agreement is admissible. This exception of part performance is an anomaly; it is based on equities resulting from the acts done; but unless we are to say that, after performance by one party, any refusal to perform by the other gives rise to them, which would in large measure write off the section, we must draw the line where those acts are referable and referable only to the contract alleged. The facts here are almost the classical case against which the statute was aimed: they have been found to be truly stated and I accept that; but it is the nature of the proof that is condemned, not the facts, and their truth at law is irrelevant. Against this, equity intervenes only in circumstances that are not present here. . . .

[The remainder of Rand J.'s judgment is reproduced on page 59. Rinfret C.J.C. and Taschereau J. concurred with Rand J. The judgment of Cartwright J., who agreed with Rand J., and with whom Estey and Locke JJ. concurrred, is omitted.]

[The judgment of the Court of Appeal included this paragraph from [1953] O.W.N. at p. 666: "A more serious argument presented by the appellant was that this agreement being an agreement whereby the aunt would leave to him at her death a particular piece of property, the acts of part performance must be such as in their own nature were referable to and affected the land in question, and he relied upon the decision and judicial views expressed in the case of *Maddison* v. *Alderson*, (1883), 8 App. Cas. 467. We have, however, been referred to the decision of this Court in *Fox* v. *White*, [1935] O.W.N. 316, where this Court distinguished the decision in *Maddison* v. *Alderson* and the principles there laid down from a case such as the case at bar, and in that case this Court held that if the acts relied upon as being acts of part performance were referable to some contract, and consistent with the contract alleged, then evidence was admissible as to the precise terms of the particular contract alleged. We are of the opinion that the acts in this case which are alleged to be acts of part performance are plainly referable to the existence of a contract and are consistent with the particular contract alleged, and that when the evidence is admitted as to the precise terms of the particular contract the plaintiff's case is made out and the acts of part performance take the case out of the statute."]

STEADMAN v. STEADMAN
[1974] 3 W.L.R. 56 (H.L.)

The parties, whose marriages had been dissolved, were negotiating a settlement of the wife's claim under section 17 of the Married Women's Property Act 1882 for a declaration that the matrimonial home was jointly owned and an order for its sale when the husband, who was £194 in arrears of maintenance, applied to the magistrates' court to vary the maintenance order. The parties met outside the magistrates' court on March 2, 1972, and agreed that the wife would surrender her interest in the house for £1,500; that the maintenance order for the wife should be discharged; that the child's maintenance order should continue and that the arrears of maintenance should be remitted save for £100 to be paid by March 31. The justices were told of the agreement, they discharged the maintenance order and remitted the arrears save for £100. The husband paid the £100 and his solicitors prepared the deed of transfer and sent it to the wife. The wife refused to sign the transfer and, on the hearing of her application under section 17 of the Act of 1882, the husband contended that the wife had compromised the suit by the agreement of March 2. The registrar held that incurring the costs of preparing the transfer was an act of part performance of an oral agreement concerning land and therefore the agreement was enforceable under section 40 of the Law of Property Act 1925, [the equivalent of s. 4 of the Statute of Frauds]. The wife appealed and the county court judge held that the agreement was unenforceable as there had been no act of part performance. The husband appealed to the Court of Appeal and, by a majority, the court allowed the appeal holding that the payment of £100 arrears of maintenance, although not referable to the term of the agreement relating to land, was an act of part performance of the contract for the purposes of section 40 (2) of the Act of 1925.

The wife appealed to the House of Lords.

LORD SIMON OF GLAISDALE: . . . The respondent ("the husband") in effect is seeking to enforce that term of what the learned registrar called "an oral package deal" (by which is meant an indivisible contract consisting of a number of obligations on each side) which relates to the disposition of an interest in land. The contract (of March 2, 1972) disposed of the various issues raised by three legal processes: (i) a summons under section 17 of the Married Women's Property Act 1882 taken out by the appellant ("the wife"); (ii) a summons under the Matrimonial Proceedings (Magistrates' Courts) Act 1960 taken out by the husband for variation of a maintenance order which had been made in favour of the wife and the child of the marriage; (iii) a summons by the wife for enforcement of payment of arrears of £194 which had accrued under the maintenance order. The terms of the contract were necessarily conditional on approval by the justices at the hearing which would immediately ensue. They were in effect as follows: (1) the wife would consent to the discharge of the maintenance order of £2 weekly in her favour; (2) the husband and wife would consent to the continuance of the maintenance order of £2.50 weekly in respect of the child; (3) the husband would, before March 30, 1972, pay £100 in part discharge of the arrears; (4) the wife would consent to the remission of the balance of the arrears; (5) the wife would surrender to the husband the interest which she claimed in the former matrimonial home; (6) the husband would pay her £1,500 for such interest.

As will appear hereafter, it is only the obligations incumbent on the husband which are relevant to the doctrine of part performance, with which your Lordships are concerned. But, in addition to his positive obligations set out under heads (2), (3) and (6) above, which would on execution involve detriment to him, there were some tacit forbearances by the husband: (a) it was open to him, on his complaint for variation of the maintenance order, to ask the justices to reduce the maintenance order in respect of the child; (b) it would be unusual, to say the least, for justices to order the discharge of maintenance arrears otherwise than by a weekly instalment order; before ordering a payment of £100 within 28 days they would require positive proof that the husband had such a sum at his immediate disposal; the husband forbore from putting the wife to proof; (c) the enforcement of arrears of maintenance is a matter of judicial discretion, so that it was open to the husband to ask the court to discharge the entire arrears; (d) it is the practice not to enforce more than a year's arrears of maintenance (*Pilcher* v. *Pilcher* (*No. 2*), [1956] 1 W.L.R. 298); the evidence does not show how long the arrears had been accumulating (this would depend mainly but not exclusively on whether the husband had been keeping up the maintenance payments in respect of the child); and it might be that the justices would have refused to enforce arrears of £100, even by instalments.

I would emphasise that the agreement generally, and various terms of it specifically, provided for the justices to be informed as to what had been agreed and to be asked to implement the matters which lay within their jurisdiction.

The justices, on being informed of the agreement between the parties and on being satisfied that the wife was a freely and knowledgeably consenting party, approved it, and implemented so much of it as lay within their jurisdiction, by varying the maintenance order on the husband's complaint and by adjourning the wife's complaint for variation, in order that the husband might pay the £100 not later than March 30, 1972; they remitted the balance of the arrears. This adjournment and remission were the only positive orders that the justices made on the wife's complaint; they did not actually order the husband to pay the £100, though the order states: "If you fail to pay as directed, further proceedings will be commenced to recover the amount due." There was, in other words, no merger of the husband's contractual obligation to pay £100 in a subsequent judgment debt. On the justices' approval the agreement between the parties became contractually binding (*Smallman* v. *Smallman*, [1972] Fam. 25), subject to any question of enforceability in view of the want of writing and signature to evidence it.

This is one of those difficult situations where two legal principles are in competition. The first legal principle is embodied in section 40 (1) of the Law of Property Act 1925, which states: "No action may be brought upon any contract for the sale or other disposition of land or any interest in land, unless the agreement upon which such action is brought, or some memorandum or note thereof, is in writing, and signed by the party to be charged or by some other person thereunto by him lawfully authorised."

This provision replaced that part of section 4 of the Statute of Frauds 1677, which related to interests in land. The preamble to the Statute of Frauds explained its object: "For prevention of many fraudulent practices, which are commonly endeavoured to be upheld by perjury and subornation of perjury . . ."

The "mischief" for which the statute was providing a remedy was, therefore, that some transactions were being conducted orally in such a way that important interests were liable to be adversely affected by a mode of operation that invited forensic mendacity. The remedy was to require some greater formality in the record of such transaction than mere word of mouth if it was to be enforced. The continuing need for such a remedy for such a mischief was apparently recognised as subsisting when the law of landed property was recast in 1925.

The second, competing, legal principle was evoked when, almost from the moment of passing of the Statute of Frauds, it was appreciated that it was being used for a variant of unconscionable dealing, which the statute itself was designed to remedy. A party to an oral contract for the disposition of an interest in land could, despite performance of the reciprocal terms by the other party, by virtue of the statute disclaim liability for his own performance on the ground that the contract had not been in writing. Common law was helpless. But equity, with its purpose of vindicating good faith and with its remedies of injunction and specific performance, could deal with the situation. The Statute of Frauds did not make such contracts void but merely unenforceable; and, if the statute was to be relied on as a defence, it had to be specifically pleaded. Where, therefore, a party to a contract unenforceable under the Statute of Frauds stood by while the other party acted to his detriment in performance of his own contractual obligations, the first party would be precluded by the Court of Chancery from claiming exoneration, on the ground that the contract was unenforceable, from performance of his reciprocal obligations; and the court would, if required, decree specific performance of the contract. Equity would not, as it was put, allow the Statute of Frauds "to be used as an engine of fraud." This became known as the doctrine of part performance—the "part" performance being that of the party who had, to the knowledge of the other party, acted to his detriment in carrying out irremediably his own obligations (or some significant part of them) under the otherwise unenforceable contract. This competing principle has also received statutory recognition, as regards contracts affecting interests in land, in section 40 (2) of the Law of Property Act 1925.

But what was in origin a rule of substantive law designed to vindicate conscientious dealing seems to have come in time sometimes to have been considered somewhat as a rule of evidence. It is easy to appreciate how this happened. Part performance could be viewed as a way of proving an agreement falling within section 4 notwithstanding the absence of writing. Seen as such, it was no doubt considered necessary to frame stringent requirements to prevent the doctrine from carting a sedan chair through the provisions of the statute. If part performance was to be evidence of a contract which could not otherwise and directly be proved, the acts of part performance should themselves intrinsically be capable of proving some such contract as that alleged. Oral evidence was not admissible to connect them with the alleged contract: otherwise, it was held, the statutory object would be defeated by allowing an interest in land to pass on mere oral testimony. As the Earl of Selborne L.C. put it in *Maddison* v. *Alderson*, 8 App.Cas. 467, 478, 479 (in a passage I label "(A)" for ease of reference later): (A) "The doctrine . . . has been confined . . . within limits intended to prevent a recurrence of the mischief which the statute was passed to suppress. . . . All the authorities show that the acts relied upon as part performance must be unequivocally, and in their own nature, referable to some such agreement as that alleged."

It may be questionable whether it was direct respect for the statute which led to such confinement of the doctrine, or whether it was not rather because part performance seems sometimes to have been regarded as an alternative way of proving an oral agreement; for equity allowed a person to prove by parol evidence that land conveyed to another was so conveyed on trust for himself, notwithstanding section 7 of the Statute of Frauds: *Rochefoucauld* v. *Boustead*, [1897] 1 Ch. 196, 206; *Bannister* v. *Bannister* [1948] 2 All E.R. 133, 136—the passages show that here, too, the guiding rule was that the court would not allow the statute to be used as a cloak for fraud. However that may be, the speech of the Earl of Selborne L.C. has always been regarded as authoritative, notwithstanding that what he said about part performance was, strictly, obiter.

But Lord Selborne went on to effect a complete reconciliation between the provisions of the statute and the doctrine of part performance in a passage (pp. 475-476) which is of crucial importance to the instant appeal, and which I have labelled "(B)":

(B) "In a suit founded on such part performance, the defendant is really 'charged' upon the equities resulting from the acts done in execution of the contract, and not (within the meaning of the statute) upon the contract itself. If such equities were excluded, injustice of a kind which the statute cannot be thought to have had in contemplation would follow . . . All the acts done must be referred to the actual contract, which is the measure and test of their legal and equitable character and consequences. . . . The matter has advanced beyond the stage of contract; and the equities which arise out of the stage which it has reached cannot be administered unless the contract is regarded. The choice is between undoing what has been done (which is not always possible, or, if possible, just) and completing what has been left undone ... it is not arbitrary or unreasonable to hold that when the statute says that no action is to be brought to charge any person upon a contract concerning land, it has in view the simple case in which he is charged upon the contract only, and not that in which there are equities resulting from res gestae subsequent to and arising out of the contract. So long as the connection of those res gestae with the alleged contract does not depend upon mere parol testimony, but is reasonably to be inferred from the res gestae themselves, justice seems to require some such limitation of the scope of the statute . . ."

The following questions arise for determination in relation to the facts of the instant case: (1) What is meant by res gestae in passage (B)? Are they different from acts of part performance of the alleged contract? If so, do they impose some limitation—e.g. contemporaneity? Or are they words of extension—permitting, for example, evidence of explanatory acts antecedent to the alleged contract (such as the correspondence between the solicitors in the instant case)? (2) In passage (A) Lord Selborne says "referable to *some such agreement* as that alleged": in passage (B), "referred to the *actual contract.*" Is there a discrepancy here? What must be the relationship between the acts of part performance and/or the res gestae (if there is a distinction), on the one hand, and the alleged contract, on the other, in order to raise an equity precluding the other party from relying on the statute? (3) Must the alleged act(s) of part performance indicate specifically the term of the alleged contract to which the statute is pleaded as a defence (e.g. the term relating to the disposition of an interest in land), or is it sufficient that the alleged act(s) indicate *some* contract? (4) What does "unequivocally" in passage (A) mean in this connection? What is the standard of proof required? (5) What does "of their own nature" in passage (A) mean? Must each act of alleged part performance "of its own nature" be separately referable to the alleged, or "some such," contract, or can they be regarded cumulatively—reinforcing each other, so to speak? (6) For what purpose, if at all, is oral evidence admissible? (7) Can payment of a sum of money ever be a relevant act of part performance? (8) What issues arise at the trial and how are they to be resolved?

These questions to some extent overlap. I do not think that it is possible to reconcile all the authorities and dicta. There seems to be an uneasy oscillation between regarding the doctrine as a principle vindicating conscientious dealing and as a rule of evidence. Concurrently with this and reinforcing the latter view, there seems to have been a hardening of equity's arteries, an increasing technicality until quite recent times. The Chancellor's foot evolves into the Vice-Chancellor's footrule.

(1) *Res gestae* (i.e. things done). The concept is more familiar in the law of evidence, where it relates to the admissibility of acts, declarations and incidents which either are constituents of, or accompany and explain, the fact or transaction in question: see *Phipson on Evidence*, 11th ed. (1970), para. 171. Lord Selborne probably had two reasons for using the words in preference to "acts of part performance of the alleged contract": (i) they are sometimes used in the law of evidence to mark the distinction between the principal fact or transaction in question, on the one hand (as to which evidence is always admissible), and ancillary facts, on the other (as to which evidence is only admissible if they are so closely connected with the principal fact is either to form one continuous transaction with it or to

be necessary to give meaning to it): Lord Selborne was emphasising that what gave rise to the equity was, not the contract itself, but what was done ancillary to it; (ii) one rationale for the res gestae rule of evidence is that the probability of an occurrence may often be tested by considering its attendant circumstances (*Dysart Peerage Case* (1881) 6 App. Cas. 489, 502): so here, once it was considered incumbent to do equity without undermining the statute, it was reasonable to look for attendant circumstances which inherently rendered it probable that there had been an antecedent contract the obligations of which it would be inequitable to allow a party to escape. But I do not think that Lord Selborne intended to import generally the rules of the law of evidence relating to res gestae. Those rules often extend to admitting acts and declarations antecedent to the principal fact where they either form one continuous transaction with it or are necessary to explain it. But an act or declaration antecedent to a contract cannot be part performance of it; and it was the doctrine part of part performance which Lord Selborne was concerned with. He speaks of "res gestae subsequent to and arising out of the contract." I do not think, therefore, that the correspondence between the solicitors before March 2, 1972, can avail the husband in obviating the plea of section 40 (1) (though it is available to aid him in establishing the alleged agreement of March 2, 1972, once the plea of the statute is obviated). Then there is authority that acts preparatory, not merely to the contract, but to the performance of a term of the contract (such as compiling an abstract of title or making a valuation) are not sufficient acts of part performance: but these certainly would seem to be res gestae pursuant to the contract involving detriment to the plaintiff. Did the preparation of the conveyance on behalf of the husband in the instant case stand alone, it might be necessary to give consideration to this line of authority: however, on the view I take of other matters it is not called for. Again, I do not think that Lord Selborne's description of acts of part performance as res gestae under the contract imports from the law of evidence into this branch of the law the requirement of substantial contemporaneity: equity's doctrine of laches and the requirement of referability provide superior and less technical safeguards against injustice. On the other hand, the fact that Lord Selborne used the term res gestae throws some light on the admissibility of oral testimony in this branch of the law, since in the law of evidence the doctrine of res gestae is very largely concerned with the question of admissibility of oral declarations.

(2) *"Some such agreement"/"the actual agreement."* I think that the discrepancy in expression foreshadows Upjohn L.P.'s formulation of the rule—the acts must be such as "prove the existence of some contract, and are consistent with the contract alleged." (*Kingswood Estate Co. Ltd.* v. *Anderson*, [1963] 2 Q.B. 169, 189, citing *Fry on Specific Performance*, 6th ed. (1921), p. 278; see also *Wakeham* v. *Mackenzie*, [1968] 1 W.L.R. 1175, 1180). Alternatively, Lord Selborne might have been drawing a distinction between the stage of part performance giving rise to equities in favour of the plaintiff which preclude the defendant from pleading the statute, and the next stage where the plaintiff may lead evidence of the oral contract with sufficient particularity that equity will enforce it. Both must now be accepted as valid ways of considering the rule.

The law here is not logical: it represents the compromise of the two principles to which I referred near the outset of this speech. If the contract alleged is such that it ought not to depend on oral testimony, it is *this* contract, not merely *some* contract, that the acts should prove. If the plaintiff has so performed his obligations under the contract that it would be unconscionable for the defendant to plead the statute, it is immaterial whether or not the plaintiff's acts prove the contract let alone some other contract. But it is the sort of illogical compromise, doing some deference to each of two competing and inconsistent principles, in which English law abounds. There is no reason to disturb it so long as it does substantial justice, as it seems to have done in all the recent reported cases. However, I have already ventured to point out that equity did not find it necessary to create the same difficulties as regards section 7 of the statute—unembarrassed by a long line of authority, it took the direct route to oral evidence.

But the law as stated by Upjohn L.J. is juridically justifiable. If the plaintiff proves that he carried out acts in part performance of *some contract* to which the defendant was a party while the latter stood by, it becomes inequitable that the latter should be allowed to plead, in exoneration of reciprocal obligations, that *any such contract* was unenforceable by reason of the statute particularly when it is borne in mind that few acts of performance point exclusively to a particular contract, least of all a particular multi-term contract.

But "some such contract" must be a contract with the defendant— otherwise no equity arises against him to preclude his pleading the statute.

(3) *Must the act of part performance indicate that term of the contract which concerns the disposition of an interest in land?* This question has often been answered in the affirmative. *Snell's Principles of Equity*, 27th ed. (1973), p. 587, for example, states: "the acts must indicate the land concerned." But where, as so often, the only term to be performed by the defendant is the transfer of the interest in land, the fulfilment of the other conditions stipulated by equity will generally involve that the effective act of part performance indicates the land concerned. The Earl of Selborne's "referable to some such agreement as that alleged" is not so specific; and it has now, in any event, received Upjohn L.J.'s gloss. In *Wakeham* v. *Mackenzie*, [1968] 1 W.L.R. 1175 a woman agreed to surrender her rent-restricted flat and keep house for an elderly widower in consideration of his oral promise to leave her his house by will: her action was held to be sufficient part performance to make the widower's oral promise binding on his personal representative. The case must be compared with *Maddison* v. *Alderson*, 8 App.Cas. 467, where the only material distinction was that the woman had no house of her own to give up. This distinction might be sufficient to justify the inference in the later case that the housekeeper's actions implied a quid pro quo, a bargain, which had not been a justifiable inference in the earlier case (see Lord Blackburn in *Maddison* v. *Alderson* at p. 487); but they could hardly be said to have indicated a bargain a term of which related to the widower's house.

It is unnecessary to determine the point in the instant case. The husband's acts of part performance included two which specifically indicated the land in question: (i) procuring his solicitor to inform the justices of the entire bargain and to invite them to implement such of its terms as concerned them; (ii) procuring his solicitor to carry out the obligation which, under the bargain, the husband had assumed of drafting the conveyance and sending it to the wife (see *Williams on Title*, 3rd ed. (1966), p. 709)—this was the performance of an obligation arising from the contract, not preparation for performance.

Other acts of part performance by the husband proved that there had been *some* contract with the wife, though without specifically indicating those terms which concerned the house. The consent to the justices' orders and the payment of £100 are, in my view, only reasonably intelligible on the hypothesis that the issues raised by the cross-summonses in the magistrates' court had been settled by agreement. As for the other limb of Upjohn L.J.'s formulation of the rule, the husband's acts were consistent with the contract alleged by him.

(4) "*Unequivocally.*" This could bear three meanings: (i) referable to the alleged contract and no other; (ii) clearly, on more than a mere balance of probabilities; (iii) not equally referable to the hypothesis of a contract or some other hypothesis, i.e. on the preponderance of probability.

The first view was apparently held at one time—in logical consistency with the principle that the doctrine of part performance should not be allowed to undermine the statutory insistence that the contract must not be proved by oral testimony. It would seem, indeed, to be a reflection of the tendency to regard the doctrine of part performance as a rule of evidence. But it must often have led to a failure of justice, to equity helplessly standing by while the statute was used as an engine of fraud; since, as *Snell* puts it (p. 587): "Few acts of part performance are so eloquent as to point to one particular contract alone." This idea is therefore now to be regarded as "long exploded," to use Upjohn L.J.'s expression in *Kingswood Estate Co. Ltd.* v. *Anderson*, [1963] 2 Q.B. 169, 189.

As for the second view, there would be nothing unique in equity requiring that the act of part performance should indicate beyond doubt that it was in pursuance of a contractual obligation. For example, for rectification, there must be "strong irrefragable evidence" of the mistake (*Countess of Shelburne* v. *Earl of Inchiquin*, (1784) 1 Bro. C.C. 338, 341): it must "leave no fair and reasonable doubt upon the mind" (*Fowler* v. *Fowler* (1859) 4 De G. & J. 250, 265); there must be "convincing proof" (*Joscelyne* v. *Nissen* [1970] 2 Q.B. 86, 98). A similar standard is probably required to establish a secret trust (*Ottaway* v. *Norman*, [1972] Ch. 698, 712). Or that persons who have lived together purporting to be husband and wife were not married, especially if there had been *some* ceremony (*Morris* v. *Davies* (1837) 5 Cl. & Fin. 163; *Piers* v. *Piers*, (1849) 2 H.L.Cas. 331 and *Hill* v. *Hill* [1959] 1 W.L.R. 127). Or to prove the abandonment of a domicile of origin (*Winans* v. *Attorney-General*, [1904] A.C. 287).

Nevertheless, the general standard of proof in civil proceedings is proof on a balance of probabilities. In some of the situations referred to in the preceding paragraph justice may call for a higher standard of proof; but I can see no reason why it should here—though no doubt, here as elsewhere, the evidence (and the nexus) will be more jealousy scrutinised where the other party to the alleged contract is deceased. In passage (B) the Earl of Selborne used the words "reasonably to be inferred." In *Wakeham* v. *Mackenzie* [1968] 1 W.L.R. 1175 the alleged acts of part performance can only on a balance of probability have been more likely to have been in pursuance of some contract than otherwise. I am therefore of opinion not only that the facts relied on to prove acts of part performance must be established merely on a balance of probability, but that it is sufficient if it be shown that it was more likely than not that those acts were in performance of some contract to which the defendant was a party.

(5) "*Of their own nature.*" This means merely that oral testimony is

not admissible to show that the acts relied on were in part performance of a contract: the acts must themselves on a balance of probability indicate this. But it does not mean that each act must be considered seriatim by itself. The acts may throw light on each other; and there is no reason to exclude light. In the instant case, for example, the payment of £100 would, standing by itself, have been equivocal: it would not even marginally have been more suggestive of performance of a contractual term than otherwise. But taken together with the other acts and forbearances of the husband in relation to the summary matrimonial proceedings it becomes strongly indicative of a bargain. So, too, the preparation of the draft conveyance when taken together with the statements made to the justices—provided that the latter were admissible in evidence.

(6) *Oral evidence.* The extent of the exclusionary rule is to preclude oral evidence to establish that the acts relied on were in part performance of a contract; in other words, the nexus between the acts and the alleged contract, or some such, cannot be established by oral testimony at the trial. But the acts themselves may be, and generally are, proved orally. Moreover, spoken words may themselves be part performance of a contract. "Words spoken are facts just as much as any other action by a human being. If the speaking of words is a relevant fact, a witness may give evidence that they were spoken." (Lord Wilberforce in *Ratten* v. *The Queen*, [1972] A.C. 378, 387, in relation to the evidentiary rule of res gestae.) As such they are to be considered as of the nature of real evidence: see Lord Normand in *Teper* v. *The Queen*, [1952] A.C. 480, 487. So, in the instant case, the bargain between the parties necessitated the justices being informed of what had been agreed, as a preliminary to the invitation to them to implement part of the agreement. The statement to the justices was part performance of the bargain, including those terms adverse to the husband; and oral evidence is admissible as to what was said to them. But "human utterance is both a fact and a means of communication": Lord Normand in *Teper* v. *The Queen*, at p. 486. When it comes to determining whether acts of part performance of their own nature indicate the contract alleged, or some such, words inevitably speak more specifically than deeds; but that is no reason for excluding them either as facts or as means of communication. The statement to the justices as an act of part performance indicated in terms that there had been an agreement between the parties and what were its provisions. Moreover, the ensuing actions of the husband (in inviting the order of the justices, instructing his solicitor to prepare the conveyance, and paying the £100) must be viewed in the light of the statement to the justices—they were integral res gestae in every sense of that expression.

(7) *Payment of money.* It has sometimes been said that payment of money can never be a sufficient act of part performance to raise the required equity in favour of the plaintiff—or, more narrowly, that payment of part or even the whole of the purchase price for an interest in land is not a sufficient act of part performance. But neither of the reasons put forward for the rule justifies it as framed so absolutely. The first was that a plaintiff seeking to enforce an oral agreement to which the statute relates needs the aid of equity; and equity would not lend its aid if there was an adequate remedy at law. It was argued that a payment could be recovered at law, so there was no call for the intervention of equity. But the payee mght not be able to repay the money (he might have gone bankrupt), or the

land might have a particular significance for the plaintiff (cf. the equitable order for specific delivery of a chattel of particular value to the owner: *Duke of Somerset* v. *Cookson*, (1735) 3 P.Wms. 390), or it might have greatly risen in value since the payment, or money may have lost some of its value. So it was sought to justify the rule, alternatively, on the ground that payment of money is always an equivocal act: it need not imply a pre-existing contract, but is equally consistent with many other hypotheses. This may be so in many cases, but it is not so in all cases. Oral testimony may not be given to connect the payment with a contract; but circumstances established by admissible evidence (other acts of part performance, for example) may make a nexus with a contract the probable hypothesis. In the instant case, for example, what was said (i.e. done) in the magistrates' court in part performance of the agreement makes it plain that the payment of the £100 was also in part performance of the agreement and not a spontaneous act of generosity or discharge of a legal obligation or attributable to any other hypothesis.

(8) *The issues at the trial.* A plaintiff alleges an oral agreement. If the defendant does not plead the statute, the plaintiff may prove the agreement by any relevant evidence, including oral testimony. But if the defendant does plead the statute, the plaintiff is barred unless he can establish that the defendant's plea of the statute should not be admitted because its maintenance would be unconscionable. To do this the plaintiff has to prove that: (i) on balance of probability he acted to his detriment: (ii) it was more probable than not he so acted because he was contractually obliged to the defendant to do so; (iii) such actions were consistent with the oral agreement which he alleges. As regards (i), the plaintiff's detrimental actions can include words; and he can prove them by any relevant evidence, including oral testimony. But he cannot lead oral or any testimony (other than a written confession by the defendant which satisfies the requirements of the statute) as to (ii) and (iii); the facts proved under (i) must themselves answer (ii) and (iii) in his favour. But if all three requirements are satisfied, an equity arises in his favour which precludes the defendant from relying on the statute; and the plaintiff can then lead evidence (including oral evidence) to establish the oral agreement on which he based his claim for relief, as if the statute had never been pleaded. He still, of course, has to prove such oral agreement on a balance of probability; and if the other party is dead the evidence will be rigorously scrutinised.

In the instant case the husband proved to the satisfaction of the registrar the following acts which were to his detriment: (i) procuring his solicitor to consent to an order by the justices which placed him under a continuing legal obligation; (ii) procuring his solicitor to forbear from seeking from the justices orders which might have been more advantageous to himself; (iii) paying £100 to the wife before March 30, 1972; (iv) procuring his solicitor to draft a conveyance for execution by the wife. Even if, contrary to my view, these matters could be considered in isolation from the statements inviting the justices to play their part in implementing them, they still, in my opinion, make it more probable than not that the husband acted as he did because he had contracted with the wife to do so; and they are consistent with the agreement which the husband alleges. This makes it inequitable for the wife to allege that the agreement was unenforceable because the formalities required by section 40 (1) were not complied with. The registrar, therefore, rightly admitted oral and affidavit evidence to establish the agreement alleged by the husband, which he found proved.

I would therefore dismiss the appeal.

[Lord Reid, Lord Salmon and Viscount Dilhorne concurred in dismissing the appeal; Lord Morris dissented.]

STATUTE OF FRAUDS
British Columbia. Revised Statutes. 1960. Chapter 369

2. (1) No agreement concerning an interest in land is enforceable by action unless evidenced in writing, signed by the party to be charged or by his agent.

5. (1) No guarantee or indemnity is enforceable by action unless evidenced in writing, signed by the party to be charged or by his agent, but any consideration given for the guarantee or indemnity need not appear in the writing.

(2) This section does not apply to a guarantee or indemnity arising by operation of law.

6. No action shall be brought whereby to charge any person upon or by reason of any representation or assurance made or given concerning or relating to the character, conduct, credit, ability, trade, or dealings of any other person, to the intent or purpose that such other person may obtain credit, money, or goods thereupon, unless such representation or assurance be made in writing, signed by the party to be charged therewith.

PROBLEM. Sections 50-54(1) of the Ontario Family Law Reform Act, 1978, are as follows:

50. In this Part,
(a) "cohabitation agreement" means an agreement entered into under section 52;
(b) "domestic contract" means a marriage contract, separation agreement or cohabitation agreement;
(c) "marriage contract" means an agreement entered into under section 51;
(d) "separation agreement" means an agreement entered into under section 53.

51.(1) Two persons may enter into an agreement, before their marriage or during their marriage while cohabiting, in which they agree on their respective rights and obligations under the marriage or upon separation or the annulment or dissolution of the marriage or upon death, including,
(a) ownership in or division of property;
(b) support obligations;
(c) the right to direct the education and moral training of their children, but not the right to custody of or access to their children and
(d) any other matter in the settlement of their affairs.

(2) Any provision in a marriage contract purporting to limit the rights of a spouse under Part III in respect of a matrimonial home is void.

52.(1) A man and a woman who are cohabiting and not married to one another may enter into an agreement in which they agree on their respective rights and obligations during cohabitation, or upon ceasing to cohabit or death, including,
(a) ownership in or division of property;
(b) support obligations;
(c) the right to direct the education and moral training of their children, but not the right to custody of or access to their children; and
(d) any other matter in the settlement of their affairs.

(2) Where the parties to an agreement entered into under subsection 1 subsequently marry, the agreement shall be deemed to be a marriage contract.
53. A man and a woman who cohabited and are living separate and apart may enter into an agreement in which they agree on their respective rights and obligations, including,

(a) ownership in or division of property;

(b) support obligations;

(c) the right to direct the education and moral training of their children;

(d) the right to custody of and access to their children; and

(e) any other matter in the settlement of their affairs.

54.(1) A domestic contract and any agreement to amend or rescind a domestic contract are void unless made in writing and signed by the persons to be bound and witnessed.

1. Albert, while travelling abroad, writes to his wife, Bertha, as follows: "I have decided to stay away for at least a few years. The land I bought for a cottage will be yours if you will make the mortgage payments." Bertha writes accepting the arrangement and subsequently makes all the mortgage payments and builds a cottage on the land at her own expense. Albert now seeks to repossess the land. Advise Bertha.

2. Ann and her husband, Bob, enter into a marriage contract duly executed under s. 54(1) whereby Ann is to pay Bob $500 a month. Subsequently Ann gives up her job and she and Bob agree informally that their agreement will be cancelled. Six years later Bob sues Ann for $36,000 arrears, and interest, under the original agreement. Advise Ann.

Index